# NTC's
## Dictionary
of
# AMERICAN
# SLANG
and
## COLLOQUIAL EXPRESSIONS

## About the Author and Editor

**Richard A. Spears, Ph.D.,** Adjunct Associate Professor of Linguistics, Northwestern University, and specialist in lexicography; English Language structure; phonetics; language standardization and codification; English as a Second Language; and American culture. Dr. Spears is also the Director of the Dictionary Department at National Textbook Company.

**Linda Schinke-Llano, Ph.D.,** Assistant Professor of English, Millikin University. Specialist in English as a second language, bilingual education, and second language acquisition.

Also available by the same author:

*NTC's American Idioms Dictionary*
*NTC's Dictionary of Phrasal Verbs and Other Idiomatic Verbal Phrases*

# NTC's
## Dictionary
of
# AMERICAN
# SLANG
and
## COLLOQUIAL EXPRESSIONS

## RICHARD A. SPEARS

Consulting Editor
**LINDA SCHINKE-LLANO**

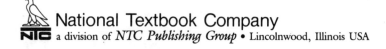

**National Textbook Company**
**NTC** a division of NTC *Publishing Group* • Lincolnwood, Illinois USA

# ACKNOWLEDGMENTS

We are grateful to Bruce Smith for his assistance with the phonetic transcription and suggested entries. Thanks also to Rachel B. Spears for adding and verifying entries.

**1993 Printing**

Published by National Textbook Company, a division of NTC Publishing Group.
©1989 by NTC Publishing Group, 4255 West Touhy Avenue,
Lincolnwood (Chicago), Illinois 60646-1975 U.S.A.
Manufactured in the United States of America.
Library of Congress Catalog Card Number: 89-60358

2 3 4 5 6 7 8 9 RD 9 8 7 6

# CONTENTS

# TO THE USER

This dictionary is a collection of slang and colloquial expressions in frequent use in the United States in the twentieth century. It contains expressions that are familiar to many Americans and other expressions that are used primarily within small groups of people. These expressions come to us from movies, novels, newspaper stories, and everyday conversation. The entries represent the language of the underworld, the nursery, the college campus, California beaches, urban back streets, and Wall Street. We hear from prisoners, surfers, junkies, Valley Girls, weight lifters, and just plain country folks. Fad words, metaphors, wordplay, and various figures of speech make up the body of the **Dictionary**.

There is no standard test that will decide what is slang or colloquial and what is not. Expressions that are identified as slang are often some type of entertaining wordplay, and they are almost always an alternative way of saying something. Colloquial expressions are usually spoken and are often thought of as being direct, earthy, or quaint. Slang and colloquial expressions come in different forms: single words, compound words, simple phrases, idioms, and complete sentences. Slang is rarely the first choice of careful writers or speakers or anyone attempting to use language for formal, persuasive, or business purposes. Nonetheless, expressions that can be called slang or colloquial make up a major part of American communication in movies, television, radio, newspapers, magazines, and informal spoken conversation.

Localized fad words usually have a short life, but other kinds of slang expressions may spread and last for a long time. The farther they spread, the longer they will last. If they last long enough, they may become so well known that, unavoidably, they become standard American English. Most such expressions simply join an enormous pool of similar expressions, and they are used until they are displaced by newer terms. At some point the old ones are put on hold until they are forgotten by everyone or revived by a new generation. Many expressions that hang around for decades will pop up again and again in novels and movies, or in sporadic use in the speech of the older generation.

For more than two hundred years the jargon of criminals has been a major source of everyday slang words. Alcohol, drugs, and crime have been firmly fixed in the public consciousness since the time of U.S. prohibition. The entertainment value of crime and law enforcement has brought a constant stream of criminal slang into novels, movies, radio, and television over the last half century. This dictionary contains many of the expressions from these areas that have been used over the years. Even more remain hidden behind closed doors. Matters of social taboo have also provided many slang expressions. Although, strictly speaking, taboo words are not slang, the major taboo words have been included in this dictionary. Young people are responsible for a high proportion of the fad expressions and collegiate wordplay found here. Clever or insulting nicknames for types of people are the major linguistic product of this subgroup.

Whereas many of the entries are humorous or clever, others simply represent the everyday turns of phrase common to informal U.S. speech. Where possible, the examples are given in natural slangy language, even if it is ungrammatical or too informal for formal writing. The examples are to be taken as representative of slang usage, not of standard English usage.

The grammar and syntax of the use of each expression are best determined from the examples that accompany each entry. The notion of "part-of-speech" is relevant to the function of individual words. The words within the clauses and phrases that are entries in the **Dictionary** can be given part-of-speech labels, but it is the grammar and syntax of the entire phrase that is important. Each expression—as well as each particular sense of an expression—in the **Dictionary** is assigned a "function code" that serves to indicate the functional potential of the entry expression. These codes represent function independently from form. That is, expressions that function the same get the same label. For instance, nouns, noun compounds, noun phrases, and noun clauses are all marked *n.* for "nominal." The codes are described and illustrated in the section "How to Use This Dictionary."

Unlike standard English, few slang or colloquial expressions are standardized in spelling or punctuation. Standard dictionaries differ considerably as to whether a standard English compound is printed as one word, two words, or a hyphenated word. The spelling of slang entries is even more variable. This dictionary usually represents slang expressions in the form in which they were found in print, except for the following. Words made up of initials that are pronounced as one word—an acronym—are spelled without periods, e.g., "AWOL." Words that are really one or more letter names, e.g., "A.W.O.L.," have a period after each letter. Rhyming compounds, such as "fat-cat, funny-money," are hyphenated.

The entries come from many sources. Many have been collected and submitted by students and other individuals. Much of the latest material has come directly from television and a lesser amount from contemporary radio. Standard reference works have been used to verify the meanings and spellings of older material. A surprising amount of old material has been verified in reruns of old movies. Many attestations have come from contemporary journalism, especially human interest and Sunday supplement material. Few of the examples are verbatim quotes of the original. Some are concocted, and many more have been edited to exemplify an expression's meaning more concisely than the original quote. The examples exist to illustrate meaning, not to prove the earliest date of print or broadcast dissemination.

# HOW TO USE THIS DICTIONARY

**1.** Entries are alphabetized according to an absolute alphabetical order that ignores all punctuation, spaces, and hyphens.

**2.** The first step in finding an expression is to try looking it up in the **Dictionary**. Entries that consist of two or more words are entered in their normal order, such as **chill someone's action**. Phrases are never inverted or reordered like **action, chill someone's** or **twitter, in a**.

**3.** If you do not find the expression you want, or if you cannot decide on the exact form of the expression, look up any major word in the expression in the Phrase-Finder Index, which begins on page 451. There you will find all the multiword expressions that contain the word you have looked up. Once you have the expression you want, look it up in the **Dictionary**.

**4.** Entry expressions appear in **boldface type**. When words or expressions that are not entries in this **Dictionary** are cited, they appear in *italics*. Function codes [see 9 below] and examples appear in *italics*.

**5.** A main entry may have one or more alternative forms. The alternatives are printed in **boldface type** and are preceded by "AND." Alternative forms containing commas are separated by semicolons. Other alternative forms are separated by commas. For example:

> **spondulicks** AND **spondulix, spondulics** [spɑn'dulɪks]
> *n.* money. □ *How much spondulicks will this set me back?* □ *I don't have enough spondulix to swing the deal.*

**6.** Definitions are in roman type. Alternative or closely related definitions are separated by semicolons. For example:

> **take a flyer** *tr.* to leave town; to depart. □ *Things got a little rough, and Marty decided to take a flyer.* □ *Bruno took a flyer when he heard about the raid.*

**7.** Some definitions contain restrictive comments in parentheses that help to clarify the definition. These comments limit the context in which the expression can be used. For example:

> **blindside** *tr.* (for someone or something) to surprise someone, as if sneaking up on the blind side of a one-eyed person (or animal). □ *The new tax law blindsided about half the population.* □ *The mugger came up and blindsided her with a blow to the head before she knew what had happened.*

**8.** A definition may be followed by comments in parentheses. These comments give additional information about the expression, including any cautions, notes on origins, or indications of cross-referencing. Each numbered sense can have its own comments. For example:

> **Stay tuned. 1.** *sent.* "Stay tuned in to this radio or television station." (A formula uttered before a commercial.) □ *I'll be right back after these announcements. Stay tuned.* □ *Stay tuned. Back in a minute.* **2.** *sent.* "Continue to pay attention to this matter."; "Watch for further developments." (From sense 1.) □ *Things are developing rapidly in this*

*area. Stay tuned.* □ *Stay tuned. Pending legislation could change all this.*

**9.** Every expression is followed by a function code that indicates the grammatical or syntactic function of the expression. These codes are in *italics*. The function codes provide a way of determining the grammatical or syntactic function of a particular expression as it occurs in its examples. Expressions functioning as nominals (nouns, noun phrases, etc.) are marked *n.* Expressions serving to modify, restrict, or qualify (adjectives, adjectives phrases, adverbs, adverb phrases, etc.) are marked *mod.* Expressions that are transitive verbs or transitive verb phrases (a transitive verb, its auxiliaries, object(s), and modifiers) are marked *tr.* Expressions that are intransitive verbs or intransitive verb phrases (an intransitive verb, its auxiliaries, and modifiers) are marked *in.* Other abbreviations are explained in the section titled "Terms and Symbols." For example:

> **ace 1.** *mod.* (of persons) best; top-rated. □ *She is an ace reporter with the newspaper.* □ *Frank is an ace swimmer.* **2.** *n.* one dollar. □ *Give me an ace. I have to get some telephone change.* □ *It only costs an ace. Buy two.* **3.** *tr.* to pass a test easily, with an A grade. (Compare to *ace out*.) □ *Man, I really aced that test.* □ *I knew I wouldn't ace it, but I never thought I'd flunk it!*

**10.** Some expressions that are modifiers (marked *mod.*) can occur before or after the things they modify. Other modifiers can occur both before and after the things they modify. The distribution of modifiers is illustrated in the examples. For example:

> **back-to-back** *mod.* in a line; in a series. □ *I can't take two days like this one back-to-back.* □ *I schedule all my appointments back-to-back to save time.* □ *These back-to-back appointments are killing me.*

**11.** Many expressions have more than one major sense or meaning. These meanings are numbered with boldface numerals. For example:

> **sting 1.** *tr.* to cheat or swindle someone; to overcharge someone. □ *That street merchant stung me, but good.* □ *They are likely to sting you in any of those hockshops.* **2.** *n.* a well-planned scheme to entrap criminals. □ *The sting came off without a hitch.* □ *It was a well-planned sting and shouldn't have failed.* **3.** *tr.* to entrap and arrest someone. □ *The feebies stung the whole gang at once.* □ *"We've been stung!" they hollered.*

**12.** Sometimes a numbered sense will have an alternative form that does not apply to the other senses. In such cases the AND and the alternative forms follow the numeral. For example:

> **birdbrain 1.** *n.* a stupid-acting person. □ *You silly birdbrain. Stop it!* □ *I'm such a birdbrain. I forgot my driver's license, officer.* **2.** AND **birdbrained**

*mod.* stupid. □ *I've never heard such a birdbrain idea in my life.* □ *Look, you birdbrained idiot, you are dead wrong!*

**13.** Some entries are followed by an asterisk (*), which indicates caution in their use. Of course, many of the entries may seem offensive or insulting because that is the nature of much slang. These cautions are usually based on social taboos or the avoidance of specific topics. For example:

> **scare the hell out of someone*** *tr.* to frighten someone badly. (Caution with *hell*.) □ *These figures scare the hell out of me.* □ *The door blew shut and scared the hell out of me.*

**14.** Where there are numbered senses in an entry and only some of the senses need caution, the asterisk is placed after the number of the sense requiring caution, as well as after the entry expression. For example:

> **butt*** [bət] **1.*** *n.* the buttocks. (Caution with *butt*.) □ *She fell right on her butt.* □ *The doctor gave her a shot in the butt.* **2.** *n.* a cigarette butt. □ *Whose butts are those in the car ashtray?* □ *Don't leave your butts in the houseplants!* **3.** *n.* a cigarette of any kind. □ *You got a butt I can bum?* □ *What kind of butt is that, anyway?*

**15.** Entries that contain unfamiliar words and entries whose spelling is misleading have an indication of pronunciation in IPA symbols. See the symbols and their values in the "Pronunciation Guide."

Pronunciation may be for the entire expression...

> **triple whammy** ['trɪpl̩'ʍæmi]

... or only part of it:

> **beer and skittles** [ . . . 'skɪdl̩z]

Alternative pronunciations are separated by OR:

> **anti** ['ænti OR 'æntɑɪ]

Pronunciations coordinated with alternative entry forms are separated by AND:

> **legal-beagle** AND **legal-eagle** ['ligl̩'bigl̩] AND ['ligl̩'igl̩].

**16.** In some entries comments direct the user to other entries for additional information through the use of the terms "compare to," "see," or "see also." The expressions mentioned are in *slanted sans serif type*. For example:

> **B-ball** *n.* basketball; a basketball. (See also *hoops.* Compare to *V-ball*.) □ *Let's go play some B-ball.* □ *Toss me the B-ball, huh?*

**17.** In some instances an expression that is an entry in the **Dictionary** is used to define another word. Such expressions are in *slanted sans serif type*. For example:

> **bear trap** *n.* a hidden speed trap that was set by a *bear.* (Citizens band radio.) □ *That whole town is a glorified bear trap.* □ *I got caught in a bear trap.*

**18.** When additional forms of an expression are to be found at another entry, a comment beginning with "More at . . . " is found at the end of the entry. For example:

> **bamboozle** [bæm'buzl] *tr.* to deceive someone; to confuse someone. □ *Don't try to bamboozle me! I know what I want!* □ *The crooks bamboozled the old man out of his life savings.* (More at *bamboozled.*)

**19.** If an entry has a grammatical structure that requires a nominal to serve as a subject or object, the nominal is represented by **someone** for human nominals or **something** for nonhuman nominals. When both human and nonhuman nominals are possible, **someone or something** is used. For example:

> **saddled with someone or something** *mod.* burdened with someone or something. □ *I've been saddled with the children all day. Let's go out tonight.* □ *I don't want to be saddled with your work.*

**20.** Sometimes the numbered senses refer to only people or things, but not both. In such cases the numeral is followed by "[with *someone*]" or "[with *something*]." For example:

> **lay someone or something out** AND **lay out someone or something** **1.** *tr.* [with *someone*] to scold someone severely. □ *Don't lay me out! I didn't do it!* □ *She really laid him out but good. What did he do, rob a bank?* (More at *laid out.*) **2.** *tr.* [with *someone*] to knock someone down with a punch. □ *The boxer laid out his opponent with a blow to the head.* □ *I can't wait to get into that ring and lay the guy out.* **3.** *tr.* [with *something*] to spend some amount of money. □ *I can't lay out that kind of money every day!* □ *She laid out about $24,000 for that beemer.*

**21.** In some entries the numbered senses differ from the entry expression in punctuation. These differences are noted in a comment. For instance:

Verbal entry expression with nominal subsenses:

> **blow up** **1.** *in.* to burst into anger. □ *I just knew you'd blow up.* □ *So she blew up. Why should that affect you so much?* **2.** *n.* an angry outburst; a fight. (Usually **blowup**.) □ *After the third blowup, she left him.* □ *One blowup after another. Yuck!* **3.** *n.* an enlarged version of a photograph, map, chart, etc. (Usually **blowup**.) □ *Here's a blowup of the scene of the crime.* □ *Kelly sent a blowup of their wedding picture to all her relatives.* **4.** *n.* the ruination of something; the collapse of something. (Usually **blowup**.) □ *The blowup in the financial world has ruined my chances for early retirement.* □ *After the blowup, they called one another to compare notes.*

Nominal entry expression with a subsense that is an exclamation:

> **big deal**   **1.** *n.* something really important. □ *Don't make such a big deal out of it!* □ *This isn't a big deal as I see it.* **2.** *exclam.* "So what!"; "What does it matter?" (Usually **Big deal!**) □ *So he snores! Big deal! Snore back!* □ *She says to me, "Your socks don't match." And I say back, "Big deal!"*

**22.** In an entry phrase, parentheses can be used to collapse two or three semantically related phrases into one. The phrase **waffle (around)** stands for **waffle** and **waffle around**. The phrase **(baby) boomer** stands for **boomer** and **baby boomer**. The phrase **come clean (with someone) (about something)** stands for **come clean, come clean with someone, come clean about something,** and **come clean with someone about something.**

# TERMS AND SYMBOLS

* (asterisk) indicates caution. Its use is explained in items 13 and 14 in the section "How to Use This Dictionary."

□ marks the beginning of an example.

**acronym** a set of initials pronounced as a single word, like *UNESCO*.

**advertising** used in advertisements or marketing jargon.

**Amerindian** related to American Indian languages or cultures.

AND indicates an alternative element, either an alternative entry form or an alternative pronunciation. See items 5, 12, and 15 in the "How to Use This Dictionary" section.

**baby talk** used by infants or children, or more typically by adults when talking to infants or children.

**black** typically used by or originated by black Americans.

**blend** made up of sounds from two other words, like *smoke* + *fog* = *smog*.

**California** originating among the young people of California, especially the Valley Girls.

**catch phrase** an expression that is meant to catch attention because of its cleverness or aptness.

**collegiate** typically heard on college campuses.

**combining form** a form of a word used only in combination with another word.

**deliberate spoonerism** a deliberate interchanging of initial consonants in a pair of words, such as "queer old dean" for "dear old queen."

**drugs** having to do with illegal drugs, and their sale and use.

**euphemistic** relatively refined and having no negative connotations.

*exclam.* exclamation.

**eye-dialect** a type of respelling of a word so that it appears to have been spoken with a regional accent, as with "sez" for "says."

**financial markets** having to do with the stock markets, the bond markets, or the sale of other financial instruments.

**folksy** in the manner of country people; rustic and quaint.

**function code** an indication of the grammatical or syntactic potential of a particular sense of an expression. See item 9 in the "How to Use This Dictionary" section and *exclam., in., interj., interrog., mod., n., phr., prep., pro., sent.,* and *tr.* in this section.

**in.** intransitive. Expressions that are intransitive verbs or intransitive verb phrases (an intransitive verb, its auxiliaries, and modifiers) are marked *in.*

**interj.** interjection.

**interrog.** interrogative.

**jargon** the specialized terminology of an occupation; shoptalk.

**journalistic** as used in popular journalism—newspapers and magazines.

**juvenile** as might be said by a child.

**mod.** modifier. Expressions serving to modify, restrict, or qualify (adjectives, adjective phrases, adverbs, adverb phrases, etc.) are marked *mod.*

**n.** nominal. Expressions functioning as nominals (nouns, noun phrases, etc.) are marked *n.*

**onomatopoetic** having to do with a word whose sound suggests the meaning of the word.

**phr.** phrase.

**Pig Latin** a form of wordplay where the second part of a word is placed before the initial part, which then ends in "ay," as with "unkjay" for "junk."

**play on** referring to wordplay that is based on a particular expression. For instance, "eagle-freak" is a play on "eco freak."

**prep.** preposition.

**pro.** pronoun.

**prohibition** indicates an expression that came into use during the U.S. prohibition of alcohol.

**see** Go to the entry indicated.

**see also** Find additional information at the entry indicated.

**sent.** sentence.

**standard English** widely known English, not usually considered slang or colloquial.

**streets** originating in the streets of urban America.

**substandard** not recognized as standard or proper English.

**taboo** indicates an expression that is regarded as out of place in public use.

**term of address** an expression that can be used to address someone directly.

**tr.** transitive. Expressions that are transitive verbs or transitive verb phrases (a transitive verb and its auxiliaries, object(s), and modifiers) are marked *tr.*

**underworld** from criminal speech or law enforcement.

**verbal weapon** an expression that is typically used to insult or malign someone.

**Western** speech typical of Western movies or other stereotypes of the Old West.

# PRONUNCIATION GUIDE

Some expressions in the **Dictionary** are followed by a phonetic transcription in IPA symbols. These expressions include words whose pronunciation is not predictable from their spellings, difficult or unfamiliar words, and words where the stress placement is contrastive or unique. The style of pronunciation reflected here is informal and tends to fit the register in which the expression would normally be used. A [d] is used for the alveolar flap typical in American pronunciations such as [wɑdɚ] "water" and [əˈnɑɪəledəd] "annihilated." The transcriptions distinguish between [ɑ] and [ɔ] and between [w] and [ʍ] even though not all Americans do so. In strict IPA fashion, [j] rather than the [y] substitute, is used for the initial sound in "yellow." The most prominent syllable in a multisyllabic word is *preceded* by a [ˈ].

The use of AND or OR in a phonetic transcription echoes the use of AND or OR in the preceding entry phrase. The use of ellipsis ( . . . ) in a transcription indicates that easy-to-pronounce words have been omitted. Parentheses used in a transcription either correspond to parentheses in the preceding entry phrase or indicate optional elements in the transcription. For instance, in [ˈɑrtsi ˈkræf(t)si] "artsy-craftsy," the "t" may or may not be pronounced.

The following chart shows the American English values for each of the IPA symbols used in the phonetic transcriptions. To use the chart, first find the large phonetic symbol whose value you want to determine. The three English words to the right of the symbol contain examples of the sound for which the phonetic symbol stands. The letters in boldface type indicate where the sound in question is found in the English word.

| | | | | | | | |
|---|---|---|---|---|---|---|---|
| [ɑ] | stop<br>top | [ɚ] | bird<br>turtle | [n] | new<br>funny | [tʃ] | cheese<br>pitcher |
| [æ] | sat<br>track | [f] | feel<br>if | [n̩] | button<br>kitten | [θ] | thin<br>faith |
| [ɑʊ] | cow<br>now | [g] | get<br>frog | [ŋ] | bring<br>thing | [u] | food<br>blue |
| [ɑɪ] | bite<br>my | [h] | hat<br>who | [o] | coat<br>wrote | [ʊ] | put<br>look |
| [b] | beet<br>bubble | [i] | feet<br>leak | [ɔɪ] | spoil<br>boy | [v] | save<br>van |
| [d] | dead<br>body | [ɪ] | bit<br>hiss | [ɔ] | caught<br>yawn | [w] | well<br>wind |
| [ð] | that<br>those | [j] | yellow<br>you | [p] | tip<br>pat | [ʌ] | wheel<br>while |
| [dʒ] | jail<br>judge | [k] | can<br>keep | [r] | rat<br>berry | [z] | fuzzy<br>zoo |
| [e] | date<br>sail | [l] | lawn<br>yellow | [s] | sun<br>fast | [ʒ] | pleasure<br>treasure |
| [ɛ] | get<br>set | [l̩] | bottle<br>puddle | [ʃ] | fish<br>sure | ['] | 'water<br>ho'tel |
| [ə] | but<br>nut | [m] | family<br>slam | [t] | top<br>pot | | |

# A

**A. 1.** *n.* *acid*, the drug *L.S.D.* (Drugs.) □ *Max went on a 4-hour trip with A.* □ *A. is just as illegal as any other drug.* **2.** *n.* amphetamines in liquid or pill form. (Drugs.) □ *Fred is shooting A. now, and gets half out of his mind.* □ *He is almost burnt out on A.*

**A-1** AND **A number 1** ['e 'wən AND 'e 'nəmbɚ 'wən] *mod.* of the highest rating. □ *This steak is really A-1!* □ *I would like to get an A number 1 secretary for a change.*

**abbreviated piece of nothing** *n.* an insignificant person or thing. □ *Tell that abbreviated piece of nothing to get his tail over here, but fast.* □ *Why don't you drive your abbreviated piece of nothing over to the service station and have a muffler put on?*

**able to cut something** *phr.* able to manage or execute something. (Often negative.) □ *He's not able to cut his responsibilities like we thought.* □ *We thought he could cut it.* □ *Do you think you're able to cut it?*

**abortion** [ə'borʃn] *n.* a travesty; a mockery. □ *This isn't a drama! It's an abortion!* □ *Move your abortion of an automobile out of my driveway!*

**above board** See *open and above board.*

**abs** [æbz] *n.* the abdominal muscles. (Bodybuilding.) □ *Look at the abs on that guy. Like a crossword puzzle.* □ *I do situps to harden my abs.*

**abso-bloody-lutely** ['æbsoblədi'lutli] *mod.* absolutely; emphatically. □ *Do I like pizza? Abso-bloody-lutely!* □ *We are abso-bloody-lutely sick to death of your wishy-washy attitude.*

**absotively (posilutely)** ['æbsə'tɪvli 'pazə'lutli] *mod.* absolutely; decidedly. □ *I will be there at ten, absotively posilutely.* □ *I am absotively exhausted!*

**Acapulco (gold)** *n.* a potent, brownish-gold marijuana from Mexico. (Drugs.) □ *John just sat there taking hits off his pipe full of Acapulco.* □ *Acapulco gold used to be the best.*

**accidentally-on-purpose** *mod.* deliberate, but meant to look like an accident. □ *Then I accidentally-on-purpose spilled water on him.* □ *I knew it was done accidentally-on-purpose. That kind of thing doesn't just happen.*

**A.C.-D.C.** AND **A.C./D.C.** *mod.* bisexual. □ *I didn't realize at first that we were in an A.C.-D.C. bar!* □ *Clare said Tom is A.C./D.C., but I don't believe it.*

**ace 1.** *mod.* (of persons) best; top-rated. □ *She is an ace reporter with the newspaper.* □ *Frank is an ace swimmer.* **2.** *n.* one dollar. □ *Give me an ace. I have to get some telephone change.* □ *It only costs an ace. Buy two.* **3.** *tr.* to pass a test easily, with an A grade. (Compare to *ace out.*) □ *Man, I really aced that test.* □ *I knew I wouldn't ace it, but I never thought I'd flunk it!* **4.** *n.* a nickname for a foolish and ineffectual person. (Sarcastic. Usually a term of address.) □ *Hey, ace, hand me that monkey wrench—if you know what one is.* □ *Look, ace, you can't expect to fix an engine without getting dirty.* **5.** *n.* a marijuana cigarette; a single marijuana cigarette. (Drugs.) □ *John just stood there with an ace dangling from his lower lip.* □ *That nut wants two bucks for an ace!* **6.** *n.* a capsule or pill of a drug. (Drugs. Black.) □ *How about you loan me a couple of aces?* □ *How much does that dude charge* *for an ace?* **7.** *tr.* to surpass someone or something; to beat someone or something; to *ace someone out.* □ *The Japanese firm aced the Americans by getting the device onto the shelves first.* □ *Fred aced Tom in the contest for the best beard.*

**aced** [est] **1.** *mod.* outmaneuvered; outscored. □ *Rebecca really got aced in the track meet.* □ *"You are aced, sucker!" shouted Rebecca as she passed Martha in the 100-yard sprint.* **2.** *mod.* alcohol intoxicated. □ *How can anybody be so aced on three beers?* □ *I've never seen anybody that aced in my life.*

**ace in the hole** *n.* something important held in reserve. □ *The twenty-dollar bill I keep in my shoe is my ace in the hole.* □ *Mary's beautiful singing voice was her ace in the hole in case everything else failed.*

**ace in (to something)** *in.* to happen onto something good; to manage to get into something. □ *I hope I can ace into the afternoon physics class.* □ *I don't know how I aced in. I guess I was just lucky.*

**ace out** *in.* to be fortunate or lucky. □ *I really aced out on that test in English.* □ *Freddy aced out at the dentist's office with only one cavity.*

**ace someone out** AND **ace out someone** *tr.* to maneuver someone out; to win out over someone. (See also *ace.*) □ *Martha aced out Rebecca to win the first-place trophy.* □ *I plan to ace you out in the first lap.* (More at *aced.*)

**acid** *n.* *L.S.D.*, lysergic acid diethylamide. (Drugs.) □ *Acid and pot! That's all you think about.* □ *Freddy got hold of some bad acid and freaked out.*

**acid funk** ['æsɪd 'fəŋk] *n.* a depression following the use of *L.S.D.* (Drugs.) □ *Freddy was in his acid funk for at least a week.* □ *This is no acid funk. I'm cracking up over a girl.*

**acidhead** *n.* someone who uses *L.S.D.* regularly and is frequently under its influence. (Drugs. See also *A-head.*) □ *None of those acidheads can hold a steady job.* □ *Sometimes acidheads look real happy.*

**(acid) mung** ['æsɪd 'məŋ] *n.* an uncomfortable oily feeling after taking *L.S.D.*

(Drugs. See *mung.*) □ *I don't mind the flashbacks. It's that old mung that gets me down.* □ *Yeah, there's nothing worse than acid mung.*

**acid rock** *n.* a style of music associated with *L.S.D.* and having lyrics that relate to *L.S.D.* use. □ *Isn't acid rock out of style?* □ *The name is, but the old acid rock just evolved a little into stuff like heavy metal.*

**acid test** **1.** *n.* a very thorough test. (From a test for true gold using acid.) □ *We put your invention through the acid test, and—I am extremely sorry to tell you—it failed miserably.* □ *I'll take this home to my kids and let them give it the acid test. If it survives them, it's a winner.* **2.** *n.* a mass introduction to the use of *L.S.D.* (Drugs. This is mostly a pun on the first sense.) □ *One time they put L.S.D. into the punch so that everyone would drink some without knowing it. If they didn't freak out, they had passed the acid test.* □ *Fred is throwing a big acid test for everybody over in the park at midnight. Wanna go?*

**action** **1.** *n.* excitement; activity in general; whatever is happening. □ *This place is dull. I want some action.* □ *How do I find out where the action is in this town?* **2.** *n.* a share of something; a share of the winnings or of the booty. (See *piece of the action.*) □ *I did my share of the work, and I want my share of the action.* □ *Just what did you do to earn any of the action?* **3.** *n.* sex; copulation. □ *Paul is over at Martha's house looking for some action.* □ *All those guys play around with girls just trying for a little action.* **4.** *n.* illegal activity; commerce in drugs; acts of crime. (Underworld.) □ *You want a fast buck, you get in on that action over on 4th Street.* □ *Things have been a little slow here, but there's some action on the East Coast.*

**activated** *mod.* tipsy; alcohol intoxicated. □ *All four of them went out and got a little activated.* □ *Will this stuff get me seriously activated?*

**active citizen** *n.* a louse. (Usually plural. Jocular.) □ *Somebody in this place is carrying around some—ah—active citizens.* □ *What can I do to get rid of these active citizens?*

**Act your age!** *exclam.* "Act more grown up!" □ *Stop whining! Act your age!* □ *You're 27 years old, and you still sleep with a teddy bear? Act your age!*

**addict** ['ædɪkt] *n.* someone showing a marked preference for something or someone. (A combining form not related to drug addiction.) □ *Sam is a real opera addict. He just loves the stuff.* □ *My uncle is a mystery addict.*

**adios muchachos** [adi'os mu'tʃatʃos] *phr.* "the end"; "goodbye, everyone." (Spanish. See examples.) □ *If you step out in front of a car like that again, it's adios muchachos.* □ *I've got a gun aimed at your navel. If you move so much as one muscle, you can just say adios muchachos.*

**adobe dollar** [ə'dobi 'dalɚ] *n.* a Mexican peso. □ *How many of these adobe dollars does it take to buy a can of pop here?* □ *One greenback will get you about 2400 adobe dollars these days.*

**afraid not** *phr.* "sorry, but no." (A polite way of saying no.) □ *Lend you $400? No, I'm afraid not.* □ BILL: *How about coming to my party?* TOM: *Afraid not. I'm tied up all weekend.*

**African black** *n.* a variety of marijuana from Africa. (Drugs.) □ *Where can I get some of that African black that everybody seems to be lighting up these days?* □ *There is no such pot as African black. It's all from California.*

**Afro** ['æfro] **1.** *n.* an American black. □ *Two Afros came in and bought a case of champagne.* □ *The earliest Afros to settle the islands spoke a mixture of African languages.* **2.** *n.* a hairstyle worn mostly by blacks of both sexes. □ *Some gal in a big fluffy Afro came in and left this note for you.* □ *I thought Afros were out this season.*

**After you.** *phr.* "Please go ahead of me." (A polite formula.) □ *As John opened the door, he turned to Paul and said, "After you."* □ *"No, no," said Paul, stepping back, "after you."*

**age out** *in.* to "outgrow" criminal and antisocial activities at about age 40. □ *Most of the young guys in the county slammer will age out and straighten up. The rest will end up in the state pen.* □ *Some of them know they will age out*

and are squeezing in all the crime they can manage before that time.

**ages** ['edʒəz] *n.* a very long time. □ *I haven't seen you in ages!* □ *That ridiculous ceremony seemed to go on for ages.* □ *I've been here just ages! I want to go home!*

**aggie** ['ægi] **1.** *mod.* agricultural. □ *She spent a year at some aggie college, but didn't like it.* □ *Her aggie interests faded fast.* **2.** *n.* a student of an agricultural (college) training program. (Specifically, Texas A & M.) □ *More and more aggies are going back for their M.B.A.s.* □ *What kind of a job can an aggie get these days?* **3.** *n.* an agricultural futures contract. (Financial markets. Usually plural.) □ *The March aggies are looking good right now.* □ *Let's take a look at the aggies and see how the bellies are doing.* **4.** *n.* an agate marble or a glass imitation of one. □ *I found the old aggies I played with when I was a kid.* □ *Somebody stole my prize aggie!*

**agin'** [ə'gɪn] **1.** *prep.* against. (Folksy.) □ *All these votes are agin' your city bred ideas.* □ *I'm agin' them and you.* **2.** *n.* someone (or something) who is against something. (Folksy.) □ *Seven people are for it, but the agin's win.* □ *So you're the agin' who keeps voting against me.*

**agonies** ['ægəniz] *n.* the extreme discomforts of drug withdrawal. (Drugs.) □ *Max is at home suffering from the agonies.* □ *The agonies start with sneezing and yawning.*

**agree to disagree** *phr.* to agree to discuss something, but retain one's opinions. □ *We have accomplished nothing except that we agree to disagree.* □ *The two political parties agreed to disagree in 1971, and that was the last agreeable thing either one of them did.*

**A-head 1.** *n.* an *acidhead*, a user of the drug *L.S.D.* □ *There was a bunch of A-heads in the alley, singing and crying.* □ *A real A-head can be a strange person.* **2.** *n.* a habitual user of amphetamines or other stimulants. (Drugs.) □ *Don't try to tell me I can become an A-head from taking pep pills!* □ *Most A-heads use speed.*

**ahead of the game** *mod.* being early; having an advantage in a competitive situation; having done more than necessary. (Especially with *get* or *keep*.) □ *Without a car telephone, I find it hard to get ahead of the game.* □ *If being ahead of the game is important to you and to your business, lease a mobile telephone from us.*

**aim for the sky** AND **reach for the sky, shoot for the sky** *in.* to aspire to something; to set one's goals high. (See a different sense at *reach for the sky*.) □ *Shoot for the sky, son. Don't settle for second best.* □ *Set your sights high. Aim for the sky!*

**ain't\*** [ent] *phr.* "is not"; "am not"; "are not"; etc. (Viewed as substandard. Frequent in slang.) □ *And that ain't hay!* □ *You ain't kiddin'.*

**ain't no good nohow\*** *phr.* "is not good, anyway." (Folksy. Caution with *ain't*.) □ *It doesn't matter if I wreck my car. It ain't no good nohow.* □ *My brother got put in jail, but he ain't no good nohow.*

**air** *n.* air conditioning. (Found in house and car advertising.) □ *I told them I wanted a four-door with air, but they didn't have one.* □ *Our house doesn't have air, and summers can be very unpleasant.*

**air-bags** *n.* the lungs. □ *Fill those air-bags with good Colorado air!* □ *I've had a cold or something in my air-bags for about three days now.*

**air ball** *n.* a basketball throw that misses everything, especially the goal. □ *Old Fred has become a master with the air ball. The net will never get worn out.* □ *Another air ball for Fred Wilson. That's his fourth tonight.*

**airbrain** See *airhead*.

**air guitar** *n.* an imaginary guitar, played along with real music. □ *Dave stood near the window while his roommate played air guitar in front of the mirror.* □ *Jed, who sees himself as some sort of rock star, plays air guitar when he's happy or sad.*

**airhead** AND **airbrain** *n.* a stupid person. (Someone with air where there should be brains.) □ *What is that loony airhead doing there on the roof?* □ *Some airbrain put mustard in the ketchup squeezer.*

**air hose** *n.* invisible socks; no socks. □ *All these kids run around campus in air hose. You'd think they'd get blisters.* □ *How do you like my new air hose? One size fits all.*

**air one's belly** *tr.* to empty one's stomach; to vomit. □ *What was in that hamburger? I think I've got to air my belly.* □ *That must have been some party. I heard you airing your belly for most of the night, after you got home.*

**air one's dirty linen in public** AND **wash one's dirty linen in public** *tr.* to allow all one's private and personal business to be known to the public. □ *I don't want you to have to air your dirty linen in public.* □ *People just try to get sympathy by washing their dirty linen in public.*

**air one's pores** *tr.* to undress oneself; to become naked. □ *I'm fixing to air my pores and take a shower.* □ *Me and Wilbur, that's my brother, both fell in the creek and had to air our pores a while so our pants could dry out.*

**airplane 1.** *n.* a device used to hold the butt of a marijuana cigarette. (Drugs.) □ *Use your little airplane, or you'll burn your fingers.* □ *Walter thought the airplane would help him get higher. Stupid burnout!* **2.** *in.* to breathe in marijuana smoke through the nose. (Drugs.) □ *Max likes to airplane, but sometimes he burns his nose.* □ *What's the advantage of airplaning? It looks wasteful.*

**airy-fairy** ['eri'feri] *mod.* insubstantial; of wishful thinking. □ *Haven't you outgrown that kind of airy-fairy thinking yet?* □ *Her ideas are too airy-fairy.* □ *I don't care to hear any more of your airy-fairy ideas.*

**ak** AND **ok** [ɑk] *n.* October. (Financial markets: options and futures trading.) □ *The ak futures are looking worse by the hour.* □ *When the oks expire on Friday, we'll start looking at the dec index.*

**alchy** AND **alkie, alky** ['ælki] **1.** *n.* alcohol; an alcoholic beverage. □ *He showed up with a week's supply of alkie.* □ *The crooks stole most of the alchy from the bar at the club.* **2.** *n.* a drunkard. □ *You see alchy after alchy all up and down Maxwell Street.* □ *Some alkie came in and asked for a quarter.*

**Alibi Ike** [ˈæləbaɪ ˈaɪk] *n.* a nickname for someone who always has excuses or alibis for failures. (Also a rude term of address.) □ *Well, Alibi Ike, what's the excuse this time?* □ *Here comes Alibi Ike, late as usual. I wonder what caused it today.*

**Alice B. Toklas brownies** [...ˈtoklas...] *n.* a small square of chewy chocolate cake with marijuana baked in it. (Alice B. Toklas, the companion of Gertrude Stein, devised the recipe.) □ *They said they were serving Alice B. Toklas brownies, but I think the whole business is a joke.* □ *Aren't Alice B. Toklas brownies just an eccentric bit of nonsense?*

**alive and kicking** *mod.* well, healthy, and functioning. (Folksy.) □ JED: *How's it going, Gary?* GARY: *Oh, I'm alive and kicking.* □ *Is your uncle still alive and kicking?*

**alive and well** *mod.* well and functioning; sound and useful. □ *Is that idea of yours about putting in a window here still alive and well?* □ *Everybody in my family is alive and well, except Freddy, who has a little cold.*

**alkie** See *alchy.*

**alkied (up)** [ˈælkid...] *mod.* alcohol intoxicated. □ *That old bum looks completely alkied up.* □ *She spends a lot of time alkied.*

**alky** See *alchy.*

**all balled up** See *balled up.*

**all bets are off** *phr.* earlier predictions are no longer valid; earlier bets are cancelled. □ *I can't figure out what's going on at work. All bets are off on this Wilson contract.* □ *The stock market just crashed. When it comes to our net worth, all bets are off.*

**all by one's lonesome** *mod.* by oneself. (Folksy.) □ *She just sat there for hours all by her lonesome.* □ *I just can't spend New Year's Eve all by my lonesome.*

**all ears** *mod.* listening eagerly; eager to hear. □ *Keep talking. I'm all ears.* □ *The lecture was so fascinating that the audience was all ears for an hour and a half.*

**alley apple** 1. *n.* a piece of horse manure. (See *road apple.*) □ *The route of the parade was littered with alley apples after about twenty minutes.* □ *Harry is*

collecting alley apples for his garden. 2. *n.* a brick or stone found in the rubble of the streets. □ *"Drop it!" the cop called to the kid with an alley apple in his hand.* □ *Kelly kicked an alley apple so that it struck a garbage can with a metallic crash.*

**all-fired** *mod.* "hell-fired"; damned. (Folksy. Euphemistic.) □ *I'm all-fired mad at you!* □ *Don't get so all-fired snooty with me!*

**all get out** 1. *mod.* very much. (Folksy. Usually with *as.*) □ *I'm as tired as all get out!* □ *She was sick as all get out for a while.* 2. *n.* Hell. (Folksy. Euphemistic. Usually with *as.*) □ *I was as mad as all get out!* □ *He crashed into the room screaming at Clare like all get out!*

**all in** 1. *mod.* exhausted. □ *I'm just all in. I can't move a muscle.* □ *The whole gang was all in and spent the day relaxing and talking about the meaning of life and the price of chicken.* 2. *mod.* alcohol intoxicated. (Euphemistic.) □ *He looks—ah—all in. I think he's had enough to drink.* □ *I'm a bit all in after last night's party.*

**all-nighter** 1. *n.* something that lasts all night, like a party or study session. □ *After an all-nighter studying, I couldn't keep my eyes open for the test.* □ *Sam invited us to an all-nighter, but we're getting a little old for that kind of thing.* 2. *n.* a place of business which is open all night. □ *We stopped at an all-nighter for a cup of coffee.* □ *I worked in an all-nighter for a month. I just couldn't keep those hours though.* 3. *n.* a person who often stays up all night. □ *Fred is an all-nighter. He's not worth much in the mornings though.* □ *I'm no all-nighter. I need my beauty sleep, for sure.*

**all right** 1. *interj.* "yes"; "okay." □ *All right. I'll do it.* □ *All right. I'm coming.* 2. *mod.* for sure; for certain. □ *He's the one who said it, all right.* □ *I was there, all right.* 3. *mod.* okay. (Usually **all-right**. Slang when used before the noun.) □ *Wally is an all-right guy.* □ *I'm all right.* □ *We had an all-right time at your party.* 4. *exclam.* "That's good!"; "Keep it up!" (A general expression of approval, often cried out from the audience during a performance or at applause time. Usually **All right!** The *right* is drawn out and falling in pitch.) □ *After the last drum beat, the entire audience exploded into a roaring "All right!"* □ *"All right!" cried the crowd when they heard the announcement about the pay increase.*

**all schnozzled up** [...ʃnɑzl̩d...] *mod.* alcohol intoxicated. □ *She spends a lot of time all schnozzled up.* □ *I've never seen anybody all schnozzled up that bad before.*

**all-star 1.** *n.* a member of a specially chosen ball team selected from a wide geographical area, or the team itself. □ *She played with the state all-stars last year.* □ *She was an all-star two years in a row.* **2.** *mod.* having to do with a player, team, or game as described in sense 1. □ *Being on the all-star team was the best thing about this year.* □ *I got tickets to the all-star game.*

**All systems are go.** *sent.* "Everything is okay." (From rocketry.) □ *I hope everything is ready for tomorrow. Tell us when all systems are go.* □ *All systems are go. Let's get on the road before the traffic builds up.*

**all that jazz** *n.* all that stuff; all that nonsense. □ *I need some glue, paper, string, and all that jazz, to make a kite.* □ *She told me I was selfish, hateful, rude, ugly, and all that jazz.*

**all (that) meat and no potatoes** *phr.* said of a tremendously fat person. (A rude catch phrase.) □ *Look at that guy—all meat and no potatoes.* □ *All that meat and no potatoes. She should go on a diet.*

**all the way** *mod.* with everything on it, as with a hamburger. (See also *go all the way*.) □ *I'd like one double cheeseburger—all the way.* □ *Make mine all the way, too.*

**all the way live** *mod.* very exciting; excellent. (California.) □ *Man, this place is all the way live.* □ *Oh, Tiffany is just, like, all the way live!*

**all thumbs** *mod.* awkward and clumsy. □ *I can't do that kind of fine work. I'm all thumbs.* □ *I'm all thumbs when it comes to needlework.*

**all-time** *mod.* record; unique. □ *The lake is at an all-time high this year.* □

*The stock market broke an all-time high record every day this week.*

**all-time favorite 1.** *n.* someone or something popular over a long period of time. □ *This recording is an all-time favorite of mine.* □ *Shirley was an all-time favorite in our town.* **2.** *mod.* popular over a long period of time. □ *Frankie is my all-time favorite singer.* □ *Who is your all-time favorite pitcher?*

**all wet** *mod.* completely wrong. □ *Wrong again! You're really all wet.* □ *If you think I'm going to take that kind of talk from you, you're all wet.*

**almighty** *mod.* terrible; damnable. (Folksy.) □ *There is an almighty argument going on next door.* □ *I'm almighty tired, and I'm going to bed.*

**almighty dollar** *n.* the dollar viewed as a symbol of power or greed. □ *You don't care about anything but the almighty dollar.* □ *The world's economy seems to depend on an adequate supply of the almighty dollar.*

**alphabet soup** *n.* initialisms and acronyms in general. □ *The names of these government offices are just alphabet soup.* □ *Just look at the telephone book! You can't find anything because it's filled with alphabet soup.*

**also-ran** *n.* a secondary performer; a contestant who loses. □ *He's just an also-ran. He'll never go anywhere.* □ *John was an also-ran in the contest for governor.*

**ambulance chaser 1.** AND **chaser** *n.* a lawyer or entrepreneur who hurries to the scene of an accident to try to get the business of any injured persons. □ *The insurance companies are cracking down on ambulance chasers.* □ *Two minutes after the spectacular wreck, seven chasers with police radios showed up and began harassing the victims.* **2.** *n.* a derogatory term for any lawyer. (Also a rude term of address.) □ *That ambulance chaser is trying to charge me for reaching his office when I called a wrong number!* □ *Look here, you ambulance chaser, I can't afford your rates.*

**amies** See *amy*.

**amigo** [əˈmigo] *n.* a friend. (Spanish. Also a term of address.) □ *Me and my amigo want to rent a couple of horses.*

6

□ *Hey, amigo, let's go somewhere for a drink.*

**ammo** ['æmo] **1.** *n.* ammunition. □ *There they were, trapped in a foxhole with no ammo, enemy all over the place. What do you think happened?* □ *I don't know. They sent out for ammo, maybe?* **2.** *n.* information or evidence that can be used to support an argument or a charge. □ *I want to get some ammo on the mayor. I think he's a crook.* □ *Try to keep my traffic tickets a secret. The opposition will use them as ammo in the next election.*

**ammunition 1.** *n.* toilet tissue. □ *Could somebody help me! We're out of ammunition in here!* □ *The ammunition in Europe is better these days than it used to be.* **2.** *n.* liquor. (See *shot*.) □ *The cowboy walked in, downed a shot, and called for more ammunition.* □ *He's had about all the ammunition he can hold.*

**amped** [æmpt] *mod.* intoxicated with amphetamines. (Drugs. See *amps*.) □ *Hank got himself amped last night.* □ *Larry was amped for a long time after his three-day run.*

**amps** *n.* amphetamines. (Drugs. Compare to *damps*.) □ *I never do any drugs except maybe a few amps now and then, and the odd downer, and maybe a little grass on weekends, but nothing really hard.* □ *Paul is on a roller coaster of amps and damps.*

**amy** ['emi] **1.** AND **amyl** ['æml] *n.* amyl nitrite, a vasodilator drug that causes the blood vessels to expand when it is inhaled. (Drugs.) □ *He seems to like amy for some reason. He won't say what it is.* □ *They use amyl for kicks.* **2.** *n.* a capsule of Amytal™, a barbiturate. (Drugs. The plural is **amies**.) □ *She had a handful of amies in her purse when she was arrested.* □ *She has to take an amy or two to bring her down after an upper.*

**amyl** See the previous entry.

**anchor-clanker** *n.* a sailor. (Army.) □ *The bar was suddenly filled with anchor-clankers, and the army guys began looking for a way out.* □ *How can you anchor-clankers stand being cooped up on those cans?*

**ancient history** *n.* someone or something completely forgotten, especially past romances. (See also *history*.)□ *Bob? I never think about Bob anymore. He's ancient history.* □ *That business about joining the army is ancient history.*

**and change** *phr.* plus a few cents; plus a few hundredths. (Used in citing a price or other decimal figure to indicate an additional fraction of a full unit.) □ *This one only costs 10 bucks and change.* □ *The New York Stock Exchange was up seven points and change for the third broken record this week.*

**and everything** *phr.* "etc."; something said when someone runs out of words or is about to be interrupted. □ *And when I'm elected you can be sure that the farm situation, the budget deficit, the trade deficit, and everything will improve.* □ *Please bring your book, pencil, handkerchief, wallet, comb, keys, watch, and everything over here, and put them on the table so we can make a list.*

**And how!** *exclam.* "I agree!" □ *I am really excited you are here. And how!* □ BILL: *I am pleased you are here.* BOB: *Me, too! And how!*

**angel 1.** *n.* a secret financier. □ *Who was the angel for your new play?* □ *I was hoping for an angel to see this project through, but all the fat-cats seem to have disappeared.* **2.** *n.* cocaine. (Drugs.) □ *One gram of angel was found in the lining of the coat of the suspect.* □ *Do you mean angel or angel dust?* **3.** *n.* phencyclidine, *P.C.P.*, an animal tranquilizer. (Drugs.) □ *Now, this pill is what we call angel. It sort of numbs you, but it's out of this world.* □ *There is a new variety on the streets now. They call it angel.* **4.** *n.* a sweetheart. (Also a term of address.) □ *See my angel standing over there? Isn't he gorgeous?* □ *Okay, angel, let's get in the car.*

**angel dust** AND **angel hair, dust of angels** *n.* the common name for *P.C.P.* (Originally drugs.) □ *Angel dust is getting to be quite a problem in this town.* □ *I thought that angel hair and stuff like that was a problem of the sixties.*

**angel hair** See *angel dust*.

**angel puke** ['endʒl 'pjuk] *n.* phencyclidine, *P.C.P.* (Drugs. Compare to *an-*

gel dust.) □ *I don't care what you call it, I call it angel puke. That stuff is deadly.* □ *Mix a little angel puke with this grass, and you'll really have a treat.*

**angie** ['ændʒi] *n.* cocaine. (Drugs. See **angel**.) □ *I didn't know that angie was addictive.* □ *Wally was the last person you would think would be hooked on angie.*

**angle** **1.** *n.* selfish motive; ulterior motive. □ *Okay, Ted, I know you better than to think that you are doing this out of the kindness of your heart. What's your angle?* □ *I don't have any angle. I have reformed.* **2.** *n.* slant; bias; focus. □ *Let's try to get a good angle on this news story so the wire service will buy it from us.* □ *I think that by studying the Maya I will be able to develop a new angle on why they disappeared.*

**animal** *n.* a male who acts like a beast in terms of manners, cleanliness, or sexual aggressiveness. (Also a term of address.) □ *You are an animal!* □ *Stop picking your nose, animal.*

**ankle** **1.** *n.* an attractive woman or *girl.* (Typically with *some.*) □ *Now, there's some ankle I've never seen around here before.* □ *Do you get ankle like that around here all the time?* **2.** *in.* to walk away from one's employment; to leave. (Compare to *walk.*) □ *One more day like this, and I'm gonna ankle.* □ *I didn't fire her. I told her she could ankle if she wanted.*

**annihilated** [ə'naɪəledəd] *mod.* alcohol or drug intoxicated. □ *Drunk, hell. He was annihilated!* □ *Those three women became totally annihilated on a bottle of wine.*

**another mouth to feed** *n.* another person in the house, especially a new baby. □ *What's another mouth to feed? Come on, sit down and eat!* □ *That's all we need, another mouth to feed.*

**another peep (out of you)** *n.* another complaint, word, or sound from someone. (Usually in the negative.) □ *I don't want to hear another peep out of you!* □ *I've heard enough! Not another peep!*

**ante** ['ænti] **1.** *n.* an amount of money that must be contributed before playing certain card games such as poker. □ *What's the ante to join this game?* □

*That's a pretty high ante. Forget it!* **2.** *n.* the charge or cost. □ *What's the ante for a used 1985 four-door?* □ *The ante is marked on the sticker.*

**ante (something) up** AND **ante up something** *tr. & in.* to pay one's share (of something); to come up with the amount of money required. □ *Come on, ante up! Pay what you owe.* □ *Are you going to ante up your part, or do I have to ask some of the boys to help you?*

**anti** ['ænti OR 'æntaɪ] **1.** *n.* someone who is against someone or something. (See also *agin'.*) □ *She's an anti. Don't even ask her.* □ *All the antis are going to vote for it this time.* **2.** *mod.* against someone or something. (Sometimes with the force of a preposition.) □ *I'm not anti the proposal, I just have some questions.* □ *Four are in favor, and two are anti.*

**antifreeze** **1.** *n.* heroin. (Drugs.) □ *Max couldn't come out till he filled up on antifreeze.* □ *He can't get through one of these cold nights without antifreeze.* **2.** *n.* liquor; any legal or illegal alcohol. □ *With enough antifreeze, I can stand the cold.* □ *Here's some antifreeze to stop your teeth from chattering.*

**antifreezed** *mod.* alcohol intoxicated. □ *Man, I feel totally antifreezed.* □ *He appears to be frozen even though he's antifreezed.*

**antinuke** ['ænti'njuk OR 'ænti'nuk] *mod.* having to do with persons who are against nuclear energy and nuclear weapons. □ *Are you antinuke or not?* □ *The antinuke crowd is picketing the power company.* □ *Who is voting for the antinuke candidate?*

**antsy** ['æntsi] *mod.* nervous; restless. (See *have ants in one's pants.*) □ *You look a little antsy. What's wrong?* □ *Who is that antsy guy?* □ *She gets antsy before a test.*

**anymore** *mod.* nowadays. (Folksy.) □ *Do you still swim anymore?* □ *Anymore, kids tell us what to do.*

**any old how** *mod.* "just any way." (Folksy.) □ *What a mess! You can't just paint the wall any old how!* □ *Do it any old how—the best you can.*

**Anytime.** *interj.* "You are welcome."; "Happy to oblige." (Sometimes said in response to "Thank you.") □ MARY:

*Thanks for the ride.* PAUL: *Anytime. Think nothing of it.* □ TOM: *You've been a real friend, Sally. I can't thank you enough.* SALLY: *Anytime.*

**A-OK** ['e'o'ke] *mod.* in the best of condition. □ *I really feel A-OK.* □ *Show me the most A-OK canary you have.*

**A.P.B.** AND **APB** *n.* "all points bulletin"; a police alert sent out over a wide area, describing a wanted criminal. □ *They sent out an A.P.B. on the smuggler.* □ *We just got an APB on that Johnson character. Keep an eye out for him.*

**ape** *n.* a hoodlum or strong-arm man, especially if big and strong. (Underworld.) □ *Tell your ape to let me go!* □ *You take your apes and get out of here!*

**aped** [ept] *mod.* alcohol intoxicated. □ *I've never seen my brother so totally aped before.* □ *He comes home aped about once a month.*

**ape hangers** *n.* long steering handles on a bicycle or motorcycle. □ *Who is that guy riding the bike with ape hangers?* □ *Aren't ape hangers sort of dangerous?*

**apple 1.** *n.* a baseball. □ *Jim slammed the apple over the plate, but the ump called it a ball.* □ *Just when I raised my arm to throw to second, the damn apple slipped out of my hand and rolled down my arm. Now, explain that!* **2.** *n.* a capsule of Seconal™, a barbiturate. (Drugs. Seconal™ is red.) □ *No more apples! No more apples! I gotta have amps!* □ *Man, you got any apples you can spare a friend?*

**apple of someone's eye** *n.* an admired or desired—but not possessed—thing or person. (Always with *the.*) □ *Martha is the apple of Larry's eye, but she hardly knows he exists.* □ *That car in the show window is the apple of my eye.*

**apple-polisher** *n.* a flatterer. □ *Doesn't that wimpy apple-polisher know how stupid he looks?* □ *Everybody at the office seems to be an apple-polisher but me.*

**applesauce** *n.* nonsense. □ *Don't give me that applesauce. I know better.* □ *That's just applesauce!*

**apps** [æps] *n.* apparatus for taking drugs. (Drugs.) □ *Where's my apps! I need my apps now!* □ *Max keeps his apps in the closet under the blue towel.*

**arb** [ɑrb] *n.* an arbitrageur, a market speculator. (Financial markets.) □ *The arbs are at it again, buying up companies like hot cakes.* □ *I wanted to be an arb, but it takes about forty million to get in the door.*

**Arctic explorer** *n.* a cocaine user; a user of *snow.* (Drugs.) □ *Three Arctic explorers trudged up to the door of the crack house.* □ *The place was full of Arctic explorers trying to lose themselves in the snow.*

**Are you holding?** AND **Are you carrying?** *interrog.* "Do you have drugs for sale?" (Drugs.) □ *The nark asked Max if he was holding, and Max just stared at him.* □ *Paul said to Max, "Are you carrying?" Then Max reached in his pocket and pulled out a handful of peppermints.*

**Are you ready for this?** *interrog.* "Isn't this exciting? Shall I go on?" □ *You wouldn't believe who is about to lose house and car in a sheriff's sale. Are you ready for this?* □ *Did you see what Gary and Jill were doing? Are you ready for this?*

**ark** [ɑrk] *n.* an old car. □ *Why don't you get rid of that old ark and get something that's easier to park?* □ *This ark is the most comfortable car I've ever had. I'll drive it till it falls apart.*

**arm** *n.* a police officer. (Underworld. See also *long arm of the law.*) □ *What'll you do if the arms come in while you're sawing the bars of your cell?* □ *So this arm says to me, "Going to a fire?"*

**armpit** *n.* any undesirable place. (A nickname for an undesirable town or city.) □ *Who wants to spend a weekend in an armpit?* □ *The town should be called the armpit of the nation.*

**arm-twister** *n.* someone who uses strong persuasion. □ *I hate to seem like an arm-twister, but I really need your help on this project.* □ *My aunt works as an arm-twister, collecting overdue bills for the telephone company.*

**arm-twisting** *n.* powerful persuasion. □ *The boss is very good at arm-twisting.* □ *If nice talk won't work, try a little arm-twisting.*

**army brat** *n.* a child born to a parent in the army. (Such a child will live in many different places.) □ *I was an army brat and went to 7 different schools before I got out of high school.* □ *We army brats tend to stick together.*

**around the bend** AND **round the bend** **1.** *mod.* crazy; beyond sanity. □ *I think I'm going around the bend.* □ *She sounds like she's round the bend already.* **2.** *mod.* alcohol or drug intoxicated. □ *One more of those, and you'll be around the bend.* □ *From the look in her eye, I'd say she is completely round the bend now.*

**artillery** **1.** *n.* guns; grenades. (Underworld.) □ *Where does Max stash the artillery?* □ *All the artillery is locked in the trunk of the getaway car.* **2.** *n.* flatware; cutlery. □ *Who put out the artillery? I didn't get a fork.* □ *Go get your own artillery. This ain't the Ritz.* **3.** *n.* equipment used to inject drugs. (Drugs.) □ *Max kept his artillery on the top shelf of his closet.* □ *The junky got all her artillery ready for a fix.*

**artist** *n.* a combining form meaning "specialist." See *beat artist, booze artist, bullshit artist, burn artist, castor oil artist, con artist, flimflam artist, goof artist, hype artist, make-out artist, off artist, rip-off artist, takeoff artist.*

**artsy-craftsy** ['ɑrtsi 'kræf(t)si] *mod.* dabbling in arts and crafts; artistic. □ *Wally is sort of artsy-craftsy.* □ *Gary's an artsy-crafty kind of guy with lots of talent.* □ *The artsy-craftsy crowd held a show in the library parking lot last Sunday.*

**A.S.A.P.** AND **ASAP** *mod.* "as soon as possible." □ *Get this thing done ASAP!* □ *A.S.A.P or not, it will get done when it gets done, period!*

**ASCII** AND **asky** ['æski] *n.* "American Standard for Computer Information Interchange." (Computers. A particular alphabetic interpretation of computer bytes.) □ *This program produces a regular ASCII file.* □ *Fred knows what the asky code for "f" is.*

**ashes** *n.* cannabis. (Drugs.) □ *Lemme have a drag of your ashes, what do you say?* □ *How much for just a little pipe full of ashes, Max?*

**as is** *mod.* in its present condition; without guarantee. □ *I'm selling this as is.*

*Look it over carefully.* □ *If I take it as is, does that mean there is no guarantee?*

**asky** See *ASCII.*

**asleep at the switch** *mod.* inattentive to duty. (Not really asleep.) □ *Donald was asleep at the switch when the call came in.* □ *He sat there reading—asleep at the switch as usual.*

**asphalt jungle** *n.* the paved landscape of the city; the city viewed as a savage place. □ *I don't look forward to spending the rest of my days in an asphalt jungle.* □ *I want to go back to Kansas. I hate the asphalt jungle.*

**ass*** **1.*** *n.* the buttocks. (Caution with *ass.*) □ *Shut up, or I'll throw you out of here on your ass.* □ *Look at the fat ass on the goalie.* **2.*** *n.* a stupid or foolish person. (Caution with *ass.* Provocative.) □ *Don't be such an ass!* □ *Who's calling who an ass?*

**asshole*** **1.*** *n.* the anus. (Caution with *ass* and topic.) □ *He threatened to kick me in the asshole, or something like that, if I didn't leave at once.* □ *He had to tell the doctor about the pain in his asshole because he simply didn't know any other word for it.* **2.*** *n.* an obnoxious person. (Caution with *ass* and topic. Crude and provocative. Also a rude term of address.) □ *Shut up and get out, you asshole!* □ *Some days it seems like only the assholes got up, and everyone else stayed in bed.*

**astronomical** *mod.* extremely expensive; of any very high figure. □ *The prices here are astronomical!* □ *The market indexes have all reached astronomical heights for the second time.*

**at a snail's pace** AND **at a snail's gallop** *mod.* very slowly. □ *Things are moving along at a snail's pace here, but we'll finish on time—have no fear.* □ *Poor old Wally is creeping at a snail's gallop because his car has a flat tire.*

**at loose ends** *mod.* nervous and anxious; bored with nothing to do. □ *Tom usually works puzzles whenever he's at loose ends.* □ *I'm at loose ends on weekends.*

**at the market** *mod.* at the current market price. (Financial markets. An instruction given to a stockbroker.) □ *I put in an order for 200 shares at the* market, but my broker placed the order wrong and it cost me a fortune. □ I never buy at the market. My orders are always a point or two under the market price.

**attic** n. the head, thought of as the location of one's intellect. □ She's just got nothing in the attic. That's what's wrong with her. □ Ken has an attic full of fear and resentment he needs to clean out before he will feel comfortable again.

**Aunt Mary** n. marijuana. (Drugs.) □ I've got some Aunt Mary in the closet under the red towel. □ We'll have a little conversation with Aunt Mary after dinner tonight.

**avs** [ævz] n. chance; the law of averages. (Streets. Always with the.) □ The avs say that I ought to be dead by now. □ It looks like the avs finally caught up with him.

**awash** mod. alcohol intoxicated. □ Sue got herself pretty much awash on gin last night. □ He showed up for his interview all awash.

**away 1.** mod. out (in baseball). □ Jim put the last one away, and that is three outs retiring the side. □ There's one away and two men left on base. **2.** mod. in prison. (Underworld.) □ My cousin

is away for a year. □ The judge wanted to put him away for two years, but decided on one instead.

**awesome 1.** exclam. "Great!"; "Excellent!" (Usually **Awesome!** Standard English, but used often in slang.) □ You own that gorgeous hog? Awesome! □ Awesome! I'm impressed. **2.** mod. impressive. □ Let me have a look at this awesome new box of yours. □ That thing is really awesome.

**A.W.O.L.** AND **AWOL** [e 'dəbḷju 'o 'ɛl OR 'ɛwɑl] mod. "absent without leave"; escaped from prison or from the military. (Acronym or initials.) □ The kid the cops picked up was AWOL. He's had it. □ If I don't get back to the base, they're going to think I'm A.W.O.L.

**Aztec** ['æztɛk] n. a clothing style based on wild Mexican patterns. □ She just doesn't look good in Aztec. □ Madam asked to see something Aztec. Is this what madam had in mind?

**Aztec two-step** n. diarrhea, specifically that contracted in Mexico or South America by tourists; Montezuma's revenge. □ I was there for only two days before I was struck down with the Aztec two-step. □ I spent a week in Cancun and never even heard of anybody with Aztec two-step.

# B

**babe 1.** AND **babes** *n.* a term of endearment for a woman or a man. (Also a term of address. See *baby*.) □ *Look, babe, get in there and tackle that guy! We're losing!* □ *Say, babes, bring me a beer, would you?* **2.** *n.* a good-looking woman. □ *Who is that babe standing on the corner over there?* □ *That babe happens to be my sister.*

**baboon** *n.* a jerk; a stupid person. (Also a rude term of address.) □ *Stop acting like a baboon! Grow up!* □ *Tell that ugly baboon to get out of here.* □ *Hey, baboon, get off my lawn!*

**baby 1.** *n.* a lover; one's sweetheart. (Also a term of address.) □ *Come over here and kiss me, baby.* □ *Look, baby, I think we can work this out.* **2.** *n.* a term of address for a friend or pal of either sex. □ *Come on, baby, push this thing— hard!* □ *Hey, baby! Getting any action?* **3.** *n.* a thing; a gadget; a machine, such as a car. (Similar to *sucker*.) □ *This baby is a real bear.* □ *Hand me that baby with the sharp point, will you?* □ *What kind of tranny does that baby have?* **4.** *n.* a project thought of as an offspring. (Always with a possessor.) □ *Whose baby is the Johnson account?* □ *You give the report. This project is your baby.* **5.** AND **baby buds** *n.* marijuana. (Drugs.) □ *She claims she only smokes baby buds and they won't affect her driving ability.* □ *Baby can set you back a lot, but there's not much to it.* **6.** *n.* a small or beginning heroin habit. (Drugs.) □ *You just have a baby. Wait a few years till the tolerance begins to build.* □ *I can remember when this monkey was a baby. I could actually take it or leave it.*

**baby bear** *n.* a beginning highway patrol officer; a *rookie* cop. (Citizens band radio. See *Smokey (the bear)*.) □ *Some baby bear tried to arrest me for speeding, but I conned him out of it.* □ *He may be just a baby bear, but he can still bite hard.*

**Baby Bell** *n.* one of the new, regional telephone companies that were formerly a part of American Telephone and Telegraph Company. (See *Ma Bell*.) □ *The Baby Bells are doing better than the parent company.* □ *"If the Baby Bells get into long distance service, say goodbye to Ma Bell," the hotshot money manager muttered in his third martini.*

**(baby) boomer** *n.* someone born during the baby boom—from the last years of World War II until the early 1960s. □ *When the baby boomers get around to saving up for retirement, you're going to see a lot of investment scams.* □ *At about age 45 the boomers will start putting money away.*

**babycakes** AND **honeycakes** *n.* a term of endearment; sweetie; dear. (Also a term of address.) □ *My babycakes gave me a flimsy nightie for my birthday.* □ *Look, honeycakes, I found some lipstick on your collar.*

**baby-kisser** *n.* a politician. □ *Once those baby-kissers get in office, they spend, spend, spend.* □ *There were lots of promises at the town square today when 4 local baby-kissers tried to rally interest in the upcoming election.*

**baby-sit** *tr. & in.* to sit with and guide a person during an *L.S.D.* session. (Drugs. Also with *with*.) □ *Max promised to baby-sit me when I took the stuff, but he wasn't there when I came down.* □ *Who* *will baby-sit with Fred?* □ *Max, you didn't baby-sit like you promised!*

**baby sitter** *n.* a guide for an *L.S.D.* session. (Drugs.) □ *Max is a lousy baby sitter.* □ *It's dangerous to trip out with a stoned baby sitter.*

**backbone** *n.* courage; integrity. □ *If you had any backbone, you would be able to deal with this.* □ *She lacks backbone, that's all.*

**back-door trot(s)** *n.* a case of diarrhea. (From the time when people had to go out the backdoor to the outhouse.) □ *I can't go out tonight. I got a case of the back-door trots.* □ *She gets the back-door trot when she drinks wine.*

**backed up** *mod.* drug intoxicated. □ *Oh my God, I am really backed up!* □ *Old Benny's really backed up.*

**backer** *n.* a supporter; a financier of a play, political campaign, etc. □ *I had a lot of generous backers for the play.* □ *I was hoping for a backer, but the project was too chancy.*

**backfire (on someone)** *in.* (for a scheme meant to cause harm to someone or something) to harm the person who runs the scheme. □ *I hope this plan doesn't backfire on me.* □ *Her attempt to frame Bill for the crime backfired.*

**backhander** *n.* a backhand slap in the face. □ *Then she gave me a powerful backhander without even looking to see who I was.* □ *Yes, officer, a perfectly strange woman came up and clobbered me with a backhander that loosened a tooth.*

**backlash** *n.* the negative response to something. □ *Was there any backlash aimed at your suggestion?* □ *We weren't prepared for the backlash we got.*

**back number** *n.* an old-fashioned person. (Like an out-of-print issue of a magazine.) □ *Some old back number wearing gaiters wants to have a word with you.* □ *Oh, Dad! You're getting to be such a back number!*

**back off (from someone or something)** **1.** *in.* to withdraw from someone or something. □ *We decided to back off from our plan.* □ *Gary was screaming at me, and I thought I'd better back off for a bit.* **2.** *in.* [with *someone*] to reduce one's anger at someone. □ *Gary began*

*to back off from me a little.* □ *Come on, man. Cool it! Back off!*

**backroom** *mod.* secret; concealed. □ *I am going to watch for backroom deals.* □ *All the candidates were selected in backroom meetings.*

**backroom boys** See *boys in the backroom.*

**backseat driver** *n.* an annoying passenger who tells the driver how to drive; someone who tells others how to do things. □ *I don't need any backseat driver on this project.* □ *Stop being a backseat driver!*

**backside** *n.* the buttocks; one's rear. □ *She fell right on her backside.* □ *There is some mustard or something on your backside.*

**backslapper** *n.* someone who is overly friendly and outgoing. □ *At election time, city hall is filled with backslappers and baby-kissers.* □ *In the used car dealership, this backslapper comes up to me and tells me he's got something that will last me a lifetime.*

**back-to-back** *mod.* in a line; in a series. □ *I can't take two days like this one back-to-back.* □ *I schedule all my appointments back-to-back to save time.* □ *These back-to-back appointments are killing me.*

**back to square one** *phr.* back to the beginning. (Often with *go.*) □ *Well, it looks like it's back to square one.* □ *We've got to get this done without going back to square one.*

**back to the salt mines** *phr.* back to the workplace. □ *Well, it's Monday morning. Back to the salt mines.* □ *Break's over! Back to the salt mines, everybody.*

**back up** *in.* to refuse to go through with something; to back out (of something). □ *Fred backed up at the last minute, leaving me with 20 pounds of hotdogs.* □ *Don't back up now, man. It's too late.*

**backwards** *n.* a barbiturate; a depressant drug. (Drugs. See *forwards.*) □ *Backwards always put me to sleep.* □ *She's hooked on backwards and forwards and has been for years.*

**bacon** *n.* the police; a police officer. (Black. Compare to *pig.*) □ *Keep an eye out for the bacon.* □ *That bacon is hassling me!*

**bad 1.** *mod.* powerful; intense. (Black.) □ *Man, that is really bad music!* □ *This grass is bad!* **2.** *mod.* suitable; excellent. (Black.) □ *I got some new silks that are really bad.* □ *That is a bad man dancing there.*

**baddy** AND **baddie** [ˈbædi] *n.* a bad thing or person. □ *Using butter is supposed to be a real baddy.* □ *Marty has become such a baddie that no one speaks to her anymore.*

**bad egg** *n.* a repellent person. □ *You're not such a bad egg after all.* □ *She's a real bad egg.*

**badger game** *n.* a type of swindle where a man is lured into a compromising position with a woman, and then blackmailed. □ *The old man was taken for a bundle by a swindle called the badger game.* □ *So Jed is up to the old badger game again!*

**bad grass** *n.* phencyclidine, *P.C.P.*, as if it were powerful marijuana. (See *grass*.) □ *Man, this is some bad grass!* □ *Stay away from bad grass. It turns you into a zombie.*

**bad-mouth 1.** *tr.* to speak ill of someone or something. (See also *dirty mouth*.) □ *I wish you would stop bad-mouthing my car.* □ *Harry bad-mouths everything he doesn't understand.* **2.** *n.* someone who speaks ill of someone or something. □ *Harry is such a bad-mouth!* □ *The world is filled with bad-mouths. We need more caring people.*

**bad news 1.** *n.* the bill for something. □ *Here comes the bad news.* □ *Okay, let's see what the bad news is.* **2.** *mod.* unpleasant; unfortunate. □ *That poor guy is really bad news.* □ *It's bad news Freddy on the phone again.*

**bad paper** *n.* bad checks; a bad check. □ *She got 6 months for passing bad paper.* □ *There is more bad paper passed in this town in one month than in all of Sweden for a whole year!*

**bad rap 1.** *n.* a false criminal charge. (Underworld. The same as *bum rap*.) □ *Freddy got stuck with a bad rap.* □ *All those guys get nothing but bad raps. Nobody's ever guilty.* **2.** *n.* unjustified criticism. □ *This car has gotten a bad rap, and I don't know why.* □ *Butter has been getting sort of a bad rap lately.*

**bad seed** *n.* peyote cactus. (Drugs. Always with *the*.) □ *I spent most of Saturday coasting around with the bad seed.* □ *She's got the bad seed at the top of her list of happy dope.*

**bad trip 1.** *n.* a bad experience with a drug. (Drugs.) □ *My first trip was a bad trip, and I never took another.* □ *The guide is supposed to talk you down from a bad trip.* **2.** *n.* any bad experience or person. □ *This class is a bad trip.* □ *Harry can be such a bad trip.*

**bafflegab** [ˈbæflgæb] *n.* confusing jargon. □ *Don't throw that bafflegab at me. Use English.* □ *Watch out for the bafflegab they use to try to sell that stuff.*

**bag 1.** *tr.* to capture and arrest someone. (Underworld.) □ *They bagged the robber with the loot still on him.* □ *We'll be able to bag the alleged killer when we have more evidence.* (More at *bagged*.) **2.** *n.* an ugly woman. (Derogatory.) □ *Tell the old bag to mind her own business.* □ *She has turned into an absolute bag.* **3.** *n.* one's preference; something suited to one's preference. □ *My bag is things with whipped cream.* □ *That kind of stuff is just not my bag.* **4.** *tr.* to obtain something. □ *I'll try to bag a couple of tickets for you.* □ *See if you can bag one of the red ones.* **5.** *tr.* to buy drugs. (Drugs.) □ *She went out to bag some grass.* □ *See if you can bag some horse.* **6.** *n.* a container of drugs. (Drugs. Not necessarily a real bag.) □ *Two bags of H. for two dimes?* □ *The man flipped a couple of bags out from a little stack he had held under his wrist by a rubber band.*

**bagged 1.** AND **in the bag** *mod.* alcohol intoxicated. □ *How can anybody be so bagged on four beers?* □ *She just sat there and got bagged.* **2.** *mod.* arrested. □ *"You are bagged," said the officer, clapping a hand on the suspect's shoulder.* □ *"I'm not bagged yet, copper," said the crook.*

**Bag it! 1.** *exclam.* "Drop dead!" (California. See also *Bag your face!*) □ *You are not rad, and you are not awesome, so, like, bag it!* □ *Bag it yourself!* **2.** *exclam.* "Shut up!" □ *Bag it! I'm reading.* □ *Oh, bag it! I've heard enough.*

**bag lady** AND **bag woman** *n.* a female drug seller. (Drugs. See *bag*.) □ *My bag lady says she can get some cheap.* □ *The cops picked up a bag woman pushing pot over on Maple Street.*

**bagman** ['bægmæn] **1.** *n.* a tramp. □ *Two old bagmen wandered slowly down the lane.* □ *The bagman asked politely for some work that he would be paid for in food.* **2.** *n.* a drug dealer. (Drugs.) □ *Sam was a bagman for a well-known dealer for a while.* □ *We don't just want the bagman. We want to arrest Mr. Big.* **3.** *n.* any racketeer. □ *Some bagman from the mob was pulled out of the river yesterday.* □ *So you think you and your bagmen can just walk in here and take over!*

**bag of bones** *n.* an extremely skinny person or animal. □ *I'm just turning into a bag of bones.* □ *Get that old bag of bones off the racetrack!*

**bag of wind** See *windbag*.

**bag some rays** See *catch some rays*.

**Bag your face!** *exclam.* "Go away!" (See also *Bag it!*) □ *You outrage me. Bag your face!* □ *You are in the way. Bag your face!*

**Bahama-mama** [bə'hɑmə'mɑmə] *n.* an obese black woman. □ *Clare has turned into a real Bahama-mama. She's gonna have to lay off eating so much.* □ *That Bahama-mama who was just in here ordered four chocolate shakes.*

**bail (out)** *in.* to resign or leave; to get free of someone or something. □ *I can't take any more. I'm going to bail out.* □ *Albert bailed just before he got fired.*

**baked** *mod.* alcohol or drug intoxicated. □ *All four of them went out and got baked.* □ *I've never seen anybody so baked.*

**baker's dozen** *n.* thirteen of something. (Compare to *long dozen*. Bakers used to give 13 when asked for a dozen of something.) □ *I had hoped to get a baker's dozen, but they don't do that anymore.* □ *There's a baker's dozen dogs in the front yard digging up your tulips.*

**baldy** AND **baldie** ['bɔldi] *n.* a bald-headed man. □ *I'm getting to be an old baldie.* □ *I turned into a baldy in my twenties.*

**bale (of hay)** *n.* a large amount of marijuana; a kilogram of marijuana or hashish. (Drugs. See *hay*.) □ *I only want a tiny bit, not a whole bale.* □ *Sam wants to buy a bale of hay for a party.*

**ball\*** **1.** *n.* a wild time at a party; a good time. □ *We really had a ball. See ya!* □ *Your birthday party was a ball!* **2.** *in.* to enjoy oneself. (Ambiguous with the next sense.) □ *The whole crowd was balling and having a fine time.* □ *We balled the whole evening.* **3.\*** *tr. & in.* to copulate (with someone). (Caution with topic.) □ *Isn't there anything more to you than balling?* □ *I hear she balled him but good.* **4.\*** *n.* a testicle. (Usually plural. Caution with *ball*.) □ *He got hit right in the balls.* □ *The teacher preferred 'testicles' to 'balls,' if they had to be mentioned at all.*

**ball and chain** *n.* a wife. (Mostly jocular.) □ *I've got to get home to my ball and chain.* □ *My ball and chain is mad at me.*

**balled up** AND **balled-up** *mod.* confused; mixed up. □ *That dame is so balled up she doesn't know anything.* □ *This is really a balled-up mess you've made.*

**ball is in someone's court** *phr.* to be someone else's move, play, or turn. (Always with *the*.) □ *The ball's in your court now. You do something.* □ *I can't do anything as long as the ball is in John's court.*

**ball of fire** AND **fireball** *n.* an energetic and ambitious person; a go-getter. □ *That guy is a real ball of fire when it comes to sales.* □ *I don't want to hire some young fireball. I need wisdom and thoughtfulness.*

**ball park estimate** AND **ball park figure** *n.* a rough estimate. □ *I can only give you a ball park estimate at this time.* □ *All I need is a ball park figure. Exactness comes later.*

**ball someone or something up** AND **ball up someone or something** *tr.* to mess someone or something up. □ *I hope I don't ball it up again!* □ *You ball up another contract, and you are finished.*

**ballyhoo** ['bælihu] **1.** *n.* publicity. □ *I have never heard so much ballyhoo for such a lousy movie.* □ *After the ballyhoo* *died down, we realized that nothing at all had really changed.* **2.** *tr.* to promote or publicize someone or something. □ *They ballyhooed this movie on television for a month before it came out.* □ *We promise to ballyhoo John at election time.*

**balmy 1.** *mod.* crazy; giddy. □ *You are totally balmy if you think I will put up with that stuff.* □ *What a balmy idea!* **2.** *mod.* alcohol intoxicated. □ *She's not just drunk, she's a little balmy.* □ *How can anybody be so balmy on four beers?*

**baloney** AND **bologna** [bə'loni] *n.* nonsense. (Also as an exclamation.) □ *Don't give me all that baloney!* □ *That's just a lot of bologna. Don't believe it for a minute.* □ *Baloney! You're nuts!*

**bamboozle** [bæm'buzl̩] *tr.* to deceive someone; to confuse someone. □ *Don't try to bamboozle me! I know what I want!* □ *The crooks bamboozled the old man out of his life savings.* (More at *bamboozled.*)

**bamboozled** [bæm'buzl̩d] **1.** *mod.* confused. (Folksy.) □ *This stuff sure has me bamboozled.* □ *I don't know who's more bamboozled, you or me.* **2.** *mod.* alcohol intoxicated. (Collegiate.) □ *She's not just drunk, she's totally bamboozled.* □ *She just sat there and got bamboozled as the dickens.*

**bambs** See *bams.*

**bammy** AND **bammies** ['bæmi(z)] *n.* marijuana; a marijuana cigarette. (Drugs.) □ *I want to get hold of some bammies to send over to my brother in jail.* □ *The guard found a bammy in his cell and sold it to another prisoner.*

**bams** [bæmz] **1.** *n.* amphetamines; amphetamine capsules. (Drugs.) □ *These bams are wearing me out.* □ *He is on a steady diet of bams and soda pop.* **2.** AND **bambs** *n.* barbiturate capsules. (Drugs.) □ *I want some bams, like, downers, you know.* □ *Bambs around here are called sec.* **3.** *n.* marijuana cigarettes. (Drugs. See *bammy.*) □ *I need some bams. Who's selling?* □ *Bams is just kid stuff.*

**banana-head** *n.* a stupid person. □ *Kelly can be such a banana-head!* □ *Ask that banana-head why she is wearing a coat like that in July.*

**banana oil** *n.* nonsense. □ *That is the silliest banana oil I have ever heard!* □ *I refuse to listen to any more of your childish banana oil.*

**banana republic 1.** *n.* a stereotypic small Central American country having continual political turmoil. (Formerly of interest to the U.S. only because it supplied bananas.) □ *This is no banana republic! Things like this aren't supposed to happen here!* □ *If you want to change governments like underwear, maybe you should emigrate to some banana republic.* **2.** *mod.* in turmoil, like a stereotypic small Central American country. □ *Who would think that you would have banana republic politics in your own backyard?* □ *We've had enough of your banana republic tactics!*

**bananas 1.** *mod.* crazy. □ *You are driving me bananas!* □ *You were bananas before I ever showed up on the scene.* **2.** *mod.* enthusiastic. □ *The audience was bananas over the new star.* □ *The kids went bananas when they saw their presents.*

**banana split** *n.* an ampoule of amyl nitrite. (Drugs.) □ *Harry found a few banana splits in his locker and wondered who put them there.* □ *She sat right in class and broke a banana split.*

**B. and B.** *mod.* "breast and buttock," having to do with entertainment featuring female nudity. □ *There were some picketers in front of the store protesting the sale of B. and B. mags over the counter.* □ *Many movies contain a little B. and B. just to get an R-rating.*

**bang 1.** *n.* a bit of excitement; a thrill; some amusement. □ *We got a bang out of your letter.* □ *What a bang the party was!* **2.** *n.* the degree of potency of the alcohol in liquor. □ *This stuff has quite a bang!* □ *The bang is gone from this wine.* **3.** *n.* an injection of a drug; any dose of a drug. (Drugs.) □ *I need a bang pretty fast.* □ *If Max doesn't have a bang by noon, he gets desperate.* **4.** *tr. & in.* to inject a drug. (Drugs.) □ *They were in the backroom banging away.* □ *She banged herself and went on with her work.* **5.** *n.* a drug rush. (Drugs.) □ *One snort and the bang will knock you over.* □ *There was one sudden bang and then nothing.*

**(bang) (dead) to rights** *mod.* in the act; (guilty) without question. □ *We caught her dead to rights with the loot still on her.* □ *There he was, bang dead to rights with the gun still smoking.*

**banger 1.** *n.* the front bumper of a vehicle. □ *Other than a dent or two in the banger, this buggy's okay.* □ *How much for a used banger like this old heap?* **2.** *n.* a hypodermic syringe. (Drugs.) □ *Jed dropped his banger and really panicked when it broke.* □ *His banger and other stuff were upstairs under a loose board.*

**bang for the buck** *n.* value for the money spent; excitement for the money spent; the cost-to-benefit ratio. □ *I didn't get anywhere near the bang for the buck I expected.* □ *How much bang for the buck did you really think you would get from a twelve-year-old car—at any price?*

**bang in the arm** *n.* an injection of narcotics. (Drugs. See *bang*. Compare to *shot in the arm*.) □ *The guy looked like he needed a bang in the arm right then!* □ *One good bang in the arm leads to another, they always say.*

**bangster** *n.* an addict who injects drugs. (Drugs.) □ *The former bangster was among the last witnesses to come before the committee.* □ *Two teenage bangsters huddled in the alley, nodding and rocking from side to side.*

**bang-up** *mod.* really excellent. □ *We had a bang-up time at your bash.* □ *I like to throw a bang-up party once or twice a year.* □ *Another bang-up day at the factory!*

**banjaxed** ['bændʒækst] **1.** *mod.* demolished; ruined. □ *My car is totally banjaxed. What a mess!* □ *Everything I worked for is now banjaxed.* **2.** *mod.* alcohol intoxicated. □ *She just sat there and got banjaxed.* □ *All four of them went out and got banjaxed.*

**banji** ['bændʒi] *n.* a type of marijuana grown in the Middle East. (Drugs.) □ *Where can I get some banji?* □ *You can't get banji around here.*

**bank bandit pills** AND **bank bandits** *n.* barbiturate capsules, especially black and white ones. (Drugs.) □ *A handful of bank bandit pills was all that the bust uncovered.* □ *Look at these bank ban-*

*dits. See the black mask over the white face?*

**banker's hours** *n.* short work hours: 10:00 A.M. to 2:00 P.M. □ *When did you start keeping banker's hours?* □ *There aren't many bankers who keep banker's hours these days.*

**bankroll 1.** *n.* a roll or wad of currency; one's cash assets. □ *My bankroll is getting a little low.* □ *Don't show that bankroll around here!* **2.** *tr.* to finance something. □ *We were hoping to find somebody who would bankroll the project.* □ *Wilson Sanderson, famous for bankrolling struggling acting companies, could not be reached for comment.*

**barb** *n.* a barbiturate; a barbiturate capsule. (Drugs.) □ *Old Joey is hooked on barbs.* □ *You got a barb I can bum?*

**barb freak** *n.* a barbiturate user; someone who injects barbiturates. (Drugs.) □ *There is an example of a real barb freak. Looks like he just got up.* □ *Most barb freaks are a little older than the typical acid user.*

**Barbie doll 1.** AND **barbies** *n.* a barbiturate tablet or capsule. (Drugs. See *Ken doll*.) □ *How about one of them Barbie dolls you got there?* □ *That guy popped a whole rack of Barbie dolls.* **2.** *n.* a pretty, giddy *girl* or woman. □ *She's just a Barbie doll.* □ *Ask that little Barbie doll if she wants a drink.*

**bare-assed*** *mod.* naked. (Caution with *ass*.) □ *Man, that little store has the biggest display of bare-assed girlie magazines I have ever seen.* □ *And she stood there at the window, drunk and bare-assed for all the world to see.*

**barf** [barf] **1.** *in.* to empty one's stomach; to vomit. □ *I think I'm going to barf!* □ *Don't barf here.* **2.** *n.* vomit. □ *Is that barf on your shoe?* □ *Whatever it is, it looks like barf.* **3.** *in.* (for a computer) to fail to function. □ *The whole system barfed about noon, and all the data was lost.* □ *My little computer barfs about once a day. Something is wrong.* **4.** AND **barfola** [barf'olə] *interj.* "dammit"; "Good grief!" (Often **Barfola!**) □ *Oh they're late. Barfola!* □ *Barfola! You're out of your mind!*

**barf bag** *n.* a bag available on an airplane for persons who are nauseated. □

*I hope I never even have to see anyone use a barf bag.* □ *What do they do with used barf bags?*

**barfly 1.** *n.* a person who frequents bars. □ *Who will trust the word of an old barfly like Wally?* □ *There were only a few of the regular barflies hanging over their drinks when I walked into Mike's place.* **2.** *n.* a drunkard. □ *You're nothing but an old barfly!* □ *Some barfly staggered out of the tavern straight into the side of a car.*

**barfola** See *barf.*

**Barf out!** *exclam.* "This is awful!" (California.) □ *Look at that scrungy wimp! Barf out!* □ *Barf out! Get a life!*

**barf-out** *n.* an unpleasant person or thing. □ *What a barf-out! I want my money back.* □ *That guy is a real barf-out.*

**barf someone out** AND **barf out someone** *tr.* to disgust someone. (California.) □ *This whole scene like, so, like, barfs me out.* □ *The movie barfed out everybody in the theatre.*

**(bargaining) chip** *n.* something to be used in negotiations. □ *I want to use this incident as a bargaining chip in future negotiations.* □ *I need a few chips to use when we get down to drawing up the contract.*

**bari** AND **bary** ['bæri] *n.* a baritone saxophone, the saxophone with a pitch range approximating that of the human baritone voice. (Musicians.) □ *Wally played the bari when he was in college.* □ *A fine bary will cost thousands of dollars.*

**barnburner** *n.* an attention-getting event or development. □ *The current barnburner in Washington is the Wilson investigation.* □ *This is a real barnburner! Everyone will want to see it.*

**barnstorm 1.** *tr. & in.* (for an entertainer) to perform in small towns for short engagements. □ *My great uncle used to barnstorm Kansas and Oklahoma with his medicine show.* □ *He barnstormed for three years before his death.* **2.** *in.* to perform stunts in a biplane in small towns. (Presumably swooping around barns.) □ *When we used to barnstorm, everybody thought we were kooks.* □ *The old biplane we used to barnstorm with is the safest plane ever built.*

**barnyard** *mod.* smutty; obscene. (Refers to the dung found in barnyards. See the following entry.) □ *Those barnyard movies belong in the barnyard.* □ *You are thinking barnyard thoughts again. I see it in your eyes.*

**barnyard language** *n.* dirty language. □ *We don't allow any barnyard language in the house!* □ *I don't care to hear so much barnyard language.*

**barrel 1.** *tr. & in.* to drink liquor to excess. □ *Those guys are barreling like beer was going out of style.* □ *Stop barreling beer and let's go home.* **2.** *n.* a drunkard. □ *The barrel was full up and through for the evening.* □ *A tired and weepy barrel staggered in and fell into a booth in the corner.* **3.** *in.* to go fast; to speed while driving. □ *He was barreling along at about 90.* □ *She barreled out of here like a bat out of hell.*

**barrel ass\*** *in.* to move or drive carelessly and rapidly. (Caution with *ass.*) □ *He was barrel assing along at nearly 90.* □ *I'm gonna barrel ass outa here in just one minute.*

**barreled (up)** *mod.* alcohol intoxicated. □ *Those guys are really barreled up!* □ *She spends a lot of time barreled.*

**barrel fever 1.** *n.* drunkenness. □ *She seems to get barrel fever about once a week.* □ *I think she has figured out what caused her barrel fever.* **2.** *n.* a hangover. □ *Man, have I ever got barrel fever.* □ *That business last night gave me a touch of barrel fever.* **3.** *n.* the delirium tremens. □ *The old man is down with barrel fever again.* □ *The barrel fever hit him in the middle of the night.*

**barrel of fun** *n.* a tremendous amount of fun. □ *Molly is just a barrel of fun on dates.* □ *We had a barrel of fun at your party.*

**bary** See *bari.*

**base 1.** *mod.* rude; *gross.* (California.) □ *You are so, like, base!* □ *What a base creep!* □ *Oh, how base!* **2.** See *free base.*

**baseballing** AND **(free) basing** *n.* using *free base,* a form of cocaine. (Drugs.) □ *Max is at Fred's, baseballing as usual.* □ *Basing is very expensive.*

**base binge** [...bɪndʒ] *n.* a binge on *free base,* a form of cocaine. (Drugs.) □ *Clare is off on another base binge.* □ *Base binges are very expensive.*

**base house** *n.* a house or other dwelling where *free base* and other cocaine products and equipment are sold and used. (Drugs.) □ *Who would expect to find a base house in Beverly Hills?* □ *The cops raided the base house at midnight.*

**baseman** *n.* someone who is using *free base*, a form of cocaine; someone who is "on *base*." (Drugs.) □ *They say that all those rich guys are basemen.* □ *Basemen shouldn't drive.*

**bash** [bæʃ] **1.** *n.* a wild party; a night on the town. □ *What a bash! I'm exhausted!* □ *There's a big bash over at Wally's place.* **2.** *in.* to *party*; to celebrate. □ *Let's go out and bash, how 'bout it?* □ *No more bashing for me till I recover from last night.*

**bashed** [bæʃt] **1.** *mod.* crushed; struck. □ *His poor car was bashed beyond recognition.* □ *Give me that bashed one, and I'll straighten it out.* **2.** *mod.* alcohol intoxicated. □ *All four of them went out and got bashed.* □ *I've never seen anybody so bashed.*

**bashing** *n.* criticizing; defaming. (A combining form which follows the name of the person or thing being criticized.) □ *I am sick of your college-bashing!* □ *I hope you'll excuse the broker-bashing, but some of these guys don't play fair.* □ *On T.V. they had a long session of candidate-bashing, and then they read the sports news.*

**basing** See *baseballing.*

**basket** *n.* the stomach. (See *breadbasket.*) □ *I got a pain in the basket.* □ *You've got a lot of something in your basket. It's huge.*

**basketballs** *n.* 250-mg capsules of Placidyl™. (Drugs.) □ *Ernie is flying on basketballs again.* □ *Basketballs are too much for me.*

**basket case** *n.* a person who is a nervous wreck. (Formerly referred to a person who is totally physically disabled.) □ *After that meeting, I was practically a basket case.* □ *The waiting was so intense that I was a real basket case.*

**Basra belly** [ˈbɑsrə ˈbɛli] *n.* diarrhea; a case of diarrhea. □ *The Basra belly hit me while I was on the bus.* □ *How do you tell Basra belly from Montezuma's revenge?*

**bastard\*** *n.* a wretched and repellent male; a *son of a bitch.* (Crude and provocative. Caution with *bastard.*) □ *You damn bastard. What the hell do ya think you're doing?* □ *He can be such a bastard!*

**basted** [ˈbestəd] **1.** *mod.* beaten; harmed. □ *The team got basted three games in a row.* □ *We were really basted in the market crash.* **2.** *mod.* alcohol intoxicated. □ *I got totally basted.* □ *I got so basted I vowed never to touch another drop.*

**bat** [bæt] **1.** *n.* a drinking bout. □ *She was on a bat that lasted over a week.* □ *What's the longest bat you've ever heard of?* **2.** *n.* a drunkard; a person on a drinking spree. □ *Somebody give that bat a hand before he falls down.* □ *A tired old bat—still waving a bottle—met me on the stairs.*

**batch (it)** AND **bach (it)** [bætʃ...] *tr. & in.* to live alone like a bachelor. □ *I tried to bach it for a while, but I got too lonely.* □ *I didn't want to batch, but I had to.*

**bathtub gin** *n.* inferior and illegal homemade gin. (Prohibition.) □ *My grandfather was an expert at making bathtub gin.* □ *Did people really make bathtub gin in bathtubs?*

**bats** [bæts] **1.** AND **batty** [ˈbædi] *mod.* crazy. □ *You're bats!* □ *You are driving me batty!* **2.** AND **batty** *mod.* alcohol intoxicated; confused and drunk. □ *The guy was bats—stewed to his ears.* □ *She was sort of batty from the wine.* **3.** *n.* the delirium tremens. (Always with the.) □ *My buddy is shaking because of a slight case of the bats.* □ *The bats getting you down again, Jed?*

**batted** **1.** *mod.* alcohol intoxicated. □ *She spends a lot of time batted.* □ *Will this stuff get me batted?* **2.** AND **batted out** *mod.* arrested. (Underworld.) □ *I got batted out on my first day as a booster.* □ *This gal got batted twice last year on the same rap.*

**battered** *mod.* alcohol intoxicated. □ *Man, was I battered. I will never drink another drop.* □ *Those guys really got battered at the party.*

**battle-ax** ['bædḷˈæks] *n.* a belligerent (old) woman. (Derogatory.) □ *Tell the old battle-ax she can go straight to blazes.* □ *I can handle any battle-ax. Send her on in.*

**battle of the bulge** *n.* the attempt to keep one's waistline normal. (Named for a World War II battle.) □ *She appears to have lost the battle of the bulge.* □ *I've been fighting the battle of the bulge ever since I had the baby.*

**battleships** See *gunboats*.

**batty** See *bats*.

**bawl someone out** AND **bawl out someone** *tr.* to scold someone loudly. □ *You know they're really going to bawl you out over this.* □ *I specialize at bawling out people.*

**bay window** *n.* a belly; an abdomen. □ *You are going to have to do something about that bay window.* □ *Your bay window is getting out of hand.*

**bazillion** [bəˈzɪljən] *n.* an indefinite enormous number. □ *Ernie gave me a bazillion good reasons why he shouldn't do it.* □ *Next year's bazillion-dollar budget should make things even worse.*

**bazoo** ['bɑˈzu OR bəˈzu] **1.** *n.* a jeer; a raspberry. □ *They gave Ted the old bazoo when he fumbled the ball.* □ *A chorus of bazoos and hoots rebuked the coach when he threw the chair on the court.* **2.** *n.* the mouth. □ *You would have to open your big bazoo and tell everything.* □ *Don't talk with a full bazoo.*

**bazoom(s)\*** *n.* the breasts. (Caution with the topic. Jocular or euphemistic.) □ *This doll has real bazooms.* □ *She has quite a—ah—bazoom.*

**B.B. 1.** *n.* a "blue bomber," a 10-mg tablet of Valium. (Drugs.) □ *Max took some B.B.s to help break a habit, then became addicted to them.* □ *There were a few B.B.s and a bottle of cough syrup in his locker.* **2.** *n.* a "base burnout," a person debilitated from the excessive use of *free base*. (Drugs.) □ *The hospital admitted 2 B.B.s in cardiac arrest last night.* □ *A couple of B.B.s spent the night in the alley behind the grocery.* **3.** *n.* "Brigitte Bardot," the movie star. □ *I used to dream of B.B. when she was younger.* □ *How many movies did B.B. actually make?*

**B-ball** *n.* basketball; a basketball. (See also *hoops*. Compare to *V-ball*.) □ *Let's go play some B-ball.* □ *Toss me the B-ball, huh?*

**B.B. brain** *n.* a stupid person; a person with a brain the size of shot. (Also a rude term of address.) □ *What B.B. brain left the door open?* □ *Look here, B.B. brain, straighten up and fly right!*

**beach bum** *n.* a young man who frequents beaches. □ *A bronzed beach bum helped me find my lotion.* □ *Some of those beach bums are getting to look sort of old.*

**beach bunny** *n.* a young woman who frequents beaches. □ *This little beach bunny bounced up and offered to put lotion on me.* □ *They say that most of those beach bunnies have some degree of sun blindness.*

**be a drag (on someone)** *phr.* to be a burden (to someone). □ *I wish you wouldn't be such a drag on your friends.* □ *I don't want to be a drag on the department.*

**beak** *n.* a nose. □ *What a beak on that guy!* □ *I want some glasses that sit in just the right place on my wonderful beak.*

**be-all, (and) end-all** *n.* an obsession. □ *For you, booze has become a be-all, end-all.* □ *She is my be-all, and end-all.*

**beam** See *I-beam*.

**bean 1.** *n.* the head. (See *bean ball*.) □ *I got a bump right here on my bean.* □ *Put your brim on your bean and cruise.* **2.** *tr.* to hit someone on the head. □ *The lady beaned me with her umbrella.* □ *A board fell off the scaffold and beaned the worker.* **3.** AND **beaner** *n.* a pill or capsule, usually of amphetamine. (Drugs.) □ *Tom came home from the party with a pocket full of beans.* □ *Beans can be just about anything, but usually they are uppers.* **4.** See *beans*.

**bean ball** *n.* a pitched baseball that strikes the batter on the head, usually by accident. (Baseball.) □ *He got hit by a bean ball and went after the pitcher with a bat.* □ *The guy is a master at throwing a bean ball and living to tell about it.*

**bean-counter** *n.* a statistician; an accountant. □ *When the bean-counters* *get finished with the numbers, you won't recognize them.* □ *The bean-counters predict a recession sometime in the next decade.*

**beaned up** *mod. high* on amphetamines. (Drugs.) □ *Ernie is beaned up again.* □ *Two students were beaned up and were sent home.*

**beaner** See *bean.*

**beanery** *n.* a cheap eating establishment. (Where baked beans are served.) □ *I stopped in for a cup of brew at a little all-night beanery on 34th. Barlowe was waiting.* □ *I'm tired of eating in beaneries.*

**beanhead** AND **bean head 1.** *n.* an oaf. □ *You are such a beanhead!* □ *Why I keep running around with a bean head like you is beyond me.* **2.** *n.* a drug user who uses pills habitually. (Drugs.) □ *You beanheads are just as much junkies as the jerks who shoot.* □ *There's no harm in being a bean head.*

**beanpole** *n.* a skinny person. □ *I'm getting to be such a beanpole.* □ *I used to be a beanpole. Look at me now—both of me!*

**beans 1.** *n.* nothing. □ *You act like you don't know beans about it.* □ *I have nothing I can give you. Nothing, zotz, beans!* **2.** *n.* nonsense. (Refers to beans which produce *gas,* which is *hot air* or nonsense.) □ *Come on, talk straight. No more beans!* □ *Stop feeding me beans.* **3.** *n.* soybean futures contracts. (Financial markets. Usually with *the.*) □ *The beans are headed south.* □ *Buy the jan beans and sell puts on the bellies.*

**bean time** *n.* dinnertime. □ *Hey, you guys! It's bean time!* □ *I'm hungry. When's bean time around here?*

**Bean Town** *n.* Boston, Massachusetts. (From *Boston baked beans.*) □ *I plan to hit Bean Town about noon.* □ *I got a lot of buddies in Bean Town.*

**bean trip** *n.* a *high* from Benzedrine™, an amphetamine. (Drugs.) □ *Man, he's on a real bean trip!* □ *I never take enough for a bean trip. After all, I really don't do drugs.*

**bear 1.** *n.* a difficult task. □ *This problem is a real bear.* □ *This is a bear of a job. I'll be glad when it's over.* **2.** *n.* an ugly woman. (Derogatory.) □ *Tell the*

old bear to hold her tongue. □ *How can a bear like that be allowed to run around loose?* **3.** *n.* a highway patrol officer. (See *Smokey (the bear).*) □ *There's a bear hiding under that bridge.* □ *A bear is overhead, watching your speed from a helicopter.*

**bear cage** *n.* a police station. (Citizens band radio.) □ *Have you ever been in a country bear cage?* □ *I sat for two hours in that stinking bear cage.*

**bear in the air** *n.* a police officer in an airplane or a helicopter. (Citizens band radio.) □ *They've got a bear in the air on duty in northern Indiana.* □ *There's a bear in the air and another regular one keeping watch over your speed.*

**bear trap** *n.* a hidden speed trap that was set by a *bear.* (Citizens band radio.) □ *That whole town is a glorified bear trap.* □ *I got caught in a bear trap.*

**beast 1.** *n.* an ugly person. □ *Who is that beast with the big hat?* □ *That beast should give the monkey back its face before it bumps into something.* **2.** *n.* a crude, violent, or sexually aggressive male; an *animal.* □ *That beast scares the hell out of me.* □ *Oh, Martin, you're such a beast!* **3.** *n.* liquor. □ *I feel a little overcome by the beast.* □ *Pour me some more of that beast.*

**beasty** *mod.* (of a person) undesirable; *yucky.* (California.) □ *You are like, so like, beasty!* □ *I can't stand that gross beasty jerk!*

**beat 1.** *mod.* exhausted; worn-out. □ *I'm just beat!* □ *The whole family was beat after the game.* **2.** *mod.* down and out; ruined. □ *This thing is beat. I don't want it.* □ *Who wants a beat hat?* **3.** *n.* the area that a worker, a police officer, reporter, etc., is assigned to cover. □ *That's not on my beat. You'll have to talk to someone else.* □ *Your store is on my beat, and I want to make sure everything is okay.* **4.** *n.* (in music) the rhythm, especially the bass. □ *Man, that is just the kind of beat I like.* □ *The notes are nice, but it has no beat!* **5.** *mod.* having to do with the Bohemian youths of the 1950s. □ *My brother looked sort of beat, but I was neat as a pin.* □ *Actually, I don't think I ever saw anybody who I would call beat.* □ *The beat guys are all* *gone now.* **6.** *mod.* broke. □ *Man, I'm beat. I got no copper, no bread.* □ *All we need is another beat mouth to feed.* **7.** *tr.* to get free from a specific criminal charge or *rap.* □ *I tried, but I couldn't beat the rap.* □ *I beat it twice, but there is no third time.* **8.** *mod.* having to do with counterfeit or bogus drugs. (Drugs.) □ *This stuff is beat. Ditch it!* □ *Whose ever it is, it's beat.* **9.** *tr.* to sell someone bogus drugs. (Drugs.) □ *My bag lady beat me again with that bull jive.* □ *Who wants to risk complaining when somebody beats you in a dope deal?* **10.** *mod.* having to do with marijuana after the smokable substance is exhausted; *cashed.* □ *This stuff is beat. Who wants it?* □ *Who sold you this beat dope?* **11.** *mod.* lousy; unfortunate. (Collegiate.) □ *This has been a beat day.* □ *What a beat deal you got!*

**beat artist 1.** *n.* an addict who beats up people to get money to buy drugs. (Drugs.) □ *Max is a beat artist and shouldn't be trusted.* □ *The streets aren't safe with all these beat artists lurking about.* **2.** *n.* a drug seller who sells bogus drugs. (Drugs.) □ *I was hit by a beat artist again.* □ *This town is full of beat artists and junkies.*

**beat box** *n.* the person who provides the (verbal) rhythmic beat in a rap song. □ *What makes him sound so good is his beat box.* □ *Let me be the beat box this time.*

**beater 1.** *n.* a junky old car. □ *I like my old beater even if it has no bumpers.* □ *I want an old beater that doesn't cost more than 800 bucks.* **2.** See *beatnik.*

**Beat it!** *exclam.* "Get out!"; "Go away!" □ *You bother me. Beat it!* □ *Beat it! I've had it with you.*

**beatnik** AND **beater** ['bitnɪk AND 'bitɚ] *n.* a member of the Bohemian subculture that flourished in the 1950s. (The *nik* is from Russian via Yiddish.) □ *Those beatniks back in the fifties were something to behold.* □ *This beater comes up to me and mumbles something I can't hear.*

**beat one's brains out (to do something)** AND **beat out one's brains (to do something)** *tr.* to work hard at a task. □ *I'm tired of beating my brains out to do what you want.* □ *He beat his brains out to get here on time!*

**beat one's gums** *tr.* to waste time talking a great deal without results. □ *I'm tired of beating my gums about this stuff.* □ *You're just beating your gums. No one is listening.*

**beats me** *phr.* (the answer is) not known to me. (The emphasis is on *me.*) □ *I don't know the answer. Beats me!* □ *Beats me how those things stay in the air.*

**beat someone or something out** AND **beat out someone or something 1.** *tr.* [with *someone*] to outdistance someone; to perform better than someone. □ *I beat out Walter in the footrace.* □ *We have to beat the other company out, and then we'll have the contract.* **2.** *tr.* [with *something*] to type something or play something on the piano. □ *It'll just take me a few minutes to beat this out.* □ *He beat out a cheery song on the old ivories.*

**beat someone's brains out 1.** *tr.* to beat someone severely. □ *She threatened to beat my brains out.* □ *Those thugs nearly beat his brains out.* **2.** *tr.* to drive oneself hard (to accomplish something). □ *I beat my brains out all day to clean this house, and you come in and track up the carpet!* □ *Don't beat your brains out. Just give it a good try.*

**beat the drum for someone or something** *tr.* to promote or support someone or something. □ *I spent a lot of time beating the drum for our plans for the future.* □ *The senator is only beating the drum for his special interests.*

**beat the living daylights out of someone** AND **beat the stuffing out of someone, beat the tar out of someone** *tr.* to beat someone very badly; to spank a child very hard. □ *Do you want me to beat the living daylights out of you?* □ *He threatened to beat the tar out of me.*

**beat the stuffing out of someone** See *beat the living daylights out of someone.*

**beat the tar out of someone** See *beat the living daylights out of someone.*

**beat up** AND **beat-up** *mod.* visibly worn; shabby. □ *Get your beat-up car painted or something!* □ *My coat is too beat up to wear to the opera.*

**beaut** [bjut] *n.* someone or something excellent, not necessarily beautiful. □ *Man, this fishing rod's a beaut!* □ *This is a beaut of a day!*

**beautiful** *mod.* very satisfying; excellent. □ *This wine is really beautiful!* □ *Man, this place is beautiful. You got your own sink and toilet right in the room and good strong bars to keep the riffraff out.*

**beauty sleep** *n.* sleep; the sleep one requires. (Usually mentioned by non-beautiful men as a joke.) □ *I gotta get home and get my beauty sleep.* □ *You really need some beauty sleep. Why don't you try a week of it and see if that works?*

**bed of roses** *n.* a luxurious situation; an easy life. □ *Who said life would be a bed of roses?* □ *If I had a million bucks, I would be in a bed of roses.*

**bedrock 1.** *n.* fundamentals; solid facts. □ *Let's get down to bedrock and quit wasting time.* □ *This is bedrock—the truth.* **2.** *mod.* fundamental. □ *You've been avoiding the bedrock issues all your life.* □ *Let's hear some more about these bedrock ideas.*

**bedroom eyes** *n.* seductive eyes. □ *Beware of bedroom eyes. They mean trouble.* □ *She batted those bedroom eyes at me, and I knew I was a goner.*

**bedtime story** See *fairy tale.*

**bee** AND **B.** *n.* a matchbox of marijuana; a small measure of marijuana. (Drugs.) □ *How much for a B.?* □ *The cops never found the bee in his coat pocket.*

**bee bites** *n.* injection sites; scars from injections of drugs. (Drugs.) □ *Look at the bee bites on her arms.* □ *If she's wearing long sleeves, it's probably to hide the bee bites.*

**beef 1.** *n.* a complaint; a quarrel. □ *I gotta beef against you.* □ *Okay, what's the beef?* **2.** *n.* a criminal charge or complaint. □ *Well, officer, what's the beef?* □ *The beef is that you appear to have left the bank Monday with about 75 grand that isn't yours. That's the beef!* **3.** *n.* a large and muscular male. □ *Let's get one of those beefs in here to help.* □ *The two beefs pushed and pushed, but couldn't budge the crate.* **4.** *in.* to complain. □ *Stop your beefing!* □ *What's he beefing about now?*

**beefcake 1.** *n.* a display of the male physique. (Compare to *cheesecake.*) □ *There was some beefcake at the party just to liven things up.* □ *There was one calendar showing beefcake rather than the usual cheesecake.* **2.** *n.* a muscularly handsome male. □ *She's been going out with a real beefcake.* □ *I prefer skinny guys to a beefcake.*

**beef-head** *n.* an oaf; a *meathead.* □ *Look you beef-head, lay off!* □ *This beef-head here thinks he knows how to do my job.*

**beef something up** AND **beef up something** *tr.* to add strength or substance to something. □ *Let's beef this up with a little more on the drums.* □ *They beefed up the offer with another thousand dollars.*

**beemer** ['bima·] *n.* a B.M.W. automobile. □ *I had to sell my beemer when the stock market crashed.* □ *Tiffany's beemer was leased, but no one was supposed to know.*

**been had** AND **was had 1.** *phr.* been copulated with; been made pregnant. □ *I've been had, and I'm going to have the baby.* □ *When she said she was had, I didn't know it was on her honeymoon.* **2.** *phr.* been mistreated, cheated, or dealt with badly. (See also *taken.*) □ *Look at this shirt! I was had!* □ *I've been had by that lousy gyp joint.*

**beeper** *n.* a portable telephone signal. □ *I have somebody call me during a meeting so my beeper will go off and get me out of it.* □ *My beeper went off, and I had to leave the meeting.*

**beer 1.** *in.* to drink beer. □ *Fred and Tom sat in there watching the game beering and belching like two old whales.* □ *Let's just sit here and beer for a while.* **2.** *tr.* to get oneself drunk on beer. □ *I beered myself, but good.* □ *Let's go beer a few.*

**beer and skittles** [...'skɪd‖z] *n.* something very easy to do; an easy time of it. □ *Did you think life was all beer and skittles?* □ *All you want is beer and skittles. Don't you know you have to work hard for what you want?*

**beer belly** AND **beer gut** *n.* a large belly. □ *You're going to end up with a real beer belly hanging over your belt if you* *don't let up on that stuff.* □ *Look at the beer gut on that guy.*

**beer blast** AND **beer bust** *n.* a beer-drinking party; a beer binge. □ *Kelly's having a beer blast at his place, starting tonight.* □ *There is a beer bust somewhere around here almost every night.*

**beerbong** ['birbɔŋ] **1.** *n.* a can of beer prepared for drinking in one gulp. (An opening is made in the bottom of a can of beer. The can, with the opening placed in the mouth, is turned upright, and the tab opener is pulled, releasing all the beer directly into the mouth.) □ *Do you know how to make a beerbong?* □ *A beerbong is a great way to liven up a party.* **2.** *in.* to drink beer as described in sense 1. □ *Those guys who were beerbonging all barfed after it was over.* □ *I tried beerbonging once, just once.*

**beer bust** See *beer blast.*

**beer gut** See *beer belly.*

**beeswax** ['bizwæks] *n.* business; concern. (See *mind your own beeswax, none of someone's beeswax.*) □ *Is this any of your beeswax?* □ *Tend to your own beeswax.*

**beetle** *n.* a Volkswagen automobile. □ *We wanted to buy a beetle, but decided on a domestic model.* □ *I remember when people used to put big windup keys on their beetles to make them look like windup toys.*

**beetlebrain** ['bidⱡbren] *n.* a stupid person. □ *Some beetlebrain left a can of paint in the hall, and guess who knocked it over?* □ *Why are you such a beetlebrain when it comes to math?*

**beeveedees** ['bi'vi'diz] *n.* men's underwear, especially underpants. □ *I'm soaked right through to my beeveedees.* □ *It's too cold for beeveedees. I want some insulated stuff.*

**beezer** ['bizɚ] *n.* the nose. □ *I've got a zit on my beezer.* □ *I was afraid he would bop me on the beezer.*

**begathon** *n.* a televised appeal for contributions, especially as conducted by U.S. public television stations. □ *It seems like this station is one long begathon all year long.* □ *They made 2 million in the begathon last month.*

**behind** *n.* the posterior; the buttocks. □ *I've got a boil on the behind that's driv-*

*ing me crazy.* □ *She needs some jeans that will flatter her behind.*

**behind acid** *mod.* using *acid*; under the influence of the drug *L.S.D.* (Drugs.) □ *The gal was behind acid for about a week.* □ *Poor kid! She spent most of her time behind acid.*

**behind bars** *mod.* in jail; in prison. □ *You belong behind bars, you creep!* □ *I've got something here that will keep you behind bars for years.*

**behind the eight ball 1.** *mod.* in trouble; in a weak or losing position. □ *I'm behind the eight ball again.* □ *John spends a lot of time behind the eight ball.* **2.** *mod.* broke. □ *Sorry, I'm really behind the eight ball this month. I can't make a contribution.* □ *I was behind the eight ball again and couldn't make my car payment.*

**beige** [beʒ] *mod.* boring; insipid. (California. See also *vanilla.*) □ *The party is beige. Let's cruise.* □ *Let's blow this beige joint!* □ *This day is way beige! Bag it!*

**be-in** ['bi ɪn] *n.* a gathering of hippies. □ *A meeting of happy people, yes; a be-in this is not.* □ *This is just like a sixties be-in. Lots of phony love.*

**being as how** *phr.* because. (Folksy.) □ *Being as how you seem to have found your car, we'll call off the search.* □ *Being as how you're the sheriff's daughter, we'll have a big party.*

**belch** [bɛltʃ] **1.** *in.* to bring up stomach gas. (See also *berp.*) □ *They swallow beer by the can and see who can belch the loudest.* □ *I belched, and everybody stared.* **2.** *n.* a burp; an upwards release of stomach gas. □ *That was the loudest belch I've ever heard.* □ *What I really need is a good belch.* **3.** *n.* beer, especially bad beer. □ *Where did you get this belch?* □ *Pass the belch. Anything's good on a hot day.*

**belcher** ['bɛltʃɚ] **1.** *n.* a beer drinker. □ *Look at the belly on that belcher!* □ *Harry is a confirmed belcher.* **2.** *n.* a hard drinker; a drunkard. □ *A couple of belchers wandered in about midnight. Other than that, the night is dead.* □ *I'm a belcher, and I know it.*

**Believe you me!** *exclam.* "You should believe me!" □ *Believe you me, that* *was some cake!* □ *This is a fine picnic. Believe you me!*

**bellies** *n.* pork bellies; pork belly futures. (Financial markets. Often with *the.*) □ *What are the dec bellies doing?* □ *Buy the bellies and sell the beans.*

**bells and whistles** *n.* extra, fancy gadgets. □ *I like machines with all the bells and whistles.* □ *All those bells and whistles add to the cost.*

**bellyache** ['bɛliek] **1.** *n.* a stomachache. □ *Oh, mama, do I have a bellyache!* □ *That stuff will give you one fine bellyache.* **2.** *in.* to complain. □ *You are always bellyaching!* □ *Don't bellyache to me about it!*

**belly button** *n.* the navel. □ *Is your belly button an insy or an outsy?* □ *Do dogs have belly buttons?*

**belly flop 1.** *n.* a failed dive where there is a loud noise when the flat of the stomach hits the water. □ *Wow, I never knew that a belly flop hurts!* □ *A belly flop gets zero points in a dive meet.* **2.** *in.* to dive into the water so that the flat of the stomach hits the water, usually making a loud noise. □ *Sam belly flopped again.* □ *I get so embarrassed when I belly flop!*

**bellyful** *n.* more than enough; more than one needs. □ *I've had a bellyful of your excuses.* □ *You've given us all a bellyful. Now, good night.*

**belly laugh** AND **belly laff** *n.* a loud, deep, uninhibited laugh. □ *I don't want to hear giggles when I tell a joke. I want long belly laughs.* □ *I let out a loud belly laff at the preacher's joke. A no-no, for sure.*

**belly up 1.** *mod.* alcohol intoxicated. □ *Sylvia was boiled—belly up— glassy-eyed.* □ *After four beers, I was belly up, for sure.* **2.** *mod.* dead. □ *That's the end. This company is belly up.* □ *After the fire the firm went belly up.* **3.** See *belly up (to something).*

**belly up (to something)** *in.* to move up to something, often a bar. □ *The man swaggered in and bellied up to the counter and demanded my immediate attention.* □ *As he bellied up, he said, "Do you know who I am?"*

**belt 1.** *n.* a blow with the fist or hand. □ *Quiet or I'll give you a belt in the*

*chops.* □ *I got a belt in the gut for my trouble.* **2.** *tr.* to strike someone. □ *Quiet or I'll belt you one!* □ *Don't belt me!* **3.** *n.* a kick or a thrill. □ *We all got quite a belt from your jokes.* □ *Kelly gets a belt from roller coasters.* **4.** *n.* the *rush* or jolt from an injection of a drug. (Drugs.) □ *This stuff has one hell of a belt.* □ *The belt nearly knocked her over.* **5.** *n.* an injection of a drug. (Drugs.) □ *I could use a belt of smack to hold off the pain.* □ *Gimme a belt in the leg, will you? My arms are finished.* **6.** *n.* a swallow of liquor. □ *He took a belt and rolled it around in his mouth before draining it down into his rumbling belly.* □ *Three more quick belts and he was ready to sit down and talk.* **7.** *tr.* to drink (something). (See *belt the grape.*) □ *He belted his drink and asked for another.* □ *Don't belt it! Savor it! Go slowly.*

**belted** *mod.* alcohol or drug intoxicated. □ *How many belts does it take to get belted?* □ *We were belted out of our minds.*

**belt something down** AND **belt down something** *tr.* to drink something down quickly. □ *She always belts down her drink—like she really needs it.* □ *Here, drink this slowly. Don't belt it down.*

**belt the grape** *tr.* to drink wine or liquor heavily and become intoxicated. □ *He has a tendency to belt the grape— twenty-four hours a day.* □ *She's been belting the grape more than she wants.*

**Be my guest.** *sent.* "Please go in front of me."; "Please make yourself comfortable in my home." □ *John stood aside at the open door and said to Walter, "Be my guest."* □ *Help yourself to whatever you need. Be my guest.*

**bench 1.** *tr.* to take someone out of a ball game. □ *The coach benched Jim, who injured his arm.* □ *If you don't stop fouling, I'll bench you!* **2.** *tr.* to retire someone; to withdraw someone from something. □ *I worked as a bridge painter for 25 years until they benched me.* □ *The manager benched the entire sales staff for cheating on their expense reports.*

**bench jockey** *n.* a player who sits on the bench and calls out advice. □ *The coach told all the bench jockeys to shut* up. □ *Do what you are told, or be a bench jockey for the rest of the season!*

**bench warmer** *n.* a ballplayer who spends most of the game on the bench waiting to play; a second-rate player. □ *You'll never be anything but a bench warmer.* □ *I do what I'm told so I can play every game. I don't want to be a bench warmer.*

**bender** **1.** *n.* a drinking binge. □ *Her benders usually last about 10 days.* □ *Paul is off on a bender again.* **2.** *n.* a heavy drinker; a drunkard. □ *This bender comes up to me and nearly kills me with his breath, asking for a match.* □ *In the dim light I could make out a few of the regular benders, but Harold wasn't there.*

**bend one's elbow** AND **bend the elbow, lift one's elbow** *tr.* to take a drink of an alcoholic beverage; to drink alcohol to excess. □ *He's down at the tavern, bending his elbow.* □ *Paul gets lots of exercise. He bends his elbow 30 times a day.*

**bend the law** *tr.* to cheat a little bit without breaking the law. (Jocular.) □ *I didn't break the law. I just bent the law a little.* □ *Nobody ever got arrested for bending the law.*

**benies** *n.* benefits. (See also *benny.*) □ *The salary is good, but the benies are almost nonexistent.* □ *Are retirement contributions one of your benies?*

**bennied (up)** *mod.* intoxicated with Benzedrine™. (Drugs. See *benny.*) □ *I got myself a little bennied on the road the other night.* □ *When a bennied up driver comes in here for coffee, I try to talk him down a little.*

**benny** AND **bennie** *n.* a Benzedrine™ capsule or tablet. □ *You got a benny or two you could spare a poor man?* □ *A couple of bennies will chase away the blues.*

**benny (jag)** *n.* an intoxication from Benzedrine™. (Drugs. See *benny.*) □ *A benny jag is like a long, very nervous day.* □ *I'm on a big benny, now.*

**bent** **1.** *mod.* alcohol or drug intoxicated. □ *I've never seen two guys so bent.* □ *I can get bent on a glass of wine.* **2.** *mod.* dishonest; crooked. □ *I'm afraid that Paul is a little bent. He cheats on*

his taxes. □ *A lot of those officeholders get bent in office—if they weren't before.* **3.** *mod.* angry. □ *He was so bent there was steam coming out of his ears.* □ *Come on, don't get bent. I was only kidding.*

**bent out of shape** **1.** *mod.* angry; insulted. □ *Man, there is no reason to get so bent out of shape. I didn't mean any harm.* □ *I got bent out of shape because of the way I was treated.* **2.** *n.* alcohol or drug intoxicated. □ *I was so bent out of shape I thought I'd never recover.* □ *I've been polluted, but never as bent out of shape as this.*

**benz** [bɛnz] **1.** *n.* Benzedrine™. (Drugs.) □ *Benz will pep you up, but you give it all back later.* □ *Stay off the benz. Coffee is enough to perk anybody up.* **2.** AND **Benz** *n.* a Mercedes Benz automobile. □ *I traded in my Benz for a beemer.* □ *My uncle had a Benz that he took back to Germany every two years for service.*

**berp** AND **burp** [bɚp] **1.** *in.* to bring up stomach gas. (See also *belch.*) □ *She burped quietly behind her hanky, so no one would notice.* □ *Try not to burp at the table.* **2.** *n.* an upward release of stomach gas. □ *The burp did not go unnoticed.* □ *What can you do when you berp in church?*

**berps** AND **burps** [bɚps] *n.* liquor; beer. (See also *belch.*) □ *Did you bring the berps for the party?* □ *Hey, this is pretty good berps.*

**berpwater** *n.* beer; ale; champagne. □ *I don't care for all that berpwater.* □ *Berpwater is for sissies.*

**berries** **1.** *n.* the best; the finest. (Always with *the.* A noun with the force of an adjective.) □ *Those people are really the berries.* □ *Man, this stuff is the berries!* **2.** *n.* wine. (Originally black. Compare to *grape(s).*) □ *Lemme stop at the liquor store for some berries.* □ *No berries for me. Where's the belch?*

**betcha\*** ['bɛtʃə] *phr.* "I bet you..." (Eye-dialect. Caution with use in writing. See also *you betcha.*) □ *Betcha can't do this!* □ *Betcha I can.*

**Bethesda gold** [bəˈθɛzdə...] *n.* a weak variety of marijuana. (Drugs.) □ *I tried to get some Bethesda gold, but I guess* *it's just local.* □ *Bethesda gold is nothing special anyway.*

**bet one's bottom dollar** *tr.* to be very certain of something; to bet in complete certainty of winning. (Need not refer to an actual bet. See examples.) □ *I bet my bottom dollar you never ever went to Alaska!* □ *He bet his bottom dollar on that horse, and it died at the gate.*

**bet someone dollars to doughnuts** *tr.* to bet something of value against something worth considerably less. □ *I bet you dollars to doughnuts that she is on time.* □ *He bet me dollars to doughnuts that it would snow today.*

**better half** *n.* one's wife, and occasionally, one's husband. □ *My better half disapproved of the movie.* □ *I gotta go home to my better half.*

**Better luck next time.** *sent.* "I wish you luck when you try again." □ *So you goofed up. Better luck next time.* □ *You blew it, you stupid twit. Better luck next time.*

**between a rock and a hard place** *mod.* in a very difficult position; facing a hard decision. □ *You got him caught between a rock and a hard place, for sure.* □ *I'm between a rock and a hard place. I don't know what to do.*

**between you, me, and the lamp post** AND **between you, me, and the bedpost** *phr.* "just between you and me." □ *Between you, me, and the lamp post, things are going to get worse before they get better.* □ *They're worse than you think now, just between you, me, and the bedpost.*

**B.F.** *n.* "best friend." (Collegiate.) □ *You would have thought you and she were B.F.s to hear her talk.* □ *Sharon is my B.F.*

**bhang** [bæŋ OR baŋ] **1.** *n.* the marijuana plant. (Drugs. From Hindi.) □ *Martha grows bhang in a pot in her room.* □ *She farms bhang for her own use.* **2.** *n.* a marijuana cigarette; the smoking of a marijuana cigarette. □ *Max had to stop for a bhang.* □ *The kids found an old bhang in Fred's car.*

**bhang ganjah** [bæŋ 'gændʒə OR baŋ 'gandʒə] *n.* marijuana; marijuana resin. (Drugs.) □ *It's the bhang ganjah that gives the stuff its kick.* □ *Can you get bhang ganjah by itself?*

**bhong** See *bong.*

**bicarb** ['baɪkarb] *n.* bicarbonate of soda, used for an upset stomach. □ *I sure could use a little bicarb after that chili she served.* □ *I can't stand that sweet-tasting stuff. I want bicarb.*

**biff** [bɪf] **1.** *tr.* to hit someone. □ *Tom biffed Fred on the snoot.* □ *Fred got biffed, and that really made him mad.* **2.** *n.* a blow. □ *The biff on the nose gave Fred a nosebleed.* □ *Tom got a biff in the gut for his trouble.*

**biffy** ['bɪfi] *n.* a toilet. □ *Where's the biffy?* □ *The house we toured has a pink biffy. Can you believe it?*

**Big Apple** *n.* New York City. (Always with *the.*) □ *The Big Apple is filled with young kids trying to get into show biz.* □ *Max and his gang went to the Big Apple to lie low for a while.*

**big as life (and twice as ugly)** AND **big as you please, large as life (and twice as ugly)** *mod.* present and real. (A way of saying that a person or a thing appeared in a particular place. Also with *as.* See examples.) □ *And there he was, big as life and twice as ugly.* □ *Seeing the actress as large as life was a real thrill.* □ *There was my fine new car, big as you please, sparkling in the sun.*

**big as you please** See the previous entry.

**big blue** *n.* the stock of International Business Machines or the company itself. (Financial markets. See also *beam.*) □ *I have 400 shares of big blue that I would like to sell.* □ *Big blue led the market lower again today.*

**big board** *n.* the New York Stock Exchange. (Financial markets.) □ *On the big board, stocks were down again today, bringing the loss this week on the Dow to nearly 175 points.* □ *Is that stock on the big board or where?*

**big brother** **1.** *n.* a personification of the totalitarian state. (From George Orwell's *1984.*) □ *Big brother has changed the tax laws again.* □ *Now big brother has fixed it so you can't even baby-sit without paying taxes.* **2.** *n.* someone who personifies the totalitarian state: the police, parents, teachers. □ *Old big brother grounded me for a week.* □ *Big brother says the paper is due tomorrow, or else.*

**big bucks** *n.* a lot of money. (See *mega-bucks*.) □ *To me, $400 is big bucks.* □ *She gets paid big bucks to worry about stuff like that.*

**big-C. 1.** *n.* cancer. (Usually with *the*.) □ *She was struck with the big-C.* □ *The big-C. will finish off quite a few of us.* **2.** *n.* cocaine. (Drugs.) □ *When she started taking big-C., she was only 8.* □ *They use kids to deliver big-C. because they know they're not going to get put in prison.*

**big cheese** *n.* the boss; the key figure; the leader. □ *Here's a note from the big cheese telling me to come in for a chat.* □ *The big cheese is giving everyone a bonus at the end of the year.*

**big chief 1.** *n.* mescaline. (Drugs.) □ *They say that Indians used big chief all the time.* □ *I don't care if it is big chief. It looks like something nobody should eat, and I won't eat it!* **2.** *n.* L.S.D. (Drugs.) □ *This is big chief because there's a little picture of a big chief on the paper.* □ *Who makes big chief anyway?*

**big-D.** *n.* Dallas, Texas. □ *Kelly is from big-D.* □ *What is big-D. famous for?*

**big deal 1.** *n.* something really important. □ *Don't make such a big deal out of it!* □ *This isn't a big deal as I see it.* **2.** *exclam.* "So what!"; "What does it matter?" (Usually **Big deal!**) □ *So he snores! Big deal! Snore back!* □ *She says to me, "Your socks don't match." And I says back, "Big deal!"*

**big doings** *n.* something exciting; preparations for something exciting. (Folksy.) □ *There's big doings over at the fairgrounds this weekend.* □ *We've got some big doings at our house.*

**big drink** *n.* the Atlantic Ocean; an ocean. □ *We flew over the big drink in an hour or two.* □ *When you're over the big drink you really get to feel how tiny we humans are.*

**big drink of water 1.** *n.* a very tall person. (Folksy.) □ *Tim is sure a big drink of water.* □ *Kelly grew into a big drink of water.* **2.** *n.* a boring person or thing. (A pun on "hard to take.") □ *She is a big drink of water, but she could be worse.* □ *The lecture was a big drink of water.*

**big enchilada** [...ɛntʃəˈlɑdə] *n.* the boss; the leader. (See also *big cheese*.) □ *I wanna see the big enchilada!* □ *The big enchilada has sent word that it's safe to return.*

**big fish** *n.* the boss; the leader. (Underworld.) □ *We took in the little guys, but the big fish got away.* □ *The big fish ordered the killing.*

**biggie 1.** *n.* something or someone important. □ *This one's a biggie. Treat him well.* □ *As problems go, this one's a biggie.* **2.** *n.* copulation. (Usually with *the*.) □ *But I don't think I'm ready for the biggie.* □ *He wanted to do the biggie!*

**biggity** [ˈbɪgədi] *mod.* haughty; aloof. □ *Kelly is too biggity for my taste.* □ *Who is that biggity guy with the moustache?*

**big gun** *n.* an important and powerful person, such as the officers of a company. (Often with *bring in* as in the example.) □ *It went up to the big guns, who said no immediately.* □ *I knew they would bring in the big guns at the last minute.*

**big-H.** *n.* heroin. (Drugs.) □ *She's on big-H. now. Soon she'll be hooked for good.* □ *The big-H. in this town is so watered down, you can joy pop for years and never get hooked.*

**(big) Harry** *n.* heroin. (Drugs.) □ *I want to know where I can find big Harry.* □ *Harry is cheaper now than you would believe.*

**bighead** *n.* a headache and other ill effects from drinking. □ *I got a case of the bighead. Too much soda in my drinks, I guess.* □ *You look like you have the bighead this morning.*

**bigheaded 1.** *mod.* conceited. □ *Now don't get bigheaded, but you are a top drummer in my book.* □ *Look at him swagger. He is so bigheaded.* □ *What a bigheaded jerk!* **2.** *mod.* having a hangover. □ *Tiffany is a little bigheaded this morning.* □ *I feel sort of bigheaded.*

**big house** *n.* a state or federal penitentiary. (Always with *the*.) □ *It's either go straight now or spend the rest of your life in the big house.* □ *Two years in the big house is like two years in a custom-made hell.*

**big iron** *n.* a large, mainframe computer. (Computers. See *iron.*) □ *We'll have to run this job on the big iron over at the university.* □ *What kind of big iron do they have over there?*

**big John** *n.* the police; a police officer. □ *Big John is going to have to deal with you.* □ *Big John took her in and hit her with a vice rap.*

**big juice** *n.* a big-time crook. (Black. See *juice.*) □ *Marty's big juice now that he's got himself a gang.* □ *So, you're the big juice around here.*

**big league** **1.** *n.* a situation where competition is keen and a high level of performance is expected. (Usually plural. Referred originally to major league sports.) □ *In the big leagues you've got to know what you're worth.* □ *You're in the big leagues now—no more penny-ante stuff.* **2.** AND **big-league** *mod.* professional; *big-time.* (From baseball.) □ *He works for one of the big-league accounting firms.* □ *When I'm a big-league star, I'll send you free tickets.*

**big-M.** *n.* morphine. (Drugs.) □ *Addiction to the big-M. dates back to the Civil War.* □ *The big-M. is relatively hard to get these days.*

**Big Mac attack** *n.* a sudden and desperate need for a Big Mac™ sandwich, a product of the McDonald's restaurant chain. □ *I feel a Big Mac attack coming on!* □ *I just can't fight off a Big Mac attack.*

**big man on campus** *n.* an important male college student. (See more examples at *B.M.O.C.*) □ *Hank acts like such a big man on campus.* □ *Let some big man on campus do the dirty work for a change.*

**big mouth** **1.** *n.* a person who talks too much or too loudly; someone who tells secrets. (Also a term of address.) □ *Okay, big mouth! Shut up!* □ *Tell that big mouth to shut up.* **2.** *tr.* to spread secrets around. □ *Why do you always have to big mouth everything around?* □ *Don't you big mouth this, but I'm going to have a baby.*

**big name** **1.** *n.* a famous and important person. □ *Lots of big names were there lending their support to the cause.* □ *One of the big names invited for the event canceled out at the last minute.* **2.** AND **big-name** *mod.* famous; important. □ *Some big-name star I've never heard of was there pretending to serve dinner.* □ *The big-name ballplayers make millions.*

**big noise** **1.** *n.* an important person. □ *If you're such a big noise, why don't you get this line moving?* □ *She's the big noise in Washington right now.* **2.** *n.* the important current news; the current scandal. □ *What's the big noise around town now?* □ *There's a big noise up on Capitol Hill. Something about budget cuts.*

**big-O.** *n.* opium. □ *The big-O. is making a comeback, I hear.* □ *Most of the users of big-O. died out 30 years ago.*

**big of someone** **1.** *mod.* magnanimous of someone. □ *That is really big of you, Fred.* □ *It was big of Tom to come back and apologize.* **2.** *mod.* nice of someone. (Often sarcastic.) □ *A whole pound. Wow, that is really big of you!* □ *Three daisies he gave me! "Oh, that's big of you!" I said, batting my eyes.*

**big shot** AND **bigshot** **1.** *n.* a very important person. □ *So, you really think you're a big shot.* □ *I'm no big shot, but I do have a little power around here.* **2.** *mod.* mighty; overbearing; overly-important. □ *If you think that a big shot title impresses me, you're wrong.* □ *Your bigshot ideas are getting us nowhere.*

**big spender** *n.* someone who spends much money. (Often sarcastic.) □ *The big spender left me a whole quarter tip!* □ *It's the big spenders who get themselves into money trouble.*

**big stink** *n.* a major issue; a scandal; a big argument. □ *There was a big stink made about my absence.* □ *Don't make such a big stink about it.*

**big talk** **1.** *n.* boasting; exaggerated claims. □ *No more big talk. I want action!* □ *I heard nothing but big talk since you got here.* **2.** *tr.* to boss other people around. □ *Don't big talk me. I know who you are.* □ *She came in and big talked everybody, and we just naturally thought she was the owner.*

**big-ticket** *mod.* having to do with something expensive. □ *Will the govern-*

ment cut back on the big-ticket programs? □ *In a survey taken last month, heads of families said they were unwilling to put big-ticket items at the bottom of their shopping lists.*

**big time 1.** *n.* the high level of success. □ *I've finally reached the big time!* □ *When the pressure in the big time got to be too much, the guy simply retired.* **2.** AND **big-time** *mod.* outstanding; extravagant. □ *This is one of your real big-time stars.* □ *I can't stand any more of this big-time living.* **3.** AND **big-time** *mod.* felonious. (Underworld.) □ *Max is into big-time stuff now.* □ *The gang pulled a real big-time job and got away with it.* **4.** *n.* heroin. (Drugs.) □ *Guess who's shooting big time?* □ *Once you hit big time, you're way hooked.*

**big-time operator** AND **B.T.O. 1.** *n.* someone who does business in a big way. □ *If you're such a B.T.O., why are we standing here in the rain?* □ *He's no big-time operator!* **2.** *n.* a man who chases women. □ *This big-time operator comes up and asks me to go home with him.* □ *That twit thinks he's a big-time operator. A stud he's not.*

**big-time spender** *n.* someone who spends a lot of money. □ *Martin is the original big-time spender.* □ *A big-time spender doesn't look at the prices on the menu.*

**big top 1.** *n.* a circus tent; the circus, in general. □ *The best acts take place under the big top.* □ *And now, one of the greatest acts under the big top.* **2.** *mod.* having to do with the circus. □ *Big top life doesn't appeal to me at all.* □ *One big top experience is enough to last me a lifetime.*

**big wheel** *n.* a very important person. □ *Some big wheel wrote the order. Don't blame me.* □ *Kelly was a big wheel with the gas company for a while.*

**bigwig** *n.* an important person; a self-important person. □ *The bigwig in charge of that sort of thing will be in tomorrow.* □ *Some bigwig in a pinstripe suit waltzed through and asked me to leave.*

**big with someone** *mod.* preferred by someone. □ *Soup is big with everybody in cold weather.* □ *This kind of ice cream is really big with my family.*

**big Z's** *n.* sleep. □ *I need me some of them big Z's.* □ *The big Z's must have set in before I could finish the movie.*

**bike 1.** *n.* a bicycle. □ *My bike's the yellow one.* □ *I got a new bike for Christmas.* **2.** *n.* a motorcycle. □ *How much did that bike set you back?* □ *You have to wear a helmet with a bike that size, don't you?*

**biker** *n.* a motorcycle rider. □ *Four bikers roared by and woke up the baby.* □ *That biker is wearing about a dozen earrings.*

**bill and coo** *in.* to kiss and cuddle. (In the manner of love birds.) □ *Keep an eye on those kids. They aren't going to be satisfied with billing and cooing forever, you know.* □ *If they bill and coo enough now, maybe they will remember how when they're older.*

**billie** AND **bill(y)** ['bɪli] *n.* paper money; a bill. (California.) □ *Do you have any billies on you?* □ *Nope, no billies on me.*

**bimbo** ['bɪmbo] **1.** *n.* a clown-like person. □ *What a silly bimbo!* □ *If that bimbo doesn't keep quiet, I'll bop him.* **2.** *n.* a giddy woman; a sexually loose woman. □ *So she's a bimbo. She still has rights. Have a heart!* □ *Now the bimbo is a star in the movies.*

**bind** *n.* a problem; a *wrinkle*. □ *I've got a little bind here I didn't anticipate.* □ *Unfortunately, a new bind has slowed down the project.*

**bindle 1.** *n.* a packet or bundle; a hobo's pack. □ *The guy had a bindle tied to a stick, just like an old-time tramp.* □ *Throw your bindle over yonder, and plunk your butt on that empty crate.* **2.** *n.* a packet of drugs. (Drugs.) □ *She had a bindle of H. in her purse.* □ *That bindle was more important than money.*

**bing** [bɪŋ] **1.** *n.* a dose of drugs; an injection of drugs. (Drugs.) □ *He needed a bing like fury.* □ *He took a bing in the arm and was okay for about 2 hours.* **2.** *n.* a drug *rush* or jolt. (Drugs.) □ *The bing from the bang made him shudder, then he started to nod.* □ *There's not much of a bing in this stuff.*

**binge** [bɪndʒ] **1.** *n.* a drinking or drugging spree. □ *Larry is the type who likes a good binge every now and then.* □ *A coke binge can cost a lot of cabbage.* **2.**

*n.* any spree of self-indulgence: emotional, gluttonous, etc. □ *About Thanksgiving time I start a month-long eating binge.* □ *The crying binge started when Marty got off the train.* **3.** *in.* to drink heavily. □ *He has been binging since June.* □ *She binges about once a month and is stone cold sober the rest of the time.*

**binged** [ˈbɪndʒd] *mod.* alcohol intoxicated. □ *She sat there, binged out of her mind.* □ *I'm gonna go out and get myself binged, but good.*

**Bingo!** [ˈbɪŋgo] *exclam.* "Yes!"; "That's right!" (From the game "Bingo.") □ *Bingo! I've got the answer!* □ *And we put this little jobber here, another one here, and bingo! We're done.*

**bird** **1.** *n.* a woman; a *girl*. □ *I like the bird you were with last night.* □ *What a bird! I want one.* **2.** *n.* a derisive noise made with the lips; a *raspberry*. □ *The third time he fumbled, he was greeted by two thousand mouths making the bird.* □ *You guys making the bird aren't perfect either.* **3.** *n.* an odd person. □ *Some old bird came up to me and tried to sell me a cookbook.* □ *This bird is too much for me. I'm leaving.* **4.** *n.* a rude gesture made with the middle finger. (See comments at *finger wave*.) □ *The kid gave me the bird, so I bopped him.* □ *A lot of little kids give people the bird all the time because they see it on television.* **5.** *n.* an airplane. □ *I like this bird. She's a dream to fly.* □ *The bird crashed on takeoff.*

**birdbrain** **1.** *n.* a stupid-acting person. □ *You silly birdbrain. Stop it!* □ *I'm such a birdbrain. I forgot my driver's license, officer.* **2.** AND **birdbrained** *mod.* stupid. □ *I've never heard such a birdbrain idea in my life.* □ *Look, you birdbrained idiot, you are dead wrong!*

**birdbrained** See the previous entry.

**bird-dog** **1.** *tr.* to take away another man's girlfriend. □ *Why'd you have to go and bird-dog me, your best buddy?* □ *I didn't bird-dog you. I'm just more lovable, that's all.* **2.** *tr.* to supervise someone; to tail someone. □ *I wish you would stop bird-dogging me!* □ *Barlowe knew somebody was bird-dogging him, but he was too smart to show it.*

**birdseed** **1.** *n.* a small amount of money. (Compare to *chicken feed*.) □ *That's just birdseed compared to what I spend.* □ *Forty billion is birdseed to a government with a 600 billion dollar budget.* **2.** *n.* nonsense. (Based on the *B.S.* of birdseed.) □ *Cut the birdseed. I'm not stupid, you know.* □ *I've heard enough birdseed here to last for a lifetime.*

**birdturd*** **1.*** *n.* an obnoxious person. (Caution with *turd*.) □ *You silly birdturd. Wake up!* □ *Clare can be such a birdturd when she wants.* **2.*** *mod.* stupid; obnoxious. (Caution with *turd*.) □ *Of all the stupid, under-handed, birdturd tricks—this takes the cake!* □ *Get your ugly birdturd car out of my driveway!*

**bird-watcher** *n.* a *girl* watcher; someone, usually a man, who enjoys watching women go by. □ *Harry is a dedicated bird-watcher.* □ *You bird-watchers should just mind your own business.*

**birdwood** *n.* marijuana. (Drugs.) □ *I asked the guy on the corner where I could find some birdwood, and he just stared at me.* □ *Max says he smokes birdwood, but I think he'll smoke anything.*

**birdy** AND **birdie** *mod.* crazy; strange. □ *She acts a little birdy from time to time.* □ *Would you kindly take your birdie friends and go?*

**biscuit** [ˈbɪskət] **1.** *n.* the head. □ *She got a nasty little bump on the biscuit.* □ *He wears a tin can on his biscuit in case he tumbles.* **2.** *n.* peyote; peyote cactus. (Drugs.) □ *I ate three biscuits, and now you tell me that's too much!* □ *Two biscuits should make you fly all the way to heaven and back.* **3.** See *(dog) biscuits*.

**bit** **1.** *n.* a jail sentence. (Underworld.) □ *I did a two-year bit in Sing Sing.* □ *He got only a four-year bit. He was afraid of getting worse.* **2.** *n.* a small theatrical part. (From *bit part*.) □ *I worked in bits for a year and then started selling used cars.* □ *It was just a bit, but I needed the money.* **3.** *n.* any part of an act; any business or presentation. □ *I didn't like that bit concerning penalties.* □ *Now, in this next bit, you are to move stage center.*

**bit-bucket** *n.* the imaginary place where lost computer data goes. (Computers.) □ *I guess my data went into the bit-bucket.* □ *I bet the bit-bucket is filled with some of the best stuff in the world.*

**bitch*** **1.** *n.* a derogatory term for a woman. (A verbal weapon.) □ *The stupid bitch doesn't know from nothing.* □ *You bitch! Stop it!* **2.*** *n.* the queen at cards and at chess. (Caution with *bitch.* Mostly jocular.) □ *You dealt me the bitch.* □ *And I take your bitch.* **3.*** *in.* to complain. (Caution with *bitch.*) □ *You are always bitching!* □ *If I couldn't bitch, I would blow my top.* **4.*** *n.* a difficult thing or person. (Caution with *bitch.*) □ *Life's a bitch.* □ *This algebra problem is a real bitch.* **5.*** *tr.* to ruin something. (Caution with *bitch.* See also *bitch something up.*) □ *You really bitched this coil of wire.* □ *Here's a clean one. Don't bitch it.* **6.*** *n.* one's girlfriend. (Caution with *bitch.* Crude and mostly jocular.) □ *She's my bitch, and I love her.* □ *Me and my bitch really like this kind of stuff.*

**bitchen** See *bitchin'.*

**(bitchen-)twitchen** ['bɪtʃn̩'twɪtʃn̩] *mod.* excellent. (California.) □ *This is a bitchen-twichen way to boogie.* □ *She is like, twichen!*

**bitchin'** AND **bitchen** ['bɪtʃn̩] **1.** *mod.* excellent; great; classy. □ *This is a totally bitchin' pair of jeans!* □ *This is a way bitchen rally, my man!* **2.** *exclam.* "Terrific!" (Usually **Bitchin'!**) □ *Bitchen! Let's do it again!* □ *Four of them? Bitchen!*

**bitch of a someone or something*** *n.* a really difficult person or thing. (Caution with *bitch.*) □ *What a bitch of a day!* □ *He is really a bitch of a boss.*

**bitch session*** *n.* an informal gathering where people gripe and air their grievances. (Caution with *bitch.*) □ *The bitch session went on for forty minutes.* □ *I learned never to open my mouth in those office bitch sessions.*

**bitch someone off*** AND **bitch off someone*** *tr.* to make someone angry. (Caution with *bitch.*) □ *You really bitch me off, do you know that?* □ *That foul temper of yours could bitch off anybody.*

**bitch something up*** AND **bitch up something*** *tr.* to ruin something; to mess something up. (Caution with *bitch.*) □ *You really bitched my day up!* □ *How can one person bitch up something this easy?*

**bitchy*** ['bɪtʃi] *mod.* spiteful; moody; rude; complaining. (Caution with *bitch.*) □ *Don't be so bitchy!* □ *Who needs a house full of bitchy kids?*

**bite** *in.* to accept a deception; to fall for something; to respond to a come-on. □ *I knew somebody would bite.* □ *We put up a sign advertising free pop, but nobody bit.*

**biters** *n.* the teeth. □ *My biters need a little work.* □ *I gotta get my biters to the dentist while there are still a few left.*

**bite the bullet** *tr.* to accept something difficult and try to live with it. □ *You are just going to have to bite the bullet and make the best of it.* □ *Jim bit the bullet and accepted what he knew had to be.*

**bite the dust** **1.** *tr.* to die. □ *A shot rang out, and another cowboy bit the dust.* □ *I'm too young to bite the dust.* **2.** *tr.* to break; to fail; to give out. □ *My car finally bit the dust.* □ *This pen has bitten the dust.*

**Bite the ice!** *exclam.* "Go to hell!" □ *If that's what you think, you can just bite the ice!* □ *Get a life! Bite the ice!*

**Bite your tongue!** *exclam.* "Be sorry you said that!"; "Take back what you said!" □ *Me a thief? Oh, bite your tongue!* □ *Why do you say that this will fail? Bite your tongue!*

**bit much** *mod.* more than enough; more than good taste allows. (Always with *a.*) □ *That was a bit much, Paul. After all there is such a thing as good taste.* □ *Your birthday card was a bit much, but thank you just the same.*

**bit of the action** See *piece of the action.*

**biz** [bɪz] **1.** *n.* a business; business. □ *What biz you in?* □ *I'm in the plumbing biz.* **2.** *n.* apparatus for injecting drugs. (Drugs.) □ *The biz is right there in the towel on top of the stack.* □ *Use your own biz. I got that disease, I think.*

**B.K.** *n.* "Burger King," the fast-food franchise. (Collegiate.) □ *Let's go over to B.K. for some fries.* □ *No B.K. for me. I need pizza!*

**blab** [blæb] **1.** *n.* talk; chatter; meaningless talk. □ *I never pay any attention to blab like that.* □ *Cut the blab and get to work.* **2.** *tr.* to tell a secret; to reveal something private in public. □ *I'll tell you if you promise not to blab it.* □ *Tiffany blabbed the whole thing.*

**blabbermouth** **1.** *n.* someone who talks too much and tells secrets. □ *You are such a blabbermouth!* □ *See if you can keep your brother—who is a blabbermouth—to keep this still.* **2.** *tr.* to tell secrets in public. □ *Don't blabbermouth this to everybody.* □ *Somebody blabbermouthed the story all over town.*

**black** **1.** *mod.* without cream or milk, said of coffee. □ *I'd like mine black, please.* □ *Black coffee, good and hot, please.* **2.** *n.* a high quality cannabis. (Drugs. See *African black, black gungeon.*) □ *I don't smoke nothing but black, ya see?* □ *Get me some black while you're out.*

**black and blue** *mod.* bruised, physically or emotionally. □ *I'm still black and blue from my divorce.* □ *What is that black and blue area on your leg?*

**black and white** **1.** *n.* the police; a black and white police patrol car; any police car. □ *A black and white pulled up to the curb.* □ *Call the black and whites. We got trouble here.* **2.** AND **(black and white) minstrel** *n.* an amphetamine capsule that is half black and half white. (Drugs. See also *bank bandit pills.*) □ *Here, pop a black and white. That'll hold you till you can fix.* □ *I don't touch minstrels. That stuff is too strong.*

**blackball** *tr.* to vote against someone in a secret ballot. □ *Someone blackballed the prospective member.* □ *I chose to blackball her, and I'm not sorry.*

**blackbirds** *n.* amphetamine capsules. (Drugs.) □ *A handful of blackbirds and a bottle of wine was all that was left.* □ *Too many blackbirds can leave you wired.*

**black eye** *n.* a moral blemish; an injury to the prestige of someone or something. □ *The library has gotten a black eye from this incident.* □ *That kind of behavior can give us all a black eye.*

**black gungeon** AND **black gunion, black gunnion** [...'gənd ʒən AND ...'gənjən] *n.* a high grade of cannabis. (Drugs.) □ *Is this black gungeon or tea?* □ *Real black gunnion is softer than this.*

**blackjack** **1.** *n.* a small leather-covered club used to knock people unconscious. (Underworld. See also *sap.*) □ *Max always carries a blackjack in his coat pocket.* □ *The thug used a blackjack to silence Barlowe.* **2.** *tr.* to hit someone with a blackjack. (Underworld.) □ *Someone blackjacked me as I came into the office.* □ *Max blackjacked the cop, and the guy crumpled up.*

**blacklist** **1.** *n.* a list of the names of banned people; a list of people undesirable to some group. □ *Am I on your blacklist?* □ *I hear they keep a blacklist on all the people they disagree with.* **2.** *tr.* to put someone's name on a list of undesirables. □ *They blacklisted me for not belonging to the right organizations.* □ *Nobody else I know was blacklisted.*

**black mo** See the following entry.

**black moat** AND **black mo(te)** ['blæk 'mot] *n.* a potent, black variety of marijuana. (Drugs.) □ *They call grass black moat on the West Coast.* □ *I heard the best kind was black mote. Is that the same?*

**(black) widow** *n.* a (black) amphetamine capsule. (Drugs.) □ *A couple of widows will cheer you up.* □ *Those black widows have quite an effect on me.*

**blade** **1.** *n.* a knife. □ *Bring your blade over here and cut this loose.* □ *What are you carrying a blade for?* **2.** *n.* a young man, witty and worldly. □ *One of those blades kept winking at me.* □ *A couple of blades from the international jet set ordered vintage wine for everyone.* **3.** *n.* a homosexual man. (From "gay blade." See *gay.*) □ *This blade comes up and says, like, "Gotta match?"* □ *Some blade came over and offered to buy me a drink.*

**blah** [blɑ] **1.** *mod.* bland; dull. □ *What a blah performance!* □ *After a blah day like this I need something really exciting like a hot bath.* **2.** *mod.* depressed; worn out. □ *When I get into a blah mood like this, I just want to cry.* □ *I'm really blah. Would you mind awfully if I just went home?* **3.** *mod.* alcohol intoxicated; very drunk. □ *I got myself blah in about 20 minutes.* □ *We are going to get totally blah tonight.*

**blah-blah** [ˈblɑˈblɑ] *phr.* a phrase echoic of gibberish or incessant chattering. (It can be repeated many times.) □ *Why all this blah-blah-blah?* □ *She's going blah-blah on the phone all the time.*

**blahs** [blɑz] *n.* a state of mental depression. (Always with *the.*) □ *I've had the blahs about as long as I can stand.* □ *You look like you've got the blahs.*

**blank 1.** *n.* white wine. (From French *blanc.* See also *plonk.*) □ *How about a nice glass of blank?* □ *She can put away blank like it was water.* **2.** *n.* bogus heroin; a portion of bogus heroin. (Drugs.) □ *This stuff is a blank.* □ *Don't let them sell you any blanks this time.* **3.** *tr.* to sell someone bogus heroin. □ *Damn! I got blanked!* □ *Somebody blanked Bruno.*

**blanket drill** *n.* a night's sleep; sleep. (Military.) □ *Fred is still on blanket drill. He's in for it.* □ *Blanket drill is the only thing I like in the army.*

**blankety-blank** AND **blankity-blank** [ˈblæŋkədiˈblæŋk] *mod.* damned. (From the past practice of printing blank spaces in place of banned words. See also *blasted.*) □ *I'm tired of your blankety-blank bad humor.* □ *Get this blankity-blank cat out of here!*

**blast 1.** *n.* an exciting party. □ *Fred knows how to put on a real blast!* □ *What a blast we had!* **2.** *n.* a thrill; a *kick.* □ *That gag gave me a blast.* □ *The roller coaster was a blast.* **3.** *tr.* to shoot someone with a gun. □ *The speeding car drove by, and somebody tried to blast him with a machine gun.* □ *The cops blasted the crook till there was nothing left.* **4.** *tr.* to attack or criticize someone or something verbally. □ *She really blasted the plan in front of the board.* □ *He blasted his brother until we all left in embarrassment.* **5.** *n.* a verbal attack. □ *The senator leveled a blast at the administration.* □ *The administration delivered an enormous blast at the senate hearing.* **6.** *tr. & in.* to take drugs; to smoke marijuana. (Drugs. See *blast a joint.*) □ *Max went out to blast some pot.* □ *Those kids will blast for the rest of their lives.* **7.** *n.* the kick or *rush* from taking or injecting a drug. (Drugs.) □ *That stuff really gives me a blast.* □ *With a blast like that, somebody's gonna get hooked fast.*

**blast a joint** AND **blast a stick, blast the weed** *tr.* to smoke a marijuana cigarette. (Drugs.) □ *Let's stop here and blast a stick or two.* □ *I don't have time to blast a joint.*

**blasted 1.** *mod.* alcohol or drug intoxicated. □ *I got myself blasted. I'm really sorry.* □ *I got so blasted I swore never to blow another joint.* **2.** *mod.* damned. □ *I asked her to get her blasted stockings off the shower curtain.* □ *Shut your blasted mouth!*

**blaster** See *(ghetto) blaster.*

**blazes** See *(blue) blazes.*

**bleed** *tr.* to drain someone of money through extortion or continuous demands for payment. □ *You can't bleed me anymore. I'm tapped.* □ *I'm going to bleed you till I get what I deserve.*

**bleed for someone** *in.* to sympathize with someone. □ *I really bleed for you, but there's nothing I can do.* □ *We bleed for you, we really do.*

**bleed someone dry** See the following entry.

**bleed someone white** AND **bleed someone dry** *tr.* to take all of someone's money; to extort money from someone. (See *bleed.*) □ *The creeps tried to bleed me white.* □ *Max got some picture of Fred and Paul together and tried to bleed both of them dry.*

**blimp** *n.* a nickname for an obese person. (Cruel.) □ *Look at that blimp who just came in.* □ *This enormous blimp managed to get on the plane, but couldn't get into a seat.*

**blimped** *mod.* alcohol intoxicated; swollen with drinking. □ *I am still a little blimped from our party last night.* □ *I'm bigheaded and still blimped this morning.*

**blimp out** *in.* to overeat. □ *I love to buy a bag of chips and just blimp out.* □ *I only blimp out on weekends.*

**blind drunk** *mod.* heavily alcohol intoxicated. □ *You came in blind drunk last night. What's going on?* □ *They drank till they were blind drunk.*

**blind(ed)** *mod.* alcohol or drug intoxicated. □ *I guess she was blinded. She couldn't stand up.* □ *They were both blind as they come.*

**(blind) munchies** *n.* a craving for food or snacks. (Originally drugs. See also *munchies.*) □ *There is nothing like potato chips when you've got the munchies.* □ *By midnight I had the blind munchies.*

**blindside** *tr.* (for someone or something) to surprise someone, as if sneaking up on the blind side of a one-eyed person (or animal). □ *The new tax law blindsided about half the population.* □ *The mugger came up and blindsided her with a blow to the head before she knew what had happened.*

**blinkers** *n.* the eyes. □ *As I opened my blinkers, guess who I saw?* □ *Look at those classy blinkers!*

**blinky** AND **winky** ['blɪŋki AND 'wɪŋki] *n.* a device for smoking *free base,* a form of cocaine. (Drugs.) □ *He broke his blinky and is desperate for a new one.* □ *Hold the winky here and wait till I tell you.*

**blip** [blɪp] **1.** *n.* an intermittently appearing light on a radar screen. □ *A blip caught the controller's eye for an instant.* □ *Did you see that blip, Freddy?* **2.** *n.* anything quick and insignificant; a onetime thing of little importance. □ *It was nothing, just a blip. The press blew it out of proportion.* □ *It wasn't really a fight. It was just a blip.*

**blissed (out)** AND **blissed-out** [blɪst...] **1.** *mod.* in a state of emotional bliss. □ *After the second movement, I was totally blissed out.* □ *What a blissed-out dame!* □ *I know a gal who can get blissed from a sunset.* **2.** *mod.* alcohol or drug intoxicated. □ *She is more than blissed. She is stoned.* □ *My friend is a little blissed out. Can she sit here?*

**bliss ninny** ['blɪs 'nɪni] *n.* a giddy and disoriented person; a *blissed out* person. □ *You silly bliss ninny. Who watches over you, anyway?* □ *Tiffany is such a bliss ninny—all heart though.*

**bliss out** *in.* to become euphoric. □ *I blissed out just because it is spring and I am with you.* □ *I always bliss out from talk like that, but I still love Wally.* (More at *blissed (out).*)

**blisterfoot** *n.* someone who walks a lot: a police patrol officer, a soldier, etc. □ *This blisterfoot puts his hand on my shoulder and says, "What's the rush, chum?"* □ *So this blisterfoot just falls down right there on the parade ground.*

**blithering idiot** ['blɪðɚɪŋ...] *n.* a crazy person; a totally disoriented person. □ *How can you be such a blithering idiot?* □ *You blithering idiot! You've buttered the tablecloth!*

**blitz** [blɪts] **1.** *n.* a devastating attack. □ *After that blitz from the boss, you must feel sort of shaken.* □ *That's my second blitz this week. I feel like London.* **2.** *tr.* to attack and defeat someone or something. □ *Two of your friends came by and blitzed my refrigerator.* □ *The team from downstate blitzed our local team for the third year in a row.*

**blitzed (out)** [blɪtst...] *mod.* alcohol or drug intoxicated. □ *To say she is blitzed out is putting it mildly!* □ *I want to go out and get totally blitzed. I'll show her who's in charge!*

**blivit** ['blɪvət] *n.* someone or something annoying and unnecessary. □ *The dame's a blivit. She adds up to one too many.* □ *Don't be a blivit. Just calm down.*

**blixed** ['blɪkst] *mod.* mildly drug intoxicated. (Drugs.) □ *He was a little blixed when I last saw him.* □ *He has been blixed for hours.*

**blob** [blɑb] **1.** *n.* a fool; an oaf. □ *Don't be a blob. Get up and get going.* □ *This blob just sits there and lets me do all the work.* **2.** *n.* a useless dishrag of a person; a *wimp.* □ *You blob! Show some spunk!* □ *I'm amazed that blob can tie his own shoes.* **3.** *n.* a very fat person. □ *What a blob!* □ *You'd think being a blob like that would get old after a while.*

**block 1.** *n.* the head. (See *knock someone's block off.*) □ *That block of yours is pretty dense.* □ *Try to get this stuff through your block before the test.* **2.** *n.* the auction block. □ *The painting went on the block and sold for nearly fifty-three million dollars.* □ *The house had just gone on the block, and the first bid was already opened.*

**blockbuster 1.** *n.* something enormous, especially a movie or book that attracts a large audience. □ *That blockbuster should make about 20 million.* □ *I need two blockbusters like that to pay for the last flop.* **2.** *mod.* (of a thing) exciting and successful. □ *The new blockbuster movie made about a zillion bucks in a month.* □ *With a blockbuster novel like that in print, you should make quite a bundle.*

**blocked** *mod.* alcohol or drug intoxicated. □ *Man, he is really blocked.* □ *How can anybody get so blocked on 4 beers?*

**blockhead** *n.* a stupid person. (See *block.*) □ *Without a blockhead like you to remind me of the perils of stupidity, I might be less efficient than I am.* □ *Why did he call me a blockhead? I didn't do anything.*

**blood** 1. *n.* catsup. □ *Somebody pass the blood.* □ *How 'bout some blood for my burger?* 2. See *blood (brother).*

**blood and guts** 1. *n.* strife; acrimony. □ *There is a lot of blood and guts around here, but we get our work done.* □ *Cut out the blood and guts and grow up.* 2. *mod.* acrimonious. □ *There are too many blood and guts arguments around here.* □ *Old blood and guts Wally is here making threats again.*

**blood bath** *n.* a battle; a great decimation. □ *What a blood bath! The whole town collapsed after the bank failed.* □ *There was a blood bath at the office when the manager fired 20 people.*

**blood (brother)** *n.* a fellow black male. □ *One of the bloods came up to say hello.* □ *This blood brother keeps asking me for money.*

**blooey** ['blui] 1. *mod.* gone; destroyed. □ *Everything is finished, blooey!* □ *All my plans are blooey!* 2. *mod.* alcohol intoxicated. □ *Bruno is totally blooey. He can't even open his eyes.* □ *Man, I'm blooey. I'm stoned to the bones.*

**blooper** ['blupɚ] 1. *n.* an embarrassing broadcasting error that must be bleeped or blooped out of the program. □ *I made a blooper, and they cut it out of the program.* □ *There is a record you can buy that lets you hear the famous bloopers of the past.* 2. *n.* an error. □ *Another day, another blooper.* □ *That was a real blooper. Did you get fired?*

**blort** [blort] *n.* heroin. (Drugs.) □ *You got any blort?* □ *Somebody watered down this blort.*

**blot someone out** AND **blot out someone** *tr.* to kill someone. (Underworld.) □ *Sorry, chum, we got orders to blot you out.* □ *They blotted out the witness before the trial.*

**blotter** 1. *n.* a drunkard. (See also *sponge.*) □ *The guy's a blotter. He'll drink anything and lots of it.* □ *They say that Mr. Franklin is a blotter and needs treatment.* 2. *n.* the drug *L.S.D.*, sold on bits of blotting paper. (Drugs.) □ *Most of the acid in this town is blotter.* □ *Blotter can bring 1 to 5 dollars a pop.* 3. *n.* a police station log of arrests; a police blotter. □ *We went downtown to have a look at the blotter. There was no Matthew Wilson on it anywhere.* □ *The blotter is full of the names of petty criminals and drunks.*

**blotto** ['blado] 1. *n.* strong liquor. □ *Let's go get a little of that blotto.* □ *Let's get some blotto and get blocked.* 2. *mod.* alcohol intoxicated; dead drunk. □ *Let's get some smash and get blotto.* □ *She just lay there—blotto.*

**blow** 1. *tr. & in.* to leave (someplace) in a hurry. (See also *blow town, blow the joint.*) □ *It's late. I gotta blow.* □ *They blew this place before you got here.* 2. *tr.* to ruin something; to ruin an opportunity. □ *You really blew it!* □ *It was my last chance, and I blew it.* 3. *n.* a setback; an attack. □ *It was a real blow to our prestige.* □ *Acme Systems Industries suffered a blow to its plans to acquire A.B.C. Steel Widgets.* 4. *tr.* to waste money; to spend money. □ *Mary blew 40 bucks on a secondhand radio.* □ *We blew it all at a fancy restaurant.* 5. *in.* to become very angry; to lose one's temper. (See *blow a fuse.*) □ *Finally I had had enough, and I blew.* □ *The brass blew, and we heard the noise all the way down here.* 6. *in.* to play a musical instrument, not necessarily a wind instrument. □ *Man, listen to her blow.* □ *She blows, and everybody listens.* 7. AND **blow-out** *n.* a drinking party. □ *What a blow over at Joe's. I'll never get sober.* □ *Man, come to my blow-out. It's the best place to go.* 8. *tr.* to snort any powdered drug; to take snuff. (Drugs.) □ *Those guys spend all their time blowing coke.* □ *Are you* *blowing something good?* **9.** *in.* to smoke marijuana. (Drugs.) □ *He sits there blowing by the hour. How can he afford it?* □ *They say that blowing that much will affect your brain.* **10.** *n.* cocaine. (Drugs.) □ *You can get some good blow over at that crack house.* □ *What's blow cost around here?*

**blow a fuse** AND **blow one's fuse, blow a gasket, blow one's cork, blow one's lid, blow one's top, blow one's stack** *tr.* to explode with anger; to lose one's temper. □ *Come on, don't blow a fuse.* □ *Go ahead, blow a gasket! What good will that do?*

**blow a gasket** See *blow a fuse.*

**blow a hype** *tr.* to overreact; to *spaz out.* □ *I was afraid she would blow a hype about the broken window.* □ *Come on, don't blow a hype. It's only a car.*

**blow beets** *tr.* to empty one's stomach; to vomit. □ *What was in that stew? I feel like I gotta blow beets.* □ *She wasted a few minutes blowing beets, just to make things worse.*

**blow chunks** *tr.* to empty one's stomach; to vomit. (Collegiate.) □ *Wilson Food Service strikes again. Time to blow chunks.* □ *The stuff makes me blow chunks every time I get near it.*

**blow cold** *in.* (for a person) to display disinterest. □ *Lately, he's sort of blown cold when I'm around.* □ *The committee blew cold as my plan unfolded.*

**blowed (away)** *mod.* alcohol or drug intoxicated. (See also *blown away.*) □ *I was so blowed away I couldn't see straight.* □ *I'm afraid I am way blowed.*

**blower** **1.** *n.* a cocaine user. (Drugs.) □ *I can spot a blower any day.* □ *Max is a blower, among other things.* **2.** *n.* cocaine. (Drugs.) □ *What's the best quality blower around here?* □ *George says he can't live without blower.* **3.** *n.* a cigarette. □ *You got a blower I can bum?* □ *That's the third blower in ten minutes!* **4.** *n.* a handkerchief. □ *He pulled a crusty blower from his back pocket.* □ *And what does he do when he doesn't have a blower?*

**blowhard** ['bloʰhard] *n.* a braggart; a big talker. □ *You're just a big blowhard.* □ *When and if this blowhard finishes, let's go.*

**blow in** *in.* to arrive. □ *I just blew in last night. Where can I find a room?* □ *When I blew in, nobody was here.*

**Blow it out your ear!** *exclam.* "Go away!"; "I don't believe it!" □ *Oh, blow it out your ear, you cornball!* □ *You are not way rad, you're just way out, twit! Blow it out your ear!*

**blow jive** [...dʒɑɪv] *tr.* to smoke marijuana. (See *jive.*) □ *Man, let's go out and blow some jive!* □ *You would rather blow jive than eat, I think.*

**blow lunch** See *blow one's lunch.*

**blown away** **1.** *mod.* dead; killed. (Underworld.) □ *Four of the mob were blown away when the cops got there.* □ *That guy was blown away weeks ago.* **2.** AND **blown** *mod.* alcohol or drug intoxicated. □ *I drank till I was blown, and then I drank some more.* □ *Whatever that pill was, Cecilia is totally blown away.* **3.** *mod.* overwhelmed; greatly impressed. (Often with *with* or *by.*) □ *We were just blown away by your good words.* □ *Like it? I was blown away.*

**blown out** *mod.* intoxicated with drugs. (Drugs.) □ *Max is blown out and making threats.* □ *I still feel sort of blown out. Is that normal, three days after?*

**blown (up)** *mod.* alcohol intoxicated. (See also *blown away.*) □ *I guess I'm a little too blown up to drive.* □ *You are blown as blazes, you twit!*

**blow off** **1.** *in.* to goof off; to waste time; to procrastinate. □ *You blow off too much.* □ *All your best time is gone—blown off.* **2.** *n.* a time-waster; a *goof-off.* (Usually **blow-off.**) □ *Fred is such a blow-off!* □ *Get busy. I don't pay blow-offs around here.* **3.** *n.* something that can be done easily or without much effort. (Usually **blow-off.**) □ *Oh, that is just a blow-off. Nothing to it.* □ *The test was a blow-off.* **4.** *n.* the final insult; an event that causes a dispute. (Usually **blow-off.**) □ *The blow-off was a call from some dame named Monica who asked for Snookums.* □ *When the blow-off happened, nobody was expecting anything.* **5.** *n.* a dispute; an argument. (Usually **blow-off.** See *blow up.*) □ *After a blow-off like that, we need a breather.* □ *There was a big blow-off at the plant today.*

**blow off (some) steam** AND **let off (some) steam** *tr.* to release emotional tension by talking or getting angry. □ *Don't worry. She's just blowing off steam.* □ *Let off some steam. Get it out of your system.*

**blow one's cookies** *tr.* to empty one's stomach; to vomit. □ *I think I'm going to blow my cookies.* □ *Okay, if any you guys gotta blow your cookies or something, do it here, not inside!*

**blow one's cool** *tr.* to become angry. □ *Now, now, don't blow your cool.* □ *I almost blew my cool when the dog wet my pants leg.*

**blow one's doughnuts** AND **lose one's doughnuts** [...'donəts] *tr.* to empty one's stomach; to vomit. □ *The stuff was so vile, I thought I would blow my doughnuts.* □ *Who lost their doughnuts in the hall?*

**blow one's fuse** See *blow a fuse.*

**blow one's groceries** *tr.* to empty one's stomach; to vomit. □ *I gotta blow my groceries. Look out!* □ *She blew her groceries all over the front seat.*

**blow one's lid** See *blow a fuse.*

**blow one's lines** *tr.* to forget one's lines in a play; to speak one's lines incorrectly in a play. □ *There I was in my first major role, and I blow my lines!* □ *If you blow your lines, just try to cover it up.*

**blow one's lunch** AND **blow lunch, lose one's lunch** *tr.* to empty one's stomach; to vomit. □ *I almost lost my lunch, I ran so hard.* □ *I wanted to blow my lunch, that's how rotten I felt.*

**blow one's own horn** AND **toot one's own horn** *tr.* to brag. □ *Gary sure likes to toot his own horn.* □ *"I hate to blow my own horn," said Bill, lying through his teeth.*

**blow one's stack** See *blow a fuse.*

**blow one's top** See *blow a fuse.*

**Blow on it!** *exclam.* "Cool it!"; "Take it easy!" □ *It's all right, Tom. Blow on it!* □ *Hey, man. Relax. Blow on it!*

**blow-out** *n.* a great spree of eating and drinking. □ *Man, what a blow-out. I'm still full!* □ *I have a nightly blow-out at 11:00 P.M. in front of the refrigerator.*

**blow smoke 1.** *tr.* to state something in a way that conceals the truth. (See *smoke and mirrors.*) □ *She is a master at blowing smoke. She belongs in government.* □ *When they began to figure him out, he began to blow smoke.* **2.** *tr.* to smoke marijuana. (Drugs.) □ *Max sits around blowing smoke when he's not selling.* □ *The whole sales force blows smoke during office hours.*

**blow snow** *tr.* to *snort* cocaine. (Drugs.) □ *See that house over there. For ten bucks you can go in and blow snow.* □ *All the guy does is blow snow. He's in love with it.*

**blow someone away** AND **blow away someone 1.** *tr.* to kill someone; to shoot someone. (Underworld.) □ *The boss said we was to blow you away if you gives us any trouble.* □ *We blow away guys like you every day.* **2.** *tr.* to overwhelm someone. □ *The music about blew me away.* □ *The whole idea just blew her away.*

**blow someone or something off** AND **blow off someone or something 1.** *tr.* to neglect or ignore someone or something. □ *Get it done now. Don't blow it off!* □ *Don't blow me off! Listen! I want it done now!* **2.** *tr.* [with *someone*] to cheat someone; to deceive someone. □ *They blew off a young couple and conned a hundred bucks out of them.* □ *Don't try to blow me off! I know what's what.*

**blow someone out of the water** *tr.* to utterly destroy someone. (As a ship is blown up by a torpedo.) □ *This is too much. I'm gonna blow that guy out of the water.* □ *How does it feel to be blown out of the water like that?*

**blow someone's cover** *tr.* to reveal someone's true identity; to ruin someone's scheme for concealment. □ *The dog recognized me and blew my cover.* □ *I didn't mean to blow your cover.*

**blow someone's doors off** *tr.* to defeat someone; to surpass someone. (As if someone were going by another vehicle on the highway at such a high speed that the doors would be blown off in passing.) □ *We're gonna really blow your doors off in the next game.* □ *They blew our doors off in sales last year.*

**blow someone's mind 1.** *tr.* to impress someone; to overwhelm someone. □

*This whole business just blows my mind.* □ *Your credentials really blow my mind!* **2.** *tr.* (for a drug) to intoxicate someone. □ *This stuff will blow your mind.* □ *That blue acid blew my mind.*

**blow someone to something** *tr.* to treat someone to something, such as a meal, a movie, a drink, etc. □ *Let me blow you to a meal.* □ *I think I'll blow myself to a fancy dessert.*

**blow something wide open** AND **bust something wide open** *tr.* to expose corrupt practices or a scheme; to put an end to corruption. □ *The press is trying to blow the town wide open, and the feebies are trying to hush them up so they can move in in secret.* □ *I'm going to bust this racket wide open.*

**blow the joint** *tr.* to get out of a place, probably in a hurry. (Underworld. See *joint.*) □ *Come on, let's blow the joint before there's trouble.* □ *They blew the joint about an hour ago.*

**blow the lid off something** *tr.* to expose a scandal or corrupt practice; to expose political dishonesty. □ *I'm going to blow the lid off another phony candidate.* □ *The reporter blew the lid off the latest city hall scandal.*

**blow town** *tr.* to get out of town, probably in a hurry. (Underworld.) □ *He blew town yesterday.* □ *I gotta pack and blow town. The cops are on to me.*

**blow up 1.** *in.* to burst into anger. □ *I just knew you'd blow up.* □ *So she blew up. Why should that affect you so much?* **2.** *n.* an angry outburst; a fight. (Usually **blow-up.**) □ *After the third blow-up, she left him.* □ *One blow-up after another. Yuck!* **3.** *n.* an enlarged version of a photograph, map, chart, etc. (Usually **blow-up.**) □ *Here's a blow up of the scene of the crime.* □ *Kelly sent a blow-up of their wedding picture to all her relatives.* **4.** *n.* the ruination of something; the collapse of something. (Usually **blow-up.**) □ *The blow-up in the financial world has ruined my chances for early retirement.* □ *After the blow-up, they called one another to compare notes.*

**blow Z's** [...ziz] *tr.* to sleep. □ *I got to blow Z's for a while; then we'll talk.* □ *Him? Oh, he's in the back blowing Z's.*

**blubber** ['bləbɚ] *in.* to cry, softly and wetly. □ *Don't sit there and blubber, dammit. Get it over and done with.* □ *By the end of the film, everyone in the place was blubbering.*

**blubber gut(s)** ['bləbɚ 'gət(s)] *n.* a fat person. (Also a rude term of address.) □ *Hey, blubber guts! Get a girdle.* □ *Why doesn't that blubber gut do something about all that weight?*

**blue 1.** *mod.* depressed; melancholy. □ *That music always makes me blue.* □ *I'm feeling sort of blue.* □ *I'm in a blue mood.* **2.** *mod.* obscene; vulgar; dirty. □ *Those blue jokes don't go over very well around here.* □ *Enough of your blue interests. Get out and take all these magazines with you.* □ *That one was really blue.* **3.** *n.* the sky; the heavens. □ *I just look up at the blue and hope for the best.* □ *The idea came to me right out of the blue.* **4.** *mod.* alcohol intoxicated. □ *What have you been drinking? You're getting a little blue.* □ *You might say I'm blue. Others might note that I am stoned.* **5.** *n.* an amphetamine tablet or capsule, especially a blue one. (Drugs.) □ *How are blues different from reds and yellows?* □ *I'm sort of wired. You got any blues?* **6.** *n.* a police officer; the police. □ *The blues will be here in a minute.* □ *One blue isn't enough to handle the job.* **7.** *n.* a 10-mg tablet of Valium™. (Drugs.) □ *A blue is enough to put most people into a stupor. Why do you want two?* □ *In treatment they kept giving me blues to calm me down. Now I can't live without them.*

**blue acid** *n.* the drug *L.S.D.* (Drugs.) □ *Blue acid is the cheapest thing around here. Toot is a lot more.* □ *Who makes this blue acid?*

**blue and white** *n.* a police car; the police. (Patterned on *black and white* and used in cities where the police cars are painted blue and white.) □ *A blue and white suddenly appeared, and I knew we were finished.* □ *I can usually spot a blue and white before anyone else.*

**blue around the gills** AND **green around the gills 1.** *mod.* ill; nauseated. □ *You are looking a little blue around the gills.* □ *How about a little air? I feel a little green around the gills.* **2.** *mod.* alcohol intoxicated. □ *In the middle of the drink, I knew I was getting blue around the gills.* □ *Marty—now thoroughly green around the gills—slid neatly under the table, and everyone pretended not to notice.*

**blue baby 1.** *n.* a baby blue from oxygen deprivation; a cyanotic baby. (Hospitals.) □ *I was a blue baby when I was born, but I got over it fast.* □ *They put the blue baby on oxygen.* **2.** *n.* the drug *L.S.D.* (Drugs.) □ *A bit of blue baby is just what this cowboy needs.* □ *Blue baby will cost you 4 clams a pop.*

**blue (barrels)** *n.* a blue tablet of the drug *L.S.D.* (Drugs.) □ *Whatever these blue barrels are, it's powerful stuff.* □ *You got any blue barrels?*

**bluebird** *n.* a capsule of Amytal™, a barbiturate. (Drugs.) □ *Here, this little bluebird will sing you to sleep.* □ *Do bluebirds make you fly?*

**(blue) blazes** *n.* hell. □ *You can go straight to blue blazes as far as I care.* □ *It's as hot as blazes here.*

**blue blood** *n.* a person of noble descent; an aristocratic person. □ *She acts like a blue blood, but we all know she comes from a long line of horse thieves and tramps.* □ *The blue bloods will never take over this neighborhood.*

**blue bomber** *n.* a 10-mg tablet of Valium™, a tranquilizer. (Drugs.) □ *A couple of blue bombers will knock you flat.* □ *How about a blue bomber just to start off the evening?*

**blue boys** AND **blue coats** *n.* the police. (Black. See *men in blue*.) □ *Four blue boys held me while a fifth slipped the cuffs on me. I ain't no pushover.* □ *The blue coats climbed out of the black and white and just stood there.*

**blue chip 1.** *n.* stock shares of a large company that has a high value. (Financial markets.) □ *The blue chips took another nose dive in today's trading.* □ *I buy nothing but blue chips.* **2.** *mod.* having to do with the stock of large, valuable companies. (Usually **blue-chip**. Financial markets.) □ *The blue-chip rally ran for a third day.* □ *It was another blue-chip led sell off.*

**blue devils 1.** *n.* melancholia; depression. □ *Hank is down with the blue*

devils again. □ *How do you get rid of the blue devils?* **2.** *n.* the delirium tremens. □ *You wouldn't think that a society dame like that would have the blue devils, would you?* □ *The shakes, or the blue devils, are a sure sign of a serious drinking problem.* **3.** *n.* capsules of Amytal™, a barbiturate. □ *How much for a little box of blue devils?* □ *Got no red devils. Will blue devils do it to you?*

**blue-eyed** *mod.* innocent. □ *Look, you little blue-eyed sweetie, I know your game!* □ *He's sure his blue-eyed wonder couldn't have hit my child.* □ *Don't try to look so blue-eyed.*

**blue flu** ['blu 'flu] *n.* an imaginary disease afflicting police officers who call in sick during a work stoppage or slowdown. (Journalistic. Done where strikes are illegal.) □ *Another epidemic of the blue flu struck the city's police officers early today.* □ *It seems that the city's criminals and lawbreakers are immune to the blue flu. Their work goes on totally unaffected.*

**blue funk** ['blu 'fəŋk] *n.* a state of depression. □ *I'm glad I'm out of my blue funk.* □ *You've got to get out of your blue funk and get back to work.*

**blue in the face** *mod.* pale from exhaustion or exertion. □ *I laughed until I was blue in the face.* □ *She worked hard enough to be blue in the face.*

**blue Johnnies** *n.* the delirium tremens. □ *The one that's shaking has the blue Johnnies. Everybody else in the tank is just drunk.* □ *Here come the blue Johnnies again!*

**blue movie** *n.* a sexually oriented or sexually explicit movie. □ *I saw my first blue movie and found it disappointing.* □ *I've got an old blue movie from the forties.*

**blues 1.** *n.* barbiturates. (Drugs. The opposite of *rhythm(s)*, amphetamines.) □ *The principal found a bottle of blues in somebody's locker.* □ *When Max said he really likes rhythm and blues, no one knew what he was really talking about.* **2.** *n.* melancholia; sadness. (Always with *the*.) □ *You look like you really have the blues. What's wrong?* □ *When I have the blues, I like sad music.*

**3.** *n.* the delirium tremens. (An extension of sense 2. Always with *the*.) □ *When I can't get wine, I get the blues.* □ *The blues don't make me shake. I can't move at all when I have the blues.*

**B.M.O.C.** *n.* "big man on campus," an important or self-important male college student. (Collegiate. See also *B.W.O.C.*) □ *Who's the B.M.O.C. who keeps trying to get elected class president?* □ *When this B.M.O.C. asked me to leave, I ignored him.*

**B.O.** **1.** *n.* (bad) "body odor." □ *Man, do you have B.O.!* □ *Now here is a product that will end your worries about B.O.* **2.** *n.* "box office," where tickets to some event are sold. □ *The show was a big hit at the B.O.* □ *If you want your money back, you'll have to go to the B.O.*

**bo** [bo] *n.* marijuana; Colombian marijuana. (Black. From *Colombo*.) □ *That bo is good stuff, babe.* □ *How much for a bee of bo?*

**boat** **1.** *n.* a big shoe. (See also *gunboats*.) □ *Whose boat is that under the coffee table?* □ *Those boats are special made, in fact.* **2.** *n.* a big car; a full-size car. □ *I don't want to drive a big boat like that.* □ *How do you stop that boat? Throw out an anchor?*

**bo-bo (bush)** ['bo'bo...] *n.* marijuana; hashish. (Drugs.) □ *She likes to blow bo-bo she says. Is that what grows on a bo-bo bush?* □ *Bo-bo bush is just another kind of hash.*

**bod** [bad] **1.** *n.* a body, especially a nice body. (Compare to *odd-bod*.) □ *You got a nice bod, Tom.* □ *If you got a good bod and enough money, why are you depressed?* **2.** *n.* a person. □ *How many bods are coming over tonight?* □ *Who's the bod with the tight slacks?*

**bodacious** [bo'deʃəs] *mod.* assertive; audacious. (Folksy.) □ *That is a bodacious plan, for sure.* □ *Yes, sir! That is really bodacious.*

**body count** **1.** *n.* the total of dead bodies after a battle. □ *The body count at Hill 49 was 3.* □ *The body count seems to go down during the rainy season.* **2.** *n.* the total of casualties after some kind of shake-up. □ *The pink slips are coming out every day. The body count on Monday was 23.* □ *Most everybody is flunk-*ing quan. The body count after the last test was in the twenties.* **3.** *n.* a count of people present. □ *The body count was about 45 at the meeting.* □ *The body count seems to go down each month.*

**body-packer** AND **body carrier** *n.* a person who swallows packets of drugs in order to smuggle them into the country. (Drugs.) □ *The guy—who they decided later was a body-packer—had just crumpled up on the floor and died.* □ *When a packet breaks inside a body carrier, that's the end.*

**body shake** *n.* a shakedown of the body; a skin-search. (Underworld. See *shakedown*.) □ *You can't give me a body shake. I want my lawyer!* □ *They give everybody who passes through these doors a body shake.*

**boff** [baf] **1.** *tr.* to punch someone. □ *I was afraid she was going to boff me.* □ *Ted boffed Harry playfully.* **2.** *in.* to empty one's stomach; to vomit. (See also *barf*.) □ *She boffed and boffed, until she was exhausted.* □ *I think I'm gonna boff!*

**boffo** ['bafo] **1.** *n.* a box-office hit; a successful play, musical, movie, etc. □ *The last one was a tremendous boffo, but we only broke even.* □ *I need a boffo just once in my life.* **2.** *mod.* successful; tremendous. □ *We had a boffo time at your rally.* □ *Another boffo success for Wally!* □ *That was really boffo!*

**bogart** AND **bogard** ['bogart AND 'bogard] **1.** *in.* to monopolize a communal marijuana cigarette; to hold a communal marijuana cigarette so long—Bogart style—that one drools on it. (From Humphrey Bogart, the actor.) □ *Come on, man. Don't bogart on us!* □ *Stop bogarding and take a hit!* **2.** *in.* to act in a tough manner like Humphrey Bogart. (Black.) □ *Look at him bogarting! Who needs tough guys?* □ *There's nothing funnier than a wimp trying to bogard around.*

**bogue** [bog] *mod.* bogus; fake. □ *Keep your bogue gold watch. I don't want it!* □ *She is so, like, bogue!*

**boheme** [bo'him] *n.* a (feminine) personal style consisting of no makeup, large baggy clothing, long skirts, and comfortable shoes. (Collegiate.) □ *She* looks so good in boheme! □ Boheme is not you.

**boiled 1.** mod. angry. □ I am so boiled at you! □ Now, don't get boiled. It was only a joke. **2.** mod. alcohol intoxicated. □ How can you get so boiled on wine? □ The two were boiled and not much use to us.

**boiling (mad)** mod. very mad. □ Mad, I'm not mad. I'm just boiling. □ She is really boiling mad.

**B.O. juice** n. a deodorant; an underarm deodorant. (Collegiate. See B.O.) □ Who took my B.O. juice? I've got to go to class. □ Help this man find his B.O. juice, fast! He really needs it.

**bokoo** AND **boku** ['bo'ku] mod. many. (A play on French beaucoup.) □ I've got bokoo things to do today. □ There are already boku people invited.

**bolus** ['boləs] n. a physician. (From the Latin name for a pill.) □ The bolus kept trying to get me to lose weight. □ There is a new bolus in town.

**bomb 1.** n. a bad performance or an inherently bad show. □ They tried as hard as they could, but the thing was a bomb from act one on. □ The latest bomb on Broadway, like all bombs, will only go off once. This one finished to a chorus of boos before the final curtain. **2.** in. to fail. □ My first try bombed, but things got better. □ It bombed the minute the first curtain went up. **3.** AND **bomb out** in. (for a computer or computer program) to fail. □ You expect a program to bomb a time or two. □ The whole thing bombed out at just the wrong time. **4.** See bomb(shell).

**bombed (out)** mod. alcohol or drug intoxicated. □ They were bombed and looked nearly dead. □ How can I drive when I'm bombed out?

**bomber 1.** n. a barbiturate capsule. □ I am so tired from that bomber you gave me. □ I didn't give you a bomber! That was horse! **2.** n. a large, thick marijuana cigarette. □ He rolled himself a bomber and lit up. □ He can go through a bomber like that in 10 minutes.

**bomb(shell)** n. a stunning piece of news that is "dropped" without warning. □ I am still recovering from your bomb of last evening. □ After you left us with the bombshell about your marriage to the Christmas tree farmer in Montana, we began to realize that it's your life and you should do what you want.

**bone** [bon] n. a trombone. (Musicians. See also bones.) □ Herman is just a wonder on the bone. □ She plays the bone like nobody's business.

**bone factory 1.** n. a hospital. □ Lemme outa this bone factory! □ After about two months in the bone factory, I was back on the job. **2.** n. a cemetery. □ We must have passed by 40 bone factories going across Missouri. □ I know I'll end up in the bone factory just like everyone else.

**bonehead 1.** n. a stupid or stubborn person. □ You are such a bonehead when it comes to buying cars. □ Don't be a bonehead. Cooperate! **2.** AND **boneheaded** mod. stupid; stubborn. □ Of all the boneheaded things to do! □ Why am I married to the world's greatest, all-time bonehead klutz? □ Don't be so boneheaded.

**boneheaded** See the previous entry.

**bone idle** mod. very lazy; completely idle or unproductive. □ Your problem is that you are bone idle. □ Take your bone idle brother and move out!

**bone orchard** n. a cemetery. □ That is a very pleasant bone orchard. □ Does it really matter how comfortable a bone orchard looks?

**boner** ['bonɚ] n. a silly error; a gaffe. (See pull a boner.) □ Well, that was a bad boner. □ What a boner! You must be embarrassed.

**bones 1.** n. dice. (See also bone.) □ Toss me the bones and get out your checkbooks. □ Throw them bones and hope for the best. **2.** n. a nickname for a ship's physician. (From sawbones. Also the nickname of the doctor on the starship Enterprise of Star Trek fame.) □ This fat bones actually wanted me to lose weight. □ This is quite a cut. You'll have to go over to the bones in Adamsville. **3.** n. a nickname for a skinny person. (Also a term of address.) □ Well, bones, how about a nice big meal? □ Ask bones there what he wants to drink.

**boneyard 1.** n. a cemetery. □ I'd like to be planted in a boneyard like that. □ I'll

*take a boneyard with a view of the lake.*
**2.** *n.* a junkyard. □ *I got a used right-hand door from a boneyard.* □ *This old car's ready for the boneyard.*

**bong** AND **bhong** [bɔŋ] **1.** *n.* a marijuana smoking device that cools the smoke by passing it through water. (Drugs.) □ *This bong is really getting sort of nasty.* □ *Fill up your bong and let's get going.* **2.** *tr. & in.* to smoke marijuana or other drugs with a *bong* or other device. (Drugs.) □ *You can't just bong for the rest of your life!* □ *Wanna go bong a bowl?* **3.** *n.* a puff or *hit* of marijuana taken through a *bong.* (Drugs.) □ *I'll take two bongs, and then I gotta go.* □ *I only got one bong!* **4.** *tr. & in.* to drink keg beer through a hose. (California. See also *beerbong.*) □ *Everybody bonged till the keg was empty.* □ *There were no cups, so people had to bong their beer.*

**bonged (out)** [bɔŋd...] *mod.* exhausted from too much marijuana. (Drugs.) □ *I was bonged all through the holidays.* □ *She was still bonged out after the first week of classes.*

**bonk** [bɔŋk] **1.** *tr.* to strike one's head. □ *He bonked his head on the shelf.* □ *I bonked my bean.* **2.** *tr.* to strike someone on the head. □ *I bonked John on the head.* □ *He wouldn't move, so I bonked him.*

**bonkers** ['bɔŋkɚz] **1.** AND **crackers** *mod.* insane; crazy. □ *Get this bonkers brother of yours out of here!* □ *I think I am going bonkers.* **2.** *mod.* slightly intoxicated. □ *I'm just a little bonkers, nothing really serious.* □ *She's too bonkers to drive.*

**bonzo** ['bɑnzo] *mod.* crazy. □ *You are completely bonzo!* □ *I want out of this bonzo place!*

**boo** AND **bu** [bu] *n.* marijuana; a marijuana cigarette. (Drugs.) □ *Gimme a drag on your boo, huh?* □ *Get your own bu, you wimp!*

**boob\*** [bub] **1.** *n.* a stupid person; a rural oaf. □ *You boob! What have you done?* □ *Why did I marry a boob like you?* **2.\*** AND **booby\*** ['bubi] *n.* a breast. (Caution with topic. Usually plural.) □ *My boobs aren't what I might have wished for.* □ *With boobs like that, she can go anywhere she likes.*

**boo-bird** ['bubɚd] *n.* a person who boos frequently at games or other public events. □ *It was a big day for the boo-birds at Wrigley field.* □ *The catcher turned and stared right at the loud-mouthed boo-bird. Everybody knew what he was thinking.*

**boo-boo** ['bubu] *n.* an error. (See *make a boo-boo.*) □ *It's only a small boo-boo. Don't stress yourself.* □ *Another boo-boo like that, and you are through.*

**boob-tube** ['bubtub] *n.* a television set. (Something for a *boob* to watch.) □ *You spend too much time in front of the boob-tube.* □ *What's on the boob-tube tonight?*

**booby** See *boob.*

**booby hatch** ['bubi...] *n.* a mental hospital. □ *I was afraid they would send me to the booby hatch.* □ *Don't you mean send you back to the booby hatch?*

**booby trap 1.** *n.* a concealed trap. (Both literal and figurative. See examples.) □ *This clause in the contract is a real booby trap. Let's rewrite it.* □ *Some kind of booby trap in the warehouse kept the robber from getting away.* **2.** *tr.* to install a concealed trap in a place. (Usually **booby-trap.**) □ *The agents booby-trapped the cellar.* □ *They booby-trapped the elevator so it turned into a cell if you didn't know the code to open the door.*

**boodie** See *boody.*

**boodle** ['budl] *n.* loot; the proceeds from a crime. (Underworld.) □ *All of the boodle was recovered in a suitcase.* □ *They divvied up the boodle and got out of town.*

**boody\*** AND **boodie\*, bootie\*** ['budi] *n.* the buttocks. (Caution with topic.) □ *Look at the nice little boody on that guy.* □ *Get your boodie out on that dance floor and shake it.*

**booger** See *boogie.*

**boogie\*** ['bugi OR 'bʊgi] **1.** *n.* a kind of rock dance. □ *I didn't like the boogie until I learned how to do it right.* □ *The boogie will tire you out, but good.* **2.** *in.* to dance rock-style. □ *I don't like to boogie.* □ *I'm too old to boogie.* **3.** *n.* a party where the *boogie* is danced. □ *There's a boogie over at Steve's tonight.* □ *One more boogie and I'm through for* the year. **4.**\* *in.* to copulate. (Caution with topic.) □ *Come on. Let's get it on! Let's boogie!* □ *When you said let's boogie, I thought you wanted to dance!* **5.** *in.* to get down to work; to get down to business. □ *All right, it's time to boogie. Cool it!* □ *The whistle blew. Time to boogie.* **6.**\* AND **booger\*** ['bʊgɚ] *n.* a piece of nasal mucus. (Caution with topic.) □ *That's no way to take care of a booger!* □ *Is that a boogie on your lip, or what?*

**boogie-board** ['bugibord OR 'bʊgibord] **1.** *n.* a surfboard. (California.) □ *Get your boogie-board out there in that tube.* □ *She cracked her boogie-board apart on that big one.* **2.** *n.* a skateboard. (Teens.) □ *He fell off his boogie-board and broke his tailbone.* □ *Can you imagine a boogie-board costing 600 dollars?*

**boogie down (to somewhere)** *in.* to hurry (to somewhere); to go (somewhere). □ *So, why don't you boogie down to the store and load up with bud and berries for the weekend?* □ *I'm gonna boogie down and see what's going on.*

**boogieman** ['bugimæn OR 'bʊgimæn] *n.* an imaginary man who is said to frighten people; a false threat of any kind. □ *Don't turn me into a boogieman. Spank the child yourself.* □ *The press has made the secretary into some sort of boogieman.*

**book 1.** *in.* to leave. □ *Time's up. Gotta book.* □ *Let's book. I'm late.* **2.** *tr.* to charge someone with a crime. □ *The cop booked him for vagrancy.* □ *She looked sort of scroungy, and they wanted to book her for something, but didn't know what.* **3.** *in.* to study. (See also **book it.**) □ *I gotta book. Bye.* □ *I hate to book all night.*

**bookie** *n.* a bookmaker for betting. □ *Max was a bookie till he got into drugs.* □ *My bookie wants his money on the spot.*

**book it** *tr.* to study hard; to spend a period of time studying. (Collegiate.) □ *I am so tired of booking it every night of my life.* □ *I've got to spend the rest of the night booking it.*

**boom box** *n.* a portable stereo radio. (See also *box*.) □ *Turn down that damn boom box, or I'll kick it in.* □ *Hey, man! You even gonna take your boom box to church, or what?*

**boomer 1.** *n.* a laborer who moves from one economic boom to another. □ *Fred's great-uncle was a boomer in the days of the Oklahoma oil rush.* □ *Most of the old boomers settled down and raised families.* **2.** See *(baby) boomer.*

**boom sticks** *n.* drumsticks. (Musicians.) □ *He always carries his boom sticks in his back pocket, and he beats on walls, radiators, desks—you name it.* □ *I need new boom sticks. They keep breaking.*

**boondocks** AND **boonies** ['bundɑks AND 'buniz] *n.* an isolated area; an area of wild terrain; suburbs distant from a city. (From the word for mountain in the Tagalog language. Since World War II.) □ *The weather out in the boonies looks cold and dry.* □ *I don't want to be stuck out in the boondocks!*

**boondoggle** ['bundɔgl] *n.* a waste of time and money; a project for spending public money. □ *Another Washington boondoggle came to light today as investigators revealed plans for a dam in a California canyon that doesn't have any water.* □ *This is another boondoggle—just the thing every single baby-kisser pledged to stop.*

**boonies** See *boondocks.*

**boost 1.** *tr. & in.* to steal or shoplift something. (Underworld.) □ *He specializes in boosting meat for resale.* □ *He boosts for a living.* **2.** *tr.* to praise or *hype* someone or something; to support someone or something. □ *She is always boosting some cause.* □ *If she would boost me as well, I wouldn't object to the time she spends hyping other people.*

**booster 1.** *n.* a shoplifter. □ *The cops hauled in two boosters by noon.* □ *Gary was a part-time booster till he got into dope.* **2.** *n.* a supporter (of someone or some cause). □ *We don't have enough boosters to have any effect.* □ *I'm a booster of lots of good causes.*

**booster pill** *n.* an amphetamine pill or capsule. (Drugs.) □ *I'm glad I don't* *need booster pills to start off the day.* □ *Are booster pills habit-forming?*

**boot 1.** *n.* a thrill; a charge. □ *I get a real boot out of my grandchildren.* □ *Their little games give me a real boot.* **2.** *tr.* to dismiss or eject someone. □ *I booted him myself.* □ *Bruno, boot that guy at once!* **3.** *n.* a dismissal or ejection. □ *I got the boot even though I had worked there for a decade.* □ *Seven people got the boot.* **4.** *tr. & in.* to start the operating system of a computer. □ *I booted the thing, but it just sat there.* □ *When I booted, all I got was the feeper going batty.* **5.** *in.* to empty one's stomach; to vomit. □ *The kid booted and booted and will probably never smoke another cigar.* □ *I think I'm gonna boot. Gangway!*

**boot someone out** AND **boot out someone** *tr.* to throw someone out; to kick someone out. □ *Are you going to boot me out?* □ *I don't boot out anybody. Bruno does that. Bruno, come here.*

**booze** [buz] **1.** *n.* beverage alcohol. (Slang since the 1500s.) □ *I don't care for booze. It makes me sneeze.* □ *Where's the booze?* **2.** AND **booze up** *in.* to drink alcohol to excess; to go on a bash. □ *Let's go out and booze up!* □ *Stop boozing for a minute and listen up, guys.*

**booze artist** *n.* a drunken person; a drunkard. □ *Tod was a booze artist for a decade before he realized what he was doing.* □ *A wobbly booze artist sat musing on the stool in the corner.*

**boozed** *mod.* alcohol intoxicated. □ *Wow, is he ever boozed!* □ *I think I am a little boozed.*

**booze it (up)** *tr.* to drink excessively; to drink to intoxication. □ *You come home every night and booze it up. How can you keep on this way?* □ *Let's go out and booze it, okay?*

**boozy-woozy** ['buzi'wuzi] *mod.* alcohol intoxicated. □ *The boozy-woozy man clung to the railing and sang at the top of his voice.* □ *I think I am just an itty-bitty boozy-woozy.*

**bop** [bɑp] **1.** *tr.* to strike someone or something. □ *I bopped the car on the hood and made a dent.* □ *You wanna get bopped in the beezer?* **2.** *n.* a style of jazz popular in the 1940s. □ *We heard*

*some bop in an old movie.* □ *Bop is not popular, but it is by no means dead.* **3.** *n.* a drug in pill form; a dose of a drug. (See *hit.*) □ *Give me a bop of that stuff, will ya?* □ *You gonna drop both of them bops?*

**border (red)** *n.* a secobarbital capsule manufactured in Mexico. (Drugs.) □ *Borders are cheap and not too safe either.* □ *People looking for secs end up with border reds.*

**bore the pants off (of) someone** *tr.* to bore someone exceedingly. □ *You bore the pants off me!* □ *The lecture bored the pants off of everybody.*

**bosh** [bɑʃ] *n.* nonsense; idle talk. (Also an exclamation, **Bosh!**) □ *That is enough of your bosh!* □ *Oh, bosh! You don't know what you're talking about.*

**bosom buddy** *n.* a very close male or female friend. □ *We are bosom buddies, but we can still get into a big fight every now and then.* □ *Oh, yes, Sharon is my bosom buddy.*

**bosom chums** AND **bosom friends** *n.* lice. □ *The old guy sat there scratching at his bosom chums.* □ *"Nobody seems to like my bosom friends," he muttered.*

**bosom friends** See the previous entry.

**boss** *mod.* excellent; powerful. □ *That is a boss tune.* □ *This rally is really boss.*

**boss habit** *n.* a very demanding addiction to heroin. (Drugs.) □ *Max has a boss habit that keeps him hustling for copper.* □ *Man, that is a boss habit. You are massively hooked.*

**boss lady** *n.* the woman in charge. □ *You'll have to ask the boss lady.* □ *The boss lady asked again for volunteers.*

**boss man** *n.* the man in charge. □ *The boss man's coming. Watch out!* □ *I guess the boss man is about ready to retire.*

**both sheets in the wind** *mod.* alcohol intoxicated. (See *three sheets in the wind.*) □ *She's both sheets in the wind at the moment.* □ *She's not just both sheets in the wind—they're all in the wind.*

**bottle 1.** *n.* a drunkard. □ *The bar was empty save an old bottle propped against the side of a booth.* □ *That old girl is just a bottle. There's more booze in her than* outside. **2.** *n.* liquor. (Always with *the* in this sense.) □ *Her only true love is the bottle.* □ *The bottle plays a big role in his life.* **3.** *in.* to drink liquor to excess. □ *I wish there was a way I could get through the day without bottling.* □ *Let's go out and bottle into oblivion.*

**bottleache** ['bɑdˌlek] *n.* a hangover; the delirium tremens. □ *A lot of these guys really suffer from the bottleache, but what can they do?* □ *I got a touch of the bottleache this morning.*

**bottle baby** *n.* an alcoholic. □ *The bottle babies sat there, waiting to be thrown out at closing time.* □ *There is help for bottle babies.*

**bottom 1.** *n.* the buttocks. □ *Ted fell on his bottom and just sat there.* □ *My bottom is sore from sitting too long.* **2.** *n.* the second half of a baseball inning. □ *It's the bottom of the second, Wilbur's up.* □ *Wilbur hit a double-bagger in the bottom of the second.*

**bottom dollar** *n.* one's last dollar. (See also *bet one's bottom dollar.*) □ *I lost my bottom dollar on that deal.* □ *I'm down to my bottom dollar. How about a little loan?*

**bottomless pit 1.** *n.* a very hungry person. □ *The guy is a bottomless pit. There isn't enough food in town to fill him up.* □ *I've got two boys, and they're both bottomless pits.* **2.** *n.* an endless source of something, usually something troublesome. □ *This house is a bottomless pit. Keeping it up is endless.* □ *Our problems come from a bottomless pit. There is just no end to them.*

**bottom line 1.** *n.* the grand total; the final figure on a balance sheet. (Financial markets. Always with *the.*) □ *The company's bottom line is in bad shape.* □ *If the bottom line is positive, everything is okay.* **2.** *n.* the result; the *nitty-gritty*; the *score.* □ *The bottom line is that you really don't care.* □ *Well, when you get down to the bottom line, it's only money that matters.*

**bottom of the barrel** AND **bottom of the heap** *n.* the location of persons or things of the very lowest quality. (Usually with *from.* See also *scrape the bottom of the barrel.*) □ *That last secretary you sent me was really from the bottom of the barrel.* □ *I don't need any candidates from the bottom of the heap.*

**bottom of the heap** See the previous entry.

**bottom out** *in.* to reach the lowest or worst point of something. □ *All my problems seem to be bottoming out. They can't get much worse.* □ *Interest rates bottomed out last February.*

**Bottoms up.** *sent.* "Let us drink up!" (A drinking toast.) □ *Well, bottoms up.* □ *They all raised their glasses, and the host said, "Bottoms up."*

**bounce 1.** *in.* (for a check) to be returned from the bank. (See also *rubber (check).*) □ *The check bounced, and I had to pay a penalty fee.* □ *If your check bounces, you'll have to bring us cash.* **2.** *tr.* (for a bank) to refuse to honor a check. □ *They bounced another of my checks today.* □ *The bank won't bounce any more checks because I closed the account.* **3.** *tr.* to throw someone out. □ *Bruno bounced me, and I ran to my car and beat it.* □ *The owner came out and bounced us.* **4.** *n.* pep; energy. □ *All these kids have a lot of bounce.* □ *I never have any bounce when I wake up early.*

**bounce for something** See *spring for something.*

**bouncer** *n.* a strong man hired to eject unruly people from a bar or similar place. (People supposedly bounce when thrown out.) □ *I saw the bouncer looking at me, and I got out of there fast.* □ *He was the biggest bouncer I've ever seen.*

**bounce something off (of) someone** *tr.* to try out an idea on someone; to get someone's opinion of an idea. □ *Let me bounce this off of you.* □ *I bounced the idea off Gary, but he wasn't at all impressed.*

**bowl 1.** *n.* a *pipe* or other device for smoking cannabis. (Drugs.) □ *Where is my bowl? I got some real Q. gold.* □ *There's somebody's bowl out in the hall. Go get it before the neighbors call the fuzz.* **2.** See *bowl (up).*

**bowl (up)** *in.* to fill a *pipe* with cannabis. (Drugs.) □ *I was just bowling up when you came in.* □ *Man, let's bowl and get on with this!*

**bow to the porcelain altar** *in.* to empty one's stomach; to vomit. (The porcelain altar is the toilet bowl.) □ *He spent the whole night bowing to the porcelain altar.* □ *I have the feeling that I will be bowing to the porcelain altar before morning.*

**bow-wow** ['bɑuwɑu] **1.** *n.* a dog. (Juvenile.) □ *The bow-wow frightened me.* □ *We're going to get you a bow-wow!* **2.** *n.* an ugly woman; a *dog.* (Derogatory.) □ *What a bow-wow!* □ *I would have chosen a better nose if I had been given a chance, but—all in all—I'm not such a bow-wow.*

**box 1.** *n.* a coffin. □ *I want the cheapest box they sell.* □ *Put him in a box and put the box in a hole. Then the matter is closed.* **2.** *n.* an accordion. (See *(squeeze-)box.*) □ *If he brings his box to the party, we'll polka all night.* □ *A box—if used right—can do something special for a band.* **3.** *n.* a phonograph player. □ *My box is old, but still good.* □ *Yours is old! My box still has tubes!* **4.** *n.* a portable stereo radio; a *(ghetto) box.* (See *(ghetto) blaster.*) □ *Where did you get that box?* □ *Does that damn box have to be so loud?* **5.** *n.* a piano. □ *Man, he plays a mean box.* □ *She sure can pound the devil out of that box!*

**boxed in** *mod.* in a bind; having few alternatives. □ *I really feel boxed in around here.* □ *I got him boxed in. He'll have to do it our way.*

**boxed (up) 1.** *mod.* alcohol or drug intoxicated. □ *I am way boxed, and I feel sick.* □ *She got boxed up on gin.* **2.** *mod.* in jail. □ *I did it, and I was boxed for a long time for it. Now lay off!* □ *Pat was boxed up for two days till we got bond money.*

**box someone in** AND **box in someone** *tr.* to put someone into a bind; to reduce the number of someone's alternatives. (See examples.) □ *I don't want to box you in, but you are running out of options.* □ *I want to box in the whole staff, so they'll have to do it my way.* (More at *boxed in.*)

**Boy howdy!** ['bɔɪ 'hɑudi] *exclam.* "Wow!" (Folksy.) □ *Boy howdy! What a game!* □ *Boy howdy! Are you ever stoned!*

**boys in blue** See *men in blue.*

**boys in the backroom** AND **backroom boys** *n.* any private male group making decisions, usually politicians. □ *The boys in the backroom picked the last presidential candidate.* □ *The backroom boys have decided too many things in the past. Their day is over.*

**bozo** ['bozo] *n.* a clown; a jerk; a fool. (Also a term of address.) □ *Look, you bozo, I've had enough of your jabber.* □ *Those bozos are at it again. Spend, spend, spend.*

**bra-burner** *n.* a nickname for a woman who supported the women's liberation movements of the 1960s-70s. (Derogatory.) □ *Didn't the bra-burners give way to whale-savers in the seventies?* □ *Mike wants to know if the bra-burners took them off first.*

**brack-brain** ['brækbren] *n.* a fool. □ *The brack-brains in Washington have done it again!* □ *One brack-brain around here is enough. Do you want me to leave?*

**brain 1.** *n.* a good student; a very intelligent person. (See also *brains.*) □ *I'm no brain, but I get good grades.* □ *Who was the brain who figured this out?* **2.** *tr.* to hit someone (in the head). □ *I ought to brain you for that!* □ *She almost brained me with her umbrella.*

**brain-burned** AND **brain-fried** *mod.* brain-damaged from drugs. (Drugs. See *burnout.*) □ *The kid is a little brain-burned, but still has a chance at an independent life.* □ *Man, you're gonna get brain-burned from this stuff.*

**brain-burners** *n.* injected amphetamines, probably methamphetamine. (Drugs.) □ *What did you think was going to happen to you when you started shooting brain-burners?* □ *The kid's a burnout all right. Brain-burners did it.*

**brainchild 1.** *n.* someone's good idea viewed as an offspring of the brain. □ *Is this your brainchild? It won't work.* □ *Listen to this. It's my best brainchild.* **2.** *n.* a person who has good ideas. □ *The boss's new brainchild seems to have gone dry.* □ *You can't just go out and hire a brainchild. They've got to want to work for you.*

**brain-drain** *n.* the movement of intellectuals from one country to another where the pay and job opportunities are better. □ *It looks like the brain-drain of the fifties is reversing with more and more academics leaving the U.S. to join British universities.* □ *Where there is a good education system, there will always be a brain-drain.*

**brain-fried** See *brain-burned.*

**brains** *n.* the person(s) in charge of thinking something through. □ *Who's the brains around this joint?* □ *Bruno is not what I would call the brains of the gang.*

**brainstorm 1.** *n.* a sudden good idea. □ *I had a sudden brainstorm and got out of bed to write it down.* □ *This brainstorm hit me while I was in the shower.* **2.** *in.* to try to think up good ideas, especially as a group. □ *Let's brainstorm on this for a little while.* □ *They are in the meeting room now, brainstorming.*

**brain-teaser** See the following entry.

**brain-twister** AND **brain-teaser** *n.* a puzzle. □ *This Maltese falcon case is a real brain-twister.* □ *Can you help me with this brain-teaser?*

**(brand) spanking new** *mod.* completely new. □ *My car is spanking new.* □ *Look at that brand spanking new car!*

**brass** *n.* high ranking military or civilian officers. (See also *top brass.*) □ *We'll see what the brass has to say first.* □ *The brass said no to your promotion.*

**brassed (off)** *mod.* angry; disgusted. □ *You look so brassed off at the world. Smile!* □ *I'm not brassed in the least, really.*

**brass hat** *n.* a member of the *brass.* □ *When are the brass hats going to start paying attention to the important things?* □ *A brass hat came up to me and asked me where I was going.*

**brass someone off** AND **brass off someone** *tr.* to make someone angry. □ *She really brasses me off!* □ *The dean brassed off the entire fraternity by putting them on probation.*

**brass tacks** *n.* essential business. (Usually in "get down to brass tacks.") □ *Now that we are talking brass tacks, how much do you really want for this watch?*

□ *Since we haven't gotten down to brass tacks, would it be unethical for me to buy you lunch?*

**bread** *n.* money. □ *I need to get some bread to live on.* □ *You got any bread you can spare?*

**bread and butter 1.** *n.* one's livelihood. □ *It's bread and butter to me. I have to do it.* □ *I can't give it up. It's my bread and butter.* **2.** *phr.* something said when two people walking along must separate to pass around a pole or something similar. (Folksy.) □ *I'll say "bread and butter" at the next post.* □ *Why do people say "bread and butter" at all?*

**bread and butter letter** *n.* a polite letter sent after a visit, meeting, or conversation. □ *I sat down after I got home and wrote a stack of bread and butter letters.* □ *I got a bread and butter letter from Frank. I should have sent him one first.*

**breadbasket** AND **dinner basket** *n.* the belly; the stomach. □ *I hit him, pow, right in the breadbasket.* □ *With a dinner basket like that, he must have a devil of a time buying clothes.*

**break 1.** *n.* a chance; an opportunity. □ *Come on, give me a break!* □ *I got my first break in show biz when I was only 12.* **2.** *n.* an escape from prison; a prison break-out. □ *I hear there's a break planned for tonight.* □ *Two cons got shot in the break.* **3.** *in.* (for a story) to unfold rapidly. (Journalism.) □ *As the story continues to break, we will bring you the latest.* □ *Something is breaking on the Wilson murder. Get over to the D.A.'s office, quick.* **4.** *n.* a solo played when the rest of the band stops. □ *This is your break, Andy. Let's hear it, man.* □ *It wasn't much of a break, but I gave it everything.*

**Break a leg!** *exclam.* "Good luck!" (A special theatrical way of wishing a performer good luck. Saying "good luck" is a jinx.) □ *"Break a leg!" shouted the stage manager to the heroine.* □ *Let's all go and do our best. Break a leg!*

**breaker 1.** *n.* a break dancer. (Break dancing is a rhythmic and energetic impromptu performance usually done by untrained urban youths.) □ *He is one of the best breakers in the city.* □ *I'm too fat to be a breaker.* **2.** *n.* someone attempting to use a citizens band radio channel. □ *There's a breaker trying to use this channel. Let's drop down to 11.* □ *You got it, breaker.*

**breakfast of champions** *n.* a first drink of the day, taken in the morning, instead of breakfast. (Collegiate.) □ *Well, here it goes—the breakfast of champions.* □ *He calls it the breakfast of champions. I call it a bad sign of something out of hand.*

**Break it up!** *exclam.* "Stop it!" (An order to two or more people to stop doing something, such as fighting.) □ *All right you two, break it up!* □ *She told the boys to break it up or get sent to the principal's office.*

**break the ice** **1.** *tr.* to be the first one to do something. □ *No one wants to break the ice. I guess I will be first.* □ *Well, I guess we should break the ice and start dancing.* **2.** *tr.* to attempt to become friends with someone. □ *He tried to break the ice, but she was a little cold.* □ *A nice smile does a lot to break the ice.*

**breathe easy** *in.* to relax; to let down one's guard and relax. □ *Now I can sit down and breathe easy.* □ *I won't breathe easy until this matter is settled.*

**breather** *n.* a rest period; a lull. □ *I really need a breather.* □ *As soon as we've had a breather, it's back to work.*

**breeder** *n.* a non-homosexual. (In a homosexual context.) □ *Don't invite Wally. He's a breeder.* □ *Why not? The breeders invited us to their party.*

**breeze** *n.* an easy task. □ *Nothing to it. It was a breeze.* □ *I went through it like a breeze.*

**breeze along** *in.* to move along rapidly in a car; to speed in a car. □ *We were breezing along at about 80 when we saw the red light.* □ *You were breezing along sort of fast there, weren't you, son?*

**breeze in** *in.* to come in casually; to come in rapidly (and go out again rapidly). □ *She breezed in, did her work, and left.* □ *You can't just breeze in here and expect to be fed!*

**breeze off** *in.* to go away; to leave quickly. □ *I hate to just breeze off, but duty calls.* □ *I knew she would breeze off like that. She is so busy.*

**breeze through (something)** *tr. & in.* to pass through something quickly. □ *I breezed right through the tax form.* □ *He breezed through on his way to Chicago.*

**breezy** *mod.* casual; light. □ *If she just wasn't so breezy about it, I wouldn't mind so much.* □ *Your breezy attitude burns me up.*

**brew** **1.** *n.* coffee; occasionally, tea. □ *I could use a nice cup of brew.* □ *This is my kind of brew—hot, black, and aromatic.* **2.** *n.* beer; a can, bottle, or glass of beer. □ *Hey, give me a cold brew, will ya?* □ *This is my favorite brew, and it's at just the right temperature.*

**brew-ha** ['bruhɑ] *n.* beer; a beer. □ *One brew-ha over here, innkeeper!* □ *How 'bout another brew-ha, Mike?*

**brew-out** *n.* a beer blast; a beer *blow-out.* □ *Were you at Tom's brew-out? I was too bombed to see who was there.* □ *Was that Tom's brew-out I was at?*

**brewski** AND **brewsky** ['bruski] *n.* beer; a beer. □ *Hey, how 'bout a brewski?* □ *I'll take a nice cold brewsky.*

**brick** **1.** AND **brick gum** *n.* a brick of unprocessed opium. (Drugs.) □ *Where would anyone get any brick gum these days? Is it coming back?* □ *He got it from some refugee, and he doesn't know what to do with it.* **2.** *n.* a kilogram of compressed marijuana; a bar of hashish. (Drugs.) □ *Don said he left a whole brick under the car seat.* □ *What does a brick cost these days?*

**bridge** *n.* a holder for a marijuana cigarette butt. (Drugs.) □ *I had a bridge in my stash, but it's gone.* □ *Gimme a bridge. I burned my finger.*

**brig** [brɪg] *n.* jail. (From the term for a naval prison or a shipboard jail.) □ *Throw this jerk in the brig.* □ *The brig in that one-horse town is a mess.*

**bright and breezy** *mod.* cheery and alert. □ *You look all bright and breezy. What happened?* □ *Bright and breezy people on a day like this make me sick.*

**bright-eyed and bushy-tailed** *mod.* alert and ready to do something; as alert and as active as a squirrel. □ *You look all bright-eyed and bushy-tailed this morning.* □ *The child—bright-eyed and bushy-*

*tailed—woke everyone up at dawn.* □ *Tell that bright-eyed and bushy-tailed brat to shut up!*

**brim** *n.* a hat. □ *Man, that is one fine brim you got.* □ *New silks call for a new brim.*

**bring-down 1.** *n.* something that depresses someone. □ *The news was a terrible bring-down.* □ *Just to see your face was a bring-down.* **2.** *n.* something that brings someone back to reality. □ *The bill for the week's stay was a real bring-down.* □ *I have had one bring-down after another today.*

**bring home the bacon** *tr.* to earn a livelihood; to earn money to buy food. □ *When I have to bring home the bacon, I hope I have an interesting job.* □ *I have to bring home the bacon for six kids.*

**bring someone down** AND **bring down someone 1.** *tr.* to terminate one's own or someone else's drug experience. (Drugs.) □ *It took a lot to bring her down.* □ *We brought down the two of them carefully.* **2.** *tr.* to depress someone. □ *The news really brought me down.* □ *The failure of the business brought down the staff.*

**bring someone on** AND **bring on someone** *tr.* to arouse sexually; to turn someone on. □ *She was trying to bring her date on, but he saw her game.* □ *This kind of music brings me on.*

**bring something up** AND **bring up something 1.** *tr.* to mention something. (Standard English.) □ *Why did you have to bring that up?* □ *Then they brought up the question of money.* **2.** *tr.* to vomit something up; to cough something up. □ *See if you can get him to bring up the penny.* □ *I did, and he brought up a nickel instead!*

**broad** *n.* a woman. (Originally derogatory. Now usually derogatory.) □ *This pushy broad comes up to me and asks if I have any manners!* □ *So—come on, what'd you tell the broad?*

**broker 1.** *n.* a dope pusher or seller. (Drugs.) □ *He said he had to meet with his broker. I thought he was talking about stocks.* □ *The guy never touches the stuff. He's a broker, though, and a rich one.* **2.** *n.* a ruined addict; a broken addict. (Drugs.) □ *He's a burnout, a*

broker. *Chill him!* □ *This broker comes up and puts a touch on me for old times' sake.*

**Bronx cheer** ['brɑŋks 'tʃir] *n.* a rude noise made with the lips; a *raspberry*. □ *The little air compressor in the corner of the parking lot made a noise like a Bronx cheer.* □ *He got only a Bronx cheer for his efforts.*

**brother Ben** *n.* A personification of Benzedrine™; the amphetamine Benzedrine™. (Drugs.) □ *With the help of brother Ben, I'll make it to L.A. by morning.* □ *Brother Ben can get you in a lot of trouble.*

**brown-bag 1.** *n.* a bag lunch. □ *Bring a brown-bag, and we'll talk and eat at the same time.* □ *I lost my brown-bag, but I'll come to talk anyway.* **2.** *in.* to carry a bag lunch. □ *He's back to brown-bagging while he saves up for his vacation.* □ *I like to brown-bag. I don't eat so much when I do.* **3.** *mod.* having to do with an event during which people eat their own bag lunches. □ *These brown-bag affairs seem so tacky.* □ *The brown-bag meeting wasn't very useful.* □ *It's brown-bag. Come if you can.*

**browned (off)** *mod.* angry. □ *I am really browned off at you!* □ *The boss is browned—to say the least.*

**brownie points** *n.* imaginary credit for doing something well. (Originally "demerits" in railroading.) □ *How many brownie points do I get for not frowning when you take my picture?* □ *No brownie points for you, twit!*

**brown-nose 1.** AND **brown-noser** *n.* a sycophant; one who flatters for self-serving motives. □ *You are just a plain old brown-nose.* □ *That brown-noser actually gave the boss a bottle of wine for her birthday.* **2.** *tr. & in.* to curry favor with someone; to be a sycophant. □ *Don't you brown-nose me!* □ *Don keeps brown-nosing, and the professor pretends not to notice.*

**brown-noser** See the previous entry.

**brown out 1.** *in.* (for the electricity) to fade and dim down. (Something less than a blackout.) □ *The power kept browning out.* □ *The lights started to brown out, and I thought maybe I didn't pay the bill for the juice.* **2.** *n.* a period of dimming or fading of the electricity. □ *There was another brown out today.* □ *They keep building all these expensive power stations, and then we still have brown outs.*

**brown someone off** AND **brown off someone** *tr.* to make someone angry. □ *That whole business with the cab really browned me off.* □ *I'm afraid I'm going to brown off everyone, but here goes anyway.* (More at *browned (off).*)

**brown sugar** *n.* a grainy, low-potency heroin. (Drugs.) □ *This stuff is brown sugar. I've been burned.* □ *Some people prefer brown sugar as long as it's cheap.*

**brown weed** *n.* marijuana; a brown variety of marijuana. □ *This brown weed is as good as gold.* □ *Brown weed is as good as anything you can get around this town.*

**bruised** [bruzd] *mod.* alcohol intoxicated. □ *I am bruised. My head hurts, and my gut feels yucky.* □ *How can anybody get so bruised on so little booze?*

**bruiser** ['bruzɚ] *n.* a big rough male. □ *That big bruiser must weigh a ton.* □ *They call that 320-pound bruiser "The Fridge."*

**brush** *n.* an encounter; a *close shave*. □ *My brush with the bear was so close I could smell its breath—which was vile, I might add.* □ *It seemed like a brush with death.*

**brushoff** ['brəʃɔf] *n.* a dismissal; an act of ignoring someone. (See also *give someone the brushoff.*) □ *No brushoff for her. I told her to beat it.* □ *I got the brushoff, but I can take it.*

**brush someone off** AND **brush off someone** *tr.* to get rid of or dismiss someone or something. (See also *give someone the brushoff.*) □ *Don't just brush me off. Answer me!* □ *They brushed off the charges without any comment.*

**brutal** *mod.* excellent; powerful. □ *Man, what a brutal tune!* □ *That last wave was brutal to the max.*

**B.S.** *n.* nonsense; *bullshit*. □ *I've heard enough of your B.S.* □ *Less B.S. and more facts, please.*

**B.T.O.** See *big-time operator*.

**bubblehead** **1.** *n.* a fool; a giddy person. □ *You silly bubblehead. Watch where you are going!* □ *If you can't say any-*

thing without coming off like a bubblehead, keep your mouth shut. **2.** *n.* a heavy drinker of champagne. □ *It takes a pretty good bankroll to be a real high-class bubblehead.* □ *Part-time bubbleheads go into operation at weddings and other celebrations.*

**bubble water** AND **bubbles** *n.* champagne. □ *More bubble water, or do you want something stronger?* □ *I want about a gallon of bubbles, thanks.*

**bubbly** *n.* champagne. (Often with *the.*) □ *I'd like a big glass of bubbly, if you don't mind.* □ *The bubbly will brighten up any party.*

**buck** **1.** *n.* a dollar. □ *Gimme a buck for a bottle of wine, will you mister?* □ *Here's a buck; get me some cigarettes.* **2.** *tr.* to resist something. □ *Don't buck it. Do what you are told.* □ *He enjoys bucking the system.* **3.** *n.* a buckskin (leather) shoe. (Usually plural.) □ *Look at my new bucks!* □ *You don't see many red bucks. Are you sure you got the right thing?*

**bucket** **1.** *n.* the goal (hoop and net) in basketball. (Sports.) □ *Freddy arced one at the bucket and missed.* □ *When he holds his arm up, his hand is as high as the top of the bucket.* **2.** *n.* a goal or basket in basketball. (Sports.) □ *Four buckets in 2 minutes. Is that a record, or what?* □ *The last bucket put Adamsville ahead by 2 points.*

**buck for something** *tr.* to work ambitiously for something, such as a promotion. □ *I'm just bucking for recognition, and of course, a 20% raise.* □ *You can tell she's bucking for promotion.*

**buck naked** *mod.* entirely naked. (Folksy. From the color of buckskin leather.) □ *He stood there buck naked, scratching his belly.* □ *They all slipped off their trousers and went swimming buck naked.* □ *Who's that buck naked dancer?*

**bucko** ['bəko] *n.* friend; pal. (Also a term of address.) □ *Hey, bucko, come here a minute.* □ *Ask your bucko there if he wants to join us.*

**buckpasser** *n.* someone who cannot accept the responsibility for something. (See *pass the buck.*) □ *You are the most irresponsible buckpasser I have ever had to deal with!* □ *When some-*

*thing really goes wrong, everybody suddenly becomes a buckpasser.*

**buck up** *in.* to cheer up; to perk up. □ *Come on, now, buck up. Things can't be all that bad.* □ *She began to buck up when I showed her the results of the tests.*

**bud** [bəd] **1.** *n.* marijuana containing the buds of marijuana flowers. (Drugs.) □ *She has a bag of buds in her stash.* □ *She takes the buds out of everybody else's stuff.* **2.** *n.* a Budweiser™ beer; any beer. (See *budhead*.) □ *How 'bout one of them buds in a green bottle?* □ *I got four kinds of bud here. Which do you want?*

**Buddha stick** ['budə 'stɪk] *n.* a marijuana cigarette. (Drugs.) □ *She says she wants a Buddha stick, which is just a fancy name for a joint.* □ *I'll show you how to make a Buddha stick. Watch!*

**buddy** ['bədi] *n.* a friend; a pal. (Also a term of address.) □ *Look, buddy, I gotta a little problem maybe you can help me with.* □ *My buddy over there is from Bean Town.*

**buddy-buddy** ['bədi'bədi] *mod.* friendly; too friendly. □ *Why is that guy so buddy-buddy with me?* □ *Don't try to get too buddy-buddy with these people. They don't like strangers.* □ *What a buddy-buddy phony!*

**buddy up to someone** *in.* to become very friendly toward someone. □ *Why are you buddying up to me? I don't even know you.* □ *Try to buddy up to him and pretend you are interested in what he is doing.*

**buddy up (with someone)** *in.* to share living space with someone; to share something with someone. □ *Let's buddy up, okay?* □ *There weren't enough to go around, so we had to buddy up.*

**budget crunch** See the following entry.

**budget squeeze** AND **budget crunch** *n.* a situation where there is not enough money in the budget. □ *Facing another budget squeeze, the legislators were forced to put off their pay increase.* □ *The budget crunch hasn't begun to affect us yet.*

**budhead** ['bədhɛd] *n.* a beer drinker. (Black. See *bud*.) □ *You're a budhead, and you're getting worse.* □ *Here comes Charlie, my favorite budhead. How about a brew, Charlie?*

**buffaloed** ['bəfəlod] *mod.* confused; stumped. □ *These tax forms really have me buffaloed.* □ *He was so buffaloed by the problem that he didn't get any work done.*

**bug 1.** *n.* a flaw in a computer program. □ *As soon as I get the bugs out, I can run my program.* □ *There is a little bug still, but it hardly causes any problems.* **2.** *n.* a combining form meaning someone who is enthusiastic about something. □ *Mary is a camera bug.* □ *Al has turned into a real compact disc bug.* **3.** *n.* an obsession or urge. □ *I've got this bug about making money.* □ *I had this bug that made me eat all shapes of pasta.* **4.** *n.* a spy device for listening to someone's conversation. □ *I found a little bug taped under my chair.* □ *The agency bulls put bugs everywhere.* **5.** *tr.* to conceal a microphone somewhere. □ *Who bugged my office?* □ *We will have to bug the bookie joint to get the goods on those guys.* **6.** *tr.* to annoy someone. □ *Stop bugging me, you twit!* □ *This kind of thing really bugs me.*

**buggy** ['bəgi] *n.* an automobile. □ *Other than a dent in the front bumper, this buggy is in A-1 condition.* □ *It's time to buy a new buggy.*

**Bug off!** *exclam.* "Get out!"; "Go away!" □ *Bug off! Get out of here!* □ *Bug off and leave me alone!*

**bug out 1.** *in.* to pack up and retreat. (Military, Korean war.) □ *Orders are to bug out by oh-nine-hundred.* □ *Okay, everybody, move it! We're bugging out.* **2.** *in.* to get out of somewhere fast. □ *I gotta find a way to bug out of here without getting caught.* □ *Okay, it's clear. Let's bug out.*

**built like a brick outhouse** AND **built like a brick shithouse\*** *mod.* (of a person who is) well built—either strong or attractive. (Caution with *shit*.) □ *That guy's built like a brick shithouse.* □ *This garage is built like a brick outhouse. It'll last for years.*

**bull 1.** *n.* nonsense; *bullshit*. □ *That's just a lot of bull.* □ *Don't give me that bull! I won't buy it.* **2.** *tr. & in.* to lie to or deceive someone. □ *Stop bulling me!* □ *Is she bulling again?* **3.** *n.* a police officer; a private detective or guard. □

*Here come the bulls. Get out.* □ *And this bull comes up and says, "Where's the fire?"*

**bulldoze** *tr.* to apply pressure or force to get someone to do something. □ *You think you can bulldoze people into doing what you want!* □ *Don't bulldoze me! I push back.*

**bullheaded** *mod.* stubborn. □ *Don't be so bullheaded.* □ *You are the most bullheaded man I've ever known.*

**bull jive** *n.* diluted or adulterated cannabis. (Drugs. See *jive*.) □ *Don't sell me no bull jive again, you hear?* □ *This is bull jive if I ever saw it.*

**bull-pucky** ['bʊlpəki] **1.** *n.* bull dung. □ *Why didn't you watch where you were going? Didn't you expect to find bull-pucky in a barnyard?* □ *How can you tell it's bull-pucky?* **2.** *n.* nonsense; *bullshit.* □ *Don't give me that bull-pucky!* □ *That's all just bull-pucky. Don't believe a word of it.*

**bull session** *n.* a session of casual conversation. □ *The gals were sitting around enjoying a bull session.* □ *The bull session ran on late into the night.*

**bullshit\*** **1.\*** *n.* nonsense; lies; deception. (Caution with *shit*.) □ *Don't give me all that bullshit!* □ *That's just bullshit.* **2.\*** *tr.* to deceive someone; to lie to someone. (Caution with *shit*.) □ *Stop bullshitting me!* □ *You wouldn't bullshit us, would you?*

**bullshit artist\*** AND **bullshitter\*** *n.* someone who excels at boasting or lying. (Caution with *shit*.) □ *Jim is such a bullshit artist!* □ *He can't talk straight—nothing but a bullshitter.*

**bullshitter** See *bullshit artist.*

**Bully for you!** *exclam.* "Very good for you!" □ *You did it! Bully for you!* □ *You are the winner! Bully for you!*

**bullyrag** ['bʊliræg] *tr. & in.* to harass someone. □ *Don't bullyrag me just because you're upset.* □ *Tod is bullyragging again.*

**bum** **1.** *n.* a vagrant; a good-for-nothing. □ *You had better get your finances in order unless you want to become a bum.* □ *There is a bunch of bums on the corner, just doing nothing.* **2.** *mod.* bad; faulty. □ *This is a bum fuse. No wonder it won't run.* □ *The screw has a bum*

head and won't turn. **3.** See *bum something (off someone).*

**bum around** *in.* to wander around; to *kick around.* □ *I thought I'd bum around a few years before I settled down.* □ *Those two kids bummed around Europe for two months.*

**bum check** *n.* a bad check; a forged check. (See *paper*.) □ *I never wrote a bum check in my life.* □ *We took in four bum checks today.*

**bummed (out)** *mod.* discouraged; depressed. □ *I feel so bummed. I think I need a nice hot bath.* □ *When you're feeling bummed out, think how many problems I have.*

**bummer** **1.** AND **bum trip** *n.* a bad drug experience. (Drugs.) □ *She almost didn't get back from a bum trip.* □ *This bummer comes from mixing pills.* **2.** *n.* a disagreeable thing or person. (Compare to *buzz-kill*.) □ *My coach is a real bummer.* □ *The game was a bummer you wouldn't believe.*

**bumming** *mod.* down; depressed; suffering from something disagreeable. (Collegiate.) □ *I'm really bumming. I think I need somebody to talk to.* □ *Everybody's bumming. It must be the weather.*

**bum out** **1.** *in.* to have a bad experience with drugs. (Drugs.) □ *I bummed out on angel dust.* □ *She bummed out once too often and gave up the stuff altogether.* **2.** *in.* to have any bad experience. □ *We bummed out at the concert. I dropped my music, and Larry broke a string.* □ *The test was horrible. I bummed out, for sure.*

**bump** *tr.* to remove someone from an airplane flight, usually involuntarily, because of overbooking. □ *They bumped me, but gave me something to make up for it.* □ *Is this airline in the habit of bumping old ladies?*

**bump someone off** AND **bump off someone** *tr.* to kill someone. (Originally underworld.) □ *The mob bumped off the witness before the trial.* □ *What am I supposed to do, bump her off?*

**bum rap** **1.** *n.* a false criminal charge. (Underworld. The same as *bad rap*.) □ *This is a bum rap, and you know it.* □ *If a crook didn't scream that he got a* bum rap, I might think he was really innocent. **2.** AND **bum-rap** tr. to talk ill about someone; to accuse someone of something falsely. □ You're always bum-rapping your car! □ Don't bum rap me! I'll sue!

**bum someone out** AND **bum out someone** tr. to discourage someone. □ The failure of his tires bummed out the race driver. □ That darn blow-out bummed me out. (More at bummed (out).)

**bum something (off someone)** tr. to beg or borrow something (from someone). □ Can I bum a cigarette off you? □ Can I bum a quarter for a phone call?

**bum's rush** n. the ejection of a person from a place. □ I got the bum's rush at that bar. Do I look that bad? □ Give this dame the bum's rush. She can't pay for nothin'.

**bum steer** ['bəm 'stir] n. a false lead; false information. □ You sure gave me a bum steer when you told me who he was. □ We spent all day checking out what turned out to be a bum steer.

**bunch of fives** n. the fist. □ How would you like a bunch of fives right in the kisser? □ He ended up with a bunch of fives in the gut.

**bunco** ['bəŋko] **1.** n. a scheme to swindle people. (From banca, the name of a card game in Spanish.) □ He's been fiddling with bunco on the West Coast. □ All the stuff relating to bunco comes across this desk. **2.** tr. to swindle someone. □ They buncoed an old lady and left her penniless. □ Fred tried to bunco a chick in Frisco, but felt sorry for her at the last minute.

**bundle** n. a large amount of money. (See make a bundle, package.) □ He still has a bundle from the sale of his house. □ You must think I have a real bundle.

**bundle of joy** AND **bundle from heaven** n. a baby. □ We are expecting a bundle of joy next September. □ When your little bundle from heaven arrives, things will be a little hectic for a while.

**bundle of nerves** n. a very nervous person. □ I'm just a bundle of nerves. I wish this were over. □ Paul's been a bundle of nerves ever since his wreck.

**bunkie** ['bəŋki] n. a roommate. □ My bunkie is from Iowa. □ I wish I had a bunkie. Things get lonely in a single room.

**bunkum** AND **buncombe** ['bəŋkəm] n. nonsense. □ That's just plain bunkum. □ Another candidate for governor means just that much more buncombe.

**buns** n. the buttocks. □ What cute little buns! □ His face looks like a mule kicked him, but have you seen his buns!

**burb** [bɚb] n. a suburb. (Usually plural.) □ I've lived in the burbs all my life. □ Our burb is too far from the city for much pollution.

**burbed out** [bɚbd...] mod. looking very middle-class and suburban; decked out like a suburban citizen. □ She's all burbed out with new clothes and a fancy car. □ He looks sort of burbed out for a city guy.

**burg** [bɚg] n. a small town. (Disdainful.) □ I can't stand another day in this burg. □ This burg is getting on my nerves.

**burger** n. a hamburger sandwich; a hamburger patty. □ You ready for another burger? □ He's cooking burgers out on the grill right now.

**burn 1.** n. a cigarette. □ Gimme a burn, huh? □ Fred just stood there with a burn on his lower lip and his hands in his pockets. **2.** tr. to smoke a cigarette. □ I need to burn a fag. Just a minute. □ This nicotine fiend needs to burn one for a fix! **3.** tr. to smoke cannabis. (Drugs.) □ Jim spent Saturday out in the field burning grass. □ The two of them sat there burning reefers for hours on end. **4.** tr. to execute someone in the electric chair. (Underworld.) □ I'll see that they burn you for this! □ The D.A. tried to burn me, but I got off with six months. **5.** in. to die by electrocution in the electric chair. (Underworld.) □ I ain't afraid I'll burn, copper! □ I'll see that you burn for this. **6.** tr. to cheat or rob someone. □ Tom tried to burn me by selling me a bum watch, but I'm too clever. □ He will burn you if you're not careful. **7.** tr. to shoot someone. (Underworld.) □ He burned the guy with a pistol, but it didn't stop him. □ Hold it! I've burned one guy tonight, and I ain't *afraid of puttin' a hole through you.* **8.** *n.* a deception; an instance of being cheated. □ *Man, that was a burn. That guy was really mad.* □ *We pulled off the burn without a hitch. It was a gas.* **9.** *n.* the charge or *rush* after the injection of a drug into a vein. (Drugs.) □ *Man, wait'll you taste the burn from this stuff.* □ *I don't want a big burn; just drag it out for about an hour.* **10.** *tr.* to cook food. (Black.) □ *Why don't you burn some chow for me?* □ *Burn your own stuff, you lazy good-for-nothing man!*

**burn artist** *n.* someone who cheats or harms someone else; an informer. (Underworld.) □ *Never trust a known burn artist.* □ *The fuzz rounded up all the burn artists in the district and pumped them for info.*

**burned 1.** *mod.* cheated; betrayed. □ *Man, did I get burned in that place!* □ *We sure got burned on that deal.* **2.** *mod.* disappointed; humiliated; put down. □ *Whenever we rap, you're never happy till I'm burned.* □ *Ha! You're burned!* **3.** AND **burned up** *mod.* very angry. □ *I've never been so burned up at anyone.* □ *Boy, was I burned!*

**burned out** AND **burnt out 1.** *mod.* tired; bored. □ *I'm burned out after all that partying.* □ *I don't want to work with burnt out people. I need energy.* **2.** *mod.* having to do with the ruined veins of an addict. (Drugs.) □ *These old ropes are just burned out. I don't know what to do.* □ *My veins are burnt out so I shoot in the jug.* **3.** *mod.* ruined by marijuana smoking. (Drugs. See *burnout*.) □ *The poor kid was burned out at the age of 12.* □ *What's left for these burned out kids?* **4.** *mod.* no longer affected by a particular drug. (Drugs.) □ *It's no good. I'm just burned out. The stuff doesn't affect me at all.* □ *She was burned out on Q.*

**burned up** See *burned*.

**burnie** ['bɚni] *n.* a marijuana cigarette. (Drugs.) □ *Light me up a burnie.* □ *Gimme a burnie, will you?*

**burnout** ['bɚnɑʊt] **1.** *n.* a person who is ruined by drugs. □ *The kid's a burnout. What can you do?* □ *Two burnouts sat on the school steps and stared at their feet.* **2.** *n.* someone no longer effective

on the job. □ *As a teacher, Fred is a burnout.* □ *We try to find some other employment for the burnouts.*

**burn rubber** *tr.* to run a car engine so fast that one spins the tires so that rubber is left on the street. □ *Man, this hog can really burn rubber.* □ *When George was at the age when the greatest thrill was burning rubber, he began to shave once a week.*

**burn someone down** AND **burn down someone** *tr.* to humiliate someone. □ *Man, don't you ever burn me down like that again!* □ *You just want to burn down everybody to make yourself seem better.*

**burn someone up** *tr.* to make someone very angry. □ *That kind of thing just burns me up.* □ *This whole business burns all of us up.* (More at *burned up*.)

**burn something in** AND **burn in something** *tr.* to "break in" the microchips in an electric device by running the device for a few hours. □ *We usually burn in all our computers for 48 hours before we ship them.* □ *Did you burn this one in? It doesn't even feep!*

**burnt offering** *n.* burned food; a badly cooked meal. □ *Everything I try to cook turns out to be a burnt offering.* □ *All I have to look forward to after work is a burnt offering.*

**burn with a low blue flame 1.** *in.* to be heavily alcohol intoxicated. □ *Yeah, he's burning with a low blue flame.* □ *He's not just drunk, he's burning with a low blue flame.* **2.** *in.* to be quietly and intensely angry. □ *She just sat there with her steak in her lap, burning with a low blue flame.* □ *She was quiet, but everyone knew she would soon burn with a low blue flame.*

**burp** See *berp*.

**burps** See *berps*.

**burst 1.** *n.* a riotous drinking bout; a *bust*. □ *What a burst we had at Clare's!* □ *You call that a burst? You should have been at Freddy's the night after.* **2.** *tr. & in.* to separate computer printout sheets. □ *Now I have to sit down and burst these things before the meeting.* □ *Don't they make a machine that will burst for you?*

**bushed** [buʃt] *mod.* exhausted. □ *I am just bushed.* □ *Another hard day! I am more bushed than ever.*

**bushes** *n.* homegrown marijuana. (Drugs.) □ *Sally has some bushes growing in a pot in her room.* □ *Take your old bushes and get out of my house.*

**bush patrol** 1. *n.* a session of necking and petting. (Here *patrol* has the military meaning of assignment.) □ *Tom is out on bush patrol tonight. I don't know who with.* □ *Martha and Paul spent the evening on bush patrol.* 2. *n.* an imaginary search through campus shrubbery to flush out the necking couples. □ *The dean of women put on her housecoat and went out on bush patrol.* □ *Bush patrol starts at midnight, so be in by then.*

**business end (of something)** *n.* the dangerous end of something; the part of something that does something as opposed to the part one holds onto. (See examples.) □ *Harry burned himself on the business end of a soldering iron.* □ *The robber pointed the business end of the gun right at Kelly.*

**bust** 1. *n.* a failure. □ *The whole project was a bust from the beginning.* □ *My whole life is a bust.* 2. *tr.* to reduce someone's rank. (Originally military, now also in civilian use as with the police.) □ *I'm going to bust you to private!* □ *The brass busted her on the spot.* 3. *n.* a riotous drinking party. (See also *burst.*) □ *There was a big bust in the park until two in the morning.* □ *There was no beer at the bust. Only wine.* 4. *n.* a raid by the police. □ *The cops staged a bust on Max's place.* □ *I knew it was a bust the minute they broke in the door.* 5. *tr.* (for the police) to raid a place. □ *The bacon busted Bill's bar and put Bill in the slammer.* □ *We're gonna bust every bookie joint in town.* 6. *tr.* to arrest someone. □ *The feds finally busted Max on a tax rap.* □ *A smokey busted Fred for not having a taillight.* 7. *n.* an arrest. □ *The bust was carried off without much stress.* □ *What a bust! The man was hollering and the kids were scoffing like mad.* 8. *tr.* to inform on someone, leading to an arrest. □ *I guess I busted Max, but they*

threatened me. □ *Tom busted Sam because there's bad blood between them.* 9. *n.* the police. □ *The bust is gonna find you no matter where you hole up.* □ *Here comes the bust. Beat it!*

**bust a gut (to do something)** AND **bust (one's) ass (to do something)*** *tr.* to make a great effort (to do something). (Caution with **ass.**) □ *I busted my ass trying to get just the thing you wanted!* □ *Don't bust a gut, but try to get here on time.*

**busted** 1. AND **bust** *mod.* arrested. □ *Max is bust again. The third time this month.* □ *I got busted for speeding.* 2. *mod.* alcohol intoxicated. □ *I went to a beer bust and got busted.* □ *Jim is busted again—really boiled.*

**buster** 1. *n.* a barbiturate. (Drugs. The opposite of *thrust(er).*) □ *I really need a buster.* □ *Don's been taking busters and thrusters off and on for nearly a year.* 2. *n.* a riotous drinking bout. □ *Let's all go on a real buster.* □ *Jed threw a real buster at his pad, but I didn't go.* 3. *n.* a heavy drinker on a spree. □ *There were two busters standing outside looking sort of sick.* □ *One old buster sat by the window, singing at the top of his lungs.* 4. *n.* a law enforcement agent. □ *The busters just left and took Max with them.* □ *The busters wrecked my furniture looking for dope.* 5. *n.* a generic nickname for a male. (Also an aggressive or stern term of address.) □ *Look, buster, get your dog off my lawn.* □ *Well, buster, it's time you learned some manners.*

**bust (one's) ass to (do something)** See *bust a gut (to do something).*

**bust someone's head open** *tr.* to damage someone's head severely; to strike someone on or about the head. □ *I ought to bust your head open for that!* □ *The jerk threatened to bust my head open!*

**bust (some) suds** 1. *tr.* to drink some beer. □ *Let's go out and bust some suds.* □ *I'm tired of busting suds. Let's play cards.* 2. *tr.* to wash dishes. □ *I don't want to spend the rest of my life busting suds.* □ *You get into that kitchen and bust some suds to pay for your meal!*

**bust something up** AND **bust up something** *tr.* to ruin something; to break something up. □ *I hate to bust up the party, but we gotta go.* □ *She tried to bust up my marriage!*

**bust something wide open** See *blow something wide open.*

**bust suds** See *bust (some) suds.*

**but** *mod.* totally; very. (Note position in the sentence.) □ *Tell him to get his tail over here but fast.* □ *This thing has to be done but good.*

**butch** [butʃ] **1.** *n.* a physician. (Derogatory. From *butcher.*) □ *The butch at the infirmary was no help at all.* □ *What does it take to be a butch besides an office and a degree?* **2.** *mod.* virile and masculine. (In a homosexual context.) □ *That's a real butch haircut, Claude.* □ *Really, Clare. How butch!*

**butcher** *n.* a surgeon; a physician. (Usually derogatory, possibly jocular.) □ *I won't go back to that butcher for anything at all.* □ *He's been a butcher for seven years and pays 80% of his income for insurance.*

**butt\*** [bət] **1.\*** *n.* the buttocks. (Caution with *butt.*) □ *She fell right on her butt.* □ *The doctor gave her a shot in the butt.* **2.** *n.* a cigarette butt. □ *Whose butts are those in the car ashtray?* □ *Don't leave your butts in the houseplants!* **3.** *n.* a cigarette of any kind. □ *You got a butt I can bum?* □ *What kind of butt is that, anyway?*

**butterfingers** *n.* someone who cannot hold on to things. (Also a term of address.) □ *I'm such a butterfingers. I dropped my papers.* □ *Hang onto this tight, butterfingers!*

**butter flower** *n.* marijuana. (Drugs.) □ *Where can I get some butter flower?* □ *There is a bag of butter flower in the closet under the red towel.*

**butt in** *in.* to interrupt. □ *Please don't butt in all the time.* □ *Mind if I butt in?*

**buttinsky** AND **buttinski** [bə'tɪnski] *n.* someone who interrupts. □ *Frank is such a buttinsky.* □ *I hate to be a buttinski, but what are you talking about?*

**buttlegging** ['bətlegɪn] *n.* the transportation of untaxed or undertaxed cigarettes across a state line. (Patterned on *bootlegging.*) □ *There's another news story about buttlegging in northern Indiana tonight.* □ *Most of the guys at the plant do buttlegging on the way home from work.*

**butt naked\*** ['bət 'nekəd] *mod.* totally nude. (Collegiate. Caution with *butt.*) □ *She just stood there butt naked, looking at us.* □ *My roommate sleeps butt naked.*

**button 1.** *n.* the termination of a recitation; the punch line of a joke; a *zinger.* (The equivalent of a button punched to signal a response.) □ *When I got to the button, I realized that I had told the whole joke wrong.* □ *When I came to the button, I knew I was really going to insult the guy.* **2.** AND **buttons** *n.* mescaline in the form of a small dried nodule of peyote cactus. (Drugs. The same as *cactus (buttons).*) □ *He ate a couple of buttons and sat down.* □ *These buttons are just what you need.* **3.** *n.* a police officer's badge or shield. □ *The guy flashed his button, so I let him in.* □ *Just because you got a button, it doesn't mean you can push innocent citizens around!*

**buttonhole** *tr.* to accost someone; to make someone listen to one. (As if grabbing someone by the coat lapel to keep them from getting away.) □ *The guy buttonholed me on my way out, and started asking me a lot of questions.* □ *See if you can buttonhole a cop and get some directions.*

**Butt out!** *exclam.* "Get out of my affairs!"; "Mind your own business!" □ *Go away! Butt out!* □ *Butt out! I'm busy.*

**buy 1.** *n.* a purchase. □ *Man, this is a great buy.* □ *What a buy, two for the price of one.* **2.** *tr.* to believe something. □ *Nobody'll buy that story.* □ *It sounds good to me, but will your wife buy it?*

**buy it** *tr.* to die. (See *buy the farm.*) □ *For a minute, I thought I was going to buy it.* □ *He lay there coughing for a few minutes, and then he bought it.*

**buy someone's wolf ticket** *tr.* to challenge someone's boast or taunt. (Black. See *sell a wolf ticket.*) □ *He wants me to buy his wolf ticket bad.* □ *He's such a fighter. He'll buy anybody's wolf ticket.*

**buy the big one** *tr.* to die. □ *I don't plan to buy the big one for at least another 30* years. □ *She conked out for good—you know, bought the big one.*

**buy the farm** *tr.* to die; to get killed. □ *He bought the farm on San Juan Hill.* □ *I'm too young to buy the farm.*

**buy time** *tr.* to use a tactic to postpone something. □ *You are just doing this to buy time.* □ *Maybe I can buy some time by asking for a continuance.*

**buy trouble** *tr.* to encourage trouble; to bring on trouble. □ *I don't want to buy trouble. I have enough already.* □ *Saying something like that is just buying trouble.*

**buzhie** ['buʒi] **1.** *n.* a middle-class person. (From *bourgeoisie.*) □ *My mother was a buzhie, but my father was a Bohemian type.* □ *I live in a neighborhood of buzhies.* **2.** *mod.* middle-class. □ *I can't stand this buzhie neighborhood.* □ *I live in a buzhie house and drive a buzhie car.* □ *She is so buzhie!*

**buzz 1.** *n.* a call on the telephone. (Usually with *give.* See also *jingle.*) □ *I'll give you a buzz tomorrow.* □ *I got a buzz from him yesterday.* **2.** *tr.* to call someone on the telephone. □ *Buzz me about noon.* □ *I'll buzz Mary and see if she can go.* **3.** *tr.* to signal someone with a buzzer. □ *I'll buzz my secretary.* □ *Did you buzz, Gloria?* **4.** *n.* a thrill. □ *I got a real buzz out of that.* □ *The dancers gave the old man a buzz.* **5.** *n.* a chuckle. □ *She gets a buzz out of reading the comics.* □ *Here's a little joke that'll give you a buzz.* **6.** *n.* the initial effects of drinking alcohol or taking certain drugs. □ *Sam got a little buzz from the wine, but he still needed something stronger.* □ *She took a hit and leaned back, waiting for the buzz.*

**buzz along 1.** *in.* to depart. □ *Well, I must buzz along.* □ *It's time to buzz along to work now.* **2.** *in.* to drive or move along rapidly. □ *We were buzzing along at about 70 when we heard a siren.* □ *"You were buzzing along at 82*

miles per hour," said the cop.

**buzzard** *n.* an old man; a mean old man. (Especially with *old.*) □ *Who's the buzzard in the wing-tip shoes?* □ *Some old buzzard is at the door asking for Mary Wilson.*

**buzzed (up)** *mod.* alcohol or drug intoxicated. □ *He gets buzzed up and then calls his friends on the phone to complain.* □ *That dame is really buzzed.*

**buzz-kill** *n.* someone or something that ruins someone's fun; someone or something that kills a *buzz;* a *bummer.* □ *John is a real buzz-kill.* □ *The news about the suspension was a buzz-kill.*

**buzz off** *in.* to leave in a hurry. (Often a command. See examples.) □ *Buzz off! You're bothering me.* □ *I have to buzz off now. I'm late.*

**buzzword** *n.* a specialist word; a technical word; a jargon word. (Compare to *fuzzword.*) □ *Your constant use of buzzwords makes your work sound quite trivial.* □ *What's the latest buzzword?*

**buzzy** *mod.* alcohol intoxicated. □ *Fred was too buzzy to drive, so I took everybody home.* □ *Man, he is really buzzy.*

**B.V.D.s** *n.* underwear; men's underwear. (The same as *beeveedees.* From *Bradley, Voorhies, and Day,* the manufacturers. Always plural.) □ *He stood there in his B.V.D.s, freezing.* □ *If you don't wear a belt, your B.V.D.s will show.*

**B.W.O.C.** *n.* "big woman on campus," an important or self-important female college student. (Collegiate. See also *B.M.O.C.*) □ *Some B.W.O.C. came in and asked us to leave.* □ *It's always the same B.W.O.C.s you see in the paper.*

**by a whisker** *mod.* by the tiniest amount. □ *My horse won by a whisker.* □ *I just barely qualified for admission by a whisker.*

**B.Y.O.(B.)** *mod.* "bring your own (booze or bottle)." □ *A note on the invitation says that the party is B.Y.O.B.* □ *I hate B.Y.O.B. parties. There's never enough to drink.*

# C

**C.** 1. *n*. the sum of one-hundred dollars, as in *C-note*. (Underworld. The "C" is the Roman numeral 100. ) □ *Four C.s for an old junker like that? You're crazy!* □ *This suit cost me 2 C.s.* 2. *n*. cocaine. (Drugs.) □ *They found a gram of C. in his coat lining.* □ *"How did this C. get in your clothes?" said the cop, scratching his head.*

**cabbage** *n*. money. (Originally underworld. See *green stuff* at *green*.) □ *How much cabbage you want for this heater?* □ *I don't make enough cabbage to go on a trip like that!*

**cabbagehead** *n*. a fool; a stupid person. □ *What cabbagehead put this thing on upside down?* □ *I'm such a cabbagehead. I mailed my paycheck back to the office by mistake.*

**cabbie** AND **cabby** *n*. a taxi driver. (Also a term of address.) □ *Ask the cabbie if he can change a twenty.* □ *Say, cabby, do you know the way to St. Joseph's Hospital?*

**caboose** [kə'bus] *n*. the buttocks. (The name of the car at the end of a railroad train.) □ *You just plunk your caboose over there on the settee and listen up to what I have to tell you.* □ *My caboose is bigger than I want it, but life is too short to fret about stuff like that.*

**caca\*** AND **kaka\*** ['kɑkɑ] 1.\* *n*. dung; feces. (Juvenile. From Spanish. Caution with topic.) □ *There's fresh caca in the front yard.* □ *Don't worry. It's dog kaka.* 2.\* *in*. to defecate. (Juvenile. Caution with topic.) □ *Jimmy kakad in his diaper!* □ *It's time you learned to caca in the potty.* 3. *n*. inferior, bogus, or adulterated heroin or marijuana. (Drugs.) □ *This stuff is just kaka. You'll be sorry*

*you tried to cheat me.* □ *Where did you get this caca? It's cheap, but not all that bad.*

**cack\*** [kæk] 1.\* *n*. dung; feces. (Caution with topic. See *caca*.) □ *Wipe that cack off your shoes before you come in here!* □ *The sidewalks are just covered with cack!* 2.\* *in*. to defecate. (Caution with topic.) □ *The dog cacked right there on Fifth Avenue.* □ *"Dogs can't cack here," hollered the police officer.* 3. *in*. to empty one's stomach; to vomit. □ *I cacked all night with the flu.* □ *I've never heard anybody cack so loud in my life!*

**cactus (buttons)** *n*. peyote cactus containing mescaline. (Drugs.) □ *Gert came back from vacation with a bag of cactus buttons.* □ *"Who ate all my cactus?" screamed Gert.*

**cactus juice** *n*. tequila. (A Mexican liquor.) □ *Ernie brought back a big jug of cactus juice from Mexico.* □ *This cactus juice will make your hair stand on end.*

**caddy** ['kædi] *n*. a Cadillac automobile. □ *What I really want is a caddy. Keep your yuppie beemer.* □ *Who's the chick in the caddy?*

**cadet** [kə'dɛt] *n*. a new drug user; a new heroin user. (Drugs.) □ *Max is always looking for cadets.* □ *The cadet who O.D.ed was pulled from the river this morning.*

**Cadillac** ['kædl̩æk] 1. *n*. the name of something powerful or superior. (From the name of the automobile.) □ *This product is the Cadillac of plastic kitchenware.* □ *Acme is the Cadillac of monochrome closed-circuit retail surveillance equipment.* 2. *n*. a powerful drug, especially cocaine. (Drugs.) □ *Just a pinch*

59

*of Cadillac in my junk seems to keep me a little more lively.* □ *Nothing but Cadillac for Max!*

**cagey** [ˈkedʒi] *mod.* sneaky; shrewd. □ *Bruno is pretty cagey. You have to keep an eye on him.* □ *He's too cagey for me. I don't trust him at all.*

**cake** *n.* money. (From *bread, dough.*) □ *I can't scrape together enough cake to do the job.* □ *I don't have cake in my pocket, in the bank, or under my mattress. What am I going to do?*

**cakewalk** *n.* something very easy. (Compare to *sleepwalk.*) □ *Nothing to it. It's a cakewalk.* □ *The game was a cakewalk from beginning to end.*

**calaboose** [ˈkæləbus] *n.* jail. (From a Spanish word.) □ *One night in the calaboose is enough.* □ *Are we going to tell what happened, or are we going to spend the night in the calaboose?*

**calendar** *n.* a month. (Black.) □ *Okay, man. I'll see you in one calendar.* □ *One more calendar, then you get your jack.*

**California cornflakes** *n.* cocaine. (Drugs.) □ *I never use California cornflakes when I'm on a sales trip.* □ *If you asked Max for California cornflakes, he'd laugh his head off.*

**California turnarounds** See *L.A. (turnabouts).*

**call** **1.** *n.* a decision; a prediction. □ *That was a good call, Mike.* □ *The market behaved just as you said it would. Good call.* **2.** *tr.* to challenge someone. □ *I called him, but he ignored me.* □ *Are you the guy who called me? Who do you think you are?* **3.** *n.* the early effects of a drug; the beginning of a rush; a rush. (Drugs.) □ *You may not get the call on this stuff for twenty minutes or more.* □ *A guy like this is only happy when he senses the call.*

**call (all) the shots** *tr.* to decide on the course of action; to be in charge. □ *Why do you have to call all the shots?* □ *Do what you're told. I'll call the shots.*

**call girl** *n.* a prostitute; a prostitute who is always on call. □ *The snatcher hauled her in because she looked like a call girl.* □ *Most of the really sharp call girls look like M.B.A.s and drive beemers.*

**call house** *n.* a brothel. □ *The cops busted a call house on 4th Street last*

*week.* □ *The madame of the call house certainly looked like a lady to me.*

**Call my service.** *sent.* "Please call me through my answering service." (Not a friendly or encouraging invitation.) □ *Good to talk to ya, babe. Call my service. Love ya!* □ *I can't talk now. Call my service.*

**call of nature** See *nature's call.*

**call someone out** *tr.* to challenge someone to a fight. □ *Max wanted to call him out, but thought better of it.* □ *Did you call me out? What are you going to do about it?*

**cam** See the following entry.

**Cambodian red** AND **cam (red)** *n.* a reddish brown marijuana grown in Cambodia. (Drugs.) □ *Where did you get cam red?* □ *Cam is hard to find in the last few years.*

**camp** **1.** *n.* something cute and out-of-fashion; something of such an anachronistic style as to be intriguing; something with as much bittersweet nostalgia as summer camp. □ *Camp is dull and was never interesting.* □ *My brother thinks camp is just a joke.* □ *Nobody really knows what style camp really is, and very few even care.* **2.** AND **campy** *mod.* having to do with the things described in sense 1. □ *Most camp entertainment is pretentious and overdrawn.* □ *Who needs camp movies?* **3.** *mod.* having to do with homosexual persons and matters. □ *What a camp way of walking!* □ *She is so camp, I could scream!*

**camp it up** **1.** *tr.* to overact. □ *Can you make it a little more lively without camping it up?* □ *She's so dull that she could camp it up and still look half asleep.* **2.** *tr.* to overdo effeminacy; (for a homosexual person) to act too effeminate in public. □ *Can't you even walk across the room without camping it up?* □ *John just loves to burst into the most sedate hotel in town and camp it up in the lobby.*

**campus** [ˈkæmpəs] *tr.* to restrict someone to the grounds of a college campus. (Collegiate.) □ *The dean threatened to campus the entire fraternity for a month.* □ *"We will campus you for a year, if necessary," shouted the dean, who really* *didn't understand young people. (More at campused.)*

**campused** ['kæmpəst] *mod.* restricted to the campus. (Collegiate.) □ *I can't go to town. I'm campused.* □ *She's campused and can only go to the library.*

**campus queen** *n.* a good-looking and popular female college student. □ *I always thought I wanted to be a campus queen, but all that has changed.* □ *I wonder what some of those campus queens look like when they get up in the morning.*

**campy** See *camp.*

**can\*** **1.** *n.* the head. □ *What do you have in your can, anyway? Lard?* □ *Jerry landed one on Frank's can. Frank crumpled.* **2.** *n.* toilet. □ *Hell, I ain't tired! Where's the can?* □ *I gotta use the can before we leave.* **3.\*** *n.* the buttocks. (Caution with topic.) □ *The guy slipped on the ice and fell on his can.* □ *Look at the can on that guy!* **4.** *n.* jail. (Usually with *the.*) □ *I had to spend the night in the can, but it wasn't too bad.* □ *You've seen one can, you've seen 'em all.* **5.** *tr.* to dismiss someone from employment. □ *The jerk canned everybody who played a part in the gag.* □ *I'll can anybody who tries a stunt like that again.* **6.** *n.* a car. □ *That's a good-looking can he's driving.* □ *Please don't park your old can in front of my house.* **7.** See *cans.* **8.\*** *n.* a breast. (Caution with topic. Usually plural.) □ *Man, look at the cans on that dame!* □ *Those cans can't be real!* **9.** *n.* a measurement of marijuana. (Drugs.) □ *How much do you want for a can?* □ *A can is too much except for a party.*

**Canadian quail** [...kwel] *n.* Quaalude™ brand of methaqualone. (Drugs. *Quail* is from the *Quaal* in Quaalude.) □ *You got some of that Canadian quail?* □ *Max can tell you who is serving Canadian quail.*

**canary** [kə'nɛri] **1.** *n.* a female singer. □ *The band had a cute canary who could really sing.* □ *The drummer and the canary just don't seem to be able to get along.* **2.** *n.* a capsule of Nembutal™, a barbiturate. (Drugs. The capsule is yellow.) □ *You got any canaries? I need a downer.* □ *There are a couple of blues, which ought to do the same as canaries.*

**cancel someone's Christmas** *tr.* to kill someone; to destroy someone. (Underworld. The dead person will miss Christmas.) □ *If he keeps bugging me, I'm gonna cancel his Christmas.* □ *Bruno threatened to cancel Max's Christmas if Max didn't pay up.*

**cancer stick** *n.* a tobacco cigarette. (From the notion that cigarette smoking is a major cause of lung cancer.) □ *Kelly pulled out his ninth cancer stick and lit it up.* □ *A lot of people are addicted to cancer sticks.*

**candied** ['kændid] *mod.* addicted to cocaine. (Drugs. See *nose (candy).*) □ *Unfortunately, Paul is candied, and he lost his job so he can't buy toot.* □ *He is one of those people who gets candied at first snort.*

**candy** **1.** *mod.* alcohol intoxicated. (See *candy store.*) □ *Isn't he a little candy?* □ *I think he's too candy to drive.* **2.** *n.* drugs in general. (Drugs. See *nose (candy).*) □ *I gotta go get some candy from the candy man.* □ *This candy is powerful stuff.*

**candy-ass\*** **1.\*** *n.* a coward. (Caution with *ass.*) □ *You are such a candy-ass! Stand up for your rights.* □ *Ralph seems tough, but he's just a candy-ass.* **2.\*** *mod.* cowardly. (Caution with *ass.*) □ *The candy-ass approach just isn't going to work.* □ *Stop the candy-ass stuff. Handle this issue directly.*

**candy man** *n.* a drug dealer. (Drugs.) □ *Lefty said he had to go meet with the candy man.* □ *Max is sort of a candy man.*

**candy store** *n.* a liquor store. □ *Let's stop at this candy store and get some bubbles.* □ *Somebody robbed the candy store on the corner.*

**cane** *n.* cocaine. (Drugs.) □ *What the hell did you pay for this cane?* □ *Even the kids can afford to buy cane now. The social problems of the 21st century are starting right here.*

**Can it!** *exclam.* "Shut up!" □ *I've heard enough. Can it!* □ *That's enough out of you! Can it!*

**canned** **1.** *mod.* alcohol intoxicated. □ *I'll drive. I'm too canned to walk.* □ *Man, am I canned!* **2.** *mod.* having to do with prerecorded laughter or applause which is added to the sound track of a television program. □ *Canned laughter really sounds phony.* □ *The dialogue was funny enough that they didn't need to have the laughter canned.*

**cannon** *n.* a gun; a revolver. (Underworld.) □ *Rocko pulled out his cannon and aimed it at Barlowe's throat.* □ *The cops found Rocko's cannon where Barlowe had kicked it during the struggle.*

**can of worms** *n.* an intertwined set of problems; an array of difficulties. (Often with *open*.) □ *This whole business is a real can of worms.* □ *When you brought that up, you opened a whole new can of worms.*

**cans** *n.* earphones. (See also *can*.) □ *The guy with the cans on his head is the radio operator.* □ *I bought a new set of cans for my stereo.*

**can-shaker** *n.* a fund-raiser. (As if a person were holding a can for the solicitation of coins from passersby.) □ *John was the mayor's can-shaker in the last election.* □ *Fred was a professional can-shaker for a museum. Maybe he has some ideas as to how we can raise some money.*

**can't hit the (broad) side of a barn** *phr.* "cannot aim something accurately." □ *You're way off. You couldn't hit the broad side of a barn.* □ *Carry the paper to the wastebasket. You can't hit the side of a barn.*

**can't win (th)em all** *phr.* (one should) expect to lose every now and then. □ *It doesn't really matter. You can't win them all.* □ *Well, I can't win 'em all.*

**cap 1.** *tr.* to exceed something; to surpass something. □ *I know I can't cap that. That's just super!* □ *Who could ever cap a joke like that?* **2.** *n.* a capsule of a drug. □ *Do you want it in caps or elixir?* □ *She spilled the caps on the floor and had to find every single one of them.* **3.** *tr.* to make a capsule. □ *I must have capped 300 placebos today.* □ *Max capped some H. for a pal.*

**caper** ['kepɚ] **1.** *n.* any stunt or event; a trick or a *scam*. □ *That little caper the kids did with the statue from the town square was a dandy.* □ *Another caper like that and I call your parents.* **2.** *n.* a criminal job: theft, kidnapping, black-

mail, etc. (Underworld.) □ *Who did you work with on that bank caper?* □ *The black and whites pulled up right in the middle of the caper.*

**capish** [kəˈpiʃ] *in.* to understand. (Usually as a question. From an Italian dialect.) □ *The matter is settled. No more talk. Capish?* □ *Now, if you don't capish, let's get it clear right now.*

**cap out** *in.* to pass out from drugs. (Drugs.) □ *The poor kid capped out in class and fell out of his chair.* □ *I was afraid that Marty would cap out in the subway.*

**capper** ['kæpɚ] *n.* the climax or *clincher* of something. □ *The capper of the evening was when the hostess got lathered before midnight and couldn't celebrate the new year.* □ *When the butler tripped and served Mr. Wilson the entire dessert, in his lap, that was the capper to an exciting evening.*

**captain of industry** *n.* a corporation officer; a capitalist. □ *The captains of industry manage to hang onto their money no matter what.* □ *It's fun to see those captains of industry drive up in their benzes.*

**carb** [karb] *n.* carburetor. □ *This can needs a new carb.* □ *I learned how to clean and adjust a carb by the time I was in high school.*

**carbos** ['karboz] *n.* carbohydrates. (Bodybuilding.) □ *You need more protein and less carbos.* □ *Too much carbos will make you fat.*

**carburetor** *n.* a device for smoking cannabis that mixes the smoke with air. (Drugs.) □ *I have a carburetor with the rest of my stash.* □ *Max showed Walter how to use a carburetor.*

**carcass** ['karkəs] *n.* one's body; a large or heavy body. □ *He hauled his carcass out of the car and lumbered into the bank.* □ *Put your carcass on a chair, and let's chew the fat.*

**card 1.** *n.* a funny person. □ *Molly is such a card. She cracks me up.* □ *Gee, Fred. You're a card. Somebody's gonna have to deal with you.* **2.** *tr.* to check people's I.D. cards for age or other eligibility. □ *They card everybody at the football games, even the parents.* □ *The bartender was carding people so we left quietly.*

**carrier** *n.* a narcotics seller or transporter. (Drugs. See also *courier.*) □ *The carrier has the most dangerous job of all.* □ *You'll never see an old carrier.*

**carrot top** *n.* a person with red hair. (Also a term of address.) □ *Sam is a carrot top with the most beautiful hair I've ever seen.* □ *Hey, carrot top, where are you going?*

**carry 1.** *in.* to carry drugs on one's person. (Drugs.) □ *If you get busted while you're carrying, you are in big trouble with the man.* □ *You gotta learn when you can carry and when you can't.* **2.** *n.* drugs carried on the person as an emergency supply in case of arrest. (Underworld.) □ *I lost my carry somewhere.* □ *The cops found my carry, and I spent three days in the clink climbing the walls.*

**carrying a (heavy) load** *mod.* alcohol intoxicated. □ *Marty is carrying a heavy load.* □ *Your father's carrying a load again. What are we going to do?*

**carry the stick** *tr.* to live as a hobo, on the streets. (Streets. From the stick that supports the hobo's bundle.) □ *I even carried the stick for a while in the sixties.* □ *I was afraid I'd be carrying the stick if I got laid off.*

**carry weight** *tr.* to have influence. □ *I don't carry much weight around here, but Walter does.* □ *Tom carries weight with the mayor. Ask him.*

**cartoon 1.** *n.* a drug-induced hallucination. (Drugs.) □ *He dropped some chief about a week ago, and he still has cartoons.* □ *Cartoons can go on for a long time.* **2.** *in.* to have a drug-induced hallucination. □ *Right in the middle of algebra, Gary began cartooning.* □ *He may go on cartooning for a few weeks.*

**cartwheel** *n.* a round, white cross-scored amphetamine tablet. (Drugs.) □ *He took cartwheels in the morning and fender-benders at night.* □ *Cartwheels were the favorite diet pill of the 1960s.*

**carved in stone** *mod.* permanent or not subject to change. (Often in the negative.) □ *Now, this isn't carved in stone yet, but this looks like the way it's going to be.* □ *Is this policy carved in stone?*

**case of the shorts** See *shorts.*

**case the joint 1.** *tr.* to look over someplace to figure out how to break in, what to steal, etc. (Underworld. See *joint.*) □ *First of all you gotta case the joint to see where things are.* □ *You could see he was casing the joint the way he looked around.* **2.** *tr.* to look a place over. □ *The dog came in and cased the joint, sniffing out friends and foes.* □ *The old lady entered slowly, casing the joint for the face of someone of her era, and finally took a seat.*

**cash cow** *n.* a dependable source of money; a good investment. □ *I put most of my money in a dependable cash cow that pays off once a month.* □ *Mr. Wilson turned out to be the cash cow we needed to start our repertoire company.*

**cashed 1.** *mod.* having to do with marijuana whose active ingredients have been exhausted. (Drugs.) □ *This stuff is cashed. Trash it.* □ *Max sold the wrong guy some cashed grass.* **2.** *mod.* exhausted. □ *I'm just cashed—really pooped.* □ *After the game, the team was cashed and couldn't even celebrate.*

**cash in one's chips** AND **cash in one's checks** *tr.* to die; to finish the game (of life). □ *He opened his eyes, said goodbye, and cashed in his chips.* □ *I'm too young to cash in my checks.*

**Casper Milquetoast** ['kæspɚ 'mɪlktost] *n.* a very timid man. (From the name of a character in a cartoon.) □ *I'm a little sensitive—not a Casper Milquetoast, but I have feelings.* □ *He's no Casper Milquetoast. He's quite a tennis player in fact.*

**casting-couch** *n.* a legendary couch found in the offices of casting directors for use in seducing young people by offering them roles. □ *They say she got the job on the casting-couch.* □ *They say the director got his job on the casting-couch, too.*

**cast-iron stomach** *n.* a very strong stomach that can withstand bad food or anything nauseating. □ *If I didn't have a cast-iron stomach, I couldn't eat this stuff.* □ *Fred—known for his cast-iron stomach—ate all of his pepper soup.*

**castor oil artist** *n.* a medical doctor. □ *This two-bit castor oil artist tried to get me to lose weight.* □ *Check with your* *personal castor oil artist to see if you should be taking this medication.*

**cat 1.** *n.* a fellow; a guy; a *dude*. □ *Now, this cat wants to borrow some money from me. What should I do?* □ *Ask the cat what he's got for security.* **2.** *in.* to empty one's stomach; to vomit. □ *I think I'm gonna cat.* □ *Looks like somebody catted in the bushes.* **3.** *n.* a gossipy woman. (See *catty.*) □ *She is such a cat!* □ *Mary can be such a cat, you know.*

**catch 1.** *n.* a drawback. □ *Okay, that sounds good, but what's the catch?* □ *There's no catch. It's all on the up and up.* **2.** *tr.* to view something; to attend something. □ *We'll take the chicks to catch a film after we eat.* □ *Did you catch "Gone with the Wind" on T.V.?*

**catch 22** *n.* a directive that it is impossible to obey without violating some other, equally important, directive. □ *There was nothing I could do. It was a classic catch 22.* □ *I had my choice between catch 22s. What do you call that kind of a dilemma?*

**catch hell (for something)** *tr.* to get severely reprimanded for (doing) something. □ *I knew I'd catch hell for it.* □ *Somebody is going to catch hell for this!*

**catch some rays** AND **bag some rays** *tr.* to get some sunshine; to tan in the sun. □ *We wanted to catch some rays, but the sun never came out the whole time we were there.* □ *I went to Hawaii to bag some rays.*

**catch some Z's** AND **cop some Z's, cut some Z's** *tr.* to get some sleep. □ *I gotta catch some Z's before I drop.* □ *Why don't you stop a little bit and try to cop some Z's?*

**catch up** *in.* to break the drug habit; to withdraw from drugs. (Drugs.) □ *Bruno never tried to catch up. He's just too far gone.* □ *I just know I can catch up, if I can just get through the first week.*

**Catch you later.** *sent.* "I will talk to you again when I next see you." □ *Can't talk now. Catch you later.* □ *Sorry, gotta rush. Catch you later.*

**cats and dogs** *n.* slow selling or undesirable merchandise. □ *During the Christmas season, the merchants try to get rid of all their cats and dogs.* □ *When people are buying up even the cats and dogs, you know business is good.*

**cat's meow** [...mi'aʊ] *n.* something really fine. □ *This stuff is really the cat's meow.* □ *Hearing all the old big band music again is the cat's meow.*

**cat-soup** ['kætsup] *n.* catsup; ketchup. □ *Do you want some cat-soup on your burger?* □ *No, I never use cat-soup.*

**cattle-rustler** *n.* a thief who steals meat from supermarkets for resale. (Underworld.) □ *Marty is a cattle-rustler, and she's got some stuff for sale.* □ *She's a cattle-rustler to support her habit.*

**catty** *mod.* spiteful; snotty. □ *You know how catty Mary is—almost as catty as Gloria—well, she told me something about you that really shocked me.* □ *How can anybody be so catty?*

**cave man** *n.* a strong, virile man. □ *He's sort of a cave man, big and hairy.* □ *I don't care for cave men.*

**cazh** [kæʒ] *mod.* casual. (California.) □ *Melissa is so, like, so, cazh!* □ *Roger can be so forceful and cazh—all at the same time.*

**cee** [si] *n.* cocaine. (Drugs. See *C.*) □ *Where can I get a little bit of cee?* □ *Ask Max for some cee, but ask him nice.*

**celeb** [sə'lɛb] *n.* a celebrity. □ *They hired a few celebs to shill for their new computer.* □ *There were celebs all over the place, but nobody I recognized.*

**cement city** *n.* a cemetery. □ *I'm too young to end up in cement city.* □ *There's a cement city outside town, and our house is just a half mile east of it.*

**cent** *n.* one dollar. (Underworld.) □ *One cent for one joint? Not bad.* □ *A cent for this thing?*

**century note** *n.* a one-hundred-dollar bill. (Underworld. The "C" is the Roman numeral for 100. See *C-note.*) □ *I got a couple of century notes for driving these guys home from the bank.* □ *Here's a century note for your trouble, young man.*

**certain party** *n.* "someone whom I do not wish to name; you can guess whom." (Always with *a.*) □ *I spoke to a certain party about the matter you mentioned.* □ *If a certain party finds out about you-know-what, what on earth will you do?*

**cets** AND **sets** [sɛts] *n.* tablets of Darvocet™, a painkiller. (Drugs.) □ *You* *got any cets I can bum off you?* □ *I don't know anything about sets or any of that stuff.*

**C-habit** *n.* a cocaine habit. (Drugs.) □ *She's had a C-habit for over a year.* □ *Her finances are totally depleted by her C-habit.*

**chain(saw)** *tr.* to destroy something; to cut something up severely. □ *The senatorial committee tried to chainsaw the nominee, but the full senate voted for confirmation.* □ *We didn't think they'd come in and chain all our plans.*

**chain(-smoke)** *in.* to smoke cigarette after cigarette. □ *I have never wanted to chain-smoke, but I got addicted.* □ *I used to chain, and my husband threatened to leave me if I didn't give it up. I quit when he left.*

**chain-smoker** *n.* someone who smokes cigarette after cigarette. □ *She was a chain-smoker for thirty years, and then suddenly, boom. She's gone.* □ *There are fewer chain-smokers now than there were just a few years ago.*

**chair** *n.* the electric chair, as used in the execution of the death penalty. (Underworld. Always with *the*.) □ *You'll fry in the chair for this, Lefty!* □ *I don't wanna go to the chair!*

**cham** AND **chammy, shammy** [ʃæm AND 'ʃæmi] *n.* champagne. □ *Would you like a little more shammy?* □ *This is a stunning cham you picked for us, Tiffany. Is it famous?*

**champ** [tʃæmp] **1.** *n.* a champion. (Also a term of address.) □ *Mark is a real champ—always there to help.* □ *Hey, champ, welcome home!* **2.** *n.* a dependable member of the underworld. (Underworld.) □ *Bruno would never sing. He's a champ.* □ *Lefty is a champ. He stood by me the whole time.*

**champers** See *shampers.*

**change** *n.* money. (See also *and change.*) □ *It takes a lot of change to buy a car like that.* □ *I don't have the change to get one of those video tape machines.*

**changes** *n.* an alteration in one's mental state. (See also *go through the changes.*) □ *The changes have sort of got me down.* □ *I'm 40 and I'm finished with the changes, and if there's anything I don't want it's to be young again.*

**change the channel** *tr.* to switch to some other topic of conversation. □ *Just a minute. I think you changed the channel. Let's go back to the part about you owing me money.* □ *Let's change the channel here before there is a fight.*

**channel 1.** *n.* a source for drugs; a connection. □ *The next slide is a diagram of the drug distribution chain. Every user has to have a "channel" to obtain drugs.* □ *Max is somebody's channel, and he has his channel, also.* **2.** *n.* a large vein into which injections are made. (Drugs.) □ *The movie showed these characters injecting into the channel, as they called it. So gross!* □ *She missed the channel and ended up skin-popping.*

**chap** *tr.* to anger or annoy someone. □ *That whole business really chapped me.* □ *I didn't mean to chap you.* (More at *chapped.*)

**chapped** *mod.* angry; annoyed. □ *I was chapped. There was no way to get around it.* □ *Don't get so chapped. Nothing can be done now.*

**chapter and verse** *mod.* in the finest detail. (From the "chapter and verse" organization of the Bible.) □ *He could recite the law concerning state-funded libraries, chapter and verse.* □ *She knew her rights, chapter and verse.*

**charge 1.** *n.* a dose or portion of a drug. (Drugs.) □ *I need a charge to tide me over.* □ *Just a little charge till I can get to my candy man.* **2.** *n.* a drug's *rush.* (Drugs.) □ *This stuff has no charge at all.* □ *What kind of charge do you expect out of half-cashed weed?* **3.** *n.* a thrill. □ *Seeing my kid up there on that stage was a real charge.* □ *I got a tremendous charge out of your last letter.*

**charged (up) 1.** *mod.* slightly overdosed with drugs. (Drugs.) □ *He was talking fast and nodding his head back and forth. I think he was charged.* □ *The kid is usually charged up by class time.* **2.** *mod.* drug intoxicated. (Drugs.) □ *The way she sat there nodding, you knew she was completely charged up.* □ *Paul was one charged up guy after the session.* **3.** *mod.* excited. □ *The audience was charged up and ready for the* star to come out. □ *The charged up quarterback made some wonderful plays.*

**Charles** 1. *n.* cocaine. (Drugs.) □ *I want to meet Charles somewhere.* □ *Is there a house where I can buy some Charles somewhere close?* 2. *n.* a Caucasian. (Black. Not necessarily derogatory.) □ *And what is Charles gonna say about what you did to his car?* □ *That brother's so backward, he's still afraid to go to Charles' front door.*

**Charley** *n.* the Viet Cong in Vietnam. (Military. From "Victor Charley" which is from "V.C.") □ *How come Charley never gets bit to death by those snakes?* □ *What if we meet up with Charley down there?*

**Charlie Irvine** *n.* a police officer. (Black. See also *Irv.*) □ *Charlie Irvine was around asking after you.* □ *Look smart, dude, here comes Charlie Irvine.*

**charmer** *n.* a seducer; a *make-out artist.* □ *You always have to act like some half-ass charmer scamming like it really mattered! Grow up!* □ *Willard is such a charmer! Too bad he's married.*

**chart** *n.* a musical score. (Musicians. See also *map.*) □ *Come on, man! Look at the chart! You're making clinkers like hot cakes.* □ *Lemme borrow your chart for a while, okay?*

**charts** *n.* the trade magazine rankings of current pop music. □ *The big one is back on the charts this week. Give it a listen.* □ *Number five on the charts again this week—it's "My Blue Heaven" with the Andrews Sisters.*

**chas** AND **chez** [tʃæz AND tʃez] *n.* matches. (Collegiate. A clipping of "matches".) □ *Where are my chas?* □ *You got a couple of chez?*

**chaser** 1. *n.* an alcoholic drink taken after a non-alcoholic one; beer, water, or some similar liquid drunk after a *shot* of hard liquor. (See also *wash.*) □ *I could use a little chaser with this soda.* □ *I'd like a double scotch and a beer chaser.* 2. See *ambulance chaser.*

**chase the dragon** *tr.* to inhale opium fumes through a straw. (Drugs.) □ *Harry thinks that chasing the dragon sounds like real fun.* □ *Chasing the dragon may sound good, but it smells awful.*

**C-head** 1. *n.* a cocaine user; a *cubehead.* (Drugs.) □ *I don't want any C-head operating on me!* □ *How much money does a C-head need to get through the day?* 2. *n.* an *L.S.D.* user who takes *L.S.D.* on sugar cubes. (Drugs.) □ *Frank was a C-head in the sixties.* □ *Why don't you C-heads grow up?*

**cheapie** *n.* a cheaply made article. (See *el cheapo.*) □ *I don't want a cheapie. I can afford better.* □ *It broke. I guess it was a cheapie.*

**cheap shot** *n.* a remark that takes advantage of someone else's vulnerability. □ *It's easy to get a laugh with a cheap shot at cats.* □ *People who wouldn't dare utter anything negative about blacks, Poles, or women just love to take a cheap shot at yuppies.*

**cheapskate** [ˈtʃipsket] *n.* a miserly person; a very cheap person. (Compare to *piker.*) □ *A 5% tip! What a cheapskate!* □ *I don't think of myself as a cheapskate, but I do try to watch my cash flow.*

**cheaters** *n.* sunglasses. (Formerly all spectacles. See also *shades, sunshades.*) □ *Get your cheaters on. The sun's really bright.* □ *Somebody sat on my cheaters!*

**check** 1. *n.* a dose of a drug in a capsule or folded in a paper. (Drugs.) □ *Max handed me a check, and I slipped him some long green.* □ *How much you want for a check?* 2. *interj.* okay; yes; "yes, it is on the list." □ BILL: *Four quarts of oil.* TOM: *Check.* □ FRED: *Are you ready?* PAUL: *Check.*

**check out the plumbing** AND **visit the plumbing** *tr.* to go to the bathroom. (See *plumbing.*) □ *I think I'd better check out the plumbing before we go.* □ *I want you kids to visit the plumbing as soon as we get there.*

**check something out** AND **check out something** *tr.* to examine something; to think about something. □ *It's something we all have to be concerned with. Check it out.* □ *Check out this Billy Biggles album.*

**check that** *tr.* cancel that; ignore that (last remark.) □ *Check that. I was wrong.* □ *At four, no, check that, at three this afternoon, a bomb exploded at the riverside.*

**cheese 1.** *n.* vomit. □ *There's cheese on the sidewalk. Look out!* □ *In there, there's cheese on the bathroom floor. So gross!* **2.** *in.* to empty one's stomach; to vomit. □ *Somebody cheesed on the sidewalk.* □ *She popped into the bushes and cheesed soundlessly.*

**cheesecake 1.** *n.* a display of the female form, probably wearing little clothing, often in photographs. (Compare to *beefcake.*) □ *Women don't like to see all that cheesecake on the walls when they bring their cars in here to be fixed.* □ *Now they're even putting the magazines with cheesecake under the counter.* **2.** *n.* a good-looking woman; good-looking women. □ *Who's the cheesecake in that low-cut job?* □ *Bring on the cheesecake!*

**cheesed off** *mod.* angry; disgusted. □ *Clare was really cheesed off at the butler.* □ *The butler was cheesed off at the cook.*

**cheese-eater** *n.* an informer; a *rat fink.* (Rats eat cheese.) □ *Some cheese-eater called the clerk and warned her we were coming.* □ *Molly, the cheese-eater, called the police.*

**cheesehead** *n.* a stupid-acting person. □ *Is this cheesehead bothering you?* □ *Why do all the cheeseheads in town ride in my cab in the same day?*

**Cheese it (the cops)!** *exclam.* "Run away, the cops are coming!" □ *Look out! Cheese it, the cops!* □ *If you see the fuzz coming, you're supposed to yell, "Cheese it, the cops!" But I don't know why. Then they know we're doing something wrong.*

**cheesy** *mod.* cheap; tacky. □ *I wouldn't live in a cheesy place like this if I could afford better.* □ *That was a cheesy trick to pull on somebody.*

**chewed** *mod.* tired; abused. □ *After that argument at the office yesterday, I really felt chewed.* □ *After an interview like that, I am too chewed to even cry.*

**chew face** *tr.* to kiss. (More jocular than crude.) □ *A couple of kids were in a doorway chewing face.* □ *Hey Molly! Wanna go chew face?*

**chew someone out** AND **chew out someone** *tr.* to scold someone. □ *I knew my dad was going to chew me out.* □ *The dean chewed out the whole fraternity.*

**chew something over** AND **chew over something 1.** *tr.* to talk something over. □ *Why don't we do lunch sometime and chew this over?* □ *We can chew it over at lunch.* **2.** *tr.* to think something over. □ *I'll have to chew it over for a while. I'm not sure now.* □ *Don't chew it over too long. The offer is only good till Friday.*

**chew the fat** AND **chew the rag** *tr.* to chat or gossip. □ *Put your carcass over on the chair, and let's chew the fat for a while.* □ *We were just chewing the rag. Nothing important.*

**chew the rag** See the previous entry.

**chez** See *chas.*

**chick 1.** *n.* a *girl* or woman. □ *Who's the chick driving the ragtop?* □ *We're gonna take some chicks to dinner and then catch a flick.* **2.** *n.* heroin. (Drugs.) □ *This chick is really stepped on.* □ *I gotta get to my channel and get some chick.*

**chicken** *n.* a coward. □ *Come on, let's go. Don't be a chicken.* □ *He's no fun. He's a chicken.*

**chicken feed** *n.* a small amount of money. (See also *peanuts.*) □ *Sure I can afford it. It's just chicken feed.* □ *It may be chicken feed to you, but that's a month's rent to me.*

**chicken-hearted** *mod.* cowardly. □ *Yes, I'm a chicken-hearted softie. I hope you don't want to make something of it.* □ *He's chicken-hearted, but I still love him.*

**chicken out (of something)** *in.* to manage to get out of something, usually because of fear or cowardice. □ *Come on! Don't chicken out now!* □ *Freddy chickened out of the plan at the last minute.*

**chicken powder** *n.* powdered amphetamine. (Drugs.) □ *Those kids seem to be satisfied with chicken powder.* □ *Nobody is satisfied with chicken powder for very long.*

**chick(en) shit habit\*** *n.* a small drug habit. (Drugs. As if it were a coward's addiction. Caution with *shit.*) □ *Paul just has a little chicken shit habit.* □ *A chick shit habit will grow and grow.*

**chief** [tʃif] **1.** *n.* the person in charge. (Also a term of address.) □ *Okay, chief, where to?* □ *You got a couple of clams* *to pay the toll with, chief?* **2.** AND **the chief** *n.* mescaline. (Drugs.) □ *I gotta go talk to the chief.* □ *He threw up all the chief he ate.* **3.** AND **the chief** *n.* *L.S.D.* (Drugs.) □ *See the little picture of the Indian? That's why they call it the chief.* □ *The chief and I are gonna go on a little trip.*

**chief cook and bottle washer** See *head cook and bottle washer.*

**chill 1.** AND **chilly** *n.* a cold can of beer. □ *Hey, toss me a chill, would ya, buddy?* □ *You ready for another chill?* **2.** *tr.* to kill someone. (Underworld.) □ *Rocko had orders to chill Barlowe or not to show his face again.* □ *I'll chill you with one blast from my cannon, you creep.* **3.** *tr.* to frighten someone. (Standard English.) □ *The specter chilled everyone who saw it.* □ *The prospect of having to go in there alone chilled Wally, but good.* **4.** *tr.* to reject someone. □ *The whole gang chilled him, and this really made him come home.* □ *She chilled me once too often. I won't take that from a dame.* **5.** See *chill (out).*

**chill (out)** *in.* to calm down; to be *cool;* to get *cool.* □ *All right now, people, chill . . . chill.* □ *Before we can debate this matter, you're all gonna have to chill out.*

**chill someone's action** *tr.* to squelch someone; to prevent someone from accomplishing something. (Black.) □ *Freddie is trying to chill my action, and I'm a little steamed about that.* □ *Just wait! I'll chill his action—just you wait.*

**chillum** [ˈtʃɪləm] *n.* a pipe or device used for the smoking of marijuana. (Drugs.) □ *He keeps a chillum in his stash.* □ *Ernie carries a chillum with him. He's trying to sell it.*

**China** *n.* the teeth. (See also *ivories.*) □ *I spent a damn fortune trying to get this China fixed up.* □ *If you would brush your China every day, you'd be okay.*

**China white 1.** AND **Chinese white** *n.* pure or nearly pure heroin. (Drugs.) □ *Beware of that China white.* □ *You never see Chinese white anymore. There's too many other kinds of junk for anybody to bother with it.* **2.** *n.* fentanyl, a synthetic narcotic analgesic. (Drugs.)

□ *That Chinese white can paralyze your lungs.* □ *All the hopheads I know of stay away from China white.*

**Chinese red** *n.* heroin. (Drugs.) □ *Chinese red is really high quality.* □ *No, Chinese red is cheap.*

**Chinese white** See *China white.*

**chin music** *n.* talk; idle chatter. □ *That's enough chin music back there.* □ *Okay, chum, make with the chin music. Let's have it.*

**chintzy** [ˈtʃɪntsi] **1.** *mod.* cheap; shoddy. □ *Nobody's gonna buy this chintzy stuff. Throw it out.* □ *What a chintzy car! The door fell off!* **2.** *mod.* stingy; miserly. □ *The chintzy guy left me no tip!* □ *Don't be chintzy. Give the man a dollar for a cup of coffee.*

**chip 1.** *in.* to take an amount of an addictive drug small enough to avoid addiction. (Drugs.) □ *He thought he could get away with chipping, but now he's hooked.* □ *It doesn't matter whether you chip or shoot. If you're meant to be a junky, you're gonna be a junkie, and that's the truth.* **2.** *tr.* to dilute a drug. (Drugs.) □ *Max chipped the bag too much and has some mad customers.* □ *Mr. Big didn't know that Max was chipping the merchandise.*

**chipper 1.** *mod.* jolly, fresh, and alert. (Standard English.) □ *Well, you look chipper this morning.* □ *This chipper young man will show you around.* **2.** *mod.* alcohol intoxicated. □ *Larry here is chipper already!* □ *A glass of wine will make her chipper almost immediately.* **3.** AND **chippie, chippy (user)** *n.* an occasional user of an addictive drug. (Drugs.) □ *The chippy users rarely end up in the hospital.* □ *Who can stay a chippie very long?*

**chippy 1.** AND **chippie** *n.* a part-time prostitute. □ *Yeah, so I'm a chippie. So what's that make you?* □ *Some little chippie stopped us to ask for a match. How amateurish.* **2.** *in.* to play around sexually. □ *She won't even chippie.* □ *So me and my boyfriend was chippying a little in the hall. Why was you watching?* **3.** See *chipper.*

**chippy around** *in.* to be sexually promiscuous. □ *She has been known to chippy around, but not with just anyone* *and never for money.* □ *She figures it's her right to chippy around.*

**chippy-chaser** *n.* a man who chases sexually loose women. □ *He tried to be such a charmer—you know, a chippy-chaser, but he is so inept.* □ *Max used to be a chippy-chaser, but the scag has him sort of debilitated these days.*

**chippy habit** *n.* a small drug habit; the occasional use of addictive drugs. (Drugs.) □ *All I have is a chippy habit. Is that illegal?* □ *A chippy habit will grow into the kind of habit any real junky would be proud of.*

**chips 1.** *n.* money. (See also *(bargaining) chip.*) □ *I managed to put away a few chips when I worked for Acme Systems.* □ *She saved some chips over the years and bought herself a little place on the beach.* **2.** *n.* a carpenter. (Also a term of address.) □ *Tell our chips to come up here and put in a new floorboard.* □ *Tell me, chips, how fast can you build a coffin?*

**chisel** ['tʃɪzl] *tr. & in.* to extort (money). □ *Lefty tried to chisel forty bucks outa me.* □ *He's always chiseling. That's his hustle.*

**chiseler** *n.* a small-time crook; a cheater. (Originally underworld. Also a rude term of address.) □ *You dirty, two-bit chiseler! Give me my money back!* □ *Why did you trust a known chiseler like him?*

**chit** [tʃɪt] **1.** *n.* a bill or tabulation of charges that one signs rather than paying. □ *I don't have any cash. Can I sign a chit for it?* □ *Fred came in to pay for his chits about once a week.* **2.** *n.* a check. □ *She wrote out a chit for the balance due.* □ *I have your chit for the full amount.*

**chitchat** ['tʃɪtʃæt] **1.** *n.* talk; idle talk. □ *That's enough chitchat. Please get to work.* □ *Please stop the chitchat there in the back row.* **2.** *n.* a short, friendly conversation. □ *I'd like to have a little chitchat with you when you have time.* □ *We had a chitchat about the problem, and I think things will work out.*

**Chi(town)** ['ʃaɪtaʊn OR 'tʃaɪtaʊn] *n.* Chicago, Illinois. □ *I can't wait to get back to old Chitown.* □ *I was born in Chi.*

**chiv** See *shiv.*

**chiz** [tʃɪz] *in.* to relax. (Collegiate.) □ *I gotta get back to my room and chiz a while.* □ *Chiz, guys, things are getting a little rough.*

**chock-full** *mod.* totally full. □ *The new musical is just chock-full of laughs.* □ *The trunk is chock-full. There's no more room.*

**chocolate** *n.* hashish. (Drugs.) □ *Get me some of that chocolate if you can.* □ *I asked Max for some chocolate, and he tossed me a cookie.*

**chocolate chips** *n.* the drug *L.S.D.* (Drugs.) □ *Some of those chocolate chips you got were impure, and they gave Terry a very scary time.* □ *The cops found a handful of chocolate chips in Paul's pocket. They didn't know what it was.*

**choke** *in.* (for a computer) to fail to take in information being fed to it. (Computers.) □ *If you don't have your modem and your software set the same way as the host, your machine will choke.* □ *I did what you told me, but it choked anyway.*

**choked** *mod.* having to do with overly diluted drugs. □ *This stuff is choked. Don't score with that guy again.* □ *Why is this stuff so stepped on—you know, choked?*

**choker 1.** *n.* a cigarette; a cigarette butt. □ *Put that damn choker out in my house!* □ *I can smell a choker the minute somebody lights it.* **2.** *n.* a tobacco cigarette laced with cocaine. (Drugs.) □ *Bruno made me a choker, but I didn't like it at all.* □ *Jim smoked a lot of chokers, but he preferred banging.*

**chop** *n.* a rude remark; a cutting remark. □ *Jerry made some chop about the way I dress.* □ *That was a rotten chop! Take it back!*

**chopper** *n.* a helicopter. □ *The chopper that monitors the traffic goes over my house every morning at 6:00.* □ *I never want to ride in a chopper. Those things scare me.*

**choppers** *n.* the teeth. □ *I may be on my last legs, but my choppers are still my own.* □ *That horse has a nice set of choppers.*

**chop-shop** *n.* a place where stolen cars are cut or broken up into car parts for resale. □ *The state is cracking down on these chop-shops.* □ *Once a stolen car gets to a chop-shop, there's no hope of identifying it.*

**chow 1.** *n.* food. □ *I need some chow before I go out and shovel snow.* □ *What time is chow served around here?* **2.** *tr. & in.* to eat (something). (See also *chow down.*) □ *I've been chowing canned tuna and stale bagels to save money.* □ *When do we chow?* **3.** See *ciao*.

**chowderhead** *n.* a stupid person. □ *Look, chowderhead, do what I told you.* □ *Don't be such a chowderhead.*

**chow down** *in.* to eat; to take a meal. □ *Over there is where we chow down.* □ *It's past my time to chow down.*

**chow hound** *n.* someone who loves to eat; a heavy eater. □ *Harry is a real chow hound, and he's got love handles to prove it.* □ *Okay, listen up all you chow hounds. There's extra beans tonight!*

**chow something down** AND **chow down something** *tr.* to eat something, probably quickly or without good manners. □ *We can chow this pizza down in about two minutes!* □ *I found a box of cookies and chowed it down before anybody knew what I was doing.*

**Christmas tree** *n.* a drunkard. (From being *lit* like a Christmas tree.) □ *Some old Christmas tree staggered by, muttering to herself.* □ *A well-dressed Christmas tree sat in the corner—lit up, of course.*

**chrome-dome** *n.* a shiny bald head; a man with a bald head. (Also a rude term of address.) □ *The guy with the chrome-dome suddenly grasped his chest and made a face.* □ *Hey, chrome-dome, you're blinding me!*

**chuck 1.** AND **chuck up** *in.* to empty one's stomach; to vomit. (See also *up-chuck.*) □ *Look! Somebody chucked.* □ *I think I gotta chuck!* **2.** *tr.* to throw something away. □ *Chuck this thing. It's no good.* □ *The wrinkle-rod was so twisted we had to chuck it.* **3.** *in.* to eat voraciously. □ *Don't just chuck, man, enjoy your food.* □ *The two guys sat guzzling and chucking till they were full.* **4.** *n.* food. □ *Man, this chuck is okay.* □ *Who cooked this chuck, man? It's garbage!*

**chuck a dummy** *tr.* to empty one's stomach; to vomit. □ *He left the room—to chuck a dummy, I guess.* □ *Somebody chucked a dummy on the patio.*

**chucked** *mod.* alcohol intoxicated. □ *I'm too chucked to drive.* □ *How did you get so chucked?*

**chuckers** AND **chucks** *n.* a great hunger; an enormous appetite. (Usually with *the.*) □ *Oh, man, I really got the chucks. What time is chow?* □ *The chuckers got my stomach asking if my throat is cut.*

**chuck it in** *tr.* to quit; to give up. (See *throw in the towel.*) □ *I was so depressed, I almost chucked it in.* □ *If I didn't have to keep the job to live, I'd have chucked it in long ago.*

**chug(-a-lug)** ['tʃəgələg] *tr. & in.* to drink down a whole beer (or other drink) without stopping. □ *The two guys tried to see who could chug-a-lug the most beer.* □ *Wally chugged two cans in a row.* □ *All four of them sat there chugging.*

**chum** *n.* a pal; a good friend. □ *This is my chum, Wally.* □ *We've been chums for years. Went to college together.*

**chummy** ['tʃəmi] *mod.* friendly. □ *I'm glad to see that you are a little more chummy this morning.* □ *Don't get too chummy with me. I'm a real son of a bitch.*

**chump** [tʃəmp] *n.* a stupid person; a gullible person. □ *You are such a chump.* □ *See if that chump will loan you some money.*

**chumphead** *n.* a stupid person. □ *John is not my favorite chumphead, but he's close.* □ *What a chumphead. You painted over the windows.*

**chunk** *in.* to empty one's stomach; to vomit. (Collegiate.) □ *I think I gotta chunk.* □ *The cat chunked all over the carpet.*

**chunky** *mod.* stout; fat. □ *Harry—the chow hound—is getting a little chunky.* □ *It's not all fat! He's always been a chunky brute.*

**church key** *n.* a beer can opener. □ *Where is the church key when I need it?* □ *I have a church key in my glove compartment.*

**churn** *tr.* (for a stockbroker) to cause a heavy turnover in the portfolio of an investor. (The broker collects commissions on each transaction.) □ *I reported my broker for churning my account.* □ *They churn accounts to earn the commissions.*

**ciao** AND **chow** [tʃɑʊ] "Goodbye"; "Hello." (Italian.) □ *See ya. Ciao.* □ *Chow, baby. Call my service.*

**cid** AND **sid** [sɪd] *n.* the hallucinogenic drug *L.S.D.* (Drugs. From *acid*. *Sid* can be capitalized.) □ *Where can I go to drop a little cid?* □ *Bruno can tell you where Sid is these days.* □ *You know where I can rap with Sid?*

**cig** [sɪg] *n.* a cigarette; a cigar. □ *Barlowe fumbled for a cig and thought better of it.* □ *Toss me my pack of cigs, will ya?*

**cigarette with no name** AND **no brand cigarette, no name cigarette** *n.* a marijuana cigarette. (Drugs. Black.) □ *You got one of them cigarettes with no name?* □ *He spends his whole life burning those no name cigarettes.*

**ciggy** AND **ciggie** ['sɪgi] *n.* a cigarette. □ *How 'bout a ciggy before we take off?* □ *Where is my pack of ciggies?*

**cinch** [sɪntʃ] **1.** *n.* something very easy. □ *No sweat! It was a cinch!* □ *What a cinch. Anybody can do it.* **2.** *tr.* to have something settled and secured. □ *He cinched it with a simple signature and date.* □ *It only took a handshake to cinch the deal.*

**cinched** [sɪntʃt] *mod.* settled; secured; *sealed (up).* (As one tightens the saddle girth on a horse.) □ *I've got it cinched! No sweat!* □ *This is a cinched deal—a done deal. No one can stop it from going through.*

**circular file** *n.* a wastebasket. □ *That letter went straight into the circular file.* □ *Most of the junk mail sits here until I can put it into the circular file.*

**city slicker** *n.* a city dweller. (Folksy.) □ *These city slickers just don't know nothing about hogs.* □ *Some city slicker came through town and tried to get us to vote for that Wilson guy.*

**civil serpent** *n.* a civil servant. □ *You have no idea the kinds of things civil serpents have to put up with.* □ *I'm a civil serpent with the state.*

**civvies** ['sɪviz] *n.* civilian clothes rather than a uniform. (Originally military.) □ *I feel sort of funny in civvies.* □ *I re-upped because I couldn't stand the thought of civvies and stuff like that.*

**C.J.** AND **K.J.** *n.* phencyclidine, P.C.P.; a *crystal joint.* (Drugs.) □ *Max tried to give me some of that C.J. stuff, but I wouldn't take it.* □ *K.J. is one of the biggest problems in the inner city.*

**C-joint** AND **coke joint** *n.* a place where cocaine is sold. (Drugs.) □ *The cops raided the C-joint and rounded up about 20 people.* □ *The gang spent a lot of time at a well-known coke joint in Frisco.*

**C.K.** *n.* cocaine. (Drugs. As if it were spelled "cokaine.") □ *Do you know where I can get some good C.K.?* □ *You can't get C.K. around here anymore.*

**clam 1.** *n.* a dollar. (Underworld.) □ *Forty clams for a sweater that doesn't even have arms!* □ *You got a couple of clams I can bum for a little bottle?* **2.** *n.* a tight-lipped person. □ *Suddenly, she became a clam and wouldn't talk anymore.* □ *Rocko's a clam. He won't say a word.*

**clam up** *in.* to get quiet. (See also *dummy up.*) □ *The minute they got him inside the cop-shop, he clammed up.* □ *You'll clam up if you know what's good for you.*

**clanked** *mod.* exhausted; pooped. □ *At the end of the race, the chick was totally clanked.* □ *I'm really clanked, man. Gotta take a rest.*

**clanks** *n.* the delirium tremens. □ *He's suffering with the clanks again.* □ *Who's the old buzzard shaking with the clanks?*

**clap\*** *n.* gonorrhea. (Caution with topic.) □ *Max has had the clap a dozen times.* □ *A case of the clap can change your life for a while.*

**claptrap** *n.* nonsense; something worthless. □ *This is enough claptrap. I'm leaving.* □ *I know claptrap when I see it, and your play was claptrap.*

**class 1.** *n.* high style; elegance. □ *The dame's got class, but no brains.* □ *Class isn't worth much in this neighborhood.* **2.** *mod.* first-rate; high-class. □ *I've always regarded the firm as a class outfit.* □ *This was a class suburb just a few years ago.*

**class act** *n.* a high-quality act; a high-quality way of doing things. □ *I like the way you move on the field, Jerry. It's a real class act.* □ *The prof puts on a real class act, but he grades very hard.*

**classis-chassis** AND **classy-chassy** ['klæsi'tʃæsi AND 'klæsi'ʃæsi] *n.* an attractive female figure. □ *Who's the classis-chassis in the mink?* □ *Now there is a classy-chassy if I ever saw one.*

**classy** *mod.* elegant; dandy. □ *Pretty classy place you got here.* □ *How much does a classy car like this cost?*

**clay** *n.* good-quality hashish. (Drugs.) □ *I like the feel of this clay. I'll take it.* □ *Ask Bruno where you can dig up some clay.*

**clay pigeon** *n.* a gullible person; a *pigeon.* (Underworld.) □ *We need a clay pigeon to divert attention from the snatch.* □ *Who's gonna be the clay pigeon for the bank caper?*

**clean 1.** *mod.* not using drugs; not involved with drugs. □ *There's a success story. Kelly is one clean guy if I ever saw one.* □ *I've been clean for over a month now.* **2.** *mod.* not intoxicated with drugs. (Almost the same as sense 1.) □ *He's clean right now, but he'll get the call in an hour or two.* □ *Just being clean for a day is an accomplishment.* **3.** *mod.* well-dressed. (Black.) □ *Now there's a clean dude!* □ *New threads, huh? Clean, baby, clean!*

**clean-cut** *mod.* having to do with a person who is neat and tidy. □ *He's a very clean-cut guy, and polite too.* □ *He's sort of clean-cut looking, but with bushy hair.*

**cleaned out 1.** *mod.* broke; with no money. □ *I'm cleaned out. Not a cent left.* □ *Tom's cleaned out. He's broke. He'll have to go home.* **2.** *mod.* with one's digestive tract emptied. □ *That medicine really left me cleaned out.* □ *I feel better now that I'm cleaned out.*

**clean someone out** AND **clean out someone 1.** *tr.* to get all of someone's money. □ *The bill for supper cleaned me out, and we couldn't go to the flick.* □ *The robbers cleaned out everybody on the train.* (More at *cleaned out.*) **2.** *tr.* to empty someone's bowels. □ *That medicine I took really cleaned me out.*

□ *A couple of those little burgers will clean me out.* (More at *cleaned out.*)

**clean sweep** *n.* a broad movement clearing or affecting everything in the pathway. (Usually figurative. See examples.) □ *The boss and everybody in the front office got canned in a clean sweep from upstairs.* □ *Everybody got a raise. It was a clean sweep.*

**clean up one's act** AND **clean one's act up** *tr.* to reform one's conduct; to improve one's performance. □ *We were told to clean up our act or move out.* □ *I cleaned up my act, but not in time. I got kicked out.*

**clean up (on something)** *in.* to make a lot of money on something. □ *The promoters cleaned up on the product.* □ *If we advertise, we can clean up.*

**clear 1.** *mod.* alcohol intoxicated. □ *Man, is she ever clear!* □ *He was clear, you know, polluted.* **2.** *mod.* (of liquor) undiluted; neat. □ *No soda. Clear, please.* □ *I like mine clear with just one ice cube.* **3.** *tr.* to earn a specific net amount of money. □ *She cleared a cool forty thousand on that Wilson deal.* □ *We just want to clear a decent profit. Nothing greedy.*

**clear as mud** *mod.* not clear at all. (Often with *as.*) □ *All of this is clear as mud to me.* □ *I did all the reading, but it's still as clear as mud.*

**clear out** *in.* to leave; to depart. □ *Time for you people to clear out. It's past midnight.* □ *The boss gave me till next week to clear out. I'm fired—canned.*

**clear sailing** *mod.* easygoing. □ *It'll be clear sailing from now on.* □ *When this is finished, it'll be clear sailing.*

**click (with someone)** *in.* to catch on with someone; to intrigue someone; to become popular with someone. □ *The pink hair and multiple earrings never really seemed to click with many kids.* □ *Sam and Mary are getting along fine. I knew they'd click.*

**cliff-dweller** *n.* someone who lives in a tall apartment building. □ *I could never survive as a cliff-dweller in a big city.* □ *The majority of cliff-dwellers wouldn't choose to live in any other way.*

**climb 1.** *n.* a marijuana cigarette. (Drugs. The means to a *high.*) □ *I need a climb* *to set me straight.* □ *Here, have a swallow of this climb.* **2.** *tr.* to scold someone. □ *The boss climbed Harry for being late.* □ *Don't climb me! The train broke down!*

**climb the wall(s)** *tr.* to do something desperate when one is anxious, bored, or excited. □ *He was home for only three days; then he began to climb the wall.* □ *I was climbing the walls to get back to work.*

**clinch** [klɪntʃ] *tr.* to settle something; to make something final. □ *I was able to clinch the deal, and I got a raise for it.* □ *I want to clinch this contract before the weekend.*

**clinched** [klɪntʃt] *mod.* alcohol intoxicated. □ *They got themselves totally clinched.* □ *Oh, brother, are you clinched!*

**clincher** ['klɪntʃɚ] *n.* the final element; the straw that broke the camel's back. (See also *capper*.) □ *The clincher was when the clerk turned up the volume.* □ *Eating garlic by the bushel was the clincher. I had to get a new roommate.*

**clink** *n.* jail. □ *We'll throw you in the clink if you don't talk.* □ *One night in the clink was enough.*

**clinker** **1.** *n.* a mistake; (in music) a misplayed note. □ *That was a bad clinker in the middle of the soft passage.* □ *Look at the score, man! That series of clinkers just isn't there.* **2.** *n.* a worthless person or thing. (From the term for a cinder.) □ *This guy is such a clinker. Who needs him?* □ *Ralph has turned out to be a real clinker. We'll have to pink slip him.*

**clip** **1.** *tr.* to cheat someone. (See *clip joint*.) □ *That guy in there clipped me for a fiver.* □ *I didn't clip you or anybody else!* (More at *clipped*.) **2.** *tr.* to kill someone. □ *Rocko had orders to clip both Max and Bruno.* □ *Max and Bruno had set out to clip Rocko first.* **3.** *n.* a holder for a marijuana cigarette butt. (Drugs. See *roach clip*.) □ *She's got a clip if you need it.* □ *My clip's at home in my stash.* **4.** *n.* a music video; a short film. □ *This next clip is something you'll all recognize.* □ *Stay tuned for more great clips.* **5.** *n.* a fast rate of speed. □ *By traveling at a good clip, we managed to get there before the wedding*

*started.* □ *You were moving at a pretty good clip when you ran into the truck.*

**clip a butt** *tr.* to pinch out a cigarette for later smoking. (Also with *the*.) □ *Like an old soldier, Wally took a puff and then clipped the butt for later.* □ *You learn to clip a butt so you won't waste what you can't finish.*

**clip joint** *n.* a business establishment that cheats customers. □ *That place is a clip joint. Stay away.* □ *The clip joint on 4th Street was busted last night.*

**clipped** **1.** *mod.* cheated. □ *When Marty counted his change, he found he'd been clipped.* □ *You weren't clipped by me. I just made a mistake.* **2.** *mod.* arrested. □ *Max got clipped as he got out of his car.* □ *He was clipped and no one read him his rights, so off he went.*

**clip someone's wings** *tr.* to restrain someone; to reduce or put an end to a teenager's privileges. □ *One more stunt like that, and I'm going to clip your wings for a couple of weeks.* □ *Her father clipped her wings for getting into trouble with the cops.*

**clobber** *tr.* to strike someone; to beat someone; to out-score someone. □ *I ought to clobber you, but good.* □ *She clobbered him over the head with her bouquet.*

**clobbered** *mod.* alcohol intoxicated. □ *He's the kind of guy who goes home and gets clobbered after work.* □ *The whole fraternity celebrated by getting themselves clobbered.*

**clock in** *in.* to record one's arrival at a set time. □ *He clocked in three minutes late.* □ *When they clock in, give them this envelope.*

**clock watcher** *n.* someone—a worker or a student—who is always looking at the clock. □ *There are four clock watchers in our office.* □ *People who don't like their jobs can turn into clock watchers.*

**clodhopper** **1.** *n.* a big shoe. □ *Wipe the mud off those clodhoppers before you come in here.* □ *Look at the clodhoppers she's wearing!* **2.** *n.* a stupid person; a rural oaf. □ *Some clodhopper came into town and fell in with the wrong crowd.* □ *You don't know it, but that clodhopper is worth about two million bucks.*

**Close, but no cigar.** [klos...] *phr.* "Close, but not close enough to win a prize!" □ *You almost did it. Close, but no cigar.* □ *Close, but no cigar! Give it another try.*

**close call** See the following entry.

**close shave** AND **close call** *n.* a narrow escape. □ *Wow, that was a close shave.* □ *The car passed this close to us—a real close call.*

**closet** *mod.* secret; concealed. □ *Marty is a closet chocolate fiend.* □ *I'm a closet hard rock fan.*

**clotheshorse** ['klozhors] *n.* someone who is obsessed with clothing and looking good in it. □ *Her brother is the real clotheshorse.* □ *Mary is such a clotheshorse! Look at her now.*

**clout** *n.* influence; power. (See also *wallop.*) □ *You have clout with the mayor. You try it.* □ *I don't have any clout at all.*

**clouted** *mod.* arrested. □ *Some old wino got clouted for spitting on the sidewalk.* □ *They do things like that to get clouted so they can have a warm place to stay overnight.*

**clown** *n.* a fool. □ *Some clown threw our paper in a puddle this morning.* □ *Tell that clown in the front row to can it.*

**clown around** *in.* to act silly; to mess around. □ *Please stop clowning around and get to sleep.* □ *We were just clowning around. We didn't mean to break anything.*

**cluck** AND **kluck** [klǝk] *n.* a stupid person; a person as stupid as a chicken. □ *Why did they send me a dumb cluck to do this work?* □ *Some kluck came in and asked for a left-handed monkey wrench.*

**cluckhead** *n.* a stupid oaf. □ *What cluckhead put sugar in the salt shaker?* □ *I'm getting to be such a cluckhead!*

**clucky** *mod.* stupid; oafish. □ *What a clucky dame!* □ *The plan you submitted to this office was rejected by the policy committee. They noted that it was the cluckiest idea they had ever seen.*

**cluelessness** *n.* total stupidity. (See *totally clueless.*) □ *I just shake my head in wonder at the cluelessness of my fellow humans.* □ *This place is just infested with juvenile cluelessness!*

**clue someone in** AND **clue in someone** *tr.* to set someone straight (about something); to inform someone of the facts. □ *I think I'd better clue in Sam about the rally.* □ *What's going on? Clue me in.*

**clunk** **1.** *tr.* to strike someone or something. □ *A small truck clunked me from behind.* □ *The branch clunked the roof as it fell.* **2.** *n.* a hit; the sound of a hit. □ *I heard a clunk on the roof. Must be reindeer.* □ *The clunk on the roof was a falling branch.*

**clunker** **1.** *n.* an old car. □ *He drives an old clunker and doesn't have any insurance.* □ *I gotta get rid of this clunker pretty soon.* **2.** *n.* someone or something worthless; a *clinker.* □ *We have to get the clunkers off the payroll.* □ *Fred? There's another clunker we don't need.*

**clunkhead** *n.* an oaf; a stupid dolt. □ *What clunkhead put sugar in the salt shaker?* □ *My brother can be such a clunkhead.*

**clunky** *mod.* ponderous and inefficient. □ *The whole plan is too clunky. Try to prune it down.* □ *I got rid of all the clunky stuff. Now it's lean and mean.*

**clutched** *mod.* nervous. □ *I get so clutched before a test.* □ *George is clutched most of the time. He's in bad shape.*

**clutch (up)** *in.* to become very tense and anxious; to freeze with anxiety. □ *I have been known to clutch up before a race.* □ *Cool it, babe! Don't clutch!*

**Clyde** [klaɪd] *n.* an oaf; a *square,* usually a male. (Also a term of address.) □ *Well, Clyde, I think you're way off base.* □ *A dull Clyde, that's my old Bill, but I still love him.*

**C-note** AND **C-spot** *n.* a one-hundred dollar bill. (The "C" is the Roman numeral for "100." See also *century note.*) □ *How much ammo will a C-note buy these days?* □ *That guy wanted a C-spot to fix my muffler.*

**coaster** *n.* someone who lives near the ocean. (California.) □ *Tiffany is a coaster now, but she was born, like, somewhere else.* □ *The coasters just don't want to be beige, that's all.*

**coast-to-coasts** *n.* long-lasting amphetamines. (Drugs. Said to be used by truck drivers.) □ *The police said the* driver had a small box of "coast-to-coasts" in his pocket. These amphetamines were thought to have contributed to the accident. □ Max sold the guy the coast-to-coasts that led to the accident.

**cocaine blues** n. depression suffered after a bout of cocaine use. (Drugs.) □ There is nothing worse than the cocaine blues. □ The trouble with the cocaine blues is that the cure is more cocaine.

**cock\*** n. the penis. (Taboo. Caution with topic.) □ He made some joke about a cock, but nobody laughed. □ The streaker covered his cock and ran across the field.

**cockamamie** ['kɑkəmemi] mod. ridiculous; inconceivable. □ What a cockamamie idea! □ That is the most cockamamie thing I ever heard of.

**cockeyed** ['kɑkaɪd] mod. crazy. □ Who came up with this cockeyed idea, anyway? □ If you didn't act so cockeyed all the time, you'd have more friends.

**cockle burrs** ['kɑkl̩ bɚz] n. amphetamines; amphetamine tablets and capsules. (Drugs.) □ Cockle burrs tend to make you alert. □ One cockle burr a day keeps the blues away.

**cocktail** n. a tobacco cigarette with a marijuana cigarette butt stuck into the end. (Drugs.) □ All I want is a little cocktail. □ Here's a roach. Make me a cocktail.

**coed** ['koɛd] n. a female college student. (From coeducational.) □ Some of these coeds are pretty strong-minded. □ My daughter is a coed at Midwest University.

**coffee and** n. coffee and a doughnut or a pastry. □ I'll have coffee and. □ We stopped at a little shop for coffee and.

**coffin-dodger** ['kɔfn̩ dɑdʒɚ] n. a heavy smoker. □ I just hate these damn coffin-dodgers who light up a cigarette in a restaurant! □ Coffin-dodgers, chain-smokers—who cares? Let 'em commit suicide—in the privacy of their own homes, of course.

**coffin nail 1.** AND **coffin tack** n. a cigarette. □ No more coffin nails for me. □ Every coffin tack you smoke takes a little off the end of your life. **2.** n. a drink of liquor. □ How about another coffin

nail? □ Coffin nail sounds bad. Drink sounds good.

**coffin varnish** n. inferior liquor. □ You want some more of this coffin varnish? □ Do you see what that coffin varnish you serve here has done to some of those guys?

**coin** n. money. (See also hard coin.) □ I'm sort of short of coin right now. Can it wait? □ He made a lot of coin on the last picture.

**cokeaholic** [kokə'hɑlɪk] n. a cocaine addict. (Drugs.) □ It's hard to get a cokeaholic to get treatment. □ When I realized I was a cokeaholic, I decided to stop, but I couldn't.

**coke fiend** AND **coke freak** n. a heavy user of cocaine. (Drugs.) □ The place was filled with coke fiends sniffing and snorting like fury. □ Do you know any coke freaks who actually call themselves coke freaks?

**coke freak** See the previous entry.

**cokehead** n. a heavy cocaine user; a cocaine addict. (Drugs.) □ We get a few depressed cokeheads in the E.R. who have tried suicide. □ As a banker, I see two or three cokeheads file for bankruptcy each year.

**coke joint** See C-joint.

**coke party** n. a gathering where cocaine is consumed. (Drugs.) □ There's a coke party in the warehouse after closing tonight. □ Tom's hosting a coke party for his yuppie friends.

**cokespoon** AND **(flake) spoon** n. a small spoon used to carry powdered cocaine to a nostril. (Drugs.) □ Wally wears a cokespoon around his neck. □ The principal wrote a letter to Mrs. Simpson telling her that Jimmy had brought a flake spoon to school.

**cola** ['kolə] n. cocaine. (Drugs. Probably from Coca-Cola™.) □ Some of these clowns want only the best cola. □ The crowd that specializes in cola doesn't usually fret about the cost—till they're almost wiped out.

**cold 1.** mod. (stopping something) suddenly and totally. □ I stopped cold—afraid to move further. □ That remark stopped her cold. **2.** mod. dead. □ This parrot is cold—pifted! □ When I'm cold and buried, I hope people will think of me fondly. **3.** See cold sober.

**cold blood** AND **cold coffee** *n.* beer. (See also *in cold blood*.) □ *How would you like a little cold blood to start things off?* □ *A nice big cold coffee would do me fine.*

**cold call** *tr.* to call a sales prospect from a list of persons one has never met. □ *The broker cold called a number of people each evening for two months.* □ *Things have to be pretty bad when the senior brokers at a major house have to cold call people to get business.*

**coldcock** *tr.* to knock someone out. □ *The guy who called Max out wanted to coldcock him for shorting him, but got coldcocked himself.* □ *The clerk cold-cocked the would-be robber with a champagne bottle.*

**cold coffee** See *cold blood*.

**cold feet** *n.* a wave of timidity or fearfulness. □ *Suddenly I had cold feet and couldn't sing a note.* □ *You sort of expect a candy-ass like that to have cold feet.*

**cold fish** *n.* a dull and unresponsive person. □ *I hate to shake hands with a cold fish like that. He didn't even smile.* □ *I hate going out with a cold fish.*

**cold shoulder** **1.** *n.* a cool reception; the brushoff. □ *I didn't expect to be greeted by such a cold shoulder.* □ *I got the cold shoulder at the office today.* **2.** *tr.* to ignore someone; to give someone a cool reception. □ *The hostess cold-shouldered me, so I spilled my appetizers in the swimming pool.* □ *Tiffany cold-shouldered the guy who was putting the moves on Roberta.*

**cold sober** *mod.* sober; completely sober. (See also *sold cober*.) □ *Of course, I'm cold sober!* □ *He had a fine head on and wanted more than anything to be cold sober and alert.*

**cold turkey** *mod.* (stopping something) suddenly, without tapering off. (Said especially of stopping an addictive drug intake. Originally drugs.) □ *Martha stopped cold turkey and survived.* □ *I stopped smoking cigarettes cold turkey and had to be hospitalized.* □ *I gave up rich desserts cold turkey and lived to tell about it.*

**coli** ['kɑli] *n.* marijuana. (Drugs. From broccoli.) □ *There's a little bag of coli in the fridge.* □ *Who got into my stash and took the coli?*

**collar** **1.** *tr.* to arrest someone. □ *The cops collared her as she was leaving the hotel.* □ *The nark tried to collar Max, but Max moved away too fast.* (More at *collared*.) **2.** *n.* an arrest. □ *It was a tough collar, with all the screaming and yelling.* □ *I made the collar in broad daylight.*

**collard greens** ['kɑlɚd...] *n.* marijuana. (Drugs. Black.) □ *This collard greens you sold me is no good.* □ *Where does a dude latch onto some collard greens in this town?*

**collared** *mod.* arrested. □ *Willard Babbit? Oh, yes. He's collared. Got him last night.* □ *Got collared during a routine traffic stop.*

**Colombian (gold)** AND **Columbian (gold)** *n.* a potent marijuana from Colombia. (*Columbian* is a misspelling.) □ *Colombian gold seems to be a favorite around here.* □ *Columbian is cheap and abundant in almost every city.*

**color of someone's money** *n.* the amount of money someone has in hand. □ *Well, I can tell if we can make a deal if I could see the color of your money.* □ *Lemme see the color of your money. Then we'll talk.*

**combo** ['kɑmbo] **1.** *n.* a small group of musicians; a small band. (From *combination*.) □ *Andy started his own combo and made money from day one.* □ *You can make a good living with a combo.* **2.** *n.* a combination of people or things. □ *Those two make an interesting combo.* □ *The dish was a combo of fish, garlic, and cream.*

**comboozelated** [kəm'buzəledəd] *mod.* alcohol intoxicated. (Collegiate.) □ *I believe I am just a little comboozelated.* □ *How did you get so comboozelated?*

**Come again?** *interrog.* "What did you say?" (Folksy.) □ *Come again? It's awful noisy in here.* □ *I didn't hear you. Come again?*

**Come and get it!** *exclam.* "Dinner is ready!" (Folksy.) □ *Dinner's ready! Come and get it!* □ *Come and get it, or we'll throw it to the hogs!*

**comeback** ['kəmbæk] **1.** *n.* a retort; back talk. □ *Hank is pretty fast with the* *comeback.* □ *One more snotty come-back like that and you're finished.* **2.** *n.* a return to a former state. □ *The aging singer tried to sober up and make a comeback.* □ *Her comeback was not a financial success, but it improved her spirits.*

**come clean (with someone) (about something)** *in.* to admit (something) to someone. □ *I wish you'd come clean with me about this problem.* □ *You're gonna have to come clean eventually.*

**come down 1.** *in.* to happen. □ *Hey, man! What's coming down?* □ *When something like this comes down, I have to stop and think things over.* **2.** *n.* a letdown; a disappointment. (Usually **comedown.**) □ *The loss of the race was a real comedown for Willard.* □ *It's hard to face a comedown like that.* **3.** *in.* to begin to recover from the effects of alcohol or drug intoxication. □ *She came down slow, which was good.* □ *It was hard to get her to come down.*

**come down hard** *in.* to come out of a drug use session badly. (Drugs.) □ *Mike came down hard, and it took them a long time to calm him down.* □ *Some kids who come down hard will need treatment, but none of them get it unless they look like they are bad off.*

**come-hither look** [kəmˈhɪðɚ lʊk] *n.* an alluring or seductive look or glance, usually done by a woman. □ *She blinked her bedroom eyes and gave him a come-hither look.* □ *She had mastered the come-hither look, but was not ready for the next part.*

**come home 1.** *in.* to return to reality. □ *I'm glad you decided to come home.* □ *Hey, wake up, you spacy clown. Come home!* **2.** AND **come home to haunt someone** *in.* (for some problem) to cause negative consequences. □ *Eventually every single problem you have avoided dealing with will come home.* □ *All these things come home to haunt you sooner or later.*

**Come off it! 1.** *exclam.* "Stop acting arrogantly!" □ *Oh, you're just one of us. Come off it!* □ *Come off it, Tiff. You're not the Queen of England.* **2.** *exclam.* "Give up your incorrect point of view!" □ *Come off it! You're wrong, and you*

know it. □ *You are arguing from a foolish position. You're dead wrong. Come off it!*

**come on** [ˈkəmɔn] **1.** *n.* a lure; bait. (Usually **come-on.**) □ *Forty people responded to the come-on published in the Sunday paper.* □ *It's just a come on. Nobody is giving away a decent color T.V. just for listening to a sales pitch.* **2.** *n.* an invitation; a sexual invitation. (Usually **come-on.**) □ *She stared at him with her bedroom eyes, giving him that age-old come-on.* □ *Who could resist a come-on like that?* **3.** *in.* to begin to perform well. □ *In the second scene, the entire cast came on, and the audience loved it.* □ *The singer came on immediately. We knew we had a star.* **4.** *in.* to begin to become friendly. □ *After a few minutes, they began to come on to each other.* □ *When the nervousness of meeting a blind date passed, Sam and Mary began to come on, and we could see it would be a success.* **5.** *in.* to feel the effects of a drug; for a drug to take effect. (Drugs.) □ *After what seemed a long time, I began to come on to the stuff.* □ *When I came on, I decided I didn't like it, but then it was too late.* **6.** [kəmˈan] *exclam.* "You are wrong!" (Usually **Come on!**) □ *Come on! This is a good set of clubs!* □ *Come on! Wasteful spending occurs at all levels of all governments! Nobody is innocent!*

**come on like gangbusters** See the following entry.

**come on strong** AND **come on like gangbusters** *in.* to seem aggressive; to impress people initially as very aggressive and assertive. (See explanation at *like gangbusters.*) □ *She has a tendency to come on strong, but she's really a softie.* □ *The new president comes on strong at first.*

**come on to someone** *in.* to make advances to a person. □ *He came on to her, but she beat it outa there fast.* □ *She didn't even know he was coming on to her, till they got to his place.*

**come out ahead** *in.* to end up with a profit; to end up with some benefit. □ *I never seem to come out ahead at the end of the month.* □ *We'll come out ahead in the end. Just you wait.*

**come out in the wash** *in.* to be dealt with in the normal chain of events. (As if someone were counselling someone who had caused a clothing stain.) □ *All of these things will come out in the wash.* □ *Whatever it is, it'll come out in the wash. Don't worry.*

**come out on top** *in.* to end up to the better; to win. □ *Tim always has to come out on top—a classic poor loser.* □ *She made all the wrong moves and still came out on top.*

**comer** ['kɔmɚ] *n.* someone with a bright future. □ *Fred is a real comer. You'll be hearing a lot about him.* □ *A comer like that can command a high salary.*

**come unglued** AND **come unstrung, come untied, come unscrewed.** *in.* to get angry or lose control. □ *I was so mad, I just knew I would come unglued.* □ *The kid sat there for a while and then just came unscrewed.*

**come unscrewed** See *come unglued.*

**come unstrung** See *come unglued.*

**come unstuck** See *come unglued.*

**come untied** See *come unglued.*

**come up for air** *in.* to pause for a break. □ *The kissers—being only human—had to come up for air eventually.* □ *They were taking in money so fast at the box office that there wasn't a minute to come up for air.*

**comeuppance** [kəm'əpənts] *n.* a well-deserved rebuke. □ *He finally got the comeuppance that he's needed for so long.* □ *I gave her a comeuppance she'll never forget.*

**comfort station 1.** *n.* a restroom; toilet facilities available to the public. □ *Do you have a comfort station in this store?* □ *We need to stop and find a comfort station in the next town.* **2.** *n.* an establishment that sells liquor. □ *Let's get some belch at a comfort station along here somewhere.* □ *There's cops all around that comfort station. Somebody must have robbed it.*

**comfy** ['kəm(p)fi] *mod.* comfortable. □ *This is a very comfy chair.* □ *I find myself in a not too comfy position with regard to your further employment here.*

**coming out of one's ears** *mod.* in great abundance. □ *Mr. Wilson has money coming out of his ears.* □ *Borrow some*

paper from Chuck. He's got it coming out of his ears.

**comma-counter** *n.* a pedantic person. □ *Comma-counters can be such a pain.* □ *When you need a proofreader, you need a comma-counter.*

**commie** ['kɑmi] *n.* a communist. □ *What are the commies up to now?* □ *The commies are selling gold today, and the price went down a lot.*

**commode-hugging drunk** *mod.* heavily alcohol intoxicated; drunk and vomiting. □ *Bruno got commode-hugging drunk in the space of two hours.* □ *I could tell by the sounds coming from the bathroom that Ernie had come home commode-hugging drunk again.*

**company bull** *n.* a detective or guard who works for a private firm. □ *Tod is company bull for Acme Systems. He works nights.* □ *The company bull asked what we were doing there.*

**company man** *n.* a man who always sides with his employers. □ *Ken's a company man—he'll always take management's side.* □ *You can depend on a company man to do as he is told.*

**comps** [kɑmps] *n.* comprehensive examinations. □ *She flunked her comps, but they let her go on anyway.* □ *I take my comps tomorrow, and I'm clutched up.*

**con 1.** *n.* a convict. □ *One of the cons keeps a snake in his cell for a pet.* □ *Is that guy in the gray pajamas one of the escaped cons?* **2.** *n.* a confidence scheme. □ *They pulled a real con on the old lady.* □ *This is an okay con you got going.* **3.** *tr.* to swindle or deceive someone. □ *Don't try to con me. I know the score.* □ *Bruno conned him out of his money.*

**con artist** See *con man.*

**conehead 1.** *n.* a fool; an oaf. □ *Some conehead put sugar in the salt shaker.* □ *You can be pretty much of a conehead yourself sometimes, you know.* **2.** *n.* an intellectual; a *pointy-head.* □ *The coneheads have decided that we are all making too much money.* □ *They build fences around universities to keep the coneheads in.*

**conga** ['kɔŋgə] *n.* marijuana from central Africa. (Drugs.) □ *A nice pipe of conga would make me very happy.* □ *Is* *this real conga or just hyped up domestic?*

**con job** *n.* an act of deception. □ *What a con job he tried to pull on us!* □ *This is not an annual report! It's a con job!*

**conk** AND **konk** *n.* the head. □ *Put your brim on your conk, and let's cruise.* □ *Where'd you get that nasty bump on your konk?*

**conk-buster** ['kɔŋkbəstɚ] *n.* inferior liquor. □ *Another shot of that conk-buster and I will just pass out.* □ *Jed kept a jar of conk-buster under his bed against night sweats.*

**conk out** **1.** *in.* (for someone) to collapse. □ *I was so tired I just went home and conked out.* □ *I was afraid I would conk out while I was driving.* **2.** *in.* (for something) to break down; to quit running. □ *My car conked out finally.* □ *I hope my computer doesn't conk out.*

**con man** AND **con artist** *n.* someone who makes a living by swindling people. □ *Gary is a con artist, but at least he's not on the dole.* □ *He looks like a con man, but he's just a sweetie.*

**connection** *n.* a seller of drugs; someone who is a source for drugs. (Originally drugs.) □ *Max's connection got rousted.* □ *This connection you keep talking about—is he dependable?*

**connect (with someone or something)** **1.** *in.* [with *someone*] to meet someone; to talk to someone on the telephone. □ *Let's try to connect on this matter tomorrow.* □ *We connected over a drink and discussed the matter fully.* **2.** *in.* [with *something*] (for a batter) to hit a ball. □ *Wally connected for a double.* □ *He swung, but didn't connect with the ball.*

**conniption (fit)** [kə'nɪpʃən...] *n.* a burst of anger; a *spaz.* □ *He had a conniption fit over the question of my marriage to Wally.* □ *Come on, don't have a conniption!*

**constitutional** *n.* the first drink or dose of drugs of the day. (See also *breakfast of champions*.) □ *He downed a constitutional and made ready to set out for the office.* □ *He never fails to drop a constitutional in the morning.*

**contact high** **1.** *n.* drug euphoria from marijuana smoke in the immediate area.

(Drugs.) □ *That place was so smoky, I almost got a contact high.* □ *Kelly—the cheapskate—tried to get a contact high at the concert.* **2.** *n.* euphoria from being in contact with people. □ *I get a contact high from just being around young people.* □ *Anyway, a contact high is legal.*

**coo-coo** AND **cuckoo** **1.** *mod.* unconscious. □ *I socked him on the snoot and knocked him coo-coo.* □ *Rocko was cuckoo for a minute; then he was up and swinging.* **2.** *mod.* insane. □ *The chick is just cuckoo, that's all.* □ *How did I ever get involved in this cuckoo scheme, anyway?* **3.** *mod.* alcohol intoxicated. □ *How'd you get coo-coo so soon?* □ *She's too cuckoo to talk. Leave her alone.*

**cook** **1.** *in.* to die in the electric chair. (Underworld.) □ *If you think I'm gonna cook for this rap, you're dead wrong.* □ *I'll see that you cook if it's the last thing I do.* **2.** *in.* to stew (over something); to worry. □ *He seemed to be cooking about the lost check.* □ *You could tell she was still cooking. The whole business was a real worry.* **3.** AND **simmer** *in.* (for something) to be considered or be thought about. □ *I'll let it cook overnight and see how I feel about it in the morning.* □ *Let this idea simmer a while, and then we'll talk about it.* **4.** *tr.* to tamper with something, such as accounts or records. □ *Somebody cooked the books, and the feds are in on it now.* □ *Cooking the accounts is a risky business.*

**cooked** *mod.* alcohol or drug intoxicated. □ *Tod is cooked, fried, boiled, baked—drunk.* □ *Gary is calling a cab. He's too cooked to drive.*

**cooked up** AND **cooked-up** *mod.* contrived. □ *The whole thing seems so cooked up.* □ *What a cooked-up story! Of course, you don't believe it.*

**cookie pusher** **1.** *n.* a bootlicker; someone who flatters other people for self-serving motives. □ *When you've got a whole office full of cookie pushers, there's always someone to take you to lunch.* □ *Another cookie pusher came in today to tell me what a great teacher I am.* **2.** *n.* a lazy do-nothing. □ *Is Martin a couch potato or a cookie pusher? That is the question!* □ *I'm just looking for a cookie pusher to fire today.*

**cooking with gas** *in.* doing exactly right. (Always with *-ing.*) □ *That's great! Now you're cooking with gas!* □ *I knew she was finally cooking with gas when she answered all the questions correctly.*

**cool 1.** *mod.* unabashed; unruffled; relaxed. □ *This chick is so cool—no matter what happens.* □ *She is totally cool and easygoing.* **2.** *mod.* good; excellent. □ *This is a really cool setup!* □ *Then this, like, cool muscleman comes over and asks Tiffany if she'd like to dance.* **3.** *mod.* (of music) mellow; smooth. □ *This stuff is so cool, I'm just floating.* □ *Doesn't he blow a cool trumpet?* **4.** *mod.* no less than (some amount of money). (See examples.) □ *He earns a cool million every year.* □ *She cleared a cool forty thousand on the Wilson deal.* **5.** See *keep one's cool, lose one's cool.*

**Cool bananas!** See the following entry.

**Cool beans!** AND **Cool bananas!** *exclam.* "Wow!" □ *Cool beans, man. That's great!* □ *You got a car? Cool bananas!*

**cool, calm, and collected** *mod.* cool; unabashed. □ *Albert is almost always cool, calm, and collected.* □ *Before a race I am anything but cool, calm, and collected.*

**cool cat** *n.* someone who is *cool,* usually a male. □ *Monty is a cool cat. I really like him.* □ *There is a shortage of cool cats on this turf.*

**cool down** *in.* to calm down. □ *Now, just cool down. Chill, chill. Everything's gonna be real cool.* □ *When things cool down around here, life will be much more liveable.*

**cooled out** *mod.* calm; unabashed. □ *Ted is a really cooled out kind of guy.* □ *When she's cooled out, she's great.*

**cooler** *n.* jail. (Usually with *the.*) □ *Do you want to talk, or do you want to spend a little time in the cooler?* □ *Let me outa this cooler!*

**Cool it!** *exclam.* "Calm down!" □ *Take it easy! Cool it!* □ *Come on, cool it, man!*

**cool off** *in.* to calm down. □ *Now, it's all right. Cool off!* □ *I knew things would cool off eventually.*

**cool out** *in.* to calm down; to relax. □ *Now, just cool out, man. This will pass.* □ *Everybody cooled out after the emergency, and everything was fine.* (More at *cooled out.*)

**cool someone out** AND **cool out someone** *tr.* to calm someone; to appease someone. □ *The manager appeared and tried to cool out everybody, but that was a waste of time.* □ *Cool yourselves out, you people. We gotta be sensible.*

**cooties** ['kudiz] *n.* real or imagined lice. □ *Randy pulled back from me like I had cooties or something. What's wrong with me?* □ *You have cooties, crotch-pheasants, and bad breath. What do you expect?*

**cop 1.** *tr.* to take or steal something. (Originally underworld.) □ *Somebody copped the statue from the town square.* □ *Who copped the salt from this table?* (More entries meaning "take" follow this one.) **2.** *n.* a theft. (Underworld.) □ *They pulled the cop in broad daylight.* □ *It was a lousy cop. No skill. No finesse.* **3.** *n.* a police officer. □ *The cop wasn't in any mood to put up with any monkey business.* □ *You call the cops. I've got enough trouble.* **4.** *tr.* to arrest someone. □ *The officer copped him and read him his rights.* □ *They copped Bruno with the evidence right on him.* (More at *copped.*) **5.** *n.* an arrest. □ *It was a smooth cop. No muss, no fuss.* □ *The cop went off without a hitch except for a few little insults.* **6.** See *cop a fix.*

**cop a buzz** *tr.* to smoke marijuana. (Drugs. See *buzz.*) □ *Let's go out and cop a buzz.* □ *If you want to cop a buzz, go talk to Bruno.*

**cop a drag** *tr.* to smoke a cigarette. (See *drag.*) □ *She kept going off to the john to cop a drag.* □ *Smokers who have to leave the office to cop a drag must cost this nation billions each year.*

**cop a fix** *tr.* to obtain a dose of drugs. □ *She was gonna, like, die if she didn't cop a fix pretty soon.* □ *She carries her apps so she can cop a fix whenever.*

**cop a head** *tr.* to become alcohol or drug intoxicated. □ *He was mad and depressed and went home having decided to cop a head.* □ *The two old codgers sat there copping a head, or trying to anyway.*

**cop an attitude** *tr.* to take a negative or opposite attitude about something. (See also *tude*.) □ *Look, chum, don't cop an attitude with me!* □ *I think you're copping an attitude. Not advised, man. Not advised.*

**cop a plea** *tr.* to plead guilty to a lesser charge. □ *Rocko copped a plea and got off with a week in the slammer.* □ *I wanted to cop a plea, but didn't have the chance.*

**copasetic** [kopə'sɛdɪk] *mod.* agreeable; satisfactory. (Originally black. Probably from French.) □ *Everything is copasetic. Couldn't be better.* □ *This is one fine copasetic day.*

**cop a squat** *tr.* to sit down. □ *Hey, man! Come in and cop a squat.* □ *Cop a squat and crack a tube.*

**cop a tube** *tr.* to catch a perfect tubular wave. (Surfers.) □ *He was a real pro at copping a tube, and always just the right one.* □ *Mark—as drunk as all get out—said he was gonna go out and cop a tube.*

**copilot** *n.* someone who sits with an *L.S.D.* user during a drug session. (Drugs.) □ *Max was supposed to be Molly's copilot, but he failed to show.* □ *Stoned copilots are not cool.*

**copilot ben** *n.* a Benzedrine™ amphetamine tablet. (Drugs.) □ *Copilot ben is not what you need.* □ *You got some copilot ben on you?*

**cop out** **1.** *in.* to plead guilty (to a lesser charge). (Underworld. See *cop a plea*.) □ *Frank copped out and got off with a night in the cooler.* □ *I decided not to cop out and got a mouthpiece instead.* **2.** *in.* to give up and quit; to *chicken out (of something).* □ *Why do you want to cop out just when things are going great?* □ *I couldn't cop out on you guys if I wanted to.* **3.** *n.* a poor excuse to get out of something. (Usually **cop-out** or **cop-out**.) □ *This is a silly copout.* □ *That's not a good reason. That's just a cop-out.*

**copped** *mod.* arrested. □ *Jed got himself copped—a speeder.* □ *I was copped for doing absolutely nothing at all.*

**copper** **1.** *n.* a police officer. (Originally underworld. Because the *copper* "cops" or "takes." See *cop*.) □ *See that copper over there? He busted me once.* □ *The coppers will catch up with you some day.*

**2.** *n.* money. (From *copper penny*. See also *rivets*.) □ *How much copper you got on you?* □ *That car takes too much copper to run.*

**cop-shop** *n.* a police station. □ *They hauled off everybody to the cop-shop.* □ *The pigs down at the cop-shop tried to act like they didn't know who Max was.*

**cop sickness** *n.* the need for drugs. (Drugs. See *cop a fix*.) □ *Molly was facing cop sickness if she didn't make a meet soon.* □ *She went into treatment because she hates that cop sickness.*

**cop some Z's** See *catch some Z's.*

**copycat** *n.* someone who mimics or copies the actions of others. □ *Don't be such a copycat. Find a style that suits you.* □ *Jim is a real copycat. He can say anything you say, just the way you say it.*

**corked (up)** AND **corky** *mod.* alcohol intoxicated. □ *You seem to be a little corked.* □ *You'd be corked up, too, if you'd drunk as much as I have.*

**corker** *n.* someone or something good, funny, or entertaining. □ *That was a real corker. I thought I'd die laughing.* □ *Molly is quite a corker. I bet she's fun at parties.*

**corkscrewed (up)** *mod.* courageous because of alcohol; with one's courage screwed by alcohol. □ *After getting himself corkscrewed up, he went into the boss's office for a word.* □ *He used a bit of vodka to get corkscrewed enough to demand a raise.*

**corky** See *corked (up).*

**corn** **1.** *n.* silly humor. □ *Enough of your corn!* □ *All he can do is juvenile corn. He has no timing and no sense of what the audience is thinking.* **2.** *n.* liquor; *moonshine.* (Folksy.) □ *Old Jed drinks more corn than he grows.* □ *You want a swallow of real country corn?*

**cornball** **1.** *n.* a stupid or corny person. □ *He's a cornball, but he's fun.* □ *Who invited this cornball to my party?* **2.** *mod.* stupid or corny. □ *What a cornball idea!* □ *Ken is such a cornball hick!*

**corned** *mod.* alcohol intoxicated. □ *The old-timer is corned on moonshine.* □ *Let's go out and get corned.*

**cornfed** *mod.* rural; backwards; unsophisticated. □ *I enjoy her honest, cornfed* humor. □ *Jed is a homey, cornfed kind of guy. Don't know anybody who bears him any ill will.*

**corn squeezings** *n.* whiskey; *moonshine.* (Folksy.) □ *Where's that jar of corn squeezings you usually keep under the counter?* □ *He puts away more corn squeezings in a month than most folks do in a year.*

**corn whiskey** *n.* whiskey made from corn mash. (Folksy.) □ *He makes his own corn whiskey and sells it to his neighbors.* □ *Most of that store-made bourbon is just corn whiskey with a pedigree.*

**corn wine** *n.* whiskey; rotgut. (Folksy.) □ *This is mighty fine corn wine, Jed.* □ *With corn wine like this, all you need is somebody to feed your hogs, and you're living in the lap of luxury.*

**corny 1.** *mod.* having to do with simpleminded, overdrawn humor. □ *This corny dialog has to be revised before I'll act in this play.* □ *Don't be corny. This is serious.* **2.** *mod.* having to do with overdone sentiment. □ *The love scenes were your corny hands-off-the-naughty-parts jobbers, but nobody laughed.* □ *Harry always laughs at corny mush in a movie.*

**corpse 1.** *n.* an empty liquor or beer bottle. (See *dead soldier.*) □ *Sam tossed another corpse out the window.* □ *Throw your corpses in the trash can, you jerk!* **2.** *n.* a cigarette butt. □ *The wino picked up the corpse and put it in a little box of them he carried with him.* □ *He is saving corpses to build a real smoke.*

**corral dust** *n.* nonsense, lies, and exaggeration. (A euphemism for *bullshit.*) □ *The way Judy handles the corral dust, she must be running for political office.* □ *That stuff is all corral dust. Don't believe a word of it.*

**cosmic** *mod.* excellent; powerful. □ *This pizza is absolutely cosmic!* □ *Who wants to see a really cosmic movie?*

**cotton-picker** *n.* a worthless person, typically a man. (Folksy.) □ *You silly cotton-picker! What do you mean?* □ *What cotton-picker put the scallops in the scalloped potatoes?*

**cotton-picking** AND **cotton-pickin'** *mod.* worthless; damned. (Folksy.) □ *What's the cotton-pickin' idea?* □ *Who*

is this cotton-picking bigwig pushing us around?

**couch-doctor** AND **couch-turkey** *n.* a psychiatrist; a psychoanalyst. □ *Some couch-doctor told her to go out and find a lover.* □ *I finally walked out on my couch-turkey. Now I'm getting it all together.*

**couch potato** *n.* a lazy, do-nothing television watcher. (See also *sofa spud.*) □ *If there was a prize for the best couch potato, my husband would win it.* □ *You are turning into a perfect couch potato.*

**couch-turkey** See *couch-doctor.*

**cough something up** AND **cough up something** *tr.* to produce something (which someone has requested), usually money. □ *Come on, buster, cough it up, now!* □ *You owe me seven stereo amplifiers. Now, cough them up!*

**country drunk** *mod.* alcohol intoxicated; drunk and disorganized. (Folksy.) □ *Them good old boys know how to get country drunk.* □ *The cowboy, really country drunk this time, got to town somehow and started a fight.*

**county-mounty** *n.* a highway patrol officer. (Citizens band radio.) □ *There's a county-mounty waiting under that bridge ahead of you.* □ *The county-mounty wrote me seven tickets in that one roust.*

**courage pill 1.** *n.* a tablet of heroin in pill form. (Drugs.) □ *Max capped about 40 courage pills for his "dependents."* □ *He used courage pills as monkey bait.* **2.** *n.* a barbiturate capsule. (Drugs.) □ *She can't face any social event without courage pills.* □ *A few courage pills and he was ready to take on the whole world.*

**courier** *n.* a small-time drug seller; a drug runner; a carrier of contraband. (Drugs.) □ *The cops can catch the couriers whenever they want. It's the big guys they're after.* □ *The couriers are expendable.*

**cover-up** *n.* an act of concealing something. □ *The cover-up drew more attention than whatever it was that was covered up.* □ *The candidate accused her opponent of a cover-up.*

**cow** *n.* a fat or ugly woman. (Cruel.) □ *That cow can hardly get through the door.* □ *Wouldn't you think a cow like that would go on a diet?*

**cowboy** *n.* a reckless and independent man; a reckless driver. (Also a term of address.) □ *Come on, cowboy, finish your coffee and get moving.* □ *Some cowboy in a new caddy cut in front of me.*

**cow chips** *n.* dried cow dung. □ *There's a whole field of cow chips out there! Why do you want to buy a bag of the stuff at a nursery?* □ *Break up these cow chips and work them into the soil around the base of the bushes.*

**cow flop** AND **cow plop** *n.* a mass of cow dung. □ *Mrs. Wilson is out in the pasture gathering cow flops for her garden.* □ *Cow plops are not all the same, you know.*

**cow juice** See *moo juice*.

**cow plop** See *cow flop*.

**coyote-ugly** ['kaɪot'əgli OR 'kaɪoti'əgli] *mod.* extremely ugly. (Said of people. See *double-bagger, triple-bagger*. Supposedly, if one woke up and found one's arm around a *coyote-ugly* person, one would chew off one's arm—in the manner of a coyote escaping from a steel-jaw trap—rather than pull it back away from this person.) □ *Is that your pet monkey, or is your date just coyote-ugly?* □ *Isn't that the most coyote-ugly creep you've ever seen?*

**cozy up (to someone)** *in.* to become overly friendly with someone in hope of gaining special favors. □ *Molly cozied up to the prof, hoping for a good grade at least.* □ *She failed to read the syllabus, which advised students not to cozy up to the professor or call him at home.*

**crab** *n.* a louse. (Usually plural.) □ *He's scratching like he's got crabs.* □ *The old wino and his crabs wandered into the flop house for a little peace and quiet.*

**crack 1.** *n.* a joke; a smart aleck remark. □ *Another crack like that and your nose will be a little flatter than it is.* □ *Who made that crack?* **2.** *n.* a try (which may or may not succeed). □ *Have another crack at it.* □ *One more crack and I'll have it.* **3.** *n.* a unit of something (for a particular price); a use (of something). (See examples.) □ *You would think twice, too, if you remembered that it's $7 a crack.* □ *At 2 dollars a crack, this is the best game on the midway.* **4.** *n.*

crystalline, smokable cocaine. (Drugs.) □ *This crack seems to have become the drug of choice for punks of all ages.* □ *Crack became popular when it became easy and cheap to process. It's been around for years in medicinal form.* **5.** *in.* to break down and talk under pressure. (Underworld.) □ *They kept at her till she finally cracked and talked.* □ *We knew you'd finally crack.* **6.** *mod.* (of a person) excellent; top-flight. □ *The dealer's crack salesman was no help at all.* □ *With our crack staff, we can have everything worked out in no time.* **7.** *tr.* to break into something. (Underworld.) □ *We almost cracked the safe before the alarm went off.* □ *His specialty is cracking car trunks and stealing tires.*

**crack a book** *tr.* to open a book to study. (Usually in the negative.) □ *I never cracked a book and still passed the course.* □ *Sally didn't crack a book all semester.*

**crack a tube** *tr.* to open a can of beer. (See *tube*.) □ *Why don't you drop over this evening, and we'll crack a few tubes?* □ *Would you crack a tube for me? My hands are too cold.*

**crackbrain** *n.* a fool; a stupid oaf. □ *Did you hear about the crackbrain who found part of the sky floating in the lake?* □ *Sometimes you are quite a crackbrain yourself.*

**crackbrained** *mod.* stupid; ridiculous. □ *I've heard enough of your crackbrained schemes.* □ *One more crackbrained idea and you're fired.*

**cracked 1.** *mod.* crazy. □ *You're cracked if you think I'll agree to that.* □ *You gotta be cracked if you think I'm going back in there.* **2.** *mod.* alcohol intoxicated. □ *I'm too cracked to drive.* □ *Two glasses of gin, and Walter was cracked beyond recognition.*

**cracked up to be** *mod.* supposed to be. □ *This pizza isn't what it's cracked up to be.* □ *I wanted to find out whether this stuff was what it is cracked up to be.*

**crackerjack** ['krækɚdʒæk] *mod.* excellent; industrious. □ *Fred is a crackerjack stockbroker, but his personal life is a mess.* □ *Clare is a crackerjack teacher, but she is looking for something that pays a real salary.*

**crackers** See *bonkers*.

**crackhead** *n.* a user of *crack*. (Drugs.) □ *They brought an eight-year-old crackhead in for treatment.* □ *Crackheads are a very serious problem in the nation's work force.*

**crack house** *n.* a house or dwelling where *crack* is sold and used. (Drugs.) □ *The police are continuing their efforts to close down crack houses in the area.* □ *In one dilapidated neighborhood, there is a crack house on every block.*

**crack open a bottle** AND **crack a bottle open** *tr.* to open a bottle of liquor. (Also with *the*.) □ *Let's crack open a bottle and celebrate.* □ *He cracked the bottle open and poured a little for everyone to try.*

**crackpot** **1.** *n.* a fake; a person with strange or crazy plans. □ *Some crackpot called to tell us that the sky is falling in.* □ *I'm no crackpot! I saw some of the sky floating in the lake. If it had fallen on land, someone might have been killed.* **2.** *mod.* having to do with crazy things, mainly ideas. □ *We need a crackpot idea around here just so we'll have something to compare your ideas to.* □ *Why not start a crackpot idea contest?*

**crack someone up** AND **crack up someone** *tr.* to make someone laugh. □ *She giggled, and that cracked us all up.* □ *The lecturer would talk along sort of boring like, and then all of a sudden he would crack up everybody with a joke.*

**crack up** [kræk'əp] **1.** *in.* to have a wreck. □ *The plane cracked up and killed two of the passengers.* □ *Whose car cracked up on the expressway?* **2.** *in.* to break out in laughter. □ *The whole audience cracked up.* □ *I knew I would crack up during the love scene.* **3.** *in.* to have a nervous breakdown. □ *The poor guy cracked up. It was too much for him.* □ *You would crack up, too, if you had been through all he went through.* **4.** ['krækəp] *n.* an accident; a wreck. (Usually **crack-up**.) □ *There was a terrible crack-up on the expressway.* □ *There were four cars in the crack-up.*

**cram** *in.* to study hard at the last minute for a test. □ *She spent the night cramming for the test.* □ *If you would study all the time, you wouldn't need to cram.*

**crank** **1.** *n.* a *crackpot*; a bothersome person with a bogus message. □ *A crank called with a bomb threat.* □ *A crank came in and offered to punch me in the nose for a quarter.* **2.** *mod.* bogus. □ *We had four crank calls threatening to blow up the Eiffel Tower.* □ *A crank letter promised us a million dollars if we would play "My Blue Heaven" for two hours each morning.* **3.** AND **cranks** *n.* amphetamines. (Drugs. See *crink*.) □ *Crank nearly wrecked that guy.* □ *Max eats cranks like candy.* **4.** *n.* a crabby person. (Collegiate.) □ *Why are you such a crank? Is something wrong in your life?* □ *The prof is such a crank; he jokes only about once a semester.*

**crank bugs** *n.* a drug-induced hallucination that insects are crawling under one's skin. (Drugs.) □ *I have crank bugs, and I'm cartooning, too.* □ *There's no such thing as crank bugs, so stop scratching them.*

**cranker** *n.* a heavy user of amphetamines. (Drugs. See *crank*.) □ *He's not just a nervous type. He's a cranker. Look at his pupils!* □ *The cranker is wired. Don't you know wired when you see it?*

**crank freak** AND **crank commando** *n.* a drug user who alternates between stimulants and depressants. (Drugs.) □ *The crank commandos are made to sit on this bench where we can keep an eye on them till they come home.* □ *When we find crank freaks on any of the athletic teams, that's it. They're gone.*

**cranking** *mod.* exciting; excellent. □ *This record is really cranking!* □ *We had a massively cranking time at your set.*

**crank something out** AND **crank out something** *tr.* to produce something; to make a lot of something. □ *She can crank mystery novels out like fury. They're all good, too.* □ *That man does nothing but crank out trouble.*

**crank something up** AND **crank up something** **1.** *tr.* to start something up. □ *I'll go out and crank the car up so it can warm up.* □ *Crank up the copying machine. We've got a big job to do.* **2.** *tr.* to increase the volume of an electronic device. □ *Kelly cranked up his stereo until we were nearly deafened.* □ *He* *cranked it up a little more and* CRACK, *there went both speakers!*

**cranky** *mod.* irritable; fretful. □ *Don't be cranky. We're almost there.* □ *Max is cranky today. The fuzz is on his tail.*

**crap\*** [kræp] **1.** *n.* junk; worthless matter. □ *Why don't you just throw this crap away?* □ *Get your crap off my bed!* **2.\*** *n.* dung. (Crude. Caution with topic.) □ *There's dog crap on the lawn.* □ *Don't step in that crap.* **3.** *n.* nonsense; lies. □ *I've had enough of your crap. Now talk straight, or out you go.* □ *Cut the crap!* **4.\*** *in.* to defecate. (Crude. Caution with topic.) □ *Your dog crapped on my lawn!* □ *I have to crap; then I'll be right with you.*

**craphouse\*** *n.* a privy. (Caution with *crap*.) □ *Wally's out in the craphouse reading, I guess.* □ *Where's the craphouse that used to be out there?*

**crap out** *in.* to evade something; to *chicken out (of something)*. □ *Now, don't crap out on me at the last minute.* □ *Fred crapped out, so there are only three of us.*

**crapper\*** **1.\*** *n.* a toilet, privy, or restroom. (Caution with topic. See *crap*.) □ *Where's the crapper around here?* □ *Old Jed never passes up a chance to use an indoor crapper.* **2.** *n.* a braggart. (Crude.) □ *The guy is a crapper and can't be trusted at all.* □ *Don't listen to the crapper.*

**crapper dick** *n.* a police officer or detective who patrols public toilets. □ *When he flubbed up the Wilson case, they made him a crapper dick in the central business district.* □ *What's a crapper dick get paid?*

**crappy** *mod.* bad; lousy; junky. □ *This is sure one crappy day!* □ *Shut your crappy mouth!*

**crapshoot** *n.* a gamble; a matter of chance. (Like a crap (dice) game.) □ *Basically, life is a crapshoot.* □ *The stock market isn't concerned with value anymore. It's just a crapshoot.*

**crash** **1.** *tr. & in.* to attend a party or other event uninvited. □ *Some clown tried to crash the rally, but my dad called the cops.* □ *The boys who tried to crash also broke a window.* (More at *crasher*.) **2.** *in.* to spend the night. (See *crash pad*.) □ *I crashed at a friend's place in the city.* □ *You have a place I can crash?* **3.** *in.* (for a computer) to stop working. □ *This thing crashes every time I hit a certain key.* □ *My machine hasn't crashed since I got it.* **4.** *n.* a total failure of a computer. □ *Most of my data was lost in the crash.* □ *Crashes are to teach you to back up your data.* **5.** *in.* (for any electronic device) to fail. □ *My stereo crashed, so I've been watching T.V.* □ *My T.V. crashed, and I had to go out to watch at somebody else's house.* **6.** *in.* (for a financial market) to lose a significant portion of its value in a short time. □ *The market crashed and scared the stuffing out of everybody.* □ *When the bond market crashed, the press didn't even realize it.* **7.** *n.* a collapse of a financial market. □ *After the crash, a lot of people swore off the market for good.* □ *A crash like that was too much for a lot of people.* **8.** AND **crash out** *in.* to come back to reality and sober up abruptly from a session of drug use. (Drugs.) □ *Sally crashed out and was a real mess for a while.* □ *We keep these pills here to help if we crash.* **9.** *in.* to pass out from drinking alcohol to excess. □ *About midnight I crashed, and I woke up here.* □ *Let's get Wilbur home before he crashes for good.*

**crash and burn** *in.* (for a young man) to fail brilliantly with a romance. (Collegiate. See *go down in flames*.) □ *I knew I would crash and burn with her.* □ *It stands to reason that if Ken hadn't shot me down, I wouldn't have crashed and burned.*

**crashed** **1.** *mod.* alcohol intoxicated. □ *Fred is crashed. Leave him alone.* □ *There were two crashed freshmen asleep on the lawn.* **2.** *mod.* raided by the police. (See *bust*.) □ *Our pad got crashed, and a lot of kids were arrested.* □ *After the place was crashed, it was a mess.*

**crasher** *n.* a person who attends a party uninvited. (See *crash*.) □ *The crashers ruined the party, and my dad called the cops.* □ *The crashers were no more rude than the guests.*

**crash pad** *n.* a place to stay the night on short notice. □ *I've got a crash pad in the city for emergencies like this.* □ *I gotta find a crash pad for tonight.*

**crate** *n.* a dilapidated vehicle. □ *Where'd you get that old crate?* □ *This crate gets me to work and back. That's good enough.*

**crater** *n.* an acne scar. □ *Ted has a nasty crater on his cheek.* □ *Walter was always sort of embarrassed about his craters.*

**crater face** *n.* someone with an acne scarred face. (Cruel. Collegiate.) □ *Who's the crater face putting the moves on Sally?* □ *Crater face over there is talking sort of loud.*

**crawling with someone or something** *mod.* covered with someone or something; alive with someone or something. □ *The place was crawling with police and F.B.I. agents.* □ *The room was just crawling with ants.*

**crazy 1.** *n.* a crazy person. □ *The guy's a crazy, and he keeps coming in here asking for money.* □ *I think the crazies are taking over the world.* **2.** *mod.* cool. □ *This stuff is really crazy, man. I love it!* □ *What a crazy dress. It makes you look like a million.*

**crazy bone** *n.* the elbow. □ *Ouch! I hit my crazy bone!* □ *Ken hit his crazy bone as he went into church, and was yelling "Oh! Oh! Oh!" as if the Spirit had got into him or something.*

**crazy in the head** *mod.* crazy. (Folksy.) □ *You're crazy in the head if you think I'm going out in this blizzard.* □ *So I'm crazy in the head. I'll go myself.*

**cream** *tr.* to beat someone; to out-score someone. □ *The other team creamed us, but we had better team spirit.* □ *We'll cream 'em next week.*

**creamed 1.** *mod.* beaten; out-scored. □ *We were really creamed in that last game, and the coach is steamed.* □ *Midwest U. got creamed again today by the Podunk Badgers.* **2.** *mod.* alcohol intoxicated. □ *Man, Tony is totally creamed!* □ *I got myself creamed last night, didn't I?*

**cream puff 1.** *n.* a weakling; a *wimp.* □ *Don't be a cream puff all your life! Join a health club!* □ *We're having a cream puff special this week for you clowns who can't climb stairs without panting.* **2.** *n.* a used car that is in very good condition. □ *This one is a real cream puff. Only driven to church by a little old lady.*

□ *This cream puff is loaded, air and everything.*

**creased** *mod.* exhausted. □ *What a day. I am totally creased.* □ *Here is one creased football player. Let him hit the rack.*

**creep** *n.* a weird person; an eerie person. □ *Charlie is such a creep when he's stoned.* □ *I thought Charlie was a creep no matter what.*

**creeping-crud 1.** *n.* any unidentified disease. □ *There is some kind of creeping-crud between my toes.* □ *I got the creeping-crud growing in my armpit.* **2.** *n.* a repellent person. □ *Wally has become such a creeping-crud since he inherited all that money.* □ *Don't be a creeping-crud. Just go back to being a plain crud.* **3.** *n.* any nasty slimy substance. □ *You got creeping-crud all over my pants leg.* □ *That's not creeping-crud! That's my pecan pie!*

**creep joint** AND **creep dive** *n.* an unpleasant place populated by creeps. □ *You shouldn't go into a creep joint like that alone.* □ *Why would anyone want to work in a creep dive like that?*

**creeps** *n.* the jitters; a case of nerves. (Always with *the.*) □ *These movies always give me the creeps.* □ *The creeps always make me have to go to the john.*

**creepy** *mod.* eerie; frightening. □ *I have this creepy feeling that someone is just this very moment reading something that I wrote.* □ *This is the creepiest old house I have ever been in.*

**crib 1.** *n.* a location where thieves gather to plot; a dwelling for thieves, prostitutes, etc. (Underworld.) □ *The police busted a crib over on 4th Street.* □ *They use a basement over there for a crib.* **2.** *n.* a dwelling. (Underworld.) □ *Where's your crib, man?* □ *My good threads are all back at my crib.*

**cricket** *mod.* acceptable. (Compare to *kosher.* See negative examples at *not cricket.*) □ *Is it really cricket to play under two different names?* □ *Who cares if it's cricket!*

**crink** *n.* amphetamines. (Drugs. Usually with *some.*) □ *He's never had anything but some crink—or so he says.* □ *Crink is just kid stuff.*

**cripple** *n.* a marijuana cigarette butt. (Drugs. See *crutch*.) □ *You got a crutch I can borrow for my cripple?* □ *Save those cripples for me.*

**crisco** ['krɪsko] *n.* a fat person. (Cruel. Also a rude term of address. The brand name of a baking shortening.) □ *Some crisco came in and ordered 10 large fries.* □ *Hey, crisco! Go on a diet!*

**crisp** *mod.* drug intoxicated. □ *The crisp guy waving the bra is the one we are after.* □ *Man, is he crisp!*

**crispo** AND **crispy** ['krɪspo AND 'krɪspi] *n.* someone burned out by marijuana use; someone who is *fried*. (Drugs.) □ *The kid's a crispo. It'll take years to make her productive.* □ *Now take a crispy like Karen. I can get her back on her feet a month after she stops using.*

**crispy** See *crispo*.

**crispy-critter** *n.* a person under the effects of marijuana. (From the brand name of a breakfast cereal.) □ *He's fried all right. A real crispy-critter.* □ *A crispy-critter came in and tried to sell me his watch.*

**croak** **1.** *in.* to die; to expire; to succumb. □ *I was afraid I'd croak.* □ *The parrot croaked before I got it home.* **2.** *tr.* to kill someone. □ *The car croaked the cat just like that.* □ *Somebody croaked my parrot.*

**croaker** *n.* a physician; a prison doctor. (Underworld.) □ *The croaker says I got the clap.* □ *I better go see that croaker.*

**crock** **1.** *n.* nonsense. (See *crock of shit*.) □ *What a crock! You don't know what you are talking about!* □ *This whole business is a crock. Hell, life's a crock!* **2.** *n.* a drunkard. □ *Give the old crock some money, anything to get him outa here before he barfs or something.* □ *The crock wants booze, not money.*

**crocked** [krɑkt] *mod.* alcohol intoxicated. □ *What do you get out of getting crocked very night?* □ *Oh, my God! You're crocked again!*

**crockery** *n.* the teeth. (See *China*.) □ *I gotta go to the dentist for some work on my crockery.* □ *Is that your own crockery?*

**crock of shit\*** **1.\*** *n.* something really awful; a great mass of nonsense. (Caution with *shit*.) □ *That whole place is just a crock of shit. Nobody knows what's what.* □ *You went on vacation and left this office with a real crock of shit.* **2.\*** *n.* a worthless person. (Caution with *shit*.) □ *Who is that crock of shit who brought in the dead cat?* □ *Some crock of shit put my coat on the floor!*

**cromagnon** [kroˈmægnən] *n.* an ugly male. (Collegiate.) □ *Who is that cromagnon you were with last night?* □ *That was no cromagnon. That was your blind date for next weekend.*

**crosses** See *crossroads*.

**cross-eyed (drunk)** *mod.* alcohol intoxicated. □ *What's the point of getting cross-eyed drunk?* □ *He sat on the bar stool, cross-eyed and crying.*

**crossroads** AND **crosses, cross tops** *n.* cross-scored amphetamine tablets. (Drugs.) □ *Does your roommate really have to have cross tops every morning in order to wake up?* □ *Usually, just one. Sometimes she has to take three crosses. Depends on how much of what she's had the night before.*

**cross someone (up)** AND **cross up someone** *tr.* to go against someone; to thwart someone. □ *Don't cross me up if you know what's good for you.* □ *I told you not to cross me again!*

**cross top** See *crossroads*.

**crotch-pheasant** ['krɑtʃfɛznt] *n.* a louse. (Usually in the plural.) □ *He appears to be afflicted with what you might call crotch-pheasants.* □ *There is a special medicine that will get rid of crotch-pheasants.*

**crotch-rot** *n.* a skin irritation or disease characterized by itching in the genital area, usually said of males. (See also *grunge*.) □ *What will get rid of crotch-rot?* □ *Here's some medicine for crotch-rot.*

**crowd** **1.** *tr.* to pressure or threaten someone. □ *Don't crowd me!* □ *Max began to crowd Bruno, which was the wrong thing to do.* **2.** *tr.* to gang up on someone. (Black.) □ *Some guys were crowding Tod, so we chased them off.* □ *They moved in from all sides, carrying clubs, and began to crowd us.*

**crown** *tr.* to hit someone on the head. □ *The clerk crowned the robber with a champagne bottle.* □ *The bride, at the* end of her patience, crowned the stuttering cleric with her bouquet, shouted "I do," and began kissing the groom.

**crud** [krəd] **1.** *n.* nastiness; junk; worthless matter. □ *This is just crud. Get rid of it.* □ *Get all that old crud out of the attic so we can have room for newer stuff.* **2.** *n.* a repellent person. □ *Don't be such a crud!* □ *That crud kept trying to paw me!*

**cruddy** AND **crudy, cruddie** ['krədi] *mod.* nasty; awful. □ *What is this cruddy stuff on my plate?* □ *It's just chocolate mousse, and it's not cruddie.*

**cruise 1.** *in.* to travel at top speed. □ *This old caddy can really cruise.* □ *We cruised all the way to Philly.* **2.** *in.* to drive around looking for friends or social activity. □ *We went out cruising, but didn't see anybody.* □ *Let's go cruise for a while.* **3.** *tr.* to pursue a member of the opposite sex. □ *Tom was cruising Tiffany, but she got rid of him.* □ *Are you cruising me, Tom? You know you just barf me, like, out!* **4.** *in.* to move on; to leave. □ *Listen, I gotta cruise.* □ *Time to cruise. Monty Python's on in ten minutes.* **5.** *in.* to move through life at a comfortable pace. □ *I just want to get a good job and cruise for a while.* *I'm cruising just the way I want now.* **6.** *tr.* to pass a course easily. □ *I'm gonna cruise that math course.* □ *Tom really cruised English this semester.*

**cruiser** *n.* a car; a fast car. □ *This old hog is a real cruiser.* □ *I don't want a yuppie cruiser, just an old family wagon.*

**cruising for a bruising** AND **cruisin' for a bruisin'** ['kruzn̩ fɔr ə 'bruzn̩] *in.* asking for trouble. □ *You are cruising for a bruising, you know that?* □ *Who's cruisin' for a bruisin'?*

**crumb** [krəm] *n.* a repellent person. □ *The old man was a crumb and tried to cheat us.* □ *Micky is a crumb, and he treats me like dirt.*

**crumbum** ['krəmbəm] **1.** *n.* a repellent person; a bum. □ *A skid row crumbum asked us for a buck.* □ *I gave the crumbum a buck and hoped he would leave.* **2.** *mod.* inferior; lousy. □ *I sent the crumbum food back to the kitchen. There was a bug in it.* □ *I want out of this crumbum place.*

**crumby** See *crummy.*

**crummy** AND **crumby** ['krəmi] *mod.* lousy; bad; inferior. □ *You know, this stuff is pretty crummy.* □ *It's worse than crumby.*

**crumped out** *mod.* alcohol intoxicated. □ *She was too crumped out to drive herself home.* □ *Are you crumped out again?*

**crum something up** AND **crum up something** *tr.* to mess something up; to make something crummy. □ *Now don't crum up this deal.* □ *Who crummed the bird feeder up?*

**crunch** *n.* a crisis; a time of pressure or tightness, especially of a budget. □ *We seem to be in a crunch of one kind or another all the time.* □ *The budget crunch meant that we couldn't take trips to Europe anymore.*

**crunchers** *n.* the feet. □ *My crunchers are sore from all this walking.* □ *New shoes can be hard on your crunchers.*

**crunchie** *n.* a soldier; a marching infantry soldier. (Military. See *crunchers.*) □ *A couple of crunchies were complaining about the Army.* □ *Crunchies have a pretty hard life.*

**crust** *n.* nerve; gall. □ *She's got a lot of crust—coming in here like that.* □ *It takes crust to sell this stuff to somebody. You really gotta push.*

**crusty** *mod.* feisty; gruff. □ *Jed is a crusty old man.* □ *Unlike most crusty, avuncular old men, Jed hasn't a single redeeming quality.*

**crutch** *n.* a device to hold a marijuana cigarette butt. (See *cripple.*) □ *Here's a crutch so you can smoke your cripple.* □ *I lost my crutch.*

**cry hughie** ['kraɪ 'hjui] *in.* to empty one's stomach; to vomit. □ *He is in the john crying hughie.* □ *I think I gotta go cry hughie.*

**crying drunk** *mod.* alcohol intoxicated and weeping. □ *She was crying drunk and feeling sorry for herself.* □ *I really hate it when they come in here crying drunk.*

**crying towel** *n.* someone or something used to comfort someone. □ *I guess I really need a crying towel today.* □ *I'm the kind of person who has to carry a crying towel at all times.*

**crying weed** *n.* marijuana. (Compare to *up pot.*) □ *I must have got hold of some crying weed. This stuff leaves me cold.* □ *On a rainy day, crying weed seems just right.*

**cry in one's beer** *in.* to feel sorry for oneself. □ *She calls up, crying in her beer, and talks on and on about her problems.* □ *Don't cry in your beer. Get yourself straightened out.*

**cry ruth** ['kraɪ 'ruθ] *tr.* to empty one's stomach; to vomit. (See *ruth.*) □ *Someone is in the bushes crying ruth.* □ *I think I have to cry ruth! Stop the car!*

**crystal** **1.** *n.* crystallized cocaine. (Drugs. See *crack.*) □ *I wonder how much crystal is used in this country each day.* □ *Crystal—an older name for crack—was a favorite many years ago.* **2.** *n.* liquid Methedrine™ in glass ampoules. (Drugs.) □ *I hear that Wally's shooting crystal. Is that true?* □ *Max has lots of crystal right now.*

**crystal joint** AND **krystal joint, crystal T.** *n.* phencyclidine, *P.C.P.,* an animal tranquilizer. (Drugs.) □ *Crystal joint is not meth, nor is it pot. These poor kids never really know what they're taking.* □ *That crystal T. stuff just makes me numb all over.*

**crystallized** *mod.* under the effects of Methedrine™. □ *Look at that kid shake. Look at his pupils. He is crystallized.* □ *She was one scared crystallized kid.*

**cube** [kjub] **1.** *n.* a very *square* person. □ *This nerd was the most unbelievable cube you have ever seen.* □ *Not just an L7, a real cube.* **2.** *n.* a die, one of a pair of dice. (Usually in the plural.) □ *Toss me the cubes.* □ *She shook the cubes, saying, "Baby needs shoes!"* **3.** *n.* a sugar cube impregnated with *L.S.D.* (Drugs. Often in the plural.) □ *First they took it on cubes. Then on little bits of paper.* □ *The cubes were usually bluish.*

**cubehead** *n.* an *L.S.D.* user who prefers to take the drug on a sugar cube. (Drugs.) □ *The kid is a confirmed cubehead.* □ *A few of the cubeheads will drop out of school each year.*

**cuckoo** See *coo-coo.*

**cuddle bunny** *n.* a female lover. □ *All you want is a cuddle bunny with big tits! Grow up, Maxwell Wilson!* □ *Who is that cuddle bunny driving the caddy?*

**cues** [kjuz] *n.* Quaalude™ tablets. (Drugs. From *Q.*) □ *Give her a couple of cues to help bring her down.* □ *Max can get all the cues you want.*

**cuff** *tr.* to put a charge on one's bill. □ *Would you cuff this for me, please?* □ *Sorry, I can't cuff anymore for you.*

**cuff quote** *n.* an off-the-cuff quote of a financial instrument price. (Financial markets.) □ *This is just a cuff quote, but I would say it's about 94.* □ *I can give you a cuff quote of 92, but don't hold me to it.*

**cuffs** *n.* handcuffs. □ *I felt the cuffs tighten and snap shut on my wrists.* □ *The cuffs carried the cold of the night to my bare skin. Of course, I was innocent, but that's not the way it works in real life.*

**cull** *n.* a socially unacceptable person. □ *Who's the cull driving the Edsel?* □ *This place is filled with culls. Let's split.*

**culture-vulture** **1.** *n.* an avid supporter of the arts. □ *A gaggle of culture-vultures gawked its way into the gallery.* □ *Many culture-vultures seem to be long on enthusiasm and short on taste.* **2.** *n.* someone who exploits the arts for monetary gain. □ *Mr. Babbit, a well-known culture-vulture in art circles, never could pass up a chance to grab up all the works of an up-and-coming young artist.* □ *Some culture-vultures are throwing a wine and cheese party on behalf of some of the young dolts they have grubstaked.*

**cume** AND **cum** [kjum] *n.* a cumulative average, such as a grade-point average. □ *My cume is not high enough to get into law school.* □ *My cum is a straight A average.*

**cupcake** *n.* an attractive woman. (Also a term of address.) □ *Hey, cupcake, what ya doing?* □ *Who is that cupcake driving the beemer?*

**cup of tea** *n.* something preferred or desired. (Often negative.) □ *This drug scene stuff is just not my cup of tea.* □ *Driving children around all afternoon is not my cup of tea.*

**curl up and die** *in.* to retreat and die. (Often figurative.) □ *I was so embarrassed, I thought I would just curl up and die.* □ *The old cat, finishing up the last of the nine lives, just curled up and died.*

**curse** *n.* the menses. (Always with *the*.) □ *The curse struck this morning.* □ *Oh, the woes of the curse!*

**curtains** *n.* death. (Underworld.) □ *It's curtains for you if you don't come across.* □ *Okay, Barlowe, this time it's curtains.*

**cushy** ['kuʃi] *mod.* soft; easy. (From cushion.) □ *He's got sort of a cushy job.* □ *That's a cushy kind of life to lead.*

**cuss** [kəs] **1.** *n.* a tough or difficult man. (Folksy.) □ *Jed can be a pretty tough cuss at times.* □ *Some old cuss wants you to sharpen this while he waits.* **2.** *in.* to curse; to swear. (Folksy.) □ *He's always cussing in public.* □ *I'll cuss if I please!*

**cuss someone out** AND **cuss out someone** *tr.* to rebuke someone; to scold someone severely. □ *Don't cuss me out! I can't take it.* □ *You can't cuss out people you don't know!*

**cut 1.** *mod.* alcohol intoxicated. □ *She's too cut to drive.* □ *He got cut on beer, which is unusual for him.* **2.** *tr.* to dilute something. □ *She always cuts her eggnog with cola. Yuck!* □ *You can cut the saltiness with a little sugar.* **3.** *n.* a share of the loot or the profits. (Originally underworld.) □ *I want my cut now.* □ *You'll get your cut when everybody else does.* **4.** *n.* a single song or section of music on a record. □ *This next cut is one everybody likes.* □ *Let's listen to another cut of the same album.* **5.** See *cut a check.* **6.** *tr.* to eliminate something; to stop (doing something). □ *Okay, chum, cut the clowning.* □ *Cut that noise! Not another peep out of you.* **7.** See *able to cut something.*

**cut a check** *tr.* to write a check. □ *We'll cut the check tonight and send it out in tomorrow's mail.* □ *Please cut a check for Mr. Babbit. Here's the amount.*

**cut a deal** *tr.* to arrange a deal; to seal a bargain. □ *Maybe we can cut a deal. Let's talk.* □ *The two lawyers cut a deal that left me with the furniture, although she got the house.*

**cut and run** *in.* to stop what one is doing and flee. □ *The cops were coming, so we cut and run.* □ *At the first warning, we cut and run.*

**cut corners** *tr.* to do something more easily; to take shortcuts; to save money by finding cheaper ways to do something. □ *They're always finding ways to cut corners.* □ *I won't cut corners just to save money. I put quality first.*

**cutie** *n.* a cute thing or person. (Also a term of address.) □ *Your baby is a real cutie.* □ *Come here, cutie, let me fix your collar.*

**cutie pie** *n.* a cute person, typically a woman or a baby. (Also a term of address.) □ *She is such a cutie pie.* □ *What's your name, cutie pie?*

**Cut it out!** *exclam.* "Stop it!" □ *That's enough! Cut it out!* □ *Get your hands off me! Cut it out!*

**cut loose** *in.* to let go; to become independent. □ *It was hard to cut loose from home.* □ *I guess it's time I cut loose.*

**cut no ice (with someone)** *tr.* to have no influence on someone; to fail to convince someone. □ *I don't care who you are. It cuts no ice with me.* □ *So you're the mayor's daughter. It still cuts no ice.*

**cut one's losses** *tr.* to do something to stop a loss of something. (See examples.) □ *I knew I had to do something to cut my losses, but it was almost too late.* □ *Sell some of the high-priced stuff to cut your losses.*

**cut one's own throat** *tr.* to do something that harms oneself. □ *If I do that, I'd be cutting my own throat.* □ *He's just cutting his own throat, and he knows it.*

**cut one's wolf loose** *tr.* to go on a drinking bout; to get drunk. □ *I'm gonna go out and cut my wolf loose tonight.* □ *You're going to cut your wolf loose too often and really get into trouble.*

**cut out** *in.* to leave; to run away. □ *It's late. I think I'll cut out.* □ *Don't cut out now. The night is young.*

**cut-rate** *mod.* cheap; low-priced. □ *I don't want any cut-rate stuff.* □ *Where are your cut-rate sweaters?*

**cut someone in (on something)** *tr.* to permit someone to share something. □ *You promised you would cut me in on this caper.* □ *We can't cut you in. There's not enough.*

**cut someone off at the pass** See *head someone off at the pass.*

**cut some Z's** See *catch some Z's.*

**cut the cheese\*** AND **cut the mustard\*** *tr.* to release intestinal gas. (Caution with topic.) □ *Who cut the cheese?* □ *People who cut the mustard in the car have to get out and walk.*

**Cut the comedy!** *exclam.* "Get serious!"; "Stop acting silly!" □ *That's enough, you guys. Cut the comedy!* □ *Cut the comedy and get to work!*

**Cut the crap!** *exclam.* "Stop the nonsense!" □ *I've heard enough. Cut the crap!* □ *Cut the crap. Talk straight or get out.*

**cut the dust** *tr.* to take a drink of liquor. □ *I think I'll stop in here and cut the dust.* □ *I want to cut the dust. Can I have a snort?*

**cut the mustard** **1.** *tr.* to be able to do something requiring youth or vigor. (Usually in the expression **too old to cut the mustard**.) □ *Do you really think he can cut the mustard?* □ *She's not too old to cut the mustard.* **2.** See *cut the cheese.*

**cut up (about someone or something)** *mod.* emotionally upset about someone or something. □ *She was all cut up about her divorce.* □ *You could see how cut up she was.*

**cyclone(s)** ['saɪklonz] *n.* phencyclidine, *P.C.P.*, an animal tranquilizer. (Drugs.) □ *I thought only kids O.D.ed on cyclones.* □ *What Sam thought was cyclones was really caffeine.*

# D

**D.A. 1.** *n.* a "drug addict." (Drugs.) □ *Some old D.A. was found in the river last night.* □ *Is Max a D.A.?* **2.** AND **DA** *n.* the "district attorney." (Originally underworld.) □ *The D.A. is anxious to put Mr. Big out of business.* □ *Why is the DA trying to get Bruno?*

**dad** *n.* one's father; any father; any old man. (Also a term of address. Capitalized when referring to one's own father.) □ *Hey, Dad, can I use the car tonight?* □ *Well, dad, how's it going?*

**daddy (of them all)** See *granddaddy (of them all).*

**daffy** ['dæfi] *mod.* silly; crazy. □ *Kelly was acting daffy because she was so happy.* □ *Oh, don't be daffy!*

**dagwood (sandwich)** ['dægwʊd...] *n.* a tall sandwich with many layers of food. (From the comic strip character *Dagwood* by Chick Young.) □ *I really like to make an old-fashioned dagwood sandwich every now and then.* □ *How many calories are there in a dagwood, on the average?*

**daily dozen** *n.* a short set of daily exercises. □ *I need to do my daily dozen before breakfast.* □ *A daily dozen would be good for you.*

**daily grind** *n.* the tedious pattern of daily work. (See also *rat race.*) □ *Well, it's Monday. Time to start another week of the daily grind.* □ *The daily grind really gets me down.*

**daisy** *n.* an excellent thing. (Compare to *doosie.*) □ *This little car is a real daisy.* □ *I want a daisy of a haircut. Something unusual with bangs or something.*

**damage** *n.* the cost; the amount of the bill (for something). (Compare to *bad news.*) □ *Okay, waiter. What's the damage?* □ *As soon as I pay the damage, we can go.*

**damfool** ['dæm'ful] *mod.* foolish. (See also *tomfool.*) □ *What a damfool idea!* □ *Stop revving up that damfool car!*

**Dammit!\*** AND **Damn!\*** ['dæmɪt AND dæm] *exclam.* a curse, usually uttered in anger or agitation. (Caution with *damn.*) □ *That's mine, dammit!* □ *Oh, damn! I'm late!*

**damn\* 1.** See *Dammit!* **2.** AND **damned\*** *mod.* cursed; rotten; infuriating. (Caution with *damn.*) □ *Get this damn mess cleaned up!* □ *Clean up the damned mess yourself!* **3.** *n.* something of little concern or value. (Caution with *damn.* Usually with *give.*) □ *I don't give a damn what you do!* □ *Who around here does give a damn?*

**damn(ed) sight better\*** *mod.* considerably better. (Folksy. Caution with *damn.*) □ *This one is a damned sight better than the old one.* □ *The weather's not great, but it's a damn sight better than yesterday.*

**damn(ed) well\*** ['dæm(d)'wɛl] *mod.* certainly; really. (Caution with *damn.*) □ *You know damned well I'm mad!* □ *I will damn well be there when I said I would.*

**dampen someone's spirits 1.** *tr.* to make someone less happy; to make someone sad. □ *The news dampened everyone's spirits.* □ *I hate to dampen your spirits, but there is a tidal wave headed for this island.* **2.** *tr.* to dilute someone's alcoholic drink with some other liquid. (A pun on sense 1.) □ *Bartender, would you dampen my spirits a bit?* □ *I hate to dampen your spirits this way, but here goes. Say when.*

**damps** *n*. barbiturates. (Drugs. The opposite of *amps*, "amphetamines.") □ *Gary dropped a few damps and felt relaxed.* □ *Max tossed Bruno a couple of damps and smiled.*

**danged** [dæŋd] *mod.* damned. (Folksy.) □ *Put your danged hat on a hook!* □ *That's a danged stupid thing to do.*

**dap** [dæp] *mod.* well-dressed. (From *dapper.*) □ *Who is that dap looking dude?* □ *Man, you look dap!*

**darb** [dɑrb] *n*. an excellent person or thing. □ *Carl is a real darb. I'm glad to know him.* □ *What a swell darb of a car!*

**dark horse** **1.** *n*. an unknown entrant into a contest; a surprise candidate for political office. □ *The party is hoping that a dark horse will appear before the election.* □ *You'd be surprised at how eagerly people will vote for a dark horse.* **2.** *mod.* previously unknown. □ *Who would vote for a dark horse candidate?* □ *A dark horse player can win if all the others are creeps.*

**Dash it all!** *exclam.* "Oh, phooey!"; "To hell with it all!" □ *Oh, dash it all! I'm late.* □ *I broke it! Dash it all!*

**day one** *n*. the first day. □ *You haven't done anything right since day one! You're fired!* □ *She was unhappy with her new car even on day one.*

**day person** *n*. a person who prefers to be active during the daytime. (Compare to *night person.*) □ *I am strictly a day person. Have to be in bed early.* □ *The Count insisted that he was not a day person, and he had to remain on his home ground until nightfall.*

**day the eagle flies** See *when the eagle flies.*

**day-tripper** *n*. a tourist who makes one-day trips. □ *At about 4:00 P.M. the day-trippers start thinning out.* □ *Being a day-tripper is hard on your feet sometimes.*

**dead** **1.** *mod.* quiet and uneventful. □ *The day was totally dead.* □ *What a dead day!* □ *Things were sure dead around this town this summer.* **2.** *mod.* very tired. □ *I am just dead from all that jogging.* □ *I went home from the office, dead as usual.* **3.** *mod.* dull; lifeless; flat. □ *This meal is sort of dead because I am out of onions.* □ *The pop went dead*

because someone left it open. □ *Who wants dead pop?* **4.** *mod.* (of a person) no longer effective; no longer of any consequence. □ *You're dead, Fred. You can't help us anymore.* □ *That guy is dead—out of power.* **5.** *mod.* (of an issue) no longer germane; no longer of any importance. □ *Forget it! It's a dead issue.* □ *The project is dead. Don't waste any more time on it.*

**dead and gone** **1.** *mod.* (of a person) long dead. □ *Old Gert's been dead and gone for quite a spell.* □ *When I'm dead and gone, I hope folks remember me at my best.* **2.** *mod.* (of a thing) gone long ago. □ *That kind of thinking is dead and gone.* □ *The horse-and-buggy days are dead and gone.*

**deadbeat** *n*. someone who doesn't pay debts or bills. □ *Some deadbeat with the same name as mine is ruining my credit rating.* □ *Pay up! Don't be a deadbeat.*

**dead broke** *mod.* completely broke; without any money. □ *I'm dead broke—not a nickel to my name.* □ *I've been dead broke for a month now.*

**dead cinch** *n*. an absolute certainty; an easy thing to do. □ *It's a dead cinch. I foresee no problems.* □ *The job was no dead cinch, but we did it on time.*

**dead drunk** *mod.* alcohol intoxicated; totally inebriated. □ *They were both dead drunk. They could only lie there and snore.* □ *Marty is dead drunk again.*

**dead duck** *n*. a person or thing doomed to failure or disaster. □ *This whole plan was a dead duck from the beginning.* □ *Wally is a dead duck because he flunked astronomy.*

**dead easy** *mod.* very easy. □ *This whole job is dead easy.* □ *It was so dead easy, Frank did it with one hand.*

**dead-end kid** *n*. a youth with no future, usually a male. □ *Kelly wasn't your typical dead-end kid.* □ *Max was a dead-end kid from the day he was born.*

**dead from the neck up** **1.** *mod.* stupid. (With a "dead" head.) □ *Merton seems dead from the neck up.* □ *She acts like she is dead from the neck up.* **2.** *mod.* no longer open to new ideas. □ *My uncle is dead from the neck up. A real fossil.* □ *Everyone on the board of directors is dead from the neck up.*

**deadhead 1.** *n.* a stupid person. □ *Who's the deadhead in the plaid pants?* □ *Wow, are you a deadhead!* **2.** *tr. & in.* (for someone) to return an empty truck, train, airplane, etc., to where it came from. □ *I deadheaded back to Los Angeles.* □ *Who is supposed to deadhead this truck to Miami?* **3.** *n.* a follower of the rock group The Grateful Dead. □ *What do these deadheads see in that group?* □ *My son is a deadhead and travels all over listening to these guys.*

**dead horse** *n.* a *dead issue*, especially one which is referred to continually. (Often with *beat, whip*.) □ *Forget it! Don't waste time whipping a dead horse.* □ *The whole business is a dead horse. Forget it.*

**dead in the water** *mod.* stalled; immobile. (Originally nautical.) □ *This whole company is dead in the water.* □ *The project is dead in the water for the time being.*

**dead issue** *n.* an issue that doesn't matter anymore. □ *It's a dead issue. Forget it.* □ *The question of my late arrival is a dead issue.*

**dead letter 1.** *n.* a letter that cannot move through the post office because the addressee does not exist or because the address is wrong or illegible. (Standard English.) □ *Every now and then they open the dead letters to see if they can figure out who they were meant for.* □ *Sometimes dead letters have return addresses in them.* **2.** *n.* an issue that does not matter anymore. □ *This contract is a dead letter. Forget it!* □ *The mayor's plan for our raises is a dead letter.*

**deadly (dull)** *mod.* very dull. □ *The lecture was deadly dull, and I went to sleep.* □ *What a deadly dull prof.* □ *Her story was really deadly. I am sorry I was awake for part of it.*

**dead man** See *dead soldier*.

**dead marine** See *dead soldier*.

**deadneck** *n.* a stupid person. □ *What deadneck put sugar in the salt shaker?* □ *Who's the deadneck who painted the fence purple?*

**dead on** *mod.* exactly right; on target. □ *That's a good observation, Tiffany. You are dead on.* □ *Your criticism is dead on!*

**deadpan 1.** *n.* an expressionless face. (See *pan*.) □ *This guy has a super deadpan.* □ *Remember the deadpan she used to put on?* **2.** *n.* a person with an expressionless face. □ *The guy's a perfect deadpan.* □ *When you come on stage, look like a deadpan.* **3.** *mod.* dull and lifeless. (Usually said of a face, expression, etc.) □ *What a deadpan expression!* □ *Her face is totally deadpan.* □ *He has such a deadpan approach to everything.*

**(dead) ringer (for someone)** *n.* someone who is an exact duplicate of someone else. □ *You are sure a dead ringer for my brother.* □ *Isn't he a ringer for Chuck?*

**dead soldier** AND **dead man, dead marine, dead one 1.** *n.* an empty liquor or beer bottle. □ *Toss your dead soldiers in the garbage, please.* □ *A dead marine fell off the table and woke up all the drunks.* **2.** *n.* a cigarette butt. (Less common than sense 1.) □ *The bum found a dead soldier on the ground and picked it up.* □ *He collected dead soldiers to use in building a whole smoke.*

**dead to rights** See *(bang) (dead) to rights, have someone dead to rights*.

**dead to the world 1.** *mod.* sound asleep. □ *After all that exercise, he's dead to the world.* □ *He's dead to the world, and I can't rouse him.* **2.** *mod.* alcohol intoxicated. □ *Six beers and he was dead to the world.* □ *By midnight almost everybody was dead to the world.*

**deadwood** *n.* nonproductive or nonfunctional persons. □ *We'll have to cut costs by getting rid of the deadwood.* □ *Is there any way to make the deadwood productive again?*

**deal 1.** *n.* a bargain. □ *This is a real deal!* □ *This is no deal. The price is too high for el cheapo.* **2.** *tr. & in.* to traffic in drugs; to sell drugs. (Drugs.) □ *Max has been dealing for years.* □ *He dealt only pills at first.*

**dealer** *n.* a drug seller or supplier. (Drugs.) □ *Yes, Max is a dealer. So what?* □ *There are a lot of dealers in this neighborhood.*

**deal stock** *n.* a stock that is a takeover candidate. (Financial markets.) □ *I try to spot the deal stocks early and buy* *them before others do.* □ *You can lose a lot of money on deal stocks, too.*

**Dear John letter** *n.* a letter a woman writes to her boyfriend in the military service telling him that she does not love him anymore. □ *Wally got a Dear John letter today.* □ *Sally sends a Dear John letter about once a month.*

**Dear me!** *exclam.* "Oh, my goodness!" □ *Dear me! I'm so sorry.* □ *Dear me! I'm late!*

**death on someone or something 1.** *n.* causing the death or destruction of someone or something. □ *This kind of road is just death on tires.* □ *This candy is death on my teeth.* **2.** *n.* [with *something*] moving very fast or skillfully on something, such as wheels. □ *He is way fast—just death on wheels.* □ *Tod is death on skis. You ought to see him go.*

**decent 1.** *mod.* good; very good. □ *This is some pretty decent jazz.* □ *Your threads are decent, all right.* **2.** *mod.* having to do with good to very high-quality drugs. (Drugs.) □ *This grass is truly decent.* □ *You got any decent dust?*

**deck 1.** *tr.* to knock someone to the ground. □ *Fred decked Bob with one blow.* □ *I was so mad I almost decked him.* **2.** *n.* a pack of cigarettes. □ *Can you toss me a deck of fags, please?* □ *Why don't you stop in there and buy a deck?* **3.** *n.* a stack of packets of a powdered drug. (Drugs.) □ *Max always carried a deck held to his wrist by a rubber band.* □ *How much for a deck of dust?*

**deduck** ['didək] **1.** *n.* a tax deduction. (From *deduct.*) □ *Interest is no longer a deduck.* □ *I need a few more deducks this year.* **2.** AND **duck** *n.* a deduction from one's paycheck. □ *More of my pay goes to deducks than I get myself.* □ *What's this duck for?*

**deejay** See *disk jockey.*

**deep pockets 1.** *n.* a good source of money. □ *We need to find some deep pockets to finance this venture.* □ *Deep pockets are hard to find since the stock market crashed.* **2.** *n.* a rich person. □ *The lawyer went after the doctor who was the deep pockets of the organization.* □ *I want to find the deep pockets who arranged all this.*

**deep six 1.** *tr.* to jettison something, including a corpse, from a ship at sea. □ *The captain had them deep six the garbage.* □ *They deep sixed the body of the first mate who had died of the shakes.* **2.** *n.* burial at sea. (Always with *the.*) □ *They gave her the deep six with full honors.* □ *I think I'd want the deep six, but I'll probably kick off on dry land.* **3.** *tr.* to kill or dispose of someone. (Underworld.) □ *Mr. Big ordered Bruno to deep six Max.* □ *The thugs tried to deep six the witness, but failed.* **4.** *tr.* to throw something away. □ *Take this old thing out and deep six it.* □ *I've got to deep six this old T.V. set.* **5.** *n.* a grave. (Always with *the.* Graves are usually six feet deep.) □ *When you know the deep six is at the end of the line no matter who you are, it makes you take life less seriously.* □ *The deep six can't be made attractive to many people.*

**def** [dɛf] *mod.* better; *cool.* (Black. From *definitive.*) □ *Man, that yogurt is def!* □ *What a def set of threads!*

**defrosted** *mod.* "even" with someone who has insulted, embarrassed, or angered one. (Black. See *chill, ice.*) □ *He yelled at her till he was defrosted, and then things settled down.* □ *Bob was finally defrosted when he insulted Alice.*

**Delhi belly** ['dɛli bɛli] *n.* diarrhea, as suffered by tourists in India. □ *I've got a touch of the Delhi belly and will have to miss the Taj Mahal.* □ *I've got something you can take for Delhi belly.*

**delish** [dəˈlɪʃ] *mod.* delicious. □ *Oh, this cake is just delish.* □ *What a delish meal.*

**delts** [dɛlts] *n.* the deltoid muscles. (Bodybuilding.) □ *Look at the delts on that dame!* □ *How do you get delts like that?*

**demo** ['dɛmo] **1.** AND **dem** [dɛm] *n.* a member of the Democratic Party. □ *A couple of dems are running for the caucus, but no other party is represented.* □ *Which demos are they?* **2.** *n.* a demonstration (of something). □ *Can I have a demo of this model?* □ *Hey, Chuck, give this man a demo.* **3.** *n.* an automobile or other machine or device which has been used by a dealer for demonstration purposes. □ *I can give you a demo for half price.* □ *Do you have any*

**demos?** **4.** *tr.* to demonstrate something (to someone). □ *Let me demo this for you so you can see how it works.* □ *Will someone please demo this computer?* **5.** *tr.* to demonstrate (something) to someone. (See examples.) □ *I've got to go demo these people on this software.* □ *Can you demo me before you go?*

**dems** [dɛmz] **1.** See *demo*, sense 1. **2.** *n.* Demerol™. (Drugs.) □ *The nurse was hooked on dems.* □ *Dems are easy to get in a hospital.*

**des** [dis] *n.* December. (Financial markets. Futures and options trading.) □ *The bean futures for des fell out of bed yesterday.* □ *Are these figures des or March?*

**desk jockey** *n.* someone who works at a desk in an office. (Patterned on *disc jockey.*) □ *I couldn't stand being a cooped-up desk jockey.* □ *The desk jockeys at our place don't get paid very well.*

**destroyed** *mod.* drug intoxicated. □ *Wow, what happened to Molly? She looks destroyed.* □ *The kid who took angel dust is destroyed most of the time.*

**deuce** [dus] **1.** *n.* the devil. (Always with *the.*) □ *I'll knock the deuce out of you if you come around here again.* □ *Get the deuce out of here!* **2.** *n.* the two in playing cards. □ *If I could only get a deuce.* □ *Ah, here's the deuce I need.* **3.** *n.* two dollars. □ *Can you loan me a deuce till payday?* □ *Sure, here's a deuce. Don't spend it all in one place.* **4.** *n.* a two-year prison sentence. (Underworld.) □ *Lefty served a deuce up the river.* □ *The D.A. made sure that Bruno got more than a deuce.*

**devil of a time** *n.* a very difficult time. (Always with *a.*) □ *I had a devil of a time with my taxes.* □ *This cold has been giving me a devil of a time.*

**devil's own time** *n.* a very difficult time; a hellish time. (Always with *the.*) □ *I had the devil's own time with these tax forms.* □ *My gout is giving me the devil's own time.*

**dew** **1.** See *(mountain) dew.* **2.** *n.* cannabis. (Drugs.) □ *Max always has some dew within a few yards of him.* □ *You got any decent dew?*

**dex** AND **dexo, dexy** [dɛks AND 'dɛkso, 'dɛksi] *n.* Dexedrine™, an amphe-

tamine. (Drugs and hospitals.) □ *They used to give away dex at the infirmary like it was aspirin.* □ *In the past, a lot of people used dexies just to get perked up.*

**dexed** [dɛkst] *mod.* *high* on Dexedrine™. (Drugs.) □ *Gert was dexed half out of her mind.* □ *Larry was sort of jumpy and dexed.*

**dexo** See *dex.*

**dexy** See *dex.*

**dialog** *tr.* to attempt to deceive someone; to attempt to seduce someone. □ *Just let me dialog her for a while; then you'll see some action.* □ *Ron was dialoging this dame when her brother came in.*

**diamond in the rough** *n.* a person who is wonderful despite a rough exterior; a person with great potential. □ *Sam looks a little tacky, but he's a diamond in the rough.* □ *He's a diamond in the rough—a little hard to take at times, but okay mostly.*

**diarrhea of the mouth** AND **diarrhea of the jawbone** *n.* an imaginary disease involving constant talking. □ *Wow, does he ever have diarrhea of the mouth!* □ *You're getting diarrhea of the jawbone again.*

**dibs on something** *phr.* a claim on something. (See examples.) □ *I've got dibs on the yellow one!* □ *Dibs on the front seat!*

**dicey** ['daɪsi] *mod.* touchy; chancy; *touch and go.* □ *Things are just a little dicey right now.* □ *I'm working on a dicey deal with the city right now.*

**dick\*** **1.** *n.* a detective; a police officer. (Underworld. From *detective.*) □ *Some dicks were around looking for you.* □ *Barlowe is a private dick who has to keep one step ahead of the cops.* **2.\*** *n.* the penis. (Caution with *dick* and topic.) □ *She told some dirty joke about a dick, but everybody just sat there and looked straight ahead.* □ *He covered his dick and stooped down, then reached up to pull down the shade.* **3.\*** *n.* a stupid person, usually a male. (Caution with *dick.* Also a provocative term of address.) □ *You stupid dick!* □ *What stupid dick put this thing here in the way?*

**dickens 1.** *n.* the devil. (Always with *the*.) □ *She was going to kick the dickens out of me.* □ *I felt as bad as the dickens, but what could I do?* **2.** *n.* a devilish or impish child. (Also a term of address.) □ *Come here, you little dickens.* □ *You are such a cute little dickens!*

**dicty** ['dɪkti] *mod.* snobbish. (Black.) □ *Those people can be so dicty!* □ *That dicty lady told me I could come to the back to get a tip if I wanted.*

**diddenwhacker** ['dɪdn̩mækɚ] *n.* a name for a gadget. □ *Where is the diddenwhacker that opens the end of this?* □ *I lost the little diddenwhacker that fits in this slot.*

**diddle\* 1.** *tr.* to cheat someone; to deceive someone. □ *The clerk diddled me so I reported her.* □ *That's a good place to get diddled. You gotta watch them in there.* **2.\*** *tr. & in.* to copulate (with someone). (Caution with topic.) □ *I didn't think they'd diddle right there in the film.* □ *I'm tired of hearing who has diddled whom in Hollywood.*

**diddle with something** *in.* to play with something; to toy with something. □ *Here, don't diddle with that watch.* □ *Stop diddling with your nose, Jimmy!*

**diddly-squat** AND **(doodly-)squat** ['dɪdliskwɑt AND 'dudliskwɑt] *n.* nothing. (Folksy. Originally black or southern.) □ *This contract isn't worth diddly-squat.* □ *I get paid almost doodly-squat for a full day's work.*

**D.I.D.O.** AND **DIDO** *phr.* "dreck in, dreck out"; garbage in, garbage out. (Computers. Acronym. See *dreck*. If you get dreck out of a computer, it's because you put dreck in. See also *G.I.G.O.*) □ *Look at this stuff that the printer put out. What is it? Oh, well. D.I.D.O.* □ *As a programmer, I specialize in DIDO.*

**die** *in.* to die (figuratively) from laughter or some other emotionally intense response. □ *The whole audience died laughing.* □ *He laughed till he died.*

**die on someone 1.** *in.* (for a patient) to die under the care of someone. □ *Get that medicine over here fast, or this guy's gonna die on me.* □ *Come on, mister, don't die on me!* **2.** *in.* (for something) to quit running for someone. □

*My car died on me, and I couldn't get it started.* □ *My stereo died on me, and I had to listen to the radio.*

**diff** [dɪf] *n.* difference. □ *Aw, come on! What's the diff?* □ *The diff is about twenty dollars worth of repairs, that's what.*

**differential** *n.* the buttocks; the *rear (end)*. □ *I got a little ache in the differential.* □ *You're walking like there's something wrong with your differential.*

**different strokes for different folks** *phr.* different things please different people. (Catch phrase.) □ *Do whatever you like. Different strokes for different folks.* □ *Different strokes for different folks. That's what I always say.*

**dig 1.** *tr. & in.* to understand something. □ *I just don't dig what you are saying.* □ *Sorry. I just don't dig.* **2.** *tr.* to appreciate something; to like something. □ *He really digs classical music.* □ *Do you dig chocolate?*

**digs** *n.* a dwelling; a dwelling and its furnishings. □ *You got some pretty swell digs, here.* □ *Nice digs. You like it here?*

**Dig up!** *exclam.* "Listen up!"; "Pay attention!" (Black.) □ *Dig up, man! This is important.* □ *Shut up and dig up!*

**dike\*** [dɑɪk] *n.* a lesbian; a homosexual woman. (Caution with *dike* and topic. Regarded as offensive.) □ *Why does she work so hard to look like a dike?* □ *Who's the dike in the cowboy boots?*

**dildo\*** ['dɪldo] *n.* a stupid person, usually a male. (From the name for a false penis. Caution with *dildo*.) □ *Hank can be such a dildo sometimes.* □ *You silly dildo!*

**dilly** *n.* something excellent. □ *This little car is a real dilly.* □ *What a dilly of an apartment!*

**dilly-dally** *in.* to waste time. □ *Stop dilly-dallying around.* □ *I like to dilly-dally over a cup of coffee.*

**dim bulb** *n.* a dull person; a stupid person. □ *George seems to be a dim bulb, but he's a straight-A student.* □ *I feel like such a dim bulb when I do things like that.*

**dime-dropper** *n.* an informer. (Underworld. Because an informer at one time could drop a dime in a public telephone and call the police or drop a dime on the sidewalk as a signal for the police to move in and make an arrest. See also *drop a dime*.) □ *I think that Molly is the dime-dropper who caused the roust.* □ *The fuzz protects its dime-droppers with everything they've got.*

**dime store** *n.* an establishment that is chaotic because of its small scale. □ *I can't stand this dime store anymore. This is no way to run a law firm.* □ *Things move so fast around here that we have become a dime store rather than an accounting office.*

**dimwit** ['dɪmwɪt] *n.* an oaf; a dullard. (Also a rude term of address.) □ *Oh, Dave, you can be such a dimwit!* □ *Come on, now, you're not really a dimwit.*

**dinero** [dɪ'nero] *n.* money. (Spanish.) □ *I don't have as much dinero as I need, but other than that, I'm doing okay.* □ *You got some dinero I can borrow?*

**ding** *tr.* to shoot, dent, or knock something. □ *The rock dinged my left fender.* □ *The bullet dinged Rocko's right arm.*

**ding-a-ling** ['dɪŋəlɪŋ] *n.* a stupid person; a giddy person who hears bells. □ *This ding-a-ling comes up and asks me for a dollar for the orphans. I tell her I got all the orphans I can use at any price.* □ *Who's the ding-a-ling who painted the windows stuck?*

**dingbat** 1. *n.* a name for a gadget. □ *Isn't there supposed to be a little red dingbat that goes in this hole?* □ *Is this the dingbat you mean?* 2. *n.* a stupid person. □ *Who is the dingbat with Merton?* □ *That's no dingbat; that's his sister.* 3. *n.* any undesirable person. (Also a rude term of address.) □ *Look, dingbat, stop laughing!* □ *I'm tired of reading about that dingbat in the paper every day.*

**dinged out** *mod.* alcohol intoxicated. □ *Gary is dinged out and can't drive.* □ *He got dinged out on a couple of quarts of foam.*

**dingus** ['dɪŋgəs] *n.* a thing or gadget. □ *I have a little dingus that helps me clean venetian blinds.* □ *Toss me one of those dinguses that holds the wire in the groove, will ya?*

**dingy** ['dɪŋi] *mod.* loony; giddy. □ *That friend of yours sure does act dingy sometimes.* □ *Tell the dingy drip to forget it.* □ *I'm not dingy, I'm just in love.*

**dinky** ['dɪŋki] *mod.* small; undersized. □ *Isn't this a little dinky for a $14 steak?* □ *I'll take the dinky one. I'm on a diet.*

**dip** 1. *n.* a drunkard. (From *dipsomaniac*.) □ *Buy the dip a drink. That'll shut him up for a while.* □ *A dip hung around outside the tavern, mooching coin for drinks.* 2. *n.* a pickpocket. (Underworld.) □ *Watch out for dips at the racetrack.* □ *The dip tried a snatch, but the dupe turned around at the wrong time.* 3. *n.* a pinch or helping of snuff. □ *He took a dip just before he picked up the bat.* □ *After the hit, he got another dip.* 4. *n.* a wad of chewing tobacco. □ *You could see he had a big dip in his cheek.* □ *I won't tell you what he did with the dip when he was finished with it.* 5. See *dipshit*.

**diphead** See *dipshit*.

**dippy** *mod.* crazy; loony. □ *Who is that dippy chick with the lamp shade on her head?* □ *Tom is dippy, but fun.*

**dipshit*** AND **dip, diphead, dipstick** *n.* an oaf; a *jerk*. (Caution with *shit*.) □ *Why are you acting like such a diphead?* □ *Is there a convention of dipsticks or something here today?*

**dipso** ['dɪpso] *n.* a drunkard; an alcoholic. (From *dipsomaniac*. See also *dip*.) □ *Oh, I didn't realize she was a dipso.* □ *She's sort of a closet dipso.*

**dipstick** See *dipshit*.

**dipsy** ['dɪpsi] *mod.* tipsy; alcohol intoxicated. (See *dip*.) □ *I think that Jed is permanently dipsy.* □ *The cop pulled the dipsy dame over and arrested her.* □ *He was too dipsy to drive.*

**dirt** 1. *n.* low, worthless people. □ *He is just dirt.* □ *I am not dirt. I'm just temporarily financially embarrassed.* 2. *n.* scandal; incriminating secrets; *dirty linen.* □ *What's the dirt on Molly?* □ *I don't want to know about anybody's dirt!*

**dirt cheap** *mod.* very cheap. □ *I picked this thing up dirt cheap.* □ *Get one of these while they're dirt cheap.*

**dirt grass** *n.* low-quality cannabis. (Drugs.) □ *This junk is just dirt grass!* □ *Max* *will buy anybody's dirt grass and sell it to some punk.*

**dirty 1.** *mod.* obscene. □ *You have a dirty mind.* □ *The movie was too dirty for me.* □ *How would you know what's dirty and what's not?* **2.** *mod.* low and sneaky. □ *What a dirty trick!* □ *That was really dirty!* □ *What a dirty thing to do!* **3.** *mod.* showing signs—such as needle marks—of being addicted to narcotics; carrying drugs. (Drugs.) □ *The cops saw that Molly was dirty and locked her up, hoping that her need for drugs would force her to "cooperate."* □ *John's dirty even though he says otherwise.*

**dirty crack** *n.* a rude remark. □ *Who made that dirty crack?* □ *Another dirty crack like that and I'll leave.*

**dirty deal** *n.* an unfair deal. □ *That was a dirty deal. I feel cheated.* □ *I got a dirty deal at that shop, and I won't go back.*

**dirty dog** *n.* a low and sneaky person. □ *What a low, dirty dog.* □ *That dirty dog tried to get fresh with me!*

**(dirty) dozens** *n.* a game of trading insulting remarks about relatives. (Black. Always with *the*.) □ *Man, what's with you? Always the dirty dozens. You just gotta start something all the time.* □ *Freddy is out giving the dozens to Marty.*

**dirty joke 1.** *n.* an obscene joke. □ *Fred told a dirty joke that shocked almost everyone.* □ *No dirty jokes around here. We get enough of that on television.* **2.** *n.* a very ugly or very stupid person. □ *Look at that face. That's a dirty joke.* □ *Merton is sort of a dirty joke that nobody can laugh at.*

**dirty laundry** See the following entry.

**dirty linen** AND **dirty laundry** *n.* scandal; unpleasant private matters. □ *I wish you wouldn't put our dirty linen out for everyone to see.* □ *I've heard enough about her dirty laundry.*

**dirty look** *n.* a frown meant to show displeasure with something that has been said or done. □ *I gave him a dirty look, and he took his arm off my shoulder.* □ *What is that dirty look meant to mean?*

**dirty-minded** *mod.* having a tendency to see the lewd or obscene aspects of anything; having a tendency to place an obscene interpretation on the words and actions of others. □ *Bruno is sort of dirty-minded, but he wouldn't do anything really vile.* □ *He's a vile, dirty-minded jerk.* □ *Most of those guys are dirty-minded.*

**dirty mouth 1.** *n.* a person who talks dirty. (See *bad-mouth*.) □ *You are getting to be quite a dirty mouth, Gary.* □ *Some dirty mouth yelled out the most obscene things during the meeting.* **2.** *tr.* to speak ill of someone or something. (See also *bad-mouth*.) □ *Please stop dirty mouthing my friends.* □ *You have dirty mouthed cats just about enough.*

**dirty old man** *n.* a lecherous old man. (Usually jocular.) □ *Jimmy, you are getting to be a dirty old man!* □ *What a terrible joke. You are a dirty old man!*

**dirty pool** *n.* activities conducted using unfair or sneaky tactics. □ *They're playing dirty pool now. This calls for a new plan.* □ *When they start playing dirty pool, it's time to get mean.*

**dirty word** *n.* a curse word; an informal word concerned with sex or excrement. □ *No dirty words are allowed on this computer bulletin board.* □ *Some kid got the microphone and yelled a dirty word into it.*

**dirty work 1.** *n.* menial work; hard work. □ *Why do I always get stuck with the dirty work?* □ *We should share the dirty work evenly.* **2.** *n.* sneaky activities. □ *I hear that Sam is up to his old dirty work again.* □ *He is a master at dirty work.*

**disc jockey** See *disk jockey*.

**discombobulate** [dɪskəm'bɑbjəlet] *tr.* to confuse or perplex someone. □ *That kind of discussion discombobulates me something awful.* □ *Don't let the heat of the argument discombobulate you.*

**discombobulated** AND **discomboobulated** [dɪskəm'bɑbjəledəd] AND dɪskəm'bubjəledəd] **1.** *mod.* confused. □ *I get completely discombobulated when I think of figures that big.* □ *I'm so discomboobulated these days!* □ *She is one discombobulated gal.* **2.** *mod.* alcohol intoxicated. □ *From the way she is*

walking, *I'd say she is discombobulated.*
□ *You'd be discomboobulated, too, if you'd drunk as much as she has.*

**dish** *n.* a good-looking woman. □ *Wow, isn't she a dish?* □ *Now there's a good-looking dish.*

**dishrag** See *limp dishrag*.

**dish something out** AND **dish out something** **1.** *tr.* to serve up food to people. (Standard English.) □ *I'll dish it out, and you take it to the table.* □ *Careful how you dish out the mashed potatoes. There may not be enough.* **2.** *tr.* to distribute information, news, etc. □ *The press secretaries were dishing out reports as fast as they could write them.* □ *The company dishes out propaganda on a regular basis.* **3.** *tr.* to give out trouble, scoldings, criticism, etc. □ *The boss was dishing out criticism this morning, and I really got it.* □ *The teacher dished out a scolding to each one who was involved in the prank.*

**dish the dirt** *tr.* to spread gossip; to gossip. □ *Let's sit down, have a drink, and dish the dirt.* □ *David goes down to the tavern to dish the dirt.*

**disk jockey** AND **deejay, disc jockey, D.J., DJ** *n.* a radio announcer who introduces music from phonograph records. (Compare to *desk jockey*.) □ *The disk jockey couldn't pronounce the name of the singing group.* □ *I was a D.J. for a while, but I didn't like it.*

**ditch** **1.** *tr.* to dispose of someone or something; to abandon someone or something. □ *The crooks ditched the car and continued on foot.* □ *The flyboy ditched the plane in the lake and waded ashore.* **2.** *tr. & in.* to skip or evade someone or something. □ *Tod ditched class today.* □ *If you ditch too often, they'll throw you out of the organization.*

**dither** ['dɪðɚ] *n.* a state of confusion. (See *in a dither*.) □ *A dither like that is hard to break out of. Maybe a good night's sleep would help.* □ *I'm too far gone with this dither to sleep.*

**ditsy** AND **ditzy** ['dɪtsi] *mod.* pretentious; haughty; snobbish. □ *Who is that ditsy old girl who just came in?* □ *This table is so ditzy—gold artillery and such—and I would just like to sit here and eat some grits or something.*

**ditz** [dɪts] *n.* a giddy, absentminded person. □ *You silly ditz!* □ *I'm getting to be such a ditz!*

**dive** *n.* a low drinking establishment; a cheap saloon. □ *I don't think I want to spend the whole evening in this dive.* □ *Hey, this dive ain't bad.*

**divot** ['dɪvət] *n.* a toupee; a partial toupee. (See also *rug*.) □ *I think that Sam is wearing a little divot.* □ *His divot slipped, but no one laughed.*

**divvy** ['dɪvi] *n.* a share of something. (See the following entry.) □ *How much is my divvy?* □ *Give me my divvy so I can go home.*

**divvy something up** AND **divvy up something** *tr.* to divide something up. □ *They divvied up the fish and drove back to the city.* □ *We had to divvy my aunt's things up after her death.*

**dizzy** *mod.* stupid; scatterbrained. □ *The prof is a little dizzy, but entertaining.* □ *Who is that dizzy dame?*

**D.J.** See *disk jockey*.

**do** **1.** *n.* a party; a social event. □ *We had a smashing time at your little do.* □ *I'm having a do for a friend this weekend. Would you like to come?* **2.** *tr. & in.* to use a drug or drugs in general. (See also *do a line, do drugs*.) □ *Is Molly doing dust again?* □ *Molly never stopped doing. She just switched from dust to splash.* **3.** AND **doo** *n.* a hairdo. □ *Nice do. Is it new?* □ *I can't go out in this rain and get my doo wet!* **4.** See *must do*. **5.** *in.* to serve (a purpose) well. (Usually with *will* or *won't*.) □ *This will do quite nicely.* □ *Oh, yes, this will do.* □ *That won't do at all!* **6.** See *doo-doo*.

**D.O.A.** AND **DOA** **1.** *mod.* "dead on arrival." (Hospitals.) □ *The kid was D.O.A., and there was nothing anybody could do.* □ *Do you want to end up D.O.A.?* **2.** *n.* a person who is dead on arrival at a hospital. □ *They brought in two D.O.A.s Saturday night.* □ *Drugs increase the number of D.O.A.s considerably.* **3.** *n.* P.C.P., phencyclidine. (Because it is deadly.) □ *Stay away from D.O.A. There's a good reason why it's called that.* □ *The kids use D.O.A. no matter what.*

**do a dump on someone or something** AND **dump all over someone or something, dump on someone or some-**

**thing** *tr.* to criticize someone or something; to destroy someone or something. □ *There is no need to do a dump on me. I didn't wreck your car.* □ *The boss—mad as a wet hen—dumped all over me.* □ *That rotten jerk really did a dump on my car. Look at that fender!*

**do a fade** *tr.* to leave; to sneak away. □ *Max did a fade when he saw the pigmobile.* □ *It's time for me to do a fade.*

**do a job on someone or something 1.** *tr.* to ruin someone or something; to give someone or something a thorough working over. □ *The cops did a job on Rocko, but he still wouldn't talk.* □ *There's no need to do a job on me, man, I'll tell you everything I know—which is zip.* □ *That punch sure did a job on my nose.* **2.** See *do a number on someone.*

**do a line** *tr.* to *snort* a dose of a powdered drug, usually cocaine. (Drugs.) □ *Max slipped into a doorway to do a line.* □ *Ernie has to do a line about every four hours—night and day.*

**do a number on someone** AND **do a job on someone** *tr.* to harm or deceive someone. □ *The IRS really did a number on me.* □ *My local friendly plumber did a job on me cleaning out my drain.*

**do a slow burn** *tr.* to be quietly angry. (See also *slow burn.*) □ *I did a slow burn while I was getting my money back.* □ *I was doing a slow burn, but I didn't let it show.*

**do a snow job on someone** *tr.* to deceive or confuse someone. □ *Don't try to do a snow job on me. I know all the tricks.* □ *She thought she did a snow job on the teacher, but it backfired.*

**doc(s)-in-a-box** *n.* a walk-in emergency health care center, as found in shopping centers. (See also *McDoctor(s).*) □ *I was cut and went immediately to the docs-in-a-box in the mall.* □ *The doc-in-the-box finally closed because of lack of customers.*

**doctor's orders** *n.* something that one is strongly advised to do. (Refers here to any advice given by anyone but a doctor.) □ *I have to spend a month in Arizona. Doctor's orders.* □ *I'm doing this on doctor's orders, but I don't like it.*

**dodge** [dɑdʒ] *n.* a swindle; a *scam*; a deception. □ *What sort of dodge did you get flimflammed with?* □ *Gary has a new dodge to make money, but he hasn't made any yet.*

**do drugs** AND **do dope** *tr.* to take drugs; to use drugs habitually. (Drugs and now general.) □ *Rocko doesn't do drugs, and he doesn't drink.* □ *Max started doing dope when he was very young.*

**dog 1.** *n.* a foot. (Usually plural.) □ *My dogs are killing me.* □ *I gotta get home and soak my dogs.* **2.** *n.* an ugly *girl*. □ *I'm no dog, but I could wish for some changes.* □ *So she's not a movie star; she's not a dog either!* **3.** *n.* something undesirable or worthless; merchandise that no one wants to buy. □ *Put the dogs out on the sale table so people will see them.* □ *They even bought all the dogs this year. Sales were great.* **4.** *n.* dog dung. (See *dog-doo.*) □ *There's some dog on the lawn.* □ *Don't step in the dog.* **5.** *tr.* to follow someone. □ *The cop dogged Lefty for a week.* □ *Stop dogging me, you twit!* **6.** *tr.* to stay with one and haunt one. □ *Will this memory dog me all the days of my life?* □ *The thought of all that cake and ice cream dogged me all during my diet.*

**dog and pony show** *n.* a demonstration; a speech, skit, or other presentation that is presented often. □ *Wally was there with his dog and pony show about water safety.* □ *I've seen that dog and pony show so many times, it's like I know all the words.*

**(dog) biscuits** ['dɑgbɪskɪts] *n.* peyote; peyote buttons. (Drugs. See also *gorilla biscuits.*) □ *Jim brought a big bag of dog biscuits into the room.* □ *He dumped the biscuits on the table and said, "Dig in!"*

**dog-doo** AND **dog-dew, dog-do** ['dɔgdu] *n.* dog dung. (See also *do.*) □ *Don't step in the dog-doo.* □ *When the snow melts, the sidewalks are covered with dog-doo.*

**dog-eat-dog** *mod.* cruel; highly competitive. □ *This is a dog-eat-dog world.* □ *It's dog-eat-dog out there.*

**dogface** *n.* infantry soldier. (World War II. Also a term of address.) □ *Get those dogfaces over here on the double.* □ *Did I see a salute, dogface?*

**doggo** ['dɔgo] *mod.* hidden away; quiet and waiting. (See *lie doggo*.) □ *This error was there, doggo, for nearly thirty years.* □ *Here is another one of your doggo deadbeats on this list.*

**doggone(d)** ['dɔ'gɔn(d)] *mod.* darn(ed); damn(ed). □ *I sort of wish my hooter wasn't so doggone big.* □ *Who made this doggoned mess?*

**doggy bag** ['dɔgibæg] *n.* a bag—supplied by a restaurant—in which uneaten food can be carried home. □ *Do you have a doggy bag for my mousse?* □ *We do not have doggy bags, but we do supply foil.*

**dog meat** *n.* a dead person. (Typically in a threat. See examples.) □ *Make one move, and you're dog meat.* □ *They pulled another hunk of gangland dog meat out of the river.*

**do-gooder** ['duguɔ-] *n.* a person who is always trying to help others. (Often derogatory.) □ *The do-gooders are demanding a bigger cut of the pie.* □ *I don't consider myself a do-gooder, but I try to help people.*

**Do I have to paint (you) a picture?** AND **Do I have to draw (you) a picture?** *interrog.* "Do you understand yet?"; "How simple do I have to make it for you?" □ *This is supposed to be easy. Do I have to paint a picture?* □ *Do I have to draw you a picture, or can you visualize this?*

**dojigger** AND **doojigger** ['dudʒigɔ-] *n.* a name for a gadget. □ *A doojigger like this is worth about a quarter, but you'll pay 100 times that for it.* □ *What's this little dojigger called?*

**doll 1.** *n.* a pretty girl or woman. □ *Who's the doll I saw you with last night?* □ *That doll was my sister, jerk.* **2.** *n.* a pill. (Drugs. Usually plural.) □ *She took stuff, yeah, but only dolls.* □ *Taking dolls is different from shooting up.*

**domajig(ger)** AND **domajiggus** ['dumədʒig(ɔ-) AND 'dumədʒigəs] *n.* a name for a gadget. □ *There is supposed to be a little domajig which fits in right here.* □ *Is this the domajiggus you're talking about?*

**dome-doctor** *n.* a psychologist or psychiatrist. □ *They sent me to a dome-doctor, but it didn't help.* □ *The dome-doctor lets me talk while he keeps score.*

**domestic** *n.* marijuana grown in the U.S. (Drugs.) □ *Most of the stuff on the streets is domestic, no matter what they call it.* □ *The South American sources are all busy smuggling in cocaine, so domestic is getting a big boost.*

**done** [don OR dɑn] *n.* methadone. (Drugs.) □ *Ernie gets done from a clinic.* □ *They make the addicts take the done right there so they won't go out and sell it.*

**done by mirrors** AND **done with mirrors** *mod.* illusory; purposefully deceptive. □ *The whole budgetary process is done with mirrors.* □ *The self-review was done by mirrors and didn't come off too bad.*

**done deal** *n.* a completed deal; something that is settled. □ *It's too late. It's a done deal.* □ *The sale of the property is a done deal. There is nothing that can be done now.*

**done for** *mod.* lost; dead; doomed. □ *I'm sorry, this whole scheme is done for.* □ *I knew I was done for.*

**done over** *mod.* beat; out-scored. □ *The other team was done over, and they knew it.* □ *Bruno felt that Max would get the idea if he was done over a little.*

**done to a turn 1.** *mod.* well-cooked; nicely cooked. □ *The entire meal was done to a turn.* □ *The turkey was done to a turn.* **2.** *mod.* beaten. □ *When Wilbur's opponent was done to a turn, Wilbur was declared the winner.* □ *Max was done to a turn, and Bruno walked away.*

**donkey's breakfast** *n.* something made of straw: a straw hat, a straw mattress, etc. □ *I don't really want to sleep on a donkey's breakfast, but it's better than the floor.* □ *The tourist was wearing a red dress and had a donkey's breakfast on her head.*

**donkey's years** *n.* a long time. □ *I haven't seen you in donkey's years.* □ *It's been donkey's years since we talked.*

**donnybrook** *n.* a big argument; a brawl. □ *There was a big donnybrook at the concert, and the police were called.* □ *Who started this donnybrook?*

**Don't ask.** *sent.* "The answer is so depressing, you don't even want to hear it." □ *How am I? Don't ask.* □ *This has been a horrible day. How horrible, you say? Don't ask.*

**Don't ask me.** *sent.* "I don't know either." (With the emphasis on *me*.) □ *I don't know. Don't ask me.* □ *Don't ask me. I wasn't there.*

**Don't call us, we'll call you.** *sent.* a formulaic expression given to job applicants who have just interviewed or auditioned for a job. □ *Thank you, Eddie Evans. Don't call us, we'll call you.* □ *Stupendous, Gloria, just stupendous. What glamour and radiance! Don't call us, we'll call you.*

**Don't give it another thought.** AND **Don't give it a second thought.** *sent.* "It's nothing. Don't worry about it." (See examples.) □ *No problem. Don't give it another thought.* □ *Yes, the vase is broken, but don't give it a second thought. It was old anyway—about 400 years.*

**Don't give it a second thought.** See the previous entry.

**Don't I know it!** *exclam.* "That is really true!" □ *It's bad all right. Don't I know it!* □ *Late? Don't I know it. I'm yawning like hot cakes.*

**Don't make me laugh!** *exclam.* "That is a stupid suggestion!" □ *You a judge? Don't make me laugh!* □ *Don't make me laugh. Tom could never do that.*

**Don't sweat it!** *exclam.* "Don't worry about it!" □ *No problem. Don't sweat it!* □ *Don't sweat it! We'll take care of it.*

**Don't you wish!** AND **You wish!** *exclam.* "I'm sure you wish it were true." □ *You think you'll win? Don't you wish!* □ *There's no school tomorrow? You wish!*

**doo** See *do*.

**doobage** ['dubɪdʒ] *n.* a *stash* of cannabis. (Drugs.) □ *The dorm counselor found my doobage.* □ *Is there a bridge in your doobage?*

**doobie** AND **dooby, duby** ['dubi] *n.* a marijuana cigarette; a fat marijuana cigarette. (Drugs.) □ *Max sells doobies like they were candy.* □ *Want a doobie?*

**doodad** ['dudæd] *n.* a name for a gadget. □ *What are these little doodads?* □ *I don't know what they're called. If they had names, they wouldn't be doodads, now would they?*

**doodly-squat** See *diddly-squat*.

**doo-doo** ['dudu] **1.** AND **(do-)do** ['dudu] *n.* dung, especially animal dung. (See *dog-doo*.) □ *Don't step in the doo-doo.* □ *There's a lot of pigeon doo-doo in the attic.* **2.** *in.* to defecate. (Juvenile.) □ *Jimmy was reminded that he had to remember to doo-doo in the potty.* □ *He has to doo-doo before he goes to bed, too.*

**doofer** AND **dufer** ['dufɚ] *n.* a (found or borrowed) cigarette saved for smoking at another time. (It will "do for" later.) □ *Sam always has a doofer stuck behind his ear.* □ *He takes two fags, one to smoke and a dufer.*

**doohickey** See the following entry.

**doojigger** AND **doohickey** ['dudʒɪgɚ AND 'duhɪki] *n.* a name for a gadget. □ *Toss me that little red doohickey, will you?* □ *Jim has one of those doohickies that will tighten the bit in the drill.*

**do one's damnedest*** *tr.* to do one's best. (Caution with *damn*.) □ *I don't know if I can, but I'll do my damnedest.* □ *I'll do my damnedest to get it done on time.*

**do oneself proud** *tr.* to have done a very fine job. □ *That's super! You've done yourself proud!* □ *I feel like I've done myself proud.*

**do one's (own) thing** *tr.* to do what one wants; to do what pleases oneself no matter what others think. □ *She's going to start doing her own thing for a change.* □ *I've always done my thing, and I don't see a great amount of benefit from it.*

**do-or-die** *mod.* having to try as hard as one can. □ *He has the obsessive do-or-die attitude.* □ *I was determined to get there—do-or-die.*

**doormat** *n.* a weak-willed person who is abused by others. □ *I always feel like a doormat.* □ *Why do people treat me like a doormat?*

**doors** AND **dors** [dorz] *n.* the sedative Doriden™. (Drugs.) □ *Dors aren't seen in this neighborhood anymore.* □ *Doors can really get you hooked.*

**doosenwhacker** ['duzn̩mækɚ] *n.* a name for a gadget. □ *Where is the doosenwhacker that opens the end of this?* □ *I lost the little doosenwhacker that fits in this slot.*

**doosie** AND **doozie, doozy** ['duzi] *n.* something extraordinary, good or bad. □ *The trade show was a real doozy this year.* □ *Old Gert was a real doozy.*

**doowacky** ['duмæki] **1.** *n.* a thing; a nameless gadget. □ *Where is the doowacky I laid here?* □ *Is this your doowacky? I was going to throw it away.* **2.** *n.* money. □ *You got some doowacky I can borrow?* □ *I'm out of doowacky myself.*

**dope 1.** *n.* a stupid person. □ *I'm not such a dope.* □ *That dope has done it again!* **2.** *n.* drugs in general; marijuana. □ *Lay off the dope, will ya?* □ *How much dope do you do in a week anyway?* **3.** *n.* news; *scuttlebutt.* □ *What's the dope on the new mayor?* □ *I got some dope on the tavern fire if you want to hear it.*

**doper** *n.* a dope user; a smoker of cannabis. (Drugs.) □ *Max is a doper, and so are all his friends.* □ *There are a lot of dopers in this neighborhood now.*

**dope something out** AND **dope out something** *tr.* to figure out something from the *dope* (information) available. □ *I think I can dope this thing out from the evidence available.* □ *We can dope out the truth from her testimony if we have to.*

**dope up 1.** *in.* to inject drugs; to take a dose of a narcotic. (Drugs.) □ *I'm hurting, man, I gotta dope up, now!* □ *She slipped into the back room to dope up.* **2.** *in.* to purchase a supply of drugs. (Drugs.) □ *Where's my old friend Max? I gotta dope up.* □ *Max is doping up, himself. He doesn't grow it himself, you know.*

**dopey 1.** *mod.* stupid. □ *What a dopey guy!* □ *That was a dopey thing to do.* **2.** *mod.* sleepy. □ *I feel sort of dopey.* □ *The soft music made him dopey.* **3.** *mod.* drug intoxicated. □ *He looks sort of dopey.* □ *The chick is too dopey to drive. See that she gets home, Ralphy, huh?*

**do-re-mi** AND **do-re-me** ['do're'mi] *n.* money. (From *dough.*) □ *It takes too much do-re-mi to live in this part of town.* □ *Do you have a little do-re-me you could loan me?*

**dorf** [dorf] *n.* a stupid person; a weird person. □ *You are a prize-winning dorf.* □ *Is there a convention of dorfs here today or something?*

**dork\*** [dork] **1.** *n.* a *jerk*; a strange person. (See also *megadork.*) □ *Ye gods, Sally! You are a dork!* □ *Here comes the king of dorks again.* **2.\*** *n.* the penis. (Caution with topic.) □ *Paul told a joke about a dork, but everybody just sat there and looked straight ahead.* □ *He covered his dork and squatted down; then he reached up and pulled down the shade.*

**dorky** ['dorki] *mod.* strange; weird; undesirable. □ *That is a real dorky idea. Just forget it.* □ *It's just too dorky.* □ *Let me out of this dorky place!*

**do's and don't's** *n.* the rules; the things which should be done and those which should not be done. □ *I must admit that a lot of the do's and don't's don't make much sense to me either.* □ *Better learn the do's and don't's immediately.*

**do some bongs** *tr.* to smoke some marijuana, usually with a water pipe. (Drugs. See *bong.*) □ *All the kids think that doing bongs is the greatest thing on earth.* □ *Hey, dude, wanna do some bongs?*

**do someone dirt** *tr.* to do ill to someone; to harm someone's reputation. □ *You really did me dirt.* □ *It seemed that the lawyer was determined to do me dirt right there in the courtroom.*

**Do tell.** *sent.* "Is that so?" (A disinterested way of holding up one end of a conversation.) □ *So, you're a dentist. Do tell.* □ *Do tell. I've never heard that before. Nice talking to you.*

**do the drink thing** *tr.* to drink alcohol heavily. □ *He's been doing the drink thing quite a lot lately.* □ *He started doing the drink thing when he got out of prison.*

**do the drug thing** *tr.* to be involved with drugs; to take drugs. □ *Man, you gotta stop doing the drug thing.* □ *All she thinks about is doing the drug thing.*

**do the trick** *tr.* to do exactly what is needed. □ *This about does the trick.* □ *Does this little dudenwhacker do the trick?*

**do time** *tr.* to serve a sentence in prison; to serve a specific amount of time in prison. (Underworld. See *hard time.*) □ *Lefty had done time on a number of occasions.* □ *You'd better talk and talk fast if you don't want to do time.*

**double** *n.* a drink consisting of two servings of liquor. □ *Make mine a double, bartender.* □ *Sam usually has two doubles on the way home.*

**double-bagger 1.** *n.* a hit good for two bases in baseball. □ *Wilbur hit a nice double-bagger in the top of the fourth.* □ *The hit was good for a double-bagger.* **2.** *n.* a very ugly person. (With a face so ugly that it takes two paper bags to conceal it. See *Bag your face!* See also *triple-bagger, coyote-ugly.*) □ *Fred is what I would call a double-bagger. What a mug!* □ *I am no double-bagger!*

**double-barreled slingshot** *n.* a brassiere. □ *Why does she wear a red double-barreled slingshot?* □ *Who dropped a double-barreled slingshot on the floor?*

**double buffalo** See *double nickels.*

**double cross 1.** *tr.* to betray someone. (Originally a more complicated switching of sides in a conspiracy wherein the *double-crosser* sides with the victim of the conspiracy—against the original conspirator.) □ *Don't even think about double crossing me!* □ *Max double crossed Mr. Big a few years back.* **2.** *n.* a betrayal. (See comments with sense 1.) □ *He always remembered that double cross.* □ *It's one double cross Max is sorry about.*

**double-crosser** *n.* a person who betrays someone. (Often with *dirty.* See comments at *double cross.*) □ *You dirty, lowdown double crosser, you!* □ *Max is the classic double-crosser.*

**double-decker 1.** *n.* a two-level bus. □ *I like to ride in double-deckers.* □ *Some double-deckers don't have tops.* **2.** *n.* a sandwich of two layers. □ *He put away a giant double-decker and a glass of milk.* □ *How can anybody eat a double-decker that is so thick?*

**double-deuces** *n.* the number 22. □ *The National Weather Service says it's going down to the double-deuces tonight.* □ *He's double-deuces today, that's right, twenty-two years old!*

**double-dipper** *n.* a person who collects two salaries; a federal employee who collects a federal pension and social security. □ *The voters of the state were shocked to learn that there were no laws against double-dippers.* □ *The double-*dippers say they weren't doing anything wrong.

**double-dome 1.** *n.* an intellectual. □ *It's not that what the double-domes say is wrong, it's that they are so sure that they are right that scares me.* □ *I'd rather be just folks than a double-dome.* **2.** *mod.* intellectual. □ *No more of your double-dome ideas.* □ *Most kids need to be exposed to double-dome profs at college for a while.*

**double-gaited** *mod.* weird; eccentric. □ *Carl is a little double-gaited at times. Tries too hard for a laugh.* □ *Wow, is he ever double-gaited!* □ *She is one of the most successful double-gaited comedians I've ever seen.*

**double nickels** AND **double buffalo** *n.* the number 55; the 55-mile-per-hour speed limit. (Originally citizens band radio. The buffalo is on one side of the nickel and accounts for the 5.) □ *You'd better travel right on those double nickels in through here. The bears are hungry.* □ *The double buffalo is enforced on this road.*

**double saw(buck)** *n.* a twenty-dollar bill. (See *sawbuck.*) □ *This whole thing only cost a double sawbuck.* □ *Can you loan me a double sawbuck till payday?*

**double take** *n.* a surprised second look at something. □ *I did a double take and blushed.* □ *Fred did a double take, then recognized Molly.*

**double-trouble** *n.* a very troublesome thing or person. □ *Oh, oh. Here comes double-trouble.* □ *That car you got is double-trouble.*

**double up (with laughter)** *in.* to laugh so hard that one bends over. □ *We all just doubled up with laughter.* □ *I doubled up when I heard the punch line.*

**double whammy** ['dəbl 'ʍæmi] *n.* a double portion of something, especially something troublesome. (From *Li'l Abner,* a comic strip by Al Capp.) □ *We got a real double whammy of trouble down at the office.* □ *This morning was bad, but this afternoon the boss gave us a double whammy.*

**douche bag** *n.* a repellent person; a disliked person. (Crude.) □ *Oh, shut up, you old douche bag!* □ *Don't be a douche bag!*

**dough** [do] *n.* money. (See *bread.*) □ *I got a lot of dough for that ring I found.* □ *I need some dough to buy groceries.*

**dove** [dəv] *n.* someone who supports a peace-seeking U.S. defense policy. (Compare to *hawk.*) □ *The doves want to sell the tanks and distribute the money to the poor.* □ *The hawks want to ignore the poor and the doves and buy tanks with the money.*

**down 1.** *mod.* depressed; melancholy. (See also *down with something.*) □ *I feel sort of down today.* □ *We're all a little down.* **2.** *mod.* (of a machine) inoperative. (Originally said of a computer.) □ *The system is down. Come back later.* □ *How long has it been down?* **3.** *tr.* to eat or drink something down quickly. □ *He downed a can of soda and burped like a thunderclap.* □ *She downed her sandwich in record time.* **4.** *tr.* to throw someone down, as in wrestling. □ *Wilbur downed his opponent and won the match.* □ *Paul downed the guy with one blow.* **5.** *mod.* behind in a score. □ *We're three points down with 2 minutes to play.* □ *They're 20 points down, and it looks like the Adamsville team has won.* **6.** *mod.* finished; completed; behind one. □ *Well, I've got the test down. Now what?* □ *One down and three to go.* **7.** *mod.* learned; memorized. (From sense 6.) □ *I got all the dates down pat.* □ *I've got the dates down, but not the names.* **8.** *mod.* prepared; knowledgeable. (Black. From sense 7.) □ *Are you down for the test tomorrow?* □ *Everything's down for the party.* **9.** *mod.* alcohol intoxicated. □ *Five beers and he was down.* □ *They were all down by midnight.* **10.** See *downer.*

**downbeat** *mod. cool;* easy going. (Compare to *upbeat.*) □ *He is sort of a downbeat character—no stress.* □ *I wish I was downbeat like he is.* □ *I had sort of a downbeat day. Not your typical Monday.*

**downer** AND **down, downie 1.** *n.* a barbiturate or a tranquilizer. (Drugs.) □ *She favors downers.* □ *Too much booze with those downers, and you're dead.* **2.** *n.* a bad drug experience; a *down trip.* (Drugs.) □ *That stuff you gave me was a real downer.* □ *Dust is a downer for most people.* **3.** *n.* a depressing event; a bad situation; a *down trip.* □ *These cloudy days are always downers.* □ *My birthday party was a downer.*

**down for the count** *mod.* inactive for the duration (of something). (From boxing.) □ *I've got a terrible cold, and I think I'm down for the count.* □ *Fred is down for the count. He's in jail.*

**down someone's way** *mod.* in someone's vicinity. (Folksy.) □ *What's happening down your way?* □ *There was a fire down your way, I hear.*

**down the drain** *mod.* gone; wasted. □ *Well, there's 400 bucks down the drain.* □ *A lot of money went down the drain in that Wilson deal.*

**Down the hatch!** *exclam.* "Let's drink it!" (A drinking toast. See *hatch.*) □ *Down the hatch! Have another?* □ *Bottoms up! Down the hatch!*

**down time** *n.* the time when a computer is not operating. (Compare to *up time.*) □ *I can't afford a lot of down time in the system I buy.* □ *We had too much down time with the other machine.*

**down to the wire** *mod.* until the very last minute. □ *It came down to the wire before I turned the proposal in.* □ *We went right down to the wire on that one.*

**downtown** *n.* heroin. (Drugs. The opposite of *uptown.*) □ *She is high on good old downtown.* □ *By the time they get on downtown, they're really hooked.*

**down trip 1.** *n.* a bad and depressing drug experience. (Drugs. Compare to *downer.*) □ *Tod is still suffering from that down trip he had.* □ *For some of them, one down trip is enough.* **2.** *n.* any bad experience. (Compare to *downer.*) □ *Today was a classic down trip.* □ *My vacation was a down trip.*

**down under** *n.* the area of Australia; Australia. □ *I've always wanted to visit down under.* □ *We spent Christmas down under.*

**down with something 1.** *mod.* comfortable with something; comfortable. (Usually with *get.*) □ *Let's get down with some good music.* □ *Tod wanted to get down with some grapes.* **2.** *mod.* ill with something; sick in bed with something. □ *I was down with the flu for two weeks.* □ *Fred and his wife were down with colds for weeks at a time.*

**doxy** ['dɑksi] *n.* a gangster's woman. (Underworld. Old.) □ *Lefty's doxy dropped off this package. It's ticking.* □ *Does Max have a doxy?*

**dozens** See *(dirty) dozens.*

**D.Q.** *n.* "Dairy Queen," a trade name for a franchise fast-food store specializing in frozen desserts. (Teens and collegiate.) □ *Let's go to D.Q., okay?* □ *The D.Q. is closed for the winter.*

**drafty** *n.* a draft beer; beer. □ *How about a cold drafty?* □ *Another drafty, Tom?*

**drag 1.** *n.* something dull and boring. □ *This day's a drag.* □ *What a drag. Let's go someplace interesting.* **2.** *n.* an annoying person; a burdensome person. (Compare to *schlep.*) □ *Gert could sure be a drag when she wanted.* □ *Clare was a drag whether she wanted to be or not.* **3.** *n.* a (female) date. □ *You got a drag for the dance yet?* □ *My drag finked out on me.* **4.** *n.* a puff of a cigarette. □ *He took a big drag and scratched at his tattoo.* □ *One more drag and he coughed for a while and stubbed out the fag.* **5.** *tr.* to pull or puff on a cigarette. □ *She dragged a couple and sat in the funk for a while.* □ *When she dragged a fag, you could see her relax and get straight.* **6.** *tr.* to race a car against someone; to race someone in a car. □ *I'm planning to drag you at the fairgrounds next Saturday. Better be there.* □ *I don't drag anybody anymore. I lost my license.*

**dragged** *mod.* anxious or frightened after smoking marijuana. (Drugs. Compare to *wired.*) □ *The kid was dragged. You could tell he didn't have much experience with the real world.* □ *Some of these burnouts really look dragged.*

**dragged out** *mod.* exhausted; worn out. □ *I feel so dragged out. I think I need some iron.* □ *After the game, the whole team was dragged out.*

**draggin'-wagon** *n.* a fast car; a car customized for racing. □ *My draggin'-wagon is in the shop.* □ *Your draggin'-wagon can't be driven in town, can it?*

**drain 1.** *n.* someone or something that exhausts one. □ *Harry is such a drain on me.* □ *What a drain these meetings are.* **2.** *tr.* to wear someone out. □ *Arguing like that drains me something*

awful. □ *Your constant bickering is meant to drain me till I submit. Is that it?*

**drain the bilge** *in.* to empty one's stomach; to vomit. □ *Fred left quickly to drain the bilge.* □ *Who drained the bilge in the bushes?*

**Drat!** [dræt] *exclam.* "Damn!" □ *Drat! I'm late!* □ *Oh, drat! Another broken nail!*

**dreamboat** *n.* just the kind of lover one has always dreamed of. (Also a term of address.) □ *Oh, Tod is my dreamboat.* □ *A face man makes a great dreamboat, as long as you never get to know him.*

**dreck** [drɛk] *n.* dirt; garbage; feces. (From German via Yiddish.) □ *What is all this dreck in the corner?* □ *I've had enough of this dreck around here. Clean it up, or I'm leaving.*

**dressed to kill** *mod.* dressed in fancy or stylish clothes to impress someone. □ *She is always dressed to kill.* □ *I'm never dressed to kill. I just try to be neat.*

**dressed to the nines** AND **dressed to the teeth** *mod.* dressed very stylishly with nothing overlooked. □ *She showed up for the picnic dressed to the nines.* □ *Clare is usually dressed to the teeth in order to impress people.*

**dressed to the teeth** See the previous entry.

**drinkies** ['drɪŋkiz] *n.* drinks; liquor. □ *Okay, kids, it's drinkies all around.* □ *What time is drinkies around here?*

**Drink up!** *exclam.* "Finish your drink!"; "Finish that drink, and we'll have another!" □ *Okay, drink up! It's closing time.* □ *Drink up, and let's get going.*

**drinkypoo** ['drɪŋkipu] *n.* a little drink of liquor. □ *Wouldn't you like just one more drinkypoo of Madeira?* □ *Just a little drinkypoo, my dear.*

**drip** *n.* an oaf; a *nerd.* □ *Oh, yuck. He's such a drip.* □ *Merton is a drip, I guess, but he's harmless.*

**drippy** *mod.* weak; ineffective; undesirable. □ *Merton can be so drippy without even trying.* □ *You are proposing some pretty drippy ideas.*

**drivers** See *truck drivers.*

**drive someone around the bend** *tr.* to drive someone crazy. (See also *around* the bend.) □ *This tax stuff is about to drive me around the bend.* □ *Gert tried to drive us all around the bend.*

**drive someone bonkers** AND **drive someone nuts** *tr.* to drive someone crazy. (See *bonkers*, *nuts*.) □ *This cold is driving me bonkers.* □ *These tax forms are driving me nuts.*

**drive someone nuts** See the previous entry.

**drive someone up the wall** *tr.* to frustrate someone; to drive someone to distraction. □ *These days of waiting drive me up the wall.* □ *Staying in the house drove us all up the wall.*

**drive the big bus** AND **drive the porcelain bus, ride the porcelain bus** *tr.* to vomit into the toilet. □ *Harry's in the john driving the big bus.* □ *Who do I hear driving the porcelain bus in the john?*

**drive the porcelain bus** See the previous entry.

**droid** [drɔɪd] *n.* a robot-like person; a nerd. (From *android*.) □ *Merton is as close to a droid as we'll ever see.* □ *The droids are taking over this campus.*

**droob** AND **drube** [drub] *n.* a dullard; an oaf. □ *Who's the droob standing by the punch bowl?* □ *That drube is my brother!*

**drool (all) over someone or something** *tr.* to show enormous desire for someone or something. □ *He was just drooling all over that new car.* □ *Sam was drooling over Martha like a lovesick calf.*

**droopy-drawers** *n.* someone—usually a child—whose pants are falling down. (Also a term of address.) □ *Hey, droopy-drawers, pull up your pants.* □ *Jimmy is a regular droopy-drawers. Maybe he needs suspenders.*

**drop** **1.** *tr.* to kill someone or something. □ *He dropped the deer with one shot.* □ *Lefty tried to drop the leader of the gang.* **2.** *in.* to get arrested. (Underworld.) □ *I'm not going to drop for you.* □ *Bruno dropped, but Mr. Big got him off.* **3.** *tr.* to knock someone down. □ *Jim dropped Willard with a punch to the shoulder.* □ *The swinging board hit him and dropped him.* **4.** *n.* a small drink of liquor; a small serving of liquor. □ *I'll take just*

another drop of that dew, if you don't mind. □ *Can I give you another drop?* **5.** *n.* a place at which drugs, alcohol, or other contraband is left to be claimed by the recipient. □ *The police discovered the drop and waited for the runner.* □ *They switched drops constantly just in case of discovery.* **6.** *tr.* to take a drug, specifically *acid*. (Drugs.) □ *Ted dropped some stuff and went on a trip.* □ *Now he doesn't drop even once a month.*

**drop a bomb(shell)** See *drop a brick*.

**drop a bop** *tr.* to take a drug in pill form. (See *bop*.) □ *Tyrone dropped a bop and went on his way.* □ *Wanna come over and drop a bop or two?*

**drop a brick** AND **drop a bomb(shell)** *tr.* to reveal startling information. □ *Molly came in and dropped a brick that scared us all.* □ *You really dropped a bombshell!*

**drop a bundle (on someone or something)** **1.** *tr.* [with *someone*] to spend a lot of money pleasing or entertaining someone. □ *I dropped a bundle on the candidate, and it didn't help me at all.* □ *Over the years, I've dropped a bundle on clients at that restaurant.* **2.** *tr.* [with *something*] to pay a lot of money for something. □ *Tod dropped a bundle on this car.* □ *I always buy el cheapo. I've never dropped a bundle on anything.*

**drop a dime** *tr.* to inform the police of criminal activity. (Underworld. See explanation at *dime-dropper*.) □ *We were pretty sure that Molly is the one who dropped the dime.* □ *No, almost anybody will drop a dime these days.*

**drop a roll** See *pop a roll*.

**Drop dead!** *exclam.* "No!"; "Beat it!"; "Go away and don't bother me!" □ *I don't care. Just drop dead!* □ *Drop dead! Beat it!*

**drop-dead list** *n.* an imaginary list of annoying people whom one could live happily without. □ *You are right at the top of my drop-dead list.* □ *I put Max on my drop-dead list.*

**Drop it!** *exclam.* "Forget it!"; "Never mind!" □ *Never mind! Just drop it!* □ *Drop it! I should never have brought it up.*

**drop one's cookies** *tr.* to empty one's stomach; to vomit. (See *toss one's cook-*

*ies.*) □ *The runner went off to the side and dropped her cookies.* □ *If you feel like you're going to drop your cookies, don't do it on the carpet.*

**drop one's teeth** *tr.* to react with great surprise. □ *I almost dropped my teeth when she told me her news.* □ *They dropped their teeth when I told them I was married.*

**drop out 1.** *in.* to withdraw from a conventional lifestyle. □ *Sometimes I just want to drop out and raise pigs or something.* □ *Ted dropped out and bought a farm.* **2.** *in.* to drop out of school or some organization. □ *I dropped out before I got promoted.* □ *Don't drop out of school. You'll regret it.* **3.** AND **dropout** *n.* someone who has dropped out of school. □ *Dropouts find it very hard to get a job.* □ *Some dropouts make great successes of themselves, but not very many.*

**dropped** *mod.* arrested. □ *Max was dropped only once last year.* □ *He got himself dropped on a speeding ticket.*

**drop someone or something like a hot potato** *tr.* to disassociate oneself with someone or something instantly. □ *When we learned of the conviction, we dropped him like a hot potato.* □ *I dropped the idea like a hot potato.*

**drop the ball** *tr.* to fail at something; to allow something to fail. □ *I didn't want to be the one who dropped the ball, but I knew that someone would flub up.* □ *Sam dropped the ball, and we lost the contract.*

**drug 1.** *in.* to use drugs. (Drugs.) □ *There is no way that she will stop drugging by herself.* □ *Why does she drug so heavily?* **2.** AND **drug out** *mod.* down; depressed. □ *Man, am I drug!* □ *We are all drug out after that meeting.*

**druggie** AND **druggy** *n.* a drug addict or user. □ *That druggy loves to hang out here.* □ *There are too many druggies in this neighborhood.*

**drughead** *n.* a heavy drug user; an addict. (Drugs.) □ *They find a drughead in the river about once a month.* □ *The drugheads are taking over this neighborhood.*

**drug lord** *n.* a drug dealer high up in the distribution chain. □ *The drug lords*

like Mr. Big seem never to get arrested. □ *Max had always admired the sheer power of the domestic drug lord.*

**drugola** [drəgˈolə] *n.* a bribe paid to police for protection by drug dealers. (Patterned on *payola*.) □ *Max pays a little drugola, but mostly the cops never come into this area anyway.* □ *A lot of drugola is simply paid in drugs.*

**drugstore cowboy** *n.* a male who hangs around drugstores and other public places trying to impress women. □ *You don't see the old drugstore cowboys around this part of town anymore.* □ *The drugstore cowboys of years ago are all hidden away shooting up something.*

**drunk back** *mod.* alcohol intoxicated; very drunk. □ *The whole bunch was drunk back by midnight.* □ *Larry was drunk back and couldn't drive us home.*

**drunk tank** *n.* a jail cell where drunks are kept. (Compare to *junk tank*.) □ *A couple of hours in the drunk tank really made me think about alcohol.* □ *They hose down the drunk tank every hour on Friday and Saturday nights.*

**dry 1.** *mod.* sober; no longer alcohol intoxicated. □ *Molly's dry, I hear.* □ *How long will Ernie stay dry?* **2.** *n.* a prohibitionist; an abstainer from alcohol. □ *The drys are in an increasing majority.* □ *Do you know even one dry?* **3.** *mod.* having to do with a region where beverage alcohol cannot be purchased. (Compare to *wet*.) □ *Is Kansas still dry?* □ *I hate to get stuck in a dry town.* □ *Some small towns are dry, but not many.*

**dry-as-dust** *mod.* dull; lifeless. □ *I can't take another one of his dry-as-dust lectures.* □ *All her ideas are dry-as-dust.* □ *Some dry-as-dust old crock talked endlessly about old bones.*

**dry high** *n.* cannabis. (Drugs. See *high*.) □ *Max always favored dry highs till crack came along.* □ *Rudy liked the dry high, although it gave him a gravelly voice.*

**Dry up!** *exclam.* "Shut up!"; "Go away and don't bother me!" □ *Aw, dry up! I've heard enough.* □ *Dry up and beat it!*

**dub** [dəb] **1.** *tr. & in.* to duplicate something; to copy something. □ *Dub this*

**ducats**

and keep a copy yourself. □ He's busy dubbing right now. **2.** n. a duplicate; a copy. □ The dub was so poor we couldn't understand the dialog. □ This is an almost perfect dub of the original.

**ducats** AND **duc-ducs** ['dəkəts AND 'dəkdəks] n. money. (See also *gold*.) □ Who's got enough ducats to pay for the tickets? □ I've got duc-ducs galore!

**duc-ducs** See *ducats*.

**duck 1.** n. a male urinal bedpan. (Hospitals.) □ Somebody in room 212 needs a duck. □ Take this duck down there quick. **2.** tr. to avoid someone or something. □ Clare is ducking her responsibility. □ You can't duck this investigation. They're on to you. **3.** See *deduck*.

**duck butt\*** AND **dusty butt\*** n. a short person, especially someone with large buttocks. (Also a rude term of address. Caution with *butt*.) □ The duck butt who just came in reminds me of somebody I once knew. □ Hey, dusty butt, where you been keeping yourself?

**ducks** n. tickets. □ You got the ducks for Friday? □ There were no ducks left.

**duck-squeezer** n. someone with strong concerns about the environment and conservation, especially rescuing oil-covered ducks. (See *eagle freak*.) □ Some duck-squeezers were complaining about what the new dam might do. □ The duck-squeezers were picketing the dam site.

**ducky** mod. okay; good. (Often used sarcastically.) □ Now, isn't that just ducky? □ That's a ducky idea!

**dud** [dəd] **1.** n. a failure; something that fails to perform as intended. □ The whole idea turned out to be a dud. □ The play was a dud from start to finish. **2.** See *duds*.

**dude** [dud] n. a male friend; a guy. (Also a term of address.) □ Who's the dude with the cowboy boots? □ Hey, dude, what's happ?

**dudenwhacker** ['dudṇʍækɚ] n. a name for a gadget. □ Where's my mustache dudenwhacker? □ Is this thing the dudenwhacker you want?

**dude up** in. to dress up. □ Let's get all duded up and go out. □ I got to dude up a little before we go.

**duds** [dədz] n. clothes. (Folksy. Always plural.) □ Are those new duds? □ I need some new duds, too.

**dufer** See *doofer*.

**duff** [dəf] n. the buttocks. □ Get off your duff and get busy. □ Don't you get tired of sitting around on your duff?

**duffer** ['dəfɚ] **1.** n. a foolish oaf; a bumbler. □ Some old duffer is weeding our garden for us. He's lost, I think. □ Tod's just a duffer—he's not really serious at it. **2.** n. an unskilled golfer. □ Those duffers up ahead are holding up the game. □ Don't call me a duffer!

**dugout** n. a type of cannabis pipe. (Drugs.) □ She keeps a little dugout in her doobage. □ Somebody dropped a dugout or something, and the cops then started searching everybody.

**duji** ['dudʒi] n. heroin. (Drugs.) □ Max slipped a packet of duji into Molly's pocket. □ Is she still on the duji?

**duke 1.** in. to empty one's stomach; to vomit. (Collegiate. Rhymes with *puke*.) □ He left to duke. I saw how green he was. □ She's in the john, duking like a goat. **2.** See *dukes*.

**dukes 1.** n. the fists. □ Okay, brother, put your dukes up. □ The guy's got dukes like hams. **2.** n. the knees. □ He went down on his dukes and prayed for all sorts of good stuff. □ He cracked one of his dukes on the railing.

**duke someone out** AND **duke out someone** tr. to knock someone out. (See *dukes*.) □ Bob duked out the mugger with a jab to the cheek. □ Wilbur tried to duke the guy out first.

**dull as dishwater** mod. very dull. □ She's cute, but dull as dishwater. □ Life can be as dull as dishwater.

**dull roar** n. a relatively quiet degree of noisiness. □ Hey, simmer down to a dull roar! □ Try to keep it at a dull roar if you can.

**dullsville** ['dəlzvɪl] **1.** n. a dull place. □ This place is just dullsville! □ Home is dullsville to a teenager. **2.** n. something dull. □ The lecture was downtown dullsville for sure. □ When each movie I see turns into dullsville, I want to give up seeing them.

**dumb-ass\*** AND **stupid-ass\*** mod. stupid. (Caution with *ass*.) □ That was a *dumb-ass thing to do!* □ *You can be such a stupid-ass jerk!*

**dumbbell** *n.* a stupid oaf. (Also a rude term of address.) □ *Look, dumbbell, pay attention!* □ *I'm afraid I come on like a dumbbell sometimes.*

**dumb bunny** *n.* a stupid person; an oaf. □ *Who's the dumb bunny in the double-knits?* □ *Don't be a dumb bunny. Pay attention to what's going on.*

**dumb cluck** *n.* a stupid oaf; a person as stupid as a chicken. □ *Sally is not a dumb cluck, but she is sort of slow.* □ *What a dumb cluck!*

**dumb-dodo** ['dəm'dodo] *n.* a very stupid person. □ *What a dumb-dodo you are!* □ *I'm no dumb-dodo!*

**dumb Dora** *n.* a stupid woman; a giddy woman. □ *I'm no dumb Dora. I'm just learning.* □ *Who's the dumb Dora with the blonde hair and long fingernails?*

**dumb-dumb** AND **dum-dum** *n.* a stupid oaf; a dullard. □ *You can be such a dumb-dumb without even trying.* □ *Merton is no dum-dum. He just looks that way.*

**dumbhead** *n.* a stupid person. □ *Merton is no dumbhead, but he sure is strange.* □ *I'm no dumbhead. Just a little slow.*

**dumbo** ['dəmbo] **1.** *n.* a stupid oaf. (Also a rude term of address.) □ *Say, dumbo, could you move out of the way?* □ *Who's the dumbo in the plaid pants?* **2.** *n.* someone with large ears. (Also a rude term of address. The name of a cartoon character elephant whose ears were large enough to fly with.) □ *Wow, look at that dumbo with size twenty ears!* □ *I better get new glasses, or I'm going to be a dumbo when my head starts growing.*

**dumb ox** *n.* a large and stupid person, usually a man. □ *What does that dumb ox want?* □ *Do you think I'm going to argue with that big dumb ox?*

**dumbski** ['dəmski] **1.** *n.* a stupid person. □ *He's not the dumbski he seems to be.* □ *They used to think Gert was a dumbski.* **2.** *mod.* stupid; dumb. □ *What a dumbski jerk!* □ *It is not a dumbski idea!*

**dummy** **1.** *n.* an empty liquor or beer bottle. □ *Toss your dummies over here, and I'll put them in the bin.* □ *That was*

*a sixty dummy party. I counted.* **2.** *n.* a cigarette butt. □ *The tramp collected dummies until he had enough for a smoke.* □ *The guy tossed a dummy out the window of his car.* **3.** *n.* a stupid person. □ *Don't be such a dummy.* □ *I'm no dummy!*

**dummy up** *in.* to refuse to talk. (Underworld. See *clam up.*) □ *Molly dummied up when they got her into the station.* □ *Rocko dummied up right away. He's a real thoroughbred.*

**dump\*** **1.** *tr. & in.* to empty one's stomach; to vomit. □ *He ran straight to the john and dumped his dinner.* □ *She turned green, and I knew she was going to dump.* **2.\*** *in.* to defecate. (Caution with topic. See also *dump one's load.*) □ *He dumped and then came back.* □ *He said he had to dump.* **3.\*** *n.* an act of defecation. (Caution with topic.) □ *He said he needed a dump.* □ *He had a dump and then came back.* **4.** *n.* a low or cheap establishment; a *joint.* □ *I want out of this dump.* □ *My mama didn't raise me to spend the rest of my days in a run-down dump like this.*

**dumped on** **1.** *mod.* maligned; abused. □ *I really feel dumped on.* □ *The jerk who designed this stupid congested stairway hasn't been dumped on enough.* **2.** *mod.* snowed on. □ *The entire Midwest was dumped on with about 10 inches of snow.* □ *Our town really got dumped on last night.*

**dump one's load\*** **1.** *in.* to empty one's stomach; to vomit. □ *He's in the john dumping his load.* □ *Why can't he learn to dump his load silently?* **2.\*** *in.* to defecate. (Caution with topic. Also with *a.*) □ *He had to go dump a load.* □ *He dumped his load and settled back down to work.*

**dump on someone or something** **1.** *in.* to snow on someone or something. □ *Well, it dumped on us again last night.* □ *The cold front dumped on the northeast again today.* **2.** See *do a dump on someone or something.*

**dupe** **1.** *n.* a potential victim of a confidence trick; a *patsy.* □ *The crooks found a good dupe and started their scheme.* □ *I don't want to be a dupe for anybody.* **2.** *tr.* to trick someone; to swindle some-*

one. □ *You tried to dupe me!* □ *I did not try to dupe you. It was an honest mistake.* **3.** *n.* a duplicate; a copy. □ *Make a dupe of this before you send it off.* □ *I've got a dupe in the files.* **4.** *tr.* to duplicate something; to copy something. □ *Dupe this and send the original back.* □ *Just a minute, I have to dupe a contract for the boss.*

**dust 1.** *in.* to leave; to depart. □ *Well, it's late. I gotta dust.* □ *They dusted out of there at about midnight.* **2.** *tr.* to defeat someone; to win out over someone. □ *We dusted the other team, 87 to 54.* □ *In the second game, they dusted us.* **3.** *tr.* to kill someone. (Underworld.) □ *The gang set out to dust the witnesses, but only got one of them.* □ *Max knew that Bruno was out to dust him.* **4.** *n.* fine tobacco for rolling cigarettes. (Prisons.) □ *How about a little dust for this candy bar?* □ *I don't want dust. I need chocolate.* **5.** *n.* a powdered drug: heroin, *P.C.P.*, cocaine; fine cannabis. (Drugs.) □ *It's the dust that can really do you damage.* □ *Wally got hold of some kind of dust and took it to the police.* **6.** *tr.* to add a powdered drug to the end of a (tobacco or cannabis) cigarette. (Drugs.) □ *Pete dusted one, then lit it up.* □ *Max never dusts them before he sells them.*

**duster** *n.* the buttocks. (See *rusty-dusty.*) □ *She fell down right on her duster.* □ *My duster is sore from all that riding.*

**dust someone off** AND **dust off someone** *tr.* to give someone a good pounding or beating. □ *Bruno threatened to dust Max off.* □ *Bob dusted off Larry; then he started for Tom.*

**dust someone's pants** *tr.* to spank someone, usually a child. □ *My dad will dust my pants if he hears about this.* □ *I'm too old for somebody to dust my pants.*

**dust-up** *n.* a fight. □ *Max got in a dust-up with Bruno.* □ *There was a dust-up at the party that ruined the evening for everyone.*

**dusty butt** See *duck butt.*

**Dutch act** AND **Dutch cure** *n.* suicide. (Always with *the.*) □ *Well, Ken took the*

Dutch cure last week. So sad. □ *She had tried the Dutch act many times in the past.*

**Dutch courage 1.** *n.* liquor; false courage from drinking liquor. □ *A couple of shots of Dutch courage, and he was ready to face anything.* □ *How about a little Dutch courage to help you through the first act?* **2.** *n.* drugs. □ *Max deals in Dutch courage, as he calls it.* □ *Too much Dutch courage and you're in permanent trouble.*

**Dutch treat** *n.* an outing for two or more where the cost is split among the participants, either evenly or in proportion to what is consumed. (See also *go Dutch.*) □ *I propose a Dutch treat to celebrate the day.* □ *We had a Dutch treat, which gave us a chance to get to know one another better.*

**Dutch uncle** *n.* someone who gives avuncular advice; a man who gives advice with the directness of one of one's own relatives. □ *If I can be a Dutch uncle for a minute, I could give you some good advice.* □ *Dutch uncles can be as big of a pain as parents.*

**dweeb** [dwib] **1.** *n.* an earnest student. (Collegiate.) □ *Don't call Merton a dweeb! Even if he is one.* □ *The dweebs get all the A's, so why work?* **2.** *n.* a strange or eccentric person; a *nerd.* □ *This place is filled with dweebs of all sizes.* □ *Here comes a dweeb. Ask him for some money.*

**dynamic duo** [daɪ'næmɪk 'duo] *n.* a very special pair of people or things. (From the "Batman" television program. Used mostly for humor.) □ *The dynamic duo, Merton and Fred, showed up late and without the beer.* □ *Next time tell the dynamic duo to come earlier.*

**dynamite** ['daɪnəmaɪt] **1.** *n.* anything potentially powerful: a drug, news, a person. □ *This chick is really dynamite!* □ *The story about the scandal was dynamite and kept selling papers for a month.* **2.** *mod.* excellent; powerful. □ *I want some more of your dynamite enchiladas, please.* □ *These tacos are dynamite, too.*

# E

**eager-beaver** *n.* a person who is very eager to do something. □ *Rocko is an eager-beaver when it comes to collecting money for Mr. Big.* □ *The eager-beavers were trying to buy tickets yesterday!*

**eagle-eye 1.** *n.* a busybody; a person who watches or monitors other people's actions: a floorwalker, a detective, a hall-monitor. □ *Some old eagle-eye across the street saw me standing in the cold and called my wife who came down and let me in.* □ *The store detective is an eagle-eye and caught the kleptomaniac.* **2.** *n.* an eye or eyes with very keen vision. □ *Keep your eagle-eye trained on the entrance.* □ *My eagle-eye tells me there's trouble over there.*

**eagle freak** *n.* someone with strong concerns about the environment and conservation, especially the preservation of the eagle. (A play on *eco freak*.) □ *The eagle freaks oppose building the dam.* □ *They call me an eagle freak, which doesn't bother me at all.*

**ear candy** *n.* soft and pleasant popular music; music that is sweet to the ear. □ *I find that kind of ear candy more annoying than heavy metal.* □ *People joke about it, but ear candy is restful.*

**ear-duster** *n.* a gossipy person. □ *Sally is sort of an ear-duster, but she's all heart.* □ *I can be an ear-duster, I know, but have you heard about Sally and her you-know-what?*

**earful** ['irful] **1.** *n.* a tremendous amount of gossip. □ *I got a big earful about Sally.* □ *I can give you an earful about the mayor.* **2.** *n.* a scolding. □ *Her mother gave her an earful when she finally got home.* □ *Tom got an earful for his part in the prank.*

**early bird 1.** *n.* a person who gets up early. □ *I never miss sunrise. I'm an early bird.* □ *The early birds saw the corpse on the street and called the cops.* **2.** *n.* a person who arrives early. □ *The early birds get the best seats.* □ *There were some early birds who arrived before the tea things were laid.* **3.** *mod.* having to do with early arrival. □ *Early bird arrivals will be given a free cup of coffee.* □ *The early bird special this week is a free six-pack of pop for the first 100 visitors.*

**earp** AND **urp** [ɚp] **1.** *in.* to empty one's stomach; to vomit. □ *Somebody earped here!* □ *I wish people could urp silently.* **2.** *n.* vomit. □ *There's earp on your shoe.* □ *Throw something over the urp in the flower bed.*

**Earp slop, bring the mop.** *phr.* "Someone has vomited." (Juvenile catch phrase.) □ *See what's in the hall? Earp slop, bring the mop.* □ *Earp slop, bring the mop. Somebody was sick.*

**Easy does it. 1.** *phr.* "Calm down."; "Relax." □ *Chill, man, easy does it.* □ *Easy does it! Relax and go slow!* **2.** *phr.* "Be gentle."; "Handle with care." □ *Easy does it. Go slow, and you won't dent anything.* □ *Easy does it. Two people can handle this heavy old thing if they go slow.*

**easy mark** *n.* a likely victim. □ *Merton looks like an easy mark, but he's really quite savvy.* □ *Mary is an easy mark because she is so unsuspecting.*

**easy money** *n.* money earned or gained with little or no difficulty. □ *You know where I can get some easy money?* □ *All you guys want easy money. Don't you want to work for it?*

**easy street** *n.* a place or position in life where living is easy. (See *fat city, on easy street.*) □ *Easy street is no place for an active guy like Sam.* □ *Easy street is exactly what I want out of life.*

**eat 1.** *tr.* (for something) to bother or worry someone. □ *What's eating you, Bill?* □ *Nothing's eating me. I'm just the nervous type.* **2.** *tr.* to absorb the cost or expense of something. □ *It was our mistake, and we'll have to eat it.* □ *We'll eat the costs on this one. It's the least we can do.*

**eat crow** *tr.* to display total humility, especially when shown to be wrong. □ *Well, it looks like I was wrong, and I'm going to have to eat crow.* □ *I'll be eating crow if I'm not shown to be right.*

**eater** *n.* a drug user or addict who takes drugs orally. (Drugs.) □ *In the opium days, some of the smokers were also eaters at the times when it wasn't possible to smoke.* □ *The eaters didn't get so heavily addicted.*

**eat nails** *tr.* to look and act really tough or angry. □ *Bruno looked mad enough to eat nails.* □ *They were all eating nails by the time the IRS got the mess straightened out.*

**eat one's hat** *tr.* to do something extraordinary. □ *If she wins, I'll eat my hat.* □ *I'll eat my hat if our advertisement actually brings us a president.*

**eat one's heart out 1.** *tr.* to suffer from sorrow or grief. □ *She has been eating her heart out over that jerk ever since he ran away with Molly.* □ *Don't eat your heart out. You really didn't like him that much, did you?* **2.** *tr.* to suffer from envy or jealousy. (Usually a command.) □ *Yeah, this one's all mine. Eat your heart out!* □ *Eat your heart out! I won it fair and square.*

**eats** *n.* food. (Folksy.) □ *You ready for some eats yet?* □ *We have enough eats, and we have a roof over our heads. What else is there?*

**eat something up** AND **eat up something 1.** *tr.* to consume something rapidly, such as food or money. □ *The car really eats up gas.* □ *Running this household eats my income up.* **2.** *tr.* to believe something. □ *Those people really eat that stuff up about tax reduction.* □

*They'll eat up almost anything you tell them.* **3.** *tr.* to appreciate something. □ *The audience really ate it up.* □ *The stuff about the federal budget went over well. They really ate it up.*

**eat up** *in.* to eat in enjoyment. (Usually a command.) □ *Come on, now. Sit down and eat up!* □ *Eat up! There's plenty more where this came from.*

**echo** *n.* repetitions of the effects of an *L.S.D.* experience after the immediate effects of the chemical have worn off. (Drugs. See also *flashback.*) □ *The kid was troubled with echoes for a month afterward.* □ *Echoes can lead to severe psychological problems.*

**eco freak** AND **eco nut** ['iko frik AND 'iko nɑt] *n.* someone with strong concerns about the environment and conservation. (Mildly derogatory. From *ecology.*) □ *They call me an eco freak, which is okay by me.* □ *It's we eco nuts who think about the future of our planet.*

**Ecstasy** ['ɛkstəsi] *n.* a hallucinogen similar to *L.S.D.* (Drugs.) □ *Chemicals with names like "Ecstasy" are being put on the streets every day.* □ *Ecstasy is just one of a dozen drugs with similar formulas.*

**edge** *n.* drunkenness; the early stage of intoxication from alcohol or drugs. (See *have an edge on.*) □ *She was beginning to show a little edge, but she obviously still could drive.* □ *The edge was starting, so Kelly slowed down her drinking.*

**edged** *mod.* alcohol or drug intoxicated. □ *They set out to be edged by midnight.* □ *We were edged and full of rich food. We needed only to sleep.*

**edgy** *mod.* nervous; anxious and uncertain. □ *I feel sort of edgy about the race.* □ *I'm just an edgy guy.* □ *Don't let yourself get so edgy.*

**eggbeater 1.** *n.* an outboard boat motor. □ *My eggbeater has been acting up, so I didn't go out on the lake today.* □ *By the time you get about twenty eggbeaters on the lake at once, it's really pretty noisy.* **2.** *n.* a helicopter. (See also *rotorhead.*) □ *The eggbeater landed on the hospital roof.* □ *I would think that eggbeaters all over the place would disturb the patients.*

**egghead** *n.* an intellectual person. □ *The eggheads aren't exactly taking over the world.* □ *My uncle was an egghead, but nobody in our family thought he knew very much.*

**eggs** *n.* pills. (Drugs.) □ *Max doesn't normally carry eggs.* □ *Most of his customers want dust rather than eggs.*

**egg-sucker** *n.* a flatterer; a sycophant. □ *The guy is a chronic egg-sucker. Ignore him.* □ *Who's the egg-sucker who brought the teacher candy?*

**ego trip** *n.* a public expression of one's feelings of importance or superiority. □ *The guy is on another ego trip. Pay no attention.* □ *Sorry, I guess I'm on another ego trip.*

**ego tripper** *n.* a person who habitually goes on an *ego trip*. □ *Not another ego tripper running for public office!* □ *You have to be an ego tripper to be a palm-presser.*

**eight** AND **8** *n.* heroin. (Drugs. The eighth letter of the alphabet is H.) □ *I asked Max for some eight, and he didn't know what I was talking about.* □ *The old-timers still call it 8.*

**eighteen wheeler** *n.* a large trailer truck. (There are a total of 18 wheels on the cab and trailer.) □ *An eighteen wheeler almost ran me off the road.* □ *The eighteen wheelers rule the road at night.*

**elbow-bending** *n.* drinking liquor; drinking liquor to excess. □ *She spends quite a bit of time at elbow-bending.* □ *That's a lot of elbow-bending for one sitting.*

**elbow-grease** *n.* effort. □ *Put out a little elbow-grease.* □ *All this job needs is a little more elbow-grease.*

**el cheapo** [ɛl 'tʃipo] **1.** *n.* the cheap one; the cheapest one. (Mock Spanish.) □ *I don't want one of those el cheapos.* □ *I can only afford el cheapo.* **2.** *mod.* cheap. □ *The el cheapo brand won't last.* □ *This is el cheapo. I don't want it.* □ *Is this the el cheapo model?*

**electric koolaid** [...'kuled] *n.* a soft drink or punch laced with *L.S.D.* (Drugs. See *electric wine.*) □ *Serving electric koolaid was a favorite event in the 1960s.* □ *Electric koolaid was a big surprise to some people.*

**electric wine** *n.* *L.S.D.* combined with a cheap sparkling wine or a soft drink.

(Drugs.) □ *Electric wine is making a comeback, I hear.* □ *In electric wine, the alcohol is more powerful than the drug.*

**electrified** *mod.* alcohol intoxicated. □ *Her eyes were staring straight ahead, and I knew she was electrified.* □ *By midnight we were all electrified.*

**elephant (tranquilizer)** *n.* phency-clidine, *P.C.P.*, an animal tranquilizer. (Drugs.) □ *Who needs elephant tranquilizer? These kids take stuff stronger than any doctor would give to an elephant.* □ *Some of them who say they like elephant really just want to die.*

**elevated** *mod.* alcohol intoxicated; tipsy. □ *Jerry was too elevated to drive home.* □ *Sam was elevated from the drinking he did.*

**elevator music** *n.* dull, uninteresting music of the type that can be heard in elevators or shops. (As compared to exciting jazz or rock.) □ *I don't want to have to hear elevator music all day.* □ *Elevator music is better than listening to someone chewing food.*

**eliminated 1.** *mod.* killed. □ *Mr. Big wanted Max eliminated.* □ *When Max is eliminated, there will be no competition.* **2.** *mod.* alcohol intoxicated. □ *By midnight, Wally was eliminated.* □ *How can anybody get eliminated on four beers?*

**(el) primo** [(ɛl) 'primo] *mod.* having to do with top-quality drugs. (Drugs. From Spanish for "the first.") □ *This stuff is primo.* □ *I want some more of that el primo C.*

**els** [ɛlz] *n.* Elavil™, an antidepressant. (Drugs.) □ *She had to have her els or else.* □ *You got any decent els?*

**em** [ɛm] **1.** *n.* AND **emm** an empty liquor bottle. □ *Put your ems in the garbage, not on the floor.* □ *Whose emms are all these?* **2.** *n.* morphine. (Drugs. Old. A spelling-out of the initial M.) □ *The addicts used to tramp from town to town begging doctors for "some em."* □ *This "em" is a very old source of addiction.*

**embalmed** *mod.* alcohol intoxicated. □ *By morning they were all embalmed.* □ *Bob was too embalmed to stand up.*

**embalming fluid** *n.* strong liquor; raw whiskey. □ *Jed seemed to favor some* *cheap embalming fluid as his poison.* □ *Bartender, pour out this embalming fluid and get me your best.*

**embroidery** *n.* scars on the arms from many drug injections. (Drugs. Old.) □ *Molly wears some embroidery as a symbol of her past.* □ *She wears long sleeves to cover up the embroidery.*

**empties** *n.* empty bottles. □ *Throw your empties in the trash.* □ *Whose empties are these, and how many are there?*

**empty-nesters** *n.* parents whose children have grown and moved out. □ *There are a few adjustments that empty-nesters have to make.* □ *I don't mind being an empty-nester. There's more room.*

**emsel** ['ɛmsəl] *n.* morphine. (Drugs. A respelling of "M. sul." morphine sulfate.) □ *The old-timer asked the doctor for some emsel.* □ *Emsel is what they called it back in the last century.*

**end** *n.* the final insult; too much; the last straw. □ *This is just the end. I'm leaving.* □ *When she poured her drink down my back, that was the end.*

**end of the ball game** *n.* the end of everything. □ *Well, the car broke down. I guess that's the end of the ball game.* □ *It looked like the end of the ball game as we sped too fast around the curve.*

**ends** **1.** *n.* money. (Streets.) □ *You got enough ends to get you through the week?* □ *We don't have enough ends to pay the gas bill.* **2.** *n.* shoes. □ *You even got holes in your ends.* □ *Could you use some new ends?*

**enforcer** *n.* a bully; a thug or bodyguard. □ *Bruno is the perfect enforcer. Meaner than all get out.* □ *Rocko is too tender-hearted to be a good enforcer.*

**English spliff** [...splɪf] *n.* a cigarette containing tobacco and cannabis. (Drugs. See *spliff*.) □ *Max favored English spliff, which is not from England, by the way.* □ *English spliff looks to be like some sort of Jamaican mojo.*

**enhanced** *mod.* high on marijuana. (Drugs.) □ *Max is sort of enhanced, as usual.* □ *Fred is enhanced by dinnertime each day.*

**Enjoy!** *exclam.* "Please enjoy it!" □ *Come! Sit! Eat! Enjoy!* □ *Welcome. Come in and enjoy!*

**equalizer** *n.* a gun; a pistol. (Underworld.) □ *Rocko carried an equalizer, but wouldn't dream of using it.* □ *An equalizer can be dangerous in Max's business.*

**E.R.** *n.* an "emergency room." (Hospitals.) □ *Get that stuff up to E.R. now, or this guy's gonna die on me.* □ *I've pulled duty in E.R. all weekend.*

**erase** *tr.* to kill someone. □ *Bruno had orders to erase Max.* □ *Mr. Big decided who was gonna erase who.*

**erb** See *herb*.

**Ervine** See *Irv*.

**eternity-box** *n.* a coffin. □ *When I'm in my eternity-box, then you can have my stereo.* □ *I have my eternity-box all picked out.*

**euchre** ['juka-] *tr.* to cheat or deceive someone. □ *Those guys'll try to euchre you, so watch out.* □ *I think the clerk euchred me.*

**evened out** *mod.* back to normal; restored to sanity. □ *When things are evened out after the holidays, we can settle down.* □ *Finally, at about age 30, you could say that Sam was evened out.*

**even-Steven** **1.** *mod.* evenly divided. □ *He made the two piles of diamonds even-Steven and then let me choose which one I wanted.* □ *The cake is not exactly cut even-Steven.* **2.** *mod.* even; balanced. □ *Now we're even-Steven.* □ *Now that we've given each other black eyes, are we even-Steven?*

**everything from soup to nuts** *n.* everything imaginable. □ *It looks like she brought everything from soup to nuts.* □ *I have everything from soup to nuts in my briefcase.*

**evidence** *n.* liquor. (Usually with *the*. Incorporated into a suggestion that the evidence be destroyed by drinking it.) □ *There is only one thing to do with evidence like this, and that's drink it.* □ *They knocked back all the evidence very quickly.*

**evil** *mod.* excellent. (See *wicked*.) □ *This wine is really evil!* □ *Man, what evil fronts!*

**ex** [ɛks] *n.* a former spouse or lover. □ *My ex is in town, but we don't talk much anymore.* □ *Her ex remarried.*

**Excellent!** *exclam.* "Fine!" (Like *awesome*, this expression is a standard word used frequently in slang contexts.) □ *A new stereo? Excellent!* □ *Excellent! Way rad!*

**exec** [ɛgˈzɛk] *n.* an executive. □ *The execs are well-treated around here.* □ *They are even firing the execs now.*

**extracted** *mod.* intoxicated with flavoring extract. (Military. Flavorings such as lemon extract have a high alcoholic content.) □ *The cook seems more than a little extracted today.* □ *Being extracted wasn't bad, he said, but the taste left in his mouth the next day was bad.*

**eyeball** *tr.* to look hard at someone or something. □ *I eyeballed the contract and saw the figures.* □ *The two eyeballed each other and walked on.*

**eyeball to eyeball** *mod.* face to face. □ *They approached each other eyeball to eyeball and frowned.* □ *Let's talk more when we are eyeball to eyeball.*

**eyeful** *n.* the sight of something that one was not meant to see. □ *I got an eyeful of that contract. Yikes! What a giveaway!* □ *She really gave us an eyeful. Shame.*

**eye-opener 1.** *n.* a real surprise. □ *Her confession was a real eye-opener.* □ *This day has been an eye-opener for me.* **2.** *n.* a wake-up drink of liquor; a strong drink any time. □ *He knocked back a quick eye-opener and finished dressing.* □ *One eye-opener led to another.* **3.** *n.* the first narcotics injection of the day. (Drugs.) □ *Now it was so bad that she was up before dawn for an eye-opener.* □ *When you're still nodding from the night before and don't need an eye-opener, that's bad!*

**eye-popper 1.** *n.* something astonishing. □ *The description of the theft was a real eye-popper.* □ *What an eye-popper of a story!* **2.** *n.* a very good-looking woman or *girl.* □ *Isn't that foxy lady an eye-popper?* □ *I may not be an eye-popper, but my virtue is exemplary.*

**eyewash 1.** *n.* nonsense; deception. □ *Aw, that's just a lot of eyewash!* □ *It's not eyewash! It's true!* **2.** *n.* liquor. □ *How about some of that nice eyewash?* □ *You've been putting away a lot of that eyewash, haven't you?*

# F

**fab** [fæb] *mod.* fabulous. □ *Man, what a fab stereo!* □ *Your pad is not what I'd call fab. Just okay.*

**face card** *n.* an important person; a self-important person. (As with the royal characters in playing cards.) □ *Who's the face card getting out of the benz?* □ *Mr. Big is the face card in the local mob.*

**faced 1.** *mod.* alcohol intoxicated. (From *shit-faced.*) □ *Lord, is he faced!* □ *Who is that guy on the corner who looks so faced?* **2.** *mod.* rejected by a member of the opposite sex. (Collegiate.) □ *I've been faced again, and I hate it!* □ *Sally was faced by Tod, and she won't speak to him or anybody else.*

**(face) fungus** ['fes fəŋgəs] *n.* whiskers; a beard. □ *If John would shave off that face fungus, he'd look a lot better.* □ *What do you need all that fungus for anyway?*

**face man** *n.* a good-looking young man with no personality. (Collegiate.) □ *Harry is just a face man and as dull as dishwater.* □ *Norm is the perfect face man—all looks and no brains.*

**face-off** ['fesɔf] *n.* a confrontation. (From hockey.) □ *For a minute it looked like we were headed toward a nasty face-off.* □ *The face-off continued for a few moments till both of them realized that there was no point in fighting.*

**face the music** *tr.* to receive the rebuke that is due one. □ *You had better go in and face the music now.* □ *You have to face the music eventually.*

**facilities** *n.* toilet facilities. □ *Where are the facilities around here?* □ *Can I use your facilities?*

**fack** [fæk] *in.* to state the facts; to tell (someone) the truth. (Black.) □ *That*

dude is not facking with me.* □ *Now is the time to start facking. Where were you?*

**facts of life 1.** *n.* an explanation of human reproduction, especially as presented to a child. □ *No one ever explained the facts of life to me. I read books about it.* □ *She is so naive. She doesn't even know the facts of life.* **2.** *n.* the truth about life's difficulties. □ *You had better face up to the facts of life and get a job.* □ *They taught me everything in college except the facts of life.*

**fade 1.** *in.* to leave. □ *I think that the time has come for me to fade. See ya.* □ *Hey, man, let's fade.* **2.** *in.* to lose power; to lose influence. □ *Ralph is fading, and someone else will have to take over.* □ *The positive effect of the weekend faded fast.*

**fadoodle** [fə'dudl] *n.* something ridiculous; nonsense. □ *Oh, stop your silly fadoodle!* □ *That's nothing but fadoodle!*

**fag\*** [fæg] **1.** *n.* a cigarette. □ *Hey, pal, gimme a fag.* □ *Go buy your own fags!* **2.\*** AND **faggot\*** *n.* a homosexual. (Caution with *fag* and *faggot.* Usually derogatory.) □ *Who's the fag with the fancy hat?* □ *Don't act like a faggot, Gary.* **3.** *n.* a repellent male. □ *You creepy fag. Stop it!* □ *Bruno is such a fag!*

**fag-busting\*** *n.* doing violence to homosexuals. (Caution with *fag.*) □ *Those bums get some kind of pleasure out of fag-busting.* □ *What's this strange need you have for fag-busting? What's your problem?*

**fagged out** *mod.* exhausted. □ *I'm really fagged out after all that running.* □ *John, you sure look fagged out.*

**faggot** See *fag.*

**fail** *n.* a failing grade; a grade of F. (Compare to *pass.*) □ *Sorry, this paper's a fail if I ever saw one.* □ *I pulled a fail in stat.*

**fair-haired boy** *n.* a promising young man; a young man who receives favoritism. □ *Ted is the boss's fair-haired boy now, but he'll be just like the rest of us in a month.* □ *He'd have been fired if he wasn't the fair-haired boy.*

**fair shake** *n.* a fair chance. (From shaking dice.) □ *I want to give you both a fair shake.* □ *All I want from you is a fair shake.*

**fair-weather** *mod.* temporary; insincere. (From "fair-weather sailor.") □ *I need something more than a fair-weather friend to help me through all this.* □ *Well, I see you are just a fair-weather golfer like me.*

**fairy\*** *n.* a homosexual. (Caution with *fairy.* Derogatory.) □ *I hear that you-know-who is a fairy.* □ *Who goes around calling people fairies?*

**fairy tale** AND **bedtime story** *n.* a simplistic and condescending explanation for something; a lie. □ *I don't want to hear a fairy tale, just the facts, ma'am.* □ *What you're telling me sounds like a bedtime story. Come back when you can be more straightforward.*

**fake book** *n.* a book with basic melody and chord changes for hundreds of popular songs. □ *Somebody lifted my fake book.* □ *I thought fake books were illegal.*

**fake it** *tr.* to pretend (to do something). □ *If you don't know the right notes, just fake it.* □ *I can't fake it anymore. I've got to be honest with you.*

**fake off** *in.* to waste time; to *goof off.* □ *Hey, you guys, quit faking off!* □ *All you clowns do is fake off. Now, get busy!*

**fake someone out** AND **fake out someone** *tr.* to deceive someone, as with a football pass. □ *They faked me out, and then I stumbled over my own feet. The coach was fuming.* □ *We faked out the teacher who thought we had gone out in the hall.*

**fakus** ['fekəs] *n.* a gadget; something with no name or a forgotten name. □ *This little fakus goes right in here.* □ *Hand me that long fakus with the hole in one end.*

**falderal** AND **folderol** ['faldɚal] *n.* wasted effort; nonsense. □ *I had about enough of your falderal.* □ *Stop the folderol and get to work.*

**fall** **1.** *in.* to be arrested; to be charged with a crime. (Underworld. See also *fall guy.*) □ *I heard that Bruno fell. Is that right?* □ *Bruno would never fall easily. Must be a frame.* **2.** *n.* one's arrest; being arrested and charged. (Underworld.) □ *Who took the fall for the bank job?* □ *Rocko will never accept a fall willingly.*

**fall apart** *in.* to become upset or distraught. □ *It looks like everything around me is falling apart.* □ *Gert almost fell apart when she got the news.*

**fall down and go boom** *in.* to fall down. (Baby talk.) □ *Poor Jimmy. Did you fall down and go boom?* □ *Careful, now. You'll fall down and go boom.*

**fall guy** *n.* a victim; a dupe. (Originally underworld.) □ *Rocko wasn't going to be the fall guy for this caper.* □ *I didn't want to be the fall guy, so I sat out the last job.*

**falling-down drunk** **1.** *mod.* alcohol intoxicated; very drunk. □ *Poor Fred's falling-down drunk and has no way to get home.* □ *She's not just tipsy; she's falling-down drunk.* **2.** *n.* a drunken person who falls down. □ *Poor old Jed is turning into a falling-down drunk.* □ *One more falling-down drunk in this neighborhood will not be anything new.*

**falling-out** *n.* a disagreement. (Always with *a.*) □ *Tom and Bill had a little falling-out.* □ *They patched up their little falling-out.*

**fall off the wagon** *in.* to resume drinking after having stopped. □ *Poor Jed fell off the wagon again.* □ *It looks to me like he wanted nothing more than to fall off the wagon.*

**fall out** *in.* to overdose; to pass out from drugs. (Drugs.) □ *Rocko took some junk and just about fell out from it.* □ *Gert is going to fall out. Watch her!*

**fallout** *n.* the results of something; the *flack* from something. □ *The fallout from this afternoon's meeting was not as serious as some expected.* □ *It's not* *the crisis itself, but the fallout from the crisis that concerns us all.*

**fall out of bed** *in.* to fall far down, as with the drop in some measurement. □ *The temperature really fell out of bed last night! It was 23 below!* □ *The stock market fell out of bed last year at this time.*

**fancy footwork** AND **fast footwork** *n.* artful maneuvering; fast and clever thinking. □ *Ken did a lot of fancy footwork to get out of that one.* □ *Fast footwork is the key to success in politics.*

**Fancy meeting you here.** *sent.* "Just imagine meeting you here!"; "I am surprised to meet you here!" □ *Well, hello, Tom. Fancy meeting you here!* □ *Fancy meeting you here, Bill. How have you been?*

**fancy-schmancy** ['fæntsi'ʃmæntsi] *mod.* fancy; very fancy. □ *This one is just too fancy-schmancy for Alice.* □ *She likes everything fancy-schmancy.* □ *I don't care for these fancy-schmancy get-togethers.*

**Fancy that!** *exclam.* "Imagine that!" □ *So, you're a bus driver now. Well, fancy that!* □ *Fancy that! There's a piece of pie left in the fridge.*

**fandangle** [fæn'dæŋgl] *n.* a gadget. □ *Where is the little fandangle that opens a can of sardines?* □ *This fandangle on this end fits into the slot on the end of this thingy.*

**fanny** *n.* the buttocks. (Euphemistic in the U.S. Taboo implications in the U.K.) □ *He fell down right on his fanny.* □ *There's dust or something on your fanny.*

**fanny-bumper** *n.* an event that draws so many people that they bump into one another. □ *The fire on 34th Street turned into a real fanny-bumper.* □ *There was a typically dull fanny-bumper in the village last night.*

**fanny-dipper** *n.* a swimmer, as opposed to a surfer. (California.) □ *The fanny-dippers are not supposed to go out that far.* □ *It's too windy for fanny-dippers, let alone surfers.*

**fan someone's behind** *tr.* to spank someone. □ *You straighten out, or I'll fan your behind.* □ *My pop threatened to fan my behind.*

**Fantabulous!** *exclam.* "Great!" (A blend of *fantastic* and *fabulous*.) □ *You're here at last. Fantabulous!* □ *Fantabulous! It's finished.*

**fan the breeze** *tr.* to chat or gossip. □ *We're just fanning the breeze, so you didn't interrupt anything.* □ *Stop fanning the breeze and get to work.*

**far gone 1.** *mod.* in an extreme state. □ *Wow, that chick is far gone. Listen to her rave.* □ *He was too far gone to make any sense.* **2.** *mod.* alcohol intoxicated. □ *Larry's far gone and looking sick.* □ *Wow, is she ever far gone!*

**far out 1.** *mod.* cool; great; extraordinary. □ *This jazz is really far out!* □ *You want to hear some far out heavy metal?* **2.** *mod.* very hard to understand; arcane; highly theoretical. □ *This stuff is too far out for me.* □ *I can't follow your far out line of reasoning.* **3.** *mod.* alcohol or drug intoxicated. □ *How'd you get so far out?* □ *Three beers and Wally was really far out.*

**fart\*** [fɑrt] **1.\*** *n.* a release of intestinal gas, perhaps with a noise. (Caution with *fart* and with topic in all senses.) □ *Did I hear a fart?* □ *Who is responsible for that fart?* **2.\*** *in.* to release intestinal gas, perhaps with a noise. □ *Who farted?* □ *Somebody farted.* **3.\*** *n.* an obnoxious or a stupid person. (Also a provocative term of address.) □ *Who's the old fart with the enormous mustache?* □ *Who called me an old fart?*

**fart sack\*** *n.* a sleeping bag; a bed. (Crude. Caution with *fart*.) □ *Well, it's time I was getting into the old fart sack.* □ *Get out of that fart sack and get up and get going!*

**fast buck** See *quick buck*.

**fast footwork** See *fancy footwork*.

**fast one** *n.* a clever and devious trick. (Usually with *a*. See *pull a fast one*.) □ *That was a fast one. I didn't know you were so devious.* □ *This was the last fast one like that you'll ever pull on me.*

**fat** *mod.* well supplied; having an overabundance of something. □ *When it comes to printer paper, this place is fat.* □ *We're fat with paper, but there's not a ribbon in sight.*

**fat-cat 1.** *n.* someone with great wealth and the accompanying success. □ *I like* to watch the fat-cats go by in their beemers. □ I'm no fat-cat. I'm usually financially embarrassed in fact. **2.** mod. having to do with wealth or a wealthy person. □ You'll never see me driving any of those fat-cat cars. □ I just have a bank account. No fat-cat investments.

**fat chance** n. a very poor chance. (Sarcastic.) □ Fat chance I'll ever get a new car. □ Me, get an A? Fat chance.

**fat city 1.** n. a state of wealth and comfort; *easy street*. □ She's living in fat city ever since she inherited her fortune. □ I could settle down in fat city without any trouble. **2.** n. fatness (expressed as a place). (See examples.) □ I've had it with fat city. I'm going on a diet. □ Sally is well on her way to fat city.

**fathead** n. a stupid person; someone who has fat where brains ought to be. □ You can be such a fathead! □ Paul, you are being a perfect fathead.

**fatheaded** mod. stupid. □ Now that is really a fatheaded idea. □ It's not fatheaded! □ Let's not come up with a fatheaded plan. This one has to make sense.

**fatso** ['fætso] n. a fat person. (Cruel. Also a rude term of address.) □ Hey, fatso! Go on a diet! □ Some fatso tried to get on the plane and couldn't even get through the door!

**fatty** n. a derogatory nickname for a fat person. (Cruel. Also a rude term of address.) □ Okay, fatty, you get the biggest piece of cake because you deserve it. □ That fatty over there is going to eat up all the snacks.

**fattygews** ['fætigjuz] n. fatigues. (Originally military.) □ I'll slip into some fattygews and be right with you. □ Whose fattygews are piled here in the corner?

**feather brain** n. a stupid person. (Also a rude term of address.) □ Gary is such a feather brain. □ Hey, feather brain. Wake up and get busy!

**feature** tr. to conceive of something; to imagine something. □ I don't feature having a replay of what happened last night. □ I can't even feature such a thing. □ Can you feature what it would be like to be fabulously wealthy?

**fed 1.** AND **the feds** n. a federal agent concerned with narcotics, tax collection, customs, etc. □ Some fed was prowling around asking questions about you. □ The feds are onto Rocko and his gang. **2.** n. the Federal Reserve Board. (Always with *the*.) □ The fed is not likely to raise interest rates very soon again. □ There is no way to predict what the fed is going to do.

**federal diploma** n. a U.S. bank note. □ I could use a few extra of those federal diplomas. □ How many federal diplomas you got with you?

**federal jug** n. a federal prison. (Underworld. See *jug*.) □ Rocko was set to spend the next twenty years in the federal jug. □ Lefty is fresh and sweet—just out of the federal jug.

**feeb** [fib] n. an oaf; a stupid person. (From *feebleminded*.) □ Don't be a feeb. Wake up! □ You are such a feeb!

**feeby** AND **feebee** ['fibi] n. the F.B.I., the Federal Bureau of Investigation. □ The locals were going to call in the feebies, but the D.A. said to wait. □ The feeby is in on this already.

**feed one's face** tr. to put food in one's mouth; to eat (something). □ You're always feeding your face. You're going to get fat. □ Stop feeding your face and listen to me.

**feel a draft** tr. to sense that one is being rejected; to sense that someone is cool toward one, possibly for racial reasons. □ Oh, man, I feel a draft in here. Let's leave. □ What a reception! I sure feel a draft.

**feel groovy 1.** in. to feel really good and mellow. □ It's a beautiful day, and I really feel groovy. □ Everybody is feeling groovy and smiling and all. **2.** in. to be alcohol or drug intoxicated. □ Looks like Kelly is feeling groovy on gin again. □ Bruno feels groovy because of what he is smoking.

**feeling no pain 1.** mod. numbed by alcohol and feeling nothing; alcohol intoxicated. □ She fell off the wagon and is feeling no pain. □ He drank the whole thing, and he's feeling no pain. **2.** mod. feeling nothing; dead. □ Now, poor Jed is feeling no pain. □ Your aunt is feeling no pain now. She slipped away before dawn.

**feep** [fip] **1.** *n.* the beep made by a computer. □ *This thing only makes a feep when I try to run my program.* □ *What does the feep mean?* **2.** *in.* (for a computer) to make a little beep. □ *It feeps when it's angry, I think.* □ *Naw! It just feeps to get your attention.*

**fella** ['fɛlə] *n.* a fellow; a guy. (Also a term of address.) □ *Who's the fella with the dark glasses?* □ *Hey, fella. Got a match?*

**feller** ['fɛlɚ] *n.* a fellow. (Folksy.) □ *Now, old John is a pretty smart feller, but I think he's wrong on this one.* □ *I knew a feller who thought he knew it all.*

**fell of a hix** ['fɛləvəhɪks] *n.* a "hell of a fix"; a hell of a mess. (A deliberate spoonerism. See *mell of a hess.*) □ *Now I'm in one fell of a hix.* □ *This is a nice fell of a hix you've gotten me into.*

**fenced** *mod.* angry. (California.) □ *Boy, was that old man fenced!* □ *Too many people around here are fenced all the time.*

**fence hanger** *n.* someone who cannot decide which side to be on. □ *We need to find a way to persuade the fence hangers to come over to our side.* □ *The senator stated he would be a fence hanger until the very minute of the vote.*

**fender-bender** ['fɛndɚbɛndɚ] **1.** *n.* a minor accident. (Compare to *rear-ender.*) □ *There are a couple of fender-benders on the expressway this morning, so be careful.* □ *A minor fender-bender blocked traffic for a while.* **2.** *n.* a reckless driver (who causes minor accidents). □ *I can't get insurance on my 17-year old, who is a hopeless fender-bender.* □ *Don't give up on young fender-benders.* **3.** *n.* a barbiturate. (Drugs.) □ *Vince popped a couple of fender-benders and went on his way.* □ *Max usually has some fender-benders on him.*

**fen(s)** *n.* the powerful painkiller, fentanyl. (Drugs.) □ *Even Max says to stay away from fens.* □ *Those fens'll lay you low.*

**fer shur** [fɚ 'ʃɚ] *phr.* "for sure"; "absolutely." (Eye-dialect. See *for sure.*) □ *This is way rad, fer shur.* □ *I'll be there. Fer shur!*

**feshnushkied** [fɛ'ʃnuʃkid] *mod.* alcohol intoxicated. □ *Wow, is that guy ever feshnushkied!* □ *Gert is too feshnushkied to drive home.*

**fetch up** *in.* to empty one's stomach; to vomit. □ *I really felt like I was going to fetch up.* □ *Somebody fetched up in here and didn't clean it up.*

**fib** [fɪb] **1.** *n.* a small lie. □ *It was just a little fib. I'm sorry.* □ *Is this another one of your fibs?* **2.** *in.* to tell a small lie. □ *Stop fibbing and tell me the truth.* □ *Did you fib to the teacher?*

**fibber** ['fɪbɚ] *n.* a liar. □ *Harry can be a fibber sometimes. You got to watch him.* □ *Jimmy is turning into a little fibber.*

**Fiddle-faddle!** AND **Fiddlesticks!** ['fɪdl̩fæd] AND 'fɪdl̩stɪks] *exclam.* "Nonsense!"; "I disagree!" □ *Oh, fiddle-faddle! That's silly!* □ *Fiddlesticks! You can't be full. Have some more.*

**Fiddlesticks!** See the previous entry.

**F.I.F.O.** *phr.* "first in, first out," the first items placed in the stack are the first items to be retrieved. (Computers. Acronym. See also *G.I.G.O., L.I.F.O.*) □ *Of course the wrong thing came out. That register is F.I.F.O.* □ *Oh, I thought this thing was F.I.F.O., and I put the stuff in in the wrong order.*

**fifth wheel** *n.* an extra and unneeded person. □ *I feel like such a fifth wheel around here.* □ *Hank is just a fifth wheel. Send him home.*

**fill-in** *n.* a substitute. □ *I was a fill-in for the receptionist today.* □ *I'm just a fill-in. I'll have to refer you to the manager.*

**filling station** *n.* a liquor store. (From an old name for an automobile service station.) □ *Please stop at the filling station and get some suds on your way home.* □ *The filling station on the corner does a big business on Fridays.*

**fill-mill** *n.* a tavern. □ *She stopped off at the fill-mill again this evening.* □ *She spends a lot of time at that fill-mill.*

**fill or kill** AND **F.O.K.** *phr.* a broker's notation advising the stock exchange to fill a stock order or kill it. (Financial markets.) □ *Get rid of this order. It was fill or kill, and it should have been killed yesterday.* □ *Where? I don't see that it's marked F.O.K.*

**filly** *n.* a young woman. (Folksy.) □ *Your daughter is getting to be a fine-looking filly.* □ *Who's that young filly who just came in?*

**filthy lucre** [...'lukɚ] *n.* money. □ *I sure could use a little of that filthy lucre.* □ *I don't want to touch any of your filthy lucre.*

**filthy rich 1.** *mod.* very wealthy. □ *I wouldn't mind being filthy rich.* □ *There are too many filthy rich people now.* □ *Ken is filthy rich because of the money his uncle left him.* **2.** *n.* people who are very wealthy. □ *The filthy rich can afford that kind of thing, but I can't.* □ *I sort of feel sorry for the filthy rich.*

**fin** AND **finn** [fɪn] *n.* a five-dollar bill. (Germanic via Yiddish.) □ *Who says I owe you a fin?* □ *I gave the old guy a finn, and he nearly passed out.*

**finagle** AND **fanigle** [fɪ'negl̩ AND fə'nɪgl̩] **1.** *in.* to plot and plan; to conspire; to arrange (something). □ *He's pretty good at finagling.* □ *She'd rather fanigle than ask outright.* **2.** *tr.* to acquire something through conniving. □ *She spent a lot of time trying to finagle a ride to work.* □ *Can I fanigle a buck from you?*

**financially embarrassed** *mod.* broke. □ *I'm a bit financially embarrassed at the moment.* □ *Gary found himself financially embarrassed when the time came to pay the bill.*

**fine and dandy** *mod.* nice; good; well. (Often sarcastic.) □ *Well, that's just fine and dandy. Couldn't be better.* □ *I feel fine and dandy, and I'm going to have a good time here.*

**finger 1.** *tr.* to point someone out; to identify someone (as having done something, been somewhere, etc.) □ *Tod fingered Marty as being the one who arrived first.* □ *Nobody would dare finger Rocko as the one who did it.* **2.** *n.* someone who identifies criminals for the police; a police informer. (Underworld.) □ *Molly has become a finger for the cops.* □ *Yup, she turned finger after her last vacation.* **3.** *n.* an amount of liquor poured into a glass equal to the width of a finger. □ *Molly said she only drank one finger, but the glass was 4 inches in diameter.* □ *No fingers for you, chum. You've had enough.* **4.** *n.*

Mediterranean hashish in stick form. (Drugs.) □ *Max, you got some fingers you can lay your hands on?* □ *Rocko has carried fingers for people, but he never uses the stuff.*

**finger wave** *n.* the act of giving someone the finger; displaying the middle finger upright as a sign of derision. (The gesture is taboo. See also *give someone the finger.*) □ *Two little kids gave the cop the finger wave.* □ *The salute turned into a finger wave when the Major turned away.*

**fink** [fɪŋk] **1.** *n.* a guard hired to protect strikebreakers. (From *Pinkerton.*) □ *Management called in the finks.* □ *We would've settled if the finks hadn't showed up.* **2.** *n.* a strikebreaker. □ *The finks moved in with clubs.* □ *Bruno used to be a fink. He'd do anything for money.* **3.** *n.* an informer; a *stool (pigeon).* (See also *rat fink.*) □ *Molly has turned into a fink.* □ *Mr. Big doesn't think much of finks.* **4.** See *fink (on someone).* **5.** *n.* any strange or undesirable person. □ *You are being such a fink. Stop it!* □ *Merton is a strange kind of fink.*

**fink (on someone)** *in.* to inform on someone. □ *You won't fink on me, will ya?* □ *Rocko never finks on his friends.*

**fink out (on someone or something)** *in.* to decide not to cooperate with someone or something (after all). □ *Come on, don't fink out on us now.* □ *Bob finked out on the plan.*

**fire a line** *tr.* to *snort* a *line* of cocaine. (Drugs.) □ *Max left to fire a line.* □ *Rocko has never fired a line in his life.*

**fire away** *in.* to start asking questions; to start talking. □ *Okay, I'm ready. Fire away.* □ *The cops fired away at him for an hour.*

**fireball** See *ball of fire.*

**fired up** *mod.* excited; enthusiastic. □ *How can you be so fired up at this time of the morning?* □ *It's impossible to get Merton fired up at all.*

**fire someone or something up** AND **fire up someone or something 1.** *tr.* [with *someone*] to motivate someone; to make someone enthusiastic. □ *See if you can fire John up and get him to paint the house.* □ *I have to fire up the electorate if I want them to vote for me.* (More at *fired up.*) **2.** *tr.* [with *something*] to start something such as an engine; to light something. □ *Andy fired up the snow blower and started to clear a path.* □ *Fire this thing up, and let's get going.*

**fire up** *in.* to light a marijuana cigarette. □ *Max fires up at every chance.* □ *Rocko says he never fired up in his life.*

**firewater** *n.* whiskey. (From cowboy and Indian talk.) □ *This firewater leaves a lot to be desired.* □ *This isn't gin; it's firewater!*

**fireworks 1.** *n.* excitement. □ *When the fireworks are over, come in and we'll talk.* □ *What're all the fireworks about around here?* **2.** *n.* trouble; a display of temper. □ *After Bruno's fireworks, we calmed down a little.* □ *Cut out the fireworks, Sally. Calm down and get back to work.*

**first-class** AND **first-rate** *mod.* fine; the best. □ *This is a first-rate za!* □ *It is really first-class.* □ *You are being a first-class feather brain.*

**firstest with the mostest** *mod.* the earliest and in the largest numbers; the earliest with more of what's needed. (Always with *the.*) □ *Tod got the prize for being the firstest with the mostest.* □ *I always like to be there early—the firstest with the mostest.*

**first-rate** See *first-class.*

**fish** *n.* a stupid and inept person. (Derogatory.) □ *The guy's a fish. He can't do anything right.* □ *Don't be such a fish, Merton. Anyone can work a can opener.*

**fish-fight** *n.* a fight between females. □ *There's a fish-fight over by the biology building.* □ *Those fish-fights can get brutal.*

**fishing expedition** *n.* an exploratory search for facts. (This involves asking questions with no preconceived notion of what they might reveal.) □ *The lawyer was on a fishing expedition. There was no real wrong committed to justify a lawsuit.* □ *Your honor, counsel is just on a clumsy fishing expedition. I move for dismissal.*

**fish-kiss 1.** *tr. & in.* to kiss (someone) with puckered-up lips. (Collegiate.) □ *He can fish-kiss like an expert, which is like being an expert at nothing.* □ *He*

*fish-kissed me, then ran back to his car.* **2.** *n.* a kiss made with puckered up lips. (Collegiate.) □ *One more fish-kiss tonight, and I am going to scream.* □ *The actor planted a big fish-kiss right on her lips and frightened her.*

**Fish or cut bait.** *sent.* "Do something or get out of the way." □ *Fish or cut bait, Chuck. There's work to be done here.* □ *Decide whether you're going to watch or help. Fish or cut bait.*

**fish story** AND **fish tale** *n.* a great big lie. (Like the fisherman who exaggerates the size of the fish that got away.) □ *That's just a fish story. Tell me another!* □ *He's a master at the fish tale. Maybe he should be a politician.*

**fishtail** *in.* (for the rear of a car) to whip back and forth like a fish moving its tail. □ *The caddy fishtailed on the curb and almost spun around.* □ *It's easy to fishtail in wet weather.*

**fish tale** See *fish story.*

**fishy** *mod.* dubious; questionable; likely to be improper or illegal. (See also *smell fishy.*) □ *Something here is fishy.* □ *That was a pretty fishy story you told us.*

**five-finger discount** *n.* the acquisition of something by shoplifting. □ *Bruno used his five-finger discount to get the kind of ring Molly wanted.* □ *I got this thingy with my five-finger discount.*

**five it** See *take the fifth.*

**fiver** ['faɪvɚ] *n.* a five-dollar bill. (See *tenner.*) □ *This thing only cost me a fiver.* □ *Give him a fiver, and let's get outa here.*

**fix 1.** AND **fix-up** *n.* a dose of a drug, especially for an addict who is in need of drugs. (Drugs. It fixes the suffering of withdrawal.) □ *It was clear that the prisoner needed a fix, but there was nothing the cops would do for him.* □ *Max arranged to get a fix-up into the con.* **2.** *in.* to buy a dose of drugs; to take drugs. (Drugs.) □ *Max had to fix before he could even talk to me.* □ *Molly was in the other room fixing.* (More at *fixed.*) **3.** *tr.* to castrate or spay an animal, especially a pet. (Jocularly of people.) □ *Get somebody to fix your cat!* □ *Sally suggested that someone ought to fix Merton—if he isn't already.* (More at *fixed.*) **4.** *n.* a bribe. □ *Rocko never took a fix in his life.* □ *The agent payed a fix to the cops.* (More at *fixed.*) **5.** *tr.* to influence the outcome of a contest or an election. □ *Who fixed this race?* □ *Bruno knows what it takes to fix an election—cash.* (More at *fixed.*) **6.** *n.* a scheme to influence the outcome of a contest or an election. □ *Something is wrong with this game. I smell a fix.* □ *Bruno planned a great fix, but the cops got wise.* **7.** *n.* a repair made to a computer program. (Computers.) □ *This little fix should make the whole program run faster.* □ *I wrote a fix to make the program more efficient.* **8.** *n.* a "cure" for a social ill. (See also *quick fix.*) □ *There is no easy fix for a problem like this.* □ *Some people think there is no fix at all.*

**fixed 1.** *mod.* doped; intoxicated. □ *Max is comfortable now that he's fixed.* □ *He was fixed and broke—in a fell of a hix, I'd say.* **2.** *mod.* (of a person) bribed. □ *Don't worry, the night watchman is fixed.* □ *The cop is fixed and won't give you guys any trouble.* **3.** *mod.* (of a contest or election) with the outcome prearranged. □ *The election was fixed, and we are going to protest.* □ *It was not fixed!* □ *The race was fixed, but we won anyway.* **4.** *mod.* neutered. □ *Now that the cat is fixed, she seems even meaner.* □ *I wouldn't buy anything but an already-fixed dog.*

**fixed up 1.** *mod.* provided with a dose of drugs. (Drugs.) □ *Max got Molly fixed up; then she felt better.* □ *Kelly saw Molly after she was fixed up, and she looked better.* **2.** *mod.* provided with a date. □ *Sam got fixed up with Martha.* □ *Okay, Sam is fixed up with a date for Saturday.*

**fixer 1.** *n.* a lawyer. □ *I'll get my fixer on it first thing in the morning.* □ *Bruno's fixer didn't show up in court.* **2.** *n.* a drug dealer. (Drugs.) □ *Max is the name of the local fixer.* □ *Molly has to get to her fixer fast.*

**fixins** ['fıksn̩z] **1.** *n.* the ingredients for something. (Folksy.) □ *Get out all the fixins before you start.* □ *Do we have the fixins we need for a spice cake?* **2.** *n.* the preparations for an event. (Folksy.) □

*Hurry up with the fixins. It's almost time for people to be here.* □ *We're about through with the fixins. Just in time, too.* **3.** *n.* the extra garnishes on a meal; the extra touches essential to a special meal. (Folksy.) □ *We had a big turkey and all the fixins.* □ *We couldn't afford all the fixins, but we had a good meal and there was enough for everyone.*

**fizzle** ['fızl] **1.** *n.* a failure; something that sputters away. □ *The whole project was a fizzle.* □ *Her first play was no fizzle.* **2.** *in.* to fail; to *peter out.* □ *The whole plan fizzled, and we had to start over.* □ *The play began to fizzle in the second act.*

**flabbergasted** ['flæbɚgæstəd] **1.** *mod.* surprised; baffled. □ *We were flabbergasted by your proposal.* □ *They all sat there flabbergasted.* **2.** *mod.* alcohol intoxicated. □ *I thought you were cutting down, and here you are totally flabbergasted again.* □ *After about six beers, Harry became flabbergasted and slid under the table.*

**flack** See *flak.*

**flack (out)** *in.* to collapse in exhaustion; to go to sleep. □ *I just have to go home now and flack out.* □ *Betsy flacked out at nine every night.*

**flag** [flæg] **1.** *tr.* to fail a course. □ *Pat flagged English again.* □ *I'm afraid I flagged algebra.* **2.** *n.* the grade of F. □ *I'll get a flag on algebra for the semester.* □ *I got three flags and an A.* **3.** *tr.* to arrest someone. □ *The cop flagged Molly for soliciting.* □ *They flagged Bob for speeding even though he was a judge.* (More at *flagged.*)

**flagged** [flægd] *mod.* arrested. □ *Max almost got himself flagged for speeding.* □ *Sally was flagged, and she called her fixer to come get her out.*

**flak** AND **flack** [flæk] **1.** *n.* complaints; criticism; negative feedback. □ *Why do I have to get all the flak for what you did?* □ *We're getting a lot of flack for that news broadcast.* **2.** *n.* publicity; hype. □ *Who is going to believe this flack about being first-rate?* □ *It's all flak and no substance.* **3.** *n.* a public relations agent or officer. □ *The flak made an announcement and then disap-*

*peared.* □ *There were flacks all over the place telling lies and making false promises.*

**flake** [flek] **1.** *n.* a person who acts silly or giddy. □ *Sally is such a flake!* □ *Who's the flake in the plaid pants?* **2.** *n.* a medicinal form of crystallized cocaine. (Drugs. Similar to *crack*.) □ *Where can I get some flake around here?* □ *Max specializes in flake.* **3.** *tr.* (for the police) to place drugs or traces of drugs on a person during an arrest. (Underworld. The person is then charged with possession of drugs.) □ *That's not mine! You flaked me!* □ *The fuzz must have flaked Rocko. He never touches the stuff.* **4.** AND **flakes** *n.* phencyclidine, *P.C.P.*, an animal tranquilizer. □ *Even Max won't sell flake, and he's not what I would call a concerned citizen.* □ *Sometimes they smoke a cigarette with flakes on it.*

**flaked out 1.** *mod.* alcohol intoxicated. □ *You are too flaked out to drive home. Give me your keys.* □ *Man, is she flaked out!* **2.** AND **flaked** *mod.* passed out because of drugs. (Drugs.) □ *Sally was flaked out on the sofa.* □ *Jerry took the stuff and ended up flaked.* **3.** *mod.* unconscious; exhausted; tired out. □ *Tom? He's upstairs flaked out from work.* □ *There are too many flaked out people working at dangerous machines.*

**flake down** *in.* to go to bed; to go to sleep. □ *Look at the time. I gotta go home and flake down.* □ *After I flake down for about three days, I'll tell you about my trip.*

**flake (out) 1.** *in.* to pass out from exhaustion; to fall asleep. □ *I just flaked out. I had had it.* □ *After jogging, I usually flake for a while.* **2.** *in.* to fall asleep after drug use. (Drugs.) □ *An hour after she took the stuff, she just flaked.* □ *Tod popped a few fender-benders and flaked out.*

**flake spoon** See *cokespoon*.

**flako** See the following entry.

**flaky** ['fleki] **1.** *mod.* unreliable. □ *She's too flaky to hold the job.* □ *He's a flaky dude.* □ *I'm getting so flaky. Must be old age.* **2.** *mod.* habituated to the use of cocaine. (Drugs.) □ *He looks a little flaky. Look at his eyes and nose.* □ *Max*

*is flaky. He's a walking advertisement for what he sells.* **3.** AND **flako** ['fleko] *mod.* alcohol intoxicated. □ *Man, is she flako!* □ *Paul was flaky and couldn't drive.*

**flamdoodle** See *flapdoodle*.

**flap** *n.* an argument; a minor scandal. □ *I'm sorry about that flap we had yesterday, but it was all your fault.* □ *Who started this flap anyway?*

**flapdoodle** AND **flamdoodle** ['flæpdudl̩ AND 'flæmdudl̩] *n.* nonsense. □ *I've heard enough of this flapdoodle.* □ *Cut out the flamdoodle and speak the truth.*

**flapjaw** ['flæpdʒɔ] **1.** *n.* a talkative person. □ *Who is the flapjaw who has Sally cornered?* □ *Merton is anything but a flapjaw. I bet he doesn't say a dozen words per hour.* **2.** *n.* chatter; gossip. □ *Too much flapjaw for me to concentrate in here.* □ *Could you all turn down the flapjaw a little?*

**flash** [flæʃ] **1.** *n.* something suddenly remembered; something suddenly thought of. □ *I had a flash and quickly wrote it down.* □ *After we talked a while, a flash hit me. Why don't we sell the house?* **2.** *n.* a very short period of time; an instant. (See *in a flash*.) □ *I'll be there in a flash.* □ *It was just a flash between the time I said I'd be there and when I showed up.* **3.** *tr.* to display something briefly. □ *You'd better not flash a wad like that around here. You won't have it long.* □ *The cop flashed her badge and made the pinch.* **4.**\* *in.* to display one's private parts briefly. (Caution with topic.) □ *The guy flashed and moved on down the street.* □ *She flashed briefly, providing the show that people came to see, and left the stage.* **5.** See *flashback*. **6.** *n.* a drink of liquor. □ *I'll have just a flash; then I've got to run.* □ *Here, have a flash, and let's chat a little longer.* **7.** *n.* a drug *rush*. (Drugs.) □ *The flash of this stuff is something to behold.* □ *Jerry's whole being is keyed to one flash after another.*

**flashback 1.** *n.* a memory of the past; a portrayal of the past in a story. □ *Suddenly, Fred had a wonderful flashback to his childhood.* □ *The next scene in the film was a flashback to the time of Ivan the Terrible.* **2.** AND **flash**

*n.* a recurrent hallucination experienced after the use of *L.S.D.* (Drugs.) □ *Gary was having flashes for a month after he took the stuff.* □ *These "flashbacks," as they call them, can occur at the most inopportune moment.*

**flasher** *n.* a man who exhibits his genitals. □ *The cops caught the flasher and took him away.* □ *Sarah said she thought she saw a flasher in the library.*

**flash on something** *in.* to remember something suddenly and vividly. □ *Then I flashed on a great idea.* □ *I was trying to flash on it, but I couldn't bring it to mind.*

**flash the hash** *tr.* to empty one's stomach; to vomit. □ *Dave left quickly to go out and flash the hash, I think.* □ *Who's in there flashing the hash?*

**flat broke** *mod.* having no money at all. □ *Sorry, I'm flat broke. Not a cent on me.* □ *You may be flat broke, but you will find a way to pay your electricity bill or you will live in the dark.*

**flatfoot** AND **flatty** ['flætfut AND 'flæti] *n.* a police officer, especially a foot-patrol officer. □ *Think about how the flatfoot on the beat is affected by this cold.* □ *The flatty stopped at the door, tried the lock, and moved on.*

**flathead** *n.* a stupid person. □ *Carl, don't act like such a flathead.* □ *He may seem slow, but Carl is no flathead.*

**flatheaded** *mod.* stupid. □ *That is really a flatheaded idea, you know?* □ *Merton seems flatheaded, but he's quite brilliant.*

**flat on one's ass\*** **1.\*** *mod.* completely exhausted. (Caution with *ass.*) □ *I'm just flat on my ass. I need some rest.* □ *After the day of the marathon, Tod was flat on his ass for a week.* **2.\*** *mod.* broke; financially destroyed. (Caution with *ass.* An elaboration of *flat broke.*) □ *Sorry, I can't help you. I'm broke—flat on my ass.* □ *The guy's flat on his ass. Can you help him out with a loan?*

**flat out** **1.** *mod.* totally. □ *She was flat out mad as hell.* □ *We were all flat out disgusted.* **2.** *mod.* at top speed. □ *They drove the thing flat out for an hour.* □ *If we run flat out, we can get there before dusk.*

**flatten** *tr.* to knock someone down with a blow. □ *Max flattened the kid with a*

jab to the nose. □ *Wilbur will flatten his opponent.*

**flatty** See *flatfoot.*

**fleabag** ['flibæg] *n.* a cheap hotel; a *flop house.* □ *I won't stay in this fleabag for one minute.* □ *Rocko never stays in fleabags. He's too proud. Bruno doesn't care.*

**fleece** *tr.* to cheat someone; to steal everything from someone. (Underworld.) □ *Bruno fleeced the kids for a lot of money.* □ *Rocko never tried to fleece anybody.*

**flesh-presser** AND **palm-presser** *n.* a politician. □ *It's that time of the year when the flesh-pressers really go to work.* □ *A palm-presser came to our door to ask us what we thought about his issues.*

**flexed out of shape** *mod.* very angry; bent out of shape. □ *The boss was completely flexed out of shape.* □ *I am truly flexed out of shape.*

**flick** [flɪk] *n.* a movie. □ *That was a pretty good flick, right?* □ *Let's go see that new Woody Allen flick.*

**flimflam** ['flɪmflæm] **1.** *n.* a confidence trick or deception. □ *The whole business sounds like a bit of flimflam to me.* □ *The crooks pulled a nasty flimflam on Betsy.* **2.** *n.* nonsense; deception. □ *Beware of the flimflam they will try to pull on you.* □ *I can spot flimflam a mile away.* **3.** *tr. & in.* to cheat or deceive (someone). □ *Don't try to flimflam me. I wasn't born yesterday, you know.* □ *She is flimflamming over at the Adamsville fair this week.*

**flimflam artist** *n.* someone who practices confidence tricks or deceptions on someone else. □ *I don't trust that flimflam artist at all.* □ *Pretty soon, you'll learn how to spot a flimflam artist.*

**fling up** *in.* to empty one's stomach; to vomit. □ *I was afraid I was going to fling up.* □ *Who flung up on the sidewalk?*

**fling-wing** *n.* a helicopter. □ *The fling-wing from the radio station is hovering over the traffic jam.* □ *There must be a dozen fling-wings up there making all that noise.*

**flip** *in.* to go crazy. □ *Wow, I've got so much to do, I may just flip.* □ *The guy flipped. He was the nervous type.*

**flip-flop 1.** *n.* a reversal. □ *The President denied making a flip-flop. He said he simply forgot his earlier position.* □ *The manager did a flip-flop on the personnel policy.* **2.** *n.* the return trip of a long journey. (Citizens band radio. See also *flip side.*) □ *Nice talking to you, Silver Streak. Catch you on the flip-flop.* □ *Didn't we chat on the flip-flop last week?* **3.** *in.* to change direction or intensity. □ *He flip-flopped again, leaving us quite confused.* □ *Jed flip-flopped twice in the evening, leaving us where we started.* **4.** *in.* to waiver in one's decisions. □ *I'm sorry I'm flip-flopping on this matter. I just can't seem to decide.* □ *Well, you just flip-flop all you want. I know what I want.*

**flip one's wig** *tr.* to go crazy; to lose control. □ *Tom nearly flipped his wig.* □ *I flipped my wig when I got the news.*

**flip (out) 1.** *in.* to lose control of oneself. □ *Wow, I almost flipped out when I heard about it.* □ *He got so mad that he flipped.* **2.** *in.* to become deranged because of a drug. (Drugs.) □ *After taking whatever it was, two kids flipped out.* □ *Why did they flip out? What did they take?*

**flipping** *mod.* damnable. (Euphemistic for *fucking.*) □ *Get this flipping dog out of here!* □ *What's the flipping idea?*

**flip side 1.** *n.* the "other" side of a phonograph record. □ *On the flip side, we have another version of "Love Me Tender" sung by Beverly Mills.* □ *Give a listen to the flip side sometime.* **2.** *n.* the "other" side of something, such as an argument. □ *I want to hear the flip side of this before I make a judgement.* □ *On the flip side, he is no bargain either.* **3.** *n.* the return trip of a long journey. (Citizens band radio.) □ *See ya. Catch you on the flip side, maybe.* □ *Didn't I talk to you on the flip side last week?*

**flip someone off** AND **flip someone out** *tr.* to *give someone the finger.* (Collegiate.) □ *Did you flip me off?* □ *Ernie flipped Tom out, and Tom flattened Ernie. Ah, life in the big city.*

**flip someone out** See the previous entry.

**flip someone the bird** *tr.* to *give someone the finger.* □ *Max flipped the cop the bird—and that was just the wrong thing to do.* □ *The little kid flipped the cop the bird and didn't even know what it meant.*

**flivver** ['flɪvɚ] *n.* an old car. (Once a nickname for the Model-T Ford.) □ *Whose flivver is that parked out in the street?* □ *I got an old flivver to get to school and back.*

**flog** [flɑg] *tr.* to promote something; to try to sell something aggressively. □ *Fred was flogging this car so hard, I figured he was trying to get rid of it.* □ *Don't flog it so hard. It makes people suspicious.*

**flooey** ['flui] *mod.* alcohol intoxicated. □ *You're flooey again. That's every night this week.* □ *Wow, is she flooey!*

**floored 1.** *mod.* surprised. □ *I was really floored by what she had to say.* □ *You looked floored when I came in. Wasn't I invited?* **2.** *mod.* knocked to the floor by a blow. □ *Wilbur was floored by his opponent.* □ *The guy was floored and didn't move a muscle—ever again.* **3.** *mod.* alcohol intoxicated. □ *He's totally floored. Can't see a hole in a ladder.* □ *You'd be floored, too, if you'd drunk a dozen beers.*

**floor it** See *put the pedal to the metal.*

**floozie** ['fluzi] *n.* a promiscuous woman. □ *Molly was enraged when Rocko called her a floozie.* □ *"I didn't call you a floozie," said Rocko. "I said you were boozy."*

**flop 1.** *n.* a failure. □ *What do you mean your life is a flop?* □ *The play was a flop. The entire audience left during the second act.* **2.** *n.* a place to sleep for the night; a bed in a *flop house.* (Streets.) □ *The old man was looking for a flop for the night.* □ *Do you know where I can find a flop?*

**flop house** *n.* a very cheap hotel offering only rows of beds. □ *This place is a flop house! I won't stay here for a moment.* □ *All some of those guys need in life is a flop in a flop house.*

**flopper-stopper** *n.* a brassiere. □ *Hey, Jimmy, does your sister wear a flopper-stopper yet?* □ *She's very shy. She won't even hang her flopper-stoppers out on the line to dry.*

**flower tops** AND **flowers** *n.* the resinous buds of marijuana plants. (Drugs.) □ *They say that flower tops are the best.* □ *Tiffany only buys flowers.*

**flub something up** AND **flub up something** *tr.* to do something incorrectly; to mess up a procedure. □ *Now don't flub this up.* □ *I never flub up anything.*

**flub the dub** ['fləb ðə 'dəb] *tr.* to fail to do the right thing. □ *Merton is flubbing the dub with the fund-raising campaign.* □ *Please don't flub the dub this time.*

**flub (up)** 1. AND **flub-up** *n.* an error; a blunder. □ *I tried not to make a flub, but I did.* □ *Who is responsible for this flub-up?* 2. *in.* to *mess up*; to *foul up.* □ *You are flubbing up again, aren't you?* □ *I do my best to keep from flubbing.*

**fluff** [fləf] 1. *n.* nonsense; irrelevant stuff; hype. □ *This is just a lot of fluff. Nothing substantial at all.* □ *Cut out the fluff and talk straight.* 2. *tr. & in.* to make an error; to do something incorrectly. □ *Tod fluffs his lines in the same place every night.* □ *Don't fluff again, please.*

**fluff-stuff** ['fləfstəf] *n.* snow. □ *There is supposed to be an inch of fluff-stuff tonight.* □ *Fluff-stuff looks pretty, but it's no fun to shovel it.*

**flunk** [fləŋk] 1. *tr. & in.* to earn a failing grade in a course. □ *I'm flunking in English lit.* □ *Wilbur is flunking everything.* 2. *tr.* to assign someone a failing grade. □ *Good grief! She flunked me!* □ *I'm sorry, but I am going to have to flunk half the class.*

**flunk out (of something)** *in.* to leave school or a course because of failure. □ *Fred flunked out of school and never tried to go back.* □ *That's it. All F's. I've flunked out.*

**flush** *mod.* wealthy; with plenty of money. □ *Today I am flush. By tomorrow, I'll be broke.* □ *I'm not exactly flush, but I can pay the bills.*

**flusher** *n.* a toilet. (Folksy. Compared to an outhouse.) □ *I hear they put in a flusher over at the Babbits'.* □ *That's silly. They've always had a flusher.*

**fly** *mod.* knowledgeable; alert and in the know. □ *This dude is fly; there's no question about it.* □ *We don't need any more fly birds around here.*

**flyboy** ['flaiboi] *n.* a pilot. (Military.) □ *Rocko was a flyboy in Korea.* □ *Those flyboys have it easy.*

**fly-by-night** *mod.* undependable; dishonest. □ *Bruno seems like such a fly-by-night character.* □ *He's not fly-by-night at all.* □ *Don't do business with fly-by-night people.*

**fly kites** *tr.* to distribute or *pass* bad checks. (Underworld. See *kite*.) □ *Marty was picked up for flying kites in three different cities.* □ *She got caught flying kites in Philadelphia.*

**fly light** *in.* to skip a meal or eating. □ *Nothing for me, thanks. I'm flying light today.* □ *I fly light until about dinnertime.*

**fly the coop** *tr.* to escape from somewhere; to get away. □ *I was afraid he would fly the coop if I didn't tie him up.* □ *I flew the coop before my dad got home.*

**fly trap** *n.* the mouth. □ *Close your fly trap. You talk too much.* □ *Don't talk with your fly trap full.*

**foam** *n.* beer. □ *How about some more foam?* □ *All the guy thinks about is foam.*

**F.O.B.** *mod.* "Fresh off the boat"; as gullible and trusting as a new immigrant. (A play on the initials of "Free on Board.") □ *That new guy is really F.O.B. What a wimp!* □ *Where did you get those F.O.B. shoes? Blue suede is back?*

**foggiest (idea)** *n.* (even) a hazy idea. (Usually in the negative. Always with *the*.) □ *I'm sorry I don't know. I haven't the foggiest.* □ *I don't have the foggiest idea of how to do this.*

**F.O.K.** See *fill or kill*.

**fold** 1. *in.* to fail; to close. □ *The play folded in the second week.* □ *I was afraid my business would fold because of the recession.* 2. *in.* to collapse from drinking. □ *Dave had just one more drink, and then he folded.* □ *She folded neatly and slid beneath the table.*

**folded** *mod.* alcohol intoxicated. □ *Tod is folded. That's the third time this week.* □ *Man, is he folded!*

**folding money** AND **folding stuff** *n.* U.S. paper bank notes, as opposed to coins. □ *Sorry, I don't have any folding money with me. Can you pick up the bill?* □ *I* *sure could use some more of that folding stuff.*

**folks** *n.* one's parents. (Always with the possessive.) □ *I'll have to ask my folks if I can go.* □ *Her folks are sort of mad at her.*

**fomp** [famp] *in.* to play around sexually. (Collegiate.) □ *Who are those two over there fomping?* □ *Jerry wanted to fomp, and I wanted to get him out of my sight.*

**fooey** See *phooey.*

**foo-foo water** ['fufuwɑdɚ] *n.* aftershave lotion; cologne. □ *Don't use so much of that foo-foo water.* □ *I got three bottles of foo-foo water for my birthday.*

**foot-in-mouth disease** *n.* the tendency to say the wrong thing at the wrong time. □ *I suffer a lot from foot-in-mouth disease.* □ *Well, Ralph has foot-in-mouth disease again.*

**foot it** *tr.* to go somewhere by foot; to walk or run. (Compare to *ankle, shank it.*) □ *I have to foot it over to the drugstore for some medicine.* □ *I'm used to footing it wherever I go.*

**footsy-wootsy** [fʊtsi'wʊtsi] *n.* a foot. (Baby talk.) □ *Your little footsy-wootsies are cold.* □ *Somebody stepped on the toes of my footsy-wootsy!*

**foozle** ['fuzl̩] **1.** *n.* an error; a messed up task. □ *Who made this foozle?* □ *What a stupid foozle!* **2.** *tr.* to mess something up; to bungle something. □ *I'm afraid I'll foozle the camera if I open it up.* □ *Who foozled the copying machine?* (More at *foozlified.*)

**foozlified** ['fuzlɪfaɪd] **1.** *mod.* bungled. □ *This job is really foozlified. Who was in charge?* □ *I've never seen such a foozlified mess in my life!* **2.** *mod.* alcohol intoxicated. □ *Why do you always come home foozlified?* □ *Fred is foozlified and can't see his hand in front of him.*

**for all I know** *phr.* "as far as I know"; "I really don't know." □ *For all I know, they just did it for a lark.* □ *She came in late because she had an accident, for all I know.*

**for (all) one's trouble** *phr.* in spite of one's efforts; in very poor payment for one's efforts. □ *He got a punch in the jaw for all his trouble.* □ *For her trouble, she got only honorable mention.*

**forbidden fruit** *n.* something that is attractive because it is denied to one. (From the Garden of Eden in the Bible.) □ *A new car became Ralph's forbidden fruit.* □ *Liquor was forbidden fruit for Jed.*

**for chicken feed** See *for peanuts.*

**For crying in a bucket!** AND **For crying out loud!** *exclam.* "Good grief!" □ *For crying in a bucket! Who did this?* □ *Look at this mess! For crying in a bucket!*

**For crying out loud!** See the previous entry.

**for free** *mod.* free from monetary charge; gratis. □ *And I get all this for free?* □ *Is all this really mine for free?*

**Forget it! 1.** *exclam.* "Never mind, it wasn't important!" □ *Forget it! It wasn't important.* □ *I had an objection, but just forget it!* **2.** *exclam.* "Never mind, it was no trouble at all!" □ *No trouble at all. Forget it!* □ *Forget it! It was my pleasure.*

**Forget you!** *exclam.* "Drop dead!"; "Beat it!" □ *Oh, yeah! Forget you!* □ *Forget you! Get a life!*

**for keeps** *mod.* forever. □ *Does that mean I'm going to have this scar for keeps?* □ *This is yours for keeps. Enjoy it.*

**for kicks** *mod.* for fun; for a thrill. □ *We just did it for kicks. We didn't mean to hurt anyone.* □ *Let's drive over to Wally's place, just for kicks.*

**fork something over** AND **fork over something** *tr.* to hand something over (to someone). □ *Okay, fork it over. It's mine!* □ *Okay, fork over the dough and be quick about it!*

**for peanuts** AND **for chicken feed** *mod.* for practically no money at all. (See *chicken feed.*) □ *I won't work for peanuts.* □ *You surely don't expect me to do this for chicken feed, do you?*

**For Pete's sake!** AND **For pity's sake!, For the love of Mike!** *exclam.* "Good grief!" □ *For Pete's sake! How've ya been?* □ *For pity's sake! Ask the man in out of the cold!*

**For pity's sake!** See the previous entry.

**for real** *mod.* genuine; not imaginary. □ *Ken is really strange. Is he for real?* □ *This whole day just isn't for real.*

**for sure** *phr.* "absolutely." (The same as *fer shur.*) □ *I'll be there, for sure.* □ *Am I happy? For sure!*

**for the birds** *mod.* undesirable. □ *This pizza is for the birds.* □ *I don't like this kind of life. It's for the birds.*

**for the devil of it** AND **for the heck of it, for the hell of it\*** *mod.* because it is slightly evil; for no good reason. (Caution with *hell.*) □ *The kids broke the window just for the devil of it.* □ *We just drove over for the heck of it.*

**for the heck of it** See the previous entry.

**for the hell of it** See *for the devil of it.*

**For the love of Mike!** See *For Pete's sake!*

**(forty) winks** *n.* a nap; sleep. (Usually with a quantifier. Either *forty* or *some, a few, a bunch of,* etc.) □ *I could use forty winks before I have to get to work.* □ *I need a few winks before I get started again.*

**forwards** *n.* amphetamines; stimulants. (Drugs. The opposite of *backwards.*) □ *Tod popped some forwards to wake himself up.* □ *Molly drops forwards around the clock.*

**fossil 1.** *n.* an old-fashioned person. □ *Some old fossil called the police about the noise.* □ *Oh, Tad, you are such a fossil.* **2.** *n.* a parent. □ *My fossils would never agree to anything like that.* □ *Would your fossils permit that?*

**fouled up** *mod.* messed up; ruined; tangled up. □ *This is sure a fouled up mess.* □ *You sure are fouled up, you know.*

**foul mouth** *n.* a person who uses obscene language habitually. □ *Terry, don't be such a foul mouth.* □ *Sally is turning into a real foul mouth.*

**foul up 1.** *in.* to blunder; to *mess up.* □ *Please don't foul up this time.* □ *The quarterback fouled up in the first quarter, and that lost us the game.* **2.** *n.* a blunder; an error. (Usually **foul-up.**) □ *That was a fine foul-up! Is that your specialty?* □ *I can produce a serious foul up with both hands tied behind me.*

**four-bagger** *n.* a home run in baseball. □ *Wilbur hit his third four-bagger of the season.* □ *Another four-bagger for Wilbur!*

**four-bits** *n.* fifty cents. (A bit is equal to 12.5 cents.) □ *You got four-bits I can borrow?* □ *Here's four-bits. Keep the change.*

**four-eyes** *n.* someone who wears glasses. (Also a rude term of address.) □ *Well, I've got to the age where I'm a four-eyes.* □ *Hey, four-eyes, betcha you can't see this!*

**four-flusher** *n.* a cheater. □ *Bruno is a lousy four-flusher, among other unpleasant things.* □ *You dirty four-flusher!*

**fours and doors** AND **four-doors** *n.* Tylenol™ No. 4 (with codeine) and Doriden™. (Drugs. See also *doors.*) □ *Any little kid around here can tell you where to get fours and doors.* □ *Max won't deal with four-doors.*

**four sheets in the wind** AND **four sheets (to the wind)** *mod.* alcohol intoxicated. (See comments at *three sheets in the wind.*) □ *She's not just tipsy. She's four sheets!* □ *After only three beers, Gary was four sheets to the wind.*

**four wheels** *n.* a car; transportation. (Compare to *wheels.*) □ *I need four wheels to get me around town.* □ *Without four wheels at my disposal, I feel trapped.*

**fox** *n.* an attractive *girl* or young woman. □ *Man, who was that fox I saw you with?* □ *That fox was my sister. Next question?*

**fox trap** *n.* an automobile customized and fixed up in a way that will attract women. □ *I put every cent I earned into my fox trap, but I still repelled women.* □ *To you it's a fox trap; to me it's a pimpmobile.*

**foxy** ['faksi] **1.** *mod.* sexy, especially having to do with a woman. □ *Man, isn't she foxy!* □ *What a foxy dame!* **2.** *mod.* smelly with perspiration odor. □ *Somebody in this taxi is a little foxy.* □ *Who's got the foxy pits?* □ *Subway cars can sure get foxy in the summer.* **3.** *mod.* alcohol or drug intoxicated. □ *Gary is a little foxy. Let him rest awhile.* □ *He's worse than foxy—he's stinking drunk.*

**foxy lady** *n.* a sexually attractive woman or *girl.* □ *You are really a foxy lady, Molly.* □ *A couple of foxy ladies stopped us on the street.*

**fracture** *tr.* to cause someone to laugh very hard. □ *Now, this joke'll fracture you.* □ *I like to tell a few that fracture everybody.*

**fractured 1.** *mod.* alcohol intoxicated. □ *This is the third night this week that Tod has rolled in fractured.* □ *He was so fractured he couldn't see.* **2.** *mod.* demolished by laughter. □ *The class was fractured, and the laughter didn't stop until the teacher managed to get up off the floor.* □ *The whole audience was fractured by the time my ten minutes was up.*

**frag** [fræg] *tr.* to assassinate an unpopular military officer in Vietnam. (Military.) □ *The guy was so certain that nobody was going to frag him that he got careless and Charlie got him.* □ *I saw some creeps frag a guy once.*

**fragged** [frægd] *mod.* destroyed; ruined. □ *Why does your room look so fragged?* □ *My clothes are fragged, and I need a haircut.*

**fraidy cat** ['fredi...] *n.* a coward; a person who is frightened of everything. (Used in children's taunts.) □ *Don't be a fraidy cat. Go ahead, jump!* □ *Carl is such a fraidy cat.*

**frame 1.** *tr.* to cause an innocent person to be blamed for a crime; to contrive evidence so that someone appears to be guilty. (Originally underworld.) □ *Jimmy tried to frame his sister for painting the cat yellow.* □ *You won't frame me and get away with it!* **2.** AND **frame-up** *n.* an act of incrimination caused by contrived evidence. (Underworld.) □ *Bruno would never fall easy. Must be a frame.* □ *The frame-up would have worked if it weren't for one little thing.*

**frame-up** See the previous entry.

**frantic** *mod.* great; wild. □ *We had a frantic time at Chez Freddy.* □ *That rally was really frantic.*

**frat** [fræt] **1.** *n.* a fraternity. (Collegiate.) □ *Are you going to join a frat?* □ *My brother is in a frat.* **2.** *mod.* having to do with fraternities and their members. (Collegiate.) □ *Is there a frat party tonight?* □ *Frat life is not for me.*

**frat-rat** ['frætræt] *n.* a member of a fraternity. (Collegiate.) □ *The frat-rats are having a rally tonight.* □ *Is Frank a frat-rat, or is he independent?*

**freak** [frik] **1.** *n.* one's drug specialty; one's preferred drug. (Drugs.) □ *Max's freak is crack.* □ *Hey, man, what's your freak?* **2.** *n.* a person devoted to doing something. (A combining form.) See *barb freak, coke freak, crank freak, eagle freak, eco freak, freon freak, frost freak, garbage freak, juice freak, kick freak, meth freak, speed freak.* **3.** See *freak (out).*

**freaked (out) 1.** *mod.* shocked; disoriented. □ *I was too freaked out to reply.* □ *Man, was I freaked.* **2.** *mod.* tired out; exhausted. □ *I'm too freaked out to go on without some rest.* □ *The chick is really freaked. Let her rest.* **3.** *mod.* drug intoxicated. (Drugs.) □ *Ye gods, you're freaked!* □ *Molly was so freaked out, she refused to keep her clothes on.* **4.** *mod.* emotionally disturbed through drug use. (Drugs.) □ *Tod was freaked out from the stuff for a month.* □ *She was so freaked that she never touched the stuff again.*

**freaker** ['frikɚ] **1.** *n.* an incident that causes someone to *freak (out).* (Collegiate.) □ *Wasn't that weird? A real freaker.* □ *Did you see that near miss? What a freaker!* **2.** *n.* a *freaked (out)* person. (Collegiate.) □ *Some poor freaker sat in the corner and rocked.* □ *Who's the freaker in the corner?*

**freak freely** *in.* to experience *L.S.D.* visions and hallucinations without using the drug. (Drugs.) □ *After about the third trip, Ernie was freaking freely, day and night.* □ *Freaking freely is no big gift at all. It's horrible.*

**freak house** *n.* a house or other dwelling where methamphetamine is sold and used. (Drugs.) □ *The cops busted a freak house over on Maple.* □ *I saw a couple of kids I know going into a freak house.*

**freaking** *mod.* damned. (Euphemistic for *fucking.*) □ *Get your freaking socks off my bed.* □ *What is this freaking mess on my plate?*

**freak (out) 1.** *in.* to panic; to lose control. □ *I was so frightened, I thought I would freak.* □ *Come on, relax. Don't freak out.* **2.** *n.* a bad drug experience; a psychotic reaction to the drug *L.S.D.* (Drugs. Usually **freak-out** or **freak-out.**) □ *The poor kid had a freak-out and never really recovered.* □ *Some of them get turned off to drugs by a really* *good freakout.* **3.** ['frikɑʊt] *n.* a wild party of any type; any exciting happening. (Usually **freak-out** or **freakout**.) □ *There is a big freak-out at Freddy's joint tonight.* □ *What a frantic freakout!* **4.** ['frikɑʊt] *n.* a *freaked (-out)* person. (Usually **freak-out** or **freakout**.) □ *Some poor freak-out sat in the corner and rocked.* □ *Who's the freakout in the corner?*

**freak someone out** AND **freak out someone** *tr.* to shock or disorient someone. □ *The whole business freaked me out.* □ *I didn't mean to freak out everybody with the bad news.*

**freaky** *mod.* strange; eccentric. □ *I get a freaky feeling whenever I hear that music.* □ *That's really freaky.* □ *What a freaky movie.*

**free base** AND **(free)base** ['fribes] **1.** *n.* a smokable, pure extract of cocaine. □ *Max is real big on free base.* □ *Bruno likes base, too.* **2.** *in.* to smoke a pure extract of cocaine. □ *Rocko has never freebased in his life.* □ *Rocko won't base, smoke, or anything.*

**free base party** *n.* a gathering where *free base* is used. (Drugs.) □ *Max has a free base party about once a week.* □ *The cops broke up a free base party in Beverly Hills.*

**free-baser** *n.* a user of *free base.* (Drugs.) □ *Of course Max is a free-baser! What doesn't he do?* □ *Some of these free-basers have heart attacks.*

**free-basing** AND **baseballing, basing** *n.* using *free base* as a recreational drug. (Drugs.) □ *Rocko refuses to try free-basing.* □ *He saw what basing did to his brother.*

**freebie** AND **freebee, freeby** ['fribi] *n.* something given away free. □ *They gave me a freebie with my purchase.* □ *I expect a freebee when I spend a lot of money like that.*

**free for all** AND **free-for-all** *n.* a brawl; a general fight. □ *A free for all started on the beach over near the concession stand.* □ *The cops broke up the free-for-all.*

**freeload** *in.* to sponge off someone else; to eat and drink at someone else's expense; to live off someone else. □ *Don't come around here and expect to freeload.*

□ *My brother-in-law has been freeloading at our house for months.*

**freeloader** *n.* someone who eats and drinks at someone else's expense; a parasitic person. □ *Ken is sort of a freeloader, but he's a lot of fun anyway.* □ *There are a lot of freeloaders here. We are going to have to ask to see tickets.*

**free lunch** *n.* something free. (Often negative.) □ *There is no such thing as a free lunch.* □ *There's always somebody who'll do anything to get a free lunch.*

**free ride** *n.* an easy time; participation without contributing anything. □ *You've had a free ride long enough. You have to do your share of the work now.* □ *No more free rides around here. Get off your duff and get a job!*

**free show** *n.* a peek at a private part of someone's body, usually a woman. □ *Merton looked like the type who was always waiting for a free show that was never to be.* □ *A true gentleman takes no notice of a "free show".*

**free trip** *n.* an *echo* or a *flashback* of an *L.S.D.* experience. (Drugs.) □ *The kid got a free trip, and it scared her to death.* □ *If these free trips continue, we may have to run some tests.*

**free-wheeling** *mod.* lacking restraint; flamboyant and uncontrolled. □ *These high-spending, free-wheeling palm-pressers appear out of nowhere at election time.* □ *She's too free-wheeling.* □ *She's a free-wheeling executive type.*

**freeze 1.** *n.* the act of ignoring someone; the *cold shoulder.* □ *Everybody seems to be giving me the freeze.* □ *I got the freeze from Julie. What did I do wrong?* **2.** *tr.* to ignore someone; to give someone the cold shoulder. □ *Don't freeze me, gang! I use a mouthwash!* □ *They froze him because he didn't send thank-you notes for his birthday presents.* **3.** *in.* to hold perfectly still. (Also a command given by a police officer which implies that there is a gun pointed at a suspect.) □ *I froze, and the bull didn't see me.* □ *The fuzz shouted, "Freeze, or you're dead meat!"*

**freeze someone out** AND **freeze out someone 1.** *tr.* to make it too cold for someone, usually by opening windows or through the use of airconditioning. (See *play freeze-out*.) □ *Are you trying to freeze out everybody? Close the door.* □ *Turn up the heat unless you're trying to freeze us out.* **2.** *tr.* to lock someone out socially. □ *They froze me out of the club. What did I do wrong?* □ *We didn't want to freeze you out. You failed to pay your dues, however.*

**freezing cold** *mod.* very cold. □ *It's freezing cold out there.* □ *I won't go out in freezing cold weather.* □ *Why does it have to be so freezing cold?*

**French kiss 1.** *n.* kissing using the tongue; open-mouth kissing. □ *What's French about a French kiss?* □ *I didn't know whether I was going to get a French kiss or a fish-kiss.* **2.** *tr.* to kiss someone using the tongue. □ *Kids like to try to French kiss each other at an early age. It's part of growing up.* □ *He tried to French kiss me, but I stopped him.*

**freon freak** AND **frost freak** ['friɑn frik AND 'frɔst frik] *n.* a drug user who breathes freon gas (from pressurized spray cans) for a *high*. (Drugs.) □ *Bill was a freon freak when he was a kid.* □ *Now those frost freaks can't get the stuff anymore. They don't sell it because it ruins the air or something.*

**fresh 1.** *mod.* cheeky; impudent. □ *Ken sure is fresh sometimes.* □ *Kids get some pretty fresh ideas.* **2.** *mod.* a little aggressive sexually; prone to caress too eagerly. □ *Hey, buster! Don't get fresh with me!* □ *He got fresh, so I slapped him.* **3.** *mod. cool*; okay. □ *Gee, that's not fresh. Too bad.* □ *That stuff's really fresh. It's a winner.*

**fresh and sweet** *mod.* just out of jail. (Streets.) □ *Molly is fresh and sweet and back on the street.* □ *Hey, Lefty, you look all fresh and sweet.*

**fresh as a daisy** *mod.* someone who is always alert and ready to go. □ *How can you be fresh as a daisy so early in the morning?* □ *I always feel fresh as a daisy.*

**freshman** ['frɛʃmən] *n.* a new drug addict; new drug user. (Drugs.) □ *Max likes to deal with freshmen. They become good customers.* □ *The freshmen replace the ones who get flagged or freak out permanently.*

**fridge** [fridʒ] *n.* a refrigerator. □ *Put this in the fridge so it won't spoil.* □ *What's in the fridge for dinner tonight?*

**fried** *mod.* alcohol or drug intoxicated. (See also *brain-fried* at *brain-burned*.) □ *How the hell did you get so fried?* □ *The chick got totally fried on three beers.*

**frigging 1.** *mod.* damnable. (A euphemism for *fucking*.) □ *Who made this frigging mess?* □ *I smashed up my frigging car!* **2.** *mod.* damnably. □ *What a frigging stupid thing to do!* □ *That is a dumb frigging thing to do!*

**Frisco** ['frisko] *n.* San Francisco, California. □ *Have you ever been in Frisco?* □ *My cousin lives in Frisco.*

**Frisco speedball** [frisko 'spidbɔl] *n.* an injectable mixture of heroin, cocaine, and *L.S.D.* (Drugs. See also *San Francisco bomb*.) □ *Wasn't it a Frisco speedball that killed what's-his-name?* □ *Frisco speedballs were popular over 40 years ago.*

**from A to Z** *mod.* of a complete and wide variety. □ *We have just about everything from A to Z.* □ *She ordered everything on the menu from A to Z.*

**from hunger** See *(strictly) from hunger*.

**from (the) git-go** *mod.* from the very start. (See *git-go, jump (street)*.) □ *This kind of thing has been a problem from the git-go.* □ *I warned you about this from git-go.*

**from way back** *mod.* for a long time; since a long time ago. (Folksy.) □ *I'm a banjo picker from way back.* □ *Tod is a woodcarver from way back.*

**front 1.** *in.* to pay out money in advance of receiving goods; to pay up front. (See *front money*.) □ *I fronted about $550 for the new computer.* □ *How much do you want her to front for this?* **2.** *n.* a respectable appearance. □ *Jan can put up a good front, but most of us know the real Jan.* □ *The front she put up collapsed as she heard the bad news.*

**front man** *n.* a respectable and well-known man who represents a less respectable person or organization. □ *The former adviser now serves as a front man for a large foundation.* □ *The front man came out and made an announcement.*

**front money** *n.* money paid in advance; earnest money. □ *How much front money do you need?* □ *I put up a lot of front money and have nothing to show for it.*

**front runner** *n.* the leader; the person or thing most likely to win. □ *The press found out some juicy secrets about the front runner and made them all public.* □ *Who is the front runner in the race for senator?*

**fronts** *n.* clothing; a sports jacket. (Black.) □ *You got some good-looking fronts there.* □ *I need some new fronts.*

**froody** ['frudi] *mod.* grand; wonderful. □ *The curtains parted to the most froody funky set I've ever seen.* □ *Man, is this froody!* □ *Oh, you have some froody ideas, all right. But can you carry them out?*

**frosh** [frɔʃ] **1.** *n.* a freshman. □ *Ken is just a frosh, but he looks older.* □ *Get some frosh to do it for you.* **2.** *mod.* having to do with freshmen. □ *The frosh dorm is full again this year.* □ *This is a frosh dance. You can't come in.*

**frost** *tr.* to make someone angry. □ *That really frosts me.* □ *The little car frosted me by zooming into my parking place.* (More at *frosted (over)*.)

**frosted (over)** *mod.* angry; annoyed. □ *The clerk was really frosted over when I asked for a better one.* □ *Why was he so frosted?*

**frost freak** See *freon freak.*

**frosty 1.** AND **frosty one** *n.* a beer; a cold beer. □ *Hey, toss me a frosty, will ya?* □ *I need a frosty one after all that work.* **2.** *mod.* cool; really cool and mellow. □ *That music is really frosty.* □ *We had a frosty time, didn't we?* **3.** AND **frost(ed)** *mod.* under the influence of cocaine. (Drugs.) □ *Max seems frosty all the time.* □ *She looked a little frosty when she came back to her desk.* **4.** AND **Frosty the Snowman** *n.* a cocaine dealer. (Drugs. Usually capitalized. From the title of a song.) □ *Don't call Max Frosty. He doesn't like that.* □ *Where can I find Frosty the Snowman in this neighborhood?*

**froth** *n.* a beer. □ *Would you like some froth?* □ *How about another pitcher of froth, innkeeper?*

**fruit 1.** *n.* a strange person. (Now overwhelmed by sense 2.) □ *Ted is such a fruit.* □ *Sam comes on like a fruit, but it's just his sense of humor.* **2.** *n.* a homosexual person. (Objected to by homosexual persons.) □ *Bob thinks that you-know-who is a fruit.* □ *Who's the fruit who just came in?*

**fruitcake 1.** AND **fruit loop** *n.* a foolish oaf. (Someone who is as *nutty as a fruitcake.*) □ *What a fruitcake! Doesn't even know where his head is at.* □ *Carl acts like such a loony fruit loop.* **2.** *n.* a homosexual person. (Objected to by homosexual persons.) □ *Ken said that you-know-who is a fruitcake.* □ *Who's the fruitcake who just came in?*

**fruit loop** See the previous entry.

**fry 1.** *in.* to die in the electric chair. (Underworld.) □ *The D.A. is determined that you will fry.* □ *I don't want to fry!* **2.** *tr.* to execute someone in the electric chair. (Underworld.) □ *They're gonna fry you for this.* □ *Nobody's gonna fry Rocko!*

**fuck\*** [fək] *tr. & in.* to copulate (with someone or some creature). (Taboo. Caution with *fuck* and with topic. A highly offensive word to many people. There are many additional meanings and constructions with the word.) □ *Two dogs were fucking out on the lawn.* □ *He actually said in public that he had—you know—fucked her.*

**fucking\*** *mod.* "damnable." (Taboo. Caution with *fuck.*) □ *Get this fucking idiot outa here!* □ *What the fucking hell do you think you are doing?*

**fud** See *fuddy-duddy.*

**fuddy-duddy** AND **fud** ['fədidədi AND fəd] *n.* a stuffy person; an old-fashioned person, especially a male. □ *Pay no attention to him. He's just an old fud.* □ *There seems to be a convention of fuddy-duddies in the park today.*

**fudge** [fədʒ] **1.** *in.* to cheat; to deceive (someone). □ *Bill, you're fudging. Wait till the starting gun fires.* □ *No fair fudging!* **2.** *n.* nonsense; deception. □ *Cut out the fudge and talk straight.* □ *I've heard enough of your fudge. Let's get honest, okay?*

**fudge factor** *n.* a margin of error. □ *I never use a fudge factor. I measure cor-*

*rectly, and I cut the material exactly the way I measured it.* □ *I built in a fudge factor of 3 inches.*

**fugly** ['fəgli] *mod.* "fat and ugly." (Collegiate.) □ *Man, is that dog of yours ever fugly! What or who did it eat?* □ *This is a real fugly problem we're facing.*

**full blast** *mod.* as strongly as possible. □ *He honked the horn full blast for a long time.* □ *The whistle blew full blast and woke everyone up.*

**full moon 1.** *n.* a large chunk of peyote cactus. (Drugs.) □ *Don dumped a sack full of full moons on the table and smiled.* □ *Within minutes, the full moons had gone, and Don had himself a fist full of clams.* **2.** *n.* hashish sold in a round shape. (Drugs.) □ *Max tossed Bruno a full moon and told him to forget where he got it.* □ *Bruno, fat with 3 full moons—the one Max gave him and the two he kiped—smiled and slowly walked away.*

**full of beans** *mod.* full of nonsense; *full of hot air.* □ *Oh, be quiet. You're just full of beans.* □ *Pay no attention to John. He's full of beans.*

**full of hops** *mod.* full of nonsense. (As if one were full of beer, which contains hops.) □ *Aw, you're just full of hops!* □ *The guy was full of hops. Nothing he said made any sense.*

**full of hot air** AND **full of bull, full of it.** *mod.* full of nonsense. □ *You're full of hot air. I don't believe you.* □ *Aw, you're just full of it! Be quiet!*

**full of Old Nick** See *full of the devil.*

**full of prunes** *mod.* full of nonsense. (Like *full of beans.*) □ *You're just silly. Completely full of prunes.* □ *Oh, you're full of prunes. Get a life!*

**full of the devil** AND **full of Old Nick** *mod.* always making mischief. □ *Little Chuckie is sure full of the devil.* □ *In this weather, the kids are always full of Old Nick.*

**full sesh** ['ful 'sɛʃ] *mod.* totally; completely. (California.) □ *He was really out of it full sesh.* □ *It was a great game. They went at it full sesh the whole time.*

**full steam ahead** *mod.* with determination. □ *We started moving full steam ahead on the project.* □ *Full steam ahead! Let's see how fast this will go!*

**fun** *mod.* pleasant; entertaining. □ *We had a real fun time.* □ *His party was fun.* □ *What a fun evening!*

**fun and games** *n.* nonsense; a waste of time. □ *I've had enough fun and games. Let's get on with the business.* □ *You spend too much time with fun and games!*

**fungus** See *(face) fungus.*

**fungus-face** *n.* a bearded man. (See also *(face) fungus.* Compare to *fuzz-face.*) □ *Who's the fungus-face in the striped blazer?* □ *Hey, fungus-face! Who is that behind all the fuzz?*

**funk** [fəŋk] **1.** *n.* a bad odor; a stench. □ *What is that ghastly funk in here?* □ *Open the windows and clear out this funk.* **2.** *n.* tobacco smoke. □ *The funk was so thick I couldn't see across the room.* □ *Most of those important decisions are made by party hacks in funk-filled back rooms.* **3.** *n.* a depressed state. □ *I've been in such a funk that I can't get my work done.* □ *As soon as I get out of my winter funk, I'll be more helpful.* **4.** *n.* cowardice; terror. □ *She suffers this terrible funk whenever she has to give a talk.* □ *The dog was in such a funk that it was crying.* **5.** *n.* a kind of blues rock; jazz based on gospel music. □ *Man, groove on that funk, would ya?* □ *Now this is the kind of funk I've been looking for.*

**funked out** *mod.* alcohol or drug intoxicated. □ *Do you think you can go through life funked out all the time?* □ *Are you funked out again?*

**funking\*** *mod.* "damnable." (Caution with *funking.* Euphemistic for *fucking.*) □ *Who put this funking milk crate in the hall?* □ *Get the funking hell out of here.*

**funky 1.** *mod.* strange; *far out.* □ *I like your funky hat.* □ *Is he funky?* □ *He's such a funky guy.* **2.** *mod.* basic and simple; earthy. □ *Everything she does is so funky.* □ *I like to be around funky people.* **3.** *mod.* smelly; obnoxious. □ *Get your funky old socks outa here.* □ *This place is really funky. Open some windows.* **4.** *mod.* unkempt. □ *Your hair is sort of funky. Comb it.* □ *John's room is funky and disorganized.*

**funky-drunk** *mod.* alcohol intoxicated; stinking drunk. □ *The guy is funky-*

drunk, and I think he's going to be sick. □ *Wow, is she ever funky-drunk!*

**funny business** See *monkey business.*

**funny-farm** *n.* an insane asylum; a mental hospital. □ *I think they ought to send you to the funny-farm.* □ *He's too far gone for the funny-farm.*

**funny-money** *n.* any substitute money: counterfeit money, military script, etc. □ *I don't want any funny-money. Real U.S. greenbacks or forget the deal.* □ *Who'll change my funny-money back to bucks?*

**fur** *n.* the police. (See *fuzz.*) □ *I think the fur is on to you, Rocko.* □ *The fur ain't never gonna get Rocko.*

**furphy** ['fɚfi] *n.* a groundless rumor. □ *I heard a furphy about you yesterday.* □ *Who started that furphy anyway?*

**fuse box** ['fjuz bɑks] *n.* the head; the brain. □ *I'm afraid she's missing a little something in the fuse box.* □ *Jed acts like his fuse box is completely blown.*

**fussbudget** ['fʌsbədʒət] *n.* someone who fusses all the time, especially a baby. □ *Oh, Gary, don't be such a fussbudget.* □ *He is such a fussbudget. Get him a passy.*

**futz** See *phutz.*

**fuzz** [fʌz] **1.** AND **fuzz man, fuzzy (tail)** *n.* the police; a jail keeper; a detective. □ *The fuzz is on to you.* □ *See if you can distract the fuzz man while I lift his keys.* **2.** AND **fuzzle** *in.* to get drunk. □ *They were just sitting there fuzzling away the day.* □ *Stop fuzzing and listen.* **3.** *n.* a drug *high*; a *buzz.* (Drugs.) □ *Just when she was beginning to feel the fuzz, her parents came home.* □ *This stuff has no fuzz at all.*

**fuzzed** AND **fuzzled, fuzzy** *mod.* alcohol intoxicated. □ *You are too fuzzed all the time to hold the job. Pack!* □ *Why do you come home every night fuzzled?*

**fuzz-face** *n.* a man with a beard. (Compare to *fungus-face.*) □ *Hey, fuzz-face, come here a minute.* □ *A couple of fuzz-faces came in and asked for mustache wax.*

**fuzz station** *n.* a police station. □ *He had to spend about an hour at the fuzz station, but nothing happened to him.* □ *Drop by the fuzz station and pick up a copy of the driving rules.*

**fuzzword** ['fʌzwɚd] *n.* a confusing term usually meant to obscure meaning. (From *buzzword.*) □ *The current crop of fuzzwords contains a few that have come back from the twenties.* □ *Don't sling those fuzzwords at me!*

**fuzzy** ['fʌzi] **1.** See *fuzz.* **2.** *mod.* alcohol intoxicated. □ *Rudy seems a bit fuzzy. Did he fall off the wagon again?* □ *She was too fuzzy to drive home.*

# G

**G.** See *grand*.

**gab** [gæb] **1.** *in.* to chatter; to gossip. □ *Can you stop gabbing just for a minute?* □ *We like to gab. Leave us alone.* **2.** *n.* mindless chatter; gossip. □ *I like to listen in on other people's gab.* □ *Enough of this gab—on with the show!*

**gabfest** ['gæbfɛst] *n.* an event where much chattering or gossip takes place. □ *There's a gabfest going on in Clare's room.* □ *Say, your gabfest is a little loud.*

**gab room** *n.* a women's restroom where women are said to chatter. □ *She went to the gab room to powder her nose.* □ *There was a small commotion in the gab room.*

**gaffer** ['gæfɚ] *n.* an old man; a rustic old man. (From *grandfather*.) □ *Nobody out there but some old gaffer with a cane.* □ *The old gaffer smiled and moved on.*

**gaffled** ['gæfl̩d] *mod.* arrested. □ *Fred got himself gaffled for speeding.* □ *I can just picture Fred gaffled and acting all humble.*

**gag** [gæg] **1.** *in.* to retch or choke, especially with much noise. (Standard English.) □ *The food was so horrible I almost gagged on it.* □ *Don't eat so fast. You'll gag.* **2.** *n.* a joke; a trick. □ *She tells the best gags.* □ *What a great gag! Everybody will love it.*

**gaga** ['gɑgɑ] **1.** *mod.* crazy; eccentric. □ *Sometimes you are so gaga!* □ *Sally is just naturally gaga.* **2.** *mod.* dazzled. □ *The family was gaga about my success.* □ *Tom was totally gaga after he got promoted.*

**gage** AND **gauge** [gedʒ] **1.** *n.* whiskey; liquor; inferior liquor. □ *This gage is vile.* □ *How about some more gauge?* **2.** *n.* tobacco; cigarettes. □ *No more gauge for me.* □ *You got any gage on you?* **3.** *n.* marijuana; a marijuana cigarette. (Drugs.) □ *Max is always smoking gauge.* □ *This is crummy gage.*

**gaged** AND **gauged** [gedʒd] *mod.* alcohol intoxicated. □ *The chick was gaged out of her mind.* □ *Wow, were they all gaged!*

**Gag me with a spoon!** *exclam.* "I am disgusted!" (A catch phrase initiated by Moon Unit Zappa in a phonograph recording about "Valley Girls" in California.) □ *So gross! Gag me with a spoon!* □ *Gag me with a spoon! You are way gross!*

**Gainesville green** ['genzvɪl...] *n.* a variety of marijuana from Gainesville, Florida. (Drugs.) □ *Gainesville green is just cheap local pot.* □ *Max will call his stuff Gainesville green, African black—whatever will sell it.*

**gallery** See *shooting gallery*.

**galloping dandruff** See *walking dandruff*.

**galumph (around)** [gəˈlʌmpf...] *in.* to walk around; to *schlep* around. □ *I spent all day galumphing around, looking for a present for Ted.* □ *Stop galumphing long enough to eat some dinner.*

**game** *mod.* willing to so something. □ *Is anybody game for some pizza?* □ *I'm game, what about you?*

**game plan** *n.* a plan of action; a scheme. (From sports.) □ *The game plan for the election was beginning to shape up.* □ *Our game plan had to be scrapped.*

**game time** *n.* time to go do what has to be done; time to go to work. (From sports.) □ *Okay, gang, let's get going.*

*It's game time.* □ *Will this report be ready by game time?*

**gams** [gæmz] *n.* a woman's legs, especially if attractive. □ *Is she the one with the gorgeous gams?* □ *Look at the gams on that chick!*

**gander** *n.* a look. □ *Let me take a gander at it and see if it's done right.* □ *We should all take a gander to see what one is like.*

**gang-bang 1.** *n.* an act of group rape. □ *The fuzz was around investigating that gang-bang on the next block.* □ *There were reports of a gang-bang in the prison.* **2.** *tr. & in.* to rape in a group. □ *The pack of thugs set out to gang-bang some innocent victim.* □ *Why can't they stop gang-banging people?* **3.** *tr. & in.* to gang up on someone or something.* □ *They looked like they were going to gang-bang me.* □ *They're always gang-banging. The punks!*

**gangbusters** ['gæŋbəstɚz] **1.** *n.* a wild, busy, and successful event. □ *Our party was truly gangbusters, for sure.* □ *The explosion and fire two streets over was really gangbusters for a while.* **2.** See *like gangbusters.*

**gangster 1.** *n.* a hoodlum; a thug. □ *The gangsters run the whole town.* □ *Doesn't Bruno just look like a gangster?* **2.** *n.* marijuana; a marijuana cigarette. (Drugs.) □ *Max flipped him a gangster and winked.* □ *How many gangsters does Max carry with him?*

**gangster pill** *n.* barbiturate tablet or capsule. (Drugs.) □ *Molly is having trouble with gangster pills.* □ *Stay off those gangster pills.*

**Gangway!** ['gæŋwe] *exclam.* "Get out of the way!" □ *Gangway! Here I come!* □ *Make way for the passengers! Gangway!*

**ganja** AND **ganjah, ghanja** ['gɑndʒə OR 'gænd ʒə] *n.* marijuana. (Drugs. See also *gunja.*) □ *All that kid thinks about is ganja.* □ *Max only deals with ganjah.*

**ganjah** See *ganja.*

**GAPO** AND **gapo** ['gæpo] *n.* "giant armpit odor"; a bad underarm odor. □ *Who's got the gapo?* □ *That cab driver really has the GAPO.*

**gapper** ['gæpɚ] *n.* a drug addict in the early stages of withdrawal. (Drugs. Refers to yawning.) □ *The junk tank has*

*a couple of gappers in it.* □ *A gapper can get sort of frantic.*

**garbage 1.** *n.* nonsense; gibberish. □ *He's just talking garbage.* □ *I've heard too much garbage here today.* **2.** *n.* jumbled computer code. □ *All I get is garbage on the screen.* □ *If you put garbage into the computer, you'll get garbage out.* **3.** *n.* low-quality drugs. (Drugs.) □ *Max would never sell anybody garbage.* □ *A lot of what's on the streets these days is just garbage.*

**garbage freak** AND **garbagehead** *n.* an addict who will take any drug. (Drugs.) □ *We don't know what she took. She was such a garbage freak.* □ *The garbageheads will take beans or anything else.*

**garbagehead** See the previous entry.

**garbage mouth** *n.* someone who uses obscene language. □ *Quiet, garbage mouth! Watch your language.* □ *Who's the garbage mouth making all the noise?*

**garbage something down** AND **garbage down something** *tr.* to gobble something up; to bolt something down. □ *Don't garbage your food down!* □ *That guy will garbage down almost anything.*

**gargle 1.** *in.* to drink liquor. □ *They sat and gargled for an hour or two.* □ *Let's go out and gargle for a while.* **2.** *n.* liquor; a drink of liquor. □ *You want some more gargle?* □ *Pour me a little of that gargle, if you please.*

**gargle factory** *n.* a saloon; a tavern. □ *Gary spends a lot of time at the gargle factory.* □ *He should open his own gargle factory.*

**gargler** *n.* a drinker; a drunkard. □ *You are going to turn into a gargler if you don't let up on your drinking.* □ *Some old gargler froze to death last night.*

**gas 1.** *n.* intestinal gas. □ *The baby has gas and will cry for a while longer.* □ *I'm not too well, but I think it's just gas.* **2.** *n.* nonsense. □ *All we got in class today was gas.* □ *Hey, that's about enough of your gas.* **3.** *in.* to talk nonsense; to brag. (See *gasbag.*) □ *Pay no attention. She's just gassing.* □ *Stop gassing for a minute and listen.* **4.** *in.* to have a good time. □ *We gassed all evening.* □ *Let's go out and gas tonight, how about it?* **5.** *n.* a joke; a prank; a wild time. □ *The party was a gas.* □ *What a gas! I had a great time.* **6.** *n.* liquor, especially inferior liquor. □ *You want some more gas?* □ *Pour me a little more of that gas, will you?* **7.** AND **gas up** *in.* to drink excessively; to get drunk. □ *Let's go out and gas up!* □ *I come home every night and find that you've been gassing all day.*

**gasbag** *n.* a braggart. □ *What's the old gasbag going on about now?* □ *Harry is such a gasbag when he gets going about himself.*

**gas-guzzler** *n.* a large automobile that uses much gasoline. □ *I got rid of my gas-guzzler and got a smaller car.* □ *The old gas-guzzlers were certainly comfortable.*

**gash bucket** *n.* a refuse bucket; a bucket used as a urinal. (Underworld and military.) □ *Don't kick over the gash bucket over there!* □ *Why don't you go dump the gash bucket?*

**gas-passer** *n.* a jocular nickname for an anesthetist. (Hospitals.) □ *My gosh! The gas-passer charged almost as much as the surgeon.* □ *The gas-passer put a needle in my arm.*

**gassed (up)** *mod.* alcohol or drug intoxicated. □ *Fred is gassed up and very wobbly.* □ *He was too gassed up to drive home.*

**gate** *n.* sending (someone) away. (Always with *the.*) □ *I could see in his eyes that it was the gate for me.* □ *I got the gate, but I was going to leave anyway.*

**gaucho** ['gautʃo] *tr. & in.* to expose the buttocks (at someone), usually through a car window; to *moon.* □ *Victor gauchoed the cops as they went by.* □ *Victor would gaucho at the drop of a hat—so to speak.*

**gauge** See *gage.*

**gauge-butt** AND **gage-butt** ['gedʒbət] *n.* a marijuana cigarette. (Drugs.) □ *You got a gage-butt?* □ *Gimme a hit off your gauge-butt, will ya?*

**gay** [ge] **1.** *mod.* alcohol intoxicated. □ *After about an hour of guzzling, we were more than a little gay.* □ *He got a little gay and slipped under the table.* **2.** *mod.* homosexual; having to do with homosexual matters or interests. □ *Is this a gay bar?* □ *Is he gay?* □ *These gay guys*

seem to be having a good time. **3.** *n.* a homosexual person. □ *The gays were a little upset at the remark.* □ *Some of the gays just got up and left.* **4.** *mod.* weird; undesirable. (Teens.) □ *Stop acting so gay.* □ *I'm not going to wear that gay parka!*

**gay as pink ink** *mod.* having to do with an obviously homosexual person, usually a male. □ *Who said Ron's as gay as pink ink?* □ *These two guys—as gay as pink ink—came in together.*

**gazinkus** AND **gazunkus** [gə'zɪŋkəs AND gə'zəŋkəs] *n.* a gadget. □ *Where is the gazinkus I use for opening paint cans?* □ *Is this the little gazinkus you were looking for?*

**gazizzey** AND **gazob** [gə'zɪzi AND gə'zɑb] *n.* a fool. □ *What gazizzey put the sugar in the salt shaker?* □ *Don't call me a gazob!*

**gazob** See the previous entry.

**gazoo** [gə'zu] *n.* the buttocks; the anus. □ *He fell down flat, smack on his gazoo.* □ *Look at the monstrous gazoo on that guy.*

**gazoony** [gə'zuni] *n.* a bully or strongarm man. (Underworld.) □ *Bruno didn't like being called a gazoony, although that is what he is.* □ *A couple of gazoonies stood outside looking menacing.*

**gazumph** [gə'zumpf] **1.** *tr.* to raise the price of a house after it is sold. □ *They tried to gazumph the price at the closing.* □ *I just knew that the owner was going to gazumph the final figure.* **2.** *tr.* to subject someone to the raising of the price of a house after it is sold. □ *They tried to gazumph me!* □ *If they try to gazumph you, tell them to forget the deal.*

**G.B.** See *goofball.*

**G.B.'ed** ['dʒi'bid] *mod.* "Goofballed"; drug intoxicated. (Drugs.) □ *Tod is G.B.'ed again.* □ *Gert got G.B.'ed fairly often before the accident.*

**gear 1.** *mod.* excellent. □ *This jazz is really gear!* □ *Man, what a gear pizza!* **2.** *n.* '*'; an asterisk. □ *Why is there a gear after this word?* □ *The gear stands for anything you want it to stand for.*

**gee** [dʒi] **1.** *n.* a portion of liquor, a gallon or a single drink. □ *You want another gee of this booze?* □ *How about* *a gee for me?* **2.** *exclam.* "Wow!" (An abbreviation of *Jesus!*, although not always recognized as such. Usually **Gee!**) □ *Gee! What a mess!* □ *Golly gee, do I have to?* **3.** *mod.* "gross"; disgusting. (The initial letter of *gross*.) □ *This is just too gee!* □ *Tiffany is acting way gee lately.*

**geedis** See *geetis.*

**geedunk** [gi'dəŋk OR 'gidəŋk] *n.* ice cream. □ *Let's go out and get some geedunk for dessert.* □ *Pineapple on chocolate geedunk? Yuck!*

**geed up** AND **gheed up** ['dʒid... AND 'gid...] *mod.* alcohol or drug intoxicated. (Drugs. Old.) □ *Everybody was geed up and singing.* □ *Old Tom was gheed up a lot.*

**geegaw** AND **gewgaw, googaw** ['gigɔ AND 'gugɔ] *n.* a gadget; a bauble. □ *Now that's a cute little geegaw.* □ *What do you do with these gewgaws? Hang them on a tree?*

**geek** AND **geke** [gik] **1.** *n.* a disgusting and repellent person; a *creep.* □ *The convention was a seething morass of pushy sales geeks and glad-handers.* □ *Who's the geek who just came in?* **2.** *n.* an earnest student; a hardworking student. □ *Merton is a geek, but he will go places with his brains.* □ *It looks like the geeks are taking over this campus. How gross!*

**geetis** AND **geedus, geetus** ['gidəs] *n.* money. □ *That kind of car takes a lot of geetis, doesn't it?* □ *I don't have the geetis to throw around on something like that.*

**geez** AND **geeze** [giz] **1.** *tr. & in.* to inject a drug. (Drugs.) □ *Gert geezed herself and lay down.* □ *She's in the back, geezing.* **2.** *n.* an injection of a drug. (Drugs.) □ *Another geez before bedtime would hold poor Gert till morning.* □ *Give her a geeze, will ya?*

**geezed (up)** AND **geesed (up)** *mod.* alcohol or drug intoxicated. □ *Gert was geezed up by ten in the evening.* □ *Why isn't Max always geesed?*

**geezer** ['gizɚ] **1.** *n.* a strange old man; an old *buzzard.* □ *Who's the old geezer with the straw hat on?* □ *He is a nice geezer, but a little talkative.* **2.** *n.* a drink of liquor. □ *Toss down a geezer of this* *stuff and see how you like it.* □ *Can I have another geezer of this firewater?* **3.** *n.* a dose of a drug. (Drugs.) □ *Gert said she needed a geezer.* □ *Just a little geezer and I'll feel great.*

**gender-bender 1.** *n.* a device that changes electrical plugs or sockets to the opposite gender—male to female, female to male. □ *You need what's called a gender-bender to match those plugs.* □ *I tried a gender-bender, but it won't work.* **2.** *mod.* having to do with something that obscures male/female distinctions. □ *Those gender-bender hair styles can be confusing.* □ *He always wears gender-bender clothes.*

**genuine article** ['dʒɛnjəwən 'ɑrtɪk] OR 'dʒɛn'ju'wɑin 'ɑrtɪk]] *n.* the real thing rather than a substitute. □ *Is this the genuine article or some cheap made-in-U.S.A. substitute?* □ *I'll take the genuine article, thanks.*

**george\* 1.\*** *tr. & in.* to seduce and copulate (with someone, usually a woman). (Caution with topic.) □ *They say he georges her a lot.* □ *They were off somewhere georging.* **2.\*** *n.* a bowel movement. (Euphemistic. Caution with topic.) □ *I gotta go take a george. Back in a minute.* □ *I'm okay. Nothing a good george wouldn't cure.*

**German goiter** See *Milwaukee goiter.*

**Geronimo!** [dʒə'rɑnəmo] *exclam.* "Here I go!" (Originally said by parachutists leaving a plane. From Spanish for *Jerome.*) □ *There's my cue. Geronimo!* □ *Here goes nothing. Geronimo!*

**get a bang out of someone or something** AND **get a kick out of someone or something** *tr.* to get a thrill from someone or something. □ *I always get a bang out of her jokes.* □ *She gets a kick out of her grandchildren.*

**get a buzz out of someone or something** *tr.* to get some humor from someone or something. (See also *give someone a buzz.*) □ *I thought you'd get a buzz out of that gag.* □ *I hope you get a buzz out of Ted. He's a funny guy.*

**get a can on** AND **get on a can** *tr.* to get drunk. (Compare to *tie one on.*) □ *Let's go out tonight and get a can on.* □ *The entire office staff got on a can to celebrate the contract.*

**get across** *in.* to project oneself (to someone); to succeed. □ *I really want to get across in life.* □ *When I meet a prospective employer, I want to do everything possible to get across.*

**get a fix** AND **get a gift** *tr.* to buy drugs; to take a dose of drugs. (Drugs.) □ *Gert had to get home and get a fix.* □ *What did Molly mean when she said she had to get a gift fast?*

**Get a life!** *exclam.* "Change your life radically!" (Compare to *Get real!*) □ *You are such a twit! Get a life!* □ *Get a life, you clown!*

**get a load off one's feet** AND **take a load off one's feet** *tr.* to sit down and relax. □ *Sit down and get a load off your feet.* □ *Take a load off your feet and have a drink.*

**get a load off one's mind** *tr.* to say what one is thinking; to speak one's mind; to talk something out. □ *I'm sorry, but I just had to get a load off my mind.* □ *I think you'll feel better after you get a load off your mind.*

**get a load of something or someone** *tr.* to look at someone or something. □ *Wow, get a load of Fred!* □ *Get a load of the chrome on that set of wheels!*

**get a toehold** *tr.* to work one's way into some association or relationship. □ *As soon as I get a toehold in the company, I'll be more relaxed.* □ *Once he gets a toehold, you'll never get rid of him.*

**getaway** ['gɛtəwe] **1.** *n.* an escape from the law. (Originally underworld.) □ *Lefty made a quick getaway.* □ *There was no time to make a getaway, so we had to talk to Mrs. Wilson.* **2.** *n.* a quick vacation. □ *We took a little getaway to the Bahamas.* □ *What you need is a weekend getaway.*

**Get away!** ['gɛt ə'we] *exclam.* "Stop being a pest!"; "I don't believe you!" □ *Don't bother me! Get away!* □ *Get away! Nobody is that stupid!*

**Get a wiggle on!** *exclam.* to hurry up. □ *Get a wiggle on! We don't have all day!* □ *Hey, you guys! Get a wiggle on! We gotta finish before nightfall.*

**get behind someone or something 1.** *in.* to support someone or something. □ *Let's all get behind the party in the next election.* □ *Everybody got behind Tod and cheered him on.* **2.** *in.* [with *something*] to enjoy something, such as a drug or music. (Originally drugs.) □ *I'm really getting behind heavy metal.* □ *Sam got behind some acid and got stuck there.*

**get down 1.** *in.* to lay one's money on the table. (Gambling.) □ *Okay, everybody get down.* □ *Get down, and let's get going!* **2.** *in.* to concentrate; to do something well. □ *I'm flunking two subjects, man. I gotta get down.* □ *Come on, Sam, pay attention. Get down and learn this stuff.* **3.** *in.* to copulate. (Black.) □ *Hey, let's get down!* □ *All Steve wants to do is get down all the time.*

**get down on someone** *in.* to be critical of someone; to *get on someone's case.* □ *Don't get down on me. I didn't do it!* □ *I'm gonna get down on him for that.*

**get down to some serious drinking** *in.* to settle down to a long session of drinking. □ *Well, now we can get down to some serious drinking.* □ *When the kids go to bed, let's get down to some serious drinking.*

**get down to the nitty-gritty** *in.* to get down to the basic facts. (See *nitty-gritty.*) □ *Stop messing around and get down to the nitty-gritty.* □ *If we could only get down to the nitty-gritty and stop wasting time.*

**get face** *tr.* to gain respect; to increase one's status. (The opposite of *lose face.*) □ *He's doing his best in life to get face.* □ *Let's do something to help her get face.*

**get hot 1.** *in.* to begin to get lucky, as in gambling. □ *I knew I was getting hot when I got all the right cards.* □ *If I could only get hot, I might win back everything I lost.* **2.** *in.* to become busy or hectic. □ *Things always get hot around here toward the end of the month.* □ *When things start getting hot, we have to hire more people.*

**get in bad (with someone)** *in.* to get into trouble with someone. □ *I tried not to get in bad with Wally.* □ *We got in bad with each other from the start.*

**get in on the act** *in.* to become involved in something. (The involvement is not necessarily welcome.) □ *Everybody wants to get in on the act.* □ *Why are you trying to get in on the act?*

**get in the groove** *in.* to become attuned to something. □ *I was uncomfortable at first, but now I'm beginning to get in the groove.* □ *Fred began to get in the groove, and things went more smoothly.*

**get into something** *in.* to become deeply involved with something. □ *I got into computers when I was in junior high school.* □ *When did you get into foreign films?*

**get it 1.** *tr.* to understand a joke; to understand a point of information. □ *Sorry. I don't get it.* □ *Don't you get it?* **2.** *tr.* to get punished. □ *I just know I'm going to get it when I get home.* □ *You're going to get it all right!*

**get it (all) together** *tr.* to get oneself organized; to get mentally adjusted. □ *When I get it together, I'll try to go back to school.* □ *Try to get it all together and come back to work next week, okay?*

**get it in the neck** *tr.* to receive something bad, such as punishment or criticism. (See *pain in the neck*.) □ *You are going to get it in the neck for that remark.* □ *Jimmy was afraid he'd get it in the neck for being late.*

**get it off\*** *tr.* to achieve sexual release; to copulate. (Caution with topic.) □ *Harry kept saying he had to get it off or die. What's wrong with Harry?* □ *The entire crew of the yacht came ashore to get it off.*

**get it on\* 1.** *tr.* to begin something. □ *Time to go back to work. Let's get it on!* □ *Get it on, you guys! Time to start your engines.* **2.** *tr.* to begin dancing. □ *Let's go out there and get it on!* □ *He wanted to get it on, but my feet hurt.* **3.\*** *tr.* (for people) to copulate. (Caution with topic.) □ *Come on, baby, let's get it on.* □ *I don't want to get it on with you or any other creep.* **4.** *tr.* to undertake to enjoy oneself. □ *I can really get it on with that slow jazz.* □ *Let's go listen to some new age and get it on.*

**get it out** *tr.* to tell (someone) about a problem; to pour out one's grief. □ *Come on, get it out. You'll feel better.* □ *He would feel better if he could get it out.*

**get it up** *tr.* to get excited about something. (Other taboo meanings, also.) □ *I just couldn't get it up about going off to college.* □ *Paul just couldn't get it up about life in general.*

**get lip** *tr.* to get some kissing; to neck. (Teens.) □ *Jim's been out getting lip again. Look at the lipstick.* □ *These kids talk about getting lip. Ye gods, how crude!*

**Get lost!** *exclam.* "Go away!"; "Beat it!" □ *Get lost, you're bothering me!* □ *Quit following me. Get lost!*

**get mad (at something)** *in.* to muster great physical strength and determination in order to do something. □ *You're gonna have to get mad at it if you want to move it.* □ *Come on, you guys. Get mad.*

**Get my drift?** AND **Do you get my drift?** *interrog.* "Do you understand me?" □ *Get my drift? Should I explain it again?* □ *Do you get my drift, or shall I run through it again?*

**get naked** *in.* to enjoy oneself thoroughly; to relax and enjoy oneself. □ *Let's all go out and get naked tonight.* □ *Man, I feel like getting naked tonight.*

**get narkied** [...'narkid] *in.* to inject drugs; to become addicted. (Drugs.) □ *Rocko only got narkied once in his life.* □ *Gert couldn't wait to get narkied.*

**get nowhere fast** *in.* to make very poor progress. □ *We are getting nowhere fast around here.* □ *I'm getting nowhere fast in this job. I quit.*

**get off 1.** *in.* to reach an understanding with someone. (Not slang.) □ *We just weren't getting off well at all.* □ *How well do you get off with Ralph?* **2.** See *get off (on something)*.

**get off one's rear** *in.* to get up and get busy. □ *It's time to get off your rear and get to work.* □ *Hey, Chuck, get off your rear! There's work to be done.*

**get off (on something) 1.** *in.* to get pleasure from something. □ *I don't get off on music anymore.* □ *I listen, but I just don't get off.* **2.** *in.* to take a drug and experience a *rush*. (Drugs.) □ *Max likes to get off, but he's got his business to run.* □ *Molly likes getting off better than anything else.*

**get off someone's back** AND **get off someone's case** *in.* to stop annoying someone. □ *I wish you'd get off my back.* □ *Get off my case! You aren't my mother.*

**get off someone's case** See the previous entry.

**get off the dime** *in.* (for something or someone) to start moving. (To get off the dime that one stopped on in "stop on a dime.") □ *I wish this organization could get off the dime.* □ *If this project gets off the dime, we'll be okay.*

**get one right here** *tr.* to affect one deeply in a specific way. (Usually accompanied with a hand gesture showing exactly where one is affected: the heart = lovingly, the stomach or bowels = sickeningly.) □ *That sort of thing gets me right here.* □ *Tod clasped his hand to his chest and said, "That sort of thing gets me right here."*

**get one's act together** AND **get one's shit together\*, get one's stuff together 1.** *tr.* to organize oneself; to get one's possessions organized. (Caution with *shit*.) □ *Let me get my act together, and I'll be right with you.* □ *I'll get my stuff together and be right with you.* **2.** AND **get one's head together** (Caution with *shit*.) *tr.* to calm down and get mentally organized. □ *As soon as I get my head together, I can be of more help.* □ *Get your act together and start living again.*

**get one's bowels in an uproar** *tr.* to become overly anxious or excited. □ *Cool it! Don't get your bowels in an uproar.* □ *Fred's always getting his bowels in an uproar about nothing.*

**get one's head together** See *get one's act together.*

**get one's hooks into someone or something 1.** *tr.* to get a hold of someone or something; to gain control of someone or something. □ *I want to get my hooks into the operation of this organization.* □ *If I could get my hooks into the control of the company, I would change things for the better.* **2.** *tr.* [with *someone*] (for a woman) to succeed in "capturing" a specific man. □ *She just can't wait to get her hooks into Chuck.* □ *When she got her hooks into him, she decided he wasn't so great after all.*

**get one's kick's (from someone or something)** *tr.* to get pleasure from someone or something. □ *Do you get your kicks from this sort of thing?* □ *I get my kicks*

*from Billy Simpson. What a great entertainer!*

**get one's lumps** *tr.* to get the result or punishment one deserves. (Compare to *take one's lumps.*) □ *If she keeps acting that way, she'll get her lumps.* □ *We will see that Dave gets his lumps.*

**get one's nose cold** *tr.* to *snort* cocaine. (Drugs.) □ *Max is always ready to get his nose cold.* □ *Rocko has never gotten his nose cold in his life.*

**get one's nose out of joint** *tr.* to feel slighted by something someone has done; to take offense at something. (See also *put someone's nose out of joint.*) □ *You get your nose out of joint too easily about stuff like that.* □ *Now, don't get your nose out of joint. She didn't mean it.*

**get one's rocks off (on something)** *tr.* to enjoy something. (Other taboo meanings, also.) □ *I really get my rocks off on heavy metal.* □ *I've listened to the stuff, but I sure don't get my rocks off on it.*

**get one's shit together** See *get one's act together.*

**get one's stuff together** See *get one's act together.*

**get one's teeth into something** AND **sink one's teeth into something** *tr.* to undertake to do something. □ *I can't wait to sink my teeth into that Wallace job.* □ *Here, sink your teeth into this and see if you can't manage this project.*

**get one's ticket punched** *tr.* to die; to be killed. (Literally, to be cancelled.) □ *Poor Chuck got his ticket punched while he was waiting for a bus.* □ *Watch out there, or you'll get your ticket punched.*

**get one's wings** *tr.* to use *heavy drugs* for the first time; to succeed in becoming a drug addict. (Drugs. See *give someone wings.*) □ *Gert got her wings after fiddling around with stuff for a long time.* □ *Max got his wings at about age 12.*

**get on someone's case** *in.* to start harassing someone about a personal problem; to annoy someone. □ *I'll get on Tom's case about being late so much.* □ *I'm sorry, I won't get on your case anymore.*

**get on the stick** *in.* to get organized and get busy. □ *Get on the stick and get this job done!* □ *Come on, you guys. Let's get on the stick!*

**Get out of my face!** *exclam.* "Stop arguing with me!"; "Stand back! Don't confront me with your arguments and challenges!" □ *Beat it! Get out of my face!* □ *Get outa my face if you know what's good for you.*

**Get out of town!** *exclam.* "Beat it!"; "Get out of here!" □ *Go away, you bother me! Get out of town!* □ *You'd better get out of town, my friend. You are a pest.*

**get (out) while the getting's good** AND **get (out) while the goin's good** *phr.* to leave while it is still safe or possible to do so. □ *I could tell that it was time for me to get while the gettin's good.* □ *I told her she should get out while the goin's good.*

**Get real!** *exclam.* "Start acting realistically!" (Compare to *Get a life!*) □ *Hey, chum! You are way off base! Get real!* □ *Get real! Wake up to reality!*

**get right** See *get straight.*

**get smart (with someone)** *in.* to become fresh with someone; to talk back to someone. □ *Don't you get smart with me!* □ *If you get smart again, I'll bop you.*

**get someone going** *tr.* to get someone excited; to get someone talking excitedly. □ *I guess I really got him going on the subject of politics.* □ *The whole business really makes me mad. Don't get me going.*

**get someone's goat** *tr.* to irritate someone. □ *Don't let Mary get your goat. She's just irritable today.* □ *Everybody seems to be getting my goat today.*

**get someone's motor running** **1.** *tr.* to get someone excited. □ *What'll I have to do to get your motor running about algebra?* □ *I've got some news that'll really get your motor running.* **2.** *tr.* to get someone sexually aroused. □ *She knows how to get his motor running.* □ *It's funny how that wild music gets her motor running.*

**get some shut-eye** *tr.* to get some sleep. □ *I need to get home and get some shut-eye before I do anything else.* □ *We all could use some shut-eye.*

**get something across (to someone)** AND **get something over (to someone)** *tr.* to succeed in making someone understand something. (Compare to *get across, put something across.*) □ *I hope I'm getting this across to you in a way you can understand it.* □ *I'll try to get it over again. This time I'll go slower.*

**get something going (with someone)** *tr.* to start a romance with someone. □ *Alice wants to get something going with Tod.* □ *Mary and Sam got something going.*

**get something over (to someone)** See *get something across (to someone).*

**get straight** AND **get right** *in.* to take a dose of a drug to end drug craving. (Drugs.) □ *Gert needed a fix to get straight.* □ *I need to get right before anything else.*

**get the ax** See *get the sack.*

**get the drop on someone** **1.** *tr.* to succeed in getting an advantage over someone. □ *I guess I got the drop on you because I was early.* □ *I got the drop on almost everybody by sending in my registration by mail.* **2.** *tr.* (for person A) to manage to get a gun aimed at person B before person B can aim back (at person A). (The gun is then "dropped" by person B.) □ *Rocko got the drop on Max in a flash.* □ *Max was too stoned to get the drop on Rocko.*

**get the goods on someone** *tr.* to uncover incriminating evidence against someone. □ *The fuzz has the goods on Mr. Big.* □ *The IRS tried to get the goods on Rocko, but Rocko knows all the angles.*

**Get the hell out (of here)!** * *exclam.* "Get out!" (Caution with *hell.*) □ *Go on, get the hell out of here!* □ *Get the hell out. Beat it!*

**Get the lead out (of your ass)!** * AND **Shake the lead out!** *exclam.* "Get moving!"; "Hurry up!" (Crude. It is assumed that one has buttocks of lead. Caution with *ass.*) □ *Come on, you turkeys. Get the lead out!* □ *Shake the lead out! I want it done today, not next week.*

**Get the message?** AND **Get the picture?** *interrog.* "Do you understand?"; "Are you able to figure out what is meant?" □ *Things are tough around here, and we need everyone's cooperation. Get the picture?* □ *We don't need lazy people around here. Get the message?*

**get the nod** *tr.* to be chosen. (See also *give someone the nod.*) □ *Fred got the nod for class treasurer.* □ *I hope I get the nod for the job.*

**Get the picture?** See *Get the message?*

**get there** *in.* to get drunk. □ *Another hour of drinking and Tod knew he was going to get there.* □ *Those guys have all got there. Now what?*

**get the sack** AND **get the ax** *tr.* to be dismissed from one's employment. □ *Poor Tom got the sack today. He's always late.* □ *I was afraid that Sally was going to get the ax.*

**get the show on the road** *tr.* to get (something) started. □ *Let's get started! Get the show on the road!* □ *Get the show on the road. We don't have all day.*

**get to someone** **1.** *in.* (for someone or something) to annoy someone. □ *The whole business began to get to me after a while.* □ *Her remark got to me after a while.* **2.** *in.* (for someone or something) to please or entice someone. □ *Lovely flowers and things like that get to me.* □ *Sad music gets to me and makes me cry.*

**get-up** **1.** *n.* an addict's first dose of the day. (Drugs.) □ *He always took a get-up first thing in the morning.* □ *He was very uncomfortable until he got his get-up.* **2.** *n.* an outfit or costume; an unusual selection of clothing. (Usually **getup**.) □ *That's the craziest looking getup I've ever seen.* □ *Where did you get that strange getup?*

**get wise to someone or something** *in.* to catch on to someone or something. □ *The goon squad is going to get wise to what you're doing and nab you.* □ *The boss is getting wise to what John is up to.*

**get with it** **1.** *in.* to modernize one's attitudes and behavior. □ *Get with it, Merton. Get real!* □ *You really have to get with it, Ernie.* **2.** *in.* to hurry up and get busy; to be more industrious with something. □ *Get with it; we've got a lot to do.* □ *Let's get with it. There's a lot of work to be done.*

**get with someone** *in.* to find out about someone; to get to know someone. (Black.) □ *I'd really like to get with her, but she's so distant.* □ *I was just beginning to get with Alice when she left.*

**gewgaw** See *geegaw.*

**ghanja** See *ganja.*

**(ghetto) blaster** AND **(ghetto) box** ['gɛdo blæstɚ AND 'gɛdo baks] *n.* a portable stereo radio. (Often carried on the shoulder, especially by blacks.) □ *Hey, turn down that ghetto blaster in here!* □ *You can't bring that box on this bus!*

**(ghetto) box** See the previous entry.

**ghost turd*** *n.* a wad of lint, as found under a bed. (Caution with *turd.*) □ *There's a lot of ghost turds under the bed.* □ *Sweep out those ghost turds and get rid of them.*

**G.I.B.*** AND **GIB*** *mod.* "good in bed"; good as a sexual partner. (Caution with topic.) □ *Tod lets on that he's G.I.B.* □ *How does he know he's GIB?*

**gibber-gabber** ['dʒɪbɚdʒæbɚ] *n.* nonsense; gossip and chatter. □ *There sure is a lot of gibber-gabber coming from your room, Jimmy.* □ *What's all this gibber-gabber about?*

**Giddy up!** ['gɪdi...] *exclam.* "Move faster!" (Said to a horse to start it moving. Also said to people or things as a joke.) □ *Giddy up, Charlie! It's time to start moving.* □ *Let's get going, chum. Giddy up!*

**giffed** [gɪft] *mod.* alcohol intoxicated. (From *T.G.I.F* "Thank God it's Friday." Said of people who celebrate the end of the work week with liquor.) □ *He left the tavern pretty giffed.* □ *She was pretty giffed for just a few beers.*

**gift of gab** *n.* the ability to speak well in public; the ability to persuade people verbally; the ability to speak well extemporaneously. □ *Gary has the gift of gab, but it doesn't get him anywhere.* □ *I wish I had the gift of gab. I'm just so shy.*

**gig** **1.** *n.* a onetime job; an engagement. (Musicians.) □ *I had a gig out on the west side, but I couldn't get there.* □ *The gig was canceled because of the snow.* **2.** *in.* to play or perform. (Musicians.) □ *I didn't gig at all last week. I'm getting hungry for a job.* □ *I'm happiest when*

*I'm gigging.* **3.** *n.* any job of an assignment nature; a onetime job such as when a newspaper reporter is assigned to write a particular story. □ *I didn't want that election gig, but I got it anyway.* □ *Wally is tired of getting the crime gigs.* **4.** *n.* a bother; an annoyance; a job. (Black.) □ *Man, this paperwork is such a gig.* □ *This day's a gig. I've had it.*

**gigamaree** [gɪgəməˈri] *n.* a gadget. □ *Toss me one of those little copper gigamarees, will ya?* □ *Is this the gigamaree you want?*

**giggle goo** [ˈgɪgl̩ gu] *n.* liquor. □ *Can I pour you a little of that giggle goo?* □ *Haven't you had about enough of that giggle goo?*

**G.I.G.O.** AND **GIGO** *phr.* "garbage in, garbage out." (Computers. Acronym. If you get garbage out of a computer, it's because you put garbage in. See also *D.I.D.O.*) □ *The program failed, and I know it's my fault. You know, GIGO.* □ *G.I.G.O. is my theme song. I get out just what I deserve.*

**gimme\*** [ˈgɪmi] *phr.* "give me." (Eye-dialect. Typical spoken English. Caution with use in writing.) □ *Do you wanna gimme the thingy and lemme go ahead with my work?* □ *Gimme another one.*

**gimp** [gɪmp] **1.** *n.* a lame person. (Originally underworld. Otherwise derogatory.) □ *Lefty tried to mug an old gimp with a cane.* □ *The gimp came hobbling along, muttering something under his breath.* **2.** *in.* to limp about. □ *I've been gimping a little bit since my accident.* □ *I'll gimp over there as soon as I can. It'll take a while on these crutches.*

**gimpy** [ˈgɪmpi] **1.** *mod.* crippled; lame. □ *I got a gimpy leg. I'll catch up in a minute.* □ *He's sort of gimpy since the football season.* **2.** *n.* a police officer. (Also a rude term of address. A pun on *lame*, an inept person.) □ *Here comes gimpy, swinging his stick.* □ *Gimpy has been around asking about you.*

**ginhead** *n.* a drunkard. □ *Gert could have ended up a ginhead, but she went another route instead.* □ *A couple of ginheads sat in the corner booth silently.*

**gin mill** AND **gin dive, gin palace** *n.* a saloon; a low liquor establishment. □ *Fred hit every gin mill on the way home.* □ *You'll find Bob in some gin dive on the west side of town.*

**girl 1.** *n.* a woman; a young woman. (Objectionable to some as demeaning to women.) □ *A bunch of us girls got together for coffee today.* □ *Would you girls care to come over to my house next week?* **2.** AND **girly** *n.* cocaine. (Drugs. See *lady.*) □ *You got any of that girly?* □ *Max is totally out of girl. It's a famine.* **3.** *n.* the queen of playing cards. (See *bitch.*) □ *What I needed in that last hand was the girl.* □ *Come on, dealer, I need that girl!*

**girlie magazine** *n.* a magazine featuring pictures of nude women. □ *The girlie magazines were hidden under the counter.* □ *Some creepy character asked Sally if she would pose for a girlie magazine.*

**girlie show** *n.* a performance featuring nude women. □ *Bob and Tod went to the city and tried to get into a girlie show.* □ *This movie has turned out to be nothing but a girlie show.*

**git-go** [ˈgɪtgo] *n.* the very beginning. (Black. See also *from (the) git-go.*) □ *Clear back at the git-go, I told you this wouldn't work.* □ *He's been gritching ever since git-go.*

**giveaway** *n.* something that reveals a fact that was meant to be concealed. (Often with *dead.*) □ *The way he was walking was a giveaway to the fact that he was the one who was injured.* □ *The look on her face was a dead giveaway.*

**Give it a rest!** *exclam.* "Shut up!" (The "it" is a mouth. Compare to *Give me a rest!*) □ *I've heard enough. Give it a rest!* □ *Give it a rest! You talk too much.*

**give it the gun** *tr.* to gun an engine; to rev an engine up. □ *Give it the gun for a minute.* □ *I gave it the gun, and it backfired.*

**Give it up!** *exclam.* "Quit now!"; "Enough is enough!" □ *Oh, give it up! You can't do it right.* □ *Give it up! You can't pitch!*

**Give me a break!** *exclam.* "That is enough!"; "Stop it!" □ *Do you have to go on and on? Give me a break.* □ *Give me a break, you guys! That's enough!*

**Give me a rest!** *exclam.* "Lay off!"; "That is enough!" (Compare to *Give it a rest!*) □ *Haven't I told you everything you need to know? Give me a rest.* □ *Give me a rest! I've heard enough.*

**Give me five!** See the following entry.

**Give me (some) skin!** AND **Give me five!, Slip me five!** *exclam.* "Shake my hand!" (A request for some form of hand touching in greeting. See *give someone five, high five.*) □ *Hey, man! Give me some skin!* □ *Give me five, my man!*

**give (out) with something** *in.* to give out information. □ *Come on, give out with the facts, man.* □ *Give with the info. We're in a hurry.*

**give someone a buzz** **1.** *tr.* to give someone a telephone call. □ *Give me a buzz sometime.* □ *I'll give her a buzz tonight and ask her.* **2.** *tr.* to give someone a chuckle or a bit of enjoyment. □ *It always gives me a buzz to watch Sally do her act.* □ *Your little joke gave me a buzz.*

**give someone a (good) talking to** *tr.* to scold someone; to lecture someone sternly. □ *I think I'll have to give Tod a good talking to.* □ *The teacher gave Jimmy a talking to.*

**give someone a (good) working over** *tr.* to scold or beat someone. □ *The boss gave me a good working over before firing me.* □ *Fred really gave her a working over about her performance on the project.*

**give someone an earful** **1.** *tr.* to scold someone. □ *I'm going to give Ralph an earful for doing that.* □ *Sally gave Sam an earful for the way he treated Mary.* **2.** *tr.* to tell someone surprising secrets. □ *Sally gave Wally an earful about Tod and the things he said about Mary.* □ *Wally gave Sally an earful about Tod's tax problems.*

**give someone a pain** *tr.* to annoy or bother someone. □ *Please don't give me a pain. I've had a hard day.* □ *You give me a pain!*

**give someone five** **1.** *tr.* to give someone a helping hand. □ *Hey, give me five over here for a minute, will ya?* □ *I gotta give this guy five with the crate. Be right with you.* **2.** *tr.* to slap hands in greeting. (See *high five, Give me five!*) □ *Jerry*

gave John five as they passed in the corridor. □ *Don tried to give me five in class, but missed.*

**give someone hell\*** **1.\*** *tr.* to bawl someone out; to scold someone severely. (Caution with *hell.*) □ *The boss just gave me hell about it.* □ *I'm really going to give Tom hell when he gets home.* **2.\*** *tr.* to trouble someone. (Caution with *hell.*) □ *My arthritis is giving me hell in this weather.* □ *This problem is giving us hell at the office.*

**give someone the ax** **1.** *tr.* to dismiss someone from employment. □ *They had to give Paul the ax because he was so unproductive.* □ *I was afraid they would give me the ax.* **2.** *tr.* to divorce someone. □ *Mary gave Fred the ax after only 6 months.* □ *She gave him the ax because he wouldn't stop smoking like he promised.*

**give someone the brushoff** *tr.* to repel someone; to ignore someone. (See *brushoff, brush someone off.*) □ *Sam was afraid that Mary was going to give him the brushoff.* □ *The manager gave her the brushoff when she asked for a raise.*

**give someone the business** **1.** *tr.* to harass someone; to scold someone. □ *The guys have been giving me the business about my haircut.* □ *Sam was giving Tom the business about being late all the time.* **2.** *tr.* to kill someone. (Underworld.) □ *Lefty wanted to give Rocko the business for being so damn perfect.* □ *Mr. Big told Bruno to give Max the business.*

**give someone the finger** **1.** *tr.* to display the middle finger upright as a sign of derision. (The gesture is taboo.) □ *Did one of you guys give Ted the finger?* □ *Somebody gave the cop the finger.* **2.** *tr.* to mistreat someone; to insult someone. □ *You've been giving me the finger ever since I started working here. What's wrong?* □ *I'm tired of everybody giving me the finger around here just because I'm new.*

**give someone the gate** *tr.* to get rid of someone. □ *The chick was a pest, so I gave her the gate.* □ *He threatened to give me the gate, so I left.*

**give someone the go-by** *tr.* to bypass someone; to ignore someone. (See *go-*

*by*.) □ *Gert gave us all the go-by when she was so sick.* □ *I didn't mean to give you the go-by. I'm preoccupied, that's all.*

**give someone the nod 1.** *tr.* to signal someone by nodding. (Not slang.) □ *I gave Tod the nod, and he started the procedure.* □ *Just give me the nod when you are ready.* **2.** *tr.* to choose someone. (See *get the nod*.) □ *The committee gave Frank the nod for the job.* □ *They gave her the nod.*

**give someone the raspberry** *tr.* to make a rude noise with the lips at someone. (See *Bronx cheer, raspberry*.) □ *The audience gave him the raspberry, which gave him some second thoughts about his choice of career.* □ *Even after his grandstand play, they gave him the raspberry.*

**give someone the shaft** *tr.* to cheat or deceive someone; to mistreat someone. (See *shaft*.) □ *The boss really gave Wally the shaft.* □ *Somebody always gives me the shaft.*

**give someone the slip** *tr.* to escape from a pursuer. □ *We were on his tail until he gave us the slip.* □ *I can give her the slip in no time at all.*

**give someone wings** *tr.* to introduce someone to heroin by injection. (Drugs.) □ *Max just loves to give new customers wings.* □ *Gert was really anxious for him to give her wings.*

**give something to someone straight** AND **give something to someone fast** *tr.* to tell something to someone immediately and concisely. □ *Come on, give it to me straight. I can take it.* □ *Give it to me fast and don't waste time.*

**gizmo** ['gɪzmo] *n.* a gadget. □ *What is this silly little gizmo on the bottom for?* □ *This gizmo turns it on.*

**gizzy** ['gɪzi] *n.* marijuana. (Drugs.) □ *The cops found a little gizzy in the guy's pocket.* □ *Where'd you get this gizzy?*

**glad** *mod.* alcohol intoxicated. □ *After a few beers she was a mite glad.* □ *In fact, she was too glad to stand up.*

**glad-hand** *tr.* to greet someone effusively. □ *The Senator was glad-handing everyone in sight.* □ *He glad-handed Ernie and got a real earful.*

**glad-hander** *n.* someone who displays effusive friendship. □ *What a morass of eager glad-handers and glitz!* □ *The glad-handers were out in full force at the Independence Day parade.*

**glad rags** *n.* fancy clothes; best clothing. (See *rag*.) □ *You look pretty good in your glad rags.* □ *I'll get on my glad rags, and we'll go out tonight.*

**glamour puss** *n.* a person with a beautiful face. □ *I'm no glamour puss, but I'm no dog either.* □ *Now, Sally is what I would call a glamour puss.*

**glass gun** *n.* a hypodermic syringe. (Drugs.) □ *Gert broke her glass gun and had to improvise.* □ *A lot of those bangsters don't even use a glass gun.*

**glassy-eyed** AND **glass-eyed** *mod.* alcohol or drug intoxicated. □ *Mary is looking sort of glassy-eyed, and it's only midnight.* □ *Ernie is usually glass-eyed, but tonight it's much worse.*

**glazed (drunk)** AND **glazed (over)** *mod.* alcohol intoxicated. □ *She has had too much. She's glazed drunk.* □ *Fred looks a little glazed. I think he's done for.*

**gleep** [glip] *n.* a fool; an oaf. □ *What a gleep! Does he know what's what?* □ *Don't act like such a gleep!*

**glitch** [glɪtʃ] *n.* a defect; a bug. □ *There is a glitch in the computer program somewhere.* □ *I'm afraid there's a glitch in our plans.*

**glitz** [glɪts] *n.* flashiness and glamour. □ *The place was a morass of eager sales geeks and phony glitz.* □ *The glitz was blinding, and the substance was invisible.*

**glitzy** ['glɪtsi] *mod.* fashionable; glamorous. □ *It was a real glitzy place to hold a meeting.* □ *Some glitzy blonde sang a couple of songs, and then the band played again.*

**glom** [glɑm] **1.** *tr.* to steal something. (Underworld.) □ *Lefty glommed a little car for the evening.* □ *He gloms just about everything he needs.* **2.** *tr.* to take a look at someone or something. (Underworld.) □ *Glom this layout for a minute.* □ *Come over here and glom the view of the bank from this window.*

**glommed** [glɑmd] *mod.* arrested. (Underworld.) □ *Max got glommed on a* *speeding charge. I didn't even know he could drive. □ Glommed again! That's the story of my life.*

**glooch** [glutʃ] *n.* a drug addict whose senses have been degraded by drugs. (Drugs.) □ *Some old glooch was lurking around outside.* □ *This poor glooch was only about twenty and was shaking like a leaf every minute.*

**gloomy Gus** *n.* a sad or dismal person; a pessimist. □ *Don't be such a gloomy Gus, Wally.* □ *Well, gloomy Gus just came in again.*

**glop** [glɑp] **1.** *n.* unappetizing food; *gunk*; anything undesirable. □ *Do we have the same old glop again tonight?* □ *No, this is different glop.* **2.** *tr.* to slop or plop something (onto something). □ *She glopped something horrible onto my plate.* □ *Don't glop any of that pink stuff anywhere near me.*

**glorified** *mod.* overblown; over-hyped; phony. □ *Why, this is just a glorified potato chip!* □ *She's just a glorified dance-hall girl.*

**Glory be!** *exclam.* "Wow!" (Folksy.) □ *Glory be! What a wonderful surprise!* □ *I'm as pleased as could be. Glory be!*

**glory seeds** *n.* morning glory seeds used as a drug. (Drugs.) □ *Some kid ate so many glory seeds to get a high that he was really sick.* □ *Glory seeds were popular in the sixties when kids would take almost anything.*

**glow** *n.* a mild state of drug or alcohol intoxication. □ *She had a nice glow, but was by no means stewed.* □ *What was supposed to be a nice glow turned out to be a terrifying hallucination.*

**glow worm** *n.* a drunkard; an alcoholic. (From *glow*.) □ *You are turning into a regular glow worm.* □ *Gary came out of the bar and tripped over a napping glow worm near the entrance to the alley.*

**glued 1.** *mod.* arrested. (Underworld.) □ *Wally got glued for having over three hundred parking tickets.* □ *Max goes to great extremes to keep from getting glued.* **2.** *mod.* alcohol intoxicated. □ *Fred is glued and can't stand up.* □ *About three more beers and I'll be glued.*

**glue factory** *n.* the place where old horses are sent so their bones can be made into glue; a similar, imaginary

place for people. □ *I'm not as young as I used to be, but I'm not ready for the glue factory yet.* □ *If you can't keep up, we'll send you to the glue factory.*

**gluey** AND **gluer** *n.* a person, usually a teenager, who sniffs glue. (Drugs.) □ *Teddy is a gluey. That's why he's failing in school.* □ *The gluers stand a chance of having brain damage.*

**glug** [gləg] *n.* a gulp or shot of liquor. □ *Have another glug of this moonshine.* □ *I took one glug and spit it out.*

**glutz** [gləts] *n.* a slut; a woman of low morals. □ *I didn't say she is a glutz!* □ *Molly knows some old dames she would call glutzes.*

**G-man** ['dʒimæn] *n.* a government investigative agent; an F.B.I. agent. □ *The G-men busted in and started shooting.* □ *When I was a kid, I wanted to be a G-man.*

**gnarly** AND **narly** ['nɑrli] *mod.* excellent; great. (California.) □ *This pizza is too gnarly for words!* □ *Who is that narly guy in the white sweater?*

**go\* 1.** *n.* a try (at something). □ *Let me have a go at it this time.* □ *I'd like to have another go at it, if I can.* **2.** *n.* a drink of liquor; a dose of a drug. □ *She had one go and then sat back for a while.* □ *Another go and she was essentially stoned.* **3.** *in.* to urinate. □ *I gotta go!* □ *Jimmy's gonna go in his pants!* **4.\*** *tr.* to say or utter something. (Mostly teens. Caution with use in writing.) □ *So I go, "Gross!"* □ *Then she goes, "Like...," and just stops talking.*

**go-ahead** *n.* permission to proceed; the signal to go ahead. (Compare to *sayso*.) □ *We're ready to go as soon as we get the go-ahead.* □ *I gave him the go-ahead, and the tanks started moving in.*

**go all the way\*** *in.* to copulate; to carry necking all the way to copulation. (Euphemistic. Caution with topic.) □ *Did they go all the way?* □ *He keeps wanting me to go all the way.*

**go ape (over someone or something)** *in.* to become very excited over something. □ *I just go ape over chocolate.* □ *Sam went ape over Mary.*

**goat** *n.* a fast and powerful car; a Pontiac GTO. □ *Hey, man, where'd you get* *that goat?* □ *His goat conked out on him.*

**gob** [gɑb] **1.** *n.* a blob or mass of something. □ *I'd like a big gob of mashed potatoes, please.* □ *Take that horrid gob of gum out of your mouth!* **2.** *n.* a large amount of something. (Often in the plural.) □ *I've just got gobs of it if you need some.* □ *I need gobs of money to get through school.*

**go bananas** *in.* to go mildly crazy. (See *bananas.*) □ *Sorry, I just went bananas for a minute.* □ *I thought he was going to go bananas.*

**gobbledygook** ['gɑbḷdigʊk] **1.** *n.* nonsense; officialese or government gibberish. □ *I can't understand all this gobbledygook.* □ *They must have a full-time staff to dream up all this gobbledygook.* **2.** *n.* any mess, especially of food. □ *Dinner was just gobbledygook again.* □ *Do we have the same old gobbledygook tonight?*

**go belly up** See *turn belly up.*

**go blooey** AND **go flooey** [go 'blui AND go 'flui] *in.* to fall apart; to go out of order. □ *Suddenly, all my plans went blooey.* □ *I just hope everything doesn't go flooey at the last minute.*

**go-by** ['gobaɪ] *n.* an instance of ignoring or passing by (someone). (See *give someone the go-by.*) □ *I got the go-by from her every time I saw her.* □ *I find the go-by very insulting.*

**Go chase yourself!** AND **Go climb a tree!, Go fly a kite!, Go fry an egg!, Go jump in the lake!, Go soak your head!, Go soak yourself!** *exclam.* "Beat it!"; "Go away!" □ *Oh, go chase yourself! Get out of my face!* □ *Go soak your head! You're a pain in the neck.*

**Go climb a tree!** See the previous entry.

**God-box 1.** *n.* a church organ. (Folksy. Compare to *groan box, (squeeze-)box.*) □ *Would you believe that the one on the left plays the God-box on Sundays?* □ *That God-box sounds like it needs tuning.* **2.** *n.* a church. (Folksy.) □ *Nobody's gonna get me into no God-box.* □ *My kids go to the God-box every now and then.*

**God only knows!** *exclam.* "Only God knows the answer to your question; no one else does." (See also *gork.*) □ *When*

*will it end? God only knows!* □ *How long it will be, God only knows!*

**go down 1.** *in.* to happen. □ *Hey, man! What's going down?* □ *Something strange is going down around here.* **2.** *in.* to be accepted. (See *swallow.*) □ *We'll just have to wait a while to see how all this goes down.* □ *The proposal didn't go down very well with the manager.* **3.** *in.* to be arrested. (Underworld.) □ *Lefty didn't want to go down for a job he didn't do.* □ *Mr. Big said that somebody had to go down for it, and he didn't care who.*

**go downhill** *in.* to decline. □ *This company is going downhill at a great rate.* □ *Things began to go downhill when the county cut the maintenance budget.*

**go down in flames** *in.* to fail spectacularly. (See also *shoot someone down in flames.*) □ *The whole team went down in flames.* □ *I'd hate for all your planning to go down in flames.*

**go down the line** *in.* to *snort* a *line* of cocaine. (Drugs.) □ *Gert had to leave the office to go down the line.* □ *They found her in the john, going down the line.*

**go down the tube(s)** AND **go down the chute** *in.* to fail totally; to be ruined. □ *The whole project is likely to go down the tubes.* □ *All my plans just went down the chute.*

**God's acre** *n.* a cemetery. □ *When I end up in God's acre, I want everything to go on without me.* □ *They're planting somebody new in God's acre.*

**go Dutch** *in.* (for two people) to split the cost of something, such as a meal. (See *Dutch treat.*) □ *How about dinner tonight? We'll go Dutch, okay?* □ *Yes, let's go Dutch.*

**go-fasters** AND **goies** ['gofæstɚz AND 'goiz] *n.* amphetamines. (Drugs.) □ *He was habituated to "go-fasters," some kind of pep pill.* □ *He just had to have his goies every morning.*

**gofer** See *gopher.*

**go flooey** See *go blooey.*

**Go fly a kite!** See *Go chase yourself!*

**go for a sleigh ride** AND **go on a sleigh ride, take a sleigh ride** *in.* to take cocaine. (Drugs. See *snow.*) □ *Sally says she heard some druggies talking* *about going for a sleigh ride in the middle of summer.* □ *Ernie left the room briefly to take a sleigh ride.*

**go for broke** *in.* to choose to risk everything; to try to succeed against great odds. □ *I feel lucky today. I'll go for broke.* □ *We decided to go for broke, and that is exactly how we ended up.*

**Go for it!** *exclam.* "Do it!"; "Try it!" □ *Go for it! Give it a try!* □ *It looked like something I wanted to do, so I decided to go for it.*

**Go fry an egg!** See *Go chase yourself!*

**go-getter** *n.* an energetic person. □ *Wally is a real go-getter. He'll go places.* □ *Sally was really cut out to be a go-getter.*

**goggle-eyed** AND **googly-eyed** ['gaglaɪd AND 'guglaɪd] *mod.* alcohol intoxicated and staring. □ *Wally was goggle-eyed and couldn't stand up.* □ *He's too googly-eyed to drive home.*

**go-go** ['gogo] **1.** *mod.* having to do with fast-dancing young women on display in a nightclub. □ *I worked as a go-go girl for a while.* □ *Those go-go places have mostly changed their style.* **2.** *mod.* vigorous; energetic; frantically moving. □ *He's a real go-go guy, always up to something.* □ *I bought some silly go-go stock, and it collapsed immediately.*

**go great guns** *in.* to do very well; to go very fast. □ *Everything is going great guns around here. We're busy and making lots of money.* □ *The project is finally going great guns, just as we planned.*

**go haywire** **1.** *in.* (for a person) to go berserk. □ *I thought for a minute that Tod was going to go haywire.* □ *Sorry, I guess I just went haywire for a minute.* **2.** *in.* (for something) to go out of order; to break down. □ *My stereo's gone haywire.* □ *I'm afraid my car's gone haywire. It won't start.*

**go hog-wild** See *run hog-wild.*

**go home in a box** *in.* to be shipped home dead. □ *Hey, I'm too young to go home in a box.* □ *You had better be careful on this camping trip, or you'll go home in a box.*

**go home to mama** *in.* to give up something—such as a marriage—and return to one's mother's home. □ *I've had it. I'm going home to mama.* □ *Mary left him and went home to mama.*

**going high** *n.* a long-lasting type of drug high. (Drugs.) □ *Freddie had a going high and was in trouble.* □ *Gert was always after a real going high.*

**going over** **1.** *n.* an examination. □ *After a thorough going over, the doctor pronounced me alive.* □ *I gave your car a good going over, and I fixed a lot of little things.* **2.** *n.* a beating. □ *Bruno gave the guy a terrible going over.* □ *After a going over like that, the guy spent two weeks in the hospital.*

**goings-on** *n.* happenings; events. □ *There are sure some strange goings-on around here.* □ *Some big goings-on downtown tied up the traffic.*

**go into orbit** *in.* to become very excited. □ *Wow, I thought the manager was going to go into orbit, she was so mad.* □ *The entire staff went into orbit when they got the news.*

**Go jump in the lake!** See *Go chase yourself!*

**gold** **1.** *n.* money. (See also *ducats.*) □ *Do you have enough gold to pay the bill?* □ *There's no gold in my pockets.* **2.** *n.* any golden or tan marijuana. (Drugs. See *Acapulco (gold).*) □ *Max can turn gold into cash.* □ *This gold looks a little green to me.*

**goldbrick** **1.** *n.* a lazy person. □ *Tod is just a lazy goldbrick.* □ *Tell that goldbrick to get back to work.* **2.** *in.* to be lazy; to shirk one's duty. □ *Stop goldbricking and get back to work.* □ *Whoever is goldbricking when I come back gets a real talking to.*

**goldbricker** *n.* a loafer. (Also a term of address.) □ *Larry is such a goldbricker!* □ *Get moving, you goldbrickers.*

**gold bud** *n.* a golden marijuana, especially the flowering heads. (Drugs.) □ *Her very favorite was gold bud.* □ *Gold bud sounds like it would be very expensive.*

**gold Colombian** See *Colombian (gold).*

**gold digger** *n.* a woman who pays attention to a man solely for his money. □ *Sam called Sally a gold digger, and she was devastated.* □ *"You little gold digger!" cried Sam.*

**gold duster** AND **golden duster** *n.* a cocaine user. (Drugs.) □ *The gold dusters are taking over this neighborhood.* □ *Who can afford to be a golden duster?*

**golden-ager** *n.* an old person; a senior citizen. □ *The golden-agers sat on the benches and chatted.* □ *When I'm a golden-ager, I'm going to have a part-time job.*

**golden handcuffs** *n.* monetary inducements to stay on the job. (Usually for highly paid executives in large corporations. See also *golden parachute.*) □ *The company provided a variety of golden handcuffs to keeps its execs happy through a takeover.* □ *The golden handcuffs included a half million in severance pay for one of the vice presidents.*

**golden leaf** *n.* a high-quality marijuana; *Acapulco (gold).* (Drugs.) □ *Max says he has a lot of golden leaf for sale.* □ *Golden leaf must be pretty high quality.*

**golden opportunity** *n.* a very good opportunity. □ *This is my golden opportunity, and I can't pass it up.* □ *You get a golden opportunity like this very rarely.*

**golden parachute** *n.* a special kind of severance pay for persons who may be forced to leave a job. (Usually for highly paid executives in large corporations. If the company is taken over and the executives are fired, they are very well provided for. See also *golden handcuffs.*) □ *My golden parachute was so attractive that I wanted to get fired.* □ *If all the golden parachutes were used at the same time, it would bankrupt the company.*

**goldie locks** *n.* a policewoman. (Citizens band radio.) □ *Goldie locks pulled me over and gave me a citation.* □ *There was a goldie locks waiting under the bridge to spring on poor unsuspecting people like me.*

**Golly!** ['gɑli] *exclam.* "Wow!" □ *Golly, I'm sorry!* □ *Oh, golly! Did I step on your toe?*

**gomer** ['gomɚ] **1.** *n.* a stupid oaf; a social reject. (From the television character Gomer Pyle.) □ *Who's that gomer in the overalls?* □ *That gomer is my uncle Ben.* **2.** AND **goomer** ['gumɚ] *n.* a person unwelcome in a hospital. (Supposedly an acronym for "Get out of my emergency room.") □ *That goomer with the allergy is back in E.R.* □ *I don't want that goomer back in the emergency room.*

**gone 1.** AND **gone under** *mod.* unconscious. □ *He's gone. Prop his feet up and call an ambulance.* □ *He's gone under. You can begin the procedure now.* **2.** AND **gone under** *mod.* alcohol or drug intoxicated. □ *Those chicks are gone—too much to drink.* □ *Ted is really gone under.* **3.** *mod.* cool, out of this world. □ *This ice cream is gone, man, gone!* □ *She is one real gone chick.*

**gone goose** *n.* someone or something finished or done for. (A play on *dead duck.*) □ *I'm afraid that your old car is a gone goose.* □ *This old thing is a gone goose.*

**goner** ['gonɚ] *n.* someone or something finished or nearly finished. □ *This one's a goner. Toss it.* □ *The horse was a goner, so it had to be destroyed.*

**gonged** [goŋd] *mod.* drug intoxicated. (Drugs. Originally on opium.) □ *Bruno found himself in the alley, gonged.* □ *Ernie was too gonged to stand up.*

**gonna\*** ['gonə OR 'gunə] *phr.* "going to." (Eye-dialect. Caution with written use.) □ *What time you gonna be home?* □ *I'm gonna get you, you little dickens!*

**gonsel** AND **gonzel, gunzel** ['gɑnzḷ AND 'gənzḷ] *n.* a slob or an oaf. (Underworld.) □ *Bruno is such a gonsel. What a jerk!* □ *Why don't you send your gunzel out after coffee and rolls?*

**gonzo** ['gɑnzo] **1.** *n.* a silly or foolish person. □ *Some gonzo is on the phone asking for the president of the universe.* □ *Tell the gonzo I'm out.* **2.** *mod.* crazy. □ *The guy is totally gonzo!* □ *Who drew this gonzo picture of me?*

**goo** [gu] *n.* some sticky substance; *gunk.* □ *What is this goo on my shoe?* □ *There is some sort of goo on my plate. Is that meant to be my dinner?*

**goob** [gub] *n.* a pimple. (Short for *guber.*) □ *The goobs are taking over my whole face.* □ *I have the world's greatest goob right on the end of my nose.*

**goober** See *guber.*

**goober-grabber** ['gubɚ'græbɚ] *n.* someone who picks peanuts. (Typically someone native to Georgia where peanuts are grown. From *guber.*) □ *My nephew moved from Chicago to Atlanta, where he became a goober-grabber in no time at all.* □ *One of the local goober-grabbers took us to a peanut boil.*

**goober-grease** ['gubə-gris] n. peanut butter. □ *Pass me some of that goobergrease, will ya?* □ *This goober-grease is stale.*

**goobrain** ['gubren] n. a fool; a stupid person. (Also a rude term of address.) □ *What silly goobrain put sugar in the salt shaker?* □ *Look, goobrain, think about it a while. You'll catch on.*

**good and something** mod. thoroughly something. (Where *something* is an adjective. See examples.) □ *I am really good and mad at you for that.* □ *We are good and ready to do something about it.*

**good buddy** n. a friend; a partner. (Citizens band radio. Also a term of address.) □ *Well, good buddy, what's new with you?* □ *John's my good buddy.*

**good-for-nothing 1.** mod. worthless. (Usually having to do with a person.) □ *Let's get rid of this good-for-nothing car right now.* □ *Tell your good-for-nothing brother to find another place to live.* **2.** n. a worthless person. (Also a rude term of address.) □ *Tell the good-for-nothing to leave.* □ *Look, you good-for-nothing. Go out and get a job.*

**good for what ails someone** mod. good for someone. (Folksy.) □ *This stuff is good for what ails you.* □ *Take some for John. Tell him it's good for what ails him.*

**Good golly, Miss Molly!** exclam. "Good grief!"; "Wow!" □ *Good golly, Miss Molly! This place is a mess!* □ *Good golly, Miss Molly, that's awful!*

**Good grief!** exclam. "My goodness!" (A mild exclamation of despair, sympathy, amazement, etc.) □ *Good grief! I'm late.* □ *It's my own car! Good grief!*

**Good heavens!** exclam. "My goodness!" (A mild exclamation of amazement, shock, etc.) □ *Good heavens! I didn't expect you to be here.* □ *Good heavens! There's a man at the window!*

**goodie** n. a person who always behaves well. □ *She is such a goodie! No fun at parties.* □ *I'm no goodie, but I didn't care for his behavior.*

**good Joe** n. a good fellow. □ *Fred's a little slow on the uptake, but he's a good Joe.* □ *Frank's a good Joe. He'll help us.*

**good old boy** AND **good ole boy** n. a good guy; a dependable companion. (Folksy.) □ *Old Tom is a good old boy. He'll help.* □ *One of these good ole boys will give you a hand.*

**good-time Charley** n. a man who is always trying to have a good experience; an optimist. □ *Wally is such a good-time Charley. Who would believe the trouble he's had?* □ *Some good-time Charlie is making a lot of noise.*

**good-time it** tr. to *party*; to spend money and have a good time. □ *You're always good-timing it. Don't you ever study?* □ *I just want to good-time it for the rest of my life.*

**good-time man** n. a man who sells drugs. (Drugs.) □ *Max is the main good-time man in this neighborhood.* □ *The fuzz wants to see all the good-time men behind bars.*

**good trip 1.** n. a good session with L.S.D. or some other drug. (Drugs.) □ *Paul said he had a good trip, but he looks like the devil.* □ *One good trip deserves another. At least that's what my guru says.* **2.** n. any good time. □ *This meeting was a good trip.* □ *Compared to the last class, this one is a good trip.*

**Goody-goody gumdrop!** exclam. "Oh, good!" (Usually juvenile.) □ *Goodygoody gumdrop! I got what I wanted for my birthday!* □ *We're here, we're here! Goody-goody gumdrop!*

**goody two-shoes** n. someone who tries to behave better than anyone else. (Also a term of address.) □ *Well, goody twoshoes, so you decided to come sit with us.* □ *I'm no goody two-shoes. I just like to keep my nose clean.*

**goof** [guf] **1.** n. a foolish oaf; a *goofy* person. □ *Sometimes I'm such a goof. I really messed up.* □ *Don't be a goof. Get with it.* **2.** in. to use heroin or some other addictive drugs without intending to become addicted; to play around (with heroin). (Drugs.) □ *Gert spent the first few years just goofing.* □ *She was goofing, and you know what that leads to.* **3.** in. to scratch, nod, and slobber after an injection of heroin. (Drugs.) □ *She just rocks and goofs for hours.* □ *She has been goofing for an hour.* **4.** AND

**goof up** *in.* to make a blunder. □ *Whoops, I goofed!* □ *This time, you goofed.* **5.** *n.* a blunder; an error. □ *Who made this silly goof?* □ *This goof is yours, not mine.*

**goof around** See *goof off.*

**goof artist** *n.* a person who experiments with drugs. (Drugs.) □ *Gert set out to be a goof artist and ended up a junky.* □ *A goof artist is playing with fire.*

**goofball** AND **goofer** **1.** *n.* a stupid person; a fool. □ *You are such a silly goofball.* □ *Chuck acts like a goofer, but he's really with it.* **2.** AND **G.B.** *n.* marijuana; a marijuana cigarette; pills made from marijuana resin. (Drugs.) □ *Can I have a hit off your goofball?* □ *Go get your own goofball, goof!* **3.** AND **goofballer** *n.* a marijuana smoker. (Drugs.) □ *The guy's a goofball. That's why he's flunking.* □ *Most of his friends are goofers, too.* **4.** *n.* barbiturate tablets or capsules; tranquilizers. (Drugs.) □ *He popped a couple of goofers and leaned back.* □ *One goofer isn't enough anymore.*

**goofed (up)** **1.** *mod.* messed up; out of order. □ *All my papers are goofed up.* □ *Everything on my desk is goofed. Who's been here?* **2.** *mod.* confused; distraught. □ *I'm sort of goofed up today. I think I'm coming down with something.* □ *I was up too late last night, and now I'm all goofed up.* **3.** *mod.* under the effects of marijuana; under the effects of a *goofball.* (Drugs.) □ *Ted has never been goofed up in his life.* □ *Max has been goofed most of his life.*

**goofer** See *goofball.*

**go off half-cocked** *in.* to proceed without knowing all the facts. □ *I waited because I didn't want to go off half-cocked.* □ *The boss went off half-cocked and exploded into a rage about the mess.*

**go off the deep end** *in.* to do or experience something in the extreme: to fall madly in love, to go crazy, to commit suicide, to fly into a rage, etc. □ *John is completely in love with Mary and wants to marry her. I was afraid he would go off the deep end, and he did.* □ *Sally was so depressed that we had to watch her day and night so she wouldn't go off the deep end.* □ *I saw what he had done, and I just went off the deep end. I was in a blind rage and didn't know what I was doing.*

**goof-off** See *goof off.*

**goof off** **1.** AND **goof around** *in.* to waste time. □ *Quit goofing off.* □ *Get busy. Stop goofing around.* **2.** *n.* a time-waster; a *jerk.* (Usually **goof-off.**) □ *Tod is such a goof-off!* □ *I'm no goof-off, but I am no scholar either.*

**goof on someone** *in.* to play a prank on someone; to involve someone in a deception. □ *Hey, don't goof on me. I'm your buddy!* □ *The kid goofed on Chuck, and he thought it was a pretty good joke.*

**goof-proof** **1.** *mod.* foolproof; not subject to misuse. □ *I want a goof-proof scheme.* □ *This scheme is not goof-proof, but it's pretty sound.* □ *Now, this time I've made it goof-proof.* **2.** *tr.* to make something foolproof; to take action to see that something cannot be misused. □ *I'll try to goof-proof my scheme.* □ *See if this can be goof-proofed by Monday evening.*

**goof something up** AND **goof up something, goof up on something** *tr.* to mess something up. □ *Now don't goof it up this time.* □ *I hope I don't goof up the report again.*

**goof up** See *goof.*

**goofus** ['gufəs] **1.** *n.* a gadget. □ *Where is that little goofus I use to pry open these cans?* □ *Here's just the little goofus you're looking for.* **2.** AND **goopus** *n.* a foolish oaf. (Also a term of address.) □ *You're just acting like a goofus. Be serious!* □ *Hey, goopus! Come here!*

**goofy** ['gufi] **1.** *mod.* silly. □ *Stop acting so goofy! What will the neighbors say?* □ *You are really a goofy chick.* **2.** *mod.* alcohol intoxicated. □ *Wow, is she goofy!* □ *They went out and got themselves good and goofy.*

**goof(y) butt** *n.* a marijuana cigarette. (Drugs.) □ *Max had a goofy butt stuck behind his ear.* □ *Ernie took a hit of the goof butt and passed it on.*

**goo-goo eyes** ['gugu 'aɪz] *n.* flirtatious eyes. (Often with *make.*) □ *Mary was making goo-goo eyes at Sam.* □ *Who's the chick over there with the goo-goo eyes?*

**gook** [guk OR gʊk] **1.** *n.* a slimy substance; a sediment or residue. □ *There was a lot of gook in my crankcase.* □ *Too much of that gook will ruin your engine.* **2.** *n.* a foolish oaf. □ *Wow, Chuck is turning into a real gook!* □ *Don't be such a gook, you twit!* **3.** *n.* a tramp. □ *Some old gook was asking for a handout.* □ *Give the gook some food and wish him well.* **4.** *n.* a prostitute. □ *Some old gook was standing around with too much leg on view.* □ *There are a lot of gooks around here in the center of town.* **5.** *n.* a derogatory nickname for various Orientals. (Crude.) □ *Nobody wanted to go to war against the gooks.* □ *Let the gooks fight it out amongst themselves.*

**goombah** ['gumbɑ] *n.* a buddy; a trusted friend. (Also a term of address. Ultimately from Italian.) □ *Hey, goombah! How goes it?* □ *He's my goombah. I can trust him.*

**goon** [gun] **1.** *n.* a stupid person; a fool. □ *Oh, Wally, you're such a goon sometimes.* □ *Tod is a silly goon, but he's a lot of fun at parties.* **2.** *n.* a hooligan; a thug or bodyguard. (Underworld.) □ *Bruno is one of Mr. Big's goons.* □ *Call off your goons!*

**Go on!** *exclam.* "I don't believe you!"; "I deny it!" □ *Go on! You don't really know what you are talking about!* □ *Go on! You weren't even there.*

**go on (and on) about someone or something** *in.* to rave about someone or something endlessly. □ *He just went on and on about the trouble he was having with the post office.* □ *Why do you have to go on about your sister so?*

**gooner** ['gunɚ] *n.* a term for an Asian. (Derogatory. Military.) □ *These gooners sure can cook.* □ *See if one of the gooners will show you how to do it.*

**goon-platoon** *n.* a platoon of misfits; a platoon which is noted for its errors. (Military.) □ *Well, the goon-platoon's done it again!* □ *Which side is the goon-platoon on?*

**goon squad** **1.** *n.* an organized group of thugs; a gang of toughs. (Underworld.) □ *Bruno and his goon squad are lurking about.* □ *The goon squad Mr. Big sent around scared the devil out of Max.* **2.**
*n.* the police. (Black.) □ *Here comes the goon squad. Watch out!* □ *My old buddy on the goon squad tells me there'll be some action over on Maple Street tonight.*

**goop** AND **goup** [gup] *n.* slop; gunk; bad food. □ *I refuse to eat this goop.* □ *You get used to this goup after a while.*

**goophead** ['guphɛd] *n.* an inflamed pimple. (Patterned on *blackhead*.) □ *Ye gods! I'm covered with goopheads.* □ *You ought to see the goophead on your nose.*

**goopus** See *goofus.*

**goopy** ['gupi] *mod.* gummy; syrupy. □ *I just love goopy desserts.* □ *This is not goopy enough.* □ *There is some goopy stuff coming out of the car's engine.*

**goose** **1.** *n.* a silly oaf; an oaf. □ *Oh, I'm such a silly goose!* □ *What a goose you are!* **2.** *tr.* to (attempt to) poke something, such as a finger, in someone's anus. □ *Freddy tried to goose me!* □ *Don't goose me!* **3.** *n.* an attempt to *goose* someone. □ *Harry is a master of the rude goose.* □ *He tried to give me a goose.* **4.** *tr.* to rev up an engine; to press down hard on the accelerator of a car. □ *Why don't you goose the thing and see how fast it'll go?* □ *Don't goose it too much.* **5.** *n.* an act of suddenly pressing down the accelerator of a car. □ *Give it a good goose and see what happens.* □ *One more goose, but don't hold it down so long.*

**goose egg** **1.** *n.* a score of zero. □ *We got a goose egg in the second inning.* □ *It was double goose eggs for the final score.* **2.** *n.* a bump on the head. □ *You've got quite a goose egg there.* □ *I walked into a door and got a big goose egg on my forehead.* **3.** *n.* a failure; a zero. (Similar to sense 1.) □ *The outcome was a real goose egg. A total mess.* □ *The result of three weeks' planning is one big goose egg.*

**go over big** *in.* to be appreciated as a success. □ *I'm sure this will go over big with the folks at home.* □ *Well, it didn't go over very big with the boss.*

**go overboard** *in.* to do far more than is necessary. □ *He has a tendency to go overboard at these parties.* □ *Now don't go overboard for us. We're just folks.*

**go over like a lead balloon** *in.* (for something meant to be good) to fail to be good. □ *The joke went over like a lead balloon.* □ *I'm afraid your plan went over like a lead balloon.*

**go over the hill** *in.* to escape from a prison or from the military service. (See also *over the hill* and the following entry.) □ *Jim went over the hill, and they caught him.* □ *Jed and Tom planned to go over the hill last night. What happened?*

**go over the wall** *in.* to escape from a prison. □ *Lefty tried to go over the wall, but the warden got wind of it.* □ *Nobody goes over the wall in this joint.*

**goozlum** ['guzləm] *n.* any gummy, sticky substance: syrup, gravy, soup. □ *Do you want some of this wonderful goozlum on your ice cream?* □ *Just keep putting that goozlum on my spuds.*

**gopher** AND **gofer** ['gofɚ] **1.** *n.* someone who goes for things and brings them back. (From *go for*.) □ *You got a gopher who can go get some coffee?* □ *Send the gofer out for cigarettes.* **2.** *n.* a dupe; a pawn; an underling. □ *The guy's just a gopher. He has no say in anything.* □ *I'll send a gopher over to pick up the papers.*

**gopher ball** *n.* a baseball pitch that is hit as a home run. (When it is hit, the batter will "go for" home.) □ *Wilbur hit another long gopher ball straight across center field.* □ *The center fielder did a belly flop on the field trying to get the gopher ball.*

**go-pills** *n.* amphetamines. (Drugs.) □ *She took go-pills to start the day.* □ *After a while, these go-pills just demand to be taken.*

**go places** *in.* to become very successful. □ *I knew that Sally would go places.* □ *I really want to go places in life.*

**go public 1.** *in.* to sell to the public shares of a privately owned company. (Financial markets.) □ *The company decided not to go public because the economy was so bad at the time.* □ *We'll go public at a later time.* **2.** *in.* to reveal something to the public. (Especially with *with*, as in the examples.) □ *It's too early to go public with the story.* □ *Just let me know when we can go public with this.*

**gorilla biscuits** AND **gorilla pills** *n.* amphetamines. (Drugs.) □ *Molly is big on those gorilla pills.* □ *Stay away from gorilla biscuits.*

**gorilla juice** *n.* steroids. (Bodybuilding. Steroids build muscle tissue rapidly.) □ *Andy really wanted to get hold of some gorilla juice, but his parents said no.* □ *Do all those muscle-bound creatures take gorilla juice?*

**gorilla pills** See *gorilla biscuits*.

**gorilla tabs** *n.* phencyclidine, *P.C.P.* (Drugs.) □ *The kid was knocked for a loop by something called gorilla tabs.* □ *Even Max won't sell gorilla tabs.*

**gork** [gork] **1.** *n.* a fool; a dupe. □ *Merton acts like such a gork sometimes.* □ *The gorks are taking over the world!* **2.** AND **GORK** *phr.* an alleged hospital chart notation of the diagnosis "God only really knows." (Hospitals.) □ *I see old Mr. Kelly is in again with a hundred complaints. His chart says GORK.* □ *He's down with gork again.* **3.** *tr.* to give a patient sedation. (Hospitals.) □ *Dr. Wilson says to gork the patient in 226.* □ *He'll quiet down after we gork him.*

**gorked (out)** [gorkt...] *mod.* heavily sedated; knocked out. (Hospitals.) □ *Once the patient was gorked, he was more cooperative.* □ *The guy in 226 is totally gorked out now.*

**Go soak your head!** See *Go chase yourself!*

**Go soak yourself!** See *Go chase yourself!*

**go sour** *in.* to turn bad or unpleasant. □ *It looks like all my plans are going sour.* □ *My whole life is going sour right now.*

**go South** AND **head South 1.** *in.* to make an escape; to disappear. □ *Lefty went South the minute he got out of the pen.* □ *The mugger headed South just after the crime.* **2.** *in.* to fall; to go down. (Financial markets.) □ *All the stock market indexes went South today.* □ *The market headed South today at the opening bell.*

**gospel bird** *n.* chicken served on Sunday. (Folksy.) □ *We used to have gospel bird every single Sunday.* □ *I remember the Sunday dinners and the gospel bird, as we called it.*

**gospel (truth)** *n.* the honest truth. □ *You gotta believe me. It's the gospel truth!* □ *He speaks nothing but gospel. You can trust him.*

**go straight 1.** *in.* to stop breaking the law. □ *Lefty thought about going straight once, but pulled himself out of it.* □ *I think I'll give all this up and go straight—some day.* **2.** *in.* to get off drugs. (Drugs.) □ *Ernie wanted to go straight more than anything else in the world.* □ *I'll go straight one of these days.*

**gotcha** ['gɑtʃə] **1.** *phr.* "I got you!"; "I've caught you!" (Usually **Gotcha!**) □ *I gotcha, and you can't get away.* □ *Ha, ha! Gotcha! Come here, you little dickens.* **2.** *n.* an arrest. (Underworld.) □ *The cop reached out, grasped Bruno's shoulder, and made the gotcha.* □ *It was a fair gotcha. Bruno was nabbed, and he went along quietly.* **3.** *phr.* "I understand you." □ *Gotcha! Thanks for telling me.* □ *Seven pounds, four ounces? Gotcha! I'll tell everybody.*

**go the limit** *in.* to do as much as possible; to get as much as possible. □ *Let's plan to do everything we can. Let's go the limit.* □ *We'll go the limit. To heck with the cost.*

**go through someone like a dose of the salts** *in.* to move through someone's digestive tract like a strong laxative. □ *That stuff they served last night went through me like a dose of salts.* □ *Careful of the coffee. It'll go through you like a dose of salts.*

**go through the changes 1.** *in.* to experience life's changes. □ *A good day, a bad day—it's all part of going through the changes.* □ *Nothing new with me, just going through the changes.* **2.** *in.* to go through a reconstruction of one's life. □ *I went through the changes all last year. It was a real bad time.* □ *I've been going through the changes lately. It's tough to grow up at this age.*

**Go to!** *exclam.* "Go to hell!" □ *Oh, you're terrible. Just go to!* □ *Go to, you creep!*

**Go to blazes!** AND **Go to the devil!** *exclam.* "Go to hell!" □ *Go to blazes! Stop pestering me!* □ *I'm sick of your complaining. Go to the devil!*

**Go to the devil!** See the previous entry.

**go to town** *in.* to do something with gusto; to do something with great speed and energy. □ *The main office is really going to town on collecting overdue payments.* □ *Man, our team is really going to town.*

**gotta*** ['gɑdə] *phr.* "got to." (Eye-dialect. Typical spoken English. Caution with use in writing.) □ *Well, I gotta be off.* □ *Ya gotta do it when ya wanna do it, or just forget it.*

**gotta go** AND **got to go** ['gɑdə 'go] **1.** *phr.* have to leave. □ *Well, I gotta go. See ya!* □ *We've got to go in ten minutes!* **2.** *phr.* have to go to the bathroom. □ *Hurry, hurry. I gotta go!* □ *I really gotta go. Please!*

**gouch off** [gɑutʃ...] *in.* to pass out under the influence of drugs. (Drugs.) □ *After taking the stuff, Gary gouched off.* □ *After the fix, Gert waited patiently to gouch off.*

**go underground** *in.* to go into hiding; to begin to operate in secret. □ *The entire operation went underground, and we heard no more about it.* □ *We'll go underground if we have to. Nothing will stop the movement.*

**go up** *in.* to start to feel the effects of a drug. (Drugs.) □ *Gert started to go up and suddenly fell asleep.* □ *The guy couldn't wait to get home and go up.*

**gourd** [gord] *n.* the head. □ *I raised up and got a nasty blow on the gourd.* □ *My gourd aches something awful.*

**gow** AND **ghow** [gɑu] *n.* drugs in general. (Drugs. Originally opium only.) □ *The cops are looking for the creeps who supply the gow that these kids get hold of.* □ *The old man used to carry his ghow in a little wooden case.*

**go West** *in.* to die. □ *Ever since Uncle Ben went West, things have been peaceful around here.* □ *When I go West, I want flowers, hired mourners, and an enormous performance of Mozart's "Requiem."*

**go with the flow** AND **go with it** *in.* to cope with adversity; to accept one's lot. □ *No, just relax and go with the flow.* □ *Go with it. Don't fight it.*

**goy** [gɔɪ] **1.** *n.* a gentile. (From Hebrew. Not necessarily derogatory.) □ *But the* *goys can do anything they want on Sunday!* □ *Leave that kind of thing to the goys.* **2.** *mod.* gentile; non-Jewish. □ *I don't care for that goy stuff.* □ *Goy pickles are sort of blah.*

**go zonkers** *in.* to go slightly crazy. □ *What a day! I almost went zonkers.* □ *I went a little zonkers there for a minute.*

**grabbers** *n.* the hands. □ *Keep your grabbers to yourself.* □ *Wash your grubby little grabbers before coming to the table.*

**grade-grubber** **1.** *n.* an earnest, hard-working student. (In the way a pig roots or grubs around for food.) □ *Merton is a grade-grubber and a real hard worker.* □ *If there are too many grade-grubbers in a class, it will really throw off the grading scale.* **2.** *n.* a student who flatters the teacher in hopes of a higher grade. □ *Toward the end of a semester, my office is filled with grade-grubbers.* □ *A few grade-grubbers help assure old professors that the world is not really changing at all.*

**grade-grubbing** **1.** *n.* working hard at one's studies in hopes of a high grade. □ *If all you're here for is grade-grubbing, you're going to miss a lot.* □ *Get a hobby. All grade-grubbing in college is no good.* **2.** *n.* flattering a teacher in hopes of a higher grade. □ *Some teachers don't mind a lot of grade-grubbing.* □ *So you've come in to do some grade-grubbing.* **3.** *mod.* having to do with students who are only concerned with getting high grades. □ *Grade-grubbing college kids are driving me crazy.* □ *Two grade-grubbing seniors came in and begged me to change their grades.*

**graduate** ['grædʒuət] **1.** *n.* a person experienced in life, especially sexually experienced. □ *Molly is a graduate. Nothing is new to her.* □ *You need someone who is a graduate for this kind of a job.* **2.** ['grædʒuet] *in.* to move from casual drug use to addiction. (Drugs.) □ *Gert graduated to smack after only a year of skin-popping.* □ *Tod graduated and went into treatment all in the same month.*

**grand** AND **G.** *n.* one thousand dollars. □ *That car probably cost about twenty grand.* □ *Four G.s for that thing?*

**Grand Central Station** *n.* any busy and hectic place. (From Grand Central Station in New York City—a very busy place.) □ *This place is Grand Central Station on a Friday night.* □ *At just about closing time, this place becomes Grand Central Station.*

**granddaddy (of them all)** AND **daddy (of them all)** *n.* the biggest or oldest of all; the patriarch. □ *This old fish is the granddaddy of them all.* □ *This one is the daddy. Been here since the place was built.*

**grandstand** *in.* to make oneself conspicuous. □ *Stop grandstanding, Sally. Everyone can see you.* □ *Don't you just hate the way that Pat grandstands all the time?*

**grandstand play** *n.* something done exceedingly well to impress an audience or a group of spectators. □ *The grandstand play caught the attention of the crowd just as they were leaving.* □ *He tried one final grandstand play, but the audience continued to give him the raspberry.*

**grape(s)** *n.* champagne; wine. (Compare to *berries.*) □ *These grapes are great!* □ *No more of the grapes for me. It tickles my nose.*

**grape shot** *mod.* alcohol intoxicated; drunk on wine. □ *After the reception, Hank found himself a little grape shot.* □ *Man, is that guy ever grape shot! How can he hold enough to get that way?*

**grapes of wrath** *n.* wine. □ *Fred had taken a little too much of the grapes of wrath.* □ *How about another dose of the grapes of wrath?*

**grapevine** *n.* a mouth-to-mouth communications network. □ *I heard on the grapevine that Sam is moving to the east.* □ *The grapevine was right. He's already left.*

**grass** **1.** *n.* marijuana. (Drugs and now widely known.) □ *These kids manage to find this grass somewhere.* □ *Almost everybody knows that grass means marijuana.* **2.** *n.* lettuce; salad greens. (See *rabbit food.*) □ *I could use a little more grass in my diet.* □ *Do you want some dressing on your grass?*

**grasser** See the following entry.

**grasshead** AND **grasser, grasshopper** n. a marijuana smoker. (Drugs.) □ *The grassheads are taking over this neighborhood.* □ *Imagine, a seven-year-old grasser!*

**grasshopper** See the previous entry.

**grass party** n. a marijuana-smoking party. (Drugs.) □ *The goon squad raided Tod's grass party without any warning.* □ *Sally tried to have a grass party, but didn't have any grass.*

**grassroots 1.** n. the common people, especially rural people. □ *We really haven't heard anything from the grassroots yet.* □ *The grassroots isn't organized on most issues.* **2.** mod. having to do with or originating with the common people. □ *A grassroots movement pushed Senator Del Monte toward the nomination.* □ *Politicians love to create grassroots movements.*

**grave-dancer** n. someone who profits over someone else's misfortune. (From *dance on someone's grave.*) □ *I don't want to seem like a grave-dancer, but his defeat places me in line for a promotion.* □ *The guy's a grave-dancer. Anything to get ahead.*

**gravel-pounder** n. an infantry soldier. (Military.) □ *Do you really want to join the Army and be a gravel-pounder?* □ *The life of a gravel-pounder is not for me.*

**graveyard shift** n. the night shift of work in a factory, usually starting at about midnight. (Compare to *swing shift.*) □ *I'd prefer not to work the graveyard shift.* □ *The pay is pretty good on the graveyard shift.*

**gravy** n. extra or easy money; easy profit. □ *Virtually every cent that came in was pure gravy—no expenses and no materials costs at all.* □ *After I pay expenses, the rest is pure gravy.*

**gravy train** n. a job that brings in a steady supply of easy money or *gravy.* □ *This kind of job is a real gravy train.* □ *The gravy train is just not for me.*

**grayhound** in. (for a black) to date Caucasians. □ *Somebody said you were grayhounding. Is that so?* □ *I am not grayhounding.*

**grease** n. protection money; bribery money. (See *grease someone's palm.*)

□ *Rocko was in charge of making sure that enough grease was spread around city hall.* □ *See that the commissioner of the park district gets a little grease to help us get the contract.*

**greased** [grizd OR grist] mod. alcohol intoxicated. □ *He went out and got himself greased, even though he knew it would probably kill him.* □ *She is way too greased to drive.*

**greased lightning 1.** n. strong liquor. □ *This greased lightning of yours nearly blew my head off.* □ *No more greased lightning for me.* **2.** n. something fast or powerful. □ *That little car is just greased lightning.* □ *That kid can run like greased lightning.*

**grease monkey** n. a mechanic. □ *I took my car to my favorite grease monkey who says I need a new something or other.* □ *How much money does a grease monkey make?*

**greaser** ['grizɚ OR 'grisɚ] n. a rough and aggressive male, usually with long greased-down hair. □ *Who's the greaser who just swaggered in?* □ *Donna has been going out with a real greaser.*

**grease someone's palm** tr. to pay someone a bribe. □ *I had to grease the clerk's palm in order to get the job done.* □ *Are you trying to grease my palm?*

**grease the skids** tr. to help prepare for the success or failure of someone or something. (Compare to *put the skids under someone or something.*) □ *Ray set out to grease the skids for the right things to happen.* □ *We need someone to grease the skids for the Wilson contract.*

**greasy spoon** n. an untidy and unappetizing diner or restaurant. □ *Let's eat at the greasy spoon over on Maple. The food is gross, but the people-watching is good.* □ *I wouldn't be caught dead in a greasy spoon like that.*

**Great!** exclam. "Excellent!"; "Wonderful!" □ *Great! I'm glad to hear it.* □ *You got married? Great!*

**great divide** n. a divorce. □ *How did Sam survive the great divide?* □ *The great divide cost over two grand.*

**Great Scott!** ['gret 'skɑt] exclam. "Good grief!" □ *Great Scott! What happened!* □ *I'm late again! Great Scott!*

**great unwashed** *n.* most of the common people; the hoi polloi. (Always with *the*.) □ *The great unwashed could probably tell us a lot about life in the big city.* □ *I usually find myself more in agreement with the great unwashed than with the elite.*

**greefo** AND **griefo** ['grifo] *n.* marijuana or a marijuana cigarette. (Drugs. Old. Mexican Spanish for *weed*. See also *reefer*.) □ *Max had a soggy greefo in his mouth.* □ *He tossed Fred a griefo and held out his hand for some bread.*

**Greek to someone** *n.* something incomprehensible to someone; something as mysterious as Greek writing. □ *I don't understand this. It's all Greek to me.* □ *She said it was Greek to her, and that it made no sense at all.*

**green 1.** AND **green folding, green paper, green stuff** *n.* money; paper money. (See also *long green*.) □ *How much green you got on you?* □ *I have so much green stuff, I don't know what to do with it.* **2.** AND **greenie** *n.* a green amphetamine tablet. (Drugs.) □ *She took greenies to wake up with in the morning.* □ *Can I have one of your greenies?* **3.** AND **greens** *n.* weak or inferior marijuana. (Drugs.) □ *I don't want any old green. Where's the good stuff?* □ *This slide shows "greens," or low-quality cannabis.* **4.** *n.* ketamine hydrochloride, a drug used like *L.S.D.* (Drugs.) □ *Now he's trying to get people to use green—after having caused so much trouble with acid.* □ *Is green likely to become as bad a problem as acid?*

**green around the gills** See *blue around the gills*.

**greenback** ['grinbæk] *n.* a dollar bill. □ *She came out of the bank and dropped this pack of greenbacks right there on the street.* □ *It's only 10 greenbacks. Anybody can afford that.*

**green bud** AND **mud-bud** *n.* homegrown marijuana. (Drugs. See *domestic*.) □ *I suspect that green bud isn't anywhere near as good as gold bud.* □ *She grows her own mud-bud.*

**green dragon** AND **green hornet** *n.* a green amphetamine tablet. (Drugs.) □ *The truck driver said he had found some green dragons outside Frisco.* □ *After*

getting wired a couple of times, Alice won't touch green hornets.

**green hornet** See the previous entry.

**greenie** ['grini] **1.** *n.* a Heineken (brand) beer. (It comes in a green bottle.) □ *Tom ordered a greenie and had it put on his tab.* □ *Can I have a couple of greenies over here, please?* **2.** See *green*.

**green light** *n.* the signal to go ahead with something; the *okay*. (Compare to *go-ahead, high sign*.) □ *She gave the green light to the project.* □ *When we get the green light, we'll start.*

**greenmail** *n.* a money-making scheme wherein a very wealthy person buys a large number of shares of a company, threatens to take control of the company, and then offers to sell the stock to the company at an exorbitant price in lieu of a takeover. (Financial markets.) □ *Mr. Smith made about 20 million in greenmail last year.* □ *One state is trying to outlaw greenmail to protect its industrial base.*

**green paper** See *green*.

**greens** See *green*.

**green stuff** See *green*.

**green tea** AND **green snow** *n.* phencyclidine, *P.C.P.*, an animal tranquilizer. (Drugs.) □ *Now the kids are taking something they call green tea, and they think it's marijuana.* □ *There's another one—green snow—that makes them think they're getting coke.*

**green thumb** *n.* a wonderful ability to garden and grow houseplants. □ *Alice has a green thumb and can work wonders with plants.* □ *If I had a green thumb, I could grow my own bananas.*

**greenwash** *tr.* to *launder* money; to obliterate the illegal sources of money by moving it through a variety of financial institutions. (Underworld.) □ *It was shown in court that the mayor had been involved in greenwashing some of the bribe money.* □ *The treasurer hired someone to greenwash the cash.*

**greldge** [grɛldʒ] **1.** *n.* something nasty or *yucky*. □ *What is this greldge on my shoe?* □ *That's not greldge, that's just plain mud.* **2.** *exclam.* "Nuts!"; "Darn!" (Usually **Greldge!**) □ *Oh, greldge! I'm late!* □ *This is the last straw! Greldge!*

**gripe one's soul** *tr.* to annoy someone. □ *That kind of thing really gripes my soul!* □ *John, have I ever told you that you gripe my soul?*

**grit** *n.* courage; nerve. □ *It takes a lot of grit to do something like that.* □ *Well, Tod has lots of grit. He can do it.*

**gritch** [grɪtʃ] **1.** *in.* to complain. (A blend of *gripe* and *bitch*.) □ *Stop gritching all the time.* □ *Are you still gritching about that?* **2.** *n.* a complainer; a griper. □ *You are getting to be such a gritch.* □ *Don't be such a gritch!*

**gritchy** ['grɪtʃi] *mod.* complaining; irritable. □ *I don't feel as gritchy today as I did yesterday.* □ *You seem quite gritchy to me.*

**groan box** *n.* an accordion. (See also *squeeze-box*.) □ *Clare is pretty good at the groan box.* □ *I used to play the groan box when I was a kid.*

**groaty** See *grody*.

**grod** AND **groddess** [grɑd AND 'grɑdəs] *n.* an especially sloppy man or woman. (Patterned on *god* and *goddess*.) □ *Hello, grods and groddesses, what's new?* □ *She is the goddess of scraggly ends.*

**grody** AND **groaty** ['grodi] *mod.* disgusting. (From *grotesque*. See *grotty*.) □ *What a grody view of the street from this window.* □ *These shoes are getting sort of groaty. I guess I'll throw them out.*

**grody to the max** ['grodi tu ðə 'mæks] *mod.* totally disgusting. (California. From *grotesque*. See also *groaty, grody*.) □ *Oo, this is grody to the max!* □ *This pizza is, like, grody to the max!*

**grog** [grɑg] *n.* liquor. □ *Here, have some more of this grog.* □ *That's enough grog for me.*

**grogged (up)** *mod.* alcohol intoxicated. □ *The two guys were totally grogged up by midnight.* □ *Let's go out and get grogged.*

**groggery** ['grɑgɚi] *n.* a tavern; a place to buy liquor. □ *Sam stopped at the groggery for a snort.* □ *All the groggeries are closed on Sundays.*

**groggy 1.** *mod.* tired; in a stupor. □ *He was too groggy to care what happened to him.* □ *Who's that groggy guy?* □ *I'm still groggy by ten in the morning.* **2.** AND **groggified** ['grɔgifaɪd] *mod.* alcohol intoxicated. □ *John was a little*

groggy—*from the grog, of course.* □ *He was too groggified to drive.*

**groghound** *n.* a drunkard. □ *I'm afraid that Ernie is getting to be a groghound.* □ *I'm an old groghound from way back.*

**grok** [grɔk] *tr.* to appreciate someone or something; to relate to someone or something. □ *I can really grok what you're saying.* □ *I don't quite grok that. Run it by again, would you?*

**gronk** [grɔŋk] *n.* a nasty substance, such as dirt which collects between the toes. □ *I don't want to hear any more at all about your gronk.* □ *What is this gronk here?*

**gronk (out)** *in.* to *conk out*; to crash, as with a car or a computer. □ *My car gronked out on the way to work this morning.* □ *The program gronks every time I start to run it.*

**grooby** See *groovy*.

**groove** *n.* something pleasant or *cool*. (See also *in the groove*.) □ *This day has been a real groove.* □ *Man, what a groove!*

**grooved** [gruvd] *mod.* pleased. □ *I am so grooved. I'll just kick back and meditate.* □ *You sure look grooved. What's been happening in your life?*

**groove on someone or something** *in.* to show interest in someone or something; to relate to someone or something. □ *Fred was beginning to groove on new age music when he met Phil.* □ *Sam is really grooving on Mary.*

**grooving** *mod.* enjoying; being *cool* and laid back. □ *Look at those guys grooving in front of the television set.* □ *They were just sitting there grooving.*

**groovy 1.** *mod. cool*; pleasant. □ *Man, this music is groovy.* □ *What a groovy day!* **2.** *mod.* drug intoxicated. (Drugs.) □ *Three beers and he was a little groovy.* □ *She's groovy, but she can still stand up.* **3.** *mod.* out of date; passe. (California.) □ *Your clothes are so groovy. It barfs me out.* □ *Oh, how groovy!*

**gross** [gros] *mod.* crude; vulgar; disgusting. (Slang only when overused.) □ *This food is gross!* □ *What a gross thing to even suggest.*

**gross-out 1.** *n.* something disgusting. □ *This whole day has been a total gross-out.* □ *That horror movie was a* *real gross-out.* **2.** *mod.* disgusting; *gross.* □ *What a gross-out day this has been!* □ *Well, it looks like another gross-out movie.*

**gross someone out** AND **gross out someone** *tr.* to disgust someone. □ *Those horrible pictures just gross me out.* □ *Jim's story totally grossed out Sally.*

**grotty** ['grɑdi] *mod.* highly undesirable. (Originally British. From *grotesque.* See *grody.*) □ *Let's not see another grotty movie tonight.* □ *What is this grotty stuff they serve here?* □ *It's not grotty!*

**grounded** *mod.* confined to one's home. (The standard punishment for a teenager. See also *campused.*) □ *Molly is grounded for a week because she came in late.* □ *You are grounded, and I don't want to hear another word about it!*

**ground-pounder** *n.* an infantry soldier. (Military.) □ *If you join the Army, it means a lot of your life spent as a ground-pounder.* □ *You won't find me among the ground-pounders. I have flat feet.*

**group-grope** *n.* a group of people engaged in sexual activities. □ *That party turned into a hopeless group-grope.* □ *The group-grope was busted up by you-know-who.*

**groupie** *n.* a young woman who follows a band seeking romance with the band members. □ *Would you believe that Sally was a groupie when she was 19?* □ *You mean all those young girls are groupies?*

**grouse** [grɑus] **1.** *in.* to complain. □ *Paul is always grousing about something.* □ *Stop grousing and look on the good side of things.* **2.** *n.* a woman; women considered sexually. □ *Who's the grouse I saw you with last night?* □ *Look at that grouse over there.* **3.** *in.* to neck; to pet and kiss. □ *They stopped grousing in order to come up for air.* □ *They were grousing in the back seat the whole trip.*

**grovel** ['grɑvl̩] *in.* to fondle or pet. □ *They spent the whole time in the back seat groveling.* □ *He always wants to go out and grovel.*

**growler** *n.* a toilet. □ *Where's the growler around here?* □ *We only have one growler in this house.*

**grub** [grəb] **1.** *n.* food. □ *Hey, this grub's pretty good.* □ *What time's grub?* **2.** *in.* to eat (a meal). (Black.) □ *When do we grub?* □ *Let's grub and get going.* **3.** *n.* an earnest student. (Collegiate. See also *grade-grubber.*) □ *Merton is not exactly a grub. He gets good grades without trying.* □ *The test was so hard, even the grubs did poorly.* **4.** *n.* a sloppy person. (From *grub worm.*) □ *Don is such a grub all the time.* □ *Sorry I look like a grub. I've been doing some plumbing.* **5.** See *grubs* in the following entry.

**grubbies** AND **grubbers, grubs** ['grəbiz AND 'grəbɚz, grəbz] *n.* worn-out clothing; clothing one wears for the occasional dirty job. □ *I have to go home, put some grubbies on, and paint the house.* □ *There I was, running around in my grubs when the Senator stops by to say hello!*

**grubby** ['grəbi] *mod.* unclean; untidy; unshaven. □ *Tod looks sort of grubby today. What's wrong?* □ *Who's that grubby guy?* □ *I feel grubby, and I want a shower.*

**gruesome-twosome** ['grusəm'tusəm] *n.* two people or things. (Jocular. Neither the things nor the people have to be "gruesome.") □ *Well, it's the gruesome-twosome. Come in and join the party.* □ *The gruesome-twosome will both start in tonight's game.*

**grunch** See the following entry.

**grunge** AND **grunch** [grəndʒ AND grəntʃ] **1.** *n.* any nasty substance; dirt; gunk. □ *There's some gritty grunge on the kitchen floor.* □ *What's that grunch on your tie?* **2.** *n.* an ugly or nasty person; a repellent person. □ *Alice thinks that Max is a grunge.* □ *Some grunch came by and dropped off this strange package for you.*

**grungy** ['grəndʒi] *mod.* dirty and smelly; yucky. □ *Get your grungy feet off the table!* □ *My feet are not grungy!* □ *What is this grungy stuff on the closet floor?*

**grunt** [grənt] **1.** *n.* a guttural sound, as made by a pig. (Not slang.) □ *Mary made a loud grunt and then threw the spear.* □ *Did I hear your grunt of assent, or did that mean no?* **2.** *n.* an infantry soldier. (Military.) □ *Hey, you grunts!*

*Get in line!* □ *Get those grunts out on the field at sunrise!* **3.** *n.* a low-ranking or subservient person. (Someone who is likely to utter a grunt because of the discomforts of menial labor.) □ *Get one of the grunts over here to clean this up.* □ *Let's hire a grunt to do this kind of work.* **4.** *n.* a belch. □ *I heard your grunt!* □ *Does that grunt mean you like my cooking?* **5.** *in.* to defecate. (Juvenile.) □ *Jimmy's got to go grunt, mom.* □ *Okay, grunt, Jimmy.* **6.** *n.* an act of defecation. □ *Jimmy's got to do a grunt, mommy.* □ *That's a good grunt, Jimmy.* **7.** *n.* a hard-working student. □ *Merton isn't a grunt. Everything's easy for Merton.* □ *The grunts got B's on the test. It was that hard!* **8.** *n.* a wrestler. (Possibly in reference to a grunting pig.) □ *Two big grunts wearing outlandish costumes performed for the television cameras.* □ *One grunt threw the other grunt out of the ring.*

**grunt work** *n.* hard, menial labor; tedious work. □ *I'm tired of doing grunt work for minimum wages.* □ *Who is supposed to do the grunt work around here? Not me!*

**gubbish** *n.* nonsense; useless information. (Computers. A combination of *garbage* and *rubbish*.) □ *There's nothing but gubbish on my printout.* □ *I can't make any sense out of this gubbish.*

**guber** AND **goober** ['gubɚ] *n.* a facial pimple. (See also *goob*.) □ *Wow, look at that giant guber on my nose.* □ *How does anybody get rid of goobers?*

**guck** [gək] *n.* a thick, sticky substance; yuck. □ *What is this guck on the bottom of my shoe?* □ *The doctor painted some nasty guck on my throat and told me not to swallow for a while.*

**gucky** ['gəki] *mod.* thick and sticky; yucky. □ *This is a gucky day. Look at the sky.* □ *Yes, it is gucky.* □ *There is a lot of gucky oil and grease on the garage floor.*

**guff** [gəf] **1.** *n.* nonsense; *bunkum.* □ *Wow, that vice president guy can sure dish out the guff!* □ *No more guff outa you, okay?* **2.** *n.* back talk; complaining. □ *I don't want to hear anymore of your guff.* □ *That's enough of your guff!*

**gug** [gəg] *n.* a repellent person. □ *Oo, he's such a gug!* □ *Rocko is not a gug!*

**gulf** *n.* heroin from the Persian Gulf region. (Drugs.) □ *This gulf is flooding the country.* □ *Those pushers can call anything gulf. How does anybody know where it's from?*

**gumdrop** *n.* a tablet or capsule of a drug. (Drugs.) □ *The kids call these things gumdrops.* □ *John's pocket broke, and a bunch of gumdrops ran down his pants leg and out on the floor.*

**gump** [gəmp] *n.* a fool; an oaf. □ *Who's the gump in the yellow slacks?* □ *Don't act like such a gump!*

**gumshoe** ['gəmʃu] *n.* a policeman or a detective. (Underworld. Also a term of address. So-named for wearing silent, gum-rubber soles.) □ *Has that gumshoe been around asking questions again?* □ *Look, gumshoe, what do you want with me?*

**gun 1.** *n.* a hired gunman; a bodyguard, assassin, or member of a gang of criminals. (Underworld and Western.) □ *Bruno and his guns came by to remind Gary of what he owed Mr. Big.* □ *Tell your guns to lay off.* **2.** *n.* a leader; the key member of a group. □ *Who's the gun around here?* □ *Bruno is the gun, and what he says goes.* **3.** *tr.* to race an engine; to rev up an engine. □ *See how loud it is when I gun it?* □ *Gun the thing again and let me hear it.* **4.** *n.* a hypodermic syringe. (Drugs.) □ *Gert broke her gun and had to get another.* □ *She shouldn't use somebody else's gun.*

**gunboats** AND **battleships** *n.* big feet; big shoes. □ *Hasn't he got the biggest gunboats you ever saw?* □ *Whose battleships are these under the coffee table?*

**gun for someone** *in.* to be looking for someone, not necessarily with a gun. □ *Bruno is gunning for Max.* □ *The French prof is gunning for you.*

**gunge** [gəndʒ] *n.* a skin irritation in the groin. (See also *crotch-rot.* Said of males.) □ *I got the gunge. What'll I do?* □ *The sawbones'll give you something for the gunge.*

**gungeon** ['gəndʒən] *n.* a potent type of marijuana from Africa or Jamaica; a cigarette made of this marijuana. (Black.) □ *Where can I get some of that gun-*

*geon?* □ *Is this gungeon really from Africa?*

**gung-ho** ['gəŋ'ho] *mod.* zealous; enthusiastic. □ *We're really gung-ho about the possibilities of this product.* □ *Tod always seems so gung-ho about everything.* □ *He's a gung-ho guy.*

**gungy** AND **grungy** ['gəndʒi AND 'grəndʒi] *mod.* messy; nasty; worn out. (See *grunge.*) □ *Get your grungy feet off the sofa.* □ *The weather is so grungy today.*

**gunja** AND **gunjah** ['gəndʒə] *n.* marijuana; Jamaican marijuana. (Drugs. See also *ganja.*) □ *Max says he sells only the best gunja.* □ *Is this gunjah guaranteed to be from Jamaica?*

**gunk** [gəŋk] **1.** *n.* any nasty, messy stuff. □ *What is this gunk on the counter?* □ *Get this gunk up off the floor before it dries.* **2.** *n.* glue sniffed as a drug. (Drugs.) □ *This kid is high on gunk.* □ *I thought that it was illegal to sell gunk.*

**gunner** *n.* an earnest student. (Collegiate.) □ *Merton is a gunner, all right.* □ *The gunners in my algebra class always get the A's.*

**gunny** ['gəni] *n.* a potent marijuana from Jamaica or Africa. (Drugs. Black.) □ *Is this gunny really from Jamaica?* □ *This gunny is just junk, plain old junk.*

**gunzel** See *gonsel.*

**gunzel-butt** ['gənz|bət] *n.* a strange looking person, usually a male. (Underworld.) □ *Bruno told the gunzel-butt where to get off.* □ *Rocko is no gunzel-butt. He's a thinker.*

**guru** ['guru] **1.** *n.* an experienced *L.S.D.* user who guides someone else on a *trip.* □ *Max volunteered to serve as a guru, but he never showed up.* □ *A guru can be a big help.* **2.** *n.* a stockbroker or other financial adviser. (Financial markets.) □ *My guru says to sell all my bonds.* □ *My guru just went bankrupt.* **3.** *n.* a psychiatrist; a psychotherapist. □ *I go to this guru who gets a lot of money just to listen.* □ *I've started using my mirror for a guru. It's cheaper.*

**gussied up** ['gəsid...] *mod.* dressed up in one's best clothing. (Folksy.) □ *She was all gussied up in her finest.* □ *I like to get gussied up and go out on the town.*

**gusto** ['gəsto] **1.** *n.* beer. (Black.) □ *Can you stop at the filling station and get some gusto?* □ *How about another tube of gusto?* **2.** *in.* to drink beer. (Black.) □ *Don't you ever do anything but gusto?* □ *Let's go out and gusto all night!*

**gut** [gət] **1.** *n.* the belly; the intestines. □ *What a gut that guy has.* □ *Tom poked Bill right in the gut.* **2.** *mod.* basic; fundamental. □ *This is a gut issue, and we have to deal with it now.* □ *We are not dealing with what I would call one of the gut matters of the day.* **3.** *mod.* (of a course in school) easy. □ *That's a gut course. Nothing to it.* □ *I won't take any more gut economics courses. Even those are hard.* **4.** *n.* an easy course in school. □ *That course is a gut.* □ *If it's a gut, it's for me.*

**gutbucket** ['gətbəkɪt] **1.** *n.* a chamber pot, especially one used in a prison cell. (Compare to *gash bucket.*) □ *You got something around here I can use as a gutbucket?* □ *I don't want any gutbucket around here.* **2.** *n.* a toilet. □ *Where's the gutbucket around here?* □ *The kid tried to flush his stash down the gutbucket.* **3.** *n.* the stomach. □ *Hey, your gutbucket's getting sort of big, isn't it?* □ *Sam poked Tod right in the gutbucket.* **4.** *n.* a fat person, usually a man. □ *Harry is getting to be a real gutbucket.* □ *Look at the gutbucket waddling down the street.* **5.** *n.* a cheap saloon; a low tavern. □ *Old Jed is probably stuck in some gutbucket someplace, talking his head off.* □ *The pinstriper needed a drink so bad he stopped at one of those gutbuckets on Maple Street.* **6.** *n.* an earthy style of music. □ *I'd like to hear some good old-fashioned gutbucket.* □ *You don't hear much gutbucket in public places these days.*

**gutless wonder** *n.* a totally spineless person. □ *George, don't be such a gutless wonder! Stand up for your rights!* □ *Here comes that gutless wonder, Merton.*

**gut reaction (to something)** *n.* a basic and immediate response to something. □ *Well, my gut reaction is quite negative.* □ *Her gut reaction to the plan is basically a good one.*

**guts** [gəts] **1.** *n.* courage; bravado. □ *Man, she's got guts!* □ *It takes guts to do something like that.* **2.** *n.* the belly; the intestines. □ *Ted poked Frank right in the guts.* □ *I've got some kind of pain in the guts.* **3.** *n.* the inner workings of anything. □ *There's something wrong in the guts of this clock.* □ *My tape recorder needs all new guts.* **4.** *n.* the essence of something. □ *Let's discuss the real guts of this issue.* □ *The guts of your proposal are really easy to understand.*

**gutsy** ['gətsi] *mod.* courageous; feisty. □ *She sure is a gutsy young thing.* □ *She is not gutsy.* □ *Ernie's acting sort of gutsy today. What happened?*

**gutter** *n.* the vein inside the elbow when used for injecting drugs. (Drugs.) □ *Gert likes to take it in the gutter.* □ *There aren't any places left in the gutter.*

**guy** *n.* a fellow; a man or boy. (Not necessarily male in the plural.) □ *Hey you guys, let's go!* □ *When you guys finish getting your makeup on, we can go back to the guys.*

**guzzle** ['gəzl] **1.** *tr. & in.* to drink alcohol in great quantities. □ *Stop guzzling for a while and pay attention.* □ *Don't guzzle all that beer, or you'll turn into a guzzle-guts.* **2.** *n.* a drinking spree. □ *Fred's out on another of his guzzles.* □ *It's one guzzle after another, day after day.*

**guzzled** ['gəzl̩d] **1.** *mod.* arrested. (Underworld.) □ *Rocko got himself guzzled on a speeding rap.* □ *Lefty is guzzled again. He's so clumsy.* **2.** *mod.* alcohol intoxicated. □ *Sam was plenty guzzled when he got home.* □ *Tod was too guzzled to drive home.*

**guzzle-guts** *n.* a drunkard; a heavy drinker. □ *Old guzzle-guts here would like another drink.* □ *Don't call me guzzle-guts. I hardly ever have a drop.*

**guzzler** *n.* a heavy drinker. □ *Harry is getting to be quite a guzzler.* □ *A couple of guzzlers at the bar were carrying on a low conversation when Barlowe came in.*

**guzzlery** AND **guzzery** ['gəzlə·i AND 'gəzə·i] *n.* a bar; a liquor store. □ *Sam hit every guzzlery on Maple Street on the way home.* □ *I wouldn't be caught dead in a guzzery like that!*

**gweeb** [gwib] *n.* a studious student. (Collegiate. A variant of *dweeb*.) □ *I'm in a physics class full of gweebs.* □ *Merton is a gweeb, all right, but he's a good guy.*

**gynie** ['gɑini] *n.* a gynecologist. □ *My gynie says I'm fine.* □ *She went to a new gynie last week.*

**gyp joint** ['dʒɪp dʒɔɪnt] *n.* a shop or business that cheats people. □ *I'm not going back into that gyp joint.* □ *Stay out of gyp joints like that.*

**gyppy tummy** ['dʒɪpi 'təmi] *n.* an upset stomach; a case of diarrhea. □ *He's got a bad case of the gyppy tummy.* □ *I need some medicine for a gyppy tummy.*

**gyve** [dʒɑɪv] *n.* marijuana; a marijuana cigarette. (Drugs. See also *jive*.) □ *Why are you always smoking gyve?* □ *How about a hit of that gyve?*

**gyvestick** ['dʒɑɪvstɪk] *n.* a marijuana cigarette. (Drugs. The same as *jivestick*.) □ *Where can I get a gyvestick like that?* □ *Max'll sell you all the gyvesticks you want.*

# H

**H.** *n.* heroin. (Drugs.) □ *Now he's shooting H.* □ *First it was M.; now it's H.*

**habit** *n.* an addiction to a drug. □ *She has to steal to support her habit.* □ *There are many treatment programs to help with drug habits.*

**hack 1.** *n.* a taxi. □ *Go out to the street and see if you can get a hack.* □ *I drove a hack for a few months; then I quit.* **2.** *n.* a cough. □ *That's a nasty hack you've got there.* □ *A hack like that can lead to pneumonia.* **3.** *n.* a professional writer who writes mediocre material to order. □ *This novel shows that even a hack can get something published these days.* □ *That hack can't even write her name!* **4.** *n.* a newspaper reporter. □ *She was a hack for the newspaper for a while.* □ *Newspaper hacks have to know a little of everything.* **5.** *tr. & in.* to write clumsy or inefficient computer programs. □ *I can hack a program for you, but it won't be what you want.* □ *Well, I can hack myself.* **6.** *tr.* to annoy someone. □ *This really hacks me.* □ *That kind of behavior hacks her a lot.* (More at *hacked (off).*) **7.** *n.* anyone who does poor or undesirable work. □ *Oh, he's just a hack. What can you expect?* □ *There's always plenty of work for a hack.*

**hack around** *in.* to waste time. □ *You guys are always hacking around. Get busy!* □ *I wanted to hack around for a year after college, but my finances disagreed.*

**hacked** [hækt] *mod.* worn out; ready to quit. □ *What a day! I'm hacked.* □ *We were all hacked at the end of the climb.*

**hacked (off)** *mod.* angry; annoyed. □ *Wally was really hacked off about the* accident. □ *Oh, Wally is always hacked about something.*

**hacker 1.** *n.* a taxi driver. □ *That hacker nearly ran into the back of my car!* □ *You wonder how some of these hackers keep their licenses.* **2.** *n.* a sloppy or inefficient computer programmer. □ *This program was written by a real hacker. It's a mess, but it works.* □ *I may be a hacker, but I get the job done.* **3.** *n.* a generally unsuccessful person. □ *Poor Tod is just a hacker. He'll never go any place.* □ *Hackers keep trying, but they never succeed.*

**hack it** *tr.* to stand up to something; to endure something. □ *It's hard, but I'm sure I can hack it.* □ *I'm afraid you can't hack it. It just isn't working out.*

**had** See *taken.*

**hairy** *mod.* hazardous; difficult. □ *That was a hairy experience!* □ *Wow, that's hairy!* □ *What a hairy ride!*

**hairy-ass(ed)\* 1.\*** *mod.* wild; exciting. (Caution with *ass*.) □ *We had a real hairy-ass time on the roller coaster.* □ *The last part of the climb was really hairy-assed.* **2.\*** *mod.* virile. (Caution with *ass*.) □ *This big hairy-ass guy started to push us around.* □ *He's not what I would call hairy-assed.* □ *Stop acting like a hairy-assed jerk.*

**half-baked 1.** *mod.* badly thought out. □ *That was a half-baked scheme. Was that the best you could do?* □ *It would have been approved if it weren't so half-baked.* **2.** *mod.* alcohol intoxicated. □ *We're getting half-baked, come hell or high water.* □ *Fred got himself sort of half-baked every Saturday night.*

**half-blind** *mod.* alcohol intoxicated. □ *Fred got himself half-blind in no time at* all. □ *Get that half-blind jerk out of here!* □ *Four cans of beer and she was half-blind.*

**half-canned** *mod.* alcohol intoxicated; tipsy. □ *He's half-canned and will be no help at all.* □ *Old Don is half-canned and can't drive home.*

**half-cocked 1.** *mod.* unprepared. (See *go off half-cocked*.) □ *So he's half-cocked. So what?* □ *You're half-cocked for everything you do.* **2.** *mod.* alcohol intoxicated. □ *He just sat there, half-cocked and singing.* □ *Old Jed got himself half-cocked at the reception.*

**half-crocked** *mod.* alcohol intoxicated. □ *Sam and John set out to get half-crocked.* □ *They came home half-crocked at midnight.*

**half in the bag** *mod.* alcohol intoxicated. □ *Jerry was half in the bag when we found him.* □ *They were all half in the bag by midnight.*

**half-lit** *mod.* alcohol intoxicated. □ *John was half-lit in no time at all.* □ *Harry was half-lit by noon.*

**half moon 1.** *n.* hashish molded in the shape of a half moon. (Drugs. See *moon*.) □ *Max is selling half moons, too.* □ *Gert pulled out a half moon and tried to tempt him with it.* **2.** *n.* peyote; a piece of peyote cactus. (Drugs. See *moon*.) □ *Gary poured out a bag of half moons on the table.* □ *These half moons look like little dead somethings.*

**half-sprung** *mod.* tipsy; alcohol intoxicated. □ *Ted was half-sprung and could hardly stand up.* □ *They were half-sprung by noon.*

**half-stewed** *mod.* tipsy; alcohol intoxicated. □ *Poor Fred was half-stewed and still had to give a speech.* □ *We were half-stewed and had a lot of drinking yet to do.*

**half under 1.** *mod.* semiconscious. □ *I was half under and could hear what the doctor was saying.* □ *I was afraid they would start cutting while I was only half under.* **2.** *mod.* alcohol intoxicated; tipsy. □ *He was half under and could barely stand up.* □ *Only four beers and she was half under.*

**half up the pole** *mod.* alcohol intoxicated; tipsy. □ *She drank till she was half up the pole.* □ *Don was half up the*

pole when we picked him up to come here.

**halvsies** ['hævziz] *mod.* with each (of two) paying half. (See *go Dutch*.) □ *Let's do it halvsies.* □ *Let's make it halvsies, and I pay for the parking, too.*

**ham 1.** *n.* an actor; a bad actor. (See also *hams*.) □ *What a ham! A real show-off.* □ *The cast was an assemblage of hams.* **2.** *n.* an amateur radio operator. □ *My brother is a ham, and he helped a lot during the emergency.* □ *The hams helped by providing communication to the outside world.*

**hamburg** *n.* a hamburger. (Compare to *burger*.) □ *I'd like a couple of hamburgs and a shake.* □ *This hamburg is as greasy as they come.*

**hamburger** *n.* a stupid and worthless person—meat. □ *The guy is just hamburger. You can't teach him anything.* □ *There is a lot of hamburger around here. Who hired them?*

**hamburgers** *n.* shares in the McDonald's corporation. (Financial markets. New York Stock Exchange jargon.) □ *I want 400 shares of hamburgers.* □ *Hamburgers just dropped a point.*

**ham-handed** *mod.* lacking dexterity; clumsy. □ *If I wasn't so ham-handed, I could probably fix the thing myself.* □ *He is the most ham-handed guy I've ever seen.*

**hammer** *n.* the accelerator of a vehicle. □ *She pressed down the hammer, and off they went.* □ *The hammer went straight to the floor.*

**hammered** *mod.* alcohol intoxicated. □ *Man, old Fred was really hammered.* □ *She got so hammered she couldn't see.*

**hammerhead 1.** *n.* a stupid person; a person whose head seems to be as solid as a hammer. □ *You can be such a hammerhead!* □ *What a hammerhead! Totally dense!* **2.** *n.* a drunkard or a drug user. □ *These hammerheads can't even hold a simple job for the most part.* □ *A couple of hammerheads stood in the alley, looking suspicious.*

**hams** *n.* legs; hips. □ *Her great hams extended over the sides of the chair.* □ *I got to do something to get the size of these hams down.*

**handful** *n.* a difficult thing or person. □ *Little Jimmy is a handful.* □ *His dad can be a handful, too.*

**hand in glove** *mod.* suiting one another naturally. □ *These two go hand in glove.* □ *The two parts went together like hand in glove.*

**hand it to someone** *tr.* to acknowledge someone's excellence (at something). □ *Well, I have to hand it to you. That was great!* □ *He had to hand it to her for her excellent performance.*

**handle 1.** *n.* a person's name or nickname. (Western jargon and then citizens band radio.) □ *Well, what's your handle so I'll know what to call you?* □ *My handle is Goober. You can call me Goob.* **2.** *n.* a way of dealing with something; a grasp of a problem. □ *As soon as I get a handle on this Wilson matter, I'll give you a buzz.* □ *I can't seem to get a handle on what's wrong.*

**handout 1.** *n.* a gift of money, food, or other goods to a needy person. (Often in the negative, as in the examples.) □ *I don't want a handout, just a loan.* □ *Give him a handout and send him on his way.* **2.** *n.* an informational sheet of paper "handed out" to people. □ *As you can see on your handout, 40 percent of those who started never finished.* □ *I didn't get a handout.*

**hand over fist** *mod.* repeatedly and energetically, especially as with taking in money in a great volume. □ *We were taking in fees hand over fist, and the people were lined up for blocks.* □ *The money came in hand over fist at the B.O.*

**hands down** *mod.* easily; unquestionably. □ *She won the contest hands down.* □ *They declared her the winner hands down.*

**hand someone something** *tr.* to tell someone something; to tell someone nonsense. □ *Don't hand me that stuff! That's silly!* □ *She handed me a line about being a famous author.*

**hands-on 1.** *mod.* having to do with an instructional session where the learners are able to handle the device they are being trained to operate. □ *Please plan to attend a hands-on seminar on computers next Thursday.* □ *After three weeks of hands-on training, I still couldn't* *add two and two.* **2.** *mod.* having to do with an executive or manager who participates directly in operations. □ *We expect that he will be the kind of hands-on president we have been looking for.* □ *John is a hands-on manager. I wish he would stay in his office.*

**Hands up!** AND **Stick 'em up!** *exclam.* "Raise your hands in the air; this is a robbery!" (Underworld and Western.) □ *Hands up! Don't anybody move a muscle. This is a heist.* □ *Stick 'em up! Give me all your valuables.*

**hang a few on** AND **hang on a few** *tr.* to take a few drinks; to have a few beers. □ *They went out to hang a few on.* □ *Let's hang on a few and then go on to the meeting.*

**hang a huey** ['hæŋ ə 'hjui] *tr.* to turn left. □ *Hang a huey at the next corner.* □ *Right here! Hang a huey!*

**hang a left** *tr.* to turn left. □ *He hung a left at the wrong corner.* □ *Hey, here! Hang a left here!*

**hang a louie** ['hæŋ ə 'lui] *tr.* to turn left. □ *You have to hang a louie at the stop sign.* □ *Go another block and hang a louie.*

**hang a ralph** ['hæŋ ə 'rælf] *tr.* to turn right. □ *He skied down the easy slope and hung a ralph near a fir tree.* □ *Don't hang a ralph until you get past the traffic light.*

**hang a right** *tr.* to turn right. □ *Hang a right about here.* □ *I told him to hang a right at the next corner, but he went on.*

**hang (around)** *in.* to loiter; to waste away time doing nothing. □ *Don't just hang around. Get busy with something.* □ *Move. Don't just hang. There's work to be done.*

**hang five** AND **hang ten** *tr.* to stand toward the front of a surfboard or diving board and hang the toes of one or both feet over the edge. (Teens and collegiate.) □ *The coach told her to hang ten and not to look down.* □ *Get out there and hang five. You can swim. Nothing can go wrong.*

**hang in there** *in.* to keep trying; to persevere. □ *Hang in there. Keep trying.* □ *I'll just hang in there. Maybe things will get better.*

**Hang it all!** *exclam.* "Damn it all!" □ *Oh, hang it all! I'm late.* □ *He's late again! Hang it all!*

**hang it up** *tr.* to quit something. □ *I finally had enough and decided to hang it up.* □ *Oh, hang it up! It's hopeless.*

**hang loose** AND **stay loose** *in.* to relax and stay cool. □ *Just hang loose, man. Everything'll be all right.* □ *Stay loose, chum. See ya later.*

**hang one on** *tr.* to get drunk. □ *Fred was hacked and went out to hang one on.* □ *Fred hangs one on about once a month.*

**hangout** ['hæŋaʊt] *n.* a place to loaf or hang (around). □ *I dropped by one of his favorite hangouts, but he wasn't there.* □ *We went over to the hangout and sat around talking.*

**hang ten** See *hang five.*

**hang tough (on something)** *in.* to stick to one's position (on something). □ *I decided I'd hang tough on it. I tend to give in too easy.* □ *Yes, just hang tough.*

**hang up** **1.** *n.* a problem or concern; an obsession. (Usually **hang-up.**) □ *She's got some serious hang-ups about cats.* □ *I don't have any hang ups at all. Well, almost none.* **2.** *in.* to say no; to cancel out of something. □ *I hung up. That's not for me anyway.* □ *If you don't want to do it, just hang up. I'll understand.*

**hanky** AND **hankie** ['hæŋki] *n.* a handkerchief, especially if lacy and feminine. □ *Do you have a hanky I can borrow?* □ *Here, use my hankie.*

**hanky-panky** ['hæŋki'pæŋki] **1.** *n.* funny business; deceitfulness. □ *There's some hanky-panky going on in the treasurer's office.* □ *I am going to get this hanky-panky straightened out.* **2.** *n.* sexual play; sexual misconduct. □ *Sam and Mary are up to a little hanky-panky, I've heard.* □ *There's some hanky-panky going on in the storeroom.*

**happening** **1.** *mod.* fashionable; trendy. (Collegiate.) □ *Oh, Tiffany, your skirt is really happening.* □ *Wow, that's happening!* **2.** *n.* an event. □ *The concert was a real happening.* □ *Well, class is never a happening, but it's never dull.*

**happy** **1.** *mod.* alcohol intoxicated; tipsy. □ *She seems a little happy. Must have had a few already.* □ *She's not*

happy. *She's stewed.* **2.** *mod.* obsessed with something. (A combining form showing a strong interest in the thing that is named before *happy.*) □ *All those guys are girl-happy at this age.* □ *Tod's car-happy right now. That's all he thinks about.*

**happy hour** *n.* cocktail time. □ *Happy hour starts at dawn for Harry.* □ *The hotel had a nice happy hour at five.*

**happy juice** *n.* liquor, beer, and wine. □ *A little more happy juice, John?* □ *Too much happy juice can make you very unhappy.*

**happy pills** *n.* tranquilizers. □ *She asked the doctor for some happy pills.* □ *She is now hooked on happy pills.*

**happy shop** *n.* a liquor store. (Black.) □ *I need something from the happy shop.* □ *Let's stop off at the happy shop.*

**hard** **1.** *mod.* fermented, as with cider. (See also *hard liquor.*) □ *This juice got hard. What shall I do with it?* □ *Where's the hard stuff?* □ *If it's hard, give it to me and I'll drink it.* **2.** *mod.* having to do with an addictive drug. (Compare to **soft.**) □ *Gert's on hard stuff now.* □ *Hard drugs are easier to get than ever before.*

**hardboiled** *mod.* tough; heartless. □ *She is a hardboiled old gal.* □ *Do you have to act so hardboiled?*

**hard candy** *n.* heroin. (Drugs.) □ *Mr. Big wants to move in on Max and peddle hard candy.* □ *Hard candy brings in a lot of cash.*

**hard case** **1.** *n.* a case of liquor. □ *Tod wanted a hard case delivered to his house.* □ *There's a lot of beer and a hard case in the van.* **2.** *n.* a person who is a real problem. □ *Jed has turned into a hard case. He's fighting us at every turn.* □ *The hard case we dealt with last week is back again.*

**hard coin** *n.* lots of money. (See *coin.*) □ *A car like that takes hard coin.* □ *Old Freddie is earning some hard coin these days.*

**hard-core** **1.** *mod.* sexually explicit; pornographic. □ *You can't sell that hard-core stuff in a store like this!* □ *You think that's hard-core?* **2.** *mod.* extreme; entrenched. □ *She spent some time teaching hard-core illiterates in a medi-*

um-sized town. □ *There are too many hard-core cases of poverty there.*

**hardhat** ['hɑrdhæt] **1.** *n.* a protective helmet worn around construction sites. (Standard English.) □ *You'll need a hardhat to come into this area.* □ *John swiped a hardhat from the construction site.* **2.** *n.* construction worker. (Usually derogatory.) □ *The hardhats didn't care much for the actress's politics.* □ *Some hardhat was waving a flag and shouting something I couldn't understand.*

**hardhead** *n.* a stubborn person. □ *You are a classic hardhead. Lighten up!* □ *I'm not really a hardhead. You bring out the worst in me.*

**hardheaded** *mod.* stubborn. □ *Gary is a real hardheaded guy.* □ *Anybody that hardheaded is going to have trouble with everybody.*

**hard-liner** *n.* a person who takes a strict position (on something). □ *Tom is sort of a hard-liner when it comes to spending public money.* □ *The mayor is a hard-liner on the question of care for the elderly.*

**hard liquor** *n.* potent liquor such as whiskey, gin, rum, etc. □ *Hard liquor makes me sick.* □ *Stay off of hard liquor until your stomach feels better.*

**hard-nosed** *mod.* stern and business-like; unsympathetic. □ *She's pretty hard-nosed and tends to put people off.* □ *It takes a hard-nosed manager to run a place like this.*

**hard sell** *n.* a high-pressure attempt to sell something. □ *I didn't want to listen to any hard sell, so I bought it from a mail-order place.* □ *I'm afraid I'm very susceptible to the hard sell.*

**hard time** **1.** *n.* a difficult experience. □ *I had a hard time at the doctor's office.* □ *She's having a hard time with her child.* **2.** *n.* a prison sentence. (Underworld.) □ *Lefty did hard time for his part in the robbery.* □ *How much hard time does he have behind him?*

**hard to swallow** *mod.* difficult to believe. □ *Your story is pretty hard to swallow, but I am beginning to believe it.* □ *The news was hard to swallow.*

**hard up** **1.** *mod.* alcohol intoxicated. □ *After a couple of six packs, Wally found himself a little hard up.* □ *The whole gang was hard up by midnight.* **2.** *mod.* in need of drugs or alcohol. □ *Gert was hard up and needed a fix.* □ *The old hobo was hard up for a drink.* **3.** *mod.* desperate for companionship. □ *Freddie said he was hard up and needed a date.* □ *Mary must be hard up to date a jerk like that.*

**hardware** **1.** *n.* whiskey; potent liquor. □ *This hardware is enough to knock your socks off.* □ *Pour me some of that hardware, will ya?* **2.** *n.* hard drugs or hard liquor. □ *No wine for me. Give me the hardware.* □ *This hardware is pretty powerful.* **3.** *n.* a weapon; a gun. (Underworld and Western.) □ *I think I see your hardware showing.* □ *Lefty keeps his hardware under his mattress.* **4.** *n.* computer parts, as opposed to computer programs. □ *What kind of hardware are you running this program on?* □ *The software is okay, so it must be the hardware that's off.*

**harpoon** *n.* a hypodermic syringe and needle. (Drugs.) □ *Gert kept her harpoon in a drawer by the bed.* □ *She dropped the harpoon and really panicked when it broke.*

**Harry** *n.* heroin. (Drugs.) □ *Gert said she was going to spend the evening with Harry.* □ *Harry isn't a person. Harry is smack.*

**harsh toke** **1.** *n.* an irritating puff of a marijuana cigarette. (Drugs.) □ *Wow, that was a harsh toke. Yuck!* □ *Pat got a harsh toke and coughed a lot.* **2.** *n.* anything or anyone unpleasant. □ *Sally can sure be a harsh toke when she wants.* □ *This meeting has been a real harsh toke.*

**has-been** ['hæzbɪn] **1.** *n.* someone who used to be important; a person whose career has ended. □ *Marty is just a has-been. There's no future for him.* □ *An old has-been was hired to host the midnight show.* **2.** *mod.* former; burnt-out. □ *Some has-been singer croaked through the "Star Spangled Banner."* □ *Now I'm a has-been football player, and nobody even knows my name.*

**hash** [hæʃ] *n.* hashish; cannabis in general. (Drugs.) □ *The amount of hash that moves into this city in a single day would astound you.* □ *Hash is still the favorite first drug other than alcohol.*

**hash brownies** See *pot brownies*.

**hash cannon** *n.* a device used in the smoking of cannabis. (Drugs. Similar to *shotgun*.) □ *Gert kept a hash cannon in her stash.* □ *Don had a hash cannon in his office as a sample of a device for smoking pot.*

**hash-head** *n.* a smoker of cannabis. (Drugs.) □ *You can't stay a hash-head all your life.* □ *Kelly was almost a hopeless hash-head.*

**hash-house** **1.** *n.* a cheap diner. □ *Tom worked for two days as a hash-slinger in a hash-house.* □ *You see a lot of interesting people go in and out of a hash-house like this one.* **2.** *n.* a place where hashish is sold and used. (Drugs.) □ *This hash-house is due for a raid. Let's hit it.* □ *The fuzz raided a hash-house over on Maple Street.*

**hash pipe** *n.* a small pipe for smoking cannabis. (Drugs.) □ *John kept a hash pipe on the shelf just for show.* □ *The cops found a hash pipe in her pocket.*

**hash-slinger** *n.* a cook, waiter, or waitress in a *hash-house*. □ *I worked as a hash-slinger in an all-night diner.* □ *The life of a hash-slinger is pretty tough.*

**hassle** ['hæsl] **1.** *n.* a dispute; a bother. □ *The whole thing was a real hassle.* □ *It's a hassle every time I come here.* **2.** *tr.* to harass someone; to bother someone; to give someone a hard time. □ *Listen, please don't hassle me. I've had a hard day.* □ *Please make this dame stop hassling me!*

**hatch** *n.* the mouth. (See also *Down the hatch!*) □ *Shut your hatch!* □ *Pop this in your hatch.*

**hatch a brick** AND **shit a brick\*** *tr.* to become very angry. (Caution with *shit*.) □ *If my father saw me doing this, he'd hatch a brick.* □ *My uncle nearly shit a brick when the roof collapsed.*

**haul** **1.** *n.* the proceeds from a theft; loot. (Underworld.) □ *They divvied up the haul from the bank job.* □ *The cops thought they must have got a pretty good haul.* **2.** *n.* the proceeds from any activity: a performance, a fishing trip, a collection of goods or money for charity, etc. □ *They got a good haul from the benefit.* □ *They surveyed the haul of cans and packages and decided they had done a pretty fair job.*

**have a ball** *tr.* to have an exciting time. (See *ball*.) □ *I plan to have a ball while I'm there.* □ *Come on, everybody! Let's have a ball!*

**have a big head** **1.** *tr.* to be conceited. (*Have got* can replace *have*.) □ *You've got such a big head, Kate.* □ *If you didn't have a big head, you'd be easier to get along with.* **2.** *tr.* to have a hangover. □ *Wow, do I have a big head this morning!* □ *He's got a big head and can't go to work.*

**have a big mouth** *tr.* to speak loudly; to tell secrets. (*Have got* can replace *have*.) □ *Boy, do you have a big mouth!* □ *He has a big mouth. Don't tell him anything you don't want everybody else to know.*

**Have a blimp!** *exclam.* "Have a good year!" (A play on *Goodyear Tire and Rubber Company*, which operates the Goodyear blimp.) □ *Goodbye. Have a blimp!* □ *Have a blimp! See you next summer.*

**have a buzz on** *tr.* to be tipsy or alcohol intoxicated. (*Have got* can replace *have*.) □ *Tod has a buzz on and is giggling a lot.* □ *Both of them had a buzz on by the end of the celebration.*

**have a crack at something** See *take a crack at something*.

**have a glow on** *tr.* to be alcohol intoxicated; to be tipsy. (*Have got* can replace *have*.) □ *Since you already have a glow on, I guess you won't want another drink.* □ *Jed had a glow on and was just becoming civil.*

**Have a good one.** AND **Have a nice one.** *sent.* "Have a good morning, afternoon, or evening," as appropriate. (A general formulaic expression used at any time of the day or night.) □ *Thank you. Have a good one.* □ *See you tomorrow, Tod. Have a nice one.*

**have a head** *tr.* to have a hangover. (*Have got* can replace *have*.) □ *Oh, man, do I have a head!* □ *Tom has a head this morning and won't be coming into work.*

**Have a heart!** *exclam.* "Be compassionate!"; "Be kind!" □ *Have a heart! Give me another chance.* □ *Come on! Have a heart!*

**have a leg up on someone**  *tr.* to have an advantage over someone; to be ahead of someone. (*Have got* can replace *have*.) □ *Tod has a leg up on Wilbur because of his physical strength.* □ *I don't have a leg up on anyone. I'm a loser.*

**have a little visitor**  *tr.* to have received the menses. (*Have got* can replace *have*.) □ *Mary said she has a little visitor.* □ *She has a little visitor and will call you later.*

**have all one's marbles**  *tr.* to have all one's mental faculties; to be mentally sound. (See also *lose (all) one's marbles. Have got* can replace *have*.) □ *I don't think he has all his marbles.* □ *Do you think Bob has all his marbles?*

**have a load on**  *tr.* to be alcohol intoxicated. (*Have got* can replace *have*.) □ *Fred has a load on and is finished for the evening.* □ *You have a load on every time I see you.*

**have a loose screw**  See *have a screw loose*.

**have a monkey on one's back**  *tr.* to have a drug addiction. (Drugs. *Have got* can replace *have*.) □ *Gert has a monkey on her back.* □ *Do you think she wants to have a monkey on her back?*

**have an ace up one's sleeve**  *tr.* to have something useful in reserve; to have a special trick available. (*Have got* can replace *have*.) □ *I still have an ace up my sleeve that you don't know about.* □ *I don't have an ace up my sleeve. If it doesn't work, it doesn't work.*

**have an edge on**  *tr.* to be alcohol intoxicated. (See also *edge. Have got* can replace *have*.) □ *I've got an edge on and shouldn't drive home.* □ *Bob has an edge on even though he hardly drank anything.*

**Have a nice day.**  *sent.* a formulaic way of saying goodbye. (See *Have a good one*.) □ *Thank you for shopping at Wallace's. Have a nice day.* □ *See you tomorrow. Have a nice day.*

**have an itch for something**  *tr.* to have a desire for something. (*Have got* can replace *have*.) □ *I have an itch for some ice cream.* □ *We had an itch for a good movie, so we went.*

**have ants in one's pants**  *tr.* to be nervous and anxious. (See *antsy. Have*

*got* can replace *have*.) □ *He seems to have ants in his pants before each game.* □ *All kids've got ants in their pants all the time at that age.*

**have a run-in (with someone or something)**  *tr.* to have trouble with someone or something. □ *I had a run-in with Mrs. Wilson. She's a hard case.* □ *We've had a run-in before.*

**have a score to settle (with someone)**  See *settle a score (with someone)*.

**have a screw loose** AND **have a loose screw**  *tr.* to be silly or eccentric. (*Have got* can replace *have*.) □ *He's sort of strange. I think he's got a loose screw.* □ *Yes, he has a screw loose somewhere.*

**have a short fuse**  *tr.* to be easy to anger. (*Have got* can replace *have*.) □ *He's got a short fuse, so watch out.* □ *Molly has a short fuse and is likely to lose her temper at any time.*

**have a skinful**  *tr.* (for someone) to contain too much alcohol; to be alcohol intoxicated. (See *skinful. Have got* can replace *have*.) □ *Tod had a skinful and just sat there quietly.* □ *What is wrong with her is that she has a skinful, that's what.*

**have a spaz**  [...spæz] *tr.* to get angry or hysterical; to have a *conniption (fit).* (Teens and collegiate.) □ *If my dad hears about this, he'll have a spaz.* □ *The teacher had a spaz when I came in so late.*

**have a tiger by the tail**  *tr.* to have become associated with something powerful and potentially dangerous. (*Have got* can replace *have*.) □ *You have a tiger by the tail. You bit off more than you could chew.* □ *You've had a tiger by the tail ever since you took office.*

**have a whale of a time**  *tr.* to have an exciting time; to have a big time. (See *whaling* at *wailing*.) □ *We had a whale of a time at your party.* □ *Yes, we really had a whale of a time.*

**have a yellow streak down one's back**  *tr.* to be cowardly. (*Have got* can replace *have*.) □ *I think that Wally has a yellow streak down his back. That's what's wrong.* □ *If you have a yellow streak down your back, you don't take many risks.*

**have bats in one's belfry** [...'bɛlfri] *tr.* to be crazy. (See *batty. Have got* can replace *have*.) □ *You must really have bats in your belfry if you think I'll put up with that kind of stuff.* □ *Pay no attention to her. She has bats in her belfry.*

**have egg on one's face** *tr.* to be embarrassed by something one has done. (As if one went out in public with a dirty face. *Have got* can replace *have*.) □ *I was completely wrong, and now I have egg on my face.* □ *She's really got egg on her face!*

**have good vibes** [...vaɪbz] *tr.* to have good feelings (about someone or something). (*Have got* can replace *have*.) □ *I've got good vibes about Alice.* □ *I know everything will go all right. I have good vibes.*

**have hell to pay** See *There will be hell to pay.*

**have it all together** *tr.* to be mentally and physically organized; to be of sound mind. (*Have got* can replace *have*.) □ *I don't have it all together today.* □ *Try me again later when I have it all together.*

**have it made** *tr.* to have succeeded; to be set for life. (*Have got* can replace *have*.) □ *I have a good job and a nice little family. I have it made.* □ *He's really got it made.*

**have it made in the shade** *tr.* to have succeeded; to be set for life. (A more casual version of the previous entry. See examples. *Have got* can replace *have*.) □ *Wow, is he lucky! He has it made in the shade.* □ *Who's got it made in the shade?*

**have kittens 1.** *tr.* to become enraged. □ *When I heard the news, I had kittens. I was hacked!* □ *I almost had kittens, I was so mad.* **2.** *tr.* to laugh very hard; to enjoy something enormously. □ *It was so funny, I had kittens laughing.* □ *She had kittens laughing about it.* **3.** *tr.* to be surprised. □ *I nearly had kittens when I heard.* □ *She had kittens when she heard about the wedding.*

**have-nots** *n.* the poor; those who have little or nothing. (Always with *the*. Compare to *haves*.) □ *The have-nots seem never to be able to get ahead.* □ *What's in it for the have-nots?*

**have one foot in the grave** *tr.* to be near death. (*Have got* can replace *have*.) □ *I feel like I've got one foot in the grave.* □ *Uncle Ben has one foot in the grave, but he's still cheery.*

**have one's ass in a crack\*** *tr.* to be stranded in a very difficult or uncomfortable state of affairs. (Caution with *ass. Have got* can replace *have*.) □ *He's got his ass in a crack and needs all the help he can get.* □ *Now he's really got his ass in a crack and doesn't know what to do.*

**have one's ass in a sling\*** *tr.* to be dejected or hurt; to be pouting. (Caution with *ass. Have got* can replace *have*.) □ *She's got her ass in a sling because she got stood up.* □ *Why do you have your ass in a sling?*

**have one's mind in the gutter** *tr.* to think or suggest something obscene. (*Have got* can replace *have*.) □ *Tiffany has her mind in the gutter. That's why she laughs at all that dirty stuff.* □ *You always have your mind in the gutter.*

**have rocks in one's head** *tr.* to be silly or crazy. (*Have got* can replace *have*.) □ *You have rocks in your head!* □ *She's got rocks in her head if she thinks that.*

**haves** *n.* the wealthy; those who have money. (Always with *the*. Compare to *have-nots*.) □ *The haves seem to be able to take care of themselves.* □ *I live in the western suburbs with the haves.*

**have someone dead to rights** *tr.* to have caught someone red-handed; to have irrefutable evidence about someone's misdeed. (*Have got* can replace *have*. See *(bang) (dead) to rights*.) □ *We've got you dead to rights on this one.* □ *The cops had him dead to rights.*

**have something cinched** *tr.* to have something settled; to have the results of some act assured. (See *cinched. Have got* can replace *have*.) □ *Don't worry. I've got it cinched.* □ *You just think you've got it cinched.*

**have something on the brain** *tr.* to be obsessed with something. (*Have got* can replace *have*.) □ *You've just got girls on the brain, you silly twit.* □ *I have money on the brain, I guess.*

**have the wrong number 1.** *tr.* to be wrong. (*Have got* can replace *have*.) □

*Boy, do you have the wrong number! Get with it!* □ *You have missed the boat again. You have the wrong number!* **2.** *tr.* to be addressing the wrong person. (This use is in addition to the same expression used for a wrong telephone number. *Have got* can replace *have.*) □ *You have the wrong number. Walter is my brother. We look alike, though.* □ *No, I'm Sally. You have the wrong number.*

**have what it takes** *tr.* to have the skills, power, intelligence, etc., to do something. (*Have got* can replace *have.*) □ *I know I've got what it takes.* □ *I guess I don't have what it takes to be a composer.*

**Hawaiian (sunshine)** *n.* marijuana grown in Hawaii. (Drugs.) □ *Max says he knows where you can get Hawaiian.* □ *Hawaiian sunshine is what they are all clamoring for now.*

**hawk 1.** *n.* someone who supports a warlike U.S. defense policy. (Compare to *dove.*) □ *The hawks want to raise taxes and buy tanks.* □ *The doves want to sell the tanks, ignore the hawks, and give the money to the poor.* **2.** *in.* to cough mightily; to cough something up. □ *The cold has had me hawking for a week.* □ *He's been hawking all night.* **3.** *n.* the cold winter wind. (Originally black. Always with *the.* See also *Mr. Hawkins.*) □ *Man, just feel the hawk cut through you!* □ *It's the time of the year when the hawk rules!*

**hay 1.** *n.* marijuana; low-quality marijuana. (Drugs.) □ *This stuff isn't anything but hay.* □ *Even if it is hay, it's still illegal.* **2.** See *That ain't hay!*

**hay burner 1.** *n.* a worthless racehorse; any old and worn-out horse. □ *Send that old hay burner to the glue factory.* □ *I went to a dude ranch, and they gave me an old hay burner to ride.* **2.** AND **hay head** *n.* a marijuana smoker. (Drugs. See *hay.*) □ *Some hay burner was around trying to sell raffle tickets that looked handmade.* □ *Another hay head came in and applied for the job.*

**hay head** See the previous entry.

**hayseed** *n.* a farmer; a rustic character, usually a male. □ *I'm not just some hayseed fresh off the farm.* □ *It's hard for these hayseeds to adjust to city life.*

**haywire** ['hewaɪr] **1.** *mod.* out of order. (Folksy.) □ *This telephone has gone haywire.* □ *My stereo is haywire, so I've been listening to the radio.* **2.** *mod.* disoriented from drugs. (Drugs. See *hay.*) □ *Wally is sort of haywire from the grass.* □ *Max has been haywire for years.*

**hazel** ['hezl] *n.* heroin. (Drugs. A variety of *H.*) □ *Gert needs some Hazel, but anything will help her.* □ *She wants to spend the evening with Hazel.*

**head 1.** *n.* a headache. □ *Man, do I have a head. You got any aspirin?* □ *Music that loud gives me a head.* **2.** *n.* a hangover. (Always with *a.*) □ *Boy, do I have a head this morning.* □ *How do you get rid of a head so you can go to work?* **3.** *n.* a toilet; a restroom. (Originally nautical. Usually with *the.*) □ *Where's the head around here?* □ *Ralph is in the head. He'll be back in a minute.* **4.** *n.* a member of the drug culture; a hippie or a person who drops out of mainstream society because of drug use. (From the 1960s and 1970s.) □ *You still see a few heads around, even today.* □ *Some of the heads became very, very straight.*

**headache 1.** *n.* an annoying person or thing. □ *Here comes that Kelly Johnson. He's a real headache.* □ *Cars can be such a headache.* **2.** *n.* liquor. □ *Pour me some more of that headache, will you?* □ *Give the man some more headache.*

**headache department 1.** *n.* a central source of unnecessary problems; a person who habitually causes problems. □ *Here's another memo from the headache department.* □ *Mrs. Wilson is my least favorite headache department.* **2.** AND **headache house** *n.* a liquor store or department. □ *I stopped in at the headache department for some supplies.* □ *The headache house is having a special on gin.*

**headache man** *n.* a male law enforcement agent. □ *The headache man was here to see you, Ernie.* □ *Who gave that hot tip to the headache man?*

**headbone** *n.* the skull. □ *I got a nasty bump on my headbone.* □ *Do you want I should conk your headbone, or will you be coming along politely?*

**head cook and bottle washer** AND **chief cook and bottle washer** *n.* someone who is in charge of something trivial. □ *I'm the head cook and bottle washer around here.* □ *I want to see the chief cook and bottle washer.*

**head drug** *n.* a drug that affects the mind rather than the body; a psychoactive drug. □ *It's these head drugs that get the kids into so much trouble.* □ *Head drugs are just as addictive as other drugs, but in a different way.*

**headfucker\*** ['hɛdfəkɚ] *n.* a potent psychoactive drug; *L.S.D.* (Drugs. Caution with *fuck*.) □ *This stuff is a real headfucker. Stay away from it.* □ *John's first experience with a headfucker was not one he's likely to forget.*

**head hunt** *tr. & in.* to recruit someone (for a job). □ *He went to the conference to head hunt a new employee.* □ *All the managers were there to head hunt.*

**headhunter** *n.* someone who recruits executives for employment. (*Head* means "boss" here.) □ *The board of directors hired a headhunter to get a new manager.* □ *The headhunter brought in a few candidates, but nobody promising.*

**head kit** *n.* equipment for using drugs. (Drugs.) □ *Gert kept her head kit hidden away.* □ *She had a little hash cannon in her head kit.*

**head shop** AND **head store** *n.* a shop that sells drug-use equipment. (Drugs.) □ *The parents kept after the mayor until the head shop was closed.* □ *They'd better not try to open a head store on our block.*

**head someone off at the pass** See *cut someone off at the pass.*

**head South** See *go South.*

**Heads up!** *exclam.* "Look out!" □ *Heads up! Watch out for the swinging bucket!* □ *Here's a rough spot on the trail. Heads up!*

**heads will roll** *phr.* someone will be punished. □ *When I find out who did this, heads will roll.* □ *Heads will roll when I get back to the office.*

**head trip** **1.** *n.* a session with a *head drug.* (Drugs.) □ *Bob had his first head trip last night.* □ *He says it will be his last head trip.* **2.** *n.* an ego trip. □ *Wally is on another of his head trips.* □ *Come*

down from your head trip and see if you can get along with the rest of us.

**heap** **1.** *n.* an old car. □ *I've got to get my heap fixed up.* □ *Is this old heap yours?* **2.** *n.* any dilapidated thing or person. □ *Marty is turning into a heap.* □ *We have to fix up this heap if we're really going to live in it.* **3.** AND **heaps** *n.* lots (of something). □ *I have a whole heap of papers for you.* □ *Mr. Wilson has heaps of money.*

**heaps** See the previous entry.

**heart** **1.** *n.* an amphetamine tablet, especially a heart-shaped tablet. (Drugs.) □ *She was taking nothing but hearts the last I heard.* □ *She takes hearts in the mornings.* **2.** *tr.* to love someone or something. (Teens.) □ *Oh, I just, like, heart your letter.* □ *She's hearting him more every day.*

**hearts and flowers** *n.* sentimentality. □ *The movie was so full of hearts and flowers that I was bored.* □ *I didn't care for the hearts and flowers part.*

**heart-to-heart (talk)** *n.* a serious and intimate discussion. □ *We sat down and had a nice heart-to-heart for about an hour.* □ *A little heart-to-heart talk is just what you need.*

**heat** **1.** *n.* the police. (Underworld. Always with *the.*) □ *The heat is gonna catch up with you, Ernie.* □ *Who tipped the heat off about me?* **2.** *n.* pressure. □ *There's a lot of heat on Fred right now.* □ *The boss put some heat on Wally, and things are moving faster now.* **3.** *n.* a gun; armaments. (Underworld. Compare to *heater.*) □ *Lefty has his heat on him at all times.* □ *Rocko never carries heat.*

**heater** *n.* a pistol. (Underworld.) □ *Lefty carried his heater with him that day.* □ *Put your heaters away, boys. This is a job for reason.*

**heave** [hiv] *in.* to empty one's stomach; to vomit. □ *He heaved and heaved and sounded like he was dying.* □ *I think I have to go heave.*

**heaven dust** *n.* cocaine. (Drugs.) □ *A little heaven dust and Pat was as good as new.* □ *She left her desk to take on a little heaven dust.*

**heavies** ['hɛviz] *n.* hard drugs; addictive drugs. (Drugs.) □ *Stay away from the* heavies. □ *Heavies will stay with you for the rest of your life.*

**heavy 1.** *n.* a villain. (Especially in movies, etc.) □ *He is well known for playing heavies in the movies.* □ *Do I always have to be the heavy?* **2.** *mod.* important; profound; serious. □ *This is a very heavy matter.* □ *This matter is too heavy.* □ *I have some heavy things to talk over with you, Sam.* **3.** *mod.* really fine. □ *Man, this is some heavy chocolate cake!* □ *This stuff is really heavy!* □ *This is a real heavy thing you're doing for me.*

**heavy artillery** *n.* powerful or persuasive persons or things. (See examples.) □ *Finally, the mayor brought out the heavy artillery and quieted things down.* □ *The heavy artillery seemed to know how to handle matters.*

**heavy bread** AND **heavy money** *n.* a great deal of money. □ *Man, that car cost some heavy bread.* □ *It takes heavy money to run a household like this.*

**heavy date** *n.* an important date with someone; a date with someone important. □ *Mary has a heavy date with Sam tonight.* □ *Tod and Sally were out on a heavy date together.*

**heavy drugs** AND **heavy stuff** *n.* addictive drugs. (Drugs.) □ *Ernie and Gert are both into heavy drugs.* □ *The heavy stuff will hook them for sure.*

**heavy-handed** *mod.* tactless; forceful; unfair. □ *Paul is a little heavy-handed at times, but mostly he's reasonable.* □ *That was a pretty heavy-handed thing to do.*

**heavy hash** *n.* potent cannabis. (Drugs.) □ *Man, you came up with some real heavy hash.* □ *This is heavy hash, and it will cost you.*

**heavy into someone or something** *mod.* much concerned with someone or something; obsessed with someone or something. (Black.) □ *Freddie was heavy into auto racing and always went to the races.* □ *Sam is heavy into Mary.*

**heavy joint** *n.* a marijuana cigarette tipped with *P.C.P.* (Drugs.) □ *He said something about smoking a heavy joint just before he passed out.* □ *Bob found something on the sidewalk he called a heavy joint.*

**heavy metal 1.** *n.* a type of rock music characterized by enormous volume and a throbbing beat. □ *I just don't care for that heavy metal.* □ *Heavy metal is just too loud.* **2.** *mod.* having to do with *heavy metal* music or musicians. □ *Heavy metal stuff is a little harsh for my old ears.* □ *Those heavy metal guys must have made a fortune.*

**heavy money** See *heavy bread.*

**heavy necking** *n.* hugging and kissing, plus intimate caresses. □ *Mary and Sam are past heavy necking.* □ *The teacher caught them at some heavy necking in the closet.*

**heavy scene** *n.* a serious state of affairs; an emotionally charged situation. □ *Man, that meeting was really a heavy scene.* □ *Another heavy scene like that and I quit.*

**heavy soul** *n.* heroin. (Black.) □ *Tyrone is hung up on some heavy soul.* □ *That heavy soul will be on your back forever.*

**heavyweight 1.** *n.* an important person; a successful person; a leader. □ *Mr. Wilson is a heavyweight in local government.* □ *They'll bring out the heavyweights next time. Just wait and see.* **2.** *mod.* important; successful. □ *Vince is one of the heavyweight operators in this business.* □ *He's good, but he's no heavyweight.*

**heebie-jeebies** AND **heeby-jeebies** ['hibi'dʒibiz] *n.* an extreme case of anxiety or fear. □ *I have the heebie-jeebies whenever I go to the dentist.* □ *These movies give me the heebie-jeebies.*

**heel** *n.* a low and despicable man. □ *You are the most impossible heel!* □ *The guy is a heel, and he seems to work at it, too.*

**heeled 1.** *mod.* alcohol intoxicated. □ *Sally was too heeled to drive home.* □ *Man, were those guys heeled!* **2.** *mod.* carrying drugs. (Drugs.) □ *Max is heeled and ready to deal.* □ *Gert was heeled when they arrested her.*

**heesh** [hiʃ] *n.* hashish; cannabis. (Drugs.) □ *Ernie started out on heesh and moved on from there.* □ *Who's dealing heesh around here?*

**Heinz 57 (variety)** [haɪnz...] *n.* a mongrel breed of dog. (From the trade name of a condiment company.) □ *We have one pedigreed dog and one Heinz 57 variety.* □ *My Heinz 57 is the greatest dog of all.*

**heist** [haɪst] **1.** *n.* a theft; a robbery; a *lift*. (Underworld.) □ *Lefty just had to pull one last heist.* □ *The heist went off without a hitch.* **2.** *tr.* to steal something; to rob a person or place; to *lift* something. (Underworld.) □ *The thugs heisted her and took her purse and watch.* □ *Lefty heisted a car and then drove around in it all evening.*

**heister** ['haɪstɚ] *n.* a drunkard. □ *Two old heisters were lifting drink after drink and tossing them down.* □ *Wally is getting to be quite a heister.*

**Helen** *n.* heroin. (Drugs.) □ *Gert said she was spending the evening with Helen, whatever that means.* □ *Max is dealing Helen and gets good stuff from the east.*

**helium head** ['hiliəm 'hɛd] *n.* a fool; an airhead. □ *Well, what's that helium head done now?* □ *You can be such a helium head without even trying.*

**hell\* 1.\*** *n.* trouble. (Caution with *hell*.) □ *I went through all sorts of hell to get this done on time.* □ *This day was real hell.* **2.\*** *exclam.* "Damn!" (Usually **Hell!** Caution with *hell*.) □ *Oh, hell. I'm late.* □ *Hell, I'm too early.*

**hellacious\*** [hɛl'eʃəs] **1.** *mod.* wild; excellent. (Caution with *hell*.) □ *What a hellacious good time we had!* □ *Sally throws one hellacious party.* **2.** *mod.* terrible. □ *The food was just hellacious. Yuck!* □ *The heat was hellacious, and the mosquitoes wouldn't leave us alone.*

**hell and half of Georgia\*** [...'dʒɔrdʒə] AND **hell's half acre\*** *n.* an enormous geographical area. (Folksy. Caution with *hell*.) □ *My family's scattered over hell and half of Georgia.* □ *My papers blew all over hell's half acre.*

**hellbender\*** ['hɛlbɛndɚ] **1.\*** *n.* a drinking bout. (Caution with *hell*.) □ *Jed is off on another of his hellbenders.* □ *One of his hellbenders can last for a week.* **2.\*** *n.* a heavy drinker; a drunkard. (The *bender* refers to bending the elbow with a drink in hand. Caution with *hell*.) □ *Wally is a hellbender from way back.* □ *Jed is a world-class hellbender.*

**heller\*** AND **hell raiser\*** *n.* a rowdy person; a hell-raising person. (Caution with *hell*.) □ *Ernie was a real heller when he was younger.* □ *A bunch of hell raisers kept me up late last night.*

**hellhole\*** *n.* a hot and crowded place; any unpleasant place. (Caution with *hell*.) □ *I want out of this hellhole.* □ *The theater was an over-crowded hellhole. Lucky there was no fire.*

**hell of a mess\*** *n.* a terrible mess. (See also *mell of a hess*. Caution with *hell*.) □ *This is really a hell of a mess you've gotten us into.* □ *I never dreamed I'd come back to such a hell of a mess.*

**hell of a note\*** *n.* a surprising or amazing piece of news. (Caution with *hell*.) □ *Well, that's a hell of a note!* □ *You forgot it. That's a hell of a note.*

**hell of a someone or something\*** AND **helluva someone or something\* 1.\*** *n.* a very bad person or thing. (Caution with *hell*.) □ *That's a hell of a way to treat someone.* □ *He's a hell of a driver! Watch out!* **2.\*** *n.* a very good person or thing. (Caution with *hell*.) □ *He is one hell of a guy. We really like him.* □ *We had a helluva good time.*

**hell on wheels\*** *n.* a very impressive person or thing; an extreme type of person or thing. (Caution with *hell*.) □ *Fred is really hell on wheels when it comes to getting those little jobs done on time.* □ *This little machine is hell on wheels for general woodworking purposes.*

**Hell's bells (and buckets of blood)!\*** *exclam.* "Dammit!" (Caution with *hell*.) □ *Oh, hell's bells and buckets of blood! I forgot my keys.* □ *Hell's bells! I'm late.*

**hell's half acre** See *hell and half of Georgia*.

**helluva someone or something** See *hell of a someone or something*.

**hemp 1.** *n.* a smelly cigar. □ *Get that vile hemp out of here!* □ *Can you imagine somebody bringing an old hemp like that in here?* **2.** *n.* cannabis. (Drugs. See also *rope*.) □ *The guy sort of smells like hemp.* □ *I smell hemp in here.*

**hen fruit** *n.* hen's eggs. □ *I always have hen fruit for breakfast.* □ *There's nothing like hen fruit and bacon.*

**hen party** *n.* a gossipy party attended by women. □ *I have a hen party every few weeks. We love to get together.* □ *I wouldn't be caught dead at one of those hen parties.*

**Henry** *n.* heroin. (Drugs.) □ *Ernie says he's going to take a vacation with Henry.* □ *Ask Max where Henry is.*

**hep** [hɛp] *mod.* aware; informed. □ *The chick is simply not hep.* □ *Fred is one of the most hep guys you're going to run into.*

**hepped (up)** *n. mod.* alcohol intoxicated. □ *Wally is a little too hepped up to drive home.* □ *Harry's too hepped to stand up.*

**her** *n.* cocaine. (Drugs.) □ *Max was trying to sell a few ounces of her before giving up for the night.* □ *You got any her on you?*

**herb** AND **erb** *n.* marijuana. (Drugs.) □ *Bruno is very fond of herb.* □ *Carl has found a way to synthesize the erb.*

**Herb and Al** *n.* marijuana and alcohol. □ *I'm afraid that Tom's best friends are Herb and Al.* □ *Wally asked us over to meet Herb and Al.*

**Here's looking at you.** *sent.* "I salute you." (A polite drinking toast.) □ *Well, here's looking at you.* □ *Here's looking at you. Bottoms up!*

**Here's mud in your eye.** *sent.* "I salute you." (A jocular drinking toast.) □ *Here's mud in your eye. Bottoms up!* □ *Well, here's mud in your eye. Care for another?*

**hero (of the underworld)** *n.* heroin. □ *Don says he knows the hero of the underworld well.* □ *Bruno stays away from hero.*

**herped up** *mod.* infected with the *herpes simplex* virus. □ *Why do all the boys treat me like I was herped up or something?* □ *They say all those frat guys are herped up.*

**herpie** ['hɚpi] *n.* a person infected with the *herpes simplex* virus. □ *Oo, somebody said he's a herpie!* □ *Stay away from that chick. She's a herpie.*

**het up** [hɛt...] *mod.* angry; agitated. (Folksy.) □ *I wouldn't want him to get all het up.* □ *Now, don't get so het up!*

**hick** [hɪk] *n.* a farmer; a rustic oaf. □ *Some hick brought his pig into town to see the doctor.* □ *That hick only shaves once a week.*

**hickey** AND **hicky** ['hɪki] **1.** *n.* a love bite; a mark on the skin caused by biting or sucking. (See also *monkey bite*.) □ *He's mad at her because she gave him a hicky.* □ *She wore a high collar to cover up a hickey.* **2.** *n.* a pimple, especially if infected. □ *There is a hickey on my nose!* □ *Wouldn't you know I'd get a hickey like this right when I have to have my picture taken!*

**hicky** See the previous entry.

**hide** *n.* the skin. □ *I need to get some rays on my hide.* □ *Your hide looks pretty pale, all right.*

**hides** *n.* drums. (See also *skins*.) □ *Andy can really bang those hides.* □ *They say his hides are worth about 4,000 clams.*

**high 1.** *mod.* alcohol or drug intoxicated. □ *Wally is a little high for so early in the evening.* □ *They went out for the evening to get high, and for no other reason.* **2.** *n.* a state of euphoria caused by drugs or alcohol. □ *His life is nothing but one high after another.* □ *Her only goal is a high.*

**high and dry** *mod.* abandoned; unsupported. (Like a ship beached or stranded ashore.) □ *He went off and left me high and dry.* □ *Here I sit high and dry—no food, no money, no nothing.*

**highbrow 1.** *n.* an intellectual person; a person with refined tastes. (The opposite of *lowbrow*. See also *longhair*.) □ *Sam used to be a highbrow, but he gave up his fancy ways.* □ *The highbrows usually congregate in there.* **2.** *mod.* having to do with an intellectual or a person with refined tastes. □ *I just don't care for highbrow music.* □ *Tod is sort of highbrow, but he's an okay guy.*

**highfalutin** ['haɪfə'lutn̩] *mod.* high-class; refined; snobbish. (Folksy.) □ *Maybe someday all that highfalutin talk will get you somewhere.* □ *She's too highfalutin.* □ *Save your highfalutin ideas for when you go to the city.*

**high five 1.** *n.* a greeting where the palm of the hand is raised and slapped against another person's palm similarly raised. (Compare to *low five*.) □ *They exchanged a high five and went on with the*

*show.* □ *How about a high five, man?*
**2.** *tr. & in.* to greet someone as described in sense 1. □ *They high fived and went off together.* □ *Ted high fived Sam, and they stopped to talk.*

**highjinks** AND **hijinks** ['haɪdʒɪŋks] *n.* tricks; capers. □ *Enough of your hijinks! Get busy.* □ *I like to hear about the kids and their latest hijinks.*

**high old time** *n.* a fine time, as at a good party. (Folksy.) □ *We had a high old time at Sally's hoochfest.* □ *We're going to have a high old time tonight.*

**high on something** *mod.* excited or enthusiastic about something. □ *Tom is really high on the idea of going to Yellowstone this summer.* □ *I'm not high on going, but I will.*

**high-res** AND **hi-res** ['haɪ'rɛz] *mod.* good; satisfying. (From *high-resolution,* referring to the picture quality of a computer monitor. Compare to *low-res.*) □ *This is a real high-res day for me.* □ *I sure feel hi-res today.*

**high roller** *n.* a big gambler who risks much money; anyone who takes risks. (Refers to rolling dice.) □ *Rocko is a high roller and isn't afraid to lose some money.* □ *He's a high roller from way back.*

**high sign** *n.* a hand signal meaning "okay." (The tip of the index or middle finger touches the tip of the thumb, and the hand is raised into the air.) □ *Tom got the high sign and began to open the door.* □ *Give me the high sign when you want me to start.*

**high tea** *n.* a session of marijuana smoking. (Drugs. A pun on (British) "high tea.") □ *Wally can't wait for high tea once or twice a week.* □ *We went over to Clare's for high tea.*

**high ups** AND **higher ups** *n.* the people in charge. □ *I have to speak to the high ups about the refund.* □ *One of the higher ups is coming down to talk to you.*

**highway robbery** *n.* a charge that is unbelievably high, but nonetheless unavoidable. (As if one had been accosted and robbed on the open road.) □ *But this is highway robbery. I demand to see the manager.* □ *Four thousand dollars! That's highway robbery!*

**high, wide, and handsome** *mod.* happy; carefree. □ *Wally is high, wide, and handsome after his great triumph.* □ *He sure looks high, wide, and handsome. I'm glad he's happy.*

**hike 1.** *n.* a monetary increase. □ *I need a pay hike.* □ *Another hike in the electric rates takes place this spring.* **2.** *tr.* to increase an amount of money. □ *I wanted them to hike my salary, but they refused.* □ *The utilities all hike their rates at least once a year.*

**Hill** *n.* the U.S. Congress; the U.S. capitol building located on Capitol Hill in Washington, D.C. (Always with *the.*) □ *I really can't tell what's happening up on the Hill.* □ *The Hill moves at its own speed.*

**hincty** ['hɪŋkti] *mod.* snobbish; fussy; aloof. (Black.) □ *Some of those people are so hincty.* □ *That hincty lady told me to turn my radio down.*

**hip 1.** *mod.* informed; aware. (See also **hep.**) □ *The guy is just not hip. He's a nerd.* □ *Get hip, Tom!* **2.** *tr.* to tell someone; to inform someone. □ *Hey, man, hip me to what's going on!* □ *What's happening? Take a minute and hip me!*

**hipe** See **hype.**

**hippy** AND **hippie** ['hɪpi] *n.* a long-haired, drug-using youth of the 1960s-70s. □ *That guy looks like a hippy left over from the sixties.* □ *Who's that has-been hippie who just came in?*

**hip-shooter** *n.* someone who talks without thinking; someone who speaks very frankly. (See *shoot from the hip.*) □ *He's just a loudmouth hip-shooter. Pay no attention.* □ *The press secretary was a hyper and a hip-shooter. She won't last long.*

**hipster** ['hɪpstɚ] *n.* a youth of the 1950s, characterized by an interest in jazz and cool things. □ *Can you imagine your father as a hipster?* □ *Were the hipsters the ones with the big shoulder pads?*

**hired gun** *n.* a hired assassin. (Underworld.) □ *Bruno is Mr. Big's hired gun.* □ *The cops are holding a well-known hired gun until they can prepare charges.*

**hi-res** See **high-res.**

**history** *n.* someone or something in the past. (See also *ancient history.*) □ *Dave?*

*Oh, he's just history. I never go out with him anymore.* □ *Susan is just history. We're through.* □ *Don't make a move! If this gun goes off, you're history.*

**hit 1.** *n.* a success; something that meets with approval. (Often with *with*.) □ *The play was a hit.* □ *The fudge with nuts in it was a great hit at the sale.* **2.** *n.* a successful result; something that is exactly as intended. □ *It was a hit—a real winner.* □ *Your idea was right on target—a hit for sure.* **3.** *n.* a drink of liquor; a dose of a drug. (See also *bop*.) □ *He had a hit of sauce and went out to finish his work.* □ *She popped a hit by the watercooler.* **4.** *tr.* to reach something; to achieve something. □ *The car hit 90 in no time at all.* □ *I hit sixty next month, and I'm going to retire.* **5.** *tr.* to kill someone; to assassinate someone. (Underworld.) □ *Bruno was told to hit Max.* □ *The thug set out to hit the mayor, but got nabbed first.* **6.** *tr.* to attack or rob someone or something. (Underworld.) □ *Lefty and his gang hit the bank for the second time.* □ *Can you believe that they tried to hit a block party on 47th Street?* **7.** *n.* a robbery; an assassination. (Underworld.) □ *There was a hit at the bank on Maple Street last night.* □ *Somebody died in the hit last night, but they don't know who yet.*

**hitched** *mod.* married. (Folksy.) □ *Sam and Mary decided to get hitched.* □ *They went out of state to get hitched.*

**hit list** *n.* a list of people to whom something is going to happen. □ *Ralph is on my hit list for contributing money for the orphans.* □ *She's on our hit list for volunteers.*

**hit man 1.** *n.* a hired killer. (Underworld.) □ *Bruno was the perfect hit man. Hardly any brains or conscience.* □ *To look at Rocko, you'd never believe he was a hit man.* **2.** *n.* a man hired by a helpless addict to inject drugs. (Drugs. See *pinch hitter*.) □ *Gert needed a hit man when she was sick.* □ *Max refuses to be a hit man. He says that's not what he does best.*

**hit me 1.** AND **hit me again** *tr.* (in gambling) "Deal me a card." □ *Hit me again, dealer!* □ *Okay, hit me.* **2.** *tr.* "Give me the high five." □ *Hit me!*

*Where you been? Hit me again!* □ *Long time, no see. Hit me, man.* **3.** AND **hit me again** *tr.* "Serve me (another) drink." □ *Hit me again, bartender.* □ *It's empty. Hit me.*

**hit on something** *in.* to discover something. □ *She hit on a new scheme for removing the impurities from drinking water.* □ *I hit on it when I wasn't able to sleep one night.*

**hit pay dirt** AND **strike pay dirt 1.** *tr.* to discover something of value. □ *At last, we hit pay dirt.* □ *When we opened the last trunk, we knew we had hit pay dirt.* **2.** *tr.* to get to the basic facts of something. □ *Now we're beginning to hit pay dirt.* □ *When we figured out the code, we really struck pay dirt.*

**hit (someone) below the belt** *tr.* to deal with someone unfairly. (From boxing.) □ *Don't hit below the belt!* □ *You were hitting Tom below the belt when you said that.*

**hit someone (up) for something** *tr.* to ask someone for something. □ *I hit Fred up for some help with the committee.* □ *He hit me up for a loan, but I said no.*

**hit someone with something** *tr.* to present someone with an idea, plan, or proposal. □ *Tod hit me with a great idea just before we left.* □ *Fred hit his boss with a plan to save a bundle in the front office.*

**hit spike** *n.* a substitute for a hypodermic needle. (Drugs.) □ *Gert always kept a hit spike in a secret place.* □ *Ernie couldn't find a hit spike.*

**hit the books** AND **pound the books** *tr.* to study hard. □ *I spent the weekend pounding the books.* □ *I gotta go home and hit the books.*

**hit the bottle** AND **hit the booze** *tr.* to go on a drinking bout; to get drunk. □ *Jed's hitting the bottle again.* □ *He's been hitting the booze for a week now.*

**hit the bricks** AND **hit the pavement 1.** *tr.* to start walking; to go into the streets. □ *I have a long way to go. I'd better hit the bricks.* □ *Go on! Hit the pavement! Get going!* **2.** *tr.* to go out on strike. □ *The workers hit the pavement on Friday and haven't been back on the job since.* □ *Agree to our demands, or we hit the bricks.*

**hit the ceiling** AND **hit the roof** *tr.* to get very angry. □ *She really hit the ceiling when she found out what happened.* □ *My dad'll hit the roof when he finds out about this.*

**hit the deck 1.** *tr.* to get out of bed. □ *Come on, hit the deck! It's morning.* □ *Hit the deck! Time to rise and shine!* **2.** *tr.* to fall down; to drop down. □ *Hit the deck. Don't let them see you.* □ *I hit the deck the minute I heard the shots.*

**hit the fan** *tr.* to become publicly known; to become a scandal. (From the phrase "when the shit hit the fan.") □ *I wasn't even in the country when it hit the fan.* □ *It hit the fan, and within ten minutes the press had spread it all over the world.*

**hit the hay** AND **hit the sack** *tr.* to go to bed. □ *I have to go home and hit the hay pretty soon.* □ *Let's hit the sack. We have to get an early start in the morning.*

**hit the jackpot 1.** *tr.* to win a large amount of money. □ *I hit the jackpot in the big contest.* □ *Sally hit the jackpot in the lottery.* **2.** *tr.* to be exactly right; to find exactly what was sought. □ *I hit the jackpot when I found this little cafe on 47th Street.* □ *I wanted a small house with a fireplace, and I really hit the jackpot with this one.*

**hit the panic button** AND **press the panic button, push the panic button** *tr.* to panic. □ *She hit the panic button and just went to pieces.* □ *Don't press the panic button. Relax and keep your eyes open.*

**hit the pipe 1.** *tr.* to smoke opium. □ *The old man told about the days when they went down to Chinatown to hit the pipe.* □ *They would hit the pipe about once a week.* **2.** *tr.* to smoke cannabis. (Drugs.) □ *Jack liked to hit the pipe every now and then.* □ *Come over, and we'll hit the pipe or something.*

**hit the road** *tr.* to leave; to begin to travel on a road. □ *We plan to hit the road about dawn.* □ *Let's hit the road. We have a long way to go.*

**hit the roof** See *hit the ceiling.*

**hit the sack** See *hit the hay.*

**hit the skids** *tr.* to decline; to decrease in value or status. □ *Jed hit the skids when he started drinking.* □ *The firm hit the skids when the dollar collapsed.*

**hit the spot 1.** AND **hit the bull's eye** *tr.* to be exactly right. (See also *ring the bell.*) □ *You really hit the spot with that prediction.* □ *Tod's prediction hit the bull's eye.* **2.** *tr.* to be refreshing. □ *This cold water really hits the spot.* □ *I want something hot—some coffee would really hit the bull's eye.*

**hit the trail** *tr.* to leave. (As if one were riding a horse.) □ *I have to hit the trail before sunset.* □ *Let's hit the trail. It's late.*

**hit under the wing** *mod.* alcohol intoxicated. (See *shot.*) □ *Jed got hit under the wing.* □ *Sally was a little hit under the wing, but she wasn't bad off at all.*

**Hiya!** [ˈhaɪjə] *exclam.* "Hi!" (From *Hi, you!*) □ *Hiya! Good to see ya!* □ *Hiya! Where you been keeping yourself?*

**hock 1.** *tr.* to pawn something. □ *I tried to hock my watch to get some money.* □ *I've got nothing left to hock.* **2.** *n.* the state of having been pawned. (Usually with *in.*) □ *My watch is already in hock.* □ *Get it out of hock or go buy a new one.* **3.** *n.* a foot. □ *My hocks are sore from all that walking.* □ *Have you ever seen such humongous hocks?*

**hockey** AND **hocky** [ˈhɑki] *mod.* dung. (See also *horse hockey.*) □ *Watch out for that hocky there in the gutter.* □ *Don't step in the fresh hockey.*

**hockshop** *n.* a pawnshop. □ *We took the watch to a hockshop, but couldn't get enough money for it.* □ *The cops checked all the hockshops in town for the murder weapon.*

**hocky** See *hockey.*

**hocus** *tr.* to falsify something; to adulterate something. □ *Who hocused the check?* □ *Somebody has hocused the booze.*

**hodad** AND **hodaddy** [ˈhodæd AND ˈhodædi] *n.* an obnoxious person; a repellent person. (California.) □ *Ted is a total hodad.* □ *Who's the hodaddy in the plaid pants?*

**hog 1.** AND **hog cadillac** *n.* a large car; a *souped up* car. (See also *road hog.*) □ *How do you like my new hog?* □ *That hog cadillac needs new shocks.* **2.** *n.* a police officer; a *pig.* □ *The hogs are on to you.* □ *Who called the hogs?* **3.** *n.* an addict who requires very large doses to sustain the habit. (Drugs.) □ *Gert isn't a hog. She tries to keep her habit small.* □ *Ernie is turning into a hog. He just can't get enough.* **4.** *n.* phencyclidine, *P.C.P.*, an animal tranquilizer. (Drugs.) □ *We're glad to learn that the demand for hog is tapering off.* □ *Max won't sell hog to kids these days.*

**hogwash 1.** *n.* bad food or drink. □ *This stuff is hogwash. Take it away.* □ *How about some more of this high-quality hogwash?* **2.** *n.* nonsense. □ *Now that's just hogwash, and you know it.* □ *Hogwash! That's about enough of your lies!*

**hog-wild** *mod.* wild; boisterous. (See *run hog-wild.*) □ *All the kids were completely hog-wild by the time I got there.* □ *Things got sort of hog-wild while you were away.*

**ho-hum** ['ho'həm] *mod.* dull; causing yawns. □ *Clare played another ho-hum concert at the music hall last night.* □ *It was a ho-hum lecture.*

**hoist one** *tr.* to have a drink. □ *Let's go out and hoist one sometime.* □ *Hey, Sam. Let's you and me hoist one.*

**ho-jo('s)** ['hodʒo(z)] *n.* a Howard Johnson's restaurant or hotel. (Collegiate. Often with *the.*) □ *Let's hit ho-jo's for some grub.* □ *We're going to meet the others at the ho-jo.*

**hokey** ['hoki] *mod.* contrived; phony. □ *What a hokey way to deal with a perfectly honest request.* □ *That idea is too hokey.* □ *That's a pretty hokey idea, but it may work.*

**hokum** ['hokəm] *n.* nonsense. □ *All that is just hokum.* □ *No more hokum. I want the truth.*

**hold** *tr. & in.* to possess drugs. (Drugs.) □ *Gert was holding coke when she was arrested.* □ *Max is holding and wants to deal.*

**hold all the aces** *tr.* to be in control of everything. □ *The boss holds all the aces on this deal.* □ *I'll come out okay. I hold all the aces.*

**Hold everything!** *exclam.* "Stop everything!" □ *Hold everything! I forgot my wallet.* □ *Hold everything! My door isn't closed.*

**Hold it!** *exclam.* "Stop right there!" □ *Hold it! Stop!* □ *That's enough! Hold it!*

**Hold it, Buster!** *exclam.* "Stop that, mister!" (Sometimes said by women in repulsing an arduous male.) □ *Hold it, Buster! Who do you think you are?* □ *Hold it, Buster! Who do you think I am?*

**hold one's high** *tr.* to behave reasonably well under the influence of drugs. □ *Gert is having a harder and harder time holding her high.* □ *Ernie can't hold his high. What a creep!*

**hold one's horses** *tr.* to wait up; to relax and slow down; to be patient. (Usually a command.) □ *Hold your horses! Don't get in a hurry.* □ *Now, just hold your horses and let me explain.*

**hold one's liquor** *tr.* to be able to drink alcohol in quantity without ill effects. □ *Old Jed can sure hold his liquor—and a lot of it, too.* □ *I asked him to leave because he can't hold his liquor.*

**hold the fort** *tr.* to remain behind and take care of things. □ *Hold the fort. I'll be there in a while.* □ *I left John there to hold the fort.*

**hold water** *tr.* (for an idea, plan, etc.) to survive evaluation or scrutiny. □ *Nothing you've said so far holds water.* □ *Her story doesn't hold water.*

**hole in the wall** *n.* a tiny shop, not much wider than its doorway. □ *I went into this little hole in the wall where they had the nicest little gifts.* □ *His office is just a hole in the wall.*

**hole up** *in.* to hide (somewhere). □ *Lefty wanted to hole up somewhere till things cooled down.* □ *I just want to hole up until the whole matter is settled.*

**holiday cheer** *n.* liquor, especially liquor drunk at Christmas and New Year's. □ *I think he had a little too much holiday cheer.* □ *Would you care for a little holiday cheer?*

**holier-than-thou** *mod.* superior in piety; condescending. □ *She has such a holier-than-thou attitude.* □ *Molly can act so holier-than-thou sometimes.*

**Hollywood 1.** *mod.* having phony glitter. □ *Who is this Hollywood dame who just came in?* □ *This whole thing is just too Hollywood.* **2.** *n.* a gaudily dressed person in sunglasses. (Also a term of address.) □ *Hey, Hollywood! What's cooking?* □ *Ask Hollywood over there to take off his shades and make himself known.*

**Holy cow!** *exclam.* "Wow!" □ *Holy cow! A red one!* □ *Give me a chance! Holy cow, don't rush me!*

**holy Joe 1.** *n.* a chaplain; a cleric; a clergyman. □ *I went to see the holy Joe, and he was a lot of help.* □ *Old holy Joe wants to see all of us at services.* **2.** *n.* a very pious person. □ *Merton looks stuffy, but he's no holy Joe.* □ *Don't let that holy Joe hear about what you've done.*

**Holy mackerel!** ['holi 'mækrəl] *exclam.* "Wow!" □ *Holy mackerel! What a day!* □ *Holy mackerel! What's this?*

**Holy moley!** ['holi 'moli] *exclam.* "Wow!" □ *Holy moley! A whole quarter!* □ *Look, here's another one! Holy moley!*

**holy stink** *n.* anything repellent. □ *You really created a holy stink with that silly remark.* □ *What is this holy stink about broken windows?*

**holy terror** *n.* a devilish person; a badly behaving child. □ *Jimmy has become a holy terror lately.* □ *Why is the boss such a holy terror today?*

**hombre** ['ambre] *n.* a man. (From Spanish.) □ *Who's that hombre who just came in?* □ *Now, he's a strange sort of hombre.*

**home-brew** *n.* homemade liquor or beer. □ *Is this your own home-brew, Wally?* □ *My uncle makes his own home-brew.*

**homegrown 1.** *mod.* local; folksy; amateur. □ *Everyone enjoyed Sally's homegrown humor.* □ *The homegrown talent at the fair was just as entertaining as anything could have been.* **2.** *n.* marijuana grown domestically or locally. (Drugs.) □ *She'd rather use homegrown than have to deal with Max.* □ *This homegrown is from the pots in her room.*

**homer** ['homɚ] **1.** *n.* a home run in baseball. □ *Wilbur hit one homer after another.* □ *Another homer for our team!* **2.** *tr. & in.* to hit a home run. □ *Wilbur homered another one and brought in two runs with him.* □ *Sam has never homered in six years of playing,*

**homespun** *n.* homemade liquor or beer. □ *Jed offered a little of his homespun round the table.* □ *How about a swig of homespun?*

**homo** ['homo] **1.** *mod.* homosexual. (Often derogatory. Resented by homosexual persons.) □ *Is this one of those homo bars?* □ *Where'd you get those homo shoes?* **2.** *n.* a homosexual person. (Often derogatory. Resented by homosexual persons.) □ *Somebody said she is a homo.* □ *So what if he's a homo? He can still vote, can't he?*

**honcho** ['hantʃo] **1.** *n.* the head man; the boss. (Usable for either sex.) □ *The marketing honcho couldn't say when the product would be on the shelves.* □ *The top honcho at the water department was no help at all.* **2.** *tr.* to manage or boss something. □ *Who's supposed to honcho this affair?* □ *I'll honcho it until Larry gets here.*

**honest injun** ['anəst 'ɪndʒən] *interj.* "It is true." □ *You actually did that? Honest injun?* □ *Sure I did, honest injun.*

**honey** ['həni] *n.* beer. □ *Let's stop at the happy shop and get some honey.* □ *You want another can of honey?*

**honeybunch** *n.* a sweetheart. (Also a term of address.) □ *Look, honeybunch, let's hurry up. We're late.* □ *I can't wait to get back and see my honeybunch.*

**honeycakes** See *babycakes*.

**honey cart** See *honey wagon*.

**honeymoon** AND **honeymoon period, honeymoon stage** *n.* an early stage in any activity, before problems set in. □ *Of course, this is still the honeymoon stage, but everything seems to be going all right.* □ *The honeymoon is over, Carl. You have to produce now.*

**honey of a something** *n.* a very special something; an excellent example of something. □ *This is a honey of a car. Wanna drive it?* □ *Now here's a honey of a little stereo receiver.*

**honey wagon 1.** AND **honey cart** *n.* any vehicle used for or designed for carrying excrement: a farm manure wagon; a tank truck used to pump out septic tanks; a tank truck used to pump out airplane toilets; a portable latrine truck used in moviemaking. □ *I drove a honey wagon in Hollywood for a year. How's that for glamour?* □ *The honey cart was stalled with a flat tire in front of the plane.* **2.** *n.* a beer truck. □ *What time does the honey wagon bring in new supplies?* □ *I drove a honey cart in the city for a while.*

**Hong Kong dog** ['hɔŋ 'kɔŋ 'dɔg] *n.* diarrhea; a case of diarrhea. □ *Andy has a touch of the Hong Kong dog and needs some medicine.* □ *I got rid of the Hong Kong dog by meditating.*

**honk 1.** *n.* a drinking spree; a *toot*. □ *Jed's last honk lasted nearly a week.* □ *The guys went off on the honk to end all honks.* **2.** *n.* a white male; a *hunky*. (Black. Not necessarily derogatory.) □ *Who's the honk who keeps driving by?* □ *There are mainly honks where I work.*

**honked AND honkers** *mod.* alcohol intoxicated. □ *Wally was too honked to stand up.* □ *Man, is that guy honkers!*

**honker 1.** *n.* a goose. (Juvenile.) □ *A whole flock of honkers settled on our pond.* □ *Can we have honker for Thanksgiving dinner?* **2.** *n.* a strange or eccentric person. □ *Clare is a real honker these days. Is she all right?* □ *Merton is a classic honker.*

**honky AND honkey, honkie** ['hɔŋki] **1.** *n.* a Caucasian. (Black. Not necessarily derogatory. Probably from *hunky*.) □ *The honkies are taking over this neighborhood.* □ *Some honky was around asking for you.* **2.** *mod.* in the manner of a Caucasian; white-like. (Black.) □ *Where'd you get that honky car?* □ *That's honky music. I want to hear soul.*

**hooch AND hootch** [hutʃ] *n.* hard liquor; any alcoholic beverage. □ *Let's go guzzle some hooch.* □ *More hootch for you?*

**hooched (up)** *mod.* alcohol intoxicated. □ *Sally is too hooched to drive.* □ *She got herself hooched up and couldn't give her talk.*

**hoocher AND hootcher** *n.* a drunkard. □ *Ernie isn't a hoocher, you can say that for him.* □ *A hootcher staggered in and staggered right out again.*

**hooch hound AND hooch head** *n.* a drunkard. □ *Jed is a classic hooch hound. He lives for the stuff.* □ *The party turned into a drinking session for hooch heads.*

**hood** *n.* a hoodlum. □ *A couple of hoods hassled us on the street.* □ *That hood should be behind bars.*

**hooey** ['hui] *n.* nonsense. □ *The whole newspaper is nothing but hooey today.* □ *What's all this hooey about getting a new car?*

**hoofer** *n.* a (professional) dancer. □ *Clare was a hoofer when she was younger and lighter.* □ *She was a hoofer on Broadway.*

**hoof it** *tr.* to run away. □ *I saw them coming and hoofed it home.* □ *Lefty hoofed it when he saw the uniform.*

**hoo-ha** ['huha] **1.** *n.* a commotion. □ *What is all this hoo-ha about?* □ *A deer created quite a hoo-ha by running frantically through the department store.* **2.** *n.* nonsense. □ *What is all this hoo-ha about your leaving the company?* □ *Stop talking hoo-ha and tell the truth.*

**hook 1.** *tr.* to cheat someone. □ *Watch the clerk in that store. He might try to hook you.* □ *They hooked me on the car deal.* **2.** *tr.* to steal something. □ *Lefty hooked a couple of candy bars just for the hell of it.* □ *What did they hook last night?* **3.** *tr.* to addict someone (to something). (Not necessarily drugs.) □ *The constant use of bicarb hooked him to the stuff.* □ *The pot hooked him.*

**hooked (on someone or something) 1.** *mod.* [with *something*] addicted (to a drug). □ *Gert is hooked on horse.* □ *Everybody knows she is hooked.* **2.** *mod.* preferring someone or something; enamored of someone or something. □ *I'm really hooked on chocolate anything.* □ *Sam is hooked on Mary for good.* **3.** *mod.* [with *something*] cheated. □ *I was really hooked on this travel deal.* □ *You were hooked all right.*

**hooker** *n.* a prostitute. □ *There were some hookers standing right on that corner.* □ *Clare dresses like a hooker.*

**hook, line, and sinker** *mod.* totally. □ *She fell for it hook, line, and sinker.* □ *They believed every word hook, line, and sinker.*

**hooks** *n.* the hands. (See also *meathooks*.) □ *Get your hooks off my newspaper!* □ *Don't stand there with your hooks in your pocket. Get busy!*

**hook shop** *n.* a brothel. (See *hooker*.) □ *Guess who I saw coming out of a hook shop?* □ *There is a secret hook shop over on Maple Street.*

**hook something down AND hook down something** *tr.* to swallow something down. □ *Hook down one of these cookies and see what you think about them.*

□ *He hooked a drink down and turned to face his brother.*

**hoopla** ['huplɑ OR 'huplə] *n.* an outcry; a fuss or a to-do. □ *What's all this hoopla about?* □ *There is too much hoopla in these elections.*

**hoops** *n.* the game of basketball. □ *You wanna go play some hoops?* □ *Welcome to another evening of college hoops, brought to you by the Nova Motor Company.*

**hoosegow** ['husgɑu] *n.* a jail. □ *Learning to read can shorten one's time in the hoosegow.* □ *The judge threw the punk in the hoosegow for a few days.*

**hoot** 1. *in.* to laugh loudly. □ *The audience screamed and hooted with their appreciation.* □ *They howled and hooted. I know they just loved it.* 2. *n.* a joke; something laughable. □ *The whole business was a terrific hoot.* □ *The skit was a hoot, and everyone enjoyed it.* 3. *in.* to boo at someone's performance. □ *The audience hooted until the performer fled the stage in disgrace.* □ *They hooted for a few minutes after she left the stage.*

**hoo(t)chfest** *n.* a drinking bout; a drinking party. □ *We stopped by Sally's to join in the hoochfest for a while.* □ *Let's throw a big hootchfest next month.*

**hooted** *mod.* alcohol intoxicated. □ *Jed got himself good and hooted.* □ *Ted is too hooted to drive.*

**hooter** 1. *n.* a nose; a big nose. □ *I sort of wish my hooter wasn't so doggone big.* □ *He blew his hooter and went back to his reading.* 2. *n.* a drink of liquor. □ *He tossed back a big hooter of booze and stood there a minute.* □ *Have another hooter?* 3. *n.* cocaine. (Drugs.) □ *Max is known for his high-quality hooter.* □ *Where can I get some hooter around here?*

**hop** 1. AND **hops** *n.* opium; any narcotic drug. (Drugs.) □ *His great-grandfather smoked hop once.* □ *All he can think about is where he can get his hops.* 2. *n.* beer. □ *Pretty good hops, Tom.* □ *How about some hop with your hamburger?* 3. *n.* a dancing party for young people. □ *The kids are out at some school-sponsored hop.* □ *The hop was a lot of fun.* 4. *tr.* to get aboard a plane or train. □ *I'll hop a plane and be there in a couple of hours.* □ *Hop a train or*

*anything, but get here as soon as you can.*

**hopfest** *n.* a beer-drinking party. □ *We went to a big hopfest over at Wally's, but it broke up early.* □ *That was some hopfest! No potato chips!*

**hophead** 1. *n.* an alcoholic or a drunkard. □ *I'm afraid that Wally is becoming a hophead.* □ *Ernie is a well-established and incurable hophead.* 2. *n.* a drug user; someone under the effects of drugs. (Drugs.) □ *The hopheads are taking over this part of town.* □ *What happens to these hopheads when they grow up?*

**hopheaded** *mod.* addicted to drugs. (Drugs.) □ *I don't want any hopheaded hay burner working for me!* □ *That whole area is populated by hopheaded hookers.*

**hopped up** 1. *mod.* stimulated by drugs. (Drugs.) □ *The two of them were hopped up most of the time.* □ *Two hopped up kids were hunkered down in the alley.* 2. *mod.* (having to do with a car that is) customized and speeded up. □ *As soon as I get this hog hopped up, you'll see some real speed.* □ *Sam drives a hopped up old Ford.* 3. *mod.* excited. □ *Paul is certainly hopped up about something.* □ *Why are you so hopped up?*

**hopping mad** *mod.* very angry; angry and jumping up and down. □ *I was hopping mad about the broken window.* □ *The boss was hopping mad at the secretary.*

**Hop to it!** *exclam.* "Get moving!"; "Hurry up!" □ *Hop to it! I don't pay you to stand around.* □ *I need it now! Hop to it!*

**horizontal** *mod.* alcohol intoxicated. □ *The boss was horizontal at the Christmas party.* □ *Stewed? No, he's totally horizontal!*

**horn** 1. *n.* the nose. □ *He scratched his horn with his pencil and opened his mouth to speak.* □ *He had the most humongous horn I have ever seen on man or beast.* 2. *n.* the telephone. □ *Get Mrs. Wilson on the horn, please.* □ *She's on the horn now. What'll I tell her?* 3. *tr.* to sniff or *snort* a narcotic. (Drugs.) □ *Ernie horned a line and paused for a minute.* □ *He'd rather horn it than shoot it.*

**horner** **1.** *n.* a heavy drinker; a drunkard. □ *Wally is a real horner. He has an enormous capacity.* □ *Jed is the king of horners around here.* **2.** *n.* a cocaine user. (Drugs.) □ *Sure, Max is a horner. He sells the stuff to support his own habit.* □ *I think the new employee is a horner.*

**horny\*** *mod.* sexually aroused. (Caution with topic.) □ *Tom said he was horny.* □ *Who is that horny jerk?* □ *All the guys in that fraternity are horny.*

**horrors** **1.** *n.* the delirium tremens. □ *The old wino had the horrors all the time.* □ *He has a bad case of the horrors.* **2.** *n.* frightening hallucinations from drugs. (Drugs.) □ *Once he had gone through the horrors, he swore off for good.* □ *Tod had the horrors and had to be hospitalized.*

**horse** **1.** *n.* heroin. (Drugs.) □ *Now, horse is all that Gert will touch.* □ *Horse is still very popular in the big cities.* **2.** *n.* horse dung. □ *I use horse on my vegetables.* □ *I got a job shoveling horse out of the stables.* **3.** See *horse (tranquilizer).*

**horse around** *in.* to work inefficiently; to *goof around.* □ *Stop horsing around and get busy.* □ *You guys are always horsing around.*

**horsed** AND **on the horse** *mod.* under the effects of heroin; addicted to heroin. (Drugs.) □ *Gert was totally horsed.* □ *How long have you been on the horse?*

**horse doctor** *n.* a doctor. (Derogatory. Refers to a veterinarian.) □ *That horse doctor says there's nothing wrong with me.* □ *My horse doctor says everything is wrong with me.*

**Horsefeathers!** *exclam.* "Phooey!"; "Nonsense!" □ *Oh, horsefeathers! You're nuts!* □ *Horsefeathers! I did no such thing!*

**horse hockey** **1.** *n.* horse dung. □ *I try to get horse hockey for my garden.* □ *You don't see horse hockey in the streets anymore.* **2.** *n.* nonsense. □ *I've heard enough of your horse hockey.* □ *The guy specializes in producing horse hockey for the gossip columns.*

**horse laugh** *n.* a mocking and sarcastic laugh. □ *He came out with a horse laugh that caused some eyebrows to raise.* □ *The horse laugh from the back of the room did not go unnoticed.*

**horse opera** *n.* a Western movie. (See also *oater.*) □ *They're showing a series of old horse operas at the theater tonight.* □ *Haven't I seen this horse opera before? About a hundred times maybe?*

**horseradish** *n.* heroin. (See *horse.*) □ *Max can get you some horseradish.* □ *Gert is hooked on horseradish.*

**horses** *n.* horsepower, as in an engine. □ *How many horses does this thing have?* □ *Isn't 400 horses a lot for just one car?*

**horse's ass\*** *n.* a fool. (Crude. Caution with *ass.*) □ *My ex-husband was a real horse's ass.* □ *Stop being such a horse's ass and listen to some sense.*

**horse (tranquilizer)** AND **horse trank** *n.* phencyclidine, *P.C.P.,* an animal tranquilizer. (Drugs.) □ *One hit of that horse trank and he was really hurt.* □ *Jim said he knows of a kid trying to sell horse trank or something like that.*

**hoser** ['hozɚ] **1.** *n.* a good guy or buddy. □ *You're a real hoser, Ted.* □ *Old Fred is a good hoser. He'll help.* **2.** *n.* a cheater or deceiver. □ *Stop acting like a hoser and tell me the truth!* □ *You dirty lying hoser!*

**hose someone down** AND **hose down someone** *tr.* to kill someone. (Underworld.) □ *Mr. Big told Bruno to hose Max down.* □ *The thugs tried to hose down the witness.*

**hoska** See *(ma)hoska.*

**hot** **1.** AND **hot under the collar** *mod.* angry. □ *Don't get so hot under the collar. Chill, man.* □ *What a hot dude!* □ *Gee, that guy is really hot. What did I do?* **2.** *mod.* wanted by the police. (Underworld.) □ *Lefty is hot because of his part in the bank job.* □ *Bruno was hot and wanted somebody to hide him.* **3.** *mod.* stolen. □ *This watch is hot. Keep it.* □ *Rocko won't touch a hot watch or anything else hot.* **4.** *mod.* carrying contraband and subject to arrest if caught. □ *Max was hot and on the run.* □ *Lefty was hot and needed a place to stay.* **5.** *mod.* having a run of good luck in gambling. □ *I'm hot tonight! Here I go again.* □ *I was hot when I started. I'm broke now.* **6.** *mod.* of great renown; doing quite well for the time being. □ *The opera tenor was hot,* *and even the lowbrows would pay to hear him.* □ *The dancer was hot and was offered movie roles and all sorts of things.* **7.** *mod.* alcohol intoxicated. □ *You could see that Wally was pretty hot from all the whisky.* □ *He was too hot to stand up.* **8.** *mod.* selling well. □ *These things are really hot this season.* □ *Now, here's a hot item.* **9.** *mod.* sexy; sexually aroused. □ *Man, is that chick hot!* □ *She's not my idea of hot.* □ *Wow, who was that hot hunk you were with?*

**hot air** *n.* boasting; lying; nonsense. □ *I've heard enough of your hot air.* □ *That's just a lot of hot air. Ignore it.*

**hotbed of something** *n.* a nest of something; a gathering place of something. □ *This office is a hotbed of lazy people.* □ *My class is a hotbed of nerds.*

**hot check** *n.* a bad check. □ *The crook got picked up after passing a hot check.* □ *The clerk got in trouble for taking a hot check.*

**Hot diggety (dog)!** [ˈhɑt ˈdɪgədi (ˈdɔg)] *exclam.* "Wow!" □ *Hot diggety dog! I won!* □ *I made it on time. Hot diggety!*

**Hot dog!** *exclam.* "Wow!" □ *Hot dog! It's my turn.* □ *Look at that! Hot dog! It's coming this way!*

**hot head** *n.* a person with a bad or quick temper. □ *Max is a hot head. Watch out.* □ *Don't be such a hot head, Chuck.*

**hot item 1.** *n.* an item that sells well. □ *This little thing is a hot item this season.* □ *Now here's a hot item that everybody is looking for.* **2.** *n.* a romantically serious couple. □ *Sam and Mary are quite a hot item lately.* □ *A hot item like Bill and Clare isn't likely to show up for the party.*

**hotkey 1.** *n.* one or more keys on a computer keyboard that will bring forth a special computer applications program. (Computers.) □ *The hotkeys for my thesaurus are "control" and "F2."* □ *Press the hotkey to bring up a calendar.* **2.** *tr.* to press one or more keys on a computer keyboard that call a program as in sense 1. (Computers.) □ *I hotkeyed my calculator and figured out the total charges as I was writing the letter.* □ *I forget how to hotkey my calendar.*

**hot number 1.** *n.* an exciting piece of music. □ *Now here's a hot number by the Wanderers.* □ *Another hot number after this message.* **2.** *n.* an attractive or sexy *girl* or woman. □ *She's quite a hot number.* □ *Who's that hot number I saw you with last night?*

**hot paper** *n.* bad checks; a bad check. (Underworld. See *hot check*.) □ *Molly got caught passing hot paper.* □ *That teller can spot hot paper a mile away.*

**hot potato** *n.* a difficult problem. □ *I sure don't want to have to deal with that hot potato.* □ *This one is a hot potato. Ignore it for a while.*

**(hot) rod** *n.* a car that has been customized for power and speed by the owner. □ *My rod'll outrun yours any day.* □ *Is that a hot rod or a junk heap?*

**hot seat 1.** *n.* the electric chair. (Underworld.) □ *Lefty, you're headed for the hot seat.* □ *The hot seat is just waiting for you, Lefty.* **2.** *n.* the position of being scrutinized. □ *I was in the hot seat for about an hour, but they didn't learn anything from me.* □ *This new information puts Tom in the hot seat, doesn't it?*

**hot-shot** AND **hotshot 1.** *n.* an important and energetic person. (Often used sarcastically. Also a term of address.) □ *If you're such a hotshot, why not straighten out the whole thing?* □ *Look, hot-shot, get busy, will you?* **2.** *mod.* brilliant; great. □ *Wally is becoming a real hot-shot tenor with the local opera company.* □ *So, you're the hot-shot guy who's going to straighten this place out?*

**hot skinny** See *skinny*.

**hot stuff** *n.* a person who acts superior (to others). (Also a term of address.) □ *What makes you think you're such hot stuff?* □ *Hey, hot stuff, come down here and say that.*

**hotsy-totsy** [ˈhɑtsiˈtɑtsi] *mod.* fine; great. □ *Well, isn't that just hotsy-totsy.* □ *I don't feel so hotsy-totsy.*

**hot tip** *n.* a special bit of information that ought to be reliable. □ *Ted got a hot tip on a horse.* □ *I phoned in a hot tip about a news story to the papers.*

**hot wire** *tr.* to start a car without a key. □ *Lefty hot wired the car and used it for an hour or two.* □ *Isn't it illegal to hot wire a car?*

**Hot ziggety!** [ˈhɑt ˈzɪgədi] *exclam.* "Wow!" □ *Hot ziggety! I made it!* □ *The plane's on time! Hot ziggety!*

**house dealer** *n.* a drug seller who lives in and sells in a private dwelling. (Drugs.) □ *This building even has its own house dealer.* □ *When the cops can't even get a line on a house dealer, there's something wrong.*

**house moss** *n.* little blobs of lint. (See also *ghost turd.*) □ *There is some house moss under the sofa.* □ *Sweep up this house moss, please.*

**How come?** *interrog.* "Why?" □ *You're late. How come?* □ *How come we never see you anymore?*

**How does that grab you?** *interrog.* "What do you think of that?" □ *Looks good, okay? How does that grab you?* □ *How does that grab you! Enough salt?*

**howdy** *interj.* "hello." (Folksy.) □ *Howdy, friend.* □ *Well, howdy. Long time, no see.*

**How goes it?** *interrog.* "How are you?"; "How are things going?" □ *Nice to see you. How goes it?* □ *How goes it? Everything okay?*

**howl 1.** *n.* something funny. (See *scream.*) □ *What a howl the surprise party turned out to be when the guest of honor didn't show up.* □ *The gag was a real howl.* **2.** *in.* to laugh very hard. □ *Everybody howled at my mistake.* □ *John howled when the joke was told.*

**howler** *n.* a serious and funny mistake. □ *Who is responsible for this howler on the Wilson account?* □ *That howler cost us plenty.*

**howling (drunk)** *mod.* alcohol intoxicated; loudly drunk. □ *Wally got howling drunk and ran in the streets with his coat off.* □ *He was just howling!*

**How's by you?** AND **How's with you?** *interrog.* "How are you?" □ *How's by you, Wilbur?* □ *I'm fine. How's with you?*

**How's tricks?** *interrog.* "How are you?"; "What are you doing lately?" □ *Hiya, Chuck. How's tricks?* □ *How's tricks? What's new?*

**How's with you?** See *How's by you?*

**how the other half lives** *n.* how poorer people live; how richer people live. □ *Now I am beginning to understand how*

the other half lives. □ *Most people don't care how the other half lives.*

**How you been?** *interrog.* "How are you?"; "How have you been?" □ *Good to see you. How you been?* □ *How you been? Long time, no see.*

**H.T.H.** *n.* "hometown honey," a sweetheart from home or still at home. (Collegiate.) □ *Wally is my H.T.H., but I think I've outgrown him.* □ *I heard that Mary is Sam's H.T.H.*

**hubbas** *n.* crystallized cocaine; *crack.* (Drugs.) □ *A ten-year-old died yesterday from hubbas.* □ *They arrested an eight-year-old for selling hubbas.*

**hubby** [ˈhəbi] *n.* a husband. □ *My hubby will be late tonight.* □ *Where is your hubby tonight?*

**huffer** [ˈhəfɚ] *n.* a person (teenager) who inhales glue vapors or some other solvent for a *high.* (Drugs.) □ *The age of the huffers has come to an end. Now they start out on crack.* □ *His schoolwork suffered because he was a huffer.*

**huffy** *mod.* angry; haughty. □ *Now, don't get huffy. I said I was sorry, didn't I?* □ *Who's the huffy old lady?* □ *She was so huffy about it.*

**hughie** [ˈhjui] *in.* to empty one's stomach; to vomit. (See also *cry hughie.*) □ *I gotta go hughie.* □ *Oo, who hughied?*

**humdinger** AND **hummer** [ˈhəmˈdɪŋɚ AND ˈhəmɚ] *n.* someone or something excellent. □ *Now, this one is a real humdinger.* □ *Yup, he's a hummer all right.*

**hummer** See the previous entry.

**humongous** [hjuˈmɑŋgəs] *mod.* huge. □ *She lives in a humongous house on the hill.* □ *Wally has a humongous nose.* □ *That nose is not humongous.*

**hump (along)** *in.* to move along in a hurry. □ *I guess I'd better hump along over there.* □ *Come on, move it! Hump to the main office and be fast about it!*

**hump it (to somewhere)** *tr.* to move rapidly (to somewhere). □ *I have to hump it over to Kate's place right now.* □ *You'll have to hump it to get there in time.*

**hung 1.** *mod.* hungover. □ *John is really hung this morning.* □ *I'm miserable when I'm hung.* **2.** *mod.* annoyed. □ *Fred is hung and looking for somebody to take it out on.* □ *How can you get so hung about practically nothing?*

**hungover** *mod.* having a hangover from too much alcohol. □ *John is really hungover today.* □ *I can't eat when I'm hungover.*

**hungries** *n.* hunger. (Always with *the*. See also *munchies*.) □ *Jimmy's crying because he's got the hungries.* □ *I get the hungries about this time every day.*

**hungry 1.** *mod.* eager to make money. □ *He doesn't sell enough because he's not hungry enough.* □ *When he gets hungry for wealth, he'll get busy.* **2.** *mod.* ambitious. □ *He gets ahead because he's hungry.* □ *We like to hire the hungry ones.*

**hung up (on someone or something) 1.** *mod.* obsessed with someone or something. □ *Mary is really hung up on Sam.* □ *Sam's hung up on his car.* **2.** *mod.* troubled by someone or something. □ *She's hung up on the new tax rules.* □ *I just read the things, and I'm hung up, too.* **3.** *mod.* addicted to a drug. (Drugs.) □ *Gert is hung up on Hazel.* □ *Ernie was hung up on pot till he discovered coke.*

**hunk** *n.* a strong and sexually attractive male. □ *Larry is a real hunk.* □ *Who was that hot hunk I saw you with?*

**hunker down (to do something)** *in.* to settle down to do something. (Folksy.) □ *I have to hunker down to finish my algebra this evening.* □ *Yes, you'd better hunker down.*

**hunky** See *honky*.

**hunky-dory** [ˈhəŋkiˈdori] *mod.* fine; okay. □ *As a matter of fact, everything is just hunky-dory.* □ *That is a hunky-dory idea all right.*

**hurl** *in.* to empty one's stomach; to vomit. (Like the *throw* in *throw up*.) □ *I think I gotta go hurl.* □ *Who's in the john hurling so loud?*

**hurry up and wait** *phr.* to be alternately rushed and delayed in a hectic situation. (Often with the force of a modifier. See examples.) □ *I hate to hurry up and wait.* □ *It's always hurry up and wait around here.*

**hurt 1.** *mod.* very ugly; damaged and ugly. (Black. Similar to *hurting*.) □ *Man, are you hurt!* □ *That poor girl is really bad hurt.* **2.** *mod.* drug intoxicated. (Black.) □ *Gert was really hurt and nodding and*

drooling. □ *One hit of that horse trank and he was really hurt.*

**hurt for someone or something** *in.* to long after someone or something; to need someone or something. □ *Sam really hurts for Mary.* □ *I sure am hurting for a nice big steak.*

**hurting 1.** *mod.* very ugly; in pain from ugliness. (Similar to *hurt*.) □ *That dog of yours is something to behold. It's really hurting.* □ *Man, is she hurting!* **2.** *mod.* seriously in need of something, such as a dose of drugs. (Drugs.) □ *Gert is hurting. She needs something soon.* □ *When Ernie is hurting, he takes barbs.*

**hush-hush** [ˈhəʃˈhəʃ] **1.** *mod.* secret; undercover. □ *The matter is so hush-hush I can't talk about it over the phone.* □ *What is all this hush-hush stuff?* **2.** *mod.* secretly. □ *They did it so hush-hush that no one knew for a long time.* □ *It was not done hush-hush. It was just private.*

**hush money** *n.* money paid to buy someone's silence. □ *They paid enough hush money to silence an army.* □ *There was some hush money paid to someone in city hall.*

**hush someone or something up** AND **hush up someone or something 1.** *tr.* [with *someone*] to kill someone. □ *Mr. Big told Bruno to hush up Max.* □ *Nobody knew how to get to Mr. Big to hush him up.* **2.** *tr.* [with *something*] to keep something a secret; to try to stop a rumor from spreading. □ *We wanted to hush up the story, but there was no way to do it.* □ *We just couldn't hush it up.*

**husky** [ˈhəski] *n.* a strong man; a thug. □ *Tell your husky to lay off, Bruno.* □ *A couple of huskies helped me get my car unstuck.*

**hustle** [ˈhəsl] **1.** *in.* to move rapidly; to hurry. □ *Come on, hustle, you guys.* □ *It's late. I've got to hustle.* **2.** *n.* hurried movement; confusion. □ *All the hustle and confusion made it hard to concentrate.* □ *I can't work when there is all this hustle around me.* **3.** *n.* a scheme to make money; a special technique for making money. (Underworld. This includes drug dealing, prostitution, and other vice activities.) □ *Each of these* punks has a hustle—a specialty in crime. □ *We all know what Max's hustle is.* **4.** *in.* to use one's special technique for making money. □ *He's out there on the streets hustling all the time.* □ *I gotta go hustle. I need some bread.* **5.** *tr.* to use a scheme on a person to try to make money; to *con* someone. □ *Don't try to hustle me, sister. I know which end is up.* □ *Sam is always trying to hustle people.* **6.** *tr.* to attempt to seduce someone. □ *Max is hustling Molly.* □ *I think that Molly's hustling Max.*

**hustler** ['hǝslɚ] **1.** *n.* a gambler in a pool hall. □ *Wasn't he the guy who played the hustler in that famous movie?* □ *He made plenty as a hustler.* **2.** *n.* a swindler; a *con artist.* □ *The chick is a real hustler. I wouldn't trust her at all.* □ *The hustler conned me out of a month's pay.* **3.** *n.* a prostitute. □ *Gert almost became a hustler to pay for a habit.* □ *A lot of hustlers are hooked on horse.* **4.** *n.* a *stud*; a man who is notoriously good with women. □ *That guy's a hustler. Watch out.* □ *He thinks he's a hustler. The chicks think he's a wimp.*

**hype** [haɪp] **1.** *n.* publicity; sales propaganda; promotion, especially if blatant and aggressive. □ *There was so much hype before the picture was released that the picture itself was a letdown.* □ *There is hype for the election all over the place.* **2.** *tr.* to publicize or promote someone or something aggressively; to overpraise someone or something. □ *Don't hype the thing to death.* □ *Let's hype it until everyone in the country has heard about it.* **3.** AND **hipe** *n.* a hypodermic syringe and needle. (Drugs.) □ *She forgot to clean the hype.* □ *He got an infection from a dirty hipe.* **4.** *n.* an injection of drugs. (Drugs.) □ *Ernie needed a hype real bad.* □ *Max told him*

who could help him with a hype. **5.** *n.* a drug addict who injects drugs. (Drugs.) □ *Gert's been a hype for about a year.* □ *The hypes have a rough time in prison.*

**hype artist** *n.* someone who produces aggressive promotional material for a living. □ *She is a hype artist for a public relations firm.* □ *How much does a hype artist get paid for all that junk?*

**hyped (up)** **1.** *mod.* excited; stimulated. □ *They were all hyped up before the game.* □ *She said she had to get hyped before the tennis match.* **2.** *mod.* contrived; heavily promoted; falsely advertised. □ *I just won't pay good money to see these hyped up movies.* □ *If it has to be hyped so much, it probably isn't very good.* **3.** *mod.* drug intoxicated. (Drugs.) □ *Gert is happiest when she's hyped.* □ *Here comes another hyped up musician.*

**hyper** ['haɪpɚ] **1.** *mod.* excited; overreacting. □ *I'm a little hyper because of the doctor's report.* □ *Here's another hyper patient.* □ *Now, now, don't get hyper.* **2.** *n.* a person who praises or promotes someone or something. □ *She's a hyper, and she doesn't always tell things the way they are.* □ *As a hyper, she is a whiz.* **3.** *n.* a person who is always overly excited or hyperactive. □ *Pat is such a hyper. Just can't seem to relax.* □ *My dad is a hyper.* **4.** *n.* a drug user who injects drugs with a hypodermic syringe. (Drugs.) □ *How long have you been a hyper, Gert?* □ *Max has been a hyper since he was 24.*

**hype something up** AND **hype up something** *tr.* to overpraise something; to propagandize something. □ *They hyped it up too much.* □ *Why do they hype up an election?*

# I

**I am so sure!** *exclam.* "I am right!" (California.) □ *You are way rad! I am so sure!* □ *This is too much. I am so sure!*

**(I-)beam** ['aɪbim AND bim] *n.* "IBM," International Business Machines stock shares. (Financial markets. See also *big blue.*) □ *I-beam fell out of bed and took the market with it.* □ *How much beam do you own?*

**(I) beg (your) pardon. 1.** *sent.* "Excuse me. I am sorry." □ *I beg your pardon. I didn't mean to step on your toe.* □ *Beg your pardon. I didn't see you.* **2.** *sent.* "I am sorry, but I did not hear what you said." □ *I beg your pardon. It's so noisy in here.* □ *Beg pardon. I didn't catch that last comment.* **3.** *sent.* "I object to what you said!" (The tone of voice indicates great dissatisfaction.) □ *I beg your pardon! I am not a clerk!* □ *I beg your pardon. Are you addressing me?*

**ice 1.** *n.* diamonds; jewels. (Underworld.) □ *That old dame has tons of ice in her hotel room.* □ *Look at the ice on her!* **2.** *n.* cocaine; crystalline cocaine. (Drugs.) □ *Max deals mostly in ice, but can get you almost anything.* □ *This ice isn't good enough.* **3.** *tr.* to kill someone; to kill an informer. (Underworld. See *chill.*) □ *Mr. Big ordered Bruno to ice you-know-who.* □ *Somebody set out to ice Molly—the dirty squealer.* **4.** *tr.* to ignore someone. (Underworld. See *chill.*) □ *Max iced Bruno for obvious reasons.* □ *The members of the gang iced Bruno, and that really made him worry.* **5.** *tr.* to embarrass someone; to make someone look foolish. □ *Don't ice me in front of my friends.* □ *Why does she feel like she has to ice everybody?* **6.** *n.*

money given as a bribe, especially to the police. (Underworld.) □ *Did you give Ervine the ice?* □ *A lot of those cops take ice.*

**iceberg 1.** *n.* a cold and unemotional person. □ *Sally can be such an iceberg!* □ *What an insensitive iceberg!* **2.** *n.* marijuana concealed in iceberg lettuce. (Drugs. California.) □ *Can you get me some iceberg?* □ *The inspectors found a load of what they call "iceberg."*

**iceberg slim 1.** *n.* a pimp. □ *When iceberg slim came by in his pimpmobile, Jed made a rude sign at him.* □ *No iceberg slim is gonna push me around!* **2.** *n.* a person who exploits others; a cold, heartless person. □ *The guy's a regular iceberg slim.* □ *Rocko is a perfect example of an iceberg slim. He's heartless.*

**iced** *mod.* settled once and for all; done easily. □ *I've got it iced. Nothing to it.* □ *The whole business is iced. Don't fret.*

**iceman** *n.* a killer. (Underworld. See *ice.*) □ *It's hard to believe that Rocko is a professional iceman.* □ *The mob employs a number of icemen.*

**ice queen** *n.* a cold and haughty woman. □ *Molly is not exactly an ice queen, but comes close.* □ *It's Jane who's the ice queen.*

**icicles** ['aɪs sɪkḷz] *n.* pure cocaine in a crystallized form. (Drugs.) □ *Are icicles the same as crack?* □ *Icicles are probably more pure than crack.*

**icing on the cake** *n.* an extra enhancement. □ *Oh, wow! A tank full of gas in my new car. That's icing on the cake!* □ *Your coming home for a few days was the icing on the cake.*

**ick** [ɪk] **1.** *n.* any nasty substance. □ *What is this ick on my shoe?* □ *That's not ick; it's good clean mud.* **2.** *exclam.* "Nasty!" (Usually **Ick!**) □ *Oh, ick! What now?* □ *Ick! I'm late!* **3.** *n.* a disliked person. □ *Tell that ick to leave. He's polluting the place.* □ *Oh, Tod, don't be an ick.*

**icky** ['ɪki] *mod.* distasteful; nasty. □ *What is this icky old stuff?* □ *This is icky.* □ *This was an icky day.*

**icky-poo** ['ɪkipu] **1.** *mod.* disgusting. □ *I don't like all this icky-poo talk.* □ *What is that icky-poo stuff in the soup bowl?* **2.** *exclam.* "Nasty!" (Usually **Icky-poo!**) □ *Icky-poo! What a mess!* □ *Oh, icky-poo! I missed my bus!*

**I couldn't care less.** AND **I could care less.** *sent.* "I don't care!" (The affirmative version does not make sense, but is widely used, nonetheless.) □ *So you're late. I couldn't care less.* □ *I could care less if you fell off a cliff.*

**I.D.** AND **ID 1.** *n.* some kind of identification card. □ *Can you show me an I.D.?* □ *I don't have any ID on me.* **2.** *tr.* to check someone for a valid identification card. □ *They IDed us at the door.* □ *I hate being I.D.ed.*

**idiot box** *n.* a television set. □ *You spend too much time watching the idiot box.* □ *What's on the idiot box tonight?*

**idiot card** *n.* a large card that shows people on television what to say. □ *The floor director held up an idiot card so I could read out the telephone number.* □ *I couldn't read the number off the idiot card.*

**idiot juice** AND **idiotic** ['ɪdiət dʒus AND ɪdi'adɪk] *n.* a mixture of ground nutmeg and water. (Prisons.) □ *Somehow a bunch of these guys got hold of some idiot juice.* □ *He drank about a gallon of idiotic to get the kick of one beer.*

**idiot light** *n.* a light (instead of a meter) on a car's dashboard that indicates the state of various things concerning the operation of the car. □ *I don't want idiot lights. I want meters!* □ *The idiot light went on, and I knew I was in some sort of trouble.*

**idiot oil** *n.* alcohol. □ *She drinks too much of that idiot oil.* □ *Idiot oil can wreck you as much as smack does.*

**idiot pills** *n.* barbiturates. (Drugs.) □ *Lay off those idiot pills, why don't you?* □ *She takes idiot pills every night.*

**I don't believe this!** *exclam.* "What is happening right now is unbelievable!" □ *Gross! I don't believe this!* □ *I don't believe this! It can't be happening.*

**I don't know.** *sent.* "I disagree." □ *I don't know. I like it. What's wrong with it?* □ *I don't know. It looks good to me.*

**I don't mean maybe!** *exclam.* "I am not kidding!" □ *You get over here right now, and I don't mean maybe!* □ *I will spank you if you ever do that again, and I don't mean maybe.*

**iffy** ['ɪfi] *mod.* marginally uncertain. □ *Things are still sort of iffy, but we'll know for sure in a few days.* □ *It's sort of an iffy matter, but things will get straightened out.*

**if I've told you once, I've told you a thousand times...** *phr.* "I know I have told you many, many times." □ *If I've told you once, I've told you a thousand times, don't lean back in that chair.* □ *If I've told you once, I've told you a thousand times, wipe your feet!*

**if one knows what's good for one** *phr.* "one had better do what is expected of one." □ *You'd better be on time if you know what's good for you.* □ *If you know what's good for you, you'll call and apologize.*

**if one's a day** *phr.* a phrase attached to an expression of someone's age. (See examples.) □ *She's fifty if she's a day!* □ *I'm sure he's forty-five if he's a day.*

**if push comes to shove** See *when push comes to shove.*

**If you can't stand the heat, keep out of the kitchen.** *sent.* "If you cannot accept the problems of involvement, do not get involved." □ *Yes, it's difficult to be a candidate. If you can't stand the heat, keep out of the kitchen.* □ *Relax. If you can't stand the heat, keep out of the kitchen.*

**if you'll pardon the expression** *phr.* "excuse the expression I am about to say." □ *This thing is—if you'll pardon the expression—loused up.* □ *I'm really jacked, if you'll pardon the expression.*

**I hear what you are saying. 1.** AND **I hear you.** *sent.* "I know just what you are trying to say." □ *Yes, yes. I hear what you are saying, and I'm with you.* □ *Yeah! I hear you!* **2.** *sent.* "I understand your position, but I am under no obligation to agree." □ *I hear you. So do what you want.* □ *I hear you, but it doesn't matter.*

**I hear you.** See the previous entry.

**I kid you not.** *sent.* "I am not kidding." (Attributed to the entertainer Jack Paar.) □ *She is a great singer. I kid you not.* □ *I kid you not. This is the best.*

**I'll bite.** *sent.* "You want me to ask what or why, so, what or why?" □ *Okay, I'll bite. What's the answer?* □ *I'll bite. Why did the chicken cross the road?*

**illuminated** *mod.* alcohol intoxicated. (A play on *lit.*) □ *Paul is a bit illuminated.* □ *He's too illuminated to drive home.*

**(I) love it!** *exclam.* "That is wonderful!" (A catch phrase.) □ *It's wonderful, Ted. I love it!* □ *Love it! More, more!* □ *You're so clever! Love it! Love it!*

**I'm listening.** *sent.* "Keep talking.";"Make your explanation now." □ *You did it wrong. I'm listening.* □ *I'm sure there's an explanation. Well, I'm listening.*

**I'm not kidding.** *sent.* "I am telling the truth." □ *Get over here now! I'm not kidding.* □ *I'm not kidding. It was this big!*

**I'm out of here.** AND **I'm outa here.** *sent.* "I am leaving this minute." □ *In three minutes I'm outa here.* □ *I'm out of here. Bye.*

**impaired** *mod.* alcohol intoxicated. (Borrowed from the euphemistic *impaired physician.*) □ *Don is a bit impaired because he drinks like a fish.* □ *He was so impaired he couldn't see his hand in front of his face.* □ *The impaired driver was arrested.*

**I'm sorry.** *sent.* "I do not understand."; "I did not hear you." □ *I'm sorry. What did you say?* □ *I'm sorry. It's noisy in here.*

**in 1.** *mod.* high on marijuana. (Drugs.) □ *Larry is really in. He's fried.* □ *The kid comes to school completely in every day.* **2.** *mod.* current; fashionable. □ *This kind of thing is in now.* □ *What's in around here in the way of clothing?* **3.** *mod.* private. □ *Is this in informa-*

tion? □ *If it's in or something, I'm sure they won't spread it around.* **4.** *n.* someone in a special position; someone who is serving in an elective office. □ *Well, now that I am an in, there's going to be some changes.* □ *When Ralph is one of the ins, he'll throw the crooks out.* **5.** *n.* a ticket or means of getting in (someplace). □ *I lost my in. Can I still see the show?* □ *Lemme see your in or give me a buck.*

**in a bad way** See *in bad shape.*

**in a big way** *mod.* very much; urgently. □ *I'm really interested in her in a big way.* □ *He plays to win—in a big way.*

**in a blue funk** *mod.* sad; depressed. □ *I've been in a blue funk all week.* □ *Don't be in a blue funk. Things'll get better.*

**in a cold sweat** *mod.* in a state of fear. □ *He stood there in a cold sweat, waiting for something to happen.* □ *I was in a cold sweat while they counted the ballots.*

**in action 1.** *mod.* healthy and getting around. □ *After I got well, I was in action again immediately.* □ *When will she be in action again?* **2.** *mod.* selling or using drugs. (Drugs.) □ *Max is in action about 20 hours a day.* □ *In this neighborhood, somebody is in action 24 hours a day.*

**in a dither** *mod.* confused; undecided. □ *Mary is sort of in a dither lately.* □ *Don't get yourself in a dither.*

**in a familiar way** *mod.* pregnant. (Euphemistic for *in a family way.*) □ *Molly is in a familiar way, have you heard?* □ *In a familiar way again?*

**in a family way** AND **in the family way** *mod.* pregnant. □ *I hear that Molly is in a family way.* □ *Is she in the family way again?*

**in a flash** *mod.* right away; immediately. (See *flash.*) □ *Get over here in a flash, or else.* □ *I'll be there in a flash.*

**in a heap** *mod.* alcohol intoxicated. □ *Poor Jed's in a heap again.* □ *The guys were all in a heap after the blast.*

**in a jam** *mod.* in a difficult situation. □ *I think I'm sort of in a jam.* □ *Sam is in a jam.*

**in a jiff(y)** *mod.* right away; immediately. (See *jiffy.*) □ *I'll be there in a jiffy.* □ *The clerk'll be with you in a jiff.*

**in a month of Sundays** *mod.* in a very long time. (Folksy.) □ *I haven't seen you in a month of Sundays.* □ *We haven't visited the city in a month of Sundays.*

**in a pinch 1.** *mod.* in difficulty; *in a jam.* □ *I'm sort of in a pinch. Can you come over?* □ *Whenever you get in a pinch, give me a ring.* **2.** *mod.* when one needs something one does not have. □ *It'll do in a pinch.* □ *You got something I can use in a pinch?*

**in a snit** *mod.* in a fit of anger or irritation. □ *Don't get in a snit. It was an accident.* □ *Mary is in a snit because they didn't ask her to come to the shindig.*

**in a tizzy** *mod.* in a state of mental disorder. □ *Fred is all in a tizzy.* □ *The whole office is in a tizzy today.*

**in a twit** *mod.* upset; frantic. □ *She's all in a twit because she lost her keys.* □ *Tod was in a twit and was quite rude to us.*

**in a twitter** *mod.* in a giddy state; silly. □ *Don't get yourself in a twitter.* □ *We were all in a twitter over the upcoming event.*

**in bad shape** AND **in a bad way 1.** *mod.* injured or debilitated in any manner. □ *Fred had a little accident, and he's in bad shape.* □ *Tom needs exercise. He's in bad shape.* **2.** *mod.* pregnant. □ *Molly's in bad shape again, I hear.* □ *Yup, she's in bad shape all right—about three months in bad shape.* **3.** *mod.* alcohol intoxicated. □ *Two glasses of that stuff and I'm in really bad shape.* □ *Fred is in bad shape. I think he's going to toss his cookies.*

**in business** *mod.* operating; equipped to operate. □ *We're in business now, and things are running smoothly.* □ *Now it works. Now we're in business.*

**incense** *n.* marijuana. (Drugs.) □ *I think I smell some incense somewhere in this building.* □ *Hank likes to burn a little incense every now and then.*

**incentive** *n.* cocaine. (Drugs. See *initiative.*) □ *Maybe a little of that incentive would make me work harder.* □ *That's pretty expensive incentive.*

**in cold blood** *mod.* without feeling; with cruel intent. (Compare to *cold blood.*) □ *Rocko kills in cold blood and never gives it a thought.* □ *The prof flunked me in cold blood.*

**in cold storage** *mod.* dead; in a state of death. □ *Rocko gets paid for putting his subjects in cold storage.* □ *Poor old Jed is in cold storage.*

**incy-wincy** ['intsi'wintsi] *mod.* tiny. (Compare to *itty-bitty, itsy-bitsy.*) □ *Just give me an incy-wincy bit. I'm on a diet.* □ *Well, maybe an incy-wincy bit more wouldn't hurt.*

**in deep 1.** *mod.* deeply involved (with someone or something). □ *Mary and Sam are in deep.* □ *Max is in deep with the mob.* **2.** *mod.* deeply in debt. (Often with *with* or *to.*) □ *Bruno is in deep with his bookie.* □ *I'm in deep to the department store.*

**Indian hay** AND **Indian hemp** *n.* marijuana. (Drugs. Refers to *Cannabis indicus.*) □ *Nobody calls pot Indian hay anymore, do they?* □ *Sure they do, and Indian hemp, too.*

**in drag** *mod.* wearing the clothing of the opposite sex. (Usually refers to women's clothing.) □ *Two actors in drag did a skit about life on the farm.* □ *Gary looks better in drag than he does in a suit.*

**in dribs and drabs** *mod.* in small portions; bit by bit. □ *I'll have to pay you what I owe you in dribs and drabs.* □ *The whole story is beginning to come in in dribs and drabs.*

**in Dutch** *mod.* in trouble. □ *I think I'm in Dutch with my folks.* □ *I didn't want to get in Dutch with you.*

**in fine feather 1.** *mod.* well-dressed; of an excellent appearance. □ *Well, you are certainly in fine feather today.* □ *I like to be in fine feather when I have to give a speech.* **2.** *mod.* in good form; in good spirits. □ *Mary is really in fine feather tonight.* □ *I feel in fine feather and ready to go!*

**in high** *mod.* drug intoxicated; at the peak of a drug high. (Drugs.) □ *Sally was in high and couldn't come to the phone.* □ *Max is in high a good part of each day.*

**initiative** *n.* cocaine. (Drugs. See *incentive.*) □ *Maybe I need some more of that initiative to get me going.* □ *That kind of initiative is pretty expensive.*

**in jail** *mod.* overdosed with drugs. (Drugs.) □ *Ernie was in jail twice last year, but he still won't give up the smack.* □ *The kid's in jail and may not get out this time.*

**ink** *n.* cheap red wine. □ *The old wino prefers ink to anything else.* □ *All I have is some ink. Is that okay?*

**ink slinger** *n.* a professional writer; a newspaper reporter. □ *The ink slingers have been at the candidates again.* □ *The problem is that there are too many ink slingers around.*

**in nothing flat** *mod.* immediately. □ *I'll be there in nothing flat.* □ *She changed the tire in nothing flat.*

**in one's blood** *mod.* inborn; part of one's genetic makeup. □ *It's in my blood. I can't help it.* □ *Running is in his blood. He loves it.*

**in orbit** **1.** *mod.* ecstatic; euphoric. □ *She was just in orbit when she got the letter.* □ *Tod was in orbit over the promotion.* **2.** *mod.* alcohol or drug intoxicated. □ *Gary is in orbit and can't see a hole in a ladder.* □ *After a six-pack all to herself, Julie was in orbit.*

**in play** **1.** *mod.* being played. (Said of a ball in a game.) □ *The ball's in play, so you made the wrong move.* □ *No, it wasn't in play, you twit!* **2.** *mod.* having to do with a company (or its stock) which is a candidate for acquisition by another company. (Financial markets.) □ *The company was in play, but nobody was buying it.* □ *These deal stocks that are in play right now offer excellent buying opportunities.*

**in power** AND **in the power** *mod.* having to do with a person who has heroin for sale. (Drugs.) □ *Who's in power around here?* □ *Max is in power, as always.*

**in rare form** **1.** *mod.* well-tuned for a good performance; at one's best. □ *He is in rare form today.* □ *We are not exactly in rare form on Monday mornings.* **2.** *mod.* alcohol intoxicated. □ *Gert is in rare form, but she'll have time to sleep it off.* □ *When Harry was finally in rare form, he slid beneath the table.*

**ins and outs** *n.* the fine points (of something); the details; the intricacies. □ *I'm learning the ins and outs of this business.* □ *My father taught me the ins and outs of hog calling.*

**inside dope** *n.* the inside story; special or privileged information. (Compare to *skinny.*) □ *Can you give me the inside dope on Marty?* □ *What's the inside dope on the candidate's drug addiction?*

**inside job** *n.* a crime perpetrated against an establishment by someone associated with the victimized establishment. (Underworld.) □ *The cops figured that it was an inside job.* □ *It was an inside job all right. The butler did it.*

**in spades** *mod.* in the best way possible; extravagantly. □ *He flunked the test in spades.* □ *They won the championship in spades.*

**insy** ['ɪnzi] *n.* a navel that recedes and does not protrude. (Compare to *outsy.*) □ *Is yours an insy or an outsy?* □ *It's an outsy. So what?*

**in tall cotton** *mod.* successful; on easy street. □ *I won some money at the track, and I'm really in tall cotton.* □ *We were in tall cotton until the IRS caught up with us.*

**intense** *mod.* serious; heavy. □ *That man is so intense!* □ *This is an intense matter.* □ *Oh, wow! Now that's what I call intense!*

**in the bag** **1.** *mod.* cinched; achieved. □ *It's in the bag—as good as done.* □ *The election is in the bag unless the voters find out about my past.* **2.** *mod.* alcohol intoxicated. □ *Kelly looks like he is in the bag.* □ *John is in the bag and mean as hell.*

**in the black** *mod.* financially solvent; profitable; not in debt. □ *Now that the company is in the black, there's a good chance it will become a deal stock.* □ *We're in the black now and making a profit.*

**in the buff** *mod.* naked. □ *You-know-who sleeps in the buff.* □ *You can save hundreds of dollars in a lifetime by not buying pajamas and sleeping in the buff instead.*

**in the catbird seat** *mod.* in a dominant or controlling position. □ *Sally's in the catbird seat—telling everybody where to go.* □ *I hold all the aces. I'm in the catbird seat.*

**in the chips** *mod.* wealthy; with lots of money. □ *I'm in the chips this month. Let's go squander it.* □ *If I was in the chips, I'd buy a jag.*

**in the driver's seat** *mod.* in control. □ *She's just not comfortable unless she's in the driver's seat.* □ *I'm in the driver's seat now, and I get to decide who gets raises.*

**in the groove** *mod. cool; groovy;* pleasant and delightful. □ *Man, is that combo in the groove tonight!* □ *Get in the groove! Relax.*

**in the gun** *mod.* alcohol intoxicated. (See also *shot.*) □ *Ted is in the gun again.* □ *When Fred is in the gun, he's mean.*

**in the hole** *mod.* in debt; running a deficit. □ *Looks like we are in the hole again this month.* □ *We always end the month in the hole.*

**in the (home) stretch** *mod.* in the last stage of the process. (From horse-racing.) □ *We're in the home stretch with this project and can't change it now.* □ *We're in the stretch. Only three more days till we graduate.*

**in the hopper** *mod.* in process; in line to be processed. (A hopper is an "in-basket" for incoming work.) □ *It's in the hopper. I'll get to it.* □ *Your job is in the hopper, and your turn is next.*

**in the know** *mod.* knowledgeable (about something); having inside knowledge (about something). □ *Ask Harry. He's usually in the know.* □ *Sure I'm in the know. But I'm not telling.*

**in the ozone** *mod.* alcohol or drug intoxicated. □ *Four beers and Tom is in the ozone.* □ *We were in the ozone, but we still made a lot of sense.*

**in the pink 1.** *mod.* feeling quite well; feeling on top of the world. □ *I'm in the pink today. Feeling great.* □ *When she's in the pink again, she'll give you a ring.* **2.** *mod.* alcohol intoxicated. □ *Tod is in the pink and singing at the top of his lungs.* □ *When he's in the pink, he's a handful.*

**in the pipeline** *mod.* backed up somewhere in a process; in process; in a queue. □ *There's a lot of goods still in the pipeline. That means no more orders for a while.* □ *Your papers are in the pipeline somewhere. You'll just have to wait.*

**in there** *mod.* sincere; likable. □ *Martha is really in there. Everybody likes her.* □ *I like a guy who's in there—who thinks about other people.*

**in the soup** *mod.* in trouble. □ *Now you're in the soup.* □ *I'm in the soup with the boss.*

**in the suds** *mod.* alcohol intoxicated. □ *Fred is in the suds and can't see.* □ *When Bob is in the suds, he's mean.*

**in the tube 1.** *mod.* in the tube of a large wave. (Surfing.) □ *Tod is in the tube and looks great.* □ *On a day like today, I want to be out there in the tube.* **2.** *mod.* at risk. □ *He's in the tube now, but things should straighten out soon.* □ *If you find yourself in the tube in this matter, just give me a ring.*

**in thing to do** *n.* the fashionable or orthodox thing to do. (Always with *the.* See *in.*) □ *Cutting your hair short on the sides is the in thing to do.* □ *Smoking is no longer the in thing to do.*

**invite** ['ɪnvɑɪt] *n.* an invitation. (Folksy.) □ *Thanks for the invite, but we can't come.* □ *Let's send an invite to the Babbits.*

**I owe you one.** *sent.* "Thank you. I owe you a favor." □ *Thanks. I owe you one.* □ *You've been a big help. I owe you one.*

**iron 1.** *n.* a gun; a revolver. (Underworld.) □ *Rocko never carries iron unless he's going to use it.* □ *What kind of iron do you carry?* **2.** *n.* computer hardware. (See also *big iron.*) □ *What kind of iron are you people running over there?* □ *This is good old compatible iron.*

**Irv** AND **Ervine, Irvine** *n.* a police officer. (Black. See also *Charlie Irvine.*) □ *Irv is after you, did you know?* □ *Tell Ervine to go catch a speeder or something.*

**It cuts two ways.** *sent.* "There are two sides, you know."; "There are two people involved." □ *You have to help, too. It cuts two ways.* □ *It cuts two ways, you know. It can't always all be my fault.*

**It's a deal.** *sent.* "Okay, it is agreed." □ *Okay, man. It's a deal.* □ *It's a deal. See you at noon.*

**itsy-bitsy** See *itty-bitty.*

**It's your funeral!** *exclam.* "If you do it, you will suffer all the consequences!" □ *Go if you want. It's your funeral!* □ *Go ahead, swim to Cuba. It's your funeral!*

**itty-bitty** AND **itsy-bitsy** ['ıdi'bıdi AND 'ıtsi'bıtsi] *mod.* tiny. □ *What an itty-bitty car!* □ *Give me an itsy-bitsy piece. I'm on a diet.*

**I've been there.** *sent.* "I know from experience what you are talking about." □ *I know what you mean. I've been there.* □ *I've been there. You don't need to spell it out for me.*

**I've got to fly.** AND **I('ve) gotta fly.** *sent.* "I have to leave right now." □ *Time's up. I've got to fly.* □ *I've gotta fly. See you later.*

**I've got to split.** *sent.* "I have to leave now." □ *See you later. I've got to split.* □ *I've got to split. Call my service.*

**ivories** ['aıvriz] **1.** *n.* the teeth. (See also *China.*) □ *I gotta go brush my ivories.* □ *Look at those nice white ivories!* **2.** *n.* piano keys. (From when piano keys were made from real elephant ivory.) □ *She can really bang those ivories.* □ *I'd say she has mastered the ivories.*

**ivory tower** *n.* an imaginary location where aloof academics are said to reside and work. □ *Why don't you come out of your ivory tower and see what the world is really like?* □ *Better yet, stay in your ivory tower.*

**I wouldn't know.** *sent.* "I don't know, and I should not be expected to know." □ *I wouldn't know. Ask your mother.* □ *Where's the mustard? I wouldn't know.*

# J

**J.** AND **jay** *n.* a marijuana cigarette; marijuana. (Drugs. From the initial letter of *joint*.) □ *Toss me a jay, huh?* □ *A jay is two clams.*

**jabber** ['dʒæbɚ] **1.** *n.* mindless chatter. □ *Stop all this jabber and get to work.* □ *I've heard enough of your jabber.* **2.** *in.* to chatter. □ *Come over and we'll jabber about things over coffee.* □ *What are those kids jabbering about?* **3.** *n.* a drug addict who injects drugs. (Drugs.) □ *The guy's a jabber. Look at those tracks.* □ *These scars show that the victim was a jabber.*

**jab pop** ['dʒæb'pɑp] *in.* to inject (drugs). (Drugs.) □ *Gert was jab popping when she died.* □ *Jab popping is a ticket to cement city.*

**jack 1.** *n.* money. □ *I don't have the jack for a deal like that.* □ *How much jack will it take?* **2.** *n.* tobacco for rolling cigarettes. □ *You got some jack I can bum?* □ *I don't use jack at all.*

**jackal** *n.* a low and devious person. □ *You are nothing but a slimy jackal!* □ *What does that jackal want here?*

**jack around** *in.* to waste time; to mess around. □ *Stop jacking around and get busy.* □ *The gang was jacking around and broke your window.*

**jacked (out)** *mod.* angry; annoyed. □ *Boy was that old guy jacked out at you.* □ *Yup, he was jacked all right.*

**jacked up 1.** *mod.* excited. □ *Don was really jacked up about the election.* □ *The gang was jacked up and ready to party.* **2.** *mod.* arrested. (Underworld.) □ *What time did Bruno get himself jacked up?* □ *He was jacked up at midnight.* **3.** *mod.* upset; *stressed.* □ *I was really jacked up by the bad news.* □

*Don't get jacked up. It'll work out.* **4.** *mod. high* on drugs. □ *He's jacked up, and he may have O.D.ed.* □ *The poor kid is jacked up most of the time now.*

**jacket** See *(yellow) jacket.*

**jack someone around** AND **jack around someone** *tr.* to hassle someone; to harass someone. (Compare to *jerk someone around*.) □ *The IRS is jacking my brother around.* □ *The boss was jacking around Gert, so she just walked out.*

**jack someone or something up** AND **jack up someone or something 1.** *tr.* [with *someone*] to motivate someone; to stimulate someone to do something. □ *I'll jack him up and try to get some action out of him.* □ *What does it take to jack you up?* **2.** *tr.* [with *something*] to raise the price of something. □ *They kept jacking the price up with various charges, so I walked.* □ *How can they jack up the published price?*

**jack-ups** *n.* capsules of a barbiturate drug. (Drugs.) □ *Walter took a few jack-ups and went on to work.* □ *Gert took her jack-ups with whiskey. She's gonna get pifted.*

**jag 1.** *n.* a Jaguar automobile. □ *What I really want is a jag.* □ *How much will a jag set me back?* **2.** *n.* a drinking bout; a prolonged state of alcohol or drug intoxication. □ *Is he off on another jag, or is this the same one?* □ *One more jag will kill her. Try to keep her away from the stuff.* **3.** *n.* a prolonged state of emotional excess. □ *I've been on a jag and can't get my work done.* □ *She's off on a jag again.* **4.** *n.* a drug *rush.* (Drugs.) □ *This stuff has no jag at all.* □ *How big a jag do you want?*

**jagged** *mod.* alcohol intoxicated. □ *Man, is that chick jagged!* □ *Let's go out and get jagged.*

**jag party** *n.* a gathering where drugs are used. (Drugs.) □ *There was a jag party scheduled at Freddy's, but Irvine got wind of it.* □ *The jag party ended in a bust.*

**jagster** *n.* someone on a drinking spree; a heavy drinker. □ *Gary is a typical jagster. Drunk for a week and sober for three.* □ *There's not a lot that a doctor can do for a jagster like that.*

**jai-by-jai** [ˈdʒɑɪbɑrˈdʒɑɪ] *mod.* this dimension by this dimension. (Folksy. Always accompanied by gestures showing approximate sizes.) □ *It wasn't very big. About jai-by-jai.* □ *The room was only jai-by-jai. Not big enough to house two people.*

**jail bait** See *(San Quentin) jail bait*.

**jake 1.** *n.* a toilet; a men's restroom. □ *Where's the jake?* □ *The jake is around the corner.* **2.** *n.* a stupid person, usually a male. □ *Some loony jake told me we are going the wrong way.* □ *Who's the jake in the plaid pants?* **3.** *mod.* okay; satisfactory. □ *All right? Then everything is jake.* □ *If you get here by nine, it'll be just jake.* **4.** *n.* illegal liquor. (Prohibition.) □ *You know where I can get some jake?* □ *Why, there's no jake around here. There's a law against it, you know.*

**jam 1.** *n.* a problem; trouble. □ *I hear you're in a bad jam.* □ *Well, it's not a bad jam.* **2.** *in.* (for musicians) to play together, improvising. □ *They jammed until the neighbors complained.* □ *Come over and let's jam, okay?* **3.** *n.* cocaine. (Drugs.) □ *Anybody got a little jam?* □ *There's no jam anywhere in town.* **4.** *n.* amphetamines. (Drugs.) □ *That kid actually shoots jam.* □ *Is there a lot of jam in this neighborhood?* **5.** *tr. & in.* to force a basketball into the basket; to *slam dunk* a basketball. □ *He tried to jam it, but blew it.* □ *Andy broke the goal by trying to jam.* **6.** *n.* an act of forcing a basketball into the basket; a *slam dunk.* □ *The jam didn't work, and Fred's team got the ball.* □ *One more jam for Wilbur!*

**Jamaican (gold)** *n.* potent marijuana grown in Jamaica. (Drugs.) □ *She says it's Jamaican gold, but I'll bet you it's domestic.* □ *Real Jamaican costs more than this.*

**jambled** [ˈdʒæmbl̩d] *mod.* alcohol intoxicated. □ *Jerry was too jambled to stand up.* □ *Let's go out and get good and jambled.*

**jammed** [ˈdʒæmd] **1.** *mod.* arrested. (Underworld.) □ *Bruno got jammed for speeding.* □ *When did he get jammed?* **2.** *mod.* alcohol intoxicated. □ *I'm a little jammed, but I think I can still drive.* □ *They were jammed by midnight.* **3.** See the following entry.

**jammed up 1.** AND **jammed** *mod.* in trouble. □ *He got himself jammed up with the law.* □ *I'm sort of jammed and need some help.* **2.** *mod.* glutted; full of food or drink. □ *I'm jammed up. I can't eat another bite.* □ *After dinner, I am so jammed up that I need a nap.* **3.** *mod.* overdosed with drugs. (Drugs.) □ *He gets high, but never jammed up.* □ *Tod is jammed up and out of commission for a while.*

**jamming** *mod.* excellent. □ *This music is really jamming.* □ *What a jamming class session.*

**jampacked** AND **jam-packed** *mod.* full. □ *This day has been jampacked with surprises.* □ *The box was jam-packed with goodies.*

**jams** See *(jim-)jams*.

**jan** [dʒæn] *n.* January in the financial futures markets. (Financial markets.) □ *The bean futures for jan fell out of bed yesterday.* □ *Are these figures jan or March?*

**jane 1.** *n.* marijuana. (Drugs.) □ *You got any jane?* □ *Max has jane coming out of his ears.* **2.** *n.* a women's restroom; the same as *ruth.* □ *Where's the jane around here?* □ *The jane is upstairs.*

**Jane Doe** [ˈdʒen ˈdo] *n.* a general term for a woman. (The mate of *John Doe.*) □ *A Jane Doe was pulled out of the river this morning.* □ *There was an accident involving a Jane Doe.*

**Jane Q. Public** [ˈdʒen ˈkju ˈpəblɪk] *n.* a general term for a female representative of the public. (The mate of *John Q.*

Public.) □ *And what does Jane Q. Public think about all this?* □ *Jane Q. Public doesn't care at all.*

**java** ['dʒɑvə] *n.* coffee. □ *How about a cup of java?* □ *Some black java would be real good.*

**jaw 1.** *n.* a chat. □ *Come over for a jaw this weekend.* □ *I could use a good jaw with my old friend.* **2.** *in.* to chat. □ *Stop jawing and get to work.* □ *Come over, and we can jaw for a while.* **3.** See *jawbone.*

**jawbone** AND **jaw** *tr.* to try to persuade someone verbally; to apply verbal pressure to someone. □ *They tried to jawbone me into doing it.* □ *Don't jaw me. I won't do it.*

**jay** See *J.*

**jay smoke** *n.* a marijuana cigarette. (Drugs. See *J.*) □ *He had a jay smoke hanging from his lower lip.* □ *He lit up a jay smoke and smiled.*

**jazzed (up) 1.** *mod.* alert; having a positive state of mind. □ *I am jazzed up and ready to face life.* □ *Those guys were jazzed and ready for the game.* **2.** *mod.* alcohol or drug intoxicated. □ *Dave was a bit jazzed up, but not terribly.* □ *Gert was jazzed out of her mind.* **3.** *mod.* enhanced; with something added; having been made more enticing. □ *The third act was jazzed up with a little skin.* □ *It was jazzed enough to have the police chief around asking questions.* **4.** *mod.* forged or altered. (Underworld. See *tinseled.*) □ *This check is jazzed. Deep six it!* □ *Better not try to cash a jazzed check at this bank.*

**jazz someone or something up** AND **jazz up someone or something** *tr.* to make someone or something more exciting or sexy; to make someone or something appeal more to contemporary and youthful tastes. □ *Let's jazz this up a little bit.* □ *They jazzed up the old girl till she looked like a teenager.* □ *Don't jazz up the first number too much.*

**jazzy** ['dʒæzi] *mod.* stimulating; appealing. □ *That's a jazzy sweater you got.* □ *He's a real jazzy guy.*

**J.C.L.** See *Johnnie-come-lately.*

**J.D. 1.** *n.* "Jack Daniels"™ whiskey. □ *He poured a little J.D. into a glass, set it aside, and drank all of what was in the*

bottle. □ *Then he poured the glass of J.D. back into the bottle.* **2.** *n.* a "juvenile delinquent." □ *Some J.D. broke my window.* □ *The J.D.s are taking over the neighborhood.*

**J. Edgar (Hoover)** ['dʒe 'ɛdgɚ ('huvɚ)] *n.* the police; federal officers. (Underworld.) □ *Max got out of town when he heard that the J. Edgars were on his tail.* □ *Well, J. Edgar Hoover, looks like you got me!*

**jeegee** See *jojee.*

**Jeepers(-creepers)!** ['dʒipɚz'kripɚz] *exclam.* "Wow!" □ *Jeepers-creepers! I'm sorry!* □ *Jeepers, she's wonderful!*

**Jeez!** See *Jesus!*

**jeff** [dʒɛf] **1.** *n.* a Caucasian. (All senses originally black. From *Jefferson Davis.* Potentially derogatory.) □ *The jeffs are coming around more often. What's up?* □ *Those jeffs like you, man.* **2.** *n.* a boring or *square* person. □ *That jeff bugs me.* □ *Don't be a jeff, man!* **3.** *tr.* to persuade or deceive someone. □ *The guy tried to jeff me!* □ *You're just jeffing us!* **4.** *in.* to gentrify; to take on the ways of whites. □ *Cool it man; stop your jeffing.* □ *I'm not jeffing.*

**jel** [dʒɛl] *n.* a stupid person with Jello™ (gelatin) where brains ought to be. □ *The guy's a jel. Forget him.* □ *Oh, Wallace, don't act like such a jel.*

**jellies** See *jelly shoes.*

**jelly babies** *n.* an amphetamine tablet or capsule. (Drugs. Another term for *jelly bean.*) □ *You got any jelly babies?* □ *Is there much of those jelly babies in this neighborhood?*

**jelly shoes** AND **jellies, jelly sandals** *n.* colorful shoes made from soft, flexible plastic. (From *jelly bean.*) □ *It's too cold to wear jelly shoes.* □ *Jellies will crack in this weather.*

**jerk** *n.* a stupid or worthless person. (Now both males and females.) □ *What a loony jerk!* □ *You are such a classic jerk!*

**jerk around** *in.* to waste time. □ *Stop jerking around and get to work.* □ *All you do is jerk around. Get a move on!*

**jerker 1.** *n.* a drunkard; an alcoholic. (See *jerker.*) □ *Some of the jerkers have the D.T.s.* □ *Ask the jerker to come in and have a drink.* **2.** *n.* a heavy user of cocaine. (Drugs.) □ *The new guy is a jerker. You can see it in his eyes.* □ *The jerkers who need immediate treatment are sent from E.R. up to detox.*

**jerks** *n.* the delirium tremens. □ *The old guy has the jerks.* □ *What can they do for the jerks—other than hospitalize the victims?*

**jerk someone around** AND **jerk around someone** *tr.* to hassle someone; to waste someone's time. □ *Stop jerking me around and give me my money back.* □ *They sure like to jerk around people in that music shop.*

**jerkwater** *mod.* backwoodsy; insignificant. (See also *one-horse town*.) □ *I'm from a little jerkwater town in the Midwest.* □ *He's sort of the jerkwater type.*

**jerry-built** *mod.* carelessly and awkwardly built. □ *This is an old, jerry-built house, but we love it.* □ *The lawyer's case was jerry-built, but the jury bought it anyway.*

**Jesus!*** AND **Jeez!** ['dʒizəs AND 'dʒiz] *exclam.* "Wow!" (Caution with *Jesus* in profane senses.) □ *Jesus, what a jerk!* □ *Jesus! I'm late.*

**Jesus boots*** *n.* sandals. (Caution with *Jesus* in profane senses.) □ *Jesus boots are okay in the summer.* □ *Who is the kook in Jesus boots?*

**jet** *n.* ketamine hydrochloride, a drug like *L.S.D.* (Drugs.) □ *Now he's trying to get kids to use jet instead of acid.* □ *Is jet that green stuff?*

**jet-set** AND **jet-setters** *n.* young and wealthy people who fly by jet from resort to resort. □ *The jet-set doesn't come here anymore.* □ *Jet-setters have turned to other kinds of excitement.*

**jibe** [dʒaɪb] *in.* to agree; to be in harmony. (Compare to *track*.) □ *Your story just doesn't jibe with the facts.* □ *These things just don't jibe.*

**jiffy** ['dʒɪfi] *n.* a very short time. (See *in a jiff(y)*.) □ *That was a pretty long jiffy I had to wait!* □ *Just a jiffy, I'll be there.*

**jig*** [dʒɪg] *tr. & in.* to copulate (with someone). (Caution with topic.) □ *He's telling everybody that he didn't jig her.* □ *She's claiming they jigged twice.*

**jigalorum** AND **jigamaree** [dʒɪgə'lorəm AND dʒɪgəmə'ri] *n.* a gadget. □ *Now, put this little jigalorum over the end, and you've got a perfect and efficient little jigamaree.* □ *This jigamaree is broken.*

**jigamy** ['dʒɪgəmi] *n.* a word used in place of a forgotten name. □ *Where is that jigamy I use for opening paint cans?* □ *I put that jigamy away the last time I used it.*

**jigger** **1.** *n.* a drink of whiskey. (The standard term for a small container used for measuring the right amount of liquor for a drink.) □ *How about another jigger of that shine?* □ *Okay, I'll have a jigger.* **2.** *n.* a cigarette. □ *You got a jigger I can bum?* □ *Here's a pack of jiggers. Help yourself.* **3.** *n.* a gadget. □ *Toss me one of those copper jiggers there in the box.* □ *This kind of jigger?*

**jiggered** **1.** *mod.* damned. □ *Get that jiggered cat out of here!* □ *Well, I'll be jiggered!* **2.** *mod.* alcohol intoxicated. (See *jigger*.) □ *Tod was more than just a little jiggered.* □ *Tod was too jiggered to stand up.*

**jiggus** AND **jiggum** ['dʒɪgəs AND 'dʒɪgəm] *n.* a gadget. □ *Toss me that jiggus, will you?* □ *Do you want this jiggum or that one?*

**jig is up** *phr.* the game is ended; the scheme has been found out. (Always with *the*.) □ *Okay, you kids. The jig's up!* □ *Who says the jig is up?*

**jillion** ['dʒɪljən] *n.* an enormous, indefinite number. □ *I've got a jillion things to tell you.* □ *This car cost me about a jillion bucks.*

**(jim-)jams** AND **jimmies** ['dʒɪm'dʒæmz AND 'dʒɪmiz] **1.** *n.* a nervous fit; a depression. □ *He got the jim-jams whenever he went out.* □ *This kind of movie gives me the jimmies.* **2.** *n.* the delirium tremens; a hangover. □ *When the jim-jams began, I knew I'd gone too far.* □ *The jimmies nearly tore him apart.*

**jimmies** See the previous entry.

**jingle** **1.** *n.* a buzz or tingle from alcohol. □ *He had a little jingle, but he wasn't even tipsy.* □ *This stuff gives me a little jingle, but that's all.* **2.** *n.* a drinking bout. □ *Jack was out on a jingle all night.* □ *The guys planned a big jingle for Friday.* **3.** *n.* a call on the telephone. (See also *buzz*.) □ *Give me a jingle when you get into town.* □ *I got a jingle from Gert today.*

**jingled** *mod.* alcohol intoxicated. □ *She was a little jingled, but not worse than that.* □ *Let's go out and get good and jingled.*

**jingler** *mod.* a drunkard; an alcoholic. □ *The jinglers have taken over the streets.* □ *Where do all these jinglers sleep?*

**jitters** ['dʒɪdəz] *n.* the nervous shakes. (Always with *the.*) □ *I get the jitters when I have to talk in public.* □ *Too much booze gives me the jitters.*

**jive** [dʒɑɪv] **1.** *n.* drugs; marijuana. (Drugs. Black. See also *gyve.*) □ *Stop using all that jive all the time.* □ *That jive is gonna be the end of you.* **2.** *n.* back talk. □ *Cut the jive, man!* □ *Don't you give me any of that jive!* **3.** *n.* lies; deception; nonsense. □ *No more of your jive. Talk straight or don't talk.* □ *I've listened to your jive for years. You'll never change.* **4.** *mod.* deceptive; insincere. □ *Don't give me all those jive excuses.* □ *I listened to her little jive speech and then fired her.*

**jive-ass*** *mod.* foolish. (Black. Caution with *ass.*) □ *You can tell that jive-ass jerk to forget it.* □ *Don't pay any attention to that jive-ass jeff.*

**jivestick** AND **gyvestick** *n.* a marijuana cigarette. (Drugs.) □ *Max flipped a jivestick to Bruno and smiled.* □ *He had a gyvestick stuck behind his ear.*

**jive talk** *n.* slang; contemporary fad words. □ *I like to hear jive talk. It's like trying to work a puzzle.* □ *He stands by the window with a pad of paper and takes down the jive talk he hears.*

**jive turkey** *n.* a stupid person. □ *What jive turkey made this mess?* □ *Get that jive turkey out of here!*

**job** *n.* a drunkard. □ *What does this old job want besides a drink?* □ *Give the job a drink and make somebody happy today.*

**jobber** AND **jobby** ['dʒɑbə AND 'dʒɑbi] **1.** *n.* a gadget. □ *Where is the little jobber I use to tighten this?* □ *Do you mean this little jobber?* **2.** *n.* a bowel movement. (Juvenile.) □ *Don't forget to jobber, Jimmy.* □ *Mommy, I gotta jobby.*

**jober as a sudge** ['dʒɑbə æz ə 'sədʒ] *mod.* sober. (A deliberate spoonerism on *sober as a judge.*) □ *Me? I'm as jober as a sudge.* □ *What I mean to shay*

*is that I am shertainly as jober as a sudge!*

**jock 1.** *n.* an athlete. (See also *strap.* See *jockstrap.* Now of either sex.) □ *The jocks are all at practice now.* □ *She's dating a jock who has to be home by ten.* **2.** *n.* an athletic supporter (garment). □ *Somebody dropped a jock in the hall.* □ *Whose jock is that out there on Molly's clothesline?*

**jockey** AND **jocky** *n.* an addictive drug. (Drugs. Because such a drug rides one like a jockey rides a horse.) □ *That jockey rode her for years.* □ *She fought that jocky, and it finally won.*

**jockstrap 1.** AND **jockstrapper** *n.* an athlete. (From the name of the supporting garment worn by male athletes.) □ *The jockstrappers are all at practice now.* □ *Here comes one of the best jockstrappers on the team.* **2.** *in.* to work as a professional athlete. □ *I jockstrapped for a few years and then lost my interest in it.* □ *I made a lot of money jockstrapping.*

**joe 1.** *n.* coffee. □ *How about a cup of joe?* □ *Yeah, a cup of black joe would be great.* **2.** *n.* an ordinary man. □ *What does the everyday joe make of all this nonsense?* □ *Do you know even one everyday joe?*

**Joe Blow** AND **Joe Doakes** ['dʒo 'blo AND 'dʒo 'doks] *n.* a typical or average male American citizen. □ *What do you think Joe Blow really thinks about all this?* □ *According to surveys, Joe Doakes can hardly read.*

**Joe Citizen** ['dʒo 'sɪtəsn̩] *n.* a general term for a male representative of the public. (Compare to *John Q. Public.*) □ *Joe Citizen hasn't spoken yet.* □ *Joe Citizen is watching T.V.*

**Joe College** *n.* a typical or average male college student. □ *You sure look like Joe College from the good old days.* □ *Joe College never had a computer or a laser-powered record player in the good old days.*

**Joe Doakes** See *Joe Blow.*

**Joe Schmo** ['dʒo 'ʃmo] *n.* a jerk. □ *Joe Schmo doesn't really care.* □ *Let's say Joe Schmo wants a new car. What does he do?*

**Joe Six-pack** *n.* the average guy who sits around drinking beer by the six-pack. □ *Joe Six-pack likes that kind of television program.* □ *All Joe Six-pack wants is a good game on T.V.*

**john** **1.** *n.* a toilet; a bathroom. □ *Somebody's in the john.* □ *Is there another john around here?* **2.** *n.* a man. □ *Some john was around asking for you.* □ *This john came up and asked if I had seen the girl in a picture he had.* **3.** *n.* a prostitute's customer. □ *She led the john into an alley where Lefty robbed him.* □ *The john looked a little embarrassed.* **4.** *n.* a victim of a crime or deception; a *sucker.* □ *The john went straight to the cops and told the whole thing.* □ *Clobber the john a good one when he turns around.*

**John Doe** ['dʒɑn 'do] *n.* a general term for a man. (The mate of *Jane Doe.*) □ *John Doe was the name at the bottom of the check.* □ *Oh, you mean John Doe isn't his real name?*

**John Hancock** *n.* one's signature. (Refers to the signature of John Hancock, one of the signers of the Declaration of Independence.) □ *Put your John Hancock right here, if you don't mind.* □ *Mr. Wilson's John Hancock is worth about 30 million.*

**Johnnie-come-lately** AND **J.C.L.** *n.* someone new to a situation or status. □ *This Johnnie-come-lately doesn't know what it was like in the old days.* □ *I'm just a Johnnie-come-lately, but I'm eager.*

**Johnny-be-good** *n.* a police officer. □ *Here comes Johnny-be-good, so be good.* □ *Johnny-be-good went through my pockets.*

**Johnny Law** AND **John Law** *n.* a law officer. □ *Johnny Law is supposed to be your friend.* □ *John Law showed up with a piece of paper that says you are in trouble.*

**John Q. Public** ['dʒɑn 'kju 'pəblɪk] *n.* a general term for a male representative of the public. (The mate of *Jane Q. Public.*) □ *John Q. Public doesn't seem to like the new tax forms.* □ *John Q. Public tends not to like regimentation.*

**johnson*** **1.** *n.* a thing. (Black. See *jones.*) □ *What is this johnson about you snitching?* □ *He's got this smack*

johnson riding him. **2.*** *n.* a penis. (Black. Again, a "thing." Caution with topic.) □ *Zip up, or your johnson'll get out.* □ *He covered his johnson and ran for the dressing room.* **3.** AND **johnson grass** *n.* marijuana; drugs; any contraband. (Drugs. Black. See the following entry.) □ *Is johnson around here?* □ *Me and johnson gonna rap tonight.*

**johnson (grass)** See *johnson.*

**joined at the hip** *mod.* closely connected; as thick as thieves. (As Siamese twins are joined.) □ *Those two are joined at the hip. They are always together.* □ *Sam and Martha are joined at the hip.*

**joint*** **1.** *n.* a tavern; a speakeasy. (Prohibition.) □ *Lefty has his own joint over on 12th.* □ *I wanted to open a joint, but I don't have the cash.* **2.** *n.* a low-class establishment; a *dive.* □ *Let's get out of this crummy joint.* □ *This joint bores me.* **3.** *n.* a tobacco cigarette. □ *You got a filter joint on you?* □ *Why are beggars being choosers about their joints all of a sudden?* **4.** *n.* a marijuana cigarette. (Drugs. Compare to *jointstick.*) □ *He always has a joint with him.* □ *The joint wasn't enough to carry him very long.* **5.*** *n.* a penis. (Caution with topic.) □ *He told some joke about a joint, but people just turned away.* □ *He covered his joint and ran for the dressing room.* **6.** *n.* equipment for preparing and injecting drugs. (Drugs.) □ *He keeps his joint at his aunt's house.* □ *His aunt found his joint and threw it out.* **7.** *n.* a concealed collection of drugs and drug equipment; a *stash.* (Drugs.) □ *Her joint was thrown out accidentally.* □ *What does a 12-year-old need with a joint anyway?* **8.** *n.* a jail; a prison. (Underworld.) □ *Lefty just got out of the joint.* □ *He learned a lot in the joint that he was anxious to try out.*

**jointstick** *n.* a marijuana cigarette. (Drugs.) □ *He had a jointstick stuck behind his ear. That was his signature.* □ *Max sold the kid a jointstick made of ragweed.*

**join up** *in.* to become addicted to a drug. (Drugs.) □ *Max is always trying to get somebody to join up.* □ *Once you join up in Max's club, you've got to be nice to Max.*

**jojee** AND **jeegee** ['dʒodʒi AND 'dʒidʒi] *n.* heroin. (Drugs.) □ *Max keeps a supply of jojee somewhere in the Bronx.* □ *Jeegee is hard to stockpile. It's a real investment.*

**joke** *tr.* to tease someone; to make fun of someone. □ *Everybody was joking my roommate because of her accent.* □ *Don't joke me, man. I do the best I can.*

**joker** *n.* a man; a guy. □ *Who was that joker I saw you with last night?* □ *Some joker was at the door selling something.*

**jollies** *n.* a charge or thrill; a sexual thrill; *kick.* □ *He got his jollies from skin flicks.* □ *This gyvestick gives Ernie all the jollies he wants.*

**jollop** ['dʒɑləp] *n.* a drink of liquor □ *She poured a big jollop into each of the glasses and then drank them one by one.* □ *"Have another jollop," she said to herself.*

**jolly** *mod.* alcohol intoxicated; tipsy. □ *Everybody was jolly and singing by the time the food arrived.* □ *Kelly was a little too jolly, and her sister told her to slow down.*

**jolly-well** *mod.* certainly. □ *You jolly-well better be there on time.* □ *I jolly-well will.*

**jolt 1.** *n.* the degree of potency of the alcohol in liquor. □ *It doesn't have much of a jolt.* □ *Watch out. This stuff has quite a jolt.* **2.** *n.* a drink of strong liquor. □ *Can you give me a little jolt of shine?* □ *He knocked back a jolt and asked for another.* **3.** *n.* a portion or dose of a drug. (Drugs.) □ *How about a little jolt as a taste?* □ *A jolt costs.* **4.** *n.* the *rush* from an injection of drugs. (Drugs.) □ *This stuff doesn't have much jolt.* □ *What kind of jolt do you want?*

**jones\* 1.** *n.* a thing. (Black. See *johnson.*) □ *There's a big turf jones down on the corner.* □ *This get-rich-quick jones will land you in the joint, Lefty.* **2.\*** *n.* a penis. (Black. Caution with topic.) □ *Zip up, man. You want your jones getting out?* □ *Cut out all this talk about joneses!* **3.** *n.* a drug habit; drug addiction. (Drugs. Black. See *skag jones.*) □ *That jones is really riding that guy.* □ *He's got a real bad jones with that dust.*

**joog** [dʒug] *tr.* to stab someone. (Prisons.) □ *Lefty jooged the screw.* □ *Man, who'd you joog?*

**josh** [dʒɑʃ] *tr. & in.* to tease someone; to kid someone. □ *Stop joshing. Be serious.* □ *You're just joshing me!*

**joybox** *n.* a piano. □ *Can you play this joybox at all?* □ *Your joybox needs some tuning.*

**joy dust** AND **joy powder** *n.* a powerful powdered drug: cocaine; heroin; morphine. (Drugs.) □ *There are old houses in that part of town where they sell joy dust to just about anybody they recognize, even kids.* □ *Amy is always trying to get hold of some joy dust.*

**joy flakes** AND **joy dust** *n.* powdered or crystallized cocaine. (Drugs. See *crack.*) □ *Is joy flakes the same as crack?* □ *Joy dust is sort of crack without the press coverage.*

**joy juice** *n.* liquor; beer. □ *Joy juice makes Ted sad.* □ *Can I pour some more of this joy juice?*

**joy pop** *in.* to inject heroin subcutaneously for pleasure, not to feed an addiction. (Drugs.) □ *What's wrong with joy popping?* □ *She started out joy popping, but the scars of real addiction looked like rows of buttons up and down her arms when they pulled her out of the river.*

**joy popper** AND **joy rider** *n.* someone who injects narcotics only occasionally. (Drugs.) □ *You could see by her arms she was a joy popper.* □ *Joy riders don't stay innocent for long.*

**joy powder** See *joy dust.*

**joy ride 1.** *n.* a drinking bout or party. □ *There's a little joy ride over at Tom's.* □ *Some joy ride! They ran out of booze.* **2.** *n.* a state of euphoria from drug use. (Drugs.) □ *This stuff is a real joy ride.* □ *Ernie's on a little joy ride right now and can't come to the phone.* **3.** *n.* a ride where the passenger does not return alive. (Underworld.) □ *Mr. Big wanted Bruno to take Max on a joy ride.* □ *You're going on a little joy ride with me. Now, get moving.*

**joy rider** See *joy popper.*

**joy smoke** AND **joy hemp, joy root** *n.* marijuana; a marijuana cigarette. (Drugs.) □ *He just wanted a little joy smoke. Nothing serious.* □ *He developed a fondness for joy root while he was in Vietnam.*

**joystick 1.** *n.* an opium pipe. (Drugs. Old.) □ *I think that old man was married to a joystick when he was a little younger.* □ *Many of the old-time joysticks were very ornate.* **2.** *n.* a marijuana cigarette; a marijuana pipe. (Drugs.) □ *Bring your joystick over, and we'll do some bongs.* □ *Tod refused the joystick, which surprised everybody.*

**joy water** *n.* liquor; strong liquor. □ *How about some more joy water?* □ *No more joy water for me, thanks.*

**joy weed** *n.* cannabis. (Drugs. See *weed*.) □ *The kids can even buy joy weed in school.* □ *Some little kids even sell joy weed in school.*

**juane** AND **juana** ['wɑnə] *n.* cannabis; marijuana. (Drugs. See *Mary Jane*.) □ *He had some juane on him when he was arrested.* □ *This juana is all dried out.*

**jug 1.** *n.* jail. (Usually with *the*.) □ *Take it easy. I don't want to end up in the jug.* □ *A couple of days in the jug would do you fine.* **2.** *n.* a jug of liquor; a jar of *moonshine*; a can of beer. □ *Where's my jug? I need a swig.* □ *Pass her the jug, Sam.* **3.** AND **jug up** *in.* to drink heavily. □ *Let's jug up and have a good time.* □ *We jugged till about noon and then went to sleep.* (More at *jugger*.) **4.** *n.* a glass vial of liquid amphetamine intended for injection. (Drugs.) □ *His mother found a jug and took it to a drugstore to find out what it was.* □ *Any kid can get jugs just by asking around.* **5.** *n.* the jugular vein, used for the injection of narcotics. (Drugs.) □ *Now Ernie has to take it in the jug.* □ *He's even got scars on his jugs.*

**jugged (up)** *mod.* alcohol intoxicated. □ *I'm not jugged up. I'm not even tipsy.* □ *Fred was too jugged to drive home.*

**jugger** *n.* an alcoholic; a drunkard. □ *A couple of old juggers sat in the alley, trying to figure out how to get some more.* □ *He's a jugger, and he will never change.*

**jughead 1.** *n.* a stupid person. □ *You can be such a jughead!* □ *I guess I'm sort of a jughead lately.* **2.** *n.* a drunkard. □ *Buy the jughead a drink. That'll shut him up.* □ *You don't see jugheads at parties as much as you used to.*

**jug man** AND **jug broad** *n.* a drug addict who has no remaining veins suitable for injection except the jugular vein. (Drugs. Either male with *man* or female with *broad*.) □ *When I got to be a jug man, something inside me screamed at me to stop.* □ *The jug broad finally bled to death trying for a big jolt.*

**jug wine** *n.* cheap wine that is sold in volume, usually in gallon jugs. □ *We're having a little do tomorrow—nothing special. A little jug wine and chips.* □ *Can you stop by the juice shop and nick some jug wine?*

**juice 1.** *n.* liquor; wine. □ *Let's go get some juice and get stewed.* □ *You got any juice in your room?* **2.** *in.* to drink heavily. (See *juiced (up)*.) □ *Both of them were really juicing.* □ *Stop juicing and listen to me.* **3.** *n.* liquid amphetamine for injecting. (Drugs.) □ *For some reason, juice has always been easy to get.* □ *Juice seems to be a favorite with the college crowd.* **4.** *n.* cough syrup containing codeine. (Drugs.) □ *Kids take juice just for fun.* □ *Howard has some juice in his stash.* **5.** *n.* electricity. □ *The juice has been off since dawn.* □ *Turn on the juice, and let's see if it runs.* **6.** *n.* energy; power; political influence. □ *The boss has the juice with the board to make the necessary changes.* □ *Dave left the president's staff because he just didn't have the juice anymore to be useful.* **7.** *n.* orange juice futures market. (Financial markets. Usually with *the*.) □ *The juice opened a little high today, but fell quickly under profit taking.* □ *It's time to sell the juice and buy bellies.*

**juice and beans** *n.* a narcotic cough syrup taken with sleeping pills. (Drugs. See *beans, juice*.) □ *All these kids know where they can get juice and beans.* □ *This juice and beans stuff can be found all over the city.*

**juiced (up)** AND **juiced to the gills** *mod.* alcohol intoxicated. (See *juice*.) □ *Let's go out and get juiced up.* □ *Man, that chick is really juiced.*

**juice freak** *n.* someone who prefers alcohol to drugs. (Drugs.) □ *Freddy is a juice freak. He won't touch dolls.* □ *Juice freaks end up with addictions, too.*

**juicehead** AND **juicer**  *n.* a heavy drinker; a drunkard. □ *Hank is turning into a regular juicehead.* □ *The tavern is always filled with juicers on Friday night.*

**juice house**  *n.* a liquor store. (Black.) □ *Would you stop by the juice house for some foam?* □ *The juice house was held up last night.*

**juice joint**  *n.* a liquor establishment; a speakeasy. (Prohibition.) □ *His grandfather ran a juice joint during prohibition.* □ *The cops raided the juice joints over and over.*

**juicer**  See *juicehead.*

**juice racket**  *n.* a racket where exorbitant interest is charged on loans. (Underworld.) □ *The cops got one of the leaders of the juice racket.* □ *The juice racket is no picnic, I guess.*

**juice something back** AND **juice back something**  *tr.* to drink alcohol. □ *He's been juicing it back since noon.* □ *Juice back your drink, and let's go.*

**juicy**  *mod.* alcohol intoxicated. □ *Mary is just a little bit juicy, I'm afraid.* □ *She's so juicy she can't stand up!*

**juju**  ['dʒudʒu] **1.** *n.* a marijuana cigarette. □ *You got a spare juju?* □ *Ernie passed the juju to Molly.* **2.** *n.* a capsule of a drug. (Drugs.) □ *The pushers call all pills "jujus."* □ *Max says that jujus are kid stuff.*

**jump**  See *jump (street).*

**jump all over someone** AND **jump down someone's throat, jump on someone**  *in.* to scold someone severely. □ *My dad jumped all over me for being late.* □ *Don't jump down my throat. I didn't do it.*

**jump bail**  *tr.* to fail to show up in court and forfeit bail. □ *Lefty jumped bail, and now he's a fugitive.* □ *Once you've jumped bail, everybody is after you.*

**jump smooth**  *in.* to give up illegal activities; to become *straight.* (Underworld.) □ *Freddy jumped smooth just in time.* □ *After a night in the junk tank, I knew I had to jump smooth.*

**jump start**  **1.** *n.* the act of starting a car by getting power—through jumper cables—from another car. □ *I got a jump start from a friend.* □ *Who can give me a jump start?* **2.** *tr.* to start a car by getting power from another car. □ *I*

*jump started her car for her.* □ *I can't jump start your car. My battery is low.*

**jump (street)**  *n.* the beginning; the start (of something). (Prisons and streets.) □ *I knew from jump that you were going to be trouble.* □ *Way back at jump street, I spotted you as a troublemaker.*

**jump the gun**  *tr.* to start too soon; to start before the starting signal. □ *Don't jump the gun again. Wait till I tell you.* □ *The secretary jumped the gun and gave out the letters too soon.*

**jumpy**  *mod.* nervous. □ *I'm a little jumpy today, and I don't know why.* □ *Now, don't be jumpy. Everything will be all right.*

**jungle**  *n.* a vicious area of confusion; the real world. □ *The place is a jungle out there. You'll grow up fast out there.* □ *Once you're out in that jungle, you'll appreciate home more.*

**jungled**  *mod.* alcohol intoxicated; affected by *jungle juice.* □ *Tod is a little jungled.* □ *He was jungled before he came here.*

**jungle juice**  *n.* homemade liquor; any strong liquor. □ *This jungle juice will knock you for a loop.* □ *Jungle juice will do in a pinch.*

**juniper juice**  *n.* gin. (From the juniper berry flavoring of gin.) □ *He just lived for his daily ounce of juniper juice.* □ *Molly used to like juniper juice before she went on the dust.*

**junk**  **1.** *n.* liquor; inferior liquor. □ *Pour this junk down the drain and get me something good.* □ *After a while the derelicts grow to prefer junk.* **2.** *tr.* to dispose of something, such as a piece of equipment. □ *Junk this thing. It's broken.* □ *I can't junk it. It's the only one I have.* **3.** *n.* drugs. (Drugs.) □ *You don't have to go downtown to buy junk anymore.* □ *You can get junk on any street corner.*

**junk bond**  *n.* a low-rated corporate bond that pays higher interest because of greater risk. (Parallel to *junk food.*) □ *Don't put all your money into junk bonds.* □ *Junk bonds pay a lot of interest.*

**junk connection**  *n.* someone who knows how and where to get drugs; a drug supplier. (Drugs.) □ *Who is Max's junk* connection? □ *Ernie has no fixed junk connection.*

**junked (up)** *mod.* drug intoxicated. □ *Fred has never been junked up even once.* □ *Paul came in junked this morning.*

**junker 1.** *n.* a drug dealer. (Drugs.) □ *Max is the best-known junker in the area.* □ *The junkers all belong behind bars.* **2.** *n.* a drug addict. (Drugs.) □ *Molly is a full-fledged junker now.* □ *Once you're a junker, it's hard to jump straight.*

**junker man** *n.* a marijuana smoker. □ *Ernie is a junker man. He doesn't like the juice.* □ *Can you imagine a 12-year-old junker man?*

**junk food** *n.* food that is typically high in fats and salt and low in nutritional value; food from a fast-food restaurant. □ *Stay away from junk food. It's bad for you.* □ *Junk food tastes good no matter how greasy it is.*

**junk heap** *n.* an old dilapidated car; a dilapidated house or other structure. □ *They lived in that junk heap for 30 years and never painted it.* □ *Why don't you fix up that junk heap?*

**junk hog** See the following entry.

**junkhound** AND **junk hog** *n.* a drug user or addict. (Drugs.) □ *Gert became a shameless junkhound.* □ *The junk hogs are taking over this neighborhood.*

**junkie** AND **junky** ['dʒəŋki] **1.** *n.* a drug dealer. (Drugs.) □ *Max is a junkie.* □ *Junkies should be put into the jug.* **2.** *n.* a drug user; an addict. (Drugs.) □ *The junkies can be helped, you know.* □ *Junkies have to steal to support their habits.*

**junk mail** *n.* unwanted or annoying advertising mail. □ *All we got was junk mail today.* □ *I read everything that comes in the mail, even the junk mail.*

**junk peddler** AND **junk pusher** *n.* a dope dealer. (Drugs.) □ *There is only one major junk peddler around here.* □ *Max is a very wealthy junk pusher.*

**junk pusher** See the previous entry.

**junk squad** *n.* police who enforce the narcotics laws. (Underworld.) □ *The junk squad has more than it can handle trying to keep up with the hard stuff.* □ *We need a bigger junk squad in this part of town.*

**junk tank** *n.* a jail cell where addicts are kept. (Compare to *drunk tank.*) □ *That junk tank is a very dangerous place.* □ *Nobody sleeps in the junk tank.*

**junky** See *junkie.*

**just off the boat** *mod.* to be freshly immigrated and perhaps gullible and naive. (See *F.O.B.*) □ *I'm not just off the boat. I know what's going on.* □ *He may act like he's just off the boat, but he's all right.*

**just the ticket** *n.* just the perfect thing. □ *This little jigger is just the ticket.* □ *A nice cup of tea will be just the ticket.*

**just what the doctor ordered** *n.* exactly what is needed. □ *This nice cool beer is just what the doctor ordered.* □ *A nice chat with friends is just what the doctor ordered.*

**juvie** ['dʒuvi] **1.** *n.* a police officer concerned with juveniles. (Underworld.) □ *I'm a juvie in the Shakespeare district.* □ *The juvies have to know juvenile law cold.* **2.** *n.* a youth; a teenager under 18. (Underworld.) □ *I work with juvies a lot. I try to get them back on the track.* □ *They brought in a juvie and charged him with shoplifting.* **3.** *mod.* juvenile. □ *That was sort of a juvie thing to do.* □ *Don't be so juvie.* □ *She still has a lot of juvie attitudes.*

# K

**K.** [ke] **1.** AND **kee, key, ki** [ki] *n.* a kilogram of cannabis. (Drugs.) □ *You want a whole K.?* □ *Well, how much is a ki?* **2.** *n.* ketamine hydrochloride, a drug similar to *L.S.D.* (Drugs.) □ *You want to try this K. stuff?* □ *What is this K. anyway?* **3.** *n.* a thousand (of anything, such as dollars, bytes, etc.) □ *This car is worth at least 20 K.* □ *I have 640 K. memory in my computer.*

**kack** AND **kak** *in.* to empty one's stomach; to vomit. □ *I thought I was going to kack when I saw that stuff.* □ *Somebody's in the jake kaking.*

**kafooster** [kəˈfustɚ] *n.* nonsense. □ *We've heard enough of your kafooster.* □ *This kafooster about me being a cheater is too much.*

**kajody** [kəˈdʒodi] *n.* a gadget. □ *Now, put this kajody right into this slot.* □ *Toss me a clean kajody, will ya?*

**kaka** See *caca.*

**kangaroo court** **1.** *n.* a bogus or extralegal court. □ *Is this a newspaper office or a kangaroo court?* □ *You have turned this interview into a kangaroo court.* **2.** *n.* a legally convened court operating unjustly. □ *"Let me out of this kangaroo court," muttered Fred.* □ *The judge held Fred in contempt for calling the proceedings a kangaroo court.*

**karma** [ˈkɑrmə] *n.* aura; *vibes.* □ *There's bad karma here.* □ *She had this exquisite karma that attracts everyone.*

**Kauai (electric)** [ˈkɑwɑi...] *n.* a variety of marijuana, presumably from Hawaii. (Drugs.) □ *Is this real Kauai electric?* □ *Sure, this is real Kauai!*

**kayo** See *K.O.*

**kee** See *K.*

**keef** AND **kef, kif** [kif] *n.* cannabis. (Drugs. From Arabic.) □ *Don't even mention keef around that guy. He kills for it.* □ *The stuff they call kif is just plain old domestic.*

**keep cool** *in.* to keep calm. □ *Now, keep cool. It's going to be all right.* □ *Just keep cool, man. Chill.*

**keeper** *n.* something that can be kept; something that qualifies. □ *This fish is a keeper. Throw the others out.* □ *The chipped one is not a keeper.*

**Keep in touch.** *sent.* "Goodbye." (Sometimes a sarcastic way of saying goodbye to someone one doesn't care about.) □ *Nice talking to you. Keep in touch.* □ *Sorry, we can't use you anymore. Keep in touch.*

**keep one's cool** *tr.* to remain calm and in control. (See *keep cool, lose one's cool.*) □ *Relax, man! Just keep your cool.* □ *It's hard to keep your cool when you've been cheated.*

**keep one's head right** *tr.* to maintain control of oneself. (Black.) □ *Chill, man, chill. You've got to keep your head right.* □ *I can keep my head right. I'm mellow.*

**keep one's nose clean** *tr.* to keep out of trouble, especially trouble with the law. □ *Okay, chum. Keep your nose clean.* □ *I can keep my nose clean. Don't worry.*

**Keep on trucking.** *sent.* "Keep doing what you are doing."; "Keep taking care of business." □ *See ya, man. Keep on trucking.* □ *Keep on trucking. Things'll get better.*

**Keep out of this!** *exclam.* "Mind your own business!" □ *This is not your affair. Keep out of this!* □ *Keep out of this! I'll settle it.*

**Keep the faith (baby)!** *exclam.* a statement of general encouragement or solidarity. □ *You said it! Keep the faith, baby!* □ *Keep the faith! See ya later.*

**Keep your hands to yourself.** **1.** *sent.* "Do not touch things that are not yours."; "Do not touch breakable things." (Said to a child.) □ *You can look, but don't touch. Keep your hands to yourself.* □ *Put that down and keep your hands to yourself.* **2.** *sent.* "Don't poke or hit other children." (Said to a child.) □ *Jimmy! Leave him alone and keep your hands to yourself.* □ *Keep your hands to yourself when you go to school.* **3.** *sent.* "No intimate caressing is allowed." (Said to an adult, usually a male.) □ *Keep your hands to yourself, Buster.* □ *Just keep your hands to yourself or take me home.*

**Keep your pants on!** See the following entry.

**Keep your shirt on!** AND **Keep your pants on!** *exclam.* "Just wait a minute!" □ *I'll be right with you. Keep your shirt on!* □ *Keep your pants on! You're next.*

**keester** AND **keyster, kiester** [ˈkistɚ] **1.** *n.* a chest; a suitcase. □ *The old lady was hauling the most enormous keester.* □ *The keester was full of cash.* **2.** *n.* the buttocks; the anus. □ *Get your keester over here!* □ *He fell flat on his keester.*

**kef** See *keef*.

**keg** **1.** *n.* a kilogram of cannabis. (Drugs.) □ *Max has a good price on a keg.* □ *How long will a keg last?* **2.** *in.* to pay attention. □ *You're not kegging. I'll try it again.* □ *Keep kegging, you guys! This is important.*

**kegger** **1.** *n.* a party where beer is served from a keg. (Teens and collegiate.) □ *Tiffany is having a kegger, and a few of her intimates are invited.* □ *Isn't there a kegger somewhere tonight?* **2.** AND **keggers** *n.* a keg of beer. (Collegiate.) □ *We need another kegger. It's only 9 o'clock.* □ *We came here because somebody said there was keggers.*

**keg party** *n.* a party where liquor, especially beer, is served. □ *There is a free keg party at Freddy's.* □ *The keg party ended early owing to the arrival of uninvited nabs.*

**keif** See *keef*.

**keister** See *keester*.

**Ken doll** *n.* a barbiturate tablet or capsule. (Drugs. See *Barbie doll*.) □ *She liked to dope up on Ken dolls.* □ *She takes Ken dolls with booze.*

**Kentucky blue** *n.* marijuana. (Drugs. From "Kentucky bluegrass.") □ *No, I don't have Kentucky blue. I'm a pusher, not a travel agent.* □ *Many of the terms for pot are really puns, like "Kentucky blue." It's just another way of saying grass.*

**Kentucky corn** *n.* corn whiskey; moonshine. (Folksy.) □ *Kentucky corn is what Jed makes back in the woods.* □ *He has a jar of Kentucky corn behind the closet door.*

**Kentucky fried** *mod.* alcohol intoxicated. (An elaboration of *fried*. Based on the trade name "Kentucky Fried Chicken.") □ *Man, is that guy really Kentucky fried!* □ *I've never seen anybody so downright Kentucky fried on six beers.*

**key** See *K*.

**keyed (up)** **1.** *mod.* nervous; anxious. □ *Sally was a little keyed up before the meet.* □ *When I get keyed, I meditate.* **2.** AND **keyed up to the roof** *mod.* alcohol or drug intoxicated. □ *He was a mite keyed, but still technically sober.* □ *She was so keyed up she could hardly stand up.*

**key figure** *n.* an important person in an event; a person central to an event. □ *Wally is a key figure in the investigation.* □ *Bruno is not exactly a key figure, but he can lead us to Mr. Big.*

**key grip** *n.* the head laborer on a movie set. (Film making.) □ *The key grip has a complaint that could hold up production.* □ *What is the key grip's beef?*

**ki** See *K*.

**kibosh** [ˈkaɪbɑʃ OR kəˈbɑʃ] **1.** *tr.* to end something; to squelch something. □ *Please don't try to kibosh the scheme this time.* □ *Fred kiboshed our plan.* **2.** *n.* the end; the final blow; the thing that terminates something. (Usually with *the*. See *put the kibosh on something*.) □ *The kibosh was a real corker.* □ *They thought the kibosh was overdone.*

**kick 1.** *n.* a charge or good feeling (from something); pleasure or enjoyment from something. (See *get a kick out of someone or something* at *get a bang out of someone or something*.) □ *That song really gives me a kick. I love it!* □ *What a kick that gives me!* **2.** *n.* the jolt from a drug or a drink of strong liquor. □ *This stuff really has a kick.* □ *The kick nearly knocked Harry over.* **3.** *tr.* to break a drug addiction voluntarily. (Drugs.) □ *I knew I had the guts in me somewhere to kick juice.* □ *It's hard to kick that stuff.* **4.** *n.* a complaint. □ *What's the kick, man?* □ *You got another kick, troublemaker?* **5.** *in.* to complain. □ *Why are you always kicking?* □ *Ernie kicks about everything.* **6.** See *kicks*.

**kick around** See *knock around*.

**kick back 1.** *in.* to relax (and enjoy something). □ *Now you just kick back and enjoy this.* □ *I like to kick back and listen to a few tunes.* **2.** *n.* money received in return for a favor. (Usually **kickback**.) □ *The kickback the cop got wasn't enough, as it turned out.* □ *You really don't believe that the cops take kickbacks!* **3.** *in.* (for an addict) to return to addiction after having been detoxified and withdrawn. (Drugs.) □ *Gert stopped and kicked back a number of times.* □ *They may kick back a dozen times before it takes.*

**kick cold (turkey)** *in.* to stop taking drugs without tapering off. (Drugs.) □ *Molly tried to kick cold turkey, but it was just too much.* □ *Kicking cold may be the only way to do it.*

**kicked by a horse** *mod.* addicted to heroin. (Drugs. See *horse*.) □ *Gert was kicked by a horse when she was very young.* □ *From the way Ernie was nodding, you could see he had been kicked by a horse.*

**kicker** *n.* a clever but stinging remark; a sharp criticism; a *zinger*. □ *I waited for the kicker, and finally it came.* □ *The kicker really made me mad.*

**kick freak** *n.* a non-addicted drug user. (Drugs.) □ *Ernie used to be a kick freak, but all that has changed.* □ *Yeah, the kick freak became a junky.*

**kickin'** ['kɪkn̩] *mod.* wild; super; excellent. □ *Your rally was really kickin'.* □ *I don't know where you get your clothes, but that jacket's kickin'.*

**kick in the guts** *n.* a severe blow to one's body or spirit. □ *The news was a kick in the guts, and I haven't recovered yet.* □ *I didn't need a kick in the guts like that.*

**kick in the (seat of the) pants** AND **kick in the ass\*, kick in the butt\*, kick in the teeth** *n.* a strong message of encouragement or demand. (Caution with *ass, butt*.) □ *All he needs is a kick in the seat of the pants to get him going.* □ *A kick in the butt will get her moving.*

**kick in the wrist** *n.* a drink of liquor. □ *You want another kick in the wrist?* □ *I'll take another kick in the wrist.*

**kick man** *n.* a (male) drug dealer. (Drugs.) □ *Max is everybody's favorite kick man.* □ *Go see the kick man about some juana.*

**kick off 1.** *in.* to die. □ *We've been waiting for years for that cat to kick off.* □ *The old girl finally kicked off.* **2.** *in.* to sleep off the effects of drugs. (Drugs.) □ *He's in the back room kicking off.* □ *He'll have to kick off for an hour or two.*

**kick party** *n.* a party where some drug is used. (Drugs.) □ *The kick party broke up early with the help of Johnny-be-good.* □ *There was a kick party at one of the crack houses, and even little children went in.*

**kicks** *n.* cleats or shoes. (Collegiate. See also *kick*.) □ *Don't you dare wear those kicks in here!* □ *Take your kicks off before coming in.*

**kick some ass (around)\*** *tr.* to take over and start giving orders; to *raise hell*. (Caution with *ass*.) □ *Do I have to come over there and kick some ass around?* □ *Bruno is just the one to kick some ass over there.*

**kickstick** AND **kick-stick** *n.* a marijuana cigarette. (Drugs.) □ *Gimme a hit off your kickstick, okay?* □ *Get your own kick-stick.*

**kick the bucket** *tr.* to die. □ *I'm too young to kick the bucket.* □ *The cat kicked the bucket last night.*

**kick the habit** *tr.* to voluntarily end any habit or custom, especially a drug habit. □ *She tried and tried to kick the habit.* □ *It's hard to kick the habit.*

**kick up a storm** *tr.* to create a disturbance; to put on an angry display. □ *My dad will just kick up a storm when he finds out.* □ *The demand made us all kick up a storm.*

**kicky** ['kɪki] *mod.* exciting and energetic. □ *Man, what a kicky idea!* □ *She is a real kicky gal.*

**kidney-buster** **1.** *n.* a rough ride; a rough road. □ *This road is a kidney-buster. I wish they'd fix it.* □ *That kidney-buster damaged my car.* **2.** *n.* an uncomfortable or poorly built seat in a vehicle. □ *I have to get this kidney-buster replaced.* □ *This kidney-buster is going to ruin my back.*

**kid stuff** *n.* marijuana, a drug for "beginners." (Drugs.) □ *That grass is kid stuff.* □ *He's still using kid stuff.*

**kid-vid** ['kɪdvɪd] *n.* children's television; television programming aimed at children. □ *Kid-vid isn't good for anything other than selling cereal.* □ *I don't know. Kid-vid is fun.*

**kif** See *keef.*

**kill** **1.** *tr.* to be very successful with an audience; to perform very well for an audience. □ *She really killed them with that last joke.* □ *She killed them, and they died with laughter.* **2.** *tr.* to eat all of something; to drink all (of a bottle) of something. □ *Kill this bottle so we can get another.* □ *We finally killed the last of the turkey.* **3.** *tr.* to douse a light. □ *Kill that light!* □ *Would you kill the light so they can't see we're home?* **4.** *tr.* to stop or terminate something; to quash a story; to stop a story from being printed in a newspaper. □ *Kill that story. It's got too many errors.* □ *This issue has gone to press. Too late to kill it.*

**killed (off)** *mod.* alcohol or drug intoxicated. (Drugs.) □ *The team went out drinking and came home killed off.* □ *Man, were those guys killed.*

**killer** **1.** *n.* a marijuana cigarette. (Drugs. See *killerstick.*) □ *How about a killer, Max?* □ *He's always smoking a killer.* **2.** *n.* a very funny joke. □ *That last one was a killer!* □ *She told a killer about a red-nosed juicer.* **3.** *n.* something extraordinary. □ *That jacket is a real killer!* □ *That car is a killer. I like it!* **4.**

*mod.* extraordinary. □ *What a killer jacket you're wearing!* □ *This is a killer hamburger all right.*

**killer-diller** *n.* an excellent thing or person. □ *She is just a real killer-diller.* □ *This story is a real killer-diller.*

**killerstick** *n.* a marijuana cigarette. (Drugs.) □ *He had a killerstick in his shirt pocket ready to light up when school was out.* □ *Hey, peddle me a killerstick, Max.*

**killer weed** **1.** *n.* very potent marijuana. (Drugs.) □ *Wow, this stuff is killer weed!* □ *This killer weed is oregano, I think.* **2.** *n.* phencyclidine, *P.C.P.*, an animal tranquilizer. (Drugs.) □ *Killer weed seems to be a favorite around here just now.* □ *Killer weed, K.J.—it's all exactly the same stuff.*

**killing** *n.* a great financial success. □ *Sally made a real killing in the stock market.* □ *Fred made a killing in real estate.*

**killjoy** *n.* a person who takes the fun out of things for other people; a *party-pooper.* □ *Don't be such a killjoy!* □ *Larry is such a killjoy when he gets nervous.*

**killmequick** AND **killemquick** ['kɪlmikwɪk AND 'kɪləmkwɪk] *n.* strong liquor; raw whisky. (Folksy.) □ *Pour me a little of that killmequick, would ya?* □ *That killemquick will knock your socks off.*

**kilo** *n.* a kilogram of a drug, usually cannabis. (Drugs.) □ *Tiffany wanted a kilo for a party.* □ *How much is a kilo?*

**kilo brick** *n.* a brick-shaped block of marijuana weighing approximately one kilogram. (Drugs.) □ *How much profit do these dealers make off a kilo brick?* □ *A kilo brick of high Q. will really set you back.*

**kilobucks** *n.* a tremendous sum of money. (See also *megabucks.*) □ *These boondoggles waste kilobucks!* □ *How many kilobucks does a set of wheels like that cost?*

**kingdom weed** *n.* marijuana; good-quality marijuana. (Drugs.) □ *Max has something he calls kingdom weed. It's just pot.* □ *Yeah, but kingdom weed sounds better and more powerful.*

**King Grod** [...grɑd] *n.* a very repellent male. (California.) □ *You are just King*

*Grod! So gross!* □ *Ralph is almost King Grod!*

**King Kong pills** AND **King Kong specials** *n.* barbiturates. (Drugs. See *gorilla pills*.) □ *Watch out for those King Kong pills.* □ *Don't mix these King Kong specials with booze.*

**kingpin** *n.* a major figure in organized crime. (Underworld.) □ *Mr. Big is not your typical kingpin. He likes to play the stock market, too.* □ *The drug kingpins are well protected.*

**kink 1.** *n.* a strange person; a *kinky* person. □ *The guy's a kink. Watch out for him.* □ *There are kinks all over this place.* **2.** *n.* a sexually deviant person. □ *He was a kink, and I broke up with him.* □ *The kinks congregate two streets over.*

**kinky 1.** *mod.* having to do with someone or something strange or weird. □ *The guy is so kinky that everyone avoids him.* □ *Who is that kinky dame in the net stockings?* **2.** *mod.* having to do with unconventional sexual acts or people who perform them. □ *She seems to have a morbid interest in kinky stuff.* □ *He showed her a picture of some kind of kinky sex thing.*

**kip** *in.* to sleep. □ *He's upstairs kipping. Can he call you back?* □ *He'll kip for about another hour.*

**kipe** *tr.* to steal something. □ *Where did you kipe this thing?* □ *The punk kiped a newspaper just for the heck of it.*

**kiper** ['kaɪpɚ] *n.* a thief; someone who steals. □ *The punk is a two-bit kiper and needs to be taught a lesson.* □ *You dirty little kiper. Give it back!*

**kiss-ass\* 1.\*** *mod.* subservient. (Caution with *ass*.) □ *Don't be such a kiss-ass jerk. Tell off your boss.* □ *He is a little kiss-ass bastard who'll do anything to get ahead.* **2.\*** *in.* to act subservient (to someone). (Caution with *ass*.) □ *Stop kiss-assing around and stand up to your employer.* □ *That guy will kiss-ass his way to the top.*

**kisser** *n.* the face; the mouth. (See also *right in the kisser*.) □ *I poked him right in the kisser.* □ *There he stood with a bloody kisser.*

**kiss Mary** AND **kiss Mari, kiss Maryjane** *tr.* to smoke marijuana. (Drugs.) □ *I'm gonna spend the evening kissing Mary.* □ *Come over and let's kiss Mari.*

**kiss of death** *n.* the direct cause of the end of someone or something. □ *The ordinance was the kiss of death for our budding jazz band.* □ *Your attitude was the kiss of death for your employment here.*

**kiss off 1.** ['kɪs ɔf] *n.* the dismissal of someone or something. (Usually **kiss-off**.) □ *The kiss-off was when I lost the Wilson contract.* □ *Tod got the kiss off and is now looking for a new job.* **2.** ['kɪs ɔf] *n.* death. (Usually **kiss-off**.) □ *When the time comes for the kiss-off, I hope I'm asleep.* □ *The kiss-off came wrapped in lead, and it was instant.* **3.** ['kɪs 'ɔf] *in.* to die. □ *The cat is going to have to kiss off one of these days soon.* □ *The cat kissed off after 18 years of joy and devotion.*

**kiss someone or something off** AND **kiss off someone or something 1.** *tr.* [with *someone*] to kill someone. □ *Bruno had instructions to kiss Max off.* □ *Max wanted to kiss off Bruno, too.* **2.** *tr.* [with *something*] to forget about something; to ignore something. □ *Just kiss off any idea you might have had about running for office.* □ *Just kiss it off. You've lost your chance.*

**kiss someone's ass\*** *tr.* to fawn over someone; to flatter and curry favor with someone. (Caution with *ass*.) □ *What does he expect me to do? Kiss his ass?* □ *I won't kiss your ass for anything.*

**kiss something goodbye** *tr.* to face and accept the loss of something. □ *Well, you can kiss that 100 bucks goodbye.* □ *I kissed my chance for success goodbye.*

**kiss the babe** AND **kiss the baby** *tr.* to take a drink of liquor. □ *He stopped off at Freddy's place to kiss the babe.* □ *The guys are in the back room kissing the baby.*

**kiss the dust** *tr.* to fall to the earth, because of death or because of being struck. (Western movies. See also *bite the dust*.) □ *I'll see that you kiss the dust before sunset, cowboy!* □ *You'll kiss the dust before I will, Sheriff.*

**kiss the porcelain god** *tr.* to empty one's stomach; to vomit. □ *He fled the room to kiss the porcelain god, I guess.*

□ *Who's in there kissing the porcelain god?*

**kiss up to someone** *in.* to flatter someone; to make over someone. □ *I'm not going to kiss up to anybody to get what's rightfully mine.* □ *If I have to kiss up to her, I guess I will.*

**kissyface** ['kɪsifes] **1.** *n.* kissing. □ *There was a lot of kissyface going on in the back seat.* □ *They're mostly involved with kissyface at this age.* **2.** *mod.* feeling the need to kiss and be kissed. □ *I feel all kissyface.* □ *They were both sort of kissyface, so they left.*

**kit** *n.* equipment for preparing and injecting drugs. (Drugs.) □ *Ernie laid his kit out and rolled up his sleeve.* □ *The parole officer found the kit under Ernie's bed.*

**kit and caboodle** ['kɪt n̩ kə'budl̩] *n.* everything; all parts and property. (Often with *whole*.) □ *I want you out of here—kit and caboodle—by noon.* □ *She moved in to stay, kit and caboodle.* □ *She plunked her whole kit and caboodle right in my way.*

**kite 1.** *n.* a drug user who is always *high*. (Drugs.) □ *The guy's a kite. He won't make any sense no matter what you ask him.* □ *Gert is a kite, and she's getting worse.* **2.** *tr.* to write worthless checks; to raise the amount on a check. (Underworld.) □ *Chuck made a fortune kiting checks.* □ *He kited a check for $50,000.* **3.** *n.* a worthless check. (Underworld. See *fly kites*.) □ *He finally wrote one kite too many, and they nabbed him.* □ *She passed kites from one end of town to the other, then dyed her hair, took off her glasses, and did it all over again.*

**kited** *mod.* alcohol intoxicated. (From "high as a kite.") □ *Molly was too kited to see her hand in front of her.* □ *Both guys were kited by midnight.*

**kitsch** [kɪtʃ] *n.* any form of entertainment—movies, books, plays— with enormous popular appeal. □ *This kitsch sells like mad in the big city.* □ *Most people prefer kitsch to art.*

**kitschy** ['kɪtʃi] *mod.* trivial in spite of enormous popular appeal. □ *A lot of people like kitschy art.* □ *This stuff is too kitschy for me.*

**K.J.** See *krystal joint*.

**klepto** ['klɛpto] *n.* a kleptomaniac; one who steals small things obsessively. □ *The cops thought Gert was a klepto until she showed them her receipts.* □ *The jury awarded Gert five grand for being falsely arrested as a klepto.*

**klotz** See *klutz*.

**kluck** See *cluck*.

**kludge AND kluge** [kləʤ OR kluʤ] **1.** *n.* a patch or a fix in a computer program or circuit. □ *This is a messy kludge, but it will do the job.* □ *Kluges that are invisible don't bother anybody.* **2.** *tr.* to patch or fix a computer program circuit. □ *I only have time to kludge this problem.* □ *The kid kluged a program for us in an hour.*

**kludgy** ['kləʤi OR 'kluʤi] *mod.* having to do with an inefficient or sloppily written computer program. □ *This program is too kludgy to be acceptable.* □ *Who wrote this kludgy mess?* □ *I don't care if it's kludgy. Does it work?*

**klutz AND klotz** [kləts AND klɑts] *n.* a stupid and clumsy person. □ *Don't be a klutz!* □ *Some klotz put mustard in the stew.*

**klutzy** ['klətsi] *mod.* foolish; stupid. □ *That was really a klutzy thing to do.* □ *You are so klutzy!* □ *Whose klutzy idea was this?*

**knee-deep in something** *mod.* having lots of something. (See also *up to one's knees*.) □ *We are knee-deep in orders and loving it.* □ *Right now, we are knee-deep in trouble.*

**knee-high to a grasshopper** *mod.* of very short stature. (Folksy.) □ *I knew you when you were knee-high to a grasshopper.* □ *I was knee-high to a grasshopper when I first heard that joke.*

**knee-jerk** *mod.* automatic; quick and without thought. □ *That was only a knee-jerk response. Pay no attention.* □ *My knee-jerk response is that you should not go.*

**knee-slapper** *n.* something very funny. (Folksy.) □ *Old Billy told a knee-slapper about the farmer down the road.* □ *I like to hear a good knee-slapper. It keeps my blood flowing.*

**knock** *tr.* to criticize someone or something. □ *Don't knock it if you haven't* *tried it.* □ *The papers are knocking my favorite candidate again.*

**knock around 1.** *in.* to waste time. □ *Stop knocking around and get to work!* □ *I need a couple of days a week just for knocking around.* **2.** AND **kick around.** *in.* to wander around; to *bum around.* □ *I think I'll knock around a few months before looking for another job.* □ *We're just knocking around and keeping out of trouble.*

**knock back a drink** *tr.* to drink a beer; to have a quick drink of liquor. □ *He knocked back three beers in a row.* □ *Let's knock back another one or two and leave.*

**knockdown drag-out fight** *n.* a prolonged and hard fight. □ *Trying to get my proposal accepted was a knockdown drag-out fight.* □ *I don't want to get involved in a knockdown drag-out fight over this business.*

**knock down something** AND **knock something down 1.** *tr.* to drink a portion of liquor. □ *He knocked down a bottle of beer and called for another.* □ *Here, knock this down and let's go.* **2.** *tr.* to earn a certain amount of money. □ *She must knock down about 40 thou a year.* □ *I'm lucky to knock down 20 thousand.*

**knocked in** *mod.* arrested. (Underworld.) □ *Would you believe that Rocko has never been knocked in?* □ *When Lefty was knocked in, they found his heater on him.*

**knocked out 1.** *mod.* exhausted. □ *We were all knocked out at the end of the day.* □ *I'm knocked out after just a little bit of work.* **2.** *mod.* overwhelmed. □ *We were just knocked out when we heard your news.* □ *Were we surprised? We were knocked out—elated!* **3.** *mod.* alcohol or drug intoxicated. □ *They were all knocked out by midnight.* □ *Gary was knocked out when we dropped by, so we tried to sober him up.*

**knocked up 1.** *mod.* battered; beaten. □ *Sally was a little knocked up by the accident.* □ *This book is a little knocked up, so I'll lower the price.* **2.** *mod.* alcohol intoxicated. □ *Bill was knocked up and didn't want to drive.* □ *Wow, was that guy knocked up!* **3.** *mod.* pregnant.

□ *Molly got knocked up again.* □ *Isn't she knocked up most of the time?*

**knockers\* 1.\*** *n.* the breasts. (Caution with topic.) □ *Nice knockers, huh?* □ *All you think about is knockers.* **2.\*** *n.* the testicles. (Caution with topic.) □ *Pow, right in the knockers. Ye gods, it hurt!* □ *He turned sideways to protect his knockers.*

**Knock it off!** *exclam.* "Be Quiet!"; "Shut up!" □ *Hey, you guys! Knock it off!* □ *I'm trying to sleep! Knock it off!*

**knock off (work)** *tr. & in.* to quit work, for the day or for a break. □ *What time do you knock off work?* □ *I knock off about five-thirty.*

**knock one over** AND **knock over one, knock one back, knock back one** *tr.* to take a drink of liquor. □ *He knocked one over right away and demanded another.* □ *He knocked back one and belched grossly.*

**knockout 1.** *n.* something that is quite stunning. □ *Your new car is a knockout.* □ *Isn't her dress a knockout?* **2.** *n.* a good-looking man or woman. □ *Your date is a real knockout.* □ *Who was that knockout I saw you with last weekend?* **3.** *mod.* very exciting. □ *It was a real knockout evening.* □ *What a knockout idea!*

**knock some heads together** *tr.* to scold some people; to get some people to do what they are supposed to be doing. □ *Do I have to come in there and knock some heads together, or will you kids settle down?* □ *I knocked some heads together and got the proposal out on time.*

**knock someone dead** *tr.* to put on a stunning performance or display for someone. □ *She knocked us dead with her stunning performance.* □ *Go out on that stage and knock them dead, Sally.*

**knock someone or something off** AND **knock off someone or something 1.** *tr.* [with *something*] to manufacture or make something, especially in haste. □ *I'll see if I can knock another one off before lunch.* □ *They knocked off four window frames in an hour.* **2.** *tr.* [with *someone*] to kill someone. (Underworld. See *bump someone off.*) □ *The mob knocked the witnesses off.* □ *The* cops would be happy if someone wanted to knock off Mr. Big. **3.** *tr.* [with *something*] to lower the price of something; to knock off some dollars or cents from the price of something. □ *The store manager knocked 30% off the price of the coat.* □ *Can't you knock something off on this damaged item?* **4.** See the following entry.

**knock someone or something out** AND **knock out someone or something 1.** *tr.* [with *someone*] to surprise someone. □ *Her stunning beauty knocked us all out.* □ *The news knocked out the entire crowd.* **2.** AND **knock something off, knock off something** *tr.* [with *something*] to write something quickly. □ *I'll knock out a letter explaining the whole thing.* □ *Would you please knock a speech out for the senator?*

**knock someone's block off** *tr.* to hit someone hard in the head. (See *block*.) □ *Wilbur almost knocked Tom's block off by accident.* □ *He threatened to knock my block off if I didn't do as I was told.*

**knock someone some skin** *tr.* to shake hands with someone. □ *Hey, man, knock me some skin!* □ *Tod knocked Sam some skin, and they left the building together.*

**knock someone's socks off** *tr.* to surprise or startle someone; to overwhelm someone. □ *Wow, that explosion nearly knocked my socks off.* □ *This news'll knock your socks off.*

**knock someone up** AND **knock up someone** *tr.* to make a woman pregnant. (Crude.) □ *They say it was Bruno who knocked her up.* □ *He did not knock up Molly. I did.* (More at *knocked up.*)

**knock something into a cocked hat** *tr.* to demolish a plan, a story, etc. □ *I knocked his plans into a cocked hat.* □ *You've knocked everything into a cocked hat.*

**knock something together** AND **throw something together** *tr.* to assemble something—such as a meal—at the last moment. □ *I knocked together a vegetable dish at the last minute.* □ *I'll see if I can throw something together.*

**knock the habit** *tr.* to stop using drugs; to break a drug addiction. (Drugs. See

kick the habit.) □ *I just can't knock the habit.* □ *He tried to knock the habit by drinking lots of booze.*

**knock up** *in.* to inject drugs; to *shoot up (on something).* (Drugs.) □ *Ernie had to leave for a minute to knock up.* □ *While he was knocking up, he broke the needle.*

**knothead** *n.* a stupid person. □ *Don't be such a knothead!* □ *You're no knothead. You're just great!*

**know all the angles** *tr.* to know all the tricks and artifices of dealing with someone or something. □ *Ask my mouthpiece about taxes. He knows all the angles.* □ *Rocko knows all the angles. That's how he keeps out of the slammer.*

**know from something** *in.* to know about something. (See also *not know from nothing.*) □ *Do you know from timers, I mean how timers work?* □ *I don't know from babies! Don't ask me about feeding them!*

**know-how** ['nohɑu] *n.* the knowledge of how to do something. □ *I don't have the know-how to do this job.* □ *You'll get the know-how on the job.*

**know-it-all** *n.* someone who gives the impression of knowing everything. □ *Tod is such a know-it-all!* □ *That know-it-all isn't of much use to our committee.*

**knowledge-box** *n.* the head. □ *Now, I want to get this into your knowledge-box once and for all.* □ *My knowledge-box is just spinning with all this information.*

**know the score** *tr.* to know the way things work in the hard cruel world. □ *Don't try to con me. I know the score.* □ *She knows the score. She wasn't born yesterday.*

**know what's what** *tr.* to be aware of what is going on in the world. □ *Alice knows what's what. She can help.* □ *We don't know what's what around here yet.*

**know where it's at** *tr.* to know the way things really are. □ *I know where it's at. I don't need to be told.* □ *We know where it's at, and we want to change it.*

**know where one is coming from** *tr.* to understand someone's motivation; to understand and relate to someone's position. □ *I know where you're coming from. I've been there.* □ *We all know* *where he's coming from. That's why we are so worried.*

**know which end is up** *tr.* to be alert and knowledgeable. □ *Don't try to hustle me, sister. I know which end is up.* □ *Poor Jed doesn't even know which end is up.*

**knuckle down (to something)** *in.* to get busy doing something. □ *Please knuckle down to your studies.* □ *You have to knuckle down if you want to get ahead.*

**knuckle-dragger** *n.* a strong, ape-like man. □ *Bruno is Mr. Big's favorite knuckle-dragger.* □ *Call off your knuckle-draggers. I'll pay you whatever you want.*

**knucklehead** *n.* a stupid person. □ *Oh, I feel like such a knucklehead!* □ *Don't worry, you're not a knucklehead.*

**knuckle sandwich** *n.* a blow struck in the teeth or mouth. □ *How would you like a knuckle sandwich?* □ *He threatened to give me a knuckle sandwich.*

**knuckle under (to someone or something)** *in.* to give in to or accept someone or something. □ *She always refused to knuckle under to anyone.* □ *You have to knuckle under to the system sometimes.*

**K.O.** AND **kayo** ['keʼo] **1.** *n.* a knockout. (Boxing.) □ *It was a quick K.O., and Wilbur was the new champ.* □ *It was a classic kayo. It was quick and effective.* **2.** *tr.* to knock someone out. (Boxing.) □ *Wilbur K.O.ed Wallace in the third round.* □ *Wilbur usually kayos his opponent.*

**K.O.ed** ['keʼod] **1.** *mod.* "knocked out." (Originally from boxing.) □ *Wilbur was K.O.ed and got a cut over his eye.* □ *He stayed K.O.ed for about two minutes.* **2.** *mod.* alcohol or drug intoxicated. □ *Both guys were K.O.ed and spent the night.* □ *How could anybody get so K.O.ed on a six-pack?*

**Kojak** ['kodʒæk] *n.* a police officer. (From the television character of the same name.) □ *Ask Kojak in for a cup of coffee.* □ *Here comes Kojak. Beat it!*

**Kona (coast) gold** ['konə...] AND **Kona** *n.* a potent form of marijuana from Hawaii. (Drugs.) □ *Is this Kona gold or just local weed?* □ *This is the genuine Kona coast gold.*

**kong** [kɔŋ] *n.* strong whiskey; illicit whiskey. (Black. From the movie ape King Kong.) □ *How about a big swallow of that kong?* □ *Here, have some kong.*

**konk** See *conk.*

**kook** [kuk] *n.* a strange person. □ *She seems like a kook, but she is just grand, really.* □ *Tod's a kook, but I love him.*

**kookish** ['kukɪʃ] *mod.* strange; eccentric. □ *There's a lot of kookish things going on around here.* □ *He is just too kookish.* □ *Who is the kookish one over there with the purple shades?*

**kosher** ['koʃɚ OR 'koʒɚ] **1.** *mod.* acceptable; orthodox; *cricket.* (From Hebrew *kasher* "proper" via Yiddish.) □ *Is it kosher to do this?* □ *It's a kosher thing, okay.* □ *Of course, it's kosher. Everybody does it.* **2.** *n.* kosher food; food prepared in accordance with the precepts of the Jewish religion. □ *Let's eat kosher tonight.* □ *They serve kosher at Monty's now.* **3.** *tr.* to make something acceptable. □ *Do you want me to kosher it with the boss for you?* □ *Look, if you can kosher this stuff with my parents, I agree.* **4.** *mod.* having to do with undiluted alcohol. □ *I'll take mine kosher with a little ice.* □ *Do you want this kosher or with soda?*

**krystal joint** AND **C.J., K.J.** *n.* phencyclidine, *P.C.P.*, an animal tranquilizer. (Drugs. See also *C.J.*) □ *Some little kid was trying to sell krystal joints right in the school hallway.* □ *That K.J. is dangerous stuff.*

**kvetch** AND **quetch** [kvɛtʃ AND kwɛtʃ] **1.** *in.* to complain. (From German *quetschen* "to squeeze" via Yiddish.) □ *Quit your kvetching!* □ *He quetches from dawn to dusk.* **2.** *n.* a complainer. □ *What a kvetch you are!* □ *We don't need another kvetch around here.*

# L

**L7** [ˈɛl ˈsɛvn̩] **1.** *n.* a *square*. □ *That guy is an L7.* □ *Who is that L7 in the wing-tip shoes?* **2.** *mod.* dull; *square*. □ *This guy was real, like, you know, L7.* □ *Who is the most L7 person you know?*

**label mate** *n.* someone who records on the same label (as the speaker). (Record industry.) □ *Frank Duke is my label mate, and we like to get together and gossip about the record industry.* □ *I feel like a real success because my label mates are so good.*

**labonza** [ləˈbɑnzə] **1.** *n.* the buttocks. □ *Good grief, what a gross labonza!* □ *She fell flat on her labonza.* **2.** *n.* the pit of the stomach. □ *That kind of beautiful singing really gets you right in the labonza.* □ *She experienced the kind of gut-wrenching anger that starts in your labonza and cuts through right to the tip of your noggin.* **3.** *n.* the belly. □ *I feel the effects of last night's celebration in my wallet and in my labonza.* □ *Look at the labonza on that creep! He's gonna deliver triplets.*

**lace 1.** *tr.* to add alcohol to coffee or tea; to add alcohol to any food or drink. □ *Who laced the punch?* □ *I think I'll lace my coffee with a little whisky.* **2.** *tr.* to add a bit of one drug to another; to add drugs to any food or drink. (Drugs.) □ *Somebody laced the ice cubes with acid.* □ *This fag is laced with opium.* **3.** *n.* money. (Underworld.) □ *You got any lace in those pockets?* □ *My lace won't reach that far. I can't afford it.*

**lacy** *mod.* feminine; effeminate. □ *He's sort of lacy, but when he settles down to work, the sparks fly.* □ *This place is too lacy.* □ *The hotel lobby is a little lacy, but it's clean.*

**ladies' room** *n.* the women's restroom. □ *Is there a ladies' room somewhere close?* □ *Sally has gone to the ladies' room.*

**lady** *n.* cocaine. (Drugs. Always with the.) □ *I'm in love with the lady.* □ *The lady is the favorite with many of the floor traders.*

**lady bear** *n.* a female officer of the law. (See *Smokey (the bear)*.) □ *This lady bear asks me if I'm going to a fire.* □ *These two lady bears walked in and took a booth by the door.*

**ladyfinger** *n.* a marijuana cigarette. (Drugs.) □ *Bruno knows how to roll a ladyfinger.* □ *Hell, any old joint is a ladyfinger. Don't be so particular.*

**Lady H.** *n.* heroin. (Drugs. See *H.*) □ *Lady H. can break your heart.* □ *You have to watch your step with Lady H.*

**lady-killer** *n.* a man who is very successful with women. □ *Bruno is anything but a lady killer.* □ *We saw an old-time lady-killer with a close-cut black mustache and everything.*

**Lady Snow** *n.* cocaine. (Drugs. See *lady*.) □ *I spent the afternoon with Lady Snow.* □ *Lady Snow is about the only friend I have left.*

**lah-di-dah** [ˈlɑˈdiˈdɑ] **1.** *mod.* casual; relaxed and uncaring. □ *He is so lah-di-dah with financial matters.* □ *She's not all that calm about her possessions, but she is very lah-di-dah with men.* **2.** *interj.* a jeer; a mocking response. □ *So you have a new car! Well, lah-di-dah.* □ *Lah-di-dah! Excuse me!*

**laid\* 1.** AND **layed\*** *mod.* drug intoxicated. (See also *laid out*.) □ *Man, did I get myself laid.* □ *Are you too layed to drive home?* **2.\*** *mod.* copulated with.

(Crude. Caution with topic.) □ *Well, you look laid, all right.* □ *If you come home laid, don't say I didn't warn you.*

**laid back 1.** *mod.* calm and relaxed. □ *Bruno is not what I would call laid back.* □ *You are really one laid back guy!* **2.** *mod.* alcohol or drug intoxicated. □ *He's a little laid back and can't come to the phone.* □ *How can those guys work when they are laid back by noon?*

**laid out 1.** *mod.* alcohol or drug intoxicated.* □ *Man, you got yourself laid out!* □ *I'm too laid out to go to work today.* **2.** *mod.* well dressed. (Black.) □ *Look at those silks! Man are you laid out!* □ *She is all laid out in her Sunday best.* **3.** *mod.* dead; having to do with a corpse arranged for a wake. (Not slang.) □ *When the remains were laid out, the children were allowed to come in.* □ *When I'm laid out and ready to be planted, make sure this little book is in my hand.* **4.** *mod.* knocked down (by a punch). □ *He was down, laid out, and the cowboy just stood there panting.* □ *There he was, laid out on the sidewalk, and no one made a move to help him.*

**laid to the bone** *mod.* alcohol intoxicated. (Black.) □ *He got himself laid to the bone.* □ *We were all laid to the bone by midnight.*

**lame** AND **laine, lane 1.** *mod.* inept; inadequate. □ *That guy's so lame, it's pitiful.* □ *This mark is about as laine as they come.* **2.** *n.* a *square* person. (Streets. Underworld.) □ *Let's see if that lame over there has anything we want in his pockets.* □ *He won't drink anything at all. He is such a lame!* **3.** *n.* an inept person. □ *The guy turned out to be a lame, and we had to fire him.* □ *Maybe the lane can work in the front office answering phones or something.*

**lamebrain** AND **lame-brain 1.** *n.* a fool. □ *Please don't call me a lamebrain. I do my best.* □ *What a lame-brain! She put scallops in scalloped potatoes!* **2.** AND **lamebrained** *mod.* foolish. □ *No more of your lamebrain ideas!* □ *My last scheme looked lamebrained at first, but it worked, didn't it?*

**lamebrained** See the previous entry.

**lame duck 1.** *n.* someone who is in the last period of a term in an elective

office. □ *You can't expect much from a lame duck.* □ *As a lame duck, there's not a lot I can do.* **2.** *mod.* having to do with someone in the last period of a term in an elective office. □ *You don't expect much from a lame duck president.* □ *Lame duck congresses tend to do things they wouldn't dare do otherwise.*

**lamps** *n.* the eyes. (Crude.) □ *His lamps are closed. He's asleep or dead.* □ *Look at them blue lamps that dame's got.*

**land a blow 1.** *tr.* to strike someone. □ *He kept moving, and I found it almost impossible to land a blow.* □ *The boxer landed a blow to the face of his opponent.* **2.** *tr.* to make a point. □ *I think I really landed a blow with that remark about extortion.* □ *The point about justice landed a blow.*

**land a job** *tr.* to find a job and be hired. □ *As soon as I land a job and start to bring in some money, I'm going to get a stereo.* □ *I managed to land a job at a factory.*

**land office business** *n.* a large amount of business done in a short period of time. □ *We always do a land office business at this time of year.* □ *We keep going. Never do land office business—just enough to make out.*

**landowner** ['lændonɚ] *n.* a corpse; a dead person. (See also *buy the farm.*) □ *Now old Mr. Carlson was a landowner for real.* □ *"How would you like to become a landowner?" snarled the mugger.*

**lane** See *lame.*

**lap of luxury** *n.* a luxurious situation. □ *I rather enjoy living in the lap of luxury.* □ *You call this pigpen the lap of luxury?*

**lapper** *n.* a drunkard. □ *The street was empty except for an old lapper staggering home.* □ *The party was ruined by the antics of a few lappers.*

**lard** *n.* the police. (Streets. Derogatory. See also *bacon, pig, pork.*) □ *Here comes the lard!* □ *If the lard catches you violating your parole, you're through.*

**lard ass*** *n.* a fat person. (Crude. Derogatory. Also a rude term of address. Caution with *ass.* Compare to *crisco.*) □ *Who's the lard ass with the 60-inch waist?* □ *Hay, lard ass, get moving!*

**lardhead 1.** *n.* a stupid person. □ *What a lardhead! Where are your brains?* □ *I'm not a lardhead. I dwell in a different dimension.* **2.** *mod.* foolish. □ *Now here's something from the lardhead department.* □ *No more of those lardhead ideas!*

**large as life (and twice as ugly)** See *big as life (and twice as ugly)*.

**last roundup** *n.* death. (Western.) □ *To everyone's surprise, he clutched the wound and faced the last roundup with a smile.* □ *When I know I'm headed for the last roundup, I'll write a will.*

**last straw** *n.* the final act or insult; the act that finally calls for a response. □ *This is the last straw. I'm calling the police.* □ *Someone's leaving the eggshells in the sink was the last straw.*

**later** *interj.* "goodbye." □ *It's time to cruise. Later.* □ *Later. Gotta go.*

**lathered** ['læðɚd] *mod.* alcohol intoxicated. □ *The two brothers sat there and got lathered.* □ *She is too lathered to drive.*

**latrine lips** [lə'trin 'lɪps] *n.* a person who uses dirty language. □ *Hey, latrine lips! Cool it!* □ *When old latrine lips finishes shocking everyone, I have something to say.*

**latrine rumor** [lə'trin 'rumɚ] *n.* any rumor, especially one that is alleged to spread at the latrine [general toilet facilities]. (Military.) □ *Somebody started spreading a latrine rumor about the Colonel's wife.* □ *That's just a latrine rumor. The Colonel isn't married.*

**latrine wireless** [lə'trin 'waɪɚləs] *n.* the free exchange of information and gossip at the general toilet facilities. (See the previous entry.) □ *It came over the latrine wireless this morning. We're all shipping out.* □ *The latrine wireless was virtually silent while you were in sick bay.*

**latrino(gram)** [lə'trino(græm)] *n.* a latrine rumor. □ *There was a latrino yesterday about the Colonel and his golf game.* □ *There's another latrinogram that says we're moving out.*

**lats** [læts] *n.* the *latissimus dorsi*; the muscles of the back. (Bodybuilding.) □ *Your lats are coming along fine. Now let's start working on your delts.* □ *Nice lats on that guy.*

**L.A. (turnabouts)** AND **California turnarounds, (L.A.) turnarounds, turnabouts** *n.* amphetamines. (Drugs. Alludes to the use of amphetamines by truck drivers.) □ *You got any of those L.A. turnabouts on you?* □ *That L.A. can get you in a whole heap of trouble.*

**laughing academy** *n.* a mental hospital; an insane asylum. □ *About four years in the laughing academy would get you straightened out.* □ *I'm not ready for the laughing academy. A little while longer around here and I will be, though.*

**laughing grass** *n.* marijuana. (Drugs.) □ *Where can I get some laughing grass?* □ *Bruno got to the point where he had to have his laughing grass once a day.*

**laughing soup** AND **laughing water** *n.* liquor; champagne. □ *Laughing soup flowed like fury at the reception.* □ *How about some more laughing water?*

**launch (one's lunch)** *tr. & in.* to empty one's stomach; to vomit. □ *When I saw that mess, I almost launched my lunch.* □ *Watch out! She's going to launch!*

**launder** *tr.* to conceal the source and nature of stolen or illicitly gotten money by moving it in and out of different financial institutions. (Underworld. See *greenwash*.) □ *The woman's sole function was to launder the money from drug deals.* □ *When you finish laundering the last job, we want you to do another.*

**laundry list** *n.* any long list of things. (Compare to *shopping list*.) □ *He came to the interview with a laundry list of things.* □ *Now I have a laundry list of items we have to discuss.*

**law** *n.* the police. (Always with *the*.) □ *She is in a little trouble with the law.* □ *Mrs. Wilson finally called the law in on her old man.*

**lawn** *n.* poor-quality marijuana. (Drugs.) □ *This isn't good grass; it's lawn.* □ *Put this lawn in your pipe and smoke it.*

**lay\* 1.** *n.* a period of time spent on one's hip for the purpose of smoking opium; an act of smoking opium; a smoked dose of opium. (Drugs.) □ *The old man limped in the door of the laundry saying, "I want a lay! I want a lay."* □ *There are not many opium smokers nowadays,* *and they call a lay a "session."* **2.** *n.* an opium den. (Drugs.) □ *There used to be a whole string of lays in New Orleans.* □ *You could spot a lay easy by the smell. Opium really reeks.* **3.** *n.* a dose of any powerful and addictive drug. (Drugs.) □ *Where can I get a lay of H.?* □ *Here's a lay of old horse. You pay me later.* **4.\*** *tr.* to copulate (with someone). (Crude. Caution with topic.) □ *She laid him on the spot.* □ *He said he was going to lay her. I thought he was just talking tough.* **5.\*** *n.* a sexual act. (Crude. Caution with topic.) □ *I could use a good lay about now.* □ *All the shipwrecked sailor could think about was a lay.* **6.\*** *n.* a person considered as a potential sex partner. (Crude. Caution with topic.) □ *He actually said that she was a good lay.* □ *If anybody said I was a good lay, I'd sue—probably.*

**lay a (heavy) trip on someone 1.** *tr.* to criticize someone. □ *There's no need to lay a trip on me. I agree with you.* □ *When he finally does get there, I'm going to lay a heavy trip on him like he'll never forget.* **2.** *tr.* to confuse or astonish someone. □ *After he laid a heavy trip on me about how the company is almost broke, I cleaned out my desk and left.* □ *After Mary laid a trip on John about her other self, he sat down and stared at his feet.* **3.** AND **lay a guilt trip on someone** *tr.* to attempt to make someone feel very guilty. □ *Why do you have to lay a guilt trip on me? Why don't you go to a shrink?* □ *Of course, she just had to lay a trip on him about being bossy, self-centered, and aloof.*

**lay an egg 1.** *tr.* (for someone) to do something bad or poorly. □ *I guess I really laid an egg, huh?* □ *The cast laid an egg in both performances.* **2.** *tr.* (for something) to fail. □ *The community theater laid an egg last night with the opening performance of* Death of a Salesman. □ *The film was fun to make, but it laid an egg at the box office.* **3.** *tr.* to laugh very hard; to cackle long and loudly. (As if one were a chicken.) □ *Half the audience laid an egg when I told this one.* □ *I didn't know whether to cry or lay an egg.*

**lay down** *in.* to give up. □ *Do you expect me to just lay down?* □ *You really think I should just lay down and let them walk all over me?*

**lay it on the line** *tr.* to speak very frankly and directly. □ *I'm going to have to lay it on the line with you, I guess.* □ *Go ahead; lay it on the line. I want to know exactly what you think.*

**lay off (someone or something)** *in.* to stop bothering or harming someone or something; to stop being concerned about someone or something. □ *Lay off the booze for a while, why don't ya?* □ *Lay off me! I didn't do anything!*

**lay one on** See *tie one on.*

**layout 1.** *n.* a place; a place to live. (Compare to *setup.*) □ *How much does a layout like this set you back a month?* □ *This is a nice layout you got here.* **2.** *n.* a floor plan. □ *Let's see if the layout is what we want.* □ *The layout looks awkward and wasteful of space.* **3.** *n.* a scheme. (Underworld.) □ *Now here's the layout. Lefty goes in this side, and Ratface comes in the other way.* □ *The layout's no good. The cops are wise to your style, boss.*

**lay rubber** AND **lay (some) rubber** *tr.* to spin one's car tires when accelerating, leaving black marks on the street. (Compare to *burn rubber.*) □ *At that age all they want to do is get in the car and lay some rubber.* □ *You wanna know how well I can lay some rubber in this thing?*

**lay someone or something out** AND **lay out someone or something 1.** *tr.* [with *someone*] to scold someone severely. □ *Don't lay me out! I didn't do it!* □ *She really laid him out but good. What did he do, rob a bank?* (More at *laid out.*) **2.** *tr.* [with *someone*] to knock someone down with a punch. □ *The boxer laid out his opponent with a blow to the head.* □ *I can't wait to get into that ring and lay the guy out.* **3.** *tr.* [with *something*] to spend some amount of money. □ *I can't lay out that kind of money every day!* □ *She laid out about $24,000 for that beemer.* **4.** *tr.* [with *something*] to explain a plan of action or a sequence of events. □ *Let me lay it out for you.* □ *Lay it out very careful-*

*ly, and don't skip anything.* **5.** *tr.* [with *someone*] to prepare someone for burial. (Not slang.) □ *The women of the town helped the young widow lay out her husband.* □ *The undertaker did not lay Aunt Fanny out to my satisfaction.* (More at *laid out.*)

**lay someone out in lavender** *tr.* to scold or rebuke someone severely. □ *She really laid him out in lavender for that.* □ *No need to lay me out in lavender. I wasn't there.*

**lay some sweet lines on someone** AND **put some sweet lines on someone** *tr.* to speak kindly to someone; to *soft soap* someone. □ *I just laid some sweet lines on her, and she let me use her car.* □ *If you put some sweet lines on him, maybe he won't ground you.*

**lay something on someone** **1.** *tr.* to present a plan or idea to someone. □ *Here is this century's greatest idea. Let me lay it on you.* □ *I'm going to lay a great idea on you.* **2.** *tr.* to attempt to make someone feel guilty about something. □ *Don't lay that stuff on me. Face your own problem.* □ *Every week she calls up to lay a guilt trip on me about something or other.*

**lazybones** *n.* a lazy person. □ *I'm just a lazybones, but I don't eat much.* □ *That lazybones is out there sleeping in the shade.*

**L.B.O.** AND **LBO** *n.* "leveraged buyout." (Financial markets.) □ *The money used for the LBO came from the issuance of junk bonds.* □ *Mr. Boone specializes in L.B.O.s. He's made a fortune at it.*

**lead poisoning** *n.* death caused by being shot with a lead bullet. (Underworld.) □ *He pifted because of a case of lead poisoning.* □ *The fourth mobster to die of lead poisoning this month was buried today in a private service.*

**leaf** *n.* cocaine. (Sometimes with *the.* Cocaine is extracted from the leaves of the *coca* plant.) □ *Sure I like plants. I am especially fond of the leaf.* □ *The entire shipment of leaf was seized by the feds.*

**lean and mean** *mod.* capable and ready for hard, efficient work. □ *Ron got himself lean and mean and is ready to play in Saturday's game.* □ *The management is lean and mean and looks to turn a profit next year.*

**leapers** *n.* amphetamines. (Drugs.) □ *You can tell Bruno's on leapers. He's wired as hell.* □ *He needs some barbs to balance the leapers, or maybe he just ought to go cold turkey and go straight.*

**leave someone cold** *tr.* to leave someone unaffected. □ *He said it was dull, and it left him cold.* □ *The music's good, but the story left the producer cold.*

**leeky store** ['liki stor] *n.* a liquor store. (Black. From *liquor*, but also see *take a leak.*) □ *Get me some grapes at the leeky store.* □ *The leeky store is closed till 10:00 A.M.*

**leerics** ['lɪrɪks] *n.* sexually suggestive song lyrics. □ *For those of you out there who go in for leerics, listen carefully to this tune.* □ *A group of parents has banded together in the eastern suburbs to fight the naughty leerics of some of the current hot rock tunes.*

**left-handed monkey wrench** *n.* a nonexistent tool. (New workers are sometimes sent to fetch nonexistent tools. See *sky hook.*) □ *Hand me the left-handed monkey wrench, huh?* □ *Do you think you can dig up a left-handed monkey wrench?*

**legal-beagle** AND **legal-eagle** ['lig!'big! AND 'lig!'ig!] *n.* a lawyer. □ *I've got a legal-beagle who can get me out of this scrape.* □ *She keeps a whole bunch of legal-eagles to handle that sort of thing.*

**legit** [lə'dʒɪt] *mod.* honest; legal. □ *If she's not legit, I won't work with her.* □ *Is this deal legit?*

**leg work** *n.* the physical work accompanying a task. □ *I don't mind making the phone calls if you do the leg work.* □ *I have a gopher to do the leg work for me.*

**lemme*** ['lɛmi] *phr.* "let me." (Eye-dialect. Typical spoken English. Caution with use in writing.) □ *Do you wanna gimme the thingy and lemme go ahead with my work?* □ *If you won't give me one of my own, make him lemme use his.*

**Let her rip!** AND **Let it roll!** ['lɛdɚ 'rɪp AND 'lɛdɪt 'rol] *exclam.* "Let it go!"; "Let it start!" □ *Time to start. Let her rip!* □ *There's the signal! Let it roll!*

**let it all hang out** *tr.* to be yourself, assuming that you generally are not. □ *Come on. Relax! Let it all hang out.* □ *I let it all hang out, but I still feel rotten.*

**Let it roll!** See *Let her rip!*

**let off steam** See *blow off (some) steam.*

**Let's do lunch (sometime).** *sent.* "Let us have lunch together sometime." □ *Great seeing you, Martin, absolutely great. Let's do lunch.* □ *Let's do lunch sometime so we can catch up.*

**Let's have it!** *exclam.* "Please tell (us) the news!" □ *What's happened? Let's have it!* □ *Don't beat around the bush. Let's have it!*

**let something ride** *tr.* to let something remain as is; ignore something (for a while). □ *Don't bother with it now. Let it ride for a day or two.* □ *Let it ride. It's not that important.*

**let's say** *phr.* introduces an estimate or a speculation. □ *I need about—let's say—20 pounds.* □ *Let's say I go over and talk to him. What do you think?*

**lettuce** *n.* money. □ *Put your lettuce on the table; then we'll talk.* □ *How much lettuce do you have left?*

**level best** *n.* one's very best effort. □ *I will do my level best to find your husband.* □ *Don't go to a whole lot of trouble. Your level best is good enough.*

**level with someone** *in.* to speak truly and honestly with someone. □ *Okay, I'm gonna level with you. This thing is a steal at this price!* □ *I want you to level with me. Did you do it?*

**libber** ['lɪbɚ] *n.* a woman who advocates woman's liberation movements; a feminist. (Usually derogatory.) □ *She sure sounds like a libber.* □ *This libber on the radio says men are unnecessary.*

**liberate** *tr.* to steal something. (Originally military.) □ *We liberated a few reams of paper and a box of pens.* □ *The privates liberated a jeep and went into town.*

**library** *n.* a bathroom; an outhouse. □ *John is in the library at the moment.* □ *He keeps stuff like that to read in the library.*

**lick and a promise** *n.* a very casual treatment. (Always with *a*.) □ *A lick and a promise isn't enough. Take some time and do it right.* □ *She gave it a lick and a promise and said she was done.*

**lickety-split** [lɪkɪdi'splɪt] *mod.* very fast. □ *They ran across the field lickety-split.* □ *We were there lickety-split in my new car.*

**lick something into shape** AND **whip something into shape** *tr.* to put something into good condition, possibly with considerable effort. □ *I've got about two days more to lick this place into shape so I can sell it.* □ *I want to whip this house into shape for Saturday night.*

**lick up a tab** AND **lick up some tabs** *tr.* to swallow a tablet or capsule. (Drugs.) □ *She leaned against the side of a building to steady herself while she licked up a tab or two.* □ *They went into the back room to lick up some tabs before going out to roam the streets.*

**licorice stick** ['lɪkrɪʃ stɪk] *n.* a clarinet. (Jazz musicians.) □ *Man, can he play the licorice stick.* □ *Frank makes the old licorice stick talk.*

**lid 1.** *n.* an eyelid. □ *Her lids began to close, and the professor raised his voice to a roar.* □ *Pop your lids open! It's morning!* **2.** *n.* one half to one ounce of marijuana. (Drugs. An amount that will fill the lid of a Prince Albert tobacco can lid. Often plural.) □ *How much a lid?* □ *It looks like a matchbox to me. Why do they call it a lid?*

**lid proppers** AND **lid poppers** *n.* amphetamine tablets or capsules. (Drugs. Refers to the eyelids.) □ *Kelly has to have a couple of lid proppers each morning.* □ *Are lid poppers habit-forming?*

**lie doggo** ['laɪ 'dɔgo] *in.* to remain unrecognized (for a long time). (See *doggo.*) □ *This problem has lain doggo since 1967.* □ *If you don't find the typos now, they will lie doggo until the next edition.*

**lifer** ['laɪfɚ] *n.* someone who is attached to an institution for life, such as a lifetime soldier or a prisoner serving a life sentence. (Prisons and military.) □ *Me a lifer? Not in this army!* □ *The lifers begin to accept their fate after a few years.* □ *Most of the lifers are kept in this cellblock.*

**L.I.F.O.** AND **LIFO** *phr.* "last in, first out." (Computers. Acronym. Refers to the order of data put in and returned from the processor.) □ *I can't remem-*

*ber whether the stack is LIFO or FIFO.* □ *This one is L.I.F.O.*

**lift 1.** *n.* the potency of alcohol in liquor. □ *This stuff doesn't have much lift!* □ *Now, this imported stuff has enough lift to raise the dead.* **2.** *n.* a brief spirit- or ego-lifting occurrence. □ *Your kind words have given me quite a lift.* □ *I could use a lift today. I am glummer than usual.* **3.** AND **lift-up** *n.* drug euphoria; a *rush.* (Drugs.) □ *This stuff'll give you quite a lift.* □ *The lift-up from the shot jarred her bones.* **4.** *tr.* to steal something. □ *She had lifted this ring. We found it on her when we arrested her.* □ *Some of these really young kids will lift something just because they like it.* **5.** *tr.* to take something away. □ *It was his third offense, so they lifted his license.* □ *They lifted the rule about not having two different jobs.* **6.** *n.* a tall heel that makes someone seem taller. (Usually plural.) □ *I feel better in my lifts.* □ *Some people wear lifts just to make them a little more confident.* **7.** *n.* a surgical face-lift. □ *He had a lift on his vacation, but his face still looked two sizes too big.* □ *We've got three lifts and a nose job in O.R. this morning.* **8.** *n.* a device—worn under the hair at the temples—which provides some of the effects of a surgical face-lift. □ *Do you think she's wearing a lift?* □ *Lift, hell, she's got a damn pair of cranes under that hairdo.* **9.** *n.* a ride; transportation. □ *Can you give me a lift?* □ *Would you like a lift over to your apartment?*

**lift one's elbow** See *bend one's elbow.*

**lift pill** *n.* a stimulant drug in pill form; amphetamines. (Drugs.) □ *They're just lift pills. They can't hurt you.* □ *First she takes a downer at night, then a lift pill in the morning, then another downer to sleep. She's never normal!*

**light 1.** *mod.* alcohol intoxicated. □ *I began to feel a little light after the fourth beer.* □ *I feel a little light. You'd better drive.* **2.** *n.* an eye. (Crude. Usually plural.) □ *You want I should poke your lights out?* □ *Open your lights and watch for the turnoff sign.*

**light artillery 1.** *n.* equipment for preparing and injecting drugs. (Drugs. Compare to *heavy artillery.*) □ *All that junk* *on the table is my light artillery.* □ *This bottle cap is part of the light artillery of an old-time addict.* **2.** *n.* equipment for using non-addictive drugs. (Drugs.) □ *The light artillery of a mugglehead is likely to include a pipe and a roach clip.* □ *Max keeps his light artillery upstairs.*

**light bulb** *n.* a pregnant woman. (Jocular. Refers to the shape of a pregnant woman.) □ *Who's the light bulb on the sofa?* □ *I can't possibly fit that light bulb out there. She'll have to wait a few months before buying expensive clothing.*

**lighten up (on someone or something)** *in.* to reduce the pressure (on someone or something); to calm down (about someone or something). □ *Cool it, man. Lighten up! We all gotta get along here.* □ *Lighten up on the guy. He only stepped on your toe.*

**light into someone** See *sail into someone.*

**lights out 1.** *n.* bedtime. □ *It's lights out, kids. Radios off, too!* □ *I was finished with it by lights out.* **2.** *n.* death; time to die. (Underworld.) □ *It's lights out for you, chum.* □ *When it's lights out, I want it to be fast.*

**light stuff 1.** *n.* low-proof liquor. □ *The light stuff is okay for parties, but not for serious drinking.* □ *Poor Sam is trying to cut down by drinking the light stuff. He drinks twice as much, though.* **2.** *n.* marijuana and non-addictive drugs. (Compare to *heavy drugs.*) □ *Sure, it's innocent. Sure, they're just kids. Do you know what kids do when they get through with the light stuff? They do coke, they shoot H., and they do the big one somewhere in an alley!* □ *The cops just found some light stuff in his pockets. They let him go.*

**light up** AND **fire up, flame up, torch up** *in.* to smoke a marijuana cigarette; to indulge in marijuana smoking. (Drugs.) □ *I just can't wait these days to get home and light up.* □ *I almost had to light up on the subway yesterday.*

**lightweight 1.** *mod.* inconsequential. □ *This is a fairly lightweight matter.* □ *We need an executive here, not just a lightweight flunky.* **2.** *n.* an inconsequential person. □ *Don't worry about her. She's just a lightweight.* □ *Those* *lightweights don't know how to run things right.*

**like\*** **1.\*** *interj.* an emphatic or meaningless word which, when said frequently, marks the speaker as speaking in a very casual or slangy mode. (Caution with *like.* Never used in writing. Compare to *okay, you know.*) □ *This is, like, so silly!* □ *She is like, so, like, way rad!* **2.\*** *interj.* a particle meaning roughly "saying." (Always with some form of be. Caution with *like.* Never used in writing.) □ *Tiffany was like, "Wow!"* □ *And I'm like, "Well, you should have put your hat on!"*

**like a bat out of hell\*** *mod.* very fast or sudden. (Caution with *hell.*) □ *The cat took off like a bat out of hell.* □ *The car pulled away from the curb like a bat out of hell.*

**like a million (dollars)** *mod.* very good or well. (Usually with *feel.*) □ *This old buggy runs like a million dollars.* □ *Man, I feel like a million.*

**like a ton of bricks** *mod.* like something very ponderous and heavy. □ *The whole thing hit me like a ton of bricks.* □ *Hitting the back end of that truck was like hitting a ton of bricks.*

**like crazy** AND **like mad** *mod.* furiously; very much, fast, many, or actively. □ *They're buying tickets like crazy.* □ *Look at those people on the bank. They're catching fish like mad!*

**like death warmed over** *mod.* horrible; deathlike. □ *Oh, my God! You look like death warmed over!* □ *A tall, black-garbed gentleman lay there, looking like death warmed over.*

**like gangbusters** *mod.* with great excitement and fury. (From the phrase "Come on like gangbusters," a radio show that "came on" with lots of noise and excitement.) □ *She works like gangbusters and gets the job done.* □ *They are selling tickets like gangbusters.*

**Like hell!\*** *exclam.* "That is not true!"; "I do not believe you!" (Caution with *hell.*) □ *You're going to a Dead concert! Like hell!* □ *Like hell, you are!*

**Like it or lump it!** *exclam.* "Give up!"; "Shut up!"; "Accept it or go away!" (Compare to *Lump it!*) □ *If you don't want to do it my way, lump it!* □ *Too bad! Like it or lump it!*

**like mad** See *like crazy.*

**like nobody's business** *mod.* very well; very much. □ *She can sing like nobody's business. What a set of pipes!* □ *My mom can cook chocolate chip cookies like nobody's business.*

**like stink** *mod.* rapidly. (As fast as a smell spreads.) □ *Those kids moved through the whole test like stink. Real eager-beavers.* □ *As long as she can run like stink, swim like stink, and smell like a flower, she gets my support.*

**like there was no tomorrow** *mod.* like there would never be another opportunity. □ *She was drinking booze like there was no tomorrow.* □ *He lived like there was no tomorrow.*

**like, you know\*** *interj.* a combining of the expressions *like* and *you know.* (Caution with use in speech or writing.) □ *She is, well, like, you know, P.G.* □ *This is, well, like, you know, too much!*

**lily-livered** *mod.* cowardly. □ *Don't be so lily-livered. Give it a try.* □ *That lily-livered guy is up hiding under his bed till this blows over.*

**limp dishrag** AND **dishrag** *n.* a totally helpless person; a cowardly and spineless person. □ *He's sweet, but he's a dishrag.* □ *A limp dishrag is no help at all in a crisis.*

**line 1.** *n.* a story or argument; a story intended to seduce someone. (See also *lines.*) □ *I've heard that line before.* □ *Don't feed me that line. Do you think I was born yesterday?* **2.** *n.* the median cephalic vein (in the arm) used for narcotics injections. (Drugs. From *mainline.*) □ *There's no place left to shoot in the line.* □ *You see, you have to find a soft spot in the line and stick the hype right in.* **3.** *in.* to inject a narcotic into the main arm vein. (Drugs.) □ *Bruno will line every now and then, but he can take it or leave it.* □ *This slide shows an addict "lining," that is, injecting into a vein.* **4.** AND **lines** *n.* a dose of finely-cut cocaine arranged in a line, ready for insufflation or snorting. (Drugs.) □ *Let's you and me go do some lines, okay?* □ *See these lines here? Watch what happens to them.*

**line one's own pocket(s)** *tr.* to make money for oneself in a greedy or dishonest fashion. □ *They are interested in lining their pockets first and serving the people second.* □ *You can't blame them for wanting to line their own pockets.*

**lines** *n.* words; conversation. (Black. See *line*.) □ *I like your lines, but I don't have the time.* □ *We tossed some lines back and forth for a while and then split.*

**lineup** *n.* (in a police station) a row of suspects arranged so that a witness can identify one of them. (Underworld.) □ *I had to stand in the lineup with this bunch of yahoos.* □ *When they round up all the likely suspects and put them in the lineup, they always stick in a desk sergeant to spy on the rest.*

**lingo** *n.* language; special vocabulary. □ *When you catch on to the lingo, everything becomes clear.* □ *If you don't like the lingo, don't listen.*

**lion's share** *n.* the largest portion. □ *I earn a lot, but the lion's share goes for taxes.* □ *The lion's share of the surplus cheese goes to school cafeterias.*

**lip** **1.** *tr. & in.* to kiss someone intimately. □ *The two of them were in the corner, lipping intently.* □ *Hey, honeycakes, I really want to lip you.* **2.** *n.* a lawyer. (Underworld. See *mouth*.) □ *So I brought in my lip, and he got me off the rap.* □ *How much do you pay your lip?* **3.** *n.* back talk; impudent talk. □ *Don't give me any more of your lip!* □ *I've had enough of her lip.*

**L.I.Q.** *n.* a liquor store. (Black. Also an acronym.) □ *Let's stop at the L.I.Q. and get some berries.* □ *I got a headache already. I don't need anything from any L.I.Q. to make it worse.*

**liquefied** *mod.* alcohol intoxicated. □ *Ten beers and I am absolutely liquefied!* □ *She is too liquefied to walk, let alone drive.*

**liquidate** *tr.* to kill someone. (Underworld.) □ *The boss wants me to liquidate Mr. Bruno.* □ *They used a machine gun to liquidate a few troublesome characters.*

**liquid cork** *n.* a medicine that stops diarrhea. □ *This nasty-tasting stuff is a good liquid cork for what you have.* □ *This liquid cork isn't so bad if you get it good and cold before you take it.*

**liquid laugh** *n.* vomit. □ *If you drink much more, you're gonna come out with a liquid laugh.* □ *There's some liquid laugh on your shoe.*

**listen up** *in.* to listen carefully. (Usually a command.) □ *Now, listen up! This is important.* □ *Listen up, you guys!*

**lit** *n.* literature, as a school subject. □ *I'm flunking English lit again.* □ *I hate lit. Give me numbers any day.*

**little black book** *n.* a book containing the names and addresses of acquaintances who are potential dates, usually put together by men. □ *I've got a nice collection in my little black book.* □ *Am I in your little black book, or can you already tell that I wouldn't go out with you?*

**little boy blue** *n.* a (male) police officer. (Black.) □ *I hear that little boy blue is looking for you.* □ *Little boy blue is coming this way, and he's mad.*

**little boys' room** *n.* the boys' restroom; the men's restroom. □ *Can you tell me where the little boys' room is?* □ *Ted's in the little boys' room. He'll be right back.*

**little girls' room** *n.* the girls' room; the women's restroom. □ *Can you please tell me where the little girls' room is?* □ *Is there an attendant in the little girls' room?*

**(little) pinkie** AND **(little) pinky** *n.* the littlest finger on either hand. (See also *pinkeye*.) □ *Ouch! I smashed my pinky.* □ *My little pinkie nearly froze because there's a hole in my glove.*

**liveware** ['laɪvwer] *n.* the human component of computer use. (Patterned on *software* and *hardware*.) □ *The hardware is okay. It's the liveware that's bad.* □ *If I don't get some sleep, you're going to see a liveware crash.*

**(live) wire** *n.* an energetic and vivacious person. □ *Molly is a real live wire.* □ *With a wire like Molly in charge, things will get done, that's for sure.*

**load** **1.** *n.* as much liquor as one can hold. □ *Harry had quite a load of booze.* □ *Mary is carrying a load.* (More at *loaded*.) **2.** *n.* a drink of liquor. □ *Can I have a load from your bottle?* □ *Help yourself to a load.* **3.** *n.* a dose of drugs; an injection of drugs. (Drugs.) □ *She* *shoots a load every day or two.* □ *He scored enough for a load only yesterday.* (More at *loaded.*) **4.** *n.* a drug supply; a *stash.* (Drugs.) □ *My load is up in the closet.* □ *If his load dwindles, he gets more easily.* **5.** *n.* a large purchase of heroin. (Drugs.) □ *I've scored a load that'll last me a few days.* □ *That load must be worth about $50,000.*

**loaded 1.** *mod.* alcohol or drug intoxicated. □ *If you're loaded, don't drive.* □ *I'm not loaded. I'm just a little tipsy.* **2.** *mod.* spiked with liquor; containing much alcohol. □ *There's a little rum in the eggnog, but it's certainly not what I would call loaded.* □ *Wow, this punch is loaded!* **3.** *mod.* (of a car) with all available accessories. □ *Did you want to see a car that's loaded, or is this to be a budget car?* □ *Now, this little gem is loaded with everything.* **4.** *mod.* wealthy; loaded with money. □ *Mr. Wilson is loaded, but he is also generous with his money.* □ *My Uncle Fred is loaded, but he's going to take it all with him.*

**loaded for bear 1.** *mod.* alcohol intoxicated. □ *He is loaded for bear, and anything else.* □ *He's been drinking mule since dawn, and he's loaded for bear.* **2.** *mod.* ready for the hardest problems. □ *Bring on the hard cases. I'm loaded for bear.* □ *I'm loaded for bear, and that's good because this is going to be a rough day.* **3.** *mod.* very angry. □ *By the time he finished talking, I was loaded for bear.* □ *I had been loaded for bear when I came into the room, and I left as meek as a lamb.*

**loaded question** *n.* a question to which an honest answer will reveal things the speaker might otherwise wish to conceal. □ *Now, that's a loaded question, and I don't think I have to answer it.* □ *I didn't mean it to be a loaded question.*

**loaded remark** *n.* a remark containing important implications. □ *Your loaded remark did not go over well with the host.* □ *In spite of your numerous loaded remarks, I do hope you will return sometime when it is convenient.*

**loaded to the gills** AND **loaded to the barrel** *mod.* alcohol intoxicated. □ *He's loaded to the gills. Couldn't see a hole in a ladder.* □ *Man, he's loaded to the barrel and fighting mad.*

**loady** AND **loadie** ['lodi] *n.* a drinker or drug user. (Teens and collegiate. One who gets *loaded* frequently.) □ *I hear that Wally is a loady. Is that true?* □ *These loadies are all very difficult to deal with.*

**local yokel** ['lok! 'jok!] *n.* a local resident of a rural place. (Mildly derogatory.) □ *One of the local yokels helped me change the tire.* □ *The local yokels all listen to the same radio station.*

**loco** ['loko] *mod.* crazy. (From Spanish.) □ *Who is that loco kid jumping up and down in the front seat?* □ *This zit is gonna drive me loco.*

**locoweed** *n.* marijuana. (Drugs. The name of a weed that upsets cows when they eat it.) □ *You got any locoweed you can spare?* □ *This locoweed is pretty powerful.*

**lollapalooza** [lɑləpə'luzə] **1.** *n.* something very big; something wondrous. □ *Look at that bump on your head. That's a lollapalooza!* □ *Her singing voice is a real dandy—a lollapalooza.* **2.** *n.* a big lie. □ *She just told a lollapalooza.* □ *What a lollapalooza! You expect me to believe that?*

**lone wolf** *n.* a man who stays to himself. □ *Fred is sort of a lone wolf until he has a few drinks.* □ *It's the lone wolves you read about in the paper when they pull a drowning person from the river.*

**long arm of the law** *n.* the police; the law. (See also *arm.*) □ *The long arm of the law is going to tap you on the shoulder some day, Lefty.* □ *The long arm of the law finally caught up with Gert.*

**long bread** AND **long green** *n.* money. (Black.) □ *Man, that must have cost you some long bread!* □ *Look at the long green you get for doing the job!*

**long dozen** *n.* thirteen; a *baker's dozen.* □ *Don't you sell a long dozen anymore?* □ *They used to give you a long dozen in that bakery.*

**long green** See *long bread.*

**longhair 1.** *n.* a *highbrow* with long hair; especially a musician. □ *There were a few longhairs at the bar, but none of the regulars.* □ *I am sort of a longhair, but I still watch T.V.* **2.** *mod.* having to do with *highbrow* tastes; (of music) classical. □ *I don't care for longhair music.*

□ *It's too longhair.* □ *Longhair stuff like symphonies and art galleries bores me to tears.* **3.** *n.* a hippie; a long-haired youth of the 1960s. (Usually derogatory.) □ *Tell that longhair to get out of here.* □ *There are fewer longhairs around here than there were in the sixties.*

**long knife 1.** *n.* an assassin. (Underworld.) □ *The boss sent one of his long knives to kill the guy.* □ *Some long knife showed up, but Marty took him out before he made his move.* **2.** *n.* a destroyer; a hatchet man. □ *The secretary was acting as a long knife for the President.* □ *One of his long knives came over to pressure us into cooperating.*

**long shot** *n.* a wild guess; an attempt at something that has little chance of succeeding. □ *Well, it was a long shot, but I had to try it.* □ *You shouldn't expect a long shot to pay off.*

**long story short** *phr.* "to make a long story short." □ *Okay, long story short: everything that goes up comes down, okay?* □ *Then the guy comes over, and—long story short—"You got a match?"*

**long tall Sally** *n.* a tall girl or woman. □ *Isn't she a gorgeous long tall Sally?* □ *She's quite a long tall Sally.*

**Long time no see.** *phr.* "I haven't seen you in a long time." □ *Hey, John! Long time no see!* □ *Long time no see! How ya been?*

**look after number one** *in.* to take care of oneself first. (See *number one.*) □ *You gotta look after number one, right?* □ *It's a good idea to look after number one. Who else will?*

**Look alive!** *exclam.* "Move faster!"; "Look and act alert!" □ *There's work to be done! Look alive!* □ *Look alive! It's a long hard day ahead!*

**look-see** *n.* a look; a visual examination. □ *Let's go and have a look-see at this monster of yours.* □ *Take a look-see at this one and see if you like it.*

**Look who's talking!** *exclam.* "You are just as guilty!"; "You are just as much at fault!" □ *Me a tax cheat? Look who's talking!* □ *Look who's talking. You were there before I was.*

**loony** AND **loonie** ['luni] **1.** *n.* a crazy person. (From *lunatic.*) □ *I'm beginning to feel like a loonie the longer I stay*

around here. □ *Don't be a loony. Use common sense.* **2.** *mod.* crazy. □ *That is a loony idea. Forget it.* □ *I'm not really as loony as I seem.* **3.** *mod.* alcohol intoxicated. □ *She's acting a little loonie. Let's get her home before she's sick.* □ *A couple of drinks and she's as loonie as hot cakes.*

**loony bin** *n.* an insane asylum; a mental hospital. □ *I feel like I'm about ready for the loony bin.* □ *Today's loony bins are far different from those just a few decades ago.*

**looped** AND **loopy** *mod.* alcohol intoxicated. □ *Sam is too looped to drive.* □ *She got loopy very quickly and had to be helped to a chair.*

**loop-legged** *mod.* alcohol intoxicated. □ *He's too loop-legged to drive.* □ *She has this strange tendency to get a little loop-legged when she has four or five drinks.*

**loose cannon** *n.* a loudmouth; a braggart. □ *As it turned out, he's not just a loose cannon. He makes sense.* □ *Some loose cannon in the State Department has been feeding the press all sorts of crap as a diversion.*

**loot 1.** *n.* stolen goods; stolen money. □ *The loot was stashed in the trunk of the getaway car.* □ *Where's the loot? I want my piece.* **2.** *n.* money in general. □ *I left home without any loot.* □ *It takes too much loot to eat at that restaurant.*

**Lord love a duck!** *exclam.* "Wow!" □ *Lord love a duck! It's Mary!* □ *Lord love a duck, I'm tired!*

**lo-res** See *low-res.*

**lorg** [lorg] *n.* a stupid person. □ *Why is Frank such a lorg? Can't he get with it?* □ *Tell that lorg to find his own chair.*

**lose (all) one's marbles** *tr.* to become crazy. (See *have all one's marbles, marbles.*) □ *Have you lost all your marbles?* □ *She acts like she lost her marbles.*

**lose it 1.** *tr.* to empty one's stomach; to vomit. (Collegiate.) □ *Oh, God! I think I'm going to lose it!* □ *Go lose it in the bushes.* **2.** *tr.* to get angry; to lose one's temper. □ *It was too much for him. Ted lost it.* □ *I sat there calmly, biting my lip to keep from losing it.*

**lose one's cool** *tr.* to lose control; to lose one's temper. (Compare to *keep* one's cool.) □ *Now, don't lose your cool. Relax.* □ *I'm trying not to lose my cool, but it's hard.*

**lose one's doughnuts** See *blow one's doughnuts.*

**lose one's grip** AND **lose one's hold** *tr.* to lose one's control over something. □ *When I begin to lose my grip, I will just quit.* □ *I'm losing my hold. It must be time to chuck it.*

**lose one's hold** See *lose one's grip.*

**lose one's lunch** See *blow one's lunch.*

**lose one's shirt** *tr.* to go broke; to lose everything of value, even one's shirt. □ *I lost my shirt on that bank deal.* □ *Try not to lose your shirt in the market again.*

**loser** ['luzɚ] *n.* an inept person; an undesirable or annoying person. □ *Dave is a real loser.* □ *Only losers wear clothes like that.*

**losing streak** *n.* a period of bad luck, especially in gambling. □ *After a prolonged losing streak, Diamond Jane retired and opened some sort of manicure parlor outside Las Vegas.* □ *I've been on a three-year losing streak in my business. I'm just about done.*

**lost cause** *n.* a hopeless or worthless thing or person. □ *The whole play began to wash out during the second act. It was a lost cause by the third.* □ *Max is just a lost cause. Just forget about him.*

**Lots of luck!** **1.** *exclam.* "Good luck!" □ *I'm glad you're giving it a try. Lots of luck!* □ *Lots of luck in your new job!* **2.** *exclam.* "You don't have a chance!"; "Good luck, you'll need it!" (Sarcastic.) □ *Think you stand a chance? Lots of luck!* □ *You a senator? Lots of luck!*

**loud mouth** *n.* a person who talks too much or too loudly. □ *I try not to be a loud mouth, but I sometimes get carried away.* □ *There are a number of loud mouths in here who are competing with one another.*

**louse** [laus] *n.* a thoroughly repellent person, usually a male. □ *You can be such a louse!* □ *Max turned out to be a louse, and his wife of two weeks left him.*

**louse something up** AND **louse up something** *tr.* to botch something up. □ *Pleare don't louse the typewriter ribbon*

up this time. □ *Jack loused up my effort to win approval for my plan.*

**lousy** ['lauzi] *mod.* rotten; poor; bad. □ *This is a lousy day.* □ *This mushy stuff is lousy. Do I have to eat it?*

**lousy with someone or something** *mod.* having lots of someone or something. (Like an infestation of lice.) □ *Old Mr. Wilson is lousy with money.* □ *Tiffany is lousy with jewels and furs, but she's got bad teeth.*

**love bombs** *n.* affirmations of affection. □ *These two were dropping love bombs on each other, even though they hate each other's guts.* □ *What a phony bunch of kooks. They were throwing love bombs all over the place!*

**love drug** *n.* a drug acting as an aphrodisiac; marijuana or some similar substance. (Drugs.) □ *I've heard a lot about this love drug stuff, but it doesn't do anything to me.* □ *Nearly every one of these substances has been called the love drug at one time or another.*

**love handles** *n.* a roll of fat around the waist. □ *I wish I could get rid of these love handles.* □ *Are you troubled with a spare tire or love handles? Here is a product which has helped thousands and will help you!*

**love-in** **1.** *n.* an event during the sixties where one or more couples made love in a public place. □ *My uncle was at one of those love-ins, and he said if anything was going on, it was going on under blankets.* □ *I think the only people who went to love-ins were reporters.* **2.** *n.* an event in the sixties where everyone became euphoric—with the help of marijuana—about love and respect for their fellow humans. □ *The meeting was no love-in, but we got along.* □ *Everyone at the annual company love-in was throwing love bombs around at each other.*

**Love it!** See *(I) love it!*

**Love you!** *exclam.* "You are great!" (Almost meaningless patter.) □ *See ya around, Martin. Let's do lunch! Love ya! Bye bye.* □ *Nice talking to you, babe. Love you!*

**low-blow** *n.* an unfair blow. (See also *hit (someone) below the belt.*) □ *No fair!*

*That was a low-blow.* □ *Coming in like that unannounced was a pretty low-blow.*

**lowbrow** ['lobrau] **1.** *n.* a nonintellectual person; an anti-intellectual person. □ *Some lowbrow came in and made a stink about not being able to find any Gene Autry records.* □ *Not that Gene Autry is lowbrow. The guy who came in was.* **2.** *mod.* nonintellectual; anti-intellectual.* □ *I like my lowbrow music and my lowbrow friends!* □ *What's lowbrow about soft rock?*

**lowdown 1.** *mod.* rotten; bad. □ *What a dirty, lowdown thing to do.* □ *You are a lowdown rat!* **2.** *n.* the facts on something; the scuttlebutt about something. □ *What's the lowdown on that funny statue in the park?* □ *Give me the lowdown on the project we just started.*

**low five** *n.* the slapping of hands at waist level as a greeting. (Compare to *high five*.) □ *They turned to each other, throwing a quick low five as they passed.* □ *The two 8 year-olds tried to give each other a low five, but they both hurt their hands.*

**low-key** *mod.* not obvious. □ *Let's try to keep this low-key so as not to upset the family.* □ *It was a very low-key meeting, but we got a lot done.*

**low-life 1.** *n.* a low person; a repellent person. □ *This low-life smells like bacon.* □ *Hey, low-life, keep out of my way.* **2.** *mod.* mean; belligerent. (Black.) □ *Don't be so low-life, man!* □ *We don't need any low-life characters around here.*

**low rent 1.** *n.* a low person; someone without grace or spirit. (Also a rude term of address.) □ *Look, low rent, where is what you owe me?* □ *This low rent here thinks he can push Bruno around, huh?* **2.** *mod.* cheap; unfashionable. □ *This place is strictly low rent.* □ *Why don't you go live with some of your low rent friends?*

**low-res** AND **lo-res** ['lo'rɛz] *mod.* poor; unpleasant. (From *low resolution* in a cathode ray tube computer terminal. Compare to *high-res*.) □ *I feel sort of low-res today.* □ *The party is lo-res. Let's cruise.*

**L.S.D.** *n.* lysergic acid diethylamide, a hallucinogenic drug. (Drugs. A mainstay of the 1960s-1970s drug culture.) □ *Is there much L.S.D. still around?* □ *L.S.D. isn't the problem it used to be, but it's far from gone.*

**L.T.** AND **LT** *in.* "living together." (A euphemism.) □ *Guess who're LT?* □ *They have been L.T. for some time.*

**lube** *n.* butter. □ *Pass the lube, will ya, huh?* □ *We're outa lube.*

**lubricated** *mod.* alcohol intoxicated. □ *They are sufficiently lubricated for the night.* □ *He's not fit to talk to until he's lubricated a bit.*

**lubrication** *n.* liquor. □ *A little lubrication would help this party a lot.* □ *Wally has had a little too much lubrication.*

**luck of the draw** *n.* the results of chance; the lack of any choice. □ *Why do I always end up with the luck of the draw?* □ *The team was assembled by chance. It was just the luck of the draw that we could work so well together.*

**luck out** *in.* to be fortunate; to strike it lucky. □ *I really lucked out when I ordered the duck. It's excellent.* □ *I didn't luck out at all. I rarely make the right choice.*

**lucky dog** *n.* a lucky person, perhaps undeserving. (Also a term of address.) □ *You lucky dog!* □ *Max was a lucky dog because he won the football pool.*

**lude** [lud] *n.* a Quaalude™ capsule. (Drugs.) □ *A couple of ludes put Max in a better mood.* □ *I don't know what he gave me. Mary said it was a lude or something.*

**luded out** *mod.* intoxicated with Quaalude™, a sedative-hypnotic. (Drugs.) □ *Max is luded out, but maybe Bruno can help you.* □ *Some students come to school luded out.*

**lug** [ləg] *n.* a stupid male. □ *Is this lug bothering you, lady?* □ *Some lug on a tractor was holding up traffic.*

**lughead** *n.* a stupid person. (Also a term of address.) □ *What a lughead! How can you be so dumb?* □ *Hey, lughead! Watch where you are going.*

**lumber** *n.* stems and debris in a portion of cannabis. (Drugs.) □ *This stuff is full of lumber!* □ *Take the lumber out, unless you want flames.*

**lumbo** AND **limbo** ['ləmbo AND 'lımbo] *n.* Colombian marijuana. (Drugs. See also *lum(s)*.) □ *He showed up with a bag of lumbo.* □ *Hey, Max! You are just in time with the limbo, man.*

**lummox** AND **lommix, lummux** ['ləmɑks AND 'ləməks] *n.* a heavy, awkward, stupid person. □ *He looks like a big lummox, but he can really dance.* □ *Bruno is what you would call a lummux—but not to his face, of course.*

**lump** *n.* a stupid clod of a man. □ *I am not a lump! I am just sedate and pensive.* □ *Who is that lump leaning over the bar?*

**Lump it!** *exclam.* "Forget it!"; "Go away!" (See also *Like it or lump it!*) □ *Well, you can just lump it!* □ *Lump it! Drop dead!*

**lumpus** ['ləmpəs] *n.* a stupid oaf. □ *You are a silly lumpus!* □ *Is this lumpus giving you any trouble, ma'am?*

**lum(s)** [ləm(z)] *n.* cannabis from Colombia. (The "lum" is based on the misspelling "Columbia.") □ *Bruno preferred lums, but he would take what he could get.* □ *If it weren't for lum, our trade deficit wouldn't be so bad.*

**lush 1.** *n.* liquor. □ *Who's bringing the lush to the party?* □ *Lead me to the lush.* **2.** AND **lush up** *in.* to drink alcohol to excess. □ *Come over sometime, and we'll lush.* □ *We sat lushing up for an hour waiting for the plane.* **3.** *n.* a drunkard. □ *I was afraid of it for some time, but now I know. Molly is a lush.* □ *There were four confirmed lushes at the party, but they all passed out and didn't bother us much.*

**lush hound** *n.* a drunkard. □ *What a lush hound you're getting to be!* □ *Give this lush hound a drink. The sooner he's tanked, the sooner he'll go home and leave us alone.*

**lush house** *n.* a pub or tavern. □ *Let's stop in at this lush house for a beer.* □ *Harry? You'll find him at the closest lush house.*

**lush merchant** *n.* a drunkard. □ *Some lush merchant sat by the door waiting for a handout.* □ *Do you think I want to see you turn into a lush merchant?*

**lush up** See *lush*.

# M

**M.** **1.** AND **M.s** *n.* morphine. (Drugs.) □ *M. is nice if you can get it. It's not nice if you can't get off it.* □ *M. is too hard to get to have to depend on it.* **2.** *n.* marijuana. (Drugs.) □ *Can you sell me some M.?* □ *Max deals mainly in M.*

**mañana** [mə'njanə] *mod.* tomorrow. (Spanish.) □ *It's always mañana with you. Isn't there any 'today' or 'now' in your vocabulary?* □ *He's a mañana kind of guy. You know—real laid back.*

**Ma Bell** *n.* American Telephone and Telegraph Company; any telephone company. (Compare to *Baby Bell*.) □ *I forgot to pay Ma Bell this month.* □ *Ma Bell is still one of the largest firms in the nation.*

**mace someone's face** [mes...] *tr.* to do something drastic to someone, such as spraying mace in the face. (Chemical Mace™ is a brand of tear gas sold in pressurized cans for personal protection.) □ *Do you want me to mace your face? Then shut up!* □ *I look at him, and suddenly I just want to mace his face or something.*

**macho** ['matʃo] **1.** *mod.* masculine; virile. (From Spanish. Used as a derogation by feminists.) □ *Does the world really need one more macho man?* □ *He's hardly macho.* □ *You know—that bright-eyed macho type.* **2.** *n.* a masculine or virile male. □ *He's such a macho. He even chews tobacco.* □ *Watch out for that macho over there. He's cruising for a bruising.*

**Machu Picchu** ['matʃu 'pitʃu] *n.* potent marijuana from Peru. (Drugs. Named for the ancient city, Machu Picchu.) □ *I got some Machu Picchu. Wanna come over?* □ *Some guy across the hall says*

he has Machu Picchu. It looks like ragweed to me.

**Mac(k)** [mæk] *n.* a generic name for a man. (Also a term of address.) □ *Look, Mac, you want to make some big money?* □ *Hey, Mack! Come here a minute.*

**mac out** *in.* to overeat, especially the type of food served at McDonald's fast food restaurants. (From the Big Mac™ sandwich. Compare to *Big Mac attack*. See also *blimp out, pig out, pork out, scarf out*.) □ *I've been in Europe for a month, and I just want to get home and mac out.* □ *I mac out every weekend. It's like going to church.*

**madam** *n.* the female keeper of a brothel. □ *The madam was caught in a sting operation.* □ *The cops led the madam away, followed by a parade of you-know-whats.*

**Madison Avenue** ['mædəsən 'ævənu] **1.** *n.* in the style or image of the major U.S. center for advertising agencies. (The agencies are located on Madison Avenue in New York City.) □ *It's too much like Madison Avenue. We want a calm, sincere mood.* □ *This is plain old Madison Avenue. I want something more subtle.* **2.** *mod.* in the manner of intense promotion; propaganda-like. □ *More and more people simply do not respond to Madison Avenue hype.* □ *Can Madison Avenue techniques sell a political candidate?*

**mad money** *n.* money to be spent in a frivolous fashion. □ *This is my mad money, and I'll do with it as I please.* □ *I got $100 in mad money for my birthday.*

**mag** *n.* magazine. □ *I gotta stop and get a computer mag.* □ *I've seen your face in the mags, haven't I?*

**maggot 1.** *n.* a cigarette. (Probably a play on *faggot* at *fag*.) □ *Can I bum a maggot off of you?* □ *Get your own maggots.* **2.** *n.* a low and wretched person; a vile person. □ *You maggot! Take your hands off me!* □ *Only a maggot would do something like that.*

**maggotty** AND **maggoty** *mod.* alcohol intoxicated; very drunk. □ *Rotten, hell. They were absolutely maggotty!* □ *How can anybody reach the state of being maggoty on three beers?*

**magic bullet** See *silver bullet*.

**magic mushrooms** AND **sacred mushrooms** *n.* mushrooms of the genus *Psilocybe*, which cause visions or hallucinations when eaten. (Drugs.) □ *Magic mushrooms are okay because they are natural, or something like that.* □ *This is the so-called "sacred mushroom," named for its use in Amerindian ritual.*

**magic pumpkin** *n.* mescaline. (Drugs.) □ *Magic pumpkin is really a chemical that comes from part of a cactus.* □ *This magic pumpkin tastes like rotten pumpkin.*

**magpie** *n.* a person who chatters; a person who annoys others by chattering. □ *Sally is such a magpie!* □ *Why do those horrendous magpies all go to the same movies I go to?*

**(ma)hoska** [mə'hɑskə] **1.** *n.* narcotics; any contraband. (Underworld.) □ *The tall pinstriper asked where he could get some mahoska.* □ *The hoska must be for a friend. He's a blower if I ever saw one.* **2.** *n.* energy; strength; *moxie*. □ *The guy's got mahoska and guts!* □ *She's quick and has lots of mahoska.*

**main drag** *n.* the main street. □ *I have a shop over on the main drag.* □ *The main drag is solid with traffic on Saturday nights.*

**mainline 1.** *n.* the median cephalic vein (in the forearm). (Drugs. The favored site for an injection. See also *line*.) □ *She pumped the stuff right into the mainline.* □ *See the scars along the mainline. Those are from abscesses.* **2.** *in.* to inject drugs into the main arm vein. (Drugs.) □ *Yesterday it was busters and thrusters—today he's mainlining.* □ *You can tell from the scars that he has been mainlining recently.*

**main squeeze 1.** *n.* one's boss; the person in charge. □ *The main squeeze has a lot of responsibility.* □ *The main squeeze is out of town for a week.* **2.** *n.* one's steady girlfriend or boyfriend. □ *My main squeeze is coming over to talk tonight.* □ *She plans to marry her main squeeze.*

**main stash** *n.* the home of a drug user described in terms of where one's major store of drugs is kept. (Drugs. See *stash*.) □ *His apps are in his main stash.* □ *My main stash is on Maple, but I'm usually not there.*

**major** *mod.* excellent. (Collegiate.) □ *This rally is, like, major!* □ *Wally is one of the most major beach guys!*

**make 1.** *tr.* to identify someone. (Underworld.) □ *We tried to make him down at the station, but came up with nothing.* □ *Given another second or two I could have made the guy—but he moved for his gun, and the shot I fired into his face will keep his name a secret for a long time.* **2.** *n.* an identification. (Underworld.) □ *We ran a make on her. She's got two priors.* □ *The make didn't come through until after she was released.* **3.** *tr.* to arrive at a place; to cover a distance. □ *Can we make Boston by sunset?* □ *We made 40 miles in 30 minutes.* **4.** *tr.* to achieve a specific speed. □ *See if this thing can make 90.* □ *This buggy will make twice the speed of the old one.*

**make a boo-boo** *tr.* to make an error. (See *boo-boo*.) □ *Everybody makes a boo-boo every now and then.* □ *Whoops! I made a boo-boo.*

**make a bundle** AND **make a pile** *tr.* to make a lot of money. (See *bundle*.) □ *I made a bundle off that last deal.* □ *I want to buy a few stocks and make a pile in a few years.*

**make a buy** AND **make a connection, make a meet, make the man** *tr.* to locate a drug dealer and purchase drugs. (Drugs.) □ *He slunk out the door saying something about making a connection.* □ *When it's time to make a buy, you'd better be there.*

**make a federal case out of something** *tr.* to exaggerate the importance of an error; to overdo something. □ *Do you* have to make a federal case out of everything? □ *I only spilled my milk. Why make a federal case out of it?*

**make a killing** *tr.* to make an enormous profit; to become an enormous success. □ *The company made a killing from the sale of its subsidiary.* □ *I wanted to make a killing as a banker, but it didn't work out.*

**Make a lap!** *exclam.* to sit down. □ *Hey, make a lap and get out of the way!* □ *Pull up a chair and make a lap!*

**make a meet** See *make a buy.*

**make a pig of oneself** *tr.* to overeat; to take more of something than anyone else gets; to be selfish. □ *Please don't make a pig out of yourself.* □ *I have a tendency to make a pig of myself at affairs like this.*

**make a pile** See *make a bundle.*

**make a score** *tr.* to do a criminal act: to buy or sell drugs, to rob someone, to perform a *scam.* (Underworld.) □ *We made a score with that bank job in Adamsville, didn't we?* □ *They made quite a score off that junky.*

**make a stink (about someone or something)** See *raise a stink (about someone or something).*

**make book on something** *tr.* to make or accept bets on something. □ *Well, she might. But I wouldn't make book on it.* □ *Don't make book on my success in this game.*

**make for somewhere** *in.* to set out for somewhere; to run or travel to somewhere. □ *Max made for Philadelphia when he heard the pigs in the Big Apple were after him.* □ *Barlowe made for the stairs, but two shots rang out, and he knew it was all over for Mary.*

**make hamburger out of someone or something** AND **make mincemeat out of someone or something** *tr.* to beat someone or something to a pulp; to destroy someone or something. □ *The puppy made mincemeat out of my paper.* □ *They threatened to make hamburger out of me.*

**make it 1.** *tr.* to achieve one's goals. (See *make (it) big.*) □ *I can see by looking around this room that you have really made it.* □ *I hope I make it someday. But if not, I tried.* **2.** *tr.* to copulate (with

someone). □ *There was no doubt in his mind that those bedroom eyes were telling him their owner wanted to make it.* □ *She wanted to make it, but he convinced her they should wait.*

**make (it) big** *tr. & in.* to become successful, especially financially. □ *I always knew that someday I would make it big.* □ *My brother made big, but it has just led to tax problems.*

**make it hot for someone** *tr.* to make things difficult for someone; to put someone under pressure. (Note the variation in the examples.) □ *The cops were making it hot for him, so he blew town.* □ *The boss is making it a little hot for me, so I had better get to work on time.*

**Make it snappy!** *exclam.* "Hurry up!"; "Make it fast!" □ *We're late, Molly. Make it snappy.* □ *Make it snappy, Fred. The cops are headed up the walk now.*

**make like someone or something** *in.* to act like someone or something. □ *Why don't you make like a bunny and run away? Beat it!* □ *Would you please make like a butler and hold the door open for me?*

**make mincemeat out of someone or something** See *make hamburger out of someone or something.*

**Make my day!** *exclam.* "Go ahead, do what you are going to do, and I will be very happy to do what I have to do!" (A catch phrase said typically by a movie police officer who has a gun pointed at a criminal. The police officer wants the criminal to do something that will justify pulling the trigger which the police officer will do with pleasure. Used in real life in any context, and especially in sarcasm.) □ *Move a muscle! Go for your gun! Go ahead, make my day!* □ *Make my day. Just try it.*

**Make no mistake (about it)!** *sent.* an expression signifying the sincerity of the speaker's previous statements. □ *Make no mistake! This is the real thing.* □ *This is a very serious matter. Make no mistake about it.*

**make one's bed** *tr.* to be the cause of one's own misery. □ *Well, I guess I made my own bed. Now I have to lie in it.* □ *"We all make our own beds," said the minister.*

**make oneself scarce** *tr.* to leave; to be in a place less frequently. □ *Here come the boys in blue. I'd better make myself scarce.* □ *I suggest that you make yourself scarce before she returns.*

**make out 1.** *in.* to neck and pet. □ *I still like to make out, but it's hard with dentures.* □ *He started making out when he was 12.* **2.** *in.* to succeed. □ *How did you make out?* □ *I hope I make out okay tomorrow.*

**make-out artist** *n.* a seducer; a lecher, usually a male. (See *lady-killer.*) □ *The guy thinks he's a make-out artist, but the women all think he's a nerd.* □ *He might have been a make-out artist in his youth, but I doubt it.*

**make the scene 1.** *tr.* to attend an event. (See also *scene.*) □ *We plan to make the scene, but you know how things are.* □ *I hope everybody can make the scene.* **2.** *tr.* to understand a situation; to appreciate the situation. (Underworld. See *make,* to identify.) □ *I can't quite make the scene, but it looks like Bruno punched the guy over here. Then he moved to the window over here, and that's when the old dame across the street saw him.* □ *I can make the scene. It's just like you said, except Bruno came in and found the guy laid out on the floor.*

**make tracks 1.** *tr.* to move out of a place fast. □ *I gotta make tracks home now.* □ *Let's make tracks. We gotta hit Adamsville before noon.* **2.** *tr.* to inject drugs and leave needle marks. (Drugs.) □ *I see you're making tracks. What are you on?* □ *Ernie had been making tracks for about a week when his place was raided.*

**make waves** *tr.* to cause difficulty. (Often in the negative.) □ *Just relax. Don't make waves.* □ *If you make waves too much around here, you won't last long.*

**make with the something** *in.* to make something visible; to use something. □ *Come on, make with the cash.* □ *I want to know. Come on, make with the answers!*

**malarky** AND **malarkey** [mə'lɑrki] *n.* nonsense; flattery. □ *Don't give me that malarkey.* □ *What ridiculous malarkey!*

**male chauvinist pig** See *M.C.P.*

**mallet** *n.* a police officer. (Black.) □ *Sam was struck by a mallet this noon.* □ *Some mallet is going around asking questions about you.*

**mama bear** *n.* a policewoman. (Compare to *lady bear.*) □ *As we came under the bridge, we saw a mama bear sitting in a pigmobile.* □ *A mama bear pulled the trucker over.*

**man 1.** *n.* one's friend; a buddy, not necessarily male. (Also a term of address.) □ *Look, man, take it easy!* □ *Hey, man. That one's mine!* **2.** *exclam.* "Wow!" (Usually **Man!**) □ *Man, what a bundle!* □ *Man, what an ugly mug.* **3.** AND **the man** *n.* a drug seller or pusher. (Drugs.) □ *The man won't give you credit, you numskull!* □ *When your man doesn't show, there's always a good reason.* **4.** AND **the man** *n.* the police; the establishment. (Black.) □ *You better check with the man before you get seen with me.* □ *We are about to rap a little with my man.*

**M. and M.s** *n.* capsules of Seconal™, a barbiturate. (From the brand name of a type of brightly-colored candy pellets.) □ *Is there somewhere around here I can get some M. and M.s?* □ *No M. and M.s for me. I'm on blues.*

**Manhattan white** AND **Manhattan silver** *n.* an imaginary, white (from lack of sunlight) marijuana that grows from seeds flushed down the New York City sewer system. (Completely jocular.) □ *Some clown on the corner was trying to sell Manhattan white to the tourists.* □ *The package was supposed to contain Manhattan silver. The lab tests show it to be some dried Boston fern.*

**manicure 1.** *tr.* to trim and clean marijuana for smoking. (Drugs.) □ *Bruno never would manicure the stuff. Some people would buy it anyway.* □ *Max wants to manicure his own dope.* **2.** *n.* good-quality, cleaned marijuana. □ *Ah, this manicure should bring some good coin.* □ *You got any high Q. manicure?*

**man on the street 1.** *n.* the common man; just anyone selected at random. □ *But what does the man on the street think about all this?* □ *The man on the street really doesn't care about most of*

*what you think is important.* **2.** *mod.*
common; everyday. (Usually **man-on-
the-street**.) □ *These man-on-the-street
interviews all seem sort of phony.* □ *The
man-on-the-street opinion spots are fun
to make, but we can't show half of them.*
**man-size(d)** *mod.* large-size, especially
in reference to the size of servings of
food. □ *This is a man-sized steak! That's
what I want.* □ *For a man-size meal,
open a can of Wallace's Chili tonight!*
**map 1.** *n.* one's face. □ *There was fear
and hatred all over his map.* □ *With a
map like that, she could really go somewhere.* **2.** *n.* sheet music. (Jazz musicians. See also *chart*.) □ *Check my
map, and see where you come in.* □ *I
left the map at home. Can I look at
yours?*
**marathons** ['mɛrəθɑnz] *n.* amphetamines. (Drugs.) □ *She is running on
marathons and no food at all.* □ *Now,
these things they call "marathons" because they keep you running day and
night.*
**marble dome** *n.* a stupid person. (Someone who has marble where brains should
be.) □ *The guy's a marble dome. He has
no knowledge of what's going on around
him.* □ *Is this marble dome giving you
any trouble?*
**marble orchard** AND **Marble City** *n.* a
cemetery. □ *I already bought a little
plot in a marble orchard.* □ *When I take
a trip to Marble City, I want truckloads
of flowers.*
**marbles 1.** *n.* capsules of Placidyl™, a
hypnotic sedative. (Drugs.) □ *I don't
like those marbles.* □ *The cops found a
couple of marbles in her purse.* **2.** *n.*
one's wits; one's reasoning power. (Always *someone's marbles.* See also *lose
(all) one's marbles*.) □ *If I had my full
quota of marbles, I could handle this.* □
*When your marbles are lost, you're done
for.*
**mari** ['mɛri] *n.* marijuana; a marijuana
cigarette. (Drugs. See *Mary*.) □ *How
about a little mari on me?* □ *How much
do you want for a mari?*
**mariholic** [mɛrɪ'hɑlɪk] *n.* a person psy-
chically addicted to marijuana. (Patterned on *alcoholic*.) □ *This child was
a mariholic at age 11!* □ *Mariholics
tend to lack ambition.*

**marijane** [mɛrɪ'dʒen] *n.* marijuana. (Drugs.)
□ *Marijane has been around since the
turn of the century.* □ *You'd be amazed
at how many country kids use marijane.*
**marijuanaful** [mɛrə'wɑnəfl]] *mod.* having to do with (wonderful) marijuana.
□ *Ah, this stuff is really marijuanaful!*
□ *Well, Bruno, it looks like you're having another marijuanaful day.*
**marine** AND **marine recruit, marine officer**
*n.* an empty beer or liquor bottle. (Another version of *dead soldier* or *dead
marine*. This implies that marines often
end up dead.) □ *Every now and then the
gentle muttering of the customers was
accented by the breaking of a marine as
it hit the floor.* □ *The guy in a uniform
tossed the marine officer in the barrel
and giggled.*
**mariweegee** [mɛrɪ'widʒi] *n.* marijuana.
(Drugs. Black.) □ *Give the man some
mariweegee for his trouble.* □ *It's just
a little mariweegee. Irvine won't mind
that one bit.*
**mark** *n.* a *dupe*; a victim selected for a
theft or a swindle. (Underworld.) □ *I
bumped the mark on the shoulder, and
he put his hand on his wallet just like
always.* □ *We picked the marks out of
the crowd in front of the two-dollar window.*
**mark time** *tr.* to wait; to do nothing but
wait. □ *I'll just mark time till things get
better.* □ *Do you expect me to just stand
here and mark time?*
**martooni** [mɑr'tuni] *n.* the martini, a
gin-based mixed drink. (As if pronounced by a drunken person.) □ *I'll
have just one more martooni, innkeeper.* □ *I am going to drink three double
martoonis, and I might as well have
them all at once.*
**Mary 1.** *n.* morphine. (Drugs.) □ *Mary
was at the root of an addiction problem
for years before the other mari came
along.* □ *Mary was first made as a cure
for opium addiction.* **2.** AND **mari**
*n.* marijuana. (Drugs. Can be used as a
code name.) □ *Max pulled a little packet of Mary out of his pocket.* □ *Somebody told me that Mary is here. Is that
right?*
**Mary Jane** AND **Mary J., Maryjane**
*n.* marijuana. (Drugs. See also *Jane*.) □

*I can't live another day without Mary Jane!* □ *I could sure rap with Mary Jane about now.*

**Mary Warner** AND **Mary Werner, Mary Worner** *n.* marijuana. □ *This guy came in and said he was looking for Mary Warner. I told him she must have been the last tenant.* □ *"Does Mary Worner live here?" he asked.*

**mash** *in.* to neck and pet. (Collegiate.) □ *Who are those two mashing in the corner?* □ *I can't spend every evening mashing with you!*

**mashed** *mod.* alcohol intoxicated. □ *Both guys were totally mashed. I called my brother, who came and rescued me.* □ *Bruno was mashed, but he wouldn't let anyone else drive.*

**massive** *mod.* excellent. (California.) □ *The bash at Tiffany's was, like, massive!* □ *That was a totally massive party, Tiff.*

**massively** *mod.* excellently; totally. □ *Max showed up for the meeting massively stoned and singing at the top of his lungs.* □ *Robert presented us with a massively gross belch that actually made the window rattle a little.*

**match(box)** *n.* a small matchbox full of marijuana. (Drugs.) □ *How much for a match of manicure?* □ *I'm looking for a matchbox for a friend.*

**Maui Waui** AND **Maui (wowee), Maui wowie** ['mɑui 'wɑui] *n.* a potent variety of marijuana grown on the island of Maui, Hawaii. (Drugs.) □ *Maui wowee is all the craze on the East Coast now.* □ *Is there any such thing as Maui Waui, or is it just a joke?*

**maven** AND **mavin** ['mevn̩] *n.* an expert; a self-proclaimed expert. (From Hebrew *mevin* via Yiddish.) □ *A maven in the stock market you are not.* □ *Harriet—a well-known clothing mavin in Rochester—keeps giving pointers on fabrics, but I don't listen.*

**maw** [mɔ] *tr. & in.* to kiss and pet; to smooch. (Probably from *maul*.) □ *Come on, don't maw me. You've been watching too many movies—or too few.* □ *Let's go out somewhere and maw.*

**max** *n.* the maximum. (See also *to the max*.) □ *Is this the max I can have?* □ *I want the max. I'm hungry.*

**maxed out 1.** *mod.* exhausted; tired. □ *I am just maxed out. I haven't been getting enough sleep.* □ *I had to stop work because I almost maxed out on the keyboard.* **2.** *mod.* alcohol intoxicated. □ *Sam was maxed out and seemed happy enough to sit under the table and whimper.* □ *I hadn't seen Barlowe so maxed out in years. He was nearly paralyzed.*

**mayo** ['meo] *n.* mayonnaise. □ *You want mayo or mustard?* □ *I'll take both mayo and mustard, thank you.*

**mazulla** See *mazuma*.

**mazuma** AND **mazulla** [mə'zumə AND mə'zulə] *n.* money. (From Hebrew *mezu* via Yiddish.) □ *How much mazuma do you want for this?* □ *She's got more mazuma than she knows what to do with.*

**McCoy** See *(real) McCoy*.

**McDoctor(s)** AND **McDoc(s)** *n.* a jocular term for a walk-in emergency medical clinic as found in shopping malls. (Compare to *doc(s)-in-a-box*.) □ *They took the kid to McDoctors, or whatever it is, over in the mall.* □ *McDocs is not cheap, but it's handy.*

**McD's** AND **McDuck's** *n.* McDonald's, the franchised fast-food restaurant. (Teens and collegiate. The *duck* is a play on the Walt Disney character "Donald Duck.") □ *Can you take McD's tonight, or do you want some slow food?* □ *I can always handle McDuck's.*

**McDuck's** See the previous entry.

**M.C.P.** AND **male chauvinist pig** *n.* a male who acts superior to and aggressively toward women. (From the women's liberation movements of the 1970s.) □ *The guy is just a male chauvinist pig, and he'll never change.* □ *Don't you just hate walking through a room filled with M.C.P.s and just knowing what they are thinking about you?*

**mean 1.** *mod.* having to do with someone or something that is very good. □ *This music is mean, man, mean. What a great sound!* □ *This is the meanest wine I ever drank.* **2.** *mod.* having to do with an excellent example of the art of doing something well habitually. (Always with *a* as in the examples.) □ *John plays the piano quite well. Fred says that*

*John plays a mean piano.* □ *You may say that your mother bakes delicious pies, but all my friends say she bakes a mean pie.* □ *Tom says that his father plays a mean game of golf.*

**mean business** *tr.* to be very, very serious. □ *Stop laughing! I mean business.* □ *I could tell from the look on her face that she meant business.*

**mean-green 1.** *n.* money. □ *How much of that mean-green do you need?* □ *Can I borrow a little mean-green till payday?* **2.** *n.* phencyclidine, *P.C.P.* (Drugs.) □ *He's stoned on mean-green.* □ *The hog that's nearly spoiled turns yellowish and is called mean-green.*

**meany** AND **meanie** *n.* a mean or grouchy person. □ *Come on! Don't be such a meany.* □ *I don't want to be a meany, but if you don't turn down that radio, I don't know what I'll do.*

**meathead** *n.* a stupid oaf. □ *Don't call him a meathead. He does his best.* □ *Is this meathead bothering you, miss?*

**meatheaded** *mod.* stupid; simpleminded. □ *Of all the meatheaded ideas. This one takes the cake!* □ *How meatheaded!* □ *When someone conducts a meatheaded operation like this, we tend to lose faith in the whole system.*

**meathooks** *n.* the hands. (See also *hooks*.) □ *Get your meathooks off my car!* □ *If your meathooks so much as brush by my jacket again, you are finished!*

**meat wagon** *n.* an ambulance. □ *The meat wagon showed up just as they were pulling what was left of Marty out of what was left of her car.* □ *When the meat wagon stops at all the traffic lights on the way to the hospital, you know somebody's pifted.*

**medico** ['mɛdɪko] *n.* a doctor. (From Spanish.) □ *The medico says I should lose some weight.* □ *It's hard to take it seriously when a fat medico tells you to shed a few pounds.*

**meet** *n.* a meeting or an appointment. (Mostly underworld.) □ *If this meet works out, we could score a cool million.* □ *What time is the meet?*

**meeting of the minds** *n.* a consensus; an agreement. □ *At last we've reached a meeting of the minds.* □ *This meeting of the minds is nothing more than a truce.*

**mega** ['mɛgə] *mod.* large. □ *Some mega beast boogied down to the front of the auditorium and started screaming.* □ *You see I have this, like, mega problem, ya know.*

**megabucks** ['mɛgəbəks] *n.* a lot of money; *big bucks*. (See also *kilobucks*.) □ *A stereo that size must cost megabucks.* □ *Mr. Wilson has megabucks in pharmaceutical stocks.*

**megadork** ['mɛgədork] *n.* a very stupid person. (See *dork*.) □ *What a wimpy megadork!* □ *Tiffany, you are, like, such a megadork!*

**megillah** [məˈgɪlə] *n.* a long and complicated story. (From Hebrew *megillah* via Yiddish.) □ *He struggled through this megillah and nobody believed him.* □ *Here you come in here with this megillah about a flat tire and how your brother-in-law stole your jack and how your arthritis is kicking up—what do you think I am, some sort of shoulder to cry on?*

**mell of a hess** *n.* "hell of a mess." (A deliberate spoonerism.) □ *What a mell of a hess you've gotten us into this time.* □ *Have you ever seen such a mell of a hess?*

**mellow 1.** *mod.* relaxed; untroubled; *laid back*. □ *Being mellow is my only goal in life.* □ *She is the mellowest fox I know.* **2.** *mod.* slightly alcohol or drug intoxicated. □ *I got mellow and stopped drinking right there.* □ *I'm only mellow, but you drive anyway.*

**mellow out 1.** *in.* to calm down; to get less angry. □ *When you mellow out, maybe we can talk.* □ *Come on, man, mellow out!* **2.** *in.* to become generally more relaxed; to grow less contentious. □ *Gary was nearly forty before he started to mellow out a little and take life less seriously.* □ *After his illness, he mellowed out and seemed more glad to be alive.*

**meltdown** *n.* a total collapse of anything. (From the term used to describe the self-destruction of a nuclear reactor.) □ *There seems to have been a meltdown in the computer center, and all our records were lost.* □ *The meltdown in the financial markets was caused by a combination of things.*

**melvin** ['mɛlvən] *n.* a studious or unattractive male. (Teens and collegiate.) □ *Gary is such a melvin!* □ *Do you think I would go out with that melvin?*

**men in blue** AND **boys in blue** *n.* the police; policemen. □ *The men in blue are looking for you.* □ *You can depend on the boys in blue to clean things up in this town.*

**mensch** [mɛntʃ] *n.* a mature and responsible person. (From German via Yiddish.) □ *Now there goes a real mensch!* □ *I am honored to invite such a mensch into my home.*

**men's room** *n.* a men's restroom. □ *Where's the men's room, please?* □ *I gotta use the men's room.*

**mental\*** **1.\*** *mod.* mentally retarded. (Caution with topic.) □ *The girl's mental. Leave her alone.* □ *Everybody in this ward is mental.* **2.\*** *n.* a mentally retarded person. (Caution with topic.) □ *He's a mental. He'll need some help.* □ *Who doesn't need help? Mentals are normal on that point.* **3.** *n.* a stupid person. □ *You're such a mental lately.* □ *Don't be a mental.*

**mental giant** *n.* a genius. □ *I'm no mental giant, but I do know trouble when I see it.* □ *Don was a mental giant, but didn't ever take advantage of it.*

**mental midget** *n.* a stupid person. □ *I hate to seem like a mental midget, but what's so great about that?* □ *This mental midget here thinks he can solve it for us.*

**mep(s)** *n.* meperdine, Demerol™, a painkiller. (Drugs and hospitals.) □ *The nurse was sneaking a little meps now and then.* □ *For some people, mep is highly addictive.*

**merchandise** *n.* any contraband. (Underworld.) □ *The merchandise is still at the boss's place.* □ *How much of the merchandise can you deliver by midnight?*

**mercy buckets** See *messy buckets.*

**merger-mania** *n.* an apparent need for companies to merge with one another. (Financial markets and journalism.) □ *Merger-mania is in the news again tonight with Ford's offer to take over GMC.* □ *The market meltdown put an end to merger-mania.*

**mesc** [mɛsk] *n.* mescaline, a hallucinatory substance. (Drugs.) □ *Tiffany is totally hooked on mesc. I don't know where she gets it.* □ *Jerry refuses to take mesc or any other dope.*

**mesh** *n.* a crosshatch or octothorpe, "#". (See *pigpen.*) □ *Put a mesh on each end of your formula.* □ *What does the mesh stand for in this equation?*

**meshuga** AND **meshugah** [məˈʃugə] *mod.* crazy. (From Hebrew *meshuggah* via Yiddish.) □ *What a meshuga day!* □ *This guy is meshugah!*

**mess 1.** *n.* a hopeless, stupid person. □ *Harry has turned into a mess!* □ *The guy's a mess!* **2.** *n.* dung. (Usually with *a.*) □ *There is a dog mess on the lawn again this morning.* □ *There's a mess in Jimmy's diapers, Mom.*

**mess around (with someone or something)** AND **mess about (with someone or something), monkey around (with someone or something) 1.** *in.* [with *someone*] to play with someone sexually. □ *Those two have been messing around.* □ *Tod was messing around with Maria, and now she's storked.* **2.** *in.* [with *someone*] to waste someone's time. □ *Don't mess around with me. Just answer the question, if you please.* □ *I don't have the time for this. Stop messing around.* **3.** *in.* [with *someone*] to waste time with someone else. □ *I was messing around with John.* □ *John and I were monkeying around.* **4.** *in.* [with *something*] to play with or fiddle with something. □ *Don't mess around with the ash tray.* □ *You'll break it if you don't stop messing about with it.*

**messed up 1.** *mod.* confused. □ *I'm sort of messed up since my divorce.* □ *Most kids are sort of messed up at this age.* **2.** *mod.* alcohol or drug intoxicated. □ *Somehow I must have got messed up. What caused it, do you think?* □ *Everybody at the party was too messed up to drive home.* **3.** *mod.* addicted; debilitated physically and mentally by drug use. (Drugs.) □ *I was a druggy, and by the age of 12 I was too messed up with H. to get anything out of school.* □ *See the needle marks on his arm? That means he's probably messed up.*

**mess someone or something up** AND **mess up someone or something** **1.** *tr.* to put someone or something into disorder. □ *Who messed this place up?* □ *You messed me up a little bit, but I know you didn't mean to bump into me.* (More at *messed up.*) **2.** *tr.* [with *someone*] to beat someone up. (Underworld.) □ *The boss says me and the boys is supposed to mess you up a little.* □ *Is that your job—going around messing up people?*

**mess someone's face up** AND **mess up someone's face** *tr.* to beat someone around the face. (Underworld.) □ *You want me to mess up your face, or do you want to come along quietly?* □ *I had to mess his face up a little, boss, but he's been real cooperative since then.*

**mess up** *in.* to make an error; to do something wrong; to *flub (up).* □ *I hope I don't mess up on the quiz.* □ *You really messed up!*

**mess with someone or something** AND **monkey with someone or something** *in.* to bother or interfere with someone or something. □ *Come on, don't monkey with it.* □ *Don't mess with me unless you want trouble.*

**messy bucket(s)** AND **mercy buckets, murky bucket(s)** *in.* "thanks." (From French *merci beaucoup.*) □ *That's very nice. Murky buckets.* □ *Messy bucket for the cookies you sent.*

**meth** **1.** *n.* denatured alcohol; methyl alcohol. (Streets. Underworld.) □ *Oh, yeah, we drank meth. We drank anything we could get.* □ *Meth used to be pink. Now they put something in it to make you vomit.* **2.** *n.* methamphetamine. (Drugs.) □ *Usually meth is injected, having almost an immediate effect.* □ *Meth comes in little glass tubes.* **3.** *n.* methadone. (Drugs.) □ *Sometimes meth means methadone, a drug used in drug treatment.* □ *Jerry gets meth from a clinic in the city.*

**meth freak** AND **methhead** *n.* a habitual user of methamphetamine. (Drugs.) □ *The guy was jumping around like a meth freak.* □ *They pulled a methfreak out of the river this morning.*

**methhead** See *meth freak.*

**meth monster** *n.* a habitual user of methamphetamine. □ *Sometimes a meth monster will do okay in school.* □ *These teenage meth monsters can be a real menace when they need juice.*

**metros** ['metroz] *n.* the police; the metropolitan police. (Not used in all metropolitan areas.) □ *The metros took ten minutes to get to the scene of the crime, and the entire city is enraged.* □ *The metros showed up and managed traffic for the fire company.*

**Mexican breakfast** *n.* a cigarette and a cup of coffee or a glass of water. □ *After a Mexican breakfast, I went to Barlowe's hotel, hoping to catch him before he went out.* □ *When some punk kid crosses the border into Mexico for a night of fun and games, all he can get to help him sober up and get out of the country the next day is a Mexican breakfast.*

**Mexican brown** **1.** *n.* a brownish Mexican marijuana. (Drugs.) □ *That Acapulco gold you scored is nothing but Mexican brown.* □ *If you burned a kilo at one time, Mexican brown wouldn't give you a decent high.* **2.** AND **Mexican mud** *n.* weak heroin from Mexico. (Drugs.) □ *Mexican brown is mostly sugar.* □ *This Mexican mud might be good in your coffee, but it's not worth much otherwise.*

**Mexican bush** *n.* low-quality marijuana from Mexico. (Drugs.) □ *You can send this Mexican bush back where you got it!* □ *You can call it Mexican bush if you want. I call it sagebrush.*

**Mexican mud** See *Mexican brown.*

**Mexican standoff** *n.* a hopeless standoff; a hopeless staring match. □ *We finally got to the point where it was a Mexican standoff. Nobody won.* □ *A Mexican standoff is better than a fight.*

**mic** AND **mike** [maɪk] *n.* a microgram. □ *There were just two mics of dust on his cuff, and they nailed him for it.* □ *How many mics do I have to grind off?*

**Michoacan** AND **Mishwacan** [mɪʃəˈwɑkən AND mɪʃˈwɑkən] *n.* potent marijuana from Michoacan, a Mexican state. (Drugs.) □ *Michoacan was good ten years ago. Now you don't know what any of this dope really is.* □ *Some of* *these rip-off artists sell ragweed as Mish-wacan.*

**mickey** AND **micky 1.** *n.* a hip flask for liquor. □ *He took a little swig out of a mickey he carries in his pocket.* □ *His micky made a clunk as he sat down.* **2.** See *Mickey Finn.* **3.** *n.* a small bottle of wine. □ *See if you can get a mickey of something for a buck.* □ *The old guy just wants to get a micky to help with his wineache.* **4.** *n.* a tranquilizer. (Drugs.) □ *Whatever that mickey was you gave me, it helped.* □ *Maybe a little mickey would help me relax.*

**Mickey D's** *n.* McDonald's fast-food restaurant. (Teens and collegiate.) □ *Let's hit Mickey D's for chow this noon.* □ *We're going to Mickey D's for dinner, too.*

**Mickey finished** *mod.* alcohol intoxicated; totally drunk. (A play on *Mickey Finn.*) □ *I guess the old guy is about Mickey finished. He's plootered!* □ *What gets into guys that makes them want to get Mickey finished before they stop?*

**Mickey (Finn) 1.** *n.* a drink containing chloral hydrate; a drink containing a fast-acting laxative. □ *He slipped her a Mickey Finn, but she switched glasses.* □ *Once you've had a Mickey, you'll never forget it.* **2.** *n.* chloral hydrate as put in drinks to knock people out. □ *There was a Mickey Finn in this drink, wasn't there?* □ *Now where would I get a Mickey?*

**mickey mouse 1.** *n.* nonsense; something trivial. (From the Walt Disney character by the same name.) □ *This is just a lot of mickey mouse.* □ *This mickey mouse is wasting my time.* **2.** *mod.* trivial; time-wasting; lousy. □ *I want out of this mickey mouse place.* □ *No more mickey mouse questions if I agree to stay?* **3.** *n.* a police officer. (Streets.) □ *Mickey mouse is hanging around asking about you.* □ *Tell mickey mouse he knows where to find me.* **4.** *n.* a bit of blotter impregnated with *L.S.D.* with a picture of mickey mouse on it. (Drugs.) □ *How much is the mickey mouse?* □ *The mickey mouse is more than you want to pay.*

**mickey mouse ears** *n.* the two lights found on top of a police car. □ *There*

*were no mickey mouse ears, but the jerk inside looked like your average ossifer.* □ *I could see the outline of the mickey mouse ears on the blue and white behind me.*

**mickey mouse habit** *n.* a trivial drug habit. (Drugs.) □ *Nothing to it. Just a little mickey mouse habit. I can stop any time I want.* □ *I don't care if it is a mickey mouse habit. It's a habit, and it's illegal.*

**middle brow** *mod.* middle-class; average or mediocre. (Between *highbrow* and *lowbrow.*) □ *She has average middle brow tastes and drives a mid-size Chevrolet.* □ *He's just too middle brow.* □ *There are some who look down on middle brow interests as trivial.*

**middle of nowhere** *n.* an isolated place. □ *I don't want to stay out here in the middle of nowhere.* □ *I was stranded in the middle of nowhere for an hour with a flat tire.*

**midi** ['mɪdi] **1.** *n.* a mid-length woman's garment. □ *Shall I wear my midi, or is it too hot?* □ *The midi is okay.* **2.** *mod.* having to do with a mid-length woman's garment. □ *This midi style is out, and the mini is back in.* □ *The midi length was just transitional. Who decides on these things anyway?*

**miffed** ['mɪft] *mod.* slighted; offended. □ *She seemed sort of miffed when I told her.* □ *Don't get so miffed. It was only a joke.*

**mighty** *mod.* very. (Folksy.) □ *I'm mighty tired of all your questions.* □ *Well, I'm mighty glad you came.*

**Mighty Joe Young** *n.* a powerful addiction to drugs. (Drugs. Named for a giant movie ape.) □ *She has a wicked habit—a Mighty Joe Young.* □ *That monkey on his back is a Mighty Joe Young.*

**mike** See *mic.*

**milk 1.** *tr.* to attempt to persuade an audience to laugh or applaud. □ *Mitzy tried to milk the audience for applause.* □ *She went on milking the crowd for adulation long after they had demonstrated their appreciation.* **2.** *tr.* to attempt to get recognition from an audience. □ *His performance was marred by an amateurish attempt to milk applause.*

□ *If you're good, they'll let you know it. If not, don't milk cheers, applause, or laughter.*

**milled** *mod.* alcohol intoxicated. (See also *cut.*) □ *She was cut up with all that booze—milled, I guess.* □ *She was too milled to drive and couldn't walk either.*

**milquetoast** ['mɪlktost] *n.* a shy coward; an effeminate male. (See *Casper Milquetoast.*) □ *This little milquetoast goes up to the biker, looks at him sort of sad-like, and then karate chops him into a quivering pulp.* □ *Some guy who looked like a milquetoast came in and asked for a set of brass knuckles.*

**Milwaukee goiter** AND **German goiter** [mɪl'wɔki 'gɔɪdɚ AND 'dʒɚmən 'gɔɪdɚ] *n.* a beer belly. (Refers to Milwaukee, Wisconsin, a major beer-brewing city, and to Germany.) □ *By the time he was 26, he was balding and had a Milwaukee goiter that would tip him over if he turned too fast.* □ *He was proud of his German goiter.*

**mind-bender** AND **mind-blower** *n.* a hallucinogenic drug, typically *L.S.D.* (Drugs.) □ *You wanna try some mind-blower?* □ *That mind-bender takes a long time to wear off.*

**mind your own beeswax** [...'bizwæks] *tr.* to "mind one's own business." (Juvenile.) □ *You just mind your own beeswax!* □ *Lay off! Mind your own beeswax!*

**mingy** ['mɪndʒi] *mod.* "mean" and "stingy." □ *Why can't you borrow it? I'm just mingy, that's all.* □ *What a mingy jerk!* □ *Aw, don't be so mingy!*

**mini** ['mɪni] **1.** *mod.* small; miniature. □ *I have a mini problem you can maybe help me with.* □ *This is just a mini office. I'll get a bigger one later.* **2.** *n.* a miniskirt. □ *I look pretty good in a mini.* □ *I'll try a mini this time. I was too plump the last time they were in style.*

**mink** *n.* a woman. (Black.) □ *I see your mink has some new silks, man.* □ *Take this home to your mink. She'll like it.*

**Minnehaha** [mɪni'hɑhɑ] *n.* champagne. (From Longfellow's *Song of Hiawatha.* *Minnehaha* means "laughing waters.") □ *Have a glass of Minnehaha.* □ *Minnehaha tickles my nose.*

**minstrel** See *black and white.*

**mint** *n.* a lot of money. □ *He makes a mint. He can afford a little generosity.* □ *That kind of car costs a mint!*

**miser** ['mɑɪzɚ] *n.* a device for holding a marijuana cigarette butt. (Drugs.) □ *I lost my miser. You got one?* □ *I'll show you how to use a miser. You're throwing the best part away.*

**mish-mash** AND **mish-mosh** ['mɪʃmæʃ AND 'mɪʃmɑʃ] *n.* a mixture; a disorderly conglomeration. □ *What a mish-mash of colors and designs!* □ *There's no theme or focus. It's just a mish-mash.*

**miss a trick** AND **miss any tricks** *tr.* to neglect or overlook something. (Usually negative.) □ *He didn't miss a trick. He tried everything.* □ *She hadn't missed any tricks when she chose her clothes.*

**missionary** *n.* a drug pusher who attempts to create new customers. (Drugs.) □ *Max is a missionary—the kind the judges want to send straight to hell.* □ *Missionaries who pass out monkey bait to young kids are going to see the inside of a house of correction for a long time.*

**miss the boat** *tr.* to have made an error; to be wrong. □ *If you think you can do that, you have just missed the boat.* □ *The guy's missed the boat. He's a lunkhead.*

**mitt** *n.* a hand. □ *Get your mitts off my glass.* □ *The kid's got mitts on him like a gorilla.*

**mixed (up)** **1.** *mod.* confused; mentally troubled. □ *I was a little mixed up after the accident.* □ *This kid's just a little mixed. She'll straighten out.* □ *She's a crazy mixed up kid.* **2.** *mod.* alcohol intoxicated. □ *I'm just a little mixed up, nothing serious. No reason you should be swaying around like that.* □ *Jerry's too mixed to drive home.*

**mix it up (with someone)** *tr.* to fight with someone; to quarrel with someone. □ *Max and Bruno mixed it up for a while, and then things calmed down.* □ *Max came out of the shop and began to mix it up with Bruno.*

**M.J.** *n.* marijuana. (Drugs. From the initials of *Mary Jane.*) □ *Let's go talk with M.J.* □ *He found a little bag of M.J. under the car seat.*

**mo** AND **M.O.** *n.* marijuana. (Drugs. Initials and acronym.) □ *You got a little mo I can bum?* □ *Where's somebody who can come up with some M.O.?*

**mob** [mɑb] *n.* the crime syndicate. (Underworld and journalistic.) □ *The mob has held this city in abject terror for years.* □ *One of the biggest fish in the mob was pulled from the river yesterday.*

**moby** ['mobi] **1.** *mod.* enormous; unwieldy. (Like Herman Melville's great white whale, *Moby Dick.*) □ *This is a very moby old car.* □ *Why does he let himself get so moby?* **2.** *n.* a "megabyte," a measurement of computer memory size. (A megabyte is whale-sized compared to a kilobyte.) □ *My fixed disks give me a capacity of over 75 mobies.* □ *My new computer has one moby of random access memory.*

**mod** [mɑd] *mod.* contemporary and fashionable in clothing and ideas. □ *Your clothes are mod, but you're just a plain, old-fashioned prude.* □ *Your mod friends might appreciate this article in the paper.*

**mod poser** ['mɑd 'pozɚ] *n.* someone who looks mod in dress only. (Collegiate.) □ *Tiffany is such a mod poser. At home it's jeans and a T-shirt.* □ *The more extreme the style gets, the more mod posers there are.*

**moist around the edges** *mod.* alcohol intoxicated. □ *Charlie is more than moist around the edges. He is soused.* □ *Didn't that guy seem a little moist around the edges?*

**mojo** ['modʒo] **1.** *n.* heroin; morphine; cannabis. (Drugs. See also *on the mojo.*) □ *This mojo is no good.* □ *Why don't you try to kick the mojo?* **2.** *n.* a narcotics addict. (Drugs.) □ *These mojos will rob you blind if you don't keep an eye on them.* □ *Bruno's no mojo, and if he was nobody'd mention it.*

**moldy fig** *n.* an old-fashioned person; a square. □ *Don't be a moldy fig! Lighten up!* □ *Some moldy fig objected to our music.*

**mom** *n.* a mother. (Also a term of address. Capitalized when used as the name of one's own mother.) □ *My mom is the greatest!* □ *Mom, can I have a bigger allowance?*

**mondo** ['mɑndo] *mod.* totally. (California.) □ *You are, like, mondo gross!* □ *This place is like, so, like, mondo beige.*

**moneybags** *n.* a nickname for a wealthy person. □ *When old moneybags does finally buy the farm, who gets the loot?* □ *When you get to be a big moneybags, don't forget those you left behind.*

**money from home 1.** *n.* easily gotten money. (Underworld.) □ *There is nothing to a simple con job like this. It's money from home.* □ *This job is like taking candy from a kid. It's money from home.* **2.** *n.* something as welcome as long-awaited money from home. □ *This cool drink is money from home right now.* □ *Having you visit like this is like getting money from home, Molly.*

**money grubber** *n.* a stingy person. □ *Why is he such a money grubber? Is he going to take it with him?* □ *The boss is such a money grubber. He still has his first paper clip.*

**money talks** *phr.* "money can buy cooperation"; "having money makes one influential." □ *I know that money talks, but I don't have the scratch to say anything with.* □ *Like they say, money talks, but don't try making it talk to a cop.*

**moniker** AND **monniker** ['mɑnəkɚ] *n.* a nickname. □ *What's your moniker, chum?* □ *With a monniker like that, you must get in a lot of fights.*

**monkey 1.** *n.* a playful child. (Also a term of address.) □ *Come here, you little monkey!* □ *Hey, monkey, where are you going?* **2.** *n.* a drug addiction. (Drugs. See *have a monkey on one's back.*) □ *That monkey of mine is getting hungry again.* □ *Why don't you try to get rid of that monkey?* **3.** *n.* a drug addict. (Drugs. Black.) □ *Some monkey lay there in the alley, rolling back and forth—in ecstasy, I guess.* □ *The guy's a monkey! He can't help himself.* **4.** *n.* a kilogram of drugs. (Drugs. An elaboration of *key.*) □ *Where can I find a monkey of grass?* □ *I don't want a whole monkey. I'm no moneybags.*

**monkey around (with someone or something)** See *mess around (with someone or something).*

**monkey bait** n. free samples of an addictive drug. (Drugs.) □ *Don't you dare take any of that monkey bait from that man!* □ *Max started out by taking monkey bait from a bunch of different pushers and selling it himself.*

**monkey bite** n. a kiss that leaves a blotch or mark. (See also *hickey.*) □ *Who gave you that monkey bite?* □ *Do you have some makeup that'll cover this monkey bite?*

**monkey business** AND **funny business** n. silliness; dishonest tricks. □ *That's enough monkey business. Now, settle down.* □ *Stop the funny business. This is serious!*

**monkeyshines** n. tricks; small acts of mischief. □ *You and your silly monkeyshines!* □ *These kids are a lot of fun despite their monkeyshines.*

**monkey swill** n. inferior liquor; strong liquor. □ *This monkey swill will probably make me blind.* □ *Where did you get this monkey swill? This would kill a monkey anyway.*

**monkey talk** n. distorted speech, as uttered while drug intoxicated. (Drugs.) □ *Max slapped the poor junky to get him to stop the monkey talk.* □ *Their pupils are pinpoint-sized, and they talk monkey talk. That's how you can tell they're on H.*

**monkey wagon** n. drug addiction. (Drugs.) □ *I've been riding this monkey wagon long enough.* □ *Some of these treatment centers won't get you off the monkey wagon unless you have insurance.*

**monkey wards** n. "Montgomery Wards," a department store chain. □ *I get that kind of stuff at monkey wards.* □ *They closed the monkey wards near us.*

**monkey with someone or something** See *mess with someone or something.*

**monolithic** [manəˈlɪθɪk] mod. heavily drug intoxicated. (Drugs. A play on *stoned.*) □ *She's not just stoned, she's monolithic!* □ *I was monolithic—dead drunk.*

**monster** 1. n. any powerful drug affecting the central nervous system. (Drugs.) □ *This P.C.P. is a monster. Why don't the cops put a stop to it?* □ *That monster just about did me in.* 2. mod. having to do with a powerful or addictive drug. (Drugs.) □ *Where the devil did you get*

that monster dust? □ *That is monster C., and it will make you its slave.*

**monster weed** n. cannabis; powerful marijuana. (Drugs.) □ *Where on earth does she get that monster weed she's been blowing?* □ *This is what they call monster weed. Stay away from it. It may have angel dust on it.*

**Montezuma's revenge** [mantəˈzuməz rɪˈvɛndʒ] n. diarrhea; tourist diarrhea. (Refers to tourists in Mexico.) □ *I had a little touch of Montezuma's revenge the second day, but other than that we had a wonderful time.* □ *Most people blame Montezuma's revenge on the water.*

**monthlies** n. the period of menstruation. □ *It's her monthlies. You know how she feels then.* □ *The monthlies have struck again!*

**mooch** [mutʃ] 1. tr. & in. to beg for money, liquor, or drugs in public places. □ *No mooching around here! Move along!* □ *Jed mooched drinks all evening.* 2. n. a beggar. □ *The guy is a mooch. Get him out of here.* □ *I don't want to be a mooch, but could I borrow your lawn mower?* 3. n. narcotics. (Drugs. Compare to *hooch.*) □ *Mooch is what Minnie the Moocher is famous for.* □ *He's gonna have to work hard to get off the mooch.*

**moocher** 1. n. a beggar. □ *What do you usually give a moocher?* □ *I try to give every moocher a little change.* 2. n. a drug addict. (Drugs.) □ *The guy's a moocher and can't be trusted.* □ *These moochers will do anything to get a few bucks for a load.*

**moo juice** AND **cow juice** n. milk. □ *How about another glass of moo juice?* □ *While you're at the store, get some more cow juice.*

**moolah** [ˈmulɑ] n. money. (Originally underworld.) □ *That is a whole lot of moolah!* □ *There was no moolah in that safe!*

**moon** 1. n. the buttocks. □ *He rubbed a plump moon where he had been kicked, but said no more.* □ *She fell square on her moon and slowly broke into a smile.* 2. tr. & in. to show (someone) one's nude posterior through a window (usually of an automobile). (Compare to *gaucho*.) □ *When the plane flew over Cuba, this guy named Victor actually mooned a Russian M.I.G. that flew by.* □ *The kids were mooning, and they got arrested for indecent exposure.* (More at *mooner*.) **3.** *n.* alcohol; whisky; *moonshine.* (Folksy.) □ *Where's my jug of moon?* □ *Some kid came in and ran off with my last jar of moon.* **4.** AND **moons** *n.* a portion of peyote cactus eaten for its mescaline content. (Drugs.) □ *You got any moons?* □ *Harry actually went to the desert to try to find some moon.* **5.** *n.* a cake of hashish. (Drugs.) □ *A whole moon ought to last you a while.* □ *How much for a moon?*

**mooner 1.** *n.* a drunkard. (From *moonshine*.) □ *This old mooner from up in the hills wandered into town last Friday and died in the town square.* □ *There must be dozens of mooners who beg in town in the day and drink in the woods at night.* **2.** *n.* an idler who stares at the moon. □ *If he ever outgrows being a mooner, he may be all right.* □ *I feel like a mooner tonight. There is nothing better to do.*

**moonlight 1.** *n.* illicit liquor; *moonshine.* □ *Where's that bottle of moonlight you used to keep under the counter?* □ *How about a sip of moonlight?* **2.** *in.* to traffic in illicit liquor. (Best done under the cover of darkness.) □ *He moonlighted during prohibition.* □ *Jed was moonlighting around the clock.* **3.** *in.* to work at a second job. □ *Larry had to moonlight to earn enough to feed his family.* □ *A lot of people have to moonlight to make ends meet.*

**moonlight requisition** *n.* a nighttime theft. (Military. See *liberate*.) □ *It took a moonlight requisition to get the medicine we needed.* □ *They got the spare part on a moonlight requisition.*

**moonlit** *mod.* alcohol intoxicated, with *moonshine.* □ *He's on the jug again. See, he's all moonlit.* □ *He's too moonlit to drive.*

**moonshine 1.** *n.* nonsense; humbug. □ *That's just moonshine! I don't believe a word.* □ *He's a master at moonshine.* **2.** *n.* homemade whisky; any cheap or inferior liquor. □ *This moonshine isn't the best you've made.* □ *Moonshine is*

supposed to be strong, not good. **3.** *in.* to distill or traffic in illicit liquor. □ *Yeah, I moonshine a little. So what?* □ *You would be amazed at how much people moonshine back in the hills.* (More at *moonshiner*.)

**moonshiner** *n.* a maker of *moonshine.* □ *Moonshiners in the Georgia hills are using sophisticated electronic warning systems to keep one step ahead of the feds.* □ *I have an uncle who was a moonshiner for a while.*

**moony** ['muni] **1.** *n.* illicit whiskey; *moonshine.* (Folksy.) □ *This here moony is good for what ails you.* □ *Where's my jar of moony?* **2.** *mod.* alcohol intoxicated; tipsy. □ *She looks a trifle moony.* □ *Who's that moony dame?* □ *Tod is too moony to drive.*

**moose** *n.* a Japanese girlfriend; any girlfriend. (Crude. Military.) □ *She's my moose, and you'd better remember it!* □ *She's one fine moose, if you ask me.*

**mooter** AND **moota, muta, mootah** ['mutɚ AND 'mutə] *n.* marijuana; a marijuana cigarette. (Drugs.) □ *He stood tall and panted over a smoldering moota.* □ *Max says this is the finest mootah I'll ever see.*

**mop** [mɑp] **1.** *n.* a drinking bout. □ *She is off somewhere on another mop.* □ *This mop lasted about a day and a half.* **2.** *n.* a heavy drinker; a drunkard. □ *The guy's a mop. There is nothing you can do till he decides he's had enough.* □ *The mops hang out here looking for handouts.* **3.** *n.* hair; a hairdo. □ *How do you like my new mop?* □ *Why don't you comb that mop?*

**mope** [mop] **1.** *n.* a tired and ineffectual person. □ *I can't afford to pay mopes around here. Get to work or get out! I feel like such a mope today.* **2.** AND **mope around** *in.* to move around slowly and sadly. □ *I feel like moping and nothing else.* □ *He just mopes around all day and won't eat anything.*

**mopped** AND **moppy** *mod.* alcohol intoxicated. □ *Jack was a little moppy to be driving.* □ *He's not mopped; he's sloshed.*

**mopping-up operation** *n.* a cleanup operation; the final stages in a project where the loose ends are taken care of. □ *It's all over except a small mopping-up operation.* □ *The mopping-up operation should cost just under 20 million.*

**mop up the floor with someone** AND **mop the floor up with someone, wipe up the floor with someone, wipe the floor up with someone** *tr.* to beat someone to a pulp. (Also with other verbs: *clean, dust,* etc.) □ *One more crack like that, and I'll have Bruno wipe up the floor with you.* □ *Bruno's job is dusting up the floor with people who don't wipe off their feet before coming in.*

**morals** *n.* tablets of Demerol™, a painkiller. (Drugs.) □ *I need a few morals to tide me over till I can score some horse.* □ *I got no morals. Check out Max or Bruno.*

**More power to you!** *exclam.* "Good for you!" □ *If you can get the job done, more power to you!* □ *Go ahead, neglect your family and make a million. More power to you!*

**more than one bargained for** *n.* (getting) more than one expected. □ *This is certainly more than I bargained for!* □ *Trouble and more trouble. I'm getting more than I bargained for when I took the job.*

**morf** See *morph.*

**morning after (the night before)** *n.* a hangover. (Always with *the.*) □ *Do worries about the morning after keep you from having a good time at parties?* □ *She's suffering from the morning after the night before.*

**morph** AND **morf** [morf] *n.* morphine. (Drugs.) □ *Morph was her drug of choice when it was easy to get.* □ *There were lots of men who wandered from town to town begging the local doctors to give them just a little morf.*

**mossback** ['mɔsbæk] *n.* an old square; a *stick in the mud.* □ *Walter, you are such an old mossback.* □ *I enjoy appearing to be a mossback. People expect so little from you.*

**most** *n.* something that is the best. (Always with *the.*) □ *This noodle stuff is the most, Mom!* □ *Sally is the most! Can she dance!*

**mother** **1.** *n.* marijuana. (Drugs. See *mother nature.*) □ *She grows her own mother in a pot in her room.* □ *This mother is way rad!* **2.** *n.* a drug dealer; one's own drug dealer, upon whom one depends. (Drugs.) □ *Bruno is my mother.* □ *If you can't trust your mother, who can you trust?*

**mother nature** AND **mother nature's** *n.* marijuana. (Drugs.) □ *No chemicals for me. I find that mother nature is everything I need.* □ *See if you can get some of mother nature's.*

**motion-lotion** *n.* gasoline; motor fuel. (Citizens band radio slang.) □ *Let's stop up ahead for some motion-lotion.* □ *I'm about out of motion-lotion.*

**motor-mouth** See *ratchet-mouth.*

**Motown** ['motaun] *n.* "motor town," Detroit, Michigan. □ *Have you ever been to Motown?* □ *We went to Motown to buy a car once.*

**(mountain) dew** **1.** *n.* Scotch whiskey. □ *Mountain dew is best when it's from the old country.* □ *The real mountain dew is smoky tasting and amber.* **2.** *n.* illicit liquor; any liquor. □ *Mountain dew is what I want. As long as it's not store bought.* □ *My pappy made his own mountain dew.*

**mouth** **1.** *n.* a hangover. (Always with *a.*) □ *I've got quite a mouth this morning. I guess I overdid it.* □ *What a mouth! It tastes like a bird slept in it!* **2.** See *mouth(piece).*

**mouth-breather** *n.* a stupid-acting person. □ *I always end up with a mouth-breather on a blind date.* □ *Who's the mouth-breather with Fred?*

**mouthful** **1.** *n.* a true statement. □ *You said a mouthful, and I agree.* □ *That is a mouthful, and I know it took courage to say it.* **2.** *n.* a tirade. □ *Paul really gave me a mouthful. I didn't know I hurt his feelings.* □ *She sure had a mouthful to say to you!*

**mouth full of South** *n.* a southern accent. □ *You sure do have a mouth full of South.* □ *I just love to hear a man with a mouth full of South.*

**mouth off** **1.** *in.* to give (someone) back talk. □ *If you mouth off, I will ground you for three weeks.* □ *Don't mouth off at me, buster!* **2.** *in.* to speak out of turn.

□ *Don't just mouth off. Wait your turn.*
□ *Hold up your hand. I won't deal with people who mouth off.*

**mouth(piece)** *n.* a lawyer specializing in criminal cases. (Underworld.) □ *The guy hired a mouthpiece and beat the rap.* □ *I won't answer anything without my mouth right here by me.*

**mouthwash** *n.* liquor; a drink of liquor. □ *I could use a shot of that mouthwash.* □ *You could use a little mouthwash after that long trip, I bet.*

**move on someone** *in.* to attempt to pick up someone; to attempt to seduce someone. (Collegiate.) □ *Don't try to move on my date, old chum.* □ *Harry is trying to move on Tiffany. They deserve each another.*

**movers and shakers** *n.* people who get things done; organizers and managers. □ *The movers and shakers in this firm haven't exactly been working overtime.* □ *Who are the movers and shakers around here?*

**movies** *n.* a case of diarrhea. □ *A case of the movies kept me going all night.* □ *I can't go too far from the little boys' room. I got the movies.*

**moxie** ['mɑksi] *n.* energy; spunk. □ *Now here's a gal with real moxie.* □ *Come on. Show some moxie!*

**Mr. Big** *n.* an important man; the boss man. □ *So you're Mr. Big. I thought you'd be taller.* □ *The office suite of Acme's Mr. Big was cold and ostentatious, as was its occupant.*

**Mr. Hawkins** *n.* the winter wind. (Black. See *hawk.*) □ *We have an appointment with Mr. Hawkins in January.* □ *Put something on your head, or Mr. Hawkins will cut you down.*

**Mr. Nice Guy** *n.* a friendly, forgiving fellow. □ *You'll find that I am Mr. Nice Guy as long as you play fair with me.* □ *Oh, my boss is Mr. Nice Guy. He'll let me off, I'm sure.*

**Mr. Right** *n.* the one man who is right for a woman. □ *Some day Mr. Right will come along and sweep you off your feet.* □ *I'm tired of waiting for Mr. Right. Where is Mr. Maybe?*

**Mrs. Murphy** *n.* a bathroom. □ *Whose turn is it at Mrs. Murphy's?* □ *When will Mrs. Murphy be free?*

**Mr. Whiskers** AND **whiskers (man)** *n.* a federal agent. (Underworld. From the whiskers of Uncle Sam.) □ *Mr. Whiskers is trying to get me to pay tax on those few bucks.* □ *Mr. Whiskers is on our tail. Let's blow town.*

**M.T.** *n.* an empty bottle. □ *Put your M.T.s in the garbage.* □ *Here's another M.T. for your collection.*

**mu** *n.* marijuana. (Drugs.) □ *This mu is stale.* □ *Are mu and bu the same thing?*

**mucho** ['mutʃo] *mod.* very. (Spanish.) □ *This is a mucho happy young man.* □ *We are mucho disgusted with your performance.*

**muck something up** AND **muck up something** *tr.* to mess something up; to ruin something. □ *Try not to muck it up this time.* □ *You seem to have mucked up this one, too.*

**mudbud** *n.* homegrown marijuana. (Drugs.) □ *Mudbud, hell! It's garbage.* □ *If you sell your mudbud, you're a pusher!*

**muddled (up)** *mod.* alcohol intoxicated. □ *I've had a little too much muddler, I think. Anyway, I'm muddled.* □ *Larry is too muddled up to drive.*

**muddler** *n.* liquor. □ *I've had a little too much muddler, I think. Anyway, I'm muddled.* □ *Let's stop here for some muddler.*

**mug 1.** *n.* the face. (Crude.) □ *Wipe that smile off your mug!* □ *What a gorgeous mug!* **2.** *n.* a thug; a *goon.* (Underworld.) □ *Call off your mugs. I'll come peacefully.* □ *Bruno is just another one of the mugs from the mob.* **3.** *tr.* to attack and rob someone. □ *Somebody jumped out of an alley and tried to mug me.* □ *Some punk mugged Mrs. Lopez last night.*

**mugger** *n.* someone, usually a male, who attacks and robs people. □ *I clobbered the mugger with a tire iron I carry just for such occasions.* □ *The muggers have the downtown almost to themselves after dark.*

**muggled (up)** *mod.* under the effects of marijuana. (Drugs. See *muggle(s).*) □ *Bruno is just a tad muggled up, but what else is new?* □ *Max was muggled up all through his senior year.*

**mugglehead** *n.* a marijuana smoker. (Drugs. See *muggle(s)*.) □ *Bruno is a mugglehead, but I wouldn't call him that to his face.* □ *Muggleheads tend to be solitary and aren't into heavy crime.*

**muggle(s)** **1.** *n.* marijuana leaves; marijuana; a marijuana cigarette. (Drugs.) □ *She is famous for the high Q. muggles she gives out at parties.* □ *You got a muggle to spare?* **2.** *n.* marijuana smoker(s). (Drugs.) □ *When you muggles get through smelling up the place, will one of you take the garbage out?* □ *We found a young muggle in the alley, blissed out amongst the garbage.*

**muggy** ['məgi] *mod.* alcohol intoxicated. □ *George is just a little muggy. It doesn't take much anymore.* □ *I'm too muggy to drive.*

**mug shot** *n.* a photograph of one's face taken for police records. (Underworld.) □ *I'm going to have to ask you to come down to the station and go through some mug shots.* □ *How can a professional photographer take a portrait that looks like a mug shot?*

**mule** **1.** *n.* raw corn whiskey. (Folksy.) □ *Man, this mule really has a kick.* □ *Where's my jug of mule?* **2.** *n.* marijuana soaked in whiskey. (Drugs.) □ *This mule is made with an old family recipe.* □ *Mule is moist and fragrant.* **3.** *n.* someone who delivers or smuggles drugs for a drug dealer. (Drugs.) □ *The jerks use a 12 year-old kid for a mule!* □ *A car drove by, and suddenly the mule was riddled with machine gun bullets.*

**munchies** **1.** See *(blind) munchies.* **2.** *n.* snacks, such as potato chips; any casual food. □ *What kind of munchies are we going to have?* □ *The munchies at the party were great!*

**munchkin** ['məntʃkən] *n.* a small or insignificant person. □ *You're not going to let that munchkin push you around, are you?* □ *Who is the munchkin holding the clipboard?*

**munch out** *in.* to eat ravenously. (Drugs. See also *pig out.*) □ *I had to munch out after the party. I can't imagine why.* □ *I can munch out for no reason at all.*

**mung** **1.** AND **MUNG** [məŋ] *n.* something that is "mashed until no good"; anything nasty or gloppy. □ *Get this mung off my plate.* □ *This mung is cruel and unusual punishment. I demand to see the warden.* **2.** *n.* an uncomfortable feeling after taking *L.S.D.* (Drugs. See also *(acid) mung, mungy.*) □ *Oh, man, I've got the mung.* □ *The mung might set in any time for a week afterwards.* **3.** *tr.* to ruin something. □ *You munged my car!* □ *Look at it! You munged it!*

**mung something up** AND **mung up something** *tr.* to mess something up. □ *Don't mung it up this time.* □ *The team munged up the play, and the coach blasted them but good.*

**mungy** ['məŋi] **1.** *mod.* gloppy; messy. □ *Get that mungy stuff off my plate!* □ *The spaghetti was cold and mungy by the time it was served.* **2.** *mod.* having to do with an oily feeling of the face of a person who has taken *L.S.D.* (Drugs.) □ *I feel so mungy after I take the stuff. Yuck!* □ *I can do without the mungy feeling and the flashbacks.*

**murder** AND **slaughter** *tr.* to overwhelm; to beat at sports. □ *The other team murdered us.* □ *We went out on the field prepared to slaughter them.*

**murky bucket(s)** See *messy bucket(s).*

**murphy\*** ['mɚfi] **1.** *n.* a potato. □ *I spent half my tour of duty peeling murphies.* □ *Look, this murphy looks like my mother-in-law.* **2.\*** *n.* a breast. (Crude. Usually plural. Caution with topic.) □ *Look at the murphies on that dame!* □ *She stood about six feet tall and was turned in the light so her murphies stood out in silhouette.*

**muscle** *in.* to inject a drug into a muscle rather than into the skin or a vein. (Drugs. See *skin.*) □ *I just muscle, so I can't get hooked.* □ *The worst of those junkies started out with the idea that they could muscle and come to no harm.*

**musclehead** *n.* a stupid man; a man who has muscle where there should be brains. (Also a rude term of address.) □ *Look, musclehead, do exactly what I tell you!* □ *An overstuffed musclehead waddled over and offered to bend me in half if I didn't beat it.*

**muscleman** **1.** *n.* a strong bully; a *goon.* (Underworld.) □ *Bruno is a muscleman for the kingpin of a local drug ring.* □ *Tell your muscleman to lay off.* **2.** *n.*

a man who builds muscles through body-building exercises. □ *That muscleman doesn't have a single ounce of fat on him.* □ *Being a muscleman requires most of your time.*

**mush 1.** *n.* nonsense. □ *What mush! Come on, talk straight!* □ *That's just mush. Don't believe it.* **2.** *n.* romance; lovemaking; kissing. □ *I can't stand movies with lots of mush in them.* □ *When an actor looks at an actress like that, you just know that there's gonna be some mush.* **3.** *n.* one's face. (Crude.) □ *Put some paint on your mush, and let's get going.* □ *With a mush like that, you ought to be in pictures. Maybe another King Kong remake.*

**mushhead** *n.* a stupid person. □ *Oh, good grief, I'm such a mushhead!* □ *Who is the mushhead in the cowboy boots?*

**mushmouth** *n.* a person who does not or cannot speak clearly. □ *Don't be a mushmouth. Talk plainly.* □ *How can a mushmouth like that get a job reading news on network television?*

**mushrooms** See *shrooms.*

**musical beds** *n.* acts of sexual promiscuity; sleeping with many people. (From the name of the game "musical chairs.") □ *Mary has been playing musical beds for about a year.* □ *She thinks that playing musical beds is the way to get ahead.*

**must do** AND **do** *n.* something that someone ought to do. (Always with *a.*) □ *Seeing the Eiffel tower is a must do in Paris.* □ *This is a do when you're in town.*

**My foot!** *exclam.* "I do not believe it!"; "Like hell!" (An exclamation of contradiction.) □ *You're the best in town, my foot!* □ *She's going to marry you? My foot!*

**my man 1.** *n.* an addict's (male) drug supplier. (Drugs.) □ *I gotta get to my man fast. I hurt.* □ *My man's been burning me with blanks.* **2.** *n.* my (black) brother or buddy. (Black.) □ *This is my man Sam who's gonna show you how to boogie.* □ *Come on, my man, we have to be taking care of business.*

**mystery meat** *n.* any unidentified meat. (Collegiate.) □ *What is the mystery meat tonight?* □ *There are no hints as to what this mystery meat is—except its strange pinkish color.*

# N

**nab** [næb] **1.** *tr.* to arrest someone. □ *They nabbed Tom with a stolen watch on him.* □ *I knew they would nab him sooner or later.* (More at *nabbed*.) **2.** AND **nabber** *n.* a police officer; a cop. □ *The nabs got him, and he had the evidence on his person.* □ *There's a nabber at the door who wants to talk to you.*

**nabbed** *mod.* caught by the police; arrested. □ *He got nabbed last night with a stolen watch on him.* □ *She's down at the police station. She's nabbed.*

**nabe** [neb] **1.** *n.* a neighborhood; one's own neighborhood. □ *I can't wait to get back to my own nabe.* □ *Hey, man, welcome back to the old nabe!* **2.** *n.* a neighborhood theater. □ *Do I have to go downtown to see that movie, or is it playing at the nabes yet?* □ *Why drive all the way out there when you can see it at the nabe for half the cost?*

**nada** ['nɑdɑ] *n.* nothing; none. (Spanish.) □ *I asked him, but he didn't say nada.* □ *The score was nada to nada.*

**nag** **1.** *tr.* to pester someone constantly. □ *Stop nagging me!* □ *I'll nag him until he remembers on his own.* **2.** *n.* a worn-out horse. □ *I bet a week's pay on that nag. Look what happened!* □ *The cowboy came riding into town on an old gray nag.*

**nail** **1.** *tr.* to arrest someone. □ *The cops nailed him right in his own doorway.* □ *"I'm gonna nail you," said the officer.* (More at *nailed*.) **2.** See *coffin nail.* **3.** *tr.* to identify someone. □ *They nailed him from his picture.* □ *The officer nailed Freddy, thanks to the description the victim provided.*

**nailed** **1.** *mod.* correctly identified. □ *The thugs sure got nailed fast.* □ *The killer was nailed with the help of the F.B.I.* **2.** *mod.* arrested. (See *nail.*) □ *Okay, chum. You are nailed. Let's go.* □ *Why am I nailed? I didn't do anything.*

**nail-em-and-jail-em** AND **nailer** *n.* the police in general; a police officer. (Black.) □ *The nailers caught Freddy last night.* □ *Old nail-em-and-jail-em is going to be knocking at your door any day now.*

**nail someone's hide to the wall** See *nail someone to a cross.*

**nail someone to a cross** AND **nail someone('s hide) to the wall** *tr.* to punish or scold someone severely. (Literally, to crucify someone or to nail someone's skin to the wall like that of a captured animal.) □ *That guy was really mad. He really nailed you to a cross.* □ *She must hate your guts. She sure nailed your hide to the wall.*

**nail someone to the wall** See the previous entry.

**naked** *mod.* undiluted; having to do with neat liquor, especially gin. (See *raw.*) □ *No ice, please. I want mine naked.* □ *Give me a naked whisky, if you don't mind.*

**naked truth** *n.* the complete unembellished truth. □ *Sorry to put it to you like this, but it's the naked truth.* □ *I can take it. Just tell me the naked truth.*

**Nam** *n.* Vietnam. □ *How long were you in Nam?* □ *Things were pretty bad in Nam.*

**Nam black** AND **Nam weed** ['næm 'blæk AND 'næm 'wid] *n.* potent black marijuana, from Vietnam or Southeast Asia. (Drugs.) □ *Max says he knows* *where you can get some of that Nam weed.* □ *That Nam black is really powerful.*

**namby-pamby** ['næmbi'pæmbi] *mod.* overly nice; effeminate and weak, when said of a male. □ *Fred is too namby-pamby when it comes to making up his mind.* □ *A real namby-pamby guy.* □ *What a namby-pamby guy!*

**name of the game** *n.* the way things are; the way things can be expected to be. (Always with *the.*) □ *The name of the game is money, money, money.* □ *I can't help it. That's the name of the game.*

**Name your poison.** *sent.* "State what you want to drink." (Refers to alcoholic drinks only.) □ *Okay, friend, name your poison.* □ *Step up to the bar and name your poison.*

**narc** AND **narco** [nɑrk AND 'nɑrko] **1.** *n.* a narcotic. (See also *nark.*) □ *She's been taking narcs.* □ *How long has he been on narcs?* **2.** *mod.* having to do with narcotics. □ *Does he have a narc problem?* □ *She is a narco officer.* **3.** *n.* a federal narcotics agent; any narcotics enforcement officer. □ *The narcs caught him.* □ *There is a narco at our school.*

**narco** See the previous entry.

**nark** AND **narc** [nɑrk] **1.** *n.* a police informer. □ *Fred is a nark. He squealed.* □ *I'm going to get that narc for squealing.* **2.** *in.* to inform (on someone) to the police; to *squeal.* (Often with *on.*) □ *Don't nark on me!* □ *All right. Who narked?* **3.** See *narc.* **4.** *tr.* to annoy someone. □ *Stop narking me!* □ *Why are you always narcing someone?* (More at *narked.*) **5.** *n.* any unpleasant person. □ *Tell that narc to get lost.* □ *Stop being such a narc. Beat it!*

**narked** [nɑrkt] *mod.* annoyed. (Usually with *at* or *with.*) □ *He's really narked at us.* □ *She is narked with you and your car.*

**narky** ['nɑrki] *n.* a narcotic drug. □ *They caught him with a lot of narky in his pockets.* □ *The mugger wanted money to buy some narky.*

**narly** See *gnarly.*

**narrow squeak** *n.* a success almost not achieved; a lucky or marginal success; a problem almost not surmounted. □

*That was a narrow squeak. I don't know how I survived.* □ *Another narrow squeak like that and I'll give up.*

**natch** [nætʃ] **1.** *mod.* of a natural state; being drug free or *straight.* (Drugs. See *on the natch.*) □ *If I could only get natch again.* □ *Max wasn't close to natch for a year.* **2.** *interj.* "yes"; "naturally." □ *I guess it's okay. She said natch.* □ *Natch, you can borrow my car.*

**natch trip** AND **natural high, natural trip 1.** *n.* drug euphoria from legal substances such as nutmeg. (Drugs. See also *rush.*) □ *He tried to get a natch trip from a banana peel.* □ *My brother had a natch trip on a banana peel.* **2.** *n.* any positive emotional feeling from everyday living. □ *That guy's music is a real natch trip.* □ *All of life is a natch trip, man.*

**natural** *n.* someone with obvious natural talent. □ *That guy is a natural!* □ *Can she ever dance. What a natural!*

**natural-born** *mod.* born with talent or skill. □ *She is really a natural-born dancer.* □ *Mary is a natural-born artist.*

**natural high** See *natch trip.*

**nature's call** AND **call of nature** *n.* the feeling of a need to go to the toilet. (See the following entry.) □ *I think I feel nature's call coming on.* □ *A call of nature forced us to stop along the way.*

**nature stop** *n.* a stop to use the toilet, especially during road travel. (Euphemistic.) □ *I think I need a nature stop when it's convenient.* □ *I left my comb back at the last nature stop.*

**nause someone out** *tr.* to nauseate someone. □ *That horrible smell really nauses me out.* □ *Things like that nause me out, too.*

**naw** *interj.* "no." □ *Naw, I didn't do that.* □ *Naw, I won't go.*

**nay** *mod.* ugly; unfavorable. (From *nasty.*) □ *She is really nay.* □ *What a nay thing to say.*

**N.B.T.** *n.* "no big thing." □ *Hey, man! Don't make a fuss! It's N.B.T.* □ *Listen up, Fred. This is N.B.T., but listen anyway.*

**neanderthal** [ni'ændɚθəl] *n.* a large and ugly male. □ *Tell that neanderthal to get out of here.* □ *Tom, don't act like such a neanderthal.*

**near-beer** *n.* beer with less than 1/2 percent alcohol content. (Originally from the prohibition era.) □ *I read in the paper that near-beer is making a comeback.* □ *You can drink a lot of near-beer without getting drunk.*

**neat 1.** *mod.* great; cool; fine. □ *What a neat idea!* □ *That was not a very neat thing to do.* **2.** *exclam.* "Wow!" (Usually **Neat!**) □ *Neat! I'm glad you came.* □ *Five of them! Neat!*

**nebbies** AND **neb, nemb** ['nɛbiz AND nɛb, nɛm] *n.* Nembutal™ barbiturate capsules. (Drugs.) □ *Susan has been taking nebbies for years in order to get to sleep.* □ *Nemb can be abused like any other drug.*

**nebbish** AND **neb** ['nɛbiʃ AND nɛb] *n.* a dull person. (From Yiddish.) □ *Molly is such a nebbish. Why doesn't she just give up?* □ *You are such a neb!*

**necessary** *n.* money; an income. (Always with *the.*) □ *I can always use more of the necessary.* □ *I gotta have more of the necessary, man.*

**neck** *in.* to cuddle and kiss. (Always in reference to lovers or boy-girl relationships.) □ *There are some teenagers in the back room necking.* □ *Let's go somewhere quiet and neck.*

**neck and neck** *mod.* almost even. (See also *nip and tuck.*) □ *The horses were neck and neck at the finish line.* □ *They ran neck and neck for the entire race.*

**needle** *tr.* to annoy someone. □ *Tom is always needling Frank.* □ *Stop needling me!*

**needle candy** *n.* narcotics that are taken by injection. (Drugs. Compare to *nose (candy).*) □ *Max likes needle candy best of all.* □ *Some people prefer needle candy to food.*

**negative 1.** *n.* any drawback or bad thing about someone or something. □ *There are too many negatives associated with your plan.* □ *I know another negative you didn't mention.* **2.** *n.* a bad drug experience. (Drugs.) □ *Max had one negative after another, and he finally O.D.ed.* □ *That stuff gave me a real negative.*

**nemb** See *nebbies.*

**nerd** AND **nurd** [nɚd] *n.* a dull and bookish person, usually a male. □ *Fred can be such a nerd!* □ *That whole gang of boys is just a bunch of nurds.*

**nerd mobile** *n.* a full-size, uninteresting car; a family car. □ *My father always buys some kind of stupid nerd mobile.* □ *There is nothing but nerd mobiles on our block.*

**nerd pack** *n.* a plastic sheath for holding pens in a pocket, protecting the cloth from ink. (This is the classic symbol of a bookish *nerd.*) □ *A lot of engineers have nerd packs.* □ *A real nerd wears a nerd pack in the pocket of a dirty shirt.*

**Nerts!** [nɚts] *exclam.* "Nuts!" (Partly euphemistic.) □ *Oh, nerts! I forgot my wallet.* □ *Nerts! I dropped my keys.*

**nervous Nellie** *n.* any nervous person, male or female. □ *Sue is such a nervous Nellie. She should calm down.* □ *Relax! Don't be such a nervous Nellie.*

**nervy 1.** *mod.* nervous. □ *Mary is so nervy. Anything will set her off.* □ *Now, don't get nervy.* **2.** *mod.* daring; courageous. □ *What a nervy guy!* □ *Don't get nervy with me!*

**nest egg** *n.* money saved for some important purpose, such as retirement. □ *I lost most of my nest egg in the market crash.* □ *It takes years to build up a nest egg.*

**net result** *n.* the final result after all the assets and liabilities have balanced out. □ *The net result was that I was fired.* □ *I don't care about the little things. What is the net result?*

**never mind** *phr.* "Forget it."; "It doesn't matter anymore." □ *Never mind. I forget what I was going to say.* □ *Oh, never mind. Nobody really cares anyway.*

**newshound** *n.* a newspaper reporter who pursues a story with the same diligence used by a bloodhound. □ *If the newshounds get hold of this story, we'll never have any peace.* □ *Tell that newshound that I'll sue her if she prints that!*

**newt** *n.* a stupid person; a dull and uninteresting person. □ *Look, you silly newt, you are wrong!* □ *Don't act like such a newt.*

**New York's finest** *n.* a New York City police officer. □ *One of New York's finest gave me a parking ticket.* □ *Three* of New York's finest were standing there at my door with my lost dog.

**nibble 1.** *n.* a cautious or preliminary response to something. (See also *nybble*.) □ *My advertisement got three nibbles this morning.* □ *We will see if anyone else gives it a nibble.* **2.** *in.* to reply cautiously or tentatively to something. □ *Someone nibbled at your want ad.* □ *I hope someone who wants to buy my car nibbles at the description I posted on the bulletin board.*

**nice meeting you** *phr.* "it is nice to have met you." (Said when leaving someone whose acquaintance you have just made.) □ *I must go now, Fred. Nice meeting you.* □ *Well, nice meeting you. I must get home now.*

**nice talking to you** *phr.* "it's been pleasant, goodbye." (A leave-taking formula, sometimes with an air of dismissal.) □ *Do tell. Well, nice talking to you.* □ *Nice talking to you. Call my service.*

**nick 1.** *tr.* to arrest someone. □ *The cops nicked Paul outside his house.* □ *They are going to nick Joe, too.* (More at *nicked*.) **2.** *tr.* to steal something. □ *The thugs nicked a couple of apples from the fruit stand.* □ *Don't ever nick anything! Do you hear me?* **3.** *tr.* to get or take something. □ *Would you please nick me a slice of bread?* □ *Tom nicked a copy of the test for Sam, who also needed one.*

**nicked** *mod.* arrested. □ *Paul was nicked last night.* □ *"Now I'm nicked," he said.*

**nickel and dime someone (to death)** *tr.* to make numerous small charges that add up to a substantial sum. □ *Those waiters nickel and dimed me to death.* □ *Just give me the whole bill at one time. Don't nickel and dime me for days on end.*

**nickel (bag)** *n.* a five-dollar bag of marijuana, heroin, or other drugs. (Drugs.) □ *Some kids found a nickel bag on the street corner.* □ *Can I borrow a fin so I can buy a nickel?*

**nifty** *mod.* neat; smart. □ *That is a pretty nifty car you have there.* □ *Yes, it is nifty.*

**night person** *n.* a person who prefers to be active in the nighttime. (The plural is with *people*. Compare to *day per-*

son.) □ *I can't function in the morning. I'm strictly a night person.* □ *Night people prefer to sleep in the daytime.*

**nineteenth hole** *n.* a place to buy an alcoholic beverage after a golf game. (Likely to be filled with golfers who have played eighteen holes of golf.) □ *All off us gathered at the nineteenth hole to celebrate a great match.* □ *I hit a hole-in-one on the first hole and went straight to the nineteenth hole to celebrate.*

**nine-to-five** *mod.* typical in terms of working hours; structured and scheduled, starting and ending at set times. (From the expression *from nine to five*, normal working hours.) □ *I work nine-to-five.* □ *I really wanted a nine-to-five job until I finally got one.* □ *I can't stand the nine-to-five rat race.*

**nip 1.** *n.* a small, quick drink of liquor. □ *Here, have a nip of this stuff.* □ *One nip is enough. That is powerful!* **2.** *in.* to take small drinks of liquor periodically. (See *nipped*.) □ *Paul has been nipping since noon.* □ *After nipping all day, Fred was pretty well stewed by dinnertime.* **3.** *tr.* to steal something. □ *The thief nipped my purse.* □ *The punk kid nipped two candy bars from the drug store.*

**nip and tuck** *mod.* so close as to be almost the same; *neck and neck*. □ *They ran nip and tuck all the way to the finish line, but Tom won the race.* □ *It was too close to call—nip and tuck all the way.*

**nipped** *mod.* alcohol intoxicated. (See *nip*.) □ *All four of them went out and got nipped.* □ *How can anybody be so nipped on four beers?*

**nippers** *n.* handcuffs; leg fetters. □ *The cops put the nippers on the crooks.* □ *No, not the nippers. They hurt my arms.*

**nitery** ['naɪtɚi] *n.* a nightclub. □ *We'll hit a few niteries and then come back to my place.* □ *There is a cheap nitery over on Twelfth Street where Chuck has a job.*

**nit-picker** *n.* a person who is hypercritical. □ *Mary is such a nit-picker.* □ *Nit-pickers drive me crazy.*

**nit-picking** *n.* too much minor criticism; overly particular criticism; nagging. □ *I* *am tired of all your nit-picking.* □ *Enough nit-picking! What are the major problems?*

**nitty-gritty** ['nɪdi 'grɪdi] *n.* the essence; the essential points. (Usually in *get down to the nitty-gritty.*) □ *What's the nitty-gritty about the broken window?* □ *Once we are down to the nitty-gritty, we can begin to sort things out.*

**nitwit** *n.* someone who behaves stupidly. (Also a term of address.) □ *You are such a nitwit!* □ *Please stop acting like a nitwit all the time.*

**nix** [nɪks] **1.** *interj.* "no." (All senses from German *nichts.*) □ *The man said nix, and he means nix.* □ *Nix, I won't do it.* **2.** *exclam.* "No!"; "Stop it!"; "I disagree!" (Usually **Nix!**) □ *Nix! I won't do it.* □ *"Nix," said Paul. "I can't permit that."* **3.** *n.* nothing. □ *What did I get for all my trouble? Nix!* □ *I got nix for a tip. And after I was so helpful!* **4.** *tr.* to put a stop to something; to say no to something; to ban something. □ *The boss nixed my plan.* □ *I wanted to say a certain word in my speech, but the management nixed it.*

**no\*** *mod.* any. (Caution in writing. Substandard, but frequent in slang and colloquial use. See also *ain't.*) □ *I don't want no trouble from you.* □ *This ain't no good.*

**no-account 1.** *mod.* worthless; no-good. □ *Her uncle is a no-account gambler.* □ *She is a no-account part-time dealer at the casino.* **2.** *n.* a worthless person. (Also a rude term of address.) □ *Ask that no-account to come over here and explain himself.* □ *Look, you no-account! Take your problems and go away!*

**no bargain** *n.* not an especially good person or thing. □ *Fred is okay, but he's no bargain.* □ *This car gets me to work and back, but it's no bargain.*

**no big deal** AND **no biggie** *n.* (something) not difficult or troublesome. (See also *N.B.T.*) □ *Don't worry. It's no big deal.* □ *No problem. It's no biggie.*

**no biggie** See the previous entry.

**nobody** *n.* an insignificant person. (Always with *a.* Compare to *somebody.*) □ *Don't pay any attention to him. He's just a nobody.* □ *That silly girl is a nobody and a pest.*

**no can do** *phr.* "It can't be done."; "I can't do it." □ *Sorry. No can do.* □ *Lend you $200? No can do.*

**nodded out** *mod.* in heroin euphoria; under the influence of heroin. (Drugs.) □ *Max was nodded out after his fix.* □ *He is upstairs nodded out.*

**no dice** *interj.* "no"; not possible. □ *When I asked about a loan, he said, "No dice."* □ *No. It can't be done, no dice.*

**no earthly reason** *n.* no conceivable reason. □ *There is no earthly reason for your behavior.* □ *I can think of no earthly reason why the repairs should cost so much.*

**no end of something** *n.* an endless supply of something. □ *Have some candy. I have no end of chocolate drops.* □ *I've had no end of trouble ever since I bought this car.*

**No fair!** *exclam.* "That's not fair!" □ *No fair! I saw it first!* □ *That's no fair! We paid full price to see this movie.*

**no flies on someone** *phr.* someone is energetic and active. (Folksy. Moving too fast for the flies to settle.) □ *Old Tom is really swift. There are no flies on him.* □ *No flies on Mary. She's very ambitious.*

**no-frills** *mod.* having no unnecessary extras. □ *I'll take the no-frills package, thank you.* □ *My no-frills flight to Mexico was most uncomfortable.*

**noggin** ['nɑgṇ] *n.* (one's) head. □ *I have a bump on my noggin.* □ *Put a hat on your noggin and let's go out.*

**no go** AND **no-go** ['no 'go] *mod.* negative; inopportune. □ *We're in a no-go situation.* □ *Is it go or no go?*

**no-good 1.** *n.* a worthless person. □ *Tell that no-good to leave.* □ *The no-good is back again.* **2.** *mod.* worthless; bad. □ *Get that no-good jerk out of here!* □ *I have never heard of such a no-good car dealership before.*

**no-goodnik** [no'gudnɪk] *n.* someone who is no good. (The *nik* is from Russian via Yiddish.) □ *That no-goodnik is pestering me again.* □ *Tell the no-goodnik to leave quietly, or I will call the police.*

**no great shakes** *n.* someone or something not very good. (There is no affirmative version of this.) □ *Your idea is no great shakes, but we'll try it anyway.* □

*Ted is no great shakes when it comes to brains.*

**no holds barred** *mod.* without restriction. (There is no affirmative.) □ *I want you to get that contract. Do anything—no holds barred.* □ *Try anything that will work, no holds barred.*

**nohow*** ['nohɑu] *mod.* anyway; anyhow. (Folksy. Generally in the negative forming the final member of a multiple negative. Caution with use in writing.) □ *It don't matter nohow.* □ *I don't care if you do nohow.*

**noid** *n.* a "paranoid" person. □ *Some of those noids write hilarious letters to the editor.* □ *Who's the noid screaming about Big Brother?*

**noise 1.** *n.* empty talk; nonsense. □ *I've had enough of your noise. Shut up!* □ *That's nothing but noise. I want the truth.* **2.** *n.* heroin. (Drugs.) □ *Man, I need some noise now! I hurt!* □ *Max is hooked on noise.*

**No kidding!** *exclam.* "I am not kidding."; "You are not kidding (are you)?" □ *No kidding! I never thought she would do that.* □ *No kidding, he's really going to join the Air Force.*

**No lie!** *exclam.* "Honest!"; "No kidding!" □ *I really did it! No lie!* □ *I was there on time. No lie! Ask my sister.*

**non compos** ['nɑn 'kɑmpos] **1.** *mod.* out of one's mind; *non compos mentis.* □ *She is strictly non compos!* □ *Don't pay any attention to her. She's non compos.* **2.** AND **non compos poopoo** *mod.* alcohol intoxicated. □ *That gal isn't just drunk. She's non compos poopoo.* □ *Two glasses and he was non compos.*

**non compos poopoo** See the previous entry.

**none of someone's beeswax** [...'bizwæks] *n.* none of someone's business. □ *It's none of your beeswax. I'm not telling.* □ *You'll never know. The answer is none of your beeswax.*

**no never mind** *n.* difference; bother. (Folksy. Especially with *don't make...*) □ *I don't care. It don't make no never mind.* □ *So what? It's no never mind with me.*

**no-no** ['nono] *n.* something that is not (to be) done. (Essentially juvenile.) □ *You can't smoke in here. That's a no-no.*

□ *She seems to delight in doing all the no-nos.*

**No nukes!** ['no 'nuks OR 'no 'njuks] *exclam.* a cry against nuclear energy, weapons, submarines, etc. □ *The marchers kept chanting, "No nukes! No nukes!"* □ *No nukes! Make my electricity the old-fashioned way.*

**noodle** *n.* (one's) head. □ *That's using your noodle.* □ *Put your hat on your noodle, and let's go.*

**nope** *interj.* "no." □ *I won't do it! Nope. I won't!* □ *She asked him to do it, but he said, "Nope."*

**no sale** *interj.* "no." □ *I wanted to go to Florida for the holidays, but my father said, "No sale."* □ *No sale. You can't do it.*

**nose-burner** AND **nose-warmer** *n.* a marijuana cigarette stub; a *roach.* (Drugs.) □ *Hey, man! Can I have a hit of that little nose-burner?* □ *The cops found a nose-warmer under the chair.*

**nose (candy)** *n.* powdered drugs that are inhaled, primarily cocaine, sometimes heroin. (Drugs. See *needle candy.*) □ *Max has some nose candy for sale.* □ *Hey, man! Where can I get some nose?*

**nosedive** *n.* a great drop; a great decline. (As with a bird or an airplane diving—nose first—toward the ground. See *take a nosedive.*) □ *This year our profits have taken a nosedive.* □ *Confidence in the government took a sudden nosedive.*

**nose habit** *n.* an addiction to sniffed drugs, usually heroin or cocaine. (Drugs.) □ *Max is suffering with his nose habit.* □ *One sniff of that white powder and she'll get a nose habit, for sure.*

**nose hit** *n.* marijuana smoke taken through the nose from the burning end of the cigarette. (Drugs.) □ *Max likes to take nose hits.* □ *Come on, Max. Give me a nose hit!*

**nose job** *n.* a plastic surgery operation to change the appearance of one's nose. □ *How much does a nose job cost?* □ *I don't want a nose job. What I got is good enough.*

**nose-warmer 1.** *n.* a short tobacco pipe. □ *Fred smokes a nose-warmer, especially in the winter.* □ *His nose-warmer* *almost set his mustache on fire once.* **2.** See *nose-burner.*

**nosh** [nɑʃ] **1.** *n.* a snack. (From German via Yiddish.) □ *How about a little nosh?* □ *I don't want a nosh. I need a whole meal.* **2.** *in.* to snack. □ *You nosh too much.* □ *Every time I see you, you're noshing.*

**nosher** ['nɑʃɚ] *n.* someone who is always eating snacks. (See *nosh.*) □ *I don't know of a single nosher who's not fat.* □ *Fred's a nosher. He's always eating.*

**no show** AND **no-show** *n.* someone who doesn't show up for something, such as an airline flight. □ *The flight was cancelled because there were too many no-shows.* □ *I have never been a no show, but my brother does it all the time.*

**No siree!** [no'sɚ'ri] *exclam.* "No!" (Folksy.) □ *Did I? No siree!* □ *That's no good. No siree, no good at all.*

**no soap** *interj.* "no." □ *I can't do it. No soap.* □ *No soap, I don't lend anyone money.*

**no stress** *interj.* "no problem"; "no bother." □ *Don't worry, man, no stress.* □ *Relax. No stress. It doesn't bother me at all.*

**no sweat** *interj.* "no problem"; "Don't worry; it is no problem." □ *It's no big deal. No sweat.* □ *No sweat, don't fret about it.*

**nosy parker** ['nozi 'pɑrkɚ] *n.* a nosy person. (Also a term of address.) □ *Mary can be such a nosy parker.* □ *Look, you nosy parker, mind your own business.*

**not able to cut something** See *able to cut something.*

**not a chance** *interj.* "no." □ *Me lend you money? Not a chance!* □ *I won't go, not a chance. Don't ask.*

**not all there** *mod.* crazy; stupid-acting. □ *Tom's not all there. Really dense.* □ *You can't depend on Paul for much help. He's really not all there.*

**notch** *tr.* to count up something; to add up or score something. □ *Well, it looks like we notched another victory.* □ *The crooks notched one more theft before they were caught.*

**not cricket** *mod.* unfair; illegitimate; unorthodox. (See affirmative examples at *cricket.*) □ *You can't do that! It's not cricket!* □ *What do you mean it's not cricket? You do it.*

**not for the world** AND **not for anything in the world, not for love nor money, not on your life** *mod.* not for anything (no matter what its value). (Note the variation in the examples.) □ *I won't do that! Not for the world, I won't.* □ *I won't do anything like that for anything in the world.* □ *I wouldn't buy anything there for love nor money.*

**not give a hoot** *tr.* to not care at all. (Folksy.) □ *Go ahead. Do it if you want. I don't give a hoot.* □ *She doesn't give a hoot if you go into town without her.*

**not grow on trees** *in.* to not be abundant; to not be expendable. (Usually said about money.) □ *I can't afford that. Money doesn't grow on trees, you know.* □ *Don't waste the glue. That stuff doesn't grow on trees, you know.*

**Nothing doing!** *exclam.* "No!" □ *Me, go to the opera? Nothing doing!* □ *Nothing doing! I refuse to do it.*

**Nothing to it!** *exclam.* "It is very easy!" □ *Look, anybody can do it! Nothing to it!* □ *Changing a light bulb is easy. Nothing to it!*

**nothing to sneeze at** *n.* no small amount of money; something not inconsequential. □ *It's not a lot of money, but it's nothing to sneeze at.* □ *She worked hard and did not accomplish much, but it's nothing to sneeze at.*

**nothing to write home about** *n.* something small or inconsequential. □ *I got a little bit of a raise this year, but it was nothing to write home about.* □ *The party was nothing to write home about.*

**nothing upstairs** *phr.* no brains; stupid. □ *Tom is sort of stupid-acting. You know—nothing upstairs.* □ *I know what's wrong with you. Nothing upstairs.*

**not just whistling Dixie** [...'dıksi] *tr.* "not talking nonsense." (Folksy. Refers to a song titled "Dixie.") □ *Man, you are right! You're not just whistling Dixie.* □ *When you say she is wrong, you're not just whistling Dixie.*

**not know beans (about something)** *tr.* to know nothing about something. □ *Don't pay any attention to her. She doesn't know beans.* □ *I don't know beans about fixing cars.*

**not know from nothing** *in.* to be stupid, innocent, and naive. (Usually with *don't,* as in the examples.) □ *Tom don't know from nothing. He is really dense.* □ *Don't pay any attention to her. She don't know from nothing.*

**not on your life** See *not for the world.*

**not too shabby 1.** *mod.* (with emphasis on *shabby*) "nice"; "well done." □ *Is that your car? Not too shabby!* □ *That play was not too shabby.* **2.** *mod.* (with emphasis on *too*) very shabby; very poor indeed. (Sarcastic.) □ *Did you see that basket she missed? Not too shabby!* □ *What a way to treat someone. Not too shabby!*

**Not to worry.** *sent.* "Don't worry." □ *You lost your ticket? Not to worry. I'll give you mine.* □ *Not to worry. Everything will be all right.*

**not worth a damn** *mod.* worthless. □ *This pen is not worth a damn.* □ *When it comes to keeping score, she's not worth a damn.*

**not worth a plugged nickel** *mod.* worth little or nothing. □ *This new battery is not worth a plugged nickel.* □ *Mary isn't worth a plugged nickel at baseball.*

**not worth beans** *mod.* worthless. □ *This paint is not worth beans. I'll have to buy another can.* □ *Sue, you're not worth beans as a painter.*

**No way!** *exclam.* "No!" □ *Me join the Army? No way!* □ *She can't do that. No way!*

**now generation** *n.* the (once current) generation of young people who seemed to want only instant gratification. □ *All those people in the now generation want to start out with fancy cars and nice houses.* □ *What will happen to the now generation when times are hard?*

**nowhere** *mod.* bad; no good; dull. □ *This place is really nowhere. Let's go.* □ *I want to get out of this nowhere party.*

**no-win situation** *n.* a situation in which there is no hope of success. □ *I find myself in a no-win situation again.* □ *The team—in a no-win situation—punted.*

**Now what?** *interrog.* "What is wrong now?" □ *I ran into the room and stopped in front of Tom. "Now what?" asked Tom.* □ *I see you standing there. Now what?*

**Now you're talking!** *exclam.* "What you are saying is making sense!" □ *Now you're talking! You've got a great idea!* □ *"Now you're talking!" said the coach when I told him I was going to win.*

**nudge** AND **noodge** [nudʒ] **1.** *n.* someone who nags. □ *Sally can be such a nudge!* □ *I really can't stand a noodge.* **2.** *in.* to nag. □ *Don't noodge all the time.* □ *Stop always noodging.* **3.** *tr.* to nag someone. □ *Stop nudging me about that.* □ *I'll noodge him a little to remind him.*

**nudie** ['nudi] *n.* a movie featuring nudes. □ *There is a nudie playing over at the Roxie Theater.* □ *I didn't know this movie was a nudie!*

**nudnik** ['nudnɪk] *n.* a bore; a pest; a crank. (From Russian via Yiddish. Also a term of address.) □ *Tell that nudnik to stay away from here. He is such a pest.* □ *Alice can be such a nudnik!*

**nuke 1.** *n.* a nuclear weapon. □ *Are there nukes aboard that ship?* □ *The military establishment is working on a number of new nukes.* **2.** *tr.* to destroy someone or something. (As with a nuclear weapon.) □ *Your cat ran through my garden and totally nuked my flowers!* □ *I'm going to nuke that cat the next time I see it.*

**numbed out** *mod.* nearly paralyzed by *P.C.P.* (Drugs.) □ *The teenager was nearly numbed out when they brought her in.* □ *Max was totally numbed out on angel dust.*

**number 1.** *n.* a girl; a sexually attractive girl. □ *Who is that cute little number I saw you with?* □ *She is really some number.* **2.** *n.* a marijuana cigarette. (Drugs.) □ *Max lit up a number just as the boss came in.* □ *Can I have a hit off your number?* **3.** *n.* any person or thing. □ *This is an interesting little number. You attach it to your bicycle handlebars.* □ *Yes, Tom can be a strange number when he wants.* **4.** *n.* an act or performance; a performance specialty. □ *Ann did her number and left the stage.* □ *I'll talk to you after my number.*

**number-cruncher 1.** *n.* someone who works with figures; an accountant. □ *The number-crunchers are trying to get the annual report ready.* □ *I enjoy being* *a number-cruncher. Math doesn't scare me.* **2.** *n.* a large and powerful computer. (Computers.) □ *They traded in the old computer for a powerful number-cruncher.* □ *The small one is reserved for minor projects. The really big and important jobs are run on the number-cruncher.*

**number crunching** *n.* using a computer to solve enormously complicated or complex mathematical problems. □ *I don't do a lot of number crunching, so I don't need a terribly fast machine.* □ *I use the big mainframe computer for number crunching.*

**number eight** AND **eight, 8** *n.* heroin. (*H* is the eighth letter of the alphabet.) □ *You got any number eight?* □ *What's 8? You mean horse?*

**number one 1.** *mod.* top rate; best; closest. (See also *numero uno.*) □ *We heard the number one high school band in the whole state last night.* □ *This is my number one buddy, Tom.* **2.** *n.* oneself. □ *I don't know who will pay for the broken window, but old number one won't!* □ *Everything always comes back to number one. I have to solve everybody's problems.*

**number thirteen** AND **thirteen, 13** *n.* morphine. (Drugs. *M* is the thirteenth letter of the alphabet.) □ *They caught her smoking old number thirteen and threw her out of school.* □ *Max has got some pretty good thirteen.*

**number three** AND **three, 3** *n.* cocaine. (Drugs. *C* is the third letter of the alphabet.) □ *He found a whole ounce of number three!* □ *Paul is hooked on 3.*

**numbhead** AND **numskull** *n.* a stupid person. □ *Stop being such a numskull!* □ *Tom can really be a numbhead if he hasn't had a good night's sleep.*

**numero uno** [ˈnumɚo ˈuno] **1.** *n.* "number one"; the best. (Spanish. See *number one.*) □ *This coffee is numero uno in my book.* □ *Mary is numero uno in our office. You'll have to ask her.* **2.** *n.* oneself; *number one.* □ *I always look out for numero uno.* □ *What's in it for numero uno?*

**numskull** See *numbhead.*

**nurts** AND **nerts** [nɚts] *n.* nonsense. □ *Don't talk that kind of nurts to me!* □

*Oh, that's just nerts. I don't believe a word of it.*

**nut 1.** *n.* an odd or strange person; a crazy person. □ *Who is that nut over there in the corner?* □ *Some nut is going to try to fly from the top of one building to another.* **2.** *n.* (one's) head. □ *A brick fell and hit him on the nut.* □ *The baseball came in fast. "Clonk!" Right on the nut!* **3.** *n.* an enthusiast (about something). □ *Paul is a nut about chocolate cake.* □ *Mary is a party nut.*

**nutcake** *n.* a stupid person. (Similar to *fruitcake.*) □ *Stop acting like such a nutcake all the time.* □ *My sister can be a real nutcake if she tries.*

**nuthouse** AND **nut factory, nut-foundry, nuthatch** *n.* an insane asylum. □ *The judge spent three years in the nuthouse.* □ *They're going to send you to the nut-foundry some day.*

**nutpick** *n.* a psychoanalyst. □ *Bill pays a nutpick about $100 an hour just to listen.* □ *What do you have to know to be a nutpick?*

**nuts 1.** *mod.* crazy. □ *You're nuts if you think I care.* □ *That whole idea is just nuts!* **2.** *exclam.* "No!"; "I don't believe you!"; "I don't care!" (Usually **Nuts!**) □ *Nuts! You don't know what you are talking about.* □ *Oh, nuts! I forgot my wallet.*

**nuts and bolts** *n.* the mundane workings of something; the basics of something. □ *I want you to learn how to write well. You have to get down to the nuts and bolts of writing.* □ *She's got a lot of good general ideas, but when it comes to the nuts and bolts of getting something done, she's no good.*

**Nuts to you!** *exclam.* "Go away!"; "Drop dead!" □ *Well, nuts to you! You are just plain rude!* □ *Nuts to you! I will NOT lend you money!*

**nutter** *n.* a nutty person. □ *Sally is such a nutter. She would forget her head if it wasn't screwed on.* □ *That guy is a real nutter. Thinks he can get a cab at this hour.*

**nuttery** *n.* an insane asylum; the place where nuts are kept. (See *nut.*) □ *If you keep acting so odd, we'll have to put you in a nuttery.* □ *This place is a nuttery! I've never seen so many silly people.*

**nutty** *mod.* silly; giddy; stupid. □ *What a nutty idea!* □ *That's nutty!* □ *Mary is a real nutty girl, but she is my best friend.*

**nutty as a fruitcake** *mod.* very silly or stupid. □ *The whole idea is as nutty as a fruitcake.* □ *Tom is as nutty as a fruitcake. They will put him in a nuttery someday.*

**nut up** *in.* to go crazy; to go nuts. □ *I've got to have a vacation soon, or I'm going to nut up.* □ *Poor Sue nutted up and had to take it easy for a few months.*

**nybble** ['nɪbl̩] *n.* four bits of computer memory. (Literally, one half of a "bite," i.e., a byte.) □ *My program wouldn't work just because I had one silly little nybble wrong!* □ *You don't program a nybble! It's just half a bite.*

# O

**O.** **1.** *n.* opium. (Drugs.) □ *Max knows an old man who used to smoke O.* □ *O. stinks to high heaven, so the cops caught the smokers.* **2.** *n.* an ounce of a drug. (Drugs. See also *O.Z.*) □ *Can you tell me where I can get an O. of stuff?* □ *Max has an O. or two on him.*

**oak(s)** [oks] *mod.* "O.K."; satisfactory; worthy. (Prisons.) □ *That guy's oaks.* □ *This stuff is oak.*

**oasis** [o'esəs] *n.* a place to buy liquor. □ *Let's go into this oasis here and pick up a few bottles.* □ *There is an oasis on almost every corner in this district.*

**oater** ['odɚ] *n.* a Western movie. (From the oats that the horses eat. See also *horse opera.*) □ *I don't want to see an oater. Isn't anything else showing?* □ *Let's go out and see a good old-fashioned oater.*

**obit** [o'bɪt] *n.* an obituary article; a public notice of someone's death. □ *I saw Mr. Wilson's obit in the paper this morning.* □ *There are no obits in the newspaper. Maybe Death has taken a holiday.*

**occifer** See *ossifer.*

**O.D.** **1.** *n.* an overdose of a drug. (Drugs.) □ *Max took an O.D. and was sent to the hospital.* □ *If you take an O.D. and no one is around, you may end up dead.* **2.** *in.* to purposely or accidentally give oneself a fatal dose of drugs. (Drugs.) □ *Max O.D.ed on heroin.* □ *I knew he would O.D. someday.* **3.** *in.* to die from an overdose of drugs. (Drugs.) □ *Two kids at my school O.D.ed last weekend.* □ *I think Max may O.D. in a week or two.* **4.** *n.* a person who has taken an overdose of drugs. (Hospitals.) □ *This O.D. has just stopped breathing.* □ *How many O.D.s did you get in here last weekend?*

**oddball** **1.** *n.* an eccentric person. □ *Tom is sure an oddball. He ordered a pineapple and strawberry milkshake.* □ *We oddballs love concoctions like that.* **2.** *mod.* strange; peculiar. □ *What an oddball combination of things!* □ *It's too oddball for me.* □ *Your oddball ideas have cost us too much money.*

**odd bird** AND **strange bird** *n.* a strange or eccentric person. □ *Mr. Wilson certainly is an odd bird.* □ *What a strange bird you are.*

**odd-bod** ['ɑdbɑd] **1.** *n.* a strange person. □ *Who is that odd-bod over in the corner?* □ *Ralph can be sort of an odd-bod now and then.* **2.** *n.* a person with a strange body. □ *I am such an odd-bod that it's hard to find clothes that fit.* □ *I've never seen anyone so tall. What an odd-bod!* **3.** *n.* a peculiar body. □ *I have such an odd-bod that it's hard to find clothes.* □ *With an odd-bod like that, he'll never make good in the movies.*

**odds-on** *mod.* having to do with the thing or person favored to win. □ *My horse is an odds-on favorite to win.* □ *My plan is odds-on to be selected.*

**Of all the nerve!** *exclam.* "I am shocked by your domineering and high-handed behavior." □ *You want me to do your laundry? Of all the nerve!* □ *Of all the nerve! Asking me to do a thing like that.*

**off** **1.** *mod.* alcohol or drug intoxicated. □ *She is truly off.* □ *Tom is so off he can't stand up.* **2.** *mod.* free from drugs; withdrawn from an addictive drug. (Drugs.) □ *She's been off for a week now.* □ *She'll have to be off for the rest of her life.* **3.** *tr.* to dispose of someone or something; to kill someone. □ *The crooks offed the witness before the trial.*

□ *Forget the whole idea! Just off it once and for all.* **4.** *in.* to die. □ *The guy just falls down and offs, right there on Main Street.* □ *I don't want to off before my time.* (More at *outed*.)

**off artist** See *rip-off artist*.

**off base** *mod.* off target; wrong; not relevant. □ *Your answer was completely off base. Try again.* □ *You are off base. I will have to deal with someone else.*

**offbeat** *mod.* strange; unconventional. □ *That is really an offbeat idea.* □ *Tom is sort of offbeat. Well, he's weird.*

**off-brand cigarette** *n.* a marijuana cigarette. (Drugs.) □ *Max smokes nothing but those off-brand cigarettes.* □ *I smell an off-brand cigarette in here.*

**off color** *mod.* dirty or smutty; *raunchy.* □ *That joke was sort of off color.* □ *Tom told an off color joke that embarrassed everyone.*

**offed** See *outed*.

**off one's chump** *mod.* crazy; nuts. □ *You silly clown. You're off your chump.* □ *Am I off my chump, or did that car suddenly disappear?*

**off one's nut 1.** *mod.* crazy; out of one's head. □ *Shut up! You're off your nut!* □ *Don't pay any attention to her. She's off her nut.* **2.** *mod.* alcohol intoxicated. □ *Those guys are really off their nuts!* □ *She just sat there and got more and more off her nut.*

**off one's rocker** *mod.* silly; giddy; crazy. (See also *rocker*.) □ *That silly dame is off her rocker.* □ *You're off your rocker if you think I believe that!*

**off one's trolley** *mod.* silly; eccentric. □ *Don't mind Uncle Charles. He's a bit off his trolley.* □ *That silly old man is just off his trolley.*

**off the hook** *mod.* no longer in jeopardy; no longer obligated. □ *I'll let you off the hook this time, but never again.* □ *We're off the hook. We don't need to worry anymore.*

**off-the-shelf** *mod.* readily available; purchasable without any special difficulties or delays. □ *This is just plain old off-the-shelf hand lotion. Isn't it great?* □ *Is it off-the-shelf?* □ *I don't use off-the-shelf software in my computer. I write my own.*

**off the track** *mod.* not on a productive course; following the wrong lead. □ *You are off the track just a little. Let me help you.* □ *I was off the track for a while, but now everything is O.K.*

**off the wagon 1.** *mod.* drinking liquor after a period of abstinence. □ *Poor John fell off the wagon again. Drunk as a skunk.* □ *He was off the wagon for a year the last time before he sobered up.* **2.** *mod.* back on drugs after a period of abstinence. □ *Max is off the wagon and shooting up again.* □ *He can't be off the wagon, because he has never stopped using, even for a day.*

**off the wall** AND **off-the-wall** *mod.* strange; improbable; nonsensical. □ *What an off-the-wall guy!* □ *Your ideas are generally off the wall, but this one makes sense.*

**Oh, boy!** *exclam.* "Wow!" □ *Oh, boy! What a mess!* □ *Oh, boy! That was a great play!*

**Oh, yeah?** ['o 'jæə] *exclam.* "Is that what you think?"; "Are you trying to start a fight?" □ *Oh, yeah? What makes you think so?* □ *Oh, yeah? You want to start something?* □ *Tom said, "Bill, you are a numskull." Bill whirled around, saying, "Oh, yeah?"*

**oiled** *mod.* alcohol or drug intoxicated. □ *Will this stuff make me really oiled?* □ *She's not just drunk; she's totally oiled.*

**oilhead** *n.* a drunkard; an alcoholic. □ *There is an old oilhead over there on the street corner.* □ *Paul gave the oilhead a quarter, knowing it would be spent on cheap wine.*

**oil it** *tr.* to study all night. (Literally, "burn the midnight oil.") □ *I have a test tomorrow, and I really have to oil it tonight.* □ *If you studied all semester long, you would still have to oil it before final exams.*

**oil someone's palm** See *grease someone's palm*.

**oink** [oɪŋk] *n.* a police officer. (A play on *pig*.) □ *There is an oink following us on a motorcycle.* □ *Here come the oinks!*

**O.J. 1.** *n.* orange juice. □ *I like to have a big glass of fresh O.J. every morning.* □ *The price of O.J. is going to go up again soon.* **2.** See *overjolt*. **3.** *n.* a marijuana cigarette dipped in opium. (Drugs. From *opium joint*.) □ *A lot of guys in Nam smoked O.J.s.* □ *Are O.J.s addictive?*

**O.K.** AND **OK, okay** **1.** *interj.* "accepted." (This may be originally from a jocular "oll kerrect," but no one really knows its origin.) □ *O.K., I'll do it.* □ *You want me to lend you $100? Okay.* □ *So, he said, like, "okay," and, like, I go "okay." So we both go "Okay." Okay?* **2.** *mod.* acceptable. □ *Fred is an O.K. guy.* □ *This cake is okay, but not what I would call first-rate.* **3.** *mod.* acceptably. □ *She ran okay—nothing spectacular.* □ *They usually do it okay.* **4.** *n.* (someone's) acceptance. □ *I won't give the final okay until I see the plans.* □ *We got her O.K. and went on with the job.* **5.** *tr.* to approve something. □ *She refused to okay our plans.* □ *Please OK this bill so I can pay it.*

**okay** See *O.K.*

**okey-dokey** ['oki'doki] *interj.* "yes"; "O.K." (Folksy.) □ *Okey-dokey, I'll be there at noon.* □ *Okey-dokey. You sure can.*

**old flame** *n.* a former sweetheart or lover. □ *Mary's old flame, Tom, will be at the party.* □ *It is best to forget an old flame.*

**old fogey** *n.* an old-fashioned person; an old man. □ *My uncle is an old fogey. He must be the most old-fashioned man in the world.* □ *Don't be such an old fogey.*

**old girl** *n.* an old lady; a lively old lady. □ *That old girl is still going.* □ *What makes an old girl like that so feisty?*

**old hand (at something)** *n.* someone experienced at doing something. □ *I'm an old hand at fixing cars.* □ *Do you need help with your painting? I'm an old hand.*

**old hat** *n.* an old-fashioned thing or person; an outmoded thing or person. □ *That's just old hat. This is the modern world!* □ *Her latest work is nothing but old hat. She's through.*

**old heave-ho** ['old 'hiv'ho] *n.* a dismissal; a physical removal of someone from a place. □ *I thought my job was secure, but today I got the old heave-ho.* □ *You had better act right, or my friend will give you the old heave-ho.*

**oldie but goodie** *n.* something (or even someone) that is old but still likeable. □ *I love that piece of music. It's an oldie but goodie.* □ *Mary is an oldie but goodie. I'm glad she's still around.*

**old lady** AND **old woman** **1.** *n.* (one's) mother. □ *I'll ask my old lady if I can go.* □ *What time does your old lady get home?* **2.** *n.* (one's) wife. □ *I wonder what my old lady is cooking for dinner tonight.* □ *My old lady doesn't like for me to go out without her.* **3.** *n.* (one's) girlfriend. □ *My old lady and I are getting married next week.* □ *I got my old lady a bracelet for her birthday.*

**old man** **1.** *n.* (one's) father. □ *I'll ask my old man if I can go.* □ *What time does your old man get home?* **2.** *n.* (one's) husband. □ *My old man is downstairs fixing the furnace.* □ *My old man is sick and can't come with me.* **3.** *n.* (one's) boyfriend. □ *Ask your old man to come to the party, too.* □ *I got my old man to take me to see that movie I told you about.* **4.** *n.* the boss; a high-ranking officer. (Always with *the*.) □ *The old man says do it, so you had better do it.* □ *Quiet! Here comes the old man.*

**old one-two** **1.** *n.* a series of two punches delivered quickly, one after another. (Always with *the*.) □ *Tom gave Bill the old one-two, and the argument was ended right there.* □ *Watch out for Tom. He's a master of the old one-two.* **2.** *n.* any destructive assault on an idea, thing, or person. □ *By the time the committee had given the plan the old one-two, there was nothing left I could do.* □ *I gave his proposal the old one-two. Next time he will be better prepared.*

**old soldier** **1.** *n.* a cigarette or cigar butt; a hunk of tobacco. □ *The tramp bent over to pick up an old soldier off the pavement.* □ *He's never had anything but an old soldier for a smoke.* **2.** *n.* an empty liquor bottle; an empty beer bottle or can. □ *Larry hid all his old soldiers under the bed.* □ *Bill hit Tom over the head with an old soldier.*

**old-timer** *n.* an old person; an old man. (Also a term of address.) □ *Hey, old-timer, how's it going?* □ *Ask that old-timer over there if it has always been this bad around here.*

**on a rip** *mod.* under the effects of *L.S.D.* (Drugs.) □ *Max is on a rip. Stay away from him.* □ *The kid started out the evening on a rip and ended up in the hospital.*

**on a roll** *mod.* in the midst of a series of successes. (See *roll.*) □ *Don't stop me now. I'm on a roll.* □ *Things are going great for Larry. He's on a roll now.*

**on a shoestring** *mod.* on practically no money; on a very tight budget. (See *shoestring.*) □ *I run my business on a shoestring. I never know from day to day whether I will survive.* □ *We live on a shoestring—hardly any money at all.*

**on a tight leash** **1.** *mod.* under very careful control. □ *My father keeps my brother on a tight leash.* □ *We can't do much around here. The boss has us all on a tight leash.* **2.** *mod.* addicted to some drug. □ *Max is on a tight leash. He has to have the stuff regularly.* □ *Gert is kept on a tight leash by her habit.*

**once and for all** *mod.* permanently. □ *I'm gonna take care of you once and for all!* □ *I would like to get this ridiculous problem settled once and for all.*

**once in a blue moon** *mod.* rarely. □ *I do this only once in a blue moon.* □ *Once in a blue moon I have a little wine with dinner.*

**once-over** *n.* a visual examination, especially of a person of the opposite sex. (Always with *the.*) □ *The way she was giving him the once-over, I knew she would say something to him.* □ *Tom, you are always giving the girls the once-over.*

**once over lightly** **1.** *mod.* quickly and superficially; carelessly; cursorily. □ *He looked at it once over lightly and agreed to do it.* □ *It needs more than a once over lightly look.* **2.** *n.* a perfunctory examination; a quick glance. □ *Please give it more than the usual once over lightly.* □ *A once over lightly is not enough.*

**one** *mod.* having to do with something unique or special. (Similar to a definite article. See examples.) □ *Molly is one fine cook.* □ *He was left with one powerful hangover.* □ *Hank? Now there is one ugly son of a gun for you.*

**one and one** *mod.* having to do with the use of both nostrils in snorting a drug, usually cocaine. (Drugs.) □ *Max always takes it one and one. It's the only way he can get enough.* □ *He does it one and one because it hits him faster that way.*

**one and only** *n.* one's lover or sweetheart. □ *I bought a gift for my one and only.* □ *She's my one and only, and I love her.*

**on easy street** *mod.* in a state of financial independence and comfort. (See *easy street.*) □ *I want to live on easy street when I grow up.* □ *When I get this contract signed, I'll be on easy street.*

**one for the road** *n.* a drink; a drink before a journey. □ *Let's have one for the road.* □ *Don't have one for the road if you are going to be the driver.*

**one-horse town** *n.* a very small town; a small and backward town. □ *I refuse to spend a whole week in that one-horse town!* □ *I grew up in a one-horse town, and I liked it very much.*

**one jump ahead of someone or something** *n.* in advance of someone or something; a step ahead of someone or something. □ *I try to be one jump ahead of the problems.* □ *You have to keep one jump ahead of the boss in order to succeed.*

**one-man show** **1.** *n.* a performance put on by one person. □ *It was a one-man show, but it was very entertaining.* □ *For a one-man show, it was very long.* **2.** *n.* an exhibition of the artistic works of one person. □ *She is having a one-man show at the Northside Gallery.* □ *I'm having a one-man show next weekend. Come and see what I have done.*

**one-night stand** **1.** *n.* a performance lasting only one night. □ *The band did a series of one-night stands down the East Coast.* □ *You can't make a living doing one-night stands.* **2.** *n.* a romance or sexual relationship that lasts only one night. □ *It was not a romance, just a one-night stand.* □ *It looked like something that would last longer than a one-night stand.*

**one of the faithful** *n.* a drunkard. □ *Here comes Mr. Franklin—one of the faithful—staggering down the street.* □

*I saw one of the faithful standing at the bar.*

**one's bag** *n.* one's preferences; one's talents. □ *Working crossword puzzles is my bag.* □ *Hey, Tom, what's your bag? What do you like to do?*

**one's best shot** *n.* one's best attempt (at something). □ *That was his best shot, but it wasn't good enough.* □ *I always try to give something my best shot.*

**one smart apple** *n.* a smart or clever person. (See *one.*) □ *That Sue is one smart apple.* □ *My brother is one smart apple.*

**one too many** *n.* one drink of liquor too many, implying drunkenness. □ *I think I've had one too many. It's time to stop drinking.* □ *Don't drive if you've had one too many.*

**one-track mind** *n.* a (person's) mind obsessed with only one thing. □ *When it comes to food, Tom has a one-track mind.* □ *Mary has a one-track mind. All she thinks about is Tom.*

**on fire** *mod.* very attractive or sexy. □ *She is really on fire!* □ *Look at those jet-set people! Each one of them is just on fire.*

**on ice** *mod.* in reserve. □ *That's a great idea, but we'll have to put it on ice until we can afford to put it into action.* □ *I have two boyfriends. One I see every weekend, and the other I keep on ice for a rainy day.*

**onliest** *mod.* only. (Folksy.) □ *This is the onliest nose I have. Please don't punch it.* □ *The cow led her onliest little calf to the stream.*

**only way to go** *n.* the best way to do something; the best choice to make. □ *Get a four-wheel-drive car. It's the only way to go.* □ *That's it! A new house. It's the only way to go.*

**on one's high horse** *mod.* in a haughty manner or mood. □ *Larry is on his high horse again, bossing people around.* □ *The boss is on her high horse about the number of paper clips we use.*

**on one's or its last legs** *mod.* about to expire or become nonfunctional. □ *This car is on its last legs. We have to get a new one.* □ *Poor old Chuck is on his last legs.*

**on one's own hook** *mod.* all by oneself. □ *I don't need any help. I can do it on my own hook.* □ *She did it on her own hook without having to call on anyone.*

**on someone's case** AND **on someone's tail** *mod.* nagging someone; annoying someone with criticism or supervision. □ *You have been on my case long enough. Mind your own business!* □ *The boss has been on my tail about the large number of telephone calls I make.*

**on someone's tail 1.** See the previous entry. **2.** *mod.* following someone closely. □ *There is a huge truck on my tail. What should I do?* □ *Keep on her tail and don't let her out of your sight.*

**on someone's watch** *mod.* while someone is on duty. □ *I am not responsible since it didn't happen on my watch.* □ *I guess I have to bear the blame since it happened on my watch.*

**on tap 1.** *mod.* having to do with beer sold from a barrel or keg. □ *Do you have any imported beers on tap here?* □ *I like beer on tap. The canned stuff tastes funny to me.* **2.** *mod.* immediately available. □ *I have just the kind of person you're talking about on tap.* □ *The cook has any kind of food you might want on tap.*

**on-target** *mod.* timely; exact; incisive. □ *Your criticism is exactly on-target.* □ *We are on-target for a December completion date.*

**on the back burner** *mod.* out of the way; aside and out of consideration. (See *on the shelf.*) □ *We will have to put this on the back burner for a while.* □ *She kept her boyfriend on the back burner until she decided what to do about him.*

**on the ball 1.** *mod.* knowledgeable; competent; attentive. □ *This guy is really on the ball.* □ *If you were on the ball, this wouldn't have happened.* **2.** *mod.* in one's head or brain; at one's disposal. (Especially with *have a lot.*) □ *He sure has a lot on the ball.* □ *When you've got it on the ball the way she does, things generally go right.*

**on the bandwagon** *mod.* with the majority; following the latest fad. (Often with *hop, get, climb, jump.*) □ *Come on! Hop on the bandwagon! Everyone* *else is joining.* □ *Tom always has to climb on the bandwagon. He does no independent thinking.*

**on the beam 1.** *mod.* homing in on an aviation radio beam. (No longer a major navigational device.) □ *The plane was on the beam and landed safely in the fog.* □ *I couldn't get on the beam, and I flew right over the airfield.* **2.** *mod.* on the right course or track. (From the previous sense.) □ *That is exactly right. You are right on the beam.* □ *You're on the beam. You will finish this with no problems.* **3.** AND **beaming** *mod.* under the effects of marijuana. (Drugs.) □ *Walter is on the beam again. How can he hold a job?* □ *The only time that Max is happy is when he is beaming.* **4.** *mod.* smart; clever. □ *That was well done, Tom. You're on the beam.* □ *She is really on the beam. Glad she came along.*

**on the bean** See *on the button.*

**on the blink 1.** *mod.* out of order; ill. (Compare to *on the fritz.*) □ *I was a little on the blink yesterday and decided to stay at home.* □ *My refrigerator is on the blink again.* **2.** *mod.* alcohol intoxicated; on a drinking spree. □ *They all went out and got on the blink.* □ *My brother is a little bit on the blink this morning.*

**on the button** AND **on the bean** *mod.* exactly the right time or place. □ *He was there on time, right on the button.* □ *I want to see you here at noon—on the bean.*

**on the chopping block** *mod.* in serious and threatening straits. □ *Our whole future is on the chopping block.* □ *Until this is resolved, our necks are on the chopping block.*

**on the double** *mod.* very fast; twice as fast. (Originally military. Refers to "double time" in marching.) □ *Get over here right now—on the double!* □ *She wants to see you in her office on the double.*

**on the fly** *mod.* while something or someone is operating or moving. □ *I'll try to capture the data on the fly.* □ *Please try to buy some aspirin somewhere on the fly today.*

**on the fritz 1.** *mod.* not functioning properly. □ *This T.V. is on the fritz again.* □ *My watch is on the fritz.* **2.**

*mod.* alcohol intoxicated. □ *Sue is a bit on the fritz.* □ *She drank till she was totally on the fritz.*

**on the hype** *mod.* addicted to injectable drugs. (Drugs. Compare to *on the needle.*) □ *Gert is on the hype. She shoots twice a day.* □ *Will she be on the hype all her life?*

**on the juice** *mod.* drinking heavily; on a drinking bout. (See *juice.*) □ *Fred spent the whole week on the juice.* □ *She won't be able to return your call. I'm afraid she's on the juice again.*

**on the junk** *mod.* on drugs; addicted to drugs. (See *junk.*) □ *Max has been on the junk for all of his adult life.* □ *He's not really on the junk. He's only addicted to cigarettes.*

**on the lam** [...læm] *mod.* running from the police. (Underworld.) □ *Max has been on the lam for a week now.* □ *When the boss found out you was on the lam, he got real mad.*

**on the level** *mod.* honest; straightforward. □ *Come on now. Be on the level with me.* □ *Is the ad on the level?*

**on the make** *mod.* ambitious; attempting to be great. □ *That young lawyer is sure on the make.* □ *This university is on the make.*

**on the mojo** [...'modʒo] *mod.* addicted to morphine; using morphine. (Drugs. See *mojo.*) □ *How long you been on the mojo?* □ *How can you hold a steady job if you're on the mojo?*

**on the money** *mod.* exactly as desired; at the right amount of money. □ *Your new idea is right on the money.* □ *The bid for the new hospital came in on the money.*

**on the natch** [...nætʃ] *mod.* free of drugs; natural and *straight.* □ *Max says he wants to get on the natch, but I don't believe it.* □ *I have been on the natch for almost a year.*

**on the needle** *mod.* addicted to injectable drugs. (Drugs. Compare to *on the hype.*) □ *My sister's on the needle, and I want to help her.* □ *Once you're on the needle, you've had it.*

**on the nod 1.** *mod.* in a drug stupor. (Drugs.) □ *Max is in the back room on the nod.* □ *The addict shot up and spent the rest of the day on the nod.* **2.** *mod.*

265

addicted to a drug, usually heroin. (Drugs.) □ *Max has been on the nod for three years now.* □ *If you take that stuff, you'll be on the nod for the rest of your life.*

**on the nose** *mod.* exactly on time; exactly as planned. □ *I want you there at noon on the nose.* □ *All three of them were at the appointed place right on the nose.*

**on the outs (with someone)** *mod.* in a mild dispute with someone; sharing ill will with someone. □ *Tom and Bill are on the outs again.* □ *Tom has been on the outs with Bill before. They'll work it out.*

**on the pill** *mod.* taking birth control pills. □ *Is it true that Mary is on the pill?* □ *She was on the pill, but she isn't now.*

**on the prod** *mod.* addicted to narcotics administered by injection. (Drugs. The same as *on the needle*.) □ *Max is on the prod and looks real sick.* □ *He thought he would just snort the stuff and never get on the prod.*

**on the prowl** *mod.* looking for someone for sexual purposes, in the manner of a prowling cat. □ *Tom looks like he is on the prowl again tonight.* □ *That whole gang of boys is on the prowl. Watch out.*

**on the road** *mod.* traveling from place to place, not necessarily on the highways. (See also *get the show on the road*.) □ *I was on the road with the circus for six months.* □ *I don't work in the main office anymore. Now I'm on the road.*

**on the rocks** **1.** *mod.* (of an alcoholic drink) with ice cubes. (See *rocks*.) □ *I'd like mine on the rocks, please.* □ *Give me a scotch on the rocks, please.* **2.** *mod.* in a state of ruin or bankruptcy. (Like a ship that has gone aground on the rocks and cannot be moved.) □ *That bank is on the rocks. Don't put your money in it.* □ *My finances are on the rocks just now.*

**on the run** **1.** *mod.* while one is moving from place to place. □ *I will try to get some aspirin today on the run.* □ *I will think about it on the run.* **2.** *mod.* running from the police. □ *Max is on the run from the cops.* □ *The gang of crooks is on the run. Probably somewhere in Florida.*

**on the safe side** *mod.* taking the risk-free path. □ *Let's be on the safe side and call first.* □ *I think you should stay on the safe side and call the doctor about this fever.*

**on the same wavelength** *mod.* thinking in the same pattern. □ *We're not on the same wavelength. Let's try again.* □ *We kept talking until we were on the same wavelength.*

**on the sauce** *mod.* drinking regularly; alcohol intoxicated. □ *Poor old Ron is on the sauce again.* □ *He is on the sauce most of the time.*

**on the shelf** **1.** *mod.* not active socially; left to oneself in social matters. □ *I've been on the shelf long enough. I'm going to make some friends.* □ *She likes being on the shelf.* **2.** *mod.* postponed. (See *on the back burner*.) □ *We'll have to put this matter on the shelf for a while.* □ *I have a plan on the shelf just waiting for an opportunity like this.*

**on the side** **1.** *mod.* extra, such as with a job or a side order of food. □ *I would like an order of eggs with toast on the side, please.* □ *She is a bank teller and works as a waitress on the side.* **2.** *mod.* extramarital: in addition to one's spouse. □ *He is married, but also has a woman on the side.* □ *She has boyfriends on the side, but her husband knows about them.*

**on the skids** *mod.* on the decline. (See also *put the skids under someone or something*.) □ *My newly started business is on the skids.* □ *Her health is really on the skids, but she stays cheery anyway.*

**on the sly** *mod.* secretly and deceptively. □ *She was stealing little bits of money on the sly.* □ *Martin was having an affair with the maid on the sly.*

**on the squiff** [...skwɪf] *mod.* on a drinking bout. (See also *squiff*.) □ *Bob is out on the squiff again.* □ *Max is always on the squiff, except when he's shooting dope.*

**on the street** **1.** *mod.* using drugs; selling drugs; looking for drugs. (Drugs.) □ *Fred spent a year on the street before he was arrested.* □ *Max will be on the street all his life.* **2.** *mod.* engaged in prostitution. □ *Mary said, "What am I supposed to do—go on the street?"* □ *All three of them went on the street to earn enough money to live.* **3.** *mod.* widely known. □ *Sue put it on the street, and now everyone knows.* □ *It's on the street. There isn't anyone who hasn't heard it.* **4.** *mod.* on Wall Street or elsewhere in the New York City financial district. (Similar to the previous sense, except that it refers to a specific street.) □ *I heard on the street today that Apple is buying IBM.* □ *It's on the street that the market is due to crash again.* **5.** *mod.* at discount prices; as available from discounters. (As if some item were being sold on the street by a peddler.) □ *It lists at $2200 and can be got for about $1650 on the street.* □ *On the street it goes for about $400.*

**on the take** *mod.* taking bribes. (Underworld.) □ *I heard that the mayor is on the take.* □ *Everyone in city hall is on the take.*

**on the tank** AND **on a tank** *mod.* on a drinking bout. □ *All the guys were on the tank last Saturday.* □ *Paul spent all weekend on a tank.*

**on the up and up** *mod.* legitimate; *open and above board.* □ *Is this deal on the up and up? What's the catch?* □ *Everything I do is on the up and up. I am totally honest.*

**on the wagon** *mod.* not now drinking alcoholic liquor. □ *How long has John been on the wagon this time?* □ *He's on the wagon again.*

**on the warpath** *mod.* very angry. □ *The boss is on the warpath again. Watch out!* □ *I am on the warpath about setting goals and standards again.*

**onto a good thing** *mod.* having found something that is to one's advantage, such as something easy, profitable, inexpensive, etc. □ *I think that Bill got onto a good thing when he opened his own store.* □ *I won't quit now. I'm onto a good thing, and I know it.*

**onto someone or something** *mod.* alerted to or aware of a deceitful plan or person. □ *The cops are onto your little game here.* □ *Max thought he was safe, but the fuzz was onto him from the beginning.*

**oodles** ['udļz] *n.* lots (of something). □ *My uncle has just oodles and oodles of money.* □ *I don't have oodles, but I have enough to keep me happy.* □ *When I have spaghetti, I just love oodles of noodles.*

**oof** [uf] **1.** *exclam.* the sound one makes when one is struck in the abdomen. (Usually **Oof!**) □ *So, then Bob hit him in the belly. Oof! □ "Oof!" cried Tom. He couldn't talk any more after that.* **2.** *n.* the potency of the alcohol in liquor; the effect of potent alcohol. □ *This stuff really has oof. How old is it?* □ *Beer doesn't have enough oof for her anymore.*

**oomph** [umpf] **1.** *n.* energy; drive and vitality. □ *Come on, you guys. Let's get some oomph behind it. PUSH!* □ *You need more oomph if you want to work at heavy labor.* **2.** *n.* sex appeal. (Euphemistic.) □ *She had a lot of oomph, but didn't wish to become a movie star.* □ *No amount of oomph can make up for a total lack of talent.*

**Oops-a-daisy!** AND **Oopsy-daisy!, Upsy-daisy!, Whoops-a-daisy!** ['upsə'dezı AND 'upsi'dezi, 'əpsi'dezi, 'ʌupsə'dezi] *exclam.* something said when a child falls down; something said when a child is physically moved from one place or position to another. □ *"Oops-a-daisy!" said Mrs. Fletcher when little Jimmy Fletcher fell down on his bottom.* □ *As her daddy lifted her up into bed, he said, "Upsy-daisy!"*

**open and above board** AND **above board** *mod.* honest and straightforward. □ *Let's keep everything open and above board. Honesty is the best policy.* □ *If all our discussions are above board, no one will question our procedures.*

**O.P.s** ['o'piz] *n.* other people's cigarettes; begged or borrowed cigarettes. □ *My favorite kind of cigarettes is O.P.s. They're the cheapest, too.* □ *Ted only smokes O.P.s.*

**O.R.** *n.* an "operating room." (Hospitals.) □ *The doctor is in O.R. now.* □ *The O.R. has to be scrubbed between each use.*

**orals** *n.* an oral examination, such as for an advanced academic degree. □ *He flunked his orals, but he got another chance.* □ *I hate orals. I'd rather write.*

**org** [ɔrg] **1.** *n.* the *rush* caused by potent drugs. (Drugs. From *orgasm*.) □ *Max hated the vomiting when he first took it, but he loved the org.* □ *Does this stuff give you a real org?* **2.** *n.* an organization. □ *She's a member of the org and can't be expected to use independent judgement.* □ *Come on, join the org.*

**ork-orks** [ˈɔrkɔrks] *n.* the delirium tremens. □ *He has the ork-orks. He's a real drunk.* □ *Whenever he gets the ork-orks, he gets himself arrested and put in jail where he can sober up.*

**or what?** *phr.* (part of a special formula that asks if something is a good example or specimen of something. The expected answer is yes. The question "Is this an X or what?" means "If this isn't a really great X, what is it then?") □ *Look at what I am wearing! Is that a great jacket or what?* □ *That's my son. Is he a superman or what?*

**O-sign** *n.* the rounded, open mouth of a dead person. (A semi-jocular usage. Hospitals. See also *Q-sign*.) □ *The guy in room 226 is giving the O-sign.* □ *That's the third O-sign we've got since noon.*

**ossifer** AND **occifer** [ˈɑsəfɚ] *n.* a police officer. (Also an ill-advised term of address.) □ *Look here, ossifer, I was just having a little fun.* □ *Ask the occifer there if he wants to step outside and discuss it.*

**ossified** [ˈɑsəfaɪd] *mod.* alcohol or drug intoxicated. (From *stoned (out)*.) □ *How can anybody be so ossified on four beers?* □ *I've never seen anybody so ossified.*

**out 1.** *mod.* alcohol or drug intoxicated. (Probably from *far out*.) □ *All four of them were totally out.* □ *Those guys are really out!* **2.** *mod.* out of fashion. (The opposite of *in*.) □ *That kind of clothing is strictly out.* □ *You need to tell me which of my dresses is out this season.*

**outa\*** [ˈaʊdə] *phr.* "out of." (Caution with use in writing.) □ *Get outa here!* □ *In two minutes I'm outa here!*

**out and out** *mod.* complete or total; blatant. □ *Fred was an out and out liar.* □ *Don't be such an out and out stinker!*

**out cold 1.** *mod.* unconscious. □ *Paul was out cold when we found him.* □ *Who knocked him out cold?* **2.** *mod.* alcohol intoxicated. □ *Four beers and he was out cold.* □ *He sat in his chair at the table, out cold.*

**outed** AND **offed** *mod.* dead; killed. □ *The witness was outed before a subpoena could be issued.* □ *The guy was offed when we found him.*

**outfit 1.** *n.* a group of people; a company. □ *That outfit cheated me out of my money.* □ *I will never deal with that outfit again.* **2.** *n.* a set of clothing. □ *You look lovely in that outfit.* □ *Should I wear my gray wool outfit?* **3.** *n.* a set of things; the items needed for some task. □ *I got a fine chemistry outfit for my birthday.* □ *My tool kit has everything I need. It's the whole outfit.*

**out in left field** *mod.* wrong; off base; loony. □ *Don't pay any attention to her. She's out in left field as usual.* □ *That guy is out in left field—a real nut.*

**out like a light 1.** *mod.* unconscious or sleeping soundly. □ *I fell and hit my head. I was out like a light for two minutes, they tell me.* □ *I closed my eyes and was out like a light in no time at all.* **2.** *mod.* heavily alcohol intoxicated. □ *Those guys are really out like a light!* □ *All four of them drank till they were out like a light.*

**out of it 1.** *mod.* not in with the real world. □ *You never pay attention to what's going on. You're really out of it.* □ *Fred is out of it most of the time. He even looks dull.* **2.** *mod.* alcohol or drug intoxicated. □ *Two drinks and she was totally out of it.* □ *When they are out of it, they are quite dangerous.*

**out of kilter 1.** *mod.* not functioning properly; *on the fritz*; *out of whack*. □ *My car's engine is out of kilter and needs some repair work.* □ *My coffee pot is out of kilter, so I have to make coffee in a pan.* **2.** *mod.* out of square. □ *That picture is out of kilter. Please straighten it.* □ *That corner is not square, and the wall even looks out of kilter.*

**out of left field** *mod.* suddenly; from an unexpected source or direction. □ *Most of your ideas are out of left field.* □ *All of his paintings are right out of left field.*

**out of line** *mod.* not in accord with what is appropriate or expected, especially in price or behavior. □ *Your behavior is quite out of line. I shall report you.* □ *Your price is out of line with the other stores.*

**out of luck** *mod.* unfortunate; in a hopeless position. □ *If you think you are going to get any sympathy from me, you're just out of luck.* □ *I was out of luck. There were no eggs left in the store.*

**out of one's head** AND **out of one's mind** **1.** *mod.* crazy; senseless; mad. □ *For a moment after the accident, I was out of my head.* □ *Don't pay any attention to him. He's out of his head.* **2.** *mod.* alcohol or drug intoxicated. □ *Who wants to go out and get out of his head?* □ *Tod is out of his head on four beers.*

**out of one's skull** *mod.* alcohol intoxicated. □ *Oh, man, I drank till I was out of my skull.* □ *Two beers and he was out of his skull.*

**out of sight** **1.** *mod.* heavily alcohol or drug intoxicated; *high.* □ *They've been drinking since noon, and they're out of sight.* □ *Man, is she ever out of sight!* **2.** *mod.* very expensive; high in price. □ *Prices at that restaurant are out of sight.* □ *The cost of medical care is out of sight.*

**out of sync** [...sɪŋk] *mod.* uncoordinated; unsynchronized. □ *Our efforts are out of sync.* □ *My watch and your watch are out of sync.*

**out of the picture** *mod.* no longer relevant to a situation; departed; dead. □ *Now that Tom is out of the picture, we needn't concern ourselves about his objections.* □ *With her husband out of the picture, she can begin living.*

**out of the way** **1.** *mod.* dead; killed. □ *The crooks put the witness out of the way before the trial.* □ *Now that her husband was out of the way, she began to get out and about more.* **2.** *mod.* alcohol intoxicated. □ *She spends a lot of time out of the way.* □ *After a few more drinks, Bill will be out of the way.*

**out of the woods** *mod.* freed from a previous state of uncertainty or danger; no longer critical. □ *As soon as her temperature is down, she'll be out of the woods.* □ *We're out of the woods now, and things aren't so chancy.*

**out of this world** **1.** *mod.* wonderful and exciting. □ *This pie is out of this world.* □ *My boyfriend is just out of this world.* **2.** *mod.* drug intoxicated. □ *Man, is she ever out of this world! What did she drink?* □ *He drank until he was out of this world.*

**out of whack** AND **out of wack** *mod.* out of adjustment; inoperative. (Compare to *out of kilter.*) □ *My watch is out of whack.* □ *I think my left eye is out of wack a little. Maybe I need glasses.*

**outsy** ['ɑutsi] *n.* a navel that protrudes. (Compare to *insy.*) □ *Is yours an insy or an outsy?* □ *I have an outsy. Why on earth do you ask?*

**out the window** *mod.* gone; wasted. □ *All that work gone out the window.* □ *My forty dollars—out the window. Why didn't I save my money?*

**out to lunch** *mod.* absentminded; giddy; stupid-acting. □ *Old Ted is so out to lunch these days. Seems to be losing his mind.* □ *Don't pay any attention to my uncle. He's out to lunch.*

**overamped** *mod.* high on amphetamines; overdosed with amphetamines. (Drugs.) □ *Max is overamped again.* □ *Two students were overamped and got sent to the counselor.*

**over and unders** *n.* amphetamines and barbiturates. (Drugs. See also *upper, downer.*) □ *They found a big pile of over and unders in Max's room.* □ *He takes over and unders day and night.*

**over easy** *mod.* turned carefully, said of cooking eggs. □ *I want mine cooked over easy.* □ *Over easy eggs are better than scrambled.*

**overjolt** AND **O.J.** **1.** *n.* an overdose of drugs, especially of heroin. (Drugs.) □ *Ted is suffering from a serious O.J.* □ *That overjolt nearly killed her.* **2.** *in.* to take an overdose of drugs, especially of heroin. (Drugs.) □ *She overjolted once too often.* □ *If you O.J. again, you will probably die.*

**overkill** *n.* too much. □ *That is enough. Any more is just overkill.* □ *Your policy of overkill is wasteful and expensive.*

**over my dead body** *phr.* "not if I can stop you"; "you won't be able to do something if I am alive to prevent you."

□ *You'll drop out of school over my dead body!* □ *Get married and move to Arizona? Over my dead body!*

**over one's head** *mod.* confusing; too difficult to understand. □ *This stuff is too hard. It's over my head.* □ *Calculus is all over my head.*

**overserved** *mod.* having to do with a drunken person in a bar; alcohol intoxicated. (Euphemistic.) □ *Four customers were overserved and had to leave.* □ *The overserved guy there in the corner is going to be sick.*

**over-the-counter 1.** *mod.* having to do with stocks that are sold through dealers rather than through a stock exchange. □ *You can make or lose a lot of money on over-the-counter stocks.* □ *Is this stock over-the-counter or available on the exchange?* **2.** *mod.* having to do with medication sold without a prescription. □ *Over-the-counter drugs can be helpful in some diseases.* □ *Is this medication over-the-counter or by prescription only?*

**over the hill 1.** *mod.* escaped from prison or the military. (See *A.W.O.L.*) □ *Two privates went over the hill last night.* □ *They broke out of jail and went over the hill.* **2.** *mod.* too old (for something). □ *You're only 50! You're not over the hill yet.* □ *Some people seem over the hill at 30.*

**over the hump 1.** *mod.* drug intoxicated. □ *Max is over the hump now. He is stoned.* □ *This stuff makes you sick at first. Then suddenly you are over the hump and floating.* **2.** *mod.* over the hard part; past the midpoint. □ *Things should be easy from now on. We are over the hump.* □ *When you get over the hump, life is much better.*

**over the long haul** *mod.* long term; over a long period of time. □ *Over the long haul, this one will prove best.* □ *This will last over the long haul.*

**O.Z.** AND **Oz., o-zee** *n.* an ounce of a drug, now usually marijuana. (Drugs.) □ *You got an Oz. I can buy?* □ *Max has an O.Z. or two to spare.*

**ozoned** *mod.* under the influence of *P.C.P.* (Drugs.) □ *Max is ozoned again. I think he's really sick this time.* □ *He's got himself ozoned again.*

# P

**P.** See *pee*.

**pack** *tr.* to carry something, usually a gun. (Underworld. Any of the slang terms for gun may be used: *rod, iron, heat,* etc.) □ *I can tell that guy's packing heat from the bulge in his jacket.* □ *I never pack a rod on Sunday.*

**package 1.** *n.* a combination of a variety of related things; a unified set of things. (See also *package deal*.) □ *You can't buy just one part. It comes as a package.* □ *The first college I applied to offered me a good aid package, so I went.* **2.** *n.* a lot of money; a *bundle.* □ *She made quite a package on that bank deal.* □ *I came away from the dog track with a nice little package.* **3.** *n.* someone who is cute or sexually attractive. (Primarily refers to females as bundles of sexual charms. Similar in meaning to sense 1.) □ *How do you like that little package who just came in?* □ *She's quite a package, if you like the giggly type.* **4.** *tr.* to position or display someone or something, as in marketing, to good advantage. □ *The agent packaged the actress so that everyone thought she only did dramatic roles.* □ *If you package your plan correctly, the committee will accept it.*

**packaged** *mod.* alcohol intoxicated. □ *Man, Max was really packaged last night!* □ *By midnight she was totally packaged.*

**package deal** *n.* a variety of goods or services sold as a unit. □ *I got all these tools in a package deal for only $39.95.* □ *What about giving me all three shirts as a package deal?*

**packed up** *mod.* drug intoxicated; ready for a *trip.* (Drugs.) □ *That guy doesn't make any sense. He's packed up.* □ *Tom is so packed up all the time that he can't get his work done.*

**pack of lies** *n.* a whole collection or series of lies. □ *I've heard you talk about this before, and it's all a pack of lies.* □ *Her story is nothing but a pack of lies.*

**pad 1.** *n.* a place to live; one's room or dwelling. □ *Why don't you come over to my pad for a while?* □ *This is a nice pad you've got here.* **2.** *tr.* to lengthen a piece of writing with unnecessary material. □ *This story would be better if you hadn't padded it with so much chitchat.* □ *I think I can pad the report enough to make it fill twenty pages.* (More at *padded.*)

**padded 1.** *mod.* (of a piece of writing) lengthened with unnecessary material. (See *pad.*) □ *Your report is padded and uninformative.* □ *Next time, don't give me a padded report. It's too long.* **2.** *mod.* having drugs (or other contraband) taped to one's body for international smuggling. (Drugs.) □ *The police examined him and found that he was padded with packets of cocaine.* □ *That guy over there looks padded. The customs officer is going to check him out.* **3.** *mod.* plump or fat. □ *He didn't hurt himself when he fell down. He's well padded there.* □ *Your clothes would fit better if you weren't so—ah—padded.*

**paddy** *n.* a police officer, especially an Irish police officer. (Usually derogative. Also an ill-advised term of address.) □ *Tell that paddy to go catch a crook or something.* □ *Look here, paddy, I wasn't doing anything.*

**paddy wagon** *n.* a police van used to take suspected criminals to the police station. □ *It took two paddy wagons to carry away the people they arrested.* □ *The cop put the woman in handcuffs and then called the paddy wagon.*

**pad out** *in.* to go to bed or to sleep. (See *pad.*) □ *Man, if I don't pad out by midnight, I'm a zombie.* □ *Why don't you people go home so I can pad out?*

**padre** ['pɑdre] *n.* any male religious cleric: priest, monk, or chaplain. (From Spanish. Typically military. Also a term of address.) □ *I went to see the padre for some advice.* □ *Hey, padre, anything new on the religion front?*

**pafisticated** [pə'fɪstəkedəd] *mod.* alcohol intoxicated. (A corruption of "sophisticated.") □ *Whenever I drink champagne, I get totally pafisticated.* □ *Look at her drive. She is a real pafisticated lady.*

**paid** *mod.* alcohol intoxicated. □ *I think I'll go out and get paid tonight.* □ *Tom went to the tavern and spent all his money on getting paid.*

**pain** *n.* a bother; an irritating thing or person. □ *That woman is such a pain.* □ *Those long meetings are a real pain.*

**pain in the ass\*** AND **pain in the butt\*, pain in the rear** *n.* a very annoying thing or person. (Crude. An elaboration of *pain.* Caution with *ass. Butt* is less offensive. *Rear* is euphemistic.) □ *That guy is a real pain in the ass.* □ *Things like that give me a pain in the butt.* □ *You are nothing but a pain in the rear.*

**pain in the butt** See the previous entry.

**pain in the neck** *n.* a difficult or annoying thing or person. (Compare to *pain in the ass.*) □ *This tax form is a pain in the neck.* □ *My boss is a pain in the neck.*

**pain in the rear** See *pain in the ass.*

**painkiller** *n.* liquor. (See also *feeling no pain.*) □ *Pass that bottle of painkiller over here. My throat hurts.* □ *He should look happy. He's full of painkiller.*

**paint remover** *n.* strong or inferior whiskey or other spirits. □ *That paint remover you gave me nearly burned out my throat.* □ *What do you call that paint remover anyway? It sure is powerful.*

**paint the town (red)** *tr.* to go out and celebrate; to go on a drinking bout; to get drunk. □ *I feel great. Let's go out and paint the town.* □ *They were out painting the town red last night.*

**pal** [pæl] **1.** *n.* a close male friend or buddy. □ *Be nice to him. He's my pal.* □ *Hey, be a pal. Give me a match.* **2.** *n.* a term of address for a stranger, usually a male. □ *Hey, pal. Got a match?* □ *Look, pal, I was in line in front of you!*

**pal around (with someone)** *in.* to be friends with someone; to move about socially with someone. □ *Tom and Alice have palled around for years.* □ *Young people like to pal around with one another.*

**palimony** ['pæləmoni] *n.* alimony—living expenses—paid to a common-law wife or to a former girlfriend. □ *He left her, and she took him to court to try to get him to pay palimony.* □ *With a good lawyer, she got more palimony than she could ever have gotten as alimony if they had been married.*

**pally (with someone)** *mod.* friendly or overly friendly with someone. □ *I don't know why Sue acts so pally. I hardly know her.* □ *She doesn't seem pally with me.*

**palm** *tr.* to conceal something in the hand as in a theft or the performance of a magic trick; to receive and conceal a tip or a bribe. □ *The kid palmed the candy bar and walked right out of the store.* □ *The waiter palmed the $20 bill and led us to a table.*

**palm-oil** *n.* a bribe; a tip. (See also *oil someone's palm.*) □ *How much palm-oil does it take to get this deed recorded in reasonable time?* □ *The messenger seemed to move his legs faster after an application of palm-oil.*

**palm-presser** See *flesh-presser.*

**palm someone or something off (on someone)** AND **palm off someone or something (on someone) 1.** *tr.* to transfer some unwanted person or thing to another person. □ *Don't palm her off on me. I don't want her.* □ *My uncle palmed off his old clothes on me.* **2.** *tr.* [with *something*] to succeed in spending counterfeit money; to succeed in cashing a bad check. (Underworld.) □

*Max palmed off four phony twenties in less than an hour.* □ *Somebody palmed off a rubber check on me yesterday.*

**palooka** AND **paluka** [pə'lukə] *n.* a stupid person; an unskilled prizefighter; any mediocre person. (Also a term of address. From the name of the comic-strip prizefighter "Joe Palooka.") □ *Tell that stupid palooka to sit down and shut up.* □ *Get out of here, you paluka. You're just in the way.*

**palsy-walsy** ['pælzi'wælzi] **1.** *n.* a good friend, *pal,* or *buddy.* (Also a term of address.) □ *Look here, palsy-walsy, let's you and me get out of here.* □ *Meet my old palsy-walsy, John. We've known each other since we were kids.* **2.** *mod.* friendly; overly friendly. (Often with *with.*) □ *Why is Tom so palsy-walsy with everyone?* □ *That guy is a little too palsy-walsy.*

**pan** *n.* the face. (See also *deadpan.*) □ *Look at that guy! I've never seen such an ugly pan in my life.* □ *I stared her right in the pan and told her to shut up.*

**panic** *n.* a very funny or exciting person or thing. □ *John's party was a real panic.* □ *Paul is a panic. He tells a joke a minute.*

**pan out** *in.* (for something) to work out or turn out all right. □ *Don't worry. Everything will pan out okay.* □ *Nothing seems to pan out for me anymore.*

**pants rabbits** *n.* lice. (See also *seam-squirrels.*) □ *Max is sure scratching a lot. Do you think he's got pants rabbits?* □ *I don't want to be around people who have pants rabbits and stuff like that.*

**paper 1.** *n.* a written document; written evidence supporting something. (Often with *some.*) □ *Don't tell me over the phone! I want paper!* □ *Come on, send me some paper. Let's make this official.* **2.** *n.* a folded paper containing a dose of drugs. (Drugs.) □ *The cops caught the guy with two papers up his sleeve.* □ *One paper isn't enough to last poor Ernie an hour. He's really hooked.* **3.** *n.* a forged check. (See also *paper-pusher, paper-hanger.*) □ *She was arrested for passing paper.* □ *The police actually lost the paper and ended up with no evidence.*

**paper-hanger** *n.* someone who tries to pass bad checks. (Underworld. See *paper, paper-pusher.*) □ *The cops caught the paper-hanger red-handed.* □ *He's wanted as a paper-hanger in four states.*

**paperhanging** *n.* writing and spending bad checks. (Underworld.) □ *She was accused of paperhanging and didn't even know what the cops were talking about, so they let her go.* □ *She is good at both paperhanging and acting.*

**paper over something** AND **paper something over** *tr.* to try to conceal something unpleasant; to try to cover up a misdeed. □ *This is a severe social problem. Don't try to paper over it.* □ *You can't paper this over. It has to be dealt with now!*

**paper-pusher 1.** *n.* a bureaucrat; a clerk in the military services; any office worker. (See also *pencil-pusher.*) □ *If those paper-pushers can't get their work done on time, make them stay late.* □ *I don't want to talk to some paper-pusher, I want to talk to the boss.* **2.** *n.* someone who passes bad checks. (See *paper, paper-hanger.*) □ *The bank teller spotted a well-known paper-pusher and called the cops.* □ *The old lady was charged as a paper-pusher and sent to jail.*

**parboiled** *mod.* alcohol intoxicated. (See also *boiled.*) □ *Sally stayed at the bar just long enough to get parboiled.* □ *She's not really stewed, just parboiled.*

**pard** *n.* partner. (From *pardner.* Also a term of address.) □ *Come on, pard, let's go find some action.* □ *This is my old pard, Clarence.*

**Pardon my French.** AND **Excuse my French.** *sent.* "Excuse my use of swear words or taboo words." (Does not refer to real French.) □ *Pardon my French, but this is a hell of a day.* □ *What she needs is a kick in the butt, if you'll excuse my French.*

**(parental) units** *n.* parents. (Teens. Also a term of address.) □ *I don't think my parental units will let me stay out late.* □ *Hey, units! I need to talk to you about something really important.*

**park** *in.* to neck or to make love, especially in a parked car. □ *Do kids still park, or do they just watch television?* □

*They still park, but they don't have a name for it anymore.*

**park it (somewhere)** *tr.* sit down somewhere; sit down and get out of the way. □ *Hey, park it! You're in the way.* □ *Max, park it over there in the corner. Stop pacing around. You make me nervous.*

**parting shot** *n.* the last word; a final comment before departing. □ *For a parting shot, she called me a miser.* □ *His parting shot concerned some comments about my ability to do simple math.*

**part that went over the fence last 1.** *n.* a piece of cooked chicken containing the tail. (Folksy. Always with *the.*) □ *If there aren't any more wings, I'll take the part that went over the fence last.* □ *My favorite piece of chicken is the part that went over the fence last. There's not much meat on it, but I don't like chicken anyway.* **2.** *n.* the tail end of any animal; the human buttocks. □ *I slipped and fell down on the part that went over the fence last.* □ *The cat caught the part that went over the fence last in the door.*

**party 1.** *n.* a combining form used in expressions to refer to certain kinds of activity carried on in groups or in pairs. (For examples, see *coke party, free base party, grass party, hen party, jag party, keg party, kick party, pot party, stag-party, tailgate party, tea party.*) **2.** *in.* to drink alcohol, smoke marijuana, or use other drugs. (May also include sexual activity.) □ *Come on, man! Let's party!* □ *If you didn't party so much, you'd get better grades.*

**party animal** *n.* someone who loves parties. □ *My boyfriend and I are real party animals. Let's party!* □ *If you weren't such a party animal, you'd have more time for studying.*

**party bowl** *n.* a marijuana pipe large enough to serve a number of smokers. (Drugs.) □ *When they arrested Max, he had two pipes and a party bowl with him.* □ *The cops thought the party bowl was a flower vase!*

**party-hearty** *in.* to have a great time; to celebrate. (Originally teenage. The past tense is variable.) □ *Let's get some stuff*

*and party-hearty.* □ *The whole class decided to celebrate and party-hearty.*

**party-pooper** *n.* the first person to leave a party; someone who ruins a party because of dullness or by leaving early. □ *Don't leave! Don't be a party-pooper!* □ *Don't invite Martha. She's such a party-pooper.*

**pass 1.** *n.* a passing grade or mark on a test. (Compare to *fail.*) □ *Did you get a pass or a fail?* □ *This is my third pass this semester.* **2.** *in.* to decline something; to decline to participate in something. □ *No, thanks. I pass.* □ *I'll have to pass. I am not prepared.* **3.** *n.* an act of declining something. □ *I'll have to take a pass.* □ *Can I have a pass on that one? There is nothing I can do.* **4.** *n.* a sexual advance or invitation. (Usually with *make.*) □ *He made a pass at me, so I slapped him.* □ *When he made a pass at me, he got a pass right back.* **5.** *tr.* to succeed in spending counterfeit money; to succeed in cashing a bad check. (As if to pass something to someone and have it accepted.) **6.** *n.* a successful drug purchase or sale. (Drugs.) □ *In four passes the dealer made $200.* □ *I didn't make the pass and was stuck carrying the stuff all night.*

**pass go** *tr.* to complete a difficult or dangerous task successfully. (From "pass go and collect $200" in the game Monopoly™.) □ *Man, I tried to get there on time, but I just couldn't pass go.* □ *You had better pass go with this job, or you've had it.*

**passion-pit** *n.* a drive-in movie theatre; any place where young people go to *neck,* such as an area where teenagers *park.* (Dated but still heard.) □ *She wanted me to drive down to the passion-pit, but I said I had a headache.* □ *My mother used to tell me about her trips to the passion-pit.*

**pass the buck** *tr.* to shift the responsibility for something to someone else; to evade responsibility. (See also *buck-passer.*) □ *When things get a little tough, do what I do. Pass the buck.* □ *Don't pass the buck. Stand up and admit you were wrong.*

**passy** *n.* a baby's pacifier. (Baby talk.) □ *Does little Johnnie want his passy?* □

*Mommy, Mary threw her passy on the floor.*

**paste 1.** *tr.* to strike someone, especially in the face. (See also *paste someone one*.) □ *I hauled off and pasted him right in the face.* □ *He tried to paste me, but I ducked.* **2.** *tr.* to defeat a person or a team, usually in a game of some type. (See *pasting*.) □ *The Warriors pasted the Rockets, 70-49.* □ *They really pasted our team in last week's game.* (More at *pasted*.)

**pasted 1.** *mod.* alcohol or drug intoxicated. (From *paste*.) □ *Poor Tom is totally pasted.* □ *Max got pasted on beer.* **2.** *mod.* beaten; out-scored. □ *Our team really got pasted.* □ *He sure looked pasted the last time I saw him.*

**paste someone one** *tr.* to land a blow on someone. (See also *paste*.) □ *I pasted him one right on the nose.* □ *Next time you do that, I'll paste you one!*

**pasting** *n.* a beating; a defeat in a game. (See *paste*.) □ *Our team took quite a pasting last weekend.* □ *I gave him a pasting.*

**patootie** See *(sweet) patootie*.

**patsy** ['pætsi] *n.* a victim of a *scam*. (Underworld. See also *dupe*.) □ *That guy over there looks like a perfect patsy.* □ *We got nearly 25 hundred bucks off that patsy.*

**pattern** *n.* a particular type of drug-induced hallucination. (Drugs.) □ *Max kept having patterns and finally had to go to the hospital.* □ *He seems to have gotten stuck in one of his patterns.*

**patter of tiny feet** *n.* the sound of young children; having children in the household. □ *I really liked having the patter of tiny feet in the house.* □ *Darling, I think we're going to be hearing the patter of tiny feet soon.*

**paw 1.** *n.* someone's hand. (Jocular.) □ *Get your paws off me!* □ *That dog bit my paw.* **2.** *tr.* to feel someone or handle someone sexually. □ *If you paw me again, I'll slap you!* □ *I can't stand men who paw you to pieces.* **3.** *tr.* to touch someone more than is necessary or desired, without any sexual intent. □ *I don't like for people to paw me while they're shaking hands. There is no reason to shake my shoulder, too.* □ *Tom*

*doesn't realize that he paws people and that it annoys them.*

**pay a call** *tr.* to go to the toilet; to leave to go to the toilet. (See also *call of nature, nature's call*.) □ *Excuse me. I have to pay a call.* □ *Tom left to pay a call. He should be back soon.*

**payola** [pe'olə] *n.* a bribe paid to a *disk jockey* by record producers to get extra attention for their records; any bribe or payoff. □ *The announcer was fired for taking payola.* □ *There was a big scandal of payola in the 1950s.*

**pay one's dues 1.** *tr.* to serve one's time in a menial role. □ *I spent some time as a busboy, so I've paid my dues in the serving business.* □ *You have to start out at the bottom. Pay your dues, and then you'll appreciate better what you have.* **2.** *tr.* AND **pay one's dues to society** to serve a prison or jail sentence. □ *I served 10 years in prison. I've paid my dues to society. The matter is settled.* □ *I took my medicine and paid my dues. Stop trying to punish me more.*

**P.C.P.** AND **PCP** *n.* phencyclidine, a veterinary anesthetic used as a numbing drug. (Drugs.) □ *PCP is okay for hogs, but it kills people.* □ *A lot of kids end up with P.C.P. when they think they're getting something else.*

**P.D.Q.** AND **PDQ** *mod.* "pretty damn quick"; very fast; very soon. □ *You get those papers over here P.D.Q.!* □ *They had better get this mess straightened out PDQ if they know what's good for them.*

**peace pill** AND **peace tab(let)** *n.* a tablet of one of the following drugs: *L.S.D.,* Methedrine™, *P.C.P.* (Drugs.) □ *Max gave me this stuff and said it was peace pills. I think it's dangerous.* □ *One peace tab and you're in heaven.*

**peach** *n.* someone or something excellent. (Usually a person.) □ *That guy's a real peach.* □ *This is a peach of a car!*

**peachy (keen)** *mod.* fine; excellent. □ *Your idea is really peachy!* □ *What a peachy keen idea!*

**peak 1.** *n.* the highest level of euphoria from drug intoxication. (Drugs.) □ *She reached the peak and then went to sleep.* □ *He freaked out before he ever got to the peak.* **2.** *in.* to reach the highest level of euphoria in drug intoxication. (Drugs.)

□ *He peaked, then passed out.* □ *With this stuff you vomit a lot before you peak.*

**peanuts 1.** *n.* practically no money at all; *chicken feed.* □ *They want me to do everything, but they only pay peanuts.* □ *The cost is just peanuts compared to what you get for the money.* **2.** *n.* barbiturate capsules. (Drugs.) □ *The cops busted him while he had a handful of peanuts.* □ *Those cheap peanuts nearly killed him.*

**peckish** *mod.* hungry. □ *I'm just a little peckish right now. I need a bite to eat.* □ *Wow, you look peckish!*

**pecks** AND **pecs, pects** [pɛks AND pɛkts] *n.* the pectoral muscles. (From weight-lifting and bodybuilding.) □ *Look at the pecks on that guy!* □ *With pects like that he needs a bra.*

**pects** See the previous entry.

**pee\*** AND **P.\* 1.** *n.* peyote cactus. (Drugs. *P.* is more common in writing.) □ *Hey, Mac. You got any P.?* □ *That P. you gave me made me sick as a dog.* **2.** *n.* pure or nearly pure heroin; very potent heroin. (Drugs.) □ *They say that real P. will kill you.* □ *He was so addicted, he had to have pee three times a day.* **3.** *n.* P.C.P., the drug phencyclidine. (Drugs.) □ *Bob's been smoking pee, and he really looks bad.* □ *P. is cheap, but deadly.* **4.\*** *n.* urine. (*Pee* is more common in writing. Caution with topic. Originally a euphemism for *piss.*) □ *Don't step in the pee.* □ *That dog got pee all over my tires.* **5.\*** *n.* an act of urination. (Usually with *take.* Caution with topic.) □ *He left to take a pee.* □ *When the dog finishes with its pee, it runs away.* **6.\*** *in.* to urinate. (Caution with topic.) □ *Stop the car! I gotta P.!* □ *You can't pee here!*

**pee'd** *mod.* alcohol intoxicated. (Euphemistic for *pissed.*) □ *This old boy is really pee'd.* □ *His old lady gets pee'd after a few beers.*

**pee'd off** *mod.* extremely angry. (Euphemistic for *pissed (off).*) □ *I certainly was pee'd off!* □ *I've never been so pee'd off in my life!*

**peel** *in.* to strip off one's clothing. □ *I had to peel for my physical examination.* □ *She stood up on the stage and peeled right down to nothing!*

**peep** *n.* a noise; an utterance. □ *Don't you make another peep!* □ *I don't want to hear another peep out of you.*

**peepers** *n.* the eyes. □ *Come on, use your peepers. Take a good look.* □ *My peepers are tired.*

**peg-leg** *n.* a rude nickname for someone with a wooden peg for a leg. (Now used primarily in reference to theatrical pirates.) □ *See that peg-leg over there? He lost his foot to a shark.* □ *Hey, peg-leg. Race you to the bar!*

**pen** *n.* a penitentiary; prison. (Underworld.) □ *Max got sent to the pen for 15 years.* □ *After a few years in the pen, he began to appreciate freedom.*

**pencil-pusher** *n.* a bureaucrat; a clerk; an office worker. (See also *paper-pusher.*) □ *Look here, you lousy pencil-pusher, I want to talk to your boss!* □ *City Hall is filled with a bunch of overpaid pencil-pushers.*

**Pennsy** *n.* Pennsylvania. □ *I went to a conference in Pennsy last year.* □ *My cousin lives in Pennsy.*

**penny** *n.* a police officer. (A play on *copper.* See the note at *cop.*) □ *The penny over on the corner told the boys to get moving.* □ *We better get going before the pennies get here.*

**penny-ante** *mod.* trivial; cheap. (See *ante.*) □ *I'm sick of this penny-ante stuff. Let's get serious.* □ *Max moved from penny-ante crimes into drugs.*

**penny-pincher** *n.* someone who is very miserly; someone who objects to the expenditure of every penny. □ *If you weren't such a penny-pincher, you'd have some decent clothes.* □ *Let's elect some penny-pinchers to Congress.*

**peonied** *mod.* alcohol intoxicated. (Related to *pee'd* and *pissed.*) □ *Man, was she peonied! Really stoned.* □ *Let's go get peonied, just for the hell of it.*

**people-watching** *n.* observing different kinds of people as a pastime. □ *Let's eat at the greasy spoon over on Maple. The food is gross, but the people-watching is good.* □ *I enjoy people-watching, especially at airports.*

**pepped (up)** AND **peppy** *mod.* alcohol intoxicated. (A euphemism. Compare to *perked (up).*) □ *That guy looks a little pepped up. Don't give him any* *more booze.* □ *I feel sort of pepped up. Time to stop drinking.*

**pepper-upper** *n.* an amphetamine tablet or capsule; a *pep-pill.* □ *I need me a little pepper-upper. Can I have a prescription?* □ *You need more sleep, not a pepper-upper.*

**pep pill** *n.* a stimulant pill or capsule, such as an amphetamine. □ *The doctor prescribed some kind of pep pills, but I refused to take them.* □ *Got any pep pills or anything?*

**peppy 1.** *mod.* vigorous; energetic. (Compare to *perky.*) □ *She's such a peppy thing.* □ *I sure don't feel very peppy right now.* **2.** See *pepped (up).*

**pep talk** *n.* an informal speech of encouragement. □ *The coach gave the team a good pep talk, but they lost anyway.* □ *The pep talk grew into a real gripe session.*

**Period!** *exclam.* "...and that's final!" (A way of indicating that there will be no more discussion or negotiation.) □ *I don't want to hear any more about it! Period!* □ *My final offer is $30.00. Period!*

**perk 1.** *n.* an extra financial benefit; a monetary inducement or reward. (From *perquisite.* See also *benies.*) □ *I don't get paid much, but the perks are good.* □ *I don't get paid much, and I don't get any perks!* **2.** *n.* a tablet of Percodan™ painkiller. (Drugs and medical. Usually plural.) □ *Hey, man, got any perks?* □ *He was secretly hooked on perks for years.*

**perked (up)** *mod.* alcohol intoxicated. (Compare to *pepped (up).*) □ *Three beers and he's perked.* □ *No more. She's done. She's perked up for good.*

**perky** *mod.* energetic; alert. (Compare to *peppy.*) □ *Most poodles are quite perky.* □ *A perky hostess keeps parties alive.*

**persuader** *n.* a gun or other weapon used to threaten someone. (Underworld.) □ *He pulls out this persuader, see, and aims it right at me, see.* □ *Maybe my little persuader will help you remember where the money is.*

**pesky** *mod.* annoying; bothersome. □ *I am going to kill that pesky fly!* □ *I've had a pesky headache all day.*

**Peter Jay** *n.* a nickname for a police officer. (Black.) □ *You walk straight, or Peter Jay is going to bust you.* □ *Here comes Peter Jay in his pigmobile.*

**peter out** *in.* to give out; to wear out. □ *I'm about to peter out. I need a rest.* □ *What'll we do when the money peters out?*

**pet peeve** *n.* a major or principal annoyance or complaint. □ *Dirty dishes in restaurants are my pet peeve.* □ *He has no pet peeve. He hates everything.*

**petrified** *mod.* alcohol intoxicated. (Literally, turned into stone. Another way of saying *stoned.*) □ *She's not drunk; she's petrified.* □ *He drank moonshine till he was petrified.*

**petting-party** *n.* a session of kissing and caressing. □ *I just want to watch the movie. I didn't come here for some teenage petting-party!* □ *We went to the passion-pit for a petting-party.*

**peyote (button)** [pe'odi...] *n.* the emergent tip of the peyote cactus, used as a source of the drug mescaline. (Drugs.) □ *They thought they were getting peyote buttons, but it was just some old dried mushrooms.* □ *The stuff they found in the desert was real peyote.*

**P.F.D.** *n.* a "potential formal date"; someone who looks good enough to be a date to a formal affair. (Collegiate.) □ *That gal is a real P.F.D.* □ *Mike is no P.F.D., but he is a great friend anyway.*

**P.G.** AND **PG 1.** *mod.* "pregnant." □ *Do you think Sally's P.G.?* □ *I think I'm PG. You know, pregnant.* **2.** *n.* paregoric. (Drugs. See *Proctor and Gamble.*) □ *Max's been drinking PG again.* □ *The cops could smell the P.G. on his breath.*

**phazed** AND **phased** [fezd] *mod.* intoxicated with marijuana. □ *Man, I was phazed out of my mind!* □ *How much booze does it take you to get really phased?*

**phedinkus** [fi'dɪŋkəs] *n.* nonsense. □ *Stop your silly phedinkus!* □ *That's just phedinkus. No one will believe you.*

**phennies** AND **phenies** ['fɛniz] *n.* phenobarbital tablets, capsules, or elixir. (Drugs and hospitals.) □ *Get that big bottle of phenies up to the third floor, stat.* □ *Hey, man, you got any phennies? I need them bad.*

**pheno** ['fino] **1.** *n.* AND **phenobarb** ['finobarb] a phenobarbital (barbiturate) tablet. (Drugs and hospitals.) □ *Pheno can wreck you as well as any street drug.* □ *They gave me phenobarb in the hospital. I really grew to like that stuff.* **2.** *n.* a habitual user of phenobarbital. (Drugs and medical slang.) □ *That guy in the next room is turning into a real pheno. Why does the doctor keep giving him that stuff?* □ *He doesn't need pheno to sleep!*

**phenobarb** See the previous entry.

**phfft** [ffft] **1.** *mod.* finished; done for. (See also *piffed*.) □ *There is my cat, and zoom comes a car. My cat is phfft.* □ *Yup. Deader than a doornail. Phfft!* **2.** *mod.* alcohol intoxicated. □ *You won't wake him up for hours yet. He's phfft.* □ *Three beers and she's phfft, for sure.*

**Philly** *n.* Philadelphia, Pennsylvania. □ *We stopped off in Philly for a day.* □ *We left Philly for the Big Apple at noon.*

**phony** **1.** *mod.* bogus; fake. □ *This money looks phony to me.* □ *I can't stand phony vanilla flavoring.* **2.** *n.* someone or something bogus. □ *That guy is a real phony!* □ *Look here, you phony, get out of my office!* □ *This is a phony. Get me a real one.*

**phony as a three-dollar bill** AND **queer as a three-dollar bill** *mod.* phony; bogus. □ *This guy's as phony as a three-dollar bill.* □ *The whole deal stinks. It's as queer as a three-dollar bill.*

**phooey** AND **fooey** **1.** *n.* nonsense. □ *Your story is just a lot of phooey.* □ *I've heard enough fooey. Let's get out of here.* **2.** *exclam.* an expression of disgust, disagreement, or resignation. (Usually **Phooey!** or **Fooey!** Used typically when something smells or tastes bad.) □ *Who died in here? Phooey!* □ *This is the worst food I ever ate. Fooey!*

**phumfed** ['fəm(p)ft] *mod.* drug intoxicated. □ *You can't get your work done when you are totally phumfed.* □ *She gets phumfed on pot every afternoon.*

**phutz** AND **futz** [fəts] *tr.* to rob, swindle, or cheat someone. □ *Don't futz me! Tell the truth!* □ *The muggers phutzed his wallet and watch.*

**pickled** *mod.* alcohol intoxicated. (Very common.) □ *She's usually pickled by*

noon. □ *It only takes a few drinks to get him pickled.*

**picklepuss** *n.* a person who has a puckered-up mouth; a child who is about to cry. □ *Don't be such a picklepuss. Smile!* □ *She is such a picklepuss. Nothing seems to please her.*

**pickler** *n.* a drunkard; an alcoholic. (See *pickled*.) □ *What a pickler. He could drink all night.* □ *The cops brought in about 30 picklers last night.*

**pick-me-up** *n.* any food or drink that boosts energy, such as a drink of liquor, candy, soda pop. □ *I'm pooped. I really need a pick-me-up.* □ *I can't finish the day without a little pick-me-up at lunch.*

**pickup** **1.** *n.* something eaten or drunk to boost energy; a *pick-me-up.* □ *Bartender, I need a little pickup.* □ *She stopped at a candy machine for a pickup.* **2.** *n.* a restoration of energy; a drug *rush.* (Drugs and colloquial.) □ *Candy always gives me a pickup.* □ *Man, that stuff really has a pickup.* **3.** *n.* a sudden increase in something, such as speed or tempo in music. □ *We need a bit of a pickup at measure 43.* □ *There will be a pickup in sales during the Christmas season.* **4.** *mod.* spontaneous; unplanned. (Especially with ball games where the members of the team are "picked up" from whoever is available. Compare to *scratch*.) □ *He stopped at the basketball court for a pickup game with the boys.* □ *A pickup game can be fun if the sides are evenly matched.* **5.** *n.* an arrest. (Underworld.) □ *Send Sergeant Townsend out to make the pickup.* □ *The cop made a pickup right across the street.* **6.** *n.* someone whose acquaintance is made solely for sexual purposes. □ *She's no date. She's just a pickup.* □ *She had the gall to show up at the dance with a pickup in street clothes.* **7.** *n.* the power of a car's engine as reflected in the car's ability to reach a high speed quickly. □ *This car has more pickup than I really need.* □ *Little cars hardly ever have enough pickup.* **8.** *n.* the act of receiving or collecting something, especially drugs or other contraband. □ *The dealer sent somebody down to make the pickup, but the cops showed up instead.* □ *The parcel* *truck driver stopped to make a pickup, but no one was at home.*

**pick up on something** *in.* to become alert to something; to take notice of something; to learn or catch onto something. □ *She's real sharp. She picks up on everything.* □ *The cop picked up on the word "persuader."*

**picky 1.** *mod.* choosy. □ *Don't be so picky. They're all the same.* □ *Red, blue, green! What's the difference? You are too picky.* **2.** *mod.* overly critical. □ *Complain, complain! What a picky old lady.* □ *I have to do it exactly right. My boss is very picky.*

**picnic** *n.* a good time; an easy time. □ *What a great class! Every day was a real picnic.* □ *Nothing to it. A real picnic.* □ *It wasn't a terrible day, but it was no picnic.*

**piddle 1.** *in.* to urinate. (Said of children and pets.) □ *Mommy! Jimmy's got to piddle!* □ *Please, Jimmy, don't piddle on the floor.* **2.** *n.* urine. □ *Where's the dog? There's piddle on the carpet.* □ *Don't step in the puppy's piddle.* **3.** See the following entry.

**piddle (around)** *in.* to waste time; to work aimlessly or inefficiently. □ *Stop piddling around! Get to work!* □ *Can't you get serious and stop piddling?*

**piddler** *n.* someone who wastes time. □ *Bob is such a piddler. He can't seem to get organized and get down to work.* □ *That piddler will never get anywhere in life.*

**piddling** *mod.* inadequate; meager; tiny. (Compare to *piss poor* and see *piddle*.) □ *What a piddling amount of money! I can't live on that.* □ *That is a piddling steak. I want a big one.*

**piece 1.** *n.* a sexually attractive (young) woman. (Crude.) □ *She's a real piece!* □ *Who's that piece I saw you with last night?* **2.** *n.* a gun, especially a revolver. (Underworld.) □ *Is that guy carrying a piece?* □ *Okay, this gun is aimed at your head. Drop your piece.* **3.** *n.* an ounce of a drug; a portion of a drug. (Drugs.) □ *I don't have enough dough to buy even one piece.* □ *Max had a couple of pieces in his pocket when he got busted.* **4.** See *piece (of the action)*.

**piece of cake 1.** *n.* something easy to do. □ *No problem. When you know what you're doing, it's a piece of cake.* □ *Glad to help. It was a piece of cake.* **2.** *exclam.* "It's a piece of cake!"; "It's easy!" (Usually **Piece of cake!**) □ *No problem, piece of cake!* □ *Rescuing drowning cats is my specialty. Piece of cake!*

**piece (of the action)** AND **bit of the action, slice of the action** *n.* a share in the activity or the profits. (Especially gambling activity.) □ *If you get in on that real estate deal, I want a piece, too.* □ *Deal Tom in. He wants a piece of the action.* □ *Don't be selfish. Give me a slice of the action.*

**pie-eyed 1.** *mod.* wide-eyed with amazement. □ *He didn't cry out. He just stood there pie-eyed.* □ *Why are all those people pie-eyed? What happened?* **2.** *mod.* alcohol intoxicated. □ *That guy is really pie-eyed. Send him home.* □ *We've got a pie-eyed bus driver. I want to get off!*

**pie-in-the-sky 1.** *n.* a reward; a special "heavenly reward." □ *Don't hold out for pie-in-the-sky. Get realistic.* □ *If he didn't hope for some heavenly pie in the sky, he would probably be a real crook.* **2.** *mod.* having to do with a hope for a special reward. □ *Get rid of your pie-in-the-sky ideas!* □ *What these pie-in-the-sky people really want is money.*

**piffed** [pɪft] **1.** AND **pifted** ['pɪftəd] *tr.* killed. (Past tense only. See also *phfft*.) □ *He piffed his goldfish by mistake.* □ *The speeding car pifted the cat yesterday.* **2.** AND **pifted** ['pɪftəd] *mod.* dead. □ *What will I do with a pifted cat?* □ *He's as piffed as they come.* **3.** *mod.* alcohol intoxicated. (See also *piffled*.) □ *That guy is really piffed.* □ *How can anybody get that piffed on four beers?*

**piffle** ['pɪfl] **1.** *n.* nonsense. □ *What utter piffle!* □ *The entire report was piffle from beginning to end.* **2.** *exclam.* a mild exclamation or expression of distress. (Usually **Piffle!**) □ *You a stockbroker? Piffle!* □ *She finished her story, and I looked her straight in the eye and said piffle!*

**piffled** ['pɪfld] *mod.* alcohol intoxicated. □ *Three glasses of booze and she was totally piffled.* □ *He was so piffled he couldn't talk!*

**pifflicated** AND **pifficated** ['pɪfləkɛdəd AND 'pɪfəkɛdəd] *mod.* alcohol intoxicated. □ *How can anybody drink so much and not get totally pifflicated?* □ *Get that pifficated stuffed shirt out of here!*

**pig 1.** *n.* someone who eats too much; a glutton. (All senses are usually derogatory.) □ *Stop being a pig! Save some for other people.* □ *I try to cut down on calories, but whenever I see red meat I make a pig of myself.* **2.** *n.* an ugly and fat woman. (Derogatory.) □ *Clare is a pig. Why doesn't she lose a ton or two?* □ *Every girl in that sorority is a pig.* **3.** *n.* a dirty or slovenly person. (Also a rude term of address.) □ *Max is a pig. I don't think he bathes enough.* □ *Jimmy, change your clothes. Look at that mud, you little pig!* **4.** *n.* an officer; a police officer or a military officer. (Derogatory. Used mostly for a police officer. Widely known since the 1960s.) □ *The pigs are coming to bust up the fight.* □ *The pigs who aren't in pig heaven are driving around in pigmobiles busting innocent people like me.* **5.** *n.* a Caucasian. (Derogatory. Black.) □ *Why do those pigs think they can walk in here like that?* □ *Who do those pigs think they are, tourists?*

**pigeon 1.** *n.* a *dupe*; a *sucker*; someone singled out to be cheated. (See also *patsy*.) □ *There's our pigeon now. Don't let him see us sizing him up.* □ *Be alert for pickpockets. Don't be some crook's pigeon.* **2.** *n.* a cute girl or woman. □ *What a cute little pigeon.* □ *Who was the dreamy little pigeon I saw you with last night?* **3.** See *stool (pigeon)*.

**pigeon-eyed** *mod.* alcohol intoxicated. □ *How can anyone get so pigeon-eyed on so little booze?* □ *Who is that pigeon-eyed guy over there who is having such a hard time standing up?*

**pighead** *n.* someone who is both stupid and stubborn. (See the following entry.) □ *Stop acting like such a pighead!* □ *She'll never change her mind. She's a real pighead.*

**pigheaded** *mod.* stupidly stubborn. (From the notion that pigs are immovable.) □ *You are unbelievably pigheaded!* □ *What a stupid pigheaded position to take.*

**pig heaven** *n.* a police station. (Chiefly black.) □ *The man came and took my brother to pig heaven.* □ *All the bacon eventually goes home to pig heaven.*

**pig in a poke** *n.* a person or object of unknown characteristics. (Folksy. Always with *a*. Refers to selling a pig in a sack (poke) so that the buyer does not know what is being bought.) □ *Know what you are getting. Don't buy a pig in a poke.* □ *Of course, he got gypped. He bought a pig in a poke. What do you expect?*

**pigmobile** *n.* a police car. (See *pig*.) □ *Look out, here comes the pigmobile.* □ *Hey, man! Have you ever ridden in a pigmobile?*

**pig out** *in.* to overeat; to overindulge in food or drink. (Compare to *blimp out, mac out, pork out, scarf out*.) □ *I always pig out on Fridays.* □ *I can't help myself when I see ice cream. I have to pig out.*

**pigpen** *n.* a crosshatch or octothorpe, "#." (Computers. See *mesh*.) □ *Put a pigpen just after the gear.* □ *There is nothing on my printout but a whole string of pigpens.*

**piker** ['paɪkɚ] **1.** *n.* a miser; a *cheapskate*. (Also a term of address.) □ *You cheap little piker! Beat it!* □ *A five percent tip? You piker!* **2.** *n.* a lazy person; a shirker. □ *All right, you pikers. Pick up your shovels and get back to work.* □ *Come on, you lazy piker. There's plenty left for you to do.*

**pile** *n.* a large amount of money. □ *She really made a pile in the stock market.* □ *That old lady has a pile of money stashed in the bank.*

**pileup** *n.* a wreck; a vehicular crash where more than one vehicle is heavily damaged. □ *There is a serious pileup on the expressway.* □ *My car was ruined in a pileup on the highway.*

**pilfered** ['pɪlfɚd] *mod.* alcohol intoxicated. □ *I've had too much. I'm beginning to feel pilfered.* □ *That old boy is really pilfered.*

**pill 1.** *n.* a birth control pill. (Always with *the*.) □ *Is Sally on the pill?* □ *The pill has really changed my life.* **2.** *n.* a tobacco cigarette; a marijuana cigarette. □ *Hey, toss me a pill, huh?* □ *I'll* *trade you a pill for a match.* **3.** *n.* a drug in capsule form. □ *Stop taking those pills!* □ *The doctor prescribed these pills.*

**pillhead** AND **pill freak** *n.* a drug user who prefers drugs in pill or capsule form. (Drugs.) □ *You pill freaks should try some of this stuff.* □ *I don't smoke. I'm strictly a pillhead.*

**pillowed** *mod.* pregnant. (Refers to the swelling in a pregnant woman's abdomen.) □ *She does look a bit pillowed, doesn't she?* □ *I think I'm more than a bit pillowed.*

**pill-popper** AND **popper, pill-dropper** **1.** *n.* anyone who takes pills frequently or habitually. □ *Poor Sue is a pill-popper.* □ *I knew she was always ill, but I didn't know she was a pill-dropper.* **2.** *n.* a drug user who prefers pills such as amphetamines and barbiturates. (Drugs.) □ *Max started out as a pill-dropper and then moved on to the needle.* □ *The pill-popper thought she wouldn't get hooked.*

**pill-pusher** AND **pill-roller, pill-peddler** *n.* a nickname for a physician. □ *That pill-peddler charges too much.* □ *I went to the infirmary, but the pill-pusher wasn't in.*

**pimp\*** *n.* a man who solicits business for a prostitute. (Caution with *pimp.*) □ *The guy with the diamond rings looks like a pimp.* □ *The cops took in three hookers and their pimp.*

**pimpish\*** ['pɪmpɪʃ] *mod.* flamboyant in dress and manner, as with a pimp. (Caution with *pimp.*) □ *Where did you get that pimpish hat, Ron?* □ *Take the feathers off it, and it won't look quite so pimpish.*

**pimpmobile\*** *n.* a gaudy automobile, as might be driven by a pimp. (Caution with *pimp.*) □ *You call that pimpmobile a car? Why all the chrome?* □ *He drove up in a pimpmobile and shocked all the neighbors.*

**pimpstick\*** *n.* a typical cigarette made by mass production. (Caution with *pimp.* From an earlier time when pimps were likely to smoke machine-made cigarettes rather than the rugged roll-your-own type.) □ *Hey, chum. Why do you smoke those pimpsticks? Can't you roll one yourself?* □ *Real cowboys never smoke pimpsticks, and they don't have tattoos, either.*

**pin** **1.** *n.* someone's leg. (Usually plural.) □ *My pins are a little wobbly.* □ *Stand up on your pins and speak your mind.* **2.** *n.* an important criminal leader. (From *kingpin.*) □ *The pin sent me. He says you're to come with me.* □ *The mob's getting careless. The cops think they caught the pin this time.*

**pinch** **1.** *n.* a small amount of a powdered substance, such as salt, snuff, a spice, etc. (Not slang.) □ *He put a pinch under his lips and walked up to home plate.* □ *Do you have any oregano? I need a pinch.* **2.** *tr.* to arrest someone. □ *The cops pinched her in front of her house.* □ *The police captain pinched her for passing bad checks.* **3.** *n.* the arresting of someone. □ *They made the pinch in front of her house.* □ *The pinch was for forgery.* **4.** *tr.* to steal something. (See also *cop.*) □ *The kid pinched a candy bar right off the counter.* □ *I pinched these paper clips from my office.*

**pinched** **1.** *mod.* arrested. (See *cop, pinch.*) □ *I got pinched for speeding.* □ *Sam got pinched for a parole violation.* **2.** See *pinched (for time).* **3.** See *pinched (for money).*

**pinched (for money)** AND **pressed (for money), pushed (for money)** *mod.* short of money. ("Money" can be *cash, funds, bucks,* etc.) □ *Sorry, I can't help you. I'm a little pinched this week.* □ *She was pressed for funds and couldn't pay her rent.* □ *I'm a bit pushed for cash at the moment.* □ *I'm out of a job and pressed for cash at the present.*

**pinched (for time)** AND **pressed (for time), pushed (for time)** *mod.* in a hurry; short of time. (See also *pushed.*) □ *Sorry, I can't talk to you now. I'm pinched for time.* □ *I know you're pressed, but could I have a word with you?* □ *She's always pushed for time. Try to catch her in the hall.*

**pinch hitter** **1.** *n.* a substitute batter in the game of baseball. □ *Sam is a pinch hitter for Ralph, who broke his wrist.* □ *Time to send in a pinch hitter.* **2.** *n.* any substitute person. □ *In school today we had a pinch hitter. Our teacher was sick.* □ *I want my own doctor, not a pinch hitter!* **3.** *n.* someone who is hired by a debilitated addict to inject drugs. (Drugs.

See *hit*.) □ *Before the addict died, he had to have a pinch hitter three times a day. He was that bad.* □ *He paid the pinch hitter with drugs.*

**pinhead 1.** *n.* a very stupid person; someone who acts idiotic. □ *Stop acting like a pinhead!* □ *That woman is such a pinhead. Not a brain in her head.* **2.** *n.* a user of injected drugs. (Drugs. See *head*.) □ *You know he's a pinhead. Look at the scars on his arms.* □ *That pinhead in cell four is screaming for a dose.*

**pink 1.** *n.* a type of *L.S.D.* (Drugs.) □ *You got any pink?* □ *This pink is full of impurities.* **2.** *n.* a capsule of Seconal™, a barbiturate. (Drugs.) □ *He had a handful of pinks when they found him.* □ *Pinks are just sleeping pills.*

**pinked** *mod.* alcohol intoxicated; tipsy. □ *She's sitting there looking a bit pinked.* □ *I want to get pinked. Fill it up, bartender.*

**pink elephants** AND **pink spiders 1.** *n.* the delirium tremens. □ *He's screaming with pink elephants again.* □ *He was shaking something awful from the pink spiders.* **2.** *n.* hallucinatory creatures seen during the delirium tremens. (See others at *seeing pink elephants*.) □ *He said pink elephants were trying to kill him. He's really drunk.* □ *If you ever find yourself surrounded with pink elephants, you've got the D.T.s.*

**pinkeye 1.** *n.* inferior whiskey; *moonshine*. (Drinking these substances causes redness of the eyes.) □ *Where's that jug of pinkeye you used to keep around here?* □ *Bartender, this stuff tastes like pinkeye. Give me something better.* **2.** AND **pinkie, pinky** *n.* denatured alcohol; cheap red wine. (Drinking these substances causes redness of the eyes. See also *(little) pinkie*.) □ *He's shaking because he drinks pinkeye.* □ *In the last stages these poor old men will drink anything—even pinkeye—to keep from shaking.* **3.** *n.* a denatured alcohol drunkard. □ *Get that old pinkie out of here before he does something awful.* □ *Most pinkies are homeless and hungry.*

**pinkie** See *(little) pinkie*.

**pink ladies 1.** *n.* barbiturates, especially Seconal™ capsules. (Drugs.) □ *You*

ever had any pink ladies? □ *He's stoned on pink ladies.* **2.** *n.* capsules of Darvon™. (Drugs. Chiefly black.) □ *How much do you want for a rack of pink ladies?* □ *He was drinking coffee and popping pink ladies like mad.*

**pinko 1.** *n.* a communist. (Popular during the 1950s.) □ *Get out of here, you pinko!* □ *He called me a pinko, so I left.* **2.** *mod.* having communist tendencies; in the manner of a communist. □ *Get that pinko jerk out of here!* □ *Take your old pinko laws and go to hell.*

**pinks** See *pink ladies*.

**pink slip 1.** *n.* a piece of paper giving notice of dismissal from employment; any dismissal from employment. □ *I got a pink slip today. I guess I had it coming.* □ *I hope I don't get a pink slip. I need this job.* **2.** *tr.* to dismiss someone from employment. □ *They pink slipped the whole office force today.* □ *If your work doesn't improve, I will be forced to pink slip you.* (More at *pink-slipped*.) **3.** *n.* a learner's permit for driving an automobile. (In some U.S. states.) □ *You can't even drive in your own driveway without a pink slip.* □ *He wrecked the car one day after getting his pink slip.*

**pink-slipped** *mod.* fired; dismissed from employment. □ *I guess I've done it. I'm pink-slipped.* □ *Now I'm a member of the young and pink-slipped crowd.*

**pink spiders** See *pink elephants*.

**pinky** See *pinkie*.

**pinned 1.** *mod.* arrested. (Underworld.) □ *The boys in blue pinned him and took him away.* □ *He had a gun in his belt when they pinned him.* **2.** *mod.* marked as a heroin addict by pinpoint-size pupils. (Drugs.) □ *He was pinned, so I knew he'd been on H.* □ *She was pinned, and she was shaking. She needed some stuff bad.*

**pins** See *pin*.

**pin someone's ears back 1.** *tr.* to scold someone severely. □ *She really pinned his ears back.* □ *The teacher pinned the kids' ears back for chewing gum.* **2.** *tr.* to beat someone, especially about the head. □ *Lefty says I'm supposed to pin your ears back.* □ *You do something like that again, and I'll pin your ears back.*

**pinstriper** *n.* a businessman or woman wearing a pinstriped suit. (Compare to *suit, vest.*) □ *Who's the pinstriper driving the beemer?* □ *Wall Street is nothing but wall-to-wall pinstripers.*

**pint-sized** *mod.* small; miniature. □ *I won't fit into one of those pint-sized cars.* □ *My car is not pint-sized.* □ *Tell that little pint-sized guy to beat it.*

**pip** *n.* a pimple; a *zit.* □ *Good grief, I've got ear-to-ear pips!* □ *Do you ever outgrow pips?*

**pipe 1.** *n.* an easy course in school. □ *Take this course. It's a pipe.* □ *I don't want a full load of pipes. I want to learn something.* **2.** *n.* a pipe for smoking marijuana, hashish, or opium. (Drugs.) □ *They found her pockets full of pipes and think she is a dealer.* □ *Can I use your pipe?* **3.** *n.* someone who smokes marijuana habitually. □ *That goof-off is a pipe. He's stoned all the time.* □ *Most pipes end up as burnouts.*

**pipe down** *in.* to become quiet; to cease making noise; to shut up. (Especially as a rude command.) □ *Pipe down! I'm trying to sleep.* □ *Come on! Pipe down and get back to work!*

**pipe dream 1.** *n.* a vision or dream experienced while under the effects of opium. (Drugs. See *pipe.*) □ *He liked the pipe dreams, but the violent nausea that opium produced made him give it up.* □ *He would come out of that opium den and try to make his pipe dreams come true.* **2.** *n.* any fantasy or daydream. □ *You a stockbroker? That's just a pipe dream.* □ *I know it's just a pipe dream, but I really want to go to Australia.*

**pipped (up)** *mod.* alcohol intoxicated. □ *I'm not drunk. Just a little pipped up.* □ *She's pipped and ready to get sick.*

**pipsqueak** *n.* a small or timid man or boy. (Also a term of address.) □ *Shut up, you little pipsqueak, or I'll hit you.* □ *I may be a pipsqueak, but I am a gentleman.*

**piss\* 1.\*** *in.* to urinate. (Caution with *piss.*) □ *He went out and pissed in the woods.* □ *Don't piss on the floor.* **2.\*** *n.* urine. (Caution with *piss.*) □ *There's piss on the rug. Where's that cat?* □ *Hey, stupid! There's piss on your pants*

*leg.* **3.\*** *n.* an act of urination. (Especially with *take.* Caution with *piss.*) □ *He went out to take a piss.* □ *Man, I gotta stop here for a piss.*

**piss-ant\*** ['pɪsænt] **1.** *n.* an insignificant person. (Also a rude term of address. Regarded as impolite. A misunderstanding of French *pis-ant,* a "step ant." Caution with *piss,* nonetheless.) □ *Get out of here, you little piss-ant.* □ *Tell that little piss-ant to come and see me.* **2.** *mod.* insignificant; unimportant. (Compare to *piss poor.*) □ *I don't have time for her little piss-ant problems.* □ *Take your piss-ant papers out of here and leave me alone.*

**piss-ant around\*** *in.* to move about in a timid fashion; to behave overly cautiously. (See the previous entry. Caution with *piss.*) □ *Don't just piss-ant around here. State your business or get out.* □ *Stop piss-anting around and get busy.*

**pissed\* 1.\*** *mod.* alcohol intoxicated. (Caution with *pissed.*) □ *He was really pissed.* □ *He was so pissed he could hardly stand up.* **2.** See the following entry.

**pissed (off)\*** *mod.* angry. (Crude. Caution with *piss.* Compare to *piss someone off.*) □ *I was so pissed off I could have screamed.* □ *He's come back, and he's sure pissed.*

**piss elegant\*** *mod.* falsely elegant; pretentious. (Crude. Caution with *piss.*) □ *Here comes Paul in his piss elegant car.* □ *Do we have to go to a party at that piss elegant apartment with its corny decor?*

**piss factory\*** *n.* a saloon or a tavern. (Crude. Caution with *piss.*) □ *What time did you leave that old piss factory?* □ *In my hometown there's a piss factory on every corner.*

**piss poor\*** *mod.* very inadequate. (Crude. An elaboration of *poor.* Caution with *piss.*) □ *This is a piss poor excuse for fried chicken.* □ *It is really piss poor.* □ *That was a piss poor performance for a professional musician.*

**piss someone off\*** AND **piss off someone\*** *tr.* to make someone angry. (Crude. Caution with *piss.*) □ *She really pissed me off!* □ *That's enough to piss off anybody.* (More at *pissed (off).*)

**pistol** *n.* a person who is bright, quick, or energetic. (Implying "hot as a pistol" or "quick as a pistol.") □ *She's a bright kid. A real pistol.* □ *Ask that pistol to step over here for a minute, would you?*

**pitch a bitch** *tr.* to make a complaint. (Crude.) □ *You really love to pitch a bitch, don't you? What makes you happy?* □ *Complain, complain! You could pitch a bitch all day long.*

**pitch in (and help)** *in.* to volunteer to help; to join in completing a task. □ *Come on, you guys! Pitch in.* □ *If more people would pitch in and help, we could get this job done in no time at all.*

**pitch jive** *tr.* to sell drugs. (Drugs. Black. See *jive.*) □ *Max is trying to make a living pitching jive.* □ *The man takes a dim view of pitching jive.*

**pitch (the) woo** *tr.* to kiss and caress; to woo (someone). (Old but still heard.) □ *They were out by the barn pitching woo.* □ *Old Ted can hardly see any more, but he can still pitch the woo.*

**pits 1.** *n.* the armpits. (Usually crude.) □ *Man, you have a problem in your pits.* □ *Who's got the smelly pits in here?* **2.** *n.* anything really bad. (Always with *the.*) □ *Life is the pits.* □ *This whole day was the pits from beginning to end.* **3.** *n.* the depths of despair. (Always with *the.* Often with *in* as in the example.) □ *It's always the pits with him.* □ *She's depressed and in the pits.*

**pit stop 1.** *n.* a pause in a journey (usually by car) to urinate. (From the name of a service stop in automobile racing.) □ *I think we'll pull in at the next rest area. I need a pit stop.* □ *Poor Max needs a pit stop every 30 miles.* **2.** *n.* an underarm deodorant. (Because it stops armpit odor.) □ *Man, do you need some pit stop!* □ *Can I borrow your pit stop? I need it bad.*

**pix** [pɪks] *n.* pictures; photographs. □ *I got my pix back from the drugstore.* □ *Hold still and let me get your pix taken. Then you can jump around.*

**pixilated** AND **pixolated 1.** *mod.* bewildered. □ *That little old lady is pixilated.* □ *She seems a bit young to be so pixolated.* **2.** *mod.* alcohol intoxicated; tipsy. □ *She seems a bit pixilated. She's probably been drinking.* □ *Martha, you mustn't drive. I think you are pixilated.*

**pizzazz** [pəˈzæz] *n.* punch; glitter and excitement. □ *Listen to the way she put pizzazz into that song!* □ *This script lacks pizzazz.*

**P.J.s** *n.* pajamas. (Usually juvenile.) □ *Get your P.J.s on and get into bed right now.* □ *I can't find my P.J.s. Where are they?*

**plant 1.** *tr.* to strike a blow (to a particular place on someone). □ *I planted one right on his nose.* □ *The boxer planted a good blow on his opponent's shoulder.* **2.** *n.* a spy who secretly participates in criminal activities in order to inform on the criminals. □ *The crooks discovered the plant and fed him bogus information.* □ *Don't tell everything you know. You don't know who's a plant and who isn't.* **3.** *n.* a secret place containing drugs or drug-use equipment. (Drugs. See also *plant something on someone.*) □ *He was hurting for a fix and had to get back to his plant as soon as he could.* □ *I can't find my plant, and all my stuff's in it!* **4.** AND **plants** *n.* peyote cactus, a source of the drug mescaline. (Drugs.) □ *Do you do plants or chemicals?* □ *Do you know where I can get some plants?*

**plant something on someone 1.** *tr.* to hide incriminating evidence on a person for later discovery and use in prosecution. (Drugs. Allegedly a police practice used to entrap drug offenders. See *flake.*) □ *The cops planted snow on Max and then arrested him for carrying it.* □ *Don't touch me! You'll plant something on me!* **2.** *tr.* to conceal narcotics or other contraband on an unsuspecting person for the purpose of smuggling. (This person will bear the risk of discovery and arrest.) □ *The crooks planted the stuff on a passenger, but couldn't find him when the plane landed.* □ *Someone had planted coke on me, and the airport security officer found it.*

**plastered** *mod.* alcohol intoxicated. □ *She's really plastered.* □ *She's so plastered she can't see.*

**plastered to the wall** *mod.* heavily alcohol intoxicated. (An elaboration of *plastered.*) □ *He's not just drunk; he's plastered to the wall!* □ *How can anybody get plastered to the wall on just four beers?*

**plastic** 1. *mod.* phony; false. □ *She wears too much makeup and looks totally plastic.* □ *I'm tired of living in such a plastic society.* 2. *n.* a plastic credit card. □ *Our economy depends on plastic.* □ *I don't carry any cash, just plastic.* 3. *mod.* having to do with credit cards and their use. □ *This plastic economy is dangerous.* □ *There is too much plastic debt in most households.*

**plastic punk** *n.* bogus *punk*; commercial *punk.* □ *Most music videos are just plastic punk.* □ *Isn't all punk really plastic punk?*

**plate** See the following entry.

**platter** 1. AND **plate** *n.* home base or home plate in baseball. (Usually with *the.*) □ *The batter stepped up to the platter.* □ *The ump dusted off the plate.* 2. *n.* a phonograph record. (Old but still heard.) □ *Now, here's an interesting platter.* □ *They call it a platter because it looks like a serving platter.*

**play** 1. *n.* a strategy; a plan of action. □ *That was a bad play, Bill. We lost the account.* □ *Here's a play that worked for us last year at this time.* 2. *n.* an attractive investment; a way to make some money in the financial markets. □ *I just heard about a good play in the options market.* □ *Not talking it over with your friends first was a bad play.* □ *Buying bonds at a discount is an interesting play.*

**play around (with someone)** 1. *in.* to waste time; to waste someone's time. □ *Stop playing around and get to work.* □ *Don't play around with me!* 2. *in.* to flirt or have an affair with someone. □ *Those two have been playing around for months.* □ *She only wants to play around with me.* 3. *in.* to tease, deceive, or try to trick someone. □ *You're playing around with me. Leave me alone.* □ *Don't pay any attention to them. They're just playing around.*

**play ball (with someone)** *tr.* to cooperate with someone. □ *Are you going to play ball, or do I have to report you to the boss?* □ *You will be better off if you will play ball with me.*

**played (out)** 1. *mod.* having to do with a portion of marijuana (in a cigarette or a pipe) which has had all of the effective substance smoked out of it. (Drugs. See also *cashed.*) □ *This stuff is played. Get rid of it.* □ *You gave me pot that was played out!* 2. *mod.* worn-out; exhausted; no longer effective. □ *This scenario is played out. It no longer makes sense.* □ *I'm played. I have no new ideas.*

**player** 1. *n.* someone who plays around, especially sexually. (See *play around (with someone).*) □ *He's a player, and I'm just a country girl who wanted to go dancing.* □ *I don't want a player. I want a good solid homemaker type.* 2. *n.* a drug seller. (Drugs.) □ *There's a big fight among the players down on 4th Street.* □ *Max is a player and makes a lot of money at it.* 3. *n.* a drug user or addict. □ *He tried the stuff a few times, and before he knew it, he was a player.* □ *Bud became a player because his girl was using.*

**play fast and loose (with someone or something)** *in.* to treat someone or something carelessly or unfairly. □ *The broker played fast and loose with our money. Now we are nearly broke.* □ *He was playing fast and loose with his girl, so she left him.*

**play for keeps** *in.* to take serious and permanent actions. (Refers to playing a game where the money won is not returned at the end of the game.) □ *Wake up and face the fact that she's playing for keeps. She wants to get married.* □ *I always play for keeps.*

**play freeze-out** *tr.* to open windows and doors, or turn down a thermostat, making someone cold. (See *freeze someone out.*) □ *Wow, it's cold in here! Who's playing freeze-out?* □ *Is someone trying to play freeze-out?*

**play hardball (with someone)** *tr.* to act strong and aggressive about an issue with someone. □ *Things are getting a little tough. The president has decided to play hardball on this issue.* □ *If he wants to play hardball with us, we can play that way, too.*

**play hell with someone or something** AND **play the devil with someone or something** *tr.* to cause difficulty for someone or something. □ *You know that this cake is going to play hell with my diet.* □ *Your decision plays hell with all my friends.*

**play hooky** [...'hʊki] *tr.* to not go to school; to not keep an appointment. □ *I played hooky today and did not go to work.* □ *Tommy is probably playing hooky from school again.*

**play in the big leagues** *in.* to become involved in something of large or important proportions. □ *You had better shape up if you want to play in the big leagues.* □ *The conductor shouted at the oboist, "You're playing in the big leagues now. Tune up or ship out."*

**play it cool 1.** *tr.* to do something while not revealing insecurities or incompetence. (See *cool*.) □ *Play it cool, man. Look like you belong there.* □ *If the boss walks in, just play it cool.* **2.** *tr.* to hold one's temper. □ *Come on now. Let it pass. Play it cool.* □ *Don't let them get you mad. Play it cool.*

**play someone for a fool** *tr.* to treat someone like a fool; to act as if someone were a fool. □ *I know what you're trying to do. Don't try to play me for a fool.* □ *We played her for a fool, and she never knew it.*

**play the devil with someone or something** See *play hell with someone or something*.

**play the dozens** AND **shoot the dozens** *tr.* to trade insulting remarks concerning relatives with another person. (Chiefly black. See also *(dirty) dozens*.) □ *They're out playing the dozens.* □ *Stop shooting the dozens and go do your homework.*

**play with a full deck** *in.* to operate as if one were mentally sound. (Usually in the negative. One cannot play cards with a partial deck.) □ *That guy's not playing with a full deck.* □ *Look sharp, you dummies! Pretend you are playing with a full deck.*

**play with fire** *in.* to do something dangerous or risky. □ *When you talk to me like that, you're playing with fire.* □ *Going out at night in a neighborhood like that is playing with fire.*

**pleasantly plastered** *mod.* mildly alcohol intoxicated; mellow with drink. (An elaboration of *plastered*.) □ *He wasn't really stoned. Just pleasantly plastered.* □ *I get to the point that I am pleasantly plastered, and then I stop.*

**pleasure jolt** *n.* a (small) dose of drugs taken by a nonaddict; a dose taken solely for pleasure and not out of need. (Drugs.) □ *All he wanted was a pleasure jolt.* □ *This stuff is okay for a pleasure jolt.*

**plonk** *n.* white wine; cheap wine; any liquor. (From French *blanc*. See *blank*.) □ *That plonk is really hard on the gut.* □ *How about a bottle of plonk?*

**plonked (up)** *mod.* alcohol intoxicated. (See *plonk*, *blank*.) □ *He sure is plonked up.* □ *She is totally plonked.*

**plonko** *n.* a drunkard. (See *plonk*.) □ *Get that smelly plonko out of here!* □ *He's a plonko if I ever saw one.*

**plootered** ['pludəd] *mod.* alcohol intoxicated. □ *We went out and got totally plootered.* □ *How can anyone get so plootered on a bottle of wine?*

**plop 1.** *n.* the sound of dropping something soft and bulky, such as a hunk of meat. □ *When the roast fell on the floor, it made a nasty plop.* □ *When I heard the plop, I looked up and saw our dinner on the floor.* **2.** *tr.* to put or place something (somewhere). □ *I don't mind cooking a turkey. You only have to plop it in the oven and forget about it.* □ *I plopped my books on the table and went straight to my room.* **3.** *tr.* to sit oneself down somewhere; to place one's buttocks somewhere. (The *it* in the examples is the buttocks.) □ *Come in, Fred. Just plop it anywhere you see a chair. This place is a mess.* □ *Just plop it down right there, and we'll have our little talk.*

**plotzed** ['platst] *mod.* alcohol intoxicated; really drunk. □ *They all came home plotzed.* □ *Two bottles and she was plotzed.*

**plowed (under)** *mod.* alcohol or drug intoxicated. □ *She was plowed under for a week.* □ *They went out and got plowed.*

**pluck** AND **plug** *n.* wine; cheap wine. (Originally black.) □ *Where can I get some plug?* □ *You spilled plug all over my car seat.*

**plug 1.** *n.* a bite-size, pressed mass of chewing tobacco. □ *He put a plug in his cheek and walked away.* □ *Hey, gimme a piece of that plug!* **2.** *n.* a drink of beer; a *slug* of beer. □ *Let me have a plug out* *of that bottle.* □ *I just want a plug, not the whole thing.* **3.** *n.* a free advertisement or a commercial boost from someone for a product. (See *plugola*.) □ *I managed to get a plug on the Mike Michael show.* □ *How about a free plug during your introduction?* **4.** *tr.* to give an advertisement or commercial boost for something without having to pay for it. □ *I want to get on that TV program and plug my new book.* □ *I can't plug your product until I have a sample I can test.* **5.** See *pluck*.

**plugged in** *mod.* excited by drugs; having to do with the drug culture; *turned on*. (Drugs.) □ *Those guys are really plugged in.* □ *That punker is plugged in, for sure.*

**plugola** ['pləgolə] *n.* a bribe paid to get a free advertising *plug* (worth far more than the amount of the bribe). □ *How much plugola did you have to pay for that mention?* □ *The announcer was charged with accepting plugola.*

**plug-ugly** *mod.* very ugly. (Compare to *pug-ugly*.) □ *Your dog is just plug-ugly.* □ *My plug-ugly dog happens to be pedigreed.*

**plum** *n.* a prize or reward; something that can be considered as the spoils of a political office. □ *That appointment was quite a plum.* □ *My plum for getting elected was a big new office.*

**plumb** [pləm] *mod.* totally; completely. (Folksy. From the standard sense of *plumb*: absolutely straight or vertical.) □ *I'm plumb fed up with this mess.* □ *He looks plumb full.*

**plumbing** *n.* the bathroom; the toilet facilities. (See also *check out the plumbing, visit the plumbing*.) □ *Where's the plumbing?* □ *I'll need the plumbing pretty soon.*

**plumb loco** ['pləm 'loko] *mod.* completely crazy. (Folksy. *Loco* is from a Spanish word meaning "mad.") □ *You're plumb loco if you think I'll go along with that.* □ *All those people were running around like they were plumb loco.*

**Podunk** ['podəŋk] **1.** *n.* an imaginary rural town where everything and everyone is backward, old-fashioned, and inferior. □ *I don't want a job in Podunk.* □ *This is the big city, not Podunk.* **2.**

*mod.* rural and backward. (Usually **podunk**.) □ *I want out of this podunk town.* □ *This podunk place is driving me crazy.*

**poindexter** ['pɔɪndɛkstɚ] *n.* a bookish person; a well-mannered good student, usually male. □ *Charles is a poindexter, but he's a good guy.* □ *I'm no poindexter. In fact, my grades are pretty low.*

**point after** *n.* the "extra" point attempted after a touchdown in football; the point after touchdown. □ *Mike Dennis will try for the point after.* □ *The point after was not made.*

**point man** **1.** *n.* a ballplayer who habitually scores points. □ *Fred is supposed to be point man for our team, but tonight he is not doing so well.* □ *Paul is our favorite point man.* **2.** *n.* anyone whose job it is to score successes against the opposition. □ *The president expects the secretary of defense to be point man for this new legislation.* □ *I am a diplomat, not a point man. Ask someone else to play your little games.*

**pointy-head** *n.* a studious thinker; an intellectual. (Compare to *conehead*.) □ *The pointy-heads seem to be living in a world of their own.* □ *Why do pointy-heads spend so much time arguing about nothing?*

**poison** **1.** *mod.* wicked; evil. □ *Stay away from her. She's poison.* □ *What a poison personality.* **2.** *n.* an alcoholic drink. □ *Name your poison.* □ *How about a drink of that poison there?*

**poison pill** *n.* an element introduced into the restructuring of a corporation so that it becomes undesirable for another corporation to take over. □ *Acme Corporation approved a poison pill to prevent a hostile takeover.* □ *Mr. Boone would have bought the company if it weren't for the poison pill.*

**poke\*** **1.** *n.* a puff of a marijuana cigarette or pipe. (Drugs. Compare to *toke*.) □ *Can I have a poke of that?* □ *Hey! One poke is enough!* **2.\*** *tr.* (for a male) to copulate (with a female). (Crude. Caution with topic.) □ *They say he poked her.* □ *Your dog poked my dog, then ran away.*

**poky 1.** *n.* jail; a jail cell. □ *She spent a day in the poky.* □ *Have you ever been in the poky?* **2.** *mod.* slow; lagging and inefficient. □ *Hurry up! Don't be so poky.* □ *What a poky old horse.*

**pol** [pɑl] *n.* a politician. □ *The pols are spending my taxes like mad again.* □ *How many pols does a democracy require anyway?*

**polecat** *n.* a mean and deceitful person, usually male. (Folksy. A polecat is another U.S. word for skunk. See also *skunk, stinker.*) □ *You dirty polecat!* □ *Tell that polecat I want to talk to him.*

**polished (up)** *mod.* alcohol intoxicated. (See also *waxed.*) □ *One glass of that stuff and I was polished up.* □ *How much of that do I have to drink to get good and polished?*

**polluted** *mod.* alcohol or drug intoxicated. □ *Those guys are really polluted.* □ *Madam, you are polluted!*

**pond scum** *n.* a mean and wretched person; a worthless male. (Collegiate. An elaboration of *scum*, less crude than *scumbag.* Also a rude term of address.) □ *Tell that pond scum to beat it.* □ *Get your hands off me, you pond scum!*

**poo\* 1.\*** AND **poo-poo\*** *n.* fecal material. (See also *poop.* Mostly juvenile. Caution with topic.) □ *Don't step in that dog poo!* □ *There's poo on your shoe, I think.* **2.\*** *in.* to defecate. (Caution with topic.) □ *That old dog pooed on our lawn.* □ *Don't let your dog poo here!* **3.** *n.* nonsense. (From sense 1.) □ *Don't give me that poo!* □ *I've heard enough of your poo.* **4.** *n.* champagne. (From *shampoo.*) □ *How about another glass of poo?* □ *Oh, I just love poo!*

**pooch** *n.* a dog. (Also a term of address to a friendly dog.) □ *Hello, pooch. My goodness, you're friendly.* □ *Please take your pooch out of my garden.*

**pooh-pooh** AND **poo-poo** ['pu'pu] *tr.* to belittle someone or something. □ *He tends to pooh-pooh things he doesn't understand.* □ *Don't always poo-poo me when I express my opinions!*

**pool-hopping** *n.* sneaking into private or public swimming pools at night or during the off-hours. □ *The kids went pool-hopping, and one of them nearly drowned.* □ *Pool-hopping is illegal.*

**poop\* 1.** *n.* information; the detailed knowledge of something. □ *What's the poop on the broken glass in the hall?* □ *Tell me all the poop.* **2.\*** *n.* fecal matter. (Caution with topic. See *poo.*) □ *Don't step in the poop.* □ *There's poop on the sidewalk.* **3.** *in.* to defecate. □ *Your dog pooped on my lawn.* □ *I tried to chase the cat away while it was pooping.*

**pooped (out) 1.** *mod.* exhausted; worn out. (Said of a person or an animal.) □ *I'm really pooped out.* □ *The horse looked sort of pooped in the final stretch.* **2.** *mod.* alcohol intoxicated. □ *How much of that stuff does it take to get pooped?* □ *He's been drinking all night and is totally pooped out.*

**pooper-scooper** *n.* a device used to pick up and carry away dog feces from public places. □ *I never leave home without my pooper-scooper.* □ *Molly actually got a ticket for walking her dog without a pooper-scooper in sight!*

**poophead** *n.* a person who acts very stupidly. (Also a term of address.) □ *Sometimes you act like such a poophead.* □ *Look here, poophead, you're making a fool of yourself.*

**poopied** *mod.* alcohol intoxicated. (A euphemism for *shit-faced.*) □ *She was so poopied that she giggled all the way home.* □ *They got real poopied last night.*

**poopkie** *n.* a pipe for smoking marijuana. (Drugs.) □ *I need a new poopkie.* □ *I lost my poopkie and had to roll a joint.*

**poo-poo** See *poo, pooh-pooh.*

**poop out** *in.* to quit; to wear out and stop. □ *He pooped out after about an hour.* □ *I think I'm going to poop out pretty soon.* (More at *pooped (out).*)

**poop sheet** *n.* a sheet containing information. □ *Where is the poop sheet on today's meeting?* □ *You can't tell one from the other without a poop sheet.*

**poor-mouth 1.** *tr.* to speak ill of someone. (See also *bad-mouth.*) □ *Please don't poor-mouth my brother.* □ *There's no need to poor-mouth your clothing.* **2.** *in.* to speak repeatedly of how little money one has; to plead poverty. □ *She's got money, but she's always poor-mouthing anyway.* □ *Spend more time looking for a job and less time poor-mouthing.*

**pop 1.** *tr.* to hit or strike someone. □ *Please don't pop me again.* □ *She popped him lightly on the shoulder.* **2.** *mod.* popular. □ *This style is very pop.* □ *I don't care for pop stuff.* **3.** *n.* popular music. □ *I like most pop, but not if it's too loud.* □ *Pop is the only music I like.* **4.** *n.* a time; a try, apiece. (Always with *a*.) □ *Twenty dollars a pop is too much.* □ *I love records, but not at $15.98 a pop.* **5.** *n.* an injection of narcotics; a subcutaneous injection of narcotics. (Drugs.) □ *He took a pop in the left arm.* □ *Give me a little. Just a pop.* **6.** *in.* to inject narcotics; to inject narcotics subcutaneously. (Drugs. See also *skin (pop)*.) □ *She's in the bathroom popping.* □ *I'm really sick, and popping just won't help.* **7.** *tr.* to take or swallow a pill, tablet, or capsule. □ *Here, pop a couple of these.* □ *He pops uppers from dawn to dusk.*

**pop a roll** AND **drop a roll** *tr.* to take a small number of pills at the same time. (Drugs.) □ *Max walked around the corner and popped a roll.* □ *How can Max afford to drop a roll so often?*

**pop-eyed** *mod.* alcohol intoxicated, with bulging eyes. □ *What's he been drinking? He's pop-eyed as hell.* □ *She drank until she was totally pop-eyed.*

**pop for something** *in.* to pay for a treat (for someone). (See *spring for something*.) □ *Let's have some ice cream. I'll pop for it.* □ *It's about time you popped for coffee.*

**pop in (for a visit)** AND **pop by (for a visit), pop round (for a visit)** *in.* to pay an unexpected visit on someone; to pay a very short visit. □ *Pop in sometime.* □ *I hope you don't mind if I pop by for a visit when I'm in the neighborhood.*

**pop off 1.** *in.* to make an unnecessary remark; to interrupt with a remark; to sound off. □ *Please don't pop off all the time.* □ *Bob keeps popping off when he should be listening.* **2.** *in.* to lose one's temper. (Compare to *pop one's cork*.) □ *Now, don't pop off. Keep cool.* □ *I don't know why she popped off at me. All I did was say hello.* **3.** *in.* to die. □ *My uncle popped off last week.* □ *I hope I'm asleep when I pop off.* **4.** *in.* to leave; to depart in haste. □ *Bye, I must pop off.* □ *Got to pop off. I'm late.*

**pop one's cork** *tr.* to release one's anger; to *blow one's top.* □ *I'm just about to pop my cork.* □ *She tried to hold it back, but suddenly she popped her cork.*

**popped 1.** *mod.* arrested. (Similar to *busted*.) □ *Tom got popped for speeding.* □ *He was popped for hardly anything at all.* **2.** *mod.* alcohol or drug intoxicated. □ *She looks glassy-eyed because she's popped.* □ *They went out last night and got good and popped.*

**popper 1.** AND **popsie** *n.* an ampoule of amyl nitrite, a drug that is inhaled when the ampoule is broken. (Drugs.) □ *You got a popper I can have?* □ *He had a popsie in his pocket that broke when he sat down.* **2.** See *pill-popper.* **3.** *n.* a handgun. (Underworld. From the sound of a gunshot.) □ *He carries a popper under his coat.* □ *It's illegal to carry a popper in this state.* **4.** *n.* a can of beer (in a pop-top can.) □ *Hey, toss me a popper, Fred!* □ *You ready for another popper, Tom?*

**poppycock** *n.* nonsense. (From Dutch.) □ *I've heard enough of your poppycock.* □ *That's nothing but poppycock.*

**pop round (for a visit)** See *pop in (for a visit).*

**pops** *n.* one's father; any older man. (Also a term of address.) □ *Hey, pops! How you doing?* □ *Well, pops, what do you think?*

**popsie** See *popper.*

**popskull** *n.* fiery liquor; inferior whiskey; *moonshine.* □ *This popskull will burn a hole in you.* □ *Where is that jug of popskull?*

**pop the question** *tr.* (for a man) to ask a woman to marry him. (Could also be used by a woman asking a man.) □ *She waited for years for him to pop the question.* □ *Finally she popped the question.*

**pop wine** *n.* a cheap flavorful sparkling wine drink. □ *Even if you don't like fine wines, you'll like pop wine.* □ *They were drinking pop wine like it was water.*

**pork** *n.* the police in general; a *pig.* (Underworld.) □ *Keep an eye out for the pork.* □ *The pork hauled all of them to the station.*

**pork out** *in.* to overindulge in food and drink. (A play on *pig out*.) □ *Whenever*

*I see french fries, I know I'm going to pork out.* □ *We porked out on pizza.*

**porky** *mod.* fat; obese; pig-like. □ *You are beginning to look a little porky.* □ *See that porky man over there?*

**pot 1.** *n.* a toilet. (Usually with *the.*) □ *Jimmy's on the pot, Mommy.* □ *Where's the pot around here?* **2.** *n.* a drinking vessel. (Old but still heard.) □ *How about a pot of beer?* □ *Care for another pot?* **3.** *in.* to drink heavily; to use a *pot* (sense 2) to excess. □ *He's been potting since dusk.* □ *Let's sit here and pot for a while.* **4.** *n.* a vessel, hat, basket, etc., used to collect or receive contributions. □ *Please pass the pot.* □ *How much is left in the pot?* **5.** *n.* a sum of money collected; a pool of money. □ *Clare won the whole pot.* □ *How large is the pot this month?* **6.** *n.* cannabis; marijuana. (Originally drugs, now widely known.) □ *She had pot on her when she was arrested.* □ *The cops found pot growing next to City Hall.*

**potato** *n.* the head. □ *I got a nasty bump on my potato.* □ *Put your hat on your potato, and let's get out of here.*

**potatohead** *n.* a stupid person. (Compare to *potato.*) □ *Stop acting like a potatohead.* □ *Look, potatohead, go home!*

**potato soup** *n.* vodka. □ *Have a bit of this potato soup, why don't you?* □ *Those Russians make fine potato soup.*

**potbelly** *n.* a big belly. □ *He got a potbelly from eating fried chicken.* □ *Everyone in her family has a potbelly.*

**pot boiler** *n.* a book or other literary work of no value except for the money it earns. □ *I can write one pot boiler every six months or so.* □ *Can you produce anything but pot boilers?*

**pot brownies** AND **hash brownies** *n.* a chocolate cake confection made with cannabis. (Drugs.) □ *She served pot brownies, but they only made people sick.* □ *Hash brownies don't do anything but add fiber to your diet.*

**pot bust** *n.* the capture and arrest of a group of marijuana users. (Drugs. See *bust.*) □ *Max got arrested in a pot bust.* □ *There was a pot bust downtown last night.*

**pot culture** *n.* the marijuana-smoking part of the drug culture. (Drugs. A pun on the expression describing plants grown in pots rather than in the ground.) □ *Tom's hobby is pot culture.* □ *Sally is studying pot culture for social science class.*

**pothead 1.** *n.* a drunkard. (See *pot.*) □ *We'd better get that pothead out of here.* □ *They are all potheads.* **2.** *n.* a marijuana smoker. (Drugs.) □ *Those potheads are headed for worse things.* □ *I started as a pothead and moved up to snow.*

**potholder** *n.* a gadget for holding the butt of a marijuana cigarette; a *roach clip.* (Drugs. A pun on name of the cloth pad used to handle hot pans. See *pot.*) □ *Max had a potholder in his pocket when they searched him.* □ *Let me use your potholder. This is getting short.*

**pot hound** AND **pot sniffer** *n.* a dog trained to sniff out cannabis. (Drugs.) □ *The pot hound at the airport is always busy finding marijuana.* □ *How do they train pot sniffers to find cannabis?*

**pot out** *in.* to smoke marijuana; to abandon everything and turn to marijuana use. (Drugs.) □ *I really feel like potting out and forgetting everything.* □ *Max pots out every Friday after work.*

**pot party** *n.* a communal marijuana smoking session; a party where marijuana is smoked. (Drugs.) □ *I didn't know you were taking me to a pot party!* □ *There was a bust at Max's pot party.*

**potshot 1.** *mod.* alcohol intoxicated. (Drugs. A pun on a term referring to a shot fired at game for the cooking pot.) □ *He's not just drunk; he's potshot.* □ *She got potshot on champagne.* **2.** *n.* a sharp criticism; a wild shot of criticism. (Usually with *take.*) □ *Please stop taking potshots at me!* □ *He took a potshot at my old car.*

**pot sniffer** See *pot hound.*

**potsville** *mod.* intoxicated with marijuana. (Drugs.) □ *That dame is always potsville.* □ *He drinks till he's potsville every night.*

**potted (up) 1.** *mod.* alcohol intoxicated. (Refers to the drinking *pot.*) □ *Three beers and he's potted up.* □ *He sure looks potted. Can't even stand up.* **2.**

*mod.* under the influence of marijuana; drug intoxicated. (Drugs. This *pot* is cannabis.) □ *Her throat is sore, and she acts potted. Must be pot.* □ *Everybody at the party was drunk or potted.*

**potty 1.** *n.* a small toilet. (Usually juvenile.) □ *Mommy, I've got to go to the potty.* □ *I need to use the potty.* **2.** *in.* to use the toilet. (Always juvenile.) □ *I've got to potty.* □ *Be sure to potty before we leave.* **3.** *mod.* crazy. □ *She is acting a little potty.* □ *Who is that potty old man?* □ *He got more potty as he grew older.*

**potty mouth** AND **toilet mouth** *n.* someone who uses obscene or profane language in most social settings. (Also a term of address.) □ *That potty mouth is offending people again.* □ *Hey, toilet mouth! Cool it!*

**pound 1.** *n.* a pound of marijuana. (Drugs.) □ *I need a pound for a friend.* □ *How long will a pound last?* **2.** *n.* five dollars worth of heroin. □ *I can only afford a pound.* □ *My habit wants about 10 pounds.* **3.** See *pounds.*

**pound a beer** AND **pound some beers** *tr.* to drink a beer. □ *On a hot day like this, I want to go home and pound a beer.* □ *Let's go down to the tavern and pound some beers.*

**pounder** *n.* a police officer; a cop on the beat. □ *The pounder gave me a parking ticket.* □ *Most pounders get sore feet.*

**pound one's ear** *tr.* to sleep. □ *I've got to spend more time pounding my ear.* □ *She went home to pound her ear an hour or two before work.*

**pounds** *n.* dollars; money. (Black.) □ *How many pounds does this thing cost?* □ *I don't have any pounds on me.*

**pound someone's head in** *tr.* to beat someone. □ *Talk nice to him, or he'll pound your head in.* □ *I was afraid that the cop was going to pound my head in.*

**pound something out** AND **pound out something 1.** *tr.* to play something loudly on the piano, perhaps with difficulty. □ *She was pounding out a nice little tune.* □ *Here, pound this one out. A little softer, please.* **2.** *tr.* to type something on a typewriter. □ *I have finished writing it. Can I borrow your typewriter so I can pound it out?* □ *All the reporters*

were pounding out stories for the next edition of the paper.

**pound the books** See *hit the books.*

**pour cold water on something** *tr.* to put an end to something; to dampen something. □ *I hate to pour cold water on your plan, but it won't work.* □ *I wanted to go to the party, but my brother poured cold water on that by taking the car.*

**powdered (up)** *mod.* alcohol intoxicated. □ *Those guys are powdered up.* □ *Most of the bums in the gutter are really powdered.*

**powder monkey** *n.* a specialist in the use of dynamite. (See also *grease monkey.*) □ *I won't stay around while the powder monkey is working.* □ *How long do powder monkeys usually live?*

**powder one's nose** AND **powder one's face** *tr.* to depart to the bathroom. (Usually said by women, or jocularly by men.) □ *Excuse me, I have to powder my nose.* □ *She just went out to powder her face.*

**powder room 1.** *n.* a small bathroom without bathing facilities in a private home, usually located for the convenience of guests. □ *Can I use your powder room?* □ *Excuse me, where is the powder room?* **2.** *n.* the ladies' restroom in a public place, especially a restaurant; the place women go to powder their noses. (The emphasis is on comforts other than toilet facilities, such as mirrors, places to rest, and even a maid to help with emergency repairs of makeup or clothing.) □ *The ladies went to the powder room. They'll be back in a minute.* □ *She went to the powder room to clean the spill off her dress.* **3.** *n.* a place where one can buy and use powdered drugs. (Drugs. From the previous sense.) □ *You head over to the powder room and see if you can get some H. at a decent price.* □ *The cops are watching my favorite powder room.*

**powder up** *in.* to drink heavily; to get drunk. □ *Let's go out and powder up.* □ *He's at the tavern powdering up.*

**power hitter 1.** *n.* a batter in the game of baseball who can hit the ball great distances. □ *Ted is a real power hitter. They'll try to walk him.* □ *I'm no power hitter, but I can run like mad.* **2.** *n.* a device for concentrating marijuana smoke, allowing it to go deep into the lungs. (Drugs.) □ *Where's my power hitter? This stuff is low-grade.* □ *The cops found a power hitter in his briefcase. He's finished.* **3.** *n.* someone who blows marijuana smoke into someone else's mouth. (Drugs.) □ *I need a power hitter over here.* □ *Who wants to be my power hitter?*

**power house** *n.* a very big strong person, usually a male. □ *Ted is a real power house. I'd hate to have him mad at me.* □ *Each member of the football team is a power house.*

**power tool** *n.* a student who studies most of the time. (An elaboration of *tool.*) □ *Willard is a power tool if there ever was one. Studies most of the night.* □ *All the power tools always get the best grades.*

**pow-wow 1.** *n.* a meeting; a conference. (From an Amerindian word.) □ *There's a big pow-wow about money at the home office.* □ *Let's have a pow-wow on that issue.* **2.** *in.* to hold a meeting or a conference. □ *Let's pow-wow on that tomorrow.* □ *The senators were pow-wowing on how to get the law passed.*

**pratfall** *n.* a fall on the buttocks; a stage fall on the buttocks. □ *I took a pratfall right on the sidewalk.* □ *If you want to be in musical comedy, you should learn to take a pratfall.*

**pratt** AND **prat** *n.* the buttocks. □ *Get out before I kick you in the pratt.* □ *Your father will spank your prat.*

**prayerbones** *n.* the knees. □ *Okay, down on your prayerbones.* □ *He pushed one of his prayerbones into my gut.*

**pray to the porcelain god** *in.* to empty one's stomach; to vomit. (Refers to being on one's knees (praying) in front of a porcelain toilet bowl.) □ *Boy, was I sick. I was praying to the porcelain god for two hours.* □ *I think I'd better go home and pray to the porcelain god.*

**preemie** *n.* a premature baby. (Medical.) □ *There were two preemies born today.* □ *I was a preemie.*

**preg** *mod.* pregnant. □ *Doesn't Sally look a little preg?* □ *Nobody is ever just a little preg.*

**prelims** *n.* preliminary examinations. (Collegiate.) □ *I hope I pass my prelims.* □ *What do you have to do to get the degree after you pass your prelims?*

**prels** *n.* tablets of Preludin™, a central nervous system stimulant. (Drugs and medical slang.) □ *He was stoned on prels for days at a time.* □ *Take this bottle of prels to three west.*

**preppie** AND **preppy 1.** *mod.* in the manner of a student at a preparatory school. □ *I just love your preppy coat.* □ *Preppy clothes are almost out of style.* **2.** *n.* a young person who dresses and acts like a student at a preparatory school. □ *Those preppies are having fun now, but how will they support themselves?* □ *Do all preppies become yuppies?*

**prescriptions** *n.* any drug available only on a prescription, compared to drugs that can be bought on the street. (Drugs. Black.) □ *I want some H., but I'll even take prescriptions if you got 'em.* □ *She doesn't do anything but prescriptions.*

**preserved** *mod.* alcohol intoxicated. (See also *pickled.*) □ *He's really preserved.* □ *He drank a quart of vodka and is totally preserved.*

**pressed (for money)** See *pinched (for money).*

**pressed (for time)** See *pinched (for time).*

**press (the) flesh** *tr.* to shake hands. (See *flesh-presser.*) □ *Hey, chum! Glad to press flesh with you!* □ *He wanted to press the flesh, but I refused even to touch him.*

**press the panic button** See *hit the panic button.*

**pretty** *mod.* very. □ *Bob's a pretty nice guy.* □ *I'm pretty busy at the moment.*

**pretty penny** *n.* a sizable amount of money. □ *I imagine that your jacket cost you a pretty penny.* □ *This watch cost me a pretty penny, and I intend to take care of it.*

**prexy** *n.* a president. □ *The prexy broke the tied vote.* □ *This year's prexy will retire in March.*

**pricey** AND **pricy** *mod.* expensive. □ *This stuff is too pricey.* □ *That's a pretty pricy car.* □ *Do you have anything less pricy?*

**primed** *mod.* alcohol or drug intoxicated. □ *The entire fraternity got primed.* □ *The whole college was primed by midnight.*

**primed to the ears** AND **primed to the muzzle** *mod.* alcohol or drug intoxicated. (An elaboration of *primed.*) □ *George was primed to the ears.* □ *Sue is walking like she is primed to the muzzle.*

**primo** See *(el) primo.*

**Prince Albert** *n.* cannabis in general, especially marijuana sold or transported in a Prince Albert™ pipe tobacco can. (From the 1960s, but still heard.) □ *I've heard that Max smokes Prince Albert.* □ *Where can I get a can of Prince Albert?*

**prior** *n.* a prior arrest. (Underworld.) □ *This guy has about 15 priors.* □ *Have you ever had a prior, young man?*

**private eye** *n.* a detective who is licensed to work privately rather than for a police department. □ *I worked for a while as a private eye.* □ *The cops don't like private eyes much.*

**privy** *n.* an outdoor toilet; any toilet. □ *Uncle Paul was out in the privy.* □ *Where's the privy around here?*

**pro 1.** *n.* a "professional" (at anything); someone as good as a professional. □ *I'm a pro at photography.* □ *When it comes to typing, he's a pro.* **2.** *mod.* professional. □ *I hope to play pro ball next year.* □ *This is not what I'd call a pro hammer.* **3.** *n.* a prostitute. □ *Do you think she's a pro or just overly friendly?* □ *This pro comes up to me and acts like she's met me before.*

**Proctor and Gamble** *n.* paregoric, a tincture of opium sometimes taken in quantity for its opium content. (Drugs. A reinterpretation of *P.G.*) □ *I can't stand the smell of that Proctor and Gamble when you cook it.* □ *Can you get me about a quart of Proctor and Gamble?*

**prod 1.** *n.* a reminder. □ *She gave me a little prod about the report that is due Monday.* □ *Call me up and give me a little prod so I won't forget.* **2.** *tr.* to remind someone (about something). □ *Call me up and prod me just before the due date.* □ *Stop prodding me about these minor matters.* **3.** *n.* a hypodermic needle. (Drugs.) □ *Clean up that prod before you use it.* □ *The cops found a couple of prods in her purse.* **4.** *n.* an injection of narcotics. (Drugs.) □ *I really need a prod. I'm hurting bad.* □ *There is no place left on her arm for a prod.*

**prof** *n.* a professor. (Collegiate.) □ *The prof was dull and the room was hot, and I kept closing my eyes.* □ *Who's the prof for that course?*

**pronto** *mod.* fast; immediately. (From Spanish. Common in Western movies.) □ *You get over here, pronto.* □ *I want to see you in my office, pronto.*

**proppers** *n.* amphetamines; amphetamine tablets. (Drugs. From *lid proppers.*) □ *I need a couple of proppers to start the day.* □ *She drops proppers from dawn to dusk.*

**prosty** AND **prostie** *n.* a prostitute. □ *The cops haul in about 40 prosties a night from that one neighborhood alone.* □ *This one prosty was high on something and started screaming.*

**pseudo** ['sudo] *mod.* false; bogus. (Used as a productive prefix with many nonce constructions.) □ *This is a very pseudo position that you are taking.* □ *She is just too pseudo.* □ *What a pseudo hairdo!*

**psychedelicatessen** AND **psychedeli** *n.* a place where drug supplies are sold. (Drugs. Referred to a specific shop in New York City. Now used generically.) □ *They sell drug stuff at the psychedelicatessen.* □ *His back room is a regular psychedeli.*

**psyched (out) 1.** *mod.* excited; overwhelmed; thrilled. □ *She's really psyched out.* □ *That's great. I'm really psyched!* □ *What a psyched out way to talk!* **2.** *mod.* alcohol or drug intoxicated. (Drugs.) □ *She's just lying there psyched out.* □ *Two beers and a red devil and he was psyched out.*

**psyched (up)** *mod.* completely mentally ready (for something). □ *I'm really psyched for this test.* □ *The team isn't psyched up enough to do a good job.*

**psycho** *n.* a psychopathic person; a crazy person. □ *Get that psycho out of here!* □ *Pat is turning into a real psycho.*

**psych out** *in.* to have a nervous or emotional trauma; to go mad for a brief time. (Compare to *freak (out)*.) □ *Another day like this one and I'll psych out for sure.* □ *He looked at the bill and psyched out.*

**psych someone out** AND **psych out someone** *tr.* to try to figure out what someone is likely to do. □ *The batter tried to psych out the pitcher, but it didn't work.* □ *Don't try to psych me out.*

**psych someone up** AND **psych up someone** *tr.* to get someone excited or mentally prepared for something. □ *The coach psyched up the team for the game.* □ *I psyched myself up to sing in front of all those people.* (More at *psyched (up)*.)

**psyl** [saɪl] *n.* psilocybin, a hallucinogenic drug. (Drugs.) □ *Max is doing psyl these days.* □ *Good psyl is hard to come by.*

**ptomaine-domain** AND **ptomaine-palace** ['tomen...] *n.* any institutional dining facility; a mess hall; a cafeteria. □ *I can't stand the food at the ptomaine-domain.* □ *Time to go over to the ptomaine-palace and eat—if you can call it that.*

**ptomaine-palace** See the previous entry.

**puddinghead** *n.* someone, usually a male, who acts very stupid. □ *Please stop being such a puddinghead.* □ *That puddinghead sold my antique table for junk!*

**puddle jumper** *n.* a small airplane. □ *I'm not going to fly 200 miles in that puddle jumper!* □ *My uncle has his own puddle jumper.*

**puff** **1.** AND **puff the dust, puff bamboo** *tr. & in.* to smoke opium, marijuana, or hashish. (Drugs. See *dust*.) □ *He's in the back room puffing.* □ *He wants to get home and puff the dust.* **2.** *in.* to get drunk. □ *Those guys go out and puff every Friday night.* □ *I've been puffing since dinnertime, and I'm done.*

**puffer** *n.* a cigar. □ *Who's smoking that foul puffer?* □ *Can you imagine anyone smoking a puffer like that in a restaurant?*

**puff the dust** See *puff*.

**puggled** **1.** *mod.* exhausted; bewildered. □ *I have had a long day, and I'm really puggled.* □ *Who is that puggled old man?* **2.** *mod.* alcohol intoxicated. □ *When he started pouring his drink down his collar, I knew he was puggled.* □ *The whole gang got puggled last night.*

**pug-ugly** **1.** *mod.* having to do with a very ugly person. □ *He is so pug-ugly.* □ *What a pug-ugly cat you have there!* **2.** *n.* a very ugly person. (Also a rude term of address.) □ *Ask that pug-ugly to leave. He will frighten the children.* □ *Hey, pug-ugly, try plastic surgery!*

**puke** [pjuk] **1.** *in.* to empty one's stomach; to vomit. □ *I think I am going to puke.* □ *Max went home and puked for an hour.* **2.** *n.* vomit. □ *There's puke on the floor!* □ *Good grief, Tom. Is that puke on your shoe, or what?* **3.** *n.* a disgusting person. □ *I can't stand that puke!* □ *Make that puke get out of here, or I will scream!*

**pukes** *n.* the feeling of nausea; the feeling of impending vomiting. (Especially with *have, get*. Always with *the*.) □ *Oh my God, I've got the pukes.* □ *I hate having the pukes.*

**pukey** AND **pukoid** *mod.* disgusting; repellent. □ *Who is that pukey-looking guy?* □ *Gosh, it's pukoid!* □ *What a pukey day!*

**pukish** *mod.* nauseated. (Folksy.) □ *Oh, I feel so pukish.* □ *That old pukish feeling came over me, and I just let go.*

**pukoid** See *pukey*.

**pull** **1.** *n.* a drink; a *swig*; a drink from a flask. □ *He took another pull and kept on talking.* □ *Can I have a pull?* **2.** *tr.* to take a drink or a mouthful of liquor from a bottle or other container. □ *He pulled a slug from the bottle.* □ *She pulled a mouthful and then spat it out.* **3.** *n.* a mouthful of smoke from a cigarette; a *drag* on a cigarette. □ *A couple of pulls and she crushed out the cigarette.* □ *After a big pull, she blew an enormous smoke ring.* **4.** *tr.* to smoke a cigarette. □ *He pulled a long filter job and then went back to work.* □ *He stopped for a minute and pulled one.* **5.** *in.* to *pull one's punches*. (Martial arts.) □ *See, he pulled just at the last minute.* □ *If you pull during a fight, you're through as a fighter.*

**pull a boner** *tr.* to make a silly error. (See comment at *boner*.) □ *That was dumb. You really pulled a boner.* □ *Tom is always pulling boners.*

**pull a fast one** *tr.* to outwit or outsmart someone by a clever and timely maneuver. □ *Don't try to pull a fast one on me.* □ *So you think you can pull a fast one?*

**pull down an amount of money** *tr.* to earn a stated amount of money. ("An amount of money" is expressed as a figure or other indication of an actual amount.) □ *She pulls down about $40,000 a year.* □ *They pull down pretty good salaries.*

**pull jive** *tr.* to drink liquor. (See *jive*. Black.) □ *Let's go pull jive for a while.* □ *Don't you ever do anything but pull jive?*

**pull one's belt in (a notch)** See *take one's belt in (a notch)*.

**pull one's punches** **1.** *tr.* to pull back during a boxing punch just before the full force of a blow is felt; to land lighter blows than normal upon an opponent. (Boxing and related sports.) □ *The boxer started pulling his punches, and the ref ended the fight.* □ *He got fined for pulling his punches.* **2.** *tr.* to hold back in one's criticism; to attenuate the intensity of one's remarks. (Also with *any* in the negative.) □ *I won't pull my punches with you. This is lousy.* □ *He never pulls any punches. He always talks straight.*

**pull out all the stops** *tr.* to use everything available; to not hold back. (Refers to pulling out all of the stops on an organ so that it will sound as loud as possible.) □ *Then the mayor decided to pull out all the stops.* □ *Don't pull out all the stops in the first round. Wait till he's tired in the third and clobber him good.*

**pull someone's leg** *tr.* to kid someone; to tease someone. □ *They're just pulling your leg. Relax!* □ *Stop it! I don't believe you! You're pulling my leg.*

**pull something off** AND **pull off something** *tr.* to make something happen. □ *I didn't think he could pull it off.* □ *It takes a lot of skill to pull off something like that.*

**pull the plug (on someone or something)** *tr.* to put an end to someone or something as a problem; to defuse a problem caused by someone or something. (As if one were disconnecting an electrical appliance.) □ *It's time to pull the plug on this problem.* □ *I've heard enough from Mr. Jones. It's time to pull the plug on him.*

**pummelled** *mod.* alcohol intoxicated. (Collegiate.) □ *Can you imagine getting pummelled on peppermint schnapps?* □ *They get pummelled every Friday night.*

**pump** **1.** *tr.* to press someone for an answer or information. □ *Pump him until he talks.* □ *Don't pump me! I will tell you nothing!* **2.** *n.* the heart. (See also *ticker*.) □ *He has the pump of a 40 year old.* □ *My pump's getting sort of weak.* **3.** *n.* a pumped up muscle. (Bodybuilding.) □ *Look at the size of that pump.* □ *He's tired and can't quite make a pump.*

**pumped** **1.** *mod.* pregnant; impregnated. (Crude.) □ *She was so pumped, she was out to here.* □ *Look at her! She's pumped and looks due any minute.* **2.** See the following entry.

**pumped (up)** *mod.* excited; physically and mentally ready. (Sports.) □ *The team is really pumped up for Friday's game.* □ *She really plays well when she's pumped!*

**pump ship** **1.** *tr.* to urinate. (Crude. From an expression meaning to pump the bilge water from a ship.) □ *He stopped and pumped ship right in the alley.* □ *I'll be with you after I pump ship.* **2.** *tr.* to empty one's stomach; to vomit. (Crude. Less well-known than the previous sense.) □ *After I pumped ship, I felt better.* □ *Oh, man! I think I gotta pump ship!*

**pump something up** AND **pump up something** *tr.* to flex and tense a muscle until it is expanded to its fullest size, as with thighs and forearms. (Bodybuilding.) □ *She pumped up her thighs and struck a pose.* □ *He really can pump up his pecs.*

**punch-drunk** AND **punchy** *mod.* unstable; stupid-acting; bewildered. (From a term describing a boxer suffering from brain damage.) □ *I feel sort of punch-drunk after a roller coaster ride.* □ *Who is that punchy jerk?* □ *I feel punchy when I drink too much coffee.*

**punch someone out** AND **punch out someone** *tr.* to knock someone out. (See also the following entry.) □ *The thug punched out the cop and ran down an alley.* □ *He threatened to punch me out.*

**punch someone's lights out** AND **put someone's lights out** *tr.* to knock someone out; to close someone's eyes with a hard blow. □ *Shut up, or I'll punch your lights out.* □ *He threatened to punch my lights out.*

**punchy** See *punch-drunk.*

**punk 1.** AND **punk kid** *n.* an inexperienced boy or youth. (Derogatory. Also a term of address.) □ *Ask that punk to come over here.* □ *Look here, punk, I need some help.* **2.** *n.* a petty (male) hoodlum; a (male) juvenile delinquent. □ *We know how to deal with punks like you.* □ *The jails are packed with crooks who were just punks a few years ago.* **3.** *mod.* poor; dull and inferior. □ *The party turned punk, and we left.* □ *This is pretty punk food.* **4.** *mod.* having to do with a *punker* or with punk music. □ *I am tired of your red punk hair. Try it brown for a change.* □ *This music sounds too punk for me.*

**punker** *n.* a punk rocker; a young person who dresses in the style of punk rockers or has the wild hairstyles. □ *It's not safe to walk on the street with all those weird punkers out there.* □ *The punkers don't even have a sense of rhythm.*

**punk out 1.** *in.* to chicken out. □ *He was supposed to ask her out, but he punked out at the last minute.* □ *Come on! Stick with it! Don't punk out!* **2.** *in.* to become a *punker.* □ *If I punked out, my parents would probably clobber me.* □ *If my kids ever punked out and looked like that, I think I'd clobber them.*

**punk pills** *n.* tranquilizers; barbiturates. (Drugs. They make one feel *punk* and listless.) □ *Hey! Calm down. Go take some punk pills.* □ *He's stoned out of his head on punk pills.*

**puppy 1.** *n.* a *wimp*; a softie. □ *That silly puppy is still waiting outside your door.* □ *Oh, Paul, you're such a puppy!*

**2.** *n.* a thing; a piece or part of something. □ *Put this little puppy right here.* □ *Where is that puppy?*

**puppy love** *n.* mild infatuation; infatuation as in a crush. □ *Is it really love or just puppy love?* □ *Look at them together. It may be puppy love, but it looks wonderful.*

**pure and simple** *mod.* basically; simply; essentially. □ *Max is a crook, pure and simple.* □ *It's a pure and simple fact. The guy is a bum.*

**(purple) haze** *n.* the drug *L.S.D.* (Drugs.) □ *Walter tripped out on purple haze and isn't down yet.* □ *That haze is powerful stuff.*

**purr (like a cat) 1.** *in.* to be in a mild state of drug euphoria. (Drugs.) □ *I was purring like a cat; then suddenly I just went crazy.* □ *Two puffs and Max just lay there purring.* **2.** *in.* (of an engine) to run well and smoothly. □ *My car really purred after I got it tuned up.* □ *New spark plugs and this old heap will really purr like a cat.*

**push 1.** *tr.* to approach a particular age (in years). □ *She looked like she was pushing 48 or 50.* □ *He's only pushing 30, but he looks much older.* **2.** *in.* to recruit new drug users and sell drugs to them; to deal in drugs. □ *He was pushing for two years before the cops got him.* □ *Man, look at that guy push. He hooks two new kids every day.* **3.** *tr.* to *hype* something or someone; to pressure something or someone. □ *She's always pushing her own interests.* □ *The clerk was pushing one brand so hard that I finally bought it.*

**pushed 1.** *mod.* alcohol intoxicated. □ *Tom is a little pushed and can't walk very straight.* □ *How can you be so pushed on so little booze?* **2.** *mod.* addicted to a drug. (Drugs. See *push.*) □ *He's pretty pushed, and he needs some stuff now!* □ *He used H. for years before he really got pushed.* **3.** See *pinched (for money).* **4.** See *pinched (for time).*

**pushed (for money)** See *pinched (for money).*

**pushed (for time)** See *pinched (for time).*

**pusher** *n.* a drug dealer who works hard to establish new addicts and customers.

(Drugs. See *push*.) □ *That pusher over on 8th Street was just mobbed by a group of angry parents.* □ *They said that pushers should be locked up forever.*

**pushing up daisies** *mod.* dead and buried. (Folksy. Usually in the future tense.) □ *I'll be pushing up daisies before this problem is solved.* □ *If you talk to me like that again, you'll be pushing up daisies.*

**push money** *n.* extra money paid to a salesperson to aggressively sell certain merchandise. (See also *spiff*.) □ *The manufacturer supplied a little push money that even the store manager didn't know about.* □ *I got about $300 last month in push money for selling some low-grade sweaters.*

**push off** AND **shove off** *in.* to leave. (As if one were pushing away from a dock.) □ *Well, it looks like it's time to push off.* □ *It's time to go. Let's shove off.*

**push shorts** **1.** *tr.* to sell drugs in small amounts on the street. (Drugs.) □ *Max tried to make a living pushing shorts.* □ *He was a small-time punk, pushing shorts on weekends.* **2.** *tr.* to cheat someone in a drug sale by selling underweight or short weights of a drug. (Drugs.) □ *The mob found out he was pushing shorts and gunned him down.* □ *Stay away from that guy. He pushes shorts.*

**push the panic button** See *hit the panic button.*

**pushy** *mod.* very aggressive in dealing with other people. □ *Stop being so pushy! Who do you think you are?* □ *Who is that pushy dame?* □ *If she weren't so pushy, she would get more cooperation.*

**puss** [PUS] *n.* the face. □ *I ought to poke you right in the puss!* □ *Look at the puss on that guy! What an ugly face!*

**pussycat** **1.** *n.* a woman or young woman; one's girlfriend. (Also a term of address.) □ *Hi, pussycat. Don't I know you from somewhere?* □ *Who was that yummy pussycat I saw you with last Friday?* **2.** *n.* a timid male; a mild-mannered and passive male. □ *That guy is a wimp, a real pussycat.* □ *He seems mean, but underneath he's a pussycat.*

**pussyfoot (around)** *in.* to behave in a very cautious manner; to (metaphorically) tread softly; to hedge or equivocate. □ *Come on and say what you mean! Stop pussyfooting.* □ *You can depend on the mayor to pussyfoot around while the crisis is on.*

**put a con on someone** *tr.* to attempt to deceive someone; to attempt to swindle someone. (Underworld.) □ *Don't try to put a con on me, Buster! I've been around too long.* □ *I wouldn't try to put a con on you. I'm not that dumb.*

**put a damper on something** *tr.* to reduce the intensity of something, such as a problem. □ *The death of the chief put a damper on the ceremony.* □ *I hate to put a damper on your party, but you are too loud!*

**put balls on something\*** *tr.* to make something more masculine or powerful; to give something authority and strength. (Caution with *ball*.) □ *Come on, sing louder. Put some balls on it.* □ *This story is too namby-pamby. Put some balls on it.*

**put-down** *n.* an insult; an intentionally cruel and deflating insult. □ *Another put-down like that and I'm going home.* □ *Don't cry. It was just a little friendly put-down.*

**put hair on someone's chest** *tr.* to jar someone into virility, usually through eating or drinking something. (Folksy. Used for males except in jest.) □ *Have a slug of this stuff. It will—I'm sorry to say, ma'am—put hair on your chest.* □ *Eat this stuff, Jimmy. It'll put hair on your chest.*

**put in a plug (for someone or something)** *tr.* to say something good about someone or something. (See *plug*.) □ *I'm seeing the boss this afternoon, and I'll put in a plug for you.* □ *Remember me when you see the dean. Put in a plug.*

**put in one's oar** AND **put one's oar in** *tr.* to add one's opinions or comments. □ *Why do you always have to put in your oar?* □ *You always put your oar in at exactly the wrong time.*

**put-on** *n.* a deception; an entertaining deception. □ *Of course, it was a joke. It was a really good put-on.* □ *Don't take it seriously. It's just a put-on.*

**put oneself straight** *tr.* to take a needed dose of drugs. (Drugs. See *straight.*) □ *I gotta get some stuff and put myself straight.* □ *Here take this and put yourself straight.*

**put one's nose in (where it's not wanted)** AND **stick one's nose in (where it's not wanted)** *tr.* to interfere in someone else's business. □ *Why do you always have to stick your nose in?* □ *Please don't put your nose in where it's not wanted!*

**put on the dog** AND **put on the ritz** *tr.* to make things extra special for a special event. □ *Frank's really putting on the dog for the big party Friday night.* □ *They really put on the ritz for us.*

**put on the feedbag** AND **put on the nosebag, put the feedbag on, tie on the nosebag** *tr.* to prepare to eat; to eat a meal. (Refers to a bag of feed tied under a horse's mouth.) □ *I'm starved. Must be time to put on the feedbag.* □ *Let's go tie on the nosebag. It's nearly noon.*

**put on the nosebag** See the previous entry.

**put on the ritz** See *put on the dog.*

**putrid** *mod.* alcohol intoxicated. (See also *rotten.*) □ *That guy is stinking drunk. Putrid, in fact.* □ *They went out last night and got putrid.*

**put some distance between someone and someone or something** *tr.* to lengthen the distance or time between oneself and someone or something (including a place). □ *I gotta put some distance between me and that cop, fast.* □ *You need to put some distance between you and your brother's death.* □ *She needed enough money to put some distance between herself and her hometown.*

**put someone on** 1. *tr.* to tease or deceive someone innocently and in fun. □ *Come on! You're just putting me on!* □ *He got real mad even though they were only putting him on.* 2. *tr.* to introduce someone to cannabis use, usually smoking. (Drugs.) □ *Where did you get that stuff? Who put you on?* □ *My brother uses it, and he put me on.*

**put someone or something away** AND **put away someone or something**

1. *tr.* [with *someone*] to put someone in prison for a long time. (Underworld.) □ *They put Max away for 15 years.* □ *The judge put away the whole gang.* 2. *tr.* [with *someone*] to knock someone unconscious. □ *One tap on the head and I put him away.* □ *The cowboy slugged the rancher in the jaw and put him away for a while.* 3. *tr.* [with *something*] to eat something. □ *Did you put away that whole pizza?* □ *Are you going to put this cake away?*

**put someone or something out of the way** 1. *tr.* to remove someone or something as a barrier. □ *I will put the whole problem out of the way.* □ *Yes, she is a problem, but you'll just have to put her out of the way and concentrate on this issue.* 2. *tr.* [with *someone*] to kill someone. □ *The crooks tried to put the witness out of the way.* □ *Sorry, my friend, we no longer need you. Bruno is going to have to put you out of the way.*

**put someone's lights out** See *punch someone's lights out.*

**put someone's nose out of joint** *tr.* to cause someone to feel slighted; to cause someone to take offense. (See also *get one's nose out of joint.*) □ *I'm sorry we didn't invite you. We didn't mean to put your nose out of joint.* □ *Now, now, that shouldn't put your nose out of joint. We're sorry.*

**put someone to bed with a shovel** *tr.* to bury someone; to kill and bury someone. □ *Shut up! You want me to put you to bed with a shovel?* □ *The leader of the gang was getting sort of tired and old, so one of the younger thugs put him to bed with a shovel.* (More at *put to bed with a shovel.*)

**put someone up** AND **put up someone** *tr.* to provide someone with temporary shelter; to let someone stay the night. □ *Can you put me up for a few days?* □ *I could put up a football team, there's so much room here.*

**put some sweet lines on someone** See *lay some sweet lines on someone.*

**put something across** 1. *tr.* to explain something clearly. □ *I have some pictures that ought to help me put it across.* □ *A good demonstration will help put it across.* 2. *tr.* to succeed with a deception; to succeed with any plan. □ *If we are very clever, we can put this across and no one will suspect.* □ *It was a brilliant plot, but they just couldn't put it across.*

**put something on the street** *tr.* to make something known publicly; to tell everyone one's troubles. □ *Man, can't you keep a secret? Don't put everything on the street.* □ *She gets a little problem, and she puts it on the street right away!*

**Put that in your pipe and smoke it!** *exclam.* "Take that!"; "See how you like that!" □ *Everybody thinks you're a phony! Put that in your pipe and smoke it!* □ *You are the one who made the error, and we all know it. Put that in your pipe and smoke it!*

**put the arm on someone 1.** *tr.* to demand something of someone, especially money. □ *I know Tom wants some money. He put the arm on me, but I said no.* □ *She put the arm on her roommate for a loan.* **2.** *tr.* to arrest someone. (Underworld.) □ *They put the arm on Max for pushing pills.* □ *They're gonna put the arm on the whole gang at once.*

**put the bite on someone** *tr.* to try to get money out of someone. □ *You're always putting the bite on me for a few bucks. Go away.* □ *Don't put the bite on me. I'm broker than you are.*

**put the chill on someone** AND **put the freeze on someone** *tr.* to ignore someone. □ *She was pretty snooty till we all put the chill on her.* □ *Let's put the freeze on Ted until he starts acting better.*

**put the finger on someone** *tr.* to identify someone (for someone else, such as the police). (Underworld.) □ *The old lady put the finger on the punk who mugged her.* □ *Tyrone put the finger on the killer, then got out of town fast.*

**put the freeze on someone** See *put the chill on someone.*

**put the heat on someone** See *put the screws on someone.*

**put the kibosh on something** *tr.* to squelch something. □ *The mayor put the kibosh on the whole deal.* □ *Tom was starting his presentation when Bob put the kibosh on the plan.*

**put the moves on someone** *tr.* to attempt to seduce someone. (With *any* in the negative.) □ *At least he didn't try to put any moves on me.* □ *If somebody doesn't try to put the moves on her, she thinks she's a failure.*

**put the pedal to the metal** *tr.* to press a car's accelerator to the floor; to *floor* it. □ *Let's go, man. Put the pedal to the metal.* □ *Put the pedal to the metal, and we're out of here.*

**put the screws on someone** AND **put the heat on someone, put the squeeze on someone** *tr.* to pressure someone; to threaten someone to achieve something. □ *He told everything about the plan when they put the screws on him.* □ *The cops put the squeeze on Harry, and he spilled the beans.*

**put the skids under someone or something** *tr.* to cause someone or something to fail. (See also *on the skids.*) □ *The mayor put the skids under my plan.* □ *Tom tried to talk, but the boss put the skids under him.*

**put the squeeze on someone** See *put the screws on someone.*

**put to bed with a shovel 1.** *mod.* dead and buried. (From *put someone to bed with a shovel.*) □ *You wanna be put to bed with a shovel? Just keep talking that way.* □ *Poor old Jake. He was put to bed with a shovel last March.* **2.** *mod.* alcohol intoxicated. (From sense 1.) □ *He wasn't just tipsy. He was put to bed with a shovel!* □ *Dead drunk? Yes, put to bed with a shovel.*

**put to it** *mod.* in trouble or difficulty; hard up (for something such as money). (As if one's back were put to the wall.) □ *Sorry, I can't lend you anything. I'm a bit put to it this month.* □ *What a day. I'm really put to it.*

**putt-putt** *n.* a small motorized vehicle, especially a small car. □ *I hear him coming in his putt-putt now.* □ *That's not a motorcycle; it's just a little putt-putt.*

**puttyhead** *n.* a stupid person. (As if the person's head were soft as putty. Also a term of address.) □ *Look, you silly puttyhead, shut up!* □ *Stop acting like a puttyhead.*

**put-up job** *n.* a deception; a deceptive event. □ *That's really phony. A put-up job if I ever saw one.* □ *No put-up job is clever enough to fool me.*

**Put up or shut up!** *exclam.* "Speak now or remain silent for good!" □ *I'm tired of your whining. What's your problem? Put up or shut up!* □ *Now is your chance. Put up or shut up!*

**Put your money where your mouth is!** *exclam.* "Stop talking big and make a bet!" (From gambling. Can also be said to someone giving investment advice.) □ *You want me to bet on that horse? Did you? Why don't you put your money where your mouth is?* □ *If this is such a good stock, you buy it. Put your money where your mouth is!*

**putz\*** [pəts] **1.\*** *n.* a penis. (Yiddish. Caution with *putz* and topic.) □ *Tell him to cover his putz and run and grab a towel.* □ *He told some joke about a putz, but nobody laughed.* **2.** *n.* a stupid person, typically a male; a *schmuck.* (Yiddish. Also a rude term of address.) □ *And this stupid putz just stood there smiling.* □ *Tell that putz to leave his card with the secretary.*

**putz around** [pəts...] *in.* to fiddle around; to mess around. (See the previous entry.) □ *Stop putzing around and get to work.* □ *Those guys spend most of their time just putzing around.*

# Q

**Q. 1.** *n.* a quart bottle of liquor. (An abbreviation.) □ *While you're there, get me a Q. of whiskey.* □ *She can knock off a Q. a day.* **2.** *n.* a pill or tablet of Quaalude™ brand of methaqualone, a hypnotic-sedative. (Drugs.) □ *A handful of Q.s would sure make my life easier.* □ *One Q. doesn't do anything for me anymore.* **3.** *n.* the quality of a drug. (Drugs.) □ *This stuff is not Q. at all.* □ *When I say high Q., I don't mean crap like this!*

**Q-sign** *n.* the rounded, open mouth of a dead person with the tongue hanging out like the tail of a capital Q. (A semijocular usage. Hospitals. See also *O-sign.*) □ *The old lady in the corner room is giving the Q-sign.* □ *I can't handle another Q-sign today.*

**quack 1.** *n.* a fraudulent physician; a derogatory term for a physician. □ *I won't go back to that quack ever again!* □ *Tell that quack to heal himself!* **2.** *n.* a tablet of methaqualone, a hypnotic sedative. (Drugs. An elaboration of the abbreviation *Q.*) □ *Got any quack on you?* □ *I need H., but some quack could save my life.*

**quaff a brew** ['kwɑf ə 'bru] *tr.* to drink a beer. (See *brew.*) □ *I went down to the bar to quaff a brew.* □ *Let's go somewhere and quaff a brew.*

**quail** *n.* any girl or woman, especially considered sexually. (Crude.) □ *Look at that cute little quail over there.* □ *Who was the quail I saw you with last night?*

**qual** [kwɑl] *n.* qualitative analysis. (Scientific.) □ *We'll have to turn to qual for that answer.* □ *She worked in qual for a while and then went on to management.*

**quality Joe** *n.* an innocent or straight (male) person. (Underworld.) □ *Lefty is not what I would call your average quality Joe.* □ *These quality Joes just don't understand how it is on the street.*

**quant 1.** AND **quan** *n.* quantitative analysis. (Scientific and collegiate.) □ *I didn't study enough for my quant test.* □ *I flunked quan twice.* **2.** *n.* a technician who works in financial market analysis. □ *He was a quant on Wall Street for two years.* □ *The quants have been warning us about the danger for a month.*

**quarterback** *tr.* to manage, lead, or direct someone or something. □ *Who is going to quarterback this organization after you go?* □ *I quarterbacked the whole company for more years than I care to remember.*

**quartzed** *mod.* alcohol intoxicated. (Related to *stoned (out).*) □ *She is really quartzed!* □ *How can anybody get so quartzed on a bottle of wine?*

**queen** *n.* a homosexual male. □ *Tom is getting to be such a queen.* □ *What kind of a queen is Tom?*

**queer\* 1.** *mod.* counterfeit. □ *This bill is queer.* □ *I don't want any queer money.* **2.** *n.* illicit liquor, especially whiskey. (Prohibition era.) □ *Can you get me a bottle of queer?* □ *This isn't queer; it's left over from before prohibition.* **3.** *mod.* alcohol intoxicated. □ *After a glass or two, he got a little queer.* □ *She was so queer she could hardly stagger home.* **4.** *n.* bogus drugs; inferior drugs. (Drugs.) □ *Get this queer out of here!* □ *He sold me a kilo of queer.* **5.** *tr.* to spoil something. □ *Please don't queer the deal.* □ *I was afraid his dirty* *look would queer his chances.* **6.\*** *mod.* homosexual. (Derogatory. Caution with *queer*. Resented by homosexuals.) □ *Who is that queer character?* □ *Isn't he queer?* □ *She doesn't like being called queer.* **7.\*** *n.* a homosexual male, occasionally a female. (Derogatory. Caution with *queer*. Resented by homosexuals.) □ *Tell that queer to get out of here.* □ *She came to the dance with a queer.*

**queer as a three-dollar bill\*** **1.** *mod.* See *phony as a three-dollar bill.* **2.** *mod.* definitely or obviously homosexual. (Usually derogatory. Caution with *queer*. Resented by homosexuals.) □ *That guy is as queer as a three-dollar bill.* □ *He's wearing makeup. He's queer as a three-dollar bill.*

**queer-beer\*** **1.** *n.* bad beer; beer of low alcohol content. □ *I hate this queer-beer. Get out the good stuff.* □ *Please don't serve me any of your queer-beer.* **2.** *n.* any strange person. (Also a term of address.) □ *Look, queer-beer, stop that right now!* □ *What does that queer-beer think he's doing?* **3.\*** *mod.* having to do with homosexuals; homosexual. (Usually derogatory. Caution with *queer*. Resented by homosexuals.) □ *I won't wear that queer-beer outfit!* □ *Don't call me a queer-beer fruitcake!* **4.** *n.* a homosexual male, possibly a female. (See the previous sense.) □ *They say she's a queer-beer.* □ *That queer-beer is staring at you.*

**queered** *mod.* alcohol intoxicated. (In the sense "made bogus.") □ *I feel sort of queered.* □ *How can anybody get so queered on two beers?*

**queer fish** *n.* a strange person; an aloof person. □ *She's a bit odd. Sort of a queer fish.* □ *He's a queer fish. Don't you agree?*

**queer for something** *mod.* in the mood for something; desiring something. □ *I'm queer for a beer right now.* □ *She's queer for him because of his money.*

**quencher** ['kwɛntʃɚ] *n.* a drink of liquor or beer. □ *I could really use a quencher about now.* □ *How about a nice cold quencher?*

**Que pasa?** [ke 'pɑsə] *interrog.* "Hello, what's going on?" (Spanish.) □ *Hey, man! Que pasa?* □ *What's happening? Que pasa?*

**quetch** See *kvetch.*

**quick-and-dirty** *mod.* rapidly and carelessly done. □ *I'm selling this car, so all I want is a quick-and-dirty repair job.* □ *They only do quick-and-dirty work at that shop.*

**quick buck** AND **fast buck** *n.* a quickly or easily earned profit. □ *I'm always on the lookout to make a fast buck.* □ *I need to make a quick buck without much effort.*

**quicker than hell** *mod.* very fast. (Probably from "quicker than hell could burn something up.") □ *You get over here quicker than hell.* □ *Be careful in the stock market. You can lose all your money quicker than hell.*

**quick fix** **1.** *n.* a quick and probably none too permanent or satisfactory solution to a problem. □ *The quick fix isn't good enough in this case.* □ *He's a master of the quick fix.* **2.** *mod.* having to do with a temporary or unsatisfactory solution or repair. (Usually **quick-fix**.) □ *Frank is a master of the quick-fix solution.* □ *This is no time for quick-fix efforts.*

**quickie** See *quick one.*

**quick one** AND **quickie** *n.* a quick drink of booze; a single beer consumed rapidly. □ *I could use a quick one about now.* □ *I only have time for a quickie.*

**quickstep** *n.* diarrhea. (Folksy. Always with *the*. From the name of a dance.) □ *Uncle Charlie has the quickstep. Get out of his way.* □ *I think that funny-tasting pudding gave me the quickstep.*

**quitter** *n.* someone who gives up easily. □ *Don't be a quitter. Get in there and finish the job.* □ *Dave has a reputation as a quitter.*

**quit while one is ahead** *in.* to stop doing something while one is successful. □ *When will I learn to quit while I'm ahead?* □ *Get into the market. Make some money and get out. Quit while you're ahead.*

**quote, unquote** *phr.* a parenthetical expression said before a word or short phrase that the speaker indicates would be in quotation marks in writing. □ *So I said to her, quote, unquote, it's time we had a little talk.* □ *I think my quote, unquote reputation is ruined.*

# R

**rabbit food** *n.* lettuce; salad greens. □ *I think I need a little more rabbit food in my diet.* □ *Rabbit food tends to have a lot of vitamin C.*

**rabbit punch** *n.* a quick little punch. (Boxing and general slang.) □ *That couldn't have hurt you! It was just a little rabbit punch.* □ *She battered him with about 40 rabbit punches on the arm. Boy, is he ever sore!*

**racing slicks** *n.* very wide tires with little or no treads. (Automobile racing.) □ *I need a new set of racing slicks. I burned up the old ones.* □ *How much do racing slicks cost?*

**rack 1.** *n.* a bed. □ *I need some more time in the rack.* □ *You don't get to see the rack very much in the army.* **2.** See *rack (out).* **3.** *n.* a set of 3 to 5 pills taken at one time. (Drugs. Probably from billiards.) □ *How much did she take? A whole rack!* □ *Not just one! I need a rack.*

**racked (up)** *mod.* alcohol or drug intoxicated. (See also *rack up.*) □ *They drank till they were good and racked.* □ *Man, are you racked. What did you drink? A gallon?* □ *They all got racked up last weekend.*

**racket 1.** *n.* noise. □ *Cut out that racket! Shut up!* □ *Who's making all that racket?* **2.** *n.* a deception; a scam. □ *He operated a racket that robbed old ladies of their savings.* □ *This is not a service station; it's a real racket!* **3.** *n.* any job. □ *I've been in this racket for 20 years and never made any money.* □ *I'm a stockbroker. What's your racket?*

**rack (out)** *in.* to go to sleep or to bed. (See *rack.*) □ *What time do you rack out?* □ *I've got to rack out or drop from*

exhaustion. □ *If I don't rack by midnight, I'm dead the next day.*

**rack something up AND rack up something 1.** *tr.* to accumulate something; to collect or acquire something. □ *We racked up a lot of money in the stock market.* □ *They all racked up a lot of profits.* □ *We racked up 20 points in the game last Saturday.* **2.** *tr.* to wreck something. □ *Fred racked up his new car.* □ *He racked up his arm in the football game.*

**rack time AND rack duty** *n.* time spent in bed. (Military.) □ *I need more rack time than I'm getting.* □ *I was on rack duty for my entire leave.*

**rack up** *in.* to become alcohol intoxicated. □ *Let's go down to the tavern and rack up.* □ *I think I'll rack up.* (More at *racked (up).*)

**rad** [ræd] **1.** *n.* a radical person. (California.) □ *He's such a rad! For sure!* □ *My brother is a rad, but he's a good guy.* **2.** *mod.* great; wonderful; excellent. (California. From *radical.*) □ *Oh my God, that's, like, really rad!* □ *What a rad swimsuit!*

**radical** *mod.* great; excellent. (California.) □ *It's so, like, radical!* □ *My boyfriend, he's, like, so radical!*

**radioland** *n.* an imaginary place where radio listeners dwell. □ *Hello out there in radioland. This is Merton Jones speaking.* □ *All you folks in radioland who enjoy country music will like this next one.*

**rag** *n.* a newspaper. □ *I'm tired of reading this rag day after day. Can't we get a different paper?* □ *What a rag! It's only good for putting in the bottom of birdcages!* **2.** *n.* ugly or badly styled clothing; an ugly garment. (Usually plural.) □ *I can't wear that rag!* □ *I need some new clothes. I can't go around wearing rags like these.* □ *I wouldn't be seen in last season's rags.* **3.** *n.* (in the plural) any clothing, even the best. (Always plural.) □ *Man, I got some new rags that will knock your eyes out!* □ *You got soda pop all over my new rags!*

**rage 1.** *n.* the current fad; an irresistible fad. (Always with *the;* often with *all the.*) □ *Get a haircut like mine. It's all the rage!* □ *One rage after another. Can't I find something that will stay the same for a while?* **2.** *in.* to *party;* to celebrate. (Collegiate.) □ *Man, are we going to rage tonight!* □ *Fred and Mary were raging over at the frat house last weekend.*

**rag out** *in.* to dress up. □ *I like to rag out and go to parties.* □ *I hate to rag out. I like comfortable clothes.*

**ragtop** *n.* a convertible car. □ *The ragtop is making a comeback.* □ *I wanted a ragtop, but they cost nearly $3,000 more.*

**ragweed** *n.* inferior marijuana. (Drugs.) □ *This stuff is ragweed. You can have it!* □ *Max just sells ragweed except to his friends.*

**rah-rah** ['rɑrɑ] *mod.* having to do with college and college enthusiasm. □ *That gal is so rah-rah. What energy!* □ *It was sort of a rah-rah party.*

**railroad tracks 1.** *n.* dental braces. □ *I can't smile because of these railroad tracks.* □ *My railroad tracks cost nearly $1,200.* **2.** *n.* rows of needle scars on the veins of the arms. □ *Look at those railroad tracks on his arm. That means he shoots drugs.* □ *Max has railroad tracks on both arms.*

**rails** *n.* powdered cocaine arranged into lines. (Drugs.) □ *Max makes the rails too messy.* □ *Max put the rails on something smooth.*

**rainbow 1.** *n.* a bowlegged person. (Also a rude term of address.) □ *Hey, rainbow! Are you a cowboy?* □ *Ask that rainbow if he has to have special trousers made.* **2.** *n.* a Tuinal™ capsule. (Drugs.) □ *They found a bunch of rainbows in his pocket.* □ *She took a rainbow and went to sleep immediately.*

**rain on someone's parade** AND **rain on someone or something** *in.* to spoil something for someone. □ *I hate to rain on your parade, but your plans are all wrong.* □ *She really rained on our parade.* □ *Did anyone rain on the meeting?*

**rain pitchforks** *tr.* to rain very hard and heavy. □ *It rained pitchforks all day long.* □ *Every time I go out to rake leaves, it rains pitchforks.*

**raise a stink (about someone or something)** AND **make a stink (about someone or something)** *tr.* to make a big issue about someone or something. □ *You can depend on Fred to raise a stink.* □ *I hope you don't plan to make a stink about the problem.*

**raise Cain** [...ken] *tr.* to make a lot of trouble; to *raise hell.* □ *Fred was really raising Cain about the whole matter.* □ *Let's stop raising Cain.*

**raise hell 1.** *tr.* to make a lot of trouble; to go on a rampage. □ *Stop raising hell so much of the time!* □ *Quiet! Don't raise hell around here.* **2.** *tr.* to go on a drinking spree and get drunk. □ *Let's go out and really raise hell.* □ *The boys went out to raise hell.*

**raise the devil (with someone or something)** AND **raise hell (with someone or something) 1.** *tr.* [with *someone*] to confront someone and complain or scold. □ *I really raised the devil with my brother for being late.* □ *It won't do any good to raise hell with me.* **2.** *tr.* [with *something*] to cause trouble with something. □ *That idea raises hell with my plan.* □ *The onions raised the devil with my stomach.*

**rake in something** AND **rake something in** *tr.* to take in a lot of something, usually money. □ *Our candidate will rake in votes by the thousand.* □ *They were raking in money by the bushel.*

**rally** ['ræli] **1.** *n.* a party or get-together of some kind. □ *There's a rally over at Tom's tonight.* □ *The rally was a flop. Everyone left early.* **2.** *in.* to hold a party of some kind; to *party.* (Collegiate.) □ *Let's rally tonight about midnight.* □ *They rallied until dawn.*

**ralph** AND **rolf** [rælf AND rɔlf] *in.* to empty one's stomach; to vomit. (Teens and collegiate.) □ *She went home and ralphed for an hour.* □ *I think I'm going to rolf.*

**ralph something up** AND **ralph up something** (Teens and collegiate.) *tr.* to vomit (something). □ *He ralphed up his dinner.* □ *The doctor gave him some stuff that made him ralph it up.*

**rambo** ['ræmbo] *tr.* to (figuratively) annihilate someone or something. (Collegiate. From the powerful film character Rambo.) □ *The students ramboed the cafeteria, and the cops were called.* □ *Please don't rambo the other team. Just win the game.*

**rammy** ['ræmi] *mod.* sexually excited or aroused. (Refers to the ram, a symbol of arousal.) □ *Fred was looking a little rammy, so I excused myself and left.* □ *Your rammy boyfriend is on the telephone.*

**ramrod** *tr.* to lead something; to act as the driving force behind something. □ *Who is going to ramrod this project?* □ *Don't ramrod us into something we don't really want.*

**ram something down someone's throat** *tr.* to force something upon someone. (Not literal.) □ *Don't try to ram that nonsense down my throat.* □ *They're always trying to ram something down our throats.*

**randy** ['rændi] *mod.* sexually excited or aroused. □ *The town is full of randy sailors when the fleet's in.* □ *Wow, does he look randy!* □ *There is a randy-looking guy at the door asking for you.*

**rank** *tr.* to give someone a hard time; to *hassle* someone. □ *Stop ranking me!* □ *The dean was ranking the boys for pulling the prank.* □ *When he finished with the boys, he started ranking their parents.*

**rank and file** *n.* the common members of something. □ *What will the rank and file think of the proposal?* □ *The rank and file will vote on it tomorrow.*

**rank someone (out)** AND **rank out someone** *tr.* to annoy or chastise someone. (Compare to *rank.*) □ *He really ranks me out. What a pest!* □ *I ranked out the whole gang, but good!*

**rap 1.** *in.* to talk or chat about something. □ *Something wrong? Let's rap about it.* □ *The kids sat down and rapped for an hour or so.* **2.** *n.* a conversation; a chat. □ *How about a rap?* □ *Let's have a rap sometime.* **3.** *n.* sweet talk; seductive talk; *line.* □ *I like your rap, but that's all I like about you.* □ *Don't lay that rap on me! You're not my type.* **4.** *n.* a criminal charge; the blame for something. (Underworld.) □ *I won't take the rap for something you did.* □ *The cops tried to make the rap stick, but they didn't have enough evidence.*

**rap session** *n.* an informal conversation session. □ *The kids settled down for a long rap session.* □ *The rap session was interrupted by a fire drill.*

**(rap) sheet** *n.* a criminal record listing all recorded criminal charges. (See *rap.*) □ *This guy has a rap sheet a mile long.* □ *The sargeant asked if there was a sheet on the prisoner.*

**rare bird** *n.* an unusual person; a person with rare talents or abilities. □ *An interesting kind of rare bird is the man who can take long vacations and still make money.* □ *She is a rare bird who enjoys opera and can understand most of it, too.*

**rare old time** *n.* a fine and enjoyable time at a party or something similar. (Folksy.) □ *That was a rare old time at Tom's the other night.* □ *I haven't had a rare old time like that in years.*

**raring to go** *mod.* anxious and eager to go. □ *Come on, I'm raring to go!* □ *The whole family is raring to go on vacation.*

**raspberry** ['ræzbɛri] *n.* the *Bronx cheer.* □ *The entire audience gave the performer the raspberry.* □ *The performer gave them a raspberry right back.*

**rasty** ['ræsti] *mod.* having to do with a harsh-looking young woman. (Collegiate.) □ *Who is that rasty dame I saw you with?* □ *That dark lipstick makes you look a little rasty.*

**rat 1.** *n.* a wretched-acting person. (Also a term of address.) □ *You dirty rat, you!* □ *Stop acting like a dirty rat!* **2.** See *rat (on someone).*

**rat around** *in.* to waste time loafing around; to *kick around.* (Collegiate.) □ *I didn't do anything but rat around all summer.* □ *If kids don't have jobs, they just rat around.*

**ratchet-mouth** AND **motor-mouth** *n.* someone who talks incessantly. (Also a term of address.) □ *Tell that ratchet-mouth to shut up!* □ *Hey, motor-mouth, quiet!*

**rat fink** *n.* an informer. (Also a term of address. See *rat.*) □ *That guy is nothing but a rat fink. A dirty squealer!* □ *Fred told the teacher about the plot, and everybody called him a rat fink for the next two years.*

**rathole 1.** *n.* a run-down place; a *dump* or a *joint.* □ *I refuse to live in this rathole any longer.* □ *Why don't you clean up this rathole?* **2.** *n.* a bottomless pit. (Typically with *throw...down* as in the examples.) □ *Why do they keep throwing money down that rathole?* □ *That rathole will absorb as much money as they can supply.* □ *The transportation system is beyond help. Giving it more subsidies is just throwing money down a rathole.*

**rat (on someone)** *in.* to inform (on someone). □ *Bill said he was going to rat on that punk.* □ *If you rat on me, I'll get you!* □ *Who ratted?*

**rat out** *in.* to quit; to *fink out (on someone or something).* □ *It's too late to rat out.* □ *He tried to rat out at the last minute.*

**rat race** *n.* a dull and repetitive situation; a dull and unrewarding job. (Compare to *daily grind.*) □ *I am really tired of this rat race—day after day.* □ *She dropped out of the rat race and moved to Vermont, where she opened a barber shop.*

**Rats!** *exclam.* "Oh, damn!" □ *Rats! I broke a nail!* □ *Oh, rats! I'm late.*

**rats** *n.* the delirium tremens. (Always with *the.*) □ *The way he was shaking, I knew he had the rats.* □ *Most of those old guys down on 4th Street have the rats.*

**rattlebones** *n.* a nickname for a very skinny person. (Also a term of address.) □ *Hey, rattlebones, come over here a minute.* □ *Ask rattlebones over there to have a seat.*

**rattlebrain** *n.* a stupid person. □ *Is that rattlebrain here again?* □ *Please try not to be such a rattlebrain! Pay attention to what you are doing.*

**rattled 1.** *mod.* confused; bewildered. □ *He tends to get a little rattled at minor things.* □ *Try not to get her rattled.* **2.** *mod.* tipsy; alcohol intoxicated. □ *After an hour of drinking, Bill was more than a little rattled.* □ *Being rattled from beer, I stopped drinking beer and began on the rum.*

**rattle-trap** *n.* a rattly (old) car; any rattly vehicle. □ *I hear Ted's rattle-trap in the driveway.* □ *I bought a rattle-trap for $400.*

**rattling** *mod.* excellent. (Collegiate. Compare to *rocking.*) □ *Her party was really rattling.* □ *What a rattling place to live!*

**raunchy** AND **raunchie, ronchie** ['rɑntʃi] **1.** *mod.* crude; tasteless; bad. □ *He told a very raunchy story at the party.* □ *Don't be so ronchie.* **2.** *mod.* alcohol intoxicated. □ *Those guys were raunchy as hell.* □ *Let's go out and get good and ronchie.* **3.** *mod.* sick; ill. □ *I feel sort of ronchy.* □ *After I ate dinner, my stomach felt a little raunchie, so I went home.*

**rave** *n.* a party; a wild celebration. □ *What a rave! A real fine party.* □ *Let's have a little rave next Friday.*

**raw 1.** *mod.* harsh and cold, especially weather. □ *What a raw day!* □ *The weather was cold and raw.* **2.** *mod.* inexperienced; brand-new. □ *The raw recruit did as well as could be expected.* □ *She'll get better. She's just a little raw.* **3.** *mod.* vulgar; crude. □ *I've had enough of your raw humor.* □ *That joke was a little raw.* **4.** *mod.* (of alcoholic spirits) undiluted; neat. □ *No ice, please. I prefer it raw.* □ *I'll drink it raw—just the way it is now.* **5.** *mod.* (of alcoholic spirits) unaged; fiery and strong. □ *My gosh, this stuff is raw! It'll burn a hole in me.* □ *Give me something to drink that isn't quite so raw.*

**raw deal** *n.* an unfair deal; unfair treatment. (Always with *a.*) □ *You really got a raw deal.* □ *My last job was a raw deal. I hope this is better.*

**rays** *n.* sunshine. (Collegiate.) □ *I'm going to go out and get some rays today.* □ *I've had too many rays. I'm cooked.*

**razz** [ræz] *tr.* to tease someone. □ *Please stop razzing me.* □ *I was just razzing you. I didn't mean any harm.*

**razzle-dazzle** ['ræzl̩'dæzl̩] *n.* flamboyant publicity; *hype.* □ *After all the razzle-dazzle dies down, we'll see what things are really like.* □ *Hollywood is filled with razzle-dazzle and excitement.*

**razzmatazz** AND **razzamatazz** ['ræzmə'tæz AND 'ræzəmə'tæz] *n.* deceptive talk; *hype.* □ *Cut out the razzamatazz. How dumb do you think I am?* □ *Don't give me all that razzamatazz!*

**reach for the sky 1.** *in.* See *aim for the sky.* **2.** *in.* (a command) to put one's hands up, as in a robbery. □ *Okay, you guys, reach for the sky!* □ *The bank teller reached for the sky without having to be told.*

**reader** *n.* a piece of paper with writing on it; a note; a prescription; an I.O.U. (Underworld.) □ *Max has my reader for $500.* □ *I got a reader for some morphine.*

**Read my lips!** See *Watch my lips!*

**real** *mod.* very; really. (Folksy and overused.) □ *This is a real fine party.* □ *You did a real good thing.*

**real bitch** *n.* a very difficult or annoying thing or person. (Can refer to male or female.) □ *This math problem is a real bitch.* □ *Fred is a true problem. A real bitch.*

**real gone** *mod.* really cool; mellow and pleasant. □ *Man, this music is real gone.* □ *That's a real gone drummer.* □ *You are something—real gone.*

**(real) McCoy 1.** *n.* something authentic. (Always with *the.*) □ *This is the real McCoy. Nothing else like it.* □ *This is no copy. It's the McCoy.* **2.** *n.* pure drugs or alcohol. (Always with *the.*) □ *Is this stuff the McCoy?* □ *If it's not the real McCoy, I don't want it.*

**ream someone out** AND **ream out someone** *tr.* to scold someone severely. □ *The teacher really reamed him out.* □ *The coach reamed out the whole team.*

**rear (end)** *n.* the tail end; the buttocks. (Euphemistic.) □ *She fell right on her rear.* □ *The dog bit her in the rear end.*

**rear-ender** AND **back-ender** *n.* an automobile wreck where one car runs into the back of another. (Compare to *fender-bender.*) □ *It wasn't a bad accident, just a rear-ender.* □ *My neck was hurt in a back-ender.*

**red devils** AND **R.D.** *n.* capsules of Seconal™ barbiturate. (Drugs.) □ *Max had a pocket full of red devils when he got busted.* □ *You got an R.D. I can borrow?*

**red hot 1.** *mod.* important; in great demand. □ *This is a red hot item. Everybody wants one.* □ *The stock market is a red hot issue right now.* **2.** *n.* a hotdog. □ *"Get your red hots right here!" shouted the vendor.* □ *In Chicago they eat red hots with catsup. Imagine!*

**red-hot mama** *n.* an exciting woman; a sexually exciting or excited woman. □ *Clare is really a red-hot mama!* □ *I'm no red-hot mama, just a country girl.*

**red ink** *n.* debt; indebtedness as shown in red ink on a financial statement. □ *There is too much red ink in my financial statement.* □ *Too much red ink and the company will collapse.*

**red-letter day** *n.* an important day that might well be marked in red on the calendar. □ *Today was a red-letter day in our history.* □ *It was a red-letter day for our club.*

**redneck 1.** *n.* a stereotypic southern bigot. (Derogatory. Also a term of address.) □ *Those rednecks can hardly read.* □ *Look, you stupid redneck, try to understand.* **2.** *mod.* in the manner of a southern bigot. □ *I don't follow that kind of redneck thinking.* □ *The candidate didn't want the redneck vote.*

**red tape** *n.* bureaucratic annoyances; bureaucratic forms and procedures. (Typically with *cut* as in the example.) □ *If you deal with the government, you will have to put up with lots of red tape.* □ *I have a friend who knows how to cut through red tape.*

**reef** See *reefer.*

**reefdogger** ['rifdɔgɚ] *n.* a marijuana cigarette. (Drugs. California.) □ *Got a reefdogger I can bum?* □ *Max just stood there with a reefdogger in his mouth.*

**reefer** ['rifɚ] **1.** *n.* a refrigerator. □ *Please put the milk in the reefer.* □ *A new reefer costs nearly $1000!* **2.** AND **reef** *n.* cannabis; a marijuana cigarette. (Drugs.) □ *He had a reefer in his hand when he was busted.* □ *Don't stall the reefer. Pass it on.* **3.** *n.* a smoker of marijuana. (Drugs.) □ *They say Max is a reefer.* □ *Both those kids are reefers.*

**ref** [rɛf] **1.** *n.* a referee. (Also a term of address.) □ *Hey, ref! Get some glasses!* □ *The ref did a fine job.* **2.** *tr.* to referee something, such as a game. □ *Are you going to ref this one, or am I?* □ *I don't like to ref night games.*

**regs** *n.* regulations. □ *Follow the regs or pay the penalty.* □ *There is a list of regs posted on the back of your door.*

**reinvent the wheel** *tr.* to make unnecessary or redundant preparations. □ *You don't need to reinvent the wheel. Read up on what others have done.* □ *I don't have time to reinvent the wheel.*

**rents** AND **rentals** *n.* one's parents. (Teens. See *(parental) units.* Also a term of address.) □ *I'll have to ask my rents.* □ *Hey, rentals, let's go out for dinner.*

**rep** [rɛp] **1.** *n.* a representative, usually a sales representative. □ *Please ask your rep to stop by my office.* □ *Our rep will be in your area tomorrow.* **2.** *n.* someone's reputation. □ *I hope this doesn't ruin my rep.* □ *I've got my own rep to think about.* **3.** *n.* repertory theater. □ *He spent a year in rep on the East Coast.* □ *Rep is the best place to get experience, but not to make connections.*

**repo** ['ripo] **1.** *n.* a repossessed car. □ *It's a repo, and I got it cheap.* □ *I'd rather have a plain used car than a repo.* **2.** *tr.* to repossess a car. □ *Some guy came around and tried to repo my car.* □ *She's good at repoing family cars.*

**repo man** ['ripo 'mæn] *n.* a man who repossess cars for a living. □ *What kind of guy is lower than a repo man?* □ *I'd rather beg than get a job as a repo man.*

**ret** [rɛt] *n.* a tobacco cigarette. (Collegiate. A front clipping.) □ *You got a ret I can bum?* □ *Give my buddy a ret, will you?*

**retard** ['ritard] **1.** *n.* a rude nickname for a retarded person. (Derogatory and unkind.) □ *That retard is having a rough time.* □ *Don't call my brother a retard!* **2.** *n.* a stupid person. (Also a term of address.) □ *Don't be a retard! Get with it!* □ *Look, you retard, get busy.*

**retread** ['ritrɛd] *n.* a burned-out person; a made-over person. □ *Chuck is just a retread. He's through.* □ *I need somebody fresh and alive, not some tired retread.*

**re-up 1.** *in.* to reenlist in the military services. □ *You going to re-up?* □ *I wouldn't re-up for a million dollars!* **2.** *in.* to take a needed dose of drugs. (Drugs.) □ *I'm a little sick. I think I'd better re-up.* □ *Max has to re-up twice a day.*

**rev something up** AND **rev up something** *tr.* to speed up an engine in short bursts. □ *Tom sat at the traffic light revving up his engine.* □ *Rev it up a few times and see if it stalls.*

**rhubarb** ['rubarb] *n.* a brawl, especially in a baseball game. □ *There's a noisy rhubarb down on the field.* □ *Ted got punched around a little bit in that rhubarb last week.*

**rhythm(s)** ['rɪðəmz] *n.* amphetamines. (Drugs. Compare to *blues*, which are depressants.) □ *Some people take rhythm to pep them up even though they are addictive.* □ *Max is loaded with rhythms.*

**rib 1.** *n.* a joke; an act of teasing. □ *I didn't mean any harm. It was just a little rib.* □ *That's a great rib, Sam!* **2.** *tr.* to tease someone. □ *Please don't rib me anymore tonight. I've had it.* □ *Let's go rib Jennifer.*

**rib-tickler** *n.* a joke; something very funny. □ *That was a real rib-tickler. I'll remember that joke.* □ *She told a rib-tickler, and everybody laughed.*

**ride shotgun** *tr.* to accompany and guard someone or something. (A term from the days of stagecoaches and their armed guards. See *shotgun.*) □ *I have to take the beer over to the party. Why don't you come along and ride shotgun?* □ *Who's going to ride shotgun with Bill?*

**ride the porcelain bus** See *drive the big bus.*

**rif 1.** *tr.* to dismiss an employee. (From the euphemism *reduction in force.*) □ *They're going to rif John tomorrow.* □ *Who'll they rif next?* **2.** *n.* a firing; a dismissal. □ *Who got the rif today?* □ *There's a rif in your future.*

**riff** [rɪf] **1.** *n.* a short, repeated line of music played by a particular performer. □ *Jim just sat there and forgot his riff.* □ *Listen to this riff, Tom.* **2.** *n.* a digression while speaking. (From the previous sense.) □ *Excuse the little riff, but I had to mention it.* □ *If she didn't* *make so many riffs while she spoke, we could understand her better.*

**riffed** [rɪft] **1.** *mod.* alcohol or drug intoxicated. □ *That guy is really riffed!* □ *I can't keep getting riffed every night like this.* **2.** AND **rift** *mod.* fired; released from employment. (From *R.I.F.*, "reduction in force.") □ *Poor Walter got riffed Friday.* □ *Most of the sales force was riffed last week.*

**rig 1.** *tr.* to arrange or tamper with the results of something. □ *The crooks rigged the election.* □ *Somebody rigged the contest so no one got first prize.* **2.** *n.* a large truck; an eighteen wheeler. □ *Jim drives a really big rig.* □ *There were three rigs sitting in the parking lot when we got there.* **3.** *n.* equipment for injecting or using drugs. (Drugs.) □ *Ernie broke his rig and nearly went crazy.* □ *The police found his rig in a drawer and busted him.*

**right as rain** *mod.* completely correct. (Folksy. Often with *as.*) □ *Yes, indeed! You are right as rain!* □ *She was right as rain about the score.*

**righteous** [ˈraɪtʃəs] *mod.* good; of good quality. (Originally black.) □ *She is a righteous mama.* □ *Max told me about some righteous grass he's got.* □ *This stuff is really righteous!*

**right guy** *n.* a good guy; a straight guy. □ *Tom is a right guy. No trouble with him.* □ *I'm glad you're a right guy. I can trust you.*

**right in the kisser** *mod.* right in the mouth or face. (See *kisser.*) □ *Max poked the cop right in the kisser.* □ *He caught one right in the kisser.*

**right up one's alley** AND **up one's alley** *mod.* exactly one's kind of thing; exactly what one is best equipped to do. □ *That job is right up her alley.* □ *It's not exactly up my alley, but I'll try it.*

**ring a bell** *tr.* to stir something in someone's memory. □ *Yes, that rings a bell. I seem to remember it.* □ *Maybe the name Marsha will ring a bell!*

**ringer (for someone)** See *(dead) ringer (for someone).*

**ring off the hook** *in.* (for a telephone) to ring endlessly or constantly. □ *The phone was ringing off the hook when I came in.* □ *We've been busy today. The phone's been ringing off the hook.*

**ringtailed snorter** *n.* someone or something energetic and powerful. □ *Old Charlie is a real ringtailed snorter.* □ *Ask that ringtailed snorter to calm down and come over here for a minute.*

**ring the bell** *tr.* to be just what is needed; to *hit the spot.* □ *This cold water really rings the bell.* □ *A good hot bowl of soup would ring the bell about now.*

**rinky-dink** [ˈrɪŋkiˈdɪŋk] *mod.* cheap; inferior; broken-down. □ *I sold my rinky-dink old car yesterday.* □ *What a rinky-dink job! I quit!*

**riot** [ˈraɪət] *n.* someone or something entertaining or funny. □ *Tom was a riot last night.* □ *Her joke was a real riot.*

**rip 1.** *n.* a drinking bout. (See *tear.*) □ *All four of them went out on a rip.* □ *Fred had another rip last night. He's rotten now.* **2.** *n.* a puff of a marijuana cigarette. (Drugs.) □ *Gimme a rip. One rip and she started laughing like mad.* **3.** *n.* the loot from a *rip-off.* □ *I want my share of the rip, now!* □ *Give him some of the rip and tell him to beat it.* **4.** *n.* a theft; a *rip-off.* □ *The crooks pulled a rip on 4th Street last night.* □ *That was the third rip there this week.* **5.** *n.* a tear in the flesh of the hand, as in an athletic event where the flesh comes in contact with solid material, such as in gymnastics and weight-lifting. □ *I keep getting rips from the bar.* □ *Sally has a rip on her palm.*

**ripe 1.** *mod.* alcohol intoxicated. □ *Yes, they were ripe all right. Stinking drunk.* □ *Bill was so ripe that they took him home.* **2.** *mod.* foul; smelly. □ *Whooey! This place is ripe. What died?* □ *Get your ripe old socks out of here!* □ *The fish seems quite ripe.* **3.** *mod.* crude; raunchy. □ *Your jokes are a bit ripe.* □ *That was a ripe one!* □ *Stop acting so ripe.*

**rip-off 1.** *n.* a theft; a deception; an exploitation. (See *rip.*) □ *This sandwich is a rip-off!* □ *What a rip-off! I want my money back.* **2.** *mod.* having to do with theft and deception. □ *I consider myself to be rip-off champion of North America.* □ *All I hear is rip-off stories. Isn't anybody honest?*

**rip-off artist** AND **off artist** *n.* a con artist. □ *Fred is such an off artist.* □ *Beware of the rip-off artist who runs that shop.*

**rip on someone** *in.* to give someone a hard time; to *hassle* someone. □ *Fred was ripping on me, and I heard about it.* □ *Stop ripping on my friend!*

**ripped (up)** AND **ripped (off)** *mod.* alcohol or drug intoxicated; under the effects of marijuana. □ *Why do you have to get ripped up like that?* □ *Max was ripped out of his mind on uppers.*

**rippers** *n.* amphetamines. (Drugs. See *ripped (up)*.) □ *Max is high on rippers as usual.* □ *Have you been on those rippers again?*

**rip snorter** *n.* a remarkable person or thing; a hilarious joke. (Folksy.) □ *Old Fred is a real rip snorter.* □ *Her new car is a rip snorter, I tell you.* □ *Let me tell you a rip snorter about a farmer and his cow.* □ *Judy can tell some rip snorters.*

**rip someone or something off** AND **rip off someone or something** 1. *tr.* [with *someone*] to assault, kill, beat, rob, rape, or cheat someone. (Note the *for* in the example.) □ *They ripped me off, but they didn't hurt me.* □ *Man, they ripped me off for three hundred dollars.* 2. *tr.* [with *something*] to steal something. □ *The crooks ripped off the hub caps of my car.* □ *They ripped them all off.*

**Rise and shine!** *exclam.* "Get up and get going!" □ *Get up! Rise and shine! It's late.* □ *Okay, you guys, rise and shine!*

**rits** [rɪts] *n.* tablets of Ritalin™ stimulant. (Drugs.) □ *That guy is hooked on rits.* □ *The cops found a bottle of rits in his pocket.*

**ritzy** ['rɪtsi] *mod.* elegant; flamboyant. □ *That is a real ritzy car.* □ *It's really ritzy!* □ *What a ritzy coat! Is it new?*

**rivets** ['rɪvəts] *n.* dollars; money. (From *copper* rivets.) □ *You got enough rivets on you for a snack?* □ *Who can come up with that many rivets?*

**roach** 1. *n.* a police officer. (Derogatory. From *cockroach*.) □ *Watch out! The roaches are coming.* □ *A roach caught him while he was at work.* 2. *n.* the butt end of a marijuana cigarette. (Drugs.) □ *The cops found a roach on the bath-*

room floor. □ *Hey, give me that roach!* 3. *n.* an ugly girl or woman. (Derogatory. From *cockroach*.) □ *Who was that roach you were with last night?* □ *That dame is a real roach.*

**roach clip** AND **roach pick** *n.* a device to hold a *roach* and make it smokable. (Drugs. Compare to *potholder*.) □ *When the cops find a roach clip on you, you've had it.* □ *They found two roach picks and a pipe.*

**roach-coach** *n.* a mobile snack truck. □ *Let's go get a sandwich at the roach-coach.* □ *Here comes the roach-coach! Let go spend some coin.*

**roached** *mod.* hungover; exhausted. □ *I'm roached. I feel lousy.* □ *What a day! I've never been so roached.*

**road apple** *n.* a lump of horse excrement. (Compare to *alley apple*.) □ *Don't step on the road apples.* □ *There must be horses around here. I see road apples.*

**road hog** *n.* someone who takes too much space on a road or highway; someone who seems to run other people off the road. □ *Get over! Road hog!* □ *A road hog nearly ran me off the road.*

**roadie** AND **roady** ['rodi] 1. AND **roadster** ['rodstɚ] *n.* a young person who helps rock groups set up for performances. □ *I want to be a roadie when I grow up.* □ *I was a roadster for a while, but I didn't like it.* 2. AND **roadster** *in.* to help rock groups set up. □ *Let's go downtown and roadie tonight. The Red Drips are in town.* □ *I hate to roady. It's, like, work!* 3. *mod.* eager to travel; eager to get on the road. □ *I get a little roady when the weather gets warm.* □ *We'd better get going. Your father looks a little roadie.*

**roast** 1. *tr.* to put on an entertaining program where the guest of honor is teased and insulted. □ *They roasted Dave when he retired.* □ *If they roast me at the dinner, I'll cry.* 2. *n.* an entertaining program where the guest of honor is insulted all in fun. □ *It was a wonderful roast. The guest of honor was pleased with the quality of the insults.* □ *It was a little too polite for a real roast.*

**roasted** *mod.* alcohol intoxicated. □ *He was stewed, roasted, and boiled.* □ *He's out getting roasted with the boys.*

**roasting-ear wine** *n.* illicit whiskey; *moonshine.* (Folksy.) □ *Where's that jug of roasting-ear wine?* □ *That roasting-ear wine will burn your throat.*

**rob someone blind 1.** *tr.* to steal freely from someone. □ *Her maid was robbing her blind.* □ *I don't want them to rob me blind. Keep an eye on them.* **2.** *tr.* to overcharge someone. □ *You are trying to rob me blind. I won't pay it!* □ *Those auto repair shops can rob you blind if you don't watch out.*

**rock 1.** AND **rock candy** *n. crack,* a crystallized form of cocaine. (Drugs. See also *rocks.*) □ *Some call it rock, and some call it crack.* □ *Rock is pretty expensive.* **2.** *n.* a crystallized form of heroin used for smoking. (Drugs.) □ *Max is hooked on rock—the kind that you smoke.* □ *Powder is everywhere, but you can hardly find rock anymore.* **3.** *n.* a diamond or other gemstone. □ *Look at the size of that rock in her ring.* □ *How many rocks are there decorating the edges of your watch?* **4.** See *rocks.*

**rock bottom 1.** *n.* the lowest point or level. □ *The value of the goods is at rock bottom right now.* □ *Prices have reached rock bottom.* **2.** *mod.* absolute lowest, especially in reference to price. □ *Prices are rock bottom this month.* □ *I am offering you the rock bottom price.* □ *You can't beat these rock bottom deals.*

**rocker 1.** *n.* a rocking chair. (Not slang.) □ *I love to spend a sunny afternoon in my rocker.* □ *Children love rockers, but they can tip over in them.* **2.** *n.* a rock and roll singer, song, or fan. (See also *off one's rocker.*) □ *Do all rockers have red hair?* □ *Let's listen to a good rocker.*

**rocket** *n.* a marijuana cigarette. (Drugs. It gets people *high.*) □ *Those rockets Max sold me are no good.* □ *Low-quality rockets aren't worth anything.*

**rocket ship** *n.* a hypodermic syringe and needle. (Drugs.) □ *She can't get high without her rocket ship.* □ *They all shared the same little rocket ship and will probably get some disease from it.*

**rockhead** *n.* someone who seems to have rocks in the head; a hardheaded or stubborn person. □ *What a rockhead! That's a stupid thing to do.* □ *Why do you always have to be such a rockhead?*

**rocking** *mod.* excellent. (Collegiate.) □ *Man, what a rocking party!* □ *This set is really rocking.* □ *We had a rocking time!*

**rock-jock** *n.* a mountain or rock climber. □ *The serious rock-jocks practice in North Wales.* □ *The sides of every mountain are covered with rock-jocks.*

**rock out** *in.* to pass out from the use of drugs. (Drugs.) □ *She rocked out on whatever she took.* □ *She always rocks out. She has no business taking any of that stuff.*

**rocks 1.** *n.* ice cubes. (See *on the rocks.* See also *rock.*) □ *No rocks, please. I like my drink warm.* □ *Can I have a few rocks in my drink, please?* **2.** *n.* Xerox Inc. (Financial markets, New York Stock Exchange.) □ *When she says, "Buy me a thousand rocks at the market," that means she wants one thousand shares of Xerox at whatever the market price is at the moment.* □ *Rocks is down a point and a half.* **3.** *n.* money; a dollar. (Underworld.) □ *How many rocks do you want for that?* □ *Twenty rocks for that?*

**rocky mountain canary** *n.* a donkey. (Folksy.) □ *The old man and his rocky mountain canary came slowly down the trail.* □ *They call a donkey a rocky mountain canary because of the sound of its braying.*

**rod 1.** *n.* a gun; a revolver. (Underworld.) □ *I got a rod in my pocket. Don't move.* □ *I don't have any bullets for my rod.* **2.** See *(hot) rod.*

**roger** ['rɑdʒɚ] *interj.* "okay"; "That is correct." □ *Roger, I'll do it.* □ *Roger. Will do.*

**rolf** See *ralph.*

**roll 1.** *n.* a bankroll; lots of money. □ *I earned a roll off that last deal.* □ *He's got a roll right there in his pocket.* **2.** *tr.* to rob a drunkard. □ *The muggers found a drunk and rolled him.* □ *Those punks can't get much money by rolling drunks.* **3.** *n.* a drug high. (Drugs.) □ *Max likes a good roll. That's why he uses.* □ *The roll from this stuff is okay.* **4.** *n.* a sustained period of luck or productivity. (See also *on a roll.*) □ *I'm doing great! What a roll!* □ *The fantastic roll that this performer is on is truly exciting.*

**roll in 1.** *in.* to pull in; to drive up; to arrive. □ *The car rolled in to the parking lot at a high speed.* □ *Four station wagons rolled in at the same time.* **2.** See *turn in.*

**rolling buzz** *n.* a long-lasting drug high. (Drugs.) □ *What I want is a nice rolling buzz.* □ *That stuff will give you a rolling buzz without putting you to sleep.*

**rolling in it** AND **rolling in money** *in.* having lots of money. □ *I'm not exactly rolling in it, but I have enough to meet my needs.* □ *John's uncle was rolling in money until the stock market crashed.*

**rolling in the aisles** *in.* clapping and cheering with approval, usually for something funny. □ *He's very entertaining. He usually has them rolling in the aisles.* □ *What a funny lady! The audience was rolling in the aisles.*

**ronchie** See *raunchy.*

**rook** [ruk] *tr.* to cheat someone. □ *She tried to rook me when I paid my bill.* □ *Don't go into that store. They'll rook you.*

**rookie** AND **rooky** ['ruki] **1.** *n.* a person new at something; a neophyte, especially a police officer or a ballplayer. □ *Tom is a rookie on the police force.* □ *The rookie tackled the old-time player and earned a lot of cheering and applause.* **2.** *mod.* new; inexperienced. □ *Fred is a rookie first baseman for the home team.* □ *A rooky cop can make arrests just like the other cops.*

**room for rent** *n.* a person who acts very stupid. (Also a term of address. This implies that one's head is so empty of brains that the space could be rented out.) □ *Hey, room for rent, wake up and pay attention.* □ *My brother is a room for rent if I ever saw one. What a dope!*

**rooster** ['rustɚ] *n.* the posterior; one's butt end. (Old. Because one roosts on it.) □ *Don't just sit there on your rooster. Get to work.* □ *I fell down smack on my rooster.*

**root 1.** *n.* a cigarette or a cigar. □ *That root you're smoking sure stinks.* □ *You got a root I can borrow?* **2.** *in.* to eat food like a pig. □ *Don't root. Slow down and enjoy your food.* □ *Max is downstairs rooting now. It won't take that slob long to eat.*

**rooting-tooting** *mod.* exciting; renowned; famous; illustrious. (A vague adjective of praise.) □ *We really had a rooting-tooting time last weekend.* □ *She's a rooting-tooting dancer from Omaha.*

**rope 1.** *n.* a cigar; a very bad-smelling cigar. □ *Get that vile rope out of here!* □ *What kind of jerk would smoke a rope like that in a restaurant?* **2.** *n.* cannabis; a marijuana cigarette. (Drugs. See *hemp.*) □ *Max has some good-quality rope for sale.* □ *The cops found some rope in her car and busted her.*

**rope someone in** AND **rope in someone 1.** *tr.* to cause someone to get involved in some project. □ *She's always trying to rope me into her club.* □ *Let's rope in someone to help with cleaning up.* **2.** See *take someone in.*

**roscoe** ['rasko] *n.* a pistol, especially a revolver. (Underworld.) □ *He's got a roscoe in his pocket.* □ *I'm going down there to talk to Max, and I'm taking my roscoe.*

**roses** *n.* tablets of Benzedrine™, an amphetamine. (Drugs. Named for their color.) □ *They caught the truck driver with a bottle of roses under the seat.* □ *He uses roses to keep awake on long journeys.*

**rosy** *mod.* good; satisfactory. □ *Things are looking rosy now that the economy is improving.* □ *Doesn't look like a very rosy future.* □ *When the stock market crashed, nothing looked rosy.*

**rot** *n.* nonsense. □ *Don't give me anymore of your rot. Speak straight with me.* □ *That's just rot. Don't believe any of it!*

**rotgut 1.** *n.* strong or inferior liquor, especially whisky. (Folksy.) □ *Where is that jug of rotgut you used to keep around here?* □ *The old man nearly went blind drinking all that rotgut.* **2.** *mod.* (of liquor) strong or fiery. □ *You've got to stop drinking that rotgut liquor and think of your health.* □ *I won't pay for this rotgut whisky. Give me something better.* **3.** *n.* weak or otherwise inferior beer. □ *I need a can of beer, and you give me this rotgut?* □ *She can afford something better, but she drinks nothing but cheap rotgut.*

**rotorhead** *n.* a helicopter pilot or member of a helicopter crew. (Military. Also a term of address.) □ *Radio those rotorheads and tell them to get back to the base, now!* □ *Hey, rotorhead, where's your eggbeater?*

**rotsee** ['rɑtsi] *n.* "R.O.T.C.," the Reserve Officers Training Corps. □ *I joined rotsee to help pay my way through school.* □ *How long have you been in the rotsee program?*

**Rots of ruck!** ['rɑtsə'rək] *exclam.* "Lots of luck!" (Mocking a Japanese pronunciation.) □ *Have a good trip, and rots of ruck!* □ *Goodbye, and rots of ruck!*

**rotten 1.** *mod.* smelly; disgusting. (Not slang.) □ *What is that rotten smell?* □ *Something rotten is under that board.* **2.** *mod.* alcohol intoxicated. (From the previous sense. See also *putrid*.) □ *It takes a case of beer to get Wilbur rotten.* □ *When he gets rotten, he's sort of dangerous.* **3.** *mod.* poor or bad. (From the first sense.) □ *We have nothing but one rotten problem after another.* □ *This is the most rotten mess I've ever been in.*

**rotten apple** *n.* a single bad person or thing. □ *There always is a rotten apple to spoil it for the rest of us.* □ *Tom sure has turned out to be the rotten apple.*

**rotten egg** *n.* a bad or despised person; a *stinker.* □ *That guy is a real rotten egg.* □ *She sure has turned out to be a rotten egg.*

**rotten luck** *n.* bad luck. □ *Of all the rotten luck!* □ *I've had nothing but rotten luck all day.*

**rotten to the core** *mod.* really bad. (See *rotten apple.*) □ *That lousy punk is rotten to the core.* □ *The entire administration is rotten to the core.*

**rough and ready** *mod.* vigorous and eager. □ *After a good night's sleep, I feel rough and ready—I could take on a bear.* □ *My friend is the rough and ready type. I'd rather sit and think about things.*

**rough and tumble** *mod.* disorderly; aggressive. □ *That was a rough and tumble football game.* □ *George is too rough and tumble for me. He doesn't know how to act around civilized people.*

**roughhouse** AND **roughneck 1.** *n.* a mean kid; a boisterous child, usually male. □ *Jimmy! Stop acting like such a roughhouse.* □ *Tell that young roughneck to straighten up and behave.* **2.** *in.* to be boisterous. □ *Stop roughnecking in my livingroom.* □ *The boys broke the lamp when they were roughnecking around in the family room.*

**rough it** *tr.* to live for a short period of time in a relatively primitive state. □ *We went camping and had to rough it for a week.* □ *With no electricity in our house, I roughed it by burning candles.*

**roughneck** See *roughhouse.*

**rough someone up** AND **rough up someone** *tr.* to beat someone up; to maltreat someone. □ *Am I going to have to rough you up, or will you cooperate?* □ *The crooks roughed up the old lady before taking her purse.*

**rough stuff** *n.* unnecessary roughness; physical violence or threats of violence. □ *Okay, let's cut out the rough stuff!* □ *There was too much rough stuff in Friday's game.*

**rough time** *n.* a hard time; a bad time. □ *I didn't mean to give you such a rough time. I'm sorry.* □ *What a rough time we had getting the car started!*

**roundhouse punch** *n.* a punch to the head made by swinging the arm in an arc rather than by a jabbing punch. □ *Jim knocked Ted down with a roundhouse punch.* □ *He let him have a roundhouse punch that would have cracked a two-by-four.*

**round the bend** See *around the bend.*

**round tripper** *n.* a home run in baseball. □ *Ted is responsible for four round trippers in Saturday's game.* □ *He hit a round tripper in the fourth inning.*

**roundup** *n.* a collection or summary of news items, such as a weather roundup, news roundup, etc. □ *Tune in at eleven for a roundup of the day's news.* □ *Now for a weather roundup.*

**roust** [rɑust] **1.** *tr.* (for a police officer) to bother or interfere with someone; to arrest someone. (Underworld.) □ *The cops rousted the gang without warning.* □ *I was walking along doing nothing, and this cop rousts me.* (More at *rousted.*) **2.** *tr.* to raid someone's residence;

to *bust* a person or place. (Underworld.) □ *They rousted Max's place last night.* □ *That bar was rousted last week.* **3.** *n.* a raid or a *bust.* □ *Okay, stand still. This is a roust!* □ *They pulled a big roust down on 4th Street.*

**rousted** ['raʊstəd] *mod.* arrested. (Underworld.) □ *Max got rousted last night.* □ *The cops rousted the dealers, but that didn't even slow down the drug trade.*

**R. & R.** *n.* "rest and recuperation"; "rest and relaxation." (Originally military.) □ *I could use about three years of R. & R. after that battle.* □ *I'll need a lot of R. & R. to recover from that stuff they fed us.*

**rubber 1.** *n.* automobile tires; the rubber of automobile tires. □ *This car has some fine rubber on it.* □ *The rubber on my car is practically ruined.* **2.** See the following entry.

**rubber (check)** *n.* a check that bounces; a forged check. (See *bounce.*) □ *The bank says I wrote a rubber check, but I'm sure there was enough money on deposit.* □ *One rubber check after another! Can't you add?*

**rubberneck 1.** *n.* one who stares at something or someone; a tourist. □ *At noon the sidewalks are crowded with rubbernecks.* □ *See if that rubberneck over there has the correct time.* **2.** *in.* to stare (at something or someone). □ *What are all those people rubbernecking at?* □ *Traffic is stalled because of all the drivers who are rubbernecking.*

**rubber sock** *n.* a timid person; a passive and compliant person. □ *What a rubber sock. She's afraid of her own shadow.* □ *Come on! Stand up for your rights. Don't be such a rubber sock!*

**rubbish** *n.* nonsense. (Also an exclamation.) □ *I'm tired of listening to your rubbish.* □ *Rubbish! That's the stupidest thing I've ever heard.*

**rub someone out** AND **rub out someone** *tr.* to kill someone. (Underworld.) □ *The crooks tried to rub out the witness.* □ *The gunman was eager to rub somebody out.*

**rub someone's nose in something** *tr.* to remind someone of something constantly; to make a big issue about someone's mistake. (From the practice of training a puppy by rubbing its nose in the messes it makes.) □ *So I made a mistake! I wish you'd stop rubbing my nose in it.* □ *Rubbing my nose in it is not going to correct the mistake.*

**ruckus** ['rəkəs] *n.* a commotion; an uproar. □ *Quiet, please. Don't raise such a ruckus.* □ *The boss kicked up quite a ruckus when I came in late.*

**rug** *n.* a wig or toupee. (See also *divot.*) □ *Is that guy wearing a rug, or does his scalp really slide from side to side?* □ *I wear just a little rug to cover up a shiny spot.*

**rug rat** *n.* a child. (Also a term of address.) □ *You got any rug rats at your house?* □ *Hey, you cute little rug rat, come over here.*

**rule** *in.* to dominate; to be the best. (Slang only in certain contexts. Typical in graffiti. See examples.) □ *The rockets rule!* □ *Pizza rules around here.*

**rumble 1.** *in.* to fight. □ *The gangs are rumbling over on 4th Street.* □ *We're going to rumble tomorrow night.* **2.** *n.* a fight; a street fight; a gang fight. □ *If there is a rumble, get out of there fast.* □ *My brother was hurt in a gang rumble.*

**rumdum** AND **rum-dumb** ['rəm'dəm] **1.** *n.* a drunkard; a ruined alcoholic. □ *Get that smelly rumdum out of here.* □ *I don't want to end up like a dirty rum-dumb.* **2.** *n.* a stupid person. □ *Hey, rumdum, wise up and do what you are told.* □ *Don't be such a rum-dumb.* **3.** *mod.* alcohol intoxicated. □ *The old lady got rumdum on gin.* □ *Two glasses and she was rumdum and asleep.*

**rummed (up)** *mod.* alcohol intoxicated. □ *Sailors like to go into town and get rummed up.* □ *Those boys are really rummed.*

**rummy** ['rəmi] **1.** *n.* a drunkard; an alcoholic; an alcoholic hobo. □ *Ask that rummy to leave before he throws up.* □ *There is a rummy at the door asking for a handout.* **2.** *mod.* alcohol intoxicated. □ *She's rummy, and she's going to be sick.* □ *Who's the rummy old girl?* □ *How long does it take a heavy drinker like Bob to get rummy?* **3.** *mod.* habitually confused and inept. □ *I get more rummy as I grow older.* □ *That rummy old man is here again.*

**rump 1.** *n.* the hindquarters; the buttocks; the posterior. □ *He fell on his rump.* □ *A dog doesn't have much rump.* **2.** *tr.* to flog someone on the buttocks. □ *They rumped him and made him run around the frat house.* □ *I'm going to get rumped when my dad gets home.*

**rumpus** ['rəmpəs] *n.* a commotion. □ *Please don't make such a rumpus.* □ *There was quite a rumpus in Jim's room.*

**rumpus room** *n.* a family recreation room. (Old but still heard.) □ *Our rumpus room has a pool table.* □ *If you kids are going to play rough, you'll have to go down to the rumpus room.*

**run 1.** *n.* a session or period of time spent doing something; a period of time when something happens. □ *The market had a good run today.* □ *We all have enjoyed a good run of luck.* □ *Max takes amphetamines and was on a run all week.* □ *A run like that can kill.* **2.** *tr.* to transport contraband, alcohol, or drugs. □ *Max used to run booze during prohibition.* □ *The soldiers were caught running guns.* **3.** *n.* an act of transporting contraband. □ *Four soldiers were killed during a run.* □ *In their final run the cocaine smugglers made over four million dollars.*

**run a make on someone** *tr.* to perform an identity check on someone. (Underworld.) □ *The cops ran a make on Lefty and learned about his prison record.* □ *We tried to run a make on him and came up with nothing.*

**run amok** ['rən ə'mək] *in.* to go awry. (From a Malay word meaning to run wild in a violent frenzy.) □ *Our plan ran amok.* □ *The whole company ran amok after the market crashed.*

**run a railroad** *tr.* to use heroin; to be addicted to heroin. (Drugs. Refers to rows of needle marks on the arm. See *railroad tracks.*) □ *Clare has been running a railroad for years. She is really hooked.* □ *Look at his arms. Does he run a railroad, or is he just a pleasure user?*

**runaround** *n.* a wild goose chase. (Especially with *give* as in the examples.) □ *The IRS gave us the runaround when we asked for a review.* □ *The customer will never get a runaround at my store!*

**rundown** *n.* a summary bringing someone up to date. □ *Can you give me a rundown on what's happened since noon?* □ *I need a rundown on the current situation in Alaska.*

**run down some lines 1.** *in.* to converse (with someone). □ *I was running down some lines with Fred when the bell rang.* □ *Hey, man, let's run down some lines.* **2.** *in.* to try to seduce someone; to go through a talk leading to seduction. (See *run one's rhymes.*) □ *Go run down some lines with someone else.* □ *I was just standing there running down some lines with Mary when those guys broke in.*

**run hog-wild** AND **go hog-wild** *in.* to go on a rampage; to proceed unattended. (Folksy.) □ *The kids are all running hog-wild. Take care of them.* □ *Don't go hog-wild while I'm away.*

**run-in** *n.* an unpleasant encounter; a quarrelsome discussion. □ *I had a run-in with the boss this morning.* □ *We tried to avoid a run-in, but it happened anyway.*

**run it down** *tr.* to tell the whole story; to tell the truth. □ *Come on! What happened? Run it down for me!* □ *I don't care what happened. Run it down. I can take it.*

**runner 1.** *n.* a messenger. □ *Send a runner over to the other office for supplies.* □ *I work as a runner in the financial district.* **2.** *n.* a person who transports contraband. (Underworld.) □ *The cops caught the runner red handed.* □ *The runners got away, but we have the goods.*

**run off** *in.* to have diarrhea. □ *Jimmy has been running off since midnight.* □ *At least I'm not running off anymore.*

**run off at the mouth** *in.* to talk too much; to have diarrhea of the mouth. □ *I wish you would stop running off at the mouth.* □ *Tom runs off at the mouth too much. I wish he would temper his remarks.*

**run-of-the-mill** *mod.* average; typical. (Referring to the typical quality of a product which comes out of a mill.) □ *He is just a run-of-the-mill guy.* □ *I don't want just run-of-the-mill ice cream.* □ *This stuff is just run-of-the-mill.*

**run on all cylinders 1.** *in.* to run well and smoothly. (Usually negative.) □ *This department is running on all cylinders now.* □ *My plan is not running on all cylinders.* **2.** *in.* to operate sensibly and intelligently. □ *Pay attention to what you are doing. Start running on all cylinders.* □ *She doesn't run on all cylinders this early in the morning.*

**run one's rhymes** *tr.* to say what you have to say; to give one's speech or make one's plea. (Collegiate.) □ *Go run your rhymes with somebody else!* □ *I told him to run his rhymes elsewhere.*

**run out of gas** *in.* to lose momentum or interest. □ *His program is running out of gas.* □ *I hope I don't run out of gas before I finish what I set out to do.*

**runs** *n.* diarrhea. (Always with *the*.) □ *That stuff we ate gave me the runs.* □ *I can't believe those cute little hamburgers could give anybody the runs.*

**run scared** *in.* to act panicked. □ *All the politicians are running scared.* □ *Don't panic. There is no reason to run scared.*

**run someone in** AND **run in someone** *tr.* to arrest someone; to take someone to the police station. □ *Don't argue with me, or I'll run you in.* □ *The cops ran in everybody in sight.*

**runt** *n.* a small person; someone whose growth has been stunted. (Also a rude term of address.) □ *He can't play basketball. He's just a runt.* □ *Hey, runt. Come here!*

**Run that by (me) again.** AND **Run that by (me) one more time.** *sent.* "Please tell it to me again." □ *I can't believe my own ears. Can you run that by again, please?* □ *It's noisy in here. Please run that by me one more time.*

**run-up** *n.* a movement upward in the value of a financial market. (Financial markets.) □ *The market's had a good run-up in the last week.* □ *I'm afraid that if it has a run-up to 3,000, it will fall to zero.*

**rush 1.** *n.* a quick print of a day's shooting of a film. (Film making. Usu-ally plural.) □ *After today's shooting, we'll watch yesterday's rushes.* □ *Rush these rushes right over to Mr. Hitchcock's office.* **2.** *n.* a period of time when fraternities and sororities are permitted to pursue new members. (Collegiate.) □ *When does rush start this year?* □ *I've got to be at school in time for rush.* **3.** *tr.* (for a fraternity or sorority member) to try to persuade someone to join. □ *The frat tried to rush me, but I'm too busy.* □ *They can't rush anyone except during rush week.* **4.** *tr.* to court or date someone, usually a woman. (From the previous sense.) □ *Tom's trying to rush Betty, but she's not interested.* □ *He spent some time trying to rush her, but had to give up.* **5.** *n.* a burst of energy or good feeling from a drug; the explosive euphoria of some kinds of drugs. (Drugs.) □ *Man, this stuff really gives me a rush.* □ *What kind of rush does this have?* **6.** *n.* any excitement; any burst of good feeling. (From the previous sense.) □ *I got a real rush from helping out.* □ *The wonderful ending to the movie gave me a rush.*

**rust belt** *n.* the industrial north of the U.S. (Patterned on *sun belt*.) □ *The economy in the rust belt is slowing down.* □ *The salt they put on the roads in the winter made my car all rusty. I guess that's why they call this area the rust belt.*

**rust bucket** *n.* a naval destroyer; any ship. (Military.) □ *I'm anxious to get off this old rust bucket.* □ *Why don't I ever get assigned to a new ship? It's always some crummy rust bucket!*

**rusty-dusty** *n.* the posterior; the buttocks. (See *duster*.) □ *I fell down right on my rusty-dusty.* □ *I almost kicked him in the rusty-dusty.*

**ruth** [ruθ] **1.** *n.* a women's restroom. (Compare to *john*.) □ *Where's the ruth?* □ *Point me toward the ruth!* **2.** *in.* to empty one's stomach; to vomit. (See also *cry ruth* and *rolf*.) □ *I gotta go ruth!* □ *I just can't stand to ruth.*

# S

**sack 1.** *n.* a bed. □ *I was so tired I could hardly find my sack.* □ *Somebody put a spider in my sack.* **2.** *tr.* to dismiss someone from employment; to fire someone. □ *The boss sacked the whole office staff last week.* □ *If I do that again, they'll sack me.* **3.** *n.* a dismissal. (Always with *the*.) □ *The boss gave them all the sack.* □ *The sack is what I am afraid of.* **4.** *tr.* to tackle someone in football. □ *I tried to sack him, but he was too fast.* □ *Sack that guy or else!* **5.** *n.* the completion of a tackle in football. □ *Andy made the sack on the 10-yard line.* □ *Who failed to make the sack?*

**sacked out** *mod.* asleep. □ *Mary is sacked out in her room.* □ *Here it is ten o'clock, and you are still sacked out!*

**sack out** *in.* to go to bed or go to sleep. □ *It's time for me to sack out.* □ *Let's sack out early tonight.* (More at *sacked out*.)

**sack rat** *n.* someone who spends a lot of time in bed; someone who does not ever seem to get enough sleep. □ *Tom is such a sack rat. He can't seem to get enough sleep.* □ *Mary is a such a sack rat that she misses classes.*

**sack time 1.** *n.* a period of time spent in bed. □ *I need more sack time than most people.* □ *How much sack time do you get?* **2.** *n.* time to go to bed. □ *Okay, gang, it's sack time. Go home so I can get some sleep!* □ *When is sack time around here?*

**sacred mushrooms** See *magic mushrooms*.

**sad** *mod.* poor; undesirable. □ *This is a sad excuse for a car!* □ *That was a sad pitch there at the end of the last inning.* □ *This steak is really sad.*

**saddled with someone or something** *mod.* burdened with someone or something. □ *I've been saddled with the children all day. Let's go out tonight.* □ *I don't want to be saddled with your work.*

**sad sack** *n.* a sad person; a listless or depressed person. □ *Tom always looks like such a sad sack.* □ *Who is that sad sack moping in the corner?*

**sail into someone** AND **light into someone** *in.* to beat or scold someone. □ *Jimmy's mother really sailed into him for breaking the window.* □ *Jimmy lit into the cat for getting in the way.*

**sail (right) through something** *in.* to get through something easily. □ *I sailed right through my homework.* □ *We sailed through the examination with no difficulty.*

**salt 1.** *n.* a sailor. (Especially with *old*.) □ *A couple of salts came ashore and asked if they could buy some beer.* □ *I've sailed a little, but you could hardly call me an old salt.* **2.** *n.* heroin; powdered heroin. (Drugs.) □ *Max has a little jar of salt on his shelf for emergencies.* □ *He mixes a little salt with his coke every now and then.*

**salt and pepper 1.** *n.* inferior or impure marijuana. (Drugs.) □ *This is just salt and pepper. I want good stuff.* □ *Max can only afford salt and pepper.* **2.** *n.* a black and white police squad car. □ *There is a salt and pepper around the corner waiting for speeders.* □ *There is a salt and pepper behind you, and it's too late to slow down.* **3.** *mod.* interracial, including black and white. □ *It was sort of a salt and pepper meeting, with representatives from all neighbor-*

hoods. □ *We achieved a salt and pepper agreement that made everyone happy.*

**salt horse** *n.* corned or salted beef. □ *We had salt horse on toast for dinner.* □ *We made spaghetti sauce with salt horse because that was the only meat we could find.*

**Sam** *n.* federal agents; federal narcotics agents. (Also a term of address. From *Uncle Sam*.) □ *Sam is on the trail of the dope smugglers.* □ *Sam is working hard to put an end to all this drug trouble.*

**Sam and Dave** *n.* the police; police officers. (Black.) □ *Mike got hit by Sam and Dave last night.* □ *And there at the door were my old buddies Sam and Dave with a warrant.*

**same difference** *n.* the same; no difference at all. □ *Pink, fuchsia, what does it matter? Same difference.* □ *Whether you go or I go, it's the same difference.*

**same here** *phr.* "me too"; "I agree." □ MARY: *I think I'll have the broiled halibut.* JANE: *Same here.* □ BILL: *I feel sort of cold. What about you?* SUE: *Same here.*

**same old story** *n.* an often repeated story or situation. □ *It's the same old story. Boy meets girl, girl gets consumption, girl dies.* □ *One after one they came in. It's the same old story with each of them, "Not enough time to do my homework."*

**same o' same o'** AND **same ol' same ol'** ['semo 'semo AND 'semol 'semol] *n.* the same old thing. □ *I'm getting tired of the same ol' same ol'.* □ *Why not something different? Do you like the same o' same o'?*

**sand** *n.* sugar. □ *Please pass the sand.* □ *Do you use sand in your coffee?*

**sandbag 1.** *tr.* to force someone to do something. □ *I don't want to have to sandbag you. Please cooperate.* □ *Don't let them sandbag you into buying something you don't need.* **2.** *tr.* to deceive someone; to fool someone about one's capabilities. □ *Don't let them sandbag you into expecting too little.* □ *The guy sandbagged me, and I wasn't expecting him to shoot the ball.*

**San Francisco bomb** *n.* a mixture of heroin, cocaine, and *L.S.D.* (Drugs. See also *Frisco speedball*.) □ *It was that*

*San Francisco bomb that killed him.* □ *Max tried a San Francisco bomb once and got really bombed.*

**(San Quentin) jail bait** AND **San Quentin quail** ['sæn 'kwentn̩...] *n.* a young woman under the legal age for copulation even with consent. (Originally underworld.) □ *Stay away from her. She's jail bait for sure.* □ *The cops smiled and said something about San Quentin jail bait as they put the cuffs on him and led him away.*

**sap 1.** *n.* a stupid person. □ *That poor sap thinks he can convince them.* □ *Who is that miserable-looking sap in the corner?* **2.** *n.* a blackjack. (Underworld.) □ *The thug bopped him on the head with a sap.* □ *Max had a sap in his pocket when they arrested him for possession.*

**Saturday night special** *n.* a small, easily obtainable pistol. □ *There was another killing last night with a Saturday night special.* □ *That's the tenth shooting done with a Saturday night special this week.*

**sauce** *n.* liquor; any alcoholic beverage. (See also *on the sauce*.) □ *Those guys have had too much sauce again.* □ *Did you bring the sauce? Can't have a good party without lots of sauce.*

**sauced** *mod.* alcohol intoxicated. □ *She went out and got herself sauced.* □ *Man, do you look sauced.*

**sauce parlor** *n.* a tavern. □ *You spend too much time in the sauce parlor, Fred.* □ *I wouldn't be caught dead in that sauce parlor.*

**savage** *mod.* excellent. (Collegiate.) □ *This is really a savage piece of music.* □ *Man, Fred is a totally savage guy.* □ *Wow, is he savage!*

**saved by the bell** *mod.* saved by the timely intervention of someone or something. □ *I was going to have to do my part, but someone knocked on the door and I didn't have to do it. I was saved by the bell.* □ *I wish I had been saved by the bell.*

**Save it!** *exclam.* "Be quiet!" □ *Save it! Keep quiet until this is over.* □ *I don't care what you think you have to say. Save it!*

**savvy** ['sævi] **1.** *tr. & in.* to understand (someone or something). (Adapted from Spanish *sabe*, "he knows.") □ *Do you savvy?* □ *Can you savvy at all what I am trying to tell you?* □ *I just can't savvy stuff like that.* **2.** *n.* knowledge; know-how. □ *She really has savvy when it comes to clocks.* □ *I don't have the savvy necessary to do the job.* **3.** *mod.* knowledgeable. □ *What a savvy gal!* □ *She is truly savvy!* □ *He is one of the most savvy directors in New York.*

**sawbones** *n.* a doctor. (Folksy. Referring to someone who amputates limbs.) □ *Call the sawbones. This is an emergency.* □ *Is there a sawbones in this town?*

**sawbuck** *n.* a ten-dollar bill. (From the time when the "10" was indicated by the Roman numeral "X," that looks like the crosspiece that supports wood that is being sawed.) □ *It cost me a sawbuck to have my car pulled out of the mud.* □ *Can I borrow a sawbuck till payday?*

**sawed** *mod.* alcohol intoxicated. (Perhaps an elaboration of *cut*.) □ *I got sawed last weekend, and I still have a headache.* □ *She drank a lot, but never got sawed.*

**sawed-off** *mod.* short of stature. □ *Mike is sawed-off.* □ *Tom called Mike a sawed-off little runt.* □ *Well, Mike is a sawed-off runt, isn't he?*

**Say cheese!** *exclam.* "Please smile!" (A phrase said by a photographer who is trying to get someone to smile for a photograph.) □ *Come on, now. Say cheese!* □ *Say cheese for the camera, please.*

**Says me!** AND **Sez me!** *exclam.* a formulaic answer to *Says who?* □ TOM: *Says who?* FRED: *Says me, that's who!* □ TOM: *You?* FRED: *You got it, buster. Says me!*

**say-so** *n.* a command; an authorization. □ *I can't do it just on your say-so.* □ *We can begin as soon as we get the boss's say-so.*

**Says who?** AND **Sez who?** *interrog.* a formulaic challenge indicating disagreement with someone who has said something. (See also the following entry.) □ TOM: *Says who?* FRED: *Says me, that's*

*who!* □ *She drew herself up to her full height, looked him straight in the eye, and said, "Says who?"*

**Says you!** *exclam.* "That's just what you say!"; "You don't know what you are talking about!" □ FRED: *You are fat and ugly.* TOM: *Says you!* □ MARY: *People who go around correcting other people were found to be very annoying in a recent survey.* BILL: *Says you!*

**say uncle** *tr.* to admit defeat; to give up. □ *He held me down until I said uncle.* □ *I never say uncle. I just keep right on going.*

**Say what?** *interrog.* "What did you say?" (Folksy. See also *What say?*) □ *Say what? I didn't hear that.* □ *The old man held his hand to his ear and said, "Say what?"*

**scabbed** ['skæbd] *mod.* cheated in a drug deal; having been sold bogus or inferior drugs. □ *Max got scabbed by a dealer who got arrested the next day.* □ *This junk is junk. I've been scabbed.*

**scads** [skædz] *n.* lots (of something). □ *I have just scads and scads of paper.* □ *Aunt Mary has scads of money.*

**scale** *n.* the regular union rate of pay; union wages. □ *Even the big stars work for scale.* □ *We pay scale and not a penny more. I don't care who you think you are!*

**scam** [skæm] **1.** *n.* a swindle; a *hustle.* □ *I lost a fortune in that railroad scam.* □ *What a scam! I'm calling the cops.* **2.** *tr.* to swindle someone; to deceive someone. □ *They were scammed by a sweet-talking southern lady who took all their money.* □ *She scammed them for every cent they had.* **3.** *in.* to seek out and pick up young women, said of males. (Collegiate.) □ *Bob was out scamming last night and ran into Clare.* □ *Those guys are always scamming around.* **4.** *in.* to copulate. □ *All you ever want to do is scam.* □ *I think those people over there are scamming.* **5.** *in.* to fool around and waste time. □ *Quit scamming and get busy.* □ *You'd get better grades if you didn't scam so much.*

**scammer** ['skæmɚ] **1.** *n.* a swindler; a *hustler.* □ *Max is a scammer if I ever saw one.* □ *There are a couple of scammers on the street corner. Watch out.* **2.**

*n.* a lecher; a fast worker with the opposite sex. □ *Bob thinks he's a great scammer, but he's just a wimp.* □ *Do scammers have a great future? What's for an encore?*

**scammered** *mod.* alcohol intoxicated. □ *She is scammered out of her mind.* □ *Two bottles of that stuff and she was scammered.*

**scamp** [skæmp] *n.* a small child. □ *Come here, you little scamp!* □ *There are three little scamps at the door saying, "Trick or treat!"*

**scandal sheet** *n.* a tabloid newspaper featuring lurid news. □ *I like to read a scandal sheet every now and then.* □ *I'm tired of this scandal sheet. Let's get a classy newspaper today.*

**scank** See *skank.*

**scared shitless\*** *mod.* very frightened. (Caution with *shit.*) □ *He wasn't just frightened. He was scared shitless!* □ *He had to go to court and was scared shitless about it.*

**scared stiff** *mod.* frightened; unable to move from fear. □ *The poor little kid stood there—scared stiff.* □ *I was scared stiff for hours after the accident.*

**scare someone or something up** AND **scare up someone or something** *tr.* to find someone or something. (As if one were flushing game.) □ *See if you can scare up a clean tablecloth.* □ *I have to scare a date up for Friday night.*

**scare the hell out of someone\*** *tr.* to frighten someone badly. (Caution with *hell.*) □ *These figures scare the hell out of me.* □ *The door blew shut and scared the hell out of me.*

**scare the pants off someone** *tr.* to frighten someone suddenly. □ *The piano lid fell and scared the pants off my parents.* □ *It takes a lot to scare the pants off a hardened criminal.*

**scarf** **1.** *tr.* to eat something. □ *Andy scarfed the whole pie.* □ *Are you going to scarf the whole thing?* **2.** *in.* to eat. □ *I'll be with you as soon as I scarf.* □ *I gotta go scarf now.* **3.** *n.* food. □ *I want some good scarf. This stuff stinks.* □ *No more fried scarf for me.* **4.** *tr.* to steal or *swipe* something. □ *The kid scarfed a candy bar, and the store owner called the cops.* □ *The plumber's assistant had*

been scarfing copper for months before they figured out what was going on. **5.** *tr.* to discard something. □ *Scarf that thing. It's no good.* □ *Bill scarfed his girl. She was seeing somebody else at the same time.*

**scarf out** *in.* to overeat. (See also *blimp out, pig out, mac out.*) □ *I scarf out every weekend.* □ *My brother scarfs out every day—around the clock!*

**scarf something down** AND **scarf down something** *tr.* to eat something, perhaps in a hurry; to swallow something, perhaps in a hurry. □ *Are you going to scarf this whole thing down?* □ *Here, scarf down this sandwich.*

**scary** *mod.* (of women) ugly. □ *Man, is she scary!* □ *Why do I always end up with a scary woman?*

**scat** [skæt] **1.** *n.* nonsense syllables sung to music. (Refers to a [primarily black] jazz practice in the jazz era.) □ *She used to do scat, but moved on to blues.* □ *He could sing scat like nobody's business.* **2.** *exclam.* "Go away!" (Usually **Scat!** Often said to a cat to get it to go away.) □ *Get out! Scat! Beat it, cat!* □ *Scat, you wretched animal!* **3.** *in.* to leave. □ *It's midnight. I gotta scat.* □ *You guys scat now. I have to go to work.* **4.** *n.* heroin. (Drugs. From *shit.*) □ *Max is trying to sell scat in the neighborhood again.* □ *That scat's gonna get that man killed.* **5.** *n.* inferior whiskey. □ *That rotten scat nearly choked me.* □ *You got anything better than that scat, bartender?*

**scatterbrain** *n.* a forgetful person; someone who is mentally disorganized. □ *I'm getting to be such a scatterbrain, I think.* □ *Aunt Martha is a real scatterbrain. She always forgets where her glasses are.*

**scattered** *mod.* drug intoxicated; confused by drug use. (Drugs. See *scat.*) □ *Those poor kids are so scattered, they can't even get themselves to class.* □ *Fred must spend half his life scattered and sleeping.*

**scene** [sin] **1.** *n.* a place; a setting. (See *make the scene.*) □ *This scene is no good. Let's split.* □ *I need a different scene. Life is too hectic here.* **2.** *n.* the drug-use environment; the drug scene.

□ *The longer you spend in a scene like this, the harder it is to sober up and go straight.* □ *This coke scene is a bad one. It will shorten your life.* **3.** *n.* one's preference. (Compare to *bag.*) □ *This nine-to-five stuff just isn't my scene. I quit.* □ *Your scene doesn't seem to involve much in the way of hard work.*

**schicker** ['ʃɪkɚ] *mod.* alcohol intoxicated. (See *shicker.*) □ *Two glasses of wine and she was totally shicker.* □ *I've never heard a more shicker tenor in my life.*

**schizo** ['skɪzo OR 'skɪtso] **1.** *mod.* schizophrenic. □ *That gal is sort of schizo, isn't she?* □ *I have never dealt with such a schizo type before.* **2.** *n.* a schizophrenic person. □ *That guy is an absolute schizo!* □ *Keep that schizo away from me.*

**schiz out** AND **schizz out** [skɪz...] *in.* to freak out; to lose mental control. □ *What a day! I nearly schizzed out.* □ *I schizzed out during the test. Got an F.*

**schlemazel** AND **schlemozzle, shlimazl** [ʃlə'mazl] *n.* an awkward, bumbling person; a *loser.* (Yiddish.) □ *And this poor schlemazel tries to get me to help him paint his fence!* □ *That schlemozzle is afraid of his own shadow.*

**schlemiel** AND **schlemihl, shlemiel** [ʃlə'mil] *n.* a gullible person; a *loser.* (From Hebrew *Shelumiel* via Yiddish.) □ *See if you can get that schlemiel to buy the Brooklyn Bridge.* □ *The stupid schlemiel says he already bought it yesterday.*

**schlemozzle** See *schlemazel.*

**schlep** AND **shlep** [ʃlɛp] **1.** *tr.* to drag or carry someone or something. (From German *schleppen* via Yiddish.) □ *Am I supposed to schlep this whole thing all the way back to the store?* □ *I am tired of shlepping kids from one thing to another.* **2.** *n.* a journey; a distance to travel or carry something. □ *It takes about 20 minutes to make the schlep from here to there.* □ *That's a ten-mile schlep, and I won't go by myself.* **3.** *n.* a stupid person; a bothersome person. (Literally, a *drag.*) □ *What a schlep! The guy's a real pain.* □ *Ask that shlep to wait in the hall until I am free. I'll sneak out the back way.*

**schlepper** AND **shlepper** [ʃlɛpɚ] *n.* an annoying person who always wants a bargain or a favor. (See *schlep.*) □ *Why am I surrounded by people who want something from me? Is this a schlepper colony or what?* □ *Tell the shleppers that they'll get their money after I close the sale on my wife and kids.*

**schlock** [ʃlak] **1.** *n.* inferior merchandise. (From German *schlacke,* "dregs" via Yiddish.) □ *That store has nothing but schlock.* □ *For this schlock I should pay good money?* **2.** AND **schlocky** ['ʃlaki] *mod.* cheap; junky; inferior. □ *Schlocky stuff like this I can get from a no overhead mail order.* □ *That place is nothing but a schlock shop.* □ *This thing is really schlock.* **3.** *n.* drugs. (Drugs. See *junk.*) □ *Max, get off the schlock. It will kill you.* □ *He keeps a four-day supply of schlock under his bed.*

**schloomp** AND **schlump, shlump** [ʃlump OR ʃlump] *n.* a stupid and lazy person. (From German via Yiddish.) □ *Tell that schloomp to get busy or get out.* □ *Do you work hard? I don't hire any schlumps.*

**schlub** AND **zhlub** [ʃləb OR ʒləb] *n.* a dull, unpolished person, usually a male. (Yiddish.) □ *I spent the whole evening listening to that schlub from New Hampshire.* □ *Hank's no zhlub. He's just eccentric.*

**schmack** See *schmeck.*

**schmaltz** AND **shmaltz** [ʃmalts] *n.* extreme sentimentality; corny sweetness. (From a Yiddish word meaning fat or oil.) □ *I didn't like that movie. Too much schmaltz.* □ *You aren't playing this piece right. It needs a little schmaltz.*

**schmaltzy** AND **shmaltzy** ['ʃmaltsi] *mod.* overly sweet and sentimental. (See the previous entry.) □ *This movie is too schmaltzy for me.* □ *What a schmaltzy movie!*

**schmear** See *whole schmear.*

**schmeck** AND **schmack, schmee, shmack, shmeck, shmee, smeck** [ʃmɛk AND ʃmæk, ʃmi, ʃmæk, ʃmɛk, ʃmi, smɛk] *n.* heroin; narcotics in general. (From German *schmecken* "taste" via Yiddish. Many variants in drug slang.) □ *That poor guy is really hooked on schmeck.* □ *The cops found a packet of schmack in his pocket. He says they put it there.*

**schmegegge** AND **schmegeggy**
[ʃməˈgegi] **1.** *n.* a stupid person. (Yiddish.) □ *Who is that schmegegge in the plaid pants?* □ *Ask the schmegegge standing over by the workbench if he's seen my sky hook.* **2.** *n.* nonsense. □ *I've heard enough of your schmegegge. Out!* □ *I don't hear anything but schmegeggy coming out of Washington.*

**schmendrick** AND **shmendrick**
[ˈʃmendrɪk] *n.* a stupid and ineffectual nobody. (Yiddish.) □ *Some schmendrick from downstairs asked if you could turn down your stereo.* □ *Tell the schmendrick to drop dead.*

**schmo** AND **shmo, shmoe, schmoe**
[ʃmo] *n.* a foolish and naive person, usually a male. (Yiddish. See also *Joe Schmo.*) □ *What a schmo! He thinks I caused the problem.* □ *Tell the silly schmoe to beat it.*

**schmooze** AND **shmooze, schmoose**
[ʃmuz] **1.** *in.* to chat; to *chew the fat.* (From Hebrew *schmuos* via Yiddish.) □ *You were schmoozing when you should have been listening.* □ *We were schmoozing before quitting time, and then the boss walked by.* **2.** *n.* a session of chatting or conversing. □ *Come over, and let's have a schmooze before you go.* □ *A good schmoose is what you need.*

**schmoozer** *n.* someone who chats or converses well. □ *Clare can't sing a note, but what a schmoozer!* □ *Two old schmoozers sat muttering to one another all afternoon by the duck pond.*

**schmuck*** [ʃmək] **1.** *n.* a jerk; a repellent male. (Also a rude term of address. Yiddish.) □ *Who is that stupid schmuck over there?* □ *Ask the schmuck how long he will be on the phone.* **2.*** *n.* a penis. (Yiddish. Caution with topic.) □ *If I hear that joke about a camel's schmuck one more time, I'm going to scream.* □ *There are probably better names than schmuck for what you are talking about.*

**schnockered** AND **schnoggered, shnockered, snoggered** [ˈʃnakərd AND ˈʃnagərd] *mod.* alcohol or drug intoxicated. □ *How can anybody be so schnockered on four beers?* □ *I've never seen anybody so schnockered.*

**schnoggered** See the previous entry.

**schnook** AND **schnuck, shnook**
[ʃnuk] *n.* a naive person; a dope. (Yiddish.) □ *The guy's a schnook with a heart of gold.* □ *What's a good-looking dame like her doing with a shnook like him?*

**schnorrer** [ˈʃnorɚ] *n.* a beggar; a person who sponges off of friends and relatives. (Yiddish.) □ *Here comes that schnorrer from down the street. Look poor.* □ *Buy your own ciggies if you don't like mine. Shnorrers can't be choosers.*

**schnozz** AND **schnozzle, schnozzola, shnozz** [ʃnaz AND ʃnazl̩, ʃnaˈzolə, ʃnaz] *n.* the nose. (From German *Schnauze* via Yiddish.) □ *Look at the schnozz on that guy!* □ *With a schnozzola like that he should be in the circus.*

**schnozzler** [ˈʃnazlɚ] *n.* a user (snorter) of cocaine. (Drugs.) □ *How long you been a schnozzler?* □ *Schnozzlers have a very expensive habit.*

**schoolboy Scotch** *n.* wine. (Black.) □ *Give me a pint of that schoolboy Scotch.* □ *Man, she is stoned out of her mind on schoolboy Scotch!*

**schtick** AND **shtik** [ʃtɪk] *n.* a routine or act that is the trademark of an entertainer, especially in vaudeville. (Yiddish.) □ *His schtick was a trained dog-and-cat act.* □ *Their shtik is so old! Maybe nobody will remember whose it was.*

**schtoonk** AND **shtoonk** [ʃtuŋk] *n.* a detestable person. (Yiddish.) □ *The schtoonk from downstairs was here to talk to you. I told him you died.* □ *Who needs a shtoonk like that?*

**scoff** [skɔf] **1.** *tr. & in.* to eat (something). (Compare to *scarf.*) □ *He's upstairs scoffing in his room.* □ *She scoffed three hamburgers and a large order of fries.* **2.** *n.* food. □ *This scoff is gross!* □ *I want some good old American scoff.* **3.** *tr.* to take drugs orally (rather than inject them). (Drugs.) □ *Max scoffed an upper and then went to work.* □ *He scoffs those things all the time.* **4.** *tr. & in.* to dispose of or conceal drugs when arrested by swallowing them. (Drugs.) □ *Max regretted that he had scoffed. He needed the stuff badly.* □ *When the cops punched him in the gut, the joints he scoffed came up.*

**scooch** [skutʃ] **1.** *in.* to move (oneself), while seated, forward, backward, or sideways by sliding. □ *Scooch over here by me.* □ *Why don't you scooch over here?* **2.** *tr.* to push or move something. □ *Scooch your chair over where the light is better.* □ *Scooch the potted palm to the edge of the deck and push it overboard.*

**scoop 1.** *n.* a news story gathered by a reporter before any other reporter hears of it. □ *I got a great scoop! I was right there when it happened.* □ *That was no scoop at all. It was on live television. Didn't you see the cameras?* **2.** *tr.* to beat someone—such as another reporter—in the race to get a news story first. □ *They scooped the other paper on both stories.* □ *Larry scooped me twice last month.* **3.** *n.* a general roundup and arrest of criminals; a *bust.* (Underworld.) □ *Max got picked up in that big drug scoop last month.* □ *There are some people who get dragged in every time there is a scoop. It cannot just be a coincidence.* **4.** *n.* liquor; a glass of beer. □ *I could use a good cold scoop about now.* □ *A little scoop helps pass the time when you're waiting.* **5.** *n.* a folded matchbook cover used to snort cocaine or heroin. □ *I need a scoop. It's no good without a scoop.* □ *I burned up the scoop by accident. Sorry.* **6.** *tr. & in.* to *snort* cocaine or heroin, using a folded matchbook cover. □ *Max is scooping for the fourth time today.* □ *He scooped two lines together.*

**scoot** *in.* to run or scurry quickly from one place to another. □ *I scooted from the bank to the cleaners and then on to the dentist's.* □ *The shoppers scooted from store to store spending money like it was going out of style.*

**scooters** ['skutɚz] *mod.* crazy; confused. □ *It's days like this that make me think I'm scooters.* □ *You are driving me totally scooters with your constant beefing.*

**scoots** *n.* diarrhea. (Always with *the.*) □ *Our vacation was ruined by a case of the scoots.* □ *I've got just the thing for the scoots. Stay at home.*

**scope on someone** See *scope someone.*

**scope someone** AND **scope on someone** *tr.* to visually evaluate a member of the opposite sex. □ *He scoped every girl who came in the door.* □ *He wouldn't like it if somebody scoped on him. Or would he?*

**scope someone out** AND **scope out someone** *tr.* to look someone over; to check someone out. □ *Dave was scoping out all the girls.* □ *Nobody was scoping Dave out, though.*

**scorched 1.** *mod.* alcohol or drug intoxicated. □ *Who wants to go out and get scorched?* □ *How can anybody get so scorched on four beers?* **2.** AND **singed** [sɪndʒd] *mod.* having to do with hair burned while smoking marijuana. (Collegiate.) □ *Guess who scorched herself last night?* □ *If you go to sleep, you'll be singed for sure.*

**scorcher 1.** *n.* a very hot day. □ *This is really a scorcher, isn't it?* □ *Wow! What a scorcher!* **2.** *n.* a caustic remark. □ *Bob made a real scorcher about Tom's shoes.* □ *He is a master at the rude scorcher.*

**scorching 1.** *mod.* really hot; about to win something big. □ *Let me roll again. I'm really scorching.* □ *Here comes a scorching runner!* □ *He says he's scorching. Get out of his way.* **2.** *mod.* caustic. □ *That remark was really scorching.* □ *What a scorching glare you got from her!*

**score\* 1.** *in.* to succeed. □ *I knew if I kept trying I could score.* □ *It takes hard work and luck to score.* **2.** *tr. & in.* to obtain something; to obtain drugs or sex. (Very close to sense 1.) □ *Max spent an hour trying to score some pot.* □ *Fred is always trying to score with women.* **3.** *n.* the result of a scoring: drugs, loot, winnings. □ *Where's the score? How much did you get?* □ *The crooks dropped the score as they made their getaway.* **4.\*** *in.* (for a male) to copulate (with a female). (Caution with topic.) □ *Fred can't think about anything but scoring with Martha.* □ *He will spend his vacation trying to score.* **5.** *n.* the client of a male or female prostitute. □ *She conked the score over the head and robbed him.* □ *Three scores was a full day's work for Molly.*

**6.** *n.* a summary; a conclusion; the sum total. (Compare to *bottom line*.) □ *The score is that you are in trouble with the Internal Revenue Service.* □ *Okay, waiter, what's the score?*

**score a connection** *tr.* to meet someone to buy drugs. (Drugs.) □ *Max left the room. He said he had to score a connection at eight.* □ *She scored a connection and got herself fixed up for a day or two.*

**scrag** [skræg] **1.** *n.* the neck. (Underworld.) □ *The cop grabbed him by the scrag and pushed him along to the squad car.* □ *It's gonna be your scrag in the noose when this thing's over.* **2.** *tr.* to kill someone or something. (Originally underworld to "strangle.") □ *The gang decided that somebody was going to have to scrag the witness.* □ *A truck almost scragged Max.*

**scraggy** ['skrægi] *mod.* bony. □ *That dame is too scraggy for me.* □ *Who is that scraggy dame?* □ *I lost weight till I was scraggy as a hungry bear.*

**scram** [skræm] *in.* to exit fast; to get out of a place in a hurry. □ *I gotta scram. I'm late.* □ *Go on, scram! Get out of here fast!*

**scrambled eggs** *n.* decorations on a (military) officer's uniform. □ *I know his rank is high because of the scrambled eggs, but I don't know how high.* □ *I'll be glad when I get some scrambled eggs on me.*

**scrape the bottom of the barrel** *tr.* to utilize the last or only things or people available, even if unsatisfactory. (See also *bottom of the barrel*.) □ *They were really scraping the bottom of the barrel when they picked you.* □ *You scraped the bottom of the barrel for this one. I want something better.*

**scratch 1.** *n.* money. □ *I just don't have the scratch.* □ *How much scratch does it take to buy a car like this one?* **2.** *tr.* to eliminate something from a list; to cancel something. □ *Scratch Fred. He can't make the party.* □ *We decided to scratch the idea of a new car. The old one will have to do.* **3.** *mod.* impromptu; temporary. (Compare to *pickup*.) □ *We started a scratch game of basketball, but most of the girls had to leave at dinner-*

*time.* □ *This is just a scratch tape. After you use it for your computer program, someone else will write something over it.*

**scratch sheet** *n.* a daily horse-racing newsletter at the racetrack. □ *I picked up a scratch sheet from Lucky Louie and proceeded to lay down my life's saving on a horse named Felicity Anne.* □ *Even the cost of a scratch sheet is going up, and I'm trying to economize!*

**scream 1.** *n.* someone or something very funny. (Always with *a*.) □ *The joke Tom told was really a scream.* □ *Tom is always a scream at parties.* **2.** *n.* ice cream. (Collegiate.) □ *How about a nice big dish of scream?* □ *It's too cold for scream. Ask me in June.*

**scream bloody murder** *tr.* to scream very loudly; to complain or protest loudly. □ *She screams bloody murder every time I get near her.* □ *Those guys scream bloody murder long before they're hurt.*

**screamer 1.** *n.* a newspaper headline. □ *Did you see the screamer in the paper today? The King died.* □ *I never read screamers.* **2.** *n.* an exclamation point. (Printing.) □ *Put a screamer at the end of the line.* □ *Clean up this copy. There are too many screamers. Looks like junior high stuff.* **3.** *n.* anything challenging. □ *What a horrible assignment I got. A classic screamer.* □ *Bring on the screamers. I can handle anything.* **4.** *n.* someone or something very exciting or attention getting. □ *This guy is a real screamer! Wait'll you meet him.* □ *Her political campaign is a real screamer.*

**screaming-meemie** AND **screamie-meemie** *n.* a screaming child or adult. □ *Oh, don't be such a screaming-meemie!* □ *Jennifer has been a terrible screamie-meemie all day long!*

**screaming-meemies** AND **scream-ing-meemies** *n.* the *willies*; a mental breakdown. □ *They sent Max away with the screaming-meemies.* □ *I need some sleep. I'm about to come down with the screaming-meemies.*

**screeching (drunk)** *mod.* alcohol intoxicated; very drunk. □ *How can anybody be so screeching drunk on four beers?* □ *She's not just drunk; she's screeching.*

**screw\*** **1.** *n.* a jailer. (Underworld.) □ *See if you can get the screw's attention.* □ *I'm sick, screw! Let me out!* **2.\*** *tr. & in.* to copulate (with someone). (Caution with *screw.*) □ *He's telling everybody that he screwed her.* □ *They screw all the time, just like bunnies.* **3.** *tr.* to cheat someone. □ *That salesman tried to screw me, but I just walked out on him.* □ *They didn't screw me. I got good value for my money.* (More at *screwed.*)

**screw around** *in.* to waste time. □ *Stop screwing around and get busy.* □ *John's always screwing around and never does anything on time.*

**screw around with someone or something** *in.* to fiddle with or *mess around (with someone or something).* □ *Andy screwed around with his clock until he broke it.* □ *Look, chum! Don't screw around with me!*

**screwball** **1.** *n.* an eccentric person; a clown or a dunce. (Also a rude term of address.) □ *Tom is such a screwball!* □ *Look, you screwball, get out!* **2.** *n.* (in baseball) a (pitched) ball that does not travel in a straight line. □ *Jim threw another screwball, but somehow the batter hit it.* □ *Larry always seemed to be able to hit a screwball, no matter what.*

**screwed** **1.** AND **screwed tight** *mod.* alcohol intoxicated. □ *She spends a lot of time screwed.* □ *She's not just drunk; she's screwed tight.* **2.** *mod.* bested; defeated; cheated. □ *I really got screwed at the garage.* □ *If you don't want to get screwed by somebody, you have to do it yourself.*

**screwed, blued, and tattooed** ['skrud 'blud æn tæ'tud] **1.** *mod.* badly mistreated; badly *screwed.* □ *I got a bad deal. I got screwed, blued, and tattooed.* □ *When John bought his wreck of a car, he got screwed, blued, and tattooed.* **2.** *mod.* alcohol intoxicated. □ *Who wants to go out and get screwed, blued, and tattooed?* □ *All four of them went out and got screwed, blued, and tattooed.*

**screwed up** *mod.* ruined; messed up. □ *This is a really screwed up schedule. Let's start over again.* □ *Your schedule is completely screwed up.*

**screw someone or something up** AND **screw up someone or something** *tr.* to interfere with someone or something; to mess up someone or something. □ *Try again and don't screw it up this time.* □ *You really screwed up my brother by not being on time.*

**screw someone out of something** *tr.* to cheat someone of something. □ *You are trying to screw me out of what is rightfully mine!* □ *I'm not trying to screw anybody out of anything!*

**screw someone over** AND **screw over someone** *tr.* to give someone a very bad time; to scold someone severely. □ *Those guys really screwed you over. What started it?* □ *Let's get those kids in here and screw over every one of them. This stuff can't continue.*

**screw up** **1.** *in.* to mess up. □ *I hope I don't screw up this time.* □ *The waiter screwed up again.* **2.** *n.* a mess; a blunder; utter confusion. (Usually **screw-up.**) □ *This is the chef's screw-up, not mine.* □ *One more screw up like that and you're fired.* (More at *screwed up.*)

**screwy** **1.** *mod.* crazy. □ *I've never heard such a screwy idea.* □ *It's really screwy.* □ *That's the screwiest-looking hat I've ever seen.* **2.** *mod.* alcohol intoxicated. □ *How can anybody be so screwy on five beers?* □ *I've never seen anybody so screwy.*

**script(t)** **1.** *n.* a note; any piece of paper with a written message. (Underworld.) □ *Hey, Mike, here's a script for you from the boss.* □ *Make him sign this script before you let him in on the deal.* **2.** *n.* a prescription for drugs. (Drugs.) □ *The druggist told me to take my script and go elsewhere.* □ *Do you know where I can buy a script for some uppers?*

**scrog\*** [skrɔg] *tr. & in.* to have sex; to copulate (with someone). (Caution with topic.) □ *You know what! I think those people over in the corner are scrogging!* □ *The movie showed scene after scene of this woman scrogging some guy.*

**scronched** [skrɔntʃt] *mod.* alcohol intoxicated. □ *She just sat there and got scronched.* □ *He spends a lot of time totally scronched.*

**scrooge** [skrudʒ] *n.* a stingy person; a penny-pincher. (From the character in Dickens' *A Christmas Carol.*) □ *Ask scrooge over there if you can borrow a* quarter to call the cops. □ Don't be such a scrooge! All I want is a buck!

**scrounge around (for someone or something)** [skraʊndʒ...] *in.* to look around for something; to seek something in every likely place. □ *Try to scrounge around for somebody to go to the party with, why don't you?* □ *I don't think there is anybody who will go with me, but I'll scrounge around.* □ *Ask John to scrounge around for a wrench.*

**scrounge someone or something up** AND **scrounge up someone or something** *tr.* to get someone or something somehow. □ *See if you can scrounge up a new carburetor by noon.* □ *I scrounged a doctor up in the middle of the night.*

**scrub** *tr.* to cancel something. □ *We had to scrub the whole plan because of the weather.* □ *The manager scrubbed the party because people wouldn't cooperate.*

**scrud** *n.* a serious disease; a venereal disease. (Military.) □ *Oh, hell! I think I got the scrud!* □ *Poor dumb Charlie can't tell scrud from crotch rot.*

**scruff(y)** ['skrəf(i)] *mod.* sloppy; unkempt. □ *Her boyfriend is a little scruffy, but he's got billies!* □ *Why don't you clean up this scruff car? It's—like—grody!*

**scrump\*** [skrəmp] *tr. & in.* to copulate (with someone). (Caution with topic.) □ *You know what! I think those people over by the garage are scrumping!* □ *The movie showed a scene of some woman scrumping her lover.*

**scrumptious** ['skrəmpʃəs] *mod.* excellent; tasty. □ *That cake is just scrumptious, Mary. What's in it?* □ *Who makes the most scrumptious chocolate chip cookies in the world—besides me, that is?*

**scrunch** [skrəntʃ] *tr.* to crush or crunch. □ *I sat on my cookies and scrunched them.* □ *I hate crowds. I am afraid people will scrunch me.*

**scrunge** [skrəndʒ] *n.* nastiness; gunk. □ *What is this scrunge on my shoe?* □ *When you find some scrunge on your shoe or something, never try to find out what it is. Just wipe it off.*

**scrungy** ['skrəndʒi] **1.** *mod.* filthy. □ *This place is too scrungy for me. I'm outa here.* □ *What a scrungy guy. Put*

him somewhere to soak for a day or two. **2.** *mod.* inferior; bad. □ *I don't need scrungy merchandise like this. I'm going elsewhere.* □ *You have a very scrungy outlook on life.* □ *Life is scrungy.*

**SCSI** AND **scuzzy** ['skəzi] *n.* "Small computer system interface." (Computers. Acronym.) □ *Come over and see my new SCSI. It lets me run a hard disc.* □ *Why do they call it a scuzzy? Why not just say what it is?*

**scuffle** See *skuffle*.

**scum** [skəm] *n.* a wretched person. (Also a rude and provocative term of address. See also *pond scum*.) □ *Who is that scum? Who does she think she is?* □ *Look, you scum, I'm gonna fix you once and for all!*

**scumbag** *n.* a mean and wretched person, usually a male. (Also a rude term of address. The term is also a nickname for a condom.) □ *That scumbag is going to get caught some day.* □ *All those guys are scumbags. I don't want to have anything to do with any of them.*

**scupper up** *in.* to drink liquor, especially beer. □ *Tom goes home to scupper up every evening.* □ *Come on, you guys. Scupper up, and let's get outa here.*

**scurvy** ['skɚvi] *mod.* repulsive; *gross.* (Collegiate.) □ *Who is that scurvy guy who just came in?* □ *That class is scurvy. You'll wish you hadn't taken it.*

**scut** [skət] *n.* a despicable person. (Teens and collegiate.) □ *How can you be, like, such a scut?* □ *It's scuts like that who give all us really rad kids a bad name.*

**scuttlebutt** *n.* gossip. □ *What's the scuttlebutt on the steeple clock? Why did it stop?* □ *Don't pay any attention to the scuttlebutt around here.*

**scuz(z)** [skəz] **1.** *n.* filth. □ *What is this scuzz all over the floor?* □ *There is some scuzz on your shoe.* **2.** *n.* a nasty person; an undesirable person; a scraggly person. □ *And this scuzz comes up to me and asks me to dance, and I'm like, "What?"* □ *I told the scuz, like, I was feeling sick, so I couldn't dance with anybody.*

**scuzzbag** *n.* a despicable person. (Also a rude term of address.) □ *Who is that scuzzbag who just came in?* □ *Look, scuzzbag, we don't want your kind around here.*

**scuzzo** *n.* a repellent person. □ *There's the scuzzo who thinks I like him.* □ *How do you get rid of a scuzzo like that?*

**scuzz someone out** AND **scuzz out someone** *tr.* to nauseate someone. □ *He had this unreal face that almost scuzzed me out!* □ *It's not nice to scuzz out people like that, especially when you hardly know them.*

**scuzzy** ['skəzi] **1.** *mod.* repellent; unkempt. □ *His clothes are always so scuzzy. He probably keeps them in a pile in his room.* □ *Whose scuzzy car is that in the driveway?* **2.** See *SCSI.*

**sea** *n.* cocaine. (Drugs. A spelling-out of *C.*) □ *There is a bunch using sea over at Fred's place.* □ *I never used sea before. I hear there's nothing like it.*

**sealed (up)** *mod.* settled; secured; *cinched.* □ *The matter was sealed by Monday morning.* □ *The contract was sealed up just in time.*

**sealed with a kiss** AND **S.W.A.K.** *mod.* written and sent with love and care. (The abbreviation is sometimes written on love letters. Also an acronym.) □ *All her letters come "S.W.A.K."* □ *I know they are sealed with a kiss, because she says so.*

**seam-squirrels** *n.* lice. (See also *pants rabbits.*) □ *I got an itch. Must be seam-squirrels.* □ *Where would you get seam-squirrels?*

**Search me.** AND **You can search me!** *sent.* "I don't know." □ TOM: *How do crickets make that chirping noise?* BILL: *Search me.* □ *You can search me. How should I know?*

**seat** *n.* the buttocks. □ *Bob fell down on his seat.* □ *I was so angry. I wanted to kick him in the seat as he left.*

**sec** [sɛk] **1.** *n.* a second. (See also *tick.*) □ *I'll be with you in a sec. Keep your pants on!* □ *Just a sec. I'm on the phone.* **2.** AND **secs** *n.* a Seconal™ barbiturate capsule. (Drugs. See also *sex.*) □ *Max likes amies better than secs.* □ *I started taking sec in the hospital and just couldn't stop.*

**second fiddle** *n.* a person in a secondary role; the second best. (Frequently with *play.*) □ *I won't stay around here playing second fiddle for someone half my age and ability!* □ *There are worse things than being second fiddle.*

**second sacker** *n.* the second baseman in baseball. □ *The second sacker missed the throw, and the runner went on home.* □ *The shortstop and the second sacker crashed into one another trying to catch a ball.*

**see** *tr.* to equal someone's poker bet or raise it in poker. □ *I see your five and raise you 10.* □ *Well, can you see me or not?*

**see a man about a dog** *tr.* to leave a place for a mysterious reason, usually to go to the toilet. □ *I gotta see a man about a dog.* □ *Fred went to see a man about a dog. I hope he remembers to put the seat down.*

**see eye to eye** *in.* (for two or more people) to agree on something or view something the same way. □ *We never seem to see eye to eye.* □ *Gary and Walter see eye to eye on this question.*

**seegar** ['sigɑr] *n.* a cigar. (Folksy. The stress is on the first syllable.) □ *This dude came into this hamburger joint with a big seegar in his mouth, and the manager called the cops.* □ *There's nothing like a fine seegar after a nice bowl of hot chili.*

**seeing pink elephants** AND **seeing pink spiders, seeing snakes** *tr.* alcohol intoxicated; recovering from a drinking bout; having the delirium tremens. □ *When I got to the point of seeing pink elephants, I knew that something had to be done.* □ *The old one who's shaking—he's probably seeing snakes.*

**seen better days** *tr.* showing signs of wear or exhaustion. (Always a past participle.) □ *This coat has seen better days.* □ *The pitcher has seen better days. He's about through on this team, I think.*

**see no further than the end of one's nose** AND **cannot see (any) further than the end of one's nose** *in.* to be narrow-minded; to lack understanding and perception. □ *She is so selfish she can see no further than the end of her nose.* □ *You don't care about anyone but yourself. You can't see any further than the end of your nose.*

**see red** *tr.* to be angry. □ *When she hung up the phone, I saw red. I've never been so angry in my life.* □ *As he continued to talk, she began to see red.*

**see stars** *tr.* to be (knocked) unconscious. □ *If you talk to me like that again, you'll be seeing stars.* □ *I saw stars for a few seconds, and then someone threw cold water in my face.*

**see ya** See *see you.*

**seeyabye** ['sijə'baɪ] *interj.* "bye." (California.) □ *Oh, that's, like, so, like, rad. Okay, seeyabye.* □ *Gotta go now. Seeyabye.*

**see you** AND **see ya** *interj.* "goodbye." □ *Good game, Tom. See ya.* □ *See you, old chum. Give me a ring.*

**see you later** *interj.* "goodbye." (Common colloquial. Also said to people one knows one will never see again.) □ *Nice talking to you. See you later.* □ *Have a great trip, Mary. See you later.*

**see you later, alligator** *interj.* "goodbye." (From the 1930s. Answered with "after while, crocodile.") □ TOM: *Bye.* BILL: *See you later, alligator.* □ BILL: *See you later, alligator.* TOM: *After while, crocodile.*

**seized** **1.** *mod.* welded together, said of an engine. □ *There I was in the middle of nowhere with a seized engine.* □ *This engine is seized. Junk it.* **2.** *in.* to become immobile, said of a joint in a human limb. □ *His knee seized during last Friday's game.* □ *Over the weekend, my elbow seized.*

**sell a wolf ticket** AND **sell wolf tickets** *tr.* to boast, bluff, or lie. (Originally black. Compare to *buy someone's wolf ticket.*) □ *Freddie is out selling wolf tickets again.* □ *Are you trying to sell me a wolf ticket?*

**sellout** **1.** *n.* the event of selling all of something. (Advertising.) □ *Come to our gigantic sellout of all name-brand merchandise!* □ *This is the sellout of the century. Everything must go.* **2.** *n.* a betrayal. (See also *sell someone out.*) □ *Any one of you could have stood up for me. What a sellout!* □ *How can you pull such a sellout?*

**sell someone out** AND **sell out someone** *tr.* to betray someone. □ *How could you sell me out like that?* □ *She would sell out her mother.*

**send someone from pillar to post** *tr.* to send someone from place to place; to give someone the runaround. □ *Red tape everywhere I went. They sent me from pillar to post until closing time.* □ *Nobody is in charge there. They send you from pillar to post, and you don't complain for fear they'll start you all over again.*

**send someone or something up** AND **send up someone or something** *tr.* to perform a parody of someone or something. □ *In his act, he sends up famous people.* □ *Last week, he sent the president up.* (More at *send-up.*)

**send someone to glory** **1.** *tr.* to kill someone. □ *One shot sent him to glory.* □ *You want me to send you to glory or something?* **2.** *tr.* to officiate at the burial services for someone. □ *The preacher sent him to glory amidst the sobs of six or seven former fans.* □ *The preacher probably gets fifty bucks for every stiff he sends to glory.*

**send someone up the river** *tr.* to send someone to prison. (Underworld. As done by a judge or indirectly by the police.) □ *They tried to send me up the river, but my lip got me off.* □ *I'm gonna send you up the river if it's the last thing I do.*

**send-up** *n.* a parody. □ *It was his delightful send-up of the current administration that catapulted Roger Rogers to national fame.* □ *I enjoy a good send-up, even if it is about me.*

**sense** See *sinse.*

**sent** **1.** *mod.* alcohol or drug intoxicated. □ *Two glasses and she's sent.* □ *He's not just sent; he's stoned.* **2.** *mod.* carried away by mellow music. □ *She's really sent. Look at her as she listens.* □ *All the musicians were sent. Maybe they were on something.*

**serious** *mod.* good; profound; excellent. (See *heavy.*) □ *He plays some serious guitar.* □ *Man, these tunes are, like, serious.*

**serious about someone** *mod.* in love, or almost in love, with someone. □ *I'm afraid I'm getting serious about Bill.* □ *Bill, unfortunately, is pretty serious about Mary.*

**serve someone right** *tr.* to be just what someone deserves. □ *It would serve you right if you lost your money.* □ *He fell down. It serves him right.*

**sess** [sɛs] *n.* seedless marijuana. (Drugs. From Spanish *sinsemilla,* "seedless." See *sinse.*) □ *He managed to get a bag of sess as far as customs.* □ *That was the end of the sess and the end of him.*

**session** **1.** *n.* a drinking bout. □ *Your father's off on another session again.* □ *He was just sobering up from a session with the bottle.* **2.** *n.* a marijuana smoking session; time spent on a drug high. (Collegiate.) □ *What a fine session that was!* □ *Max was terribly hungry after the session.*

**set** **1.** *n.* a period of time that a band plays without a break; a thirty-minute jam session. □ *I'll talk to you after this set.* □ *We do two sets and then take a twenty-minute break.* **2.** *n.* a combination of amphetamine and barbiturate capsules; a small number of any capsules. (Drugs. See also *cets.*) □ *Harriet tossed him a set, and he gave her the high sign in return.* □ *I'm a little wired—ya know. You got, like, a set I can drop?* **3.** *n.* a party. □ *Your set was a totally major bash!* □ *Let's throw a set tonight and invite some chicks.*

**set of pipes** *n.* a very loud voice; a singing voice. □ *She has a nice set of pipes.* □ *With a set of pipes like that, she's a winner.*

**set of wheels** *n.* a car. □ *I need a new set of wheels.* □ *Man, look at that set of wheels that chick has!*

**set someone back** *tr.* to cost someone. □ *That must have set you back a mint!* □ *This bracelet set me back plenty.*

**set someone up (for something)** AND **set up someone (for something)** *tr.* to set the scene for something to happen to someone. □ *His buddies set him up for the gag—which ended up injuring two of them severely.* □ *Who set me up for this anyway?*

**settle a score (with someone)** AND **have a score to settle (with someone)** *tr.* to settle a dispute; to redress a personal injustice. (Note the variations in the examples.) □ *I had to settle a score with Willard.* □ *I had a score to settle with Willard.* □ *Once this score is settled, I can begin living my own life again.*

**settle someone's hash** *tr.* to calm someone down, perhaps by threats or by violence. □ *If he comes in here, I'll settle his hash.* □ *Now, that ought to settle your hash.*

**setup** **1.** *n.* a place to live. □ *She's got a little setup over on Maple.* □ *This is a pretty nice setup. What's the rent?* **2.** *n.* a scheme; a plot. (Underworld.) □ *Okay, what's the setup for the bank job?* □ *I got a good little setup for earning some money.* **3.** *n.* a person who is set up for some swindle; a *mark.* (Underworld.) □ *Is he the setup? He's a cop!* □ *The setup got wise at the last minute.* **4.** *n.* a glass with ice for an alcoholic beverage. (Usually plural.) □ *Can we have a couple of setups brought to our room, please?* □ *Who ordered the setups?*

**seven-year itch** *n.* a real or imagined longing for other women in a man's seventh year of marriage. □ *Looks like Jack has the seven-year itch.* □ *The seven-year itch is just a rumor.*

**sewed up** **1.** *mod.* completed. □ *I've just about got this contract sewed up.* □ *When we get it sewed up, we'll go out for a drink.* **2.** *mod.* alcohol intoxicated. □ *She's not just drunk; she's sewed up.* □ *Will this stuff get me sewed up?*

**sewer hog** *n.* a ditchdigger; a sewer worker. □ *A sewer hog doesn't get a lot of chances to pal around with the gentry, but the pay's plenty good.* □ *Fred worked as a sewer hog and made a fortune.*

**sewermouth** *n.* someone who uses vile language constantly. (Also a rude term of address.) □ *If you're going to be a sewermouth, I wish you would leave.* □ *Who's the sewermouth in the plaid jacket?*

**sew something up** AND **sew up something** *tr.* to finalize something; to conclude. □ *Let's sew this up and get out of here.* □ *I'm about ready to sew this thing up.* (More at *sewed up.*)

**sex** *n.* Seconal™ barbiturate capsules. (Drugs. See *secs* at *sec.*) □ *Sex is a kind of downer. It's red.* □ *The druggies mean pills when they say sex.*

**sex goddess** *n.* a sexy-looking female movie or television star. □ *I wonder what these sex goddesses look like when* *they get up in the morning.* □ *Sex goddesses get up in the afternoon.*

**sex kitten** *n.* a woman with enormous sexual potential. □ *He thought he was getting a sex kitten, but she turned out to be just a plain cat.* □ *Clare does everything she can to look like a sex kitten.*

**sex pot** *n.* one who flaunts one's sexuality, usually a woman. □ *Tiffany is such a sex pot.* □ *About 20,000 young sex pots hit Hollywood every year hoping to be discovered.*

**sexy 1.** *mod.* having great sex appeal. □ *What a sexy chick!* □ *He's not what I would call sexy, but I suppose it's a matter of taste.* **2.** *mod.* neat; exciting. □ *That's a sexy set of wheels.* □ *You play really sexy music.* □ *Your idea is real sexy.*

**S.F.** *mod.* alcohol intoxicated. (From *shit-faced*.) □ *Fred was really S.F. last night.* □ *How can that guy get so S.F.?*

**shack up (with someone) 1.** *in.* to have a *one-night stand* with someone; to copulate (with someone). □ *Those two just wanted to shack up for a while.* □ *He only wanted to shack up with me.* **2.** *in.* to move in with someone temporarily, presumably for sexual purposes. □ *They shacked up for over a year until her parents found out and stopped sending her money.* □ *They decided to shack up.*

**shades** *n.* dark glasses. (See *sunshades*.) □ *Where are my shades? The sun is too bright.* □ *The guy stood there—wearing shades and carrying a violin case. Barlowe grimaced.*

**shaft 1.** *n.* a bad deal; unfair treatment. □ *He really gave me the shaft.* □ *It's the shaft whenever you go into that place.* **2.** *tr.* to do wrong to someone. □ *The jerk shafted me, but good.* □ *We are going to shaft this guy in a way that he will remember.* (More at *shafted*.)

**shafted** *mod.* beaten; bested; cheated. □ *I really got shafted in that deal.* □ *I've been shafted!*

**shagged** *mod.* alcohol intoxicated. □ *She is mucho shagged!* □ *Nobody is not too shagged to drive—or something like that.*

**shagged out** *mod.* exhausted. □ *What a day! I'm shagged out!* □ *You guys look sort of shagged out.*

**shag-nasty** *mod.* nasty. □ *What a shag-nasty jerk!* □ *I want out of this shag-nasty mess.*

**shag (off)** *in.* to depart. □ *I gotta shag. It's late.* □ *Go on! Shag off!* □ *I gotta shag. Somebody's calling my name.*

**shake** *n.* a milkshake. □ *I'd like a chocolate shake, please.* □ *A shake only costs 60 cents.*

**shake a leg 1.** *tr.* to hurry; to move faster. (Often as a command.) □ *Let's shake a leg, you guys. We gotta be there in 20 minutes.* □ *She told me to shake a leg, so I hurried the best I could.* **2.** *tr.* to dance. □ *Let's shake a leg. The music's great.* □ *Hey, Molly! You wanna shake a leg with me?*

**shakedown** *n.* an act of extortion. (Underworld.) □ *Mary was giving Bruno the shakedown, so he tried to put her out of the way.* □ *Those bums are masters at the shakedown.*

**Shake it (up)!** *exclam.* "Hurry!"; "Move faster!" □ *Get going, chum! Shake it up!* □ *We're late. Shake it!*

**shakeout** *n.* an event that eliminates the weak or unproductive elements from a system. □ *After a shakeout that lasted a month, we went into full production.* □ *There was a big shakeout at the plant, and a whole lot of people got pink slipped.*

**shakes** *n.* the delirium tremens. □ *I got the shakes again. That's what I get for putting soda water in my whisky.* □ *In the last stages, they have the shakes all the time.*

**shake someone down** AND **shake down someone 1.** *tr.* to blackmail someone. (Underworld.) □ *Fred was trying to shake Molly down, but she got the cops in on it.* □ *The police chief was trying to shake down just about everybody in town.* **2.** *tr.* to put pressure on someone to lend one money. □ *We tried to shake them down for a few hundred, but no deal.* □ *If you're trying to shake me down, forget it. I got a case of the shorts.*

**Shake the lead out!** See *Get the lead out (of your ass)!*

**shake-up** *n.* a reorganization. □ *After a shake-up like the one we've just been through, everybody's a little upset.* □ *Fred and Clare both survived the shake-up.*

**sham** AND **cham** [ʃæm] *n.* champagne. □ *Pour me some sham, will you?* □ *No cham for Tom. He's driving.*

**shammy** AND **chammy** [ʃæmi] *n.* champagne. □ *No more chammy for me, thanks.* □ *Nothing makes a party happier than shammy.*

**shampers** AND **champers** [ʃampɚz] *n.* champagne. □ *I could live on shampers.* □ *My dad sent us a bottle of French champers.*

**shampoo** *n.* champagne. (See also *poo.*) □ *I just love this bubbly shampoo!* □ *There is nothing like shampoo to liven up a party!*

**shamus** AND **shammus** [ʃeməs] *n.* a police officer or a detective. (Probably from Yiddish.) □ *One thing that a shamus always knows is when another shamus is following him.* □ *This is it, shammus, say your prayers.*

**shank** **1.** *n.* a knife. □ *The mugger pulled a shank on the victim.* □ *The cops found the shank in the bushes.* **2.** *in.* to dance. □ *They were busy shankin' and didn't hear the gunshots.* □ *We were all shankin' to a great reggae band.*

**shank it** *tr.* to use one's legs to get somewhere; to walk. □ *My car needs fixing so I had to shank it to work today.* □ *I like to shank it every now and then.*

**shank's mare** *n.* foot travel. □ *You'll find that shank's mare is the quickest way to get across town.* □ *Is there a bus, or do I have to use shank's mare?*

**shape up** **1.** *in.* to improve; to reform. □ *I want to get things shaped up around here.* □ *I guess I'd better shape up if I want to stay in school.* **2.** *in.* to assume a final form or structure. □ *The game plan for the election was beginning to shape up.* □ *Her objectives began to shape up in her senior year.*

**shape up or ship out** *phr.* "improve or get out." □ *I'll tell you one more time. Shape up or ship out!* □ *They told me I had to shape up or ship out.*

**shark** **1.** *n.* a swindler; a confidence operator. (Underworld.) □ *The sharks were lined up ten deep to get at the blue-eyed new owner of the bowling alley.* □ *The guy's a shark, and he's after your hard-earned money!* **2.** *n.* a lawyer. (Derogatory.) □ *Some shark is trying*

to squeeze a few grand out of me. □ *Hire another shark to go after him.*

**shark repellent** *n.* something that prevents corporate takeovers. (Financial markets.) □ *Acme Systems tried again to get its board to approve a shark repellent to keep the Widget cartel from acquiring it.* □ *The shark repellent wasn't enough.*

**sharp** **1.** *mod.* clever; intelligent. □ *She's a real sharp chick! Got lots of savvy.* □ *She's sharp enough to see right through everything you say.* **2.** *mod.* good-looking; well-dressed. □ *You really look sharp today.* □ *That's a sharp set of wheels you got there.*

**sharpie** *n.* a clever operator; a clever person. □ *She's a real sharpie. She'll take you for everything you've got.* □ *A young sharpie in the first row got the answer right away.*

**shave** *tr.* to reduce or lessen something. □ *They shaved the waiting time to six months.* □ *The coach thought that the other team was shaving points, so he complained the next day.*

**shaved** *mod.* alcohol intoxicated. □ *I feel a tad shaved.* □ *So what if I'm a bit shaved? I shtill have all my shenses.*

**shavetail** *n.* a second lieutenant; a non-commissioned officer in the army; any inexperienced person. (Military. From a nickname for an untrained mule that is marked by a shaved tail.) □ *This shavetail here is trying to tell me my job.* □ *Who's the shavetail dancing with the Colonel's daughter?*

**Shazzam!** [ʃəˈzæm] *exclam.* "Wow!"; "Would you believe?" □ *And there was my ring—Shazzam!—right on the sidewalk!* □ *Shazzam! I passed the test!*

**sheen** [ʃin] *n.* a car. (From *machine.*) □ *You have one fine sheen there.* □ *I have to get my sheen's oil changed today.*

**sheepskin** *n.* a high school or college diploma. □ *When you get that sheepskin on the wall, you'll feel like it was all worth something.* □ *Where is your sheepskin from?*

**sheet** See *(rap) sheet.*

**shekels** [ʃɛklz] *n.* dollars; money. □ *You got a few shekels you can spare?* □ *These things cost plenty of shekels.*

**shellac** [ʃəˈlæk] *tr.* to beat someone; to out-score someone. □ *We're gonna shellack those bums Friday night.* □ *We'll be shellacking every team in the league this year.* (More at *shellacked, shellacking*.)

**shellacked 1.** *mod.* beaten; out-scored. □ *They were shellacked, and they knew it.* □ *The team got shellacked in last week's game.* **2.** *mod.* alcohol intoxicated; overcome by booze. □ *Ernie was so shellacked he couldn't see.* □ *How did he get so shellacked? I didn't see him drink anything.*

**shellacking** *n.* a beating. □ *We gave them a shellacking they'll never forget.* □ *Our team took a real shellacking.*

**shell out (an amount of money)** AND **shell an amount of money out** *tr. & in.* to spend a certain amount of money. □ *I'm not going to shell $400 out for that!* □ *Come on. You owe me. Shell out!*

**shicker** [ˈʃɪkɚ] **1.** AND **schickered** [ˈʃɪkɚd] *mod.* alcohol intoxicated. (From Hebrew *shiqor* via Yiddish.) □ *It took her about 10 minutes to get schicker and three days to get sober.* □ *He's schickered, and he's not going anywhere tonight.* **2.** *n.* liquor; beer. □ *Fill it up with shicker again.* □ *How do you know when you've had enough shicker?* **3.** *in.* to tipple; to become alcohol intoxicated. □ *I'm gonna go out and shicker till I'm silly.* □ *Fred is shickering again this weekend.*

**shield** *n.* a police officer's badge. □ *The fuzz flashed his shield, and I knew the game was over.* □ *If you're a cop, where's your shield?*

**shill** [ʃɪl] **1.** *n.* someone planted in the crowd to urge others to buy something, participate in something, etc. □ *The guy's a shill! Don't fall for this setup!* □ *There were more shills than suckers on the midway that day.* **2.** *in.* to advertise for something; to give a sales pitch for something. □ *Four stars of an old television show were there shilling for a major computer firm.* □ *They pay them a mint to shill like that.*

**shindig** [ˈʃɪndɪɡ] *n.* a party; a dance. (Folksy.) □ *What a fancy shindig! They even have glass glasses!* □ *What time do*

we have to be at that shindig Saturday night?

**shined** *mod.* alcohol intoxicated, especially by *moonshine*. □ *Tipsy? He's shined from dawn to dusk.* □ *The old farmer seemed a bit shined.*

**shiner** *n.* a black eye. □ *Wow, look at Marty's shiner!* □ *I got this shiner by walking into a door.*

**shishi** [ˈʃiʃi] *n.* hashish; marijuana. (Drugs.) □ *The cops busted his place and found some shishi under the bed.* □ *I got a bag of shishi. You wanna go get wasted?*

**shit\* 1.\*** *n.* dung. (Caution with *shit*.) □ *Don't step in that shit there.* □ *There's dog shit in my yard!* **2.\*** *n.* something poor in quality; junk. (Caution with *shit*.) □ *This stuff is shit. Show me something better.* □ *What do you keep all this shit around here for?* **3.\*** *n.* nonsense; *bullshit*. (Caution with *shit*.) □ *Don't give me that shit! I know you're lying.* □ *I'm tired of your shit!* **4.\*** *n.* drugs in general; heroin; marijuana. (Drugs. Caution with *shit*.) □ *Lay off the shit, Harry! You're gonna end up hooked.* □ *So Marty scores a bag of shit—I mean skag—you know, H.—and we get out the apps to shoot.* **5.\*** *tr.* to deceive someone; to lie to someone. (Caution with *shit*.) □ *Stop shittin' me, you bastard!* □ *You wouldn't shit me, would you?* **6.\*** *n.* a despicable person. (Crude. Also a rude and provocative term of address. Caution with *shit*.) □ *Tell that stupid shit to get out of here, or I'll bust him one.* □ *What a shit you are!*

**shit a brick** See *hatch a brick*.

**shit-faced\*** AND **shitty\*** *mod.* alcohol intoxicated. (Caution with *shit*. See also *poopied, S.F.*) □ *I'm shit-faced, and I know it.* □ *Move over. You're too shitty to drive.*

**shithead\*** *n.* a despicable person. (Crude. Also a rude and provocative term of address. Caution with *shit*.) □ *You stupid shithead!* □ *The guy is somewhere between an asshole and a shithead.*

**shitsky\*** [ˈʃɪtski] **1.** *n.* dung. (Caution with *shit*.) □ *There's some shitsky on your shoe.* □ *Some rude dog has left a little pile of grade-A shitsky on the side-*

*walk.* **2.** *n.* a despicable person. (Provocative. Caution with *shit*.) □ *The stupid shitsky is back on skag again.* □ *With a shitsky like that on your side, who needs enemies?*

**shiv** AND **chiv** [ʃɪv] **1.** *n.* a knife. (Underworld.) □ *Swiftly and silently his shiv found its way up under Rocko's ribs. All for a silly dame.* □ *I could tell from the way his cuff broke that there was a chiv strapped to his leg.* **2.** *tr.* to stab someone. (Underworld.) □ *He shivved Rocko, and Rocko deserved it.* □ *The boss told Bruno to get Rocko one way or the other—shiv him, burn him, clobber him—but get him.*

**shlemiel** See *schlemiel.*

**shlemihl** See *schlemiel.*

**shlepper** See *schlepper.*

**shlimazl** See *schlemazel.*

**shlook** [ʃluk] **1.** *n.* a puff of a marijuana cigarette. (Drugs.) □ *Come on! Give me just a shlook!* □ *You get one shlook for a buck, okay?* **2.** *tr. & in.* to puff a marijuana cigarette. (Drugs.) □ *That man could sit under a palm tree all day, just shlooking.* □ *Tiffany shlooked her rather expensive joint like an old pro.*

**shlub** See *schlub.*

**shlump** See *schloomp.*

**shmack** See *schmeck.*

**shmaltz** See *schmaltz.*

**shmear** See *schmear.*

**shmeck** See *schmeck.*

**shmecker** See *smecker.*

**shmee** See *schmeck.*

**shmegegge** See *schmegegge.*

**shmen** [ʃmɛn] *n.* freshmen. □ *A couple of shmen wandered by—looking sort of lost.* □ *The shmen are having a party all to themselves this Friday.*

**shmendrick** See *schmendrick.*

**shmo** See *schmo.*

**shmooze** See *schmooze.*

**shmuck** See *schmuck.*

**shnazzy** See *snazzy.*

**shnockered** See *schnockered.*

**shnook** See *schnook.*

**shnozz** See *schnozz.*

**shocker** *n.* something shocking. □ *Now, here's a shocker for you.* □ *Her news was quite a shocker.*

**shocks** *n.* shock absorbers in an automobile. □ *That hog Cadillac needs new*

*shocks.* □ *How much is a set of shocks for a buggy like this?*

**shoe polish** *n.* liquor; whiskey; inferior whiskey. □ *Why don't you give that cruddy shoe polish to the cat?* □ *The old lush would be delighted to get some of your shoe polish.*

**shoestring** *mod.* low-cost; cheap. (See also *on a shoestring*.) □ *This is just a shoestring operation. There is no capital involved.* □ *We have nothing but a shoestring budget this year.*

**shoo-in** [ʃuɪn] *n.* an easy winner. □ *She's a shoo-in. Nobody can touch her.* □ *My horse was a shoo-in. It won by a mile.*

**shook up** AND **all shook up** *mod.* excited; disturbed; upset. □ *She stole my heart, and I'm all shook up.* □ *They were pretty shook up after the accident.*

**shoot 1.** AND **shoot up** *tr. & in.* to inject a specific drug into the bloodstream. (Drugs.) □ *He actually had to leave the meeting to shoot.* □ *The two of them were shooting up skag.* **2.** *n.* an injection of heroin. (Drugs. Usually **shoot-up**.) □ *The way Ernie was yawning, I knew he needed a shoot-up.* □ *"Just one more shoot up. That's all. Then, never again!" moaned Ernie, rather unconvincingly.* **3.** *tr.* to *spike* a drink with liquor. □ *I'm gonna shoot the punch with rum.* □ *Harry shot his date's coke with vodka.* **4.** *in.* to tell (something). □ *We're ready. Go ahead. Shoot!* □ *Okay, shoot. I'm all ears.* **5.** See *Shoot!*

**Shoot!** *exclam.* "Darn!" (An exclamation or a very mild curse.) □ *Oh, shoot! I left my shades in the car.* □ *Shoot! I'm late!*

**shoot 'em up 1.** *n.* a western action movie. □ *I like a good shoot 'em up every now and then.* □ *Most films are more sophisticated nowadays than the old shoot 'em ups.* **2.** *mod.* having to do with a western action film. □ *He was a shoot 'em up star in the thirties.* □ *I like the good old shoot 'em up movies.*

**shoot for the sky** See *aim for the sky.*

**shoot from the hip** *in.* to speak quickly and without thinking. (See *hip-shooter*.) □ *She has a tendency to shoot from the hip, but that's not really a problem.* □ *I shot from the hip when I spoke. I'm sorry.*

**(shooting) gallery** *n.* a place where addicts can go to inject drugs. (Drugs.) □ *You could go to this hole in the wall they called a shooting gallery, buy some skag, and shoot up right there.* □ *One of the cleverest names for a joint like that was "shooting gallery."*

**shooting iron** *n.* a pistol. (Cowboy and folksy.) □ *Millard "Shorty" Wilson always carried his shooting iron with him, except for one fateful day back in '92— 1892, that is.* □ *He pulled out his shooting iron and got down to cleaning it.*

**shoot one's cookies** AND **shoot one's breakfast, shoot one's supper** *tr.* to empty one's stomach; to vomit. □ *I think I'm gonna shoot my cookies.* □ *I shot my supper, and I was glad to get rid of it.*

**shoot oneself in the foot** *tr.* to cause oneself difficulty; to be the author of one's own doom. □ *I am a master at shooting myself in the foot.* □ *Again, he shot himself in the foot with his open and honest dealings with the press.*

**shoot one's mouth off** AND **shoot off one's mouth** *tr.* to brag; to tell secrets. □ *Stop shooting your mouth off. Nobody believes you anymore.* □ *So you had to go and shoot off your mouth about the bankruptcy proceedings!*

**shoot one's wad** *tr.* to spend or use everything. □ *I shot my wad on junk food.* □ *I can't afford a cab. I shot my wad at the restaurant.*

**shoot-out 1.** *n.* a gunfight. □ *There was a big shoot-out at the end of the movie.* □ *In this shoot-out, there were no survivors—not even a horse!* **2.** *n.* an argument. □ *When the shoot-out was over, the boss—confident she had won—went back into her office.* □ *A big public shoot-out like that sours morale a lot.*

**shoot someone down in flames** *tr.* to ruin someone; to bring about someone's downfall. (See also *go down in flames.*) □ *It was a bad idea, okay, but you didn't have to shoot me down in flames.* □ *I didn't mean to shoot you down in flames.*

**shoot someone or something down** AND **shoot down someone or something** *tr.* to ruin someone or something; to debunk someone or something. □ *The*

*boss shot down my plan immediately.* □ *Just as I was making the final point, she shot me down with a simple fact I should have remembered.* (More at *shot down.*)

**shoot the breeze** *tr.* to chat casually and without purpose. □ *We spent the entire afternoon just shooting the breeze.* □ *It was good to shoot the breeze with you, Mary.*

**shoot the bull** AND **shoot the crap\*, shoot the shit\*** *tr.* to chat and gossip. (The same as *throw the bull.* Caution with *crap, shit.*) □ *Let's get together sometime and shoot the bull.* □ *You spend too much time shooting the crap.*

**shoot the cat** *tr.* to empty one's stomach; to vomit. □ *I must have shot the cat a dozen times during the night.* □ *Shooting the cat is no fun when you're weak and dizzy.*

**shoot the dozens** See *play the dozens.*

**shoot the works 1.** *tr.* to do everything; to use everything; to bet all one's money. □ *Okay, let's go out to dinner and shoot the works.* □ *Don't shoot the works! Save some for a cab.* **2.** *tr.* to empty one's stomach; to vomit. □ *Suddenly she turned sort of green, and I knew she was going to shoot the works.* □ *After she shot the works, she looked fine—but I was sort of pale.*

**shoot up (on something) 1.** *in.* to inject (a drug). (Drugs. See *shoot.*) □ *About that time we both began shooting up on skag.* □ *He couldn't wait to get home and shoot up.* **2.** *n.* an injection of narcotics. (Drugs. Usually **shoot-up.**) □ *Barlowe watched the dame do a shoot-up on H. and settle down so they could talk.* □ *A quick shoot-up was all she needed.*

**shopping list** *n.* a list of things, especially questions or things one wants. (Compare to *laundry list.*) □ *I have a shopping list of absolute musts.* □ *He showed up for the interview with a shopping list so long that it took two pages.*

**short 1.** *n.* a small drink of hard liquor or of beer. □ *One short, bartender.* □ *I'll have a short and a pack of cigarettes.* **2.** *mod.* having to do with a single drink of undiluted liquor. □ *I'll take mine short, innkeeper.* □ *Who ordered a short one?* **3.** *n.* a purchase of drugs that counts or weighs out less than the amount agreed upon. □ *You gave me a short. Fix it now, or this thing goes off accidentally in your ear.* □ *Max knew that Bruno ended up with a short, and Bruno wasn't stable enough to talk about things like that. Max blew.* **4.** *tr.* to give someone less of something than was agreed upon. □ *You shorted me!* □ *They shorted us on the last order, so we switched suppliers.* **5.** *n.* a car. (Streets.) □ *Man, that's some short you got!* □ *Max gets his money cracking shorts.* **6.** *n.* the sale of borrowed shares of stock; a short sale. (Financial markets.) □ *I think that IBM is a good short in here. The high-tech companies are in for a pullback.* □ *There is a lot of covering of shorts this week. After that the market is in for a steady decline.* **7.** *tr.* to sell borrowed stock. (Financial markets.) □ *I wouldn't short IBM. It's a long-term hold.* □ *The way the deficit is running, I'd short the whole market.*

**short end of the stick** *n.* the burden, responsibility, blame, etc. for something. (Always with *the.*) □ *Here I am stuck with the short end of the stick again.* □ *I am the one who plans all this stuff, and when you jerks drop the ball, I'm left holding the short end of the stick.*

**short fuse** *n.* a quick temper. □ *Fred's got a short fuse. Watch out.* □ *I knew she'd blow. She's got a short fuse.*

**short one** *n.* a small or quickly drunk drink of liquor, including beer. (Compare to *tall one.*) □ *How about a short one, innkeeper?* □ *Give my friend here a short one.*

**shorts** AND **case of the shorts** *n.* the lack of money. (Always with *the.*) □ *Here I am with a case of the shorts again.* □ *The shorts always come around at the end of the month.*

**short-snort 1.** *n.* a quick drink of whiskey from a bottle, flask, or jug. □ *He grabbed a short-snort and went back to his carving.* □ *Jed offered the visitor a short-snort from a jar of shine.* **2.** *n.* a portion or *snort* of a powdered drug. (Drugs.) □ *The guy was leaving the office every thirty minutes for a short-snort.* □ *A short-snort every now and*

then can lead to more and more and more.

**shot 1.** *n.* a try at something. □ *Go ahead. Give it another shot.* □ *Have a shot at this problem.* **2.** *mod.* exhausted; ruined. □ *I really feel shot today.* □ *Here's your pen back. It's shot anyway.* □ *This thing is shot. Let's get a new one.* **3.** *n.* a rocket launching. □ *The shot was canceled because of the weather.* □ *This shot, like the last, was a total failure.* **4.** *n.* a small or quickly drunk drink of liquor, usually whiskey. □ *Here, have a shot of this stuff.* □ *He stopped at every bar on the strip for a quick shot.* **5.** *n.* an injection of drugs. □ *Just one shot of that stuff and you're hooked for life.* □ *A shot of skag put the poor guy straight for a while.* **6.** *mod.* alcohol intoxicated. □ *They are a little noisy, I guess, but after all they are shot, you know, plastered.* □ *I am half shot now. I'll quit before I'm shot.*

**shot down 1.** *mod.* demolished; destroyed. □ *Her idea was shot down after all her work.* □ *I felt shot down, even though I was sure of what I was getting into.* **2.** *mod.* rejected by a young woman. □ *Tiffany is a cruel chick. I was shot down from day one.* □ *Fred's shot down, thanks to his best girl. He'll get over it.* **3.** *mod.* drug intoxicated. (Drugs.) □ *Ernie is shot down every day by early in the afternoon. He's hooked.* □ *Bruno is in the alley—shot down as usual.*

**shotgun 1.** *mod.* broad; general. □ *It was a shotgun attempt to include everyone.* □ *A shotgun approach to a problem like this is useless. You must get specific.* **2.** *exclam.* a phrase called out by someone who claims the privilege of riding in a car's passenger seat. (Usually **Shotgun!**) □ *"Shotgun!" cried Jimmy, heading for the car.* □ *Whoever yelled "shotgun" has to sit holding the cake all the way.* **3.** *n.* a pipe designed to aid a person in blowing marijuana smoke into someone else's mouth. (Drugs.) □ *This next slide shows a "shotgun," a simple device for driving smoke into the lungs.* □ *There was this store, see, where you could buy fancy pipes and shotguns and stuff.* **4.** *tr.* to blow a puff of marijuana smoke into someone else's mouth. (Drugs.)

☐ *Molly was shotgunning Fred when the bust came.* ☐ *She likes to shotgun people.*

**shotgun wedding** *n.* a forced wedding, presumably because the bride is pregnant. ☐ *It was a shotgun wedding, but they sure are in love.* ☐ *I thought shotgun weddings went out with feuds and things like that.*

**shot in the arm 1.** *n.* a drink of liquor. ☐ *I could use a little shot in the arm.* ☐ *How about a little shot in the arm, bartender?* **2.** *n.* an injection of narcotics. (The same as *bang in the arm.*) ☐ *You might say that I really needed this shot in the arm.* ☐ *It's nothing. Just a little shot in the arm.* **3.** *n.* a boost or act of encouragement. ☐ *The pep talk was a real shot in the arm for all the guys.* ☐ *The good test grade was a shot in the arm for Gary.*

**shot in the dark** *n.* a very general attempt; a wild guess. ☐ *It was just a shot in the dark. I had no idea I was exactly correct.* ☐ *Come on, try it. Even a shot in the dark may win.*

**shot in the neck 1.** *n.* a drink of straight whiskey. ☐ *Wally took a little shot in the neck before heading out into the cold.* ☐ *A shot in the neck was just what was needed.* **2.** *mod.* alcohol intoxicated. ☐ *He's shot in the neck, but he's not bleeding.* ☐ *What's wrong with Harry is that he's shot in the neck every day by supper.*

**shot to hell** *mod.* ruined; decimated. (An elaboration of *shot.*) ☐ *This thing is shot to hell. Let's get a new one.* ☐ *My car is shot to hell.*

**shot up 1.** *mod.* severely injured by gunshots. ☐ *Tom got himself shot up in a hunting accident.* ☐ *He was pretty badly shot up in the police action.* **2.** *mod.* alcohol or drug intoxicated. (Usually **shot-away.**) ☐ *Well, you see, he's shot up and can't come to the phone.* ☐ *How can anybody get so shot-away in so little time?*

**shouldn't happen to a dog** *phr.* describes something that is so bad that no creature deserves it. ☐ *Poor guy. That shouldn't happen to a dog.* ☐ *This cold I got shouldn't happen to a dog.*

**shout** *n.* an exclamation point. (See also **screamer, shriek.**) ☐ *Put a shout at the end of the line. Make this dull story more sexy.* ☐ *This gal uses shouts like they were salt and pepper.*

**shove 1.** *tr. & in.* to sell drugs. (Drugs.) ☐ *Who would suspect that Tiffany was shoving?* ☐ *She's shoving coke.* **2.** *tr.* to pass counterfeit money. (Underworld.) ☐ *She got sent up for three years for shoving funny-money.* ☐ *He got away with shoving the stuff for months before they got onto him.*

**shove off** See *push off.*

**show and tell** *n.* a session where objects are presented and described. (Essentially a kindergarten or grade school activity.) ☐ *It was a short lecture with lots of show and tell.* ☐ *I can't take another show and tell session.*

**show biz** *n.* show business. ☐ *Well, that's show biz for you.* ☐ *Anybody who can make a living in show biz has to be clever and talented.*

**show someone or something up** AND **show up someone or something** *tr.* to make someone appear bad by comparison. ☐ *Her carefully rehearsed performance showed up my hasty efforts.* ☐ *I didn't mean to show you up.*

**shpleef** See *spliff.*

**shredded** *mod.* alcohol intoxicated. (Collegiate.) ☐ *We are all too shredded to drive home. What shall we do?* ☐ *I believe that each of us is shredded enough to fly home. Let's vote on that.*

**shriek** *n.* an exclamation point. (Printers. Compare to *screamer, shout.*) ☐ *Where is there a shriek at the end?* ☐ *Take off that shriek. You use too many of those things.*

**shrimp** *n.* a small person. ☐ *Who's the little shrimp over by the door?* ☐ *I'm such a shrimp. I just have short genes.*

**shrink** *n.* a psychoanalyst or psychotherapist. ☐ *I dropped a bundle on a shrink, but that didn't help—me anyway.* ☐ *The shrink says I have to take these pills to help me get off the drug habit.*

**shroom** [ʃrum] *in.* to take or eat peyote cactus. (Drugs.) ☐ *They spent all afternoon shrooming.* ☐ *You shroom too much.*

**shrooms** [ʃrumz] *n.* the tips of the peyote cactus that contain mescaline. (Drugs. From *mushrooms.* Not really a mushroom.) □ *I got some shrooms. Ya wanna come over?* □ *Shrooms and me don't mix.*

**shtik** See *schtick.*

**shtoonk** See *schtoonk.*

**shuck** [ʃək] **1.** *n.* an insincere person. □ *The guy's a shuck. Don't believe a thing he says!* □ *Who needs a shuck for a legislator?* **2.** *tr. & in.* to kid someone; to tease someone. □ *Cool it! I'm just shucking.* □ *Stop shucking me!* **3.** *tr.* to swindle someone; to deceive someone. □ *The con man shucked a number of people in the town before moving on.* □ *He was going to shuck the mayor, but people were beginning to talk, so he blew town.* **4.** *n.* a hoax. □ *What a stupid shuck!* □ *How could you fall for that old shuck?* **5.** AND **shuck down** *tr. & in.* to undress oneself; to remove one's clothing. □ *He shucked himself quickly and jumped into bed.* □ *He shucked and showered and was at work in twenty minutes.*

**shuck down** See the previous entry.

**Shucks!** AND **Aw shucks!** *exclam.* a mild oath. (Folksy.) □ *Shucks, ma'am. It wasn't anything at all.* □ *Aw shucks, I ain't never been this close to a woman before.*

**shuffler** *n.* a drunkard; a tippler. □ *The tavern was full of aged shufflers hoping for a handout.* □ *Some shuffler barfed in the shrubbery.*

**shush (up)** *in.* to be quiet. □ *Shush! I want to hear the weather.* □ *Shush up and listen to the lecture.*

**shut-eye** *n.* sleep. □ *It's about time to get some shut-eye.* □ *I could use about another hour of shut-eye.*

**shutout 1.** *n.* a game where one team prevents the other from scoring any points at all. □ *He was still reveling from last week's shutout.* □ *It was another shutout at Klum Field House last night.* **2.** *mod.* having to do with a game where one team has no score. □ *Another shutout game gave the fans nothing to cheer about this afternoon.* □ *I was hoping for a shutout contest, and I got one.*

**shutters** *n.* the eyelids. □ *Her shutters dropped slowly, and she was asleep.* □ *She blinked those yummy shutters over those bedroom eyes, and my knees turned to mush.*

**shut up** *in.* to be quiet. □ *Shut up and listen!* □ *Shut up yourself.*

**Shut your face!** *exclam.* "Shut up!"; "Be quiet!" □ *Oh, shut your face. I've heard enough.* □ *Can't you shut your face, you motor-mouth?*

**shwench** [ʃʍentʃ] *n.* a female freshman. (Collegiate.) □ *A couple of giggling shwenches showed up to cheer on the team.* □ *There's a shwench in my English class who knows more than the prof.*

**shyster** [ˈʃɑɪstɚ] *n.* an unethical or unscrupulous lawyer. (Also a rude term of address.) □ *Look, you cheap shyster, I paid you to help me, not ruin me!* □ *My ex-wife's shyster called again today to say she wants more money.*

**Siberian express** *n.* an enormous mass of very cold air moving from Siberia, across the North Pole, and down onto North America. □ *The country braced itself for a return Friday of the Siberian express with temperatures dropping to 20 below in many areas.* □ *The Siberian express seems to be aimed right at our state.*

**sicks** *n.* nausea; vomiting. □ *Oh man, I got the sicks.* □ *He's at home with the sicks.*

**sick to death (of someone or something)** *mod.* totally disgusted with someone or something. □ *I am sick to death of your constant bickering.* □ *This whole bribery business just has me sick to death.*

**sick (up)** *in.* to empty one's stomach; to vomit. □ *I think I'm going to sick up. Isn't there supposed to be a barf bag in one of these seat pockets?* □ *He's got to sick, and there's no air sickness bag. Help!*

**sicky** *n.* someone who seems mentally deranged. □ *The dame's a sicky. Watch out for yourself.* □ *Some sicky drew these obscene pictures on the wall.*

**sid** See *cid.*

**side** *n.* a side of a record. □ *Let's cruise over to Sam's pad and hear some sides.*

□ *Now here's a side you may remember.*

**sidewalk superintendent 1.** *n.* someone who—out of curiosity—watches excavations being dug and buildings being built. □ *All day, the lines of sidewalk superintendents oozed by.* □ *I don't want any advice from a sidewalk superintendent.* **2.** *n.* any critic. □ *If another sidewalk superintendent comes in here and tries to tell me how to manage this office, heads will roll.* □ *I hate to be a sidewalk superintendent, but this plan is all wrong.*

**sidewinder** *n.* a sneaky and despicable man. (Western jargon. From the name of the sidewinder rattlesnake.) □ *You dirty, lowdown sidewinder! That's too much!* □ *What sidewinder spilled my drink?*

**sidney** *n.* the hallucinogenic drug *L.S.D.* (Drugs. Also capitalized. See *sid*.) □ *Is Sidney working tonight?* □ *Sidney and I have a little business trip planned.*

**sight for sore eyes** *n.* a welcome sight. (Folksy. Often refers to a person.) □ *Oh boy, are you a sight for sore eyes.* □ *This glass of water is a sight for sore eyes.*

**signify 1.** *in.* to cause trouble for fun; to stir things up. (Black.) □ *Why's that dude signifying over there?* □ *What are all these cats signifying about anyway?* **2.** *in.* to try to look more important than one really is; to brag; to *strut one's stuff.* (Black.) □ *See that dude signify like somebody important?* □ *First you gotta learn to signify.*

**silk** *n.* a Caucasian. (Black.) □ *Some silk was over here, looking around sort of suspicious.* □ *He told his mama that if she doesn't treat him better, he's gonna bring some silk home for dinner and let her see what the neighbors think.*

**silks** *n.* clothing. □ *Look at the silks on that dude!* □ *I gotta get some new silks before spring.*

**silky** *mod.* smooth; unctuous. □ *Beware of anybody that silky.* □ *What a silky character. He could talk his way into the heart of some unsuspecting chick.*

**silly putty** *n.* psilocybin. (Drugs.) □ *Harry has some silly putty he doesn't want. Wanna buy it?* □ *Silly putty and silo are the same thing.*

**silo** ['saɪlo] *n.* psilocybin. (Drugs.) □ *The kid has been having hallucinations with silo. He'll recover.* □ *Where do they get stuff like silo and all that? You mean they can buy it right in our own town?*

**silo drippings** *n.* alcohol allegedly obtained at the base of a silo containing fermenting corn. □ *You actually drink this stuff? This is silo drippings.* □ *The old-timer called his moonshine "silo drippings."*

**silver** *n.* money. □ *What kind of silver is that going to take?* □ *I have some silver stashed at home if you need it.*

**silver bullet** AND **magic bullet** *n.* a specific, failsafe solution to a problem. (From the notion that a silver bullet is required to shoot a werewolf.) □ *I'm not suggesting that the committee has provided us with a silver bullet, only that their advice was timely and useful.* □ *Okay, I've got the silver bullet you need for this. Your vote on the pork storage units for my district would be greatly appreciated, of course.*

**simmer (down) 1.** *in.* to reduce one's anger. □ *Now, now! Just simmer! Cool it!* □ *Simmer down, you guys.* **2.** *in.* to get quiet. □ *I waited till things began to simmer down, and then I started.* □ *Hey, simmer down to a dull roar!* **3.** See **cook**.

**simoleon** [sɪ'molɪən] *n.* a dollar. (Underworld.) □ *How many simoleons is this going to cost me?* □ *For only one simoleon, you get a ticket to the greatest show on earth.*

**Simon Legree** ['saɪmən lə'gri] *n.* a very hard taskmaster; a hard boss. (From the name of the slave driver in *Uncle Tom's Cabin*.) □ *She's a regular Simon Legree.* □ *Ask Simon Legree if I will be able to stop work and go home for breakfast now.*

**simp** *n.* a simpleton. □ *You are such a simp!* □ *Why did some simp feel it necessary to do this?*

**simple Simon 1.** *n.* someone free of drugs; a *square.* (Drugs.) □ *Max will never be a simple Simon. The guy is hooked for life.* □ *A simple Simon stopped Bruno to ask for directions, and Bruno thought she was a cop.* **2.** *n.* psilocybin, a hallucinogenic substance. (Drugs.) □ *Is simple Simon habit-forming?* □ *You got any of that simple Simon?*

**sin** *n.* synthetic marijuana; *T.H.C.* (Drugs. From *synthetic.*) □ *Most of this stuff the kids put down good money for is not sin, but angel dust.* □ *Max was caught up in the quest for sin.*

**sin-bin** *n.* a van fitted with bedding as a place for necking and love-making. □ *Wally said he was saving his money to buy a sin-bin so he could have more fun on dates.* □ *Some rusty old sin-bin was parked in front of the house when I got there.*

**sing** *in.* to inform (on someone). (Underworld.) □ *Rocko knew the stoolie would sing. He had to do something to stop her.* □ *Bruno would never sing. He's a champ.*

**singed** See *scorched.*

**single 1.** *n.* one dollar; a dollar bill. □ *I don't have enough singles in the register to get me through the morning.* □ *I got a couple of singles I can lend you.* **2.** *n.* an unmarried person. (Usually plural.) □ *I'm holding a little party for singles.* □ *Tod's a single—just recently.*

**sink** *tr.* to swallow some food or drink. □ *Here, sink a bite of this stuff.* □ *Larry stopped at a tavern to sink a short one.*

**sinker** *n.* a doughnut. □ *This sinker must be four days old.* □ *All our sinkers are brought in fresh on Monday.*

**sink one's teeth into something** See *get one's teeth into something.*

**sinse** AND **sense (bud)** [sɪnts AND 'sɛnts(bəd)] *n.* seedless marijuana. (Drugs. From Spanish *sinsemilla,* "seedless.") □ *Where's the sinse I was saving?* □ *Sense bud is all that Tiffany will touch.*

**sip 1.** *n.* a puff of a marijuana cigarette. (Drugs.) □ *How about a sip of your joint?* □ *He took a big sip and held it so long he almost turned blue.* **2.** *tr. & in.* to take a puff of a marijuana cigarette. (See *sip tea.*) □ *He sipped a big one, stopped a minute, then spoke.* □ *The alley was populated by a bunch of teenyboppers sipping away the afternoon.*

**sipster** *n.* a tippler; a drunkard. □ *The old lady is a sipster who says she drinks a little wine to help her arthritis.* □ *Most*

*sipsters have a really fine excuse like that.*

**sip tea** *tr.* to draw a puff of marijuana smoke. (Drugs.) □ *Kelly would never sip tea. He's too square.* □ *Max sips tea when he's not high on skag.*

**sis** [sɪs] *n.* sister. (Also a term of address and a common pet name for one's sister.) □ *Come on, sis. We're going to be late.* □ *Well, sis, good luck.*

**sissified** ['sɪsɪfaɪd] *mod.* effeminate; sissy-style. □ *Don't act so sissified.* □ *I'm not comfortable in a sissified place like that.*

**sister 1.** *n.* a (female) friend. (Originally underworld. Sometimes a term of address.) □ *Hi, sister! How ya doing?* □ *Come here, sister. I gotta have a word with you.* **2.** *n.* a fellow sorority member. □ *One of my sisters let me borrow her car.* □ *The junior sisters are putting on a skit.* **3.** *n.* a fellow feminist. □ *We can do this thing, sisters, we can do it!* □ *The sisters will be discussing it at tonight's meeting.* **4.** See *(soul) sister.*

**sitcom** ['sɪtkɑm] *n.* a situation comedy as found on television. (Compare to *kid-vid.*) □ *These sitcoms are made for juvenile minds.* □ *Sitcoms can be fun.*

**Sit down and take a load off your feet.** AND **Come in and take a load off your feet.** *sent.* "Please make yourself at home." (Folksy.) □ *You look tired. Why don't you sit down and take a load off your feet?* □ *Come in and take a load off your feet. We'll beer awhile and talk over old times.*

**sit on a gold mine** *in.* to have something very valuable in one's control. □ *She's sitting on a gold mine and doesn't even know it.* □ *Fred is sitting on a gold mine and intends to get every cent out of it that he can.*

**sit on someone or something** *in.* to hold someone down (figuratively); to hold someone back (figuratively). □ *We had to sit on him to get him to do his work.* □ *They were holding him back—sort of sitting on him—until he was ready for the election.*

**sit right (with someone)** *in.* to seem right to someone; to rest easy with someone. (Usually in the negative.) □ *The whole business didn't sit right with* me. □ *Something in the witness's story just didn't sit right.*

**sit still for something** *in.* to tolerate something. □ *I will not sit still for that kind of behavior.* □ *Do they expect us to sit still for that kind of abuse?*

**sitter 1.** *n.* a person who attends another person during an *L.S.D.* session. (Drugs.) □ *Max was supposed to be a sitter for some student, but Max was stoned somewhere and didn't show.* □ *Who's my sitter?* **2.** *n.* the buttocks; the posterior. □ *My sitter always gets tired in these meetings.* □ *There's dust or something all over your sitter.*

**sit tight** *in.* to wait (for the best time to do something). □ *Just sit tight. Everything will be all right.* □ *I guess I'll just have to sit tight until it's settled.*

**sitting duck** *n.* someone who waits unsuspectingly for doom or destiny; an easy target for something bad. □ *Get out of the way! You're a sitting duck.* □ *The guy was a sitting duck for a mugging.*

**sitting pretty** *mod.* doing very nicely; in a very pleasant and secure position. □ *If I get the job, I'll be sitting pretty for a long time.* □ *She married a millionaire, and now she's sitting pretty.*

**six-bits** *n.* seventy-five cents. (A *bit* is equal to 12.5 U.S. cents.) □ *You got six-bits I can borrow?* □ *Just try one of these things. It's only six-bits.*

**six feet under** *mod.* dead and buried. □ *Fred died and is six feet under.* □ *They put him six feet under two days after he died.*

**six-pack** *in.* to while away a specified period of time drinking a six-pack of beer. (See also *Joe six-pack*.) □ *He sat in front of the television and six-packed the entire afternoon.* □ *He's in the back—six-packing, as usual.*

**sixty-four-dollar question** *n.* the most important question; the question that everyone wants to know the answer to. (Always with *the*.) □ *When? Now, that is the sixty-four-dollar question.* □ *Now for the sixty-four-dollar question. What's the stock market going to do this year?*

**sizzled** *mod.* alcohol intoxicated. (Compare to *fried*.) □ *I'd like to go out tonight and get sizzled—maybe that*

would help me forget Tiffany. □ *Harold got himself sizzled and couldn't drive to the dance.*

**sizzler** *n.* a very hot day. □ *Today will be another sizzler. A low-pressure center over Alabama is pumping hot and humid air into the area.* □ *What a sizzler! I'm sweating like a horse.*

**skag** AND **scag** [skæg] **1.** *n.* a rotten thing or person. □ *Don't be such a skag. Who do you think you are?* □ *Gary has become more of a scag than I can stand.* **2.** *n.* a very ugly woman. (Collegiate.) □ *What a skag! I wouldn't be seen with her.* □ *She looks like a scag without makeup.* **3.** *n.* a tobacco cigarette; a tobacco cigarette butt. (Military.) □ *Can I bum a scag off you?* □ *Here, have a scag on me.* **4.** *in.* to smoke (a tobacco cigarette). □ *He stopped scagging for about a week.* □ *I'll scag till I die.* **5.** *n.* heroin, especially poor-quality heroin; any powerful drug. (Drugs.) □ *Just lay off the skag—if you can.* □ *Scag has sent a lot of my friends to the bone orchard.* **6.** *n.* hard liquor. □ *No beer for me. Tonight it's scag.* □ *The two of them put away a quart of my finest skag.*

**skagged out** *mod.* drug intoxicated; very high. (Drugs. See *skag*.) □ *Max was rocking back and forth on the top step—skagged out, as usual.* □ *He got to the point where being skagged out was more important than eating.*

**skag jones** AND **scag jones** *n.* an addiction to heroin. (Drugs. Here *Jones* is a "thing.") □ *It's the scag jones that's got her down.* □ *She has a serious skag jones.*

**skank** AND **scank** [skæŋk] **1.** *n.* an ugly (young) woman. (Collegiate.) □ *What a skank she is! Give her a comb or something.* □ *Look at her! Is she a skank or what?* **2.** *in.* to appear ugly. □ *My face is skanking like mad. Must be the zits.* □ *Both sisters skank. Must be hereditary.*

**skanky** [skæŋki] *mod.* ugly; repellent, usually said of a woman. (Collegiate.) □ *She is so skanky! That grody hairdo doesn't help either.* □ *What's wrong with being a little skanky? It's what you can do with your brain that counts.* □ *She's skanky, nonetheless.*

**skat** [skæt] *n.* beer. □ *How about some skat, chum?* □ *You got any pretzels to go with the skat?*

**skate 1.** *n.* a drinking bout. □ *He's off on another 3-day skate.* □ *Jerry hopes that this will be his last skate. He wants to dry out for good.* **2.** *n.* a drunkard; a person on a drinking spree. □ *Jerry's a skate and he knows it.* □ *A couple of skates celebrating the new year ran into my car.* **3.** *in.* to get drunk. □ *Jerry's skating again. It's his whole life.* □ *Let's go out and skate, okay?*

**skating** *mod.* drug intoxicated. □ *He's high all right—I'd say he's skating.* □ *He took some wicked silo and is totally skating.*

**skedaddle** [skə'dædl] *in.* to get out; to leave in a hurry. (Folksy.) □ *Go on, skedaddle! Out!* □ *Well, I'd better skedaddle on home.*

**skeet** *n.* a blob of nasal mucus. (Collegiate.) □ *God, Fred, there's a gross skeet hanging outta your nose!* □ *That wasn't stew; that was skeets!*

**skeeter** ['skidɚ] *n.* a mosquito. (Folksy.) □ *A skeeter bit me on the arm.* □ *There are a lot of skeeters out tonight.*

**skeevy** ['skivi] *mod.* sleazy and disgusting. □ *This is a skeevy joint. Let's get out.* □ *Your coat looks so skeevy. Is it old?*

**skid-lid** *n.* a motorcycle helmet. □ *The law has no business telling me I gotta wear a skid-lid.* □ *Don't you use a skid-lid?*

**skid marks** *n.* unclean, brownish marks on one's underpants. □ *Just looking at him, you know he's the type who has skid marks and enjoys popping zits.* □ *There is hardly anything a genteel person can say about skid marks that is acceptable in public.*

**skid row** *n.* the name for a place populated with ruined alcoholics and other down-and-out people. □ *I don't want to end up on skid row. How can I get rid of this monkey?* □ *Just because they're on skid row, it doesn't mean they're beyond help.*

**skid row bum** *n.* a down-and-out person; a low alcoholic beggar. □ *Do you want to end up a skid row bum?* □ *Even a skid row bum has some pride.*

**skillion** ['skɪljən] *n.* an imaginary enormous number. □ *I have a skillion reasons why I won't marry you.* □ *About a skillion people are running in the marathon.*

**skin 1.** *n.* a dollar bill. □ *This ticket cost me a couple of skins—and it's not worth it.* □ *You got a skin for the tollbooth?* **2.** AND **skinhead** *n.* someone with a shaved or bald head. □ *Who's the skin with the earrings?* □ *That skinhead looks stoned.* **3.** *tr.* to cheat or overcharge someone. □ *The guy who sold me this car really skinned me.* □ *We skinned him on that stock deal.* **4.** *n.* a rolling paper used for tobacco and marijuana cigarettes. □ *Can I borrow your pipe? The cat ate my skins.* □ *Here's some skins—get rid of that cat.* **5.** *tr. & in.* to *skin (pop)*, either by accident or on purpose. (Drugs.) □ *They start out skinning and move on to the big stuff.* □ *She skinned the first one because she was so nervous.* **6.** See *skins.*

**skin a goat** *tr.* to empty one's stomach; to vomit. □ *Ralph went out to skin a goat.* □ *Was my cooking so bad that everybody had to skin a goat?*

**skin flick** *n.* a movie featuring nudity. (See also *nudie.*) □ *We took in a skin flick when we were in the city.* □ *Max likes skin flicks better than real girls.*

**skinful** *n.* an intoxicating quantity of liquor; enough liquor. (See also *have a skinful.*) □ *He's got a skinful and can't drive.* □ *She knows enough to stop drinking before she gets a skinful.*

**skin game** *n.* any swindle. (Underworld.) □ *Bruno was mixed up in a skin game for a while.* □ *The con running the skin game got out of town.*

**skinhead** See *skin.*

**Skin me!** *exclam.* "Give me some skin!"; "Shake my hand!" (Originally black.) □ *Hey, man, skin me!* □ *Hey, old buddy. Don't walk on! Skin me!*

**skinny 1.** *n.* marijuana. □ *Where's the rest of the skinny that was here last night?* □ *That was my skinny, and I took it home.* **2.** AND **hot skinny** *n.* inside information. □ *What's the skinny on the tower clock?* □ *I've got the hot skinny on Mary and her boyfriend.*

**skinny dip** 1. *in.* to swim in the nude. □ *We used to go skinny dipping when I was a kid.* □ *There was an old creek on the farm where we used to skinny dip.* 2. *n.* a swim in the nude. □ *A nice skinny dip in a quiet glade takes you back to nature.* □ *Randy, who fears fish, didn't take a skinny dip with the others.*

**skin (pop)** 1. *n.* an injection of a drug, usually heroin, into the flesh rather than into a vein. (Drugs.) □ *One little skin pop shouldn't have affected him that way.* □ *She did a skin just to hold her over.* 2. *tr. & in.* to inject drugs subcutaneously or intramuscularly. (Drugs. See *pop.*) □ *He started skin popping, and that led—as it always does—to the real thing.* □ *He was skin popping his friend when the cops came in.*

**skin pumping** *n.* taking a *skin (pop).* □ *Some stupid kids were playing around, skin pumping in the alley.* □ *You know what skin pumping can lead to, don't you?*

**skins** *n.* drums. (Musicians. The same as *hides.*) □ *Andy can really make the skins talk.* □ *Buddy could beat those skins like nobody's business.*

**skin-search** *n.* a search of the naked body by legal authorities. (See also *strip-search.*) □ *These clowns were actually doing skin-searches on traffic offenders!* □ *Aren't there laws against frivolous skin-searches?*

**Skip it!** *exclam.* "Forget it!"; "Never mind!" □ *I won't bother you with my question again. Skip it!* □ *Oh, skip it! It doesn't matter.*

**skip (out)** *in.* to leave; to run away without doing something, such as paying a bill. □ *The guy skipped when I wasn't looking.* □ *Fred skipped out, leaving me with the bill.*

**skirt** *n.* a woman. □ *Some skirt comes up to me and asks where the police station is.* □ *Who's the skirt I saw you with last night?*

**skivvies** ['skɪviz] *n.* underpants; underwear. □ *He stood there chattering in his skivvies waiting for additional indignities.* □ *I don't have any clean skivvies!*

**skoofer** AND **skoofus** ['skufɚ AND 'skufəs] *n.* a marijuana cigarette. (Drugs. Black.) □ *Got a skoofus?* □ *How much for one of those skoofers?*

**skrag** [skræg] *tr.* to murder someone. (Underworld.) □ *These thugs tried to skrag me, I swear.* □ *Barlowe wanted to skrag him right then and there.*

**skrungy** ['skrəndʒi] *mod.* disgusting. □ *What is this skrungy stuff they are serving here?* □ *That movie was too skrungy for me.*

**skuffle** AND **scuffle** ['skəfl] *n.* the drug *P.C.P.* (Drugs.) □ *Something called skuffle has become popular in Adamsville in the last few months.* □ *Kids buy scuffle and put it on the end of a cigarette.*

**skull-buster** 1. *n.* a difficult course in school or college. □ *The course was a skull-buster, and I had to drop it.* □ *All the courses in that department are skull-busters.* 2. *n.* a police officer. (Black.) □ *Two skull-busters came up and started asking questions.* □ *Watch out for the skull-buster over there.*

**skullduggery** ['skəl'dəgɚi] *n.* deceitful doings; dirty work. □ *It took a lot of skullduggery to bring it off, but that was no problem for Janice.* □ *Without skullduggery, politics wouldn't be interesting.*

**skulled** *mod.* alcohol or drug intoxicated. □ *He's too skulled to drive.* □ *He got himself skulled in less than 20 minutes.*

**skunk** 1. *n.* a mean and hateful person. (Compare to *polecat, stinker.*) □ *What a skunk!* □ *Must you be such a skunk in front of my friends?* 2. *tr.* to outwit someone. □ *I skunked them. They'll never find me.* □ *That fish skunked me. I thought I caught him for sure this time.*

**skunk-drunk** *mod.* alcohol intoxicated. □ *He was skunk-drunk and didn't want to be bothered.* □ *Some skunk-drunk character came in and started talking big.*

**skunked** 1. *mod.* alcohol intoxicated. □ *Kelly got skunked on suds—very unusual for him.* □ *He was so skunked he couldn't find his house.* 2. *mod.* outwitted; out-scored; defeated. □ *The home team skunked the visitors for the third year in a row.* □ *I was skunked on this year's fishing trip. Not even a bite.*

**skurf** [skɚf] *in.* to skateboard. (From the words *skate* and *surf.*) □ *He skurfed from city hall to the post office.* □ *My mom won't let me skurf anymore.*

**sky** *in.* to travel (to somewhere) in an airplane. □ *I decided to sky down to Orlando for the weekend.* □ *Let's sky to New York and then go on to London.*

**sky hook** *n.* an imaginary tool. □ *I can't get this thing outa here without a sky hook.* □ *Go get me a sky hook, would ya?*

**sky-pilot** *n.* a chaplain. □ *The sky-pilot says we can park in the church's lot, if we don't mess anything up or make too much noise.* □ *The sky-pilot's a good guy.*

**sky rug** *n.* a toupee; a man's wig. □ *I think he is wearing a sky rug.* □ *He looks better in his sky rug, but that's not necessarily good.*

**sky's the limit** *phr.* "there is no upper limit." (Always with *the.*) □ *I can afford it. The sky's the limit.* □ *You can do anything you set your mind to, Billy. The sky's the limit.*

**slam** **1.** *tr.* to criticize someone or something. □ *Please don't slam my car. It's the best I can do.* □ *The secretary was slamming the boss in one room, and the boss was slamming the secretary in another.* **2.** *n.* a criticism. □ *Harry took another slam at the sales record the sales force had produced for the meeting.* □ *I don't want to hear another nasty and hateful slam at my sister. Is that clear?*

**slam-bang** *mod.* wild; exciting. □ *It was a slam-bang weekend, and I loved every minute of it.* □ *Wow, did we ever have a slam-bang time!*

**slam-dancing** *n.* a style of punk dancing where the dancers jump about, bumping into each other, trying to knock each other down. □ *Haven't you about had enough of that juvenile slam-dancing?* □ *I hurt my shoulder doing some slam-dancing.*

**slam dunk** **1.** *tr. & in.* to force a basketball into the basket from above. (See also *jam.*) □ *Wilbur slam dunked another one, raising the score from 108 to 110.* □ *Wilbur slam dunked his way to fame and riches.* **2.** *n.* an act of making a basket as in sense 1. □ *Another slam dunk and Wilbur ties the score again!* □ *The goal will probably not withstand another slam dunk.*

**slammer** **1.** *n.* a jail. □ *I got out of the slammer on Monday and was back in by Wednesday.* □ *The slammer in this town is like a hotel.* **2.** *n.* a *slam dunk.* □ *He really has that slammer perfected!* □ *It's another slammer for Wilbur!*

**slam some beers** *tr.* to drink beer; to drink a number of beers. □ *Fred and Larry went out to slam some beers.* □ *Let's slam some beers sometime.*

**slant** *n.* a biased view; a unique perception. □ *You can probably give us yet another slant on this problem.* □ *You provided us with a fresh slant on this question.*

**slap-dab** *mod.* directly. (See also *smack (dab) in the middle.*) □ *We put it slap-dab on his head.* □ *I found this pop bottle slap-dab on top of the car! How'd it get there?*

**slap-dash** *mod.* fast and careless. □ *I wish you hadn't done it in such a slap-dash fashion.* □ *This is a very slap-dash way to do something.*

**slap happy** *mod.* silly; giddy. □ *I get slap happy when I have to stay up this late.* □ *She's a little slap happy, but a tremendous dear.*

**slap in the face** *n.* an insult; a rejection. □ *That remark was a real slap in the face.* □ *Her departure was a slap in the face to the manager, who had refused to give her a raise.*

**slap someone's wrist** AND **slap someone on the wrist** *tr.* to administer a minor reprimand. □ *The judge only slapped her wrist.* □ *The courts only slap them on the wrist and send them back out on the streets.*

**slash** *n.* a drink of liquor. □ *Just one slash, and I have to be going.* □ *How about a slash? You ready yet?*

**slaughter** See *murder.*

**slave away (at something)** *in.* to work very hard (doing something). □ *I'm tired of slaving away at this and getting nowhere.* □ *I'm slaving away for $7.00 an hour and have no prospects for the future.*

**slave market** *n.* a job market where many candidates for jobs come face to face with potential employers. □ *I gotta go to the annual slave market this year. We're hiring for a change.* □ *There* *was little hope at the annual slave market. There were 6 jobs and 432 applicants.*

**slay** *tr.* to overwhelm someone with one's performance or other excellence. □ *These jokes always slay the audience.* □ *Oh, you slay me with your silly remarks.*

**sleaze** AND **sleez** [sliz] **1.** *n.* a low and despicable person. □ *God, what a sleaze! How can anybody be so skanky?* □ *You'd expect to find a sleaze like that in a sleazoid joint like this.* **2.** *n.* any junk. □ *I won't sell sleez like that! I won't even have it in my store.* □ *Look at this sleaze—and look at the price! Outrageous!* **3.** *in.* to act low; to be sexually promiscuous. □ *She looks like the type who will sleaze and lie to get her own way.* □ *She earned quite a reputation sleazing around with just anybody.*

**sleazebag** *n.* a repellent person or place. □ *I won't go into a sleazebag like that.* □ *Who is the sleazebag leaning against the wall?*

**sleazeball** *n.* a repellent person. □ *He's okay if you're into sleazeballs.* □ *Who is that sleazeball with the earring?*

**sleaze-bucket** *n.* a repellent person, thing, or place. □ *Gad, what a sleaze-bucket! Let me out of here!* □ *Gee, Sue, your date's a real sleaze-bucket!*

**sleazo** AND **sleazoid** ['slizo AND 'slizoɪd] *mod.* low; disreputable; sleazy. □ *Let's get out of this sleazo joint.* □ *This place is really sleazo.* □ *Who wants a sleazoid car with no back seat?*

**sleazoid** ['slizoɪd] **1.** *n.* a sleazy person. □ *Who is this sleazoid?* □ *Who was that sleazoid I saw you with last night?* **2.** See *sleazo.*

**sleeper** **1.** *n.* a sleeping pill. (Drugs.) □ *I just took one little sleeper.* □ *She took a handful of sleepers with a glass of booze, and that was it.* **2.** *n.* someone or something that achieves fame after a period of invisibility. □ *The movie "Red Willow" was undoubtedly the sleeper of the year, winning 6 awards.* □ *My candidate had been a sleeper, but he finally began to pull ahead in the polls.*

**sleep it off** *tr.* to sleep while the effects of drugs or alcohol wear off. □ *I'm polluted, I guesh. Have to get home and shleep it off.* □ *She'll be okay when she sleeps it off.*

**sleepwalk** *n.* a movement toward something without effort. (A movement that could be done "in one's sleep." See *cakewalk, walk.*) □ *Getting the degree was a sleepwalk. Getting a job was hell.* □ *It was no sleepwalk, but it didn't make me slave away either.*

**sleez** See *sleaze.*

**slew** **1.** *in.* to drink to intoxication. □ *They must have been slewing for an hour before one got up and left.* □ *Let's go out and slew till we forget who we are.* **2.** AND **slews** *n.* a lot; lots. □ *I have a whole slew of old computer programs at home in a box somewhere.* □ *She's got slews of money.*

**slewed** AND **slewy, slued, sloughed (up)** [slud AND 'slui, slud...] *mod.* alcohol intoxicated. □ *Wallace is too slewed to drive.* □ *She knows how to stop drinking before she gets slewy.*

**slice of the action** See *piece of the action.*

**slick** **1.** *mod.* clever; glib. □ *He is a slick operator.* □ *His talk is slick, but his action is zotz.* **2.** *mod.* excellent. □ *This is a real slick setup you got here.* □ *That is a slick idea.* □ *The idea is not so slick!* **3.** *n.* a high-quality magazine printed on slick [coated] paper. □ *The slicks are all carrying ads for products and services that couldn't even be mentioned a few years ago.* □ *Most of the price increase for the slicks has been because of postage increases.* **4.** *n.* a racing tire. (Auto racing. See *racing slicks.*) □ *That set of wheels has slicks. I wonder why.* □ *I have some slicks at home in the garage.*

**slick-chick** *n.* an attractive and cute (young) woman. □ *Tiffany is a slick-chick. I wonder if she'd go out with me.* □ *Who was that slick-chick I saw you with the other night?*

**slickum** ['slɪkəm] *n.* hair dressing, especially if thick and heavy. □ *What kind of slickum do you have on your hair—bear grease?* □ *His hair was plastered down with slickum, and he looked like something in an old movie.*

**slightly rattled** **1.** *mod.* upset; confused. □ *Tom was slightly rattled by the trouble at the door.* □ *I'm slightly rattled. I'll get over it.* (More at *rattled.*) **2.** *mod.*

tipsy; alcohol intoxicated. □ *He's only slightly rattled. He'll recover by morning.* □ *She can be stone blind and still seem only slightly rattled.*

**slim** *n.* a tobacco cigarette. (The same as *straight*, as opposed to a marijuana cigarette, which may be thicker.) □ *I'll take a slim and a little mist, thanks.* □ *You got a slim I can borrow?*

**slime 1.** *n.* a worthless person; a low and wretched person. □ *What a slime that guy is!* □ *Who is the slime over there with the greasy hair?* **2.** *n.* degrading matters; corrupt people or situations. □ *I don't want to be involved in slime like that.* □ *The press uncovered even more slime at city hall.*

**slime bag** AND **slime bucket, slimebag, slimeball** *n.* a despicable person, usually a male. (See *slime*.) □ *Gee, a slime bag like that in the same room with me! Yuck!* □ *Who's the slime bucket in the 1962 Bonneville?*

**slimeball** See the previous entry.

**slime bucket** See *slime bag*.

**sling the cat** *tr.* to empty one's stomach; to vomit. □ *Suddenly Ralph left the room to sling the cat, I guess.* □ *That stuff will make you sling the cat.*

**Slip me five!** See *Give me five!*

**slip one's trolley** *tr.* to become a little crazy; to lose one's composure. (See also *off one's trolley*.) □ *I was afraid I would slip my trolley.* □ *He slipped his trolley and went totally bonkers.*

**slip someone a Mickey** *tr.* to secretly put a *Mickey Finn* in someone's alcoholic drink. (This drug either makes the victim ill or causes immediate diarrhea.) □ *Somebody slipped Barlowe a Mickey and sent him into action.* □ *For a ten-spot, the bartender slipped Rocko a Mickey.*

**slip someone five** *tr.* to shake someone's hand. □ *Billy slipped me five, and we sat down to discuss old times.* □ *Come on, man, slip me five!*

**slipstick** *n.* a slide rule. □ *Who carries a slipstick these days?* □ *Who even knows what a slipstick is these days?*

**slip (up) 1.** *in.* to make an error. □ *Don't slip up and pay this bill twice, please.* □ *I slipped and gave the guy a 35% tip.* **2.** AND **slip(-up)** *n.* an error.

□ *That was a silly slip-up. I'm sorry.* □ *That slip cost us nearly $2,000.*

**slob** [slɑb] *n.* a rude, fat, and unpleasant person. □ *What a slob! Comb your hair, if you can get a comb through it!* □ *Why doesn't that slob go on a diet or something? Anything!*

**slobber** *n.* nonsense. (From the term for saliva running out of the mouth.) □ *I've heard enough of your slobber. Can it!* □ *Another hour of professorial slobber!*

**slopped** *mod.* alcohol intoxicated. □ *I've never seen a senior citizen so inelegantly slopped as was Walter.* □ *He was so slopped, he could walk without his cane.*

**slop(s)** *n.* bad beer; inferior liquor. □ *Why do we have to drink slops like this? Can't Tom afford to give his guests something decent?* □ *Tom's slop is better than water—dishwater anyway.*

**slosh 1.** *n.* beer; liquor. □ *How about a glass of slosh?* □ *No slosh for me. Just plain water.* **2.** *tr. & in.* to drink liquor, including beer; to drink to excess. □ *Are you going to slosh gin all night?* □ *I slosh just because I like the taste.*

**sloshed (to the ears)** *mod.* alcohol intoxicated. □ *Man, is he sloshed to the ears!* □ *He is as sloshed as they come.*

**slow boat** *n.* a marijuana cigarette. (Drugs. See also *steamboat*.) □ *Tiffany stood there looking at the carefully made slow boat with a pained look on her face.* □ *Max yanked the slow boat from her and took an enormous swallow hit.*

**slow burn** *n.* the act of becoming angry very slowly or being resentful for a long period of time. (See *do a slow burn*.) □ *His lips were pressed together and he was angry, but just having a slow burn.* □ *She wasn't angry yet, but she was doing a slow burn.*

**sludgeball** ['slʌdʒbɑl] *n.* a despicable and repellent person. □ *Mike is such a sludgeball! Why do you keep seeing him?* □ *He's no sludgeball; he's eccentric.*

**sluff (off)** *in.* to waste time; to *goof off*. □ *Watch him. He will sluff off if you don't keep after him.* □ *He won't sluff. I know I can trust him.*

**slug 1.** *n.* a drink of liquor; a shot of whiskey. □ *Have a slug of this stuff. It* *will—I'm sorry to say, ma'am—put hair on your chest.* □ *A couple more slugs and he was ready to face the huge bull-necked ruffian.* **2.** *n.* a bullet. □ *Barlowe sent a couple of slugs into Rocko's chest. Rocko crumpled soundlessly.* □ *The medico dug out the slugs like he had done it a thousand times—which he probably had.*

**slugfest 1.** *n.* a fight; a festival of slugging. □ *They went out in the alley for a real slugfest.* □ *You wanna see a slugfest, just stick around.* **2.** *n.* a festival of arguing. □ *The slugfest went on until both sides were willing to compromise.* □ *The president emerged from the slugfest with control of the company still hers.*

**slugged** *mod.* alcohol intoxicated. □ *I'm slugged—skunked, you know, corned. And I think I am going to sick up.* □ *Ted realized that he was slugged out of his mind, but tried to get the bartender to serve him another drink.*

**slug it out** *tr.* to fight something out; to fight about something figuratively. □ *They finally went outside to slug it out.* □ *We'll just have to sit down in the conference room and slug it out.*

**slumgullion** ['sləm'gəljən] *n.* a meat stew; any food. □ *What is this slumgullion tonight? It looks like what we had last night, only thinner.* □ *This is the best slumgullion I've ever had—which puts it right up there with dishwater.*

**slummy** ['sləmi] *mod.* lousy. □ *What a slummy place!* □ *This place is not slummy!* □ *That was a slummy trick to pull on her.*

**slushed (up)** *mod.* alcohol intoxicated. □ *I hate to come home slushed and wake up everybody. I have to sing, you see.* □ *This chick is so slushed that she doesn't know her name.*

**slush fund** *n.* a fund of money that can be used for various unofficial and discretionary purposes. □ *How much is left in the slush fund?* □ *The slush fund is bankrupt.*

**slush up** *in.* to drink liquor; to get drunk. □ *They slushed up for a while and went out to look for some chicks.* □ *Don't you ever get tired of going out and slushing up with those guys?*

**smack 1.** AND **smak** *n.* heroin; a dose of heroin or opium. (Drugs. From *schmeck*.) □ *There's only one part of town where smack is sold, and you're in it.* □ *Max is the chief pusher of smack around here.* **2.** *n.* hell. □ *It's hotter than smack in here!* □ *Where in the smack are my skivvies?*

**smack (dab) in the middle** *mod.* exactly in the middle. (See *slap-dab*.) □ *I came in smack dab in the middle of the play.* □ *Not too big and not too small. Just smack in the middle.*

**smacker 1.** *n.* the face. (Compare to *kisser*.) □ *What a gorgeous smacker on that chick.* □ *She ought to give that ugly smacker back to the horse before it runs into something.* **2.** *n.* a dollar. (Underworld.) □ *You got a couple of smackers for the tollbooth?* □ *Don't waste your hard-earned smackers like that. Run on through.* **3.** *n.* a kiss. □ *He planted a smacker square on her lips. She kicked him in the shins for his trouble.* □ *Barlowe was greeted at the door by a lovely, cuddly chick in a nightie—eyes closed and lips parted for a better-than-average smacker. He really wished—just for a moment—that he hadn't rung the wrong doorbell.*

**smackhead** *n.* a heroin addict. (Drugs. See *smack*.) □ *She was a smackhead and had to sell herself to pay for her habit.* □ *After the first shoot-up, she was a smackhead for life.*

**small beer** *n.* nothing or next to nothing; an insignificant person. □ *The guy is just small beer. Pay him no mind.* □ *Small beer or not, he's my customer, and I will see that he is taken care of.*

**small change** *n.* an insignificant person. (Also a rude term of address.) □ *Look, small change, why don't you just move along?* □ *The guy you think is small change happens to own this building you seem to be guarding so well.*

**small fortune** *n.* a rather sizable amount of money. □ *This set of wheels cost me a small fortune.* □ *I've got a small fortune tied up in test equipment.*

**small fry** *n.* anything or anyone small or unimportant. (*Fry* are juvenile fish.) □ *Forget the small fry. I'm going after Mr. Big.* □ *Don't worry about the small fry. You have to please the fat-cats.*

**small potatoes** *n.* something or someone insignificant. □ *This contract is small potatoes, but it keeps us in business till we get into the real money.* □ *Small potatoes are better than no potatoes at all.*

**small-time** *mod.* insignificant; petty. □ *I was in a lot of small-time stuff at home, but never a Broadway hit before.* □ *Broadway is not small-time.* □ *Max was involved in a lot of small-time crime when he was 12.*

**smarmy** ['smɑrmi] *mod.* insincere and obsequious. □ *He's obnoxious, but brazen rather than smarmy.* □ *He's a smarmy creep.* □ *The guy is so smarmy, I can't stand him.*

**smart aleck** ['smɑrt 'ælək] *n.* someone who is saucy and acts cocky. □ *A smart aleck like you ought to have no trouble at all getting his face mashed in.* □ *Don't be such a smart aleck.*

**smart ass** *n.* someone who makes wisecracks and acts cocky. □ *Some smart ass came in here and asked for a sky hook.* □ *Don't be such a smart ass!*

**smart cookie** *n.* a clever person. □ *She's really a smart cookie if you give her a chance.* □ *Fred is a smart cookie and really ought to go far.*

**smart guy** *n.* a man who acts cocky; a *wise guy.* □ *All right, smart guy, see if you like this one.* □ *Some smart guy put fresh paint on this bench.*

**smart money** *n.* money belonging to smart or clever people. □ *Most of the smart money is going into utility stocks right now.* □ *Watch and see what the smart money is doing.*

**smart mouth** *n.* someone who makes wisecracks; a cocky person who speaks out of turn. □ *Don't be a smart mouth with me!* □ *Mr. Atkins is going to get a reputation as a smart mouth.*

**smarts** *n.* intelligence. □ *She's got plenty of smarts, but no spunk.* □ *I got the smarts to do the job. All I need is someone to trust me.*

**smarty** *n.* a cocky person. (Also a term of address.) □ *Well, if you're such a smarty, why aren't you rich?* □ *Okay, smarty, do it yourself.*

**smarty-pants** *n.* a cocky person; a *smart aleck.* □ *Look, smarty-pants, let's cut the clowning around.* □ *That smarty-pants is going to get herself into big trouble.*

**smash** *n.* wine. (Black. Because it is made from smashed grapes.) □ *I got a bottle of smash in my car.* □ *This is great smash for a buck twenty-five.*

**smashed** *mod.* alcohol or drug intoxicated. □ *He was so smashed he couldn't stand up.* □ *Molly can drink a lot without ever getting smashed.*

**smash hit** *n.* a play, movie, musical, etc., that is a big success. □ *Her first book was a smash hit. The second was a disaster.* □ *A smash hit doesn't always make people rich.*

**smashing** *mod.* excellent; really tremendous. □ *We had a smashing time at your little do.* □ *This whole meal has been smashing.*

**smear** *tr.* to defeat someone; to outscore someone. □ *We smeared them 50 to 20.* □ *They said they would smear us, but we smeared them.*

**smeared** *mod.* alcohol or drug intoxicated. □ *I feel sort of smeared. Maybe I should have drunk less.* □ *Bob and Jim found themselves smeared at the end of the day.*

**smeck** See *schmeck.*

**smecker** AND **smeaker, schmecker** ['smɛkɚ AND 'smikɚ, 'ʃmɛkɚ] *n.* a heroin addict. □ *Most of these schmeckers know where to get skag.* □ *A smeaker lives a hard life.*

**smell a rat** *tr.* to suspect that something is wrong. □ *He smelled a rat the minute he came into the room.* □ *Keep everything normal. I don't want her to smell a rat. She has never had a surprise party before.*

**smell blood** *tr.* to be ready for a fight; to be ready to attack; to be ready to act. (Like sharks that are sent into a frenzy by the smell of blood.) □ *Lefty was surrounded, and you could tell that the guys from the other gang smelled blood.* □ *The lawyer heard the crash and came running—smelling blood and bucks.*

**smeller** *n.* (one's) nose. □ *I think my smeller's gone bad because of my cold.* □ *He's got a fine strawberry on the end of his smeller.*

**smell fishy** *in.* to seem suspicious. (See also *fishy*.) □ *Barlowe squinted a bit. Something smells fishy here, he thought.* □ *Something about the deal smelled fishy.*

**smell it up** AND **smell the stuff** *tr.* to sniff or *snort* powdered drugs, usually cocaine. (Drugs.) □ *One of those guys shoots it; the other smells it up.* □ *You don't breathe it in; you just smell the stuff.*

**smell like a rose** *in.* to seem innocent. □ *I came out of the whole mess smelling like a rose, even though I caused all the trouble.* □ *Tiffany pretended that she was the only one who should smell like a rose, but I knew different.*

**smell the stuff** See *smell it up*.

**smell to (high) heaven** 1. *in.* to smell very bad. □ *This kitchen smells to high heaven. What besides garlic are you cooking?* □ *Where has this dog been? It smells to heaven.* 2. *in.* to give signals that cause suspicion. □ *This deal is messed up. It smells to high heaven.* □ *Something's wrong here. Somebody blabbed. This setup smells to high heaven.*

**smidgen** ['smɪdʒn̩] *n.* a tiny bit. □ *I just want a smidgen of cake. I'm on a diet.* □ *Oh, come on, more than a smidgen. Just a little?*

**smile** AND **smiler, smiley** *n.* a drink of liquor; liquor. □ *Come over and join me for a smiley.* □ *Here, have a smiler on me.*

**Smile when you say that.** *sent.* "Give some sort of a signal that you are only joking when you say something potentially offensive." □ *That's pretty rude. You'd better smile when you say that.* □ *I told him he'd better smile when he says that, or he's going to get in trouble.*

**smithereens** ['smɪðɚinz] *n.* many tiny pieces or splinters. □ *The mirror was broken to smithereens.* □ *I broke my crystal bell to smithereens.*

**smizz** [smɪz] *n.* heroin. (Drugs.) □ *It looks like it was the smizz that killed him.* □ *This smizz has something else in it. Probably cyanide.*

**smoke** 1. *n.* a tobacco cigarette; a pipe; a cigar. □ *I think I'll have a smoke now.* □ *You got a smoke I can owe you?* 2.

*n.* the act of smoking anything smokable, including drugs. □ *I need a smoke— of anything.* □ *I'm going to stop here for a smoke.* 3. *n.* marijuana; a marijuana cigarette. (Drugs.) □ *Some kid was passing out smokes in the middle of class.* □ *Some pusher got into the school and handed out smokes to the students.* 4. *in.* to smoke a marijuana cigarette; to smoke marijuana. (Drugs.) □ *He's smoking now because that's all he can get.* □ *Does that chick smoke?* 5. *n.* methyl alcohol; bad liquor; any liquor. □ *The old guy was drinking smoke, and it blinded him.* □ *They call it smoke because when you mix it with water and shake it, it's cloudy.* 6. *n.* exaggeration; deception. (See *blow smoke*.) □ *That's not a report. That's just smoke.* □ *If the smoke is too obvious, they'll just get suspicious.* 7. *tr.* to annihilate someone; to shoot someone. (Underworld.) □ *Rocko tried time and time again to smoke Barlowe, always without success.* □ *You want me to smoke you on the spot, or are you gonna cooperate?*

**smoke and mirrors** *n.* a strategy of deception and cover-up. □ *Her entire report was nothing but smoke and mirrors. Who could believe any of it?* □ *There is no plan. It's all just smoke and mirrors.*

**smoke eater** *n.* a fire fighter. □ *A couple of off-duty smoke eaters wandered around the store doing a little shopping.* □ *The smoke eaters took a long time getting there.*

**smoke-filled room** *n.* a room where a small group of people make important decisions. (Usually used in reference to political parties.) □ *The smoke-filled rooms are still producing the candidates for most offices, even as we approach the year 2000.* □ *The deal was cut in a smoke-filled room.*

**smoke-in** *n.* a young peoples' public gathering of the 1960s where marijuana was smoked in open defiance of the law. □ *My uncle was at a smoke-in. He says the reporters were getting kids to pose for shots.* □ *They say you could get a high just by being near a smoke-in.*

**smoke like a chimney** *in.* to smoke a great deal of tobacco or other smokable substances. □ *My uncle smoked like a chimney when he was living.* □ *Somebody who smokes like a chimney in a restaurant ought to be thrown out.*

**Smokey (the Bear)** *n.* a highway patrol officer; a police officer. (Citizens band radio. See also *bear, lady bear.*) □ *A Smokey was hiding behind a billboard!* □ *Smokey the bear is after you!*

**smokin'** ['smokən] *mod.* really hot; overpowering. □ *Those threads on that dude are really smokin'.* □ *If you wanna hear some smokin' vinyl, just stay tuned.*

**smoking gun** *n.* the indisputable sign of guilt. □ *Mr. South was left holding the smoking gun.* □ *The chief of staff decided that the Admiral should be found with the smoking gun.*

**smooch** [smutʃ] **1.** *in.* to kiss and *neck.* □ *Too much smooching in a movie ruins it for me.* □ *I like to smooch myself, but I don't enjoy watching somebody else.* **2.** *n.* a kiss. □ *I like a good smooch from my hubby.* □ *Hey, sweetie, how about a smooch?*

**smoothie** See the following entry.

**smooth operator** AND **smoothie** *n.* a clever and quiet person, especially in reference to romantic involvement. □ *Clare is an old smoothie till she thinks she's got everything the way she wants. Then you see the real Clare.* □ *Hank is a smooth operator. The girls just love him.*

**smurf** [sməf] **1.** *n.* someone who "cleans" ill-gotten money by buying cashier's checks at banks and shifting funds from place to place. (Underworld. From the name of a type of cartoon character. See also *greenwash, launder.*) □ *I think the guy at the first window is a smurf. He's in here twice week with $9,500 in cash each time.* □ *Did you get a good look at this alleged smurf?* **2.** *tr. & in.* to shift illicit money from place to place to conceal its origin. (Underworld.) □ *I smurf for a living. It doesn't pay much, but you meet some very interesting people.* □ *I smurfed a fortune for a famous drug kingpin and got 14 years up the river—with some very interesting people.*

**smurfbrain** ['sməfbren] *n.* a simpleminded person. (A smurf is an innocent little cartoon character.) □ *You can be such a smurfbrain!* □ *You're not a smurfbrain, I suppose?*

**smurfed** [sməft] *mod.* having to do with a bank that has been used to *launder* money. (See *smurf.*) □ *The teller came slowly into the office. "I think we were smurfed," she said.* □ *See that this dough is smurfed by Friday.*

**snafu** AND **SNAFU** [snæˈfu] *n.* an accident; a foul-up. (From *situation normal, all fouled (fucked) up.*) □ *Your being last is not just a snafu. It's a disaster.* □ *What a SNAFU! All the power went off when you turned on the coffee pot.*

**snag 1.** *n.* a difficulty. □ *There's a little snag in our plan.* □ *We ran into a little snag, I'm sorry to say.* **2.** *n.* an ugly (young) woman. □ *She's not a snag! She's lovely.* □ *Who's the snag your brother is running around with?* **3.** *tr.* to grab or steal something. □ *Somebody snagged the jacket I just bought.* □ *See if you can snag a couple of good seats while I get the popcorn.*

**snake** *in.* to scheme; to plot and plan. (Prisons.) □ *Lefty is always snaking.* □ *He spent a lot of time snaking about that job.*

**snakebite medicine** *n.* inferior whiskey; strong whiskey; homemade whiskey. □ *That old-time snakebite medicine is good for what ails you.* □ *Snakebite medicine is a tremendous protection against snakebites if you can get the snake to drink the stuff before it bites you.*

**snake eyes** *n.* the two in dice, one spot on each die. □ *Well, it's snake eyes again. That's all for me.* □ *The baby needs shoes, and all I get is snake eyes.*

**snake in the grass** *n.* a sneaky and despised person. □ *How could I ever have trusted that snake in the grass?* □ *John is such a snake in the grass.*

**snap 1.** *n.* a snapshot. □ *I got some good snaps of the fish you caught.* □ *Here's a snap of my brother.* **2.** *in.* to go crazy. □ *Suddenly Rocko snapped and began beating her savagely.* □ *His mind snapped, and he's never been right since.*

**3.** *n.* an easy thing to do. (Always with *a*.) □ *Nothing to it. It's a snap.* □ *The whole thing was a snap.*

**snap course** *n.* an easy course (in school). □ *I took a snap course in algebra and flunked it.* □ *I need at least one snap course a semester to pass.*

**Snap it up!** *exclam.* "Hurry up!" □ *We're late. Snap it up!* □ *Come on, snap it up! I don't have all day.*

**snap one's cookies** *tr.* to vomit; to regurgitate. □ *I think I'm gonna snap my cookies.* □ *Some jerk snapped his cookies on the sidewalk.*

**snap out of something** *in.* to recover from something. □ *I'll snap out of it in a while.* □ *It was an emotional blow, but he'll snap out of it in a while.*

**snapped (up) 1.** *mod.* alcohol intoxicated. □ *Let's go out and get ourselves good and snapped.* □ *Tod was snapped up by 8:30.* **2.** *mod.* arrested. □ *He got snapped up on a vag charge.* □ *The bacon busted the joint and snapped everybody in sight.*

**snapper** AND **snap** *n.* an ampoule of amyl nitrite, a stimulant vapor. (Drugs.) □ *Walter only wanted a couple of snappers, but Max made him buy a bindle of skag, too.* □ *"I only wanted a snap, but this guy wanted to make a big sale," lamented Walter.*

**snappers** *n.* the teeth. □ *I couldn't talk to you on the phone till I got my snappers in.* □ *You got a mouthful of fine-looking snappers.*

**snappy 1.** *mod.* quick. □ *You can get there if you're snappy.* □ *Make it snappy. I'm in a hurry.* **2.** *mod.* sharp-looking. □ *That's a real snappy outfit you're wearing.* □ *Who's driving that snappy car over there?* □ *That car's not snappy!*

**snap something up** AND **snap up something** *tr.* to buy up something. □ *People were snapping these things up like hot cakes.* □ *The customers snapped up all the humidifiers on the second day of the cold spell.* (More at *snapped (up)*.)

**snap to (attention)** *in.* to come to attention; to look alert, immediately. □ *When they realized what was happening, they began to snap to.* □ *Snap to attention when the sarge comes in!*

**Snap to it!** *exclam.* "Get busy!" □ *Come on, snap to it!* □ *Snap to it, we've got lots to do.*

**snatch 1.** *tr.* to kidnap someone. (Underworld.) □ *We're gonna snatch the kid when the baby sitter comes out to see what happened.* □ *The mob snatched Mrs. Davis and held her for ransom.* **2.** *n.* a kidnaping. (Underworld.) □ *The Bradley snatch had the detectives up all night for weeks.* □ *The snatch went off without a hitch.* **3.** *tr.* to grab something; to steal something. □ *Snatch me the paper there on the table as you walk by, would you please?* □ *Somebody snatched my car.* **4.** *n.* a theft. (Underworld.) □ *The snatch went off without a hitch except that the safe was empty.* □ *Are you the guys who pulled off that First National snatch?*

**snatched** *mod.* arrested. □ *Everybody in the crack house got snatched in the bust.* □ *Bruno was snatched for the umpteenth time yesterday.*

**snatcher** *n.* a police officer; a detective. (Underworld.) □ *One of the local snatchers came around to see if the door was locked.* □ *A snatcher hauled her away to the station.*

**snaved in** [snevd...] *mod.* drug intoxicated. □ *The poor guy was as snaved in as they come. Really fried.* □ *By midnight they were so snaved in they couldn't walk.*

**snazz** AND **shnazz** [snæz AND ʃnæz] *n.* class; glitter and excitement. □ *The curtain opened on a dazzling display of snazz and bright lights.* □ *There was lots of snazz and glitz, but no real substance.*

**snazz something up** AND **snazz up something** *tr.* to make something classy or exciting. □ *Come on, let's try to snazz this up.* □ *What can I do to snazz up my face?*

**snazzy** AND **shnazzy** ['snæzi AND 'ʃnæzi] *mod.* elegant; classy. □ *This is a snazzy place all right.* □ *This place is sure snazzy.* □ *Whose shnazzy new car is this?*

**sneak** *n.* a sneak preview of a movie. □ *There was a good sneak at the Granada last night.* □ *The sneak was better than the flick they had advertised.*

**sneaks** *n.* sneakers. □ *Are those sneaks new?* □ *She wore red sneaks and a mini.*

**sneaky** *mod.* unfair and sly. □ *That was a sneaky thing to do!* □ *Jerry is sneaky. Don't trust him.*

**snerf** [snɚf] *tr.* to sniff or *snort* cocaine. (Black. Drugs.) □ *You wanna go snerf a line or two?* □ *I don't snerf anything anymore.*

**snide remark** *n.* a caustic, haughty, or insulting remark. □ *You're really quick with the snide remark. Ever say anything nice to anybody?* □ *I did not appreciate that snide remark.*

**sniff 1.** *n.* a drink of liquor. (See *snort.*) □ *I'd like just a sniff of that Scotch.* □ *Sure, have a sniff of whatever you want.* **2.** *tr.* & *in.* to take cocaine nasally; to *snort* cocaine. (Drugs.) □ *I could hear somebody in there sniffing you-know-what.* □ *Max sniffs, shoots, and drops. He doesn't miss a trick.* **3.** *n.* cocaine; a nasal dose of cocaine. (Drugs.) □ *She needs a little sniff almost every hour.* □ *How about a sniff of your toot?*

**sniffer** AND **sniffler, snuffy** *n.* a drug user who habitually takes cocaine or heroin nasally. (Drugs.) □ *That judge goes pretty hard on sniffers—first time or not.* □ *Who's the sniffer with the spoon around his neck?*

**sniffles** AND **snuffles** *n.* the runny nose associated with crying, a cold, or an allergy. □ *I had the sniffles and couldn't go out.* □ *Marty stayed home because she had the snuffles.*

**snipe** [snaɪp] *n.* a cigarette or cigar butt. □ *Down on skid row, a snipe won't be on the sidewalk for 10 seconds.* □ *He saves a bunch of snipes until he gets enough for a real smoke.*

**snit** [snɪt] *n.* a state of resentment. □ *Don't work yourself into such a snit.* □ *She threw quite a snit.*

**snitch** [snɪtʃ] **1.** *n.* an informer. □ *Who needs a snitch? If he can't keep his mouth shut, he can beat it.* □ *The snitch went and told the teacher.* **2.** *in.* to inform (on someone). (Often with *on.*) □ *The cops were waiting for us. Who snitched?* □ *Molly snitched on Bruno, and he nearly snuffed her.* **3.** *tr.* to steal something. □ *Who snitched my cake?* □ *Why don't you snitch the salt from*

one *of the other tables?* **4.** *n.* a theft. (Underworld.) □ *The snitch went off without a hitch.* □ *How much loot did we get in the snitch?*

**snitcher** [ˈsnɪtʃɚ] *n.* an informer. (Originally underworld.) □ *There's nothing worse than a snitcher.* □ *Clare is a snitcher. Watch what you say around her.*

**snitzy** [ˈsnɪtsi] *mod.* classy; ritzy. □ *This is a pretty snitzy place—tablecloths and everything.* □ *Tiffany is too snitzy for me.*

**snoggered** See *schnockered*.

**snookered** [ˈsnʊkɚd] *mod.* cheated; deceived. □ *I was snookered skillfully and quickly. It was almost a pleasure.* □ *I got snookered at the service station.*

**snookums** [ˈsnʊkəmz OR ˈsnukəmz] *n.* a nickname for a child or a lover. (Also a term of address.) □ *Now, now, snookums, it's all right.* □ *Does my little snookums want to play?*

**snoop 1.** *in.* to prowl around looking for something. □ *What are you snooping around here for?* □ *Somebody was around here snooping and asking questions.* **2.** *n.* someone who prowls around looking for something. □ *Don't be a snoop.* □ *Fred is just a snoop. He went through my desk!*

**snoot** [snut] *n.* the nose. □ *You wanna get bopped on the snoot?* □ *That's one fine zit you got on your snoot.*

**snooted** [ˈsnudəd] *mod.* alcohol intoxicated. □ *He got himself thoroughly snooted.* □ *She's snooted and will never get home by herself.*

**snooty** *mod.* haughty; conceited. □ *Don't be so snooty!* □ *Tiffany can be snooty if she wants to, and she usually wants to.* □ *What a snooty waiter!*

**snoozamorooed** [ˈsnuzəməˈrud] *mod.* alcohol intoxicated. □ *Man, was she snoozamorooed!* □ *He went and got himself snoozamorooed before the wedding.*

**snooze** [snuz] **1.** *in.* to sleep; to take a little nap. □ *You can't snooze every afternoon!* □ *I snoozed a little bit before the party.* **2.** *n.* a little nap. □ *I need a little snooze.* □ *Why not go up and take a little snooze?* **3.** *n.* something that is boring enough to put someone to sleep.

□ *The play was a snooze. I left before it was over.* □ *It wasn't a lecture; it was a snooze.*

**snop** [snɑp] *n.* marijuana. (Drugs.) □ *You've got to quit smoking that snop.* □ *My mom found my snop and threw it out.*

**snork** [snork] *in.* to smoke marijuana or hashish. (Drugs.) □ *Let's get down to some serious snorking.* □ *They snorked until they could snork no more.*

**snort 1.** *tr. & in.* to sniff (insufflate) a powdered drug, now usually cocaine. (Drugs.) □ *Here, snort this.* □ *You're snorting every time I see you.* **2.** *n.* a nasal dose of a drug, usually cocaine. □ *Here, take a snort.* □ *I don't want a snort. I'm clean, and I'm going to stay that way.*

**snot\* 1.\*** *n.* nasal mucus. (Crude. Caution with *snot*.) □ *Oh, God, there's snot on your cheek.* □ *He sneezed and got snot all over the newspaper.* **2.\*** *n.* a nasty person; an obnoxious person. □ *You needn't be such a snot about it.* □ *What a snot!*

**snotnose(d) (kid)\*** *n.* a young child; a relatively young person. (Derogatory. Caution with *snot*.) □ *Some little snotnose swiped my wallet.* □ *A little snotnosed kid came in and asked for money.*

**snotrag\*** *n.* a handkerchief. (Crude. Caution with *snot*.) □ *I guess I should use my snotrag.* □ *Don't you carry a snotrag?*

**snotted\*** *mod.* alcohol intoxicated. (Caution with *snot*.) □ *He got himself totally snotted in two hours.* □ *He was too snotted to stand up.*

**snotty** AND **snottie** ['snɑdi] **1.\*** *mod.* nasty with nasal mucus. (Caution with *snot*.) □ *Keep your snotty old handkerchief to yourself.* □ *Don't leave your snotty tissues all over the house!* **2.\*** *mod.* *bitchy*; rude. (Caution with *snot*.) □ *What makes her so snotty?* □ *What a snotty waiter!* □ *Now, there's no reason to get snottie with me.*

**snow 1.** *n.* deceitful talk; deception. □ *No snow, okay? I want straight talk.* □ *All I heard for an hour was snow. Now, what's the truth?* **2.** *tr.* to attempt to deceive someone. □ *Don't try to snow me!* □ *You can try to snow me if you want, but I'm onto your tricks.* (More at *snowed.*) **3.** AND **snowball, snowflakes, snow stuff** *n.* a powdered or crystalline narcotic: morphine, heroin, or cocaine. (Now almost always the latter.) □ *Now, snow is almost old-fashioned.* □ *The price of snow has come down a lot as South America exports more of it.*

**snowball** *in.* to grow at an increasing rate. (As a snowball rolling down a hill might increase in size.) □ *The problem began to snowball, and we had to close down for a while.* □ *Offers to help with money and prayers began to snowball, and we had to get volunteers to help answer the phones.*

**snowball's chance in hell** *n.* a very poor chance. (Usually in the negative.) □ *She doesn't have a snowball's chance in hell of getting it done on time.* □ *I know I don't have a snowball's chance in hell, but I'll try anyway.*

**snow bunny 1.** *n.* someone learning to ski. □ *This little slope is for snow bunnies.* □ *Most of the snow bunnies come here to socialize.* **2.** *n.* a female skier. □ *Some cute little snow bunny came over and sat beside me.* □ *This place is swarming with snow bunnies who have never even seen a ski.*

**snowed** *mod.* deceived. □ *He was one snowed coach. He still doesn't know what really happened.* □ *We really had him snowed!*

**snow job** *n.* a systematic deception. □ *You can generally tell when a student is trying to do a snow job.* □ *This snow job you call an explanation just won't do.*

**snozzled** ['snɑzld] *mod.* alcohol intoxicated. □ *How can anybody be so snozzled on four beers?* □ *Those guys are really snozzled!*

**snozzle-wobbles** ['snɑzl'wɑblz] *n.* a hangover; the delirium tremens. □ *Freddy had the snozzle-wobbles this morning. He has no idea what caused it.* □ *They say that a big glass of milk is good for the snozzle-wobbles.*

**snuff 1.** *tr.* to kill someone. (Underworld.) □ *The mob tried to snuff Max, but he moved too fast for them.* □ *Somebody snuffed my cat!* **2.** *mod.* having to do with death or killing. □ *Those snuff acts ought to be outlawed.* □ *All this snuff stuff is for sickies.*

**snuff film** *n.* a film that vividly portrays death or killing. □ *Who would watch a snuff film anyway?* □ *Some of these snuff films have a loyal following of real sickies.*

**snuff it** *tr.* to die. □ *The cat leapt straight up in the air and snuffed it.* □ *I was so sick they thought I was going to snuff it.*

**snuffles** See *sniffles*.

**snuffy** ['snəfi] *mod.* alcohol intoxicated. □ *She was a little snuffy, but nothing debilitating.* □ *Who's the snuffy little guy in the corner booth?*

**soak 1.** *in.* to drink heavily; to get drunk. □ *The two old ladies put on their coats and went out to soak.* □ *They sat quietly soaking for an hour.* (More at *soaked.*) **2.** *n.* a drinking bout. □ *They sat there quietly enjoying their soak.* □ *Both guys declined to go out and stayed home and enjoyed a soak in front of the T.V.* **3.** *n.* a drunkard. □ *Some old soak lay moaning in the gutter.* □ *Hank is getting to be a real soak.* **4.** *tr.* to overcharge someone; to extort money from someone.* □ *They soaked me $20 for the parts, but at least it runs now.* □ *The cleaners soaked me for the cleaning job.*

**soaked** *mod.* alcohol intoxicated. □ *All the guys came home soaked.* □ *Frank was too soaked to drive home.*

**soaker** *n.* a drunkard; a tippler. □ *Uncle Charlie was a soaker, and the family never realized it.* □ *Give the old soaker a drink to shut him up.*

**soak one's face** *tr.* to drink heavily. □ *They're down at the tavern soaking their faces.* □ *Well, I guess I'll go soak my face for a while.*

**so-and-so** *n.* a euphemistic way of addressing someone with an insulting term of address. (This is usually euphemistic for "son of a bitch." However, it is also used for good friends, especially male to male, to show affection.) □ *This lousy so-and-so tried to take me for 400 bucks.* □ *Terry, you old so-and-so, how ya been?*

**soap 1.** *n.* a soap opera. □ *She won't schedule anything when her soap is on.* □ *Soaps are very popular on college campuses these days.* **2.** See the following entry.

**soaper** AND **soap** *n.* a methaqualone hypnotic-sedative tablet. (Drugs. From the drug's name, Sopor™.) □ *His all-time favorite is soapers.* □ *You got a soap I can drop?*

**S.O.B.** *n.* a "son of a bitch"; a despised person, usually a male. (Crude. Also a rude and provocative term of address. Never an acronym.) □ *Tell that S.O.B. to mind his own business.* □ *Look here, you S.O.B., get out!*

**so bad one can taste it** *mod.* very much, indeed. □ *I want that car so bad I can taste it.* □ *He had to get to Philadelphia so bad he could taste it.*

**sober as a judge** *mod.* as sober (free from alcohol) as it is possible to be. □ *Kelly—who was starched as could be—claimed to be sober as a judge.* □ *The judge was not always sober as a judge, but he could get through his court call.*

**sobersides** *n.* a very serious person; a grumpy old man. □ *Old sobersides can't manage to laugh at anything.* □ *Some sobersides came over and asked us to watch our language.*

**sober up** *in.* to recover from alcohol or drug intoxication. □ *Barlowe had one hour to sober up and get to the station.* □ *It took him a while to sober up.*

**sob sister** *n.* a weak woman who is prone to crying. □ *Mary is a sob sister. She wears you out fast.* □ *I had another sob sister in the office today. Went through half a box of tissues.*

**sob story** *n.* a sad story that is likely to draw tears. □ *I've heard nothing but sob stories today. Isn't anybody happy?* □ *She had quite a sob story, and I listened to the whole thing.*

**social disease** *n.* a venereal disease. □ *Many people find things like—ah—social diseases difficult to discuss in public.* □ *Others talk about private matters like social diseases till you're sick to death of it.*

**sock** *tr.* to punch someone or something. □ *Wally was so mad, he tried to sock Paul.* □ *He socked the door with his fist and began to howl with pain.*

**socked** *mod.* alcohol intoxicated. □ *I don't know what was in that punch, but I was socked.* □ *She got socked out of her mind.*

**socked in** *mod.* fogged in. □ *The airport was completely socked in.* □ *We couldn't take off because we were socked in.*

**sock hop** *n.* a dance party where everyone dances in stocking feet. (From the 1950s.) □ *My mother told us about a sock hop she went to. It doesn't sound like fun at all.* □ *Sock hops were popular in schools that had new and expensive floors in their gymnasiums.*

**Sock it to me!** *exclam.* "Come on, let me have it!" (Refers to bad news.) □ *Come on! I can take it. Sock it to me!* □ *Sock it to me, man. I'm ready.*

**sofa spud** ['sofə 'spəd] *n.* someone who spends a great deal of time sitting and watching television. (A play on *couch potato.*) □ *Sofa spuds have been getting a lot of attention in the newspapers.* □ *These sofa spuds usually watch sports on television.*

**soft 1.** *mod.* alcohol intoxicated. □ *After a few hours at the party, it appeared that most people were getting soft.* □ *Hard liquor makes people soft.* **2.** *mod.* having to do with non-addictive drugs. □ *The soft stuff just leads to hard stuff.* □ *This acid is not exactly soft.* □ *Soft drugs just take longer to turn you into a zombie.* **3.** *mod.* stupid. □ *The guy's soft in the head. He just can't think straight.* □ *She seems a little soft, but she's really bright.*

**soft berth** *n.* an easy situation; employment at an easy job. □ *Fred ended up with a real soft berth.* □ *I hope I can arrange a soft berth for my brother, who just applied for a job here.*

**soft core 1.** *mod.* referring to a mild type of pornography. □ *There are more and more soft core movies on cable television.* □ *This stuff I saw was just soft core.* □ *Now even the soft core stuff is getting harder to find at newsstands.* **2.** *n.* mild pornography. □ *They keep some soft core under the counter.* □ *The movie was a bit of soft core, but people still walked out.*

**soft-hearted** *mod.* tender-hearted; sympathetic. □ *She is too soft-hearted to handle this job.* □ *He is a soft-hearted guy who can help our cause a lot.*

**softie** AND **softy 1.** *n.* a gentle person; a very agreeable person. □ *He shouldn't give you much trouble. He's such a softie.* □ *The judge who tried the case was anything but a softie.* **2.** *n.* a weakling; a coward. □ *He's too much of a softie to fight back.* □ *Don't worry—he's a softie.*

**soft in the head** *mod.* stupid; witless. □ *George is just soft in the head. He'll never get away with his little plan.* □ *You're soft in the head if you think I'll go along with that.*

**soft money** *n.* easy money; money obtained without much effort. □ *Don't become dependent on soft money.* □ *There's not even very much soft money around now.*

**soft on someone or something 1.** *mod.* [with *someone*] romantically attracted to someone. □ *Fred is soft on Martha, I've heard.* □ *He looked like he was getting a little soft on Sally.* **2.** *mod.* too easy on someone or something. □ *The judge was viewed as being too soft on pushers.* □ *The cops are soft on speeders in this town.*

**soft pedal something** *tr.* to play something down; to de-emphasize something. (Refers to the soft pedal on the piano.) □ *Try to soft pedal the problems we have with the cooling system.* □ *I won't soft pedal anything. Everyone must know the truth.*

**soft sell** *n.* a polite attempt to sell something; a very gentle sales pitch. □ *Some people won't bother listening to a soft sell. You gotta let them know you believe in what you are selling.* □ *I tried the soft sell, but that didn't work.*

**soft soap 1.** *n.* flattering talk; sweet talk. □ *I don't mind a little soft soap. It won't affect what I do, though.* □ *Don't waste my time with soft soap. I know you don't mean it.* **2.** *tr.* to attempt to convince someone (of something) by gentle persuasion. □ *We couldn't soft soap her into it.* □ *Don't try to soft soap her. She's an old battle-ax.*

**soft touch 1.** *n.* a gentle way of handling someone or something. □ *Bess has a soft touch and can bring both sides together.* □ *Kelly lacks the kind of soft touch needed for this kind of negotia-*

*tion.* **2.** *n.* a gullible person; a likely victim of a scheme. □ *John is a soft touch for a few bucks.* □ *Here comes the perfect soft touch—a nerd with a gleam in his eye.*

**software rot** *n.* an imaginary disease that causes computer programs to go bad over a long period of time. (Computers.) □ *I guess software rot finally got to my program!* □ *What you have here is not a bug, but just plain old software rot.*

**soggy** ['sɑgi] *mod.* alcohol intoxicated. □ *The two old ladies got a little soggy, but nothing uncouth.* □ *They weren't sopping wet, just soggy.*

**So gross!** *exclam.* "How disgusting!" (California.) □ *He put chocolate syrup on his pie! So gross!* □ *He's barfing! So gross!*

**sold cober** ['sold 'kobɚ] *mod.* sober. (A spoonerism on *cold sober.* Similar to *jober as a sudge.*) □ *What do you mean drunk? Why, I'm sold cober.* □ *Ted is always as sold cober as the next guy.*

**soldier** **1.** *n.* a liquor bottle; an empty liquor bottle. (Compare to *dead soldier.*) □ *Toss your soldier into the garbage, please.* □ *There was a broken soldier on the floor and a cap on the table.* **2.** *n.* a whole tobacco cigarette. □ *The old man almost fell over trying to pick up the soldier from the sidewalk.* □ *"Look, Jed. A soldier. My lucky day!" said the old soak to his buddy.*

**sold on someone or something** *mod.* convinced of the value of someone or something. □ *I'm not sold yet on your idea.* □ *The crowd was sold on Gary. Nothing he had done or could do would cool their enthusiasm.*

**solid** **1.** *mod.* good; great; *cool.* □ *Man, this music is solid!* □ *Listen to that solid beat.* **2.** *mod.* consecutive; consecutively. □ *Larry ate for four solid days.* □ *Then he "had the flu" for three days solid.*

**so long** *interj.* "goodbye." □ *So long, see ya later.* □ *It's been good talking to you. So long.*

**somebody** *n.* an important person. (Often with *a.* Compare to *nobody.*) □ *Aren't you a somebody?* □ *If she was somebody, you wouldn't have to ask.*

**some pumpkins** AND **some punkins** *n.* someone great or special. □ *That chick is some punkins!* □ *Isn't this little gadget really some pumpkins?*

**something awful** *mod.* very much; extremely. □ *I wanted that car something awful.* □ *He threw a fit and screamed something awful.*

**something else** *n.* someone or something beyond compare. □ *Wow, she's something else. What a looker!* □ *That cake you baked is something else!*

**Something's got to give.** *sent.* "Things cannot go on like this."; "The stalemate will be broken." □ *The pressure on me is getting to be too much. Something's got to give.* □ *They keep arguing about money. Something's got to give.*

**So much for that.** *sent.* "That is all for that." (Also in other variants as in the examples.) □ *It's gone, ruined, broken—so much for that.* □ *He's finished as a friend of mine. So much for him!* □ *So much for you! Goodbye!*

**son of a bitch*** **1.*** *n.* a despicable person, usually a male. (Crude and provocative. Also a very insulting term of address. Abbreviated *S.O.B.*) □ *Tell that son of a bitch to get out of here, but fast.* □ *Look, you son of a bitch. I'm going to paste you one.* **2.** *n.* old buddy. (Used between close male companions.) □ *Why, you old son of a bitch! How are you?* □ *Where you been keeping yourself, you son of a bitch?* **3.*** *exclam.* "Dammit!" (Usually **Son of a bitch!**) □ *Son of a bitch! Look at that drip!* □ *Look at that place burn. Son of a bitch!* □ *Son of a bitch! I didn't even see that car pull out.*

**son of a gun** **1.** *n.* a despicable person, usually a male. (Euphemistic for *son of a bitch.*) □ *If that son of a gun thinks he can boss me around like that, he's got another think coming.* □ *Some son of a gun tried to sell me a used car with no engine.* **2.** *n.* old buddy. □ *You old son of a gun! How are you?* □ *I went to school with this son of a gun! He's my old buddy.* **3.** *exclam.* "I am totally surprised!"; "I am shocked!" (Usually **Son of gun!**) □ *Son of a gun! He did it!* □ *The thing just blew up! Son of a gun!*

**sop 1.** *n.* a drunkard; an alcoholic. □ *What does the old sop want, a handout?* □ *Give the old sop a buck and tell him to beat it.* **2.** *tr. & in.* to guzzle (liquor). □ *Let's go out and do some serious sopping.* □ *You've sopped booze long enough. Go home.*

**sope** See *soaper.*

**soph** [sɔf] *n.* a sophomore. □ *The sophs are holding a meeting to decide on a plan.* □ *He's just a soph, so he still might grow a little.*

**sopping (wet)** AND **soppy** *mod.* alcohol intoxicated. (Compare to *wet.*) □ *After about 6 beers, Ralph found himself a little soppy.* □ *He's soused—you know, sopping wet.*

**sore** *mod.* angry. □ *Come on! Don't get sore! I was only kidding.* □ *She is one sore old lady. You should give her teeth back.*

**sorehead 1.** *n.* a grumpy person. (Also a term of address.) □ *She's sort of a sorehead right now. Wait a day or two and then ask her.* □ *The boss is a sorehead, but she's all we have.* **2.** *n.* a poor loser. □ *Don't be a sorehead. You knew what you were getting into.* □ *Some sorehead at the track tried to punch a cashier.*

**sorry about that** AND **sorry 'bout that** *interj.* "sorry"; "whoops." (A gross understatement, said more as a self-deprecating joke than as an apology.) □ *You spill hot cocoa on my coat, and all you can say is "Sorry 'bout that?"* □ *When the passenger stepped on my toe, she said, "Sorry about that."*

**sorry-ass\*** *mod.* inadequate. (Caution with *ass.*) □ *This is a sorry-ass mess you've gotten us into.* □ *What a sorry-ass day this has been.*

**sosh** [sɔʃ] *n.* a (young female) socialite. □ *A young sosh in a beemer kept trying to get around me.* □ *Tiffany looks like a sosh, but she's just a working girl.*

**so-so 1.** *mod.* average; mediocre. □ *It was just so-so. Nothing to write home about.* □ *I don't need to pay $5.50 to see a so-so movie.* **2.** *mod.* tipsy; alcohol intoxicated. □ *They were so-so after a while—in front of the television with all that beer and stuff.* □ *He's so-so, but he can still stand up.*

**sossled** See *sozzled.*

**So's your old man!** *exclam.* "The same to you!"; "Drop dead!" (A catch phrase indicating basic disagreement or hostility.) □ *BILL: You're acting like an idiot! TOM: So's your old man!* □ *I don't know what you said, but so's your old man!*

**(soul) brother** *n.* a black person's male black friend. □ *Another brother took a fall last night.* □ *Terry's a soul brother, and I'll do anything for him.*

**soul kiss 1.** *n.* a kiss where the kissers' tongues interact; a *French kiss.* □ *He tried to give me a soul kiss, but I pulled away.* □ *Yes, a soul kiss sounds silly—till you try it with somebody you really like.* **2.** *in.* (for two people) to kiss with interacting tongues. □ *They were soul kissing and making noises.* □ *The creep has bad breath and wanted to soul kiss!*

**(soul) sister** *n.* a black person's female black friend. (See also *sister.*) □ *One of the soul sisters dropped by to talk.* □ *A sister called, but didn't leave her name.*

**sound off (about something) 1.** *in.* to complain about something; to gripe about something. □ *You are always sounding off about something that gripes your soul.* □ *Just sound off if you've got a beef.* **2.** *in.* to speak out of turn about something. □ *Who asked you to sound off about this?* □ *Don't just sound off without raising your hand.* **3.** *in.* to announce something. □ *Why did you have to go and sound off about the surprise party?* □ *Keep it a secret. Don't sound off about it.*

**sounds** *n.* music; records. □ *I got some new sounds. Ya wanna come over and listen?* □ *Man, these sounds are massive!*

**soup** *n.* nitroglycerin, a liquid explosive. (Underworld.) □ *Lefty was a master with the soup till he blew off his hand.* □ *Take care of that soup and treat it like eggs.*

**souped up** *mod.* made more powerful. □ *That souped up car of John's sure makes a lot of noise.* □ *Why do all cars driven by males under the age of twenty have to be souped up?*

**soup something up** AND **soup up something** *tr.* to increase the power of something. □ *He souped his car up so it will do nearly 120.* □ *If only I could soup up this computer to run just a little faster.* (More at *souped up*.)

**soup-strainer** *n.* a mustache. □ *Jerry had a big bushy soup-strainer that he was very proud of.* □ *It's not a soup-strainer—just a neat little black line.*

**soupy** ['supi] *mod.* alcohol intoxicated; drunk and vomiting. □ *Then he got sort of soupy and broke up the party.* □ *These young kids tend to get soupy rather than pass out.*

**sourpuss** ['sɑuɚpʊs] *n.* a grouchy or frowning person. (Compare to *pick-lepuss*.) □ *What a sourpuss! He makes King Kong look sweet.* □ *Don't be a sourpuss, babycakes.*

**souse** [sɑus] **1.** *in.* to drink excessively; to go on a drinking bout; to get drunk. (From a word meaning to soak or pickle.) □ *They sat sousing quietly in the corner.* □ *Let us retire from the table and souse in the parlor.* (More at *soused*.) **2.** *n.* a drinking bout. □ *The souse lasted longer than anyone would have thought.* □ *That was one fine souse we had.* **3.** *n.* a drunkard. □ *The best thing you can do for a souse like John is to take away his car keys.* □ *It's hard to live with a souse.*

**soused** *mod.* alcohol intoxicated. (See *souse*.) □ *We were really soused.* □ *All we need right now is a soused bus driver.*

**southpaw** *n.* a left-handed person. □ *Micky's a southpaw and writes sort of funny.* □ *My sister is a southpaw, but I'm not.*

**So what?** *interrog.* "What does it matter?"; "What is the point of what you are saying?" □ *So what if I'm too old? Did that stop Rudolph Drew from trying it?* □ *I'm a crook. So what?*

**sozzle** ['sɑzl] *in.* to drink to excess. □ *The guys are sozzling over at John's place.* □ *I wish you'd stop coming home every night and sozzling to oblivion.* (More at *sozzled, sozzler, sozzly*.)

**sozzled** AND **sossled, sozzly** ['sɑzld AND 'sɑzld, 'sɑzli] *mod.* alcohol intoxicated. □ *Man, was she sozzled.* □ *She was so sozzly she didn't even know her name, or my name, or anybody's name.*

**sozzler** ['sɑzlɚ] *n.* a drunkard. □ *The sozzler leaned against the tavern window. I thought he would break it.* □ *A sozzler staggered by—reeking of gin.*

**sozzly** See *sozzled*.

**space** See *space out*.

**space cadet 1.** *n.* a person who is always silly or giddy. □ *Mom, you are such a space cadet.* □ *Here comes a space cadet who looks like he has more money than he needs.* **2.** *n.* a person who is always high on drugs. □ *Max has been a space cadet since he was 12.* □ *The space cadets can usually be found sitting on a bench outside the principal's office.*

**spaced (out)** AND **spacy 1.** *mod.* silly; giddy. □ *I have such spaced out parents!* □ *He's so spaced!* □ *I love my spacy old dad.* **2.** AND **spaced-out** *mod.* drug intoxicated, especially from marijuana smoking. (Drugs.) □ *A lot of accidents are caused by spaced-out kids.* □ *They looked so spaced out—you can be sure of what they had been doing all afternoon.*

**space out 1.** *n.* a giddy person. (Usually **space-out**.) □ *Terry is becoming such a space-out!* □ *What a space out you are!* **2.** AND **space** *in.* to become giddy; to become disoriented. □ *She is spacing again. She doesn't even know where she is.* □ *I spaced out after the long climb.* **3.** *in.* to become euphoric under the influence of a drug. (Drugs.) □ *Whenever I see you, you are on your way somewhere to space out.* □ *Lots of people space out every day.* (More at *spaced (out)*.)

**space someone out** AND **space out someone** *tr.* to cause someone to become giddy. □ *The whole business just spaced me out.* □ *The spectacle spaced out the entire audience.*

**spacy** See *spaced (out)*.

**spaghetti western** *n.* a Western action film made in Italy. □ *I like the old spaghetti westerns. Lots of action.* □ *If you could read lips, you could see that the actors in the spaghetti western were speaking a number of different languages.*

**spanking new** See *(brand) spanking new*.

**spare tire 1.** *n.* a thickness in the waist; a roll of fat around one's waist. □ *I've got to get rid of this spare tire.* □ *The spare tire started when I was 26.* **2.** *n.* an unneeded person; an unproductive person. □ *Gary is a spare tire. Send him home.* □ *You spare tires over there! Get to work.*

**sparkler 1.** *n.* a drink of liquor. □ *The bartender slid a short sparkler down to Molly.* □ *She downed the sparkler and called for another.* **2.** *n.* an amphetamine capsule. (Drugs.) □ *She drops a couple of sparklers every morning to start off the day.* □ *Sparklers in the morning and stums at night!* **3.** *n.* a diamond; gemstones. □ *Look at the sparklers on that old dame.* □ *Janice has a new sparkler on her finger.*

**spastic** *mod.* overly responsive; out of control. □ *She can get so spastic when I come in late.* □ *Tell the spastic jerk to shut up.* □ *My dad's spastic when it comes to drugs.*

**spaz** [spæz] **1.** *n.* a fit or an attack; a strong reaction to a bad or funny situation. □ *My father had a spaz when he heard.* □ *Take it easy! Don't have a spaz.* **2.** *n.* a total jerk; someone who overreacts to something. (Not used for a congenitally spastic condition.) □ *Some spaz is in the other room screaming about a stolen car.* □ *Relax! You don't need to be a spaz.*

**spaz around** *in.* to waste time; to mess around. □ *You kids are always spazzing around. Why don't you get a job?* □ *We're just spazzing around. Leave us alone.*

**spaz out 1.** *in.* to overreact to something; to become overly excited about something. □ *I knew you would spaz out! It's not that bad!* □ *Come on, don't spaz out!* **2.** *n.* an emotional display. (Usually **spaz-out**.) □ *There's no need for a spaz-out!* □ *She threw a hell of a spaz-out.*

**speakeasy** *n.* a nightclub during prohibition. □ *My grandfather remembers speakeasies. They were pretty crude places.* □ *You weren't supposed to talk about speakeasies so their locations would remain a secret.*

**speak of the devil** *phr.* said when someone whose name has just been mentioned appears or is heard from. (A catch phrase.) □ *And speak of the devil, here's Ted now.* □ *Speak of the devil, that was Mary on the phone.*

**speak someone's language** *tr.* to say something that one agrees with or understands. □ *I gotcha. Now you're speaking my language.* □ *Mary speaks Fred's language. They get along fine.*

**specs** [spɛks] *n.* eyeglasses; spectacles. □ *I broke my specs.* □ *I need specs to find where I left my specs.*

**speed 1.** *n.* methamphetamine; amphetamine in general. (Drugs.) □ *Speed is a monstrous problem in some cities.* □ *Kids think that speed won't get them into trouble.* **2.** *in.* to use methamphetamine; to be high on methamphetamine or amphetamine. (Drugs.) □ *Kids who speed think it is a harmless blow-off.* □ *If they speed rather than study—speed is a problem.*

**speedball 1.** *n.* (in baseball) a fast (pitched) ball. □ *The pitcher threw a speedball, and I didn't even see it!* □ *Tom can hit almost any speedball that Mike can throw.* **2.** *n.* a mixture of two drugs injected together. (Drugs.) □ *Somebody gave him a speedball, and it killed him.* □ *I know it was a speedball, but what was in it?* **3.** *n.* methamphetamine. (Drugs.) □ *I need a speedball to get me through the day.* □ *My sister got hooked on speedballs.*

**speed demon 1.** *n.* a fast runner; a fast driver. □ *Tom is a speed demon. He qualified for the Olympics.* □ *Watch out, here comes another speed demon!* **2.** *n.* amphetamines; methamphetamine. (Drugs.) □ *These speed demons are of the highest Q.* □ *No more speed demons for me.* **3.** *n.* a habitual user of methamphetamine. (Drugs.) □ *A couple of speed demons mugged the old lady.* □ *When they are high, most speed demons don't know what they are doing.*

**speeder 1.** *n.* a speeding ticket. □ *The cop that gave Mary a speeder Wednesday gave her another one Friday.* □ *Actually, that's three speeders in one week counting the one she got Monday.* **2.** *n.* an amphetamine or methamphetamine tablet, capsule, or ampoule. (Drugs.

See *speed*.) □ *Somebody dropped some speeders on the floor of the car, and my father spazzed out.* □ *Fred took a speeder before the exam, but he went to sleep anyway.* **3.** AND **speedster** *n.* a user of amphetamines or methamphetamine; a person who is hyperactive from amphetamine use. (Drugs.) □ *That kid is really hyped up—must be a speeder.* □ *The speeders can seem crazy when they're on a run.*

**speed freak** AND **speedhead** *n.* a drug user who injects methamphetamine; an amphetamine user. (Drugs and general slang.) □ *Hank is a speed freak, but he's not on skag.* □ *Speed freaks, not heroin addicts, account for a high proportion of drug-related crime.*

**speed merchant** *n.* someone who does something fast: a runner, pitcher, swimmer, driver, etc. □ *Look at her go! What a speed merchant!* □ *What a pitch! That guy is a speed merchant for sure.*

**speedster** See *speeder*.

**spending money** *n.* cash, as opposed to money in the bank. □ *I'm a little short of spending money at the present. Could I borrow ten dollars?* □ *I don't have any spending money either.*

**spent 1.** *mod.* (of a person) burned out on drugs. (Drugs.) □ *She has been on pot since the seventh grade. Now, at the age of 14, she's totally spent.* □ *When a kid is spent at that age, there isn't much anybody can do.* **2.** *mod.* having to do with marijuana from which the active ingredient has been burned off. (Drugs.) □ *This stuff is spent. Where's some more?* □ *The bush in my pipe is spent, too.*

**spew** *in.* to empty one's stomach; to vomit. □ *After dinner, I suddenly had the urge to spew.* □ *Fred is up in the john spewing like mad.*

**spew one's guts (out) 1.** *tr.* to empty one's stomach; to vomit. □ *Fred is spewing his guts out because of that lousy fish you served.* □ *He's spewing his guts because he has the flu, cabbagehead.* **2.** *tr.* to tell everything that one knows; to confess everything. (Underworld.) □ *Lefty was sitting there in the cop-shop spewing his guts out about*

the bank job. □ *If he really is spewing his guts, the mob will cancel his Christmas.*

**spiff** *n.* extra money paid to a salesperson to aggressively sell certain merchandise. (See also *push money*.) □ *The manufacturer supplied a little spiff that even the store manager didn't know about.* □ *I got about $300 last month in spiff for selling some low-grade shoes.*

**spiffed out** *mod.* nicely dressed up; decked out. □ *I like to get all spiffed out every now and then.* □ *Wow, you look spiffed out! Where are you going?*

**spiffed up** *mod.* dressed up, brushed up, and polished up nicely. □ *See if you can get yourself a little spiffed up before we get to the front door. We wouldn't want the Wilmington-Thorpes to think you only have one suit.* □ *The house doesn't have to be too spiffed up for the Franklins. They are used to clutter.*

**spifflicated** AND **spificated** ['spɪfləkedəd AND 'spɪfəkedəd] *mod.* alcohol intoxicated. □ *Mrs. Wilmington-Thorpe drank champagne until she was nearly spifflicated.* □ *Being spificated on champagne is not as bad as it sounds.*

**spiffy** ['spɪfi] *mod.* excellent. □ *This is a real spiffy place you've got here, Sam.* □ *Come have a look at my spiffy new car.* □ *Doesn't look so spiffy to me.*

**spike 1.** *n.* a hypodermic needle; a hypodermic syringe and needle; a medicine dropper and a needle. (Drugs.) □ *The addict caught some strange disease from a dirty spike.* □ *What'll I do? I broke my spike.* **2.** *tr.* to add ether or alcohol to beer, originally by injecting it through the cork with a hypodermic needle; to add alcohol to a non-alcoholic drink. (From prohibition times.) □ *He found a man who would spike his beer for a small fee.* □ *He spiked the beer with ether, which is a dangerous thing to do.* (More at *spiked*.) **3.** *tr.* to puncture an idea. □ *I explained the plan, but the boss spiked it immediately.* □ *I hate to see my ideas spiked like that.*

**spiked 1.** *mod.* having to do with a drink with alcohol added; having to do with a punch with an alcoholic content. □ *Is the punch spiked? I want some without.* □ *We only have spiked punch.*

□ *Max's breakfast orange juice is usually spiked.* **2.** *mod.* having to do with a tobacco cigarette with dope added. (Drugs.) □ *Max offered me a spiked cigarette for no charge.* □ *How can you tell that a cigarette is spiked?* **3.** *mod.* alcohol or drug intoxicated. □ *I knew that Mrs. Wilmington-Thorpe was spiked when she belched like a real country thunder-boomer.* □ *Her old man was just as spiked, and he made worse noises.* **4.** *mod.* having to do with hair that stands up straight. □ *His spiked hair wouldn't look so bad if it wasn't orange.* □ *Both orange and spiked is too much.* □ *Is spiked hair a fad or the way of the future?*

**spill** *in.* to confess. (Underworld.) □ *The cops tried to get her to spill, but she just sat there.* □ *The gang was afraid she would spill, but she's a tough old thing.*

**spill one's guts** *tr.* to tell all; to confess. (Compare to *spew one's guts (out)*.) □ *I had to spill my guts about the broken window. I didn't want you to take the blame.* □ *Mary spilled her guts about the window. She confessed that she was trying to shield Bob.*

**spill the beans** AND **spill the works** *tr.* to give away a secret or a surprise. □ *There is a surprise party for Alice on Wednesday. Please don't spill the beans.* □ *Paul spilled the beans about Alice's party.*

**spill the works** See the previous entry.

**spinach** *n.* money. (Because it is green. See *cabbage, lettuce*.) □ *How much spinach you got on you?* □ *Look at this! One hundred dollars in good old American spinach!*

**spin one's wheels** *tr.* to waste time; to remain in a neutral position, neither advancing nor falling back. □ *I'm just spinning my wheels in this job. I need more training to get ahead.* □ *The whole project was just spinning its wheels until spring.*

**spit and polish** *n.* orderliness; ceremonial precision and orderliness. □ *I like spit and polish. It comes from being in the military.* □ *There is no such thing as too much spit and polish.*

**Spit it out!** *exclam.* "Say it!" □ *Come on, don't be shy! Spit it out!* □ *Say what you have to say and leave. Hurry up! Spit it out!*

**spizzerinktum** [spɪzɚˈrɪŋktəm] *n.* energy; vitality. □ *The kid's got spizzerinktum! I like that.* □ *Put more spizzerinktum into it!*

**splash 1.** *n.* liquor. □ *How about a little more splash in your glass?* □ *No splash for me, thanks.* **2.** *n.* amphetamines; methamphetamine. (Drugs.) □ *The stuff that comes in little glass tubes is called splash. They inject it for a high.* □ *I hear you've been shooting splash.*

**spleef** See the following entry.

**spliff** AND **shpleef, spleef, splim** [splɪf AND ʃplif, splif, splɪm] *n.* marijuana; a marijuana cigarette; hashish. (Originally Jamaican. See also *English spliff, sploff*.) □ *They consume an enormous amount of spliff and try to sell it to the tourists.* □ *It's really high-quality splim.*

**splint** *n.* a marijuana cigarette. (Drugs.) □ *He slipped a splint out of his pocket and lit up.* □ *You got a splint I can owe you?*

**split** *in.* to leave. □ *Look at the clock. Time to split.* □ *Let's split. We're late.*

**split a gut 1.** *tr.* to laugh very hard. □ *He laughed until he nearly split a gut.* □ *The audience split a gut laughing.* **2.** *tr.* to work very hard. □ *I split a gut to get this place fixed up in a week.* □ *Don't split a gut for me. I love things that are falling apart.*

**splitting headache** *n.* a severe headache, as if one's head were splitting open. □ *I'm sorry, I can't. I have a splitting headache. Maybe Fred will play bridge with you.* □ *This splitting headache has been going on for hours.*

**split up** [splɪt ˈəp] **1.** *in.* to separate. □ *The two split up and went their separate ways.* □ *They couldn't get along, so they split up.* **2.** [ˈsplɪtəp] *n.* an act of separating or breaking up. (Usually **split-up**.) □ *Everyone was mentally prepared for the company's split-up.* □ *The split-up caused neither surprise nor grief.*

**sploff** [splɑf] *n.* cannabis; a marijuana cigarette; a puff of a marijuana cigarette. (Drugs. See also *spliff*.) □ *My mother found all the seeds I save from* *the sploff, and she planted them.* □ *"Lady," said the narc, "Do you know you are growing sploff in this garden?"*

**splurge** *in.* to indulge oneself with much spending or eating. □ *I have to splurge every now and then. I deserve it.* □ *I splurge every weekend.*

**spoil** *tr.* to kill someone. □ *It was Bruno's job to make sure that nobody got close enough to Mr. Big to spoil him.* □ *Rocko was determined to spoil Barlowe.*

**spoiled rotten** *mod.* indulged in; greatly spoiled. □ *This kid is spoiled rotten!* □ *I was spoiled rotten when I was a child, so I'm used to this kind of wasteful luxury.*

**spoiling for a fight** *phr.* argumentative; asking for a fight. □ *They were just spoiling for a fight, and they went outside to settle the matter.* □ *She was grouchy, and you could tell she had been spoiling for a fight all day.*

**spondulicks** AND **spondulix, spondulics** [spɑn'dulɪks] *n.* money. □ *How much spondulicks will this set me back?* □ *I don't have enough spondulix to swing the deal.*

**sponge** AND **spunge** **1.** *in.* to drink heavily. □ *She was sponging like there was no tomorrow.* □ *What can you do with a woman who sits and spunges all day long?* **2.** *n.* a drunkard; a tippler. (See also *blotter.*) □ *She was a spunge, and she wasn't going to do anything about it.* □ *Is there treatment for spunges like her?* **3.** *n.* a parasitic person. □ *Don't be a sponge. Get your own!* □ *Here comes that sponge, Wally. Hide your wallet, pencils, glasses, and any clothes in his size.*

**spoof** [spuf] **1.** *n.* a parody. □ *The first act was a spoof of a Congressional investigation.* □ *The second act was a spoof of the first act.* **2.** *tr.* to make a parody of someone or something. □ *The comedian spoofed the executive branch by sitting in a big chair and going to sleep.* □ *I like to spoof myself. It helps break the ice at parties.*

**spook** **1.** *tr.* to frighten or startle someone or something. □ *Something I did spooked the teller, and she set off the silent alarm.* □ *Don't spook the cattle. They'll stampede.* (More at *spooked.*)

**2.** *n.* a spy; a C.I.A. (U.S. Central Intelligence Agency) agent. □ *I just learned that my uncle had been a spook for years.* □ *Fred is training to be a spook, but don't tell anybody.*

**spooked** *mod.* frightened or startled. □ *The guy looked sort of spooked. He was sweating and panting like someone had scared him to death.* □ *The horse was spooked and rolled its eyes and snorted a lot.*

**spook factory** *n.* the C.I.A. (U.S. Central Intelligence Agency) in Washington, D.C., where spies are said to be trained. □ *Tom got a job in the spook factory.* □ *Does the spook factory pay very well?*

**spoon** **1.** *in.* to neck and pet. □ *They like to go out and spoon under the stars.* □ *Do you remember spooning with me years ago?* **2.** See *cokespoon.*

**sport** *n.* friend; chum. (A term of address.) □ *Well, sport, looks like we have a little problem here.* □ *Hey, sport, what's new?*

**spot** **1.** *n.* a small drink of liquor. □ *I'll just have a spot, please.* □ *Just a spot for me, too.* **2.** *n.* a nightclub; a night spot. □ *It was a nice little spot, with a combo and a canary.* □ *We went to a spot with a jukebox for entertainment.* **3.** See *spot someone (something).*

**spot market** *n.* the open market where deals are made on the spot. (Financial markets.) □ *Oil reached nearly 25 dollars a barrel on the spot market.* □ *Gold prices on the spot market finally reached $600 per ounce and then promptly collapsed.*

**spot of lunch** *n.* a small amount of lunch. □ *How about a spot of lunch?* □ *I had a spot of lunch at my desk, thanks.*

**spot someone (something)** **1.** *tr.* to give an advantage to someone. □ *I'll spot you 20 points.* □ *No need to spot me. I'm the greatest!* **2.** *tr.* to lend someone something. □ *Can you spot me a few bucks?* □ *I can spot you a whole hundred!*

**sprain one's ankle** *tr.* to become pregnant. □ *She has, ah, sprained her ankle.* □ *From the looks of her, she must have sprained her ankle some months ago.*

**spring chicken** *n.* a young and naive person, especially a young woman. (Usually in the negative.) □ *Well, I may not be a spring chicken, but I got some spizzerinktum left.* □ *I am a spring chicken, but I lie about my age to get served in bars.*

**spring for something** AND **bounce for something** *in.* to treat (someone) by buying something. (See also *pop for something.*) □ *I'm bouncing for pizza. Any takers?* □ *Ralph sprang for drinks, and we all had a great time.*

**spring someone** *tr.* to get someone out of jail, on bond or permanently. □ *My wife came down and sprung me; otherwise, I'd still be in the slammer.* □ *The guy's mouthpiece tried to spring him, but the D.A. nixed it.*

**sprout** *n.* a child. □ *Where are the sprouts?* □ *A little sprout came up and tried to sell me a ticket to a game.*

**sprout wings** 1. *tr.* to die and become an angel. □ *I'm not ready to sprout wings yet. I've got a few more years.* □ *You wanna sprout wings, you just keep talking like that.* 2. *tr.* to be so good as to become an angel. □ *The kid is not about to sprout wings, but he probably won't get into jail again.* □ *He was so good and helpful, I thought he would sprout wings.*

**spud** [spəd] 1. *n.* a potato. □ *I'd like a few more spuds.* □ *Mashed spuds are the best of all.* 2. *n.* vodka, presumed to be made from potatoes. □ *How about a glass of spud?* □ *She keeps a big jug of spud in the reefer and drinks it like water.* 3. *n.* a vodka drunkard. □ *That silly spud thinks we can't smell what's on her breath.* □ *The old spud on the third floor fell down a flight or two and broke his hip.*

**spunge** See *sponge.*

**spunk** [spəŋk] *n.* courage. □ *Show some spunk. Get in there and stand up for your rights.* □ *I have the spunk, but I don't have the brains.*

**spunky** ['spəŋki] *mod.* gutsy; courageous. □ *I like a spunky girl—one who can really dance.* □ *The guy's a shrimp, but he's spunky.*

**square** 1. *mod.* old-fashioned; law-abiding; stodgy. □ *Man, you are really square.* □ *I come from a very square family.* 2. *n.* a person who behaves properly. □ *You are a square if I ever saw one.* □ *Ask that square what her favorite kind of music is.* 3. AND **square joint** *n.* a tobacco cigarette, compared to a marijuana cigarette. (Black.) □ *You got a square on you?* □ *I'll take a reefer. I've heard that squares will give you cancer.* 4. *tr.* to settle or to make something right. □ *Let's talk about squaring this matter.* □ *Will twenty bucks square the matter?* 5. See *square (meal).*

**squared away** *mod.* straightened out. □ *I'm not really squared away on this stuff, but I'm beginning to see the light.* □ *We'll get everything squared away in a few days.*

**squared up** *mod.* no longer taking drugs. (Drugs.) □ *Walter is squared up now and spends a lot of time trying to help others.* □ *Max'll never get himself squared up.*

**square John** AND **square apple** *n.* someone who obeys the rules; a *square.* □ *Fred is a square John. There's no point in worrying about him.* □ *All those square apples can take care of themselves.*

**square joint** *n.* a tobacco cigarette. (Drugs.) □ *Max doctored a square joint for Walter.* □ *Nothing but square joints for me anymore.*

**square (meal)** *n.* a good and nutritious meal. (Always with quantifier when *square* is used without *meal.*) □ *I need three squares a day—at least.* □ *The old soak looks like he could use a square meal.*

**square off** *in.* to prepare to fight; to prepare to argue or compete. □ *They were squaring off, so I asked them if they'd like to step outside.* □ *Let's square off and debate this thing properly.*

**square peg (in a round hole)** *n.* someone who does not fit in. □ *I'm a square peg in a round hole. Maybe I am meant to be eccentric.* □ *Kelly seems to be a square peg. What'll we do with him?*

**square shooter** *n.* an honest person. (See also *straight shooter.*) □ *I trust Sam. He's a square shooter.* □ *He wouldn't do anything shabby. He's a square shooter.*

**square with someone** *in.* to become honest with someone. □ *I want you to square with me. Tell the truth this time.* □ *Okay, I'll square with you. Terry did it.*

**squat 1.** *in.* to sit (down). □ *Come on in and squat for a while.* □ *Squat over here by the fire.* **2.** *n.* nothing. (See *diddly-squat.*) □ *I worked all day on this, and she didn't pay me squat.* □ *I earn just a little more than squat, but I am very pleased with my life.*

**squawk 1.** *in.* to complain. □ *Come on, don't squawk all the time!* □ *Some people squawk because they don't have anything else to do.* **2.** *n.* a complaint. □ *Here's another squawk from the lady on the third floor.* □ *I have a list of squawks from the mayor's office.* **3.** *tr. & in.* to reveal or *blab* something. □ *Watch Molly. She may decide to squawk.* □ *She squawked the whole business to the fuzz.*

**squawk box** *n.* a public address system; a loudspeaker, especially if installed in a box or other housing. □ *A raspy voice came over the squawk box announcing the arrival of what we had been waiting for.* □ *The squawk box was strangely quiet through the night.*

**squeaky clean** *mod.* very clean. (Like a clean glass that squeaks when one rubs a finger on it.) □ *I got this floor squeaky clean. Don't spill anything on it.* □ *Somebody tracked mud on my squeaky clean floor!*

**squeal** *in.* to inform (someone about something). □ *Who squealed to the cops?* □ *Molly squealed on us.*

**squealer 1.** *n.* an informer. (Underworld.) □ *Molly is a terrible squealer.* □ *Some squealer let the cops know what was going to happen.* **2.** *n.* a pig; a piglet. □ *They sent their squealers to market at just the right time.* □ *I was horrified to learn that bacon comes from squealers.*

**squeeze 1.** *n.* liquor. (Black. See *grape(s).*) □ *Let's stop on the way and get some squeeze.* □ *Freddie, where is your squeeze?* **2.** *tr.* to put pressure on someone. □ *The mob began to squeeze Max for money.* □ *The tight schedule squeezed us all.* **3.** *n.* a tight situation; a situation

where pressure is felt. □ *I'm in sort of a squeeze. Can you wait a month?* □ *When the squeeze is over, we'll be able to get squared away.* **4.** *n.* one's lover. (Black. See *main squeeze.*) □ *I'll see if my squeeze wants to go.* □ *Get your squeeze, and let's go sink a few.*

**(squeeze-)box** *n.* an accordion. (Compare to *groan box.*) □ *My brother plays the squeeze-box—not very well, but who can tell?* □ *The band consisted of drums, clarinet, and a box. A real winner.*

**squeeze play** *n.* a special play in baseball where there is a runner on third base and the batter bunts. With an early start the runner may reach home plate. □ *They pulled off that squeeze play like the professionals they are.* □ *The crowd roared as the squeeze play paid off.*

**squib** [skwɪb] *n.* a notice; a small advertisement. □ *There was a squib in the paper about your project.* □ *I read a squib about that yesterday.*

**squid** [skwɪd] *n.* an earnest student. (Collegiate.) □ *This whole campus is populated by squids and nerds.* □ *I'm no squid. I went out on a date last month.*

**squiff** [skwɪf] *n.* a drunkard. (See also *on the squiff.*) □ *It's no fun living with a squiff.* □ *Is there anything that can be done for a confirmed squiff?*

**squiffed** AND **squiffy** [skwɪft AND 'skwɪfi] *mod.* alcohol intoxicated. □ *She was a little squiffed, but still entertaining.* □ *The hostess was so squiffed she could hardly stand.*

**squiff out** *in.* to collapse from drink. □ *Hank squiffed out at midnight, right on the dot.* □ *She kept from squiffing out because she didn't trust her date.*

**squiffy** See *squiffed.*

**squiggle** ['skwɪgl] *n.* a wiggly mark. □ *What does this squiggle mean?* □ *That squiggle is my signature.*

**squirrel 1.** *n.* a strange or eccentric person. □ *Martin can be such a squirrel.* □ *Freddie is a squirrel, but I love him.* **2.** *n.* a car engine's horsepower. □ *What kind of squirrels you got under the hood?* □ *I got 440 squirrels and a gaggle of carburetors.*

**squirrel-food** *n.* a *nut;* a loony person. □ *The driver of the car—squirrel-food,* *for sure—just sat there smiling.* □ *Some squirrel-food came over and asked for a sky hook.*

**squirrel out of something** *in.* to wiggle out of something; to manage to extricate oneself from a situation one does not wish to be in. □ *He will do anything he can to squirrel out of going to the dance.* □ *Don't try to squirrel out of it. Go through with it.*

**squirrel something away** AND **squirrel away something** *tr.* to hide something in reserve. □ *She had squirreled away quite a fortune.* □ *Here is some food. I squirreled it away in my suitcase.*

**squirrely** *mod.* loony. □ *Who wrote this squirrely play?* □ *Good old squirrely Tom! Isn't he a wonder?* □ *No, he's just squirrely.*

**squirt** 1. *n.* a small person; a young child, especially a young boy. (Also a term of address.) □ *Hey, squirt, come over here.* □ *He sure is a cute little squirt.* 2. *n.* beer or champagne. □ *I like squirt and things. It tickles my nose.* □ *How about a nice bubbly glass of squirt?*

**squirts** *n.* a case of diarrhea. (Always with *the.*) □ *He's got the squirts and can't go out.* □ *What do you take for the squirts?*

**squooshy** ['skwuʃi AND 'skwuʃi] *mod.* soft; squishy. □ *I can't stand squooshy food!* □ *Mush is supposed to be squooshy.* □ *I like to walk barefooted in squooshy mud.*

**stacked** *mod.* having to do with a person with a sexually attractive body, usually a female. □ *Wow, is she ever stacked!* □ *I like to see stacked dames like that starting to do business in this place.*

**stack the deck** *tr.* to arrange things secretly for a desired outcome. (From card playing where a cheater may arrange the order of the cards that are to be dealt to the players.) □ *The president stacked the deck so I would be appointed head of the finance committee.* □ *It's not fair when somebody stacks the deck.*

**stag** 1. *mod.* having to do with someone going to a party without a date. (Originally said of a male.) □ *He decided to ignore her and go stag.* □ *A bunch of the*

guys got together and went stag to the dance. 2. *mod.* having to do with a gathering for men only. □ *The party is stag, so Tom and I are going together.* □ *Stag parties cease to be fun after a while.*

**staggers** 1. *n.* liquor. □ *He couldn't seem to get enough staggers.* □ *She poured herself a huge glass of staggers and mumbled something about cough medicine.* 2. *n.* drunkenness; the delirium tremens. (Always with *the.*) □ *He seems to have a little touch of the staggers.* □ *Larry's laid up with the staggers again.*

**stag line** *n.* a line of dateless men at a dance. □ *She looked over the stag line and saw nobody she knew.* □ *The guys in the stag line looked so forlorn. She suddenly wanted to do something to make them all happy.*

**stag-party** *n.* a party for men only. (Thought to be *raunchy.*) □ *Sally was hired to dance at a stag-party.* □ *They hired a stripper for the stag-party—you know, the kind that jumps out of a cake.*

**stakeout** 1. *n.* a person who is positioned to observe someone or something. (See *stake someone or something out.*) □ *The stakeout stuck out like a sore thumb—standing there under the streetlight reading a paper.* □ *The stakeout was one of Barlowe's best operatives.* 2. *n.* a (police) assignment where someone is positioned to observe someone or something. □ *The two top cops were out on a stakeout.* □ *The stakeout at the warehouse backfired. They only found cats.*

**stake someone or something out** AND **stake out someone or something** 1. *tr.* to position a person so that someone or something can be observed or followed. □ *The cops staked out the car and made the arrest.* □ *Barlowe staked out the apartment building and watched patiently for an hour.* 2. *tr.* to position a person to observe someone or something. □ *He staked his best operative out in front of the building.* □ *We staked out two men to keep watch.*

**stake someone to something** 1. *tr.* to lend or give someone money to buy something. □ *Can you stake me to a* *decent meal?* □ *Stake the man to a meal and a flop, and he'll tell us what we want to know.* **2.** *tr.* to treat someone to something. □ *Can I stake you to a drink to celebrate?* □ *Let me stake you to a big ice cream cone.*

**stale drunk** *n.* a long-standing and frequently renewed drunken state. □ *The guy's on a stale drunk. He is a mess.* □ *Are you on a stale drunk again, or is this the same one?*

**stallion** *n.* a tall, good-looking woman. (Black.) □ *Dana is really a stallion!* □ *Who is the stallion with that dude?*

**stamping ground** *n.* one's favorite or customary location. □ *Adamsville is my old stamping ground. I was born there, you know.* □ *I like to go back and look at my old stamping ground every now and then.*

**standee** *n.* someone who must stand (at some event). □ *There were about 40 standees in addition to the full house.* □ *Can I get in as a standee, or do I have to wait for the next showing?*

**stand-in** *n.* a substitute; a temporary replacement. □ *I was a stand-in for the lead soprano, who had the sniffles.* □ *The audience booed the stand-in. They had paid to hear a star.*

**standoffish** [stænd'ɔfɪʃ] *mod.* aloof. □ *Bob is sort of standoffish until he gets to know you.* □ *Don't be so standoffish! Join in the fun.* □ *I am a standoffish guy.*

**stand-out** *n.* an extraordinary thing or person. □ *Bob is a real stand-out in our bowling league.* □ *This car is a real stand-out as a speed machine.*

**stand pat (on something)** *in.* to stick firmly to one's position or opinions. □ *I am going to stand pat on this issue.* □ *I thought you would stand pat in the absence of new information.*

**stand someone up** AND **stand up someone** *tr.* to break a date by not showing up. □ *She stood him up, and he was really angry.* □ *He stood up his date while he played basketball with the guys.*

**stand tall** *in.* to be brave and proud. □ *I can still stand tall. I'm innocent.* □ *Our athletes stand tall in the knowledge that they did their best.*

**stand there with one's bare face hanging out** *phr.* to stand someplace looking helpless and stupid. □ *Say something. Don't just stand there with your bare face hanging out.* □ *She just stood there with her bare face hanging out while they took away everything she owned.*

**stanza** ['stænzə] *n.* an inning in baseball or some other division of a ball game. □ *He's doing better than he was in the last stanza.* □ *Jerry Clay is pitching again in this stanza.*

**starched** AND **starchy** *mod.* alcohol intoxicated. (Compare to *stiff.*) □ *Man, was he starched!* □ *No, he wasn't quite stiff, but he was starched.*

**stash 1.** *n.* a mustache. □ *Jerry has this enormous stash that he keeps waxed and trimmed.* □ *I cut my stash off because it was too much trouble to remember not to cut it off.* **2.** *tr.* to hide something (somewhere). □ *Stash this under the chair until I can think of a place to put it.* □ *Fred stashed his coat in a heap in the corner.* **3.** *n.* a concealed supply of drugs, especially marijuana; drugs and equipment to use them stored in a secret place. (Drugs.) □ *Max's stash was never located by the fuzz.* □ *My stash is down to nothing.*

**stash bag** AND **stash box** *n.* a container for marijuana and smoking supplies. (Drugs.) □ *He pulled out a stash bag full of goodies and smiled a lurid smile.* □ *Jimmy found somebody's stash box on the curb and took it to his mother.*

**stat** [stæt] *n.* a thermostat. (See also *stats.*) □ *Who turned down the stat?* □ *I'm afraid you need a new stat.*

**static** *n.* complaints. □ *I don't expect any static because of the noise. I warned the neighbors about the party.* □ *Is this guy giving you any static?*

**stats** [stæts] *n.* statistics. □ *They're working out the stats now.* □ *The stats are expected to show that the trade balance is growing steadily worse.*

**stay loose** See *hang loose.*

**Stay tuned. 1.** *sent.* "Stay tuned in to this radio or television station." (A formula uttered before a commercial.) □ *I'll be right back after these announcements. Stay tuned.* □ *Stay tuned. Back in a minute.* **2.** *sent.* "Continue to pay steady

attention to this matter."; "Watch for further developments." (From sense 1.) □ *Things are developing rapidly in this area. Stay tuned.* □ *Stay tuned. Pending legislation could change all this.*

**steady** *n.* a boyfriend or girlfriend. □ *She showed up with Tom, her steady for the last few months.* □ *My steady is laid up with a cold. I'll come alone.*

**steal** *n.* a bargain. (Always with *a.*) □ *At this price, it's a steal.* □ *This car wasn't exactly a steal at this price, but it's still a good value.*

**steam** **1.** *tr.* to anger someone. □ *She steamed him by being 2 hours late.* □ *The prof steamed the class with the long assignment.* **2.** *in.* to be angry. □ *She was absolutely steaming.* □ *They steamed for a while and then did as they were told.*

**steamboat** **1.** AND **steamroller** *n.* a toilet paper roll tube used as a chamber that cools marijuana smoke and mixes it with air. (Drugs. See also *slow boat.*) □ *There's an old steamroller in my stash you can use.* □ *Do you know how to use a steamboat?* **2.** *in.* to use a toilet paper roll tube in the smoking of marijuana. (Drugs.) □ *We tried to steamboat, but it didn't do anything for us.* □ *Bruno was steamboating when the bust came down.*

**steamed (up)** **1.** *mod.* angry. □ *Now, now, don't get so steamed up!* □ *She is really massively steamed.* **2.** *mod.* alcohol intoxicated and fighting. □ *He was really steamed—and could hardly stand up.* □ *By midnight, Larry was too steamed to drive home, and he had to spend the night.*

**steamroller** **1.** See *steamboat.* **2.** *tr.* to force something to be approved; to force something to happen. □ *He plans to steamroller this bill through Congress, but it just won't work.* □ *When you can't steamroller something, try soft soap.*

**steam someone's beam** *tr.* to make someone angry. □ *Being stood up really steams my beam!* □ *Come on, don't steam your beam. Remember how hard times are now.*

**steam someone up** AND **steam up someone** **1.** *tr.* to get someone excited. □

*Steam yourselves up and get in there and win this game!* □ *The coach can really steam up those guys.* **2.** *tr.* to get someone angry. □ *This whole mess steamed me up but good.* □ *The long critical statement simply steamed up the opposition.* (More at *steamed (up).*)

**steam up** *in.* to drink heavily; to get drunk. □ *Fred and Mike were steaming up in the back room.* □ *Let's go down to the tavern and steam up, okay?* (More at *steamed (up).*)

**steamy** *mod.* lewd; sensuous; passionate. □ *They cut a couple of steamy scenes out of the movie because of complaints.* □ *Hank and Bess were having a steamy session on the couch.* □ *The session was really steamy.*

**steenth** [stinθ] *n.* "one sixteenth," used in quoting securities prices. (Financial markets. See also *teenie.*) □ *This issue was only up a few steenths for the whole week.* □ *Acme Systems was down a steenth at midday.*

**steep** *mod.* (of a price) high; expensive. □ *Isn't that price sort of steep?* □ *I don't have steep prices here.* □ *Their prices are pretty steep, but their goods are of high quality.*

**stellar** ['stɛlɚ] *mod.* excellent; grand. □ *It was a stellar performance, and the applause was thunderous.* □ *Ronald Simpson gave us a stellar characterization of Boris, but the chorus was a disappointment.* □ *The chorus was stellar!*

**stems** *n.* legs. □ *Look at the stems on that dame!* □ *My feet are sore, and my stems ache all the time.*

**step off the curb** *in.* to die. □ *Ralph almost stepped off the curb during his operation.* □ *I'm too young to step off the curb.*

**step out on someone** *in.* to betray one's lover by going out with someone else. □ *Hank has been stepping out on Bess, and she doesn't know it yet.* □ *She would never step out on him.*

**step outside** *in.* to leave the present area and go to another place, presumably to fight. □ *The two—who had been arguing—stepped outside to settle the matter.* □ *Do you want to step outside, smart ass?*

**stepped on** *mod.* having to do with diluted drugs. (Drugs.) □ *That smack you bought was really stepped on.* □ *This stuff is too stepped on. It's sugar, and it won't do.*

**step right up** *phr.* "come forward and do not be bashful." □ *There are still a few of these left. Step right up and get yours.* □ *Step right up and buy a ticket to the greatest show on earth!*

**stern** *n.* the posterior. □ *The little airplane crashed right into the stern of an enormous lady who didn't even notice.* □ *Haul your stern over here and sit down.*

**stet** [stɛt] *mod.* just as it was originally. (Proofreading.) □ *No, mark that one stet. It was right the way it was.* □ *This says stet, but it's wrong.* □ *This one should look just like the other one, so mark one stet and ignore the other.*

**stew 1.** *n.* a drinking bout. □ *One more stew like that and I'll need a vacation to recover.* □ *These frequent stews must stop. You will ruin your health.* **2.** *n.* a drunkard. □ *Who is that stew in the corner?* □ *There are three stews sleeping in the alley.* **3.** See *stewed (up).* **4.** *n.* a stewardess or steward on an airplane. □ *The stew brought the coffee and rolls.* □ *My sister is a stew for a major airline.* **5.** *in.* to fret. □ *It's bad, but don't stew about it.* □ *I spent most of last night stewing about my job.* **6.** *n.* a fretful state. □ *Don't work yourself into a stew.* □ *Look at her face. That is the result of a dreadful stew. I wonder what's wrong.*

**stew bum** *n.* a drunkard; an alcoholic. □ *You're going to end up a stew bum if you don't lay off the moonshine.* □ *Those stew bums could use a bath.*

**stewed to the gills** AND **stewed to the ears** *mod.* alcohol intoxicated. □ *Why does a grown man have to get stewed to the gills every night of his life if there isn't something a little wrong with him?* □ *Here's old Charlie—stewed to the ears, as always.*

**stewed (up)** AND **stew** *mod.* alcohol intoxicated. □ *Gary was too stewed to remember his name.* □ *The kid was stewed up and scared to death of what his parents were going to do to him.*

**stick 1.** *n.* a baseball bat. (Baseball.) □ *He started to run and tripped over the stick.* □ *He holds the stick up higher than most batters.* **2.** *n.* a pool cue. □ *He drew the stick back slowly, sighted again, and gave the cue ball a sharp knock.* □ *The guy was so mad he broke the stick over his knee!* **3.** *n.* a golf club. □ *These aren't my sticks, and you aren't my caddy. What's going on around here?* □ *I wanted a new set of sticks for Christmas, but I got a snowmobile instead.* **4.** *n.* the lever that controls the horizontal and vertical surfaces of the tail of an aircraft. □ *The pilot pulled back on the stick, and the plane did nothing—being that he hadn't even started the engine or anything.* □ *You pull back on the stick, which lowers the tail and raises the nose, and up you go.* **5.** *n.* a gearshift lever in a car. □ *I keep reaching for the stick in a car with automatic.* □ *Put the stick in reverse and move back slowly.* **6.** *n.* a marijuana cigarette. (Drugs.) □ *Who's got a stick I can buy?* □ *He's pushing sticks again.* **7.** *n.* a drunkard. □ *Some stick threw up on my car.* □ *Get that stick out of here before he makes a mess.* **8.** *n.* (in the plural) a person's legs. (Always plural.) □ *Get those sticks moving! Get over here now!* □ *He's got good sticks under him, but he won't use them.* **9.** *n.* (in the plural) a rural or backwoods area. (Always with *the* and always plural.) □ *I hated living in the sticks.* □ *You hear a lot about how things are in the sticks. They're worse.*

**stick around** *in.* to remain nearby. □ *Stick around. Things are bound to get better.* □ *I think if you'll stick around, you'll get a seat sooner or later.*

**Stick 'em up!** *exclam.* "Put your hands in the air; this is a robbery!" □ *Okay, you people, stick 'em up! And not a peep out of you!* □ *When he said "stick 'em up," I thought it was a joke till I saw the gun.*

**sticker shock** *n.* the shock at seeing just how much a new automobile costs as determined by looking at the price tag or sticker. □ *I went to a car dealer today, and I am still suffering from sticker shock.* □ *If sticker shock is get-*

*ting you down, think about getting a used car.*

**stick in the mud** *n.* a dull and old-fashioned person. □ *Don't be such an old stick in the mud.* □ *Some stick in the mud objected to the kind of music we wanted to play in church.*

**stick it to someone** *tr.* to give someone a problem; to confront someone. □ *They stuck it to me about the stopped-up drain.* □ *He was late, and the boss really stuck it to him.*

**stick man 1.** *n.* a police patrol officer (who carries a stick.) □ *The stick man is due here in about three minutes. Hurry.* □ *I was a stick man for a few years till my feet went bad.* **2.** *n.* a smoker of marijuana cigarettes. (Drugs.) □ *Bruno is a stick man. He doesn't like pipes.* □ *Ernie was a stick man till he started being less particular.*

**stick of tea** *n.* a marijuana cigarette. (Drugs.) □ *He had a stick of tea hanging out of his mouth just like a slim.* □ *How about a stick of tea for a friend?*

**stick one's nose in (where it's not wanted)** See *put one's nose in (where it's not wanted).*

**stick out like a sore thumb** *in.* to be very obvious. □ *That zit really sticks out like a sore thumb.* □ *Do you think I would stick out like a sore thumb at the party if I wear this coat?*

**stick shift 1.** *mod.* having to do with a non-automatic transmission or a car that has one. □ *I prefer a stick shift car—I don't know why.* □ *The stick shift models are cheaper—that's why.* □ *This one's stick shift.* **2.** *n.* a non-automatic transmission. □ *I can't drive a stick shift!* □ *My husband took the other car and stuck me with the stick shift.*

**stick someone with something** *tr.* to burden someone with something. □ *Please don't stick me with the stick shift again.* □ *He left town and stuck me with the bill.*

**sticktoitiveness** [stɪk'tuɪtɪvnəs] *n.* tenacity. □ *The kid has sticktoitiveness. I like that in a kid.* □ *If I had more sticktoitiveness, maybe I could get a job.*

**stickum** ['stɪkəm] **1.** *n.* glue. □ *Put some stickum on this paper and paste it up where it can be seen.* □ *There's no stickum left on this stamp.* **2.** *n.* any thick and sticky substance, especially hair dressing. (Compare to *slickum.*) □ *Use some stickum on your hair!* □ *He uses too much stickum on his hair.*

**sticky 1.** *mod.* gooey. (Standard English.) □ *This stuff sure is sticky.* □ *What is this sticky stuff on my shoe? Oh, no!* **2.** *mod.* chancy; awkward. □ *Things began to get a little sticky, and Barlowe began to move toward the door.* □ *When the going got sticky, Freddy disappeared.* **3.** *mod.* sentimental. □ *Things were getting a little sticky the more Harriet drank. She tried to kiss me, and I left.* □ *There's a sticky part in the movie, but other than that it's pretty good.* **4.** *mod.* having to do with hot and humid weather. □ *It's so sticky today!* □ *I can't take another sticky day like this.*

**sticky fingers** *n.* a tendency to steal. □ *Bruno has sticky fingers and likes wallets especially.* □ *Watch these young kids with sticky fingers who come in here "just looking."*

**stiff 1.** AND **stiffed** *mod.* alcohol intoxicated; dead drunk. □ *Kelly was too stiff to find his keys.* □ *She knows how to stop drinking before she gets stiff.* **2.** *n.* a drunkard. □ *Some stiff staggered by—belching clouds of some beery smell.* □ *The guy's a stiff, and you want to run him for mayor? Even in this town that's going too far.* **3.** *mod.* dead. (Originally underworld.) □ *He's stiff. There's nothing that can be done.* □ *Yeah, he's stiff. Don't hit him no more.* **4.** *n.* a corpse. (Underworld.) □ *They pulled another stiff out of the river last night. Looks like another mob killing.* □ *They took me into a room full of stiffs to identify Rocko's bod.* **5.** *n.* a fellow worker; a fellow tramp. (Originally hobos.) □ *He's just another working stiff like me.* □ *This stiff wants some help finding a flop for the night.* **6.** *tr.* to fail to tip someone who expects it. □ *Ya know, you can tell right away when a guy's gonna stiff you—ya just know.* □ *I guess I get stiffed two—three times a day.* **7.** *tr.* to cheat someone. □ *The clown selling hotdogs stiffed me for about 40 cents.* □ *I really got stiffed on that deal. Look at this cheap junk.*

**sting 1.** *tr.* to cheat or swindle someone; to overcharge someone. □ *That street merchant stung me, but good.* □ *They are likely to sting you in any of those hockshops.* **2.** *n.* a well-planned scheme to entrap criminals. □ *The sting came off without a hitch.* □ *It was a well-planned sting and shouldn't have failed.* **3.** *tr.* to entrap and arrest someone. □ *The feebies stung the whole gang at once.* □ *"We've been stung!" they hollered.*

**stinger** *n.* the drawback; the catch; the hitch. □ *Now, here's the stinger.* □ *Sounds good, but what's the stinger?*

**stink 1.** *in.* to be repellent. □ *This whole setup stinks.* □ *Your act stinks. Try another agent.* **2.** *n.* a commotion. (See also *raise a stink (about someone or something).*) □ *The stink you made about money has done no good at all. You're fired.* □ *One more stink like that and out you go.*

**stinker 1.** *n.* an unpleasant or wicked person. □ *Jerry is a real stinker. Look what he did!* □ *What stinker messed up my desk?* **2.** *n.* a serious problem. □ *This whole business is a real stinker.* □ *What a stinker of a problem.*

**stinking 1.** See the following entry. **2.** *mod.* lousy; rotten. □ *What a stinking mess you've got yourself into.* □ *That was a mean stinking thing to do. Really stinking!*

**stinking (drunk)** *mod.* alcohol intoxicated. □ *He was really stinking.* □ *She came within an inch of getting stinking drunk.*

**stinking rich** *mod.* very rich. □ *I'd like to be stinking rich for the rest of my life.* □ *Tiffany is stinking rich, and she acts like it.*

**stinking with something** *mod.* with lots of something. □ *Mr. Wilson is just stinking with dough.* □ *Those guys are stinking with grass.*

**stink on ice** *in.* to be really rotten. (So rotten as to reek even when frozen.) □ *This show stinks on ice.* □ *The whole idea stank on ice.*

**stinkpot 1.** *n.* a baby with a dirty diaper. (Also a term of address.) □ *Jimmy's a stinkpot. Better change him.* □ *Come here, you little stinkpot. I'll fix you.* **2.**
*n.* anything smelly. □ *What are you barbecuing in this old stinkpot?* □ *Why don't you drive this stinkpot into a service station and get it tuned?* **3.** *n.* a motorboat. (Because the engine smells bad, especially when compared to a sailboat.) □ *Those guys in their stinkpots sure make a lot of noise.* □ *Those stinkpots just have to be polluting the lake.*

**stinky** *mod.* bad. □ *That was a stinky thing to do.* □ *You have a very stinky attitude. Really stinky.*

**stir** *n.* prison. (Underworld.) □ *I can't stand being in stir!* □ *Stir is very dull—and dangerous.*

**stir crazy** *mod.* anxious and mentally disturbed from being confined, as in prison. (See *stir.*) □ *I was going stir crazy in my little room, so I moved to a bigger place.* □ *I get sort of stir crazy in the winter.*

**stitch 1.** *n.* a very funny person. (Always with *a.*) □ *Harry is a stitch. What a sense of humor!* □ *Clare is a stitch, too. Her jokes can slay you.* **2.** *n.* a sharp pain, usually in the side. □ *I got a stitch and had to drop out of the marathon.* □ *A stitch in the side can be very painful.*

**stocking-stuffer** *n.* a small gift that is suitable for putting inside a Christmas stocking. □ *This will make the perfect stocking-stuffer.* □ *I got some little stocking-stuffers for the kids.*

**stogie** ['stogi] *n.* a cigar. □ *Then this guy pulls out a big stogie and starts to smoke it right there in the restaurant.* □ *Some activist type tried to get the customers to walk out if the manager didn't make the jerk put out his stogie.*

**stoked (on someone or something)** *mod.* excited by someone or something. (Compare to *stokin'.*) □ *We were stoked on Mary. She is the greatest.* □ *Everyone is stoked on spring.* □ *Now, don't get too stoked, you are the one who has to run.*

**stoked out** *mod.* exhausted. □ *I ran all the way and got stoked out.* □ *Alex is totally stoked out.*

**stokin'** *mod.* excellent; wild. □ *That car is really stokin'.* □ *We had a stokin' time at Fred's house.*

**stomach** *tr.* to tolerate someone or something. (Usually negative.) □ *Bruno couldn't stomach the opera, and he left after the first ten minutes.* □ *I can't stomach movies like that.*

**stomp (on) someone** *tr. & in.* to beat someone; to misuse someone. □ *We are gonna stomp you guys next game.* □ *One team stomped on the other so hard and fast, the scoreboard couldn't keep up.*

**stone** *mod.* completely; totally. (See additional examples in the following entries.) □ *This lecture is stone dull.* □ *I am stone mad at you.*

**stone blind** *mod.* heavily alcohol intoxicated. □ *Jerry drank the sauce till he was stone blind.* □ *When he was stone blind, he drank some more.*

**stone broke** *mod.* completely broke. □ *I'm sorry, I'm stone broke. Can I send you a check?* □ *What could I do? She was stone broke.*

**stone (cold) sober** *mod.* absolutely sober. □ *I am stone cold sober, or I will be by morning anyway.* □ *I found the secret to being stone sober. Don't drink.*

**stone dead** *mod.* dead; unquestionably dead; long dead. □ *The cat was stone dead and stiff as a board by the time we got to him.* □ *Old Tom is stone dead and in the ground.*

**stoned (out)** *mod.* alcohol or drug intoxicated. □ *Fred is really stoned out.* □ *I have never seen anybody so stoned who could still talk.*

**stoned out of one's head** AND **stoned out of one's gourd** *mod.* under the effects of marijuana. □ *Tiffany was stoned out of her head and started giggling.* □ *The guy was stoned out of his gourd and should never have been driving.*

**stoned out of one's squash** *mod.* alcohol or drug intoxicated. □ *Molly will drink a little now and then, but she never gets stoned out of her squash.* □ *Well, she was stoned out of her squash last night!*

**stoned silly** *mod.* alcohol or drug intoxicated. □ *I hate to get stoned silly in public. At home—ah, that's a different matter.* □ *He got stoned silly at the rally, and for all I know he is still there on the floor in the corner.*

**stone fox** *n.* an attractive woman; a very sexy woman. □ *She is a stone fox if I ever saw one.* □ *Who is that stone fox I saw you with last night?*

**stone groove** *n.* something really cool; a fine party or concert. □ *This affair is not what I would call a stone groove. Stone beige, maybe.* □ *Ted's do was a stone groove.*

**stoner** *n.* a teenager who prefers smoking marijuana to anything else. (Drugs.) □ *The kid's a stoner and will probably stay that way till he comes to his senses.* □ *What becomes of these young stoners?*

**stone's throw** *n.* a relatively short distance. (Folksy.) □ *It's just a stone's throw from here. You can walk it in five minutes.* □ *The bank is just a stone's throw from the post office.*

**stonewall** **1.** *tr.* to obstruct something or someone. □ *And again, the mayor tried to stonewall the investigation.* □ *If you continue to stonewall, we'll call in the FBI.* **2.** *n.* an obstructionist act. □ *His answer to the committee was another stonewall that caught them all by surprise.* □ *The stonewall they were faced with was almost too much.*

**stonkered** ['stɔŋkɚd] **1.** *mod.* killed. □ *The car crashed into him and he was stonkered for sure.* □ *He was stonkered before the plane hit the ground.* **2.** *mod.* alcohol intoxicated. □ *My buddy here is stonkered and needs a ride, and can I have one, too?* □ *Wally was stonkered beyond any help.*

**stony bush** *n.* marijuana. (Drugs. Because it can make you *stoned.*) □ *They celebrated with a little of the stony bush.* □ *Where do you get this stony bush stuff?*

**stooge** [studʒ] **1.** *n.* someone's pawn; someone controlled or maneuvered by someone else. □ *I'm not going to be your stooge!* □ *The guy's a stooge for the mob's Mr. Big. Ignore him.* **2.** *in.* to work as someone's underling; to serve as someone's pawn. □ *I'm not gonna stooge for you, no sirree!* □ *You will do what I tell you, and if it's stooging you will do it, and you will smile and say thank you.*

**stoolie** See *stool (pigeon)*.

**stool (on someone)** *in.* to inform (on someone). □ *Molly would stool on anybody, even her own mother.* □ *Somebody stooled and ruined the whole layout.*

**stool (pigeon)** AND **stoolie** ['stul 'pɪdʒən AND 'stuli] *n.* an informer. (Originally underworld.) □ *Some stool spilled the works to the boys in blue.* □ *There's nothing I hate worse than a stoolie.*

**stoop** See *stupe*.

**stop on a dime** *in.* to stop immediately. □ *This thing will stop on a dime.* □ *Imagine a bus that could stop on a dime.*

**stoppers** *n.* barbiturates. (Drugs.) □ *There was a real drugstore there: stoppers of all kinds, reds, yellows, blues, even some cheap borders.* □ *He had these stoppers hidden in his watch pocket. He won't miss them when he comes to.*

**Stop the music!** *exclam.* "Stop"; "Stop whatever is happening!" (From an old radio game show called "Stop the music!") □ *Stop the music! I have an announcement.* □ *"Stop the music!" hollered the conductor, making a little joke.*

**storked** *mod.* pregnant. □ *She got herself good and storked. Now what?* □ *I hear that Molly is storked again.*

**story stock** *n.* shares in a company that are bought because of an appealing story about the company. □ *I never buy a story stock. By the time I hear about it, it's already gone up as much as it ever will.* □ *Acme Widgets is another story stock that I advise all my clients to buy.*

**Stow it!** *exclam.* "Shut up!" □ *Okay, stow it! I've heard enough.* □ *Stow it! That is enough of your applesauce.*

**stozzled** ['stɑzl̩d] *mod.* alcohol intoxicated. □ *My buddy is too stozzled to drive home. Can you give him a lift?* □ *Marty can drink and drink and never get stozzled or even tipsy.*

**straddle the fence** *tr.* to support both sides of an issue. □ *The mayor is straddling the fence on this issue, hoping the public will forget it.* □ *The legislator wanted to straddle the fence until the last minute, and that alone cost her a lot of votes.*

**straight 1.** *mod.* honest; unembellished. □ *This is the straight truth.* □ *Have I ever been anything but straight with you?* **2.** *n.* a tobacco cigarette; a tobacco cigarette butt. (As opposed to a marijuana cigarette. See *slim*.) □ *No, I want a straight. That spliff makes me sneeze.* □ *Can I bum a straight off you?* **3.** *mod.* having to do with undiluted liquor. □ *I'll take mine straight.* □ *Make one straight with a little ice.* **4.** *mod.* relieved and satisfied by a dose of drugs. (Drugs.) □ *It only takes a few bucks and a little time to get straight.* □ *She will be straight for a few hours, and then the same struggle all over again—all through the night.* **5.** *mod.* off drugs; no longer addicted to drugs. □ *I'm straight now, and I'm gonna stay that way.* □ *I'm a straight guy.* □ *See how long you can stay straight, how 'bout it?* **6.** *n.* a square person (who does not use drugs, etc.). □ *The guy's a straight. He's gonna turn us over to the cops!* □ *The straights are putting pressure on city hall to clean up this neighborhood.* **7.** *n.* a non-homosexual. □ *Walter invited a few straights to the affair, just to keep things calm.* □ *The straights really get upset if you camp it up too much.*

**straight arrow** *n.* an honest person; a law-abiding citizen. (See *straight*.) □ *Wally is really a straight arrow at heart—as long as he's not around Max.* □ *Max is not a straight arrow. Slime is more like it.*

**straight dope** *n.* the true information. □ *He gave us the straight dope.* □ *I want the straight dope. I can take it.*

**straighten up and fly right** *in.* to get serious and start behaving properly. □ *It's time for you to straighten up and fly right!* □ *Straighten up and fly right before you get into difficulty.*

**straight-faced** *mod.* with a serious, unsmiling face. □ *Mary couldn't stay straight-faced very long. It was just too funny.* □ *He is a very straight-faced prof, but he has a tremendous sense of humor.*

**straight from the horse's mouth** *mod.* directly from the source. (As if a racehorse were giving racing tips.) □ *Of course it's true. I got it straight from the horse's mouth.* □ *This came straight* *from the horse's mouth. It's Zeerocks Copy in the sixth race.*

**straight from the shoulder** *mod.* very direct, without attenuation or embellishment. □ *Okay, I'll give it to you straight from the shoulder.* □ *Right straight from the shoulder: clean out your desk; you're through.*

**straight low** *n.* the absolute truth; the true *lowdown.* (Prisons.) □ *Can you give me the straight low on this mess?* □ *Nobody ain't gonna tell no warden the straight low; you can be sure of that.*

**straight man** *n.* someone who sets up jokes or gags so that someone else can say the punch line. □ *I need a straight man to pick up on all my jokes.* □ *I'm tired of being a straight man for a has-been comic.*

**straight shooter** 1. *n.* an honest person. (Compare to *straight arrow.*) □ *'I trust Mike; he's a straight shooter.* □ *We need a straight shooter in office who will work for the people rather than some political party.* 2. *n.* an addict who injects drugs. (Drugs.) □ *At 17 he turned into a straight shooter and used pills only as a stopgap.* □ *Max is a straight shooter, and he'll shoot anything.*

**straight talk** *n.* direct and honest talk. □ *It's about time for a little straight talk around here.* □ *If they want straight talk and can handle straight talk, give 'em straight talk.*

**straight up** 1. *mod.* upright. □ *A fine guy—really straight up.* □ *She is one of the most straight up brokers in town.* 2. *mod.* without ice; neat. □ *I'll have a bourbon, straight up, please.* □ *No, not straight up. Just a little ice.* 3. *mod.* *sunny-side up*; having to do with eggs cooked with yellow yolks facing straight up. □ *Two eggs, straight up, and a cup of coffee.* □ *I like my eggs straight up, but the white part has to be cooked solid.*

**strange bird** See *odd bird.*

**strap** *n.* an athlete, not necessarily male. (From *jockstrap.*) □ *A whole gang of straps came in the bar and ordered milk.* □ *The guy's a strap all right, but he's not dumb.*

**straphanger** *n.* a subway passenger. □ *I didn't think I could get used to being a straphanger.* □ *Straphangers learn to blot out their surroundings.*

**strapped** *mod.* broke; short of money. □ *I'm sorry I can't pay you right now. I'm strapped.* □ *They're really strapped for money at the present time.*

**straw** 1. *n.* marijuana. (Drugs. Probably a play on *hay.*) □ *He stood right on the corner, selling straw by the handful from a bucket at his feet—and nobody even called the cops.* □ *This straw is not the best quality I've seen.* 2. *n.* papers for rolling marijuana cigarettes. (Drugs.) □ *I need some straw.* □ *I can't manage the straw with one hand. How do these cowboys do it?*

**strawberry** 1. *n.* a pimple from drinking excessively. (See also *toddy blossom.*) □ *His disability made itself manifest by the occasional strawberry.* □ *That's a fine strawberry on your snoot.* 2. AND **strawberry tablets** *n.* a pink tablet of mescaline. (Drugs.) □ *The guards were smuggling strawberries and mushrooms into the prison right under the warden's nose.* □ *Do you know where I can get strawberries at this time of year?* 3. AND **strawberry fields** *n.* L.S.D. (Drugs.) □ *I just know I will love strawberry fields forever.* □ *I don't like this strawberry stuff.*

**straw boss** *n.* a foreman; anyone who is second in command. □ *The straw boss gave the order, and off we went.* □ *I don't mind being a straw boss as long as they pay me.*

**streak** 1. *in.* to move rapidly from one place to another. □ *The train streaked into the station and came to a stop just inches from the end of the track.* □ *I've got to streak over to the library in a big hurry.* 2. *in.* to run about in a public place naked. □ *This kid was streaking back and forth until the cops caught him.* □ *He streaked on a dare.* 3. *tr.* to grace or ornament a public place or event with a naked run. □ *Charles streaked the baseball game, but nobody noticed him.* □ *I wanted to streak her party, but decided against it.* 4. *n.* a naked run in a public place. □ *There was a streak at the end of the game, but people were leaving then and didn't see it.* □ *That was no streak; that was the coach in his long underwear being chased by the owner of the team.* (More at *streaker*.) **5.** *n.* an exciting time; a wild party. □ *That rally was a streak!* □ *We had a streak at Tom's.*

**streaker** *n.* someone who runs naked in public places. □ *The streaker ran through a glass door and was severely injured.* □ *Streakers seemed to take over the whole country in 1973.*

**street** **1.** *n.* the real, free world, as opposed to prison. (Always with *the*.) □ *The street just isn't the same as stir.* □ *It's good to be back on the street.* **2.** *n.* Wall Street in New York City. (Always with *the*.) □ *The street doesn't seem to believe the policymakers in Washington.* □ *If you want excitement and stress, the street is the place to be.*

**street-casting** *n.* selecting amateurs to be performers or models. □ *I do a lot of street-casting. Almost everybody can act a little.* □ *Street-casting is fun, and it's cheap.*

**streeter** *n.* an urban "street person." □ *These streeters have to be bright and clever just to survive.* □ *A couple of streeters taught me how to get a meal for nothing.*

**street people** *n.* people who live in the streets; homeless people. □ *There are a lot of cold street people at this time of the year.* □ *Some of the street people prefer that kind of life.*

**street pusher** *n.* a drug dealer who works at the retail level on the streets. □ *It's the street pushers who take the risk and end up doing a few months in the pen.* □ *Max was a street pusher until he got busted.*

**street smart** *mod.* wise in the ways of urban life; wise in the ways of tough neighborhoods. □ *Freddy was street smart at age 8.* □ *Bess wasn't street smart enough to survive by herself.*

**street smarts** *n.* the knowledge and ability to survive on the urban street. □ *If you don't have street smarts, you won't last long out there.* □ *You either pick up street smarts, or you don't.*

**street time** *n.* time not spent in prison. (Underworld.) □ *I had three months street time; then they nailed me again.* □ *I want out of this place. I need a little street time to renew some old acquaintances.*

**stress** **1.** *in.* to suffer annoyance; to experience stress. □ *I'm stressing again! Please don't annoy me!* □ *Clare finds that she is stressing more and more about little things.* **2.** *tr.* to annoy or bother someone. □ *Don't stress Wally! He's had a hard day.* □ *The whole affair about my beemer stressed me a whole lot.* (More at *stressed*.)

**stressed** *mod.* upset; annoyed. □ *Come on, man, don't get stressed! It's only a gag.* □ *I am really stressed. I need a vacation.*

**stretch** **1.** *n.* a period of time. (Folksy.) □ *Let's talk here for a stretch and then go up and see if dinner's ready.* □ *I sat there for a stretch and then got up and kept going.* **2.** *n.* a prison term. □ *I was away for a stretch of about seven years.* □ *That's quite a stretch for tax evasion.* **3.** *in.* to hang (as with a death sentence). □ *You will stretch for this, Lefty!* □ *I'll live to see you stretch, you rat!* **4.** *tr.* to cut or dilute a drug. □ *Max was known for stretching the smizz a little too much.* □ *Let's stretch this stuff, sell it, and then blow town.* **5.** *n.* a nickname for a tall person, usually male. □ *Well, stretch, think you'll go out for basketball this season?* □ *Come on, stretch, let's get it in the basket!*

**stretchies** *n.* an early symptom of drug withdrawal where one feels like stretching all of the time. (Drugs.) □ *The stretchies were beginning to happen more often, and Max knew he needed a fix.* □ *Things like yawning and the stretchies are signs to the addict that withdrawal is beginning.*

**stretch one's legs** *tr.* to stand up and perhaps walk about. □ *I need to get out of here and stretch my legs for a while.* □ *Most of us stood up to stretch our legs at intermission.*

**(strictly) from hunger** *mod.* very strange; acceptable only when nothing else is available. □ *This kind of entertainment is from hunger.* □ *The singer was strictly from hunger.*

**strike** *n.* a dose of drugs. (Drugs. Compare to *hit*.) □ *I need a strike. You got any stumbles?* □ *Just one strike, Max, come on, just one. I'll pay you tomorrow, Max, come on, just one little strike. Anything, Max. I really hurt, Max.*

**strike it rich** *tr.* to become rich suddenly. □ *I never thought I would strike it rich.* □ *Tod is the kind of guy who wants to strike it rich and live in the lap of luxury for the rest of his life.*

**strike out 1.** *in.* (for a baseball batter) to be declared out after three strikes. (Baseball.) □ *And so Drew Wilson strikes out for his second time in this game!* □ *He struck out in the second inning, and manager Willy "Herky" Simpson read him out then.* **2.** *in.* to fail. □ *Well, we struck out again, but we'll keep trying.* □ *I hear you struck out on that Acme proposal. Better luck next time.*

**strike pay dirt** See *hit pay dirt.*

**stringbean** *n.* a thin person. (Also a term of address.) □ *Wow, is he a stringbean.* □ *Who's the stringbean standing by the punch bowl? Somebody ought to feed him.*

**stripper** *n.* a striptease artist. □ *Molly worked for a while as a stripper.* □ *Strippers from all over assembled here for their fourth annual convention and immediately took off on a sight-seeing tour.*

**strip-search** *tr.* to search someone's entire naked body. (Compare to *skin-search*.) □ *The cops strip-searched the good-looking chick who ran a red light.* □ *Now it takes a court order to strip-search someone.*

**stroke** *tr. & in.* to flatter someone; to soothe and comfort someone. □ *She strokes everybody to keep them on her side during the bad times.* □ *She learned long ago that stroking puts people at ease.*

**strong-arm 1.** *tr.* to force someone (to do something). □ *Bruno tried to strong-arm Frank into cooperating.* □ *Don't strong-arm me, you creep!* **2.** *mod.* forceful; by physical force. □ *The strong-arm approach got him nowhere.* □ *Too much strong-arm stuff isn't good.*

**strong-arm man** *n.* a bully; a man who is employed to use physical power to force someone to do something. □ *Bruno is Mr. Big's strong-arm man.* □ *The mob employs hundreds of strong-arm men.*

**strong-arm tactics** *n.* tactics based on the use of force. □ *No more strong-arm*

tactics. *You need to be more subtle.* □ *Strong-arm tactics are out. The boss says be gentle and don't break anybody.*

**strung out 1.** AND **strung (up)** *mod.* drug intoxicated and bewildered. (Drugs.) □ *Bruno is really strung out lately. What's he shooting now?* □ *Tim is sort of strung out and doesn't even remember what he took.* **2.** *mod.* badly addicted to heroin; dissipated by heroin. (Drugs.) □ *Harry's strung out for good, I guess.* □ *Clare is strung out and can't deny her problem any longer.* **3.** *mod.* depressed; nervous. □ *I get strung out before tests and other traumatic things.* □ *I'm a little strung out—because of the accident, I guess.* **4.** *mod.* in love and disoriented. □ *Mary is strung out, and all because of Sam.* □ *Sam is strung out over Mary.*

**strung-out shape** *n.* a tired and exhausted condition. □ *They were sort of in strung-out shape, tired and ready for the sack.* □ *I've never been in such strung-out shape, but I've never run a marathon before.*

**strut one's stuff** *tr.* to walk proudly and show off one's best features or talents. □ *Get out there on that stage and strut your stuff!* □ *I'm going to strut my stuff and become a star.*

**stuccoed** ['stəkod] *mod.* alcohol intoxicated. (A play on *plastered*.) □ *The guy was too stuccoed to drive and couldn't stand up to walk.* □ *I can drink without getting stuccoed, mainly because I drink soda.*

**stuck on someone or something** *mod.* enamored with someone or something; obsessed with someone or something. □ *Tom is stuck on himself—as conceited as can be.* □ *I'm really stuck on this stuff. It's just yummy.*

**stuck-up** *mod.* conceited. □ *Tom is really stuck-up.* □ *What a stuck-up jerk.* □ *Don't be so stuck-up. Unbend a little.*

**stuck with someone or something** *mod.* burdened with someone or something; left with the burden of someone or something. □ *It's your problem, and you're stuck with it.* □ *Am I stuck with this kid forever?*

**stud** [stəd] **1.** *n.* a male horse used for breeding purposes. (Not slang.) □ *Last* *spring, we rented out all our studs and made some money.* □ *The mare kicked the stud and put us all out of business for a while.* **2.** *n.* a human male viewed as very successful with women. (Parallel to sense 1.) □ *Fred thinks he is a real stud.* □ *Man, look at that stud over there. Think he's going steady with anyone?* **3.** *n.* dope. (Drugs.) □ *I gotta have some stud now. I really hurt.* □ *You know where I can get some stud?*

**student** *n.* a new drug user. (Drugs.) □ *When Max was a student, he never thought he would end up a junky.* □ *Fred was a sitter for a student.*

**studhammer** *n.* a male who is successful sexually with women. □ *Alex is a real studhammer.* □ *The guy thinks he is a studhammer, but he is just a jerk.*

**stud-muffin** *n.* a really good-looking guy; a *stud.* □ *Who's the stud-muffin with Sally?* □ *Did you see that stud-muffin come in?*

**Stuff a sock in it!** *exclam.* "Shut up!" □ *I've heard enough. Stuff a sock in it!* □ *Stuff a sock in it! You are a pain.*

**stuffed shirt** *n.* a dull and stuffy person, usually a male. □ *Mr. Wilson is a stuffed shirt, and people would tell him so if he didn't have so much money.* □ *I don't want to listen to that stuffed shirt anymore.*

**stum** [stəm] **1.** *n.* marijuana. (Drugs.) □ *Where can I get some stum?* □ *This stum is cashed. Trash it.* **2.** See *stumbles.*

**stumblebum** *n.* a tramp or bum, especially drunk and stumbling. □ *The poor old stumblebum got to the other side of the street the best he could.* □ *You are headed toward being a stumblebum if you don't lay off the sauce.*

**stumbles** ['stəmbl̩z] **1.** AND **stum, stumble-bumbles** [stəm, 'stəmbl̩'bəmbl̩z] *n.* barbiturates; sedatives; tranquilizers; alcohol. (Drugs.) □ *Kelly was shocked to find a handful of stumble-bumbles in his brother's jeans.* □ *I need a strike. You got any stum?* **2.** *n.* the inability to stand up and walk straight. □ *I guess I have the stumbles today. Not enough sleep, I guess.* □ *Whoops! I have a case of the stumbles.*

**stump 1.** *tr.* to confuse or puzzle someone. □ *That one really stumped me.* □ *I like to stump people with hard questions.* **2.** *tr.* to visit or tour a place. □ *We stumped all of Europe this summer.* □ *The team stumped the countryside before even practicing for the game.* **3.** *n.* a visit or tour. □ *The old girl is off on another stump.* □ *It was a fine stump; we didn't miss anything.* **4.** See *stumps.*

**stumper** *n.* a shoe. (Black. Usually plural.) □ *Make those stumpers shine!* □ *You like my new stumpers?*

**stumps** *n.* a person's legs. □ *My stumps are sore from all that walking.* □ *You need good strong stumps to do that kind of climbing.*

**stung** *mod.* alcohol intoxicated. □ *I'm a little stung by the mule, but I can find my way home if you'll just remind me how to open this door.* □ *She can drink that stuff all evening and never get stung.*

**stunned** *mod.* alcohol intoxicated. □ *I was simply stunned with the stuff.* □ *Kelly was stunned and had to be carried home to recover.*

**stunner** *n.* a stunningly good-looking woman. □ *Did you see that stunner who just came in?* □ *I think that she is a stunner, and I go to all her movies—over and over.*

**stupe** AND **stoop** *n.* a stupid person. (Also a term of address.) □ *Look, stoop, just do what you are told.* □ *Don't be a stupe! Use your head!*

**stupehead** *n.* a stupid person; a blockhead. (Also a term of address. See *stupe.*) □ *What a stupehead!* □ *This stupehead keeps trying to sell me something.*

**stupid-ass** See *dumb-ass.*

**style** *in.* to show off; to strut around. (Black. See *strut one's stuff.*) □ *Look at that brother style!* □ *Why don't you style over here and meet my man?*

**stymie** ['staɪmi] *tr.* to obstruct someone or something. □ *He did everything he could to stymie the investigation.* □ *The nose guard stymied the play all by himself.*

**suave** [swav] *n.* personal polish and smoothness. □ *Man, does that guy ever have suave!* □ *You need some suave to carry off this sham.*

**sub 1.** *n.* a substitute. □ *I was a sub in the school system for a while.* □ *The coach sent in a sub for Wilbur.* **2.** *in.* to serve as a temporary replacement. □ *I subbed for Mary in a couple of games.* □ *Then she subbed for me to even the score.* **3.** *n.* a submarine. □ *I was aboard a sub for 20 minutes—and that was at Disney World.* □ *You have to have a special kind of personality to live on a sub.* **4.** See *submarine.* **5.** *n.* a subscription, as to a magazine. □ *I got a sub to a computer magazine for my birthday.* □ *Would you like to buy a sub to the local newspaper?*

**submarine 1.** AND **sub** *n.* a long sandwich containing many different foods. □ *He ordered a submarine, but he couldn't finish it.* □ *He took what was left of the sub home with him.* **2.** *n.* a large marijuana cigarette. □ *Look at the size of that sub!* □ *Max makes a sub when he's got low-power straw.*

**suck 1.** AND **suction** *n.* liquor; wine; beer; strong drink. □ *How about a little glass of suck before we leave?* □ *This is powerful suction!* **2.** AND **suck something up, suck up something** *tr.* to drink beer or liquor. □ *Let's go out and suck a few up.* □ *Yeah, I'll suck one with ya.* **3.** *in.* (for someone or something) to be bad or undesirable. □ *This movie sucks!* □ *I think that the whole business sucks.* **4.** AND **suction** *n.* influence. □ *He thinks he has suck, but he's just a pain in the neck.* □ *Who has some suction with the boss?*

**sucker 1.** *n.* a dupe; an easy mark. □ *See if you can sell that sucker the Brooklyn Bridge.* □ *The sucker says he doesn't need a bridge, thank you.* **2.** *tr.* to trick or victimize someone. □ *That crook suckered me. I should have known better.* □ *They suckered him into selling half interest in his land.* **3.** *n.* an annoying person. (Also a rude term of address.) □ *Look, sucker, get out of my way!* □ *I am really sick of that sucker hanging around here.* **4.** *n.* a gadget; a thing. □ *Now, you put this little sucker right into this slot.* □ *Where is that sucker that looks like a screw?*

**sucker for someone or something** *n.* someone who is prejudiced in favor of someone or something. □ *I'm a sucker for a pretty face.* □ *Ted is a sucker for any dessert with whipped cream on it.*

**sucker list** *n.* a list of potential dupes; a list of people who might be taken in by deception. □ *I'm sure on their sucker list. They are trying to get me to go to a lecture and receive a free clock or something.* □ *Here's the sucker list. Call them all and try to get them interested.*

**suck face** *tr.* to kiss. (Compare to *swap spits.*) □ *The kid said he was going out to suck face. It sounds awful.* □ *Sally said she didn't want to suck face.*

**suck (some) brew** AND **suck (some) suds** *tr.* to drink beer. □ *Wanna go suck some brew?* □ *I'm tired of sucking suds. Got any staggers?*

**suck someone's hind tit\*** *tr.* to do someone's bidding no matter how unpleasant or impossible; to *kiss someone's ass.* (Caution with *tit.* See *tits.*) □ *What am I supposed to do—suck his hind tit?* □ *She acts like everybody has to suck her hind tit to keep their jobs.*

**suck (some) suds** See *suck (some) brew.*

**suck up to someone** *in.* to attempt to gain influence with or favor from someone. □ *In school, Max was always sucking up to the teacher.* □ *Don't suck up to me. It won't do any good.*

**sucky** *mod.* poor; undesirable. □ *This is the suckiest movie I ever saw.* □ *This food is sucky. It really sucks!*

**suction** See *suck.*

**sudden death** *mod.* having to do with something short, quick, and decisive. □ *The game ended in a sudden death playoff.* □ *Okay, you've got just one more sudden death chance.*

**suds 1.** *n.* beer. □ *How about some suds, Bill?* □ *I can't get enough suds.* **2.** *in.* to drink beer. □ *How 'bout going out and sudsing for a while?* □ *They were sudsing when they should have been studying.*

**sue the pants off (of) someone** *tr.* to sue someone for a lot of money. □ *If they do it, I'll sue the pants off of them.* □ *He sued the pants off his landlord.*

**sugar 1.** *n.* powdered drugs, especially heroin. (Drugs.) □ *This kilo of sugar is worth about $80,000 on the street.* □ *Where is sugar like this manufactured?* **2.** *n.* inferior or bogus heroin which is overly diluted with sugar. (Drugs.) □ *The mob's shoving sugar again.* □ *This stuff is sugar. Find the creep and get some real scag.* **3.** See *sugar (cube).* **4.** *n.* money. (See *sweetener.*) □ *Gimme a little sugar to tide me over.* □ *Congress started off the year by sprinkling sugar over all the land again.*

**sugarcoated** *mod.* palatable; inoffensive; easy to take. □ *Math is so sugarcoated these days. Even I could learn it.* □ *Stop giving them sugarcoated knowledge.*

**sugar (cube)** AND **sugar lump** *n.* the hallucinogenic drug *L.S.D.* (Drugs. Refers to an *L.S.D.*-impregnated sugar cube.) □ *I didn't know what a sugar cube was till I dropped one.* □ *I want a hit of sugar lump.*

**sugar daddy** *n.* an older man who takes care of a younger person, especially a young athlete or a young woman. □ *Mr. Wilson is sort of a sugar daddy to the whole team.* □ *I thought sugar daddies were illegal.*

**suit** *n.* a businessman or businesswoman; someone who is in charge. □ *This suit comes up and asks to go to the airport.* □ *A couple of suits checked into a working-class hotel and caused some eyebrows to raise.*

**summer complaint** *n.* diarrhea, especially that experienced in the summer. □ *I've got a touch of the summer complaint.* □ *Does summer heat cause the summer complaint?*

**sun belt** *n.* the southern U.S. states, where it is generally warm and sunny. (Compare to *rust belt.*) □ *I want to retire to the sun belt.* □ *The population of the sun belt is exploding.*

**Sunday best** *n.* one's best clothing, which one would wear to church. □ *We are in our Sunday best, ready to go.* □ *I got mud on my Sunday best.*

**Sunday driver** *n.* a slow and leisurely driver who appears to be sightseeing and enjoying the view and holds up traffic in the process. (Also a term of address.) □ *I'm a Sunday driver, and I'm sorry. I just can't bear to go faster.* □ *Move over, you Sunday driver!*

**Sunday punch** *n.* a very solid and destructive blow; one's best blow. □ *Barlowe sent a Sunday punch straight into Rocko's gut. Rocko's eyes bugged out; then he crumpled to the floor and wretched.* □ *Ralph aimed a Sunday punch at Frederick's nose, but missed and spun about, striking his elbow on the banister.*

**sunny-side up** *mod.* (of eggs) with yolks facing up and still yellow and hot, but not cooked through; *straight up.* □ *I'll have my eggs sunny-side up, with toast and coffee.* □ *People who like sunny-side up eggs wouldn't dream of eating a whole raw egg.*

**sunshades** *n.* sunglasses. (See also *shades.*) □ *Where are my sunshades? Did you borrow them again?* □ *I left my sunshades in the car.*

**super 1.** *mod.* fine; excellent. □ *This report is just super!* □ *Who made the super pie?* **2.** *n.* superintendent. □ *The super comes by every now and then to check on things.* □ *Call the super and ask for some help.*

**super-duper** AND **super-dooper** *mod.* excellent. □ *That's just super-duper. Couldn't have asked for better.* □ *Where is this super-dooper car of yours?*

**superfly** *mod.* excellent; wonderful. □ *This dude is really superfly.* □ *I don't care about this superfly gent of yours. If he doesn't have a job, I don't want you seeing him anymore. Ya hear?*

**supergrass 1.** *n.* high-quality marijuana. □ *Tiffany picked up some pot she called supergrass. It looks like alfalfa to me.* □ *The cannabis that is the richest in resin is sometimes called supergrass.* **2.** AND **super, super cools, superjoint** *n.* phencyclidine, *P.C.P.*, an animal tranquilizer. (Drugs.) □ *Another way of pushing P.C.P. off on these kids is by calling it supergrass or just super.* □ *Officer Wilson asked you where you got this supergrass, son. You tell us, or we call your parents. Is that clear?*

**superjock 1.** *n.* an excellent athlete. □ *Mike is a real superjock. He plays four sports.* □ *All those superjocks get special* *meals and tutors to help them pass their classes.* **2.** *n.* a very well-built man regardless of athletic ability. □ *My boyfriend is a superjock, and does he look good!* □ *No nerd has ever been a superjock.*

**super-strap** *n.* an earnest and hardworking student. (As compared to a *jock, strap, superjock.*) □ *He's a Melvin, a super-strap, and he doesn't do anything but study.* □ *I couldn't be a super-strap even if I had the brains. I just don't care that much.*

**sure as hell*** *mod.* absolutely certain. □ *I'm sure as hell he's the one.* □ *You sure as hell better get yourself over here.*

**surefire** *mod.* certain; effective; failsafe. □ *I've got a surefire method of fixing cracks in drywall.* □ *Good, yes; surefire, no.* □ *This stuff is a surefire cure.*

**sure thing** *n.* something that is absolutely certain. □ *It's a sure thing! You can't lose!* □ *Well, it looks like the sure thing didn't turn out to be so sure, after all.*

**surf** *mod.* wonderful; with it. (California.) □ *This party is, like, surf.* □ *This is not what I would call a surf day.*

**Suzy** *n.* a U.S. one-dollar coin bearing a likeness of Susan B. Anthony. □ *I've got two Suzys I want to get rid of.* □ *Someday I'm going to buy a car or something with a barrel of Suzys.*

**swacked** [swækt] *mod.* alcohol intoxicated. □ *Molly is too swacked to drive home. Can somebody give her a lift?* □ *He walked straight out of the office and went straight into the bar with the intention of getting swacked.*

**S.W.A.K.** See *sealed with a kiss.*

**swallow** **1.** *n.* a puff of cigarette smoke. (See also *swallow hit.*) □ *He took just one swallow and started coughing.* □ *Can I have a swallow of your fag?* **2.** *tr.* to believe or accept something. (Compare to *eat.*) □ *Did they actually swallow that?* □ *Nobody's gonna swallow that nonsense.*

**swallow a watermelon seed** *tr.* to become pregnant. (Folksy. Usually in the past tense.) □ *Looks like Sandra swallowed a watermelon seed.* □ *She—well, ah—you know—ah, swallowed a watermelon seed.*

**swallow hit** *n.* a puff of marijuana smoke which is swallowed. (Drugs.) □ *Two swallow hits and Hank began coughing like fury.* □ *Things like steamboats or swallow hits aim to get the chemicals deep into the lungs.*

**swallow the dictionary** *tr.* to acquire an enormous vocabulary. (Usually in the past tense.) □ *My uncle says I've swallowed the dictionary. That's because I know so many big words.* □ *Did you just go to college to swallow the dictionary?*

**swamped** **1.** *mod.* very, very busy. □ *I can't handle it now. I'm swamped.* □ *We're always swamped at this time of the year.* **2.** *mod.* alcohol intoxicated. □ *Look at him! He's swamped—stoned out of his mind.* □ *Those old boys used to go out and get swamped every Saturday night.*

**swamper** *n.* a truck driver's helper or assistant. □ *This guy and his swamper showed up to deliver the stuff, but neither one of them would touch it.* □ *He told the swamper to get some coffee for everybody.*

**swank** [swæŋk] *n.* class; visible quality. □ *He doesn't have swank. He's a cornball!* □ *This place has swank. I like it.*

**swanky** ['swæŋki] *mod.* classy; *ritzy.* □ *What a swanky joint!* □ *This place is too swanky. I like to eat where I can pronounce the names of the food.*

**swap notes (on someone or something)** *tr.* to share information on someone or something. □ *The two chicks sat around swapping notes on guys they knew.* □ *The mechanics were swapping notes on rude customers they had dealt with in the last month.*

**swap spits** *tr.* to kiss with someone. □ *A couple of kids were in the car swapping spits.* □ *Tiffany and Wilbur were off somewhere swapping spits, I guess.*

**swear like a trooper** *in.* to curse and swear with great facility. □ *Mrs. Wilson was known to swear like a trooper on occasion.* □ *The clerk started swearing like a trooper, and the customer started crying.*

**swear on a stack of Bibles** *in.* to make a very solemn pledge of one's honesty. (Folksy. Official oaths are sometimes taken with one hand on a Bible. This phrase implies that more Bibles make an even stronger oath.) □ *I swear on a stack of Bibles that I was in Atlanta on the night of January 16.* □ *It's true! I swear on a stack of Bibles it's true!*

**sweat 1.** *tr. & in.* to fret (about something) while waiting for an outcome. □ *Come on, don't sweat it. It'll work out.* □ *This whole promotion business really has me sweating.* **2.** *n.* trouble; bother. (See *No sweat.*) □ *I can handle it. It won't cause me any sweat.* □ *You really caused a lot of sweat around here.*

**sweat blood** *tr.* to work very hard at something; to endure distress in the process of accomplishing something. □ *And here I sweated blood to put you through college, and you treat me like a stranger.* □ *Everybody in the office had to sweat blood that week.*

**sweat bullets** *tr.* to suffer about something; to be anxious or nervous about something; to *sweat blood.* □ *They were sweating bullets, waiting for the results.* □ *The kid sat in the waiting room, sweating bullets while the surgeons worked on his brother.*

**sweat-shop** *n.* a workplace where employees work long hours for low pay in poor conditions. □ *This office is a sweat-shop! I only got a 2% raise.* □ *The bank manager is unfair! I've been a teller in this sweat-shop for 13 years, and I've never had a new carpet in my office.*

**sweat something out** AND **sweat out something** *tr.* to wait out something; to fret and worry until the end of something. □ *You'll just have to sweat it out. There's no way to hurry it up.* □ *We'll sweat it out like everybody else.*

**sweep** *tr.* to *snort* cocaine. (Drugs. See the following entry.) □ *Let's sweep some toot.* □ *He swept the stuff with the skill of someone well practiced.*

**sweep with both barrels** *in.* to *snort* (a line of cocaine) with both nostrils. (Drugs.) □ *How she can sweep with both barrels is beyond me.* □ *I don't have the lung capacity to sweep with both barrels.*

**sweeten** *tr.* to make a bargain or agreement better or more attractive. □ *Okay, I'll sweeten the deal. I'll throw in a lighted mirror on the visor.* □ *Sweeten the deal with air, and I'll buy the car.*

**sweetener** *n.* extra encouragement, usually in the form of money. □ *Money makes the best sweetener around.* □ *Let me add a little sweetener, and we'll see if he goes for it.*

**sweetheart** AND **sweetie(-pie)** *n.* (one's) dear child, husband, wife, lover, etc. (Often a term of address.) □ *Look, sweetheart, can't we afford a new car?* □ *Pick up your toys, sweetie. Aunt Matilda is coming over for a visit.*

**sweetheart deal** *n.* a deal made between friends so that both may profit well. (Most such deals involve illegal or unethical practices.) □ *They found that the mayor was involved in a number of sweetheart deals.* □ *Most of the general contractors in town would be out of business if they didn't offer sweetheart deals to the politicians.*

**sweetie** See *sweetheart.*

**sweetie-pie** See *sweetheart.*

**sweet nothings** *n.* loving comments; pleasant remarks between lovers. □ *They are out on the porch swing whispering sweet nothings in each other's ears.* □ *Thank heavens most married people never remember the sweet nothings they were once told.*

**sweet on someone** *mod.* favoring someone romantically. (Folksy.) □ *Sally is sort of sweet on Walter.* □ *Are you getting sweet on me?*

**(sweet) patootie** ['swit pə'tudi] **1.** *n.* an attractive (young) woman; a girlfriend. □ *Me and my patootie went over to the dance hall.* □ *Ask your sweet patootie if she wants some of this pop.* **2.** AND **patoot** *n.* the buttocks. (See also *You bet your sweet patootie.*) □ *I've never seen such a fat patoot in my life.* □ *You get your sweet patootie out of here this minute!*

**sweet potato** *n.* an ocarina, a type of popular music instrument. □ *I play the sweet potato, but not very well.* □ *There is not much music written specifically for the sweet potato.*

**sweet talk 1.** *n.* pleasant romantic talk; seductive talk. □ *I like your sweet talk, but I don't much like you.* □ *Stop that sweet talk and kiss me, you beast.* **2.** *tr.* to persuade someone to do something through kind words. □ *Do you really* think you can sweet talk me into being naughty? □ She sweet talked him into putting up her storm windows, fixing the toaster, and mowing the grass.

**sweet tooth** 1. *n.* a craving for sugary sweets. □ *Harry has quite a sweet tooth.* □ *Your sweet tooth will benefit only your dentist.* 2. *n.* an addiction to narcotics. (Drugs.) □ *Max has a sweet tooth, but he takes care of it well.* □ *She has what you might call a sweet tooth. She can't pass the stuff up.*

**swell** *mod.* fine; excellent. (Also sarcastic use.) □ *Where did you get that swell hat?* □ *Oh that's just swell! Yuck!*

**swellelegant** ['swɛl'ɛləgənt] *mod.* really fine. (From *swell* and *elegant*.) □ *Gee, this place is sure swellelegant!* □ *It is not swellelegant.* □ *Her car is just swellelegant.*

**swellhead** *n.* a conceited person. □ *Tom is getting to be such a swellhead.* □ *I wish that swellhead would spend more time elsewhere!*

**swift** 1. *mod.* smart and clever. □ *Excuse my brother. He's not too swift.* □ *Dave is doing well in school. He's swift, and he likes his classes.* 2. *mod.* sexually fast or easy, usually said of a woman. □ *Molly is swift they say, but I find her to be a perfect lady.* □ *Clare is not only swift, she has a reputation.*

**swig** 1. *n.* a deep drink of liquor; a swallow of liquor. □ *She took a swig of rum and leaped into the lagoon.* □ *One swig of that stuff was enough for me.* 2. *tr.* to drink liquor deeply. □ *He nearly swigged the whole bottle before he needed to take a breath.* □ *She swigged a big gulp and just stood there—bottle in her hand—and became paralyzed.*

**swigged** AND **swiggled** [swɪgd AND 'swɪgld] *mod.* alcohol intoxicated; tipsy. □ *Man, is she ever swigged!* □ *He is too swiggled to drive.*

**swill** 1. *n.* liquor. □ *This swill is awful. Please give me some beer.* □ *The swill they serve here is better than you can get elsewhere.* 2. *n.* a drink of liquor. □ *How about a swill out of your glass?* □ *Here, you can have a little swill of mine.* 3. *tr. & in.* to drink liquor. □ *Ted is in his room swilling like a madman.* □ *He swilled a whole case of beer yesterday.*

*Isn't he joyful yet?* 4. *n.* any nasty food or drink. □ *Let's go over to the ptomaine-domain and get our evening swill.* □ *Man does not live by swill alone. Let's go to McDuck's instead.*

**swill-up** *n.* a drinking bout. □ *There was a swill-up at the frat house last week.* □ *I never miss a swill-up.*

**swimming in something** *in.* having lots of something. □ *Right now we are swimming in merchandise. In a month it will be gone.* □ *The Wilmington-Thorpes are just swimming in money.*

**swimmingly** *mod.* quite nicely. □ *I'm having a fine time here. Everything is going along just swimmingly.* □ *The plans are moving ahead swimmingly.*

**swindle sheet** *n.* an expense account record sheet or book. □ *I turned in my swindle sheet yesterday, and no one challenged the $400 for new shoes.* □ *The government makes it hard to put just anything on your swindle sheet these days.*

**swing** 1. *in.* (for a person) to be up to date and modern. □ *Tom really swings. Look at those blue suede shoes!* □ *I used to swing, but then age and good taste overtook me.* 2. *in.* (for a party or other event) to be fun or exciting. □ *This party really swings!* □ *I've never been to a gathering that swings like this one.* 3. *in.* to be involved in sexual fads, group sex, or the swapping of sexual partners. □ *Carol says that Tom, Ted, and Alice swing. How does she know?* □ *There is a lot less swinging going on since these strange diseases have spread.* 4. *tr.* to bring something off; to execute a deal. □ *This is a very important deal. I hope I can swing it.* □ *They want to elect me president of the club. I hope they can swing it.*

**swing both ways** *in.* to be bisexual. □ *They say that Gary swings both ways, but I wouldn't know.* □ *Since he swings both ways, he may stand a better chance at finding a date.*

**swinger** 1. *n.* a person who participates in innovative sexual activities. (See *swing*.) □ *Is Gary a swinger? I've heard talk about him.* □ *We watched a movie about a swinger, but everything interesting happened in dim blue light.* 2. *n.* a youthful, socially active, and knowledgeable person. □ *Those kids are real swingers.* □ *Tom is a swinger. Look at those mod shoes.* **3.** *n.* a person who uses many different kinds of drugs. (Drugs.) □ *Paul is a swinger who will use anything. They say he can trip on a banana peel.* □ *Eventually swingers settle down to an overwhelming addiction to just one thing.*

**swinging** *mod.* great. □ *We had a swinging time at John's rally.* □ *The concert was swinging—nothing like it, ever.*

**swing into high gear** *in.* to begin operating at a fast pace; to increase the rate of activity. □ *During the winter season we swing into high gear around here.* □ *The chef swings into high gear around eight o'clock in preparation for the theater crowd.*

**swingman** *n.* a drug seller; a drug *connection.* □ *Max couldn't deliver till he met with his swingman.* □ *Bruno wants to be a swingman with the mob.*

**swing shift** *n.* an evening work shift in a factory, usually from mid-afternoon to midnight. (Compare to *graveyard shift.*) □ *I don't mind the swing shift. I'm a night person anyway.* □ *My brother works the swing shift, so I never get to see him.*

**swing with someone or something** *in.* to appreciate someone or something. (See *swing.*) □ *Man, I can really swing with that color. Glorious!* □ *I can really swing with John. He and I are real close.*

**swipe 1.** *tr.* to drink liquor rapidly and to excess; to bolt a drink of liquor. □ *Ted swiped a quick one and ran out the door.* □ *Fred sat at the bar and swiped two gins and ate an egg.* **2.** *n.* moonshine; inferior liquor. □ *This swipe is gross. I'd rather drink water.* □ *I can't stand the swipe they serve here.* **3.** *tr.* to steal something. □ *Max swiped a pack of cigarettes from the counter.* □ *Somebody swiped my wallet!* **4.** *n.* a blow or an act of striking someone or something. (See *take a swipe at someone or something.*) □ *Bob got a nasty swipe across the face.* □ *The cat gave the mouse a swipe with its paw.*

**swish** [swɪʃ] **1.** *mod.* overly fancy; effeminate; displaying effeminacy. □ *The lobby of the theater was a little swish, but not offensive.* □ *Who is your swish little friend?* **2.** *n.* elaborate decoration; effeminacy. □ *There's a little too much swish here. Get rid of the gold drapes.* □ *What this place needs is more swish. Hang some baubles here and there.*

**switch** *n.* a switchblade knife. □ *They found a switch in his pocket when they searched him.* □ *Max was arrested for carrying a switch.*

**switched on 1.** *mod.* introduced to drug use; awakened to the use of hallucinogenic drugs. (Drugs.) □ *All my friends are switched on.* □ *Look at that switched on kid.* □ *I'd rather not be switched on, so I joined a treatment program to help.* **2.** *mod.* drug intoxicated. (Drugs.) □ *That guy is so switched on he can hardly walk.* □ *Who wants to go out and get switched on?* **3.** *mod.* alert and up to date; with it. □ *My brother is switched on and has lots of friends.* □ *I'm not switched on. In fact, I am pretty dull.* **4.** *mod.* excited. □ *I get switched on by that kind of music.* □ *I am never switched on by raucous music.*

**switcheroo** ['swɪtʃə'ru] *n.* a reversal; a switching around. □ *He pulled a switcheroo on us and showed up at the other door, so we missed getting his autograph.* □ *She is a master at the old switcheroo.*

**switch-hitter** *n.* a player who bats either right- or left-handed. (Baseball.) □ *Monty is a switch-hitter, but he's batting right-handed today.* □ *I'm not a switch-hitter. In fact, I can hardly hit the ball at all.*

**switch off** *in.* to become oblivious to everything. □ *I want to go home and switch off—just forget this whole day.* □ *I have to switch off when I go home.*

**switch on 1.** *in.* to come alive. □ *She saw her child and immediately switched on.* □ *I don't switch on until about noon.* **2.** *in.* to become modern and participate in current fads and events. □ *I am too old to switch on.* □ *Most kids I know switched on when they went to high school.* **3.** *in.* to get high on drugs; to begin taking *L.S.D.* or some other hallucinogens. (Drugs. See *turn on*.) □ *One by one, each of my friends switched on.* □ *There was some old man who seemed to get pleasure from getting kids to switch on. Maybe he was a dealer.* (More at *switched on*.)

**swizzle** ['swɪzl] **1.** *tr.* & *in.* to drink (liquor), probably to excess; to tipple. □ *Have you been swizzling again?* □ *Fred's uncle is always swizzling a little drink.* **2.** *n.* liquor; beer; a drink of an alcoholic beverage. □ *What a hot day. I could use some swizzle.* □ *What I need is a nice cold swizzle.*

**swizzled** ['swɪzld] *mod.* alcohol intoxicated. □ *Fred went out and got himself swizzled.* □ *Man, he is really swizzled!*

**swizzle-stick** *n.* a drunkard. (From the name of a short stick used to stir an alcoholic drink.) □ *That guy is a swizzle-stick. Don't give him any more.* □ *You had better slow down, or you will*

turn into a swizzle-stick.

**swoozled** AND **swozzled** ['swuzld AND 'swɑzld] *mod.* alcohol intoxicated. □ *How can anybody be so swozzled on three beers?* □ *Those guys are really swoozled!*

**swozzled** See the previous entry.

**syrup head** *n.* a drug user or addict who takes cough syrup containing codeine. (Drugs.) □ *Max is turning into a syrup head. Why does he drink that stuff?* □ *All those kids were syrup heads before they took up coke.*

**syrupy** *mod.* overly sentimental. □ *I can't stand syrupy movies.* □ *That music is too syrupy.* □ *All this syrupy talk is making me tired.*

**sysop** ['sɪsɑp] *n.* the "systems operator" of a computer. □ *I talked to the sysop, who said that the system will be back up soon.* □ *The sysop got in trouble for distributing copyrighted software.*

# T

**T.** *n.* marijuana. (Drugs. From *tea*.) □ *Can't you stay off that tea? □ All she thinks about is smoking T. and where she's gonna get more of it.*

**tab 1.** *n.* a bill (for something). (From *tabulation.* See also *chit.*) □ *What's the tab for this? □ Barlowe paid the tab and left quietly.* **2.** *n.* a tablet (of medicine). □ *Take a couple of aspirin tabs and call me in the morning. □ These tabs must have got wet. They're ruined.* **3.** *tr.* to identify someone. □ *I couldn't quite tab her, but when she started talking I knew right away who she was. □ I tabbed him right away.*

**tabbed** *mod.* well-dressed. (Black.) □ *That dude is well tabbed. □ She's really tabbed in some nice threads.*

**table-hop** *in.* to move from table to table in a restaurant, nightclub, bar, etc. □ *We used to table-hop, but nobody knows us anymore. □ They would table-hop—to the great dismay of the waiters.*

**tac** See *tic.*

**tacky 1.** *mod.* cheap; crude. □ *That was a tacky thing to do to her. □ That was so tacky! □ This is sort of a tacky gift for a wedding.* **2.** *mod.* alcohol intoxicated. □ *Tom was a little tacky, so he gave me his car keys. □ Bruno seems tacky, but that's just the way he is.*

**tad** *n.* a bit; a small bit. □ *I'll take just a tad. I'm on a diet. □ That's a little more than a tad, but it's all right.*

**tag 1.** *n.* a name. □ *I know the face, but I forgot the tag. □ Everybody knows that tag well.* **2.** *n.* euphoria from drug use; a drug *rush.* □ *This tag from this mojo is something to behold. □ This trash has no tag at all.* **3.** *n.* a car license plate or sticker. □ *The car had Kansas tags and was towing a trailer. □ Don't forget to get a new tag for this year.* **4.** *n.* a blow to the body in boxing. □ *Wilbur landed another tag to the right shoulder before the gong sounded. □ Another tag on the head and Wilbur will be down.* **5.** *tr.* to punch someone in boxing. □ *Sam tagged his opponent on the cheek. □ The guy tagged him back right in the gut.* **6.** *tr.* (in baseball) to touch a runner with the baseball. □ *Wilbur tagged the runner and fell flat on his face. □ The catcher tagged the runner, but it was too late.* **7.** *n.* the coda or ending section of a piece of music. □ *Now, I want everybody to slow down and watch me on the tag. □ Give everything you've got on the tag.* **8.** *tr.* to charge someone with a crime. □ *The cop tagged him with the bank caper immediately.* □ *The cop tagged me with a ticket before I knew what hit me.*

**Tah-dah!** [tə'dɑ] *exclam.* "Look at this!"; "Look at me!"; "Presenting..." □ *Tah-dah! How do you like my new haircut? □ And here is—tah-dah!—our ever-late and never-punished executive secretary.*

**tail bone** *n.* the base of the spine. □ *He fell square on his tail bone. □ A bruised tail bone is a real annoyance.*

**tail-end** *n.* the back end of something or someone. □ *He was at the tail-end of the long line. □ Molly fell down on her tail-end.*

**tailgate 1.** *tr. & in.* to follow (someone) too closely in a car. □ *That guy tailgating me is drunk, I think. □ Ease off a little; you're tailgating.* **2.** *in.* to have a *tailgate party.* □ *We planned to tailgate before the game, but it was massively cold. □ The people who were tailgating next to us asked to borrow our salt.*

**tailgate party** *n.* a small party held on the folded down tailgate of a station wagon in a parking lot. (Something that is done before a ball game.) □ *They had a tailgate party before the Bears game.* □ *The tailgate party was a success, except for the cold.*

**tailor made 1.** *mod.* having to do with something that is custom made. (Standard English.) □ *This lovely garment is tailor made.* □ *I have to have tailor made clothes because of my long arms and legs.* **2.** *n.* a machine made cigarette. □ *They used to call these things tailor made, meaning professionally made, as opposed to homemade.* □ *The cowboy in the movie refused to smoke a tailor made.*

**tails** *n.* a tuxedo with long tails. □ *Shall I wear my tails?* □ *Ralph had to rent tails for the evening.*

**take 1.** *n.* a section of a film that is pronounced acceptable just after it is shot. □ *It's a take. Get it over to the lab.* □ *After seven straight takes the crew demanded a break.* **2.** *n.* the amount of money taken in at some event; the money received for the tickets that have been purchased. □ *What was the take for the concert?* □ *The take was much larger than we expected.* **3.** *tr.* to cheat or deceive someone. □ *That clerk tried to take me.* □ *When they think you're going to count your change, they won't try to take you.* **4.** *tr.* to defeat someone, as in a fight. □ *Max thought he could take the guy, but he wasn't sure.* □ *I know I can take you. Make my day!*

**take a bath (on something)** *tr.* to have large financial losses on an investment. □ *Fred took a bath on that gold mining stock.* □ *The broker warned me that I might take a bath if I bought this stuff.*

**take a beating** *tr.* to be beaten, bested, or defeated. □ *The candidate took a beating in the runoffs.* □ *The team took quite a beating.*

**take a break** *tr.* to stop working for a rest period. □ *Let's take a break here. Be back in five minutes.* □ *I've got to take a break before I drop.*

**take a crack at something** AND **have a crack at something** *tr.* to take a try at something. □ *She had a crack at food*

preparation, but that wasn't for her. □ *Let me take a crack at it.*

**take a dig at someone** AND **take a jab at someone** *tr.* to insult or needle someone. □ *Why did you take a jab at Sam?* □ *You're always taking digs at people who think they're your friends.*

**take a dirt nap** *tr.* to die and be buried. □ *I don't want to end up taking a dirt nap during this operation.* □ *Isn't Tom a little young to take a dirt nap?*

**take a dive** See the following entry.

**take a fall** AND **take a dive 1.** *tr.* to fake being knocked out in a boxing match. □ *Wilbur wouldn't take a fall. He doesn't have it in him.* □ *The boxer took a dive in the second round and made everyone suspicious.* **2.** *tr.* to get arrested. (Underworld.) □ *Bruno took a fall for the bank robbery.* □ *I didn't wanna take a dive, but the cop left me no choice.*

**take a flyer** *tr.* to leave town; to depart. □ *Things got a little rough, and Marty decided to take a flyer.* □ *Bruno took a flyer when he heard about the raid.*

**take a gander (at someone or something)** *tr.* to look at someone or something. (See also *gander*.) □ *Wow, take a gander at this chick!* □ *I wanted to take a gander at the new computer before they started using it.*

**take a hike** AND **take a walk** *tr.* to leave; to beat it. □ *Okay, I've had it with you. Take a hike! Beat it!* □ *I had enough of the boss and the whole place, so I cleaned out my desk and took a walk.*

**take a jab at someone** See *take a dig at someone.*

**take a leak\*** *tr.* to urinate. (Crude. Caution with topic. Usually in reference to a male.) □ *I gotta go take a leak. Back in a minute.* □ *He just went out to take a leak.*

**take a lot of nerve 1.** *tr.* to be very rude; to require a lot of rudeness (to behave so badly). □ *He walked out on her, and that took a lot of nerve!* □ *That took a lot of nerve! You took my parking place!* **2.** *tr.* to require courage. □ *He climbed the mountain with a bruised foot. That took a lot of nerve.* □ *It took a lot of nerve to go into business for himself.*

**take a nosedive** *tr.* to collapse; to fail. □ *The market took a nosedive again* *today.* □ *She slipped on the ice and took a nosedive.*

**take a page from someone's book** *tr.* to copy or emulate. □ *I took a page from Edison's book and began inventing useful little things.* □ *Mind if I take a page from your book and apply for a job here?*

**take a pop at someone** *tr.* to punch at someone. □ *Bruno took a pop at me, but I ducked.* □ *The drunk took a pop at the cop—which was the wrong thing to do.*

**take a powder** *tr.* to leave; to leave town. (Underworld.) □ *Why don't you take a powder? Go on! Beat it!* □ *Bruno took a powder and will lie low for a while.*

**Take a running jump (in the lake)!** *exclam.* "Go away!"; "Get away from me!" □ *You know what you can do? You can take a running jump. Beat it!* □ *You can just take a running jump in the lake, you creep!*

**take a shot (at something)** *tr.* to try (to do) something. □ *I don't think I can do it, but I'll take a shot at it.* □ *Go ahead. Take a shot.*

**take a sleigh ride** See *go for a sleigh ride*.

**take a sweep (with both barrels)** *tr.* to *snort* cocaine (with both nostrils). (Drugs. See *sweep*.) □ *She was afraid at first, but now she takes a sweep with both barrels every time, and she's hooked.* □ *She left her desk to go take a sweep in the women's john.*

**take a swipe at someone or something** *tr.* to poke at someone or something. (See *swipe*.) □ *Max took a swipe at Bruno.* □ *The cat took a swipe at the ball.*

**take a walk** See *take a hike*.

**take a whack at someone or something** **1.** *tr.* to have a try at something. □ *Let me take a whack at it.* □ *Why don't you practice a little while and take a whack at it tomorrow?* **2.** *tr.* to hit at someone or something. □ *Wilbur took a whack at Martin and missed.* □ *Jerry got an ax and took a whack at the tree, but didn't do much damage.*

**Take care.** *phr.* "Goodbye, be careful." □ *See you later. Take care.* □ *Take care. See you in Philly.*

**take care of number one** AND **take care of numero uno** *tr.* to take care of oneself. (See *number one, numero uno*.) □ *Arthur, like everybody else, is most concerned with taking care of number one.* □ *If you don't take care of numero uno, who will?*

**take care of someone** *tr.* to kill someone. (Underworld.) □ *The boss told Bruno to take care of Max.* □ *I'm gonna take care of you once and for all.*

**take five** *tr.* to take a five-minute break. □ *Okay, gang, take five. Be back here in five minutes, or else.* □ *She told them to take five, but they turned the five into fifty.*

**take it** *tr.* to endure something, physically or mentally. (See also *take it on the chin*.) □ *I just can't take it anymore.* □ *If you can't take it, quit.*

**take it easy** **1.** *phr.* "relax and take care." □ *See you later. Take it easy.* □ *They told me to take it easy for a few days.* **2.** *exclam.* "Let up!"; "Not so hard!"; "Be gentle!" (Usually **Take it easy!**) □ *Take it easy! That hurts!* □ *Take it easy; he's just a kid!*

**take it on the chin** AND **take it on the nose** **1.** *tr.* to stand up to something adverse, such as criticism. □ *They laid some rude chops on him, but he took it on the chin.* □ *I knew he could take it on the nose.* **2.** *tr.* to receive the full brunt of something. □ *Why do I have to take it on the chin for something I didn't do?* □ *If you did it, you have to learn to take it on the chin.*

**take it on the lam** *tr.* to get out of town; to run away. (Underworld.) □ *Both took it on the lam when things got hot.* □ *Bruno knew that the time had come to take it on the lam.*

**Take it or leave it.** *sent.* "There are no other choices."; "It is this or nothing." □ *This is what you get for the money. Take it or leave it.* □ *I told her that there was a shortage of these things and she had to take it or leave it.*

**take it out on someone or something** *tr.* to punish or harm someone or something because one is angry or disturbed about something. □ *I'm sorry about your difficulty, but don't take it out on me.* □ *Don't take it out on the cat.*

**take it slow** *tr.* to go slowly and carefully. □ *Just relax and take it slow. You've got a good chance. □ You'll make it. Take it slow and keep your spirits up.*

**take it through the nose** *tr.* to snort cocaine. (Drugs. A play on *take it on the nose* which is at *take it on the chin*.) □ *Max liked taking it through the nose better than anything, except maybe a shot in the arm. □ He went into the john, and most of us knew he had to take it through the nose right then.*

**take it to the street** *tr.* to tell everyone about your problems. (Black. See also *on the street*.) □ *If there's something bothering her, she's gonna take it to the street, first thing. □ Come on, don't take it to the street.*

**taken** AND **had, took** 1. *mod.* cheated; deceived. □ *I counted my change, and I knew I was taken. □ You were really took, all right.* 2. *mod.* drug intoxicated; unconscious from drugs. □ *The guy in the corner booth was taken and crying in his beer. □ His eyes were bloodshot, his hands were shaking—he was had.* 3. *mod.* dead. □ *I'm sorry, your cat is taken—pifted. □ Your cat's took, lady, tough luck.* 4. *mod.* already claimed as someone's mate or lover. □ *Sorry, Bill, I'm already taken. Sam and I are engaged. □ Forget it. She's taken.*

**take names** *tr.* to make a list of wrongdoers. (Often figuratively, as with a schoolteacher, whose major weapon is to take names and send them to the principal.) □ *The boss is madder than hell, and he's taking names. □ Gary is coming by to talk about the little riot last night, and I think he's taking names.*

**take off** 1. *in.* (for someone) to leave in a hurry. □ *She really took off outa there. □ I've got to take off—I'm late.* 2. *in.* (for something) to start selling well. □ *The fluffy dog dolls began to take off, and we sold out the lot. □ Ticket sales really took off after the first performance.* 3. See the following entry.

**take-off** 1. *n.* an imitation of something; a copy of something. □ *This robot is capable of producing 200 circuit board take-offs per hour. □ My machine is a take-off of the real thing.* 2. *n.* a parody of someone or something.

(Usually with *on*.) □ *The comedian did a take-off on the wealthy senator. □ The take-off on the dean didn't go over well.* 3. *n.* a robbery. (Underworld.) □ *That was some take-off Lefty pulled, huh? □ Yeah, Lefty sure knows take-offs.*

**take-off artist** *n.* a thief. (Underworld.) □ *A take-off artist known as the Cat is cleaning out closets and jewel boxes all over town. □ He's not a sales agent. He's a take-off artist, pure and simple.*

**take off (on something)** *in.* to get a high from a particular drug. (Drugs.) □ *He couldn't wait to take off on some shrooms. □ All Tom cares about is taking off.*

**take one's belt in (a notch)** AND **pull one's belt in (a notch)** *tr.* to prepare for lean times. (See also *tighten one's belt*.) □ *It was clear that we would have to bite the bullet and take our belt in a notch. □ We were able to take our belt in a notch, unlike other people who were already strained to the maximum.*

**take one's lumps** *tr.* to accept the result or punishment one deserves. (Compare to *get one's lumps*.) □ *You've got to learn to take your lumps if you're going to be in politics. □ I hate taking my lumps. I'd rather pretend nothing had happened.*

**take on fuel** AND **take fuel on** *tr.* to drink alcohol to excess. □ *They stopped at the tavern to take on fuel. □ They went inside to take fuel on and then came back out to watch the horses.*

**take on (so)** *in.* to whine, cry, and be in great despair. (Folksy.) □ *I know it hurts, but don't take on so. □ Nobody knew why she took on so.*

**takeover** *n.* a company that has been or is likely to be taken over by new owners. (Financial markets.) □ *Acme is not—I repeat, not—a possible takeover. You can make book on it. □ Acme Systems is the latest in a series of successful takeovers.*

**take pictures** *tr.* for a highway patrol officer to use radar. (Citizens band radio.) □ *There's a smokey under the bridge taking pictures. □ I didn't see the creep was taking pictures. I got nabbed.*

**taker** *n.* one who accepts an offer; a buyer. □ *Are there any takers for this* *fine, almost new caddy?* □ *Here's a taker. You'll not be sorry.*

**take some doing** *tr.* to require added effort and planning. □ *It'll take some doing, but it'll get done.* □ *It's not impossible. It'll just take some doing.*

**take someone in** AND **take in someone 1.** AND **rope someone in, rope in someone** *tr.* to cheat or deceive someone. □ *He might try to take you in. Keep an eye on him and count your change.* □ *The con artists tried to rope the old lady in, but she was too clever.* **2.** *tr.* to give shelter to someone. □ *We took her in and gave her some soup and a place to stay.* □ *Mrs. Wilson takes in almost every young person who needs her help.*

**take someone or something apart 1.** *tr.* to criticize or defame someone or something. □ *They really took me apart, but what the hell?* □ *The editorial took the whole board apart.* **2.** *tr.* to beat or damage someone or something. □ *The mugger really took the old lady apart.* □ *The wreck took both cars apart.*

**take someone or something off** AND **take off someone or something 1.** *tr.* [with *someone*] to kill someone. (Underworld.) □ *Barlowe didn't want to have to take off Lefty—like hell, he didn't.* □ *The mob took the witness off a week before the trial.* **2.** *tr.* to rob someone or something. (Underworld.) □ *Weren't you in that bunch that took the bank off in Philly?* □ *No, we never took off no bank, did we, Lefty?*

**take someone or something on** AND **take on someone or something** *tr.* to accept the task of handling a difficult person or thing. □ *Nobody wanted to take on Mrs. Franklin, but it had to be done.* □ *I'll take it on if nobody else will do it.*

**take someone or something out** AND **take out someone or something 1.** *tr.* [with *someone*] to block someone, as in a football game. □ *I was supposed to take out the left end, but I was trapped under the center.* □ *Okay, Andy, you take out the center this time.* **2.** *tr.* [with *someone*] to kill someone. (Underworld.) □ *The boss told Rocko to take out Barlowe.* □ *Barlowe was sure he could keep Rocko from taking him out.*

**3.** *tr.* [with *something*] to bomb or destroy something. □ *The enemy took out one of the tanks, but not the one carrying the medicine.* □ *The last flight took out two enemy bunkers and a radar installation.* **4.** *tr.* [with *someone*] to date someone. □ *I hope he'll take me out soon.* □ *She wanted to take him out for an evening.*

**take someone to the cleaners 1.** *tr.* to take all of someone's money. □ *The lawyers took the insurance company to the cleaners, but I still didn't get enough to pay for my losses.* □ *The con artists took the old man to the cleaners.* **2.** *tr.* to defeat or best someone. □ *We took the other team to the cleaners.* □ *Look at the height they've got! They'll take us to the cleaners!*

**take something public 1.** *tr.* to make something known to the public. □ *You gotta take it public—put it on the street—even when it's none of your business.* □ *Don't take it public. You'll just get talked about.* **2.** *tr.* to sell shares in a company to the general public. (Financial markets.) □ *The board decided not to take the company public.* □ *We're going to take it public whenever the market looks good.*

**takes two to tango** *phr.* "requires two people to do certain things." □ *No, he didn't do it all by himself. Takes two to tango, you know.* □ *There's no such thing as a one-sided argument. It takes two to tango.*

**take the cake** *tr.* to be amazing or surprising in some way, as if there were a prize for this excellence. (Folksy.) □ *That joke really takes the cake. I wish I'd told it.* □ *I've seen some messes in my day, but this one takes the cake.*

**take the cure** *tr.* to enter into any treatment program or treatment center. (Especially those dealing with drugs and alcohol.) □ *I wanted to take the cure, but I just couldn't bring myself to do it.* □ *It's hard to get them to realize that they are the ones who have to decide to take the cure.*

**take the fifth 1.** AND **five it** *tr.* to refuse to testify to a U.S. legislative committee under the protection of the fifth amendment to the U.S. Constitution.

□ *His lawyer told him to take the fifth.* □ *The lawyer just sat there and said, "Five it" after every question.* **2.** *tr.* to decline to answer any questions. □ *I'll take the fifth on that one. Ask Fred.* □ *Don't ask me. I take the fifth.*

**take the heat** AND **take some heat** *tr.* to receive criticism (for something). □ *The cops have been taking some heat about the Quincy killing.* □ *If you can't take the heat, stay out of the kitchen.*

**take the heat off someone** *tr.* to relieve the pressure on someone; to free someone from suspicion, responsibility, a deadline, etc. □ *The confession by Rocko took the heat off the cop-shop for a while.* □ *They took the heat off us by moving the deadline.*

**take the (long) count** *tr.* to die. □ *The poor cat took the long count at last.* □ *I'm too young to take the count.*

**take the pipe 1.** AND **take the gas pipe** *tr.* to commit suicide. (Originally by inhaling gas.) □ *The kid was dropping everything in sight and finally took the pipe.* □ *Some poor old guy took the gas pipe and nearly blew the place up.* **2.** *tr.* to fail to perform under pressure; to cave in. (From sense 1.) □ *He tends to take the pipe when the going gets rough.* □ *Don't take the pipe, man. Stick in there!*

**take the pledge** *tr.* to promise to abstain from beverage alcohol. □ *I'm not ready to take the pledge yet, but I will cut down.* □ *My aunt tried to get me to take the pledge.*

**take the plunge** *tr.* to marry someone. □ *I'm not ready to take the plunge yet.* □ *Sam and Mary took the plunge.*

**take the rap (for something)** *tr.* to take the blame for something. (Originally underworld. See *rap*.) □ *I didn't want to take the rap for the job, but, after all, I was guilty.* □ *I threw the rock, but John took the rap.*

**take the spear (in one's chest)** *tr.* to accept full blame for something; to accept the full brunt of the punishment for something. □ *The Admiral got the short straw and had to take the spear in his chest.* □ *I sure didn't want to take the spear.*

**take the starch out of someone** *tr.* to reduce someone's self-assurance; to reduce someone's conceit. □ *I took the starch out of Kelly by telling him where he was headed if he didn't change his ways.* □ *That remark really took the starch out of him.*

**take the wind out of someone's sails** *tr.* to put a barrier in someone's path; to reduce the effectiveness of someone. □ *When the cops showed Max the evidence, it took the wind out of his sails.* □ *It really took the wind out of his sails when he didn't get promoted.*

**take things easy 1.** *tr.* to live well and comfortably. □ *I'll be glad when I can make enough money to take things easy.* □ *I make enough to take things easy.* **2.** *tr.* to relax temporarily and recuperate. □ *The doctor says I'm supposed to take things easy for a while.* □ *I want you to take it easy until the stitches heal.*

**take (to) the needle** *tr. & in.* to inject drugs; to begin taking drugs by injection. (Drugs.) □ *First it was pot, and then she took to the needle.* □ *They ended up taking the needle and catching some disease.*

**taking care of business** *tr.* doing what one is meant to do; coping with life as it is. (Black. See *T.C.B.*) □ *If the dude is taking care of business, what else do you want out of him?* □ *Walter is taking care of business. Back in a minute.*

**tale of woe** *n.* a sad story; a list of personal problems; an excuse for failing to do something. □ *I listened to her tale of woe without saying anything.* □ *This tale of woe that we have all been getting from Kelly is just too much.*

**talk a blue streak** *tr.* to talk fast or a lot. □ *This crazy bird suddenly began talking a blue streak.* □ *Some parrots never talk. Others talk a blue streak whenever it's light.*

**talk big** *in.* to brag; to make grandiose statements. □ *She talks big, but can't produce anything.* □ *He has some deep need to talk big. He can't do anything.*

**talking head** *n.* a television news reader or announcer whose head and neck appear on the screen. □ *I've had it with talking heads. I can read the paper and learn as much in twenty minutes.* □

*Some of those talking heads make millions a year.*

**talk like a nut** *in.* to say stupid things. □ *You're talking like a nut! You don't know what you are saying.* □ *Don't talk like a nut! We can't afford a trip to Florida!*

**talk on the big white phone** *in.* to vomit into a toilet. □ *One more beer and I'm gonna have to go talk on the big white phone.* □ *She was talking on the big white phone all night.*

**talk someone ragged** *tr.* to talk to someone too much; to bore someone. □ *That was not an interview. She talked me ragged.* □ *He always talks me ragged, but I always listen.*

**talk someone's ear off** AND **talk someone's head off** *tr.* to talk too much and bore someone. □ *I didn't mean to talk your ear off.* □ *I had to get out of that place before she talked my head off.*

**talk someone's head off** **1.** *tr.* (for someone) to speak too much. □ *I talked my head off trying to convince them.* □ *Don't waste time talking your head off to them.* **2.** See *talk someone's ear off.*

**talk through one's hat** *in.* to say baseless things; to speak carelessly and tell lies. □ *Pay no attention to my friend here. He's just talking through his hat.* □ *You don't know what you are talking about. You're just talking through your hat.*

**talk to hear one's own voice** *in.* to talk far more than is necessary; to talk much, in an egotistical manner. □ *Oh, he's just talking to hear his own voice.* □ *Am I just talking to hear my own voice, or are you listening to me?*

**talk to Herb and Al** *in.* to use marijuana and drink alcohol. (See *herb. Al* is alcohol.) □ *I've been out talking to Herb and Al—that's where I've been.* □ *Let's go talk to Herb and Al while we're waiting.*

**talk turkey** *tr.* to talk serious business; to talk frankly. □ *We've got to sit down and talk turkey—get this thing wrapped up.* □ *It's time to talk turkey and quit messing around.*

**talk until one is blue in the face** *in.* to talk until one is exhausted. □ *You can talk till you're blue in the face, but it*

won't do any good. □ *She talked until she was blue in the face, but could not change their minds.*

**talk up a storm** See *up a storm.*

**tall** **1.** *mod.* high on drugs; intoxicated with marijuana. (Drugs.) □ *When Jerry gets a little tall, he gets overwhelmed with a sense of guilt.* □ *She seems a little tall. What's she on?* **2.** *mod.* high quality. □ *This is one tall pizza, man.* □ *You're bringing in some tall ideas, man.*

**tall in the saddle** *mod.* proud. (Often with *sit.*) □ *I'll still be tall in the saddle when you are experiencing the results of your folly.* □ *Despite her difficulties, she still sat tall in the saddle.*

**tall one** *n.* a large drink; a long drink. (Compare to *short one.*) □ *She ordered a tall one and sat back to cool off.* □ *Give me a tall one, John.*

**tall order** *n.* a request that is difficult to fulfill. □ *That's a tall order. Do you think anyone can do it?* □ *Well, it's a tall order, but I'll do it.*

**tall story** *n.* a story that is hard to believe; a lie. (Folksy.) □ *That's a mighty tall story. I don't believe a word of it.* □ *Who can believe his tall stories?*

**tall timbers** *n.* some remote well-forested place; the *boondocks.* □ *Oh, Chuck lives out in the tall timbers somewhere. He only has a post office box number.* □ *You're not going to move me out into the tall timbers somewhere!*

**tamale** [tə'mɑli] *n.* a poorly made marijuana cigarette. (Drugs. From Mexican Spanish.) □ *Who made this tamale anyway?* □ *Who's the guy with the tamale hanging off his lip like a movie hero?*

**tambourine man** *n.* a drug seller. (Drugs.) □ *Max is the local tambourine man.* □ *A tambourine man and a candy man are essentially the same thing.*

**T. and A.\*** **1.** *n.* an operation to remove one's tonsils and adenoids. (Hospitals.) □ *She was scheduled for a T. and A. this morning at six sharp.* □ *The T. and A. went off without a hitch.* **2.\*** AND **tits and ass\*** *n.* a display of "tits and ass," breasts and buttocks. (See *B. and B.* Caution with topic.) □ *The magazines featuring tits and ass flourish in their under-the-counter trade.* □ *These silly*

*T. and A. movies have no plot to interfere with the leers.*

**tang** *n.* an addiction to a drug. (Drugs. From *orangutan*, one of the monkeys that can be on an addict's back. See *have a monkey on one's back*.) □ *That dude really has a tang on his back.* □ *My tang is hungry.*

**tangerine** *n.* Methedrine™, an amphetamine. (Drugs.) □ *Ken said that Kelly's been shooting tangerine.* □ *Ken is sort of fond of tangerine, too.*

**tangle with someone or something** *in.* to quarrel or fight with someone or something. □ *I didn't want to tangle with her, so I did what she wanted.* □ *It's like tangling with a grizzly.*

**tank 1.** AND **tank up** *in.* to drink too much beer; to drink to excess. □ *The two brothers were tanking up and didn't hear me come in.* □ *Let's go out this Friday and tank awhile.* **2.** *n.* a drunkard. (Usually **tank-up**.) □ *You're turning into a real tank, Harry.* □ *Who's the tank-up carrying the thermos of whiskey?* **3.** *n.* a jail cell for holding drunks. □ *Maybe a night in the tank would give you a chance to think about being a full-time drunk.* □ *One night in the tank was enough to make John take the pledge.* **4.** *n.* one's capacity or need for drugs. (Drugs.) □ *Harry's got quite a big tank.* □ *Her tank is big enough for a chippy habit.* **5.** *tr. & in.* to lose a game deliberately. □ *Wilbur would never tank.* □ *The manager got wind of a plan to tank Friday's game.* **6.** *in.* for something to fail. □ *The entire stock market tanked on Friday.* □ *My investments did not tank when the market collapsed.*

**tanked 1.** AND **tanked up** *mod.* alcohol intoxicated. □ *She was too tanked to drive.* □ *That old codger is really tanked.* **2.** *mod.* defeated; out-scored. □ *The team was tanked again—20 to 17.* □ *I just knew we'd get tanked today.*

**tanker** *n.* a drinker; a drunkard. □ *When I came into the bar, a few tankers were in the back.* □ *Who's the tanker carrying the thermos of gin?*

**tank up** See *tank.*

**tanky** *mod.* alcohol intoxicated. □ *The guy was just a little tanky.* □ *He found a way to slow down and keep from getting tanky at parties.*

**tanned** *mod.* alcohol intoxicated. (Preserved like a *tanned* hide of an animal.) □ *She was completely tanned.* □ *Tom is too tanned to drive. Get him out of that car.*

**tan someone's hide** *tr.* to spank someone. (Folksy.) □ *My dad is going to tan my hide.* □ *If you do that again, I'll tan your hide!*

**tap** See *tap someone (for something).*

**tap dance like mad** *in.* to be busy continuously; to have to move fast to distract someone. □ *When things get tough, the whole Congress tap dances like mad.* □ *Any public official knows how to tap dance like mad without getting out of breath or sweating.*

**taped** [tept] *mod.* finalized; *sealed (up); cinched.* (As if one were taping a package.) □ *I'll have this deal taped by Thursday. Then we can take it easy.* □ *Until this thing is taped, we can't do anything.*

**tap out** *in.* to lose one's money in gambling or in the financial markets. □ *I'm gonna tap out in about three more rolls—just watch.* □ *I really tapped out on that gold mining stock.* (More at *tapped.*)

**tapped** [tæpt] **1.** AND **tapped out** *mod.* broke. □ *The consumer is just about tapped. Don't expect much buying in that sector.* □ *I'm tapped out. Nothing left for you or anybody else this month.* **2.** AND **tapped out** *mod.* exhausted. □ *I need a nap. I'm tapped out.* □ *I've had it. I'm tapped.* **3.** AND **tapped out** *mod.* ruined. □ *We are tapped. That really did it to us.* □ *The project is completely tapped out.* **4.** *mod.* arrested. (As if one were tapped on the shoulder by a police officer.) □ *I knew I was gonna get tapped eventually, but I just couldn't stop stealing.* □ *The whole gang was tapped in a police raid.*

**tap someone (for something)** *tr.* to select someone for some purpose or position. □ *The committee tapped John to run for Congress.* □ *I had thought they were going to tap Sally.*

**tarantula juice** [təˈræntʃələ dʒus] *n.* potent or inferior whisky. □ *What is in this tarantula juice anyway?* □ *Do you have anything in this joint but tarantula juice?*

**tarnation** *n.* "damnation"; "(the) hell." (Folksy. A euphemism.) □ *Tarnation, man! What are you doing?* □ *What in tarnation is this mess in the closet?*

**tarred with the same brush** *mod.* having achieved guilt by association; sullied by the same agent. □ *Those guys were tarred with the same brush. Stay away from both of them.* □ *Both of the two-bit cons were tarred by the same brush and sent up the river.*

**taste 1.** *n.* a small drink of liquor. □ *Just a taste for me, thanks.* □ *How about another taste in your glass?* **2.** *n.* a sample portion of a drug; a bit of heroin. (Drugs. See *schmeck*.) □ *He wanted a taste to test it for quality.* □ *No, I don't give tastes.* **3.** *tr.* to test a sample of a drug. (Drugs.) □ *She tasted it and nodded her approval.* □ *Harry wanted to take some home and taste it.* **4.** *n.* whiskey; wine. □ *Let's hit the leeky store for some taste.* □ *I need some taste right now.* **5.** *n.* a share; a *piece of the action.* □ *I want a taste, too.* □ *Whatever the deal is, I want a taste.*

**taste blood** *tr.* to experience something exciting, and perhaps dangerous, for the first time. □ *She had tasted blood once, and she knew that the life of a race-car driver was for her.* □ *Once you taste blood, you're hooked.*

**ta-ta** ['tɑ'tɑ] *interj.* "goodbye." □ *See ya later. Ta-ta.* □ *Ta-ta. Take care.*

**tater** ['tedɚ] *n.* a potato. (Folksy.) □ *More taters, anybody?* □ *Nothing beats taters and gravy.*

**tawny** ['tɔni] *mod.* excellent. □ *Who is throwing this tawny party anyway?* □ *This pizza is, like, tawny!*

**T.C.B.** AND **TCB** *phr.* "taking care of business"; doing things that have to be done. (Black.) □ *He's TCB; that's where he is.* □ *If I am T.C.B. and keeping my nose clean, I know I'm gonna be all right.*

**tea\* 1.** *n.* liquor; alcoholic drink. □ *Would you care for more tea?* □ *Give the lady some more tea.* **2.\*** *n.* urine. (Caution with topic.) □ *There is some tea on the floor.* □ *Is that tea on your pants leg?* **3.** *n.* marijuana. (Drugs.) □ *Max has tea and canaries on him now.*

*No dust.* □ *Can't you lay off that tea awhile?*

**tea accessories** *n.* apparatus for marijuana use. (Drugs.) □ *The shops advertised tea accessories in the window. I knew what that meant.* □ *I even saw tea accessories listed in the telephone book.*

**tea bag** AND **teastick** *n.* a marijuana cigarette. (Drugs.) □ *Max slipped her a teastick in thanks for her help.* □ *Don't forget to bring the tea bags to the tea party.*

**tea-blower** See *tea-sipper.*

**tea'd up** AND **tead up, (teed) up** *mod.* alcohol or drug intoxicated. □ *It took them twenty minutes to get tea'd up.* □ *When they were teed, they started singing, and that's when the cops came.*

**teahead** AND **tea hound** *n.* a marijuana smoker. (Drugs.) □ *A lot of teaheads gather there on weekends.* □ *You tea hounds have been getting off easy. The feds are cracking down, and you're in for it.*

**tea party 1.** *n.* a wild drinking party. (Like the Mad Hatter's party in Lewis Carroll's *Alice in Wonderland*.) □ *There was a loud tea party going on in the corner booth when Barlowe came in.* □ *I'm having a little tea party Friday. Wanna come?* **2.** *n.* something easy; a pleasant and unstressful event. □ *It was not a tea party, but it wasn't bad either.* □ *The test was a real tea party. No sweat.* **3.** *n.* a session of communal marijuana use. (Drugs.) □ *Don't forget to bring the tea bags to the tea party.* □ *Some sort of a tea party was going on downstairs.*

**tear** [ter] *n.* a wild drinking bout. (See *rip*.) □ *Sally is off on a tear again.* □ *What a tear it was at Paul's on Saturday night!*

**tear into someone or something 1.** *in.* [with *someone*] to scold someone severely; to attack someone. □ *I was late, and the super tore into me like a mad dog.* □ *I don't know why she tore into me. I was at work when the window was broken.* **2.** *in.* [with *something*] to begin eating food with gusto. □ *The family tore into the mountain of food like they hadn't eaten since breakfast—which was true, in fact.* □ *Jimmy tore into the*

*turkey leg and cleaned it off in no time.*
**3.** *in.* [with *something*] to rush into a place. □ *I tore into the office and answered the phone.* □ *They tore into town and held up the bank.*

**tear-jerker** ['tɪrdʒɚkɚ] *n.* a very sad story or film. □ *The film was a real tear-jerker.* □ *I don't care to read a steady diet of tear-jerkers.*

**tear loose (from someone or something)** [tɛr...] *in.* to manage to break away from someone or something. □ *The quarterback tore loose and took 20 yards for a first.* □ *Barlowe tore loose from Rocko and made for the door.*

**tear off** *in.* to break away; to run away. □ *I hate to tear off, but I'm late.* □ *Don't tear off without having some of my pie.*

**tear someone or something apart** *tr.* to criticize someone or something severely. □ *I was late, and the boss tore me apart.* □ *I thought my paper was good, but the prof tore it apart.*

**tear someone or something up** AND **tear up someone or something 1.** *tr.* to rip someone or something to pieces. □ *The two drunks tore up the bar the best they could.* □ *The dog tore up the robber, and the robber sued.* **2.** *tr.* [with someone] to cause someone much grief. □ *I know this news will tear him up.* □ *The situation really tore him up.* (More at *torn (up)*.)

**teaser** ['tizɚ] **1.** *n.* a (found) cigarette butt. □ *The hobo picked up the teaser from the street and put it in a little bag.* □ *He saves up teasers to make a big smoke out of them.* **2.** *n.* a brief sample of something, such as a performance. □ *The teaser didn't look very promising, but the reviews were great.* □ *The teasers they showed before the film were the best part of the evening.*

**tea-sipper** AND **tea-blower** *n.* a marijuana smoker. (Drugs. See *tea*.) □ *The tea-sippers take over this neighborhood at lunchtime.* □ *A couple of tea-blowers were in the alley lighting up.*

**teastick** See *tea bag.*

**techie** ['tɛki] **1.** *n.* a student in a technical or engineering college. □ *Does one guy like Merton prove that all techies are nerds?* □ *Of course, one groovy guy*

*proves that techies aren't nerds, right?* **2.** *n.* a person with technical skills or knowledge. □ *We'll have to take this problem to a techie.* □ *The techies say it should work, theoretically, that is.* **3.** *mod.* having to do with technical people or things. □ *I don't like this techie jargon.* □ *This is the techie lounge. See how messy it is?*

**technicolor yawn** *n.* vomit. □ *This garbage will bring on a few technicolor yawns if we serve it.* □ *Who did the technicolor yawn in the bushes?*

**teed off** *mod.* angry. □ *I'm not teed off! I'm enraged.* □ *I was so teed off I could have spit!*

**teed (up)** *mod.* alcohol or drug intoxicated. □ *She was totally teed up by midnight.* □ *Tom was too teed to drive.*

**teenie** AND **teeny** *n.* a sixteenth. (Financial markets. From six*teenth*. One sixteenth of a point in a stock price. See also *steenth*.) □ *It's going at 3 and two teenies at the moment.* □ *My forty thousand shares have dropped to 3 teenies each, and I think I am going to go down to the beach and jump.*

**teenie-weenie** See *teeny-weeny.*

**teensy-weensy** See *teeny-weeny.*

**teenybopper** ['tinibapɚ] *n.* a young teenager, usually a girl. □ *The teenyboppers moved around the mall in droves, not buying and not causing any trouble, just being available for anyone who wanted to see them.* □ *Somebody called Mary a, like, teenybopper, and she went, like, "So gross!"*

**teeny-weeny** AND **teenie-weenie, teensy-weensy** ['tini'wini AND 'tintsi'wintsi] *mod.* tiny. □ *It was just a teeny-weeny sin.* □ *This one is too teeny-weeny.* □ *Could you move just a teenie-weenie bit to the left?*

**tee someone off** AND **tee off someone** *tr.* to make someone angry. □ *That really teed me off!* □ *Well, you sure managed to tee off everybody!* (More at *teed off*.)

**tee-tee*** ['titi] **1.** *in.* to urinate. (Juvenile. Caution with topic.) □ *Jimmy, please go tee-tee before we leave.* □ *Jimmy, you are supposed to flush it when you tee-tee.* **2.*** *n.* urine. (Juvenile. Caution with topic.) □ *There's tee-tee on the floor.* □ *Why is tee-tee yellow?*

**telegraph one's punches 1.** *tr.* to signal, unintentionally, what blows one is about to strike. (Boxing.) □ *Wilbur used to telegraph his punches until his coach beat it out of him.* □ *Don't telegraph your punches, kid! You'll be flat on your back in twenty seconds.* **2.** *tr.* to signal, unintentionally, one's intentions. □ *When you go in there to negotiate, don't telegraph your punches. Don't let them see that we're broke.* □ *The mediator telegraphed his punches, and we were prepared with a strong counterargument.*

**Tell it like it is.** *sent.* "Speak frankly."; "Tell the truth no matter how much it hurts." □ *Come on man, tell it like it is!* □ *Well, I've got to tell it like it is.*

**Tell me another (one)!** *exclam.* "Tell me another fairy tale!"; "That was a lie. Tell me another just as good!" □ *You a stockbroker? Tell me another one!* □ *There's no improvement in this problem! Tell me another!*

**tell someone what to do with something** *tr.* to tell someone to do something rude with something. (With the unspoken notion that one should stick it up one's ass.) □ *I'll tell you what you can do with it.* □ *If that's the way he wants to be, you can just tell him what to do with it.*

**tell someone where to get off** *tr.* to tell someone when enough is enough; to tell someone off. □ *I was fed up with her bossiness. I finally told her where to get off.* □ *He told me where to get off, so I walked out on him.*

**tell the (whole) world** *tr.* to spread around private business. □ *Well, you don't have to tell the whole world.* □ *Go ahead, tell the world!*

**telly** ['tɛli] *n.* a television set. (Originally British.) □ *What's on the telly tonight?* □ *I mean, what's showing on the telly tonight?*

**ten** *n.* the highest rank on a scale of 1 to 10. (Always with *a.*) □ *She's definitely a ten.* □ *On a scale of one to ten, this pizza's a ten.*

**ten-four** AND **10-4** *interj.* "okay." (Citizens band radio.) □ *Ten-four, old buddy. I will do that.* □ *Please, where the answer to the question is yes or no, don't write 10-4 for yes.*

**tenner** *n.* a ten-dollar bill. (See *fiver.*) □ *For a tenner, the bum lead Barlowe to the place where the crate still lay in the alley.* □ *Barlowe slipped him a tenner and faded into the fog.*

**tennies** *n.* tennis shoes; sneakers. □ *Let me get my tennies on, and I'll be right with you.* □ *What is that stuff on your tennies?*

**ten percenter** *n.* an agent who collects ten percent. □ *I've been supporting that ten-percenter for years, and he was robbing me blind.* □ *The life of a ten percenter is not easy.*

**ten-spot** *n.* a ten-dollar bill. □ *I slipped him a ten-spot, and suddenly there was a table available.* □ *It will cost you a ten-spot to get the book, in paperback, that is.*

**terrific** *mod.* excellent. □ *Glad to hear it. That's just terrific.* □ *What a terrific idea!*

**test** *n.* a small quantity of a drug. (Drugs.) □ *All I can afford is a test.* □ *Can I have a test of this stuff?*

**test-smoke 1.** *tr.* to try out a batch of marijuana before buying it. (Drugs.) □ *I wanna test-smoke this stuff first, okay?* □ *You can test-smoke anything you are willing to pay for.* **2.** *n.* an act of test-smoking marijuana before purchase. (Drugs.) □ *No, you can't have another test-smoke.* □ *Do you think a test-smoke is gonna be free?*

**Texas (tea)** *n.* marijuana. (Drugs.) □ *A little bag of Texas was all they could find.* □ *For Max, Texas tea makes the world go round.*

**T.G.I.F.** AND **TGIF 1.** *interj.* "Thank God it's Friday." □ *It was a rough week. T.G.I.F.* □ *Everybody was muttering TGIF by Friday afternoon.* **2.** *n.* a party held on Friday in honor of the end of the workweek. □ *Everyone is invited to the TGIF tonight.* □ *Terry has a T.G.I.F. in his room every evening.*

**Thaistick** AND **T-stick** *n.* a combination of strong marijuana and opium or heroin. □ *Max found an old lady who could make T-sticks for his friends.* □ *Thaisticks are pretty powerful stuff for the amateur.*

**thanks a bunch** *phr.* "thanks." □ *Thanks a bunch for your help.* □ *He said "thanks a bunch" and walked out.*

**thank you very much** *phr.* a (sometimes sarcastic) tag added to a statement for emphasis. (Often used when there is really nothing to thank anyone for.) □ *I will manage somehow to find my own way out, thank you very much.* □ *We are probably the only people in town who might be able to help you, thank you very much.* □ *You've been quite annoying, thank you very much!*

**that 1.** *mod.* a stylistic replacement for *the.* (Especially in citizens band radio jargon and much daily colloquial speech. It is the pervasive overuse of this form that makes it notable as colloquial.) □ *Can you tell me where that next rest stop is?* □ *Put that can of stuff on that shelf and sweep that floor.* **2.** *mod.* a stylistic modifier of personal and place names and some other nouns that do not normally take modifiers. (Citizens band radio.) □ *How do I get to that Kansas City?* □ *That John Silverflash is making good time.*

**That-a-boy!** *exclam.* "That is the way to do it." (Said to a boy or man.) □ *Come on, Chuck. That-a-boy!* □ *That-a-boy, Chuck. You can do it!*

**That ain't hay!** *exclam.* "That is no small amount of money!" (Folksy.) □ *I spent twenty bucks on this stuff, and that ain't hay.* □ *My jacket cost $200, and that ain't hay!*

**That does it!** *exclam.* "That is the end!"; "That is too much!" □ *Okay! That does it! Out you go, you wretched cat!* □ *That does it! I'm leaving!*

**That'll be the day!** *exclam.* "That will never happen!" □ *You win a medal? That'll be the day!* □ *When he gets his own car—that'll be the day!*

**That'll teach someone.** *sent.* "That is what someone deserves." □ *That'll teach you to pull out in front of me.* □ *I hit him on the head. That'll teach him.*

**That's about the size of it.** *sent.* "That is the way things are."; "That's all there is to tell." □ *Well, that's about the size of it. See you tomorrow.* □ *That's about the size of it. You've understood it perfectly.*

**That's all she wrote.** AND **That's what she wrote.** *sent.* "That is all of it." □ *Here's the last one we have to fix. There,*

*that's all she wrote.* □ *That's what she wrote. There ain't no more.*

**That's all someone needs.** *sent.* "That is too much."; "That is the last straw." □ *Now the sewer's backing up. That's all I need.* □ *A new mouth to feed. That's all we need!*

**That's a new one on me.** *sent.* "That is truly amazing."; "I did not know that." □ *A machine that copies in 4 colors. That's a new one on me.* □ *A talking camera? That's a new one on me.*

**That's my boy.** *sent.* "That is my son of whom I am proud."; "I'm proud of this young man." □ *After the game, Tom's dad said, "That's my boy!"* □ *That's my boy! Always a winner!*

**That's show business (for you).** *sent.* "That is the way that life really is." (Also with *biz* and *show biz*.) □ *And now the car won't start. That's show business for you.* □ *Too bad about the bad investment. That's show biz.*

**That's that!** *exclam.* "That is final!"; "That is the end of it!" □ *I said no, and that's that!* □ *I won't go, and that's that!*

**That's the stuff!** *exclam.* "That is good work!" □ *Good shot, Wally! That's the stuff!* □ *That's the stuff! Way to go!*

**That's the ticket!** *exclam.* "That is exactly what is needed!" □ *Good! That's the ticket! Now you're cooking with gas.* □ *That's the ticket! Perfect!*

**That's the way the ball bounces.** *sent.* "That is life." □ *It's tough, I know, but that's the way the ball bounces.* □ *That's the way the ball bounces. It could be worse.*

**That's the way the cookie crumbles.** *sent.* "That is life." □ *I lost my job. Oh, well. That's the way the cookie crumbles.* □ *Oh, gee! Too bad. That's the way the cookie crumbles.*

**That's the way the mop flops.** *sent.* "This is the way things happen." (Contrived.) □ *Sorry to hear about that, but that's the way the mop flops.* □ *That's tough, but that's the way the mop flops.*

**That's the way to go!** AND **Way to go!** *exclam.* "Nicely done!" □ *Way to go, Charlie!* □ *That's the way to go! You did it!*

**That's what I say.** *sent.* "I agree with you." □ *Of course, Mary. That's what I say.* □ *That's what I say. The way to cut spending is just to do it.*

**That's what she wrote.** See *That's all she wrote.*

**That tears it!** [...tɛrz...] *exclam.* "That is too much!" □ *Well, that tears it! I'm leaving!* □ *I thought yesterday's error was bad enough, but that tears it!*

**that way 1.** *mod.* in love. □ *Sam and Martha are that way. They look so happy.* □ *Well, Martha's that way, but Sam's just out for a good time.* **2.** *mod.* alcohol intoxicated. □ *Daddy's that way again.* □ *I'm sorry, but Fred's that way again and can't drive to work.* **3.** *mod.* homosexual. □ *Ken said that you-know-who was acting sort of that way. What a gossip!* □ *Somebody said that Ken talks that way because he is that way.*

**thawed** *mod.* alcohol intoxicated. □ *Tad is sort of soppy, you might say, thawed.* □ *Do you think he's too thawed to drive us home?*

**T.H.C.** AND **THC** *n.* tetrahydrocannabinol, the active ingredient in marijuana. (Drugs. See *tic.*) □ *There was a period in the drug culture heyday when the quest for pure T.H.C. was quite evident.* □ *Most of this THC stuff is really PCP or caffeine and stuff like that.*

**The baby needs shoes.** *sent.* "Give me luck." (Said in games of chance, such as dice or bingo.) □ *He shook the bones, saying, "The baby needs shoes."* □ *All the players in the crap game must be poor, because they kept saying that the baby needs shoes.*

**then and there** *mod.* right then. □ *He dropped the box right then and there and walked out on us.* □ *Right then and there, he pulled up his shirt and showed everyone the jagged scar.*

**There's nobody home.** *sent.* "There are no brains in someone's head." (See examples.) □ *There's lots of goodwill in that head, but there's nobody home.* □ *You twit! There's nobody home—that's for sure.*

**There's no such thing as a free lunch.** AND **No such thing as a free lunch.** *sent.* "Nothing is really free of charge or obligation." □ *I knew it looked too easy. Oh, well. There's no such thing as a free lunch.* □ *No such thing as a free lunch. I was just too gullible.*

**There will be hell to pay.*** *sent.* "Things will be so bad that one will have to bribe the devil to straighten them out." (Caution with *hell.*) □ *If I don't get this done on time, there will be hell to pay.* □ *There'll be hell to pay if we miss the plane.*

**There you are.** *sent.* "This is the result."; "This is the way things turned out." □ *There you are. Didn't I warn you?* □ *Well, there you are. Another first class mess.*

**There you go. 1.** *sent.* "Hooray! You did it right!" (Usually **There you go!**) □ *There you go! That's the way!* □ *Good shot, Chuck! There ya go!* **2.** *sent.* "That is the way things are, just like I told you."; "Isn't this just what you would expect?" □ *There you go. Isn't that just like a man!* □ *There you go, acting rude and ugly!* **3.** *sent.* "You are doing it again." □ *There you go! You said it again.* □ *I just told you not to put that junk on the table, and there you go.*

**the way it plays** *phr.* the way it is; the way things are. □ *The world is a rough place, and that's the way it plays.* □ *It's tough, but it's the way it plays.*

**thick 1.** *mod.* stupid; *thickheaded.* □ *She's sort of thick, but she means well.* □ *Why are you so thick about money?* **2.** *mod.* involved (with someone). □ *Sam and Mary are really thick.* □ *They're thick as can be.* **3.** *mod.* unbelievable. □ *This stuff is getting thick.* □ *This story is too thick for me. I'm cruising outa here.*

**thickheaded** *mod.* stupid; with more bone than brain in the head. □ *He's so thickheaded he can play football without a helmet.* □ *What thickheaded dolt put scallops in the scalloped potatoes?*

**thick-skinned** *mod.* able to withstand much criticism. (Compare to *thin-skinned.*) □ *You gotta be more thick-skinned if you want to be a cop.* □ *He's a real thick-skinned guy.* □ *I'm thick-skinned enough; I just don't like violence.*

**thin dime** *n.* a dime, thought of as a very small amount of money. (A concept eroded by inflation.) □ *For only one thin dime you will receive our exciting catalog of novelties and tricks.* □ *This whole mess isn't worth one thin dime.*

**thing 1.** *n.* one's interest; one's *bag.* □ *This isn't exactly my thing, but I'll give it a try.* □ *This is just your thing! Enjoy it!* **2.** *n.* a drug such as marijuana or heroin. (Drugs.) □ *You got some of that thing?* □ *I need that thing to straighten me out.*

**thingamajig** AND **thingy** [ˈθɪŋəmədʒɪg AND ˈθɪŋi] *n.* a gadget for which the proper name has been forgotten or is unknown. □ *Hand me that thingamajig with the copper base, will you?* □ *What're ya supposed to do with this thingy?*

**thingy** See the previous entry.

**think-box** *n.* the skull; the head. □ *A little weak in the think-box, but other than that, okay.* □ *Use your think-box for something other than to hold your ears apart.*

**think-piece** *n.* a thoughtful piece of writing in a newspaper or magazine. □ *Mr. Wilson's think-piece about the need for more concern for the middle class was not well received.* □ *This is plain propaganda disguised as a think-piece.*

**think-tank** *n.* a place where great minds are assembled to try to think up solutions to problems or to envision the future. □ *She spent a few months in a California think-tank, then came back to teach.* □ *What sort of solutions are coming out of the think-tanks of the nation?*

**thin-skinned** *mod.* sensitive to criticism. (Compare to *thick-skinned.*) □ *Don't be so thin-skinned. You can't expect everyone to like you.* □ *He's a thin-skinned guy.* □ *I'm too thin-skinned to be a bill collector.*

**third degree** *n.* a session of questioning, usually by the police. □ *Max got the third degree, but—being the thoroughbred he is—he was a clam.* □ *They gave Bruno the third degree, but he refused to say anything.*

**third wheel** *n.* an extra person; a person who gets in the way. (Such a person is as useful as a third wheel on a bicycle. See also *spare tire.*) □ *I feel like such a third wheel around here.* □ *Well, let's face it. We don't need you. You are a third wheel.*

**thirst-aid station** *n.* a place to purchase liquor. (From *first-aid station.*) □ *Let's stop at the next thirst-aid station and get a snort.* □ *Wally stopped by the thirst-aid station for a quick snort.*

**thirsty soul** *n.* a drunkard; a person in need of a drink. □ *Yes, I'd call Bill a thirsty soul—he always seems thirsty for booze.* □ *There was a long line of thirsty souls waiting for the liquor joint to open.*

**thirteen** *n.* marijuana. (Drugs. Old. From *M,* which is the thirteenth letter of the alphabet.) □ *Who's carrying thirteen?* □ *Thirteen can hook you.*

**This is it! 1.** *exclam.* "This is exactly what I have been looking for!"; "I have found it!" □ *This is it! I got it right this time.* □ *This is it! The world's best pizza!* **2.** *exclam.* "This is the crucial moment!" □ *Okay, this is it, the last chance!* □ *Get ready, this is it! Jump now!*

**This is where I came in.** *sent.* "This all seems very familiar." □ *Okay, that's enough. This is where I came in.* □ *This is where I came in. It's the same thing all over again.*

**thoroughbred** *n.* an underworld person who is trustworthy and loyal to the underworld. (Underworld.) □ *Max is an A-1 thoroughbred.* □ *The thoroughbred clammed up during the third degree.*

**thou** [θaʊ] *n.* one thousand. □ *I managed to get a couple of thou from the bank, but I need a little more than that.* □ *It only costs four thou. I could borrow it from my uncle.*

**threads** *n.* clothing. □ *When'd you get new threads, man?* □ *Good-looking threads on Wally, huh?*

**three bricks shy of a load** *mod.* stupid; dense; shortchanged on intelligence. □ *I would never say she was dense. Just three bricks shy of a load.* □ *Why do you act like you're three bricks shy of a load?*

**three fingers** *n.* a measurement of liquor in a glass. (Compare to *two fingers.*) □ *I'll take three fingers. It's been a hard day.* □ *Your wife told me not to give you three fingers anymore.*

**three point two**  See *three-two*.

**three sheets in the wind** AND **three sheets (to the wind), two sheets to the wind** *mod.* alcohol intoxicated and unsteady. (Sheets are the ropes used to manage a ship's sails. It is assumed that if these ropes were blowing in the wind, the ship would be unmanageable.) □ *He was three sheets to the wind and didn't pay attention to my warning.* □ *By midnight, he was three sheets.*

**three squares** *n.* three square meals a day. □ *I was glad to get back home to three squares.* □ *If I could limit myself to three squares, I could lose some weight.*

**three-two** AND **three point two** *n.* a weak beer containing 3.2% alcohol. □ *Three-two is just no good for serious sousing.* □ *James likes three point two because he can drink more of it without getting stoned.*

**thriller-diller** ['θrɪlɚ'dɪlɚ] *n.* something like a movie, book, or television program that is thrilling. (Compare to *whodunit*.) □ *The film was a real thriller-diller. I remember having to force myself to exhale.* □ *I can read one of these thriller-dillers in a couple of hours.*

**thrill-pills** *n.* barbiturate pills. (Drugs.) □ *Thrill-pills, trees, dolls—whatever you call them, Max has them.* □ *How much for some thrill-pills?*

**throat** *n.* an earnest student; a "cutthroat" student. (Collegiate.) □ *Merton is not a throat! He's not that smart.* □ *All the throats got A's, of course.*

**throat gag** *n.* liquor; strong liquor. □ *Pour me another of that throat gag, barkeep.* □ *That throat gag nearly choked me.*

**throne** *n.* a toilet; a toilet seat. □ *And there was the cat—right on the throne, just staring at me.* □ *Somebody'd better clean the throne pretty soon.*

**throne room** *n.* a restroom; a bathroom. (See the previous entry.) □ *Hank is in the throne room, reading, I think.* □ *Where's your throne room?*

**through and through** *mod.* thoroughly; throughout. □ *She's a born fighter, through and through.* □ *He is totally dishonest. A crook through and through.*

**through the mill** *mod.* abused; well-worn. □ *That was some convention.*

*I've really been through the mill.* □ *I feel like I've gone through the mill. I'm pooped.*

**throw 1.** *n.* a try; a time. □ *Have another throw at it, why don't you?* □ *Just one more throw, then I'll quit.* **2.** *tr.* to confuse someone. □ *The question really threw me.* □ *When the light fixture fell, it threw us a little.*

**throw a fight** *tr.* to lose a boxing match on purpose. (Boxing. Other words can replace *a*. See examples.) □ *I just know that Wilbur didn't throw that fight.* □ *The guy would never throw a fight.*

**throw a fit** *tr.* to have a display of bad temper. □ *I knew you'd throw a fit when I told you.* □ *Oh, boy, did she ever throw a fit.*

**throw a game** *tr.* to lose a game on purpose. (See *throw a fight*.) □ *I know Wilbur. He could never throw a game.* □ *There's a couple of those guys who would throw a game if they got enough money to do it.*

**throw a map** *tr.* to empty one's stomach; to vomit. □ *Somebody threw a map on the sidewalk.* □ *I felt like I was going to throw a map.*

**throw a punch** *tr.* to jab; to punch. □ *She tried to throw a punch at me, but I blocked it.* □ *Wilbur threw a punch at the thug.*

**throw-away 1.** *n.* a flyer or handbill. □ *The throw-away announced a big, citywide T.G.I.F.* □ *I passed out the throw-aways, but not many people would take them.* **2.** *n.* a comedian's quickly uttered one-line joke. □ *He tossed off his best throw-away of the evening just as the curtain fell.* □ *She was an expert at the one-line throw-away.*

**throw in the sponge**  See the following entry.

**throw in the towel** AND **throw in the sponge, toss in the sponge** *tr.* to quit; to give up. (From boxing where a towel or sponge thrown into the ring indicates that a boxer has given up.) □ *I can tell when it's time to throw in the towel, and this is that time.* □ *The candidate who was exposed by the press as a former pickpocket tossed in the sponge in a tearful press conference.*

**thunder-boomer** *n.* a thunderstorm. □ *There will be thunder-boomers in the boonies tonight.* □ *A few thunder-boomers may wake you up tonight.*

**thunderbox** *n.* a portable stereo radio, often played very loudly in public. □ *Someday I'm going to smash one of these thunderboxes!* □ *Why not get a thunderbox of your own?*

**thunder-cookie** *n.* a marijuana cigarette. (Drugs.) □ *Max slipped Tom a thunder-cookie as a reward for throwing the cops off the scent.* □ *How much for a thunder-cookie?*

**thunder-thighs** *n.* big or fat thighs. (Cruel. Also a rude term of address.) □ *Here comes old thunder-thighs.* □ *Here, thunder-thighs, let me get you a chair or two.*

**thunder weed** *n.* marijuana. (Drugs.) □ *There's enough thunder weed here for a whole tea party.* □ *Who wants some of this thunder weed?*

**tic** AND **tick, tac** *n.* T.H.C., tetrahydrocannabinol, the active ingredient in marijuana. (Drugs.) □ *This isn't real tic!* □ *This tick is as real as you'll ever see.*

**tick 1.** *n.* a minute; a second. (See also *sec.*) □ *I'll be with you in a tick.* □ *This won't take a tick. Sit tight.* **2.** See *tic.*

**ticked (off)** *mod.* angry. □ *Wow, was she ticked off!* □ *Kelly was totally ticked.*

**ticker 1.** *n.* a heart. □ *I've got a good strong ticker.* □ *His ticker finally gave out.* **2.** *n.* a watch. □ *My ticker stopped. The battery must be dead.* □ *If your watch runs on a battery, can you really call it a ticker?*

**ticket 1.** *n.* the exact thing; the needed thing. (Always with *the.*) □ *Her smile was her ticket to a new career.* □ *This degree will be your ticket to a bright and shining future.* **2.** *n.* a license. □ *I finally got a ticket to drive a big truck.* □ *I showed her my ticket, and she let me off with a warning.*

**ticket agent** See *travel agent.*

**tickled (pink)** *mod.* amused; utterly delighted; pleased. □ *I am tickled pink you could come this evening.* □ *We were tickled that you thought of us.*

**tickle one's smokestack** *tr.* to snort a powdered drug. (Drugs. The "smokestack" is the nose.) □ *To Larry there was nothing better than tickling his smokestack.* □ *He's in the john, tickling his smokestack.*

**tickle the ivories** *tr.* to play the piano. □ *I used to be able to tickle the ivories real nice.* □ *She sat down to tickle the ivories for a while.*

**tick someone off** AND **tick off someone** *tr.* to make someone angry. □ *That really ticks me off!* □ *Doesn't that tick you off?* (More at *ticked (off).*)

**tick-tock** ['tɪktɑk] **1.** *n.* a heart. (See also *ticker.*) □ *My tick-tock is as strong as an ox's.* □ *How long does an ox's tick-tock last anyway?* **2.** *n.* a watch or clock. (Juvenile.) □ *Wind your tick-tock before you forget.* □ *The tick-tock in the kitchen has broken.*

**ticky-tacky** ['tɪkitæki] *n.* cheap and shabby material. □ *Those houses are just made of ticky-tacky, and they won't even be here in twenty years.* □ *That stuff is just ticky-tacky. No one will buy it.*

**tiddled** *mod.* alcohol intoxicated. □ *He had a tendency to get a little tiddled.* □ *Jack's too tiddled to drive.*

**tied up** *mod.* busy. □ *I was tied up and couldn't get to the phone.* □ *The phone was tied up for over an hour.*

**tie-in** *n.* a connection; a liaison. □ *And who is your tie-in with the Acme Systems Company?* □ *I got a call from Mary—my tie-in with the mayor's office—who says it's all set.*

**tie one on** AND **lay one on, tie it on** *tr.* to get drunk. □ *The boys went out to tie one on.* □ *They laid one on, but good.*

**tie on the nosebag** See *put on the feedbag.*

**tie the knot 1.** *tr.* to marry a mate. □ *We tied the knot in a little chapel on the Arkansas border.* □ *They finally tied the knot.* **2.** *tr.* (for a cleric) to unite a couple in marriage. □ *It was hard to find somebody to tie the knot at that hour.* □ *It only took a few minutes for the ship's captain to tie the knot.*

**tiffled** ['tɪfld] *mod.* alcohol intoxicated. □ *Harry was too tiffled to drive.* □ *Mary got a little tiffled, but nothing really gross.*

**tiger** *n.* a strong and virile man. □ *The guy's a tiger. Watch out for him.* □ *Isn't Bruno a tiger!*

**tiger juice** *n.* a strong alcoholic drink. □ *What is this tiger juice anyway?* □ *You want some more tiger juice?*

**tiger milk** AND **tiger's milk** *n.* raw whiskey; moonshine. □ *Jed called his shine tiger's milk, and assured all his friends it was as dangerous as its name.* □ *This tiger milk would kill a tiger of any age or disposition.*

**tiger sweat** AND **tiger juice** *n.* bad liquor; any beer or liquor. □ *What is this tiger sweat anyway?* □ *How about some more of this tiger juice?*

**tight 1.** *mod.* stingy. □ *She's really tight with her cash.* □ *You're just too tight. Gimme a fiver, Dad, come on.* **2.** *mod.* alcohol intoxicated. □ *Frank was tight and didn't want to drive.* □ *The host got tight and had to go to bed.* **3.** *mod.* stressful; with little margin for error. □ *In a tight situation Merton can be sort of a wet rag.* □ *When the schedule is tight and we are busy as all get out, the telephone won't stop ringing.*

**tight as a tick 1.** *mod.* very tight. □ *This lid is screwed on tight as a tick.* □ *The windows were closed—tight as a tick—to keep the cold out.* **2.** *mod.* alcohol intoxicated. □ *The old man was tight as a tick, but still lucid.* □ *The host got tight as a tick and fell in the pool.*

**tighten one's belt** *tr.* to prepare for economies. (As if one would not be able to afford enough food to make one's stomach press against one's belt. Compare to *take one's belt in (a notch)*.) □ *Get ready to tighten your belt. I lost my job.* □ *The entire country will have to tighten its belt.*

**tighten someone's wig** *tr.* to introduce someone to marijuana smoking. (Drugs.) □ *Max is a master at tightening kids' wigs.* □ *Here, smoke this. It'll tighten your wig.*

**tight money** *n.* money that is hard to get. □ *This is tight money. Go easy on it. It's hard to get.* □ *In these days of tight money, no new expenditures will be approved.*

**tight spot** *n.* a difficulty. □ *I'm in sort of a tight spot and wonder if you can help*

me out. □ *Sure, I like helping people out of tight spots as long as it doesn't cost me any money.*

**tight wad** *n.* a stingy person; a miser. (See *wad*.) □ *There's no need to be such a tight wad.* □ *My dad's a tight wad.*

**Tijuana taxi** ['tiəwɑnɑ 'tæksi] *n.* a police car. (Citizens band radio.) □ *There's a Tijuana taxi back a few cars watching you awful close.* □ *It's not a Tijuana taxi; it's a park ranger!*

**till hell freezes over** *mod.* forever. □ *That's all right, boss; I can wait till hell freezes over for your answer.* □ *I'll be here till hell freezes over.*

**till the cows come home** *mod.* for a long time; until nightfall. (Folksy.) □ *You can sit there till the cows come home, but Mr. Wilson cannot see you without an appointment.* □ *I will wait till the cows come home then. This is important.*

**till the fat lady sings** AND **when the fat lady sings** *mod.* at the end; a long time from now. (Supposedly from a tale about a child—sitting through an opera—who asks a parent when it will be over. "Not until the fat lady sings" is the answer.) □ *Relax. It won't be over till the fat lady sings.* □ *We can leave with everybody else when the fat lady sings.*

**timber** *n.* stems and stalks of the hemp plant in a batch of cannabis. (Drugs.) □ *This stuff is full of timber.* □ *Show me something without timber, and then we'll talk.*

**Time (out)!** *exclam.* "Stop talking for a minute!" (A way of interrupting someone.) □ *Time! I have something to say.* □ *Just a minute! Time out! I want to speak!*

**Time's a wasting.** *sent.* "Hurry up; it's getting late." (Folksy.) □ *Come on, Tom, time's a wasting!* □ *Shake a leg! Time's a wasting.*

**time to cruise** *n.* "Time to leave." □ *See ya. It's time to cruise.* □ *Time to cruise. We're gone.*

**tin** *n.* a can of marijuana. (Drugs. See also *can*.) □ *I don't have the coin for a tin.* □ *Hank's got a tin. Let's go visit him.*

**tin cow** *n.* canned milk. □ *This tin cow is okay in coffee or something, but you* *can't drink it.* □ *Tin cow was all we could get.*

**tin hat** *n.* a soldier's helmet. □ *Where's my tin hat?* □ *You use your tin hat for everything—washing, hauling water—you name it.*

**tinkle\*** **1.\*** *in.* to urinate. (Mostly juvenile use. Caution with topic.) □ *I gotta tinkle!* □ *Jimmy, be sure and tinkle before we leave.* **2.\*** *n.* urine. (Essentially juvenile. Caution with topic.) □ *There's tinkle on the bathroom floor.* □ *Mommy, why is tinkle warm?*

**tinklebox** *n.* a piano. (See also *joybox*.) □ *She's okay on the tinklebox.* □ *The tinklebox in the bar seemed to be a bit loud.*

**tinseled** *mod.* forged or "decorated," as with a bad check. (Underworld.) □ *Gert got caught passing tinseled checks.* □ *He almost got caught kiting tinseled checks.*

**tinsel-teeth** *n.* a nickname for someone who wears dental braces. (Also a rude nickname.) □ *Tinsel-teeth is having a hard time talking.* □ *Well, tinsel-teeth, today's the day your braces come off.*

**tinseltown** *n.* Hollywood, California. □ *Tinseltown is a very glitzy place.* □ *She's talented and has her eye on tinseltown.*

**tints** *n.* sunglasses. □ *Somebody sat on my tints.* □ *I have to get some prescription tints.*

**tip-off** *n.* a clue; an indication. □ *The tip-off was when the dog started wagging his tail. We knew you were hiding somewhere close.* □ *The broken twig was just the tip-off Barlowe needed.*

**tip one's hand** *tr.* to reveal what one is going to do; to reveal one's secrets. (From card playing.) □ *I didn't tip my hand at all. I left them guessing.* □ *They tried to get me to tip my hand.*

**tipple** **1.** *n.* liquor; strong liquor. □ *This is mighty fine tipple.* □ *A little more tipple, Tom?* **2.** *tr. & in.* to drink liquor; to sip at a vessel of liquor. □ *He's been tippling beer since early morning.* □ *Actually, he's been tippling since 1943.* **3.** *n.* a drink of liquor. □ *How about a little tipple?* □ *I'll take just a little tipple—for my arthritis, you know.* **4.** *n.* a drinking bout. □ *Well, Uncle Harry's*

*off on a tipple again.* □ *No, that's the same tipple.*

**tippler** **1.** *n.* a tavern keeper. □ *Another beer, faithful tippler.* □ *John is the best tippler this place has ever seen. Tip me another, John.* **2.** *n.* a drunkard. □ *Uncle Ben was a tippler—a harmless one.* □ *He started drinking at 15 and has been a tippler ever since.*

**tipply** *mod.* alcohol intoxicated. □ *Ben is too tipply to drive home.* □ *I feel a little tipply.*

**tipster** *n.* someone who gives special information; an informer. □ *We got this from a tipster who has usually proven reliable in the past.* □ *The cops got this info from their favorite tipster.*

**tits\*** *n.* the breasts. (Crude. Caution with *tits* and topic.) □ *Wow, nice tits, huh, Fred?* □ *All you think about is tits!*

**tits and ass** See *T. and A.*

**tits up\*** *mod.* upside down; on its or someone's back. (Caution with *tits*.) □ *He landed tits up in a cornfield.* □ *Her lousy pie fell tits up onto the kitchen floor.*

**tizzy** ['tɪzi] *n.* a state of confusion. (See *twit*.) □ *The kind of tizzy that this place gets into drives me up the wall.* □ *The office was a tizzy when I left.*

**T.L.C.** AND **TLC** *n.* "tender loving care." □ *All he needs is a little TLC.* □ *This old car will keep running as long as I give it lots of T.L.C.*

**T-man** **1.** *n.* a federal narcotics agent; a treasury agent. (The "T" is from *treasury*.) □ *The T-men were at the front while Bruno crept out the back.* □ *It's curtains for you, T-man!* **2.** *n.* a marijuana smoker. (Drugs. The "T" is from *tea*.) □ *Bruno is a T-man, but he likes dolls, too.* □ *A collection of T-men puffed away over by the wading pool. Some of the mothers called the police.*

**toak** AND **toat** [tok AND tot] *n.* a puff of marijuana smoke. (Drugs. See *toke*.) □ *She took a toak and looked a little dizzy.* □ *Just one toat, how 'bout it?*

**toast** **1.** *n.* a drunkard. □ *The old toast stumbled in front of a car.* □ *A couple of toasts tried to get us to buy them drinks.* **2.** *mod.* excellent. (Black.) □ *This stuff is toast!* □ *Your silks are real toast.* **3.** *mod.* burned; done for. □ *If* *you don't get here in 20 minutes, you're toast.* □ *I told him he was toast for not being there.*

**toasted** *mod.* alcohol intoxicated. □ *The chick got toasted on two glasses of cheap white wine.* □ *I'm not toasted, just a little breathless.*

**to beat the band** *mod.* very hard and very fast. □ *He's selling computers to beat the band since he started advertising.* □ *She worked to beat the band to get ready for this.*

**to boot** *mod.* in addition. □ *For graduation, I got a new suit and a coat to boot.* □ *She got an F on her term paper and flunked the final to boot.*

**today** *mod.* now; immediately. (Sarcastic.) □ *I want it done, now—today.* □ *Come on. Sam. Move it. Today!*

**toddle off** *in.* to depart; to walk away. □ *She said goodbye and toddled off.* □ *The old man toddled off somewhere and got lost.*

**toddy blossom** *n.* a large pimple from too much drinking. (See also **strawberry**.) □ *He was sporting a toddy blossom that would be the envy of any bum on skid row.* □ *There was nothing she could do to hide her toddy blossom.*

**to-do** *n.* a commotion. □ *Don't make such a to-do when you come in late.* □ *They made quite a to-do about the broken window.*

**together** *mod.* organized. □ *I'm not together yet. Lemme call you back.* □ *That chick's really got it together.*

**to go** *mod.* packaged to be taken out; packaged to be carried home to eat. □ *Do you want it to go, or will you eat it here?* □ *This stuff is to go.*

**to hell and gone** *mod.* gone; ruined. □ *Fred was to hell and gone before anybody figured out what he had done.* □ *The whole plan is to hell and gone. Nothing can be salvaged.*

**To hell with that!\*** *exclam.* "That's the end of that!"; "No more of that!" (Caution with *hell*.) □ *To hell with that! That's no excuse!* □ *I've heard stories like that before, and I don't believe any of them. To hell with that.*

**toilet mouth** See *potty mouth*.

**toilet water** *n.* beer; draft beer. (Alludes to the term for cologne.) □ *This toilet*

*water has me running back and forth to the john.* □ *You want another pitcher of toilet water?*

**toke** [tok] **1.** *n.* a puff of marijuana smoke. (Drugs. The same as *toak*.) □ *After a big toke, he settled back to drift.* □ *Harry took a big toke and sighed.* **2.** *tr. & in.* to puff a marijuana cigarette. (Drugs.) □ *He sat on a stone to toke one before bean time.* □ *He tokes for a good bit of every day.* **3.** *n.* a cigarette. □ *You got a toke I can bum?* □ *I left my tokes in my jacket.* **4.** *in.* to *free base*. (Drugs.) □ *She almost blew herself up toking.* □ *They were toking when her mother called on the phone.* **5.** *n.* a token. □ *Yeah. Just a little toke of my approval.* □ *Nothing much. Just a toke.*

**toke pipe** *n.* a small clay pipe for smoking cannabis. (Drugs.) □ *He sat on his toke pipe and broke it.* □ *You got a toke pipe I can use?*

**toker 1.** *n.* someone who smokes marijuana. □ *There's a bunch of tokers gonna get together tonight at Wally's. Wanna come?* □ *Those guys are just tokers. They don't do anybody any harm or any good.* **2.** *n.* a water pipe for smoking marijuana. (Drugs.) □ *She dropped the toker and broke it.* □ *I know a place that sells "tea accessories." You can get another toker there.*

**toke up** *in.* to light up a marijuana cigarette. (Drugs.) □ *He would toke up at the drop of a hat.* □ *A kid toked up in the middle of my algebra class.*

**tokus** AND **tukkis, tuchus** ['tokəs AND 'tukəs] *n.* the buttocks; the *rump*. (Yiddish.) □ *She fell right on her tokus!* □ *Look at the tukkis on that fat guy.*

**tomato** *n.* an attractive *girl* or woman. □ *There's a nice-looking tomato.* □ *A good-looking tomato brought me my change.*

**tomcat 1.** *n.* a sexually active male; a *stud*. □ *Old Fred's getting to be quite a tomcat.* □ *His goal in life is to die a tomcat at age 90.* **2.** *in.* (for a man) to prowl around searching for sex. □ *Harry was out tomcatting again last night.* □ *He's gonna tomcat around till he catches something.*

**tomfool 1.** AND **Tom Fool** *n.* a "damn fool"; a stupid person, usually a male.

□ *What tomfool put sugar in the salt shaker?* □ *Why are you such a Tom Fool when it comes to money?* **2.** *mod.* foolish. □ *That is a Tom Fool idea if I ever heard one.* □ *Get your tomfool nonsense out of here!*

**tomfoolery** ['tɑm'fulɚi] *n.* foolishness. (See the previous entry.) □ *That's enough of this tomfoolery!* □ *The entire evening was devoted to tomfoolery.*

**tongue oil** AND **tongue loosener** *n.* liquor. □ *She had a little too much tongue oil and was telling all about everybody.* □ *Barlowe poured the pigeon another shot of tongue loosener.*

**tongue-tied 1.** *mod.* unable to speak from fear or confusion. (Standard English.) □ *I was tongue-tied and useless.* □ *Why do you get tongue-tied in front of a crowd?* **2.** *mod.* alcohol intoxicated. □ *He was tongue-tied and couldn't stand up.* □ *She's not just tipsy; she's tongue-tied.*

**tonic** *n.* liquor. □ *How about some more tonic?* □ *Just a bit of tonic. I'm cutting down.*

**tonsil bath** *n.* liquor; a drink of liquor. □ *I could use a little tonsil bath about now.* □ *You want some more of that tonsil bath?*

**tonsil paint** AND **tonsil varnish** *n.* liquor; whiskey. □ *This tonsil varnish would take the paint off a barn.* □ *Give the man a cup of tonsil paint.*

**tons of something** *n.* lots of something. □ *We got tons of fried chicken, so help yourself.* □ *You are in tons of trouble.*

**toodle(-oo)** ['tudl('u)] *interj.* "goodbye." □ *Take it easy. Toodle-oo.* □ *See ya! Toodle!*

**tooie** AND **tooey, tuie** ['tui] *n.* a capsule of Tuinal™, a barbiturate. □ *You got any tooies?* □ *The cops saw a few tuies on the sidewalk and made the arrest.*

**took** See *taken.*

**tool 1.** *n.* an earnest student. (Compare to *power tool.*) □ *Of course he's a tool. See the plastic liner in his pocket?* □ *Merton is a tool, and he's proud of it.* **2.** *n.* a dupe; someone who can be victimized easily. □ *They were looking for some tool to drive the getaway car.* □ *Who's the tool with the briefcase?* **3.** *in.* to speed along (in a car). (Compare to

*tool around.*) □ *We were tooling along at about 75 when the cop spotted us.* □ *I was tooling, and nobody could catch me.*

**tool around** *in.* to drive or cruise around. (Compare to *tool.*) □ *We tooled around for a while and then rented a horror movie.* □ *Let's tool around on the way home.*

**too much** *mod.* overwhelming; excellent. □ *It's wonderful. It's just too much!* □ *You are so kind. This is too much.*

**too rich for someone's blood 1.** *mod.* too expensive for one's budget. □ *This hotel is too rich for my blood.* □ *Europe is getting too rich for our blood.* **2.** *mod.* too high in fat content for one's diet. □ *This dessert is too rich for my blood.* □ *Most ice cream is too rich for my blood.*

**toot 1.** *n.* a binge or a drinking spree. □ *Harry's on a toot again.* □ *He's not on one again. It's the same old toot.* **2.** *tr. & in.* to drink copiously. □ *She could toot booze from dusk to dawn.* □ *They tooted and tooted till they could toot no more.* **3.** *n.* an emotional *jag* of some kind. □ *She's on a toot about how nobody loves her anymore.* □ *Those toots wore everybody out.* **4.** *n.* a line or dose of cocaine; cocaine. □ *These tootheads get sort of frantic when they can't get a toot.* □ *What do you spend on a toot, anyway?* **5.** *tr. & in.* to *snort* a portion of cocaine. □ *She had to leave the office to toot.* □ *She tooted a couple of lines and came back.*

**tooter 1.** *n.* a person on a drinking spree. □ *A couple of tooters were making a lot of noise.* □ *The streets belong to the tooters on New Year's Eve.* **2.** *n.* a drunkard. □ *Hank offered the tooter a drink, which was gratefully accepted, of course.* □ *I think you are turning into a tooter.* **3.** *n.* a tube to aid in the snorting of cocaine. (Drugs.) □ *She made a tooter from a playing card. This was not her first time.* □ *Somebody gave him a silver tooter for his birthday.*

**toothead** *n.* a cocaine user. (Drugs.) □ *These tootheads get sort of frantic when they can't get a toot.* □ *Where do tootheads get enough money to carry their habits?*

**toothpick** *n.* a long, thin marijuana cigarette. (Drugs. Black.) □ *Walter specializes in making toothpicks.* □ *Some people prefer toothpicks for a quick high.*

**tootle along** *in.* to depart. □ *I think I'd better tootle along now.* □ *Nice talking to you. Must tootle along.*

**toot one's own horn** See *blow one's own horn.*

**tootonium** ['tu'toniəm] *n.* an imaginary, potent type of cocaine. (Drugs. A play on *titanium.*) □ *He called it tootonium. She called it trouble.* □ *You want some real tootonium, babe?*

**tootsie** ['tutsi] **1.** *n.* a capsule of Tuinal™, a barbiturate. (Drugs.) □ *You want a buster? Here's a tootsie.* □ *What'll a pair of tootsies set me back?* **2.** AND **tootsy** *n.* a foot. (Baby talk.) □ *My tootsies are cold.* □ *Don't step on my tootsy.*

**tootsie roll** *n.* a marijuana cigarette; a marijuana cigarette rolled in brown paper. (Drugs. Named for the brand of chocolate candy.) □ *Max whipped out a big tootsie roll and started waving it around.* □ *He lit the tootsie roll and took a big hit.*

**tootsy** See *tootsie.*

**tootuncommon** [tutn̩'kamən] *n.* an imaginary, potent type of cocaine; any potent cocaine. (Drugs. A play on *King Tutankhamen.*) □ *Max laughed when the student asked for tootuncommon.* □ *Which is better, tootonium or tootuncommon?*

**top 1.** *tr.* to surpass someone or something. □ *Can you top this one?* □ *I'll try to top your joke.* **2.** *tr.* to kill someone. □ *Max was out to top Bruno.* □ *Bruno was gonna top Max first.* **3.** *n.* the first half of a baseball inning. □ *Wilbur hit a nice double-bagger in the top half of the fourth.* □ *It's the third inning at the top; Wilbur's up.*

**top banana 1.** *n.* the lead comedian in a burlesque or vaudeville act. □ *The top banana didn't show up for the gig.* □ *Let me be top banana tonight.* **2.** *n.* the boss; the leader or head of something. (See *big cheese, big enchilada.*) □ *You'll have to ask the top banana. He's out right now.* □ *Who's top banana around here?*

**top brass** *n.* the highest leader(s); the boss(es). (Originally military.) □ *The top brass turned thumbs down on the proposal.* □ *You'll have to check it out with the top brass. She'll be home around five.*

**top dog** *n.* the person in charge or in power; a company officer. □ *The reporter tried to get hold of one of the top dogs, but couldn't get past the secretary.* □ *A top dog from the executive suite read a prepared statement.*

**top-drawer** *mod.* top-quality. □ *Podunk U. is a really top-drawer school.* □ *I want to hire a young M.B.A. who's top-drawer.*

**top-flight** *mod.* of the highest caliber. □ *This candy is top-flight in every sense.* □ *We are looking for a top-flight manager for our new division.*

**top heavy** *mod.* heavy breasted; buxom. □ *Molly gets a little top heavy when she is gaining weight.* □ *Who's the top heavy number in the red tent?*

**topless** *mod.* having to do with someone wearing no clothing above the waist, usually a woman. □ *The topless places are beginning to dress up a little.* □ *The cops closed down the topless joint on Maple Street.*

**top of the heap** *n.* a position superior to everyone else. □ *For some reason, Jerry has to be at the top of the heap.* □ *She fought her way to the top of the heap and means to stay there.*

**tops and bottoms** *n.* a mixture of a painkiller and an antihistamine. (Drugs.) □ *Every kid in this neighborhood knows where to get tops and bottoms. All of them take it, and half of them sell it.* □ *To make tops and bottoms, you need a certain kind of barb.*

**top story** AND **upper story** *n.* the brain. □ *A little weak in the upper story, but other than that, a great guy.* □ *He has nothing for a top story.*

**topsy-boozy** AND **topsy-boosy** ['tapsi'buzi] *mod.* alcohol intoxicated. □ *Gary drank until he was topsy-boozy.* □ *She was so topsy-boosy she couldn't stand up.*

**topsy-turvy** ['tapsi'tɚvi] **1.** *mod.* upside down; in disarray. □ *The whole office is topsy-turvy.* □ *He came in and turned* *everything topsy-turvy.* **2.** *mod.* alcohol intoxicated. □ *Four glasses of gin and the jerk was totally topsy-turvy.* □ *She was too topsy-turvy to stand up.*

**torch** **1.** *n.* a marijuana cigarette. (Drugs.) □ *You never see Bruno without a torch.* □ *That torch is huge! What's it weigh?* **2.** *tr.* to set fire to someone or something. □ *Somebody torched the old house, and it burned to the ground.* □ *He torched himself as a protest.*

**torch up** *in.* to light up and smoke a marijuana cigarette. (Drugs.) □ *Max torched up and toked away the rest of the day.* □ *If I don't torch up every now and then, I begin to feel really rotten.*

**tore (up)** AND **torn (up)** **1.** *mod.* distraught; emotionally upset. □ *I knew you'd be tore up.* □ *Fred's really torn up about the accident.* **2.** *mod.* alcohol or drug intoxicated. □ *He wasn't just drunk—he was massively tore up.* □ *Boy, was she torn.*

**tornado juice** *n.* whiskey; strong whiskey. □ *You want another round of tornado juice?* □ *This "tornado juice" smells like antifreeze.*

**torn (up)** See *tore (up).*

**torpedo** *n.* a drink containing chloral hydrate; a knockout drink. □ *Barlowe signaled the bartender to give the stoolie a torpedo.* □ *The stoolie never knew it was a torpedo that wrecked him.*

**torqued** [torkt] *mod.* angry; *bent.* □ *Sure I was torqued. Who wouldn't be?* □ *Now, now! Don't get torqued!*

**toss** **1.** *in.* to empty one's stomach; to vomit. □ *I was afraid I was going to toss.* □ *She tossed right there on the steps and ran away.* **2.** *tr.* to throw something away. □ *Toss it. It's no good.* □ *I'll toss this one. It's all scratched.* **3.** *tr.* to search someone. (Underworld.) □ *The cops tossed him and found nothing.* □ *The feds have a special way of tossing somebody for drugs.* **4.** *tr.* to drink some liquor; to take a drink of liquor. □ *He tossed some whiskey and left.* □ *Toss that drink, and let's get out of here!*

**toss in the sponge** See *throw in the towel.*

**toss one's cookies** AND **throw one's cookies, toss one's lunch, toss one's tacos** *tr.* to empty one's stomach; to vomit. □ *Right then and there, with no warning, he tossed his cookies.* □ *If you feel like tossing your cookies, please leave quietly.*

**toss one's lunch** See the previous entry.

**toss one's tacos** See *toss one's cookies.*

**toss something off** AND **toss off something** **1.** *tr.* to do something quickly without much time or effort. □ *It was no big deal. I tossed it off in 30 minutes.* □ *We can toss off the entire order in—let's say—three hours.* **2.** *tr.* to drink something quickly. □ *She tossed off a scotch in one big swig.* □ *He tossed it off and ordered another.* **3.** *tr.* to ignore criticism; to ignore defeat or a setback. □ *She just tossed it off like nothing had happened.* □ *How could she just toss it off?* **4.** *tr.* to resist or fight off a disease. □ *I caught a little cold, but tossed it off right away.* □ *I can't toss off these viruses like I used to.*

**toss-up** *n.* a matter of chance. (As predictable as the outcome of the toss of a coin.) □ *Nobody knew what to do. It was a toss-up.* □ *Who knows what will happen? It's a toss-up.*

**totalled** **1.** *mod.* wrecked; damaged beyond repair. (From *totally wrecked.*) □ *The car was totalled. There was nothing that could be saved.* □ *There's a place in the city that will buy totalled cars.* **2.** *mod.* alcohol intoxicated. □ *Tom was too totalled to talk.* □ *Jed was totalled and couldn't see to pay the bill.*

**totally** *mod.* absolutely; completely. (Standard. Achieves slang status through overuse.) □ *How totally gross!* □ *This place is totally beige.*

**totally clueless** *mod.* ignorant (of something). (See *cluelessness.*) □ *Everybody was totally clueless as to what to do.* □ *Sorry, I'm totally clueless as to what to do.*

**tote** **1.** *n.* someone who abstains from alcohol. (From *teetotal.*) □ *I'm not a tote, but I do have a limit—rather low by your standards.* □ *Have a drink, or are you still a tote?* **2.** *n.* a small portion of cannabis. (Drugs.) □ *The cops found a tote when they tossed Max, but that was all.* □ *How much do you want for* *just a tote?* **3.** *n.* a small pipe for smoking cannabis. (Drugs.) □ *Her father found a tote in her room and really hit the ceiling.* □ *The cops found a tote in her purse and called in her father.*

**to the max** *mod.* maximally. (California. See *max.*) □ *She is happy to the max.* □ *They worked to the max their whole shift.*

**to the tune of something** *phr.* for the sum of a specific amount of money. □ *The whole thing set me back to the tune of $400.* □ *You will end up paying to the tune of twenty dollars a month.*

**touch 1.** *n.* a likely target for begging; someone who is asked for a loan. (See *soft touch.*) □ *He was just the kind of touch we were looking for, not too bright and not too poor.* □ *The touch looked around him and gave the stiff two-bits.* **2.** *n.* a request for money (from a beggar); a request for a loan. □ *I ignored the touch and walked on by.* □ *Here comes Fred, and he looks like he wants to make a touch.* **3.** *tr.* to ask someone for a loan. □ *He touched me for a hundred bucks.* □ *The wino touched Merton for a fiver.* **4.** *n.* a small portion of something to eat or drink. (Folksy.) □ *I'll have just a touch. I'm on a diet, you know.* □ *Can I have another touch of that pie, please?* **5.** *tr.* to deal with or handle someone or something. (Usually in the negative.) □ *I wouldn't touch that problem.* □ *Mr. Wilson is a real pain, and I wouldn't touch his account. Find somebody else to handle it.*

**touch and go** *mod.* chancy. □ *It was touch and go for a while, but we are out of the woods now.* □ *The place was in a real tizzy. Everything was touch and go.*

**touch a sore point** *tr.* to mention something that upsets someone. □ *I touched a sore point with Larry when I mentioned taxes.* □ *That touched a real sore point with me.*

**touch base (with someone)** *tr.* to make contact with someone. □ *I wanted to touch base with you just in case something had gone wrong.* □ *Let's touch base on Wednesday and check on things.*

**touched 1.** *mod.* flattered; honored. (Standard English.) □ *I was touched by your*

comments. □ *We were both touched by your thoughtfulness.* **2.** See *touched (in the head).* **3.** *mod.* alcohol intoxicated. □ *She was acting a little touched, but we didn't smell anything on her breath.* □ *Jed is a mite touched, wouldn't you say? Can't talk, walk, or see.*

**touched (in the head)** *mod.* slightly crazy. (Folksy.) □ *You're touched in the head if you think I'll help.* □ *I think that guy was a little touched in the head.*

**touch of the brewer** *n.* a hangover. □ *Fred's suffering from a touch of the brewer.* □ *The touch of the brewer I had was more like the hammering of the blacksmith.*

**tough break** *n.* a bit of bad luck. □ *Tough break. Sorry about that.* □ *You've had a lot of tough breaks lately.*

**tough cookie** *n.* a tough person. □ *He's a tough cookie, but I can handle him.* □ *There was a tough cookie in here this morning who demanded to see the manager.*

**tough cookies** See *tough luck.*

**tough customer** *n.* someone who is difficult to deal with. □ *Some of those bikers are really tough customers.* □ *Bruno is a tough customer. Just keep away from him.*

**tough egg to crack** AND **tough egg to crack** *n.* a person or thing that is hard to figure out or hard to deal with. □ *This problem is a tough nut to crack.* □ *I wish Jill wasn't such a tough nut to crack.*

**tough guy** *n.* a tough man; a man who might be part of the underworld. □ *He was your typical tough guy—jutting chin, gruff voice—but he was just our decorator checking up on the drapes.* □ *So, you want to be a tough guy, huh?*

**tough luck** AND **tough cookies** *interj.* "That is too bad." □ *Tough luck, but that's the way the cookie crumbles.* □ *That's too bad, tough cookies.*

**tough nut to crack** See *tough egg to crack.*

**tough row to hoe** *n.* a difficult task to carry out; a heavy set of burdens. □ *It's a tough row to hoe, but hoe it you will.* □ *This is not an easy task. This is a tough row to hoe.*

**tough something out** *tr.* to carry on with something despite difficulties or setbacks. □ *Sorry, you'll just have to tough it out.* □ *I think I can tough it out for another month.*

**Tough titty!\*** AND **Tough titties!\*** *exclam.* "That's too bad!" (Crude. Caution with *titty*.) □ *Tough titty! I told you it wouldn't be easy.* □ *So you missed the bus. Tough titty!*

**tour guide** *n.* a person who guides someone else through an *L.S.D.* experience. (See *baby sitter*.) □ *Tour guides are supposed to be dependable.* □ *A careless tour guide can frighten a tripper into a bad state.*

**tourist trap** *n.* a place set up to lure tourists in to spend money. (Can be a shop, a town, or a whole country.) □ *It looked like a tourist trap, so we didn't even stop the car.* □ *What keeps these tourists traps going?*

**townie** ['tɑuni] *n.* a permanent (non-student) resident of a college town. □ *The townies get upset when we make a lot of noise on Sundays.* □ *A couple of townies won the bicycle race.*

**toxicated** AND **toxy** ['tɑksəkedəd AND 'tɑksi] *mod.* alcohol intoxicated. □ *He was just a tad toxy, but no one in the audience could tell.* □ *The boss showed up toxicated after lunch and shocked the secretaries.*

**toxy** See the previous entry.

**toys** *n.* equipment for injecting drugs. (Drugs. Black.) □ *Somebody swiped my toys.* □ *She keeps her toys in a little box in a drawer.*

**T.P.** AND **teepee** **1.** *n.* "toilet paper." □ *There's no T.P. in the john.* □ *Don't forget to get teepee at the store.* **2.** *tr.* to festoon the trees and shrubbery of a residential yard with toilet paper. (A teenage prank.) □ *All the swimmers' houses get teepeed the night before a meet.* □ *Who teepeed my spruce tree?*

**track** **1.** *in.* (for a laser beam, a phonograph stylus, a tape head, etc.) to successfully transfer information to or from a recording medium. □ *Something here won't track. Must be the stylus.* □ *This thing won't track. What's wrong?* **2.** *in.* (for a person) to make sense. (Usually in the negative.) □ *She wasn't tracking.*

*There was no sense in trying to talk to her before she came out of it.* □ *I gave up on the lecturer. He wasn't tracking.* **3.** *in.* to coincide; to agree; to *jibe*. □ *These two things don't track. I don't know what's wrong.* □ *Your figures don't track with mine. What's wrong?* **4.** *n.* a needle mark in the flesh, indicating a recent drug injection. (Drugs. Usually plural.) □ *The tracks were a dead giveaway.* □ *Those shooters will carry those tracks all their lives.*

**tracks** See *track*.

**trad** [træd] *mod.* "traditional." □ *The approach is sort of trad, but so what?* □ *A more trad style might make the grown-ups more comfortable.*

**tragic-magic** *n.* heroin. □ *This tragic-magic, which has swept over the land, has taken too many of our youth.* □ *This tragic-magic stuff has hurt lots of my friends.*

**trammeled** ['træml̩d] *mod.* alcohol intoxicated. (Collegiate.) □ *Jim came home trammeled and was sick on the carpet.* □ *Wow, is she trammeled!*

**tranks** AND **trancs, tranx** [træŋks] *n.* tablets or capsules of a tranquilizing drug. (Drugs.) □ *He seems to like tranks better than anything.* □ *Kelly was hooked on tranx for a while.*

**tranny** ['træni] *n.* an automobile transmission. □ *It looks like you get a new tranny, and I get 900 bucks.* □ *What kind of tranny does that baby have?*

**trans** [trænts] *n.* an automobile. (From transportation.) □ *I don't have any trans— I can't get myself anywhere.* □ *What are you using for trans these days?*

**tranx** See *tranks*.

**trap** **1.** *n.* the mouth. (Crude.) □ *Shut your trap!* □ *Put this in your trap and chew it up.* **2.** *n.* a low place; a *dive*. □ *I want out of this trap!* □ *This trap is a mess. Clean it up!*

**trash** **1.** *tr.* to throw something away. □ *Trash this stuff. Nobody will ever use it.* □ *I'll take it. Don't trash it.* **2.** *n.* a low, worthless person; worthless people. □ *The guy is trash! Stay away from him.* □ *Running around with that trash—no wonder he's in trouble.* **3.** *tr.* to vandalize something. □ *Somebody trashed the statue with spray paint.* □ *Who* *trashed my room?* **4.** *n.* an act of vandalism. □ *Who quarterbacked the bus trash?* □ *The trash the other night was a real travesty.* **5.** *tr.* to beat, as in a ball game. □ *You trashed us this game, but watch out next season!* □ *The Jets trashed the Wallbangers, 48 to 13.* **6.** *tr.* to libel someone. □ *He seemed content to trash the mayor.* □ *Who is the chick who was trashing Max in the newspapers?*

**trashed** *mod.* alcohol or drug intoxicated. (Collegiate.) □ *They were trashed beyond help.* □ *Let's all get trashed and raid the girl's dorm.*

**trash mouth** *n.* someone who uses obscene language. □ *Shut up, trash mouth.* □ *Some trash mouth is making everybody mad over in the park.*

**trashy** *mod.* crude; obscene. □ *What a trashy movie!* □ *Cut out the trashy talk, you guys.*

**travel agent** **1.** *n. L.S.D.* (Drugs.) □ *Where can I get some travel agent?* □ *Max has a meeting with a travel agent. He plans to go on a trip.* **2.** AND **ticket agent** *n.* a seller of *L.S.D.* (Drugs.) □ *She served as a ticket agent for some of the kids.* □ *These travel agents are viewed as pushers, but most of them are just kids.* **3.** *n.* someone who guides another person through an *L.S.D.* experience. (Drugs.) □ *The travel agent can be a source of trouble for a "tripper."* □ *Max is the only travel agent I know of who charges.*

**trees** *n.* multicolored pills and capsules of drugs. (Drugs. See *Christmas tree.*) □ *They just take anything—trees, uppers, hell, even aspirin. Those kids are doll happy.* □ *He helped himself to a handful of trees and a can of suds.*

**trekkie** ['trɛki] *n.* a fan of *Star Trek*, the television series and the movies. □ *There is a convention of trekkies in Milwaukee this weekend.* □ *The trekkies seem to have their own language.*

**trial balloon** *n.* a test of someone's reaction. □ *It was just a trial balloon, and it didn't work.* □ *The trial balloon was a great success.*

**tric (acid)** [trɪk...] *n.* high-quality *L.S.D.* (Drugs. From *electric acid.*) □ *I tried tric acid once. That was enough.* □ *You got some of that blue tric?*

**tricks of the trade** *n.* special skills and knowledge associated with any trade or profession. □ *I know a few tricks of the trade that make things easier.* □ *I learned the tricks of the trade from my uncle.*

**trigger** **1.** *n.* a hired gunman. (Underworld.) □ *Rocko was a mob trigger for a while.* □ *Get your triggers outa here—then we can talk.* **2.** *tr.* to start something; to set something off. □ *The noise triggered an avalanche.* □ *One little thing triggered that blow-up, and I want to find out what it is.*

**trigger-happy** *mod.* eager to fire a gun; eager to shoot someone or something. □ *Rocko is sort of trigger-happy. Watch out.* □ *Ask your trigger-happy hunters to be careful this year.*

**trip** **1.** *n.* a prison sentence; a trip *up the river.* (Underworld.) □ *Yeah, me and Lefty both was on a little trip for a few years.* □ *I had a short trip, so what?* **2.** *n.* a *high* from a drug. (Drugs.) □ *Me and Sid went on a little trip.* □ *The trip was great, but once was enough.* **3.** *in.* to experience a *high* from a drug, especially *L.S.D.* (See also *trip out.*) □ *Don't bother Max. He's tripping.* □ *He trips about every other day.* **4.** *n.* a bad drug experience. (Drugs.) □ *Boy, did I ever have a trip with that stuff!* □ *What a trip! I thought I would die.* **5.** *n.* an annoying person or thing. □ *Class was a trip today.* □ *She is such a trip.* **6.** *in.* to leave. (Black.) □ *I gotta trip, man.* □ *Time to trip. See ya.*

**tripe** **1.** *n.* nonsense. □ *I don't want to hear any more of that tripe.* □ *That's just tripe. Pay no attention.* **2.** *n.* a bad performance; something worthless. □ *I know tripe when I see tripe, and that was tripe.* □ *The reviewer thought your play was tripe.*

**triple** **1.** *n.* a large alcoholic drink containing three measures of hard liquor. □ *It was a hard day. Make it a triple, John.* □ *One triple, but no more. You're cutting down, remember?* **2.** See the following entry.

**triple-bagger** **1.** AND **triple** *n.* a hit in baseball that gets the batter to third base. □ *Wilbur connected for another triple-bagger in the fifth.* □ *It's a triple for Wilbur!* **2.** *n.* a person whose ugly face is so frightful that three bags are required to conceal it. (See also **double-bagger, coyote-ugly**.) □ *That guy is just a triple-bagger.* □ *He's worse than a triple-bagger—if that's possible.*

**triple whammy** ['trɪpl 'ʍæmi] *n.* a powerful treatment; a powerful shock. □ *The market crash, the trade figures, and the death of the Secretary of Defense was a powerful triple whammy in Washington politics this week.* □ *The tax bill served as a triple whammy to the family purse.*

**trip out** *in.* to become intoxicated with a drug; to pass out from drug use. (Drugs.) □ *Sid and I are going to trip out tonight.* □ *The whole bunch of them tripped out and almost woke up the dead.*

**tripped out** *mod.* drug intoxicated. (Drugs.) □ *I refuse to listen to some tripped out poet slobber through his stuff no matter how famous he is.* □ *David found himself in an alley—tripped out—and feeling like bugs were crawling under his skin.*

**tripper** *n.* an *L.S.D.* user; a drug user. (Drugs.) □ *How do these trippers afford to do it?* □ *Sometimes trippers have to "borrow" from other people.*

**tripping heavy** *mod.* drug intoxicated and emotional. (Drugs.) □ *Her eyes were red, and you could tell she had been tripping heavy.* □ *She loves tripping heavy. She could do it without the mojo, in fact.*

**trippy** **1.** *mod.* drug intoxicated. (Drugs.) □ *The guy is always a little trippy.* □ *This town is full of trippy people.* **2.** *mod.* weird; bizarre. (As if one were on drugs.) □ *Sort of a trippy guy, but just eccentric, not tripped out.* □ *That's sort of a trippy chick you were with. Is she clean?*

**trip weed** *n.* marijuana. (Drugs.) □ *You got the trip weed with you?* □ *I have a full kilo of trip weed.*

**trots** *n.* diarrhea; a case of diarrhea. (Always with *the.*) □ *I got the trots and can't go out tonight.* □ *There's a lot of the trots going around.*

**trotters** **1.** *n.* pig's feet. □ *Trotters are okay if you can't tell what they are.* □ *Pickled trotters are good in the summer.* **2.** *n.* the feet. □ *My trotters are sort of aching.* □ *Sit down and give your trotters a rest.*

**trounce** [traunts] *tr.* to beat someone; to out-score someone. (Sports.) □ *They really trounced us.* □ *Western trounced Eastern for the 47th year in a row.*

**(truck) drivers** AND **truckers** *n.* amphetamines. (Drugs. See also *L.A. (turnabouts).*) □ *Jimmy got hold of some truck drivers and had to have his stomach pumped.* □ *You got any drivers in that mess of dolls?*

**trumped up** **1.** *mod.* heavily promoted; overly praised. □ *I don't care for trumped up stuff like that movie.* □ *That movie was so trumped up. I expected to see something much better than it turned out to be.* **2.** *mod.* made up; contrived. □ *They put Larry in the slammer on some trumped up charge.* □ *It was a silly, trumped up idea. Just forget it.*

**trump something up** AND **trump up something** *tr.* to promote or boost something. □ *They trumped up the movie so much that many people were disappointed when it finally came out.* □ *They think they have to trump something up to get people to see it.* (More at *trumped up.*)

**Trust me!** *exclam.* "Believe me!"; "Honestly!" □ *It's true! Trust me!* □ *He actually said it just like Tom told you. Trust me!*

**try someone back (again)** *tr.* to call someone back on the telephone (again) later. □ *I'll try her back later.* □ *When should I try back?*

**T-stick** See *Thaistick.*

**Tsup?** *interrog.* "What's up?"; "What is happening?"; "What have you been doing?" □ *Hi! Tsup?* □ TONY: *Tsup?* TIFFANY: *Like, nothing.*

**tube** **1.** *n.* a can of beer. (See *crack a tube.*) □ *Toss me a tube, will ya?* □ *How many tubes do you think we ought to get for tonight?* **2.** *n.* the inner curve of a tall wave. (Surfing. See *tubular.*) □ *I'm waiting for the best tube.* □ *A good tube will do, won't it?* **3.** *in.* to fail; to *go down the tube(s).* □ *The whole plan tubed at the last minute.* □ *I tubed, and I'm sorry.* (More at *tube it.*) **4.** *n.* a television set. □ *What's on the tube tonight?* □ *The tube is in the shop, so I read a book.* **5.** *n.* a cigarette. □ *You got a tube I can bum?* □ *There's a pack of tubes in my jacket.*

**tubed** *mod.* alcohol intoxicated. (See *tube*, sense 1.) □ *They were both tubed and giggling.* □ *You really look tubed, man!*

**tube it** *tr.* to fail a test. (See *tube*.) □ *I tubed it, and I'll probably get a D in the course.* □ *I was afraid I'd tube it, so I studied my head off.*

**tube steak** *n.* a frankfurter or a wiener. □ *Are we having tube steak again for dinner?* □ *I could live on tube steak. Nothing is better!*

**tub of lard** AND **tub of guts** *n.* a fat person. (Cruel. Also a rude term of address.) □ *Who's that tub of guts who just came in?* □ *That tub of lard can hardly get through the door.*

**tubular** *mod.* excellent. (Surfing and later general youth slang. Having to do with a *tube* [wave] that is good to surf in.) □ *That pizza was totally tubular!* □ *This whole week is, like, tubular.*

**tuckered out** *mod.* exhausted. (Folksy.) □ *I am really tuckered out tonight.* □ *She was too tuckered out to go to the reception.*

**tuck into something** *in.* to attack a meal. (Folksy.) □ *Now you just tuck into that fried chicken, and I'll see about a place for you to stay tonight.* □ *He tucked into the meal like it was his last.*

**tude** [tud] *n.* a bad "attitude." □ *Hey, you really got a tude, dude.* □ *Are you pulling a tude with me?*

**tukkis** See *tokus.*

**tummyache** ['təmiek] *n.* a stomachache. (Essentially baby talk.) □ *Jimmy has a little tummyache, but it's just gas, I think.* □ *That stuff will give you a tummyache.*

**tum-tum** *n.* tummy; stomach. (Baby talk.) □ *I have a pain in my tum-tum.* □ *Is your tum-tum better?*

**tune in (to something)** *in.* to become alert to something. □ *She tuned in to the comments about acid rain.* □ *When I heard my name, I tuned in.*

**tunes** *n.* a record; a record album. □ *I got some new tunes. Wanna come over and listen?* □ *The old tunes are good enough for me.*

**tune someone or something out** AND **tune out someone or something, tune out** *tr.* to ignore or disregard someone or something. □ *I heard enough and tuned her out.* □ *I managed to tune out the constant clamor in the streets.*

**turd\*** **1.\*** *n.* a lump of fecal material. (Caution with *turd*.) □ *There is a dog turd on the lawn.* □ *There are some little mouse turds in the kitchen.* **2.\*** *n.* a wretched person. (Caution with *turd*. Also a provocative term of address.) □ *You stupid turd!* □ *The guy acts like a real turd most of the time.*

**turf** *n.* (one's) ground or territory. □ *When you're on my turf, you do what I say—savvy?* □ *This is my turf, and what I say goes.*

**turistas** [tu'ristəs] *n.* diarrhea; a case of diarrhea. (From Spanish.) □ *Nobody ever died of the turistas—right away, anyway.* □ *Turistas can be very unpleasant.*

**turkey** **1.** *n.* a failure; a sham. □ *This whole business is a turkey.* □ *The turkey at the town theater closed on its first night.* **2.** *n.* a stupid person. □ *Who's the turkey who put the scallops in the scalloped potatoes?* □ *You are such a turkey!*

**turn** *in.* to go over to the other side, as with a spy or a criminal turning into an informer. (Underworld.) □ *Is there a chance that Max would turn?* □ *Max turn? Ha!*

**turn** *tr.* to corrupt someone. □ *It was the booze that turned him.* □ *Max was trying to turn a young kid.*

**turnabouts** See *L.A. (turnabouts).*

**turn around** AND **turn over** *in.* (for something) to undergo a major, dynamic change. □ *Things turned around for Willard and went okay for a while.* □ *When life turned over and things went more smoothly, Frank was happier.*

**turn a trick\*** *tr.* to perform an act of prostitution. (Caution with topic.) □ *She can turn a trick and be on the streets again in 6 minutes flat.* □ *She's upstairs, turning a trick.*

**turn belly up** AND **go belly up** **1.** *in.* to fail. □ *I sort of felt that the whole thing would go belly up, and I was right.* □ *The computer—on its last legs anyway—turned belly up right in the middle of an important job.* **2.** *in.* to die. (As a fish does when it dies.) □ *The cat was* friendly for a moment before she turned belly up. □ Every fish in Greg's tank went belly up last night.

**turned off** *mod.* uninterested. □ I'm sort of turned off to stuff like that these days. Part of getting older, I guess. □ I can't pay attention if I'm turned off, now can I?

**turned on 1.** *mod.* made alert to what is new and exciting. □ I want to hire someone who's really turned on—a real comer. □ A young, turned on M.B.A. would be just right. **2.** *mod.* drug intoxicated. (Drugs.) □ Jerry's turned on by noon—every day. □ The kid over there looks sort of turned on. Let's go talk to him a bit.

**turned out** *mod.* made aware of the pleasures of drug use. (Drugs.) □ Max was turned out before he could walk. It was all around him. □ From the minute I was turned out, I felt guilty about the whole mess.

**turn in** AND **roll in** *in.* to go to bed. □ Well, it's about time to turn in. □ I can't wait to roll in tonight.

**Turn me on!** *exclam.* "Sell me some drugs!" (Drugs.) □ Come on, Max, turn me on! □ Somebody's gotta turn me on!

**turn-off** *n.* something that repels someone. □ The movie was a turn-off. I couldn't stand it. □ What a turn-off!

**turn on 1.** *in.* to become interested or excited. □ She turned on when she heard her name called. □ He really turned on when he saw the cake. **2.** *in.* to take a drug. (Drugs.) □ Tod just can't wait to light up and turn on. □ He will turn on with anybody at the drop of a hat. **3.** *n.* someone or something that excites someone. (Usually **turn-on.**) □ The concert was a real turn-on. □ David can be a real turn-on when he's in a good mood.

**turn on a dime** *in.* to turn sharply; to turn in a small radius. □ This baby will turn on a dime. □ A car that will turn on a dime at high speed without turning turtle is what I want.

**turn on the waterworks** *in.* to begin to cry. □ His lower lip was quivering, and I knew he was going to turn on the waterworks. □ Now, now! Don't turn on the waterworks. Cheer up!

**turn onto someone or something** *in.* to become interested in someone or something. □ Jeff turned onto electronics at the age of 14. □ I tried to get her to turn onto me, but she could only think of John.

**turn on, tune in, drop out** *phr.* a slogan promoting the use of *L.S.D.* among young people. (Drugs.) □ The key phrase in the heyday of acid was "turn on, tune in, drop out." □ Millions heard "turn on, tune in, drop out" and did just that.

**turnout** *n.* an audience that has assembled for some purpose. □ How was the turnout at the benefit? □ The turnout was great. We had a full house.

**turn over** *in.* to get off of drugs. (Like *turn over a new leaf.*) □ He wanted to turn over, but just couldn't. □ There is a clinic on Maple Street that'll help heads turn over.

**turn someone off** AND **turn off someone** *tr.* to dull someone's interest in someone or something. □ The prof turned me off to the subject. □ The preacher set out to turn off the congregation to sin.

**turn someone on** AND **turn on someone** *tr.* to excite or interest someone. (See *turn on.*) □ Fast music with a good beat turns me on. □ That stuff doesn't turn on anyone.

**turn someone or something upside down** *tr.* to upset someone or something; to confuse someone or something. □ We turned his place upside down, but never found the gun. □ The whole business turned me upside down. It'll take days to recover.

**turn someone out** AND **turn out someone 1.** *tr.* to send someone away; to refuse hospitality to someone. (Standard English.) □ I wouldn't turn out anybody on a night like this. □ They turned her out to make her own way in life. **2.** *tr.* to introduce someone to drugs, prostitution, homosexuality, etc. (Underworld.) □ Mac tried to turn the kid out. □ There are laws against turning out people the way Max was doing.

**turn someone's stomach** *tr.* to nauseate someone. □ That stuff turns my stomach. Do I have to eat it? □ Whatever that smell is, it's turning my stomach.

**turn someone's water off** AND **turn off someone's water** *tr.* to deflate someone; to silence someone. □ *He said you were stupid, huh? Well, I guess that turns your water off!* □ *That really turned off her water.*

**turn tail (and run)** *tr.* to flee; to run away in fright. □ *I couldn't just turn tail and run, but I wasn't going to fight that monster either.* □ *Sometimes turning tail is the only sensible thing to do.*

**turn thumbs down (on someone or something)** *tr.* to reject someone or something. □ *The board turned thumbs down on Rocko's application for parole.* □ *The committee examined the proposal and turned thumbs down.*

**turn turtle** *in.* to turn over, as with a ship. □ *The old dog finally turned turtle, and that was the end.* □ *The car struck a pole and turned turtle.*

**turn up one's nose at someone or something** AND **turn one's nose up at someone or something** *tr.* to show disdain or disgust at someone or something. □ *This is good, wholesome food. Don't turn your nose up at it.* □ *She turned up her nose at Max, which was probably a good idea.*

**turn up one's toes** AND **turn one's toes up** *tr.* to die. □ *The cat turned up its toes right after church. Ah, the power of prayer.* □ *I'm too young to turn my toes up.*

**turps** AND **terps** [tɚps] *n.* liquor. (From turpentine.) □ *Don't forget to stop at the comfort station and get the turps.* □ *You got enough terps for the party?*

**tuskee** ['təski] *n.* a very large marijuana cigarette. (Drugs. Black.) □ *Who's the dude with the tuskee in his face?* □ *Why do you always make a tuskee? There's enough weed in it to get you rousted as a pusher.*

**tux** [təks] *n.* a tuxedo. □ *Do I have to wear a tux?* □ *Rent your tux well in advance.*

**tweak** [twik] *tr.* to adjust something slightly. □ *I just need to tweak this program a little bit; then I'll be with you.* □ *Tweak the tuner a little and see if you can get that station just a little bit clearer.*

**tweased** [twizd] *mod.* alcohol intoxicated. □ *Jim came in a little tweased last night.* □ *How tweased can anybody get on two beers?*

**tweeked** [twikt] *mod.* alcohol intoxicated. (Collegiate.) □ *They're not really bombed—just tweeked a little.* □ *Fred was too tweaked to stand up.*

**twenty-twenty hindsight** AND **20/20 hindsight** *n.* an ability to figure out what one should have done after it is too late to do it. □ *Everybody has twenty-twenty hindsight!* □ *Your 20/20 hindsight is just great.*

**twerp** See *twirp*.

**twiddle one's thumbs** *tr.* to do nothing; to wait nervously, playing with one's fingers. □ *I sat twiddling my thumbs while you were out doing I don't know what-all!* □ *Don't just sit home twiddling your thumbs.*

**twig** *n.* a marijuana cigarette. (Drugs.) □ *He called the joints twigs so no one else would know that he was talking about.* □ *How many twigs for a fiver?*

**twinkie** ['twɪŋki] *n.* a cute teenage girl. (California.) □ *The mall up from the beach is usually wall-to-wall twinkies.* □ *These twinkies ought to be a little more grown-up than they seem to be.*

**twirp** AND **twerp** [twɚp] *n.* an annoying runt of a person. (Also a term of address.) □ *Look, you twirp, get out!* □ *Some little twerp threatened to kick me in the shin.*

**twist** 1. *n.* a marijuana cigarette. (Drugs.) □ *Max whipped out a twist and lit up.* □ *How much does Max get for a twist?* 2. *n.* a girl; a woman. (Underworld.) □ *This good-looking twist comes over to the table and asks Lefty if he'd like to dance.* □ *He says "yes," and the twist says, "Go ahead, I bet it's a scream!"*

**twisted** 1. *mod.* alcohol intoxicated. □ *She was so twisted she couldn't see.* □ *That chick is really twisted bad.* 2. *mod.* suffering from drug withdrawal. (Drugs.) □ *Frank was twisted and hurting bad.* □ *When you're twisted, your head spins, and you feel like screaming.*

**twister** 1. *n.* a key. (Underworld.) □ *You got the twister for this joint?* □ *Bruno snatched the jailer's twisters and waited until midnight to try something.*

**2.** *n.* a tornado. □ *A twister touched down yesterday at an isolated farm 70 miles north of Adamsville.* □ *The twister didn't damage any homes.* **3.** *n.* a drunken spree. (See *bender*.) □ *Harry's off on a twister again.* □ *Not again. It's the same old twister.* **4.** *n.* a marijuana cigarette. (Drugs.) □ *Max rolled a quick twister and tossed it my way.* □ *How much for the twister?* **5.** *n.* a marijuana smoker. (Drugs.) □ *Who's the twister over there by Bruno?* □ *That twister designs clever tea accessories and sells them at flea markets.*

**twist (slowly) in the wind** *in.* to suffer the agony of some punishment, such as hanging. (Figurative only.) □ *I'll see you twist in the wind for trying to frustrate this investigation.* □ *The prosecutor was determined that Max would twist slowly in the wind for the crime.*

**twist someone's arm** *tr.* to pressure someone. □ *I had to twist her arm a little, but she agreed.* □ *Do I have to twist your arm, or will you cooperate?*

**twit 1.** *n.* a nervous or frantic state. □ *The twit I was in made me seem sort of silly, I'm afraid.* □ *My confused state became a serious twit, and I didn't know what to do.* **2.** *n.* a stupid person. (Also a term of address.) □ *What a yuppie twit!* □ *Hey, you twit, get off my lawn!*

**twitchen** See *(bitchen-)twitchen*.

**two-arm habit** *n.* an addiction where both of the addict's arms are used for injections. (Drugs.) □ *He had reached the limit on his two-arm habit. There wasn't any place left to hit the channel.* □ *Bruno was a two-fisted drinker with a two-arm habit.*

**two-bagger** See *double-bagger*.

**two-bit** *mod.* cheap; small-time. □ *Max is just a two-bit pusher. I want Mr. Big.* □ *I'm tired of your two-bit efforts to run this office.*

**two-bits** *n.* twenty-five cents; a quarter coin. □ *Can I bum two-bits for the phone?* □ *Here's two-bits for your piggy bank.*

**two-by-four** *mod.* small. □ *A two-by-four office with a chair and a desk was where Barlowe hung out.* □ *I can't stand living in this two-by-four room!*

**twofer** ['tufɚ] *n.* an item that is selling two for the price of one. □ *Here's a good deal—a twofer—only $7.98.* □ *Everything in this store is a twofer. I only want one of these. Do I have to bring a friend who wants one, too?*

**two fingers** *n.* a measurement of liquor in a glass. (See *three fingers*.) □ *I'll take two fingers of that tiger milk, John.* □ *Just two fingers tonight, John?*

**two-fisted drinker** *n.* a heavy drinker; someone who drinks with both hands. □ *Harry was a two-fisted drinker, a cave man, and a lady-killer.* □ *The world is filled with guys who aspire to be two-fisted drinkers.*

**two shakes of a lamb's tail** *mod.* quickly; rapidly. □ *I'll be there in two shakes of a lamb's tail.* □ *In two shakes of a lamb's tail, the entire pile of bricks had collapsed.*

**two sheets to the wind** See *three sheets in the wind*.

**two-time** *tr.* to deceive one's lover. □ *Sam wouldn't two-time Martha. He just wouldn't!* □ *Sam would and did two-time Martha!*

**two-time loser** *n.* a confirmed *loser*. □ *Poor Max is a two-time loser.* □ *Merton is a two-time loser, or at least he looks like one.*

**two-timer** *n.* one who deceives one's lover. □ *Sam just isn't my idea of the typical two-timer.* □ *Of course not. Two-timers rarely look like two-timers.*

**two umlauts** ['tu 'umlɑuts] *n.* a Löwenbräu (brand) beer. □ *I'll take a two umlauts.* □ *Calling a beer "two umlauts" is the most contrived bit of slang I have ever heard of.*

**two-way street** *n.* a reciprocal situation. □ *This is a two-way street, you know. You will have to help me someday in return.* □ *Friendship is a two-way street.*

**type** *n.* a combining form indicating a specified type of person. □ *He's a cave man type. You know, sort of hairy and smelly.* □ *Ted's the brainy type, but has no guts.*

# U

**ugly as sin**  *mod.* very ugly. □ *This car's as ugly as sin, but it's cheap and dependable.* □ *My old hound dog is ugly as sin, but faithful as the dickens.*

**uke** AND **yuke**  [juk] **1.** *in.* to empty one's stomach; to vomit. (Collegiate. Compare to *puke*.) □ *I think somebody yuked in the back seat, Tom.* □ *My friends wouldn't uke in my car!* **2.** *n.* vomit. (Collegiate.) □ *That is uke on the floor, isn't it?* □ *Tell me that the stuff in the back seat isn't uke!*

**ump**  [əmp] *n.* an "umpire." □ *The ump was gonna get killed if he didn't open his eyes.* □ *The ump has a pretty rough job.*

**umpteen**  ['əmptin] *mod.* many; innumerable. □ *I've told you umpteen times not to feed the cat right out of the can.* □ *There are umpteen ways to do this right. Can you manage to do one of them?*

**umpteenth**  See the following entry.

**umpty-umpth**  AND **umpteenth** ['əmpti'əmpθ AND 'əmp'tintθ] *mod.* thousandth, billionth, zillionth, etc. (Represents some very large, but indefinite number.) □ *This is the umpty-umpth time I've told you to keep your dog out of my yard.* □ *This is the umpteenth meeting of the joint conference committee, but still there is no budget.*

**ums**  [əmz] *n.* Valium™ tablets. (Drugs.) □ *I started the ums to try to get off the barbs.* □ *Now I don't need the barbs, but I'll die without the ums—no, I really will.*

**Uncle nab**  *n.* a policeman. (Black.) □ *Uncle nab is coming. Look sharp!* □ *Watch out for Uncle nab. He's been asking about you.*

**Uncle (Sam)** AND **Uncle Sugar**  **1.** *n.* the personification of the U.S. □ *Uncle Sugar wants a little more of your money this year.* □ *Tell Uncle to spend a little less.* **2.** *n.* a federal agent; federal agents. □ *The cops called in Uncle Sam to help in the investigation.* □ *Uncle has some pretty strong ideas about who's in charge of this investigation.*

**Uncle Sugar**  See the previous entry.

**Uncle Whiskers**  See *whiskers*.

**uncool**  *mod. square*; dull and orthodox. □ *Oh, what an uncool weirdo!* □ *This place is uncool. Let's cruise.*

**underpinnings**  *n.* the legs. □ *He has good underpinnings—ought to be able to run faster.* □ *With underpinnings like that, he ought to be able to win the marathon.*

**under someone's thumb**  *mod.* under someone's control. □ *You can't keep your kids under your thumb all their lives.* □ *I don't want all this under my thumb. I have to delegate a lot of it.*

**understanding**  *n.* the feet. (A pun. Always singular.) □ *The boy has a good understanding. Really big gunboats, in fact.* □ *I always had a good understanding—even when I was a kid.*

**under the affluence of incohol**  *mod.* alcohol intoxicated. (A deliberate spoonerism on *under the influence of alcohol*.) □ *Perhaps I am under the affluence of incohol just a little bit.* □ *You are very, very much under the affluence of incohol, as you have so aptly put it.*

**under the gun**  *mod.* under pressure; under scrutiny. □ *I've been under the gun on this one long enough.* □ *They've got the boss under the gun to get this thing wound up by Saturday.*

414

**under the table 1.** *mod.* alcohol intoxicated. □ *Jed was under the table by midnight.* □ *By 3:00 in the morning, everyone was under the table.* **2.** *mod.* secret; clandestine. □ *It was strictly an under the table deal.* □ *The mayor made a few bucks under the table, too.*

**under the weather 1.** *mod.* ill. □ *I feel sort of under the weather today.* □ *Whatever I ate for lunch is making me feel a bit under the weather.* **2.** *mod.* alcohol intoxicated. □ *Daddy's under the weather again.* □ *Wally's just a tad under the weather.*

**under the wire** *mod.* at the very last minute. □ *I got it in just under the wire.* □ *It was in under the wire. Another ten minutes and it would not have counted.*

**underwhelm** *tr. & in.* to fail to impress (someone). □ *Your talents simply underwhelm me.* □ *As we were being underwhelmed by a buxom soprano, my thoughts drifted to more pleasant matters.* □ *We know you tried, but you just underwhelm.*

**under wraps** *mod.* (held) in secret. □ *We kept it under wraps until after the election.* □ *The plan we had under wraps had to be scrapped anyway.*

**undies** *n.* underclothing; underpants, especially women's. □ *I like red undies.* □ *Where are my clean undies?*

**unearthly** *mod.* weird; terrible. □ *What was that unearthly noise?* □ *There was an unearthly smell coming out of the kitchen.* □ *That's not unearthly!*

**unflappable** *mod.* not subject to distraction; imperturbable. □ *Isn't he great? Truly unflappable.* □ *She is totally unflappable.* □ *I wish I was that unflappable.*

**ungodly** *mod.* horrendous; inconceivable. □ *What is that ungodly noise?* □ *What do you want at this ungodly hour?*

**unit** ['junət] *n.* a gadget. □ *Now, take one of the red units—put the copper strip in the slot—place the whole thing in this larger unit—and you're done.* □ *Hand me that unit on the thingy there.*

**units** See *(parental) units.*

**unk-jay** *n.* dope; *junk.* (Underworld. Pig Latin for *junk.*) □ *The creep deals in unk-jay, you know—narcotics.* □ *Stay away from the unk-jay.*

**unlax** [ən'læks] *in.* unwind and relax. □ *I just can't wait to get home and unlax.* □ *Unlax, man. Take it easy.*

**unload** *tr.* to get rid of someone or something. □ *We're gonna unload all the cats and dogs during the Christmas rush.* □ *Lemme unload this dame, and then we can go out and have a little fun.*

**unreal** *mod.* unbelievable. □ *Your hairdo is so yummy—almost unreal.* □ *Who started this unreal argument?*

**until kingdom come** *mod.* until the end of the world; forever. □ *Do I have to keep assembling these units till kingdom come?* □ *I'll hate her guts till kingdom come.*

**up 1.** *mod.* happy; cheery; not depressed; *upbeat.* □ *I'm up today. Let's celebrate.* □ *This is not an up party. Let's cruise.* **2.** *tr.* to increase something. □ *She tried to up the price on me, thinking I wouldn't notice.* □ *The bank upped its rates again.* **3.** *mod.* *high* on drugs, especially amphetamines or cocaine. (Drugs.) □ *Fred's up again. Don't let him drive.* □ *She arises at eight, but isn't up until nine.* **4.** *n.* an amphetamine. (Drugs.) □ *She needs an up every morning!* □ *You got a couple of ups I can have?* **5.** *in.* to take a stimulant drug. (Drugs.) □ *She has to up every morning.* □ *Ted upped before going in to take the test.*

**up a creek** See *up the creek (without a paddle).*

**up against it 1.** *mod.* having a personal crisis; having a financial crisis. □ *This is my bad season. I'm really up against it.* □ *Can I bum a few bucks? I'm up against it this week.* **2.** *mod.* addicted to a narcotic, usually heroin. (Drugs.) □ *The man is suffering. He's really up against it.* □ *Finally when I knew I was up against it, I decided to do something about it.*

**up and at them** AND **up an' at 'em, up an' Adam** *phr.* to get up and go at people or things; to get active and get busy. ("Adam" is a misunderstanding of "at 'em.") □ *Come on, you guys! Up and at 'em! Can't sleep all day.* □ *Up and Adam! The sun is shining.*

**up and leave** *in.* to get up and leave; to leave suddenly. (Folksy. *Up* has the force of a verb.) □ *I didn't want to just up and leave, but I had been sitting there for two hours.* □ *Half the audience up and left after the controversial scene.*

**up and up** *mod.* fair; honest. □ *Everything seemed to be on the up and up.* □ *Is this establishment on the up and up?*

**up a storm** *mod.* with an enthusiastic spirit. (Note syntax in examples. Usually with *sing, dance, talk, blow, play.*) □ *We talked up a storm until past midnight.* □ *Can't she dance up a storm?*

**up a tree 1.** *mod.* confused; without an answer to a problem; in difficulty. □ *This whole business has me up a tree.* □ *I'm up a tree, and I need some help.* **2.** *mod.* alcohol intoxicated. □ *Only two glasses of booze and he was up a tree for sure.* □ *My buddy here is up a tree and needs a crash for the night.*

**upbeat** *mod.* bright and cheery; not negative. □ *I'd prefer to open the conference with an upbeat topic.* □ *That topic is not upbeat.* □ *This piece of music has an upbeat flavor to it.*

**upchuck** [ˈəptʃək] **1.** *tr. & in.* to vomit (something). □ *Wally upchucked his whole dinner.* □ *Who upchucked over there?* **2.** *n.* vomit. □ *Is that upchuck on your shoe?* □ *There is still some upchuck on the bathroom floor.*

**up for grabs 1.** *mod.* available for anyone; not yet claimed. □ *It's up for grabs. Everything is still very chancy.* □ *I don't know who will get it. It's up for grabs.* **2.** *mod.* in total; chaos. □ *This is a madhouse. The whole place is up for grabs.* □ *When the market crashed, the whole office was up for grabs.*

**up for something** *mod.* agreeable to something. □ *I'm up for a pizza. Anybody want to chip in?* □ *Who's up for a swim?*

**up front 1.** *mod.* at the beginning; in advance. □ *She wanted $200 up front.* □ *The more you pay up front, the less you'll have to finance.* **2.** *mod.* open; honest; forthcoming. □ *She is a very up front gal—trust her.* □ *I wish the salesman had been more up front about it.* **3.** *mod.* in the forefront; under fire (at the front). □ *You guys who are up front are gonna get the most fire.* □ *You two go up front and see if you can help.*

**up high** *n.* a stimulating rather than a depressing drug *high.* (Drugs. See also *up pot.*) □ *She was always looking for a good up high. When she couldn't find quality, she went after quantity.* □ *Many of them have to have an up high. They are too close to clinical depression to chance anything else.*

**upholstered** [əˈpolstɚd] **1.** *mod.* alcohol intoxicated. □ *She was a little upholstered, but not seriously impaired.* □ *He drank till he was comfortably upholstered.* **2.** See *(well-)upholstered.*

**up in arms** *mod.* angry; excited. □ *The whole town was up in arms about the planned highway.* □ *Now, don't get up in arms about it.*

**up in the air** *mod.* (of an issue) undecided. □ *The whole matter is still up in the air.* □ *The question of who will attend is still up in the air.*

**up in the air (about someone or something)** *mod.* undecided about someone or something. □ *I'm sort of up in the air about whether to marry Mary or not.* □ *Mary's up in the air, too.*

**up one's alley** See *right up one's alley.*

**upper 1.** AND **uppy** *n.* a tablet or capsule of amphetamine. (Drugs. See *downer.*) □ *An upper in the morning and a downer at night. That's the way big things start.* □ *Some people get hooked on diet pills, which are really uppers.* **2.** *n.* (in the plural) the upper teeth; upper dentures. (Always plural.) □ *My uppers are giving me a little trouble.* □ *My uppers have been slipping.* **3.** *n.* (in the plural) one's betters; people who are superior to oneself. (Folksy. Always plural.) □ *Now, don't embarrass yourself in front of your uppers.* □ *I don't believe that anybody really has "uppers."*

**upper crust 1.** *n.* the highest level of society. □ *Actually the real upper crust is mostly just plain folks.* □ *If I was part of the upper crust, I'd move to Hawaii.* **2.** *mod.* snobbish. □ *Your upper crust attitude seems sort of phony to me.* □ *Why are you so upper crust?*

**uppers** See *upper.*

**upper story** See *top story.*

**uppity** [ˈəpədi] *mod.* haughty. (Folksy.) □ *Why is she so uppity?* □ *Don't be uppity. Remember who you are!*

**up pot** *n.* stimulating marijuana, as opposed to relaxing marijuana. (Drugs. See also *up high*.) □ *I can only handle up pot. Everything else makes me cry.* □ *Tell him you really don't want up pot unless it's cheap.*

**upshot (of something)** *n.* the result of something; the outcome of something. (Always with *the*.) □ *The upshot of it all was that we don't get the new coffee pot.* □ *And the upshot was a new manager and raises for everyone.*

**upside 1.** *prep.* at the side of; alongside. (Folksy.) □ *I'll hit you upside the head if you say that again.* □ *Lean this upside the barn, if you don't mind.* **2.** *n.* the good side. □ *On the upside, things might get better.* □ *There's not much to look forward to on the upside.*

**up stakes** *tr.* to prepare for leaving and then leave. (*Up* has the force of a verb here. The phrase suggests pulling up tent stakes in preparation for departure.) □ *They just upped stakes and left without saying goodbye.* □ *It's that time of the year when I feel like upping stakes and moving to the country.*

**Upsy-daisy!** See *Oops-a-daisy!*

**up the creek (without a paddle)** AND **up a creek** *mod.* in an awkward position with no easy way out. (This creek is called "shit creek.") □ *I'm sort of up the creek and don't know what to do.* □ *You are up a creek! You got yourself into it, so get yourself out.*

**up the pole** *mod.* alcohol intoxicated. □ *You sound a little up the pole. Why don't you call back when you're sober?* □ *She's up the pole and shouldn't drive.*

**up the river** *mod.* in prison. (Underworld.) □ *Gary was up the river for a couple of years, but that doesn't make him a criminal, does it?* □ *The judge who sent him up the river was indicted for accepting bribery. If Gary had only known sooner!*

**up the wall** *mod.* in a very bad situation. □ *He's really up the wall about Mary's illness.* □ *We were all up the wall until the matter was resolved.*

**uptight** *mod.* anxious. □ *Dave always seems uptight about something.* □ *He is one uptight guy.* □ *Don't get uptight before the test.*

**up time** *n.* the time when a computer is running. (Compare to *down time*.) □ *You'll get the maximum up time with this machine.* □ *On some systems the down time is longer than the up time.*

**up to here** *mod.* having as much as one can bear. □ *I'm up to here with your excuses!* □ *We are all up to here with this mystery.*

**up to one's ears** See the following entry.

**up to one's eyeballs** AND **up to one's ears** *mod.* filled up with something. □ *She's up to her ears in marriage proposals.* □ *We're up to our eyeballs in spare parts.*

**up to one's knees** *mod.* deep in something, such as paperwork or water. (See also *knee-deep in something*.) □ *We're up to our knees with orders and getting more all the time.* □ *The orders are up to our knees.*

**up to one's neck** *mod.* filled up with something. □ *I am up to my neck in other people's grief and anguish.* □ *We are all up to our necks in your problems.*

**up to scratch** AND **up to snuff** *mod.* satisfactory; up to what is expected. □ *This just isn't up to scratch. You'll have to do it again.* □ *The food was up to snuff, but the hotel staff was not at its usually efficient best.*

**up to snuff** See the previous entry.

**uptown 1.** *mod.* in or from the more expensive part of town. □ *Your uptown ideas won't do much good around here. People just don't care.* □ *What do you expect from an uptown boy?* □ *That is okay uptown, but not here.* **2.** *n.* cocaine, because of its cost. (Drugs.) □ *These days every junkie can afford uptown.* □ *You might say that uptown has moved downtown—and to the burbs.*

**urp** See *earp*.

**use** [juz] *tr. & in.* to use (drugs); to take drugs habitually. (Drugs and now widely known.) □ *I tried to stop using, but I couldn't.* □ *I couldn't face myself if I started using the stuff again.*

**user** *n.* a drug user; a drug addict. (Drugs.) □ *I want to stop being a user, but I can't do it by myself.* □ *I'm no user! Maybe a joint now and then, and an upper on a dreary morning—but I'm no user!*

**Use your head!** AND **Use your noggin!, Use your noodle!** *exclam.* "Think!"; "Think it through!" □ *You know the answer. Use your head!* □ *Use your noggin! It's there for more than hanging your hat on.*

**Use your noggin!** See the previous entry.

**Use your noodle!** See *Use your head!*

**U.V.s** ['ju'viz] *n.* "ultraviolet" rays from the sun; sunshine. □ *I wanna get some U.V.s before we go home.* □ *Watch out for those U.V.s.*

**uzz-fay** ['əzfe] *n.* a law enforcement officer. (Pig Latin for *fuzz.*) □ *The uzz-fay is at the door.* □ *Quiet, I think I hear the uzz-fay!*

# V

**V.** **1.** *n.* Valium™, a muscle relaxant. (Drugs.) □ *You got any V.s? My legs are cramping like mad.* □ *I don't give V.s away.* **2.** *n.* marijuana. (Drugs. From an old term for marijuana, *viper.*) □ *Charlie was burning some V. when the Duke came in.* □ *Gimme a puff of that V., will you?*

**vac** **1.** *n.* a vacuum cleaner. □ *Where's the vac?* □ *Bring the vac and clean this place up.* **2.** *tr. & in.* to clean with a vacuum cleaner. □ *Vac while you have time!* □ *You are supposed to vac the whole house, not just your room!*

**vacation** *n.* a prison sentence. (Underworld.) □ *I had a little vacation upstate for a while.* □ *It was a three-year vacation, with time off for good behavior.*

**vag** [væg] **1.** *n.* a vagrant person; a person who does not work and who wanders from place to place. □ *A couple of vags on the curb were trying to hitch a ride.* □ *You vags, move on. Go on, move it!* **2.** *mod.* having to do with a charge of vagrancy. □ *They booked him on a vag charge and gave him a nice warm place to sleep that night.* □ *The vag scam didn't work like it was planned.*

**vals** [vælz] *n.* Valium™ tranquilizers. □ *I'm taking vals for this, but the doctor says to get off of them as soon as possible.* □ *Vals really calm you down.*

**Vamoose!** [væ'mus] *exclam.* "Beat it!"; "Go away!" (From Spanish.) □ *Go on, beat it! Vamoose!* □ *Vamoose! Go home!*

**vanilla** **1.** *mod.* plain; dull. □ *The entire production was sort of vanilla, but it was okay.* □ *No more vanilla music, please.* □ *The vacation was vanilla, but restful.* **2.** *n.* a Caucasian. □ *Some vanilla's on the phone—selling something, I guess.*

□ *That vanilla is looking at you sort of cop-like.*

**varnished** *mod.* alcohol intoxicated. (Compare to *shellacked.*) □ *Really varnished, he was. Couldn't see a hole in a ladder.* □ *That lady is too varnished to drive. If you see her getting into a car, call the cops.*

**Vatican roulette** *n.* the rhythm method of birth control. □ *My parents lost at Vatican roulette, and I am the booby prize.* □ *Father John tried to get us to refer to it as something other than Vatican roulette.*

**V-ball** *n.* volleyball. (Compare to *B-ball.*) □ *You wanna play some V-ball?* □ *Playing V-ball is one of the best forms of exercise.*

**veep** [vip] *n.* a vice president. □ *The veep is going to preside today.* □ *Now we have to elect a veep. Any nominations?*

**vees** [viz] *n.* Valium™ tranquilizer tablets. (Drugs.) □ *You got a whole big bottle of vees? How?* □ *Vees are pretty easy to come by.*

**veg** [vɛdʒ] **1.** *n.* a vegetable. (See *veggy.*) □ *You want a veg with this?* □ *That's not my favorite veg.* **2.** *n.* a stupid person. □ *Where is your brain, you veg?* □ *Some veg put scallops in the scalloped potatoes.* **3.** See *veg (out).*

**vegetable** **1.** *mod.* alcohol intoxicated. □ *He's a tad vegetable, but not in a stupor.* □ *Helen drank till she was totally vegetable.* **2.** *n.* a person almost totally destroyed by drugs. □ *And now she's a vegetable, and there's nothing that can be done.* □ *You want to end up a vegetable? Just keep shooting that stuff.* **3.** *n.* someone who is brain-dead; someone who acts brain-dead. □ *You are such a vegetable!* □ *Cable T.V. is turning me into a vegetable.*

**vegged out** *mod.* debilitated by drugs or alcohol. (Drugs.) □ *Ernie is vegged out and has quit his job and everything.* □ *Won't be long till Larry is vegged out altogether.*

**veggy** ['vedʒi] **1.** *n.* a vegetarian. □ *We have a lovely salad bar for the veggies among you.* □ *She's a veggy, so make sure there's a nice selection of appropriate goodies.* **2.** *n.* a vegetable. (Usually plural.) □ *Do you want any veggies with this?* □ *No veggies for me.*

**veg (out)** *in.* to cease working and take it easy; to vegetate. □ *Someday, I just want to veg out and enjoy life.* □ *I think I'll just veg this weekend.* (More at *vegged out.*)

**vent one's spleen** *tr.* to release one's anger. □ *No need to vent your spleen at me. I wasn't in on it.* □ *I just feel like I have to vent my spleen at somebody.*

**verboten** [vɚ'botn̩] *mod.* forbidden. (German.) □ *That is strictly verboten.* □ *You said a verboten word around here.*

**vest** *n.* an important businessman or businesswoman. (See *suit.*) □ *One of the vests complained to the management about the way I cleaned his office.* □ *Some vest jumped out the window this afternoon.*

**vet 1.** *n.* a veterinarian. (Standard English.) □ *I took the cat to the vet.* □ *The vet didn't charge much to look at the turtle.* **2.** *tr.* to give a medical examination to and treat a person (or an animal). □ *The doctor vetted me quickly and charged an unbelievable sum for it.* □ *When they vet you these days, most of the work is done in a lab.* **3.** *n.* a (war) veteran. □ *The vets in the hospitals across the land appreciate your kindness.* □ *The Vietnam vets had a very bad time of it.*

**vette** [vɛt] *n.* a Corvette automobile. □ *I'd rather have a vette than a caddy.* □ *Vettes aren't as popular as they once were.*

**vibes** [vaɪbz] *n.* vibrations; atmosphere; feelings. (Usually with *good* or *bad.*) □ *I just don't get good vibes about this deal.* □ *The vibes are just plain bad.*

**vic** [vɪk] **1.** *n.* a victim. (Streets. See *vivor.*) □ *We're all vics, but we all keep going.* □ *Harry is a con artist, not a vic.* **2.** *n.* a convict. □ *Max is a vic, but nobody cares much.* □ *We try to give the vics a chance at employment where they won't be treated badly.*

**vicious** ['vɪʃəs] *mod.* great; excellent. □ *Man, this burger is really vicious.* □ *That guy is one vicious driver, all right.*

**vicious circle** *n.* a set of actions that lead to ever more unsatisfactory consequences; a set of bad actions that are repeated in a cycle. (See *catch 22.*) □ *It's a vicious circle, and I want out of it.* □ *Life has become one vicious circle after another.*

**video jock** *n.* someone who plays music videos on television. □ *Wally tried out to be a video jock, but he's too uptown.* □ *Some of these video jocks have real class.*

**Vietnik** [vi'ɛtnɪk] *n.* someone—looking like a *beatnik*—who opposed the Vietnam war. □ *The Vietniks' message was sort of distorted by the press.* □ *I knew a Vietnik who moved to Canada.*

**vim and vigor** *n.* energy; enthusiasm; moxie. □ *Show more vim and vigor! Let us know you're alive.* □ *She's sure got a lot of vim and vigor.*

**vines** *n.* clothing. (Black.) □ *I like those smokin' vines you're in.* □ *Good-looking vines on that guy, right?*

**vinyl** ['vaɪnl̩] *n.* phonograph records. □ *This is one of the best tunes on vinyl.* □ *I got some new vinyl. Come over and listen.*

**V.I.P. 1.** *n.* a "very important person." □ *Who's the V.I.P. in the Mercedes?* □ *That's no V.I.P.; that's the boss.* **2.** *mod.* something reserved for a *V.I.P.* □ *My smile and casual manner didn't get me into the V.I.P. lounge.* □ *They gave us the V.I.P. treatment.*

**visit from the stork** *n.* the birth of a baby. □ *The last visit from the stork was in March.* □ *We are expecting a visit from the stork next June.*

**visiting fireman** *n.* someone paying a visit to observe one's workplace. □ *We have a couple of visiting firemen coming today.* □ *Be sure to have these plans out when the visiting firemen come by.*

**visit the plumbing** See *check out the plumbing.*

**vital statistics** *n.* the measurements of a person's body. □ *Her vital statistics must require higher math to work out!* □ *Here are his vital statistics for those who are interested.*

**vivor** ['vɑɪvɚ] *n.* a survivor; a street person who manages to survive. (Streets. Compare to *vic.*) □ *Harry's a vivor, and I like him.* □ *She's no champ, but she's a vivor.*

**viz** [vɑɪz] *n.* Levis; blue jeans. □ *How do you like my new viz?* □ *Those viz are too tight for her.*

**volume** *n.* Valium™, a tranquilizer. (Drugs.) □ *Max, you got any of that volume?* □ *Naw, volume is something you get from a drugstore.*

**vomity** ['vɑmɪdi] *mod.* nasty. (Crude.) □ *What is this vomity stuff on my plate?* □ *Is that what you call vomity?* □ *That is a really vomity idea!*

**vote with one's feet** *in.* to show one's displeasure by walking out. □ *A lot of people are voting with their feet. Customers clearly don't like our goods.* □ *When the audience votes with its feet, you know you don't have a hit.*

**vroom** AND **varoom** [vrum AND vɑ'rum] **1.** *interj.* the noise of a loud engine. (Onomatopoetic.) □ *Vroom, varoom went the engine as Vic gunned it over and over.* □ *Suddenly, vroom, a plane passed low overhead.* **2.** *in.* to move rapidly from place to place; to travel at high speed, making the noise of a loud engine. □ *Let's vroom over to Larry's and see what's happening.* □ *The little boy varoomed down the sidewalk on his tricycle.*

# W

**wack** See *whack*.

**wacky** *mod.* loony; silly and giddy. □ *You are about the wackiest guy I ever met.* □ *I got a real kick out of that wacky movie we saw last night.*

**wacky-tabbacky** ['wækitə'bæki] *n.* marijuana. (Collegiate.) □ *You got any of that wacky-tabbacky?* □ *He gets that silly look in his eye from smoking wacky-tabbacky.*

**wad** [wɑd] *n.* a bundle of money; a bankroll. (Originally underworld.) □ *I lost my wad on a rotten horse in the seventh race.* □ *You'd better not flash a wad like that around here. You won't have it long.*

**waffle (around)** *in.* to be indecisive. □ *Don't waffle around so long. Make up your mind.* □ *She spent three days waffling over the color of the car and finally decided on red.*

**wagon** *n.* the police wagon. □ *I called the wagon. It'll come and get these two thugs in about 15 minutes.* □ *Look out, you guys, the wagon's coming. Don't let 'em see you!*

**wag one's chin** *tr.* to talk or jabber; to chatter aimlessly. □ *The two old buzzards sat on the park bench wagging their chins all afternoon.* □ *Stop wagging your chin for a minute and listen up!*

**wailing** AND **whaling** *mod.* excellent. (Teens.) □ *Man, that's wailing!* □ *What a whaling guitar!*

**waker-upper** See *eye-opener*.

**walk** **1.** *n.* something easy. (Always with a. See *cakewalk, sleepwalk*.) □ *That game was a walk!* □ *What a walk! I've never had such an easy time of it!* **2.** *in.* to walk out on someone. □ *They had*

a big fight, and he walked. □ *Much more of this and I'm going to walk.* **3.** *in.* to walk away from something unharmed. □ *It couldn't have been much of an accident. Both drivers walked.* □ *It was a horrible meeting, but when it was over I just walked.* **4.** *in.* to get out of prison; to get off from a criminal charge. (Underworld.) □ *They thought they had Bruno on a vice rap, but he walked.* □ *I showed them my license; then I walked.*

**walk away with something** AND **walk off with something** **1.** *in.* to steal something. □ *Did you see that kid walk away with that candy bar?* □ *The crook just walked off with a $30 necktie.* **2.** *in.* to win first place easily. □ *The other team walked away with the game.* □ *The Redskins walked off with it.*

**walk heavy** *in.* to be important. (Black.) □ *Harry's been walking heavy since he graduated.* □ *Why have you been walking heavy, man?*

**walk-in** **1.** *mod.* having to do with a customer who just comes in off the street. □ *Two walk-in customers wanted morning papers, but nothing more.* □ *We were hoping for more walk-in trade.* **2.** *n.* a customer who walks in off the street. □ *We had a couple of walk-ins this morning, but none of the hotel residents came.* □ *We have a new sign outside to attract walk-ins.*

**walking dandruff** AND **galloping dandruff** *n.* lice. (See also *pants rabbits*.) □ *He's hopping around like he's got walking dandruff.* □ *I don't know anybody with galloping dandruff—I hope.*

**walking on rocky socks** *mod.* alcohol intoxicated. □ *She's sort of walking on* *rocky socks.* □ *He looks like he's walking on rocky socks.*

**walking papers** *n.* a notice of being fired, released, divorced, etc. □ *I hope I don't get my walking papers today. I need this job.* □ *Well, I got my walking papers today.*

**walking wounded 1.** *n.* soldiers who are injured but still able to walk. (Standard English.) □ *There were enough walking wounded to start another division.* □ *Many of the walking wounded helped with the more seriously injured cases.* **2.** *n.* a person who is injured—mentally or physically—and still able to go about daily life. □ *As one of the walking wounded who has suffered the things you described, I have to disagree with you.* □ *The outpatient clinic was filled with the walking wounded.*

**walk off with something** See *walk away with something.*

**walk on eggs** AND **walk on thin ice** *in.* to walk very cautiously; to be in a very precarious position. □ *I have to remember that I'm walking on eggs when I give this speech.* □ *Careful with ideas like that. You're walking on thin ice.*

**walk on thin ice** See the previous entry.

**walkover** *n.* an easy victory; an easy task. (From sports.) □ *The game was a walkover. No problem.* □ *Learning the computer's operating system was no walkover for me.*

**walk soft** *in.* to take it easy; to be gentle and humble. □ *I try to walk soft and not rock the boat.* □ *The guy's a tyrant. He walks soft just to mislead people.*

**walk tall** *in.* to be brave and self-assured. (See also *stand tall.*) □ *I know I can walk tall because I'm innocent.* □ *You go out on that stage and walk tall. There is no reason to be afraid.*

**wallet** *n.* a college student's father and financial source. □ *My wallet won't send me another penny this semester.* □ *Why don't you tell your wallet you are starving?*

**wall-eyed** *mod.* alcohol intoxicated. □ *Wow, is he ever wall-eyed!* □ *Who's the wall-eyed guy carrying the ham sandwich?*

**wallflower** *n.* a shy person. □ *Clare was sort of a wallflower, until she graduated.* □ *Don't be a wallflower. Come to the reception.*

**wall job** *n.* a car—in the shop for repairs—that is parked against the wall with no repairs done. (The customer is charged anyway.) □ *Places like those we surveyed may charge hundreds of dollars for what they call "wall jobs."* □ *Okay, Lefty, the caddy looks like another wall job. Throw some plastic over it, and we'll call the old girl and tell her it needs parts.*

**wallop** ['wɑləp] **1.** *n.* a hard blow. □ *She planted a hard wallop on his right shoulder.* □ *I got quite a wallop when I walked into the door.* **2.** *tr.* to strike someone or something hard. □ *I walloped him hard on the shoulder, but he kept on laughing.* □ *The door swung open and walloped me in the back.* **3.** *n.* influence; pull; *clout.* □ *The gal has a lot of wallop in city hall.* □ *I don't have enough wallop to make that kind of demand.*

**wallpaper** *n.* worthless checks. (Underworld.) □ *This flimflam artist has spread a lot of wallpaper in her day.* □ *The feds followed a trail of wallpaper from St. Louis to San Francisco and made the pinch.*

**walls have ears** *phr.* "Someone may be listening." (Sometimes with *the.*) □ *Talk softly. Walls have ears.* □ *The walls have ears, so be careful about what you say.*

**wall-to-wall** *mod.* expansive and comprehensive. (From "wall-to-wall carpeting.") □ *The guy doesn't exactly have wall-to-wall generosity.* □ *Old Tom is wall-to-wall hostility these days. What's wrong?*

**waltz** *n.* an easy task. □ *The job was a waltz. We did it in a day.* □ *The coach promised them that the game would be a waltz.*

**waltz off (with something)** *in.* to take something away easily. □ *The thieves waltzed off with a giant-screen television in broad daylight.* □ *They just picked the thing up and waltzed off. Nobody asked them any questions.*

**waltz through something** *in.* to get through something easily. □ *I waltzed through my comps and started on my research in my second year.* □ *I tried to waltz through my assignment, but it was too hard.*

**wampum** ['wɑmpəm] *n.* money. (From an Amerindian word.) □ *I don't have enough wampum to swing the deal.* □ *How much wampum do you want for this thing?*

**wana** ['wɑnə] *n.* marijuana. (Drugs. Black.) □ *Got any wana on you?* □ *How much is this wana, man?*

**wanabe** AND **wanna be** ['wɑnə bi OR 'wɑnə bi] *n.* someone who wants to be something or someone. (Associated with Madonna, the singer.) □ *All these teenyboppers are wanabes, and that's why we can sell this stuff to them at any price.* □ *A wanna be came by selling chances on a raffle.*

**wanna\*** ['wɑnə OR 'wɑnə] *phr.* "want to." (Eye-dialect. Typical spoken English. Caution with use in writing.) □ *I will if I wanna.* □ *Do you wanna gimme the thingy and lemme go ahead with my work?*

**want list** *n.* a list of things that someone wants. (See also *laundry list, shopping list*.) □ *Some of the things on her want list we can take care of easily.* □ *Send me your want list, and I'll see what we can do.*

**want out** *in.* to want to remove oneself from some association or relationship. □ *Ted had had as much as he could stand, and he wanted out.* □ *I want out. This relationship is stifling me.*

**Want to make something of it?** AND **Wanna make sumpin' of it?** *interrog.* "Do you want to fight about it?" □ *So, I'm a little ugly. Wanna make sumpin' of it?* □ *I'm warped and smelly. Want to make something of it?*

**war chest** *n.* a political campaign fund. □ *They say the Vice President has over nine million dollars in his war chest.* □ *When the war chest gave out, the candidate dropped out of the race.*

**warhorse** *n.* a tough old thing, person, or idea. □ *The conductor loves to have us play that old warhorse as an encore.* □ *What time does the old warhorse's train get in, and how long is she staying this time?*

**warm body** *n.* just anyone who can be counted on to stay alive. □ *See if you can get a couple of warm bodies to stand at the door and hand out programs.* □ *You mean among all these warm bodies nobody knows calculus?*

**warmed over** *mod.* not very original; rehashed. □ *I am not interested in reading warmed over news on a computer screen.* □ *The lecture sounded sort of warmed over, but it wasn't too dull.*

**warm someone up** AND **warm up someone** *tr.* to prepare an audience for another—more famous—performer. □ *A famous singer came out to warm us up for Jack Benny.* □ *This man Bennett is a superb choice to warm up the audience.*

**war paint** *n.* a woman's makeup. □ *She'll be ready when she gets on her war paint.* □ *She doesn't look half bad without war paint.*

**warped** *mod.* drug intoxicated. (A variant of *bent*.) □ *Too many yellows made Jerry warped as the dickens.* □ *I think Max is permanently warped.*

**wart** 1. *n.* an annoying person. (Also a rude term of address.) □ *Who is that wart with the inch-thick glasses?* □ *Tell the wart to leave, or we will be forced to call Bruno, who doesn't care for such persons.* 2. *n.* a problem or an obstruction in a plan. □ *Okay, now we come to the wart. We don't have the money to carry out this plan.* □ *It's okay except for a little wart.*

**warts and all** *mod.* even with the flaws. □ *It's a great performance—warts and all.* □ *Yes, we admire each other very much, warts and all.*

**war zone** *n.* an area where things get rough; a tough neighborhood. □ *Unfortunately our offices are in a war zone, and we have to be on the way home before dark.* □ *The drug dealers and the gangs have turned many of our neighborhoods into war zones.*

**wash** 1. *in.* to be believed. (As if untruth were a stain which will not *come out in the wash*.) □ *It sounds phony. It won't wash.* □ *That'll never wash! It's totally unbelievable.* 2. *n.* a drink that follows a previous drink; a *chaser.* □ *He ordered a beer wash with his snort.* □ *Can I have a wash with this, bartender?* **3.** *n.* the almost simultaneous sale and purchase of the same stock, usually to make the stock appear to be trading actively. (Financial markets. The practice is illegal. Tax loss selling must be done in such a way to avoid appearing to be a *wash.*) □ *I sold the stock and couldn't buy it back for 30 days to avoid an illegal wash.* □ *The IRS ruled that the sale was a wash and that I couldn't take the tax loss.* **4.** *n.* a whitewash or covering up (of a problem). □ *What the administration presented was not an explanation, but a wash.* □ *We don't want a wash. We want the truth.*

**washed out** *mod.* exhausted; tired. □ *I feel too washed out to go to work today.* □ *Poor Ted really looks washed out.*

**washed up** **1.** *mod.* finished; ruined. □ *That's it! The end. You're washed up! Goodbye.* □ *Tom's all washed up at the grocery store.* **2.** *mod.* off drugs; withdrawn from drug addiction. (Drugs. Compare to *clean.*) □ *Ken did everything he could to get washed up.* □ *Being washed up is what I want more than anything.*

**wash one's dirty linen in public** See *air one's dirty linen in public.*

**wash out** **1.** *in.* to fail and be removed from something, such as school. (See *washout.*) □ *I studied all I could, but I still washed out.* □ *I don't want to wash out. It's my whole future.* **2.** *in.* to have a serious wreck; to *wipe out.* □ *The little car washed out on the curve.* □ *The vehicles have a tendency to wash out when cornering.* **3.** *in.* to lose a large amount of money. □ *Fred washed out on that stock deal.* □ *Lefty and Bruno washed out at the track.* **4.** *in.* to slow down or collapse from exhaustion. □ *The whole play began to wash out during the second act. It was a lost cause by the third.* □ *Finally, after a long day, I just washed out. They had to call the paramedics.* (More at *washed out.*)

**washout** *n.* a failure; a fiasco. □ *The whole project was a washout. A lost cause from beginning to end.* □ *I am beginning to think that Sally's specialty is washouts.*

**wash someone away** AND **wash away someone** *tr.* to kill someone. (Underworld.) □ *Bruno was charged with trying to wash Max away.* □ *The mob triggers came by and tried to wash away a druggy type.*

**WASP** AND **W.A.S.P.** **1.** *n.* "white Anglo-Saxon protestant." (Usually derogatory. Acronym.) □ *Would you call Tod a WASP?* □ *Not really. The west side is where the W.A.S.P.s live.* **2.** *mod.* having to do with white Anglo-Saxon protestants; *waspish.* □ *They preferred to live in a WASP neighborhood.* □ *What a silly old WASP idea.*

**waspish** *mod.* in the manner of a *WASP.* □ *She looks sort of waspish, but she's not.* □ *Sally is a waspish kind of yuppie.*

**waste** *tr.* to kill someone. (Underworld.) □ *Bruno had orders to waste Max.* □ *The mob's triggers sped by in a car and wasted four pushers.*

**wasted** **1.** *mod.* dead; killed. □ *Max didn't want to end up wasted.* □ *That's silly. We all end up wasted one way or another.* **2.** *mod.* alcohol or drug intoxicated. □ *I really feel wasted. What did I drink?* □ *I've never seen a bartender get wasted before.*

**Watch it!** *exclam.* "Be careful!"; "Watch your step!"; "Careful of what you say!" □ *Watch it, buster!* □ *You're walking on thin ice. Watch it!*

**Watch my lips!** AND **Read my lips!** *exclam.* "I am going to say something rude to you that I will not say out loud!" □ *You jerk! Watch my lips!* □ *Hey, chum! Read my lips!*

**Watch your mouth!** AND **Watch your tongue!** *exclam.* "Pay attention to what you are saying!"; "Do not say anything rude!" □ *Hey, don't talk that way! Watch your mouth!* □ *Watch your tongue, garbage mouth!*

**Watch your tongue!** See the previous entry.

**watering hole** *n.* a tavern. □ *Now this place is one of my favorite watering holes.* □ *I think you live down at that watering hole.*

**wax** **1.** *tr.* to beat or defeat someone; to assault someone. □ *Those guys look like they're gonna wax us, but good.* □ *The muggers waxed the vest and swiped* his briefcase. **2.** *n.* a phonograph recording; a substance onto which a recording is put. (Never singular or plural.) □ *This is one of the finest pieces of music ever put on wax.* □ *Now here's some wax I'll bet you've never heard before.*

**waxed** *mod.* alcohol intoxicated. (See also *polished (up)*.) □ *Tom is too waxed to talk.* □ *Sam got waxed and had to be taken home.*

**way** *mod.* extremely; totally. □ *Oh, this is way gross!* □ *I feel way tired today.*

**way down** *mod.* very depressed. □ *Poor Clare is way down. I think she has something wrong with her.* □ *Tod sure looks way down.*

**way off (base)** *mod.* on the wrong track; completely wrong. □ *I think you're way off base. Try again.* □ *Sorry. You are way off. You should just give up.*

**way out** AND **way-out 1.** *mod.* extreme; arcane. □ *Some of your ideas are really way out.* □ *What a way-out hairdo.* **2.** *mod.* heavily alcohol or drug intoxicated. □ *That guy is way out—can't even walk.* □ *She was so way-out, she was almost unconscious.*

**way rad** *mod.* quite excellent. (California. See *rad*.) □ *Oh, Tiff! That's way rad!* □ *You are? Way rad!*

**Way to go!** See *That's the way to go!*

**weak sister** *n.* a timid person, usually a male. □ *It looks like Dave is the weak sister on the team.* □ *Another weak sister and we'll have to quit. We've got to pull together.*

**wear** *tr.* to tolerate something. (Usually negative.) □ *That's no good. I won't wear it.* □ *I don't mind, but my wife won't wear it.*

**wear the pants (in the house)** *tr.* to be the boss in the house; to run a household. □ *All right, if you have to wear the pants, have it your way.* □ *Well, somebody has to wear the pants.*

**weasel 1.** *n.* a sneaky person. □ *You slimy weasel! How could you!* □ *If Fred weren't such a weasel, we could get along better.* **2.** *n.* an earnest student. (Collegiate.) □ *Who's the weasel who always gets A's?* □ *Merton is your classic weasel.*

**weasel out of something** *in.* to get out of doing something; to wiggle out of a

responsibility. □ *I know how to weasel out of something like that. You get a headache.* □ *You can't just weasel out now when we need you!*

**weed 1.** *n.* tobacco; a cigarette or cigar. □ *I've about given up weed.* □ *This weed is gonna be the death of me.* **2.** *n.* marijuana; a marijuana cigarette. (Drugs.) □ *This is good weed, man.* □ *This weed is green, but decent.*

**weedhead** AND **weed-eater** *n.* a smoker of marijuana. □ *Max is a confirmed weed-eater.* □ *The weedheads are taking over this neighborhood.*

**weed out** *in.* to escape from life into marijuana smoking. (Drugs.) □ *Gary started out by going home and weeding out every day after school.* □ *Jim liked to torch up and weed out.*

**weeds** *n.* clothing. □ *Good-looking weeds you're wearing.* □ *These weeds came right out of the wish book. Would you believe?*

**weekend warrior** *n.* a member of the military reserves. □ *I wanted to be a weekend warrior and get some of the educational benefits.* □ *The weekend warriors were called into active duty.*

**weenie\* 1.** *n.* a wiener (sausage), as in a hotdog (sandwich). □ *They gave us some yucky beans with weenies in them.* □ *It's weenies again for dinner.* **2.\*** *n.* the penis. (Essentially juvenile and jocular. Caution with topic.) □ *Tell him to cover his weenie and run and grab a towel.* □ *He told some joke about a weenie, but nobody got it.* **3.** *n.* a stupid person. □ *Gee, you can be such a weenie!* □ *Who's the weenie driving the old car?* **4.** *n.* an earnest student. (Collegiate.) □ *That weenie keeps getting A's and raising the grade scale.* □ *Who's the weenie with the thick glasses?*

**weeper** *n.* a sad movie, novel, television program, etc. □ *I can't seem to get enough of these weepers.* □ *Not another weeper!*

**wee-wee\*** ['wiwi] **1.\*** *in.* to urinate. (Baby talk. Caution with subject.) □ *Mommy, I have to wee-wee.* □ *Jimmy, please go and wee-wee before we leave.* **2.\*** *n.* urine. (Baby talk. Caution with subject.) □ *There's wee-wee on the floor, Mommy.* □ *Why is wee-wee warm, Mommy?*

**weirded out** *mod.* disturbed or unnerved by drugs or events. □ *I was totally weirded out and couldn't control myself.* □ *After the blow-up, Fred was really weirded out.*

**weirdo** ['wɪrdo] *n.* a strange person. □ *She is sure a weirdo lately.* □ *Don't be such a weirdo!*

**weird out** *in.* to become emotionally disturbed or unnerved; to *flip (out).* □ *The day was just gross. I thought I would weird out at noon.* □ *I weirded out at the news of Frankie's death.* (More at *weirded out.*)

**weisenheimer** AND **wiseacre** ['waɪzn̩haɪmɚ AND 'waɪzekɚ] *n.* a presumptuous smart aleck. (Also a term of address.) □ *Who's the wiseacre who put sugar in the salt shaker?* □ *Look, weisenheimer, watch your tongue!*

**welcher** ['wɛltʃɚ] *n.* someone who does not pay gambling debts. □ *It was Bruno's job to let the welchers know that Mr. Big was angry.* □ *Bruno set out to teach the welcher a lesson. He didn't mean to hurt him very much.*

**well-fixed** AND **well-heeled** **1.** *mod.* rich. □ *His father died and left him pretty well-fixed.* □ *Her well-fixed uncle left her a lot of money.* □ *Tod is well-fixed for life.* **2.** *mod.* alcohol intoxicated. □ *By midnight, he was pretty well-fixed.* □ *You might say he is well-fixed. You might say he's dead drunk, too.*

**well-oiled** **1.** *mod.* alcohol intoxicated. □ *He was well-oiled and couldn't stand up.* □ *Get him well-oiled and break the news to him.* **2.** *mod.* talkative. □ *She was sure well-oiled. I thought she'd never stop talking.* □ *Get him well-oiled, and you'll find out about everything.*

**(well-)upholstered** *mod.* chubby; plump. □ *Fortunately, he was upholstered enough that the fall didn't really hurt.* □ *My well-upholstered brother has to go on a diet.*

**wenchy** AND **whenchy** ['wɛntʃi AND 'ʍɛntʃi] *mod.* bitchy; snotty. (Collegiate.) □ *I really wish you wouldn't be so wenchy with me!* □ *What's the matter with that wenchy chick?* □ *Then she began to get whenchy, so I left.*

**Were you born in a barn?** *interrog.* "Weren't you trained to close the door by yourself?" □ *Close the door! Were you born in a barn?* □ *You sure are careless with that door. Were you born in a barn?*

**wet** **1.** *mod.* alcohol intoxicated. □ *The jerk is wet and can't drive home.* □ *He's been drinking since noon and is pretty wet.* **2.** *mod.* having to do with an area where is it legal to sell alcohol. (Compare to *dry.*) □ *Kansas became wet just a few years ago.* □ *Is it wet or dry in this county?*

**wet blanket** *n.* someone who ruins a good time. (In the way that a wet blanket is used to put out a fire.) □ *Oh, Merton! Why do you have to be such a wet blanket?* □ *Don't be a wet blanket! Have some fun!*

**wet noodle** *n.* a dupe; a *wimp.* □ *Don't be such a wet noodle. Don't let them push you around.* □ *Merton is such a wet noodle.*

**wet one** *n.* a cold beer. □ *How about a wet one, Fred?* □ *I could sure use a wet one about now.*

**wet one's tonsils** AND **wet one's whistle** *tr.* to have a drink of liquor or beer. (Folksy.) □ *Yup, I think I could wet my tonsils after that long ride.* □ *Try wetting your whistle with this.*

**wet one's whistle** See the previous entry.

**wet rag** See the following entry.

**wet sock** AND **wet rag** *n.* a *wimp*; a useless *jerk.* (See also *rubber sock.*) □ *Don't be such a wet sock! Stand up for your rights!* □ *Well, in a tight situation, Merton is sort of a wet rag.*

**wetware** ['wetwer] *n.* the human brain. (Computers. As compared to *hardware* and *software.*) □ *This isn't a hardware problem; it's a wetware problem.* □ *You need to update your wetware.*

**whack** AND **wack** **1.** *tr.* to strike someone or something. □ *Jed whacked the kid upside the head.* □ *Larry reached down and wacked the dog across the snout.* **2.** *n.* a blow or hit (at someone or something). □ *She tried to take a whack at me!* □ *She landed a nasty wack on his thigh.* **3.** *n.* a drink of liquor. □ *Take a whack of this stuff.* □ *Hey, give me another wack of that. It helps.*

**whacked (out)** *mod.* alcohol or drug intoxicated. □ *Gee, is he ever whacked!* □ *Dave was so whacked out he couldn't stand up.*

**whack someone or something (out)** AND **whack out someone or something** **1.** *tr.* [with *someone*] to kill somebody. (Underworld.) □ *Bruno made another try at whacking Max out last evening.* □ *He really wants to whack Mr. Big.* **2.** *tr.* [with *something*] to rob a place; to swindle a business establishment. (Underworld.) □ *Bruno's gang whacked out the bank on Maple Street.* □ *Did your guys whack the church collection box?*

**whale** **1.** *n.* a very fat person. (Cruel.) □ *Molly is getting to be such a whale.* □ *Well, Gert's the whale if you ask me.* **2.** *n.* a drunkard; a person with an enormous capacity for liquor. □ *Arthur is getting to be a regular whale. What does he drink?* □ *A pair of whales was in the corner booth tanking up.*

**whale into someone or something** *tr.* to attack someone or something. □ *Jimmy's dad really whaled into him.* □ *The guy whaled into the logs and had a nice woodpile by noon.*

**whale the tar out of someone** *tr.* to spank or beat someone. (Sometimes said to a child.) □ *My father threatened to whale the tar out of me.* □ *I'll whale the tar out of you when we get home if you don't settle down.*

**whaling** See *wailing.*

**wham-bang** ['ʌæm'bæŋ] *mod.* large; boisterous. □ *We had a really wham-bang time at your party.* □ *The overture was just too wham-bang for the tone of the play itself.*

**wham-ditty** ['ʌæm'dɪdi] *n.* a gadget. □ *That's a pretty clever little wham-ditty you have there. Fits right on the end, does it?* □ *Now, this wham-ditty can be bought for a few cents at any hardware store.*

**whangdoodle** AND **whangydoodle** ['ʌæŋ'dudl̩ AND 'ʌæŋi'dudl̩] **1.** *n.* a gadget. □ *Toss me one of the little whangdoodles, would ya?* □ *This whangydoodle is a little bent.* **2.** *n.* nonsense. □ *Now that's enough of your whangdoodle.* □ *All I ever hear out of you is whangydoodle.*

**What (a) nerve!** *exclam.* "What insolence!"; "How rude and presumptuous!" □ *Did you hear what she said? What nerve!* □ *What a nerve! Have you ever seen such gall?*

**What can I do you for?** *interrog.* "How can I help you?"; "How can I serve you?" □ *Good morning. What can I do for you?* □ *Now it's your turn. What can I do for you?*

**whatchamacallit** ['ʌɑtʃəməkɑlɪt] *n.* a name for a person or thing whose real name has been forgotten or is being avoided. □ *Did you invite whatchamacallit to the party?* □ *I lost my—you know—my whatchamacallit—my watch!*

**What do you say?** **1.** *interrog.* "Hello, how are you?" (Most often [wədəjə'se].) □ *Hi, Jim. What do you say?* □ *What do you say, man?* **2.** *interrog.* "What is your answer?" □ *Well, what do you say?* □ *Come on, I need an answer now. What do you say?*

**What else is new?** *interrog.* "But isn't that what you expect?"; "What you said isn't new, so what is new?" □ *Yes, there is trouble around the world. What else is new?* □ *So, there's not enough money this week. What else is new?*

**whatever turns you on** *phr.* "It's all right if it excites you or interests you." (Said originally about sexual matters.) □ *You really like pickled pigs feet? Whatever turns you on.* □ *I can't stand that kind of music, but whatever turns you on.*

**What gives?** *interrog.* "What is going on?"; "What is happening?" □ *Hey! What gives? Who left this here?* □ *What gives? Who's made this mess?*

**What (in) the devil?** *interrog.* "What has happened?"; "What?" (Often with the force of an exclamation.) □ *What in the devil? Who put sugar in the salt shaker?* □ *What the devil? Who are you? What are you doing in my room?*

**What (in) the hell?*** . . . **1.** *interrog.* "What has happened?"; "What?" □ *What (in) the hell? Who did this?* □ *What the hell happened here?* **2.** *interrog.* "What does it matter?" (Usually with the force of an exclamation.) □ *Give her a new one. What the hell!* □ *Don't be such a cheapskate. Get the nice one. What the hell!*

**What in (the) Sam Hill?** *interrog.* "What has happened?"; "What?" (An elaboration of *what*. *Sam Hill* is *hell*. Often with the force of an exclamation. See examples for variations.) □ *What in Sam Hill is going on around here?* □ *What in the Sam Hill do you think you are doing?*

**What in the world?** *interrog.* "What has happened?"; "What?" (Often with the force of an exclamation. See examples for variations.) □ *What in the world! What's this?* □ *There's money in this box. What in the world happened!*

**What'll it be?** *interrog.* "What do you want?" (Typically said when offering someone drinks. See also *What's yours?*) □ *Okay, Mac, what'll it be?* □ *What'll it be, chum?*

**What now? 1.** *interrog.* "What can be happening now?" □ *Somebody's at the door. What now?* □ *Is that a leak under the sink? What now?* **2.** *interrog.* "What is your next request?"; "Why are you bothering me again?" □ *It's you again. What now?* □ *What now? Is something really wrong?*

**What of it?** *interrog.* "Why does it matter?"; "So what?" □ *So I'm late. What of it?* □ *What of it? How does it affect you?*

**What say?** *interrog.* "What did you say?" (Folksy. See also *Say what?*) □ *What say? I didn't hear.* □ *What say? Talk louder.*

**What's buzzin' (cousin)?** *interrog.* "What's happening?" □ *Hey, chum! What's buzzin' cousin?* □ *What's buzzin' around here?*

**What's cooking?** *interrog.* "What is happening?"; "What's about to happen?" □ *What's cooking? Anything interesting?* □ *What's cooking anyway?*

**What's eating someone?** *interrog.* "What is bothering someone?" □ *Gee, Tom, what's eating you?* □ *What's eating Fred? He's in a rotten humor.*

**What's going down?** *interrog.* "What's happening?" □ *I can't figure out what's going down around here.* □ *Hey, man, what's going down?*

**What's going on?** *interrog.* "What is happening here?" □ *I hear a lot of noise. What's going on?* □ *What's all this broken glass? What's going on?*

**What's happening?** AND **What's happ?** *interrog.* "Hello, what's new?" □ *Hey, dude! What's happening?* □ *What's happ? How's it goin'?*

**what's his face** AND **what's his name** *n.* someone whose name has been forgotten; someone whose name is being avoided. □ *Was what's his name there? I never can remember his name.* □ *I can't remember what's his face's name either.*

**what's his name** See the previous entry.

**What's in it for me?** *interrog.* "How do I benefit from it?" □ *I might help out. What's in it for me?* □ *I might be able to contribute a little. What's in it for me?*

**whatsis** AND **whatsit, whatzit, whazzit** ['ʍɑtsɪs AND 'ʍɑtsɪt, 'ʍɑtsɪt, 'ʍɑzɪt] *n.* a name for a person or thing whose real name has been forgotten or is being avoided. □ *Hand me that whatsis, will you?* □ *Put this little whatzit on the top and another on the bottom.*

**What's it to you?** *interrog.* "What does it matter to you?"; "Is it any of your business?" □ *What's it to you if I don't do it?* □ *So I broke my glasses. What's it to you?*

**What's new?** *interrog.* "Hello, how are you?"; "What has happened since I last saw you?" □ *Hi, Jim! What's new?* □ *What's new with you?*

**What's shakin' (bacon)?** *interrog.* "How are you?"; "What is new?" □ *What's shakin' bacon? What's going down?* □ *Hi, Jim. What's shakin'?*

**What's the catch?** *interrog.* "What is the drawback?"; "It sounds good. Are there any hidden problems?" □ *Sounds too good to be true. What's the catch?* □ *This looks like a good deal. What's the catch?*

**What's the deal?** See *What's the scam?*

**What's the good word?** *interrog.* "Hello, how are you?" □ *Hi, Jim! What's the good word?* □ *Haven't seen you in a long time. What's the good word?*

**What's the scam?** AND **What's the deal?** *interrog.* "What is going on around here?" □ *There's a big rumpus down the hall. What's the scam?* □ *I gave you a twenty, and you give me five back? What's the deal? Where's my other five?*

**What's up?** *interrog.* "What is going on?"; "What is happening?" (See also *Tsup?*) □ *Hi, Jim! What's up?* □ *Haven't seen you in a month of Sundays. What's up?*

**What's with someone or something?** *interrog.* "What is wrong with someone or something?" □ *Hey, chum! What's with you?* □ *What's with this can opener? It won't turn.*

**What's yours?** *interrog.* "What (or which) do you want?" (Typically said on offering drinks. See also *What'll it be?*) □ *"What's yours?" asked the bartender.* □ *The nice young man behind the counter looked to the right and left at all 140 flavors and asked, "What's yours?"*

**What the deuce?** *interrog.* "What has happened?"; "What?" (*Deuce* is an old word for devil.) □ *What the deuce! Who are you?* □ *What the deuce! Who did this?*

**What the heck!** *exclam.* "It doesn't matter!" (Often with the force of an exclamation.) □ *Oh, what the heck! Come on in. It doesn't matter.* □ *Oh, what the heck! I'll have another beer. Nobody's counting.*

**What you see is what you get. 1.** *sent.* "The product you are looking at is exactly what you get if you buy it." □ *It comes just like this. What you see is what you get.* □ *What you see is what you get. The ones in the box are just like this one.* **2.** AND **WYSIWYG** ['wɪsiwɪg] *sent.* "What you see on the screen is what will print on the printer." (Computers.) □ *This program gives you that "what you see is what you get" feature that everyone wants.* □ *I need something that's WYSIWYG. I have no imagination.*

**whazood** AND **waa-zooed** ['ʍɑzud AND 'wɑzud] *mod.* alcohol intoxicated. □ *Man, is she whazood!* □ *Tod was too waa-zooed to stand up.*

**wheat** *n.* marijuana. (Drugs. See also *hay, straw.*) □ *Any high Q. wheat to be had around here?* □ *Whose wheat is this anyway?*

**wheel** *tr. & in.* to drive a car. (Black.) □ *I'm gonna wheel over later this afternoon.* □ *Let's wheel my heap over to Marty's place.*

**wheel and deal** *in.* to negotiate, cajole, and connive—aggressively. (See *wheeler-dealer.*) □ *If you can't wheel and deal, you can't run for elective office.* □ *Any crook can wheel and deal!*

**wheeler-dealer** *n.* someone who bargains aggressively. (See *wheel and deal.*) □ *She has turned into a real wheeler-dealer.* □ *Who's the wheeler-dealer who set up this deal?*

**wheel man** *n.* the (male) driver of a criminal escape car. (Underworld.) □ *Lefty was the wheel man for the bank job.* □ *We need a new wheel man while Lefty's away.*

**wheels** *n.* transportation by automobile. □ *I gotta get some wheels pretty soon.* □ *I'll need a ride. I don't have any wheels.*

**wheely** AND **wheelie** *n.* an act of rearing up on a bike or motorcycle. □ *Can you do wheelies?* □ *The kid did a wheelie and scared his mother to death.*

**when push comes to shove** AND **if push comes to shove** *phr.* "when things get a little pressed"; "when the situation gets more active or intense." □ *When push comes to shove, you know I'll be on your side.* □ *If push comes to shove, the front office can help with some statistics.*

**when the eagle flies** AND **day the eagle flies** *phr.* payday. (The "eagle" is the one found on U.S. currency.) □ *I'll pay you back when the eagle flies.* □ *I'll find you the day the eagle flies.*

**when the fat lady sings** See *till the fat lady sings.*

**Where (have) you been keeping yourself?** *interrog.* "I haven't seen you in a long time. Where have you been?" □ *Long time no see. Where've you been keeping yourself?* □ *I haven't seen you in a long time. Where you been keeping yourself?*

**Where in (the) Sam Hill?** *interrog.* "Where?" (An intensive form of *where.* *Sam Hill* is *hell.* See examples.) □ *Where in Sam Hill did I put my hat?* □ *Where in the Sam Hill were you?*

**Where in the world?** *interrog.* "Where?" (An intensive form of "where." See examples for variations.) □ *Where in the world have you been?* □ *Where in the world did I put my glasses?*

**where it's at** *phr.* "what one is aiming for"; "what is needed." (This does not refer to a place. See examples.) □ *Keep on trying. That's where it's at!* □ *Good strong friends. That's where it's at.*

**Where on (God's green) earth?** *interrog.* "(Exactly) where...?" (An intensive form of "where." See examples for variations.) □ *Where on God's green earth did you get that ridiculous hat?* □ *Where on earth is my book?* □ *Where on God's green earth were you?*

**where someone is at** *phr.* "what mental condition someone is in." (See examples.) □ *I know where you're at. I know what you are talking about.* □ *You said it! I know just where you're at!*

**where someone lives** *phr.* "at one's core"; "in one's own personal situation." (See examples.) □ *That really hits you where you live, doesn't it?* □ *Yes, that gets me where I live.*

**where someone's head is at** *phr.* the state of one's mental well-being. (See examples.) □ *As soon as I figure where my head is at, I'll be okay.* □ *He doesn't know where his head is at.*

**Where's the beef?** *interrog.* "Where is the substance?"; "Where is the content?" (From a television commercial where someone is looking for the meat in a fast-food hamburger.) □ *That's really clever and appealing, but where's the beef?* □ *Where's the beef? There's no substance in this proposal.*

**Where's the fire?** *interrog.* "Why are you going so fast?"; "What's the hurry?" □ *Going a little fast there, weren't you? Where's the fire?* □ *Where's the fire? We have an hour to get there.*

**where the action is** *phr.* "where important things are happening." □ *I want to be where the action is.* □ *Right there in city hall. That's where the action is.*

**wherewithal** ['ʍɛrwɪθəl] **1.** *n.* money. □ *I don't have the wherewithal to invest in anything like that.* □ *I've got the interest, but not the wherewithal.* **2.** *n.* motivation; gumption. □ *I just don't have the wherewithal to do the job.* □ *As soon as I get some wherewithal, I'll get a new computer.*

**whiffled** ['ʍɪfld] *mod.* alcohol intoxicated. □ *Jed found himself a mite whiffled,* but nobody else knew. □ *That guy really looks whiffled.*

**whiff-sniffer** AND **wiff-sniffer** *n.* a prohibitionist; someone always alert for the smell of alcohol on someone's breath. (Prohibition.) □ *Merton is something of a whiff-sniffer.* □ *No wiff-sniffer is going to tell me what to do.*

**whing-ding** AND **wing-ding 1.** *n.* a love affair; a sexual affair. □ *Sam and Martha brought their little whing-ding to an end.* □ *Somebody found out about their little wing-ding.* **2.** *n.* a gadget. □ *This whing-ding is broken. Where can I find another?* □ *I've never seen one of these little wing-dings so banged up.* **3.** AND **whinger** *n.* a wild drinking party; drinking spree. □ *Fred had one of the best whing-dings this town has ever seen.* □ *Yes, it was some whinger.*

**whipped** *mod.* alcohol intoxicated. □ *He slid under the table—whipped, for sure.* □ *She was too whipped to find money to pay her bill.*

**whippersnapper** ['ʍɪpɚˌsnæpɚ] *n.* a young, inexperienced person; an upstart, usually a male. (Folksy. Typically encountered in Western movies where an old man addresses a younger one as *whippersnapper.*) □ *Look here, you young whippersnapper, when I was your age I walked wherever I went. If it was too far to walk, I didn't go!* □ *Tell that young whippersnapper to mind his own business.*

**whippets** ['ʍɪpəts] *n.* nitrous oxide dispensed from a pressurized can of whipped cream, used to get *high.* (Drugs.) □ *The silly kid—looking for whippets—got a nose full of whipped cream and nearly sneezed himself to death.* □ *Do you mean that whippets is just old-fashioned laughing gas?*

**whips and jingles** See *whoops and jingles.*

**whipsaw 1.** *tr.* to assault a person; to gang up and beat a person. □ *The gang whipsawed the old man for about ten minutes.* □ *What kind of creeps would whipsaw an old buzzard like that?* **2.** *tr.* (for the stock market) to reduce the capital of investors by frightening them into selling when stock prices are low and encouraging them to buy when prices are high. (Financial markets.) □ *A lot of people were whipsawed in the recent market volatility.* □ *The market will whipsaw the investor who is not cautious.*

**whip something off** AND **whip off something** *tr.* to finish something quickly, especially food or drink. □ *Did you just whip that whole pizza off?* □ *Lemme whip off this sandwich, and I'll be right with you.* □ *She whipped off the dishes in 10 minutes.*

**whirly bird** *n.* a helicopter. □ *See that whirly bird up there? It's timing your speed. Slow down.* □ *The whirly bird landed on the roof of the hospital.*

**whiskers 1.** *n.* an old man, especially one with whiskers. □ *Some old whiskers came by handing out flyers.* □ *Ask whiskers over there where the john is.* **2.** AND **Mr. Whiskers, Uncle Whiskers** *n.* a federal agent; federal agents. □ *Uncle Whiskers is getting suspicious, I think.* □ *Mr. Whiskers is big brother's father.* □ *Who does whiskers think he is?*

**whiskey tenor** *n.* a strained tenor. □ *He's a whiskey tenor, but a good one.* □ *Four whiskey tenors do not a barbershop quartet make.*

**whistle-blower** *n.* someone who calls a halt to something; an informer; an enforcer; a *stool (pigeon).* □ *I don't know who the whistle-blower was, but a good time was really ruined.* □ *Some whistle-blower put Max behind bars for a few days.*

**whistle in the dark** *in.* to guess aimlessly; to speculate as to a fact. □ *Am I close, or am I just whistling in the dark?* □ *She was whistling in the dark. She has no idea of what's going on.*

**whistler** *n.* someone who informs to the police; a *stoolie.* (Underworld. More specialized than *whistle-blower.*) □ *Molly turned into a whistler after her last little vacation.* □ *Who's the whistler who squealed?*

**whitebread** *mod.* plain; dull. □ *Naw, the whole thing is too whitebread.* □ *If I wanted a whitebread vacation, I'd have gone to the beach.*

**white elephant** *n.* a useless or unwanted object. □ *How can I get rid of this white elephant?* □ *Take all those white elephants to the flea market.*

**white hat** *n.* a good guy; a hero. (From Western movies where you could tell the good guys from the bad guys by the color of their hats: white for good, black for bad.) □ *He seems like a white hat, but he's a worm.* □ *The white hats don't always win, you know.*

**white-knuckle 1.** *mod.* having to do with an event that creates a lot of tension, especially an airplane flight. □ *I had a real white-knuckle session with the boss today.* □ *We came in during the storm on a white-knuckle flight from Chicago.* **2.** *mod.* a person who is made tense by something such as flying or sailing. □ *I'm afraid I'm a white-knuckle sailor, and you'd all be much happier if I stay on dry land.* □ *My cousin is a white-knuckle flyer and would rather take the train.*

**white knuckler 1.** *n.* a tense and nervous person. □ *You white knucklers are just going to have to relax.* □ *I'm such a white knuckler before a test.* **2.** *n.* a suspenseful event, such as an exciting movie or a rough airplane flight. □ *The movie was a real white knuckler.* □ *We sat through the white knuckler even without popcorn.*

**white lightning 1.** *n.* raw liquor; strong liquor; inferior liquor. □ *Jed was put in the slammer for selling white lightning.* □ *That white lightning is hard on your insides.* **2.** *n.* L.S.D. mixed with some other drug, such as methamphetamine. (Drugs.) □ *This is white lightning because it will strike you dead.* □ *Who sells white lightning around here?*

**whitewash 1.** *tr.* to make something look better than it really is; to conceal something bad. □ *Now, don't try to whitewash this incident. Open up about it.* □ *The mayor's office tried to whitewash the whole affair.* **2.** *n.* an act or campaign of covering up something bad. □ *They tried to give the scandal the old whitewash, but it didn't work.* □ *It was a good whitewash, but nobody believed it for a minute.*

**whittled 1.** *mod.* alcohol intoxicated; filled with liquor. (Compare to *cut.*) □ *Fred's whittled and can't hardly see.* □

*Why does he keep getting so whittled?*
**2.** *mod.* overdosed with drugs. (Drugs.)
□ *Max got himself whittled and is off the streets for a while.* □ *I don't want to get whittled.*

**whiz\* 1.** *n.* a talented or skilled person. □ *She's a real whiz with stats.* □ *I'm no math whiz, but I can find your errors.* **2.\*** *in.* to urinate. (Caution with topic.) □ *I gotta stop here and whiz.* □ *You can't whiz in the park!*

**whiz-bang** AND **whizz-bang** *n.* a mixture of drugs—heroin and cocaine or cocaine and morphine—that is injected. (Drugs.) □ *The singer took a whiz-bang before going on stage and pifted before curtain time.* □ *Wasn't it one of those whizz-bangs that killed what's his face?*

**whiz kid** *n.* a young *whiz*. □ *The boss's new whiz kid doesn't seem to be doing the job very well.* □ *We need a whiz kid to get things brought up to date around here.*

**Whoa!** [wo] *exclam.* "Stop!" (Said to a horse or any person or thing.) □ *You've gone about far enough. Whoa!* □ *Whoa, you've gone about far enough.*

**whodunit** [hu'dənɪt] *n.* a detective story. □ *I love to read a good whodunit every now and then.* □ *I go through about 3 whodunits a week.*

**Who (in) the hell?** AND **Who (in) the devil?** *interrog.* "Who...?" (An elaboration of *who*. See examples for variations.) □ *Who in the hell was that masked man?* □ *Who the hell are you?*

**whole bag of tricks** *n.* everything; every possibility. (Always with *my*.) □ *Well now, I've used my whole bag of tricks, and we still haven't solved this.* □ *It may take my whole bag of tricks to do it, but I'll try.*

**whole ball of wax** *n.* everything; the whole thing. (Always with *the*.) □ *Well, that just about ruins the whole ball of wax, that's what.* □ *Your comments threatened the whole ball of wax, that's what.*

**whole bunch(es)** *mod.* a whole lot; very much. (Always with *a* in the singular.) □ *I like to spend evenings at home a whole bunch.* □ *I like pizza whole bunches.*

**whole enchilada** [...ɛntʃə'lɑdə] *n.* the whole thing; everything. (From Spanish. Always with *the*.) □ *Nobody, but nobody, ever gets the whole enchilada.* □ *Max wants the whole enchilada.*

**whole fam damily** [...'fæm 'dæmli] *n.* the entire family. (Always with *the*. A deliberate spoonerism for "whole damn family.") □ *The whole fam damily has had this virus. Yuck!* □ *There's enough here for the whole fam damily.*

**whole new ball game** *n.* a completely different situation; something completely different. (Always with *a*.) □ *Now that you're here, it's a whole new ball game.* □ *With a faster computer, it's a whole new ball game.*

**whole nine yards** *n.* the entire amount; everything. (Always with *the*. Origin unknown.) □ *For you I'll go the whole nine yards.* □ *You're worth the whole nine yards.*

**whole 'nother thing** *n.* something completely different. (Folksy. Always with *a*.) □ *Well, now, tax problems. That's a whole 'nother thing.* □ *You want a refund? Well, that's a whole 'nother thing.*

**whole schmear** [...ʃmɪr] *n.* the entire amount; the entire affair. (Yiddish. Always with *the*.) □ *You just wrecked the whole schmear, that's what.* □ *I'll take a hamburger with everything on it—the whole schmear.*

**whole shebang** AND **whole shooting match** [...ʃə'bæŋ] *n.* the whole affair; everything and everyone. (Folksy. Always with *the*.) □ *The whole shebang is just about washed up.* □ *I'm fed up with the whole shooting match.*

**whole shooting match** See the previous entry.

**whole wide world** *n.* everywhere; everywhere and everything. (Always with *the*.) □ *It's the best in the whole wide world.* □ *I've searched the whole wide world for just the right hat.*

**whomp something up** AND **whomp up something** [ʍɑmp...] *tr.* to whip something up; to come up with something. (Folksy.) □ *Gert'll whomp up some fried chicken, and we'll all have a fine time.* □ *I'll whomp up something for dinner. You just relax.*

**whoomp(h)** [ʍump(f)] *n.* the sound of falling, striking, or blowing. □ *A terrible whoomph came from the direction of the garage.* □ *I heard the whoomp and feared for the worst.*

**Whoopee!** [ˈwuˈpi] *exclam.* "Wow!" □ *Whoopee! I'm accepted at Harvard College of Commerce! □ I made it! Whoopee!*

**whoopee(-water)** *n.* champagne; liquor used for celebrating. □ *Whoopee-water was flowing like—water.* □ *Have some more whoopee?*

**whooper-up(per)** *n.* a drinking bout; a wild drinking party. □ *I hear that Fred's having a big whooper-up at his place tonight.* □ *Are you going to Fred's whooper-upper?*

**Whoops-a-daisy!** See *Oops-a-daisy!*

**whoops and jingles** AND **whips and jingles** *n.* the delirium tremens. □ *The moocher had the shakes from the whoops and jingles.* □ *The whips and jingles get going along about dawn.*

**whoosh** [ʍuʃ] *n.* the sound of rushing air or a liquid. □ *I heard a loud whoosh when I opened the door.* □ *You could hear the water whooshing in the pipes.*

**whooshed** *mod.* alcohol intoxicated. □ *Jerry was totally whooshed by midnight.* □ *Hank was whooshed, but thought he could drive home.*

**whoozis** AND **whoozit** [ˈhuzɪs AND ˈhuzɪt] *n.* a name for a person whose real name is forgotten or being avoided. □ *I met whoozis—you know, with the big whatsis—today.* □ *Is whoozit coming to my birthday party?*

**whopper** **1.** *n.* something that is of relatively great size. □ *That thing's really a whopper!* □ *It was a whopper of an argument.* **2.** *n.* a very big lie. □ *That one's a whopper. I don't believe a word of it.* □ *She sure told a whopper, didn't she?*

**whopping (great)** *mod.* enormous. □ *Somebody showed up with a whopping great basin of chunks of pickled fish. Yummy!* □ *What a whopping fool he is!*

**who shot John** *n.* moonshine; illicit whiskey. (Prohibition.) □ *You know where I can get a little of that who shot John?* □ *He's had too much of that who shot John.*

**Who the deuce?** *interrog.* "Who...?" (An elaboration of *who*. The *deuce* is the devil. See examples for variations.) □ *Who the deuce do you think you are?* □ *Who the deuce is making all that noise?*

**whump** AND **whomp, womp** [ʍəmp AND ʍamp, wamp] **1.** *tr.* to beat or out-score someone. □ *They set out to whump us, and they sure did.* □ *The Redskins womped the Walleyes.* **2.** *n.* the sound made when two flat surfaces fall together. □ *I heard the whump when the shed collapsed.* □ *The whomp woke everyone up.*

**whup** [ʍəp] *tr.* to spank or beat someone. (Folksy.) □ *Jed said he was gonna whup me, Ma. Don't let him.* □ *I'll whup you if you don't stop carrying on.*

**Why (in) the devil?** AND **Why (in) the hell?\*** *interrog.* "Why?" (An elaboration of *why*. See examples for variations. Caution with *hell*.) □ *Why the devil didn't you call and tell me you were in town?* □ *Why the hell doesn't he sit down?*

**Why (in) the hell?** See the previous entry.

**wicked** *mod.* excellent; impressive. □ *Now this is what I call a wicked guitar.* □ *Man, this wine is wicked!*

**wide** *mod.* drug intoxicated. (Black.) □ *Who is that wide dude?* □ *How'd you get so wide, man?*

**wide open** **1.** *mod.* as fast as possible; at full throttle. □ *I was driving along wide open when I became aware of a flashing red light.* □ *It was wide open and still wouldn't do better than 80.* **2.** *mod.* vice-ridden. □ *This town is wide open!* □ *Because the prison is understaffed, it is wide open.*

**wide place in the road** *n.* a very small town. □ *The town is little more than a wide place in the road.* □ *We stopped at a wide place in the road called Adamsville.*

**widget** [ˈwɪdʒɪt] **1.** *n.* a gadget. □ *Now, try to fit this widget into this slot here.* □ *What is the real name of this widget?* **2.** *n.* a hypothetical product made by a hypothetical company. (See examples.) □ *Someone said that your company is manufacturing widgets.* □ *No, we stopped* *making widgets last year. Too much foreign competition.*

**widow** See *(black) widow.*

**widow-maker** *n.* a dangerous horse; anything dangerous: a gun, strong alcohol, etc. □ *I call this stuff widow-maker. It's really strong.* □ *That horse is a widow-maker. I won't ride it.*

**wife** *n.* a girlfriend. (Collegiate.) □ *Me and my wife are going to Fred's this Friday.* □ *Ask your wife if she wants to come along.*

**wig** *in.* to take an overdose of drugs. (Drugs. From *flip one's wig.*) □ *Poor Max nearly wigged last night.* □ *Carl almost wigged, and his parents are wise to him.*

**wigged (out)** AND **wiggy 1.** *mod.* alcohol or drug intoxicated. □ *How did you get so wigged out?* □ *The kid got a little wigged and slipped under the table.* **2.** *mod.* having lost control of oneself; having flipped one's wig. □ *The kid is just too wigged to do anything these days.* □ *After the bad news, she was totally wigged out.*

**wiggle out of something** *in.* to successfully avoid doing something. □ *We wiggled out of the appointment.* □ *Don't try to wiggle out of it. I saw you with her.*

**wig out 1.** *in.* to lose control of oneself; to *flip one's wig.* □ *I was afraid I would wig out if I stayed any longer.* □ *Take it easy, man. Don't wig out.* (More at *wigged (out).*) **2.** *in.* to have a good time at a party, etc. □ *We wigged out at John's do.* □ *Come on, let's wig out!*

**wild** *mod.* exciting; eccentric; *cool.* □ *Things are really wild here.* □ *We had a wild time.*

**wild and wooly** *mod.* exciting; *hairy.* □ *Things get a little wild and wooly on a Friday evening at Wally's place.* □ *The ride home was a little wild and wooly.*

**will do** *phr.* "I will do it." □ *Will do. I'll get right on it.* □ *Fix the stuck window? Will do.*

**willies** *n.* a case of fear or anxiety. (Compare to *screaming-meemies.*) □ *That kind of movie always gives me the willies.* □ *I got the willies before the test.*

**wimp** [wɪmp] *n.* a weak and retiring person; a *square.* □ *Don't be a wimp. Stand up for your rights.* □ *What a wimp. People walk all over her.*

**wimp out (of something)** *in.* to *chicken out (of something);* to get out of something, leaving others to carry the burden. □ *Come on! Don't wimp out now that there's all this work to be done.* □ *Ted wimped out on us.*

**wimpy** *mod.* weak; inept; square. □ *You are just a wimpy nerd!* □ *Come on, don't be so wimpy.*

**Win a few, lose a few.** *phr.* "Sometimes one wins; other times one loses." □ *Too bad. Sorry about that. Win a few, lose a few.* □ *"Win a few, lose a few," doesn't mean you never win at all.*

**windbag** AND **bag of wind** *n.* a talkative person; a braggart. □ *Quiet, you windbag!* □ *She's nothing but a big bag of wind.*

**windy 1.** *mod.* talkative. □ *She's so windy! Won't she ever let up?* □ *Here comes old windy Charlie. Once he gets started, he never stops.* **2.** *mod.* flatulent; having intestinal gas. □ *I feel a little windy.* □ *If you're windy, why don't you take the day off?*

**wing** *in.* to travel by airplane. □ *We winged to Budapest and attended the conference.* □ *They winged from there to London.*

**wing-ding** See *whing-ding.*

**wingdoodle** [ˈwɪŋˌdudl̩] *n.* a gadget. □ *Do you have any of those little wingdoodles that hold screens in place?* □ *Tighten that little wingdoodle there, and I bet it will work.*

**winged 1.** *mod.* alcohol intoxicated. □ *She was completely winged by midnight.* □ *Winged, he sank beneath the table like a ship going beneath the waves.* **2.** *mod.* under the effects of cocaine; addicted to cocaine. (Drugs.) □ *She came back to her desk looking a little winged.* □ *She was too winged to do any more work.*

**wing heavy** *mod.* alcohol intoxicated. □ *Ken's a little wing heavy and can't fly straight.* □ *From the way he's staggering, I'd say he's more than a little wing heavy.*

**wing it** *tr.* to improvise; to do something extemporaneously. □ *I lost my lecture notes, so I had to wing it.* □ *Don't worry. Just go out there and wing it.*

**wings** *n.* a powdered drug—cocaine, morphine, heroin—that makes a person float. (Drugs. Compare to *give someone wings*.) □ *Where can I find me some wings?* □ *Max has wings of all kinds.*

**winks** *n.* some sleep. (See *(forty) winks*.) □ *I gotta have some winks. I'm pooped.* □ *A few winks would do you good.*

**winky** See *blinky*.

**winner** *n.* an excellent person or thing. □ *This one is a real winner.* □ *He's no winner, but he'll do.*

**wino** ['waɪno] **1.** *n.* wine. □ *How about a little more wino?* □ *This is excellent wino.* **2.** *n.* a wine drunkard. □ *By midnight the winos had gone into their stupors, and we got that part of town to ourselves.* □ *I gave the wino some money to help him stop the shakes.*

**wipe** *n.* a murder; a killing. (Underworld. See *wipe-out* at *wipe out*.) □ *Who's responsible for that wipe downtown last night?* □ *The victim of the latest mob wipe was hauled out of the river this morning.*

**wiped (out) 1.** AND **wiped over** *mod.* alcohol or drug intoxicated. □ *Harry was too wiped out to drive.* □ *Oh, man! I'm really wiped.* **2.** *mod.* (of a person or thing) exhausted. □ *I'm so wiped out that I just want to go home and go to bed.* □ *Wow, am I wiped out!* **3.** *mod.* broke. □ *I'm totally wiped out. Not enough bread for grub.* □ *Medical bills left us totally wiped out.*

**Wipe it off!** *exclam.* "Wipe that smile off your face!" □ *It's not funny. Wipe it off!* □ *Wipe it off! Nothing funny here, soldier.*

**wipe out 1.** *in.* to crash. □ *I wiped out on the curve.* □ *The car wiped out on the curve.* **2.** *in.* to fall off or away from something, such as a bicycle, skates, a surfboard, a skateboard, etc. □ *I wiped out and skinned my knee.* □ *If I wipe out again, my mother says I'm through.* **3.** ['waɪpaʊt] *n.* a wreck. (Usually **wipe-out**.) □ *There was a four-car wipe-out on the expressway when I came in this morning.* □ *It was a pretty serious wipe-out, but no one was killed.* **4.** *n.* an accident on a bicycle, skates, surfboard, skateboard, etc. (Usually **wipe-out**.) □

*I had a nasty wipe-out, but I only bruised my elbow.* □ *That last wipe-out wrecked my bike.* **5.** *n.* a loser; someone who is likely to *wipe out*. (Usually **wipe-out**.) □ *The guy's a wipe-out, for sure.* □ *Please don't call my friend a wipe-out.*

**wipe someone or something out** AND **wipe out someone or something 1.** *tr.* [with *someone*] to eliminate someone; to kill someone. (Underworld.) □ *Max almost wiped Bruno out.* □ *Who wiped out Lefty?* **2.** *tr.* [with *someone*] to exhaust or tire someone. □ *The game wiped me out.* □ *Jogging always wipes me out.* **3.** *tr.* [with *someone*] to ruin someone financially. □ *The loss of my job wiped us out.* □ *The storm ruined the corn crop and wiped us out.* **4.** *tr.* [with *something*] to use up all of something. □ *Who wiped out the strawberry preserves?* □ *I wiped the cookies out—not all at once, of course.* (More at *wiped (out)*.)

**wipe up the floor with someone** See *mop up the floor with someone*.

**wire 1.** *n.* a spy smuggled into a place. □ *Bruno thought Lefty was a wire.* □ *How do we know Lefty isn't a wire?* **2.** *tr.* to install electronic eavesdropping equipment. □ *Somebody wired the mayor's office.* □ *They say the mayor wired his own office to make himself look like a victim.* **3.** See *(live) wire*.

**wired 1.** *mod.* nervous; extremely alert. □ *The guy is pretty wired because of the election.* □ *I get wired before a test.* **2.** AND **wired up** *mod.* alcohol or drug intoxicated. □ *Ken was so wired up he couldn't remember his name.* □ *Tiff is, like, totally wired up.*

**wired into someone or something** *mod.* concerned with someone or something; really involved with someone or something. □ *Mary is really wired into classical music.* □ *Sam and Martha are totally wired into one another.*

**wiseacre** See *weisenheimer*.

**wise guy** *n.* a foolish person; a smart aleck. (Compare to *smart guy*. Also a term of address.) □ *Look, wise guy, mind your own business!* □ *Some wise guy messed up my work.*

**wise to someone or something** *mod.* having found out about someone or something. (Underworld.) □ *The cops are wise to the plan.* □ *I'm wise to Lefty. He's a wire.*

**wise up (to someone or something)** *in.* to (finally) begin to understand someone or something; to realize and accept the facts about someone or something. (Also as a command.) □ *Sally finally wised up to Max.* □ *Come on, Sally! Wise up!*

**wish book** *n.* a large mail-order catalog. □ *The new wish book just came in the mail.* □ *Where's the wish book? I have to order something.*

**wish list** *n.* a list of things one wishes to have. (Compare to *want list*.) □ *I put a new car at the top of my wish list.* □ *I have a CD player on my wish list.*

**wishy-washy** ['wɪʃi'waʃi] *mod.* indecisive; insipid; weak. □ *Don't be such a wishy-washy wimp.* □ *She is so wishy-washy!*

**with a bang** *mod.* in a flamboyant or exciting manner. (Especially with *go out, quit, finish.*) □ *The party started off with a bang.* □ *The old year went out with a bang.*

**with bells on** *mod.* ready to go; eager. □ *She was here on time with bells on.* □ *I promise to be there at five in the morning with bells on.*

**with flying colors** *mod.* flamboyantly; boldly. □ *Alice won first place with flying colors.* □ *Paul came home with flying colors after the match.*

**within an ace of (doing) something** *mod.* very close to doing something. □ *I came within an ace of getting stoned.* □ *We were within an ace of beating the all-time record.*

**with it** *mod.* up-to-date; contemporary. □ *Merton is not exactly with it.* □ *Come on, chum. Get with it.*

**with (one's) eyes (wide) open** *mod.* totally aware of what is going on. □ *I went into this with my eyes open.* □ *We all started with eyes open, but didn't realize what could happen to us.*

**without a hitch** *mod.* with no problem(s). □ *Everything went off without a hitch.* □ *We hoped the job would go off without a hitch.*

**woefits** AND **woofits** ['wofɪts AND 'wufɪts] *n.* a hangover. □ *The poor guy*

is suffering from the woefits. □ *That's a bad case of the woofits.*

**wolf** *n.* a bold and aggressive male. □ *He sees himself as a lady-killer. The chicks see him as an old-fashioned wolf.* □ *And this wolf comes up to me and starts holding my hand.*

**wolf something down** AND **wolf down something** *tr.* to gobble something up; to bolt down food or drink. □ *Enjoy your food. Don't just wolf it down.* □ *But I enjoy wolfing down food more than anything.*

**wombat** ['wambæt] *n.* a strange person; a *geek.* (Collegiate.) □ *Why does everybody think Merton is such a wombat?* □ *Who's the wombat in the 1957 Chevy?*

**womp** See *whump.*

**wonk** [wɔŋk] *n.* an earnest student. (Collegiate.) □ *Who's the wonk who keeps getting the straight A's?* □ *Yes, you could call Merton a wonk. In fact, he's the classic wonk.*

**wonky** ['wɔŋki] *mod.* studious. (Collegiate.) □ *Merton is certainly the wonky type.* □ *You ought to get a little wonky yourself.*

**wood butcher** *n.* a carpenter. □ *See if you can get a wood butcher to fix this broken panel.* □ *The wood butcher tracked sawdust up the stairs.*

**wood-pussy** *n.* a skunk. □ *Do I smell the faint perfume of a wood-pussy?* □ *The dog had a nasty run-in with a wood-pussy.*

**woods are full of....** *phr.* "there are lots and lots of...." (Always with *the.*) □ *The woods are full of cheap compatible computer clones.* □ *The woods are full of nice-looking guys who'll mug you when it's too late.*

**woody** *n.* a wooden surfboard; a surfboard. □ *Who's the guy with the woody on his head?* □ *Get your woody, and let's get moving.*

**woof** [wuf] *in.* to boast; to *sell a wolf ticket*; to chatter. (Black.) □ *They're just woofing. Ignore them.* □ *Stop woofing, Fred. You sound silly.*

**woofits** See *woefits.*

**woofled** ['wufld] *mod.* alcohol intoxicated. □ *Good grief, was he woofled!* □ *Did I get woofled last night? I just don't remember.*

**woofle-water** AND **wozzle-water** *n.* whiskey; liquor. □ *Haven't you had just about enough woofle-water?* □ *No more wozzle-water for me.*

**woolies** *n.* long underwear. □ *It's the time of the year for woolies!* □ *I wish I'd worn my woolies today.*

**woozle-water** See *woofle-water.*

**woozy** ['wuzi] **1.** *mod.* sleepy; disoriented. □ *Aren't you woozy at this time of day?* □ *Who is that woozy gal by the window?* □ *I'm still sort of woozy. Give me a minute or two to wake up.* **2.** *mod.* alcohol intoxicated. □ *I felt a little woozy, but that didn't stop me from having more.* □ *Woozy as I am, I can still drive. Now, give me back my keys.*

**workaholic** *n.* someone who is obsessed with work. □ *Jerry is a workaholic. He can't enjoy a vacation.* □ *Are workaholics really productive?*

**working stiff** *n.* a working man; a man who must work to live. (See *stiff.*) □ *But does the working stiff really care about all this economic stuff?* □ *All the working stiffs want is a raise.*

**work one's butt off** See *work one's tail off.*

**work oneself up** *tr.* to allow oneself to become emotionally upset. □ *Tod worked himself up, and I thought he would scream.* □ *Don't work yourself up over Molly. She's not worth it.*

**work oneself (up) into a lather 1.** *tr.* to work very hard and sweat very much. (Like a horse works up a lather.) □ *Don't work yourself up into a lather. We don't need to finish this today.* □ *I worked myself into a lather getting this stuff ready.* **2.** *tr.* to get excited or angry. (An elaboration of *work oneself up.*) □ *Now, now, don't work yourself up into a lather.* □ *He had worked himself into such a lather, I was afraid he would have a stroke.*

**work oneself up to something** *tr.* to get oneself mentally ready to do something. □ *I spent all morning working myself up to taking the driver's test.* □ *I had to work myself up to it little by little.*

**work one's tail off** AND **work one's butt off*** *tr.* to work very hard. (Caution with *butt.*) □ *I worked my tail off to get*

done on time. □ *You spend half your life working your butt off—and for what?*

**works 1.** *n.* the entire amount; everything. (Always with *the.*) □ *I'd like my hamburger with onions, pickles, catsup, mustard—the works.* □ *She's getting the works at the beauty shop—cut, wash, dye, and set.* **2.** *n.* equipment used for preparing and injecting drugs. (Drugs. Often with *the.*) □ *He had the works hidden in a drawer.* □ *His father found his works and raised holy hell.*

**work someone over** AND **work over someone 1.** *tr.* to threaten, intimidate, or beat someone. □ *Bruno threatened to work Sam over.* □ *Bruno had worked over Terry, and Sam knew that this was no idle threat.* **2.** *tr.* to give someone's body a thorough examination or treatment. □ *The doctors worked her over to the tune of $1,500, but couldn't find anything wrong with her.* □ *The dermatologist worked over her entire body looking for moles.*

**world-beater** *n.* an aggressive and ambitious person. □ *She's not a world-beater, but she's efficient.* □ *They hired an alleged world-beater to manage the office.*

**world-class** *mod.* absolutely top-rate. □ *Now this is a world-class computer. Lots and lots of memory.* □ *I want to see one of your world-class automobiles, whatever that might mean.* □ *This one isn't world-class.*

**world is one's oyster** *phr.* one rules the world; one is in charge of everything. (Always with *the.*) □ *I feel like the world is my oyster, today.* □ *The world is my oyster! I'm in love!*

**worm** *n.* a repellent person, usually a male. □ *Gad, you are a worm, Tom.* □ *I'd like Fred better if he wasn't such a worm.*

**worm-food** *n.* a corpse. □ *You wanna end up worm-food? Just keep smarting off.* □ *In the end, we're all worm-food.*

**worms** *n.* noodles; spaghetti. □ *Let's have worms tonight.* □ *Are the worms ready for the sauce yet?*

**worms in blood** *n.* spaghetti in tomato sauce. □ *We're having worms in blood for dinner tonight.* □ *I'm getting tired of worms in blood every Wednesday.*

**worry wart** *n.* someone who worries all the time. □ *Don't be such a worry wart.* □ *I'm sorry I'm such a worry wart.*

**worship the porcelain god** *tr.* to empty one's stomach; to vomit. (Collegiate.) □ *Somebody was in the john worshiping the porcelain god till all hours.* □ *I think I have to go worship the porcelain god. See ya.*

**worst-case scenario** *n.* the worse possible future outcome. □ *Now, let's look at the worst-case scenario.* □ *In the worst-case scenario, we're all dead.*

**worth one's salt** *mod.* worth (in productivity) what it costs to keep one. □ *We decided that you are worth your salt, and you can stay on as office clerk.* □ *You're not worth your salt. Pack up!*

**would not be seen dead....** *phr.* would not do something under any circumstances. □ *I wouldn't be seen dead going out with Bruno!* □ *Martha would not be seen dead going into a place like that.*

**wouldn't touch someone or something with a ten-foot pole** *phr.* would not get involved with someone or something. □ *Forget it. I wouldn't touch it with a ten-foot pole.* □ *Tom said he wouldn't touch Molly with a ten-foot pole.*

**Would you believe?** *interrog.* "Isn't it amazing?" □ *He actually tried to get me to scratch his bare back! Would you believe?* □ *Would you believe? A three cent per hour raise?*

**wow 1.** *exclam.* an indication of amazement or surprise. (Usually **Wow!**) □ *Wow! Is he ever ugly!* □ *A whole quarter! Wow! Thanks, mister.* **2.** *tr.* to delight or impress someone. □ *She wowed them with her cleverness.* □ *That ought to wow them right out of their seats.* **3.** *n.* something exciting. □ *The game was a real wow.* □ *For a pretty good wow, try the Empire Theater's production of "Mame" this weekend.* **4.** *n.* an exclamation point. □ *Put a wow at the end of this sentence.* □ *Almost every sentence you write has a wow at the end of it.*

**wrap one's car around something** *tr.* to drive one's car into something at fairly high speed. □ *She wrapped her car around a light pole.* □ *If he hadn't wrapped his car around a tree, he'd be here to read his own poetry tonight.*

**wrapped up (in someone or something)** *mod.* concerned or obsessed with someone or something. □ *Sally is pretty wrapped up in herself.* □ *I'm too wrapped up in my charity work to get a job.*

**wrapped up (with someone or something)** *mod.* busy with someone or something. □ *He's wrapped up with a client right now.* □ *I'll talk to you when I'm not wrapped up.*

**wrap something up** AND **wrap up something** *tr.* to finish something; to bring something to a conclusion. □ *Well, that about wraps up our little session together.* □ *Let's wrap this up and go home.*

**wreck** *n.* a person or thing in wrecked condition. □ *I'm a wreck. I think I'll join one of those health clubs and get back into shape.* □ *This house is a wreck!*

**wrecked** *mod.* alcohol or drug intoxicated. □ *Four beers and I was wrecked.* □ *Larry was far too wrecked to drive.*

**wrinkle 1.** *n.* a new idea; a new aspect of something. □ *Fred came up with a new wrinkle for the ad campaign.* □ *Here's a wrinkle for you. Nobody has ever tried this one.* **2.** *n.* a minor problem. □ *A wrinkle has developed in the Wilson proposal.* □ *What are we going to do about this wrinkle in the computer system?*

**wrinkle-rod** *n.* the crankshaft of an engine. □ *You need a new wrinkle-rod, lady.* □ *A wrinkle-rod'll set you back about $199, plus installation charges, of course.*

**wrongo** ['rɔŋo] **1.** *mod.* wrong. □ *You are totally wrongo.* □ *Wrongo, wrongo! You lose!* **2.** *n.* an undesirable thing or person; a member of the underworld. □ *The guy's a total wrongo. He's got to be guilty.* □ *This whole business is a complete wrongo. Something's fishy.*

**wrong side of the tracks** *n.* the poor side of town. □ *Fred's ashamed that he's from the wrong side of the tracks, so to speak.* □ *I'm glad I'm from the wrong side of the tracks. I know what life is really like.*

**wuss** AND **wussy** [WUS AND 'WUSi] *n.* a *wimp*; a weak person. □ *Don't be such a wuss. Stand up for your rights.* □ *Wussies like you will never get ahead.*

**WYSIWYG** See *What you see is what you get.*

# X

**X.** *n.* an injection of drugs. (Drugs.) □ *I just need one little X. to set me straight.* □ *He's gotta have an X., just one.*

**X'd out 1.** *mod.* eliminated; crossed-out. □ *But the Babbits are X'd out.* □ *Put the X'd out Babbits back where they were.* **2.** *mod.* killed. (Underworld.) □ *Mr. Big wanted Max X'd out.* □ *He wanted Bruno to see that all these small-time punks were X'd out.*

**X marks the spot.** *sent.* "This is the spot!" (A catch phrase.) □ *This is where it happened. X marks the spot.* □ *X marks the spot where we first met.*

**Xmas** ['ɛksməs] *n.* drug euphoria; a drug rush. (Drugs. *Xmas* means *Christmas.* From *Xmas rush.*) □ *It's that Xmas that keeps them coming back for more.* □ *The syringe flopped aside, and she waited for Xmas.*

**X something out** AND **X out something** *tr.* to cross something out; to strike something out. □ *We had to X the Babbits out. They can't come.* □ *Sam X'd out the first item on the list.*

**X.Y.Z.** AND **XYZ** *tr.* "examine your zipper"; make sure your fly is zipped up. (Said to men when necessary.) □ *I say there, Wally, X.Y.Z.* □ *X.Y.Z., Fred.*

# Y

**ya*** *pro.* you. (Eye-dialect. Typical spoken English. Caution with use in writing.) □ *See ya!* □ *Is this all ya want?*

**yack** AND **yock, yuck, yuk** [jæk AND jɔk, jək] **1.** *n.* a foolish person. □ *Who's the yock wearing the red bandana?* □ *Get some yuk to do it. I'm busy.* **2.** *n.* idle chatter. □ *I've heard enough yack to last me a lifetime.* □ *Too much yock. Where's the beef?*

**yackety-yak** [ˈjækədiˈjæk] *n.* chatter; gossip. □ *No more yackety-yak* □ *That's enough yackety-yak. Quiet!*

**yahoo** [ˈjɑhu] *n.* a rustic oaf; an uncouth jerk. □ *Ask that yahoo to close the door after him.* □ *What yahoo brought this dog in here?*

**yak** AND **yack** [jæk] **1.** *in.* to talk. □ *Stop yakking for a minute.* □ *I need to yack with you about something.* **2.** *n.* a chat. □ *We had a nice little yack and then left for work.* □ *Drop by for a yak sometime.* **3.** *n.* a joke. □ *That was a lousy yack.* □ *Don't tell that yack again. It's not a winner.* **4.** *n.* a laugh from a joke. □ *We had a good yack over it.* □ *The audience produced a feeble yak that was mostly from embarrassment.*

**yak it up** *tr.* to talk incessantly or a lot. □ *Why don't you all just yak it up while I get ready to give the talk?* □ *Stop yakking it up and listen.*

**yakky** [ˈjæki] *mod.* talkative. □ *He's a yakky old man, but I like him.* □ *Isn't she yakky today?*

**yank** **1.** *tr.* to harass someone. (See also *yank someone around.*) □ *Stop yanking me!* □ *Yank the welcher a little, and see what that does.* **2.** *n.* a Yankee; a U.S. soldier. □ *I don't care if you call me a yank. That's what I am.* □ *Hey, Yank! What's new?*

**yanked** *mod.* arrested. (Underworld.) □ *Lefty got himself yanked one too many times.* □ *Everybody in the gang got yanked at least once last week.*

**yank someone around** *tr.* to harass someone; to give someone a hard time. (Compare to *jerk someone around.*) □ *Listen, I don't mean to yank you around all the time, but we have to have the drawings by Monday.* □ *Please stop yanking me around.*

**yank someone's chain** *tr.* to harass someone; to give someone a hard time. (As if one were a dog wearing a choker collar, on a leash.) □ *Stop yanking my chain!* □ *Do you really think you can just yank my chain whenever you want?*

**yap** **1.** *n.* the mouth. □ *Shut your yap!* □ *You have a big yap, you know?* **2.** *in.* to chatter; to gossip. □ *Who's yapping so much in here?* □ *Did you just come here to yap?* **3.** *n.* nonsense; gibberish. □ *That's just yap. Forget it. They mean no harm.* □ *That windbag can produce an enormous amount of yap.* **4.** *in.* to empty one's stomach; to vomit. □ *Who yapped in the bushes?* □ *Ye gods, do I hear one of our guests yapping in the powder room?* **5.** *n.* a naive person; a dupe. □ *The poor yap was made a fool of.* □ *See if you can get that yap to bring over a left-handed monkey wrench.*

**yard** *n.* a one-hundred-dollar bill. (Underworld.) □ *The guy wanted a yard just to fix a little dent in the fender.* □ *Pay him a yard to shut up about what he saw.*

**yardbird** **1.** *n.* a convict. □ *Who's the yardbird with the headphones on his noodle?* □ *So, Charlie was a yardbird. So what?* **2.** *n.* an inept soldier. (Military.) □ *You yardbirds are going to learn discipline one way or another.* □ *How many of you yardbirds would like to go home in one piece?*

**yard dog** *n.* a repellent person; an uncouth person. □ *Is that lousy yard dog hanging around the neighborhood again?* □ *Yup. It's that yard dog, Max.*

**yatata-yatata** [ˈjætətəˈjætətə] *n.* the sound of chatter or *yak.* □ *All I ever hear around here is yatata-yatata.* □ *He gets on the phone, and it's yatata-yatata for hours.*

**yawner** *n.* a boring show or performance. □ *It was a yawner from the opening curtain straight through to the end.* □ *Your lecture, sir, was a total yawner.*

**yazzihamper** [ˈjæzihæmpɚ] *n.* an obnoxious person. □ *You are the most annoying yazzihamper I know!* □ *Who's the yazzihamper in the double knit?*

**yea big** [ˈje ˈbɪg] *mod.* about so big. (Accompanied by a hand gesture.) □ *Oh, it was about yea big.* □ *Do you have a panel that is about yea big?*

**yeah** [ˈjæə OR ˈjæɔ] *interj.* "yes." □ LEFTY: *You okay?* BRUNO: *Yeah.* □ LEFTY: *Yeah?* BRUNO: *Yeah! I said yeah! Did you hear me say yeah?*

**yeaster** *n.* a beer-drinker. □ *A couple of yeasters in the back of the tavern were singing a dirty song.* □ *Who's the yeaster with the bloodshot eyes?*

**Yech! AND Yecch!** [jɛk OR jɛtʃ] *exclam.* "Horrible!"; "It's yucky!" □ *Oh, yech! What's that stuff?* □ *Yecch! It's moving!*

**yegg** [jɛg] **1.** *n.* a tramp, thief, or safecracker. (Underworld.) □ *The cops hauled in the usual yeggs, but they all had alibis.* □ *See if you can find that yegg we worked with in the bank job. He'll do.* **2.** *n.* an obnoxious male. □ *Don't act like such a yegg, Bill.* □ *A couple of drunken yeggs were talking a little too loud, so Bruno showed them the door.*

**Ye gods!** *exclam.* "Good grief!" □ *Ye gods! What is this stuff here?* □ *Ye gods! My hair is falling out.*

**yell one's guts out** See the following entry.

**yell one's head off AND yell one's guts out** **1.** *tr.* to yell loud and long. □ *I was yelling my head off at the game.* □ *Stop*

yelling your guts out and listen to me. **2.** *tr.* to complain bitterly and loudly. □ *Some lady is yelling her head off about shoddy workmanship out in the lobby.* □ *I yell my guts out about tripe when I see tripe!*

**yellow** **1.** *mod.* cowardly. □ *Who says I'm yellow?* □ *Bruno says you're yellow. Wanna make something of it?* **2.** *n.* a capsule of the barbiturate Nembutal™. (Drugs. See also *(yellow) jacket.*) □ *I've got yellows, blues, and reds. They all do the same thing.* □ *Try a yellow. They're a little stronger.*

**yellow-bellied** *mod.* cowardly. □ *You are a yellow-bellied coward!* □ *I'm not yellow-bellied!* □ *What yellow-bellied skunk ran off with my horse?*

**yellow-belly** *n.* a coward. □ *He's not a yellow-belly. He's cautious.* □ *Tell the yellow-belly to come outside and say that.*

**(yellow) jacket** *n.* a capsule of the barbiturate Nembutal™. (Drugs.) □ *Max had a few jackets with him when he dropped by.* □ *Yellow jackets are the prettiest of all the barbs.*

**yellow streak (down someone's back)** *n.* a tendency toward cowardice. □ *Tim's got a yellow streak down his back a mile wide.* □ *Get rid of that yellow streak. Show some courage.*

**yelper** *n.* the whooping (electronic) siren on emergency vehicles. □ *The black and white rounded the corner, yelper blasting.* □ *Turn off the yelper, Chuck, we hear you.*

**yench** [jɛntʃ] *tr.* to swindle someone; to victimize someone. (Underworld.) □ *The flimflam artist yenched a couple of banks and then moved on.* □ *Somebody tried to yench the wrong guy at the circus.*

**yenta** [ˈjɛntə] *n.* a gossip, usually a woman. (Regarded as Yiddish.) □ *She can be such a yenta when she's got news.* □ *Molly is a yenta if ever there was one.*

**yep** See *yup.*

**yesca** [ˈjɛskə] *n.* marijuana. (Drugs. Spanish for *twigs, tinder.*) □ *Where can I get some of that yesca?* □ *Max can get you yesca, or something a little better.*

**yes indeedy (do)** *interj.* "yes, indeed." □ *Do I have chocolate? Yes indeedy do!* □ *Yes, indeedy, I will be there at noon.*

**Yes siree (Bob)!** AND **Yessiree (Bob)!** *exclam.* "Yes, indeed!" □ *Yessiree! That's the secret to doing it right!* □ *Yes siree, Bob! That's what I call hootch!*

**Yikes!** See the following entry.

**Yipes!** AND **Yikes!, Yipe!** *exclam.* "Good grief !" (Expresses mild alarm.) □ *Yipes! This branch looked like a snake!* □ *Yipe! This branch is a snake!*

**Yippee!** *exclam.* "Hooray!" (Essential juvenile.) □ *Yippee! I did it!* □ *School's out! Yippee!*

**yock** AND **yok** [jɔk] **1.** *in.* to laugh loudly. (Compare to *yak*.) □ *Everybody yocked at the joke, and when things calmed down, I announced the mass firings.* □ *Stop yocking and listen to this.* **2.** *n.* a loud laugh. □ *Sue let out an enormous yock and quickly covered her mouth.* □ *Who came out with that uncivil yock?* **3.** See also *yack*.

**yodeling in a canyon** *in.* talking aimlessly. □ *You are just yodeling in a canyon if you think I really care about it.* □ *Stop yodeling in a canyon and start making sense.*

**yo mama** *interj.* "so you say." (Black.) □ *Not enough bread! Yo mama.* □ *Yo mama! The hell you say!*

**york** [jork] **1.** *in.* to empty one's stomach; to vomit. □ *He ate the stuff, then went straight out and yorked.* □ *Who yorked in the flower pot?* **2.** *n.* vomit. □ *Is that york I see on the living-room window?* □ *Hey, Jimmy! Come out in the snow and see the frozen york!*

**You and what army?** See the following entry.

**You and who else?** AND **You and what army?** *interrog.* "Who besides you is threatening me?" □ *You're gonna whup me? You and who else?* □ *You and what army are gonna yank my chain?*

**You asked for it!** *exclam.* "Here it comes, and you deserve it!" □ *So you want the full treatment? You asked for it!* □ *So, you wanted to hear both sides of the record? You asked for it!*

**you bet** *interj.* "yes"; "you can bet on it." □ *Can you have two? You bet.* □ *You bet; it's all settled.*

**you betcha** [ˈju ˈbɛtʃə] *interj.* "yes"; "you can be sure of it." (See *betcha*. Literally, You bet, you.) □ *Will I be there? You betcha.* □ *Can I? You betcha!*

**You bet your boots!** *exclam.* "You can be absolutely certain!" □ *Am I happy? You bet your boots!* □ *You bet your boots I'm mad.*

**You bet your sweet life!** *exclam.* "You are absolutely correct!" □ *Happy? You bet your sweet life!* □ *You bet your sweet life I am glad!*

**You bet your sweet patootie!** AND **You bet your sweet patoot!** *exclam.* "You can be absolutely certain!" (See *patootie*, which is the posterior.) □ *You bet your sweet patootie I'm serious!* □ *I'll be there! You bet your sweet patoot!*

**You can say that again!** *exclam.* "I agree!" □ *You can say that again! It's really hot!* □ *You can say that again! You hit the nail right on the head.*

**You can't fight city hall.** *sent.* "You cannot fight a bureaucracy." □ *I finally gave up. You can't fight city hall.* □ *You can't fight city hall. Pay the parking ticket and forget it.*

**You can't get there from here.** *sent.* "Where you want to go is in a very remote location." (A catch phrase.) □ *Well, you can't get there from here.* □ *Adamsville? Sorry, you can't get there from here.*

**You can't take it with you.** *sent.* "You cannot take wealth with you when you die." □ *Enjoy it now. You can't take it with you.* □ *My uncle doesn't believe that saying, you know, "You can't take it with you." He's going to try.*

**You can't win them all.** *sent.* "No one succeeds all the time." (Said when someone fails.) □ *Don't fret about it, Tom. You can't win them all.* □ *You can't win 'em all, but you can't lose 'em all, either.*

**You could have knocked me over with a feather.** *sent.* "I was completely surprised." □ *I was shocked. You could have knocked me over with a feather.* □ *You could have knocked me over with a feather, I was so zapped!*

**You don't know the half of it.** *sent.* "Things are far more complicated than you think." □ *You think that's bad? You don't know the half of it.* □ *You don't know the half of it, and I'm too much a lady to tell.*

**You got it!** **1.** *exclam.* "I agree to what you asked!"; "You will get what you want!" □ *You want a green one? You got it!* □ *This one? You got it!* **2.** exclam. "You are right!" □ *That's it! You got it!* □ *That's the answer. You got it!*

**You (had) better believe it!** exclam. "It is true without question!" □ *It's true. You better believe it.* □ *Yes, this is the best, and you had better believe it!*

**You hear?** interrog. "Do you understand, and will you comply?" (Folksy.) □ *Now have a good time, you hear?* □ *I want you home by midnight, you hear?*

**You heard the man.** sent. "Do what the man tells you." (See *man*.) □ *You heard the man. Get over there and stand still.* □ *Shut up! You heard the man.*

**you know\*** phr. as you are aware, or should be aware. (Not used in writing.) □ *It was like, well, you know, grody.* □ *It's, you know, so, you know, old and, you know, like, yucky.*

**you-know-what** n. "you know what, but I won't say what." (The vaguest of euphemisms.) □ *Did you bring a you-know-what?* □ *I have a you-know-what, but it may not be the same one you are thinking about.*

**you-know-where** n. hell. □ *You can just go to you-know-where!* □ *This place is hotter than you-know-where.*

**you-know-who** n. some unnamed person. □ *Did you invite you-know-who to the party?* □ *If you-know-who is coming, I'm staying home.*

**you name it** n. everything; everything else. □ *I brought food, drink, and you name it.* □ *What do I have here? You name it.*

**young blood 1.** n. a newcomer. □ *The young blood gets a desk by the window.* □ *We keep young bloods so busy they never have a chance to look out the window.* **2.** n. a young black male. (Black. See *blood*.) □ *A young blood from two streets over came around asking for trouble today.* □ *Tell that young blood to beat it.*

**young Turk** n. a contentious young person who goes against the system. □ *The young Turks are acting up again.* □ *Not another young Turk!*

**You're dern tootin'!** AND **You're durn tootin'!** [...'dɚn 'tutn̩] exclam. "You are absolutely right!" (Folksy.) □ *You're*

dern tootin' I'm mad!* □ *Am I mad? You're durn tootin'!*

**You're the doctor.** sent. "I will do anything you say!"; "You are in charge!" □ *I'll do it if you say. You're the doctor!* □ *Put it over here. Okay, you're the doctor.*

**Your guess is as good as mine.** sent. "I don't know either." □ *I don't know. Your guess is as good as mine.* □ *Your guess is as good as mine as to when the train will get in.*

**Your place or mine?** interrog. "Shall we carry on an affair at your dwelling or mine?" □ *Then I said to her, "Your place or mine?" Then she clobbered me.* □ *Your place or mine? It doesn't matter.*

**yours truly** n. "me," the speaker. □ *If yours truly had a problem like that, it would be settled by nightfall.* □ *If it was up to yours truly, there wouldn't be any such problem.*

**You said a mouthful.** sent. "What you say is absolutely true." (Always in the past tense.) □ *That's right, man. You said a mouthful.* □ *You said a mouthful, and I agree!*

**You said it!** exclam. "That's true, and I agree!" □ *You said it! I agree with you one hundred percent.* □ *You said it! It's really hot.*

**You've got another think coming.** sent. "You have made an error. Think again." (Note the formula in the example.) □ *If you think I'm going to let you get away with that, you've got another think coming.* □ *You've got another think coming if you think I'll do it.*

**You want to step outside?** interrog. "Do you intend to start a fight?"; "Shall we go outside and fight?" □ *So, you don't like the way I talk! You want to step outside?* □ *You want to step outside? We can settle this once and for all.*

**You wish!** See *Don't you wish!*

**yo-yo** AND **yoyo** ['jojo] **1.** n. a fool; an obnoxious person. □ *Who's the yo-yo in the plaid pants?* □ *Some yoyo wants to talk to you on the phone.* **2.** mod. stupid. □ *Ask that yo-yo jerk to move along.* □ *That is the world's yoyoest joke!* **3.** in. to vacillate; to be *wishy-washy*. □ *Stop yo-yoing and make up* *your mind.* □ *He's always got to yoyo a little before deciding.*

**yuck** AND **yuk** [jək] **1.** *n.* someone or something disgusting. (Also a term of address.) □ *I don't want any of that yuck on my plate!* □ *Who is that yuk in the red bandana?* **2.** *exclam.* "Horrible!" (Usually **Yuck!**) □ *Oh, yuck! Get that horrible thing out of here!* □ *Yuck! It looks alive!* **3.** *n.* a joke. □ *Come on! Chill out! It was just a yuck.* □ *Not a very good yuk if you ask me.*

**yucky** ['jəki] *mod.* nasty. □ *What is this yucky pink stuff on my plate?* □ *This tastes yucky.*

**yuke** See *uke.*

**yummy** ['jəmi] **1.** *mod.* delicious. □ *This stuff is really yummy.* □ *Who made this yummy cake?* **2.** *mod.* delightful; beautiful. □ *Who is that yummy blonde?* □ *This evening was just yummy.*

**yup** AND **yep** [jəp AND jɛp] *interj.* "yes." (Folksy.) □ *Yup, I'd say so.* □ *I think so. Yep, that's right.*

**yuppie** ['jəpi] **1.** *n.* a "young urban professional." □ *The yuppies are getting a lot of flack these days.* □ *Why pick on yuppies?* **2.** *mod.* having to do with yuppies. □ *I don't want to drive one of those yuppie cars.* □ *You got something against yuppie beemers?*

# Z

**za** [zɑ] *n.* pizza. (Collegiate.) □ *I'm gonna spring for some za.* □ *Who wants some of this za?*

**zagged** *mod.* alcohol intoxicated. □ *How can anybody get so zagged on three beers?* □ *Wow, is she zagged!*

**zany** ['zeni] *mod.* silly. □ *What a zany chick!* □ *Clare is so zany.* □ *That's a zany idea, but I like it.*

**zap 1.** *tr.* to shock someone. □ *That fake snake zapped me for a minute.* □ *The incident zapped me, but good.* **2.** *tr.* to kill someone. □ *The stress from it all nearly zapped him.* □ *I was afraid that one of those thugs would zap me.* **3.** *tr.* to impress someone. □ *My big idea really zapped the boss. I may get a raise.* □ *I like to have something to zap the board with at every meeting.* **4.** *tr.* to stun someone with an imaginary ray gun. □ *Jimmy swung around the corner and zapped me.* □ *He zapped me with a water gun.* **5.** *exclam.* "Wow!" (Usually **Zap!**) □ *Zap! I did it again!* □ *He said, "Zap!" indicating that he really liked the present, I guess.* **6.** *tr.* to defeat someone or a team. □ *They zapped us 10 to 8.* □ *Fred zapped Molly in the spelling bee.* **7.** *in.* to *zip* or move to somewhere very fast. □ *I'll zap over and see if the duplicating is ready yet.* □ *He's zapping to the drugstore for some aspirin.*

**zapped 1.** *mod.* tired; exhausted. □ *I'm too zapped to go on.* □ *I'm way zapped. Good night.* **2.** *mod.* alcohol or drug intoxicated. □ *We all got zapped and then went home.* □ *Marty is too zapped to stand up.*

**zappy** *mod.* energetic; *zippy.* □ *How can you be so zappy at this time of the* morning? □ *That music is a little too zappy for me.*

**zarf** [zɑrf] *n.* an ugly and repellent male. □ *Ooo, who is that zarf who just came in?* □ *That zarf is Merton, and he makes all A's, and he helps me with my homework, so just shut up!*

**zebra** *n.* a referee. (Because of the black and white striped shirt.) □ *The zebra blew the whistle on almost every play.* □ *There were not enough zebras to start the game.*

**zeek out** [zik...] *in.* to lose control of oneself. □ *I was in a pretty bad state. I almost zeeked out.* □ *Fred zeeked out and had to be calmed down.*

**Zelda** ['zɛldə] *n.* a dull and ugly female. (Compare to *Clyde.*) □ *I'm not as much of a Zelda as you think.* □ *Nobody's gonna call my sister a Zelda and get away with it.*

**zerk** [zɚk] *n.* a stupid person; a *jerk.* □ *Who's the zerk in the plaid pants?* □ *Don't be a zerk! Do what you're told.*

**zerked (out)** *mod.* heavily drug intoxicated. (Drugs.) □ *Whatever they took, they sure got zerked out from it.* □ *Who's the zerked guy over there in his undershirt?*

**zerking** *mod.* strange; *zerk*-like. □ *Who is that zerking nerd over there?* □ *That zerking little guy is Merton, and I like him.*

**zero** *n.* an insignificant person; a nobody. (Always with *a.*) □ *Pay her no mind. She is a zero around here.* □ *I want to be more in life than just another zero.*

**zhlub** See *schlub.*

**zhlubby** ['ʒləbi] *mod.* dull; boorish. (See *schlub.*) □ *Who is the zhlubby type with* *the plaid pants?* □ *That guy is so zhlubby!* □ *I can't sit through this zhlubby thing one more minute.*

**zilch** [zɪltʃ] *n.* nothing. □ *And what do I get? Zilch, that's what!* □ *"Even zilch is too much," said the clerk.*

**zing 1.** *n.* energy; dynamism. □ *Put some zing into this dance number. You wanna put the audience to sleep?* □ *This whole business needs more zing.* **2.** *tr.* to make something penetrate; to shoot or fire something. □ *The crook zinged a couple of slugs into the floor and scared everyone to death.* □ *The kid zinged a paper clip into the wall.* **3.** *tr.* to verbally assault someone. □ *She zinged him with another clever remark.* □ *He zinged her back till he decided they were even.*

**zinger 1.** *n.* something nice or fine. □ *That set of wheels is a real zinger.* □ *What a zinger of a hat!* **2.** *n.* a stinging remark. □ *She got off another zinger at her brother.* □ *I did not appreciate that zinger.*

**zings 1.** *n.* the delirium tremens. □ *The old guy was suffering from the zings.* □ *What can they do for the zings?* **2.** *n.* amphetamines. (Drugs.) □ *She looks wired on zings.* □ *Got any zings?*

**zip 1.** *n.* nothing. □ *There was no mail today. Nothing. Zip.* □ *I got zip from the booking agency all week.* **2.** *n.* a score or grade of zero. □ *Well, you got zip on the last test. Sorry about that.* □ *The prof said that zip is better than nothing, but I don't see how it could be.* **3.** *n.* vigor; spunk. □ *Put some zip into it. It's too ho-hum.* □ *This whole thing lacks the zip it needs to survive.* **4.** *in.* to move to a place fast. □ *I'll zip to the office and get a new form.* □ *He's just zipped out to get pizza.*

**zip along** *in.* to move along rapidly. □ *Things are really zipping along here.* □ *Days are zipping along, and we're all getting lots done.*

**zip gun** *n.* a homemade handgun. (Underworld.) □ *The kid had a zip gun, so I didn't argue.* □ *Can he handle anything other than a zip gun?*

**Zip it up!** See *Zip (up) your lip!*

**zipped** *mod.* drug intoxicated. (Drugs.) □ *That tootsie left them zipped.* □ *The kid is too zipped to talk.*

**zippy** [zɪpi] *mod.* lively; active. □ *Wow, is that kid zippy! Look at him dance!* □ *This is a real zippy number.*

**Zip (up) your lip!** AND **Zip it up!** *exclam.* "Be quiet!"; "Zip up your mouth!" □ *Shhhh! Zip up your lip!* □ *Zip your lip!* □ *Zip it up and listen!*

**zissified** [zɪsɪfɑɪd] *mod.* alcohol intoxicated. □ *Two of them were zissified on rum. The rest just got a little wrecked.* □ *Man, is she zissified!*

**zit** [zɪt] *n.* a pimple. □ *Don't squeeze your zits on my mirror!* □ *That is one prize-winning zit on your nose.*

**zit doctor** *n.* a dermatologist. □ *The zit doctor I went to was a crater face!* □ *My zit doctor wears rubber gloves and has for years.*

**ziv** [zɪv] *tr. & in.* to make a drug purchase. (Drugs.) □ *Kelly zivved some wings and came back to the office.* □ *Max is always available for those who want to ziv.*

**zob** [zɑb] *n.* a worthless person; a nobody. □ *Another zob came in to try out for the part.* □ *Who's the zob in the plaid pants?*

**zod** [zɑd] *n.* any repellent thing or person. (California.) □ *Wally is such a total zod.* □ *Is this grody zod yours or mine?*

**zombie** [zɑmbi] **1.** *n.* a weird and frightening person. □ *Merton is practically a zombie. Doesn't he ever go out—in the daylight, I mean?* □ *Molly's getting to look like a zombie. Is she well?* **2.** *n.* a very stupid person. □ *Is this some kind of gathering of zombies and mouthbreathers or something?* □ *Please ask one of those zombies to stand by the door.* **3.** *n.* a very tired person. □ *I feel like such a zombie. Maybe I'm not eating right.* □ *I'm just a zombie at this hour of the morning.* **4.** *n.* a drug addict. (Drugs.) □ *They pulled another zombie out of the river this morning.* □ *The neighborhood is overrun with these zombies.*

**zone 1.** *n.* a giddy and disorganized person. □ *Who's the zone wearing two different colored socks?* □ *Some zone keeps turning the lights on in the hall.* **2.** *n.* someone on drugs. (Drugs.) □ *Some zone is gonna mug you if you go*

out late at night. □ *This kid is a hopeless zone. Send him away somewhere.*
**zoned (out) 1.** *mod.* alcohol or drug intoxicated. □ *What's the matter with your eyes? Get a little zoned last night?* □ *Yeah, I'm sort of zoned out.* **2.** *mod.* exhausted. □ *After a day like this, I'm really zoned.* □ *Gotta get to bed. I'm just zoned out.*
**zonk** [zɔŋk] **1.** *tr.* to overpower someone or something. □ *We zonked the dog with a kick.* □ *It took two cops to zonk the creep.* **2.** *tr.* to tire someone out. □ *The pills zonked me, but they made my cold better.* □ *Jogging always zonks me.* (More at *zonked (out)*.)
**zonked (out)** AND **zounked (out)** [zɔŋkt... AND zɑuŋkt...] **1.** *mod.* alcohol or drug intoxicated. □ *She's too zonked to drive.* □ *Jed was almost zounked out to unconsciousness.* **2.** *mod.* exhausted; asleep. □ *She was totally zonked out by the time I got home.* □ *I'm zounked. Good night.*
**zonker** ['zɔŋkɚ] **1.** *n.* a drunkard. □ *The zonker just can't help himself.* □ *If I had known she was a confirmed zonker, I never would have given her a drink.* **2.** *n.* a marijuana smoker. (Drugs.) □ *A lot of these zonkers may take 6 years to get through high school.* □ *You are turning into a first-class zonker.*
**zonk out** *in.* to collapse from exhaustion; to go into a stupor from drugs or exhaustion. □ *I'm gonna go home and zonk out.* □ *I went home after the trip and just zonked out.*
**zoo** *n.* a confusing and chaotic place. □ *This place is a zoo on Monday mornings.* □ *Where is the person in charge of this zoo?*
**zoobang** ['zubæŋ] *mod.* alcohol intoxicated. □ *Boy howdy! Are you ever zoobang!* □ *So, you think I'm zoobang? You want to step outside?*
**zooie** AND **zooey** ['zui] **1.** *mod.* confusing and chaotic. (See *zoo*.) □ *I can't get anything done in this zooie place.* □ *It's never zooey in my office, except for a little rowdiness at closing time.* **2.** *n.* a device for holding the end of a marijuana cigarette. (Drugs. See *roach*.) □ *Here, use this zooie before you burn your fingers.* □ *I left my zooie in my stash.*

**zoom 1.** *tr.* to gain entry to someplace without paying. □ *Both of them zoomed the circus, and both of them got arrested.* □ *Let's go zoom Martha's party!* **2.** AND **zoom off** *in.* to have a drug *rush*. (Drugs.) □ *Sam zoomed off and thought he had gone to heaven.* □ *Max knows how to keep zooming for about 20 minutes.* **3.** AND **zoom off** *in.* to depart; to leave in a hurry. □ *Time's up. I've gotta zoom.* □ *Oh, you don't have to zoom off, do you?* **4.** *n.* an amphetamine. (Drugs.) □ *Without zooms, she'd never be able to get up in the morning.* □ *You got any zooms, Max?*
**zoom in (on someone or something)** *in.* to focus or concentrate narrowly on someone or something. □ *The conversation zoomed in on Sally and her recent narrow escape from drowning.* □ *Let's zoom in on the question of salary.*
**zoom off** See *zoom*.
**zoom out** *in.* to lose control. □ *I nearly zoomed out when I got the news.* □ *Fred zoomed out and started screaming at Ernie.*
**zoom someone out** AND **zoom out someone** *tr.* to impress someone. (Black.) □ *Freddie is trying to zoom out Tiffany again.* □ *You can't zoom me out, you twit!*
**zoom up** *in.* to drive or pull up to a place. □ *A car zoomed up, and 7 kids got out.* □ *Let's zoom up to the door and see if she's home.*
**zooted** ['zudəd] *mod.* alcohol intoxicated. □ *Both of them were zooted to the max.* □ *She was too zooted to even see straight.*
**zorked** ['zɔrkt] *mod.* alcohol intoxicated. □ *She was zorked beyond help.* □ *Everybody was essentially zorked by midnight.*
**zot** AND **zotz** [zɑt AND zɑts] *n.* zero; nothing. □ *I went out to get the mail, but there was zot.* □ *All I got for a raise was little more than zotz.*
**zotz** [zɑts] **1.** *tr.* to kill someone. □ *Bruno had orders from Mr. Big to zotz Max.* □ *Finally, Bruno succeeded in zotzing Max. It was in all the papers this morning.* **2.** See the previous entry.
**zowie** ['zɑui] **1.** *n.* energy; sparkle; zest. □ *This one sounds better because the*

drummer has more zowie. □ *Put some zowie into it. It's not raining inside tonight.* **2.** *exclam.* "Wow!" (Usually **Zowie!**) □ *Zowie! They just pulled Mr. Big out of the river.* □ *Bruno had enough of the guy and wasted him, but good. Zowie!*

**zunked** [zəŋkt] *mod.* drug intoxicated; drug addicted. (Drugs.) □ *That poor guy is so zunked he can't see.* □ *The party went on and on. When the preacher got himself zunked on the punch, I knew it had reached the end.*

# PHRASE-FINDER INDEX

Use this index to find the form of a phrase that you want to look up in the **Dictionary**. First, pick out any major word in the phrase you are seeking. Second, look that word up in this index to find the form of the phrase used in the **Dictionary**. Third, look up the phrase in the **Dictionary**. See **Uses** and **Hints** below. Single words should be looked up in the **Dictionary** directly.

Some of the words occurring in the **Dictionary** entries do not occur as entries in this index. Entries that are only single words are not indexed here. Some words are omitted because they occur so frequently that their lists cover many pages. In these instances, you should look up the phrase under some other word. The following words and most personal pronouns do not occur as entries in the index:

| | |
|---|---|
| a | on |
| an | one's |
| and | or |
| at | out |
| but | someone |
| for | something |
| get | that |
| have | to |
| in | up |
| of | what |
| off | with |

## Uses

A very high percentage of slang and colloquial expressions are noun compounds or other sequences of two or more words. This index provides a convenient way to find the words that follow the first word in a phrasal entry. Without the index there would be no way to find these "included" words.

The entries in the index allow you to find additional instances of the single-word entries in the **Dictionary**. For instance, there are a number of **Dictionary** entries beginning with "john," but the index lists an additional five entries that include "john" in some form: **big John; blue Johnnies; Dear John letter; square John; and who shot John.**

If you were trying to find an expression that includes something about a blue flame, you could look up either word in the index. At both *blue* and *flame* you would find listed "burn with a low blue flame." Then you turn to the **B** section of the **Dictionary** to find the entry for this expression. In fact, the index lists this expression at *burn, low, blue,* and *flame.* The words *with* and *a* are not indexed.

You may be seeking an entry that explains the phrase *cut bait,* which you have heard in the sentence "It's time you decide whether you want to fish or cut bait." If you look up *cut* or *bait,* you will find that the full entry expression is "Fish or cut bait!" which you would then look up. This phrase is also listed at *fish.*

# Hints

1. When you are trying to find a slang or colloquial expression in this index, look up the noun first, if there is one.

2. When you are looking for a noun, try first to find the singular form or the simplest form of the noun.

3. When you are looking for a verb, try first to find the present tense form or the simplest form of the verb.

4. In most expressions where a noun or pronoun is a variable part of an expression, it will be represented by the words "someone" or "something" in the form of the expression used in the **Dictionary**. If you do not find the noun you want in the index, it may, in fact, be a variable word.

5. This is an index of forms, not meanings. The expressions in an index entry do not usually have any meanings in common. Consult the **Dictionary** for information about meaning.

**22**
□ catch 22
**57**
□ Heinz 57 (variety)
**ABBREVIATE**
□ abbreviated piece of nothing
**ABLE**
□ able to cut something □ not able to cut something
**ABOUT**
□ come clean (with someone) (about something) □ cut up (about someone or something) □ go on (and on) about someone or something □ make a stink (about someone or something) □ Make no mistake (about it)! □ nothing to write home about □ not know beans (about something) □ raise a stink (about someone or something) □ see a man about a dog □ serious about someone □ sorry about that □ sound off (about something) □ That's about the size of it. □ up in the air (about someone or something)
**ABOVE**
□ above board □ open and above board
**ABSO**
□ abso-bloody-lutely
**ABSOTIVELY**
□ absotively (posilutely)
**ACADEMY**
□ laughing academy
**ACAPULCO**
□ Acapulco (gold)
**ACCESSORY**
□ tea accessories
**ACCIDENT**
□ accidentally-on-purpose
**ACCOUNT**
□ no-account
**ACE**
□ ace in the hole □ ace in (to something) □ ace out □ ace someone out □ have an ace up one's sleeve □ hold all the aces □ within an ace of (doing) something
**ACID**
□ acid funk □ (acid) mung □ acid rock □ acid test □ behind acid □ blue acid □ tric (acid)
**ACRE**
□ God's acre □ hell's half acre

**ACROSS**
□ get across □ get something across (to someone) □ put something across
**ACT**
□ Act your age! □ class act □ clean up one's act □ Dutch act □ get in on the act □ get one's act together
**ACTION**
□ bit of the action □ chill someone's action □ in action □ piece (of the action) □ slice of the action □ where the action is
**ACTIVE**
□ active citizen
**ADIOS**
□ adios muchachos
**ADOBE**
□ adobe dollar
**AFFLUENCE**
□ under the affluence of incohol
**AFRAID**
□ afraid not
**AFRICAN**
□ African black
**AFTER**
□ After you. □ look after number one □ morning after (the night before) □ point after
**AGAIN**
□ Come again? □ Run that by (me) again. □ try someone back (again) □ You can say that again!
**AGAINST**
□ up against it
**AGE**
□ Act your age! □ age out □ golden-ager
**AGENT**
□ ticket agent □ travel agent
**AGREE**
□ agree to disagree
**AHEAD**
□ ahead of the game □ come out ahead □ full steam ahead □ go-ahead □ one jump ahead of someone or something □ quit while one is ahead
**AID**
□ thirst-aid station
**AIL**
□ good for what ails someone
**AIM**
□ aim for the sky □ ain't no good nohow □ That ain't hay!

## AIR
☐ air-bags ☐ air ball ☐ air guitar ☐ air hose ☐ air one's belly ☐ air one's dirty linen in public ☐ air one's pores ☐ bear in the air ☐ come up for air ☐ full of hot air ☐ hot air ☐ up in the air ☐ up in the air (about someone or something)

## AIRY
☐ airy-fairy

## AISLE
☐ rolling in the aisles

## ALECK
☐ smart aleck

## ALIBI
☐ Alibi Ike

## ALIVE
☐ alive and kicking ☐ alive and well ☐ Look alive!

## ALKY
☐ alkied (up)

## ALL
☐ all balled up ☐ all bets are off ☐ all by one's lonesome ☐ all ears ☐ all-fired ☐ all get out ☐ all in ☐ all-nighter ☐ all right ☐ all schnozzled up ☐ all-star ☐ All systems are go. ☐ all that jazz ☐ all (that) meat and no potatoes ☐ all the way ☐ all the way live ☐ all thumbs ☐ all-time ☐ all-time favorite ☐ all wet ☐ be-all, (and) end-all ☐ call (all) the shots ☐ can't win (th)em all ☐ daddy (of them all) ☐ Dash it all! ☐ drool (all) over someone or something ☐ for all I know ☐ for (all) one's trouble ☐ free for all ☐ get it (all) together ☐ go all the way ☐ granddaddy (of them all) ☐ Hang it all! ☐ have all one's marbles ☐ have it all together ☐ hold all the aces ☐ jump all over someone ☐ know all the angles ☐ know-it-all ☐ let it all hang out ☐ lose (all) one's marbles ☐ not all there ☐ Of all the nerve! ☐ once and for all ☐ pull out all the stops ☐ run on all cylinders ☐ That's all she wrote. ☐ That's all someone needs. ☐ warts and all ☐ You can't win them all.

## ALLEY
☐ alley apple ☐ right up one's alley ☐ up one's alley

## ALLIGATOR
☐ see you later, alligator

## ALMIGHTY
☐ almighty dollar

## ALONG
☐ breeze along ☐ buzz along ☐ hump (along) ☐ tootle along ☐ zip along

## ALPHABET
☐ alphabet soup

## ALSO
☐ also-ran

## ALTAR
☐ bow to the porcelain altar

## AMBULANCE
☐ ambulance chaser

## AMOK
☐ run amok

## AMOUNT
☐ pull down an amount of money ☐ shell out (an amount of money)

## ANCHOR
☐ anchor-clanker

## ANCIENT
☐ ancient history

## ANGEL
☐ angel dust ☐ angel hair ☐ angel puke

## ANGLE
☐ know all the angles

## ANIMAL
☐ party animal

## ANKLE
☐ sprain one's ankle

## ANOTHER
☐ another mouth to feed ☐ another peep (out of you) ☐ Don't give it another thought. ☐ Tell me another (one)! ☐ You've got another think coming.

## ANT
☐ have ants in one's pants ☐ piss-ant ☐ piss-ant around

## ANTE
☐ ante (something) up ☐ penny-ante

## ANY
☐ any old how

## APART
☐ fall apart ☐ take someone or something apart ☐ tear someone or something apart

## APE
☐ ape hangers ☐ go ape (over someone or something)

## APPLE
☐ alley apple ☐ apple of someone's eye ☐ apple-polisher ☐ Big Apple ☐ one smart apple ☐ road apple ☐ rotten apple

**ARCTIC**
□ Arctic explorer

**ARE**
□ all bets are off □ All systems are go.
□ Are you holding? □ Are you ready
for this? □ I hear what you are saying.
□ There you are. □ woods are full of....

**ARM**
□ arm-twister □ arm-twisting □ bang
in the arm □ long arm of the law □ put
the arm on someone □ shot in the arm
□ strong-arm □ strong-arm man □
strong-arm tactics □ twist someone's
arm □ two-arm habit □ up in arms

**ARMY**
□ army brat □ You and what army?

**AROUND**
□ around the bend □ blue around the
gills □ bum around □ chippy around
□ clown around □ drive someone around
the bend □ galumph (around) □ goof
around □ green around the gills □
hack around □ hang (around) □ horse
around □ jack around □ jack someone
around □ jerk around □ jerk someone
around □ kick around □ kick some ass
(around) □ knock around □ mess around
(with someone or something) □ moist
around the edges □ monkey around
(with someone or something) □ pal
around (with someone) □ piddle (around)
□ piss-ant around □ play around (with
someone) □ pussyfoot (around) □ putz
around □ rat around □ screw around
□ screw around with someone or something □ scrounge around (for someone
or something) □ spaz around □ stick
around □ throw one's weight around
□ tool around □ turn around □ waffle
(around) □ wrap one's car around something □ yank someone around

**ARROW**
□ straight arrow

**ARTICLE**
□ genuine article

**ARTILLERY**
□ heavy artillery □ light artillery

**ARTIST**
□ beat artist □ booze artist □ bullshit
artist □ burn artist □ castor oil artist
□ con artist □ flimflam artist □ goof
artist □ hype artist □ make-out artist
□ off artist □ rip-off artist □ take-off
artist

**ARTSY**
□ artsy-craftsy

**AS**
□ as is □ being as how □ big as life
(and twice as ugly) □ big as you please
□ clear as mud □ dry-as-dust □ dull
as dishwater □ fresh as a daisy □ gay
as pink ink □ jober as a sudge □ large
as life (and twice as ugly) □ nutty as a
fruitcake □ phony as a three-dollar bill
□ queer as a three-dollar bill □ right
as rain □ sober as a judge □ sure as hell
□ There's no such thing as a free lunch.
□ tight as a tick □ ugly as sin □ Your
guess is as good as mine.

**ASK**
□ Don't ask. □ Don't ask me. □ You
asked for it!

**ASLEEP**
□ asleep at the switch

**ASPHALT**
□ asphalt jungle

**ASS**
□ bare-assed □ barrel ass □ bust (one's)
ass to (do something) □ candy-ass □
dumb-ass □ flat on one's ass □ Get the
lead out (of your ass)! □ hairy-ass(ed)
□ have one's ass in a crack □ have
one's ass in a sling □ horse's ass □
jive-ass □ kick some ass (around) □
kiss-ass □ kiss someone's ass □ lard ass
□ pain in the ass □ smart ass □ sorry-
ass □ stupid-ass □ tits and ass

**ATTACK**
□ Big Mac attack

**ATTENTION**
□ snap to (attention)

**ATTITUDE**
□ cop an attitude

**AUNT**
□ Aunt Mary

**AVENUE**
□ Madison Avenue

**AWAY**
□ blowed (away) □ blown away □
blow someone away □ fire away □ Get
away! □ put someone or something
away □ slave away (at something) □
squared away □ squirrel something away
□ throw-away □ walk away with something □ wash someone away

**AWFUL**
□ something awful

**AX**
□ battle-ax □ get the ax □ give someone the ax

**AZTEC**
□ Aztec two-step

**BABE**
□ kiss the babe

**BABY**
□ baby bear □ Baby Bell □ (baby) boomer □ baby-kisser □ baby-sit □ baby sitter □ blue baby □ bottle baby □ jelly babies □ Keep the faith (baby)! □ The baby needs shoes.

**BACK**
□ back-door trot(s) □ backed up □ back number □ back off (from someone or something) □ back-slapper □ back-to-back □ back to square one □ back to the salt mines □ back up □ drunk back □ from way back □ get off someone's back □ have a monkey on one's back □ have a yellow streak down one's back □ juice something back □ kick back □ knock back a drink □ laid back □ on the back burner □ pin someone's ears back □ set someone back □ throw something back □ try someone back (again) □ yellow streak (down someone's back)

**BACKFIRE**
□ backfire (on someone)

**BACKROOM**
□ backroom boys □ boys in the backroom

**BACKSEAT**
□ backseat driver

**BACON**
□ bring home the bacon □ What's shakin' (bacon)?

**BAD**
□ bad egg □ bad grass □ bad-mouth □ bad news □ bad paper □ bad rap □ bad seed □ bad trip □ get in bad (with someone) □ in a bad way □ in bad shape □ so bad one can taste it

**BADGER**
□ badger game

**BAG**
□ air-bags □ Bag it! □ bag lady □ bag of bones □ bag of wind □ bag some rays □ Bag your face! □ barf bag □ brown-bag □ doggy bag □ douche bag □ half in the bag □ in the bag □ nickel (bag) □ one's bag □ slime bag □ stash bag □ tea bag □ whole bag of tricks

**BAGGER**
□ double-bagger □ four-bagger □ triple-bagger □ two-bagger

**BAHAMA**
□ Bahama-mama

**BAIL**
□ bail (out) □ jump bail

**BAIT**
□ Fish or cut bait. □ jail bait □ monkey bait □ (San Quentin) jail bait

**BAKE**
□ half-baked

**BAKER**
□ baker's dozen

**BALE**
□ bale (of hay)

**BALL**
□ air ball □ all balled up □ ball and chain □ balled up □ ball is in someone's court □ ball of fire □ ball park estimate □ ball someone or something up □ B-ball □ bean ball □ behind the eight ball □ drop the ball □ end of the ball game □ gopher ball □ have a ball □ on the ball □ play ball (with someone) □ put balls on something □ That's the way the ball bounces. □ V-ball □ whole ball of wax □ whole new ball game

**BALLOON**
□ go over like a lead balloon □ trial balloon

**BANANA**
□ banana-head □ banana oil □ banana republic □ banana split □ Cool bananas! □ go bananas □ top banana

**BAND**
□ to beat the band

**BANDIT**
□ bank bandit pills

**BANDWAGON**
□ on the bandwagon

**BANG**
□ (bang) (dead) to rights □ bang for the buck □ bang in the arm □ bang-up □ gang-bang □ get a bang out of someone or something □ slam-bang □ wham-bang □ whiz-bang □ with a bang

**BANK**
□ bank bandit pills □ banker's hours

**BAR**
□ behind bars

**BARB**
□ barb freak

**BARBIE**
□ Barbie doll
**BARE**
□ bare-assed □ stand there with one's bare face hanging out
**BARF**
□ barf bag □ Barf out! □ barf someone out
**BARGAIN**
□ (bargaining) chip □ more than one bargained for □ no bargain
**BARN**
□ can't hit the (broad) side of a barn □ Were you born in a barn?
**BARNYARD**
□ barnyard language
**BARRED**
□ no holds barred
**BARREL**
□ barrel ass □ barreled (up) □ barrel fever □ barrel of fun □ blue (barrels) □ bottom of the barrel □ double-barreled slingshot □ scrape the bottom of the barrel □ sweep with both barrels □ take a sweep (with both barrels)
**BASE**
□ base binge □ base house □ free base □ free base party □ free-baser □ free-basing □ off base □ touch base (with someone) □ way off (base)
**BASKET**
□ basket case
**BASRA**
□ Basra belly
**BAT**
□ have bats in one's belfry □ like a bat out of hell
**BATCH**
□ batch (it)
**BATH**
□ blood bath □ take a bath (on something) □ tonsil bath
**BATHTUB**
□ bathtub gin
**BATTLE**
□ battle-ax □ battle of the bulge
**BAWL**
□ bawl someone out
**BAY**
□ bay window
**BE**
(See also *BEEN, IS, WAS, WERE.*) □ be a drag (on someone) □ be-all, (and) end-all □ be-in □ being as how □ Be

my guest. □ cracked up to be □ Glory be! □ Johnny-be-good □ That'll be the day! □ There will be hell to pay. □ What'll it be? □ would not be seen dead....
**BEACH**
□ beach bum □ beach bunny
**BEAGLE**
□ legal-beagle
**BEAM**
□ (I-)beam □ on the beam □ steam someone's beam
**BEAN**
□ bean ball □ bean-counter □ beaned up □ bean time □ Bean Town □ bean trip □ Cool beans! □ full of beans □ juice and beans □ not know beans (about something) □ not worth beans □ on the bean □ spill the beans
**BEAR**
(See also *BORN.*) □ baby bear □ bear cage □ bear in the air □ bear trap □ lady bear □ loaded for bear □ mama bear □ Smokey (the Bear)
**BEAT**
□ beat artist □ beat box □ Beat it! □ beat one's brains out (to do something) □ beat one's gums □ beats me □ beat someone or something out □ beat someone's brains out □ beat the drum for someone or something □ beat the living daylights out of someone □ beat the stuffing out of someone □ beat the tar out of someone □ beat up □ to beat the band
**BEATER**
□ eggbeater □ world-beater
**BEATING**
□ take a beating
**BEAUTY**
□ beauty sleep
**BEAVER**
□ eager-beaver
**BED**
□ bed of roses □ fall out of bed □ make one's bed □ musical beds □ put someone to bed with a shovel □ put to bed with a shovel
**BEDROOM**
□ bedroom eyes
**BEDTIME**
□ bedtime story
**BEE**
□ bee bites

**BEEF**
□ beef-head □ beef something up □ Where's the beef?

**BEEN**
□ been had □ has-been □ How you been? □ I've been there. □ Where (have) you been keeping yourself?

**BEER**
□ beer and skittles □ beer belly □ beer blast □ beer bust □ beer gut □ cry in one's beer □ near-beer □ pound a beer □ queer-beer □ slam some beers □ small beer

**BEESWAX**
□ mind your own beeswax □ none of someone's beeswax

**BEET**
□ blow beets

**BEFORE**
□ morning after (the night before)

**BEG**
□ (I) beg (your) pardon.

**BEHIND**
□ behind acid □ behind bars □ behind the eight ball □ fan someone's behind □ get behind someone or something

**BELFRY**
□ have bats in one's belfry

**BELIEVE**
□ Believe you me! □ I don't believe this! □ Would you believe? □ You (had) better believe it!

**BELL**
□ Baby Bell □ bells and whistles □ Hell's bells (and buckets of blood)! □ Ma Bell □ ring a bell □ ring the bell □ saved by the bell □ with bells on

**BELLY**
□ air one's belly □ Basra belly □ beer belly □ belly button □ belly flop □ belly laugh □ belly up □ belly up (to something) □ Delhi belly □ go belly up □ turn belly up □ yellow-bellied □ yellow-belly

**BELOW**
□ hit (someone) below the belt

**BELT**
□ belt something down □ belt the grape □ hit (someone) below the belt □ pull one's belt in (a notch) □ rust belt □ sun belt □ take one's belt in (a notch) □ tighten one's belt

**BEN**
□ brother Ben □ copilot ben

**BENCH**
□ bench jockey □ bench warmer

**BEND**
□ around the bend □ bend one's elbow □ bend the law □ bent out of shape □ drive someone around the bend □ elbow-bending □ fender-bender □ gender-bender □ mind-bender □ round the bend

**BENNY**
□ bennied (up) □ benny (jag)

**BERTH**
□ soft berth

**BEST**
(See also *BETTER, GOOD*.) □ level best □ one's best shot □ Sunday best

**BET**
□ all bets are off □ bet one's bottom dollar □ bet someone dollars to doughnuts □ you bet □ You bet your boots! □ You bet your sweet life! □ You bet your sweet patootie!

**BETCHA**
□ you betcha

**BETHESDA**
□ Bethesda gold

**BETTER**
(See also *BEST, GOOD*.) □ better half □ Better luck next time. □ damn(ed) sight better □ seen better days □ You (had) better believe it!

**BETWEEN**
□ between a rock and a hard place □ between you, me, and the lamp post □ put some distance between someone and someone or something

**BHANG**
□ bhang ganjah

**BIBLE**
□ swear on a stack of Bibles

**BIG**
□ Big Apple □ big as life (and twice as ugly) □ big as you please □ big blue □ big board □ big brother □ big bucks □ big cheese □ big chief □ big deal □ big doings □ big drink □ big drink of water □ big enchilada □ big fish □ big gun □ (big) Harry □ big house □ big iron □ big John □ big juice □ big league □ Big Mac attack □ big man on campus □ big mouth □ big name □ big noise □ big of someone □ big shot

☐ big spender ☐ big stink ☐ big talk ☐ big-ticket ☐ big time ☐ big-time operator ☐ big-time spender ☐ big top ☐ big wheel ☐ big with someone ☐ buy the big one ☐ drive the big bus ☐ go over big ☐ have a big head ☐ have a big mouth ☐ in a big way ☐ make (it) big ☐ Mr. Big ☐ no big deal ☐ no biggie ☐ play in the big leagues ☐ talk big ☐ talk on the big white phone ☐ yea big

**BILGE**
☐ drain the bilge

**BILL**
☐ bill and coo ☐ phony as a three-dollar bill ☐ queer as a three-dollar bill

**BIN**
☐ loony bin ☐ sin-bin

**BINGE**
☐ base binge

**BIRD**
☐ bird-dog ☐ bird-watcher ☐ boo-bird ☐ early bird ☐ flip someone the bird ☐ for the birds ☐ gospel bird ☐ odd bird ☐ rare bird ☐ strange bird ☐ whirly bird

**BISCUIT**
☐ (dog) biscuits ☐ gorilla biscuits

**BIT**
☐ bit-bucket ☐ bit much ☐ bit of the action ☐ four-bits ☐ six-bits ☐ two-bit ☐ two-bits

**BITCH**
☐ (bitchen-)twitchen ☐ bitch of a someone or something ☐ bitch session ☐ bitch someone off ☐ bitch something up ☐ pitch a bitch ☐ real bitch ☐ son of a bitch

**BITE**
☐ bee bites ☐ bite the bullet ☐ bite the dust ☐ Bite the ice! ☐ Bite your tongue! ☐ I'll bite. ☐ monkey bite ☐ put the bite on someone

**BITSY**
☐ itsy-bitsy

**BITTY**
☐ itty-bitty

**BIZ**
☐ show biz

**BLACK**
☐ African black ☐ black and blue ☐ black and white ☐ black eye ☐ black gungeon ☐ black mo ☐ black moat ☐ (black) widow ☐ in the black ☐ little black book ☐ Nam black

**BLAH**
☐ blah-blah

**BLANK**
☐ blankety-blank

**BLANKET**
☐ blanket drill ☐ wet blanket

**BLANKETY**
☐ blankety-blank

**BLAST**
☐ beer blast ☐ blast a joint ☐ full blast ☐ (ghetto) blaster

**BLAZE**
☐ (blue) blazes ☐ Go to blazes!

**BLEED**
☐ bleed for someone ☐ bleed someone dry ☐ bleed someone white

**BLIMP**
☐ blimp out ☐ Have a blimp!

**BLIND**
☐ blind drunk ☐ (blind) munchies ☐ half-blind ☐ rob someone blind ☐ stone blind

**BLINK**
☐ on the blink

**BLISS**
☐ blissed (out) ☐ bliss ninny ☐ bliss out

**BLITHER**
☐ blithering idiot

**BLITZ**
☐ blitzed (out)

**BLOCK**
☐ knock someone's block off ☐ on the chopping block

**BLOOD**
☐ abso-bloody-lutely ☐ blood and guts ☐ blood bath ☐ blood (brother) ☐ blue blood ☐ cold blood ☐ Hell's bells (and buckets of blood)! ☐ in cold blood ☐ in one's blood ☐ scream bloody murder ☐ smell blood ☐ sweat blood ☐ taste blood ☐ too rich for someone's blood ☐ worms in blood ☐ young blood

**BLOOEY**
☐ go blooey

**BLOSSOM**
☐ toddy blossom

**BLOT**
☐ blot someone out

**BLOW**
☐ blow a fuse ☐ blow a gasket ☐ blow a hype ☐ blow beets ☐ blow chunks ☐ blow cold ☐ blowed (away) ☐ blow in

□ Blow it out your ear! □ blow jive □ blow lunch □ blown away □ blown out □ blown (up) □ blow off □ blow off (some) steam □ blow one's cookies □ blow one's cool □ blow one's dough-nuts □ blow one's fuse □ blow one's groceries □ blow one's lid □ blow one's lines □ blow one's lunch □ blow one's own horn □ blow one's stack □ blow one's top □ Blow on it! □ blow-out □ blow smoke □ blow snow □ blow someone away □ blow someone or something off □ blow someone out of the water □ blow someone's cover □ blow someone's doors off □ blow someone's mind □ blow someone to something □ blow something wide open □ blow the joint □ blow the lid off something □ blow town □ blow up □ blow Z's. □ Joe Blow □ land a blow □ low-blow □ tea-blower □ whistle-blower

**BLUBBER**
□ blubber gut(s)

**BLUE**
□ big blue □ black and blue □ blue acid □ blue and white □ blue around the gills □ blue baby □ blue (barrels) □ (blue) blazes □ blue blood □ blue bomber □ blue boys □ blue chip □ blue devils □ blue-eyed □ blue flu □ blue funk □ blue in the face □ blue Johnnies □ blue movie □ boys in blue □ burn with a low blue flame □ co-caine blues □ in a blue funk □ Ken-tucky blue □ little boy blue □ men in blue □ once in a blue moon □ screwed, blued, and tattooed □ talk a blue streak □ talk until one is blue in the face

**BO**
□ bo-bo (bush)

**BOARD**
□ above board □ big board □ boogie-board □ open and above board

**BOAT**
□ just off the boat □ miss the boat □ slow boat

**BOB**
□ Yes siree (Bob)!

**BOD**
□ odd-bod

**BODY**
□ body count □ body-packer □ body shake □ over my dead body □ warm body

**BOIL**
□ boiling (mad) □ pot boiler

**BOLT**
□ nuts and bolts

**BOMB**
□ blue bomber □ bombed (out) □ love bombs □ San Francisco bomb

**BOMBSHELL**
□ drop a bomb(shell)

**BOND**
□ junk bond

**BONE**
□ bag of bones □ bone factory □ bone idle □ bone orchard □ crazy bone □ laid to the bone □ tail bone

**BONER**
□ pull a boner

**BONG**
□ bonged (out) □ do some bongs

**BONKERS**
□ drive someone bonkers

**BOO**
□ boo-bird □ boo-boo □ make a boo-boo

**BOOB**
□ boob-tube

**BOOBY**
□ booby hatch □ booby trap

**BOOGIE**
□ boogie-board □ boogie down (to somewhere)

**BOOK**
□ book it □ crack a book □ fake book □ hit the books □ little black book □ make book on something □ pound the books □ take a page from someone's book □ throw the book at someone □ wish book

**BOOM**
□ (baby) boomer □ boom box □ boom sticks □ fall down and go boom □ thunder-boomer

**BOOST**
□ booster pill

**BOOT**
□ boot someone out □ Jesus boots □ to boot □ You bet your boots!

**BOOZE**
□ booze artist □ booze it (up)

**BOOZY**
□ boozy-woozy □ topsy-boozy

**BOP**
□ drop a bop

**BORDER**
☐ border (red)
**BORE**
☐ bore the pants off (of) someone
**BORN**
☐ natural-born ☐ Were you born in a barn?
**BOSOM**
☐ bosom buddy ☐ bosom chums ☐ bosom friends
**BOSS**
☐ boss habit ☐ boss lady ☐ boss man ☐ straw boss
**BOTH**
☐ both sheets in the wind ☐ sweep with both barrels ☐ swing both ways ☐ take a sweep (with both barrels)
**BOTTLE**
☐ bottle baby ☐ chief cook and bottle washer ☐ crack open a bottle ☐ head cook and bottle washer ☐ hit the bottle
**BOTTOM**
☐ bet one's bottom dollar ☐ bottom dollar ☐ bottom line ☐ bottom of the barrel ☐ bottom of the heap ☐ bottom out ☐ Bottoms up. ☐ rock bottom ☐ scrape the bottom of the barrel ☐ tops and bottoms
**BOTTOMLESS**
☐ bottomless pit
**BOUNCE**
☐ bounce for something ☐ bounce something off (of) someone ☐ That's the way the ball bounces.
**BOW**
☐ bow to the porcelain altar ☐ bow-wow
**BOWELS**
☐ get one's bowels in an uproar
**BOWL**
☐ bowl (up) ☐ party bowl
**BOX**
☐ beat box ☐ boom box ☐ boxed in ☐ boxed (up) ☐ box someone in ☐ doc(s)-in-a-box ☐ eternity-box ☐ fuse box ☐ (ghetto) box ☐ God-box ☐ go home in a box ☐ groan box ☐ idiot box ☐ knowledge-box ☐ squawk box ☐ (squeeze-)box ☐ think-box
**BOY**
☐ backroom boys ☐ blue boys ☐ Boy howdy! ☐ boys in blue ☐ boys in the backroom ☐ fair-haired boy ☐ good old boy ☐ little boy blue ☐ little boys'

room ☐ Oh, boy! ☐ That-a-boy! ☐ That's my boy.
**BRA**
☐ bra-burner
**BRACK**
☐ brack-brain
**BRAIN**
☐ B.B. brain ☐ beat one's brains out (to do something) ☐ beat someone's brains out ☐ brack-brain ☐ brain-burned ☐ brain-burners ☐ brainchild ☐ brain-drain ☐ brain-fried ☐ brain-teaser ☐ brain-twister ☐ feather brain ☐ have something on the brain
**BRAND**
☐ (brand) spanking new ☐ off-brand cigarette
**BRASS**
☐ brassed (off) ☐ brass hat ☐ brass someone off ☐ brass tacks ☐ top brass
**BRAT**
☐ army brat
**BREAD**
☐ bread and butter ☐ bread and butter letter ☐ heavy bread ☐ long bread
**BREAK**
(See also *BROKE*.) ☐ Break a leg! ☐ Break it up! ☐ break the ice ☐ Give me a break! ☐ take a break ☐ tough break
**BREAKFAST**
☐ breakfast of champions ☐ donkey's breakfast ☐ Mexican breakfast
**BREATHE**
☐ breathe easy ☐ mouth-breather
**BREEZE**
☐ breeze along ☐ breeze in ☐ breeze off ☐ breeze through (something) ☐ fan the breeze ☐ shoot the breeze
**BREEZY**
☐ bright and breezy
**BREW**
☐ brew-ha ☐ brew-out ☐ home-brew ☐ quaff a brew ☐ suck (some) brew ☐ touch of the brewer
**BRICK**
☐ built like a brick outhouse ☐ drop a brick ☐ hatch a brick ☐ hit the bricks ☐ kilo brick ☐ like a ton of bricks ☐ shit a brick ☐ three bricks shy of a load
**BRIGHT**
☐ bright and breezy ☐ bright-eyed and bushy-tailed
**BRING**
☐ bring-down ☐ bring home the bacon

☐ bring someone down ☐ bring someone on ☐ bring something up ☐ Earp slop, bring the mop.

**BROAD**
☐ can't hit the (broad) side of a barn

**BROKE**
☐ dead broke ☐ flat broke ☐ go for broke ☐ stone broke

**BRONX**
☐ Bronx cheer

**BROTHER**
☐ big brother ☐ blood (brother) ☐ brother Ben ☐ (soul) brother

**BROW**
☐ middle brow

**BROWN**
☐ brown-bag ☐ browned (off) ☐ brown-nose ☐ brown-noser ☐ brown out ☐ brown someone off ☐ brown sugar ☐ brown weed ☐ Mexican brown

**BROWNIE**
☐ Alice B. Toklas brownies ☐ brownie points ☐ hash brownies ☐ pot brownies

**BRUISE**
☐ cruising for a bruising

**BRUSH**
☐ brush someone off ☐ tarred with the same brush

**BRUSHOFF**
☐ give someone the brushoff

**BUBBLE**
☐ bubble water

**BUCK**
☐ bang for the buck ☐ big bucks ☐ buck for something ☐ buck naked ☐ buck up ☐ fast buck ☐ pass the buck ☐ quick buck

**BUCKET**
☐ bit-bucket ☐ For crying in a bucket! ☐ gash bucket ☐ Hell's bells (and buckets of blood)! ☐ kick the bucket ☐ mercy buckets ☐ messy bucket(s) ☐ murky bucket(s) ☐ rust bucket ☐ sleaze-bucket ☐ slime bucket

**BUD**
☐ gold bud ☐ green bud

**BUDDHA**
☐ Buddha stick

**BUDDY**
☐ bosom buddy ☐ buddy-buddy ☐ buddy up to someone ☐ buddy up (with someone) ☐ good buddy

**BUDGET**
☐ budget crunch ☐ budget squeeze

**BUFF**
☐ in the buff

**BUFFALO**
☐ double buffalo

**BUG**
☐ Bug off! ☐ bug out ☐ crank bugs

**BUILD**
☐ built like a brick outhouse ☐ jerry-built

**BULB**
☐ dim bulb ☐ light bulb

**BULGE**
☐ battle of the bulge

**BULL**
☐ bull jive ☐ bull-pucky ☐ bull session ☐ company bull ☐ shoot the bull ☐ throw the bull

**BULLET**
☐ bite the bullet ☐ magic bullet ☐ silver bullet ☐ sweat bullets

**BULLSHIT**
☐ bullshit artist

**BULLY**
☐ Bully for you!

**BUM**
☐ beach bum ☐ bum around ☐ bum check ☐ bummed (out) ☐ bum out ☐ bum rap ☐ bum someone out ☐ bum something (off someone) ☐ bum's rush ☐ bum steer ☐ skid row bum ☐ stew bum

**BUMP**
☐ bump someone off ☐ fanny-bumper

**BUNCH**
☐ bunch of fives ☐ thanks a bunch ☐ whole bunch(es)

**BUNDLE**
☐ bundle of joy ☐ bundle of nerves ☐ drop a bundle (on someone or something) ☐ make a bundle

**BUNNY**
☐ beach bunny ☐ cuddle bunny ☐ dumb bunny ☐ snow bunny

**BURBED**
☐ burbed out

**BURN**
☐ bra-burner ☐ brain-burned ☐ brain-burners ☐ burn artist ☐ burned out ☐ burned up ☐ burn rubber ☐ burn someone down ☐ burn someone up ☐ burn something in ☐ burnt offering ☐ burn with a low blue flame ☐ crash and burn

☐ do a slow burn ☐ hay burner ☐ nose-burner ☐ on the back burner ☐ slow burn

**BURR**
☐ cockle burrs

**BUS**
☐ drive the big bus ☐ drive the porcelain bus ☐ ride the porcelain bus

**BUSH**
☐ bo-bo (bush) ☐ bright-eyed and bushy-tailed ☐ bush patrol ☐ Mexican bush ☐ stony bush

**BUSINESS**
☐ business end (of something) ☐ funny business ☐ give someone the business ☐ in business ☐ land office business ☐ like nobody's business ☐ mean business ☐ monkey business ☐ taking care of business ☐ That's show business (for you).

**BUST**
☐ beer bust ☐ bust a gut (to do something) ☐ bust (one's) ass to (do something) ☐ bust someone's head open ☐ bust (some) suds ☐ bust something up ☐ bust something wide open ☐ bust suds ☐ conk-buster ☐ fag-busting ☐ Hold it, Buster! ☐ kidney-buster ☐ pot bust ☐ skull-buster

**BUTCHER**
☐ wood butcher

**BUTT**
☐ butt in ☐ butt naked ☐ Butt out! ☐ clip a butt ☐ duck butt ☐ dusty butt ☐ gauge-butt ☐ goof(y) butt ☐ gunzel-butt ☐ pain in the butt ☐ work one's butt off

**BUTTER**
☐ bread and butter ☐ bread and butter letter ☐ butter flower

**BUTTON**
☐ belly button ☐ cactus (buttons) ☐ hit the panic button ☐ on the button ☐ peyote (button) ☐ press the panic button ☐ push the panic button

**BUY**
☐ buy it ☐ buy someone's wolf ticket ☐ buy the big one ☐ buy the farm ☐ buy time ☐ buy trouble ☐ make a buy

**BUZZ**
☐ buzz along ☐ buzzed (up) ☐ buzz-kill ☐ buzz off ☐ cop a buzz ☐ get a buzz out of someone or something ☐ give someone a buzz ☐ have a buzz on

☐ rolling buzz ☐ What's buzzin' (cousin)?

**BY**
☐ all by one's lonesome ☐ by a whisker ☐ done by mirrors ☐ fly-by-night ☐ give someone the go-by ☐ go-by ☐ have a tiger by the tail ☐ How's by you? ☐ jai-by-jai ☐ kicked by a horse ☐ Run that by (me) again. ☐ saved by the bell ☐ two-by-four

**CABOODLE**
☐ kit and caboodle

**CACTUS**
☐ cactus (buttons) ☐ cactus juice

**CADET**
☐ space cadet

**CAGE**
☐ bear cage

**CAIN**
☐ raise Cain

**CAKE**
☐ icing on the cake ☐ piece of cake ☐ take the cake

**CALIFORNIA**
☐ California cornflakes ☐ California turnarounds

**CALL**
☐ call (all) the shots ☐ call girl ☐ call house ☐ Call my service. ☐ call of nature ☐ call someone out ☐ close call ☐ cold call ☐ Don't call us, we'll call you. ☐ nature's call ☐ pay a call

**CALM**
☐ cool, calm, and collected

**CAMBODIAN**
☐ Cambodian red

**CAMP**
☐ camp it up

**CAMPUS**
☐ big man on campus ☐ campus queen

**CAN**
☐ Can it! ☐ can of worms ☐ can-shaker ☐ can't hit the (broad) side of a barn ☐ can't win (th)em all ☐ get a can on ☐ half-canned ☐ If you can't stand the heat, keep out of the kitchen. ☐ no can do ☐ so bad one can taste it ☐ What can I do you for? ☐ You can say that again! ☐ You can't fight city hall. ☐ You can't get there from here. ☐ You can't take it with you. ☐ You can't win them all.

**CANADIAN**
☐ Canadian quail

**CANARY**
□ rocky mountain canary
**CANCEL**
□ cancel someone's Christmas
**CANCER**
□ cancer stick
**CANDY**
□ candy-ass □ candy man □ candy store □ ear candy □ hard candy □ needle candy □ nose (candy)
**CANNON**
□ hash cannon □ loose cannon
**CAN'T**
(See *CAN*.)
**CANYON**
□ yodeling in a canyon
**CAP**
□ cap out
**CAPTAIN**
□ captain of industry
**CAR**
□ wrap one's car around something
**CARD**
□ face card □ idiot card
**CARE**
□ I couldn't care less. □ Take care. □ take care of number one □ take care of someone □ taking care of business
**CARROT**
□ carrot top
**CARRY**
□ carrying a (heavy) load □ carry the stick □ carry weight
**CART**
□ honey cart
**CARVE**
□ carved in stone
**CASE**
□ basket case □ case of the shorts □ case the joint □ get off someone's case □ get on someone's case □ hard case □ make a federal case out of something □ on someone's case □ worst-case scenario
**CASH**
□ cash cow □ cash in one's chips
**CASPER**
□ Casper Milquetoast
**CAST**
□ casting-couch □ cast-iron stomach □ street-casting
**CASTOR**
□ castor oil artist

**CAT**
□ cats and dogs □ cat's meow □ cat-soup □ cool cat □ fat-cat □ fraidy cat □ purr (like a cat) □ shoot the cat □ sling the cat
**CATBIRD**
□ in the catbird seat
**CATCH**
□ catch 22 □ catch hell (for something) □ catch some rays □ catch some Z's □ catch up □ Catch you later. □ What's the catch?
**CATTLE**
□ cattle-rustler
**CAUSE**
□ lost cause
**CAVE**
□ cave man
**CEILING**
□ hit the ceiling
**CEMENT**
□ cement city
**CENTRAL**
□ Grand Central Station
**CENTURY**
□ century note
**CERTAIN**
□ certain party
**CHAIN**
□ ball and chain □ chain(-smoke) □ chain-smoker □ yank someone's chain
**CHAMPION**
□ breakfast of champions
**CHANCE**
□ fat chance □ not a chance □ snowball's chance in hell
**CHANGE**
□ and change □ change the channel □ go through the changes □ small change
**CHANNEL**
□ change the channel
**CHAPTER**
□ chapter and verse
**CHARGE**
□ charged (up)
**CHARLEY**
□ good-time Charley
**CHARLIE**
□ Charlie Irvine
**CHASE**
□ ambulance chaser □ chase the dragon □ chippy-chaser □ Go chase yourself!

**CHASSIS**
□ classis-chassis
**CHAUVINIST**
□ male chauvinist pig
**CHEAP**
□ cheap shot □ dirt cheap □ el cheapo
**CHECK**
□ bum check □ check out the plumbing □ check something out □ check that □ cut a check □ hot check □ rubber (check)
**CHEER**
□ Bronx cheer □ holiday cheer
**CHEESE**
□ big cheese □ cheesed off □ cheese-eater □ Cheese it (the cops)! □ cut the cheese □ Say cheese!
**CHEST**
□ put hair on someone's chest □ take the spear (in one's chest) □ war chest
**CHEW**
□ chew face □ chew someone out □ chew something over □ chew the fat □ chew the rag
**CHICK**
□ slick-chick
**CHICKEN**
□ chicken feed □ chicken-hearted □ chicken out (of something) □ chicken powder □ chick(en) shit habit □ for chicken feed □ spring chicken
**CHIEF**
□ big chief □ chief cook and bottle washer
**CHILD**
□ brainchild
**CHILL**
□ chill (out) □ chill someone's action □ put the chill on someone
**CHIMNEY**
□ smoke like a chimney
**CHIN**
□ chin music □ take it on the chin □ wag one's chin
**CHINA**
□ China white
**CHINESE**
□ Chinese red □ Chinese white
**CHIP**
□ (bargaining) chip □ blue chip □ cash in one's chips □ chocolate chips □ cow chips □ in the chips
**CHIPPY**
□ chippy around □ chippy-chaser □ chippy habit

**CHOCK**
□ chock-full
**CHOCOLATE**
□ chocolate chips
**CHOP**
□ chop-shop □ on the chopping block
**CHOW**
□ chow down □ chow hound □ chow something down
**CHRISTMAS**
□ cancel someone's Christmas □ Christmas tree
**CHROME**
□ chrome-dome
**CHUCK**
□ chuck a dummy □ chuck it in
**CHUG**
□ chug(-a-lug)
**CHUM**
□ bosom chums
**CHUMP**
□ off one's chump
**CHUNK**
□ blow chunks
**CHURCH**
□ church key
**CIGAR**
□ Close, but no cigar.
**CIGARETTE**
□ cigarette with no name □ off-brand cigarette
**CINCH**
□ dead cinch □ have something cinched
**CIRCLE**
□ vicious circle
**CIRCULAR**
□ circular file
**CITIZEN**
□ active citizen □ Joe Citizen
**CITY**
□ cement city □ city slicker □ fat city □ You can't fight city hall.
**CIVIL**
□ civil serpent
**CLAM**
□ clam up
**CLANKER**
□ anchor-clanker
**CLASS**
□ class act □ first-class □ world-class
**CLASSIS**
□ classis-chassis
**CLAY**
□ clay pigeon

465

**COMPOS**
□ non compos □ non compos poopoo
**CON**
□ con artist □ con job □ con man □ put a con on someone
**CONK**
□ conk-buster □ conk out
**CONNECT**
□ connect (with someone or something) □ junk connection □ score a connection
**CONNIPTION**
□ conniption (fit)
**CONTACT**
□ contact high
**COO**
□ bill and coo □ coo-coo
**COOK**
□ chief cook and bottle washer □ cooked up □ cooking with gas □ head cook and bottle washer □ What's cooking?
**COOKIE**
□ blow one's cookies □ cookie pusher □ drop one's cookies □ shoot one's cookies □ smart cookie □ snap one's cookies □ That's the way the cookie crumbles. □ throw one's cookies □ thunder-cookie □ toss one's cookies □ tough cookie □ tough cookies
**COOL**
□ blow one's cool □ Cool bananas! □ Cool beans! □ cool, calm, and collected □ cool cat □ cool down □ cooled out □ Cool it! □ cool off □ cool out □ cool someone out □ keep cool □ keep one's cool □ lose one's cool □ play it cool
**COOP**
□ fly the coop
**COP**
□ Cheese it (the cops)! □ cop a buzz □ cop a drag □ cop a fix □ cop a head □ cop an attitude □ cop a plea □ cop a squat □ cop a tube □ cop out □ cop-shop □ cop sickness □ cop some Z's
**COPILOT**
□ copilot ben
**CORE**
□ hard-core □ rotten to the core □ soft core
**CORK**
□ corked (up) □ liquid cork □ pop one's cork

**CORKSCREW**
□ corkscrewed (up)
**CORN**
□ corn squeezings □ corn whiskey □ corn wine □ Kentucky corn
**CORNER**
□ cut corners
**CORNFLAKE**
□ California cornflakes
**CORRAL**
□ corral dust
**COTTON**
□ cotton-picker □ cotton-picking □ in tall cotton
**COUCH**
□ casting-couch □ couch-doctor □ couch potato □ couch-turkey
**COUGH**
□ cough something up
**COULD**
□ I couldn't care less. □ You could have knocked me over with a feather.
**COUNT**
□ body count □ down for the count □ take the (long) count
**COUNTER**
□ bean-counter □ comma-counter □ over-the-counter
**COUNTRY**
□ country drunk
**COUNTY**
□ county-mounty
**COURAGE**
□ courage pill □ Dutch courage
**COURSE**
□ snap course
**COURT**
□ ball is in someone's court □ kangaroo court
**COUSIN**
□ What's buzzin' (cousin)?
**COVER**
□ blow someone's cover □ cover-up
**COW**
□ cash cow □ cow chips □ cow flop □ cow juice □ cow plop □ Holy cow! □ till the cows come home □ tin cow
**COWBOY**
□ drugstore cowboy
**COYOTE**
□ coyote-ugly
**COZY**
□ cozy up (to someone)

□ cut the mustard □ cut up (about someone or something) □ Fish or cut bait. □ It cuts two ways. □ not able to cut something

**CUTIE**
□ cutie pie

**CYLINDER**
□ run on all cylinders

**DAB**
□ slap-dab □ smack (dab) in the middle

**DADDY**
□ daddy (of them all) □ sugar daddy

**DAGWOOD**
□ dagwood (sandwich)

**DAH**
□ lah-di-dah □ Tah-dah!

**DAILY**
□ daily dozen □ daily grind

**DAISY**
□ fresh as a daisy □ Oops-a-daisy! □ pushing up daisies □ Upsy-daisy! □ Whoops-a-daisy!

**DALLY**
□ dilly-dally

**DAMILY**
□ whole fam damily

**DAMN**
□ damn(ed) sight better □ damn(ed) well □ do one's damnedest □ not worth a damn

**DAMPEN**
□ dampen someone's spirits

**DAMPER**
□ put a damper on something

**DANCE**
□ grave-dancer □ slam-dancing □ tap dance like mad

**DANDRUFF**
□ galloping dandruff □ walking dandruff

**DANDY**
□ fine and dandy

**DARK**
□ dark horse □ shot in the dark □ whistle in the dark

**DASH**
□ Dash it all! □ slap-dash

**DATE**
□ heavy date

**DAVE**
□ Sam and Dave

**DAY**
□ day one □ day person □ day the eagle flies □ day-tripper □ Have a nice day. □ if one's a day □ Make my day! □ red-letter day □ seen better days □ That'll be the day!

**DAYLIGHT**
□ beat the living daylights out of someone

**DAZZLE**
□ razzle-dazzle

**DEAD**
□ (bang) (dead) to rights □ dead and gone □ dead broke □ dead cinch □ dead drunk □ dead duck □ dead easy □ dead-end kid □ dead from the neck up □ dead horse □ dead in the water □ dead issue □ dead letter □ deadly (dull) □ dead man □ dead marine □ dead on □ (dead) ringer (for someone) □ dead soldier □ dead to rights □ dead to the world □ Drop dead! □ drop-dead list □ have someone dead to rights □ knock someone dead □ over my dead body □ stone dead □ would not be seen dead....

**DEAL**
□ big deal □ cut a deal □ deal stock □ dirty deal □ done deal □ house dealer □ It's a deal. □ no big deal □ package deal □ raw deal □ sweetheart deal □ What's the deal? □ wheel and deal □ wheeler-dealer

**DEAR**
□ Dear John letter □ Dear me!

**DEATH**
□ death on someone or something □ kiss of death □ like death warmed over □ nickel and dime someone (to death) □ sick to death (of someone or something) □ sudden death

**DECK**
□ double-decker □ hit the deck □ play with a full deck □ stack the deck

**DEEP**
□ deep pockets □ deep six □ go off the deep end □ in deep □ knee-deep in something

**DEGREE**
□ third degree

**DELHI**
□ Delhi belly

**DEMON**
□ speed demon

**DEPARTMENT**
□ headache department

**DERN**
- [ ] You're dern tootin'!

**DESK**
- [ ] desk jockey

**DEUCE**
- [ ] double-deuces [ ] What the deuce?
- [ ] Who the deuce?

**DEVIL**
- [ ] blue devils [ ] devil of a time [ ] devil's own time [ ] for the devil of it [ ] full of the devil [ ] Go to the devil! [ ] play the devil with someone or something [ ] raise the devil (with someone or something) [ ] red devils [ ] speak of the devil [ ] What (in) the devil? [ ] Why (in) the devil?

**DEW**
- [ ] (mountain) dew

**DI**
- [ ] lah-di-dah

**DIAMOND**
- [ ] diamond in the rough

**DIARRHEA**
- [ ] diarrhea of the mouth

**DIBS**
- [ ] dibs on something

**DICE**
- [ ] no dice

**DICK**
- [ ] crapper dick

**DICTIONARY**
- [ ] swallow the dictionary

**DIDDLE**
- [ ] diddle with something

**DIDDLY**
- [ ] diddly-squat

**DIE**
- [ ] curl up and die [ ] die on someone [ ] do-or-die

**DIFFERENCE**
- [ ] same difference

**DIFFERENT**
- [ ] different strokes for different folks

**DIG**
- [ ] Dig up! [ ] gold digger [ ] take a dig at someone

**DIGGETY**
- [ ] Hot diggety (dog)!

**DILLER**
- [ ] killer-diller [ ] thriller-diller

**DILLY**
- [ ] dilly-dally

**DIM**
- [ ] dim bulb

**DIME**
- [ ] dime-dropper [ ] dime store [ ] drop a dime [ ] get off the dime [ ] nickel and dime someone (to death) [ ] stop on a dime [ ] thin dime [ ] turn on a dime

**DING**
- [ ] ding-a-ling [ ] dinged out [ ] whing-ding [ ] wing-ding

**DINK**
- [ ] rinky-dink

**DIP**
- [ ] double-dipper [ ] fanny-dipper [ ] skinny dip

**DIPLOMA**
- [ ] federal diploma

**DIRT**
- [ ] dirt cheap [ ] dirt grass [ ] dish the dirt [ ] do someone dirt [ ] hit pay dirt [ ] strike pay dirt [ ] take a dirt nap

**DIRTY**
- [ ] air one's dirty linen in public [ ] dirty crack [ ] dirty deal [ ] dirty dog [ ] (dirty) dozens [ ] dirty joke [ ] dirty laundry [ ] dirty linen [ ] dirty look [ ] dirty-minded [ ] dirty mouth [ ] dirty old man [ ] dirty pool [ ] dirty word [ ] dirty work [ ] quick-and-dirty [ ] wash one's dirty linen in public

**DISAGREE**
- [ ] agree to disagree

**DISC**
- [ ] disc jockey

**DISCOUNT**
- [ ] five-finger discount

**DISEASE**
- [ ] foot-in-mouth disease [ ] social disease

**DISH**
- [ ] dish something out [ ] dish the dirt

**DISHRAG**
- [ ] limp dishrag

**DISHWATER**
- [ ] dull as dishwater

**DISK**
- [ ] disk jockey

**DISTANCE**
- [ ] put some distance between someone and someone or something

**DITHER**
- [ ] in a dither

**DITTY**
- [ ] wham-ditty

**DIVE**
- [ ] take a dive

**DIVIDE**
□ great divide
**DIVVY**
□ divvy something up
**DIXIE**
□ not just whistling Dixie
**DO**
(See also *DONE*.) □ beat one's brains out (to do something) □ big doings □ bust a gut (to do something) □ bust (one's) ass to (do something) □ do a dump on someone or something □ do a fade □ do a job on someone or something □ do a line □ do a number on someone □ do a slow burn □ do a snow job on someone □ do drugs □ do-gooder □ Do I have to paint (you) a picture? □ Don't ask. □ Don't ask me. □ Don't call us, we'll call you. □ Don't give it another thought. □ Don't give it a second thought. □ Don't I know it! □ Don't make me laugh! □ Don't sweat it! □ Don't you wish! □ do one's damnedest □ do oneself proud □ do one's (own) thing □ do-or-die □ do-re-mi □ do's and don't's □ do some bongs □ do someone dirt □ Do tell. □ do the drink thing □ do the drug thing □ do the trick □ do time □ Easy does it. □ How does that grab you? □ hunker down (to do something) □ I don't believe this! □ I don't know. □ I don't mean maybe! □ in thing to do □ Let's do lunch (sometime). □ must do □ no can do □ Nothing doing! □ take some doing □ tell someone what to do with something □ That does it! □ to-do □ What can I do you for? □ What do you say? □ will do □ within an ace of (doing) something □ yes indeedy (do) □ You don't know the half of it.
**DOAKES**
□ Joe Doakes
**DOC**
□ doc(s)-in-a-box
**DOCTOR**
□ couch-doctor □ doctor's orders □ dome-doctor □ horse doctor □ just what the doctor ordered □ You're the doctor. □ zit doctor
**DODGER**
□ coffin-dodger
**DODO**
□ dumb-dodo

**DOE**
□ Jane Doe □ John Doe
**DOG**
□ bird-dog □ cats and dogs □ dirty dog □ dog and pony show □ (dog) biscuits □ dog-doo □ dog-eat-dog □ doggy bag □ dog meat □ Hong Kong dog □ Hot diggety (dog)! □ Hot dog! □ lucky dog □ put on the dog □ see a man about a dog □ shouldn't happen to a dog □ top dog □ yard dog
**DOGGO**
□ lie doggo
**DOKEY**
□ okey-dokey
**DOLL**
□ Barbie doll □ Ken doll
**DOLLAR**
□ adobe dollar □ almighty dollar □ bet one's bottom dollar □ bet someone dollars to doughnuts □ bottom dollar □ like a million (dollars) □ phony as a three-dollar bill □ queer as a three-dollar bill □ sixty-four-dollar question
**DOMAIN**
□ ptomaine-domain
**DOME**
□ chrome-dome □ dome-doctor □ double-dome □ marble dome
**DONE**
□ done by mirrors □ done deal □ done for □ done over □ done to a turn
**DONKEY**
□ donkey's breakfast □ donkey's years
**DON'T**
(See *DO*.)
**DOO**
□ dog-doo □ doo-doo
**DOODLY**
□ doodly-squat
**DOOR**
□ back-door trot(s) □ blow someone's doors off □ fours and doors
**DOPE**
□ dope something out □ dope up □ inside dope □ straight dope
**DORA**
□ dumb Dora
**DORY**
□ hunky-dory
**DOSE**
□ go through someone like a dose of the salts

## DOUBLE
☐ double-bagger ☐ double-barreled sling-shot ☐ double buffalo ☐ double cross ☐ double-crosser ☐ double-decker ☐ double-deuces ☐ double-dipper ☐ double-dome ☐ double-gaited ☐ double nickels ☐ double saw(buck) ☐ double take ☐ double-trouble ☐ double up (with laughter) ☐ double whammy ☐ on the double

## DOUCHE
☐ douche bag

## DOUGHNUT
☐ bet someone dollars to doughnuts ☐ blow one's doughnuts ☐ lose one's dough-nuts

## DOWN
☐ belt something down ☐ boogie down (to somewhere) ☐ bring-down ☐ bring someone down ☐ burn someone down ☐ chow down ☐ chow something down ☐ come down ☐ come down hard ☐ cool down ☐ down for the count ☐ down someone's way ☐ down the drain ☐ Down the hatch! ☐ down time ☐ down to the wire ☐ down trip ☐ down under ☐ down with something ☐ fall down and go boom ☐ falling-down drunk ☐ flake down ☐ garbage some-thing down ☐ get down ☐ get down on someone ☐ get down to some serious drinking ☐ get down to the nitty-gritty ☐ go down ☐ go down in flames ☐ go down the line ☐ go down the tube(s) ☐ hands down ☐ have a yellow streak down one's back ☐ hook something down ☐ hose someone down ☐ hunker down (to do something) ☐ knock down something ☐ knuckle down (to some-thing) ☐ lay down ☐ pipe down ☐ pull down an amount of money ☐ put-down ☐ ram something down some-one's throat ☐ run down some lines ☐ run it down ☐ scarf something down ☐ shake someone down ☐ shoot some-one down in flames ☐ shoot someone or something down ☐ shot down ☐ shuck down ☐ simmer (down) ☐ Sit down and take a load off your feet. ☐ thumbs down ☐ turn someone or some-thing upside down ☐ turn thumbs down (on someone or something) ☐ way down ☐ What's going down? ☐ wolf some-thing down ☐ yellow streak (down some-one's back)

## DOWNHILL
☐ go downhill

## DOZEN
☐ baker's dozen ☐ daily dozen ☐ (dirty) dozens ☐ long dozen ☐ play the dozens ☐ shoot the dozens

## DRABS
☐ in dribs and drabs

## DRAFT
☐ feel a draft

## DRAG
☐ be a drag (on someone) ☐ cop a drag ☐ dragged out ☐ draggin'-wagon ☐ in drag ☐ knockdown drag-out fight ☐ knuckle-dragger ☐ main drag

## DRAGON
☐ chase the dragon ☐ green dragon

## DRAIN
☐ brain-drain ☐ down the drain ☐ drain the bilge

## DRAW
☐ luck of the draw

## DRAWER
☐ droopy-drawers ☐ top-drawer

## DREAM
☐ pipe dream

## DRESS
☐ dressed to kill ☐ dressed to the nines ☐ dressed to the teeth

## DRIBS
☐ in dribs and drabs

## DRIFT
☐ Get my drift?

## DRILL
☐ blanket drill

## DRINK
☐ big drink ☐ big drink of water ☐ do the drink thing ☐ Drink up! ☐ get down to some serious drinking ☐ knock back a drink ☐ two-fisted drinker

## DRIPPINGS
☐ silo drippings

## DRIVE
☐ backseat driver ☐ drive someone around the bend ☐ drive someone bon-kers ☐ drive someone nuts ☐ drive someone up the wall ☐ drive the big bus ☐ drive the porcelain bus ☐ in the driver's seat ☐ Sunday driver ☐ (truck) drivers

## DROOL
☐ drool (all) over someone or some-thing

**DROOPY**
☐ droopy-drawers
**DROP**
☐ dime-dropper ☐ drop a bomb(shell)
☐ drop a bop ☐ drop a brick ☐ drop
a bundle (on someone or something) ☐
drop a dime ☐ drop a roll ☐ Drop
dead! ☐ drop-dead list ☐ Drop it! ☐
drop one's cookies ☐ drop one's teeth
☐ drop out ☐ drop someone or something like a hot potato ☐ drop the ball
☐ get the drop on someone ☐ turn on,
tune in, drop out
**DRUG**
☐ do drugs ☐ do the drug thing ☐ drug
lord ☐ head drug ☐ heavy drugs ☐
love drug
**DRUGSTORE**
☐ drugstore cowboy
**DRUM**
☐ beat the drum for someone or something
**DRUNK**
☐ blind drunk ☐ commode-hugging
drunk ☐ country drunk ☐ cross-eyed
(drunk) ☐ crying drunk ☐ dead drunk
☐ drunk back ☐ drunk tank ☐ falling-
down drunk ☐ funky-drunk ☐ glazed
(drunk) ☐ howling (drunk) ☐ punch-
drunk ☐ screeching (drunk) ☐ skunk-
drunk ☐ stale drunk ☐ stinking (drunk)
**DRY**
☐ bleed someone dry ☐ dry-as-dust ☐
dry high ☐ Dry up! ☐ high and dry
**DUB**
☐ flub the dub
**DUC**
☐ duc-ducs
**DUCK**
☐ dead duck ☐ duck butt ☐ duck-
squeezer ☐ lame duck ☐ Lord love a
duck! ☐ sitting duck
**DUDDY**
☐ fuddy-duddy
**DUDE**
☐ dude up
**DUES**
☐ pay one's dues
**DUKE**
☐ duke someone out
**DULL**
☐ deadly (dull) ☐ dull as dishwater ☐
dull roar

**DUMB**
☐ dumb-ass ☐ dumb bunny ☐ dumb
cluck ☐ dumb-dodo ☐ dumb Dora ☐
dumb-dumb ☐ dumb ox
**DUMMY**
☐ chuck a dummy ☐ dummy up
**DUMP**
☐ do a dump on someone or something
☐ dumped on ☐ dump one's load ☐
dump on someone or something
**DUNK**
☐ slam dunk
**DUO**
☐ dynamic duo
**DUPER**
☐ super-duper
**DUST**
☐ angel dust ☐ bite the dust ☐ corral
dust ☐ cut the dust ☐ dry-as-dust ☐
dust someone off ☐ dust someone's
pants ☐ dust-up ☐ dusty butt ☐ ear-
duster ☐ gold duster ☐ heaven dust ☐
joy dust ☐ kiss the dust ☐ puff the dust
☐ rusty-dusty
**DUTCH**
☐ Dutch act ☐ Dutch courage ☐ Dutch
treat ☐ Dutch uncle ☐ go Dutch ☐ in
Dutch
**DWELLER**
☐ cliff-dweller
**DYNAMIC**
☐ dynamic duo
**EAGER**
☐ eager-beaver
**EAGLE**
☐ day the eagle flies ☐ eagle-eye ☐
eagle freak ☐ when the eagle flies
**EAR**
☐ all ears ☐ Blow it out your ear! ☐
coming out of one's ears ☐ ear candy
☐ ear-duster ☐ mickey mouse ears ☐
pin someone's ears back ☐ pound one's
ear ☐ primed to the ears ☐ roasting-ear
wine ☐ sloshed (to the ears) ☐ talk
someone's ear off ☐ throw one out on
one's ear ☐ up to one's ears ☐ walls
have ears
**EARFUL**
☐ give someone an earful
**EARLY**
☐ early bird
**EARP**
☐ Earp slop, bring the mop.

**EARTH**
☐ no earthly reason ☐ Where on (God's green) earth?
**EASY**
☐ breathe easy ☐ dead easy ☐ Easy does it. ☐ easy mark ☐ easy money ☐ easy street ☐ on easy street ☐ over easy ☐ take it easy ☐ take things easy
**EAT**
☐ cheese-eater ☐ dog-eat-dog ☐ eat crow ☐ eat nails ☐ eat one's hat ☐ eat one's heart out ☐ eat something up ☐ eat up ☐ smoke eater ☐ What's eating someone?
**ECO**
☐ eco freak
**EDGAR**
☐ J. Edgar (Hoover)
**EDGE**
☐ have an edge on ☐ moist around the edges
**EGG**
☐ bad egg ☐ eggbeater ☐ egg-sucker ☐ Go fry an egg! ☐ goose egg ☐ have egg on one's face ☐ lay an egg ☐ nest egg ☐ rotten egg ☐ scrambled eggs ☐ tough egg to crack ☐ walk on eggs
**EGO**
☐ ego trip ☐ ego tripper
**EIGHT**
☐ behind the eight ball ☐ number eight
**EIGHTEEN**
☐ eighteen wheeler
**EL**
☐ el cheapo ☐ (el) primo
**ELBOW**
☐ bend one's elbow ☐ elbow-bending ☐ elbow-grease ☐ lift one's elbow
**ELECTRIC**
☐ electric koolaid ☐ electric wine ☐ Kauai (electric)
**ELEGANT**
☐ piss elegant
**ELEPHANT**
☐ elephant (tranquilizer) ☐ pink elephants ☐ seeing pink elephants ☐ white elephant
**ELEVATOR**
☐ elevator music
**ELSE**
☐ something else ☐ What else is new? ☐ You and who else?
**EM**
☐ nail-em-and-jail-em ☐ shoot 'em up ☐ Stick 'em up!

**EMBALM**
☐ embalming fluid
**EMBARRASS**
☐ financially embarrassed
**EMPTY**
☐ empty-nesters
**ENCHILADA**
☐ big enchilada ☐ whole enchilada
**END**
☐ at loose ends ☐ be-all, (and) end-all ☐ business end (of something) ☐ dead-end kid ☐ end of the ball game ☐ go off the deep end ☐ know which end is up ☐ no end of something ☐ rear (end) ☐ rear-ender ☐ see no further than the end of one's nose ☐ short end of the stick ☐ tail-end
**ENGLISH**
☐ English spliff
**ESTIMATE**
☐ ball park estimate
**ETERNITY**
☐ eternity-box
**EVEN**
☐ evened out ☐ even-Steven
**EVERYTHING**
☐ and everything ☐ everything from soup to nuts ☐ Hold everything!
**EXPEDITION**
☐ fishing expedition
**EXPLORER**
☐ Arctic explorer
**EXPRESS**
☐ Siberian express
**EXPRESSION**
☐ if you'll pardon the expression
**EYE**
☐ apple of someone's eye ☐ bedroom eyes ☐ black eye ☐ blue-eyed ☐ bright-eyed and bushy-tailed ☐ cross-eyed (drunk) ☐ eagle-eye ☐ eye-opener ☐ eye-popper ☐ four-eyes ☐ get some shut-eye ☐ glassy-eyed ☐ goggle-eyed ☐ goo-goo eyes ☐ Here's mud in your eye. ☐ pie-eyed ☐ pigeon-eyed ☐ pop-eyed ☐ private eye ☐ see eye to eye ☐ shut-eye ☐ sight for sore eyes ☐ snake eyes ☐ wall-eyed ☐ with (one's) eyes (wide) open
**EYEBALL**
☐ eyeball to eyeball ☐ up to one's eyeballs
**FACE**
☐ Bag your face! ☐ blue in the face ☐

chew face □ crater face □ face card □ (face) fungus □ face man □ face-off □ face the music □ feed one's face □ fungus-face □ fuzz-face □ get face □ Get out of my face! □ have egg on one's face □ mace someone's face □ mess someone's face up □ shit-faced □ Shut your face! □ slap in the face □ soak one's face □ stand there with one's bare face hanging out □ straight-faced □ suck face □ talk until one is blue in the face □ what's his face

**FACT**
□ facts of life

**FACTOR**
□ fudge factor

**FACTORY**
□ bone factory □ gargle factory □ glue factory □ piss factory □ spook factory

**FADDLE**
□ Fiddle-faddle!

**FADE**
□ do a fade

**FAG**
□ fag-busting □ fagged out

**FAIR**
□ fair-haired boy □ fair shake □ fair-weather □ No fair!

**FAIRY**
□ airy-fairy □ fairy tale

**FAITH**
□ Keep the faith (baby)!

**FAITHFUL**
□ one of the faithful

**FAKE**
□ fake book □ fake it □ fake off □ fake someone out

**FALL**
□ fall apart □ fall down and go boom □ fall guy □ falling-down drunk □ falling-out □ fall off the wagon □ fall out □ fall out of bed □ take a fall

**FAM**
□ whole fam damily

**FAMILIAR**
□ in a familiar way

**FAMILY**
□ in a family way

**FAN**
□ fan someone's behind □ fan the breeze □ hit the fan

**FANCY**
□ fancy footwork □ Fancy meeting you here. □ fancy-schmancy □ Fancy that!

**FANNY**
□ fanny-bumper □ fanny-dipper

**FAR**
□ far gone □ far out

**FARM**
□ buy the farm □ funny-farm

**FART**
□ fart sack

**FAST**
□ fast buck □ fast footwork □ fast one □ get nowhere fast □ play fast and loose (with someone or something) □ pull a fast one

**FASTER**
□ go-fasters

**FAT**
□ chew the fat □ fat-cat □ fat chance □ fat city □ till the fat lady sings □ when the fat lady sings

**FAVORITE**
□ all-time favorite

**FAY**
□ uzz-fay

**FEATHER**
□ feather brain □ in fine feather □ You could have knocked me over with a feather.

**FEDERAL**
□ federal diploma □ federal jug □ make a federal case out of something

**FEED**
□ another mouth to feed □ chicken feed □ feed one's face □ for chicken feed

**FEEDBAG**
□ put on the feedbag

**FEEL**
□ feel a draft □ feel groovy □ feeling no pain

**FELL**
□ fell of a hix

**FENCE**
□ fence hanger □ part that went over the fence last □ straddle the fence

**FENDER**
□ fender-bender

**FER**
□ fer shur

**FETCH**
□ fetch up

**FEVER**
□ barrel fever

**FEW**
□ hang a few on □ Win a few, lose a few.

**FLOP**
☐ belly flop ☐ cow flop ☐ flip-flop ☐ flop house ☐ flopper-stopper ☐ That's the way the mop flops.

**FLOW**
☐ go with the flow

**FLOWER**
☐ butter flower ☐ flower tops ☐ hearts and flowers

**FLU**
☐ blue flu

**FLUB**
☐ flub something up ☐ flub the dub ☐ flub (up)

**FLUFF**
☐ fluff-stuff

**FLUID**
☐ embalming fluid

**FLUNK**
☐ flunk out (of something)

**FLUSHER**
☐ four-flusher

**FLY**
☐ day the eagle flies ☐ fly-by-night ☐ fly kites ☐ fly light ☐ fly the coop ☐ fly trap ☐ Go fly a kite! ☐ I've got to fly. ☐ no flies on someone ☐ on the fly ☐ straighten up and fly right ☐ take a flyer ☐ when the eagle flies ☐ with flying colors

**FOGEY**
☐ old fogey

**FOGGIEST**
☐ foggiest (idea)

**FOLD**
☐ folding money

**FOLKS**
☐ different strokes for different folks

**FOO**
☐ foo-foo water

**FOOD**
☐ junk food ☐ rabbit food ☐ squirrel-food ☐ worm-food

**FOOL**
☐ play someone for a fool

**FOOT**
☐ cold feet ☐ foot-in-mouth disease ☐ foot it ☐ get a load off one's feet ☐ have one foot in the grave ☐ My foot! ☐ patter of tiny feet ☐ shoot oneself in the foot ☐ Sit down and take a load off your feet. ☐ six feet under ☐ vote with one's feet ☐ wouldn't touch someone or something with a ten-foot pole

**FOOTSY**
☐ footsy-wootsy

**FOOTWORK**
☐ fancy footwork ☐ fast footwork

**FORBIDDEN**
☐ forbidden fruit

**FORGET**
☐ Forget it! ☐ Forget you!

**FORK**
☐ fork something over

**FORM**
☐ in rare form

**FORT**
☐ hold the fort

**FORTUNE**
☐ small fortune

**FORTY**
☐ (forty) winks

**FOUL**
☐ fouled up ☐ foul mouth ☐ foul up

**FOUR**
☐ four-bagger ☐ four-bits ☐ four-eyes ☐ four-flusher ☐ fours and doors ☐ four sheets in the wind ☐ four wheels ☐ sixty-four-dollar question ☐ ten-four ☐ two-by-four

**FOX**
☐ fox trap ☐ foxy lady ☐ stone fox

**FRAIDY**
☐ fraidy cat

**FRAME**
☐ frame-up

**FRANCISCO**
☐ San Francisco bomb

**FRAT**
☐ frat-rat

**FREAK**
☐ barb freak ☐ coke freak ☐ crank freak ☐ eagle freak ☐ eco freak ☐ freaked (out) ☐ freak freely ☐ freak house ☐ freak (out) ☐ freak someone out ☐ freon freak ☐ frost freak ☐ garbage freak ☐ juice freak ☐ kick freak ☐ meth freak ☐ speed freak

**FREE**
☐ for free ☐ freak freely ☐ free base ☐ free base party ☐ free-baser ☐ free-basing ☐ free for all ☐ free lunch ☐ free ride ☐ free show ☐ free trip ☐ free-wheeling ☐ There's no such thing as a free lunch.

**FREEZE**
☐ freeze someone out ☐ freezing cold ☐ play freeze-out ☐ put the freeze on someone ☐ till hell freezes over

**GANG**
- □ gang-bang

**GANGBUSTERS**
- □ come on like gangbusters □ like gangbusters

**GANGSTER**
- □ gangster pill

**GANJAH**
- □ bhang ganjah

**GARBAGE**
- □ garbage freak □ garbage mouth □ garbage something down

**GARGLE**
- □ gargle factory

**GAS**
- □ cooking with gas □ gas-guzzler □ gas-passer □ gassed (up) □ run out of gas

**GASH**
- □ gash bucket

**GASKET**
- □ blow a gasket

**GATE**
- □ give someone the gate

**GAUGE**
- □ gauge-butt

**GAY**
- □ gay as pink ink

**GEAR**
- □ swing into high gear

**GEED**
- □ geed up

**GEEZED**
- □ geezed (up)

**GENDER**
- □ gender-bender

**GENERATION**
- □ now generation

**GENUINE**
- □ genuine article

**GEORGIA**
- □ hell and half of Georgia

**GERMAN**
- □ German goiter

**GHETTO**
- □ (ghetto) blaster □ (ghetto) box

**GHOST**
- □ ghost turd

**GIANT**
- □ mental giant

**GIBBER**
- □ gibber-gabber

**GIDDY**
- □ Giddy up!

**GIFT**
- □ gift of gab

**GIGGLE**
- □ giggle goo

**GILL**
- □ blue around the gills □ green around the gills □ loaded to the gills □ stewed to the gills

**GIN**
- □ bathtub gin □ gin mill

**GIRL**
- □ call girl □ girlie magazine □ girlie show □ little girls' room □ old girl

**GIT**
- □ from (the) git-go □ git-go

**GIVE**
- □ Don't give it another thought. □ Don't give it a second thought. □ Give it a rest! □ give it the gun □ Give it up! □ Give me a break! □ Give me a rest! □ Give me five! □ Give me (some) skin! □ give (out) with something □ give someone a buzz □ give someone a (good) talking to □ give someone a (good) working over □ give someone an earful □ give someone a pain □ give someone five □ give someone hell □ give someone the ax □ give someone the brushoff □ give someone the business □ give someone the finger □ give someone the gate □ give someone the go-by □ give someone the nod □ give someone the raspberry □ give someone the shaft □ give someone the slip □ give someone wings □ give something to someone straight □ not give a hoot □ Something's got to give. □ What gives?

**GLAD**
- □ glad-hand □ glad-hander □ glad rags

**GLAMOUR**
- □ glamour puss

**GLASS**
- □ glass gun □ glassy-eyed

**GLAZED**
- □ glazed (drunk)

**GLOOMY**
- □ gloomy Gus

**GLORY**
- □ Glory be! □ glory seeds □ send someone to glory

**GLOVE**
- □ hand in glove

## GLOW
□ glow worm □ have a glow on
## GLUE
□ glue factory
## GO
(See also *GONE*.) □ All systems are go. □ fall down and go boom □ from (the) git-go □ get someone going □ get something going (with someone) □ git-go □ give someone the go-by □ go-ahead □ go all the way □ go ape (over someone or something) □ go bananas □ go belly up □ go blooey □ go-by □ Go chase yourself! □ Go climb a tree! □ go down □ go downhill □ go down in flames □ go down the line □ go down the tube(s) □ go Dutch □ go-fasters □ go flooey □ Go fly a kite! □ go for a sleigh ride □ go for broke □ Go for it! □ Go fry an egg! □ go-getter □ go-go □ go great guns □ go haywire □ go hog-wild □ go home in a box □ go home to mama □ going high □ going over □ goings-on □ go into orbit □ Go jump in the lake! □ go off half-cocked □ go off the deep end □ Go on! □ go on (and on) about someone or something □ go over big □ go overboard □ go over like a lead balloon □ go over the hill □ go over the wall □ go-pills □ go places □ go public □ Go soak your head! □ Go soak yourself! □ go sour □ go South □ go straight □ go the limit □ go through someone like a dose of the salts □ go through the changes □ Go to! □ Go to blazes! □ Go to the devil! □ go to town □ gotta go □ go underground □ go up □ go West □ go with the flow □ go zonkers □ How goes it? □ no go □ only way to go □ part that went over the fence last □ pass go □ raring to go □ That's the way to go! □ There you go. □ to go □ touch and go □ Way to go! □ What's going down? □ What's going on?
## GOAT
□ get someone's goat □ skin a goat
## GOD
□ God-box □ God only knows! □ God's acre □ kiss the porcelain god □ pray to the porcelain god □ Where on (God's green) earth? □ worship the porcelain god □ Ye gods!

## GODDESS
□ sex goddess
## GOGGLE
□ goggle-eyed
## GOITER
□ German goiter □ Milwaukee goiter
## GOLD
□ Acapulco (gold) □ Bethesda gold □ Colombian (gold) □ gold bud □ gold Colombian □ gold digger □ gold duster □ Jamaican (gold) □ Kona (coast) gold □ sit on a gold mine
## GOLDEN
□ golden-ager □ golden handcuffs □ golden leaf □ golden opportunity □ golden parachute
## GOLDIE
□ goldie locks
## GOLLY
□ Good golly, Miss Molly!
## GONE
(See also *GO*.) □ dead and gone □ far gone □ gone goose □ real gone □ to hell and gone
## GOO
□ giggle goo □ goo-goo eyes
## GOOBER
□ goober-grabber □ goober-grease
## GOOD
(See also *BEST, BETTER*.) □ ain't no good nohow □ do-gooder □ get (out) while the getting's good □ get the goods on someone □ give someone a (good) talking to □ give someone a (good) working over □ good and something □ good buddy □ good-for-nothing □ good for what ails someone □ Good golly, Miss Molly! □ Good grief! □ Good heavens! □ good Joe □ good old boy □ good-time Charley □ good-time it □ good-time man □ good trip □ Goody-goody gumdrop! □ goody two-shoes □ Have a good one. □ have good vibes □ if one knows what's good for one □ Johnny-be-good □ no-good □ oldie but goodie □ onto a good thing □ What's the good word? □ Your guess is as good as mine.
## GOODBYE
□ kiss something goodbye
## GOODNIK
□ no-goodnik
## GOOF
□ goof around □ goof artist □ goofed

(up) □ goof off □ goof on someone □ goof-proof □ goof something up □ goof up □ goof(y) butt
**GOON**
□ goon-platoon □ goon squad
**GOOSE**
□ gone goose □ goose egg
**GOPHER**
□ gopher ball
**GORILLA**
□ gorilla biscuits □ gorilla juice □ gorilla pills □ gorilla tabs
**GORK**
□ gorked (out)
**GOSPEL**
□ gospel bird □ gospel (truth)
**GOT**
□ I've got to fly. □ I've got to split. □ Something's got to give. □ You got it! □ You've got another think coming.
**GOUCH**
□ gouch off
**GRAB**
□ goober-grabber □ How does that grab you? □ up for grabs
**GRADE**
□ grade-grubber □ grade-grubbing
**GRAND**
□ Grand Central Station
**GRANDDADDY**
□ granddaddy (of them all)
**GRANDSTAND**
□ grandstand play
**GRAPE**
□ belt the grape □ grape shot □ grapes of wrath
**GRASS**
□ bad grass □ dirt grass □ grass party □ johnson (grass) □ laughing grass □ snake in the grass
**GRASSHOPPER**
□ knee-high to a grasshopper
**GRAVE**
□ grave-dancer □ have one foot in the grave
**GRAVEL**
□ gravel-pounder
**GRAVEYARD**
□ graveyard shift
**GRAVY**
□ gravy train
**GREASE**
□ elbow-grease □ goober-grease □ greased lightning □ grease monkey □ grease

someone's palm □ grease the skids □ greasy spoon
**GREAT**
□ go great guns □ great divide □ Great Scott! □ great unwashed □ no great shakes □ whopping (great)
**GREEK**
□ Greek to someone
**GREEN**
□ collard greens □ Gainesville green □ green around the gills □ green bud □ green dragon □ green hornet □ green light □ green paper □ green stuff □ green tea □ green thumb □ long green □ mean-green □ Where on (God's green) earth?
**GRIEF**
□ Good grief!
**GRIND**
□ daily grind
**GRIP**
□ key grip □ lose one's grip
**GRIPE**
□ gripe one's soul
**GRITTY**
□ get down to the nitty-gritty □ nitty-gritty
**GROAN**
□ groan box
**GROCERIES**
□ blow one's groceries
**GROD**
□ King Grod
**GRODY**
□ grody to the max
**GROG**
□ grogged (up)
**GRONK**
□ gronk (out)
**GROOVE**
□ get in the groove □ groove on someone or something □ in the groove □ stone groove
**GROOVY**
□ feel groovy
**GROPE**
□ group-grope
**GROSS**
□ gross-out □ gross someone out □ So gross!
**GROUND**
□ ground-pounder □ stamping ground
**GROUP**
□ group-grope

**GROW**
□ not grow on trees
**GRUB**
□ grade-grubber □ grade-grubbing □ money grubber
**GRUESOME**
□ gruesome-twosome
**GRUNT**
□ grunt work
**GUESS**
□ Your guess is as good as mine.
**GUEST**
□ Be my guest.
**GUIDE**
□ tour guide
**GUITAR**
□ air guitar
**GUM**
□ beat one's gums
**GUMDROP**
□ Goody-goody gumdrop!
**GUN**
□ big gun □ give it the gun □ glass gun □ go great guns □ gun for someone □ hired gun □ in the gun □ jump the gun □ smoking gun □ son of a gun □ under the gun □ zip gun
**GUNG**
□ gung-ho
**GUNGEON**
□ black gungeon
**GUNZEL**
□ gunzel-butt
**GUS**
□ gloomy Gus
**GUSSIED**
□ gussied up
**GUT**
□ beer gut □ blood and guts □ blubber gut(s) □ bust a gut (to do something) □ gut reaction (to something) □ guzzle-guts □ kick in the guts □ spew one's guts (out) □ spill one's guts □ split a gut □ yell one's guts out
**GUTLESS**
□ gutless wonder
**GUTTER**
□ have one's mind in the gutter
**GUY**
□ fall guy □ Mr. Nice Guy □ right guy □ smart guy □ tough guy □ wise guy
**GUZZLE**
□ gas-guzzler □ guzzle-guts

**GYP**
□ gyp joint
**GYPPY**
□ gyppy tummy
**HA**
□ brew-ha □ hoo-ha
**HABIT**
□ boss habit □ C-habit □ chick(en) shit habit □ chippy habit □ kick the habit □ knock the habit □ mickey mouse habit □ nose habit □ two-arm habit
**HACK**
□ hack around □ hacked (off) □ hack it
**HAD**
□ been had □ You (had) better believe it!
**HAIR**
□ angel hair □ fair-haired boy □ hairy-ass(ed) □ put hair on someone's chest
**HALF**
□ better half □ go off half-cocked □ half-baked □ half-blind □ half-canned □ half-cocked □ half-crocked □ half in the bag □ half-lit □ half moon □ half-sprung □ half-stewed □ half under □ half up the pole □ hell and half of Georgia □ hell's half acre □ how the other half lives □ You don't know the half of it.
**HALL**
□ You can't fight city hall.
**HAM**
□ ham-handed
**HAMBURGER**
□ make hamburger out of someone or something
**HANCOCK**
□ John Hancock
**HAND**
□ glad-hand □ glad-hander □ ham-handed □ hand in glove □ hand it to someone □ hand over fist □ hands down □ hand someone something □ hands-on □ Hands up! □ heavy-handed □ Keep your hands to yourself. □ left-handed monkey wrench □ old hand (at something) □ tip one's hand
**HANDCUFF**
□ golden handcuffs
**HANDLE**
□ love handles

**HANDSOME**
☐ high, wide, and handsome
**HANG**
☐ hang a few on ☐ hang a huey ☐ hang a left ☐ hang a louie ☐ hang a ralph ☐ hang a right ☐ hang (around) ☐ hang five ☐ hang in there ☐ Hang it all! ☐ hang it up ☐ hang loose ☐ hang one on ☐ hang ten ☐ hang tough (on something) ☐ hang up ☐ hung up (on someone or something) ☐ let it all hang out ☐ stand there with one's bare face hanging out
**HANGER**
☐ ape hangers ☐ fence hanger ☐ paper-hanger
**HANKY**
☐ hanky-panky
**HAPPEN**
☐ shouldn't happen to a dog ☐ What's happening?
**HAPPY**
☐ happy hour ☐ happy juice ☐ happy pills ☐ happy shop ☐ slap happy ☐ trigger-happy
**HARD**
☐ between a rock and a hard place ☐ come down hard ☐ hard candy ☐ hard case ☐ hard coin ☐ hard-core ☐ hardhead ☐ hard liquor ☐ hard-nosed ☐ hard sell ☐ hard time ☐ hard to swallow ☐ hard up
**HARDBALL**
☐ play hardball (with someone)
**HARRY**
☐ (big) Harry
**HARSH**
☐ harsh toke
**HAS**
☐ has-been
**HASH**
☐ flash the hash ☐ hash brownies ☐ hash cannon ☐ hash-head ☐ hash-house ☐ hash pipe ☐ hash-slinger ☐ heavy hash ☐ settle someone's hash
**HAT**
☐ brass hat ☐ eat one's hat ☐ knock something into a cocked hat ☐ old hat ☐ talk through one's hat ☐ throw one's hat in the ring ☐ tin hat ☐ white hat
**HATCH**
☐ booby hatch ☐ Down the hatch! ☐ hatch a brick

**HAUL**
☐ over the long haul
**HAWAIIAN**
☐ Hawaiian (sunshine)
**HAWKINS**
☐ Mr. Hawkins
**HAY**
☐ bale (of hay) ☐ hay burner ☐ hay head ☐ hit the hay ☐ Indian hay ☐ That ain't hay!
**HAYWIRE**
☐ go haywire
**HAZE**
☐ (purple) haze
**HEAD**
☐ A-head ☐ banana-head ☐ beef-head ☐ bust someone's head open ☐ C-head ☐ cop a head ☐ crazy in the head ☐ get one's head together ☐ Go soak your head! ☐ hardhead ☐ hash-head ☐ have a big head ☐ have a head ☐ have rocks in one's head ☐ hay head ☐ head cook and bottle washer ☐ head drug ☐ head hunt ☐ head kit ☐ head shop ☐ head someone off at the pass ☐ head South ☐ Heads up! ☐ heads will roll ☐ head trip ☐ helium head ☐ hot head ☐ keep one's head right ☐ knock some heads together ☐ out of one's head ☐ over one's head ☐ pointy-head ☐ pound someone's head in ☐ soft in the head ☐ stoned out of one's head ☐ syrup head ☐ talking head ☐ talk someone's head off ☐ touched (in the head) ☐ Use your head! ☐ where someone's head is at ☐ yell one's head off
**HEADACHE**
☐ headache department ☐ headache man ☐ splitting headache
**HEAP**
☐ bottom of the heap ☐ in a heap ☐ junk heap ☐ top of the heap
**HEAR**
☐ I hear what you are saying. ☐ I hear you. ☐ talk to hear one's own voice ☐ You hear? ☐ You heard the man.
**HEART**
☐ chicken-hearted ☐ eat one's heart out ☐ Have a heart! ☐ hearts and flowers ☐ heart-to-heart (talk) ☐ soft-hearted
**HEARTY**
☐ party-hearty

## HEAT
☐ If you can't stand the heat, keep out of the kitchen. ☐ put the heat on someone ☐ take the heat ☐ take the heat off someone

## HEAVE
☐ old heave-ho

## HEAVEN
☐ Good heavens! ☐ heaven dust ☐ pig heaven ☐ smell to (high) heaven

## HEAVY
☐ carrying a (heavy) load ☐ heavy artillery ☐ heavy bread ☐ heavy date ☐ heavy drugs ☐ heavy-handed ☐ heavy hash ☐ heavy into someone or something ☐ heavy joint ☐ heavy metal ☐ heavy money ☐ heavy necking ☐ heavy scene ☐ heavy soul ☐ lay a (heavy) trip on someone ☐ top heavy ☐ tripping heavy ☐ walk heavy ☐ wing heavy

## HECK
☐ for the heck of it ☐ What the heck!

## HEEBIE
☐ heebie-jeebies

## HEINZ
☐ Heinz 57 (variety)

## HELIUM
☐ helium head

## HELL
☐ catch hell (for something) ☐ for the hell of it ☐ Get the hell out (of here)! ☐ give someone hell ☐ have hell to pay ☐ hell and half of Georgia ☐ hell of a mess ☐ hell of a note ☐ hell of a someone or something ☐ hell on wheels ☐ Hell's bells (and buckets of blood)! ☐ hell's half acre ☐ like a bat out of hell ☐ Like hell! ☐ play hell with someone or something ☐ quicker than hell ☐ raise hell ☐ scare the hell out of someone ☐ shot to hell ☐ snowball's chance in hell ☐ sure as hell ☐ There will be hell to pay. ☐ till hell freezes over ☐ to hell and gone ☐ To hell with that! ☐ What (in) the hell? ☐ Who (in) the hell? ☐ Why (in) the hell?

## HELLUVA
☐ helluva someone or something

## HELP
☐ pitch in (and help)

## HEN
☐ hen fruit ☐ hen party

## HEP
☐ hepped (up)

## HERE
☐ Fancy meeting you here. ☐ get one right here ☐ Get the hell out (of here)! ☐ Here's looking at you. ☐ Here's mud in your eye. ☐ I'm out of here. ☐ same here ☐ up to here ☐ You can't get there from here.

## HERO
☐ hero (of the underworld)

## HERPED
☐ herped up

## HESS
☐ mell of a hess

## HET
☐ het up

## HI
☐ hi-res

## HIDE
☐ nail someone's hide to the wall ☐ tan someone's hide

## HIGH
☐ contact high ☐ dry high ☐ going high ☐ high and dry ☐ high five ☐ high old time ☐ high on something ☐ high-res ☐ high roller ☐ high sign ☐ high tea ☐ high ups ☐ high, wide, and handsome ☐ hold one's high ☐ in high ☐ knee-high to a grasshopper ☐ natural high ☐ on one's high horse ☐ smell to (high) heaven ☐ swing into high gear ☐ up high

## HIGHWAY
☐ highway robbery

## HIKE
☐ take a hike

## HILL
☐ go over the hill ☐ over the hill ☐ What in (the) Sam Hill? ☐ Where in (the) Sam Hill?

## HIND
☐ suck someone's hind tit

## HINDSIGHT
☐ twenty-twenty hindsight

## HIP
☐ hip-shooter ☐ joined at the hip ☐ shoot from the hip

## HIRE
☐ hired gun

## HISTORY
☐ ancient history

## HIT
(See also *HITTER*.) ☐ can't hit the

(broad) side of a barn □ hit list □ hit man □ hit me □ hit on something □ hit pay dirt □ hit (someone) below the belt □ hit someone (up) for something □ hit someone with something □ hit spike □ hit the books □ hit the bottle □ hit the bricks □ hit the ceiling □ hit the deck □ hit the fan □ hit the hay □ hit the jackpot □ hit the panic button □ hit the pipe □ hit the road □ hit the roof □ hit the sack □ hit the skids □ hit the spot □ hit the trail □ hit under the wing □ nose hit □ smash hit □ swallow hit

**HITCH**
□ without a hitch

**HITHER**
□ come-hither look

**HITTER**
□ pinch hitter □ power hitter □ switch-hitter

**HIX**
□ fell of a hix

**HO**
□ gung-ho □ ho-hum □ ho-jo('s) □ old heave-ho

**HOCKEY**
□ horse hockey

**HOE**
□ tough row to hoe

**HOG**
□ go hog-wild □ hog-wild □ junk hog □ road hog □ run hog-wild □ sewer hog

**HOIST**
□ hoist one

**HOLD**
□ Are you holding? □ hold all the aces □ Hold everything! □ Hold it! □ Hold it, Buster! □ hold one's high □ hold one's horses □ hold one's liquor □ hold the fort □ hold water □ lose one's hold □ no holds barred

**HOLE**
□ ace in the hole □ hole in the wall □ hole up □ in the hole □ nineteenth hole □ square peg (in a round hole) □ watering hole

**HOLIDAY**
□ holiday cheer

**HOLY**
□ holier-than-thou □ Holy cow! □ holy Joe □ Holy mackerel! □ Holy moley! □ holy stink □ holy terror

**HOME**
□ bring home the bacon □ come home □ go home in a box □ go home to mama □ home-brew □ in the (home) stretch □ money from home □ nothing to write home about □ There's nobody home. □ till the cows come home

**HONEST**
□ honest injun

**HONEY**
□ honey cart □ honey of a something □ honey wagon

**HONG**
□ Hong Kong dog

**HOO**
□ hoo-ha

**HOOCH**
□ hooched (up) □ hooch hound

**HOOF**
□ hoof it

**HOOK**
□ get one's hooks into someone or something □ hooked (on someone or something) □ hook, line, and sinker □ hook shop □ hook something down □ off the hook □ on one's own hook □ ring off the hook □ sky hook

**HOOKY**
□ play hooky

**HOOT**
□ not give a hoot

**HOOVER**
□ J. Edgar (Hoover)

**HOP**
□ full of hops □ hopped up □ hopping mad □ Hop to it! □ pool-hopping □ sock hop □ table-hop

**HOPPER**
□ in the hopper

**HORN**
□ blow one's own horn □ toot one's own horn

**HORNET**
□ green hornet

**HORSE**
□ dark horse □ dead horse □ hold one's horses □ horse around □ horse doctor □ horse hockey □ horse laugh □ horse opera □ horse's ass □ horse (tranquilizer) □ kicked by a horse □ one-horse town □ on one's high horse □ salt horse □ straight from the horse's mouth

## INDUSTRY
☐ captain of industry
## INJUN
☐ honest injun
## INK
☐ gay as pink ink ☐ ink slinger ☐ red ink
## INS
☐ ins and outs
## INSIDE
☐ inside dope ☐ inside job
## INTO
☐ get into something ☐ get one's hooks into someone or something ☐ get one's teeth into something ☐ go into orbit ☐ heavy into someone or something ☐ knock something into a cocked hat ☐ lick something into shape ☐ light into someone ☐ sail into someone ☐ sink one's teeth into something ☐ swing into high gear ☐ tear into someone or something ☐ tuck into something ☐ whale into someone or something ☐ wired into someone or something ☐ work oneself (up) into a lather
## IRON
☐ big iron ☐ cast-iron stomach ☐ shooting iron
## IRVINE
☐ Charlie Irvine
## IS
(See also *BE, BEEN, WAS, WERE*.) ☐ as is ☐ ball is in someone's court ☐ jig is up ☐ know where one is coming from ☐ Put your money where your mouth is! ☐ quit while one is ahead ☐ talk until one is blue in the face ☐ Tell it like it is. ☐ This is it! ☐ This is where I came in. ☐ What else is new? ☐ What you see is what you get. ☐ where someone is at ☐ where someone's head is at ☐ where the action is ☐ world is one's oyster ☐ Your guess is as good as mine.
## ISSUE
☐ dead issue
## ITCH
☐ have an itch for something ☐ seven-year itch
## ITEM
☐ hot item
## ITSY
☐ itsy-bitsy
## ITTY
☐ itty-bitty

## IVORIES
☐ tickle the ivories
## IVORY
☐ ivory tower
## JAB
☐ jab pop ☐ take a jab at someone
## JACK
☐ jack around ☐ jacked (out) ☐ jacked up ☐ jack someone around ☐ jack someone or something up ☐ jack-ups
## JACKET
☐ (yellow) jacket
## JACKPOT
☐ hit the jackpot
## JAG
☐ benny (jag) ☐ jag party
## JAI
☐ jai-by-jai
## JAIL
☐ in jail ☐ jail bait ☐ nail-em-and-jail-em ☐ (San Quentin) jail bait
## JAM
☐ in a jam ☐ jammed up ☐ (jim-)jams
## JAMAICAN
☐ Jamaican (gold)
## JANE
☐ Jane Doe ☐ Jane Q. Public ☐ Mary Jane
## JAY
☐ jay smoke ☐ Peter Jay ☐ unk-jay
## JAZZ
☐ all that jazz ☐ jazzed (up) ☐ jazz someone or something up
## JEEBIES
☐ heebie-jeebies
## JEEPERS
☐ Jeepers(-creepers)!
## JELLY
☐ jelly babies ☐ jelly shoes
## JERK
☐ jerk around ☐ jerk someone around ☐ knee-jerk ☐ tear-jerker
## JERRY
☐ jerry-built
## JESUS
☐ Jesus boots
## JET
☐ jet-set
## JIFFY
☐ in a jiff(y)
## JIG
☐ jig is up
## JIM
☐ (jim-)jams

**JINGLE**
□ whips and jingles □ whoops and jingles

**JIVE**
□ blow jive □ bull jive □ jive-ass □ jive talk □ jive turkey □ pitch jive □ pull jive

**JO**
□ ho-jo('s)

**JOB**
□ con job □ do a job on someone or something □ do a snow job on someone □ inside job □ land a job □ nose job □ put-up job □ snow job □ wall job

**JOBER**
□ jober as a sudge

**JOCK**
□ rock-jock □ video jock

**JOCKEY**
□ bench jockey □ desk jockey □ disc jockey □ disk jockey

**JOE**
□ good Joe □ holy Joe □ Joe Blow □ Joe Citizen □ Joe College □ Joe Doakes □ Joe Schmo □ Joe Six-pack □ Mighty Joe Young □ quality Joe

**JOHN**
□ big John □ blue Johnnies □ Dear John letter □ John Doe □ John Hancock □ Johnnie-come-lately □ Johnny-be-good □ Johnny Law □ John Q. Public □ square John □ who shot John

**JOHNSON**
□ johnson (grass)

**JOIN**
□ joined at the hip □ join up

**JOINT**
□ blast a joint □ blow the joint □ case the joint □ C-joint □ clip joint □ coke joint □ creep joint □ crystal joint □ get one's nose out of joint □ gyp joint □ heavy joint □ juice joint □ krystal joint □ put someone's nose out of joint □ square joint

**JOKE**
□ dirty joke

**JOLLY**
□ jolly-well

**JOLT**
□ pleasure jolt

**JONES**
□ skag jones

**JOY**
□ bundle of joy □ joy dust □ joy flakes □ joy juice □ joy pop □ joy popper □ joy powder □ joy ride □ joy rider □ joy smoke □ joy water □ joy weed

**JUDGE**
□ sober as a judge

**JUG**
□ federal jug □ jugged (up) □ jug man □ jug wine

**JUICE**
□ big juice □ B.O. juice □ cactus juice □ cow juice □ gorilla juice □ happy juice □ idiot juice □ joy juice □ juice and beans □ juiced (up) □ juice freak □ juice house □ juice joint □ juice racket □ juice something back □ jungle juice □ juniper juice □ moo juice □ on the juice □ tarantula juice □ tiger juice □ tornado juice

**JUMP**
□ Go jump in the lake! □ jump all over someone □ jump bail □ jump smooth □ jump start □ jump (street) □ jump the gun □ one jump ahead of someone or something □ puddle jumper □ Take a running jump (in the lake)!

**JUNGLE**
□ asphalt jungle □ jungle juice

**JUNIPER**
□ juniper juice

**JUNK**
□ junk bond □ junk connection □ junked (up) □ junker man □ junk food □ junk heap □ junk hog □ junk mail □ junk peddler □ junk pusher □ junk squad □ junk tank □ on the junk

**JUST**
□ just off the boat □ just the ticket □ just what the doctor ordered □ not just whistling Dixie

**KANGAROO**
□ kangaroo court

**KAUAI**
□ Kauai (electric)

**KEEN**
□ peachy (keen)

**KEEP**
□ for keeps □ If you can't stand the heat, keep out of the kitchen. □ keep cool □ Keep in touch. □ keep one's cool □ keep one's head right □ keep one's nose clean □ Keep on trucking. □ Keep out of this! □ Keep the faith

(baby)! ☐ Keep your hands to yourself. ☐ Keep your pants on! ☐ Keep your shirt on! ☐ play for keeps ☐ Where (have) you been keeping yourself?

**KEG**

☐ keg party

**KEN**

☐ Ken doll

**KENTUCKY**

☐ Kentucky blue ☐ Kentucky corn ☐ Kentucky fried

**KEY**

☐ church key ☐ keyed (up) ☐ key figure ☐ key grip ☐ low-key

**KIBOSH**

☐ put the kibosh on something

**KICK**

☐ alive and kicking ☐ for kicks ☐ get one's kick's (from someone or something) ☐ kick around ☐ kick back ☐ kick cold (turkey) ☐ kicked by a horse ☐ kick freak ☐ kick in the guts ☐ kick in the (seat of the) pants ☐ kick in the wrist ☐ kick man ☐ kick off ☐ kick party ☐ kick some ass (around) ☐ kick the bucket ☐ kick the habit ☐ kick up a storm

**KID**

☐ dead-end kid ☐ I kid you not. ☐ I'm not kidding. ☐ kid stuff ☐ kid-vid ☐ No kidding! ☐ snotnose(d) (kid) ☐ whiz kid

**KIDNEY**

☐ kidney-buster

**KILL**

☐ buzz-kill ☐ dressed to kill ☐ fill or kill ☐ killed (off) ☐ killer-diller ☐ killer weed ☐ lady-killer ☐ make a killing

**KILO**

☐ kilo brick

**KILTER**

☐ out of kilter

**KING**

☐ King Grod ☐ King Kong pills

**KINGDOM**

☐ kingdom weed ☐ until kingdom come

**KISS**

☐ baby-kisser ☐ fish-kiss ☐ French kiss ☐ kiss-ass ☐ kiss Mary ☐ kiss of death ☐ kiss off ☐ kiss someone or something off ☐ kiss someone's ass ☐ kiss something goodbye ☐ kiss the babe ☐ kiss the dust ☐ kiss the porcelain god ☐ kiss up to someone ☐ right in the kisser ☐ sealed with a kiss ☐ soul kiss

**KIT**

☐ head kit ☐ kit and caboodle

**KITCHEN**

☐ If you can't stand the heat, keep out of the kitchen.

**KITE**

☐ fly kites ☐ Go fly a kite!

**KITTEN**

☐ have kittens ☐ sex kitten

**KNEE**

☐ knee-deep in something ☐ knee-high to a grasshopper ☐ knee-jerk ☐ knee-slapper ☐ up to one's knees

**KNIFE**

☐ long knife

**KNOCK**

☐ knock around ☐ knock back a drink ☐ knock down something ☐ knocked in ☐ knocked out ☐ knocked up ☐ Knock it off! ☐ knock off (work) ☐ knock one over ☐ knock some heads together ☐ knock someone dead ☐ knock someone or something off ☐ knock someone or something out ☐ knock someone's block off ☐ knock someone some skin ☐ knock someone's socks off ☐ knock someone up ☐ knock something into a cocked hat ☐ knock something together ☐ knock the habit ☐ knock up ☐ You could have knocked me over with a feather.

**KNOCKDOWN**

☐ knockdown drag-out fight

**KNOT**

☐ tie the knot

**KNOW**

☐ Don't I know it! ☐ for all I know ☐ God only knows! ☐ I don't know. ☐ if one knows what's good for one ☐ in the know ☐ I wouldn't know. ☐ know all the angles ☐ know from something ☐ know-how ☐ know-it-all ☐ know the score ☐ know what's what ☐ know where it's at ☐ know where one is coming from ☐ know which end is up ☐ like, you know ☐ not know beans (about something) ☐ not know from nothing ☐ You don't know the half of it. ☐ you know ☐ you-know-what ☐ you-know-where ☐ you-know-who

## LEFT
☐ hang a left ☐ left-handed monkey wrench ☐ out in left field ☐ out of left field

## LEG
☐ Break a leg! ☐ have a leg up on someone ☐ leg work ☐ loop-legged ☐ on one's or its last legs ☐ peg-leg ☐ pull someone's leg ☐ shake a leg ☐ stretch one's legs

## LEGAL
☐ legal-beagle

## LEGREE
☐ Simon Legree

## LESS
☐ I couldn't care less.

## LET
☐ Let her rip! ☐ let it all hang out ☐ Let it roll! ☐ let off steam ☐ Let's do lunch (sometime). ☐ Let's have it! ☐ let something ride ☐ let's say

## LETTER
☐ bread and butter letter ☐ dead letter ☐ Dear John letter ☐ red-letter day

## LEVEL
☐ level best ☐ level with someone ☐ on the level

## LICK
☐ lick and a promise ☐ lick something into shape ☐ lick up a tab

## LICKETY
☐ lickety-split

## LICORICE
☐ licorice stick

## LID
☐ blow one's lid ☐ blow the lid off something ☐ lid proppers ☐ skid-lid

## LIE
☐ lie doggo ☐ No lie! ☐ pack of lies

## LIFE
☐ big as life (and twice as ugly) ☐ facts of life ☐ Get a life! ☐ large as life (and twice as ugly) ☐ low-life ☐ not on your life ☐ You bet your sweet life!

## LIFT
☐ lift one's elbow ☐ lift pill

## LIGHT
☐ fly light ☐ green light ☐ idiot light ☐ light artillery ☐ light bulb ☐ lighten up (on someone or something) ☐ light into someone ☐ lights out ☐ light stuff ☐ light up ☐ once over lightly ☐ out like a light ☐ punch someone's lights out ☐ put someone's lights out

## LIGHTNING
☐ greased lightning ☐ white lightning

## LIKE
☐ built like a brick outhouse ☐ come on like gangbusters ☐ drop someone or something like a hot potato ☐ go over like a lead balloon ☐ go through someone like a dose of the salts ☐ like a bat out of hell ☐ like a million (dollars) ☐ like a ton of bricks ☐ like crazy ☐ like death warmed over ☐ like gangbusters ☐ Like hell! ☐ Like it or lump it! ☐ like mad ☐ like nobody's business ☐ like stink ☐ like there was no tomorrow ☐ like, you know ☐ make like someone or something ☐ out like a light ☐ purr (like a cat) ☐ smell like a rose ☐ smoke like a chimney ☐ stick out like a sore thumb ☐ swear like a trooper ☐ talk like a nut ☐ tap dance like mad ☐ Tell it like it is.

## LILY
☐ lily-livered

## LIMIT
☐ go the limit ☐ sky's the limit

## LIMP
☐ limp dishrag

## LINE
☐ blow one's lines ☐ bottom line ☐ do a line ☐ fire a line ☐ go down the line ☐ hook, line, and sinker ☐ lay it on the line ☐ lay some sweet lines on someone ☐ line one's own pocket(s) ☐ out of line ☐ put some sweet lines on someone ☐ run down some lines ☐ stag line

## LINEN
☐ air one's dirty linen in public ☐ dirty linen ☐ wash one's dirty linen in public

## LING
☐ ding-a-ling

## LION
☐ lion's share

## LIP
☐ get lip ☐ latrine lips ☐ Read my lips! ☐ Watch my lips! ☐ Zip (up) your lip!

## LIQUID
☐ liquid cork ☐ liquid laugh

## LIQUOR
☐ hard liquor ☐ hold one's liquor

## LIST
☐ drop-dead list ☐ hit list ☐ laundry list ☐ shopping list ☐ sucker list ☐ want list ☐ wish list

**LISTEN**
- I'm listening. □ listen up

**LIT**
- half-lit

**LITTLE**
- have a little visitor □ little black book □ little boy blue □ little boys' room □ little girls' room □ (little) pinkie

**LIVE**
- all the way live □ beat the living daylights out of someone □ how the other half lives □ (live) wire □ where someone lives

**LIVERED**
- lily-livered

**LO**
- lo-res

**LOAD**
- carrying a (heavy) load □ dump one's load □ get a load off one's feet □ get a load off one's mind □ get a load of something or someone □ have a load on □ loaded for bear □ loaded question □ loaded remark □ loaded to the gills □ Sit down and take a load off your feet. □ three bricks shy of a load

**LOCAL**
- local yokel

**LOCK**
- goldie locks

**LOCO**
- plumb loco

**LONE**
- lone wolf

**LONESOME**
- all by one's lonesome

**LONG**
- long arm of the law □ long bread □ long dozen □ long green □ long knife □ long shot □ long story short □ long tall Sally □ Long time no see. □ over the long haul □ so long □ take the (long) count

**LOOK**
- come-hither look □ dirty look □ Here's looking at you. □ look after number one □ Look alive! □ look-see □ Look who's talking!

**LOONY**
- loony bin

**LOOP**
- fruit loop □ loop-legged □ throw someone for a loop

**LOOSE**
- at loose ends □ cut loose □ cut one's wolf loose □ hang loose □ have a loose screw □ have a screw loose □ loose cannon □ play fast and loose (with someone or something) □ stay loose □ tear loose (from someone or something)

**LORD**
- drug lord □ Lord love a duck!

**LOSE**
(See also LOST.) □ lose (all) one's marbles □ lose it □ lose one's cool □ lose one's doughnuts □ lose one's grip □ lose one's hold □ lose one's lunch □ lose one's shirt □ losing streak □ Win a few, lose a few.

**LOSER**
- two-time loser

**LOSS**
- cut one's losses

**LOST**
(See also LOSE.) □ Get lost! □ lost cause

**LOT**
- Lots of luck! □ take a lot of nerve

**LOTION**
- motion-lotion

**LOUD**
- For crying out loud! □ loud mouth

**LOUIE**
- hang a louie

**LOUSE**
- louse something up

**LOUSY**
- lousy with someone or something

**LOVE**
- For the love of Mike! □ (I) love it! □ Lord love a duck! □ love bombs □ love drug □ love handles □ love-in □ Love it! □ Love you! □ puppy love

**LOW**
- burn with a low blue flame □ low-blow □ low five □ low-key □ low-life □ low rent □ low-res □ straight low

**LUCK**
- Better luck next time. □ Lots of luck! □ luck of the draw □ luck out □ lucky dog □ out of luck □ rotten luck □ tough luck

**LUCRE**
- filthy lucre

**LUDE**
- luded out

**LUG**
- chug(-a-lug)

**LUMP**
- get one's lumps □ Like it or lump it! □ Lump it! □ take one's lumps

**LUNCH**
- blow lunch □ blow one's lunch □ free lunch □ launch (one's lunch) □ Let's do lunch (sometime). □ lose one's lunch □ out to lunch □ spot of lunch □ There's no such thing as a free lunch. □ toss one's lunch

**LUSH**
- lush hound □ lush house □ lush merchant □ lush up

**LUTELY**
- abso-bloody-lutely

**LUXURY**
- lap of luxury

**MAC**
- Big Mac attack □ mac out

**MACE**
- mace someone's face

**MACHU**
- Machu Picchu

**MACKEREL**
- Holy mackerel!

**MAD**
- boiling (mad) □ get mad (at something) □ hopping mad □ like mad □ mad money □ tap dance like mad

**MADE**
- have it made □ have it made in the shade □ tailor made

**MADISON**
- Madison Avenue

**MAGAZINE**
- girlie magazine

**MAGIC**
- magic bullet □ magic mushrooms □ magic pumpkin □ tragic-magic

**MAIL**
- junk mail

**MAIN**
- main drag □ main squeeze □ main stash

**MAKE**
- Don't make me laugh! □ make a boo-boo □ make a bundle □ make a buy □ make a federal case out of something □ make a killing □ Make a lap! □ make a meet □ make a pig of oneself □ make a pile □ make a score □ make a stink (about someone or something)
- make book on something □ make for somewhere □ make hamburger out of someone or something □ make it □ make (it) big □ make it hot for someone □ Make it snappy! □ make like someone or something □ make mincemeat out of someone or something □ Make my day! □ Make no mistake (about it)! □ make one's bed □ make oneself scarce □ make out □ make-out artist □ make the scene □ make tracks □ make waves □ make with the something □ on the make □ run a make on someone □ Want to make something of it? □ widow-maker

**MALE**
- male chauvinist pig

**MAMA**
- Bahama-mama □ go home to mama □ mama bear □ red-hot mama □ yo mama

**MAN**
- big man on campus □ boss man □ candy man □ cave man □ company man □ con man □ dead man □ dirty old man □ face man □ front man □ G-man □ good-time man □ headache man □ hit man □ jug man □ junker man □ kick man □ man on the street □ man-size(d) □ men in blue □ men's room □ my man □ old man □ one-man show □ point man □ repo man □ see a man about a dog □ So's your old man! □ stick man □ straight man □ strong-arm man □ tambourine man □ T-man □ wheel man □ You heard the man.

**MANHATTAN**
- Manhattan white

**MANIA**
- merger-mania

**MANY**
- one too many

**MAP**
- throw a map

**MARBLE**
- have all one's marbles □ lose (all) one's marbles □ marble dome □ marble orchard

**MARE**
- shank's mare

**MARINE**
- dead marine

## MARK
☐ easy mark ☐ mark time ☐ skid marks ☐ X marks the spot.

## MARKET
☐ at the market ☐ slave market ☐ spot market

## MARY
☐ Aunt Mary ☐ kiss Mary ☐ Mary Jane ☐ Mary Warner

## MASH
☐ mish-mash

## MATCH
☐ whole shooting match

## MATE
☐ label mate

## MAUI
☐ Maui Waui

## MAX
☐ grody to the max ☐ maxed out ☐ to the max

## MAYBE
☐ I don't mean maybe!

## MCCOY
☐ (real) McCoy

## MEAL
☐ square (meal)

## MEAN
☐ I don't mean maybe! ☐ lean and mean ☐ mean business ☐ mean-green

## MEAT
☐ all (that) meat and no potatoes ☐ dog meat ☐ meat wagon ☐ mystery meat

## MEDICINE
☐ snakebite medicine

## MEEMIE
☐ screaming-meemie

## MEET
☐ Fancy meeting you here. ☐ make a meet ☐ meeting of the minds ☐ nice meeting you

## MELL
☐ mell of a hess

## MELLOW
☐ mellow out

## MENTAL
☐ mental giant ☐ mental midget

## MEOW
☐ cat's meow

## MERCHANT
☐ lush merchant ☐ speed merchant

## MERCY
☐ mercy buckets

## MERGER
☐ merger-mania

## MESS
☐ hell of a mess ☐ mess around (with someone or something) ☐ messed up ☐ mess someone or something up ☐ mess someone's face up ☐ mess up ☐ mess with someone or something ☐ messy bucket(s)

## MESSAGE
☐ Get the message?

## METAL
☐ heavy metal ☐ put the pedal to the metal

## METH
☐ meth freak ☐ meth monster

## MEXICAN
☐ Mexican breakfast ☐ Mexican brown ☐ Mexican bush ☐ Mexican mud ☐ Mexican standoff

## MI
☐ do-re-mi

## MICKEY
☐ Mickey D's ☐ Mickey finished ☐ Mickey (Finn) ☐ mickey mouse ☐ mickey mouse ears ☐ mickey mouse habit ☐ slip someone a Mickey

## MIDDLE
☐ middle brow ☐ middle of nowhere ☐ smack (dab) in the middle

## MIDGET
☐ mental midget

## MIGHTY
☐ Mighty Joe Young

## MIKE
☐ For the love of Mike!

## MILK
☐ tiger milk

## MILL
☐ fill-mill ☐ gin mill ☐ run-of-the-mill ☐ through the mill

## MILLION
☐ like a million (dollars)

## MILQUETOAST
☐ Casper Milquetoast

## MILWAUKEE
☐ Milwaukee goiter

## MINCEMEAT
☐ make mincemeat out of someone or something

## MIND
☐ blow someone's mind ☐ dirty-minded ☐ get a load off one's mind ☐ have one's mind in the gutter ☐ meeting of

the minds □ mind-bender □ mind your own beeswax □ never mind □ no never mind □ one-track mind

**MINE**

□ back to the salt mines □ sit on a gold mine

**MIRROR**

□ done by mirrors □ smoke and mirrors

**MISH**

□ mish-mash

**MISS**

□ Good golly, Miss Molly! □ miss a trick □ miss the boat

**MISTAKE**

□ Make no mistake (about it)!

**MIX**

□ mixed (up) □ mix it up (with someone)

**MO**

□ black mo

**MOAT**

□ black moat

**MOBILE**

□ nerd mobile

**MOD**

□ mod poser

**MOIST**

□ moist around the edges

**MOJO**

□ on the mojo

**MOLDY**

□ moldy fig

**MOLEY**

□ Holy moley!

**MOLLY**

□ Good golly, Miss Molly!

**MONEY**

□ color of someone's money □ easy money □ folding money □ front money □ funny-money □ heavy money □ hush money □ mad money □ money from home □ money grubber □ money talks □ on the money □ pinched (for money) □ pressed (for money) □ pull down an amount of money □ pushed (for money) □ push money □ Put your money where your mouth is! □ shell out (an amount of money) □ smart money □ soft money □ spending money □ throw money at something □ tight money

**MONKEY**

□ grease monkey □ have a monkey on one's back □ left-handed monkey wrench □ monkey around (with someone or something) □ monkey bait □ monkey bite □ monkey business □ monkey swill □ monkey talk □ monkey wagon □ monkey wards □ monkey with someone or something □ powder monkey

**MONSTER**

□ meth monster □ monster weed

**MONTEZUMA**

□ Montezuma's revenge

**MONTH**

□ in a month of Sundays

**MOO**

□ moo juice

**MOON**

□ full moon □ half moon □ once in a blue moon

**MOONLIGHT**

□ moonlight requisition

**MOP**

□ Earp slop, bring the mop. □ mopping-up operation □ mop up the floor with someone □ That's the way the mop flops.

**MORE**

□ More power to you! □ more than one bargained for

**MORNING**

□ morning after (the night before)

**MOSS**

□ house moss

**MOST**

□ firstest with the mostest

**MOTHER**

□ mother nature

**MOTION**

□ motion-lotion

**MOTOR**

□ get someone's motor running □ motor-mouth

**MOUNTAIN**

□ (mountain) dew □ rocky mountain canary

**MOUNTY**

□ county-mounty

**MOUSE**

□ mickey mouse □ mickey mouse ears □ mickey mouse habit

**MOUTH**

□ another mouth to feed □ bad-mouth □ big mouth □ diarrhea of the mouth □ dirty mouth □ foot-in-mouth disease □ foul mouth □ garbage mouth

**NELLIE**
☐ nervous Nellie
**NERD**
☐ nerd mobile ☐ nerd pack
**NERVE**
☐ bundle of nerves ☐ Of all the nerve!
☐ take a lot of nerve ☐ What (a) nerve!
**NERVOUS**
☐ nervous Nellie
**NEST**
☐ empty-nesters ☐ nest egg
**NET**
☐ net result
**NEVER**
☐ never mind ☐ no never mind
**NEW**
☐ bad news ☐ (brand) spanking new
☐ New York's finest ☐ spanking new
☐ That's a new one on me. ☐ What else
is new? ☐ What's new? ☐ whole new
ball game
**NEXT**
☐ Better luck next time.
**NICE**
☐ Have a nice day. ☐ Mr. Nice Guy
☐ nice meeting you ☐ nice talking to
you
**NICK**
☐ full of Old Nick
**NICKEL**
☐ double nickels ☐ nickel and dime
someone (to death) ☐ nickel (bag) ☐
not worth a plugged nickel
**NIGHT**
☐ all-nighter ☐ fly-by-night ☐ morning after (the night before) ☐ night
person ☐ one-night stand ☐ Saturday
night special
**NINE**
☐ dressed to the nines ☐ nine-to-five
☐ whole nine yards
**NINETEENTH**
☐ nineteenth hole
**NINNY**
☐ bliss ninny
**NIP**
☐ nip and tuck
**NIT**
☐ nit-picker ☐ nit-picking
**NITTY**
☐ get down to the nitty-gritty ☐ nitty-
gritty
**NO**
☐ ain't no good nohow ☐ all (that)

meat and no potatoes ☐ cigarette with
no name ☐ Close, but no cigar. ☐ cut
no ice (with someone) ☐ feeling no
pain ☐ like there was no tomorrow ☐
Long time no see. ☐ Make no mistake
(about it)! ☐ no-account ☐ no bargain
☐ no big deal ☐ no biggie ☐ no can do
☐ no dice ☐ no earthly reason ☐ no
end of something ☐ No fair! ☐ no flies
on someone ☐ no-frills ☐ no go ☐
no-good ☐ no-goodnik ☐ no great shakes
☐ no holds barred ☐ No kidding! ☐
No lie! ☐ no never mind ☐ no-no ☐
No nukes! ☐ no sale ☐ no show ☐ No
siree! ☐ no soap ☐ no stress ☐ no
sweat ☐ No way! ☐ no-win situation
☐ see no further than the end of one's
nose ☐ There's no such thing as a free
lunch.
**NOBODY**
☐ like nobody's business ☐ There's
nobody home.
**NOD**
☐ get the nod ☐ give someone the nod
☐ nodded out ☐ on the nod
**NOGGIN**
☐ Use your noggin!
**NOHOW**
☐ ain't no good nohow
**NOISE**
☐ big noise
**NON**
☐ non compos poopoo
**NONE**
☐ none of someone's beeswax
**NOODLE**
☐ Use your noodle! ☐ wet noodle
**NOSE**
☐ brown-nose ☐ brown-noser ☐ get
one's nose cold ☐ get one's nose out of
joint ☐ hard-nosed ☐ keep one's nose
clean ☐ nose-burner ☐ nose (candy) ☐
nose habit ☐ nose hit ☐ nose job ☐
nose-warmer ☐ on the nose ☐ powder
one's nose ☐ put one's nose in (where
it's not wanted) ☐ put someone's nose
out of joint ☐ rub someone's nose in
something ☐ see no further than the
end of one's nose ☐ stick one's nose in
(where it's not wanted) ☐ take it through
the nose ☐ turn up one's nose at someone or something
**NOSEBAG**
☐ put on the nosebag ☐ tie on the
nosebag

Tell me another (one)! □ That's a new one on me. □ tie one on □ wet one

**ONLY**

□ God only knows! □ one and only □ only way to go

**ONTO**

□ onto a good thing □ onto someone or something □ turn onto someone or something

**OOPS**

□ Oops-a-daisy!

**OPEN**

□ blow something wide open □ bust someone's head open □ bust something wide open □ crack open a bottle □ eye-opener □ open and above board □ wide open □ with (one's) eyes (wide) open

**OPERA**

□ horse opera

**OPERATION**

□ mopping-up operation

**OPERATOR**

□ big-time operator □ smooth operator

**OPPORTUNITY**

□ golden opportunity

**ORBIT**

□ go into orbit □ in orbit

**ORCHARD**

□ bone orchard □ marble orchard

**ORDER**

□ doctor's orders □ just what the doctor ordered □ tall order

**ORK**

□ ork-orks

**OTHER**

□ how the other half lives

**OUTHOUSE**

□ built like a brick outhouse

**OUTS**

□ ins and outs □ on the outs (with someone)

**OUTSIDE**

□ step outside □ You want to step outside?

**OVER**

□ chew something over □ done over □ drool (all) over someone or something □ fork something over □ frosted (over) □ get something over (to someone) □ give someone a (good) working over □ go ape (over someone or something) □ going over □ go over big □ go over like a lead balloon □ go over the hill □ go over the wall □ hand over fist □ jump all over someone □ knock one over □ like death warmed over □ once-over □ once over lightly □ over and unders □ over easy □ over my dead body □ over one's head □ over-the-counter □ over the hill □ over the hump □ over the long haul □ paper over something □ part that went over the fence last □ screw someone over □ till hell freezes over □ turn over □ warmed over □ work someone over □ You could have knocked me over with a feather.

**OVERBOARD**

□ go overboard

**OWE**

□ I owe you one.

**OWN**

□ blow one's own horn □ cut one's own throat □ devil's own time □ do one's (own) thing □ line one's own pocket(s) □ mind your own beeswax □ on one's own hook □ talk to hear one's own voice □ toot one's own horn

**OX**

□ dumb ox

**OYSTER**

□ world is one's oyster

**OZONE**

□ in the ozone

**PACE**

□ at a snail's pace

**PACK**

□ body-packer □ Joe Six-pack □ nerd pack □ packed up □ pack of lies □ six-pack

**PACKAGE**

□ package deal

**PAD**

□ crash pad □ pad out

**PADDLE**

□ up the creek (without a paddle)

**PADDY**

□ paddy wagon

**PAGE**

□ take a page from someone's book

**PAIN**

□ feeling no pain □ give someone a pain □ pain in the ass □ pain in the butt □ pain in the neck □ pain in the rear

**PAINT**
- ☐ Do I have to paint (you) a picture?
- ☐ paint remover ☐ paint the town (red) ☐ tonsil paint ☐ war paint

**PAL**
- ☐ pal around (with someone)

**PALACE**
- ☐ ptomaine-palace

**PALLY**
- ☐ pally (with someone)

**PALM**
- ☐ grease someone's palm ☐ oil someone's palm ☐ palm-oil ☐ palm-presser ☐ palm someone or something off (on someone)

**PALSY**
- ☐ palsy-walsy

**PAMBY**
- ☐ namby-pamby

**PAN**
- ☐ pan out

**PANIC**
- ☐ hit the panic button ☐ press the panic button ☐ push the panic button

**PANKY**
- ☐ hanky-panky

**PANTS**
- ☐ bore the pants off (of) someone ☐ dust someone's pants ☐ have ants in one's pants ☐ Keep your pants on! ☐ kick in the (seat of the) pants ☐ pants rabbits ☐ scare the pants off someone ☐ smarty-pants ☐ sue the pants off (of) someone ☐ wear the pants (in the house)

**PAPER**
- ☐ bad paper ☐ green paper ☐ hot paper ☐ paper-hanger ☐ paper over something ☐ paper-pusher ☐ walking papers

**PARACHUTE**
- ☐ golden parachute

**PARADE**
- ☐ rain on someone's parade

**PARDON**
- ☐ (I) beg (your) pardon. ☐ if you'll pardon the expression ☐ Pardon my French.

**PARENTAL**
- ☐ (parental) units

**PARK**
- ☐ ball park estimate ☐ park it (somewhere)

**PARKER**
- ☐ nosy parker

**PARLOR**
- ☐ sauce parlor

**PART**
- ☐ parting shot ☐ part that went over the fence last

**PARTY**
- ☐ certain party ☐ coke party ☐ free base party ☐ grass party ☐ hen party ☐ jag party ☐ keg party ☐ kick party ☐ party animal ☐ party bowl ☐ party-hearty ☐ party-pooper ☐ petting-party ☐ pot party ☐ stag-party ☐ tailgate party ☐ tea party

**PASA**
- ☐ Que pasa?

**PASS**
- ☐ cut someone off at the pass ☐ gas-passer ☐ head someone off at the pass ☐ pass go ☐ pass the buck

**PASSION**
- ☐ passion-pit

**PASTE**
- ☐ paste someone one

**PAT**
- ☐ stand pat (on something)

**PATOOTIE**
- ☐ (sweet) patootie ☐ You bet your sweet patootie!

**PATROL**
- ☐ bush patrol

**PATTER**
- ☐ patter of tiny feet

**PAY**
- ☐ have hell to pay ☐ hit pay dirt ☐ pay a call ☐ pay one's dues ☐ strike pay dirt ☐ There will be hell to pay.

**PEACE**
- ☐ peace pill

**PEACH**
- ☐ peachy (keen)

**PEANUT**
- ☐ for peanuts

**PEDAL**
- ☐ put the pedal to the metal ☐ soft pedal something

**PEDDLE**
- ☐ junk peddler

**PEEP**
- ☐ another peep (out of you)

**PEEVE**
- ☐ pet peeve

**PEG**
- ☐ peg-leg ☐ square peg (in a round hole)

**PENCIL**
- [ ] pencil-pusher

**PENNY**
- [ ] penny-ante [ ] penny-pincher [ ] pretty penny

**PEOPLE**
- [ ] people-watching [ ] street people

**PEP**
- [ ] pepped (up) [ ] pep pill [ ] pep talk

**PEPPER**
- [ ] pepper-upper [ ] salt and pepper

**PERCENTER**
- [ ] ten percenter

**PERK**
- [ ] perked (up)

**PERSON**
- [ ] day person [ ] night person

**PET**
- [ ] pet peeve [ ] petting-party

**PETE**
- [ ] For Pete's sake!

**PETER**
- [ ] Peter Jay [ ] peter out

**PEYOTE**
- [ ] peyote (button)

**PHEASANT**
- [ ] crotch-pheasant

**PHONE**
- [ ] talk on the big white phone

**PHONY**
- [ ] phony as a three-dollar bill

**PICCHU**
- [ ] Machu Picchu

**PICK**
- [ ] cotton-picker [ ] cotton-picking [ ] nit-picker [ ] nit-picking [ ] pick-me-up [ ] pick up on something

**PICTURE**
- [ ] Do I have to paint (you) a picture? [ ] Get the picture? [ ] out of the picture [ ] take pictures

**PIDDLE**
- [ ] piddle (around)

**PIE**
- [ ] cutie pie [ ] pie-eyed [ ] pie-in-the-sky [ ] sweetie-pie

**PIECE**
- [ ] abbreviated piece of nothing [ ] piece of cake [ ] piece (of the action) [ ] think-piece

**PIG**
- [ ] make a pig of oneself [ ] male chauvinist pig [ ] pig heaven [ ] pig in a poke [ ] pig out

**PIGEON**
- [ ] clay pigeon [ ] pigeon-eyed [ ] stool (pigeon)

**PILE**
- [ ] make a pile

**PILL**
- [ ] bank bandit pills [ ] booster pill [ ] courage pill [ ] gangster pill [ ] go-pills [ ] gorilla pills [ ] happy pills [ ] idiot pills [ ] King Kong pills [ ] lift pill [ ] on the pill [ ] peace pill [ ] pep pill [ ] pill-popper [ ] pill-pusher [ ] poison pill [ ] punk pills [ ] thrill-pills

**PILLAR**
- [ ] send someone from pillar to post

**PILOT**
- [ ] sky-pilot

**PIN**
- [ ] pin someone's ears back

**PINCH**
- [ ] in a pinch [ ] penny-pincher [ ] pinched (for money) [ ] pinched (for time) [ ] pinch hitter

**PINK**
- [ ] gay as pink ink [ ] in the pink [ ] (little) pinkie [ ] pink elephants [ ] pink ladies [ ] pink slip [ ] pink-slipped [ ] pink spiders [ ] seeing pink elephants [ ] tickled (pink)

**PINT**
- [ ] pint-sized

**PIP**
- [ ] pipped (up)

**PIPE**
- [ ] hash pipe [ ] hit the pipe [ ] pipe down [ ] pipe dream [ ] Put that in your pipe and smoke it! [ ] set of pipes [ ] take the pipe [ ] toke pipe

**PIPELINE**
- [ ] in the pipeline

**PISS**
- [ ] piss-ant [ ] piss-ant around [ ] pissed (off) [ ] piss elegant [ ] piss factory [ ] piss poor [ ] piss someone off

**PIT**
- [ ] bottomless pit [ ] passion-pit [ ] pit stop

**PITCH**
- [ ] pitch a bitch [ ] pitch in (and help) [ ] pitch jive [ ] pitch (the) woo

**PITCHFORKS**
- [ ] rain pitchforks

**PITY**
- [ ] For pity's sake!

the porcelain bus ☐ worship the porcelain god

**PORES**

☐ air one's pores

**PORK**

☐ pork out

**POSER**

☐ mod poser

**POSILUTELY**

☐ absotively (posilutely)

**POST**

☐ between you, me, and the lamp post
☐ send someone from pillar to post

**POT**

☐ pot boiler ☐ pot brownies ☐ pot bust ☐ pot culture ☐ pot hound ☐ pot out ☐ pot party ☐ pot sniffer ☐ potted (up) ☐ sex pot ☐ up pot

**POTATO**

☐ all (that) meat and no potatoes ☐ couch potato ☐ drop someone or something like a hot potato ☐ hot potato ☐ potato soup ☐ small potatoes ☐ sweet potato

**POTTY**

☐ potty mouth

**POUND**

☐ gravel-pounder ☐ ground-pounder ☐ pound a beer ☐ pound one's ear ☐ pound someone's head in ☐ pound something out ☐ pound the books

**POUR**

☐ pour cold water on something

**POW**

☐ pow-wow

**POWDER**

☐ chicken powder ☐ joy powder ☐ powdered (up) ☐ powder monkey ☐ powder one's nose ☐ powder room ☐ powder up ☐ take a powder

**POWER**

☐ in power ☐ More power to you! ☐ power hitter ☐ power house ☐ power tool

**PRAY**

☐ pray to the porcelain god

**PRESS**

☐ flesh-presser ☐ palm-presser ☐ pressed (for money) ☐ pressed (for time) ☐ press (the) flesh ☐ press the panic button

**PRETTY**

☐ pretty penny ☐ sitting pretty

**PRIME**

☐ primed to the ears

**PRIMO**

☐ (el) primo

**PRIVATE**

☐ private eye

**PROCTOR**

☐ Proctor and Gamble

**PROD**

☐ on the prod

**PROMISE**

☐ lick and a promise

**PROOF**

☐ goof-proof

**PROP**

☐ lid proppers

**PROUD**

☐ do oneself proud

**PROWL**

☐ on the prowl

**PRUNE**

☐ full of prunes

**PSYCH**

☐ psyched (out) ☐ psyched (up) ☐ psych out ☐ psych someone out ☐ psych someone up

**PTOMAINE**

☐ ptomaine-domain ☐ ptomaine-palace

**PUBLIC**

☐ air one's dirty linen in public ☐ go public ☐ Jane Q. Public ☐ John Q. Public ☐ take something public ☐ wash one's dirty linen in public

**PUCKY**

☐ bull-pucky

**PUDDLE**

☐ puddle jumper

**PUFF**

☐ cream puff ☐ puff the dust

**PUG**

☐ pug-ugly

**PUKE**

☐ angel puke

**PULL**

☐ pull a boner ☐ pull a fast one ☐ pull down an amount of money ☐ pull jive ☐ pull one's belt in (a notch) ☐ pull one's punches ☐ pull out all the stops ☐ pull someone's leg ☐ pull something off ☐ pull the plug (on someone or something)

**PUMP**

☐ pumped (up) ☐ pump ship ☐ pump something up ☐ skin pumping

**PUMPKIN**
☐ magic pumpkin ☐ some pumpkins
**PUNCH**
☐ get one's ticket punched ☐ pull one's punches ☐ punch-drunk ☐ punch someone out ☐ punch someone's lights out ☐ rabbit punch ☐ roundhouse punch ☐ Sunday punch ☐ telegraph one's punches ☐ throw a punch
**PUNK**
☐ plastic punk ☐ punk out ☐ punk pills
**PUPPY**
☐ puppy love
**PURE**
☐ pure and simple
**PURPLE**
☐ (purple) haze
**PURPOSE**
☐ accidentally-on-purpose
**PURR**
☐ purr (like a cat)
**PUSH**
☐ cookie pusher ☐ if push comes to shove ☐ junk pusher ☐ paper-pusher ☐ pencil-pusher ☐ pill-pusher ☐ pushed (for money) ☐ pushed (for time) ☐ pushing up daisies ☐ push money ☐ push off ☐ push shorts ☐ push the panic button ☐ street pusher ☐ when push comes to shove
**PUSS**
☐ glamour puss
**PUSSY**
☐ wood-pussy
**PUSSYFOOT**
☐ pussyfoot (around)
**PUT**
☐ put a con on someone ☐ put a damper on something ☐ put balls on something ☐ put-down ☐ put hair on someone's chest ☐ put in a plug (for someone or something) ☐ put in one's oar ☐ put-on ☐ put oneself straight ☐ put one's nose in (where it's not wanted) ☐ put on the dog ☐ put on the feedbag ☐ put on the nosebag ☐ put on the ritz ☐ put some distance between someone and someone or something ☐ put someone on ☐ put someone or something away ☐ put someone or something out of the way ☐ put someone's lights out ☐ put someone's nose out of joint ☐ put someone to bed with

a shovel ☐ put someone up ☐ put some sweet lines on someone ☐ put something across ☐ put something on the street ☐ Put that in your pipe and smoke it! ☐ put the arm on someone ☐ put the bite on someone ☐ put the chill on someone ☐ put the finger on someone ☐ put the freeze on someone ☐ put the heat on someone ☐ put the kibosh on something ☐ put the moves on someone ☐ put the pedal to the metal ☐ put the screws on someone ☐ put the skids under someone or something ☐ put the squeeze on someone ☐ put to bed with a shovel ☐ put to it ☐ put-up job ☐ Put up or shut up! ☐ Put your money where your mouth is!
**PUTT**
☐ putt-putt
**PUTTY**
☐ silly putty
**PUTZ**
☐ putz around
**QUAFF**
☐ quaff a brew
**QUAIL**
☐ Canadian quail
**QUALITY**
☐ quality Joe
**QUE**
☐ Que pasa?
**QUEEN**
☐ campus queen ☐ ice queen
**QUEER**
☐ queer as a three-dollar bill ☐ queer-beer ☐ queer fish ☐ queer for something
**QUENTIN**
☐ (San Quentin) jail bait
**QUESTION**
☐ loaded question ☐ pop the question ☐ sixty-four-dollar question
**QUICK**
☐ quick-and-dirty ☐ quick buck ☐ quicker than hell ☐ quick fix ☐ quick one
**QUIT**
☐ quit while one is ahead
**QUOTE**
☐ cuff quote ☐ quote, unquote
**RABBIT**
☐ pants rabbits ☐ rabbit food ☐ rabbit punch

**RACE**
□ racing slicks □ rat race
**RACK**
□ racked (up) □ rack (out) □ rack something up □ rack time □ rack up
**RACKET**
□ juice racket
**RAD**
□ way rad
**RAG**
□ chew the rag □ glad rags □ rag out □ talk someone ragged □ wet rag
**RAH**
□ rah-rah
**RAILROAD**
□ railroad tracks □ run a railroad
**RAIN**
□ rain on someone's parade □ rain pitchforks □ right as rain
**RAISE**
□ raise a stink (about someone or something) □ raise Cain □ raise hell □ raise the devil (with someone or something)
**RAKE**
□ rake in something
**RALPH**
□ hang a ralph □ ralph something up
**RAM**
□ ram something down someone's throat
**RAN**
□ also-ran
**RANK**
□ rank and file □ rank someone (out)
**RAP**
□ bad rap □ bum rap □ rap session □ (rap) sheet □ take the rap (for something)
**RARE**
□ in rare form □ rare bird □ rare old time □ raring to go
**RASPBERRY**
□ give someone the raspberry
**RAT**
□ frat-rat □ rat around □ rat fink □ rat (on someone) □ rat out □ rat race □ rug rat □ sack rat □ smell a rat
**RATCHET**
□ ratchet-mouth
**RATE**
□ cut-rate □ first-rate
**RATTLE**
□ rattle-trap □ slightly rattled
**RAW**
□ raw deal

**RAY**
□ bag some rays □ catch some rays
**RAZZLE**
□ razzle-dazzle
**RE**
□ do-re-mi □ re-up
**REACH**
□ reach for the sky
**REACTION**
□ gut reaction (to something)
**READ**
□ Read my lips!
**READY**
□ Are you ready for this? □ rough and ready
**REAL**
□ for real □ Get real! □ real bitch □ real gone □ (real) McCoy
**REAM**
□ ream someone out
**REAR**
□ get off one's rear □ pain in the rear □ rear (end) □ rear-ender
**REASON**
□ no earthly reason
**RED**
□ border (red) □ Cambodian red □ Chinese red □ paint the town (red) □ red devils □ red hot □ red-hot mama □ red ink □ red-letter day □ red tape □ see red
**REINVENT**
□ reinvent the wheel
**REMARK**
□ loaded remark □ snide remark
**REMOVER**
□ paint remover
**RENT**
□ low rent □ room for rent
**REPELLENT**
□ shark repellent
**REPO**
□ repo man
**REPUBLIC**
□ banana republic
**REQUISITION**
□ moonlight requisition
**RES**
□ high-res □ hi-res □ lo-res □ low-res
**REST**
□ Give it a rest! □ Give me a rest!
**RESULT**
□ net result

**REV**
☐ rev something up
**REVENGE**
☐ Montezuma's revenge
**RHYME**
☐ run one's rhymes
**RIB**
☐ rib-tickler
**RICH**
☐ filthy rich ☐ stinking rich ☐ strike it rich ☐ too rich for someone's blood
**RIDE**
☐ free ride ☐ go for a sleigh ride ☐ joy ride ☐ joy rider ☐ let something ride ☐ ride shotgun ☐ ride the porcelain bus ☐ take a sleigh ride ☐ thumb a ride
**RIGHT**
☐ all right ☐ (bang) (dead) to rights ☐ dead to rights ☐ get one right here ☐ get right ☐ hang a right ☐ have someone dead to rights ☐ keep one's head right ☐ Mr. Right ☐ right as rain ☐ right guy ☐ right in the kisser ☐ right up one's alley ☐ sail (right) through something ☐ serve someone right ☐ sit right (with someone) ☐ step right up ☐ straighten up and fly right
**RING**
☐ (dead) ringer (for someone) ☐ ring a bell ☐ ringer (for someone) ☐ ring off the hook ☐ ring the bell ☐ throw one's hat in the ring
**RINGTAILED**
☐ ringtailed snorter
**RINKY**
☐ rinky-dink
**RIP**
☐ Let her rip! ☐ on a rip ☐ rip-off ☐ rip-off artist ☐ rip on someone ☐ ripped (up) ☐ rip snorter ☐ rip someone or something off
**RISE**
☐ Rise and shine!
**RITZ**
☐ put on the ritz
**RIVER**
☐ send someone up the river ☐ up the river
**ROACH**
☐ roach clip ☐ roach-coach
**ROAD**
☐ get the show on the road ☐ hit the road ☐ one for the road ☐ on the road ☐ road apple ☐ road hog ☐ wide place in the road

**ROAR**
☐ dull roar
**ROAST**
☐ roasting-ear wine
**ROB**
☐ rob someone blind
**ROBBERY**
☐ highway robbery
**ROCK**
☐ acid rock ☐ between a rock and a hard place ☐ get one's rocks off (on something) ☐ have rocks in one's head ☐ on the rocks ☐ rock bottom ☐ rock-jock ☐ rock out ☐ rocky mountain canary ☐ walking on rocky socks
**ROCKER**
☐ off one's rocker
**ROCKET**
☐ rocket ship
**ROD**
☐ (hot) rod ☐ wrinkle-rod
**ROLL**
☐ drop a roll ☐ heads will roll ☐ high roller ☐ Let it roll! ☐ on a roll ☐ pop a roll ☐ roll in ☐ rolling buzz ☐ rolling in it ☐ rolling in the aisles ☐ tootsie roll
**ROOF**
☐ hit the roof
**ROOM**
☐ gab room ☐ ladies' room ☐ little boys' room ☐ little girls' room ☐ men's room ☐ powder room ☐ room for rent ☐ rumpus room ☐ smoke-filled room ☐ throne room
**ROOT**
☐ rooting-tooting
**ROPE**
☐ rope someone in
**ROSE**
☐ bed of roses ☐ smell like a rose
**ROT**
☐ crotch-rot ☐ Rots of ruck! ☐ rotten apple ☐ rotten egg ☐ rotten luck ☐ rotten to the core ☐ software rot ☐ spoiled rotten
**ROUGH**
☐ diamond in the rough ☐ rough and ready ☐ rough and tumble ☐ rough it ☐ rough someone up ☐ rough stuff ☐ rough time
**ROULETTE**
☐ Vatican roulette

**ROUND**
□ pop round (for a visit) □ round the bend □ round tripper □ square peg (in a round hole)

**ROUNDHOUSE**
□ roundhouse punch

**ROUNDUP**
□ last roundup

**ROW**
□ skid row □ skid row bum □ tough row to hoe

**RUB**
□ rub someone out □ rub someone's nose in something

**RUBBER**
□ burn rubber □ lay rubber □ rubber (check) □ rubber sock

**RUCK**
□ Rots of ruck!

**RUG**
□ rug rat □ sky rug

**RUMMED**
□ rummed (up)

**RUMOR**
□ latrine rumor

**RUMPUS**
□ rumpus room

**RUN**
(See also *RAN*.) □ cut and run □ front runner □ get someone's motor running □ have a run-in (with someone or something) □ on the run □ run a make on someone □ run amok □ run a railroad □ run down some lines □ run hog-wild □ run-in □ run it down □ run off □ run off at the mouth □ run-of-the-mill □ run on all cylinders □ run one's rhymes □ run out of gas □ run scared □ run someone in □ Run that by (me) again. □ run-up □ Take a running jump (in the lake)! □ turn tail (and run)

**RUSH**
□ bum's rush

**RUST**
□ rust belt □ rust bucket □ rusty-dusty

**RUSTLER**
□ cattle-rustler

**RUTH**
□ cry ruth

**SACK**
□ fart sack □ get the sack □ hit the sack □ sacked out □ sack out □ sack rat □ sack time □ sad sack □ second sacker

**SACRED**
□ sacred mushrooms

**SAD**
□ sad sack

**SADDLE**
□ saddled with someone or something □ tall in the saddle

**SAFE**
□ on the safe side

**SAIL**
□ clear sailing □ sail into someone □ sail (right) through something □ take the wind out of someone's sails

**SAKE**
□ For Pete's sake! □ For pity's sake!

**SALE**
□ no sale

**SALLY**
□ long tall Sally

**SALT**
□ back to the salt mines □ go through someone like a dose of the salts □ salt and pepper □ salt horse □ worth one's salt

**SAM**
□ Sam and Dave □ Uncle (Sam) □ What in (the) Sam Hill? □ Where in (the) Sam Hill?

**SAME**
□ on the same wavelength □ same difference □ same here □ same old story □ same o' same o' □ tarred with the same brush

**SAN**
□ San Francisco bomb □ (San Quentin) jail bait

**SANDWICH**
□ dagwood (sandwich) □ knuckle sandwich

**SATURDAY**
□ Saturday night special

**SAUCE**
□ on the sauce □ sauce parlor

**SAVE**
□ saved by the bell □ Save it!

**SAW**
□ sawed-off

**SAWBUCK**
□ double saw(buck)

**SAY**
□ I hear what you are saying. □ let's say □ Say cheese! □ Says me! □ say-so □ Says who? □ Says you! □ say uncle □ Say what? □ Smile when you say

that. □ That's what I say. □ What do you say? □ What say? □ You can say that again! □ You said a mouthful. □ You said it!

**SCAM**
□ What's the scam?

**SCANDAL**
□ scandal sheet

**SCARCE**
□ make oneself scarce

**SCARE**
□ run scared □ scared shitless □ scared stiff □ scare someone or something up □ scare the hell out of someone □ scare the pants off someone

**SCARF**
□ scarf out □ scarf something down

**SCENARIO**
□ worst-case scenario

**SCENE**
□ heavy scene □ make the scene

**SCHIZ**
□ schiz out

**SCHMANCY**
□ fancy-schmancy

**SCHMEAR**
□ whole schmear

**SCHMO**
□ Joe Schmo

**SCHNOZZLED**
□ all schnozzled up

**SCHOOLBOY**
□ schoolboy Scotch

**SCOOPER**
□ pooper-scooper

**SCOPE**
□ scope on someone □ scope someone □ scope someone out

**SCORE**
□ have a score to settle (with someone) □ know the score □ make a score □ score a connection □ settle a score (with someone)

**SCOTCH**
□ schoolboy Scotch

**SCOTT**
□ Great Scott!

**SCRAMBLE**
□ scrambled eggs

**SCRAPE**
□ scrape the bottom of the barrel

**SCRATCH**
□ scratch sheet □ up to scratch

**SCREAM**
□ scream bloody murder □ screaming-meemie

**SCREECH**
□ screeching (drunk)

**SCREW**
□ have a loose screw □ have a screw loose □ put the screws on someone □ screw around □ screw around with someone or something □ screwed, blued, and tattooed □ screwed up □ screw someone or something up □ screw someone out of something □ screw someone over □ screw up

**SCROUNGE**
□ scrounge around (for someone or something) □ scrounge someone or something up

**SCUM**
□ pond scum

**SCUPPER**
□ scupper up

**SCUZZ**
□ scuzz someone out

**SEAL**
□ sealed (up) □ sealed with a kiss

**SEAM**
□ seam-squirrels

**SEARCH**
□ Search me. □ skin-search □ strip-search

**SEAT**
□ hot seat □ in the catbird seat □ in the driver's seat □ kick in the (seat of the) pants

**SECOND**
□ Don't give it a second thought. □ second fiddle □ second sacker

**SEE**
□ Long time no see. □ look-see □ see a man about a dog □ see eye to eye □ seeing pink elephants □ seen better days □ see no further than the end of one's nose □ see red □ see stars □ see ya □ see you □ see you later □ see you later, alligator □ What you see is what you get. □ would not be seen dead....

**SEED**
□ bad seed □ glory seeds □ swallow a watermelon seed

**SELL**
□ hard sell □ sell a wolf ticket □ sell someone out □ soft sell □ sold on someone or something

**SEND**
□ send someone from pillar to post □ send someone or something up □ send someone to glory □ send someone up the river □ send-up

**SERIOUS**
□ get down to some serious drinking □ serious about someone

**SERPENT**
□ civil serpent

**SERVE**
□ serve someone right

**SERVICE**
□ Call my service.

**SESH**
□ full sesh

**SESSION**
□ bitch session □ bull session □ rap session

**SET**
□ jet-set □ set of pipes □ set of wheels □ set someone back □ set someone up (for something)

**SETTLE**
□ have a score to settle (with someone) □ settle a score (with someone) □ settle someone's hash

**SEVEN**
□ seven-year itch

**SEW**
□ sewed up □ sew something up

**SEWER**
□ sewer hog

**SEX**
□ sex goddess □ sex kitten □ sex pot

**SHABBY**
□ not too shabby

**SHACK**
□ shack up (with someone)

**SHADE**
□ have it made in the shade

**SHAFT**
□ give someone the shaft

**SHAG**
□ shagged out □ shag-nasty □ shag (off)

**SHAKE**
□ body shake □ can-shaker □ fair shake □ movers and shakers □ no great shakes □ shake a leg □ Shake it (up)! □ shake someone down □ Shake the lead out! □ shake-up □ two shakes of a lamb's tail □ What's shakin' (bacon)?

**SHANK**
□ shank it □ shank's mare

**SHAPE**
□ bent out of shape □ flexed out of shape □ in bad shape □ lick something into shape □ shape up □ shape up or ship out □ strung-out shape

**SHARE**
□ lion's share

**SHARK**
□ shark repellent

**SHAVE**
□ close shave

**SHEBANG**
□ whole shebang

**SHEET**
□ both sheets in the wind □ four sheets in the wind □ poop sheet □ (rap) sheet □ scandal sheet □ scratch sheet □ swindle sheet □ three sheets in the wind □ two sheets to the wind

**SHELF**
□ off-the-shelf □ on the shelf

**SHELL**
□ shell out (an amount of money)

**SHIFT**
□ graveyard shift □ stick shift □ swing shift

**SHINE**
□ Rise and shine!

**SHIP**
□ pump ship □ rocket ship □ shape up or ship out

**SHIRT**
□ Keep your shirt on! □ lose one's shirt □ stuffed shirt

**SHIT**
□ chick(en) shit habit □ crock of shit □ get one's shit together □ scared shitless □ shit a brick □ shit-faced

**SHOCK**
□ sticker shock

**SHOE**
□ goody two-shoes □ jelly shoes □ shoe polish □ The baby needs shoes.

**SHOESTRING**
□ on a shoestring

**SHOO**
□ shoo-in

**SHOOK**
□ shook up

**SHOOT**
□ hip-shooter □ shoot 'em up □ shoot for the sky □ shoot from the hip □

and take a load off your feet. □ sit on a gold mine □ sit on someone or something □ sit right (with someone) □ sit still for something □ sit tight □ sitting duck □ sitting pretty

**SITUATION**
□ no-win situation

**SIX**
□ deep six □ Joe Six-pack □ six-bits □ six feet under □ six-pack

**SIXTY**
□ sixty-four-dollar question

**SIZE**
□ man-size(d) □ pint-sized □ That's about the size of it.

**SKAG**
□ skagged out □ skag jones

**SKETCH**
□ thumbnail sketch

**SKID**
□ grease the skids □ hit the skids □ on the skids □ put the skids under someone or something □ skid-lid □ skid marks □ skid row □ skid row bum

**SKIN**
□ Give me (some) skin! □ knock someone some skin □ skin a goat □ skin flick □ skin game □ Skin me! □ skin (pop) □ skin pumping □ skin-search □ thick-skinned □ thin-skinned

**SKINFUL**
□ have a skinful

**SKINNY**
□ hot skinny □ skinny dip

**SKIP**
□ Skip it! □ skip (out)

**SKITTLE**
□ beer and skittles

**SKULL**
□ out of one's skull □ skull-buster

**SKUNK**
□ skunk-drunk

**SKY**
□ aim for the sky □ pie-in-the-sky □ reach for the sky □ shoot for the sky □ sky hook □ sky-pilot □ sky rug □ sky's the limit

**SLAM**
□ slam-bang □ slam-dancing □ slam dunk □ slam some beers

**SLAP**
□ back-slapper □ knee-slapper □ slap-dab □ slap-dash □ slap happy □ slap in the face □ slap someone's wrist

**SLAVE**
□ slave away (at something) □ slave market

**SLEAZE**
□ sleaze-bucket

**SLEEP**
□ beauty sleep □ sleep it off

**SLEEVE**
□ have an ace up one's sleeve

**SLEIGH**
□ go for a sleigh ride □ take a sleigh ride

**SLICE**
□ slice of the action

**SLICK**
□ city slicker □ racing slicks □ slick-chick

**SLIGHT**
□ slightly rattled

**SLIM**
□ iceberg slim

**SLIME**
□ slime bag □ slime bucket

**SLING**
□ hash-slinger □ have one's ass in a sling □ ink slinger □ sling the cat

**SLINGSHOT**
□ double-barreled slingshot

**SLIP**
□ give someone the slip □ pink slip □ pink-slipped □ Slip me five! □ slip one's trolley □ slip someone a Mickey □ slip someone five □ slip (up)

**SLOP**
□ Earp slop, bring the mop.

**SLOSH**
□ sloshed (to the ears)

**SLOW**
□ do a slow burn □ slow boat □ slow burn □ take it slow □ twist (slowly) in the wind

**SLUFF**
□ sluff (off)

**SLUG**
□ slug it out

**SLUSH**
□ slushed (up) □ slush fund □ slush up

**SLY**
□ on the sly

**SMACK**
□ smack (dab) in the middle

**SMALL**
□ small beer □ small change □ small

fortune □ small fry □ small potatoes □
small-time

**SMART**
□ get smart (with someone) □ one
smart apple □ smart aleck □ smart ass
□ smart cookie □ smart guy □ smart
money □ smart mouth □ smarty-pants
□ street smart □ street smarts

**SMASH**
□ smash hit

**SMELL**
□ smell a rat □ smell blood □ smell
fishy □ smell it up □ smell like a rose
□ smell the stuff □ smell to (high)
heaven

**SMILE**
□ Smile when you say that.

**SMOKE**
□ blow smoke □ chain(-smoke) □
chain-smoker □ jay smoke □ joy smoke
□ Put that in your pipe and smoke it!
□ smoke and mirrors □ smoke eater
□ smoke-filled room □ smoke-in □
smoke like a chimney □ Smokey (the
Bear) □ smoking gun □ test-smoke

**SMOKESTACK**
□ tickle one's smokestack

**SMOOTH**
□ jump smooth □ smooth operator

**SNAIL**
□ at a snail's pace

**SNAKE**
□ snake eyes □ snake in the grass

**SNAKEBITE**
□ snakebite medicine

**SNAP**
□ Make it snappy! □ snap course □
Snap it up! □ snap one's cookies □
snap out of something □ snapped (up)
□ snap something up □ snap to (attention) □ Snap to it!

**SNAVED**
□ snaved in

**SNAZZ**
□ snazz something up

**SNEEZE**
□ nothing to sneeze at

**SNIDE**
□ snide remark

**SNIFF**
□ pot sniffer □ whiff-sniffer

**SNIT**
□ in a snit

**SNORT**
□ ringtailed snorter □ rip snorter □
short-snort

**SNOTNOSED**
□ snotnose(d) (kid)

**SNOW**
□ blow snow □ do a snow job on
someone □ Lady Snow □ snow bunny
□ snow job

**SNOWBALL**
□ snowball's chance in hell

**SNOZZLE**
□ snozzle-wobbles

**SNUFF**
□ snuff film □ snuff it □ up to snuff

**SO**
□ I am so sure! □ say-so □ so-and-so
□ so bad one can taste it □ So gross!
□ so long □ So much for that. □ so-so
□ So's your old man! □ So what? □
take on (so)

**SOAK**
□ Go soak your head! □ Go soak
yourself! □ soak one's face

**SOAP**
□ no soap □ soft soap

**SOB**
□ sob sister □ sob story

**SOBER**
□ cold sober □ sober as a judge □
sober up □ stone (cold) sober

**SOCIAL**
□ social disease

**SOCK**
□ knock someone's socks off □ rubber
sock □ socked in □ sock hop □ Sock
it to me! □ Stuff a sock in it! □ walking
on rocky socks □ wet sock

**SOFA**
□ sofa spud

**SOFT**
□ soft berth □ soft core □ soft-hearted
□ soft in the head □ soft money □ soft
on someone or something □ soft pedal
something □ soft sell □ soft soap □
soft touch □ walk soft

**SOFTWARE**
□ software rot

**SOLD**
(See also *SELL*.) □ sold cober

**SOLDIER**
□ dead soldier □ old soldier

**SOME**
□ bag some rays □ blow off (some)

steam □ bust (some) suds □ catch some rays □ catch some Z's □ cop some Z's □ cut some Z's □ do some bongs □ get down to some serious drinking □ get some shut-eye □ Give me (some) skin! □ kick some ass (around) □ knock some heads together □ knock someone some skin □ lay some sweet lines on someone □ put some distance between someone and someone or something □ put some sweet lines on someone □ run down some lines □ slam some beers □ some pumpkins □ suck (some) brew □ suck (some) suds □ take some doing

**SOMETIME**
□ Let's do lunch (sometime).

**SOMEWHERE**
□ boogie down (to somewhere) □ hump it (to somewhere) □ make for somewhere □ park it (somewhere)

**SON**
□ son of a bitch □ son of a gun

**SOP**
□ sopping (wet)

**SORE**
□ sight for sore eyes □ stick out like a sore thumb □ touch a sore point

**SORRY**
□ I'm sorry. □ sorry about that □ sorry-ass

**SOUL**
□ gripe one's soul □ heavy soul □ (soul) brother □ soul kiss □ (soul) sister □ thirsty soul

**SOUND**
□ sound off (about something)

**SOUP**
□ alphabet soup □ cat-soup □ everything from soup to nuts □ in the soup □ laughing soup □ potato soup □ souped up □ soup something up □ soup-strainer

**SOUR**
□ go sour

**SOUTH**
□ go South □ head South □ mouth full of South

**SPACE**
□ space cadet □ spaced (out) □ space out □ space someone out

**SPADE**
□ in spades

**SPAGHETTI**
□ spaghetti western

**SPANK**
□ (brand) spanking new □ spanking new

**SPARE**
□ spare tire

**SPAZ**
□ have a spaz □ spaz around □ spaz out

**SPEAK**
□ speak of the devil □ speak someone's language

**SPEAR**
□ take the spear (in one's chest)

**SPECIAL**
□ Saturday night special

**SPEED**
□ speed demon □ speed freak □ speed merchant

**SPEEDBALL**
□ Frisco speedball

**SPEND**
□ big spender □ big-time spender □ spending money

**SPEW**
□ spew one's guts (out)

**SPIDER**
□ pink spiders

**SPIFF**
□ spiffed out □ spiffed up

**SPIKE**
□ hit spike

**SPILL**
□ spill one's guts □ spill the beans □ spill the works

**SPIN**
□ spin one's wheels

**SPIRIT**
□ dampen someone's spirits

**SPIT**
□ spit and polish □ Spit it out! □ swap spits

**SPLEEN**
□ vent one's spleen

**SPLIFF**
□ English spliff

**SPLIT**
□ banana split □ I've got to split. □ lickety-split □ split a gut □ splitting headache □ split up

**SPOIL**
□ spoiled rotten □ spoiling for a fight

**SPONGE**
□ throw in the sponge □ toss in the sponge
**SPOOK**
□ spook factory
**SPOON**
□ flake spoon □ Gag me with a spoon! □ greasy spoon
**SPOT**
□ hit the spot □ spot market □ spot of lunch □ spot someone (something) □ ten-spot □ tight spot □ X marks the spot.
**SPRAIN**
□ sprain one's ankle
**SPRING**
□ half-sprung □ spring chicken □ spring for something □ spring someone
**SPROUT**
□ sprout wings
**SPUD**
□ sofa spud
**SQUAD**
□ goon squad □ junk squad
**SQUARE**
□ back to square one □ squared away □ squared up □ square John □ square joint □ square (meal) □ square off □ square peg (in a round hole) □ square shooter □ square with someone □ three squares
**SQUASH**
□ stoned out of one's squash
**SQUAT**
□ cop a squat □ diddly-squat □ doodly-squat
**SQUAWK**
□ squawk box
**SQUEAK**
□ narrow squeak □ squeaky clean
**SQUEEZE**
□ budget squeeze □ corn squeezings □ duck-squeezer □ main squeeze □ put the squeeze on someone □ (squeeze-)box □ squeeze play
**SQUIFF**
□ on the squiff □ squiff out
**SQUIRREL**
□ seam-squirrels □ squirrel-food □ squirrel out of something □ squirrel something away
**STACK**
□ blow one's stack □ stack the deck □ swear on a stack of Bibles

**STAG**
□ stag line □ stag-party
**STAKE**
□ stake someone or something out □ stake someone to something □ up stakes
**STALE**
□ stale drunk
**STAMP**
□ stamping ground
**STAND**
□ If you can't stand the heat, keep out of the kitchen. □ one-night stand □ stand-in □ stand-out □ stand pat (on something) □ stand someone up □ stand tall □ stand there with one's bare face hanging out
**STANDOFF**
□ Mexican standoff
**STAR**
□ all-star □ see stars
**STARCH**
□ take the starch out of someone
**START**
□ jump start
**STASH**
□ main stash □ stash bag
**STATION**
□ comfort station □ filling station □ fuzz station □ Grand Central Station □ thirst-aid station
**STATISTICS**
□ vital statistics
**STAY**
□ stay loose □ Stay tuned.
**STEAK**
□ tube steak
**STEAM**
□ blow off (some) steam □ full steam ahead □ let off steam □ steamed (up) □ steam someone's beam □ steam someone up □ steam up
**STEER**
□ bum steer
**STEP**
□ Aztec two-step □ step off the curb □ step out on someone □ step outside □ stepped on □ step right up □ You want to step outside?
**STEVEN**
□ even-Steven
**STEW**
□ half-stewed □ stew bum □ stewed to the gills □ stewed (up)

## STICK
☐ boom sticks ☐ Buddha stick ☐ cancer stick ☐ carry the stick ☐ get on the stick ☐ licorice stick ☐ short end of the stick ☐ stick around ☐ Stick 'em up! ☐ sticker shock ☐ stick in the mud ☐ stick it to someone ☐ stick man ☐ stick of tea ☐ stick one's nose in (where it's not wanted) ☐ stick out like a sore thumb ☐ stick shift ☐ stick someone with something ☐ sticky fingers ☐ swizzle-stick ☐ T-stick

## STIFF
☐ scared stiff ☐ working stiff

## STILL
☐ sit still for something

## STINK
☐ big stink ☐ holy stink ☐ like stink ☐ make a stink (about someone or something) ☐ raise a stink (about someone or something) ☐ stinking (drunk) ☐ stinking rich ☐ stinking with something ☐ stink on ice

## STIR
☐ stir crazy

## STOCK
☐ deal stock ☐ stocking-stuffer ☐ story stock

## STOKE
☐ stoked (on someone or something) ☐ stoked out

## STOMACH
☐ cast-iron stomach ☐ turn someone's stomach

## STOMP
☐ stomp (on) someone

## STONE
☐ carved in stone ☐ stone blind ☐ stone broke ☐ stone (cold) sober ☐ stone dead ☐ stoned (out) ☐ stoned out of one's head ☐ stoned out of one's squash ☐ stoned silly ☐ stone fox ☐ stone groove ☐ stone's throw ☐ stony bush

## STOOL
☐ stool (on someone) ☐ stool (pigeon)

## STOP
☐ flopper-stopper ☐ nature stop ☐ pit stop ☐ pull out all the stops ☐ stop on a dime ☐ Stop the music!

## STORAGE
☐ in cold storage

## STORE
☐ candy store ☐ dime store ☐ leeky store

## STORK
☐ visit from the stork

## STORM
☐ kick up a storm ☐ talk up a storm ☐ up a storm

## STORY
☐ bedtime story ☐ fish story ☐ long story short ☐ same old story ☐ sob story ☐ story stock ☐ tall story ☐ top story ☐ upper story

## STOW
☐ Stow it!

## STRADDLE
☐ straddle the fence

## STRAIGHT
☐ get straight ☐ give something to someone straight ☐ go straight ☐ put oneself straight ☐ straight arrow ☐ straight dope ☐ straighten up and fly right ☐ straight-faced ☐ straight from the horse's mouth ☐ straight from the shoulder ☐ straight low ☐ straight man ☐ straight shooter ☐ straight talk ☐ straight up

## STRAIN
☐ soup-strainer

## STRANGE
☐ strange bird

## STRAP
☐ super-strap

## STRAW
☐ last straw ☐ straw boss

## STREAK
☐ have a yellow streak down one's back ☐ losing streak ☐ talk a blue streak ☐ yellow streak (down someone's back)

## STREET
☐ easy street ☐ jump (street) ☐ man on the street ☐ on easy street ☐ on the street ☐ put something on the street ☐ street-casting ☐ street people ☐ street pusher ☐ street smart ☐ street smarts ☐ street time ☐ take it to the street ☐ two-way street

## STRESS
☐ no stress

## STRETCH
☐ in the (home) stretch ☐ stretch one's legs

## STRICTLY
☐ (strictly) from hunger

## STRIKE
☐ strike it rich ☐ strike out ☐ strike pay dirt

**STRIP**
- □ strip-search

**STROKE**
- □ different strokes for different folks

**STRONG**
- □ come on strong □ strong-arm □ strong-arm man □ strong-arm tactics

**STRUNG**
- □ strung out □ strung-out shape

**STRUT**
- □ strut one's stuff

**STUCK**
- □ stuck on someone or something □ stuck-up □ stuck with someone or something

**STUD**
- □ stud-muffin

**STUFF**
- □ beat the stuffing out of someone □ fluff-stuff □ get one's stuff together □ green stuff □ hot stuff □ kid stuff □ light stuff □ rough stuff □ smell the stuff □ stocking-stuffer □ strut one's stuff □ Stuff a sock in it! □ stuffed shirt □ That's the stuff!

**STUPID**
- □ stupid-ass

**SUCH**
- □ There's no such thing as a free lunch.

**SUCK**
- □ egg-sucker □ sucker for someone or something □ sucker list □ suck face □ suck (some) brew □ suck someone's hind tit □ suck (some) suds □ suck up to someone

**SUD**
- □ bust (some) suds □ bust suds □ in the suds □ suck (some) suds

**SUDDEN**
- □ sudden death

**SUDGE**
- □ jober as a sudge

**SUE**
- □ sue the pants off (of) someone

**SUGAR**
- □ brown sugar □ sugar (cube) □ sugar daddy □ Uncle Sugar

**SUMMER**
- □ summer complaint

**SUN**
- □ sun belt

**SUNDAY**
- □ in a month of Sundays □ Sunday best □ Sunday driver □ Sunday punch

**SUNNY**
- □ sunny-side up

**SUNSHINE**
- □ Hawaiian (sunshine)

**SUPER**
- □ super-duper □ super-strap

**SUPERINTENDENT**
- □ sidewalk superintendent

**SURE**
- □ for sure □ I am so sure! □ sure as hell □ sure thing

**SWALLOW**
- □ hard to swallow □ swallow a watermelon seed □ swallow hit □ swallow the dictionary

**SWAP**
- □ swap notes (on someone or something) □ swap spits

**SWEAR**
- □ swear like a trooper □ swear on a stack of Bibles

**SWEAT**
- □ Don't sweat it! □ in a cold sweat □ no sweat □ sweat blood □ sweat bullets □ sweat-shop □ sweat something out □ tiger sweat

**SWEEP**
- □ clean sweep □ sweep with both barrels □ take a sweep (with both barrels)

**SWEET**
- □ fresh and sweet □ lay some sweet lines on someone □ put some sweet lines on someone □ sweetie-pie □ sweet nothings □ sweet on someone □ (sweet) patootie □ sweet potato □ sweet talk □ sweet tooth □ You bet your sweet life! □ You bet your sweet patootie!

**SWEETHEART**
- □ sweetheart deal

**SWILL**
- □ monkey swill □ swill-up

**SWIM**
- □ swimming in something

**SWINDLE**
- □ swindle sheet

**SWING**
- □ swing both ways □ swing into high gear □ swing shift □ swing with someone or something

**SWIPE**
- □ take a swipe at someone or something

**SWITCH**
☐ asleep at the switch ☐ switched on ☐ switch-hitter ☐ switch off ☐ switch on

**SWIZZLE**
☐ swizzle-stick

**SYNC**
☐ out of sync

**SYRUP**
☐ syrup head

**SYSTEM**
☐ All systems are go.

**TAB**
☐ gorilla tabs ☐ lick up a tab

**TABBACKY**
☐ wacky-tabbacky

**TABLE**
☐ table-hop ☐ under the table

**TACK**
☐ brass tacks

**TACKY**
☐ ticky-tacky

**TACOS**
☐ toss one's tacos

**TACTIC**
☐ strong-arm tactics

**TAIL**
☐ bright-eyed and bushy-tailed ☐ have a tiger by the tail ☐ on someone's tail ☐ tail bone ☐ tail-end ☐ turn tail (and run) ☐ two shakes of a lamb's tail ☐ work one's tail off

**TAILGATE**
☐ tailgate party

**TAILOR**
☐ tailor made

**TAKE**
☐ double take ☐ have what it takes ☐ on the take ☐ Sit down and take a load off your feet. ☐ take a bath (on something) ☐ take a beating ☐ take a break ☐ take a crack at something ☐ take a dig at someone ☐ take a dirt nap ☐ take a dive ☐ take a fall ☐ take a flyer ☐ take a gander (at someone or something) ☐ take a hike ☐ take a jab at someone ☐ take a leak ☐ take a lot of nerve ☐ take a nosedive ☐ take a page from someone's book ☐ take a pop at someone ☐ take a powder ☐ Take a running jump (in the lake)! ☐ take a sleigh ride ☐ take a sweep (with both barrels) ☐ take a swipe at someone or something ☐ take a shot (at something)

☐ take a walk ☐ take a whack at someone or something ☐ Take care. ☐ take care of number one ☐ take care of someone ☐ take five ☐ take it ☐ take it easy ☐ take it on the chin ☐ take it on the lamb ☐ Take it or leave it. ☐ take it out on someone or something ☐ take it slow ☐ take it through the nose ☐ take it to the street ☐ take names ☐ take off ☐ take-off ☐ take-off artist ☐ take off (on something) ☐ take one's belt in (a notch) ☐ take one's lumps ☐ take on fuel ☐ take on (so) ☐ take pictures ☐ take some doing ☐ take someone in ☐ take someone or something apart ☐ take someone or something off ☐ take someone or something on ☐ take someone or something out ☐ take someone to the cleaners ☐ take something public ☐ takes two to tango ☐ take the cake ☐ take the cure ☐ take the fifth ☐ take the heat ☐ take the heat off someone ☐ take the (long) count ☐ take the pipe ☐ take the pledge ☐ take the plunge ☐ take the rap (for something) ☐ take the spear (in one's chest) ☐ take the starch out of someone ☐ take the wind out of someone's sails ☐ take things easy ☐ take (to) the needle ☐ taking care of business ☐ You can't take it with you.

**TALE**
☐ fairy tale ☐ fish tale ☐ tale of woe

**TALK**
☐ big talk ☐ give someone a (good) talking to ☐ heart-to-heart (talk) ☐ jive talk ☐ Look who's talking! ☐ money talks ☐ monkey talk ☐ nice talking to you ☐ Now you're talking! ☐ pep talk ☐ straight talk ☐ sweet talk ☐ talk a blue streak ☐ talk big ☐ talking head ☐ talk like a nut ☐ talk on the big white phone ☐ talk someone ragged ☐ talk someone's ear off ☐ talk someone's head off ☐ talk through one's hat ☐ talk to hear one's own voice ☐ talk to Herb and Al ☐ talk turkey ☐ talk until one is blue in the face ☐ talk up a storm

**TALL**
☐ in tall cotton ☐ long tall Sally ☐ stand tall ☐ tall in the saddle ☐ tall one ☐ tall order ☐ tall story ☐ tall timbers ☐ walk tall

## TAMBOURINE
☐ tambourine man
## TAN
☐ tan someone's hide
## TANGLE
☐ tangle with someone or something
## TANGO
☐ takes two to tango
## TANK
☐ drunk tank ☐ junk tank ☐ on the tank ☐ tank up ☐ think-tank
## TAP
☐ on tap ☐ tap dance like mad ☐ tap out ☐ tap someone (for something)
## TAPE
☐ red tape
## TAR
☐ beat the tar out of someone ☐ tarred with the same brush ☐ whale the tar out of someone
## TARANTULA
☐ tarantula juice
## TARGET
☐ on-target
## TASTE
☐ so bad one can taste it ☐ taste blood
## TATTOO
☐ screwed, blued, and tattooed
## TAXI
☐ Tijuana taxi
## TEA
☐ cup of tea ☐ green tea ☐ high tea ☐ sip tea ☐ stick of tea ☐ tea accessories ☐ tea bag ☐ tea-blower ☐ tea'd up ☐ tea party ☐ tea-sipper ☐ Texas (tea)
## TEACH
☐ That'll teach someone.
## TEAR
☐ tear into someone or something ☐ tear-jerker ☐ tear loose (from someone or something) ☐ tear off ☐ tear someone or something apart ☐ tear someone or something up ☐ That tears it! ☐ tore (up) ☐ torn (up)
## TEASE
☐ brain-teaser
## TECHNICOLOR
☐ technicolor yawn
## TEE
☐ teed off ☐ teed (up) ☐ tee someone off ☐ tee-tee
## TEENIE
☐ teenie-weenie

## TEENSY
☐ teensy-weensy
## TEENY
☐ teeny-weeny
## TELEGRAPH
☐ telegraph one's punches
## TELL
☐ Do tell. ☐ if I've told you once, I've told you a thousand times... ☐ show and tell ☐ Tell it like it is. ☐ Tell me another (one)! ☐ tell someone what to do with something ☐ tell someone where to get off ☐ tell the (whole) world
## TEN
☐ hang ten ☐ ten-four ☐ ten percenter ☐ ten-spot ☐ wouldn't touch someone or something with a ten-foot pole
## TENOR
☐ whiskey tenor
## TERROR
☐ holy terror
## TEST
☐ acid test ☐ test-smoke
## TEXAS
☐ Texas (tea)
## THAN
☐ holier-than-thou ☐ more than one bargained for ☐ quicker than hell ☐ see no further than the end of one's nose
## THANK
☐ thanks a bunch ☐ thank you very much
## THERE
☐ get there ☐ hang in there ☐ in there ☐ I've been there. ☐ like there was no tomorrow ☐ not all there ☐ stand there with one's bare face hanging out ☐ then and there ☐ There's nobody home. ☐ There's no such thing as a free lunch. ☐ There will be hell to pay. ☐ There you are. ☐ There you go. ☐ You can't get there from here.
## THICK
☐ thick-skinned
## THIGH
☐ thunder-thighs
## THIN
☐ thin dime ☐ thin-skinned ☐ walk on thin ice
## THING
☐ do one's (own) thing ☐ do the drink thing ☐ do the drug thing ☐ in thing to do ☐ onto a good thing ☐ sure thing

□ take things easy □ There's no such thing as a free lunch. □ whole 'nother thing
**THINK**
□ think-box □ think-piece □ think-tank □ You've got another think coming.
**THIRD**
□ third degree □ third wheel
**THIRST**
□ thirst-aid station □ thirsty soul
**THIRTEEN**
□ number thirteen
**THIS**
□ Are you ready for this? □ I don't believe this! □ Keep out of this! □ out of this world □ This is it! □ This is where I came in.
**THOU**
□ holier-than-thou
**THOUGHT**
□ Don't give it another thought. □ Don't give it a second thought.
**THOUSAND**
□ if I've told you once, I've told you a thousand times...
**THREE**
□ number three □ phony as a three-dollar bill □ queer as a three-dollar bill □ three bricks shy of a load □ three fingers □ three point two □ three sheets in the wind □ three squares □ three-two
**THRILL**
□ thriller-diller □ thrill-pills
**THROAT**
□ cut one's own throat □ ram something down someone's throat □ throat gag
**THRONE**
□ throne room
**THROUGH**
□ breeze through (something) □ go through someone like a dose of the salts □ go through the changes □ sail (right) through something □ take it through the nose □ talk through one's hat □ through and through □ through the mill □ waltz through something
**THROW**
□ stone's throw □ throw a fight □ throw a fit □ throw a game □ throw a map □ throw a punch □ throw-away □ throw in the sponge □ throw in the

towel □ throw money at something □ throw one out on one's ear □ throw one's cookies □ throw one's hat in the ring □ throw one's voice □ throw one's weight around □ throw someone for a loop □ throw something back □ throw something together □ throw the book at someone □ throw the bull □ throw up one's toenails
**THUMB**
□ all thumbs □ green thumb □ stick out like a sore thumb □ thumb a ride □ thumbs down □ thumbs up □ turn thumbs down (on someone or something) □ twiddle one's thumbs □ under someone's thumb
**THUMBNAIL**
□ thumbnail sketch
**THUNDER**
□ thunder-boomer □ thunder-cookie □ thunder-thighs □ thunder weed
**TICK**
□ ticked (off) □ tick someone off □ tick-tock □ tight as a tick
**TICKET**
□ big-ticket □ buy someone's wolf ticket □ get one's ticket punched □ just the ticket □ sell a wolf ticket □ That's the ticket! □ ticket agent
**TICKLE**
□ rib-tickler □ tickled (pink) □ tickle one's smokestack □ tickle the ivories
**TICKY**
□ ticky-tacky
**TIE**
□ tied up □ tie-in □ tie one on □ tie on the nosebag □ tie the knot □ tongue-tied
**TIGER**
□ have a tiger by the tail □ tiger juice □ tiger milk □ tiger sweat
**TIGHT**
□ on a tight leash □ sit tight □ tight as a tick □ tighten one's belt □ tighten someone's wig □ tight money □ tight spot □ tight wad
**TIJUANA**
□ Tijuana taxi
**TILL**
□ till hell freezes over □ till the cows come home □ till the fat lady sings
**TIMBER**
□ tall timbers

**TIME**
☐ all-time ☐ all-time favorite ☐ bean time ☐ Better luck next time. ☐ big time ☐ big-time operator ☐ big-time spender ☐ buy time ☐ devil of a time ☐ devil's own time ☐ do time ☐ down time ☐ game time ☐ good-time Charley ☐ good-time it ☐ good-time man ☐ hard time ☐ have a whale of a time ☐ high old time ☐ if I've told you once, I've told you a thousand times... ☐ Long time no see. ☐ mark time ☐ old-timer ☐ pinched (for time) ☐ pressed (for time) ☐ pushed (for time) ☐ rack time ☐ rare old time ☐ rough time ☐ sack time ☐ small-time ☐ street time ☐ Time (out)! ☐ Time's a wasting. ☐ time to cruise ☐ two-time ☐ two-time loser ☐ two-timer ☐ up time

**TIN**
☐ tin cow ☐ tin hat

**TINSEL**
☐ tinsel-teeth

**TINY**
☐ patter of tiny feet

**TIP**
☐ hot tip ☐ tip-off ☐ tip one's hand

**TIRE**
☐ spare tire

**TIT**
☐ suck someone's hind tit ☐ tits and ass ☐ tits up ☐ Tough titty!

**TIZZY**
☐ in a tizzy

**TOCK**
☐ tick-tock

**TODDLE**
☐ toddle off

**TODDY**
☐ toddy blossom

**TOE**
☐ turn up one's toes

**TOEHOLD**
☐ get a toehold

**TOENAIL**
☐ throw up one's toenails

**TOGETHER**
☐ get it (all) together ☐ get one's act together ☐ get one's head together ☐ get one's shit together ☐ get one's stuff together ☐ have it all together ☐ knock some heads together ☐ knock something together ☐ throw something together

**TOILET**
☐ toilet mouth ☐ toilet water

**TOKE**
☐ harsh toke ☐ toke pipe ☐ toke up

**TOKLAS**
☐ Alice B. Toklas brownies

**TOMORROW**
☐ like there was no tomorrow

**TON**
☐ like a ton of bricks ☐ tons of something

**TONGUE**
☐ Bite your tongue! ☐ tongue oil ☐ tongue-tied ☐ Watch your tongue!

**TONSIL**
☐ tonsil bath ☐ tonsil paint ☐ wet one's tonsils

**TOO**
☐ not too shabby ☐ one too many ☐ too much ☐ too rich for someone's blood

**TOODLE**
☐ toodle(-oo)

**TOOL**
☐ power tool ☐ tool around

**TOOT**
☐ rooting-tooting ☐ toot one's own horn ☐ You're dern tootin'!

**TOOTH**
☐ dressed to the teeth ☐ drop one's teeth ☐ get one's teeth into something ☐ sink one's teeth into something ☐ sweet tooth ☐ tinsel-teeth

**TOOTLE**
☐ tootle along

**TOOTSIE**
☐ tootsie roll

**TOP**
☐ big top ☐ blow one's top ☐ carrot top ☐ come out on top ☐ cross top ☐ flower tops ☐ top banana ☐ top brass ☐ top dog ☐ top-drawer ☐ top-flight ☐ top heavy ☐ top of the heap ☐ tops and bottoms ☐ top story

**TOPSY**
☐ topsy-boozy ☐ topsy-turvy

**TORCH**
☐ torch up

**TORE**
(See *TEAR.*)

**TORN**
(See *TEAR.*)

**TORNADO**
☐ tornado juice

**TOSS**
☐ toss in the sponge ☐ toss one's cookies ☐ toss one's lunch ☐ toss one's tacos ☐ toss something off ☐ toss-up

**TOTALLY**
☐ totally clueless

**TOTSY**
☐ hotsy-totsy

**TOUCH**
☐ Keep in touch. ☐ soft touch ☐ touch and go ☐ touch a sore point ☐ touch base (with someone) ☐ touched (in the head) ☐ touch of the brewer ☐ wouldn't touch someone or something with a ten-foot pole

**TOUGH**
☐ hang tough (on something) ☐ tough break ☐ tough cookie ☐ tough cookies ☐ tough customer ☐ tough egg to crack ☐ tough guy ☐ tough luck ☐ tough nut to crack ☐ tough row to hoe ☐ tough something out ☐ Tough titty!

**TOUR**
☐ tour guide

**TOURIST**
☐ tourist trap

**TOWEL**
☐ crying towel ☐ throw in the towel

**TOWER**
☐ ivory tower

**TOWN**
☐ Bean Town ☐ blow town ☐ Get out of town! ☐ go to town ☐ one-horse town ☐ paint the town (red)

**TRACK**
☐ make tracks ☐ off the track ☐ one-track mind ☐ railroad tracks ☐ wrong side of the tracks

**TRADE**
☐ tricks of the trade

**TRAGIC**
☐ tragic-magic

**TRAIL**
☐ hit the trail

**TRAIN**
☐ gravy train

**TRANQUILIZER**
☐ elephant (tranquilizer) ☐ horse (tranquilizer)

**TRAP**
☐ bear trap ☐ booby trap ☐ fly trap ☐ fox trap ☐ rattle-trap ☐ tourist trap

**TRASH**
☐ trash mouth

**TRAVEL**
☐ travel agent

**TREAT**
☐ Dutch treat

**TREE**
☐ Christmas tree ☐ Go climb a tree! ☐ not grow on trees ☐ up a tree

**TRIAL**
☐ trial balloon

**TRIC**
☐ tric (acid)

**TRICK**
☐ do the trick ☐ How's tricks? ☐ miss a trick ☐ tricks of the trade ☐ turn a trick ☐ whole bag of tricks

**TRIGGER**
☐ trigger-happy

**TRIP**
☐ bad trip ☐ bean trip ☐ day-tripper ☐ down trip ☐ ego trip ☐ ego tripper ☐ free trip ☐ good trip ☐ head trip ☐ lay a (heavy) trip on someone ☐ natch trip ☐ round tripper ☐ trip out ☐ tripped out ☐ tripping heavy ☐ trip weed

**TRIPLE**
☐ triple-bagger ☐ triple whammy

**TROLLEY**
☐ off one's trolley ☐ slip one's trolley

**TROOPER**
☐ swear like a trooper

**TROT**
☐ back-door trot(s)

**TROUBLE**
☐ buy trouble ☐ double-trouble ☐ for (all) one's trouble

**TRUCK**
☐ Keep on trucking. ☐ (truck) drivers

**TRULY**
☐ yours truly

**TRUMP**
☐ trumped up ☐ trump something up

**TRUST**
☐ Trust me!

**TRUTH**
☐ gospel (truth) ☐ naked truth

**TRY**
☐ try someone back (again)

**TUB**
☐ tub of lard

**TUBE**
☐ boob-tube ☐ cop a tube ☐ crack a tube ☐ go down the tube(s) ☐ in the tube ☐ tube it ☐ tube steak

## WALK
☐ take a walk ☐ walk away with something ☐ walk heavy ☐ walk-in ☐ walking dandruff ☐ walking on rocky socks ☐ walking papers ☐ walking wounded ☐ walk off with something ☐ walk on eggs ☐ walk on thin ice ☐ walk soft ☐ walk tall

## WALL
☐ climb the wall(s) ☐ drive someone up the wall ☐ go over the wall ☐ hole in the wall ☐ nail someone's hide to the wall ☐ nail someone to the wall ☐ off the wall ☐ plastered to the wall ☐ up the wall ☐ wall-eyed ☐ wall job ☐ walls have ears ☐ wall-to-wall

## WALSY
☐ palsy-walsy

## WALTZ
☐ waltz off (with something) ☐ waltz through something

## WANT
☐ put one's nose in (where it's not wanted) ☐ stick one's nose in (where it's not wanted) ☐ want list ☐ want out ☐ Want to make something of it? ☐ You want to step outside?

## WAR
☐ war chest ☐ war paint ☐ war zone

## WARD
☐ monkey wards

## WARM
☐ bench warmer ☐ like death warmed over ☐ nose-warmer ☐ warm body ☐ warmed over ☐ warm someone up

## WARNER
☐ Mary Warner

## WARPATH
☐ on the warpath

## WARRIOR
☐ weekend warrior

## WART
☐ warts and all ☐ worry wart

## WAS
☐ like there was no tomorrow

## WASH
☐ chief cook and bottle washer ☐ come out in the wash ☐ head cook and bottle washer ☐ washed out ☐ washed up ☐ wash one's dirty linen in public ☐ wash out ☐ wash someone away ☐ wishy-washy

## WASTE
☐ Time's a wasting.

## WATCH
☐ bird-watcher ☐ clock watcher ☐ on someone's watch ☐ people-watching ☐ Watch it! ☐ Watch my lips! ☐ Watch your mouth! ☐ Watch your tongue!

## WATER
☐ big drink of water ☐ blow someone out of the water ☐ bubble water ☐ dead in the water ☐ foo-foo water ☐ hold water ☐ joy water ☐ pour cold water on something ☐ toilet water ☐ turn someone's water off ☐ watering hole ☐ whoopee(-water) ☐ woofle-water ☐ woozle-water

## WATERMELON
☐ swallow a watermelon seed

## WATERWORKS
☐ turn on the waterworks

## WAUI
☐ Maui Waui

## WAVE
☐ finger wave ☐ make waves

## WAVELENGTH
☐ on the same wavelength

## WAX
☐ whole ball of wax

## WAY
☐ all the way ☐ all the way live ☐ down someone's way ☐ from way back ☐ go all the way ☐ in a bad way ☐ in a big way ☐ in a familiar way ☐ in a family way ☐ It cuts two ways. ☐ No way! ☐ only way to go ☐ out of the way ☐ put someone or something out of the way ☐ swing both ways ☐ That's the way the ball bounces. ☐ That's the way the cookie crumbles. ☐ That's the way the mop flops. ☐ That's the way to go! ☐ that way ☐ the way it plays ☐ two-way street ☐ way down ☐ way off (base) ☐ way out ☐ way rad ☐ Way to go!

## WEAK
☐ weak sister

## WEAR
☐ wear the pants (in the house)

## WEASEL
☐ weasel out of something

## WEATHER
☐ fair-weather ☐ under the weather

## WEDDING
☐ shotgun wedding

## WEE
☐ wee-wee

## WEED
□ brown weed □ crying weed □ joy weed □ killer weed □ kingdom weed □ monster weed □ thunder weed □ trip weed □ weed out

## WEEKEND
□ weekend warrior

## WEENIE
□ teenie-weenie

## WEENSY
□ teensy-weensy

## WEENY
□ teeny-weeny

## WEIGHT
□ carry weight □ throw one's weight around

## WEIRD
□ weirded out □ weird out

## WELL
□ alive and well □ damn(ed) well □ jolly-well □ well-fixed □ well-oiled □ (well-)upholstered

## WERE
□ Were you born in a barn?

## WEST
□ go West

## WESTERN
□ spaghetti western

## WET
□ all wet □ sopping (wet) □ wet blanket □ wet noodle □ wet one □ wet one's tonsils □ wet one's whistle □ wet rag □ wet sock

## WHACK
□ out of whack □ take a whack at someone or something □ whacked (out) □ whack someone or something (out)

## WHALE
□ have a whale of a time □ whale into someone or something □ whale the tar out of someone

## WHAM
□ double whammy □ triple whammy □ wham-bang □ wham-ditty

## WHATEVER
□ whatever turns you on

## WHEEL
□ big wheel □ eighteen wheeler □ fifth wheel □ four wheels □ free-wheeling □ hell on wheels □ reinvent the wheel □ set of wheels □ spin one's wheels □ third wheel □ wheel and deal □ wheeler-dealer □ wheel man

## WHEN
□ Smile when you say that. □ when push comes to shove □ when the eagle flies □ when the fat lady sings

## WHERE
□ know where it's at □ know where one is coming from □ put one's nose in (where it's not wanted) □ Put your money where your mouth is! □ stick one's nose in (where it's not wanted) □ tell someone where to get off □ This is where I came in. □ Where (have) you been keeping yourself? □ Where in (the) Sam Hill? □ Where in the world? □ where it's at □ Where on (God's green) earth? □ where someone is at □ where someone lives □ where someone's head is at □ Where's the beef? □ Where's the fire? □ where the action is □ you-know-where

## WHICH
□ know which end is up

## WHIFF
□ whiff-sniffer

## WHILE
□ get (out) while the getting's good □ quit while one is ahead

## WHING
□ whing-ding

## WHIP
□ whips and jingles □ whip something off

## WHIRLY
□ whirly bird

## WHISKER
□ by a whisker □ Mr. Whiskers □ Uncle Whiskers

## WHISKEY
□ corn whiskey □ whiskey tenor

## WHISTLE
□ bells and whistles □ not just whistling Dixie □ wet one's whistle □ whistle-blower □ whistle in the dark

## WHITE
□ black and white □ bleed someone white □ blue and white □ China white □ Chinese white □ Manhattan white □ talk on the big white phone □ white elephant □ white hat □ white-knuckle □ white knuckler □ white lightning

## WHIZ
□ whiz-bang □ whiz kid

## WHO
□ Look who's talking! □ Says who? □

Who (in) the hell? □ who shot John □
Who the deuce? □ You and who else?
□ you-know-who
**WHOLE**
□ tell the (whole) world □ whole bag
of tricks □ whole ball of wax □ whole
bunch(es) □ whole enchilada □ whole
fam damily □ whole new ball game □
whole nine yards □ whole 'nother thing
□ whole schmear □ whole shebang □
whole shooting match □ whole wide
world
**WHOMP**
□ whomp something up
**WHOOP**
□ whooper-up(per) □ Whoops-a-daisy! □ whoops and jingles
**WHOOPEE**
□ whoopee(-water)
**WHOP**
□ whopping (great)
**WHY**
□ Why (in) the devil? □ Why (in) the
hell?
**WIDE**
□ blow something wide open □ bust
something wide open □ high, wide,
and handsome □ whole wide world □
wide open □ wide place in the road □
with (one's) eyes (wide) open
**WIDOW**
□ (black) widow □ widow-maker
**WIG**
□ flip one's wig □ tighten someone's
wig □ wigged (out) □ wig out
**WIGGLE**
□ Get a wiggle on! □ wiggle out of
something
**WILD**
□ go hog-wild □ hog-wild □ run hog-
wild □ wild and wooly
**WILL**
□ heads will roll □ There will be hell
to pay. □ will do
**WIMP**
□ wimp out (of something)
**WIN**
□ can't win (th)em all □ no-win situation □ Win a few, lose a few. □ You
can't win them all.
**WINCY**
□ incy-wincy
**WIND**
□ bag of wind □ both sheets in the

wind □ four sheets in the wind □ take
the wind out of someone's sails □ three
sheets in the wind □ twist (slowly) in
the wind □ two sheets to the wind
**WINDOW**
□ bay window □ out the window
**WINE**
□ corn wine □ electric wine □ jug
wine □ pop wine □ roasting-ear wine
**WING**
□ clip someone's wings □ fling-wing
□ get one's wings □ give someone
wings □ hit under the wing □ sprout
wings □ wing-ding □ wing heavy □
wing it
**WINK**
□ (forty) winks
**WIPE**
□ wiped (out) □ Wipe it off! □ wipe
out □ wipe someone or something out
□ wipe up the floor with someone
**WIRE**
□ down to the wire □ hot wire □ (live)
wire □ under the wire □ wired into
someone or something
**WIRELESS**
□ latrine wireless
**WISE**
□ get wise to someone or something □
wise guy □ wise to someone or something □ wise up (to someone or something)
**WISH**
□ Don't you wish! □ wish book □
wish list □ wishy-washy □ You wish!
**WITHIN**
□ within an ace of (doing) something
**WITHOUT**
□ up the creek (without a paddle) □
without a hitch
**WOBBLE**
□ snozzle-wobbles
**WOE**
□ tale of woe
**WOLF**
□ buy someone's wolf ticket □ cut
one's wolf loose □ lone wolf □ sell a
wolf ticket □ wolf something down
**WONDER**
□ gutless wonder
**WOO**
□ pitch (the) woo
**WOOD**
□ out of the woods □ wood butcher □
wood-pussy □ woods are full of....

**WOOFLE**
☐ woofle-water
**WOOLY**
☐ wild and wooly
**WOOTSY**
☐ footsy-wootsy
**WOOZLE**
☐ woozle-water
**WOOZY**
☐ boozy-woozy
**WORD**
☐ dirty word ☐ What's the good word?
**WORK**
☐ dirty work ☐ give someone a (good) working over ☐ grunt work ☐ knock off (work) ☐ leg work ☐ shoot the works ☐ spill the works ☐ working stiff ☐ work one's butt off ☐ work oneself up ☐ work oneself (up) into a lather ☐ work oneself up to something ☐ work one's tail off ☐ work someone over
**WORLD**
☐ dead to the world ☐ not for the world ☐ out of this world ☐ tell the (whole) world ☐ What in the world? ☐ Where in the world? ☐ whole wide world ☐ world-beater ☐ world-class ☐ world is one's oyster
**WORM**
☐ can of worms ☐ glow worm ☐ worm-food ☐ worms in blood
**WORRY**
☐ Not to worry. ☐ worry wart
**WORSHIP**
☐ worship the porcelain god
**WORST**
☐ worst-case scenario
**WORTH**
☐ not worth a damn ☐ not worth a plugged nickel ☐ not worth beans ☐ worth one's salt
**WOULD**
☐ I wouldn't know. ☐ would not be seen dead.... ☐ wouldn't touch someone or something with a ten-foot pole ☐ Would you believe?
**WOUND**
☐ walking wounded
**WOW**
☐ bow-wow ☐ pow-wow
**WRAP**
☐ under wraps ☐ wrap one's car around something ☐ wrapped up (in someone or something) ☐ wrapped up (with someone or something) ☐ wrap something up
**WRATH**
☐ grapes of wrath
**WRENCH**
☐ left-handed monkey wrench
**WRINKLE**
☐ wrinkle-rod
**WRIST**
☐ kick in the wrist ☐ slap someone's wrist
**WRITE**
☐ nothing to write home about
**WRONG**
☐ have the wrong number ☐ wrong side of the tracks
**WROTE**
☐ That's all she wrote. ☐ That's what she wrote.
**YA**
☐ see ya
**YACKETY**
☐ yackety-yak
**YAK**
☐ yackety-yak ☐ yak it up
**YANK**
☐ yank someone around ☐ yank someone's chain
**YARD**
☐ whole nine yards ☐ yard dog
**YATATA**
☐ yatata-yatata
**YAWN**
☐ technicolor yawn
**YE**
☐ Ye gods!
**YEA**
☐ yea big
**YEAH**
☐ Oh, yeah?
**YEAR**
☐ donkey's years ☐ seven-year itch
**YELL**
☐ yell one's guts out ☐ yell one's head off
**YELLOW**
☐ have a yellow streak down one's back ☐ yellow-bellied ☐ yellow-belly ☐ (yellow) jacket ☐ yellow streak (down someone's back)
**YES**
☐ yes indeedy (do) ☐ Yes siree (Bob)!
**YO**
☐ yo mama ☐ yo-yo